# Australia

## THE ROUGH GUIDE

KT-370-967

There are more than eighty Rough Guide titles
covering destinations from Amsterdam to Zimbabwe

Forthcoming titles include
Jamaica • New Zealand • South Africa • Southwest USA

Rough Guide Reference Series
Classical Music • The Internet • Jazz • Rock Music • World Music • Opera

Rough Guide Phrasebooks
Czech • French • German • Greek • Hindi & Urdu • Indonesian •Italian
Mandarin Chinese • Mexican Spanish • Polish • Portuguese
Russian • Spanish • Thai • Turkish • Vietnamese

Rough Guides on the Internet
http://www.roughguides.com/
http://www.hotwired.com/rough

## ROUGH GUIDE CREDITS

| | |
|---|---|
| Text Editor: | Alison Cowan |
| Series Editor: | Mark Ellingham |
| Editorial: | Martin Dunford, Jonathan Buckley, Jo Mead, Samantha Cook, Amanda Tomlin, Ann-Marie Shaw, Vivienne Heller, Paul Gray, Sarah Dallas, Chris Schüler, Helena Smith, Alan Spicer (Online UK), Andrew Rosenberg (Online US) |
| Production: | Susanne Hillen, Andy Hilliard, Melissa Flack, Judy Pang, Link Hall, Nicola Williamson, David Callier, Helen Ostick |
| Publicity: | Richard Trillo, Simon Carloss, Niki Smith (UK), Jean-Marie Kelly |
| Finance: | John Fisher, Celia Crowley, Catherine Gillespie |
| Administration: | Tania Hummel, Mark Rogers |

### Acknowledgements

The editor would like to thank Susanne Hillen and Nicola Williamson for forbearance and humour, Paul Gray for the last-minute rescue in Victoria and Martin Dunford for Tasmania against the odds, Andy Hilliard and Link Hall for trouble-free typesetting, Gareth Nash and Susannah Walker for proofreading, and Micromap and Melissa Flack for cartography. Many thanks, too, for the invaluable contributions of readers of the previous edition; due to lack of space, the roll of honour appears on p.863.

**All the authors** would like to thank *YHA Australia* for their hospitality, *Australian Coachlines International*, staff at all the tourist bureaux for help along the way, Jeanne Muchnick for her work on *Basics*, and Alison Cowan for calm, kindness – and relentless editing. Individually, the authors would like to thank:

**Margo**: Special thanks to Henry Jones for re-visiting Tasmania, and Kathleen Daly for Outback company and updating. To all the Dalys – Margaret, Tony, Michael and Brigitte, Bettina, Mary and Janine (Bondi!) – plus Hervé Bethuel and Anaïs; Tracey Schirmer and Brenton Gardner; Sha Sha Kwa and Caleb Gardner; Beth Yahp and Paul Gillen; Matthew Buchanan; Nick Szentkuti; Michael McCusker; Kirsten Tilgals; Michael Schofield; Peta Donald; Rosanna Arciuli; Gillian Mears and Helen; Chris Scott; Silke Bader; Peter Burke; Don MacMillan; Janet McGarry; Sandra Hickman; David Moon and Jane Morgan of *Tasmanian Wilderness Transport*.

**Anne**: Thanks (long overdue) to Colin and Ginny, Diana and Jothi in Sydney; also to Silke Bader. In Melbourne, to Katharina (great Christmas present) and Helga, for helping me out of a few tight corners. In Castlemaine, to Gitesha and Daniel for advice and peaches. For good company, Renate and Stefan from Berlin (do drop in more often!). To staff at various information offices for patient assistance, notably in Hamilton and Lakes Entrance. And, as ever, thank you Peter, for your support (moral and otherwise).

**David**: For Narrell and Leaf, with love; Barry and Linda; Cath Budden; Brenton Arnold; Bob Cameron; Colin and Jan Forge; John Hams; Liz and Frank; Stephen Marsh; Polar Bear distilleries for OP; Martin and John for little sleep in Sydney; continuing thanks to Peter and Brigitte for technical links with the twentieth century.

**Chris**: Colin at *U-Rent*, Ross, Cameron, Don, all at Wittenoom, Andrew and Liesje, Peter Wood.

This second edition published 1995 by Rough Guides Ltd, 1 Mercer Street, London WC2H 9QJ.
Reprinted in February and October 1996 and March 1997.

Distributed by The Penguin Group:

Penguin Books Ltd, 27 Wrights Lane, London W8 5TZ
Penguin Books USA Inc., 375 Hudson Street, New York 10014, USA
Penguin Books Australia Ltd, 487 Maroondah Highway, PO Box 257, Ringwood, Victoria 3134, Australia
Penguin Books Canada Ltd, 10 Alcorn Avenue, Toronto, Ontario, Canada M4V 1E4
Penguin Books (NZ) Ltd, 182–190 Wairau Road, Auckland 10, New Zealand

Typeset in Linotron Univers and Century Old Style to an original design by Andrew Oliver
Printed in the UK by Cox & Wyman Ltd, Reading, Berks
**Illustrations** in Part One and Part Three by Edward Briant
Illustration on p.1 by Henry Jones and on p.821 by Henry Iles

896pp includes index.
A catalogue record for this book is available from the British Library.
ISBN 1-85828-141-5

# Australia

## THE ROUGH GUIDE

Written and researched by

**Margo Daly, Anne Dehne,
David Leffman and Chris Scott**

contributing editors
John Fisher and Jess Search

with additional contributions by
Jon Willis, Bruce Cameron,
Kathleen Daly and Henry Jones

THE ROUGH GUIDES

# LIST OF MAPS

---

## MAP SYMBOLS

| | | | |
|---|---|---|---|
| ┼┼┼ | Railway | ☼ | Viewpoint |
| ▬▬ | Main road | ⚓ | Lighthouse |
| ─── | Road | ▒ | Beach |
| ----- | Footpath | | |
| ─ ─ | Ferry route | **TOWN MAPS** | |
| ─── | Waterway | ▬▬ | Railway |
| ▬ ▬ ▬ | Chapter division boundary | ▭ | Road |
| ---- | International borders | ▥▥▥ | Footpath |
| ▨ | Aboriginal land | ⓘ | Tourist Office |
| ▨ | National Park | ⊠ | Post Office |
| ✕ | Airport | ℭ | Telephone |
| ⌃⌃ | Mountains | ■ | Building |
| ▲ | Peak | ⊞ | Church |
| △ | Campsite | ▨ | Park |
| ⌂ | Cave | ┼┼ | Christian Cemetery |

# CONTENTS

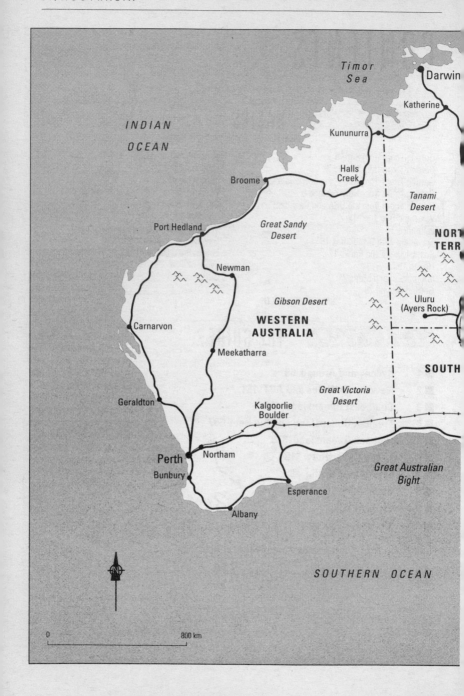

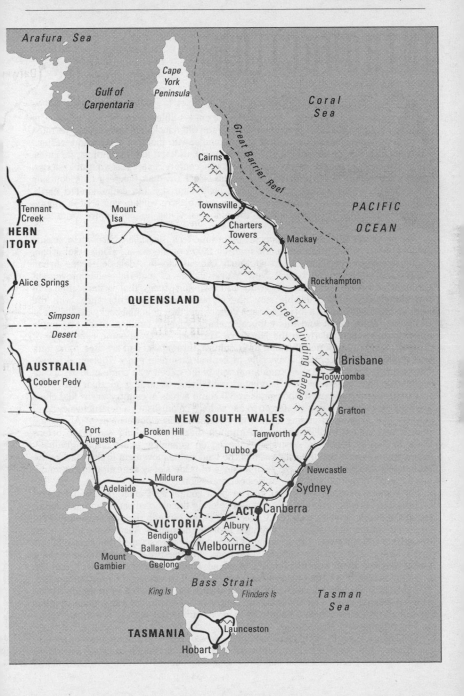

# INTRODUCTION

A ustralia is massive, and very sparsely peopled: in size it rivals the USA, yet its population is barely seventeen million – little more than that of The Netherlands. This is an ancient land, and often looks it: in places, it's the most eroded, denuded and driest of continents, with much of central and western Australia, the bulk of the country, overwhelmingly arid and flat. In contrast, its cities, most founded as recently as the mid-nineteenth century, express a youthful energy. Yet it's the interior, the Outback, west of the Great Dividing Range, which contains Australia's most memorable scenes. Here, vivid blue sky and cinnamon-red earth, deserted gorges, striking geological features and bizarre wildlife comprise a unique ecology – one that has played host to the oldest surviving human culture for at least the last 50,000 years.

The harsh interior wilderness has prompted modern Australia to become a coastal country. Most of the **population** lives within 20km of the ocean, along a suburban, southeastern arc stretching from southern Queensland to Adelaide. These urban Australians celebrate the typical New World values of material self-improvement through hard work and hard play, with an easygoing vitality that visitors often find refreshingly hedonistic. Reliable sunshine certainly aids this exuberance, with the outdoor life celebrated by a thriving beach culture and the congenial backyard "barbie".

While visitors might find this cultural mélange blandly familiar, there are ample opportunities – particularly in the Northern Territory – to gain some experience of Australia's **indigenous peoples** and their culture, through ancient art sites, tours and, less easily, personal contact. Especially in central Australia, many Aboriginal people have managed to maintain their traditional way of life (albeit with some modern accoutrements), speaking their own languages and living according to their Law (the *tjukurpa*). Conversely, most Aborigines you'll come across in country towns and cities are prey to what is scathingly referred to as "welfare colonialism": a destructive cycle of poverty and alcoholism arising from the systematic disempowerment of Aboriginal people, and funded by dole cheques. Although there's still a long way to go before black and white people in Australia can exist on genuinely equal terms, gradually improving prospects and the successes of the land rights movement in the wake of the momentous Mabo Decision have seen a sense of pride slowly returning to communities battered by more than two centuries of oppression.

For visitors, deciding **where to go** can be a complicated affair. You could spend months here, driving around the Outback, exploring the national parks, or just hanging out at the beach; or you can take a three-week swing through the populous southeast, checking out the main cities. Both options provide thoroughly Australian experiences; but neither will leave you with a feeling of having more than scraped the surface of this vast country. The two big natural attractions are the two-thousand-kilometre-long **Great Barrier Reef**, with its complex of islands and underwater splendour, and the brooding monolith of **Uluru (Ayers Rock)**, in the Red Centre. As the most impressive, and justifiably the best known, of Australia's attractions, they often form the backbone of pre-packaged tours. You should certainly try to see them, but exploration in other directions will bring you into contact with more subtle but equally rewarding sights and opportunities.

The cities are surprisingly cosmopolitan: waves of post-war immigrants from southern Europe and, more recently, southeast Asia have done much to erode Australia's Anglocentrism. Each Australian state has a capital stamped with its own personality, nowhere more apparent than in New South Wales where glamorous **Sydney** sports almost iconic landmarks in its splendid Opera House and Harbour Bridge. Elsewhere, the sophisticated café society of **Melbourne** (Victoria) contrasts with the vitality of **Brisbane** (Queensland), and **Adelaide**, in South Australia, has a human scale and old-fashioned charm; while in Western Australia, **Perth** camouflages its isolation with a leisure-orientated urbanity. Purpose-built, administrative **Canberra** at the centre of the Australian Capital Territory often fails to grip visitors, but **Darwin**'s frontier eccentricities enliven a visit to the distant lands of the Northern Territory, while in **Hobart**, capital of Tasmania, you'll encounter fine heritage streetscapes and a distinct maritime feel.

Away from the suburbs, with their satellite shopping centres and quarter-acre residential blocks, is the transitional "**bush**" and beyond that the wilderness of the **Outback** – the quintessential Australian experience. Protected from the drier interior, the **East Coast** has the pick of the country's greenery and scenery, from the north's **tropical rainforests** and the Great Barrier Reef to the endless, surf-lined beaches further south. The east coast is backed by the **Great Dividing Range**, which, peaking at the 2228-metre Mount Kosciusko in New South Wales, steadily loses height as it reaches north into tropical Queensland. With time to spare, contemplate a trip to often-forgotten **Tasmania**, across the Bass Strait, an island with vast tracts of wilderness alongside a bucolic, almost English landscape.

## When to go

Australia's **climate** has become less predictable in recent times, although records show that the country has rarely had stable weather patterns over the last few thousand years. Recently observed phenomena, such as an extended drought in the eastern Outback, the cyclic *El Niño* effect, and even the hole in the ozone layer – which is disturbingly close to the country – may in fact be part of a long-term pattern.

Visitors from the northern hemisphere should remember that, as early colonials observed, in Australia "Nature is horribly reversed": when it's winter or summer in the northern hemisphere, the opposite **season** prevails Down Under. Although this is easy to remember, the principle becomes harder to apply to the transitional seasons of spring and autumn. To confuse things further, the four seasons only really exist outside of the tropics in the **southern half of the country**. Here, you'll find reliably warm summers at the coast with regular, but thankfully brief, heatwaves in excess of 40°C. Head inland and the temperatures rise further. Winters, on the other hand, can be miserable, particularly in Victoria, where the short days add to the gloom. Tasmania's highlands make for unpredictable weather all year round, although summer is the best time to explore the island's outdoor attractions.

In the **coastal tropics**, weather basically falls into two seasons. The best time to visit is during the hot and cloudless **Dry** (from April to November), with moderate coastal humidity maintaining a pleasant temperature day and night, and cooler nights inland. In contrast, the **Wet** – particularly the "Build Up" in November or December before the rains – is very uncomfortable, marked by stifling, near-total humidity and plagues of insects. As storm clouds gather, mounting tension, temperatures and humidity can provoke irrational behaviour in the psychologically unacclimatized – known as "going troppo". Nevertheless the mid-Wet's daily downpours and enervating mugginess can be quite intoxicating, compelling a hyper-relaxed inactivity for which these regions are known; furthermore the countryside – when you can reach it – is at its best at this time.

Australia's **interior** is an arid semi-desert with very little rain, high summer temperatures and occasionally freezing winter nights. Unless you're properly equipped to cope with these extremes, the moderate seasons, between April and June, and from October to November, are the most comfortable times to visit.

**In general**, the best time to visit the south is in the Australian summer, from December to March; though long summer holidays from Christmas through January mean higher prices and crowded beaches. In the tropical north, May to October are the best months, and in the Centre, spring and autumn. If you want to tour widely, keep to the southern coasts in summer and head north for the winter.

## AVERAGE TEMPERATURES (°C)

|            | Jan | Feb | Mar | Apr | May | June | July | Aug | Sept | Oct | Nov | Dec |
|------------|-----|-----|-----|-----|-----|------|------|-----|------|-----|-----|-----|
| **Sydney**   | 25 | 25 | 24 | 23 | 20 | 17 | 16 | 17 | 19 | 22 | 23 | 24 |
| **Canberra** | 27 | 25 | 23 | 20 | 15 | 13 | 12 | 13 | 15 | 18 | 22 | 25 |
| **Brisbane** | 27 | 27 | 26 | 25 | 23 | 21 | 23 | 22 | 24 | 25 | 26 | 27 |
| **Cairns**   | 31 | 31 | 30 | 29 | 28 | 25 | 25 | 27 | 27 | 28 | 30 | 31 |
| **Darwin**   | 31 | 30 | 31 | 32 | 31 | 30 | 30 | 31 | 32 | 32 | 33 | 32 |
| **Alice**    | 36 | 35 | 32 | 27 | 22 | 21 | 19 | 21 | 25 | 30 | 32 | 35 |
| **Perth**    | 30 | 30 | 28 | 25 | 22 | 20 | 19 | 19 | 20 | 22 | 25 | 28 |
| **Adelaide** | 28 | 27 | 25 | 22 | 18 | 16 | 14 | 15 | 17 | 21 | 22 | 25 |
| **Melbourne**| 26 | 26 | 24 | 21 | 16 | 15 | 14 | 15 | 17 | 19 | 21 | 23 |
| **Hobart**   | 21 | 21 | 20 | 17 | 14 | 12 | 11 | 12 | 15 | 18 | 19 | 20 |

## AVERAGE RAINFALL (mm)

|            | Jan | Feb | Mar | Apr | May | June | July | Aug | Sept | Oct | Nov | Dec |
|------------|-----|-----|-----|-----|-----|------|------|-----|------|-----|-----|-----|
| **Sydney**   | 100 | 105 | 125 | 130 | 125 | 130 | 110 | 75  | 60  | 75  | 70  | 75  |
| **Canberra** | 55  | 50  | 50  | 45  | 50  | 30  | 30  | 50  | 50  | 70  | 65  | 55  |
| **Brisbane** | 160 | 160 | 150 | 80  | 70  | 60  | 55  | 50  | 50  | 75  | 100 | 140 |
| **Cairns**   | 400 | 440 | 450 | 180 | 100 | 50  | 30  | 25  | 35  | 35  | 90  | 160 |
| **Darwin**   | 400 | 430 | 435 | 75  | 50  | 10  | 5   | 10  | 15  | 70  | 110 | 310 |
| **Alice**    | 35  | 40  | 25  | 20  | 25  | 25  | 20  | 20  | 10  | 25  | 30  | 35  |
| **Perth**    | 10  | 15  | 25  | 50  | 125 | 185 | 175 | 145 | 80  | 75  | 25  | 20  |
| **Adelaide** | 20  | 20  | 25  | 45  | 65  | 70  | 65  | 60  | 55  | 40  | 25  | 20  |
| **Melbourne**| 45  | 50  | 55  | 60  | 55  | 50  | 50  | 50  | 55  | 65  | 55  | 55  |
| **Hobart**   | 50  | 45  | 50  | 55  | 50  | 50  | 45  | 50  | 50  | 55  | 55  | 50  |

# PART ONE

## THE

# BASICS

# GETTING THERE FROM BRITAIN

The market for flights between Britain and Australia is one of the most competitive in the world, and in real terms prices have never been lower. Modern aircraft can now reach the north Australian coast from London in just fifteen hours flying time, though in practice the journey to Sydney or the other eastern cities takes a minimum of twenty-one hours by the time you've stopped and refuelled. If you take a bit longer, breaking the journey in Southeast Asia or North America, it need not be the tedious, seat-bound slog you may have imagined.

A word of warning: don't actually buy your ticket until you're sure that you've been granted a visa (see p.12 for more).

Before booking, you need to decide where you want to fly to in Australia, where you would like to stop en route (or on the way back) and whether you want to use flights to get around once you're there. Sydney and Melbourne are served by the greatest number of airlines, and carriers such as *Qantas* offer the same price to fly to any east coast city from Cairns to Adelaide; flights to Darwin and Perth are often slightly cheaper, but you need to consider the expense of the overland journey from here. An **open-jaw ticket** (flying into one city and out from another) usually costs no more than an ordinary return.

In Britain, all direct **scheduled flights** to Australia depart from London's two main airports, Gatwick and Heathrow, although *Singapore*

*Airlines* have thrice-weekly flights from Manchester to Singapore which connect with onward flights to Sydney. The advent of **charter flights** to Australia hasn't made a huge difference to the flight scene, except perhaps to make prices even more keen. The two charter companies, *Britannia* and *Airtours*, fly from Manchester and London Gatwick, but their flights are bound with restrictions (you must stay for a minimum of 2 weeks but no longer than 8 weeks, and no stopovers are allowed), which can make them a less attractive option.

## FARES

Some eye-catching low fares will be evident in the masses of small ads in the newspapers (the quality Sundays are the best place to start your search), or, in London, in *Time Out* or *TNT*, but in practice these are often unavailable by the time you call. **Booking ahead** as far as possible is the best way to secure the most reasonable prices: it is almost invariably cheaper to buy tickets through **agents**, but we've also given a selection of airlines to show the variety of routes available (see box on p.4).

In the end, you'll find the available flights at much the same price everywhere, the main differential being between the plusher airlines like *Qantas*, *British Airways (BA)* and *Singapore Airlines* – which offer more movies, meals, drinks and comforting accessories – and *Garuda Indonesia* or *Royal Brunei* (to Darwin and Perth only), which are generally the least expensive. The wildcard on the fares scene is held by *Virgin Atlantic*, which will start flying from London to Sydney and Melbourne in 1996 and plans to undercut the prestige airlines' prices.

Tourists and those on one-year working visas (see p.12 for the lowdown on visas) are generally required by Australian immigration to arrive with a ticket out of the country, so one-way tickets are really only viable for Australian and New Zealand residents. If you've purchased a return ticket and find you want to stay longer or head off on a totally different route, it's sometimes possible to cash in the return half of your ticket (though you'll make a loss on the deal) at the travel agent where you bought it: either post it back to them or arrange for someone in the UK to do it on your

## AIRLINES FLYING FROM THE UK TO AUSTRALIA

**Aerolineas Argentinas**, 54 Conduit St, London W1 (☎0171/494 1001). Sydney via Buenos Aires and Auckland.

**Air New Zealand**, *Travel Centre*, ground floor New Zealand House, Haymarket, London SW1 (☎0171/741 2299). To Sydney via Los Angeles 2–4 times a week. Their popular Pacific routing enables a choice of stopovers in Honolulu, Fiji, Western Samoa, the Cook Islands, Tahiti, Tonga and New Zealand.

**Airtours**, Wavell House, Holcombe Rd, Hemshore, Rossendale, Lancashire (☎01706/260 0000). Charter flights from London Gatwick or Manchester, November–April only; package holidays, too – see box on p.6.

**All Nippon Airlines**, Anna House, 6–8 Old Bond St, London W1 (☎0171/355 1155). Daily flights from London Heathrow to Tokyo, with connecting flights daily to Sydney and twice-weekly to Brisbane (Tues and Sat).

**Britannia Airways**, London Luton Airport, Luton, Bedfordshire LU2 9ND (☎01582/424155). Charter flights from London Gatwick and Manchester to Adelaide, Brisbane, Cairns, Melbourne, Perth and Sydney; also London Gatwick to Alice Springs; November–April only.

**British Airways**, 156 Regent St, London W1 (☎0345/22 2111), plus branches throughout the UK. Daily scheduled flights from London Heathrow to all major Australian airports (except Cairns and Darwin) via Bangkok, Singapore or Hong Kong; discounted internal flights with *Ansett, Australian Airlines* and *Qantas*.

**Garuda Indonesia**, 35 Duke St, London W1 (☎0171/486 3011). Three flights a week from London Gatwick via Abu Dhabi and Jakarta (additional stopovers possible in Bangkok and Bali), flying into all major Australian airports.

**Japan Airlines**, 5 Hanover Square, London W1 (☎0171/408 7770). From London Heathrow, daily non-stop flights to Tokyo, 3–4 times weekly to Osaka, with daily connecting flights to Sydney from both airports. Connecting flights to Brisbane and Cairns daily from Tokyo, thrice-weekly from Osaka.

**KLM Royal Dutch Airlines**, Plesman House, 190 Great Southwest Rd, Felton, Middlesex TW6 3RW (☎0181/750 9200). Daily from London Heathrow to Sydney via Amsterdam with an optional stopover in Singapore.

**Malaysia Airlines**, 61 Piccadilly, London W1 (☎0181/740 2600). Thrice weekly flights from London Heathrow to major Australian airports (excluding Cairns) via Kuala Lumpur.

**Qantas**, 182 The Strand, London WC2 (☎0800/ 747 767), plus branches in Birmingham, Leeds and Manchester. Twice-daily flights from London Heathrow to all the mainland Australian state capitals and Cairns, via Singapore and Bangkok; plus discounted internal flights.

**Royal Brunei Airlines**, 49 Cromwell Rd, London (☎0171/584 6660). Twice-weekly flights from London Heathrow to Perth (Wed and Sun); also flights to Darwin or Brisbane – all via Brunei.

**Singapore Airlines**, 143–147 Regent St, London W1 (☎0181/747 0007). Twice daily flights from London Heathrow, and thrice-weekly from Manchester (Tues, Fri & Sat), to Singapore, with connections to Perth, Darwin, Sydney, Melbourne and Adelaide. Discounted internal flights with *Ansett* and *Australian Airlines*.

**South African Airways**, St Georges House, 61 Conduit St, London W1 (☎0171/312 5000). Daily flights to Johannesburg, with thrice-weekly connecting flights to Perth and Sydney.

**Thai International**, 41 Albermarle St, London W1 (☎0171/491 7953). Daily flights to Bangkok from London Heathrow, with connections to Sydney, Melbourne, Brisbane and Perth.

**United**, 193 Piccadilly, London W1 (☎0181/990 9900). Flights from London Heathrow via Los Angeles to Sydney, Melbourne and Brisbane.

**Virgin Atlantic**, Virgin Megastore, Tottenham Court Rd, London W1 (☎01293/747 747). Plans to launch direct flights from London to Sydney and Melbourne in late 1996.

---

behalf. With any international ticket, you can buy a *Qantas Explorer Pass* or an *Ansett G'Day Pass*, both of which entitle you to cheap internal flights, but must be purchased before you leave the UK (see p.23).

The cheapest **scheduled fare** you're likely to find is around £575 return, available during the **low-season** months of April to June; if you insist on flying with *Qantas*, *BA* or *Singapore Airlines*, expect to pay around £730 for a flight in this off-peak period. The most expensive time to fly is in the two weeks before **Christmas**, when you'd be lucky to find anything for less than £1000 return: to stand a chance of getting one of the cheaper tickets, aim to book at least six months in advance. If you do need to make last-minute arrangements at this time of year, enquire about *Garuda* business class, which compares quite favourably with some other airlines' economy fares. In between times (the **shoulder seasons** of July to Nov and Jan to March), you should expect to pay £650–750 (or around £975 with one of the prestige airlines). The lowest **charter fares** start at £499 return, rising through £609–779, up to £909 in the peak Christmas period.

## STOPOVERS AND RTW TICKETS

An excellent alternative to a long direct flight is a **multi-stopover ticket**, which can cost little more than the price of an ordinary return; check out the routing to Australia of the airlines detailed in the box opposite for some ideas. Unusual routes are inevitably more expensive, but it's also possible to fly **via South America** with *Aerolineas Argentinas*, who offer stops in

## DISCOUNT FLIGHT AGENTS

**Auspac Travel**, 3rd floor, Kent House, 87 Regent St, London W1 (☎0171/437 2328). Cheap direct flights, plus round-the-world combinations.

**Austravel**, 50 Conduit St, London W1R 9FB (☎0171/734 7755); 45 Colston St, Bristol, BS1 5AX (☎0117/927425); 3 Barton Arcade, Deansgate, Manchester, M3 2BB (☎0161/832 2445); 16–18 Country Arcade, Victorian Quarter, Leeds LS1 6BN (☎0113/244 8880); 107 Old Christchurch Rd, Bournemouth BH1 1EP (☎01202/311 488). Specialists in *Britannia Airways* charter flights costing from as little as £499, rising to £969 at Christmas. *Austravel* also lays on audio-visual presentations all over the UK to help you make up your mind, including special "Great Escape" events aimed at independent travellers heading round the world via Australia.

**Campus Travel**, 52 Grosvenor Gardens, London SW1W 0AG (☎0171/730 3402); 541 Bristol Rd, Selly Oak, Birmingham (☎0121/414 1848); 39 Queen's Rd, Clifton, Bristol BS8 1QE (☎0117/929 2494); 5 Emmanuel St, Cambridge CB1 1NE (☎01223/324283); 53 Forest Rd, Edinburgh EH1 2QP (☎0131/668 3303); 166 Deansgate, Manchester M3 3FE (☎0161/2731721); 105–106 St Aldates, Oxford OX1 1DD (☎01865/242067). Student/youth travel specialists, with further branches in YHA shops and on university campuses all over Britain.

**Connections**, 93 Wimpole St, London W1M 7DA (☎0171/495 5545). Competitive discount flights to Australia, including *Airtours'* seasonal charters.

**Jupiter Travel**, 14 Rathbone Place, London W1 (☎0171/436 2711). Dingy offices but cheap and reliable with multi-stopover and RTW tickets to Australia; often special charter flight deals to Australia with *Airtours*.

**The London Flight Centre**, 131 Earls Court Rd, London (☎0171/244 6411); 47 Notting Hill Gate, London (☎0171/727 4290); 118 Gloucester Road, London (☎0171/244 0475). Long-established agent

dealing in discount flights; vaccinations and Australian visas arranged at the Earls Court office.

**Quest Worldwide**, 29 Castle St, Kingston, Surrey, KT1 1ST (☎0181 547 3322). Specialists in RTW and Australian discount fares.

**South Coast Student Travel**, 61 Ditchling Rd, Brighton BN1 4SD (☎01273/570226). Student experts, but plenty to offer non-students as well.

**STA Travel**, 74 Old Brompton Rd, London SW7 3LH (☎0171/937 9962); 25 Queen's Rd, Bristol BS8 1QE (☎0117/929 3399); 38 Sidney St, Cambridge CB2 3HX (☎01223/66966); 75 Deansgate, Manchester M3 2BW (☎0161/834 0668); and personal callers at 117 Euston Rd, London NW1; 28 Vicar Lane, Leeds LS1 7JH; 36 George St, Oxford OX1 2OJ; plus offices at the universities of Birmingham, London, Kent and Loughborough. Discount fares, with particularly good deals for students and young people; Australian experts, with branches in Australia.

**Trailfinders**, 42–50 Earls Court Rd, London W8 6FT (☎0171/938 3366); 194 Kensington High St, London, W8 7RG (☎0171/938 3939); 58 Deansgate, Manchester M3 2FF (☎0161/839 6969); 48 Corn St, Bristol BS1 1HQ (☎0117/929 9000); 254–284 Sauchiehall St, Glasgow G2 3EH (☎0141/353 2224). Excellent for multi-stop and RTW tickets, including some unusual routings via South Africa, the Pacific and the USA. Well-informed and efficient – visa service available at the Kensington High Street branch.

**Travel Bag**, 373–375 The Strand, London WC2 (☎0171/497 0515). Discount flights.

**Travel Bug**, 125A Gloucester Rd, London, SW7 (☎0171/835 2000); 597 Cheetham Hill Rd, Manchester (☎0161/721 4000). Particularly good deals with *All Nippon Airlines* and *Japan Airlines*; *Austravel* charter flights also sold.

**Travelmood**, 246 Edgware Rd, London W2 (☎0171/258 0280). Direct and RTW flights.

Brazil, Buenos Aires and New Zealand – at least £900 return – or **via Africa** with *South African Airways*, who offer return fares via Johannesburg to Perth and Sydney from close to £900, with the added bonus of discounted internal flights to Harare (Botswana), Victoria Falls, Nairobi and many other African destinations. You can also often get good deals via **Japan** on *All Nippon Airlines* and *Japan Airlines*.

More expensive, but still good value, **round the world** (RTW) tickets incorporating Australia provide a chance to see the world on your way to and from down under. RTW flights come prepackaged in a tantalizing variety of permutations, with stopovers chiefly in Asia, the Pacific and North America, but you can pretty much devise your fantasy itinerary and get it priced. A good agent should be able to piece together sector fares from various airlines: prices range from around £750 to well over £1000. It's also possible to incorporate substantial overland segments for variety, such as London–Delhi–overland to Kathmandu–Bangkok–Sydney–overland to Cairns–Western Samoa–Honolulu–Los Angeles–Calgary–Toronto–London from £980.

## PACKAGES AND ORGANIZED TOURS

There are relatively few traditional **package holidays** available – nobody's going to fly all the way to Australia just to spend a couple of weeks on the beach – but if your time is short and you're reasonably sure of what you want to do, it may not be a bad idea to pre-book some of your accommodation, tours and vehicle rental. Many companies offer minimal packages, consisting of a flight with some accommodation and a couple of tours. Full "see-it-all" packages can work out quite expensive – to say nothing of being rather tame and controlled – but aren't bad value, considering what you'd be spending anyway.

The ultimate package must be the sea trip to Australia from England: both *Cunard Line* and *P&O* sail from Southampton in mid-December or early January, arriving in February. To arrive in style, cruising into Sydney Harbour, you'll need somewhere in the region of £4000 (or £8000+ for *Cunard's QE2*, including return flight) to spare…

Many of the Australian specialists also offer such things as **bus and train passes** (see p.24–25), discounted hotel vouchers, and the like, all of which are worth considering.

### PACKAGE-TOUR AND SPECIALIST OPERATORS

*Some discount flight agents also arrange tours and accommodation – check out* Austravel *and* Trailfinders, *among others – see box on p.5.*

**Airtours** (☎01706/260 0000). Basic charter-flight packages from £499 for 14 nights with two nights' accommodation in Sydney.

**Contiki** (☎0181/290 6422). Big group, country-wide bus tours for 18–35 year olds "thriving on good times and loads of fun". All transport and most meals covered; plenty of additional excursions (hot-air ballooning, diving, etc) at extra cost.

**Cunard Line** (☎01703/634166). Cruises to Sydney, Adelaide, Brisbane or Perth, including a yearly excursion on their flagship *QE2*.

**Explore Worldwide** (☎01252/319448). Bus and four-wheel-drive tours right across Australia through desert, rainforest and reef, ranging from two weeks to five-week treks for £2500.

**Jetabout** (☎0181/741 3111). *Qantas'* package-holiday arm, specializing in tailor-made itineraries, as well as vehicle rentals and a couple of see-it-all deals.

**Newmans Travel** (☎01252/734644). Australian-based company offering two-day to two-week escorted bus tours costing around £100 a day, self-drive tours (including self-contained motorhomes from £50 a day), as well as *Flag* hotel passes.

**P&O** (☎0171/800 2345). Cruises to Australia, via Africa and Southeast Asia.

**Travel Bag** (☎0171/497 0515). Everything from flights to car and campervan rental, farmstays and tours all over the country, including a whistlestop seven-day Sydney–Rock–Reef trip for £2600.

**Travelmood** (☎0171/258 0280). Flights, quality accommodation, car and campervan rental.

**Twickers World** (☎0181/892 8164). Tours of Australia's environmentally significant areas such as the Queensland rainforest and reef (nine days from £870), the Territory's Top End (five days from £264), the central deserts and Western Australia's wildflower regions.

## GETTING THERE FROM IRELAND

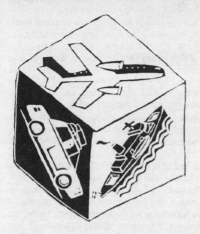

**Flying from Ireland, prices are rather higher, but since you can't fly direct anyway, the choice of routes and airlines is if anything even wider.**

Although most of the cheaper routings involve a stopover in London and transfer to one of the airlines listed above, there are also often good deals on *Air France* flying Dublin–Paris–Sydney,

*Olympic* via Greece, or with *Garuda Indonesia*. Shannon and Cork airports are also served by *British Airways, Qantas, Singapore Airlines* and *Malaysia Airlines,* with fares starting from around IR£850 for an open one-year return in low season. For youth and student discount fares, the best first stop is *USIT* (see box below for address).

When it comes to **packages**, you're best off contacting one of the UK-based companies listed above, or booking through one of the agents in the box below.

---

### FLIGHTS, PACKAGES AND TOURS

**Budget Travel**, 134 Lower Baggot St, Dublin (☎01/661 1866). Discount flights.

**Thomas Cook**, 118 Grafton St, Dublin (☎01/677 1721). Mainstream package-holiday and flight agent, with occasional discount offers.

**Unijet**, Unit 3, Lyndon Court, Queen St, Belfast (☎01232/314656). Discount scheduled fares.

**USIT**, Branches at: Aston Quay, O'Connell Bridge, Dublin (☎01/679 8833); 10–11 Market Parade, Cork (☎021/270 900); Fountain Centre, College St, Belfast (☎01232/324073). Student and youth specialist.

---

## GETTING THERE FROM ASIA – THE OVERLAND ROUTE

**A satisfying way of getting to Australia and really getting some impression of the distance you've travelled is to make your way overland through Southeast Asia. Bangkok, in Thailand, is a popular starting-point. Return flights to Bangkok are available from around £400 in the UK and US$600 in the USA.**

Plenty of people make this journey, especially Australian backpackers heading in the other direction at the start of their travels. Southeast Asia won't be as straightforward or relaxing as Australia (and you'll need to take appropriate health precautions), but it'll certainly be a fascinating, eye-opening experience and it won't make a big dent in your budget. From Bangkok an inexpensive **bus** service leaves twice-daily for

Singapore, though it's a gruelling two-day journey unless you make a stop or two along the way. First-time visitors might find it more comfortable to take the daily **train** to Singapore, taking 28 hours for the near-2000km journey and costing £60/US$S90; book a day or two in advance to be sure of a seat.

From Singapore, you can cross to Sumatra or Kalimantan (both islands in the Indonesian archipelago) and from there continue south to Java and then island-hop, via Bali, to Kupang in East Timor using the extensive network of low-cost country buses and ferries. From Kupang an inexpensive twice-weekly *Merpati* flight can be caught to Darwin, though you can just as easily take a regular flight to Australia from Singapore, Jakarta or Denpasar if you've had enough by this stage. Allow about a month from Bangkok to Kupang, and count on living expenses of at least £5/US$7.50 a day, not including flights.

For more information and advice to help you plan your travels in this area, consult the **Rough Guides** to *Thailand; Malaysia, Singapore and Brunei*, and *Bali*.

## GETTING THERE FROM NEW ZEALAND

**Flights from New Zealand to Australia are subject to an ever-changing range of deals and special offers, so you might well find fares to beat those below.**

The cheapest scheduled return **fares** to Sydney are with *Thai* (3 weekly, NZ$559 low season/NZ$618 high season), and to Brisbane with *Malaysian Airways* (3 weekly, NZ$625–690, depending on season), but these tend to be booked up well in advance. Because they each fly twice daily, *Qantas* and *Air New Zealand* seldom have this problem: they fly direct to Sydney (NZ$625/690), Brisbane (NZ$725/800), and Cairns (NZ$955/1055). Sample **open-jaw** fares from Auckland – flying into one city and out of another, and making your own way between – with *Qantas* or *ANZ* – are as follows: into Sydney and out of Brisbane, NZ$825 (low season); into Sydney and out of Cairns, NZ$1190; into Brisbane and out of Cairns, NZ$1110. There are also various internal flight deals available for purchase with your main ticket (see "Getting Around", p.23–24, for details).

There are no courier flights to Australia anymore – and no regular trans-Tasman ferries either. Cruise **ships** do come down from the Pacific between November and January, but again they're not on a regular basis and you'll need to consult a travel agent to find out what's available.

### DISCOUNT AGENTS AND SPECIALIST OPERATORS

**Australia Travel Bureau**, 145 Kitchener Rd, Milford, Auckland (☎09/486 2549).

**Budget Travel**, 16 Fort St, Auckland; other branches around the city (free call ☎0800/80 8040).

**Flight Centres**, National Bank Towers, 205–225 Queen St, Auckland (☎09/309 6171); Shop 1M, National Mutual Arcade, 152 Hereford St, Christchurch (☎09/379 7145); 50–52 Willis St, Wellington (☎04/472 8101); other branches countrywide.

**Go Travel**, 151 Victoria St West, Auckland (☎09/379 5520).

**Mister Travel**, AA Centre, 99 Albert St, Auckland (☎09/309 6152).

**STA Travellers' Centre**, 10 High St, Auckland (☎09/309 0450); 233 Cuba St, Wellington (☎04/385 0561); 223 High St, Christchurch (☎03/379 9098); other offices in Dunedin, Palmerston North and Hamilton.

# GETTING THERE FROM THE USA AND CANADA

From Los Angeles it's possible to fly non-stop to Sydney in fifteen hours. **Qantas, United, Continental, Canadian Airlines** and **Air New Zealand** all operate direct to the east coast of Australia. Most other flights stop at Honolulu, the hub for trans-Pacific connections, Papeete or Auckland – usually at more than one of these. You can also travel via Southeast Asia; Bangkok, Singapore and Kuala Lumpur are the main interchanges in this area.

Most major airlines offer "**Pacific Circle**" deals which allow four extra stopovers at Pacific rim destinations such as Tokyo, Honolulu or Kuala Lumpur, at no extra cost if tickets are bought at least two weeks in advance. **Round the world** (RTW) tickets offer very good value for an extended trip, lasting up to a year and allowing stopovers in Southeast Asia and Europe before returning to the USA or Canada.

## FARES

Fares vary significantly according to **season** – most airlines regard December to February as the high season, April to August as the low season, and other times as shoulder; note also that midweek fares tend to be cheaper than weekend departures. Inevitably, prices are at their highest over Christmas and New Year, and seats are at a premium.

Typical lowest standard **scheduled fares** to Sydney, Melbourne or Cairns (not including airport tax) for low/high seasons are as follows: Chicago ($1348/$1548); Los Angeles ($1048/$1348); Montréal (CDN$1818/$2188); New York ($1398/$1758); San Francisco ($1048/$1348); Seattle ($1208/$1498); Toronto (CDN$1818/$2188); Vancouver (CDN$1538/$1908). For Perth or Darwin add about $400. The price of an **open-jaw ticket** (flying into one city and returning from another) should be approximately the average of the round trip fares to the two cities.

**Charter flights** to Australia, a recent arrival on the scene, are mostly available through agents such as *Jetset Vacations* (☎1800-NET-FARE or 638 3273), *Qantas Vacations* (☎1800/641 8772) and *Pacific Experience* (☎1800/233 4255). Fares may slightly undercut those on scheduled flights, but this is offset by more restrictions to contend with, so check conditions carefully. There are **no courier flights** to Australia.

---

### AIRLINES FLYING FROM THE USA & CANADA TO AUSTRALIA

**Air New Zealand** (☎1800/262 1234; in Canada, ☎1800/563 5494). Flights from LA with stopovers throughout the Polynesian isles.

**Canadian Airlines** (in Canada, ☎1800/665 1177; in US, ☎1800/426 7000). Flights from Canadian cities via Vancouver.

**Continental** (☎1800/231 0856). Services from many US cities (via Los Angeles/San Francisco) to Sydney, Brisbane and Melbourne.

**Garuda Indonesia** (☎1800/342 7832; in Canada, ☎1800/663 2254). Eastbound connections from Los Angeles, stopping in Jakarta.

**Malaysian Airlines** (☎1800/421 8641). Flights from LA to Perth via Kuala Lumpur.

**Qantas** (☎1800/227 4500). Services from Los Angeles and San Francisco with direct feeds from many other cities; discounted internal flight coupons available.

**Singapore Airlines** (☎1800/742 3333). Australian connections from Los Angeles, via Singapore.

**Thai International** (☎1800/426 5204; in Canada, ☎1800/668 8103). Flights from LA via Bangkok.

**United** (☎1800/538 2929). Flights from most US cities via Los Angeles, San Francisco and Honolulu.

## SHOPPING FOR TICKETS

A specialist flight agent is generally the best starting point – either a **consolidator**, who buys up blocks of tickets from the airlines and sells them at a discount, or a **discount agent**, who wheels and deals in blocks of tickets offloaded by the airlines, and often offers special student and youth fares and a range of other travel-related services such as travel insurance, bus and train passes, car rentals, tours and the like. Bear in mind, though, that penalties for changing your plans can be stiff. Remember too that these companies make their money by dealing in bulk – don't expect them to answer lots of questions.

If you travel a lot, **discount travel clubs** are another option – the annual membership fee may be worth it for benefits such as cut-price air tickets and car rental. Many airlines offer youth or student fares to **under 26s**; a passport or driving licence are sufficient proof of age, though these tickets are subject to availability and can have eccentric booking conditions.

Don't automatically assume that tickets purchased through a travel specialist will be cheapest – once you get a quote, check with the airlines and you may turn up an even better deal. Be advised also that the pool of travel companies is swimming with sharks – exercise caution and *never* deal with a company that demands cash up front or refuses to accept payment by credit card.

Price isn't the only criterion when shopping for a ticket. Some specialists offer stopovers in any of a number of exotic South Pacific ports of call for $100 each (the first may be free), or interesting routings through Far Eastern cities for little or no extra money. Some also sell "**Pacific Circle**" deals, which allow up to four stopovers each way (from $2450 from the West Coast, $2770 from the East Coast). There are also deals on *Qantas* involving free or low-price flights within Australia (see "Getting Around", p.23, for more on these and internal air passes). **Round the world tickets** start at around $2550, are valid for a maximum of a year, and allow stopovers in Southeast Asia and Europe, although they do tend to limit flexibility.

## PACKAGE TOURS

Organized **tours** of Australia are usually tailored for those short on time and long on funds; that

## DISCOUNT FLIGHT AGENTS, TRAVEL CLUBS AND CONSOLIDATORS IN THE USA AND CANADA

**Air Brokers International**, 323 Geary St, Suite 411, San Francisco, CA 94102 (☎1800/883 3273). West Coast consolidator.

**Austravel**, 51 E 42nd St, New York, NY 10017 (☎1800/633 3404 or 212/972 6880), with other locations in Chicago, Houston and San Francisco. Full-service agency offering flights and customized tours.

**Council Travel**, 205 E 42nd St, New York, NY 10017 (☎1800/743 1823), and branches in many other US cities. Student travel organization.

**Interworld Travel**, 800 Douglass Rd, Miami, FL 33134 (☎305/443 4929). Southeastern US consolidator.

**Moment's Notice**, 425 Madison Ave, New York, NY 10017 (☎212/486 0503). Travel club good for last-minute deals.

**New Frontiers/Nouvelles Frontières**, 12 E 33rd St, New York, NY 10016 (☎1800/366 6387); 1001 Sherbrook East, Suite 720, Montréal, H2L 1L3 (☎514/526 8444 ); and other branches in LA, San Francisco and Québec City. French discount travel firm.

**STA Travel**, 48 E 11th St, New York, NY 10003 (☎1800/777 0112), and other branches in the Los Angeles, San Francisco and Boston areas. Worldwide specialist in independent travel.

**Travel Avenue**, 10 S Riverside, Suite 1404, Chicago, IL 60606 (☎1800/333 3335). Rebate travel agency offering the lowest possible fares for independent travellers who have already worked out their itinerary and are ready to book.

**Travel CUTS**, 187 College St, Toronto, Ontario, M5T 1P7 (☎416/979 2406), and other branches all over Canada. Student travel organization.

**Travelers Advantage**, 3033 S Parker Rd, Suite 900, Aurora, CO 80014 (☎1800/548 1116). Full-service travel agency providing guaranteed low prices to members; discounts on airlines and hotels around the world.

**UniTravel**, 1177 N Warson Rd, St Louis, MO 63132 (☎1800/325 2222). Reliable consolidator.

**Worldwide Discount Travel Club**, 1674 Meridian Ave, Miami Beach, FL 33139 (☎305/534 2082). Discounted prices for members on tours and cruises; five percent off airline tickets, but you have to make your own reservations.

said, even independent travellers may want to build their stay around one or two planned activities arranged through a tour company. Several of the operators below offer so-called **city modules**, providing three or four nights' accommodation, cab vouchers and perhaps a day tour, all for as little as $200. Though **fly/drive** deals don't always make sense in sprawling Australia, they're worth considering if you plan to explore just one part of the country closely. Typical prices for the smallest class of car work out at about $65 a day. And even if a package tour is the furthest thing from your mind, you may want to check out tour or specialist operators before you leave home for **rail** or **bus passes** (see p.24–25 for some of the options).

## US AND CANADIAN TOUR OPERATORS

**Abercrombie and Kent International** (☎1800/323 7308). Offers 13- and 21-day general interest tours of Australia, plus a 20-day "Natural Wonders" package exploring the Outback and Aboriginal culture.

**ATS Tours** (☎1800/423 2880). Huge Australasian specialist; ask for the *Sprint* department for diving deals, fly/drives, rail/bus passes, motel vouchers and other independent add-ons.

**Australian Pacific Tours** (☎1800/290 8687). General interest escorted tours and safaris.

**Destination World** (☎1800/426 3644). Off the beaten track tours – including a pub-crawling expedition, among others.

**Down Under Direct** (☎1800/642 6224). Specialist in independent budget tours.

**Earthwatch** (☎617/926 8200). Arranges placements for paying volunteers in scientifc projects around the country.

**Explore Worldwide** (☎1800/227 8747; in Canada, ☎1800/661 7265). Bus and four-wheel-drive tours right across Australia through desert, rainforest and reef, ranging from two weeks to five-week treks for US$3800.

**Globus and Cosmos Tourama** (☎1800/851 0722). Escorted tours, several combining Australia with Fiji and Tahiti.

**Maupintour** (☎1800/255 4266). A variety of general interest and specialist tours.

**Mount Cook Line** (☎1800/468 2665). New Zealand-based company that also offers city modules and tours in Australia.

**Mountain Travel Sobek** (☎1800/227 2384). Trips include sea kayaking in Queensland, river rafting in Tasmania and natural history tours.

**Nature Expeditions International** (☎1800/869 0639). Natural history tours accompanied by a lecturer; three-week itineraries take in the Outback and the Great Barrier Reef.

**Qantas Vacations** (☎1800/641 8772). *Qantas*' tour arm.

**See and Sea Travel Service Inc** (☎1800/348 9778). Independent diving excursions to Australia.

**Swain Australia Tours** (☎1800/22 SWAIN). Australian company offering custom itineraries and tours.

**Tauck Tours** (☎1800/468 2825). 15- and 21-day tours, with optional extensions to Fiji.

**Tropical Adventures** (☎1800/247 3843). Specialists in scuba-diving vacations to Australia and neighbouring islands.

**United Vacations** (☎1800/351 4200). Varied assortment of individual tours.

**World Travelers** (☎1800/426 3610). A selection of Australia packages including watersports, wine tours and cycling.

## VISAS AND RED TAPE

All visitors to Australia, except New Zealanders, require a visa; and, if you're heading overland, you'll obviously need to check visa requirements for countries en route. Three-month tourist visas for Australia are issued free and processed over the counter providing all your documentation and other details are in order, or returned in three weeks by mail. Visits from three to six months incur a fee (in the UK, £16; in the US, $25); if you think you might stay more than three months it's best to get the longer visa before departure as extensions once in Australia cost A$200 (around £93 or $US150). Once issued, a visa is usually valid for multiple entries so long as your passport is valid.

An important condition for all visa applications is that you have **adequate funds** both to support yourself during your stay – around A$1000 a month – and eventually to get yourself home again. As a precaution, you shouldn't actually buy your airline ticket until you're sure that you have been granted a visa. Citizens of the United States can get Australian visas from *Qantas* offices in San Francisco or Los Angeles when they buy their tickets.

**Working Holiday Visas**, valid for one year, are available easily for anyone over 18 and under 26 (and with a little more difficulty for those under 30), who are citizens of the UK, Ireland, the Netherlands, Canada or Japan, who have no children and who have not previously applied for such a visa. In the UK working holiday visas cost £71 and applicants must show evidence of at least £2000 to help support them during their stay. The sort of work you're expected to undertake is temporary and casual labour such as fruit-picking or station work, though your own experience or panache may briefly secure you more career-orientated employment.

If you're visiting immediate family who live in Australia – parent, spouse, child, brother or sister – you can apply for a **Close Family Visa**, which has fewer restrictions.

Having a visa is not an absolute guarantee that you'll be allowed into Australia – immigration officials may well check again that you have enough money to cover you during your stay, and that you have a return or onward ticket. In extreme cases they may refuse entry, or more likely restrict your visit to a shorter period.

### CUSTOMS

Australia has strict **quarantine** laws that apply to fruit, vegetables, fresh and packaged food, seed and some animal products, among other things; there are also strict laws prohibiting drugs, steroids, firearms, protected wildlife and associated products. Those over 18 can take advantage of a **duty-free allowance** on entry of one litre of alcohol and 250 cigarettes or 250g of tobacco.

### AUSTRALIAN EMBASSIES AND CONSULATES ABROAD

**United Kingdom**

**London** Australian High Commission, Australia House, Strand, London WC2B 4LA (☎0171/379 4334).

**Manchester** Australian Consulate, Chatsworth House, Lever St, Manchester M1 2DL (☎0161/228 1344).

**United States**

**Washington** Australian Embassy, 1601 Massachusetts Ave NW, Washington DC 20036 (☎202/797 3000).

**Chicago** Australian Consulate-General, Suite 2930, 321 N Clark St, Chicago, IL 60610 (☎312/645 9440). **continues**

## EMBASSIES AND CONSULATES (continued)

**Honolulu** Australian Consulate-General, 1000 Bishop St, Honolulu, HI 96813 (☎808/524 5050).

**Houston** Australian Consulate-General, Suite 800, 3 Post Oak Central, 1990 South Post Oak Blvd, Houston, TX 77056–9998 (☎713/629 9131).

**Los Angeles** Australian Consulate-General, 611 N Larchmont Blvd, Los Angeles, CA 90004 (☎213/469 4300).

**New York** Australian Consulate-General, International Bldg, 636 Fifth Ave, New York, NY 10111 (☎212/245 4000).

**San Francisco** Australian Consulate-General, 1 Bush St, San Francisco, CA 94104 (☎510/362 6160).

### Canada

**Ottawa** Australian High Commission, Suite 710, 50 O'Connor St, Ottawa, Ontario K1P 6L2 (☎613/236 0841).

**Toronto** Australian Consulate-General, Suite 2200, Commerce Court W, corner of King and Bay streets, Toronto, Ontario M5 1B9 (☎416/367 0783).

**Vancouver** Australian Consulate-General, World Trade Office Complex, 602–999 Canada Place, Vancouver, BC V6C 3E1 (☎604/684 1177).

### Denmark

Australian Embassy, Kristianagade 21, DK-2100 Copenhagen (☎3526 2244).

### Indonesia

**Jakarta** Australian Embassy, Jalan Thamrin 15, Jakarta (☎021/32 3109).

**Bali** Australian Consulate, Jalan Prof Moh Yamin 51, Renon, Denpasar, Bali (☎0361/35 092).

### Ireland

Australian Embassy, Fitzwilton House, Wilton Terrace, Dublin 2 (☎01/76 1517).

### Malaysia

Australian High Commission, 6 Jalan Yap Kwan Seng, Kuala Lumpur 50450 (☎242 3122).

### Netherlands

Australian Embassy, Carnegielaan 12, 2517 KH Den Haag (☎310 8200).

### New Zealand

**Wellington** Australian High Commission, 72–78 Hobson St, Thorndon, Wellington (☎473 6411).

**Auckland** Australian Consulate-General, Union House, 32–38 Quay St, Auckland 1 (☎09/303 2429).

### Singapore

Australian High Commission, 25 Napier Rd, Singapore 1025 (☎737 9311).

### South Africa

Australian Embassy, Mutual and Federal Bldg, 220 Vermuelen St, Pretoria 001 (☎12/342 3740).

### Sweden

Australian Embassy, Sergels Torg 12, Stockholm (☎08/613 2900).

### Thailand

Australian Embassy, 37 South Sathorn Rd, Bangkok 10120 (☎02/287 2680).

# INSURANCE

If you're entitled to free emergency **healthcare** from *Medicare* (see p.19 for details of reciprocal arrangements), you may feel that the need for the health element of travel insurance is reduced, but check carefully what is included (ambulance trips, among other things, will not be reimbursed). In any case, some form of **travel insurance** can help plug the gaps and will cover you in the event of losing your baggage, missing a plane and the like. Check, also, what cover you already have in other areas: some **home** policies cover your possessions abroad, for example, and if you pay for your trip with a **credit card**, some limited cover may well be provided by the credit card company (check the small print on this, though, as it may not be much use).

Note that very few insurers will arrange on-the-spot payments in the event of a major expense or loss; you will usually be reimbursed only after going home. In all case of loss or theft of goods, you will have to contact the local police

to have a report made out so that your insurer can process the claim. If you plan to participate in any **"high-risk" activities** – and, depending on the insurer, this can extend to watersports (especially diving), skiing or even just hiking – you'll probably have to pay an extra premium; check carefully that any policy you are considering will cover you in case of an accident.

In **Britain and Ireland**, travel insurance schemes are sold by almost every travel agent or bank, and by specialist insurance companies (see box below). Decent single-trip policies start at around £35 a month, but *Columbus* and some banks also offer a multi-trip policy for an annual fee of around £125.

## US AND CANADIAN TRAVELLERS

Before buying an insurance policy, check that you're not already covered. **Canadians** are usually covered for medical mishaps overseas by their provincial health plans. Holders of official **student/teacher/youth cards** are entitled to accident coverage and hospital in-patient benefits. **Students** will often find that their student health coverage extends during the vacations and for one term beyond the date of last enrolment. Bank and credit cards (particularly *American Express*) often have certain levels of medical or

---

### UK TRAVEL INSURANCE COMPANIES

**Columbus Travel Insurance**, 17 Devonshire Square, London EC2M 4SQ (☎0171/375 0011).

**Endsleigh Insurance**, 97–107 Southampton Row, London WC1B 4AG (☎0171/436 4451).

**Frizzell Insurance**, Frizzell House, County Gates, Bournemouth, Dorset BH1 2NF (☎01202/292 333).

**Note**: *Good-value policies are also available through* **Campus Travel** *and* **STA** *(see p.5 for addresses).*

---

### TRAVEL INSURANCE COMPANIES IN NORTH AMERICA

**Access America**, PO Box 90310, Richmond, VA 23230 (☎1800/284 8300).

**Carefree Travel Insurance**, PO Box 310, 120 Mineola Blvd, Mineola, NY 11501 (☎1800/323 3149).

**International Student Insurance Service (ISIS)** – sold by *STA Travel*, which has several branches in the US (head office is 48 E 11th St, New York, NY 10003; ☎1800/777 0112).

**Travel Assistance International**, 1133 15th St NW, Suite 400, Washington, DC 20005 (☎1800/821 2828).

**Travel Guard**, 1145 Clark St, Stevens Point, WI 54481 (☎1800/826 1300).

**Travel Insurance Services**, 2930 Camino Diablo, Suite 300, Walnut Creek, CA 94596 (☎1800/937 1387).

other insurance included, and travel insurance may also be included if you use a major credit or charge card to pay for your trip. **Homeowners' or renters'** insurance often covers theft or loss of documents, money and valuables while overseas, though conditions and maximum amounts vary from company to company.

After exhausting the possibilities above, you might want to contact a specialist **travel insurance** company; your travel agent can usually recommend one, or see the box opposite. Policies generally cover accidents, illnesses, delayed or lost luggage, cancelled flights and so on, but most exclude theft, covering only items lost, stolen or damaged while in the custody of an identifiable and responsible third party – hotel porter, airline, luggage consignment, etc. Premiums vary, so shop around. The best deals are usually from student/youth travel agencies – ISIS policies, for example, cost $48–69 for fifteen days (depending on coverage), $80–105 for a month, $149–207 for two months, on up to $510–700 for a year.

# TRAVELLERS WITH DISABILITIES

**The vast distances between Australia's cities and popular tourist resorts present visitors with mobility difficulties with a unique challenge, but overall travel in Australia for people with disabilities is rather easier than it would be in the UK and Europe.**

The federal government provides information and various nationwide services through the **National Information Communications Awareness Network** (NICAN) and the **Australian Council for the Rehabilitation of the Disabled** (ACROD) – see box below for contact details. The **Australian Tourist Commission** offices provide a helpline service and publish a factsheet, *Travelling in Australia for People with Disabilities*, available from its offices worldwide (see p.17 for addresses and phone numbers).

Disability needn't interfere with your sightseeing: the attitude of the management at Australia's major tourist attractions is excellent, and they will provide assistance where they can. For example, you can view the rock art at Kakadu National Park, do a tour around the base of Uluru (Ayers Rock), snorkel unhindered on the Great Barrier Reef (contact *Great Adventures* at Cairns, ☎1800/079 080 or *Quicksilver* at Port Douglas, ☎070/31 4299), do a cruise around Sydney Harbour, or see the penguins at Phillip Island.

## PLANNING A HOLIDAY

There are **organized tours and holidays** specifically for people with disabilities: the contacts in the box will be able to put you touch with any specialists for trips to Australia; several are listed in the ATC factsheet. If you want to be more independent, it's important to become an authority on where you must be self-reliant and where you may expect help, especially regarding transport and accommodation. It is also vital to be honest – with travel agencies, insurance companies and travel companions. Know your limitations and make sure others know them. If you do not use a wheelchair all the time but your walking capabilities are limited, remember that you are likely to need to cover greater distances while travelling (often over rougher terrain and in hotter temperatures) than you are used to. If you use a wheelchair, have it serviced before you go and carry a repair kit.

Read your **travel insurance** small print carefully to make sure that people with a pre-existing medical condition are not excluded. And use your travel agent to make your journey simpler: airline or bus companies can cope better if they are expecting you, with a wheelchair provided at airports and staff primed to help. A **medical certificate** of your fitness to travel, provided by your doctor, is also extremely useful; some airlines or insurance companies may insist on it. Make sure that you have extra supplies of drugs – carried with you if you fly – and a prescription including the generic name in case of emergency.

## ACCOMMODATION

Much of Australia's tourist accommodation is well set up for people with disabilities: partly because buildings tend to be built outwards rather than upwards, partly because any new constructions have to comply with legal minimum **accessibility standards**. This standard requires that bathrooms contain toilets at the appropriate height, circulation space, wheel-in showers

## BEFORE YOU LEAVE: USEFUL ORGANIZATIONS

### UK

**Holiday Care Service**, 2 Old Bank Chambers, Station Rd, Horley, Surrey RH6 9HW (☎01293/ 774535). Information on all aspects of travel.

**Mobility International**, 228 Borough High St, London SE1 1JX (☎0171/403 5688). Information, access guides, tours and exchange programmes.

**RADAR**, 25 Mortimer St, London W1N 8AB (☎0171/637 5400). A good source of advice on holidys and travel abroad.

### USA

**Directions Unlimited**, 720 N Bedford Rd, Bedford Hills, NY 10507 (☎1800/533 5343). Tour operator specializing in custom tours for people with disabilities.

**Mobility International USA**, PO Box 10767, Eugene, OR 97440 (Voice and TDD: ☎503/343 1284). Information and referral services, access guides, tours and exchange programs. Annual membership $20 (includes quarterly newsletter).

**Society for the Advancement of Travel for the Handicapped** (SATH), 347 5th Ave, New York, NY 10016 (☎212/447 7284). Non-profit travel-industry referral service; allow plenty of time for a response.

**Travel Information Service**, Moss Rehabilitation Hospital, 1200 West Tabor Rd, Philadelphia, PA 19141 (☎215/456 9600). Telephone information and referral service.

**Twin Peaks Press**, Box 129, Vancouver, WA 98666; ☎206/694 2462 or 1800/637 2256). Publisher of the *Directory of Travel Agencies for the Disabled* ($19.95), listing more than 370 agencies worldwide; *Travel for the Disabled* ($14.95); the *Directory of Accessible Van Rentals* and *Wheelchair Vagabond* ($9.95), loaded with personal tips.

### CANADA

**Jewish Rehabilitation Hospital**, 3205 Place Alton Goldbloom, Montréal, PQ H7V 1R2 (☎514/ 688 9550, ext 226). Guidebooks and travel information.

(sometimes with fold-down seat, but if this is lacking, proprietors will provide a plastic chair), and grab rails. The best place to start is the *A–Z Australian Accommodation Guide* published by the *Australian Automobile Association* (*AAA*) – the umbrella organization for state- and territory-based motoring associations that rate accommodation. They also offer some specialized services, a centralized **booking service** and a repair service for motorized wheelchairs, with reciprocal rights if you are a member of an affiliated overseas motoring organization. The guide is available from any of the state organizations; *NICAN* also has access to their database via computer, so you can choose your accommodation over the phone.

In the **cities** the hotels at the top of the price range – the *Hyatt, Sheraton, Accor* and other big chains – have rooms with wheelchair access. Some of the smaller hotels do provide accessible accommodation and a large proportion of suburban motels will have one or two suitable rooms. In the **country** there are fewer specially equipped hotels, but many motels (which tend to be on one level anyway) have accessible units; this is particularly true of those that belong to a chain such as *Flag* – consult their directories for locations (see p.32 for contact details). The latest YHA **hostels** are all accessible, and a review of

all hostels is attempting to improve facilities; accessible hostels are detailed in the *YHA Handbook*, or contact them direct (see box). **Caravan parks** are also worth considering, since some have accessible cabins.

In all cases, you should check what facilities are available rather than assuming it will be OK for your particular needs. An example of the **progressive attitude** found in the country's more popular areas is the *Wheel Resort*, 39–51 Broken Head Road, Byron Bay, NSW 2481 (☎066/ 85 6139, fax 066/85 8754), which was developed by and for wheelchair users, with totally accessible accommodation and other personal and professional care on offer; and the *YAL Tropicana Lodge*, 158c Martyn St, Cairns, QLD (☎070/51 1727), with seven accessible rooms.

## TRANSPORT

**Interstate** buses and trains are generally not an option, although in Victoria *V/Line* operates "Sprinter" trains and buses with wheelchair access on country routes and to Adelaide; and in New South Wales, *Countrylink* run "XPT" and "Xplorer" trains providing access to some country areas and between Sydney and Melbourne. Information on both services on ☎13 2232. However, the two main ways of getting around are plane and car. Both *Qantas* and *Ansett* welcome disabled travellers without a fuss; *Qantas* staff undergo special disability-awareness training and on international flights their aircraft carry the sky chair and are equipped with a larger toilet cubicle.

Of the major car rental agencies, *Hertz* and *Avis* offer **vehicles with hand controls** at no extra cost, but advance notice is required. Reserved **parking** is available for vehicles displaying the wheelchair symbol (available from local council offices) in all major centres, and temporary parking permits are often available from the city council. A specially adapted **taxi service** operates from all the major national airports, booked in advance toll free on ☎1800/043 187; in addition there are taxi companies in all the major cities that have some adapted vehicles. Some **suburban rail services**

can just about be used with a wheelchair: Melbourne's *MET* leads the way with Disability Services, ☎03/9619 2355.

All capital cities and most regional centres produce **Mobility Maps** showing accessible paths, car parking, toilets etc. which can be obtained from local councils. Other cities have gone further and their tourist authorities produce comprehensive books such as *Access Brisbane* and *Darwin City without Steps*, while *ACROD* in NSW publishes *Accessing Sydney* (available from them at 55 Ryde St, Ryde, NSW 2112). *Easy Access Australia – A Travel Guide to Australia* is a comprehensive guide written by wheelchair-users for anyone with a mobility difficulty and is available in the UK c/o Prawles Oast, Ewhurst Green, Nr Robertsbridge, E. Sussex TN32 5RG, for £14.95.

## USEFUL CONTACTS IN AUSTRALIA

**ACROD (Australian Council for the Rehabilitation of the Disabled)**, PO Box 60, Curtin, ACT 2605 (☎06/282 4333, fax 06/281 3488). Regional offices provide lists of state-based help organizations, accommodation, travel agencies and tour operators.

**Barrier-Free Travel**, 36 Wheatley St, North Bellingen, NSW 2454 (☎066/551 733). Fee-based travel access information service.

**NICAN**, PO Box 407, Curtin, ACT 2605 (☎06/285 3713 or free call 1800/806 769, fax 06/285 3714).

An Australia-wide directory on recreation and sport for people of all ages and disabilities.

**Para Quad Ass (Paraplegic and Quadriplegic Association)** has offices in each state capital (see "Listings" sections of city accounts), serving the interests of the spinally injured.

**YHA Travel & Membership**, 205 King Street, Melbourne, VIC 3000 (☎03/9670 7991).

*Note: see also "Listings" sections throughout the Guide for regional contacts.*

# COSTS, MONEY AND BANKS

If you've travelled down from Asia you'll find Australia expensive on a day-to-day basis, but fresh from Europe or the US you'll find prices comparable or cheaper. Australia is well set up for independent travellers, and with a student, YHA or VIP backpackers' card (see p.33) you can get discounts on a wide range of travel and entertainment.

Australia's currency is the Australian dollar, or "buck", divided into 100 cents. There are $100, $50, $20, $10 and $5 paper notes, and plastic $20, $10 and $5 notes with forgery-proof clear windows. Coins come in $2, $1, 50, 20, 10 and 5 cent denominations.

**Exchange rates** fluctuate around an over-the-counter rate of $2.10 for £1; $1.30 for US$1.

## SOME BASIC COSTS

You could keep to around **$55** a day for food, board and transport if you stay in hostels, travel on coaches and eat and drink carefully. If you're prepared to camp you might get by on as little as **$35** a day; on the other hand if you're staying in motels and B&Bs, and eating out regularly, reckon on **$70–90**: **extras** like scuba-diving courses, clubbing, car rental and tours will all add to this.

Hostel accommmodation costs $10–20 a person, while a double room in an inexpensive **motel** costs between $35 and $50 – most, though, are in the $50–70 bracket. **Food**, on the whole, is good value: counter meals in hotels rarely cost more than $10; restaurants cost upwards of $20 for a reasonable three-course feed, and many let you **BYO** (Bring Your Own) wine or beer. Buying your own ingredients is not always the cheapest way to eat in the bigger cities, where there's sure to be a range of budget diners and food halls, but overall you'll save; fruit and fresh produce in season, especially, are inexpensive. **Drinking** out is always expensive – say $2.50 or more a beer – compared with buying in bulk from a bottle shop.

Given the size of the country, **transport** can make a major dent in your budget, and is perhaps the area you're most likely to overspend on. Pre-planning makes sense here – consider an open-jaw plane ticket, for example, which saves you having to get back to where you started, or pay a little extra for an international flight that includes some internal ones. You may also be able to save by buying one of the huge variety of bus and train **passes** before you leave home (see "Getting Around", pp.24–25, for more on the options available). **Driving** yourself may not always save money, but it does give you a great deal more flexibility; finding passengers willing to share costs is one way to minimize expenses, and is usually not too hard – try the noticeboards at hostels and other meeting places. **Buying a used car** will, realistically, set you back $4000 or more for a guaranteed mechanically sound vehicle on which you can expect to get a reasonable resale value (see p.28 for more advice). On the other hand, for as little as $1000 you should be able to find something that will get you around –

if not in the greatest of style. **Rental cars** starts at $20 a day for local hire to at least $70 a day for longer distances; **fuel** averages 70 cents a litre.

## TRAVELLERS' CHEQUES, CREDIT AND CASH CARDS

**Travellers' cheques** are the best way to bring your funds into Australia, as they can be replaced if lost or stolen (remember to keep a list of the serial numbers separate from the cheques). They can be easily exchanged at any bank and at most post offices, and at many hotels and tourist shops, albeit at a worse exchange rate or higher **commission**. Obviously if your cheques are in Australian dollars that makes life slightly easier, but cheques in US dollars and UK pounds are also widely accepted, and banks should be able to handle all major currencies. It's worth checking both the rate and the commission when you come to change your cheques (as well as when you buy them), as these can vary quite widely – many places charge a set amount for every cheque, in which case you're better off with relatively large denominations.

**Credit cards** can come in very handy as a backup source of funds, and they can even save on exchange-rate commissions. They're also invaluable when used to leave a deposit, for a rental car or a hotel booking, for example, even if you settle the final bill with cash. *Mastercard/ Access*, *Visa* and *American Express* are the most widely recognized (though supermarkets tend not to take credit cards at all). In addition, with an **international debit card** you may be able to pay for goods via EFTPOS (see below) and gain direct access to your home funds via ATM machines displaying the *Cirrus* symbol; check with your bank before leaving.

## BANKS AND EXCHANGE

You'll find a branch of one of the main **banks** in every town of any size, and in smaller places there will be a local **agency** which handles bank business, usually based at the general store or roadhouse. The major banks, with branches countrywide, are *Westpac*, *ANZ*, and the *Commonwealth* and *National* banks.

**Banking hours** are Monday to Thursday 9.30am to 4pm, Friday 9.30am to 5pm: in country areas some agencies will be open later, and some big city branches might also have extended hours; **autotellers** or **ATM**s are generally open 24 hours. Bureaux de change are only found in major tourist centres and airports, so make sure you exchange your currency during banking hours. All post offices act as *Commonwealth Bank* agents for passbook accounts, although in country areas there may be a limit on weekly withdrawals.

If you're spending some time in Australia – say a month or more – and plan to move around, and especially if you plan to work, it makes life a great deal easier if you open a **bank account**. To open an account in Australia, you'll need to take every piece of ID documentation you possess; a passport may not be enough. Having said this, it's a surprisingly easy process, and can usually be done on the spot. A *Commonwealth*

*Bank* **passbook** account is one of the best bets, as virtually all post office agencies double as *Commonwealth Bank* agents, which means you can be fairly sure to find one at the general store in even the smallest Outback settlement.

Some banks issue **cash cards**, or key cards, for their ATMs, which give you a lot more flexibility in taking money out (there are often machines even where there are no branches) and can also be used anywhere that offers **EFTPOS** facilities (Electronic Funds Transfer at Point of Sale). This includes many service stations and supermarkets, where you can use your card to pay directly for goods; some of them will also give you cash. Key cards come into their own on long journeys where you may not want to carry large amounts of cash, but they are rather harder to obtain than a simple passbook account.

# HEALTH

**Australia is a pretty healthy place, with high standards of hygiene and few exceptional health hazards – at least in terms of disease. No vaccination certificates are required unless you've come from a yellow-fever zone within the past week. Standards in Australia's hospitals are also very high, and medical costs reasonable by world standards.**

The national healthcare scheme, *Medicare*, offers a reciprocal arrangement – **free essential healthcare** – for citizens of the UK, New Zealand, Italy, The Netherlands and Sweden. This free treatment is limited to public hospitals and casualty departments (though the ambulance ride to get you there isn't covered); at GPs you pay up front ($30 minimum) and have two-thirds of your fee reimbursed from *Medicare*.

The whole process is made easier by the production of a **Medicare Card**, available from any Medicare Centre, which anyone eligible staying in Australia a while, particularly those on extended working holidays, is advised to get. Dental treatment is not included: if you find yourself in need of dental treatment in one of the larger cities, try the Dental Hospital where dental students offer to practise their craft cheaply or for free.

## THE SUN

Australia's biggest health problem for fair-skinned visitors is also one of its chief attractions: **sunshine**. A sunny day in London, Toronto or even Miami is not the same as a cloudless day in Darwin, and the intensity of the Australian sun's damaging ultra-violet rays is far greater. Whether this is because of Australia's proximity to the reputed **ozone hole** is a matter of debate, but there's absolutely no doubt that the southern sun burns more fiercely than anything in the northern hemisphere; at least at first, you need to take extra care.

Australians of European origin, especially those of Anglo-Saxon or Celtic decent, could not be less suited to Australia's fierce sun, which – together with an outdoor lifestyle – is why the country now has one of the world's highest instances of **skin cancer**, a disfiguring and potentially fatal disease. The appearance of some older, pre-skin-cancer-aware Australians' ravaged complexions should be enough to make you cover yourself with lashings of the highest factor (SPF 15+) sunblock, widely used and sold just about everywhere.

These days, Australians are more aware of the dangers, and you're constantly reminded to

"**Slip, Slop, Slap**", the government-approved catchphrase reminding you to slip on a T-shirt, slop on some sun block and slap on a hat – sound advice. Pay attention to any moles on your body: if you notice any changes, either during or after your trip, see a doctor; cancerous **melanomas** are generally easily removed if caught early. To prevent headaches and, in the long term, cataracts, wearing **sunglasses** is also a good idea; look for "UV block" ratings when you buy a pair.

## DANGEROUS AND ANNOYING WILDLIFE

Although **mosquitoes** are found across the whole of the country, malaria is not endemic; however, there are rare outbreaks of similarly-transmitted Ross River Fever and Dengue Fever, both of which can be debilitating and recur for life – a good reason not to be too blasé about mozzie bites. *Aeroguard* or *Rid* are the popular brands of insect repellent, while the dangling netting designed to hang from hat rims – available in outdoor stores and supermarkets – is surprisingly effective at keeping **flies** away from your face.

The danger from other **wildlife** is much overrated: the snake and spider bites, crocodile and shark attacks are widely publicized and an essential part of the perilous Outback myth – nonetheless all are extremely rare.

Apart from never smiling at them, the way to minimize danger from **saltwater crocodiles** (which actually range far inland) is to keep your distance. If you're camping in the bush within 100km of the northern coast between Broome and Rockhampton, make sure your tent is at least 50m from waterholes or creeks, don't collect water at the same spot every day or leave any rubbish around, and always seek local advice. Four-wheel drivers should take extra care when walking creeks prior to driving across.

**Snakes** almost always do their best to avoid people and you'll probably never see one – treat them with respect and you'd be very unlucky to receive a bite. However, it's always prudent to wear boots and long trousers when hiking through undergrowth, collect firewood carefully and, in the event of a confrontation, back off. **Sea snakes** sometimes find divers intriguing, wrapping themselves around limbs or staring into masks, but they're seldom aggressive. If **bitten**, use a crepe bandage to bind the limb firmly, then splint to immobilize it (this slows the distribution of venom into the lymphatic system) and get to a hospital for treatment. Don't clean the bite area (venom around the bite can identify the species, making treatment easier), slash the bite or employ a tourniquet. Despite what you might hear, death from snakebite is extremely rare.

Two **spiders** whose bites can be fatal are the **Sydney funnel-web**, a black, stocky creature found in the Sydney area, and the **redback**, a relative of the notorious black widow of the Americas, usually found in dark, dry locations. Treat funnel-web bites as for snakebite, and apply ice to redback wounds to relieve pain; if bitten by either, get to a hospital as soon as you can – antivenenes are available. **Other spiders** and **scorpions** can deliver painful wounds but are only a problem if you're allergic.

**Ticks** and **leeches** are the bane of bushwalkers. Some ticks are poisonous and you may want to check yourself over after a hike, but you'll often feel them anyway – look for local irritation and swelling (usually just inside hairlines), and you'll find a tiny black dot. Kill the tick with kerosene and then, using tweezers, twist and pull it off. Pulling alone will leave the head behind, which might fester. Leeches are gruesome but harmless; insect repellent, fire or salt gets them off. Spraying repellent over shoes and leggings might keep both pests away in the first place.

The menace from **box jellyfish** (also known as stingers or sea wasps) in summertime tropical sea waters is more realistic – especially as it occurs at a place and time of year when a cooling dip in the sea is just about all you can think of. Their stings leave permanent red weals and can kill if serious (covering more than half a limb). Treat victims by dousing the sting area (front and back) with liberal amounts of **vinegar** (*never* rub with sand or towels, or attempt to remove tentacles from the skin – both could trigger the release of more venom); apply mouth-to-mouth resuscitation if needed, and get the victim to hospital for treatment. Don't risk swimming on tropical beaches during the **stinger season** (roughly October to May). Specific **reef hazards** are covered at the start of the chapter on Queensland's tropical coast (p.312).

For more background on Australian fauna, see "Wildlife" in *Contexts*.

## OTHER HEALTH HAZARDS

Australia has one of the lowest rates of **AIDS** infection around the world, largely because they caught on very early to the need for safe sex, which has been promoted heavily – "No glove? No love!" is the local inducement to wear a condom. Infected needles are also a danger, not only among intravenous drug users but from ear-piercing and tattooing. The *Australian National Council on AIDS (ANCA)* has centres all over the country, and you'll find AIDS helplines listed in the major cities in this guide: otherwise call ☎1800/011144.

Other health hazards are far less pressing. **Tap water** is safely drinkable everywhere – it doesn't always taste good, though, in which case bottled water is commonly available. Although you're unlikely to find yourself in the path of a raging **bushfire**, it helps to know how to survive

one. If you're in a car, don't attempt to drive through smoke but park at the side of the road in the clearest spot, put on your headlights, wind up the windows and close the air vents. Although it seems to go against commonsense – and your natural instincts – it is safer to **stay inside the car**. Lie on the floor and cover all exposed skin with a blanket or any covering at hand. The car won't explode or catch on fire, and a fast-moving wildfire will pass quickly overhead. If you smell or see smoke and fire while **walking**, find a cleared rocky outcrop or an open space: if the terrain and time permits, dig a shallow trench, but in any event lie face down and cover all exposed skin.

## INFORMATION AND MAPS

Australian tourism abroad is represented by the Australian Tourist Commission, who produce an annual, glossy *Traveller's Guide* which gives an excellent introduction to Australia. It details the country region by region, offers travel tips and ways of getting around, and has a useful directory of addresses. The ATC now also caters to the booming (and lucrative) backpacker market, producing the excellent *Australian Unplugged* guide for the young independent traveller. While not as practical as parts of the *Traveller's Guide*, it gives a colourful overview of the country's best-known attractions and themes.

### AUSTRALIAN TOURIST COMMISSION OFFICES

**New Zealand** Visit Australia Information Centre, Shop 7, Ground Floor, National Bank Centre, corner of Elliot and Victoria streets (PO Box 1365), Auckland 1 (☎09/302 7721).

**United Kingdom** Gemini House, 10-18 Putney Hill, Putney, London SW15 6AA (☎0181/780 2227).

**USA** 31st Floor, 489 Fifth Ave, New York, NY 10017 (☎212/687 6300); Suite 1200, 2121 Avenue of the Stars, Los Angeles, CA 90067 (☎310/552 1988); plus a dedicated "helpline" for tourism-related inquiries (☎708/296 4900).

### STATE TOURIST OFFICES IN LONDON

**New South Wales** Tourism Commission, 75 King William St, London EC4N 7HA (☎0171/283 2124).

**Queensland** Tourist & Travel Corporation, Queensland House, 392/3 Strand, London WC2R 0LZ (☎0171/836 7142).

**Tourism South Australia**, South Australia House, 50 Strand, London WC2N 5LW (☎0171/930 7471).

**Western Australian Tourist Commission,** Western Australia House, 115 Strand, London WC2R 0AJ (☎0171/240 2881).

**More detailed information** is available by the bagful once you're in the country; each state or territory has its own tourist authority, which runs information offices throughout its own area and in major cities in other parts of Australia – some are even represented abroad (almost all have London offices, detailed below). A level below this are a host of regional and community-run visitors' centres and information kiosks. Even the smallest Outback town seems to have one, or at the very least a pamphlet rack at the local service station, while bigger places will often have two or more rival offices.

A final source of handy tips not to be forgotten is fellow travellers. One of the best things about hostels, apart from the inexpensive accommodation they offer, is that they act as gathering points for information. Almost all of them have noticeboards where you'll find local bus schedules, offers of cheap excursions or ride shares, and comments and advice from people who've passed this way before.

## MAPS

If you want to get hold of maps before you go, the *GeoCenter* (including NZ) and *Nelles* **maps of Australia**, both 1:4,000,000, are finely produced, with good topographical detail: the *Nelles* (printed in northern and southern halves on both sides of the sheet) includes additional detail of major city environs. The *Bartholomew* and the new *Globetrotter* (both 1:5,000,000) are the best of the rest. Any of the specialist map shops listed in the box below should have all of these, together with a reasonable selection of more detailed local maps.

### SPECIALIST BOOK AND MAP SUPPLIERS

**London**
*Daunt Books*, 83 Marylebone High St, W1 (☎0171/224 2295).
*National Map Centre*, 22–24 Caxton St, SW1 (☎0171/222 4945).
*Stanfords*, 12–14 Long Acre, WC2 (☎0171/836 1321); 52 Grosvenor Gardens, London SW1W 0AG; 156 Regent St, London W1R 5TA.
*The Travel Bookshop*, 13–15 Blenheim Crescent, London W11 2EE (☎0171/229 5260).
*The Travellers Bookshop*, 25 Cecil Court, WC2 (☎0171/836 9132).

**Edinburgh**
*Thomas Nelson and Sons Ltd*, 51 York Place, EH1 3JD (☎0131/557 3011).

**Glasgow**
*John Smith and Sons*, 57–61 St Vincent St (☎0141/221 7472).

Maps by **mail or phone order** are available from *Stanfords*; ☎0171/836 1321.

**USA**
**Book Passage**, 51 Tamal Vista Blvd, Corte Madera, CA 94925 (☎415/927 0960).
**The Complete Traveler Bookstore**, 199 Madison Ave, New York, NY 10016 (☎212/685 9007); 3207 Fillmore St, San Francisco, CA 92123 (☎415/923 1511).
**Elliot Bay Book Company**, 101 S Main St, Seattle, WA 98104 (☎206/624 6600).

**Forsyth Travel Library**, 9154 W 57th St, Shawnee Mission, KS 66201 (☎1800/367 7984).
**Map Link Inc**, 25 E Mason St, Santa Barbara, CA 93101 (☎805/965 4402).
**Phileas Fogg's Books & Maps**, #87 Stanford Shopping Center, Palo Alto, CA 94304 (☎1800/233 FOGG in California; ☎1800/533 FOGG elsewhere in US).
**Rand McNally**,* 444 N Michigan Ave, Chicago, IL 60611 (☎312/321 1751); 150 E 52nd St, New York, NY 10022 (☎212/758 7488); 595 Market St, San Francisco, CA 94105 (☎415/777 3131); 1201 Connecticut Ave NW, Washington, DC 2003 (☎202/223 6751).
**Sierra Club Bookstore**, 730 Polk St, San Francisco, CA 94109 (☎415/923 5500).
**Traveler's Bookstore**, 22 W 52nd St, New York, NY 10019 (☎212/664 0995).

*Note: *Rand McNally* now has 24 stores across the US; call ☎1800/333 0136 (ext 2111) for the location of your nearest store, or for **direct mail** maps.

**CANADA**
**Open Air Books and Maps**, 25 Toronto St, Toronto, ON M5R 2C1 (☎416/363 0719).
**Ulysses Travel Bookshop**, 4176 St-Denis, Montréal (☎514/289 0993).
**World Wide Books and Maps**, 714 Granville St, Vancouver, BC V6Z 1E4 (☎604/687 3320).

In Australia *UBD*, *Gregory's* and *AusMap* produce national, state, regional and city maps of varying sizes and quality: the first two are the most widely available. *BP* annually update a 500-page touring guide to Australia (*Explore Australia*, Penguin) with regional maps and detailed things to see and do, state by state – something for the back shelf of the car rather than a backpack.

If you're a member of a **motoring organization** or automobile association, there's a good chance you'll have reciprocal rights with the Australian equivalent and be entitled to **free maps** and other discounted services. Each state

has its own organization (they're listed in the Australian Tourist Commission's guide), and most are excellent – you'll need to bring proof of membership along to take advantage.

The whole country is now covered by 1:50,000 **topographical sheets**, suitable for hiking or other travel in remote areas. You can get them at government mapping agency offices or official government bookshops (in major cities) or take a look at them at a library in the nearest major town; they're also available by mail from the **National Mapping Agency**, PO Box 31, Belconnen, ACT 2616.

# GETTING AROUND

Australia's huge scale makes the distances, and how you conquer them, a major feature of any stay in the country. In general, public transport will take you only along the major highways to capital cities, the bigger towns between them, and popular tourist destinations; to get off the beaten track you'll have to consider driving or hitching. Regular long-distance bus, train and plane services can be found under "Travel Details" at the end of each chapter, with local buses and trains covered in the main text. Another useful guide to bus, train and ferry timetables and fares is *Travel Times Australia*, updated twice a year and available at most newsagents for $4.95.

## PLANES

**Flying** isn't particularly cheap, but can begin to seem a bargain when you take into account the time saved, and the money you'll spend on incidentals during a long bus or train journey. The **best value** flights are, not surprisingly, the most

popular – between state capitals and major towns in the southeast; flying to remote Outback locations on private local services such as **mail runs** can be an expensive business.

If you do expect to fly a fair amount, there are a number of **passes** that can save money, such as the *Qantas Explorer Pass* or *Ansett G'Day Pass*. These entitle you to discounted internal flights: both passes must be purchased outside Australia, and you need to book a minimum of two flight coupons (up to a maximum of eight). Coupons cost £80 for destinations within the same zone: for example, Sydney to Hobart, and £105 for longer flights like Sydney to Perth. You may also make substantial **savings** by booking internal flights before you leave, especially as add-ons to an international ticket.

Travellers from New Zealand can take advantage of the *Qantas/ANZ See Australia* pass, which gives substantial discounts on flights within the eastern states of Australia, such as Sydney–Melbourne for A$148 instead of A$247. For longer flights, or simply more flexibility, *Airpass* coupons (minimum purchase two) allow single, direct flights, with each coupon costing A$170 (excluding Western Australia, Alice Springs and Ayers Rock) or A$220 (with no restrictions).

Once you're in Australia, there's the usual range of APEX and other restricted **fares**, including student and pensioner **reductions**. *Qantas* and *Ansett's* backpacker fares are available to anyone with a YHA or VIP card (see p.33), and represent a substantial discount if you buy a minimum of three flights, all heading in the same direction – a useful adjunct to an open-jaw ticket.

One other type of flight offered all over Australia is brief **sightseeing** or joy-rides. Everything is covered, from biplane spins above cities (cricket lovers may wish to recreate David Gower's infamous escapade) to excursions to the Great Barrier Reef and flights over famous landscapes. The latter, especially, can be worthwhile, enabling you to see things that are inaccessible or impractical overland.

## TRAINS

**Trains** are not the most obvious way to get around Australia, which has a fairly limited network, but there are a couple of wonderful, epic journeys to be made, while the populous southeast, at least, does have a reasonably comprehensive service. **Interstate railways** link the entire east coast from Cairns to Sydney, and on to Melbourne and Adelaide. The two great journeys, though, are the coast-to-coast **Indian Pacific** (Sydney to Perth) and the **Ghan** from Adelaide north to Alice Springs. Other than these, there are a couple of inland tracks in Queensland – to Mount Isa and Longreach – and suburban networks around some of the major cities. Only around Sydney does this amount to much, with decent services to much of New South Wales.

The **advantages** of train over bus travel are comfort, conversation and leisure; disadvantages are the slower pace, higher price and potential booking problems – Queensland trains, for instance, travel at about 60kph and require at least a month's notice to buy a ticket during the holiday season. The famous long-distance journeys can also be booked solid, so you'd be wise to reserve a place before you leave home if this is a major part of your plans (*Rail Australia* agents are listed below). **Fares** tend to be a little higher than comparable bus fares: sample fares from Sydney are Melbourne $93, Adelaide $99, Perth $290, Alice Springs $244, Brisbane $98, Cairns $227.

**Rail passes** include the *Australpass*, which must be bought outside Australia and gives unlimited travel for between 14 and 90 consecutive days on all state-owned railways, including suburban links around state capitals; prices range from $435 for 14 days to $1125 for 90 days. The *Austrail Flexipass* lets you linger without wasting your ticket: 8 days of travel within a 60-day period, for example, costs around $320. To be sure that you can make full use of your pass, it's advisable to book your route when you buy it. Western Australia, Victoria, New South Wales and Queensland also have their own passes available through main stations, but check any travel restrictions before buying – interstate routes do not overlap as far as passes are concerned.

## BUSES

Travelling by **bus** is almost certainly the cheapest way to get around, although it's not always a very satisfactory one. There's a lot to be said against spending much of your trip staring at the passing

---

## TRAIN AND BUS REPRESENTATIVES ABROAD

### RAIL AUSTRALIA

**UK and Ireland**: *Long Haul Leisurail*. PO Box 113, Peterborough PE1 1LE, UK (☎01733/33 5599).

**USA**: *ATS Tours*, 100 N 1st St, Suite 3101, Burbank, CA 91502 (☎818/841 1030).

**Canada**: *Goway Travel Ltd*, Suite 409, 402 W Pender St, Vancouver, BC V68 1T6, and 2300 Yonge St, Suite 2001, Toronto, ON, M4P 1E4 (☎1800/387 8850).

### AUSTRALIAN COACHLINES

**UK and Ireland**: *Greyhound International*, Sussex House, London Rd, East Grinstead, West Sussex RH19 1LD, UK (☎01342/31 7317).

**USA**: *Austravel*, 51 E 42nd Street, New York, NY 10017, and in Chicago, Houston and San Francisco (☎1800/633 3404 or 212/972 6880); *Swains*, 6 W Lancaster Ave, Ardmore PA 19003, and in LA (☎1800/22 SWAIN or 215/896 9595).

**Canada**: *Goway Travel Ltd*, Suite 409, 402 W Pender St, Vancouver, BC V68 1T6, and 2300 Yonge St, Suite 2001, Toronto, ON, M4P 1E4 (☎1800/387 8850 or 416/322 1034).

**Note**: *Passes can also be purchased from many travel agents – see boxes on p.5 and p.10.*

landscape from a cramped seat. And even though the bus network is a great deal more comprehensive than the rail one, it will still let you down if you hope to escape the tourist trail. Relying on the major operators (as you may have to do if you have a bus pass) will restrict you to the main highways between cities, and may mean arriving at smaller places in the middle of the night. On the other hand bus services are regular and good value, and vehicles are about as comfortable as they could be, with reclining seats, air-conditioning, bathrooms, videos and cold drinks: the real problem is journeys are just so long.

The main **interstate bus company** on the mainland is *Greyhound.Pioneer Australia*, although *McCafferty's* is gradually expanding its network westwards across the country. **Tasmania** is thoroughly covered by *Redline*, *Hobart Coaches* and *Wilderness Transport*. **Fares** vary according to the popularity of the route and quality and speed of the road, and also between operators – it's always worth shopping around; sample fares from Sydney are: Melbourne $61, Adelaide $95, Perth $257, Alice Springs $214, Darwin $307, Brisbane $73, Cairns $190. **Return** fares are, at best, only marginally cheaper than two singles.

The most popular option is to buy a **bus pass**. The *Aussie Pass* is the most comprehensive, allowing unlimited travel on *Greyhound.Pioneer Australia* for up to 90 days of travel within a specified period of time: prices range from $380 for 7 days, to $890 for 21 days, and $2225 for 90 days. There are also "travel only" options that allow either 6 or 12 months (depending on distance) to cover a specified route (Melbourne–Cairns for $255, for example, or even a circuit right round Australia, with limitless stopovers, for

$1350), and "value packages" that incorporate regional tours. *McCafferty's* has a similar range of passes: the *Visit Australia Pass* includes their entire network on the mainland, is valid for twelve months and costs $700; there are also a number of point-to-point passes, such as Melbourne–Cairns for $240. Tasmania has its own passes, from $111 a week to $177 a month.

Substantial **discounts** (ten to fifteen percent on *Greyhound.Pioneer*, ten percent on *McCafferty's*) on many fares are available if you have a YHA, ISIC or recognized backpacker card (see p.33).

## ONE-WAY TOURS

The big bus companies exist to transport as many passengers as quickly as possible from A to B. If you want more than a fleeting look at what you're passing, a **one-way tour** may be the answer: usually in minibuses, these tours tend to be more leisurely and detour to attractions along the way; groups are usually quite small (ten to eighteen people), and the driver/guides are mostly knowledgeable locals – see box below for a selection of operators. More conventional tours, starting from and returning to the same place, are mentioned in the "Listings" sections of the relevant accounts throughout the *Guide*.

## DRIVING

Having **your own vehicle** really opens up Australia, filling the public transport void away from the cities and allowing you to get to the national parks, the isolated beaches, the gold-mining ghost towns, that make it such a special place. If your trip is a long one – six weeks or more – then it's worth giving serious considera-

---

### SAFARIS AND ONE-WAY TOURS

**Aussie Expeditions Australia** (☎1800/63 5058). Circuit from Sydney via Brisbane, Cairns, the Gulf of Carpentaria, Darwin, Kakadu, Alice, Ayers Rock, Oodnadatta, Coober Pedy, Adelaide and Melbourne. You can join or leave at any stage; buses run from mid-June to early October, and the price is $199 per week.

**Heading Bush** (☎1800/63 9933). Adelaide to Alice Springs in ten days, via Flinders Ranges, Oodnadatta Track, Simpson Desert, Ayers Rock, the Olgas, Kings Canyon and Alice; departures every three weeks, $659.

**Oz Experience** (☎02/9907 0522). Sydney to Cairns – with plenty of stops at wineries, beaches, national parks, cattle stations etc. Passengers can do the whole trip in one go, or get off and travel for up to 6 months, all for a flat fare of $225.

**Straycat** (☎1800/80 0840). Melbourne to Sydney in three days, via the Highlands and Canberra, for $125.

**Wayward Bus** (☎1800/88 2823). Melbourne to Adelaide via the Great Ocean Rd and the Coorong (3 days for $125), plus Adelaide–Perth Outback and coastal camping adventure (14 days, $770).

tion to **buying a vehicle.** You need some money upfront, but if you're lucky and you know what you're doing this can actually be the cheapest way to see Australia, since you can resell the car at the end. On shorter trips you should consider **renting** a vehicle, if not for the whole time, then at least for short periods to allow you to explore a concentrated area in depth.

Most foreign **licences** are valid for a year in Australia, but it still makes sense to get hold of an International. Driving Permit (available from national motoring organizations) before arrival, especially if your national licence does not include your photograph. **Fuel** prices average around 70c per litre for "super" (standard) or unleaded, with diesel slightly cheaper: this can vary drastically from place to place, however, and remote service stations make a killing. **Road rules** are similar to those in the US and UK, but there's enough variation to make picking up a booklet from the nearest Transport Department worthwhile (a major deviation is that there are no "priority roads" and in the absence of Stop or Give Way signs, you give way to traffic coming from the right). Most importantly, **drive on the left** (as in Britain), remember that seatbelts are compulsory for all occupants, and maximum **speed limits** outside built-up areas are around 100kph, except in the Northern Territory where common sense and horsepower are the only limits between towns; in all built-up areas, the speed limit is 60kph. Whatever else you do in a vehicle, avoid **drunk driving**. In what has been a relatively successful campaign to lower Australia's frighteningly high road death toll, random breath tests are common.

Other **hazards**, apart from poor surfaces and fatigue, are livestock and kangaroos on the road, a serious problem at night – not only in the bush – when they feed along verges or lie on the bitumen for warmth. And beware of 50m-long **road trains**: these colossal trucks can't stop quickly or pull off the road safely, so if there's the slightest doubt, get out of the way; it's always a better idea to let a road train get ahead by pulling over and having a rest, than to try and overtake it.

## ROADS, OUTBACK DRIVING AND BREAKDOWNS

Though around cities the only problem you'll face is inept signposting, interstate main roads – even Highway 1, which circles the country – aren't always the best, and some of the minor routes

are awful. **Road conditions**, especially on unsealed roads, are unpredictable and can change on a daily basis, so always seek reliable advice (from the local police or a garage) before starting out. Make it clear what sort of vehicle you're driving and remember that their idea of a "good" or "bad" road may be radically different from yours. Some "4WD only" tracks *might* be navigable in lesser transport with a skilled driver – high ground clearance, rather than four driven wheels, is often the crucial factor.

Rain and floods – particularly in the tropics and central Australia – can close roads to all vehicles within minutes, so driving through remote regions in the wet season can be prone to delays. Several remote and unsealed **roads through central Australia** (the Sandover and Plenty highways, Oodnadatta, Birdsville and Tanami tracks, and others) are theoretically open to all vehicles, but unless you're part of an expedition, don't attempt a crossing during the summer, when extreme temperatures place extra strain on both driver and vehicle.

On poor roads and dirt tracks, the rules are to **keep your speed down** to a maximum of 80kph, stick to the best section and never assume that the road is free from potholes, eroded cattle grids, sand, rocks or oncoming traffic. Long **corrugated** stretches are a major bugbear, and can literally shake the vehicle apart – check radiators and fuel tanks for cracks afterwards; reducing tyre pressures softens the ride but can cause the tyres to overheat at high speeds, making them more puncture-prone. Windscreens can be shattered by flying stones from passing traffic, so slow down and pull over to the left. Fine "**bulldust**" fills potholes, obscures hazards and invades the car. Dirt tracks are often deeply rutted, and exposed tree roots can burst tyres if you drive over them too fast.

At all times carry plenty of **drinking water, fuel** and food, and tell someone reliable your timetable, route and destination, so that a **rescue** can be organized if you don't report in. Carry a detailed, recent **map** and don't count on finding regular signposts. In the event of a breakdown in the Outback, **always stay with your vehicle**: it's visible to potential rescuers and you can use it for shade; in any case, you risk finding it stripped when you return with a tow truck if you're stranded on an isolated road. As a last resort only, burn a tyre – property owners never ignore smoke.

## FOUR-WHEEL-DRIVING: SOME HINTS

The Outback is not the place to learn to handle a 4WD, and you should know what you're doing before disappearing off the map. Many novice four-wheel drivers assume that their vehicles are unstoppable all-terrain machines and soon get stuck through lack of technique and experience. In addition to the **spares** listed on p.28, you'll want a shovel, hi-lift jack and gloves. A copy of *Gregory's Four Wheel Drive Handbook* or Jack Absolom's *Safe Outback Travel* (Five Mile Press) is invaluable for preparing, driving and, in an emergency, fixing any vehicle in the Outback. If you're heading for remote areas you may want to rent a **two-way UHF radio** tuned to the Royal Flying Doctor Service – contact the state motoring association or National Parks and Wildlife Service for details. The following basic hints should help; see also the advice on creek crossings on p.373.

- Be aware of your limitations, and those of your vehicle.
- Know how to operate everything *before* you need it.
- Assess rivers and sandy or muddy sections on foot first.
- Admit you're stuck early – avoid wheelspin and reverse out.
- Reducing tyre pressure by up to 70 percent dramatically increases traction in mud or sand, but causes overheating at higher speeds.
- If stuck, clear all the wheels and create a shallow ramp to drive out.
- Keep to tracks – avoid unnecessary damage to the environment.
- Beaches can be treacherous – take care, especially if the tide is coming in.

## CAR RENTAL

To **rent** a car you need a full, clean driver's licence; usually, a minimum age of 21 is stipulated by the major car-rental companies, rising to 25 for 4WDs. Check on any mileage limits or other restrictions, extras, and what you're covered for in an accident, before signing. Multinational operators *Hertz*, *Budget* and *Avis* are widespread, but outside the big cities lack of competition makes their **standard rates** expensive at $70–90 a day for a sedan; long-term hire, specials and even plain bargaining can bring this down to a more affordable level. **Local firms** – of which there are lots in the cities – are almost always better value, and the bottom-line "rent-a-bomb" agencies go as low as $15 a day; however, these places often have restrictions on how far away from base you're allowed to go. **One-way rental** is handy, but expensive: usually about $200 extra for the drop-off fee. If you're simply trying to get from one place to another, you could try offering to **relocate** any vehicles they may have from other cities (ie returning someone else's one-way). They'll have regular drivers to do this, but being politely persuasive and claiming previous experience might get you massive reductions.

 **Four-wheel drives** are best used for specific areas rather than long term, as rental costs are steep, starting at around $100 per day. Some 4WD agents actually don't allow their vehicles to be driven off sealed roads, so check the fine print first. There are also plenty of places that offer **campervans** and **motorhomes** to rent. These are pricey – from around $900 a week for a camper that sleeps two, to $1400 a week for a six-berth motorhome – but not so bad when you start to consider the freedom and savings on accommodation they offer, especially for a family. A good compromise is to rent a van kitted out for camping: *Freedom Car Rentals* (in England ☎01707/26 3181; in Australia ☎07/3362 8739) rents out old but sound Ford or Holden panel wagons (small vans) for extended trips. The vehicles come equipped with mattresses, a water container and pots and pans: they cost around $260 a week, and between three people this can work out as cheap as bus passes while being far more versatile.

### CAR RENTAL RESERVATIONS

**UK**
**Avis** ☎0181/848 8733.
**Budget** ☎0800/181 181.
**Hertz** ☎0181/679 1799.
**Holiday Autos** ☎0171/491 1111

**USA AND CANADA**
**Avis** ☎1800/331 1084.
**Budget** ☎1800/527 0700.
**Hertz** ☎1800/654 3001; Canada ☎1800/263 0600.

*Branches of the big chains and local firms are detailed in "Listings" sections throughout the Guide.*

## BUYING A CAR

**Buying a used vehicle** needn't be an expensive business and a well-kept car should resell at about two thirds of the purchase price at the end of your trip – if you're lucky, or a skilful negotiator, you might even make a profit.

If you don't know your axle from your big end, **car yards** can save you a lot of hassle and provide welcome advice: in Sydney, they're the most common place to buy a used vehicle, and some even cater specifically to travellers (see p.116). Assuming you have a little time and some mechanical knowledge, however, you'll save money by buying **privately**; unless you're returning to your starting point, a **buy-back guarantee** (offered by some car yards and dealers) is not worth much. Adverts in the local newspapers and hostel noticeboards in main exit points from Australia are about the best places to start. One of the great advantages of buying off a **fellow traveller** is that you are might get all sorts of gear thrown in – jerrycans, camping gear and many of the spares listed below. The disadvantage is that the car may have been thrashed to death on its way round the country.

A thorough **inspection** is worthwhile. **Rust** is one thing to watch for, especially in the tropics where humidity and salt air will turn scratches to holes within weeks – look out for poorly patched bodywork. Take cars for a spin and check the engine, gearbox, clutch and brakes for performance, unusual noises, vibration and leaks; repairs on these items are costly. Don't expect perfection, though: leaking clutch cylinders, worn brakes, grating wheel bearings and defective electricals are less expensive to fix. If repairs are needed, it gives you a good excuse to haggle over the price. All **tyres** should be the same type and size, especially on 4WDs. If you lack faith in your own abilities, the various state automobile associations offer rigorous **pre-purchase inspections** for about $90 – not much if it saves you from buying a wreck.

If you're buying privately (or from an unscrupulous dealer) you should also check with Transport Departments for state requirements: in most states you'll need a **roadworthiness certificate** to have the vehicle transferred from its previous owner's name to yours. This means having a garage check it over; legally, the previous owner should do this, and theoretically it guarantees that the car is mechanically sound – but don't rely on it. You then proceed to the local Department of Transport with the certificate, a receipt, your driver's licence and passport; they charge a percentage of the price as stated on the receipt to register the vehicle in your name.

If the annual **vehicle registration** is due, or you bought an interstate or deregistered vehicle ("as is", without plates), you'll have to pay extra for registration, which is dependent on the engine size and runs into hundreds of dollars. Note that cars with interstate registration can be difficult to sell: if possible, go for a car with the registration of the state where you anticipate selling. Registration includes the legal minimum third-party personal **insurance**, but you might want to increase this cover to protect you against theft of the vehicle (for around $70), or if you've bought something more flash go the whole way with comprehensive motor insurance. Joining one of the **automobile clubs** for another $30 or so might be worth considering too, for free roadside assistance within certain limits of cities. Each state has their own, but membership is reciprocal: you also get benefits like free or discounted maps.

## EQUIPPING YOUR CAR

Even if you expect to stick mostly to the main highways, you'll need to carry a fair number of **spares**: there are plenty of very isolated spots even between Sydney and Melbourne. A proper tow rope is vital; passing motorists are far cheaper than tow trucks. In addition you should have a set of spark plugs, points, complete set of fuses, fuel filters, fuel lines, fan belt and radiator hoses – you need to check all these anyway and might want to replace them as a matter of course and keep the originals as backups. A selection of hose clamps, radiator sealant, putty for leaking tanks, water-dispersing spray, jump leads and a board to support the jack may also come in handy. If you're confident, get a *Gregory's* workshop manual for your vehicle; even if you're not, carry these spares anyway – someone who knows how to use them might stop. Whatever else, always carry **jerrycans** with enough oil, water and fuel to get you to the next garage after a mishap. For common cars, the cheapest place to **buy spares** is at a supermarket – head for any branch of *K-Mart* or *Coles*.

Before you set off, check battery terminals for corrosion, and the battery for charge – buy a new one if necessary but don't waste money on a secondhand dud. Carry *two* spare tyres; **off-road**

## BEST SECONDHAND BUYS

Mid-70s or later, big-engined *Holden Kingswood* or *Ford Falcon* station wagons are the **ideal travellers' cars**: roomy, reliable, mechanically straightforward and durable, with spares available in just about any city supermarket, roadhouse or wrecker's yard. At the bottom end, **$1000** plus some luck (or skill) should find you some kind of old car that goes reliably. Chances are, if a vehicle has survived this long, there's nothing seriously wrong with it and you should be able to nurse it through a bit further. Also, real bargains can be secured from travellers desperate to get rid of their vehicle before flying out. Ideally though, you should plan to pay at least **$4000** in total for a sound, fully prepared and equipped vehicle. Manual transmission models are more economical than automatic, with the four-speed versions superior to the awkward, three-speed, steering-column-mounted models. Smaller and less robust but much more economical to run are old *Toyota Corolla* or other Japanese station wagons, suitable for one or two people travelling light.

**Four-wheel drives** are expensive, and, with poor fuel economy and higher running costs, only worth it if you have some serious off-roading planned. **Toyota FJ** or **HJ** *Land Cruisers* are Outback legends, especially the long-wheelbase (LWB) models: tough, reliable and with plenty of new and used spares all over the country. If nothing goes wrong, a **diesel** (HJ) is preferable to a **petrol** (FJ) engine, being more economical, sturdier and using less expensive fuel, although all Toyota engines, particularly the six cylinder FJs, seem to keep on running, even if totally clapped-out. The trouble with diesels is that problems, when they occur, tend to be serious and repairs expensive; also, lower revs mean slower acceleration which can cause a problem in mud or up hills. Generally, you're looking at **$6000–12,000** for a reliable twelve-year-old model. **Government auctions** (city councils should have details of when and where) occasionally turn up bargains; mid-80s ex-army Series III **Landrovers** in usable condition sell from about $3500.

---

**drivers** should add a puncture repair kit, bead breaker and tubes. Keeping tyres at the correct pressure and having a wheel balance/alignment will cut down wear. Change the oil and filter, clean or replace the air filter and check the radiator for coolant/anti-freeze.

### MOTORBIKING

**Motorbikes**, especially large capacity trail bikes, are perfect for the Australian climate and an inexpensive compromise between conventional vehicles and 4WDs, although long distances place a premium on their comfort and fuel range. Mid-1980s 600cc Japanese trail bikes, such as **Yamaha**'s trendsetting XT600 *Ténéré*, sell for around $2500 and allow 100kph on-road cruising with adequate off-road agility and readily available spares.

If it's likely that you'll return to your starting-point, look out for dealers offering **buy-back** options, which guarantee a resale at the end of your trip; bikes can be more difficult to sell than cars. You're going to need a helmet and, especially if you're heading **off-road**, plenty of water-carrying capacity. It's also essential that you know what you're doing: the Outback is not somewhere you can afford to have things go

wrong. Travelling alone is generally ill-advised, while **night riding** is also hazardous, with poor surfaces hard to judge and kangaroos liable to bounce out of nowhere.

Motorbike **rental** – usually available only in the cities – is expensive: at least the same price as a car. One unusual alternative is a **motorbike tour**: these take various forms, from ones where you provide the bike and the tour consists of an itinerary, company on the road and a support vehicle, to a quick blast on the back of a Harley Davidson (see "Listings" section throughout the *Guide* for details of operators).

### CYCLING

**Cycling**, and especially cycle-racing, is popular in Australia, and even if you're not a triathlete bent on pedalling between Sydney and Perth, bicycles are easily ferried between places where you'd want to use them. Mountain bikes are ideal for rougher country, but lighter and more efficient tourers are better if you're attempting any long-distance travel on main roads. Most cities have well-defined cycle routes and bike lanes; helmets are compulsory. **Renting** and finding **spares** is no trouble in capital cities and larger country towns.

If you're **bringing your own** bike, international airlines usually overlook the odd extra kilo if the bike is properly packaged; ask first — though it's often the airport check-in counter which has the last word. **Internal flights** insist on having the handlebars and pedals turned in, the front wheel removed and strapped to the back, and the tyres deflated; some consider bikes as two pieces of excess baggage and charge accordingly (excess baggage is usually insured up to a maximum of $1600 damages; you might want to extend this). **Trains** have fixed rates for carrying bikes depending on the route and you'll save on **bus** charges by disassembling and packing them flat. See "Books" (p.849) for specialist guides to cycling in Australia.

## HITCHING

Recent events — primarily the 1992 "backpacker murders" — have drastically changed Australian attitudes to hitching. The gruesome murders attracted worldwide publicity, both for their shock value and for the seemingly indiscriminate choice of victims: men and couples seemed as likely a target as lone women, allaying several hitchhiking myths. The official advice is **don't**: with so many affordable forms of transport available, there's no real need to take the risk.

If you must do it, never hitch **alone**, and always avoid being dropped in the middle of nowhere between settlements. In rural areas people seem more willing to stop, but long, isolated stretches of road don't make this the safest country to hitch in; as usual, **women** are at greatest risk. Remember that you don't have to get into a vehicle just because it stops: choose who to get in with and don't be afraid to ask questions before you do get in, making the arrangement clear from the start. Ask the driver where he (or she) is going rather than saying where you want to go. Try to keep your pack with you; having it locked in the boot makes a quick escape more difficult.

A safer and more predictable method is to try lining up lifts through **hostel noticeboards** (though this means sharing fuel costs). This option gives you the chance to meet the driver in advance and being fellow travellers they'll most likely be stopping to see the sights along the way. In out-of-the-way locations, filling stations are a good place to head, as the owners often know of people who'll be heading your way.

The best way to ensure your **safety**, apart from exercising your judgement and common sense, is to make concrete arrangements before your departure and stick to them. Hostel managers are well aware of the possible danger to young women departing across the Outback with new acquaintances or undertaking work on remote stations, and will gladly receive or better still make calls to ensure your safe arrival. In response to increasing concerns, **Travelwatch** (free call ☎1800/673 305; $15 to join, and then $5 per month) has been formed. It operates as a phone-in security service with two functions: electronic mail where others can leave messages for you to collect; and security messages, where you can leave details of your travel plans and expected time of arrival, which will be handed to the police if you don't report in — a useful service not just for hitching, but also for journeying in remote regions.

# ACCOMMODATION

**Australians love to move around, and finding somewhere to bed down is rarely a problem, even in the smallest of places. However, on the east coast it's a good idea to book ahead for Christmas and Easter holidays, and in some places (the Gold Coast for instance), even weekends see price rises and room shortages.**

Watch out for the term "**hotel**", which does not necessarily mean the same in Australia as it does everywhere else in the world. Traditionally, an Australian hotel was a place to drink, a pub, and although there was a legal requirement that they all provided somewhere for customers to sleep off a skinful, the accommodation was not necessarily salubrious. Today, plenty of hotels have cleaned up their act and do offer pleasant rooms; these are the ones we've highlighted in the *Guide*. However, the majority of them are still primarily places to drink, can be loud and

drunken, and are not necessarily enticing places to stay.

The other side of this coin is that many places that would call themselves hotels anywhere else prefer to use another name – hence so many **motels** and **resorts**, and in the cities "**private hotels**" or, especially in Sydney, "**boutique hotels**" that tend to be smaller and more characterful places to stay, more like guesthouses than hotels. There are also a growing number of **bed and breakfast** places and **farmstays** where you can join in the farm life. Other categories of accommodation worth looking into are the huge array of excellent **hostels** and "**backpackers**", **caravan parks** that offer accommodation in the form of permanent **on-site vans** and **cabins** or chalets as well as campervan facilities and tent spaces, and **self-catering apartments** or, in country areas, cabins and cottages.

## HOTELS AND MOTELS

Cheaper Australian **hotels** are generally pubs and offer only rudimentary lodgings. Rooms tend to be basic – no TV, shared bathrooms and plain furnishings – but they are good value at around $30–50 double, $20–35 single, with rates usually including breakfast. Quite a lot of motels and hotels also offer special **backpacker deals**, either in newly kitted-out dorms or simply sharing a room. Hotels aren't always the best choice for peace and quiet: in country areas they're often the social centre of town, especially on Friday and Saturday nights. **Motels** are typically a comfortable, bland choice, often found on the edge of town to catch weary drivers, and priced

## ACCOMMODATION PRICES

All the accommodation listed in this book has been categorized into one of eight price bands, as set out below. The rates quoted are normally for the cheapest available double or twin room in **high season**; single rooms are generally about two-thirds the price of doubles. However, there's a variety of different types of accommodation on offer – sometimes under the same roof: band ① refers only to hostels and backpacker accommodation, where the price quoted is per bed in a dorm; for units, cabins and vans the price quoted is for the entire unit, which may sleep as many as six people.

In the lower categories, most rooms will be without private bath, though there's usually a washbasin in the room. From the ⑤ band upwards you'll probably have private facilities. Remember that many of the cheaper places may also have more expensive rooms including en suite facilities.

| | | | |
|---|---|---|---|
| ① Under $16 | ② $16–26 | ③ $ 27–36 | ④ $ 37–54 |
| ⑤ $55–74 | ⑥ $75–94 | ⑦ $95–124 | ⑧ $ 125 upwards |

on average at $50–70 for a double room with TV and bath, not including breakfast; they rarely have single rooms, but they may have larger units for families, often with basic cooking facilities.

In **cities**, you're far more likely to come across a hotel in the conventional sense. The cheaper of these may well describe themselves as **private hotels** to distinguish themselves from pubs, the decisive factor being the absence of a public bar. Some of these, especially in inner cities, can be rather sleazy, but others are very pleasant, family-run guesthouses; rooms might cost anything from $35 to $70 double, and there are often singles available at about two-thirds the price. **More expensive hotels** are much as you'd expect: in the cities most of them are standard places aimed at the business community with all the usual facilities; in resorts and tourist areas, they're more like upmarket motels. Prices might be anything from $70 double to $300 or more for five-star establishments: a typical city three-star will probably cost you $100–150; similar standards in a resort or country area cost $80–120 (though resort prices can soar at peak times and be brilliant value out of season).

There are numerous nationwide **hotel and motel chains** that give certain guarantees of standards, among them familiar names like *Best Western* and *Travelodge*, as well as Australian ones such as *Budget*, *Golden Chain* and *Flag*. All have directories of their members, which you can use to plan ahead. *Flag* go one further, with a discounted **hotel pass** – actually pre-paid vouchers in one of six categories for *Flag*'s 400

or so properties across the country. While these would be rather restrictive to use for your whole stay, they can be a good way of ensuring that you have a reservation immediately you arrive, or anywhere else you know you'll be spending some time.

## RESORTS AND SELF-CATERING UNITS

You'll find things calling themselves **resorts** all over Australia, but the term is not a very clearly defined one. At the bottom end, price, appearance and facilities may be little different to those of a motel, while top-flight places can be exclusive hideaways costing hundreds of dollars a night. Originally the name implied that the price was all-inclusive of accommodation, drinks, meals, sports and anything else on offer, but this isn't always the case. They tend to be set in picturesque locations – the Barrier Reef islands swarm with them – and are often good value if you can wrangle a standby or off-season price.

Self-catering or self-contained **units** or **apartments** or country **cabins** can be a very good deal for families and larger groups. The places themselves range from larger units at a motel to purpose-built apartment hotels, but are usually excellent value. Cooking facilities are variable, but there'll always be a TV and fridge; linen (generally not included) can sometimes be rented for a small extra charge.

## FARMSTAYS AND BED & BREAKFASTS

Another option in rural areas are **farmstays** on working farms and **B&Bs** or **guesthouses**, the latter predominantly in the south and east. Both offer a more homely atmosphere, though B&Bs especially can be anything from someone's large home to your own colonial cottage – ask what the "breakfast" actually includes. Farmstays are even more variable: at some you'll get a chance to involve yourself in the working of the farm and join the farmworkers or family at mealtimes, and accommodation might be fairly basic. Others, though, are effectively luxurious resorts where you can sit back and watch if that's all you want to do, while tours and activities like horse-riding are laid on.

## HOSTELS

The tourist boom of the past few years has seen a sudden glut of **budget accommodation** springing up, and though the more shambolic

### ACCOMMODATION CHAINS

The following organizations represent **chains** of independent hotels, motels or farmstays, and can provide information and make reservations before you leave home.

#### Flag International

*UK Flag International Ltd* (☎0800/89 2407 or 0181/543 4400).

*USA and Canada Flag International Ltd* (☎1800/ 624 3524).

*New Zealand Flag International* (☎0800/803 524 or 09/379 9444).

#### Australian Farmhost and Farm Holidays

*UK Sprint Representation* (☎0181/579 8648).

*USA ATS Sprint* (☎1800/423 2880 or 818/841 1030).

## YHA AND VIP PASSES

An International **YHA card**, best obtained before you leave from your national youth hostel association (though you can also buy one in Australia), is well worth having, as is the *BRA* equivalent, a **VIP card** ($15 from any member hostel). The *YHA* card gives you members' rates at *YHA* hostels (not all have different rates for members, though), while the *VIP* card is good for ten percent off at all BRA hostels. Both of them also qualify you for a wide range of other **discounts**, on everything from bus tickets and tours to museum entry fees and meals.

operations don't survive for long, standards are still wildly variable. Official **youth hostels** are pretty dependable – a few still require membership or charge a supplement to non-members, and some allocate chores and have awkward opening hours. Most restrictive rules and regulations have been dropped in the face of competition, however, especially from the **Backpacker Resorts of Australia** network, whose **VIP cards** are as useful and widely known as the *YHA* equivalent.

At their best, **hostels and backpackers** – both names are widely used, and don't necessarily imply membership of either organization – are excellent value, and good places to meet other travellers and plug into the grapevine. There's often a choice of dormitories, double or family rooms, bike rental, kitchen, games room, TV, a pool, and help with finding work or organizing trips; many have useful noticeboards, organized activities and tours. At their worst, they're

grubby, rapid-turnover dives. *VIP* listing, or even *YHA* affiliate membership, is not necessarily an assurance of quality.

Most hostels provide blankets, but they don't always include **sheets**; you can usually pay extra to rent them, but it's a wise precaution to carry a sleeping sheet, if not a full sleeping bag. Expect to **pay** between $10 and $16 per night for a bed in a dorm; $25 to $40 for a double room.

## CAMPING, CARAVAN PARKS AND ROADHOUSES

Perhaps because Australian hostels are so widespread and inexpensive, simple tent camping is a little-used option by foreign travellers. Australia has some remarkably hard ground so vital **equipment** includes ground mats and a range of pegs – some wide for sand, others narrow for soil. A hatchet is fairly light and doubles as a hammer. Fuel stoves are recommended, but if you do build a fire, make sure it doesn't get out of control and observe any fire bans. In national parks, **bushcamping** is often the only option for staying overnight: some park sites have hot showers, drinking water and toilets; others provide absolutely nothing. Prices depend on state policy and site facilities, and you'll usually need a permit from the local NPWS (National Parks and Wildlife Service) office.

**Camping rough** by the road, even if you take the usual precautions of setting up away from the roadside and avoiding dry river beds, is not a good idea. If you have to do it, try and ensure you're not too visible: having a group of drunks pitch into your camp at midnight is not an enjoyable experience. Animals are unlikely to pose a threat except to your food – keep it in your tent or

## YOUTH HOSTEL ASSOCIATIONS

**England and Wales** *Youth Hostel Association (YHA)*, Trevelyan House, 8 St Stephen's Hill, St Alban's, Herts AL1 (☎017278/45047). London shop and information office: 14 Southampton St, London WC2 (☎0171/836 1036).

**Northern Ireland** *Youth Hostel Association of Northern Ireland*, 56 Bradbury Place, Belfast, BT7 (☎01232/324733).

**Scotland** *Scottish Youth Hostel Association*, 7 Glebe Crescent, Stirling, FK8 2JA (☎01786/51181).

**Ireland** *An Oige*, 39 Mountjoy Square, Dublin 1 (☎01/363111).

**USA** *Hostelling International-American Youth Hostels (HI-AYH)*, 733 15th St NW, Suite 840, PO Box 37613, Washington, DC 20005 (☎202/783 6161).

**Canada** *Hostelling International/Canadian Hostelling Association*, Room 400, 205 Catherine St, Ottawa, ON K2P 1C3 (☎613/237 7884 or ☎1800/663 5777).

**Australia** *Australian Youth Hostels Association*, Level 3, 10 Mallett St, Camperdown, NSW (☎02/565 1325).

**New Zealand** *Youth Hostels Association of New Zealand*, PO Box 436, Christchurch 1 (☎03/799 970).

a secure container or be prepared to be woken by their nocturnal shenanigans.

In towns, there's often a choice between basic council campsites and better **caravan parks**, which as well as space to pitch a tent, will also have hook-up facilities for campervans and probably a store; some even offer pools and all the facilities of a mini-resort. Many have **on-site vans** (caravans with cooking facilities but no toilet) or **cabins** (with bath or shower and often

a TV): these can be very good value, and are often available even when all the hotel and motel rooms have gone. The main problem is that **linen** – sheets, towels, etc – is usually not included, though you may be able to rent it. Expect to pay $3–10 for an unpowered site, upwards of $15 per person for a van or cabin. Highway **roadhouses** are similar, combining a range of accommodation with fuel and restaurants for long-distance travellers.

# FOOD AND DRINK

**Australia is almost two separate nations when it comes to food. In the cities of the southeast – especially Melbourne – there's a range of fantastic, cosmopolitan and above all inexpensive restaurants and cafés featuring almost every imaginable cuisine. Here there's an exceptionally high ratio of eating places to people, and they survive because people eat out so much – three times a week is not unusual. Remote country areas are the complete antithesis of this, where the only advance on meat pies and microwaveable fast-food are the meat-and-three-veg counter meals served at the local hotel or, if you're lucky, a slightly more upmarket bistro or basic Chinese restaurant.**

Traditionally, Australian food found its roots in the English overcooked meat and three veg "commonsense cookery" mould. Two things have rescued the country from its culinary destitution:

immigration and an extraordinary range of superb fresh ingredients, locally produced, that not even the most ham-fisted chef can ruin. Various ethnic cuisines are briefly discussed below, but in addition to introducing their own cuisine, immigrants have had at least as profound an effect on mainstream Australian food. "Modern Australian" cuisine is an exciting blend of tastes and influences from around the world – particularly Asia and the Mediterranean – and many not specifically "ethnic" restaurants will have a menu that includes properly prepared curry, dolmades and fettuccini alongside the steak and prawns. This healthy, eclectic and above all fresh, contemporary Australian cuisine has been compared to Californian cooking styles.

## AUSTRALIAN FOOD

**Meat** is plentiful, cheap and excellent: steak forms the mainstay of the pub counter meal, and of the ubiquitous "**barbie**", or barbecue – as Australian an institution as you could hope to find. Even if no one invites you along to one, you can still enjoy a barbie: free or coin-operated electric barbecues can be found in car parks, campsites and beauty spots all over the country. As well as beef and lamb, you may also find **exotic meats**, especially in more upmarket restaurants. Emu, buffalo, camel and witchetty grubs are all served, but the two most common are **kangaroo** (at least in states where the cattle lobby hasn't prevented its sale), a delicious, tender and virtually fat-free meat, and **crocodile**, which tastes like a mix of chicken and pork, and is at its best plain grilled. At the coast, and elsewhere at specialist restaurants, there's tremendous **seafood** too: prawns and oysters, mud crabs, Moreton Bay "bugs" and yabbies (sea- and freshwater crayfish), lobsters, and a wide variety of fresh- and seawater fish – barramundi has a reputation as one of the finest.

**Fruit** is good too, from Tasmanian apples and pears to tropical bananas, pawpaw (papaya), mangoes, avocados, citrus fruits, custard apples, lychees, pineapples, passion fruit, star fruit and coconuts – few of them native, but delicious nonetheless. **Vegetables** are also fresh, cheap and good; note that aubergine is known as eggplant, courgettes as zucchini and red or green peppers as capsicums.

**Vegetarians** might assume that they'll face a narrow choice of food in "meatocentric" Australia, and in the country areas that's probably true. But elsewhere most restaurants will have one vegetarian option at least, and in the cities veggie cafés have cultivated a wholesome, trendy image that suits Australians' active, health-conscious nature.

## PLACES TO EAT

**Restaurants** are astonishingly good value compared with Britain and North America. Many restaurants are **BYO**, which stands for bring your own, another substantial factor in keeping your costs down: you buy your own wine or beer and bring it with you – you're rarely far from a bottle shop (the Australian term for an off-licence or liquor store). There may be a small corkage fee, but it's still better than paying inflated restaurant prices for your drink: even many licensed restaurants also allow you to BYO. You should have no problem finding an excellent two- or even three-course meal in a BYO restaurant for $20 or less. There are also lots of excellent **cafés and coffee shops** – Italian ones (see below), continental patisserie/bakeries, or places that serve English-style "Devonshire (cream) teas" and cakes. In the cities and resorts, cafés will be open from early in the morning till late at night, serving food all day; in the country, they may stick more or less to shop hours.

The hotel **counter meal** is another mainstay, and at times may be all that's available: if it is, make sure you get there in time – meals in pubs are generally served only from noon to 2pm and again from 6 to 8pm, and rarely at all on Sunday evenings. The food – served at the bar – will be simple but substantial and inexpensive (usually under $10): steak, salad and chips and variations on this theme. Slightly upmarket from this is the hotel **bistro** or restaurant in a motel, where you sit down to be served much the same food; these places often have a help-yourself salad bar too, which is always a good alternative for vegetarians.

**Fast food** is widely available, with all the usual burger, pizza and chicken places offering a quick bite for as little as $5. Fish (usually shark or snapper) and chips can be excellent in coastal

---

## INFAMOUS AUSTRALIAN FOODS AND THE "ESKY"

**Damper**. Sounding positively wholesome in this company, **"damper"** is the swagman's staple – soda bread baked in a pot buried in the ashes of a fire. It's not hard to make after a few attempts – the secret is in the heat of the coals and a splash of beer.

**Lamington**. A chocolate-coated sponge cake rolled in shredded coconut.

**Pavlova** or "pav". Named after the eminent Russian ballerina, a pavlova is a dessert concoction of meringue with layers of cream and fruit.

**Pie floater**. The apotheosis of the meat pie; found especially in Queensland and South Australia, a "pie floater" is an inverted meat pie swamped in mashed green peas and tomato sauce.

**Witchetty (or *witjuti*) grubs**. About the size of your little finger, witchetty grubs are dug from the roots of mulga trees and are a well-known Australian bush delicacy. Eating the plump, fawn-coloured caterpillars live (as is traditional) takes some nerve, so try giving them a brief roasting in embers. They're very tasty either way – reminiscent of peanut butter.

**Vegemite**. Regarded by the English as an inferior form of Marmite and by almost every other nationality with total bemusement, Vegemite is an Australian institution – a strong, dark, yeast spread for bread and toast.

**Esky**. A brand name which has been adopted to describe all similar products, Eskies are insulated food containers varying from handy "six-pack" sizes to cavernous sixty-litre trunks capable of refrigerating a weekend's worth of food or beer. No barbie or camping trip is complete without a couple of eskies.

regions. In cities and bigger resorts you'll find fantastic fast food in **food courts**, often in the basements of office blocks or in shopping malls, where dozens of small stalls compete to offer Thai, Chinese, Japanese or Italian food as well as burgers, steaks and sandwiches. On the road, you may be reduced to what's available at the **roadhouse**, usually the lowest common denominator of reheated meat pies and microwaved ready meals.

## ETHNIC FOOD

Wave after wave of immigrants since World War II have brought a huge variety of **ethnic cuisines** to Australia: first north European, then Mediterranean and finally Asian.

### CHINESE

**Chinese** restaurants were on the scene early in Australia – a result of post-goldrush Chinese enterprise – and Sydney, Melbourne and Darwin have Chinese connections dating as far back as the 1850s. The Chinese restaurants you'll find in most of the country tend to be rather old-fashioned and heavily reliant on MSG, but they're often the only alternative to Australian food. In contrast, the Chinatown area of big cities will provide a chance to sample some regional Chinese dishes as well as the usual Cantonese.

### ITALIAN – AND COFFEE

The **Italian** influence on Australian cooking is enormous, perhaps the most important of all – Italians and their language are second only to the English as an ethnic group. Italians brought with them their love of food as a lifestyle, which fitted beautifully with the Australian climate and way of life, and from the Fifties on pizzerias, espresso and gelati bars and the then exotic taste of garlic were conquering palates countrywide. One particularly Australian metamorphosis is **focaccia**, now a staple of every city café and beginning to make an appearance in country towns. A flat bread with a nubbly golden top, it's cut horizontally, filled and toasted to make delicious sandwiches.

The country can also thank the Italians for elevating **coffee** to a pastime rather than just a hot drink. Nowadays every suburban café has an espresso machine, and it's not just used to make *cappuccino*. Other **styles of coffee** have adopted uniquely Australian names: a *flat white* is a plain white coffee, *cafe latte* a milkier version usually served in a glass (like cappuccino without the froth), a *long black* is a regular cup of black coffee, *short black* is an espresso – transformed by a splash of milk into a *macchiato*.

## OTHER EUROPEAN AND MIDDLE EASTERN

Melbourne is Australia's food capital, with its legendary **Greek** population among the many European influences in the city. As well as taverna-style Greek restaurants, *souvlaki* bars abound, with spiced lamb rotating on a spit. **Turkish** and **Lebanese** takeaways use a similar ingredient for their spicy filled rolls, while some Turkish places also offer *pides*, small, simple but spicy variants on a pizza. Lebanese restaurants are especially good for **vegetarians**, with falafel rolls (pitta bread stuffed with chick-pea patties, hoummous and tabbouleh) making an inexpensive, filling meal.

Central European influences are most obvious in baking: particularly in Melbourne, Jews (mostly from pre-war Poland) contribute a strong **Jewish** flavour, and there are also a few **Polish** restaurants serving solid, peasant-style dishes. **German** influences are most prominent around Adelaide and at deli counters countrywide, where you'll find an abundance of Australian-made salamis and sausages.

## OTHER ASIAN CUISINES

Since the 1970s a new wave of immigrants, from southeast Asia, has further energized Australian cuisine. **Vietnamese** restaurants not only offer some of the cheapest meals anywhere but also combine fresh ingredients with sophisticated French influences from colonial days; with your meal comes a plate of red chillies, lemon wedges and crunchy beansprouts.

**Malaysian** and **Indonesian** restaurants or market stalls are also commonly seen, with hearty noodle soups and satays with hot peanut sauce. Hawker-style stalls in city food courts often serve *laksa*, a huge bowl of hot and spicy coconut-milk-based soup full of noodles, tofu and chicken or prawns.

**Thai** restaurants are probably the biggest success of them all, and it's hard to believe that they've been around for little more than ten years. Dishes can be fiery yet subtly-flavoured with lemongrass, garlic, chilli and coriander.

**Japanese** food in Australia is made more accessible – and less expensive – by the availa-

## BUSH TUCKER

The first European colonists decided that the country was not "owned" by the Aborigines because they didn't systematically farm the land. As many frustrated pastoralists later came to realize, this was a wise adaptation to Australia's erratic seasons, which don't lend themselves to European farming methods with any degree of long-term security. Instead, Aborigines followed a nomadic lifestyle within extensive tribal boundaries, following seasonal game and plants and promoting both by annually burning off grassland.

**Along the coast** people speared turtles and dugong from outrigger canoes, caught fish in stone traps, piled oyster shells into giant middens, and even co-operated with dolphins to herd fish into shallows. Other **animals** caught all over the country were possums, snakes (highly prized), goannas, emus and kangaroos. These animals were thrown straight onto a fire and cooked in their own juices with the skins, bones and fat sometimes used as clothing, tools and ointment respectively. More meagre pickings were provided by honey and green ants, water-holding frogs, moths and various grubs – the witchetty (or *witjuti*) being only the best known. Foot-long ooli worms were drawn out of rotten mangrove trunks and tiny native bees were tagged with strands of spider web and then followed to their hives for honey; another sweet treat was mulga resin, picked off the tree trunk.

**Plants**, usually gathered by women, were used extensively and formed the bulk of the diet. The cabbage palm, sea almond, mangrove seeds, pandanus and dozens of fruits, including tropical coconuts, plums and figs, all grew along the coast. Inland were samphire bush, wild tomatoes and "citrus", grasstree hearts, cycad nuts (very toxic until washed, but high in starch), native millet, wattle seeds, waterlily tubers, *nardoo* seeds (a water fern), fungi, macadamia nuts, cashews and bunya pine nuts – the last had great social importance in southern Queensland, where they were eaten at huge feasts. In Queensland's far north you'll find one of the few surviving traditional styles of cooking, the Torres Strait Islander *kup maori* – meat and vegetables wrapped in banana leaves and roasted in an underground oven.

It's tempting to **taste** some bush foods and a few outlets (see p.101 and p.723 for a couple of places to try) are now experimenting with them as ingredients; otherwise you'll need expert guidance as many plants are poisonous. A few tours and safaris (particularly in the Northern Territory) give an introduction to living off the land; for further reading, try *Bush Tucker: Australia's Wild Food Harvest* by Tim Low (Angus & Robertson).

bility of so much fresh seafood. There may not be much of a Japanese population, but there are a huge number of Japanese visitors – and plenty of places catering for them (you'll find lots on the Gold Coast, for example).

**Mongolian barbeques** sound like a short-lived novelty but in fact are quite good: an unusual, fast and inexpensive complement to the already diverse Asian food culture. Thinly sliced meat or seafood is added to a selection of sliced vegetables and stir-fried in a soy-type sauce before your eyes on a giant wok – a Mongol warrior's shield is said to have been the original cooking utensil.

### DRINKING

Australians have a reputation for enjoying a drink, and **hotels** (also sometimes called taverns, inns, pubs and bars) are mostly where it all happens. Traditionally, public bars are male enclaves, the place where mates meet after work on their way home, with the emphasis more on the beer and banter than the surroundings. While changing attitudes have converted some city hotels into comfortable, relaxed bars, many Outback pubs are still pretty spartan and daunting for strangers of either sex, but you'll find barriers will come down if you're prepared to join in the conversation.

Friday and Saturday are the serious **party nights**, when there's likely to be a band and – in the case of some Outback establishments – literally everybody for a hundred kilometres around jammed into the building. **Opening hours** vary from state to state; usually 11am to 11pm, closing early on Sunday.

### BEER

As anyone you ask will tell you, the proper way to drink **beer** in a hot country like Australia is ice cold (the English can expect to be constantly berated for their warm beer preferences) and fast, from a small container so it doesn't heat up before you can down the contents. Tubular foam or polystyrene **coolers** are often supplied for

**tinnies** (cans) or **stubbies** (short-necked bottles) to make sure they stay icy. Glasses are always on the small side, and are given confusingly different names state by state. The standard 10oz (half-pint) serving is known as a **pot** in Victoria and Queensland, and a **middie** in NSW and WA, where the situation is further complicated by the presence of 15oz **schooners** (a "Darwin stubby", with typically Territorian eccentricity, is two litres of beer in an oversized bottle). Buying in bulk from a bottle shop, a **carton** or slab is a box of 24 tinnies or stubbies, and is always cheaper warm.

Australian beers are lager- or pilsner-style, and even the big mass-produced ones are pretty good, at least once you've worked up a thirst. They're considerably stronger than their US equivalents, and marginally stronger than the average British lager at just under 5 percent alcohol. *Fosters* is everywhere of course, but each state has its own label and there are fierce local loyalties, even though most are sold nationwide: *Fourex* (*XXXX*) and *Powers* in Queensland; *Swan* in Western Australia; *Coopers* in South Australia; *VB* in Victoria; *Tooheys* in New South Wales; *Bogues* in Tasmania. Almost all of these produce more than one beer – usually a light (or lite) low-alcohol version and a premium "gold" or bitter brew. There are also a number of smaller "boutique" breweries and specialist beermakers: Tasmania's *Cascade*, WA's *Redback* or *Matilda Bay*, Cairns' *Draught* and *Eumundi* from Queensland are more distinctive but harder to find. Larger bottle shops might have **imported beers**, but outside the southern capitals (where Irish pubs serve *Guinness*) it's rare that you'll find anything foreign on tap.

## WINES AND SPIRITS

Australian **wines** have long been appreciated at home, and it's not hard to see why; even an inexpensive bottle (around $8.50) will be better than

just drinkable, while pricier varieties compare favourably with fine French wines. The secret is to be a bit adventurous: you're extremely unlikely to be disappointed. Even the "chateau cardboard" 4-litre bladders or wine casks that prevail at parties and barbecues are perfectly palatable.

The biggest wine-producing regions are New South Wales' Hunter Valley and the Barossa Valley in South Australia, but you'll find smaller commercial vineyards as far north as Stanthorpe in Queensland and in southwest Western Australia. **Buying** here you'll be able to sample in advance, though there's occasionally a charge for tasting to discourage over-enthusiastic visitors from just trying everything and leaving. Most bottle shops will in any case have a good range of very reasonably priced options.

The Australian wine industry also makes **port** and **brandy** as a sideline, though it's not up to international standards on the whole. Two excellent dark **rums** from Queensland's sugar belt are well worth a go, however: the sweet, deliciously smoky *Bundaberg*, and the more conventionally flavoured *Beenleigh*. They're of average strength, normally 33 percent alcohol, but beware of "overproof" variations, which will have you flat on your back if you try to drink them like ordinary spirits.

## SOFT DRINKS

Various colas, *Sprite*, *7-Up*, *Fanta* and a couple of home-produced brands – *Bundaberg* ginger beer and *Cascade*'s Tasmanian apple juice – are the soft alternatives to alcohol. Bottled **fruit juices** come in every style, and in the tropics (and trendy city cafés) you can often get the familiar and unfamiliar freshly squeezed. Next to these, there's a range of **spring waters** from several sources along the Great Dividing Range – a relief at times from the heavily chlorinated tap water. Sickly **flavoured milk** is another national institution: every store with a fridge will have it packed with different flavoured cartons.

# COMMUNICATIONS

## MAIL

Every town of any size will have a **post office**, and where there isn't one there'll be an **Australia Post** agency, usually at the general store. Post offices and agencies are officially open Mon–Fri 9am–5pm; agencies might have an hour off during the day for lunch or close early and big city **GPOs** sometimes open late or on Saturday mornings. **Postboxes** are rare out in the country, so you'll usually have to take your mail to the nearest post office or agency.

Domestically, the mail service has a poor reputation, at least for long distances: it can take a week for a letter to get from Wittenoom (WA) to Wagga Wagga (NSW). On the other hand **international mail** is extremely efficient, taking 5–10 days to reach Europe, Asia and the States, depending on where it's posted. **Stamps** are sold at some newsagents and general stores, as well as post offices and agencies; a standard letter or postcard within Australia costs 45c (more for Express, which is worth it for anything important); printed **aerogrammes** for international letters anywhere in the world cost 70c; postcards cost 95c to the USA and Canada, $1 to Europe; regular letters start at $1.05 to the USA and Canada, $1.20 to Europe. If you're sending anything bigger in or outside Australia, there's a huge range of different ways to do it at different prices; get some advice from the post office. Large parcels are reasonably cheap to send home by surface mail, but you'll have to wait up to three months for them to get there.

You can receive mail at any post office or agency: address the letter to **Poste Restante** (add "GPO" or "Central Post Office" for cities, unless you have the address of a particular branch), followed by the town, state and post code. You need a passport or other ID to collect mail, which is kept for a month and then returned; it's possible to get poste restante redirected if you change your plans – ask for a form at any post office. Some smaller post offices will allow you to ring and check if you have any mail waiting.

Most **hostels and hotels** will also hold mail for you if it's clearly marked, preferably with a date of arrival, or holders of Amex cards or travellers' cheques can have it sent to **American Express** offices (addresses are given in the "Listings" sections throughout the *Guide*). Another option is *Travellers' Contact Point*, 428 George St, Sydney (☎02/221 8744; ☎02/9221 8744 from July 1996) which operates a mail and message service: for a $35 fee, they'll hold and forward your mail as you are travelling around Australia, up to a maximum of 12 months, and offer more flexibility than poste restante – just call them to get your mail redirected if your plans change.

## PHONES

Post offices (but not agencies) always have a bank of **telephones** outside; otherwise head for the nearest bar or service station – you'll even find solar-powered, satellite-connected booths in the Outback. Most public telephones now take **phone cards**, which are sold through newsagents and other stores for $2, $5, $10 or $20; there are also some older coin-operated boxes, and newer call boxes which take credit cards (though many do not take *Mastercard*) and bank cards. You can make **international calls** from virtually any of them, though it's a great deal easier with a card; instructions are provided. Many bars, shops and restaurants also have pay phones, although they may cost more than a regular call box. In the cities there are **telecom offices** with calling rooms, where you can find a bit of peace while you ring home, and also check phone directories and time differences; elsewhere post offices may be able to help.

## CHANGES TO PHONE NUMBERS AUSTRALIA-WIDE

Over the next three years, up to 1998, there will be a progressive change to all Australian telephone numbers: every number will gain an extra one or two digits, so that all numbers will eventually consist of **eight digits** plus a two-digit area code. When completed, the **area codes** for the regions will be:

* Central East, covering New South Wales and ACT ☎02

* South East, covering Victoria, Tasmania and South West New South Wales ☎03

* North East, covering Queensland ☎07

* Central and West, covering Western Australia, Western New South Wales, Northern Territory and South Australia ☎08.

The numbers given in the guide take account of all the changes that had been made by end-1995, and boxes indicate changes planned up until end-1997. If in doubt, you can call Telstra's free **Information Hotline** on ☎1800/88 8888. For eight months after the changeover, if you accidentally call the old number you will be automatically connected to the new number at no extra charge; for a further three months you will hear a recorded message advising you that the number has been changed.

Following deregulation, **Telstra** (formerly Telecom Australia) has been joined by **Optus**, but so far their service is only available from private phones in certain areas.

Call boxes do not accept **incoming calls**. You can make **reverse charge** calls through the operator (☎0176 from public phones, ☎011 from private ones), but it's easier with **Country Direct** which, for the price of a local call, will connect you directly to an operator in the country you're calling (numbers are listed in the box below).

Calls **within Australia** are cheapest in the evenings from Monday to Saturday, and all day Sunday; local calls cost only 40c and you can talk for as long as you like. Many businesses and services operate **free call** numbers, prefixed ☎1800, while others have six-digit numbers beginning ☎13 that are charged at the **local-call rate**. Numbers starting ☎0055 are private information services (often recorded), costing between 35c and 70c per minute, but with a minimum charge of 40c from public phones. **International calls** have different hours for cheap rates, depending on the destination, but weekends will almost always be cheaper: prices are very reasonable – a call to Britain or North America costs between $1.03 and $1.35 a minute.

## MASS MEDIA

*The Australian* is Australia's only **national daily newspaper**; aimed mainly at the business community, it has good overseas coverage but local news is often built around statistics. Each state (or more properly, each state capital) has its own daily paper – sometimes more than one –

ranging from Queensland's vapid, reactionary *Courier Mail* to the more thoughtful *Sydney Morning Herald* or Melbourne's venerable *The Age*. The last two are probably the most objective of Australia's papers, and are also widely sold across much of the country. **Local papers** are always a good source of listings, if not news. You should be able to track down some **international papers** – British, American, Asian and European – in capital cities.

The weekly *Time Australia* and *Newsweek/ Bulletin* are the **current affairs** magazines, along with the more **arts**-orientated monthly *Independent*; if you're interested in **wildlife**, pick up a copy of *Geo* or the bi-monthly *Australian Geographic* (related only in name to the US magazine) for some excellent photography and in-depth coverage of Australia's remotest corners.

Australian **television** isn't particularly exciting unless you're into sport, of which there's plenty; there are three predictable commercial stations plus the somewhat stodgy ABC – a national, advertisement-free station – and the livelier SBS, a government-sponsored, multicultural station, which has the best world news coverage, as well as interesting current affairs programmes and plenty of foreign-language films. Not all of these are nationally available; in more remote regions there may be only two stations, though an increasing number of people subscribe to satellite.

The best **radio** is mostly on local stations, although **ABC Radio National** around the country offers a popular mix of arty intellectual topics and **2JJJ** ("Triple J"), a former Sydney-based alternative rock station, is available across the country in only slightly watered-down form.

## OPERATORS AND INTERNATIONAL CODES

### Operator Services

Local Directory Assistance ☎013
National Directory Assistance ☎0175
International Directory Assistance ☎0103

Operator ☎0176 from payphone; ☎011 from private phone
International Operator ☎0107 from payphone; ☎0101 from private phone

### International Calls

To **call Australia** from overseas dial the international access code (☎00 from the UK, ☎011 from the US and Canada), followed by ☎61, the area code minus its initial zero, and the number. To **dial out** of Australia it's ☎0011, followed by the country code, then the area code (without the zero if there is one), followed by the number:

UK ☎0011 44   US and Canada ☎0011 1   Ireland ☎0011 353   New Zealand ☎0011 64

### Country Direct

UK   British Telecom operator ☎1800/881 440
     automatic ☎1800/881 441
     Mercury ☎1800/881 417

US   AT&T ☎1800/881 011
     LDDS Worldcom ☎1800/881 212
     MCI ☎1800/881 100
     Sprint ☎1800/881 877

Canada   Teleglobe ☎1800/881 490
Ireland   Telecom ☎1800/881 353
New Zealand   Clear ☎1800/124 333
          Telecom ☎1800/881 640

# OPENING HOURS, HOLIDAYS AND FESTIVALS

In remote country areas **roadhouses** provide all the essential services for a traveller and, on the major highways, are open 18 or even 24 hours a day. In tourist areas – even ones well off the beaten track – **tourist offices** are often open every day or at least through the week plus weekend mornings; urban information centres are more likely to conform to normal shopping hours. **Tourist attractions** – museums, galleries and attended historic monuments – are often open daily, although rural communities may adopt odd hours to exhibit their pride and joy, particularly during the tropical north's wet season; specific opening hours are given throughout the *Guide*.

Shops and services are generally open Monday to Friday 9am to 5pm and till lunchtime on Saturdays. In addition many shops in cities and larger towns are open late on Thursday or Friday evenings – usually till 9pm – and all day Saturday.

## HOLIDAYS

Contrary to popular opinion and Australia's commendably relaxed interpretation of the work ethic, there are surprisingly few nationwide **public holidays** – and even when you add in the state ones (two or three per state, or about eight

## NATIONAL HOLIDAYS

In addition to the holidays listed below, every state has its own bank holidays – generally two or three more a year. When the official holidays fall at the weekend, there may be an extra day off immediately before or after, and these can again vary from state to state.

New Year's Day
Australia Day (Jan 26 or Monday following)
Good Friday
Easter Monday
Anzac Day (April 25)
Christmas Day
Boxing Day

and-spade war zones and the roads are jammed with stationwagons full of holidaying families. Dates vary from year to year and state to state, but generally people are on the move for six weeks from mid-December (January is worst, as many people stay home till after Christmas), a fortnight around Easter, and another couple of weeks in June or July.

## FESTIVALS

The nationwide selection of **festivals** listed below all include, necessitate, and are in some cases the imaginative product of prolonged beer swilling. Why else would you drive to the edge of the Simpson Desert to watch a horse race (see "Birdsville", below)?

At the serious level, each mainland capital tries to elevate its sophistication quotient with a regular celebration and showcase of **art and culture**, of which the biennial *Adelaide Arts Festival* is the best known.

in the Northern Territory), Australia lags behind most European countries in official days off.

Watch out for **school holidays**, when seaside resorts can be transformed into bucket-

## FESTIVALS

Besides the major events which are listed below, there's a host of smaller, local events, many of which are detailed in the text. The Christmas and Easter holiday periods, especially, are marked by celebrations at every turn, all over the country.

### JANUARY

**Festival of Sydney**, NSW. A month of festivities with something for absolutely everyone.

**Montsalvat Jazz Festival**, Eltham, VIC. Australia's premier jazz festival takes place on the Montsalvat Estate over Australia Day weekend: book well ahead.

**Tamworth Country Music Festival**, Tamworth, NSW. Ten days of Slim Dusty and his ilk, culminating in the Australian Country Music Awards.

### FEBRUARY

**Sydney Gay and Lesbian Mardi Gras**, NSW. Sydney's proud gay community's festival lasts three weeks, ending with an extravagant parade and an all-night dance party.

**Festival of Perth**, WA. A month of "low-brow arts" at venues all over the city.

**Bindoon Rock Festival**, Bindoon, WA. WA's answer to Woodstock or Reading, with some visiting overseas bands.

### MARCH

**Adelaide Arts Festival**, SA. The country's best-known and most innovative arts festival (biennial, in even years), not to be missed.

**Melbourne Moomba Festival**, VIC. Eleven days of partying beginning and ending with fireworks and lots of fun in between.

### APRIL

**Barossa Valley Vintage Festival**, SA. Biennial (odd years) Germanic festival set in the country's viticultural heart.

**Melbourne International Comedy Festival**, VIC. Opening on April Fools Day, comics from around the world gather for three weeks.

### MAY

**Bougainvillea Festival**, Darwin, NT. A laidback fortnight of music, performance and food.

**Bangtail Muster**, Alice Springs, NT. Nutty parades and Outback silliness.

### JUNE

**Melbourne International Film Festival**, VIC. The country's largest and most prestigious film festival, lasting two weeks and with prizes in many categories.

**Barunga Sports Festival**, Beswick Aboriginal Land, NT. A rare and enjoyable chance to encounter Aboriginal culture in the NT. No alcohol.

## FESTIVALS (continued)

**Cape York Aboriginal Dance Festival**, QLD. Three-day, alcohol-free celebration of authentic Aboriginal culture. Biennial in odd-numbered years.

### JULY

**Camel Cup**, Alice Springs, NT. Camel racing down the dry Todd River.

**Darwin Beer Can Regatta**, NT. Mindil Beach is the venue for the recycling of copious empties into a variety of nutty seacraft. Also a thong-throwing contest; Territorian eccentricity personified.

### AUGUST

**Shinju Matsuri Festival**, Broome, WA. Probably the most remote big festival, which doesn't stop the town being packed for this Oriental-themed pearl festival.

**Mount Isa Rodeo**, Mount Isa, QLD. Australia's largest rodeo – a gritty, down-to-earth encounter with bulls, horses and their riders.

### SEPTEMBER

**Bathurst 1000 Road Races**, Bathurst, NSW. Australia's premier weekend of car and bike street racing.

**Henley-on-Todd Regatta**, Alice Springs, NT. Wacky races in bottomless boats run down the dry Todd riverbed – the event is heavily insured against the river actually flowing.

**Birdsville Races**, QLD. Once a year the exceedingly remote Outback town of Birdsville (pop. 120) comes alive for a weekend of horse racing – a well-known and definitive Australian oddity.

**Warana**, Brisbane, QLD. Huge, two-week arts festival centred in the city's Botanical Gardens with food, wine, beer, music, writing and children's events topped off with fireworks and a wacky *Concours de Decadence*.

**Melbourne International Festival of the Arts**, VIC. Two-week celebration of visual, performing and written arts in venues all over the city.

### OCTOBER

**Manly Jazz Festival**, Sydney, NSW. Three-day jazz festival with artists from all over the world.

### NOVEMBER

**Australian Grand Prix**, Melbourne, VIC. Formula One street-racing around the city follows a week of partying. The Grand Prix's relocation from Adelaide to peaceful Albert Park in Melbourne has been hotly protested.

**Melbourne Cup**, Flemington Racecourse, VIC. 130-year-old horse race brings the entire country to a standstill around the radio or TV.

### DECEMBER

**Sydney to Hobart Yacht Race**, Sydney NSW. Crowds flock to the harbour to witness the start of this classic regatta.

The **Christmas holidays** and **New Year's Eve** are celebrated with gusto everywhere.

# OUTDOOR ACTIVITIES

Though the cities are fun, what really makes Australia special is the great outdoors: the vast and remote wilderness of the bush, the legendary Outback, and the thousands of kilometres of unspoilt coastline. There's tremendous potential here to indulge in a huge range of outdoor pursuits – hiking, fishing, surfing, diving, even skiing – especially in the multitude of national parks that cover the country. Further information on all of these is available from tourist offices who will publicize what's available in their area, from the National Parks and Wildlife Service, who have detailed maps of parks with walking trails, climbs, swimming holes and other activities, and from specialist books (see pp.848–849 for a selection). In addition, virtually any activity can be done as part of an organized excursion, often with all the gear supplied; or if you want to go it alone you'll find plenty of places ready to rent or sell you the necessary equipment, along with some friendly advice. Before indulging in adventure activities, check your insurance cover (see p.14–15).

As with any wilderness area, the Australian interior does not suffer fools, and the coast too conceals **dangers**: sunstroke and dehydration are risks everywhere, with riptides, currents and unexpected king waves to be wary of on exposed coasts. In the more remote regions isolation and lack of surface water compromise energetic outdoor activities such as bushwalking or mountain biking, which are probably better indulged in the cooler climes and more populated locations of the south.

## BUSHWALKING

**Bushwalking** in Australia doesn't mean just a stroll in the bush, but relates specifically to extended and self-sufficient outdoor hikes, from a day to a week or longer. It's an extremely popular activity nationwide, and you'll find trails marked in almost every national park, as well as local **bushwalking clubs** whose trips you may be able to join. In any tourist area you'll also find experienced **guides**. It's essential to be properly **equipped** for the conditions you'll encounter – and to know what those conditions are likely to be. Stick to the track. If your trip is a long one, let someone know where you're going, and confirm to them that you're back safely – park rangers are useful contacts for this, and some will insist on it anyway. The essentials, even for a short walk, are adequate clothing including a wide-brimmed hat, enough food, and, above all, **water**. Other things you really shouldn't be without are a map, torch, matches or lighter, penknife, sunblock, insect repellent, toilet paper, first-aid kit, and a whistle or mirror to attract attention if you get lost. A lot of this gear can be rented, or bought cheaply at disposal stores.

Long-distance tracks exist mostly in the south of the country, with Tasmania's wilderness areas being perhaps the most rewarding bushwalking location; the 85km **Overland Track** from Cradle Mountain to Lake St Clair is the island's best-known trail. On the mainland, the **Blue Mountains**, a two-hour train ride from Sydney, the **Snowy Mountains** further south, and Victoria's spectacular **Grampians** are all popular regions for longer, marked walks.

South Australia's Flinders Ranges, 300km north of Adelaide, are accessible along the **Heysen Trail** from the Fleurieu Peninsula, the walk into the 1000m-high natural basin of Wilpena Pound being the highlight. In vast Western Australia, only the southwestern corner can offer extended walks: the 640km **Bibulman Track**, an old Aboriginal trail passing through the region's giant eucalypt forests, is signed all the way from Walpole to Perth. An hour's drive north of Albany, the near-1000m peaks of the Stirling Ranges also offer some spectacular trails. In the Northern Territory, **Litchfield Park**, two hours south of Darwin, is

---

### BUSH ESSENTIALS

Three things above all:

**Bushfires**: the driest continent on earth is always at risk from bushfires and nowhere is exempt. Sydney's **Black Friday** fires of 1994 saw the city ringed with fire and the continuing drought conditions have meant a constant red alert in summer months. When there is a **total fire ban**, the law prohibits any fire in the open, including wood, gas or electric barbecues, with fines of up to $1000. Never discard burning cigarette butts from cars. If fires are permitted, take great care, using an established fireplace if possible and make absolutely sure it's out before going to sleep or moving on. Check on the local fire danger before you go **bushwalking** – some walking trails are closed in the riskiest periods (summer in the south; the end of the dry season – Sept/Oct – in the north). If **driving**, carry blankets and a filled water container, listen to your car radio and watch out

for roadside fire danger indicators. If the worst happens, there are practical ways of surviving a bushfire.*

**Water**: do not contaminate scarce water resources. Soaps and detergents especially can render water undrinkable and kill livestock and wild animals. Avoid washing in standing water, especially tanks and small lakes or reservoirs.

**Waste**: take only photographs, leave only footprints. That means carrying all your rubbish out with you, and making sure you urinate (and bury your excrement) at least 50m from a campsite or water source.

---

*See "Health", pp.20–21, for perils likely to afflict bushwalkers and advice on how to deal with them – including practical ways of surviving a bushfire.

a croc-free tableland fringed with perennial springs enabling some satisfying bushwalks in the dry season, while the **Larapinta Trail**, along the MacDonnell Ranges west of Alice, is being extended year by year. Queensland's coastal strip offers plenty more opportunities, from the **Mount Tamborine-Lamington** area in the south, to the **Atherton Tablelands** in the north, and especially on **Hinchinbrook Island**.

## WATERSPORTS

The oceans and seas around Australia are a national playground, and not just for tanning or volleyball on the beach. Always take local advice on the waves, which must be treated with respect. If possible, **swim** from a patrolled beach, between the flags: raise one hand if you get into difficulty, and clear the water if a siren sounds – it could signal dangerous waves, a shark sighting or a swarm of blue bottles (tiny, stinging jellyfish). Enjoying the water doesn't necessarily involve any special effort or equipment, but if you want it, there are plenty of activities on offer. Probably the easiest to get into is **surfing**, starting with body-surfing and progressing to boogie-boards (small boards that you lie on) and then on to full-scale surfboards. Surfing is popular everywhere, but don't expect the local surfie community to be too friendly at first – they're often very cliquey. Seaside hostels often have boards which they loan out free. **Windsurfing** and **sailing** are also extremely big, and you'll be able to rent equipment or get instruction in almost any resort. **White-water rafting**, **sea kayaking** and **canoeing** are also widely available.

The Great Barrier Reef is one of the world's great **scuba diving** meccas, with extensive and highly developed facilities. Scuba **courses** on the Reef tend to be expensive, and if you really want to make the most of it you might consider learning before you come rather than spending a week taking lessons. On the other hand there could be nowhere better to learn – and if you simply want to try it once there are plenty of people offering closely supervised "resort dives". If you're bringing your own gear, check on the compatibility of connections to Australian tanks – you may need an adaptor. **Snorkelling** is the low-tech alternative, and still allows you to get dramatically close to the aquatic life around the reef.

**Fishing** is another obsession – on rivers and lakes, off piers or small boats ("tinnies"), or heading out to sea for marlin and other game fish. Again all the equipment – even boats – can be hired in most good fishing areas. Barramundi, renowned for its fighting qualities as well as its taste, is the thing to go for up north.

## OTHER PURSUITS

The craze for **bungee jumping** has, not surprisingly, caught on with Australia's hard-core thrill-seekers: Cairns in northern Queensland is a good place to try it in a spectacular setting, or there are cranes to jump from in plenty of other places. **Rap jumping** is a newer version that essentially involves abseiling head-first at very high speed down sheer cliff faces. Alice Springs' wide-open spaces make it the country's **hot air ballooning** centre and also a base for **camel treks** through the surrounding desert.

More regular **riding**, on horseback, is offered all over the country – anything from a gentle hour at walking pace to a serious cattle round-up. **Cycling** and mountain biking are tremendously popular too, as well as being a good way of getting around resorts; many hostels rent out bikes, and we've listed other outlets throughout the text.

Australia's wilderness is an ideal venue for extended **off-road driving** or dirt-bike riding, although station- and Aboriginal-owned lands, as well as the fragile desert ecology, should be respected at all times. Northern Queensland's Cape York and WA's Kimberley are the most adventurous destinations, 4WD accessible in the dry season only. The great Outback **tracks**, pushed out by explorers or drovers, such as the Gunbarrel and Sandover Highways and the Tanami, Birdsville and Oodnadatta Tracks, are technically mostly two-wheel driveable in dry conditions, but can be hard on poorly-prepared vehicles; only WA's 2000km Canning Stock Route demands 4WD and an enormous fuel range, effectively ruling out motorbikes.

Finally, you may not associate Australia with **skiing**, but there's plenty of it in the 1500m-high Australian Alps around the border of Victoria and New South Wales, based around the winter resorts of Thredbo, Mt Hotham and Perisher. Europeans tend to be sniffy about Australian skiing, and certainly it's limited, with a season that lasts barely two months – July and August –

and few very challenging runs. The one thing that does match Europe is the prices. On the other hand it's fun if you're here, and the relatively gentle slopes of the mountains are ideal for **cross-country skiing**, which is increasingly being developed alongside downhill.

## NATIONAL PARKS

The Australian **National Parks and Wildlife Service** (NPWS) is split into federal and state bodies, the federal organization dealing with international problems such as whaling and how to use Antarctica, and occasionally arbitrating between the otherwise independent state departments. The state bodies actually run the parks day to day – and each tends to be called some-

thing slightly different. The 600-odd national parks range from suburban commons to the Great Barrier Reef, and from popular hiking areas in easy reach of the big cities to wilderness regions which require days in a 4WD simply to reach. They protect everything within their boundaries: flora, fauna and landforms as well as Aboriginal art and sacred sites.

**Fees** are variable. Some parks or states have no fees at all, some charge for use of camping facilities, others require permits bought in advance. If you're **camping** you can usually pay on site, but booking ahead might be a good idea during Christmas and Easter holidays. Nearby resorts or alternative accommodation are always independently, rather than NPWS-run.

## SPORT

**Australians are sports mad, especially for the ostensibly passive spectator sports of cricket, Aussie Rules football, rugby (league or union), tennis or any type of racing, from cockroach to camel. It really doesn't matter what it is, it'll draw a crowd – with thousands more watching on TV – and a crowd means a party. Even unpromising-sounding activities like surf lifesaving and yacht racing (the start of the Sydney to Hobart race just after Christmas is a massive social event) are tremendously popular.**

It's hard to escape sport in Australia: people talk about it constantly, it's all over the papers, TV and radio, and it's a huge source of national pride. The wintertime **football** (footy) season in Australia lasts from March till September; in summer **cricket** is played from October to March.

Footy comes in several varieties. **Soccer** is reasonably popular as a participatory sport but not very big otherwise, while amateur **rugby union**, despite the huge success of the *Wallabies* national team, is also very much a minority interest domestically. **Aussie Rules** football dominates Victoria, South Australia and Western Australia: an extraordinary, anarchic, no-holds-barred, eighteen-a-side brawl, most closely related to Gaelic football. The ball can be propelled by any means necessary, and the fact

that players aren't sent off for misconduct ensures a lively, skilful and above all gladiatorial confrontation. The game is mostly played on cricket grounds, with a rugby or American football type ball, the idea being to cross the opposition's line for a "behind" (one point) or kick it through the uprights for a goal (six points). There are four 25-minute quarters, plus lots of time added on for injury. Despite the violence on the pitch (or perhaps because of it), Aussie Rules fans tend to be loyal and well behaved. Victoria has traditionally been the home of the game, and Victorian sides are expected to win the AFL Cup, decided at the Grand Final in September, as a matter of course. In New South Wales and Queensland **Rugby League** attracts the fanatics especially for the hard-fought **State of Origin** matches. The thirteen-a-side game is one of which the Australians seem permanent world champions, despite having a relatively small professional league.

Summertime **cricket** is a great spectator sport – for the crowd, the sunshine and the beer as much as the play. Every state is involved, and the three- or four-day Sheffield Shield matches of the interstate series are interspersed with one-day games and internationals, as well as full five-day international Test Matches.

Minor sports are followed with no less avid attention, and there are plenty of them, including horse racing and trotting, motor-racing, swimming, athletics, tennis – you name it. One peculiarly Australian institution is the **surf carnival**, when teams of volunteer lifesavers demonstrate their skills – a great day out on the beach. **Surfing** itself can also be a competitive sport, with the Eastertime World Championships, held at Bell's Beach, southwest of Melbourne, and

November's Margaret River Classic, south of Perth, both good opportunities to catch some hot wave-riding action. Inland, many rural towns have a **speedway track** occupying a tract of wasteland, where at weekends motor-headed hoons demonstrate their dirt-tracking skills in souped-up utes or motorbikes; a dusty, noisy and merry focus for the entire community and passers-by.

# WOMEN ... AND SEXUAL HARASSMENT

from groups of mem in the street can be intimidating. The best policy is to appear confident, avoid making eye contact when passing a group of men or, better still, discreetly cross the street if you see a group ahead. Above all, ignore the comments to avoid giving them the reaction they seek.

Meeting Australian men **socially**, as individuals, you'll often find that under a brusque, offhand exterior, they're surprisingly helpful and kind; they're also, on the whole, honest and upfront.

## SEXUAL EQUALITY AND ATTITUDES

In public life, Australia has one of the best records for **sexual equality** in the world. It was the second country to give women the vote (after New Zealand in 1893), and the fact that this happened a year after federation in 1901 shows that the intention was for women to take a full role in the new nation. In the Seventies and Eighties Australia kept pace with the worldwide **feminist movement** (indeed, with Germaine Greer, it helped lead it): the first big milestone, equal pay for equal work, was finally achieved in 1974. Equal opportunities legislation and affirmative action schemes for employment have been widely adopted: today, non-sexist language is the norm for newspapers and officialdom.

**The stereotyped image of the Aussie male is of a boozy bloke interested in sport, his car and his mates, with his girlfriend a poor fourth. And it's not far wrong: the Australian ethos of mateship has traditionally excluded women – the hard tough life of the early days of white settlement, when women were scarce, fostered a male culture that's to some extent still current. Another legacy of pioneering times is the reputation of Australian women for being robust and practical.**

In the main **cities**, attitudes are generally enlightened and "new men" are gaining ground, but in the more remote country and **Outback areas**, the older attitudes are more tenacious and sexual harassment can be commonplace – if rarely threatening. Men in cars in particular are notorious for shouting out crude comments and sexual remarks as you walk by, and catcalling

However, with all of this has not always gone a corresponding change in attitudes. Around the same time women achieved equal pay, **public bars** of hotels which had traditionally refused to serve women were stormed by women's groups. Now, you can get a drink anywhere, but the whole way Australian pubs are set up with two bars continues to reflect the old bias; you'll still see signs saying "Ladies' Lounge", and you'll have to walk a long way from the public bar to the women's toilets. **Outback and country pubs** are still very much male bastions, and any woman travelling on her own would do well to avoid them, thus escaping the full misogynistic blast.

## WOMEN ALONE

Avoiding pubs is all very well, but **hotels** are often the cheapest and sometimes the only places to stay in **small towns**. The major drawback is that pub accommodation is often full of single male workers from other towns, or old men boarding, so late-night roaming of corridors in search of the toilet can be unpleasant. That said, the management is usually friendly, and most country pubs are family-run. **Bed and breakfast** establishments and **guesthouses** provide a more home-like, friendly environment unlike the inevitably impersonal and potentially lonely experience of staying in a **motel**. **Caravan parks** and **campsites** tend to be safe, family-dominated environments, and are a good bet if you have your own transport – and sleeping bag. In larger towns and cities, **hostels** are where you're most likely to meet like-minded women travelling solo. Easy-going Australian attitudes mean that dorms in backpackers hostels (never YHA hostels) are often mixed sex; there's usually at least one female-only dorm, but you should ask in advance or at least as you check in if this is important to you.

Best of all for making contact with locals and generally getting involved are **farmstays**, which needn't be expensive if you stay in shearers' quarters and the like, or the experience of being a WWOOF (Willing Workers on Organic Farms; see p.53). Before going to work or stay on remote **Outback stations**, try to find out as much about the set up as possible as you could end up being the only woman among a group of men – a potentially uncomfortable situation.

## RAPE AND SERIOUS TROUBLE

**Rape** figures highly in Australian crime statistics. If the worst happens, it's best to contact a Rape Crisis Line before going straight to the police; all major cities (see "Listings" sections of city accounts in the *Guide*) have them and there's always a free-call line if you're in the country. Women police officers form a large part of the force, and in general the police deal sensitively with sexual assault cases.

To **avoid** physical attack, don't get too relaxed about Australia's friendly, easy-going attitude. In the cities, buses or trams are generally safer than trains at night – on the train, always sit in the carriage next to the guard. Pick somewhere to stay that's close to public transport so you don't have to walk far at night – a busy nightlife area may well be safer than a dead suburban backstreet. If you're going to have to walk for long stretches at night, take a cab unless the streets are busy with traffic, restaurants and people.

The 1992 "backpacker murders" of hitching travellers just outside Sydney prove that it's not only in remote areas or alone that **hitchhiking** is dangerous – and that even male company is no safeguard. Hitching is doubly inadvisable for women and, with the wide variety of inexpensive transport options available, is hard to justify. If you must do it, never do it alone – and heed the general advice and warnings given on p.30.

## WOMEN'S CONTACTS

All the major cities have good **women's contacts**, from resource centres and information lines to health centres, where you can often get free pregnancy testing and other help. There's also a lively culture of women's galleries and bookshops; as well as stocking the hundreds of great Australian women writers (see "Books" in *Contexts* for suggested reading), they'll have copies of feminist journals and good noticeboards which often have information about **women-only accommodation**. Lesbian magazines also carry ads for women's bed and breakfasts and the like – you don't have to be gay to stay. In March, **International Women's Day** provides an excuse for a month-long series of women's events in the cities, culminating in enthusiastically attended street marches.

Specific women's contacts are listed in the city sections of this book. For more, check out the *White Pages* under "Women", or the Citizen's Advice Bureau in each city should be able to refer you to relevant organizations.

# GAY AND LESBIAN AUSTRALIA

**Year by year Australia grows in popularity as a Queer destination. Even as far back as 1832 a Select Committee of the British Parliament noted the popularity of "alternative lifestyles" among the colonists. Today, the beautiful people flock Down Under, lured by the conducive climate and laidback lifestyle and eager to hang with the homeboys on balmy beaches and sun-kissed city streets.**

Despite its reputation as a macho culture, Australia revels in a large and active **scene**: you'll find an air of confidence and a sense of community that is often missing in other countries — and, what's more, it's friendly and accessible.

The colonists transported English **law** to Australia, but in 1972 South Australia was the first state to enact decriminalization, followed the next year by the ACT and Northern Territory. Surprisingly, Victoria and New South Wales (generally thought of as liberal states) delayed similar legislation until the 1980s. Less surprisingly, Queensland only took the plunge in 1991. In Western Australia there's still an age of consent of 21 and Tasmania, despite constant petitioning, has so far opted to remain in the dark ages in its attitude and laws concerning homosexuality.

Today, Australia is testimony to the power of the pink dollar, and there's an abundance of gay venues, services, businesses, travel clubs, country retreats and the like. Even *McDonald's* advertise their family restaurants in Sydney's Mardi Gras magazine and Penguin Books have teamed up with *Outrage* magazine to promote gay and lesbian fiction.

## LESBIAN AUSTRALIA

Australian **dykes** are refreshingly open and self-possessed — a relief after the more closed and cliquey scenes in Europe. The flip side of their fearlessness is the predominance of S&M on the scene. Maybe the climate has something to do with it, but you'll see a good deal of tattoos and pierced flesh around.

Dyke **scenes** are nothing if not mercurial, and Australia is no exception. We've done our best to list bars, clubs and meeting places, but be warned that venues open, change name, change hands, shut for refurbishment, get relaunched at a new address and finally go out of business with frightening rapidity.

## GAY AUSTRALIA

Australia is definitely the place to watch Men At Work, and at play. **Aussie boys** get a lot of sun and sport — although the scene is a lot more diverse than simply tan and toned muscle, and the community is so large that there's bound to be something for everyone. One thing's for certain, you won't be bored. Just remember to pack your trunks, snorkel and fins, your clubbing gear and some barbecue tongs. You'll also need some cowboy boots if you want to take part in the **bootscooting** (Country and Western Line Dancing) craze currently sweeping the country.

## WHERE AND HOW TO GO

**Sydney** is the jewel in Australia's luscious navel. Firmly established as one of the world's great gay cities — only San Francisco can really rival it — it attracts lesbian and gay visitors from around the world. And if this can be overwhelming at times (the gossip alone has been known to drive people to the other side of the continent), Australia has plenty more to offer. In Melbourne the scene stays close on Sydney's heels. For a change of pace, take a trip to Brisbane and the Gold Coast; Perth, Adelaide and Darwin all have smaller, quieter scenes.

Away from the cities, things get more discreet, but a lot of **country areas** do have very friendly local scenes, impossible to pinpoint, but easy to stumble across. Australians on the city scene are a friendly bunch, but in a small country town they get *really* friendly, so if there's anything going on you'll probably get invited along.

The **Outback** covers the vast majority of the Australian continent and is, in European terms, barely populated. Mining and cattle ranching are the primary employers and they help to create a culture not famed for its tolerance of homosexuality. Tread carefully: bear in mind that Ayers Rock may be 2000km from Sydney as the crow flies, but in many ways it's a million miles.

A couple of organizations exist specifically to help lesbian and gay travellers. The **Australian Gay and Lesbian Tourism Association**

## GAY AND LESBIAN CONTACTS

**AGLTA** PO Box 208, Darlinghurst, NSW 2010. Produce *Gay and Lesbian Tourism Services Directory*, available free direct from them, but there's a small charge for overseas postage.

**AIDS Organizations** *ACON (AIDS Council of NSW) Rural Outreach Project*, PO Box 350, Darlinghurst, NSW 2010 (☎02/9283 3222 or 1800/802 612); *ACT UP*, Sydney (☎02/9281 0362), Melbourne (☎03/9419 5670) and Canberra (☎06/258 3154); *AFAO (Australian Federation of Aids Organizations)*, PO Box 525, Woden, ACT 2606 (☎06/285 4464); *AFAO National Legal Project*, PO Box 350, Darlinghurst, NSW 2010 – free legal advice; *AIDS Trust of Australia*, PO Box 1272, Darlinghurst, NSW 2010 (☎02/9211 2044); *Australian National Council on AIDS*, PO Box 9848, Canberra, ACT 2061 (☎06/289 7767); *National Association of People Living with HIV/AIDS*, PO Box 525, Woden, ACT 2606 (☎06/257 4985).

**Australian Gay Hospitality Exchange** PO Box 108, Newtown, NSW 2042. Network of gay men who will host overseas visitors. Write well in advance and send a small donation in any currency to cover postage.

**Country Network** PO Box 4488, Kingston, ACT 2604 (☎06/288 5454). Mainly urban gay and lesbian friendship network.

**Press** Two monthly gay and lesbian magazines are widely available: *Campaign*, PO Box A228, Sydney South, NSW 2000; and *Outrage*, 85 King William St, Fitzroy, VIC 3065. *Lesbian Network*, PO Box 215, Rozelle NSW 2039, is a quarterly magazine, available by mail order.

**Travel Agents** *Destination Downunder*, PO Box 429, North Sydney, NSW 2060 (☎02/957 3811, fax 02/957 1385); *Friends of Dorothy Travel*, 2nd Floor, 77 Oxford St, Darlinghurst (☎02/360 3616); *Outrage Travel Service* ☎03/9596 3566 or free call ☎1800/06 1427; *Pride Travel*, Shop 3A, 28 Hindley St, Adelaide, SA 5000 (☎08/212 3833, ☎08/8212 3833 from Aug 1996); *Silke's Travel*, 263 Oxford St, Darlinghurst, NSW (☎02/380 6244, fax 02/361 3729); *Triangle Vacations*, PO Box 186, Alderley, QLD 405 (☎07/3221 7527, fax 07/3229 7661).

(AGLTA, see box above for details) is a dynamic organization dedicated to turning Australia into *the* premier destination for the world's gay and lesbian tourists. They give their seal of approval to accommodation, resorts, travel agents and promoters that provide the attitude or atmosphere that today's gay globetrotter demands – and their *Gay and Lesbian Tourism Services Directory* covers retreats, guesthouses and country lodges across Australia, not just in the cities. AGLTA also help produce handy *Gay and Lesbian Maps* for Sydney, Melbourne and Brisbane – available from gay venues and from the travel agents listed above.

**Australia and Beyond** is an annually updated, pocket-sized gay and lesbian guide. A mine of information about where to shop, eat, drink, dance and sleep in Australia and New Zealand, it's published by the *Sydney Star-Observer* and is widely available, priced at about $15.

Each chapter has specific gay and lesbian listings, with a wealth of information – check out *Sydney and Around* in particular, which has you need to know to join in the Mardi Gras celebrations (see p.110).

### AIDS

Australia is, by and large, very **AIDS** aware. Safe sex has a prominent place on the scene and you'll probably find that you have an amazing variety and quantity of safe-sex gear thrust upon you on your travels. Australia responded early to the AIDS threat: the federal and most state governments have been relatively progressive, funding a range of AIDS organizations.

As you might expect, Sydney has the majority of Australia's AIDS cases, and the support networks are well established here and in the other major cities; again, you'll find local listings in the major city accounts as well as those included in the box above.

# POLICE, PREJUDICE AND TROUBLE

**"Transportation across the seas"**, to which judges condemned the petty criminals of two centuries ago, seems to have been a successful policy; Australia today can pride itself on being a relatively crime-free country, although increasingly it is following the American trend in gun-related incidents.

This is not to say there's no petty crime, or that you can leave normal caution behind, but there is less violent crime and theft in Australia, even in the big cities, than in most of Europe or North America, and even so-called "heavy" downtown areas can appear pretty tame. You're perhaps more likely to fall victim to a fellow traveller or an opportunist: **thefts** in some hostels are pretty common, while if you leave valuables lying around, or on view in cars, you can expect them to go. Exercise normal caution, don't forget your normal streetwise precautions, and you should be fine; in cities at night stay in the light and busy areas, walk with confidence and don't carry excess cash or anything else you can't afford to lose.

One place **violence** is commonplace is at the ritual pub "blue" (fight) among known protagonists on a Friday or Saturday night, but strangers are seldom involved without at least some apparent provocation.

## POLICE AND THE LAW

Australia's **police** – all armed – have a thoroughly poor public image and perhaps as a result tend to keep a low profile, and you should have no trouble with them. Indeed you'll hardly see

them, unless you're out on a Friday or Saturday night when they cruise in search of drink-related brawls.

Things to watch out for, above all, are **drugs**. Marijuana grows easily and its use is widespread, but you'd be foolish to carry it when you travel, and crazy to carry any other illicit narcotic: each state has its own penalties, and though a small amount of grass may mean no more than confiscation or an on-the-spot fine, they're generally pretty tough – especially in Queensland. Crossing **state borders** you may find your vehicle searched – not just for "firearms, pornography or drugs" but also for fruit and fresh produce, which often cannot be carried from one state to the next (you'll see big signs warning you, and places to dispose of your life-threatening bananas). Driving in general makes you more likely to have a confrontation of some kind, if only for a minor traffic infringement: **drunk driving** is regarded extremely seriously, so don't do it.

Lesser potential problems are **alcohol** – there are all sorts of controls on where and when you can drink, and taking alcohol onto Aboriginal Lands can be a serious offence; **smoking**, which is increasingly being banned in public places; **littering** (ditto); and nude or **topless** sunbathing, which is quite acceptable in many places, but absolutely not in a few others – follow the locals' lead.

If for any reason you are **arrested** or need help (and you can be arrested merely on suspicion of committing an offence), you are entitled to contact a friend or lawyer before answering any questions. You could call your consulate, but don't expect much sympathy. If necessary, the police will provide a lawyer, and you can usually get legal aid to settle the bill.

## PREJUDICE, POLICE AND THE TRAVELLER

Given Australia's record on treatment of its Aboriginal population, and the history of the White Australia policy, it comes as little surprise to find that this is a nation where **racial prejudice** is ingrained. As a **black traveller** you're likely to attract attention when you don't particularly want it, and be unable to get it when you do – even to the extent of being refused service in an Outback bar, or being unable to flag down a cab in a city. Certainly in remote areas, where Aboriginal people are still often treated as second-class citizens at best, black travellers may have an uncomfortable time.

**Asians** are far more accepted (in Australia, "Asian" usually means southeast Asian – the Indian and Pakistani populations are negligible), although in recent years there have been protests against continuing Asian immigration. Again it's the cities which have long-established Asian populations, and in the country you're likely to be up against more ignorance and bigotry.

Despite the foregoing, Australia does have powerful anti-discrimination laws. Any racial discrimination can be reported to the **Human Rights and Equal Opportunities Commission**, who have offices in each state capital (listed in the "Government" section at the front of the *White Pages* phone book). Although you might not have time (or desire) to go through the whole long complaints process, the threat is a useful one, as their powers are considerable. Just don't expect a country policeman to help you – many are part of the problem rather than its solution.

---

### EMERGENCIES

☎000 is the free emergency telephone number which summons the police, ambulance or fire service.

---

# WORK

**Most Australian visitors' visas clearly state that no employment of any kind is to be undertaken during their visit to the country. However, if you've succeeded in getting a Working Holiday Visa (see "Visas and Red Tape", pp.12–13) and are prepared to try anything – officially for no more than three months at a time – there are plenty of possibilities for finding work. There are also organized work programmes – both paid and voluntary.**

In practice this means that the only jobs officially open to you are unskilled, temporary ones. Certainly this is what you'll be offered if you go to the *Commonwealth Employment Service* (**CES**), the government employment agency that has a branch in every major town and in rural areas where there's a lot of seasonal work (sometimes represented by a temporary agency in a shop or post office): look them up in the phone book. What they offer will usually be either **harvesting or farm-labouring jobs** (see box opposite), or in the cities **clerical**, **bar** and **restaurant** jobs, or occasional **factory** work.

While the CES can usually offer you some kind of work (though it may take a few days, and it may be menial), finding a job yourself may be ultimately more rewarding. Private **employment agencies** are worth a try in the cities, especially if you have a marketable skill (computer training, accountancy, nursing, cooking and the like): they'll almost always have better, higher-paid jobs than the CES, though they may be looking for full-time or at least longer-term commitment. Newspaper **job ads** are also worth checking out, especially in smaller local papers. And finally, fellow travellers and **hostel** staff and noticeboards may be the best source of all, especially in remote areas. This is where you'll find out about local opportunities, while the hostels themselves may occasionally offer free nights in lieu of cleaning work – or even pay you for more complex duties.

Significant long-term **unemployment** is prevalent in recession-struck Australia, and the

## SEASONAL PICKING AND HARVESTING WORK

Listed below are the major **harvest seasons** around the country: once you're into the harvest season it's possible to move with it around the country, from one product to another, as many people do. There may be lesser harvests and other work in all of these places at any time.

**NEW SOUTH WALES**

**Summer** Nov–Apr, peaking in Feb, in central eastern district around Bathurst, Dubbo and Orange; orchard and other fruits, cotton, onions and asparagus.

**Year-round** North coast around Coffs Harbour; bananas.

**VICTORIA**

**Summer** Nov–Apr, peaking in Feb, in central northern areas around Shepparton; orchard fruits, tomatoes, tobacco, grapes and soft fruits.

**QUEENSLAND**

**Summer** Dec–Mar, around Warwick, inland on the NSW border; stone and orchard fruits, grapes.

**Year-round** Southern central coast around Bundaberg and Childers; all kinds of fruit and vegetables.

**May–Dec** Central coast around Bowen; fruit and vegetables, especially mangoes at end of year.

**May–Nov** Northern Coast around Ayr and Ingham; sugar cane, bananas and tobacco.

**TASMANIA**

**Summer** Dec–Mar; orchard and soft fruits, grapes and hops.

**SOUTH AUSTRALIA**

**Feb–April** Barossa Valley; grapes.

**Year-round** Riverland; picking, pruning and packaging citrus and soft fruits.

**WESTERN AUSTRALIA**

**Oct–June** Southwest; grapes and orchard fruits (Feb–April), plus tractor-driven grain harvesting.

**Mar–Nov** West coast from Fremantle to Carnarvon; crayfish, prawn and scallop fishing and processing.

**May–Oct** Northeast around Kununurra; fruit and vegetable picking and packing.

---

days of legendary wages for relentless hard work in mines, on the roads or on prawn trawlers are long gone. Nonetheless, work is still available if you're prepared to do anything (for poor wages) and make a bit of an effort finding it – and plenty of people still even manage to work **illegally**, though visa checks in the major harvest areas and tax reforms have made this much harder than it used to be.

## ORGANIZED WORK PROGRAMMES

To streamline the process of procuring a working visa, getting to Australia and orientating yourself on arrival, there are several packages aimed at working travellers. BUNAC organize a **Work Australia** programme that can be combined with their North American programmes, with departures from London between August and October and from Los Angeles in September and October. As well as a work/travel programme, WTN programmes also help to arrange **voluntary work** with a **conservation** bias (including the ATCV "Echidna Package" aimed at overseas travellers and WWOOF placements) – see box above for contact details.

### WORK PROGRAMME CONTACTS

**ATCV** (Australian Trust for Conservation Volunteers), PO Box 423, Ballarat, Victoria 3350 (free call ☎1800/03 2501 or 0061/53 32 7490; 0061/3 5332 7490 from March 1997).

**BUNAC** (British Universities North America Club), 16 Bowling Green Lane, London EC1R 0BD (☎0171/251 3472).

**WTN** (World Travellers Network). Head office: 3 Orwell St, Potts Point, Sydney, NSW 2011 (☎0061/2357 4477). European administration office: Postbus 107, 5800 AC Vernay, The Netherlands (☎0031/4780 88074).

**WWOOF** (Willing Workers on Organic Farms), Mount Murrindal Reserve, W Tree, Via Buchan, Victoria 3885 (☎0061/5155 0235; 0061/3 5155 0235 from April 1997).

## TAX

In recent years employers have been threatened with huge fines for offering cash-in-hand labour and, as a result, it's difficult to avoid paying **tax,** which is levied at 29 percent for earnings under about $26,000 per annum and deducted at source. To become part of the system you need a **tax file number** (form available at post offices or taxation offices), which is pretty easy to obtain on presentation of a passport with relevant visa – or even without one if you're lucky. Your employer will give you a couple of weeks' grace, but not much more – if you don't have a number

after that you'll be taxed at 49 percent. Nowadays it's hard to claim a tax **rebate**, no matter how little you earn; however, it's worth a try, and possibly a visit to a tax advisor. One tip is to tick the "resident" box on the rebate form: you're resident if you're planning to stay a day over six months.

# DIRECTORY

**BIG THINGS** Don't be surprised if on a long, hot stretch of Queensland highway you find yourself hitchhiking next to Captain Cook . . . and no, that enormous pineapple on the horizon isn't an alien spacecraft, it's real. Real fibreglass that is. Big Things are an Australian obsession, a way for a small town to make a mark on the tourist map. Travelling the country you'll find giant fruit – the Big Apple, the Big Banana, the Big Strawberry; animals and fish – the Big Lobster, the Big Penguin, the Big Cow; and tourist attractions – the Big Gold Panner and even Big Ayers Rock (far smaller than the real thing, of course). They're places to stop and get a drink or a bite, buy joyously tacky souvenirs and look at an exhibition – but above all they're places to take a photo. No Australian holiday is complete without at least one Big Thing in your album.

**CONTRACEPTION** The Pill is available on prescription only from doctors, medical centres, hospital outpatient departments and family plan-

ning clinics; keep your old packet, as brands (like all drugs) may have different names here. Condoms are sold at pharmacies and from vending machines in public toilets.

**DEPARTURE TAX** Everyone over twelve years of age must pay a $27 departure tax on leaving Australia.

**ELECTRICITY** Australia's electrical current is 240/250v, 50Hz AC. British appliances will work with an adaptor for the Australian three-pin plug; American 110v appliances will also need a transformer.

**EMERGENCIES** Dial ☎000.

**GAMBLING** Australians are obsessive about gambling, though legalities vary from state to state. Even small towns have their own race-tracks and there are government *TAB* betting agencies everywhere; you can often bet in pubs too. Many states have huge "casinos" and clubs, open to anyone, with wall-to-wall one-armed bandits (poker machines or "pokies"); there are also big state lotteries.

**KIDS** Children are well catered for in Australia, and are welcome in the bistros of hotels, with kids' menus and often a children's playroom. Nearly every park has a playground. Many attractions have reduced rates for children or families, and most motels and self-catering accommodation can provide family rooms and special rates.

**LAUNDRIES** Known as laundromats these are rare outside urban centres. Hostels, motels and caravan parks will often have a laundry area with a washing machine (coin-op). Fancy hotels, of course, will do it for you.

**PUBLIC TOILETS** Towns and cities are very well supplied with public facilities in civic-minded Australia. They're found in parks and at council and tourist offices in country areas, in shopping arcades, train stations and department stores in the city. Most roadhouses offer showers as well as toilets, often free, or for a small payment.

**SEASONS** Don't forget that in the southern hemisphere the seasons are reversed. Summer lasts from November to February, winter from June to September. But of course it's not that simple: in the tropical north the important seasonal distinction is between the wet (effectively summer) and the dry (winter) – the *Introduction* has more on their significance to travellers.

**STUDENT CARDS** are well worth having if you're eligible, for discounts on travel, tours, museum entry, etc: many of these are open to backpackers of any age or status who can produce a YHA or VIP membership card (see p.33).

**TAX** There is no sales tax or VAT in Australia.

**TIME ZONES** Australia has three time zones: Eastern Standard Time (Tas, VIC, NSW, QLD), Central Standard Time (SA, NT) and Western Standard Time (WA). Eastern Standard Time is ten hours ahead of GMT, fifteen hours ahead of US Eastern time. (At 10pm in Sydney, it's noon in London, 7am in New York, 4am in Los Angeles – but don't forget daylight saving, which can affect this by two hours either way.) Central Standard Time is 30 minutes behind Eastern Standard, Western Standard two hours behind Eastern. Daylight saving (Oct–March) is adopted everywhere except QLD, NT and WA; clocks are put forward one hour.

**TIPS** Tipping is not customary in Australia, where cab drivers and bar staff don't expect anything (unbelievably, cab drivers often round the fare down rather than bother with change). In cafés and restaurants you might tell them to keep the change – only very fancy establishments expect ten percent.

**WEIGHTS AND MEASURES** Australia has been fully metric since the early 1970s, and is thoroughly adapted to kilometres, kilograms, litres and degrees Celsius. Shoe sizes are unique to Australia, dress sizes the same as the UK (US 8 is equivalent to Australian 10). See the conversion table below.

| METRIC CONVERSION TABLE | | |
|---|---|---|
| | 1 centimetre (cm) = 0.394in | 1 inch (in) = 2.54cm |
| | | 1 foot (ft) = 30.48cm |
| 1 metre (m) = 100cm | 1 metre = 39.37in | 1 yard (yd) = 0.91m |
| 1 kilometre (km) = 1000m | 1 kilometre = 0.621 miles | 1 mile = 1.610km |
| 1 hectare = 10,000 square metres | 1 hectare = 2.471 acres | 1 acre = 0.4 hectares |
| | 1 litre = 0.22 UK gal | 1 UK gallon (gal) = 4.55 litres |
| | 1 litre = 0.26 US gal | 1 US gallon (gal) = 5.46 litres |
| | 1 gramme (g) = 0.035oz | 1 ounce (oz) = 28.57 g |
| 1 kilogramme(kg) = 1000g | 1 kilogramme = 2.2lb | 1 pound (lb) = 454g |

INDIAN
OCEAN

PACIFIC
OCEAN

CHAPTER 4
TROPICAL
QUEENSLAND
AND THE REEF

CHAPTER 6
NORTHERN
TERRITORY

CHAPTER 5
OUTBACK
QUEENSLAND

CHAPTER 7
WESTERN
AUSTRALIA

CHAPTER 3
SOUTHEAST
QUEENSLAND

CHAPTER 8
SOUTH AUSTRALIA

CHAPTER 2
NEW SOUTH WALES
AND ACT

CH. 1
SYDNEY
AND
AROUND

CHAPTER 9
VICTORIA

SOUTHERN OCEAN

CHAPTER 10
TASMANIA

0          800 km

# CHAPTER ONE

# SYDNEY AND AROUND

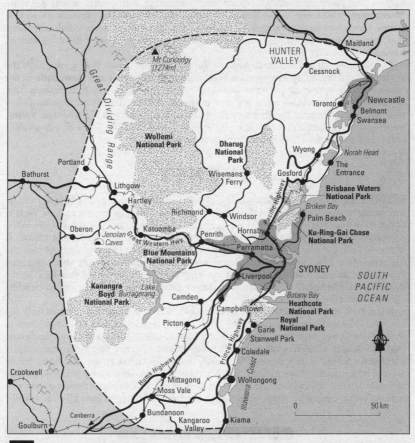

F lying into **Sydney** provides the first close-up snapshot of Australia for most
overseas visitors: toy-sized images of the Harbour Bridge and the Opera
House, tilting in a glittering expanse of blue water. The Aussie city par excel-
lence, Sydney stands head and shoulders above any other in Australia: taken
together with its surrounds, it's in many ways a microcosm of Australia as a whole – if
only in its ability to defy your expectations and prejudices as often as it confirms them.
A thrusting, high-rise business centre, a high-profile gay community, and inner-city
deprivation of unexpected harshness are as much part of the scene as the beaches,
the bodies and the sparkling harbour. The sophistication, cosmopolitan population

and exuberant nightlife of Sydney are a long way from the Outback, and yet Sydney has the highest Aboriginal population of any Australian city.

The area around – everything in this chapter is within day-trip distance – offers a taste of virtually everything you'll find in the rest of the country, with the possible exception of desert. There are magnificent **national parks** and native wildlife – Ku-Ring-Gai Chase and Royal being the best known of the parks, each a bare hour's drive from the centre of town – and beyond them stretch endless ocean **beaches**, great for surfers, and more enclosed waters for safer swimming and sailing. Inland the **Blue Mountains**, with three more National Parks, offer isolated bushwalking as well as scenic viewpoints easily reached by cable-car. On the way lie historic colonial towns that were among the earliest foundations in the country: Sydney itself, of course, having been the very first.

The commercial and industrial heart of the state of New South Wales, especially the central coastal region, is bordered by **Wollongong** in the south and **Newcastle** in the north – both synonymous with coal and steel, the smokestack industries that supported them for decades but are now in severe decline. This is far from an industrial wasteland, though: the heart of the coal-mining country is the **Hunter Valley**, northwest of Newcastle, but to visit it you'd never guess, because this is also Australia's oldest and arguably its best-known wine-growing region.

# SYDNEY

**SYDNEY** has all the vigour of a world-class city – and the year 2000 Olympics will be its coming of age ceremony. Yet those who place it on the same footing as New York or London do Australia's premier city an injustice, for Sydney's unique atmosphere is the combination of fast-moving city life with a seductive, smalltown, easygoing charm. It seems to have the best of both worlds – twenty minutes from Circular Quay by bus, the high-rise office blocks and skyscrapers give way to colourful inner-city suburbs where you can get an eyeful of sky and watch the lemons ripening above the sidewalk. In the summer the city's hot offices are abandoned for the remarkably unspoilt beaches strung around the eastern suburbs.

It's also as beautiful a city as any in the world, with a **setting** that perhaps only Rio can rival. The water is what makes the city's setting so special, and no introduction to Sydney would be complete without paying tribute to one of the world's great harbours. Port Jackson is a sunken valley which twists inland to meet the fresh water of the Parramatta River; in the process it washes into a hundred coves and bays, winds around rocky points, flows past the small harbour islands, slips under bridges and laps at the foot of the Opera House. If Sydney is seen at its gleaming best from the deck of a harbour ferry, especially at weekends when the harbour's jagged jaws fill with a flotilla

---

### TELEPHONE NUMBERS

The **telephone code** for Sydney is ☎02.

Unless otherwise specified, all phone numbers in this chapter are in the ☎02 code region.

**Note** Some Sydney telephone numbers are due to be changed in July 1996, as follows:

- 2xx xxxx and 8xx xxxx numbers will be prefixed by an additional 9, to become 92xx xxxx and 98xx xxxx.
- 3x xxxx and 8x xxxx numbers will be prefixed by an additional 91, to become 913x xxxx and 918x xxxx.

*(For more on changes to phone numbers Australia-wide, see p.40)*

## OLYMPIC CITY: 2000

Sydney beat Beijing and Manchester in the chase for the Olympics in the year 2000 – and is she proud. "Building a better Sydney" is the keynote of the Olympic Committee, *Sydney 2000* (☎02/931 2000), and the focus of beautification is bound to be Circular Quay – the showcase location for the Harbour Bridge and the Opera House, marred by the 1960s eyesore of the Cahill Expressway and a noisy above-ground train station. The Australian Tourist Commission predicts that an extra 2.1 million tourists will arrive in Australia between 1994 and 2004 on the crest of the Olympic wave, and if there isn't room in all the new hotels currently being thrown up, plans are afloat to anchor cruise ships in the harbour to increase capacity.

The main focus of events, however, will be far removed from the glamour of Sydney's harbour at **Homebush**, a fairly down-at-heel working-class suburb in the city's west. Serviced by trains and situated on the Parramatta River, there's a certain logic to the choice, with extensive riverfront Bicentennial Park and some heavy-duty sporting facilities already in place just across on Australia Avenue. If you want to check out where the action will be, head here for the **State Sports Centre** (daily 8.30am–10pm; ☎02/763 0111, 24-hr information line ☎02/746 2855) where you can visit the **NSW Hall of Champions** (same hours as centre; free) devoted to the state's sporting heroes. Also on Australia Avenue is the **Sydney International Aquatic Centre** (Mon–Fri 5am–10pm, Sat–Sun 7am–7pm; $3.50; ☎02/752 3666) where the swimming events will be based; to get here, take a train to Strathfield, then the #401 bus. Other Olympic venues around town will be the Entertainment Centre and the Exhibition Centre at Darling Harbour, with the yachting based at Rushcutters Bay and rowing at Penrith Lakes.

of small vessels, racing yachts and cabin cruisers, it's seen at its most varied in its lively neighbourhoods. Getting away from the city centre and exploring them is an essential part of Sydney's pleasures.

It might seem surprising that Sydney is not Australia's capital: the creation of Canberra in 1927 – intended to stem the intense rivalry between Sydney and Melbourne – has not affected the view of many Sydneysiders that their city remains the *true* capital of Australia, and certainly in many ways it feels like it. The city has a tangible sense of history: the old stone walls and well-worn steps in the backstreets around The Rocks are an evocative reminder that Sydney has more than two hundred years of history behind it.

Although the city's sophistication and exuberance may seem a long way from the Outback, Sydney is closer to its roots than it sometimes feels. To the centre's north and south are corridors of largely intact **bushland**, where many have built their dream homes. The scale of January 1994's **Black Friday** fires stunned the world, with front-page images of those two icons of Australiana, the Sydney Harbour Bridge and the Opera House, silhouetted against an orange, smoke-filled sky, while the leafy and affluent North Shore, only kilometres from the city centre, blazed out of control. Amazingly, although 250 homes were destroyed, only four people lost their lives; the already declining wildlife bore the brunt of the tragedy, but rapid regeneration of the bush has left few visible scars.

## Some history

The early history of Sydney is very much the history of white Australia, right from its founding as a penal colony, amid brutality, deprivation and despair. In January 1788 the **first fleet**, carrying over a thousand people, 736 of them convicts, arrived at **Botany Bay** expecting the "fine meadows" that Captain Cook had described eight years earlier. In fact what greeted them was mostly swamp, scrub and sand dunes: a desolate sight even for sea-weary eyes. An unsuccessful scouting expedition prompted Commander

Arthur Phillip to move the fleet a few miles north, to the well-wooded Port Jackson, where a stream of fresh water was found. Based around the less than satisfactory Tank Stream, the settlement was named **Sydney Cove** after Viscount Sydney, then Secretary of State in Britain. In the first three years of settlement, the new colony nearly starved to death several times; the land around Sydney Cove proved to be barren and the shotgun became the answer to the plough, with evasive kangaroos providing a meagre diet. When ships did arrive with supply, they inevitably came with hundreds more convicts to further burden the colony. It was not until 1790, when land was successfully farmed further west at Parramatta, that the hunger began to abate. Measure this suffering with that of the Iora Aborigines: their land had been invaded, their people virtually wiped out by smallpox, and now they were stricken by hunger as the settlers shot at their game – and aimed their guns at the Iora themselves as the colonists moved further inland.

By the early 1800s Sydney had become a stable colony and busy trading post. Army officers in charge of the colony, exploiting their access to free land and cheap labour, became rich farm-owners and virtually established a currency based on rum. The military, known as the New South Wales Corps (or more familiarly as "the rum corps") soon became the supreme political force in the colony, even overthrowing the governor in 1809 (mutiny-plagued Captain Bligh himself). This was the final straw for the government back home, and the rebellious officers were finally brought to heel when the reformist Governor Macquarie arrived from England with forces of his own. He liberalized conditions, supported the prisoners' right to become citizens after they had served their time, and appointed several to public offices.

By the 1840s, the explorers Lawson and Blaxland had found a way through the Blue Mountains to the Western Plains and gold had been struck in Bathurst. The population boomed as free settlers arrived in ever increasing numbers. Victorian times saw Sydney's populace even more starkly divided into the haves and the have-nots: self-consciously replicating life in the mother country, the genteel classes took tea on their verandahs and erected grandiloquent monuments such as the Town Hall, the Strand Arcade and the Queen Victoria Building in homage to English architecture of the time. Meanwhile, the poor lived in slums where disease, crime, prostitution and alcoholism were rife. An outbreak of the plague in The Rocks at the turn of the century made wholescale slum clearances unavoidable, and with the demolitions came a change in attitudes. Strict new vice laws meant the end of the bad old days of backstreet knifings, drunken taverns and makeshift brothels.

Over the next few decades, Sydney settled into comfortable suburban living. The metropolis sprawled westward, creating a flat, unremarkable city with no real centre, an appropriate symbol for the era of Bruce and Sheila, of shorts and knee socks – an international image which still plagues Australians. Sydney has come a long way since the parochialism of the 1950s, however: the cultural clichés of cold tinnies of beer and meat pies with sauce have at last been tossed out, giving way to a city confident in itself and its attractions. Skyscrapers at the city's centre have rocketed heavenward and constructions like the Sydney Tower and the Opera House reflect the new dynamism. Today, Sydney's citizens don't look inward – or even to England. Thousands of immigrants from around the globe have given Sydney a truly international air and it's a city as thrilling and alive as any.

# Arrival and information

The classic way to **arrive** in Sydney is, of course, by ship, cruising in under the great coathanger of the Harbour Bridge to tie up at the docks alongside Circular Quay. Unfortunately you're not likely to be doing that, and the reality of the functional airport, bus and train stations is a good deal less romantic.

## The airport

Sydney's **Kingsford Smith Airport**, commonly known as either Sydney Airport or "Mascot" after the suburb where it's located, near Botany Bay, is barely 8km south of the city (international flight arrivals and departures ☎0055 51850). Domestic and international terminals are on opposite sides of the airport, linked by various buses; *Qantas* and *Ansett* passengers can use a free shuttle – see box for details of **bus services** into the city. A **taxi** ride from the airport to the city or Kings Cross costs from $20 to $25 depending on traffic; between the domestic and international terminals it's $6, but drivers are reluctant to oblige.

**Bureau de change** offices at both terminals are open daily from 5am until last arrival: although exchange rates tend to be more advantageous at city banks, you'd be better off changing money at the airport if you arrive at night or on the weekend. On the ground floor of the international terminal, the helpful **Travellers' Information Service** (daily 5am until last arrival; ☎669 1583 or 1584) can book hotels (but not hostels) anywhere in Australia free of charge. Hostels do, however, advertise on a noticeboard; there's a free phone line for reservations, and many of them will also provide complementary pick-ups or else refund your bus fare.

---

### AIRPORT BUSES

**Airport Express** buses (green-and-yellow) link the two terminals ($2.50), and shuttle to and from the city: #300 runs to Circular Quay via Central Station and George Street and back; #350 runs to Central Station and Kings Cross. Every ten to twenty minutes, from the airport between 5.53am and 10.55pm, and from the city between 5.15am and 10.05pm; $5 single, $8 return valid for two months; approx. half-hour journey.

**Kingsford Smith Transport** (KST; phone ☎667 3221 to book a pick-up from your accommodation), a private bus service, will drop you right at the door of your hotel or hostel along one of two routes: via Kings Cross and Darling Harbour, or Glebe and Double Bay. At least every half-hour, but in practice they leave whenever the vehicle is full; $5, terminal shuttle $3.

**Manly Airport Bus** serves the northern beaches area. Four times daily Mon–Sat; from airport 8am, 11am, 2pm & 5pm, from Manly 7am, 10am, 1pm & 4pm; $10.

**State Transit** also has a couple of useful routes serving the airport: #305 runs to Railway Square near Central Station half-hourly from around 6am to 7pm; Metroline #400 goes to Bondi Junction via Maroubra and Randwick. Both cost $4 single; passes can be used.

Tickets can be bought on board and at the **Travellers' Information Service** in the international terminal; the latter also sells tourist bus passes – the *Sydney Pass* (see p.66) includes return airport–city transfer.

## Central Station

All local and interstate **trains** arrive at the Central Railway Station on Eddy Avenue, south of the city centre. From here and neighbouring **Railway Square**, you can hop onto nearly every major bus route. From Central you can take a CityRail train to any city or suburban stations: handy lines are the city loop via Town Hall, Wynyard, Circular Quay, St James and Museum, and the Eastern Suburbs line to Town Hall, Martin Place, Kings Cross, Edgecliff and Bondi Junction. The last trains leave at midnight, after which night buses run. See "City Transport", below, for more details.

## Long-distance bus depots

Most buses to Sydney terminate at the **Sydney Coach Terminal**, on the corner of Eddy Avenue and Pitt Street (daily 6am–10pm; ☎281 9366) down the side of Central Station. However, the **Australian Coachlines Depot** is at the corner of Oxford and Riley streets, handy for Surry Hills and Darlinghurst; from here, bus #389 will take you via the city to Circular Quay, while #378 goes to Central Station. *McCafferty's* operate out of 179 Darlinghurst Road in Kings Cross, but usually stop at Central Station first.

# Information

There's no shortage of places offering **information** about Sydney; you'll find some kind of information kiosk at all the main points of arrival to the city and many of the major attractions. The **NSW Travel Centre**, 19 Castlereagh Street in the city, just near Martin Place (Mon–Fri 9am–5pm; ☎231 4444), offers the most comprehensive service, with maps and brochures, accommodation reservations and transport bookings for Sydney and the rest of New South Wales. Ask for *The Official Sydney Map*, a free booklet with seven excellent maps of Sydney and NSW plus a *CityRail* plan.

The **Rocks Heritage and Information Centre**, 106 George Street (Mon–Fri 8.30am–5.30pm, Sat & Sun 10am–5pm; ☎255 1788 or free call ☎1800/067 676), is a good weekend-opening option near Circular Quay. Otherwise try **Sydney Visitors Information** (Mon–Fri 9am–5pm; ☎235 2424), a small information kiosk at Martin Place in the heart of the business district, or similar kiosks at Darling Harbour and Sydney Tower. **Recorded information** can be obtained from the *Tourist Information Service* (daily 8am–6pm; ☎669 5111), and free **listings magazines** are widely available: *Where Magazine* and *This Week in Sydney* are probably the best for general info; or *Index* for details of cultural pursuits. *For Backpackers By Backpackers* gives the lowdown on Sydney on the cheap, while hostel noticeboards act as an informal network, advertising everything from cars and international plane tickets to backpacks, camping gear and rides to other cities.

# City transport

Sydney's public transportation network is reasonably good, but as many Sydneysiders choose to drive to work and the system relies heavily on buses, **traffic jams** can be a problem. Small as the inner city is, you'll need to use public transport to get around comfortably, particularly on summer days when it's too hot to walk far. There are buses, trains, ferries and the city monorail to choose from, plus plentiful licensed taxis (flag them down – they're vacant if the rooftop light is on, but can be difficult to find around 3pm when the shifts change over; see "Listings", p.118, for cab rank locations and phone numbers). After the regular buses and trains finish at night, around midnight, there's a pretty good network of **night buses** that will get you around the city centre and to most of the surrounding suburbs. If you're staying more than a couple of days, a weekly **Travelpass** is a worthwhile investment (see box overpage).

## Buses

Within the central area, **buses** are much the most convenient and widespread mode of transport, and in general they reach more of the city than the trains. Buses must be hailed from yellow-signed bus stops. Major interchanges are located at Railway Square near Central, especially for the southwest routes; at Circular Quay for a range of routes; Wynyard for the North Shore; and Bondi Junction for the Eastern suburbs. The only bus route which crosses from the west to the east is the Metroline 400 which goes from Burwood through to Bondi Junction via the airport.

Single tickets, costing from $1.20 to $4 and calculated according to the distance travelled, can be bought on board from the driver, but if you're going to use the bus network more than occasionally, substantial discounts are available with TravelTen and other travel passes (see box overpage).

## Trains

Trains will get you where you're going faster than buses, especially at rush hour and heading out to the suburbs, but you need to transfer to a bus or ferry to get to most harbourside or beach destinations, and services are mainly aimed at commuters. The underground city loop is very useful, stopping at Central Station, Town Hall, Wynyard, Circular Quay, St James and Museum, and allowing you to connect with the rail system from almost anywhere in the centre. The lines out to the suburbs all run from Central Station, and most pass through Town Hall station as well. Trains run from around 5am to midnight, with single fares starting at around $1.20 on the City Loop and for short hops; you can save money by buying off-peak returns after 9am and all weekend.

Automatic ticket machines and barriers have been introduced just about everywhere; no excuses will be accepted if you don't have a ticket and fines are high. Following several incidents on late evening trains, all platforms have been painted with designated "nightsafe" waiting areas; at all times, women travelling alone (or anyone feeling vulnerable) are advised to sit in the carriage nearest the guard.

## Ferries

**Ferries** are the fastest means of transport from Circular Quay to the North Shore, and indeed to most places around the harbour; even if you don't want to go anywhere, a ferry ride is a must, just to get out on the water and see the city from the harbour. The Manly Ferry service, the most legendary, commenced in 1854, and the huge old boats come complete with snack bars selling the ubiquitous meat pie. There's also a hydrofoil which goes to Manly, the *JetCat*, a speedy catamaran that gets you there in half the time, but with less charm. Of course, if you want to see the harbour in more luxury, there are plenty of cruises available – at a price (see box on p.76).

The main ferry connections are from Circular Quay to Darling Harbour, Neutral Bay, Mosman, Cremorne, Watsons Bay, Manly, Taronga Zoo, Balmain, North Sydney, Hunters Hill, McMahon's Point and Lavender Bay. On weekends and public holidays there are services to Double Bay and Rose Bay too. In 1993, the *RiverCat* service was introduced, heading from Circular Quay up the Parramatta River as far as Parramatta.

A single fare is $2.60, or $3.40 for the Manly Ferry; the pricier *JetCat* to Manly is $4.60, while the *RiverCat* to Parramatta is $4. Once again, the various *Travelpasses* and *FerryTen* tickets can be a good deal – see box overpage for the lowdown.

## Monorail

The **Monorail** is still a controversial addition to the transport network, especially as it's essentially a tourist shuttle designed to loop around Darling Harbour, connecting it with the city centre. Thundering along tracks set above the older city streets, the monster rail – as many locals know it – doesn't exactly blend in with its surroundings.

## TRAVEL PASSES

In addition to single-journey tickets, which range from $1.20 to $4.60, there's a vast array of **travel passes** available. The most useful for visitors are outlined below; for more **information** on the full range of tickets and timetables, phone the *Bus, Train, Ferry InfoLine* (☎13 1500; daily 6am–10pm) or consult the State Transit Guide in the front of the Sydney *White Pages* phone book.

Passes are sold at most **newsagents** and at **train stations**; the more tourist-oriented *Sydney Passes* and *Sydney Explorer Passes* can be bought at the **airport** (from the Travellers Information Service in the international terminal and the State Transit counter in the domestic terminal), on the *Airport Express Bus*, the *Explorer Bus*, the *Tramway Bus*, at the **NSW Travel Centre** (19 Castlereagh St) or at *Countrylink* offices.

### Tourist passes
**Sydney Pass** (3-day $60, 5-day $80, 7-day $90, family rates from £170) is valid for all buses and ferries including the *Explorers* (see above), the *Rocks–Darling Harbour Tramway Bus*, the *JetCat* to Manly and a return trip to the airport with the *Airport Express* bus. It also includes three harbour cruises, one of them in the evening.

**Sydney Explorer Pass** (one-day $25, two-day $35, family pass $45 per day) will save you poring over schedules and may reduce time-consuming transfers. The pass comes with a map and description of sights, and includes free travel on any State Transit bus on the *Explorer* routes. The red #111 *Sydney Explorer* (daily, every 20min, 9am–7pm), takes in all the important sights in the city and inner suburbs, and you can hop on and off at any of the 26 stops. The blue #222 *Bondi & Bay Explorer* (daily, every 30min, 9am–6pm) covers the waterside Eastern suburbs; 20 stops en route include Kings Cross, Paddington, Double Bay, Vaucluse and the beaches of Bondi, Bronte, Clovelly and Coogee.

### Buses, trains and ferries
**Travelpasses** buy unlimited use of buses, trains and ferries within numbered zones. The *Red Travelpass* ($19 a week) is valid for the city and inner suburbs, but not on the Manly Ferry or the RiverCat beyond Meadowbank; a *Green Travelpass* ($25) allows use of all Sydney Ferries – except JetCats before 7pm. Passes further afield cost between $29 and $43 per week, and monthly passes are also available.

### Buses and ferries
**Travelpasses**: *Blue Travelpass* ($16.10 per week) gives you unlimited travel on buses in the inner-city area and on inner harbour ferries but is no good for Manly or beyond Meadowbank; the *Orange Travelpass* ($22.20) gets you further on the buses and is valid on all ferries.
**Bus and Ferry Tripper** ($12) gives a day's unlimited travel.

### Buses only
**TravelTen** tickets represent a 45 per cent saving over the single fares. The blue version ($7.70 a week) lets you ride 1–2 sections per validation in the on-board machine (it's one section from Central Station to Circular Quay, for example, and two sections from Queen Woollahra to Bondi Junction) while a *Red TravelTen* ($15.40) allows you to travel 3–10 sections per ride (Leichhardt to Town Hall is five sections).
**Two Zone Travelpass** comes in a bus-only variant for $16.20 per week.
**Bus Tripper** offers a day's unlimited bus travel for $7.50.

### Ferries only
**FerryTen** tickets, valid for ten single trips, start at $15.70 for Inner Harbour Services, go up to $23.50 for the Manly Ferry, and peak at $39.60 for the *JetCat* services.

### Trains only
**Cityhopper** tickets ($3) give one day's unlimited train travel in the area between Central, Kings Cross, Circular Quay and North Sydney after 9am Mon–Fri and anytime at weekends.

Still, the elevated view of the city, particularly from Pyrmont Bridge, makes it worth investing $2.50 and ten minutes to do the whole circuit; an all-day ticket costs $6. The stops are City Centre (near Centre Point), Park Plaza, World Square, Haymarket (near the Entertainment Centre and the Powerhouse Museum), Convention (by the Convention Centre), Harbourside (for the Maritime Museum and Harbourside Mall), then across Pyrmont Bridge and back to the beginning of the circuit.

# Accommodation

There are a tremendous number of places to stay in Sydney, and fierce competition helps keep prices down. Finding somewhere to stay is usually only a problem just before Christmas and throughout January, when you'll definitely need to **book ahead**. All types of accommodation offer a (sometimes substantial) discount for **weekly bookings**, and may also cut prices considerably during the **low season** (from autumn to spring, school holidays excepted); it's always worth asking.

The larger **hotels** in the centre are pretty standard – bland and international on the whole, and rarely charging less than $80 double; motels often have similar facilities at lower rates, but may not be so conveniently located. There is now an increasing number of mid-range "boutique" hotels and **guesthouses**, mostly in the suburbs, which tend to be smaller, more characterful paces to stay. **Serviced holiday apartments** can be very good value for a group, but are generally heavily booked.

Despite the number of **hostels** all over Sydney and the rivalry between them, standards are very variable and, in Kings Cross especially, can be very low. Special offers such as the first night's accommodation free or half price, with a free beer or three thrown in for good measure, are best treated with suspicion; and, as the scene changes rapidly, it's worth getting the latest news from other travellers. Rates are pretty standard – in summer about $15–17 for a dorm bed and $16–22 for a double per person, with rates dropping as low as $11 in winter, plus $10–20 key deposit which will be refunded upon departure. Theoretically, hostels have separate dorms for males and females, but in practice they often tend to be mixed, so if you don't want to spend the night in a mixed dorm, let the hostel know when you book. Most hostels will store **luggage**; some also have a safe for valuables, which you should use.

The listings below are arranged by area. For short stays, you'll want to stay in the **city centre** or the immediate vicinity. **Kings Cross** is still very much the travellers' centre, with the greatest concentration of both backpacker accommodation and more expensive hotels – a ten-minute walk from the city and with its own train station, it makes a convenient base if you don't mind the sleaze and the all-night partying. The adjacent suburbs of **Woolloomooloo**, **Potts Point** and **Elizabeth Bay** move gradually upmarket, and what little you lose in terms of accessibility, you gain in peace and quiet. To the west, **Glebe** is another slice of prime backpacker territory, featuring both of Sydney's large YHA hostels, as well as several other backpacker places and a number of small guesthouses.

If you're staying longer, consider somewhere further out – on the **North Shore**, or in the **eastern suburbs**, where you'll get more for your money and more of a feel for Sydney as a city. **Kirribilli**, **Neutral Bay** or **Cremorne Point** offer some serenity and maybe an affordable water view as well: they're only a short ferry ride from Circular Quay and job-hunters might find that their chances are better (especially where office work is concerned) in North Sydney than on the other side of the harbour. **Manly**, tucked away in the northwest corner of the harbour, is a seaside suburb with ocean and harbour beaches, just thirty minutes from Circular Quay by ferry.

Nowhere but Sydney could you stay at such great beachside locations as **Bondi** so close to the city. **Coogee Beach** seems to specialize in active hostels – many offer a free pick-up service from the airport and the city, and most organize beach parties, barbecues and inter-hostel sports competitions. **Randwick** is where the University of New South Wales is located and has a lively student feel. The high turnover here and at Bondi makes fertile ground for **flat-shares** – check out noticeboards in cafés and the university. There are no caravan parks or **campsites** anywhere close to the centre; the nearest are at the suburbs of Rockdale, 13km south of the city, and North Ryde, 14km northwest (see p.72).

## City centre

**C.B. Hotel**, 417 Pitt St (☎211 5115). Absolutely huge private hotel, very central with basic rooms; singles are especially cheap. Shared toilets and showers, TV lounge and laundry facilities. ④.

**Golden Gate International**, 169–179 Thomas St (☎281 6888). Extravagant four-star, handy for Central Station and Darling Harbour; heated pool and 24hr room service; rates include breakfast. Mardi Gras reductions. ⑧.

**Grand Hotel**, 30 Hunter St (☎232 3755). B&B in a small, private hotel near Wynyard Station, rooms with TV, fan and heating; shared bathrooms. ⑥.

**Harbour View Hotel**, 18 Lower Fort St, Miller's Point (☎252 3769). Very near the bridge, which means some noise (and more from the bar), but good pub accommodation in this location at this price is worth it. ⑤.

**Lord Nelson Brewery Hotel**, corner of Argyle and Kent streets, The Rocks (☎251 4044). B&B in historical, renovated pub. ⑥–⑦.

**Nikko**, 161 Sussex St, Darling Harbour (☎299 1231). Well-located five-star with views; undercover parking. ⑧.

**Old Sydney Park Royal**, 55 George St, The Rocks (☎252 0524). If you're going to spend $250 or more on a room, make it here, right in the heart of The Rocks, and small enough to have a personal touch. ⑧.

**Oxford Koala Hotel**, corner of Oxford and Pelican streets (☎269 0645). Multi-storey motel over-looking Hyde Park. Its fully equipped apartments are good for families, and the complex boasts room service and swimming pool. ⑦.

**Regent**, 199 George Street (☎251 3755). One of Australia's best hotels, this classy modern five-star emphasizes personal service and is superbly located by The Rocks with views of the Harbour Bridge and the Opera House. All this comes at a price – $200 minimum. ⑧.

**Russell**, 143a George St, The Rocks (☎241 3543). Charming historic hotel; continental breakfast included; restaurant. ⑧.

**Sydney City Centre Serviced Apartments**, 7 Elizabeth St, Martin Place ☎223 3529 or 233 6677. Fully equipped flats with kitchenette, TV, video etc. ⑥.

**Sydney Traveller's Rest**, 37 Ultimo Rd, Haymarket (☎281 5555). Big, renovated private hotel opposite Paddy's Markets and near Darling Harbour with simple rooms and comfortable, well furnished en suites, some large enough for families; the first two children under 19 stay free. ⑤–⑥.

**Westend Hotel**, 412 Pitt St (☎211 4822). Opposite the *C.B. Hotel* and considerably classier, old-style pub with air-conditioned motel-style units. ⑤.

## Kings Cross

**Alice's Tudor Hotel**, 64 Darlinghurst Rd (☎358 5977). Very central – opposite the train station – with clean motel-style rooms and car park. ④–⑤.

**Barclay Hotel**, 17 Bayswater Rd (☎358 6133). A good standard of private hotel, very reasonably priced; most rooms are en suite with air-con, telephone, colour TV. Other services include room service and a licensed restaurant and bar. ⑥.

**Barncleuth House (the Pink House)**, 6–8 Barncleuth Sq (☎358 1689). Attractive art-deco mansion with big dorms and a few doubles. Friendly and in a great location, though maybe a bit on the sloppy side. Guests have 24hr access via a combination lock, and there's a café in the front garden. Rooms ③, dorms ①.

**Bernly Private Hotel**, 15 Springfield Ave (☎358 3122). Good-value rooms here have TV, fridge, tea and coffee-making facilities, but shared bathrooms; big sun-roof with deck chairs and a view of the Harbour Bridge. ④.

**Carnarvon Lodge**, 16 Ward Ave (☎358 6611). A renovated old mansion with comfortable units and mini-apartments with kitchens. ⑥.

**Highfield House**, 166 Victoria St (☎358 1552). Scandinavians run this very clean, slightly impersonal place which feels more like a large hotel than a hostel. Rooms ③–④, small dorms ①.

**Jolly Swagman**, 144 Victoria St (☎357 4733), 16 Orwell St (☎358 6600) and 14 Springfield Mall (☎358 6400). These three hostels are all run by the same team. Colourful, clean and lively, they make a real effort to provide information for travellers, with good noticeboards and work connections, their own events and tour programme. Rooms ③, dorms ①.

**Kanga House**, 141 Victoria St (☎357 7897). Popular with British backpackers on working holiday visas; rough and ready but cheerful and one of the cheapest, with rock-bottom weekly rates too. Rooms ③, dorms ①.

**Kings Cross Holiday Apartments**, 169 William St (☎361 0637). Flats in this very central location accommodate up to five, and include a laundry. ⑤.

**Kirketon Hotel**, 229–231 Darlinghurst Rd (☎360 4333). Nice place with basic rooms (shared bathrooms) or en suites; all rooms with TV and hot drinks. ⑤–⑥.

**Original Backpackers**, 162 Victoria St (☎356 3232). Friendly backpacker hostel (the first in the Cross) in a lovely 1887 mansion, with a choice of simple, well-maintained rooms and 4-bed dorms – the best one leading off the huge balcony. Ask about rooms in the two terrace houses they own next door where there are some very pleasant singles and doubles. Pleasant outdoor courtyard, and lots of job contacts. Rooms ③, dorms ①.

**Plane Tree Lodge**, 172 Victoria St (☎356 4551). A combination hotel and backpackers, slightly fusty but clean and well run. All rooms and dorms have TV and fridge, and most are en suite; doubles are good and spacious, with chairs and tables. Communal facilities are limited to a tiny kitchen and common room, but there's 24hr access and good security. Rooms ③–④, dorms ①.

**Springfield Lodge**, 9 Springfield Ave (☎358 3222). Quiet location with pleasant rooms, all with fridge, TV and tea and coffee-making facilities. Good single and weekly rates. ④.

**Traveller's Rest**, 156 Victoria St (☎358 4606). Decent singles and doubles; triple rooms available on a share basis as dorms – all with colour TV, fan, fridge, kettle, sink and table and chairs. Small communal kitchen and laundry. Long-stayers are well provided for, and there are reasonable weekly rates. Rooms ③, dorms ①.

## Woolloomooloo, Potts Point and Elizabeth Bay

**Challis Lodge**, 21–23 Challis Ave, Potts Point (☎358 5422). Nice old mansion, friendly and in a quiet location. En suite and share-facility rooms, all with TV, fridge, sink, tea and coffee-making equipment; laundry available. Good single and family rooms, as well as the usual twins/doubles. ④.

**Eva's Backpackers**, 6–8 Orwell St, Potts Point (☎358 2185). This recommended family-run hostel has recently been renovated; some of the colourfully painted, clean rooms even have en suites. 24hr reception and rooftop garden with BBQ – and fantastic views over the city. Rooms ③, dorms ①.

**Florida Motor Inn**, 1 McDonald St, Potts Point (☎358 6811). Self-catering facilities, free parking, sauna, swimming pool. ⑦.

**Forbes Terrace**, 153 Forbes St, Woolloomooloo (☎358 4327). Top-class hostel, well run and clean; very friendly, with good weekly terms. Rooms ③, dorms ①.

**Gazebo Hotel Tower**, 2 Elizabeth Bay Rd, Elizabeth Bay (☎358 1999). Once one of the city's finest, this circular high-rise has come down in the world a bit but it's still pretty swish. Worth it if you get one of the rooms with a harbour view. ⑧, including breakfast.

**Madison's Ward Avenue**, 6–8 Ward Ave, Elizabeth Bay (☎357 1155). Slickly modern three-star hotel with correspondingly contemporary rooms, all en suite with baths to soak in; room service; undercover parking. Continental breakfast included in rates. ⑥.

**Montpelier Private Hotel**, 39a Elizabeth Bay Rd, Elizabeth Bay (☎358 6960). Long-established private hotel, moderately priced, simple and clean. Singles and doubles both come with colour TV and coffee-making facilities, the shower and toilets are situated just down the hall. Great value and central location; cheaper weekly rates. ④.

**Rucksack Rest**, 9 McDonald St, Potts Point (☎358 2348). Small, well-run private hostel which benefits from a friendly atmosphere and quiet location. Facilities include a backyard and barbie, a communal kitchen, and there's a laundrette around the corner. Rooms ③, dorms ①.

**Victoria Court Sydney**, 122 Victoria Street, Potts Point (☎357 3200). Boutique hotel in two inter-linked Victorian terraced houses; en suite rooms with all mod cons, some with balconies. Security parking a bonus. ⑤–⑧, including breakfast.

**Woolloomooloo Waters**, 88 Dowling St, Woolloomooloo (☎358 3100). Studio apartments with balcony views over Woolloomooloo Bay or the city; pool and spa. ⑧.

## Surry Hills, Darlinghurst, Paddington and Woollahra

**Alfred Park Budget Accommodation**, 207 Cleveland St, Surry Hills (☎319 4031). Small, well-managed private hotel with a friendly atmosphere close to Central Station. TV lounge, communal kitchen and laundry, car park. Recommended. ④–⑤; backpacker room share ①.

**Camelot Inn**, 358a Victoria St, Darlinghurst (☎331 7555). Studio apartments for up to 6 people located on a lively restaurant-filled street; parking. ⑥.

**Centennial Park Lodge**, 14 Queen St, Woollahra (☎363 4863). Old-fashioned guesthouse built in 1876 opposite Centennial Park. Moderately priced singles and doubles with shared bathroom; breakfast included in rates. ④–⑥.

**Cron Lodge Motel**, 289 Crown St, Surry Hills (☎331 2433). A fairly typical motel, well located; units with en suite, heating, fan, and small kitchenette. Some parking space. ⑤.

**Kangaroo Bakpak**, 635 South Dowling St, Surry Hills (☎319 5915). Clean and really friendly back-packer hostel. The dorms are enormous and generally untidy, but the atmosphere compensates. ①.

**Sullivans Hotel**, 21 Oxford St, Paddington (☎361 0211, free call 1800/62 0211). Small private hotel in a fun location, with comfortable rooms. Everything is laid on for guests: pool, bicycles, in-house movies, 24hr reception and restaurant. ⑥.

**YWCA**, 5–11 Wentworth Ave, Darlinghurst (☎264 2451). Great location just off Oxford Street, with café (open 7am–7.30pm) and TV lounge. Both sexes welcome. Motel-style units ⑤, dorms ②.

## Glebe and Newtown

**Alishan International Guesthouse**, 100 Glebe Point Rd (☎566 4048). Very well looked-after, beau-tifully restored old villa; rooms, mainly en suite, have a Japanese aesthetic and futon beds. Mainly doubles, a number of larger family rooms and a few squeaky-clean 4-bed dorms. Facilities on-site include a spa, cosy common room and well-equipped kitchen. ②–⑥.

**Australian Sunrise Lodge**, 485 King St, Newtown (☎550 4999). Inexpensive, small, tastefully furnished and well-managed private hotel with guest kitchen. The on-the-ball owner will set you straight on the best places to eat on King Street. Sunny single and double rooms, all with colour TV, fridge, toaster and tea and coffee facilities, most with bath and balcony. ④–⑤.

**Billabong Gardens**, 5–11 Egan St, Newtown (☎550 3236). Top-class hostel with clean dorms and some rooms. Peaceful inner courtyard with pool and spa; pool table and table tennis; good kitchen, TV lounge and undercover car park. Very friendly and helpful. Rooms ③, dorms ①.

**Glebe Point Village**, 256 Glebe Point Rd (☎660 8878 or 660 8133; free call ☎1800/801 983). These big old houses have a mellow atmosphere and feel more like a guesthouse than a hostel. The people who run the place know what's going on around town. Double and twin rooms as well as dorms; good kitchen facilities, shady courtyard, café/restaurant and sitting areas. Travel agency too. Rooms ④, dorms ①.

**Glebe Point YHA**, 262 Glebe Point Rd (☎692 8418). Reliable YHA standard with impeccably help-ful, patient staff. Private rooms as well as 4-bed dorms. Sun-roof, TV lounge and a lot of activities. Rooms ④, dorms ①.

**Hereford Lodge YHA**, 51 Hereford St, just off Glebe Point Rd (☎660 5577). Much fancier than Glebe Point YHA in a quiet residential street. All rooms, even dorms, have en suites and more mod cons are found in the motel-style doubles, many with balconies. Big sun-roof with swimming pool and sauna; travel agency; bistro serving breakfast and dinner; undercover parking. Motel-style ⑤, doubles ④, dorms ①.

**Rooftop Motel**, 146 Glebe Point Road, Glebe (☎660 7777). Reasonably priced motel with 24hr reception right in the thick of things; barbecue, swimming pool and babysitting. ⑥.

**University Motor Inn**, 25 Arundel St, Glebe (☎660 5577). Well-equipped motel handy for Sydney University, which is opposite. The playground is a bonus if you've got kids. ⑥.

**Wattle House Hostel**, 44 Hereford St, Glebe (☎692 0879). Small, cosy and clean privately owned hostel in a restored terrace house in quiet street. Rooms ③, dorms ①.

## GAY AND LESBIAN ACCOMMODATION

There are no specifically lesbian **hotels** and surprisingly few gay ones in Sydney – those listed below are reliable. In practice any hotels in Darlinghurst, Paddington or Surry Hills are bound to be used to gay and lesbian customers; hassle-free places from our main listings include the *Golden Gate International*, *Metro Motor Inn* and *Westend* in the city, *Kirketon* in Kings Cross and *Sullivans* in Paddington. If you don't want to stay in a hotel, or are planning a **longer stay**, the *Australian Gay Hospitality Exchange* (PO Box 108, Newtown, NSW 2042) is a network of gay men who will host overseas visitors; write well in advance and send a small donation in any currency to cover postage. For **flat-shares** check the community press and café noticeboards or try an agency: *Share-A-Home* (☎267 9824) deals with gay and lesbian shares only for a $50 fee.

**The Barracks**, 164b Bourke St, Darlinghurst (☎360 5823, fax 361 4584). Men only; price includes breakfast. ⑤.

**415 On Bourke**, corner Church Lane and Bourke St, Darlinghurst (☎331 5344, fax 331 3150). Run by the *Pelican Hotel*, all rooms have TV, cooking facilities and fridge, and prices include breakfast. Both sexes welcome. ⑤.

**Governors on Fitzroy**, 64 Fitzroy St, Surry Hills (☎331 4652, fax 361 5094).

Small and friendly, close to Oxford St. Full cooked breakfast included. Both sexes welcome. ⑦.

**Pelican Private Hotel**, 411 Bourke St, Darlinghurst (☎331 5344, fax 331 3150). Sydney's oldest-established gay guesthouse is friendly and central. Rooms have TV and fridge, with a guest kitchen downstairs. Breakfast is included, and you can hang out on the subtropical patio and sundeck. Women very welcome. ⑤.

## Bondi

**Bondi Beach Guesthouse**, 11 Consett Ave, off Lamrock Ave (☎389 8309). Central but surprisingly quiet location. Clean and simple rooms with TV, fridge, tea-making facilities and communal bathrooms; there's also a guest kitchen and laundry. Sharing available for backpackers. ④.

**Bondi Beach Motel**, 68 Gould St (☎365 5233). One street back from the main drag of Campbell Parade, a friendly well-run place with 24hr reception and undercover parking. ⑥.

**Bondi Beachside Inn**, 152 Campbell Parade (☎305 311). Multi-storey motel that's positioned right on the beach and boasts many rooms with ocean views. Clean, modern and air-con; two-bedroom apartments are also available and there are cheaper weekly rates. ⑥–⑧.

**Lamrock Hostel**, 7 Lamrock Ave (☎365 0221). The sea at your door makes up for rather grotty common areas. Central and quiet, with sun-roof, 24hr reception, clean dorms and one nice twin with balcony and en suite. Enquire here also about **Lamrock Flats** and **Lamrock Apartments**, both good value for longer-term rentals (usually one month minimum). Rooms ⑤, dorms ①.

**Ravesi's**, corner of Campbell Parade and Hall St (☎365 4422). Swanky boutique hotel: most rooms have sea views and small balconies; best – if you can afford them – are the top-floor split-level suites with their own private terraces. ⑦–⑧.

**Thelellen Beach Inn**, 2 Campbell Parade (☎30 5333). Simple, good and moderately priced private hotel on several floors is friendly in that old-fashioned way. Single and double rooms with fridge, tea and coffee facilities, toasters, fan, heating and colour TV, but toilets and shower down the hall. The best rooms look down on Bondi Beach and even if yours doesn't, the huge sundeck does. ④.

**Thelellen Lodge**, 11a Consett Ave (☎30 1521). Run by the same people as the *Thelellen Beach Inn*, this lodge in a bungalow has the same style rooms as the above, with the advantage of guest kitchen and laundry facilities, plus it's slightly cheaper. ④.

## Coogee Beach and Randwick

**Aegean**, Coogee Bay Rd, Coogee (☎398 4999). Holiday apartments converted into dorms and double rooms. Sun-roof with barbecue. ①–②.

**Coogee Beach Backpackers**, 94 Beach St, up the hill from the Coogee Palace complex (☎315 8000 or 665 7735). Clean, attractive rooms and dorms in four characterful neighbouring houses, blessed with many balconies overlooking the ocean. Each house has a well-equipped kitchen, and common room, and there are several gardens. Congenial and well managed, it's the best of the bunch. Rooms ④, dorms ①.

**Holiday Inn**, 242 Arden St, Coogee (☎315 7600). Swish four-star seven-storey modern hotel with 24hr room service, pool, gym and tennis courts; restaurant and bar; babysitting available. ⑧.

**Indy's Beachside Backpackers**, 302 Arden St, Coogee (☎315 7644). Small hostel with a laid-back, gently casual atmosphere; huge video collection for couch potatoes. Rates include a light breakfast. Cheap day trips to the countryside. ①.

**Metro**, 171 Arden St, Coogee (☎665 1162). Small old-fashioned private hotel opposite the beach with rec room; shared facilities; breakfast included. ④.

**The Royal**, corner Perouse and Cuthill St, Randwick (☎399 3006 or 399 5659). Big, historic pub (listed by the National Trust), with fairly upmarket rooms, mostly sharing bathrooms. Good transport to city and beaches. ⑤.

**Surfside Backpackers Coogee**, 186 Arden St, Coogee (☎315 7888). On Coogee's main drag, above *McDonalds* and absolutely opposite the beach, with great views from its high balconies. However, its tower-block feel, tiny kitchen and common room aren't great. Rooms ③, dorms ①.

## North Shore

**Cremorne Point Manor**, 6 Cremorne Rd, Cremorne Point (☎953 7899). Restored villa with very cheap singles and good-value doubles. All rooms have colour TV, fridge and coffee-making facilities. ⑤.

**Elite Private Hotel**, 133 Carabella St, Kirribilli (☎929 6365). Rooms with TV, fridge and coffee-making facilities, some with harbour view. Communal cooking facility and laundry; budget weekly rates. Only minutes by ferry from the city and just near the train station. ⑤.

**Harbourside Hotel**, 41 Cremorne Rd, Cremorne Point (☎953 7977). Hostel with no maximum stay attracts lots of local workers as well as backpackers so it doesn't feel like a real travellers hostel. Great location, though, in a bush-filled well-heeled harbour suburb one ferry stop from the city. ①.

**Tielgreen Lodge**, 310 Miller St, North Sydney (☎955 1012). Two-storeyed mansion with balconies in a quiet location opposite a park has en suite rooms or family studios, all with air-con, colour TV, hot drinks and telephone; breakfast available; share kitchens and laundry facilities. ⑤–⑥.

**Wallaringa Mansions**, 19 Lower Wycombe Rd, Neutral Bay (☎953 5231). Two old mansions near the water, attracting a mixed clientele of Australian and international travellers. Simple, quiet and clean, with affordable singles. Excellent-value weekly rates. Take the ferry to Hayes St wharf, or train to North Sydney. ③.

## Manly

**Manly Beach Resort Backpackers**, 6 Carlton St (☎977 4188). One block from the beach has clean, smoke-free 5-bed dorms with en suite; *Dukes Café*, attached, is good for breakfast. ①.

**Manly Guesthouse**, 56 Whistler St (☎977 0884). Simple, good-value clean rooms. ④.

**Manly International Beachside Backpackers**, 28 Raglan St (☎977 3411). Brand new hostel one block from the surf beach. Clean and modern twin rooms, plus dorms. Rooms ④, dorms ①.

**Manly Pacific Park Royal**, 55 North Steyne (☎977 7666). Beachfront multi-storied four-star hotel has 24hr reception, room service, spa, sauna, gym and heated pool. ⑧.

**Periwinkle Guesthouse**, 19 East Esplanade (☎977 4668). B&B near Manly Cove, close to the ferry terminal and shops. Rooms have fridge and fans; communal kitchen; car park; larger rooms suitable for families or groups. ⑤.

**Hotel Steyne**, 75 The Corso (☎977 4977). Opposite the surf beach; good rooms above a pub, with tea-making facilities; shared bathrooms and TV lounge; B&B available. ⑤.

## Camping and caravan parks

**Lakeside Caravan Park**, Lake Park Rd, Narrabeen, 26km north (☎913 7845). Great spot by Narrabeen Lakes on Sydney's northern beaches. Sites only $15–18.

**Easts Lane Cove River Van Village**, Plassey Rd, North Ryde, 14km northwest (☎805 0500). Nice location near a nature reserve, with pool. Cabins ⑤, on-site vans ④.

**Harts Caravan Park**, 215 Port Hacking Rd, Miranda, 24km south (☎22 7143). Cabins and on-site vans ③.

**Meriton Tourist Park**, cnr Lane Cove and Fontenoy Roads, North Ryde, 14km northwest of the city (☎887 2177). Pool and tennis court. Cabins ④–⑥.

**Sheralee Tourist Caravan Park**, 88 Bryant St, Rockdale, 13km south (☎567 7161). Small park with camp kitchen.

# The City

Port Jackson carves Sydney in two halves, linked by the Harbour Bridge and Harbour Tunnel. The **South Shore** is the hub of activity, and it's here that you'll find the **city centre** and most of the things to see and do. Many of the classic images of Sydney are within sight of **Circular Quay**, making this busy waterfront area on Sydney Cove a logical – and pleasurable – point to start discovering the city with the **Opera House** and the expanse of the Royal Botanic Gardens to the east of Sydney Cove and the historic area of **The Rocks** to the west; by contrast, **Darling Harbour**, at the centre's western edge, was redeveloped in the late eighties as a tourist and entertainment area and is a gleaming, if slightly tawdry, showcase for the new Sydney.

## Circular Quay

At the southern end of Sydney Cove, **Circular Quay** is the launching pad for harbour and river ferries and sightseeing boats, the terminal for buses from the eastern and southern suburbs, and a major suburban railway station to boot. With the Olympics in sight, there are frenzied plans to improve Circular Quay's appearance before it is subject to international scrutiny in the year 2000, with attention focussing on the Cahill Expressway – a public competition was launched in late 1994 with the aim of finding a way of masking its ugliness. The contention is that the railway and expressway block views to the city, particularly impeding a cohesiveness between the quay and Alfred Place with its neglected architectural gem, the **Customs House**.

The quay is always bustling, with commuters during the week, and people simply out to enjoy themselves at the weekend. Restaurants, cafés and fast-food outlets stay open until late at night and buskers entertain the crowds, while vendors of newspapers and trinkets add to the general hubbub. The sun reflecting on the water and its heave and splash as the ferries come and go make for a dreamy setting – best appreciated

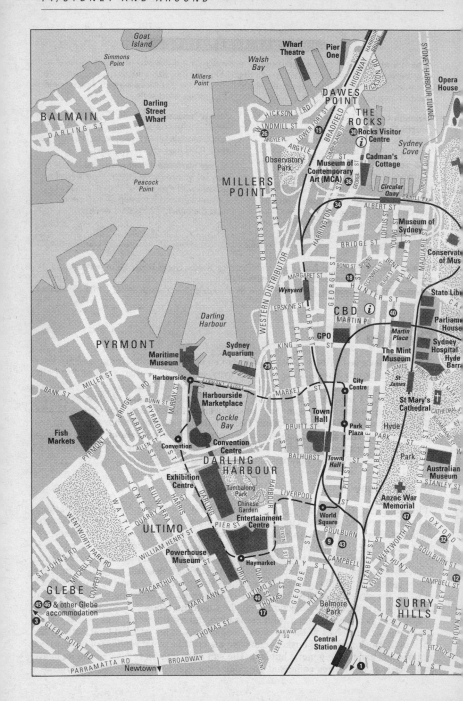

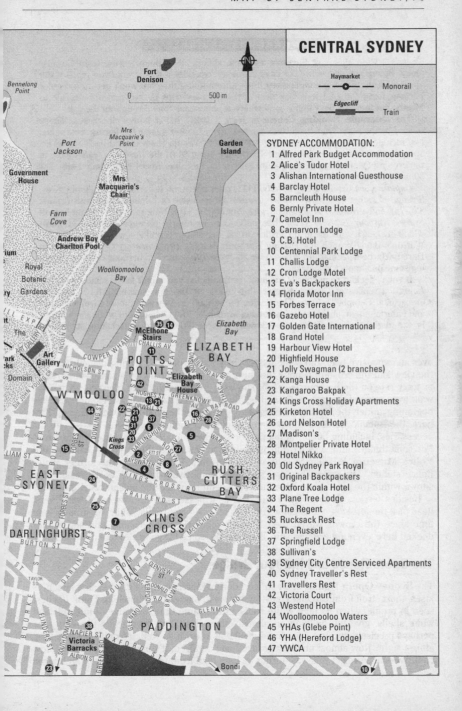

# CENTRAL SYDNEY

Haymarket ──●── Monorail

Edgecliff ──■── Train

SYDNEY ACCOMMODATION:
1 Alfred Park Budget Accommodation
2 Alice's Tudor Hotel
3 Alishan International Guesthouse
4 Barclay Hotel
5 Barncleuth House
6 Bernly Private Hotel
7 Camelot Inn
8 Carnarvon Lodge
9 C.B. Hotel
10 Centennial Park Lodge
11 Challis Lodge
12 Cron Lodge Motel
13 Eva's Backpackers
14 Florida Motor Inn
15 Forbes Terrace
16 Gazebo Hotel
17 Golden Gate International
18 Grand Hotel
19 Harbour View Hotel
20 Highfield House
21 Jolly Swagman (2 branches)
22 Kanga House
23 Kangaroo Bakpak
24 Kings Cross Holiday Apartments
25 Kirketon Hotel
26 Lord Nelson Hotel
27 Madison's
28 Montpelier Private Hotel
29 Hotel Nikko
30 Old Sydney Park Royal
31 Original Backpackers
32 Oxford Koala Hotel
33 Plane Tree Lodge
34 The Regent
35 Rucksack Rest
36 The Russell
37 Springfield Lodge
38 Sullivan's
39 Sydney City Centre Serviced Apartments
40 Sydney Traveller's Rest
41 Travellers Rest
42 Victoria Court
43 Westend Hotel
44 Woolloomooloo Waters
45 YHAs (Glebe Point)
46 YHA (Hereford Lodge)
47 YWCA

## ◄HARBOUR CRUISES

There's a wide choice of **harbour cruises**, almost all of them leaving from Circular Quay. Before you part with your cash, however, consider if this is what you really want: apart from the running commentary, they offer nothing that you won't get on a regular harbour **ferry** for a lot less. The best of the ordinary trips is the thirty-minute ride to **Manly**, but there's a ferry going somewhere at almost any time throughout the day.

The **Quayside Booking Centre** at Jetty 2 (☎247 5151) books all cruises. Those offered by the State Transit – *Sydney Harbour Ferry Cruises* – seem to offer the best value, and include an afternoon *Main Harbour Cruise* to Middle Harbour and back (Mon–Fri 1pm, Sat & Sun 1.30pm; 2hr 30min; $16, family ticket $44), the *Harbour Lights Cruise* in the evening (Mon–Sat 8pm, 1hr 30min; $14) or the morning *River Cruise* (daily 10am, 2hr 30min; $16, family ticket $44).

*Captain Cook Cruises* (Jetty 6; ☎206 1111) offer afternoon tea cruises (2hr 20min; $28), a range of rather expensive *Dinner Cruises* (all inclusive of 3-course meal with drinks; $56–75), and a *Harbour Highlights Cruise* (1hr 30min; $16). Note that their hop-on hop-off *Sydney Harbour Explorer* ($18), has only four two-hourly pick-ups (9.30am–3.30pm), which makes it difficult to do justice to all the stops: Circular Quay, Opera House, Watson's Bay, Taronga and Darling Harbour. *Matilda Bay Discovery Cruises*, based in Darling Harbour (Aquarium Wharf, Pier 26; ☎264 7377), run $25 harbour cruises, including some on a replica sailing ship.

If you're feeling romantically inclined, or mutinous, you might fancy sailing with the *Bounty*, a replica of Captain Bligh's ship made for the film starring Mel Gibson. It embarks at Campbell's Cove, The Rocks, for various cruises daily, most involving food and entertainment; cheapest is the Sunday brunch (9.30–11.30am; $35) while the splurge is the nightly dinner cruise (7–9.30pm; 3-course buffet and entertainment; $55).

over an expensive beer and some oysters at a waterfront bar. Having dallied, taken in the view and the crush of people, the thing to to do is embark on a sightseeing cruise or ferry ride on the harbour (see box above). Staying on dry land, you're only a short walk from most of the city-centre sights, along part of a continuous foreshore walkway beginning under the Harbour Bridge and extending beyond the Opera House. Past here, the Botanic Gardens boast some wonderfully picturesque picnic spots – all the necessaries, including bubbly and a barbecued chicken, can be purchased at the quay. For something a little less life-affirming, just across Alfred Place is the **Justice and Police Museum**, 8 Phillip St (Sun only 10am–4pm; $4) housed in the former Water Police station. The crime displays, including some truly macabre death masks, are shown within the context of a late-nineteenth-century police station and court mock-up.

Besides ferries, Circular Quay still acts as a passenger terminal for ocean liners; head past the *Museum of Contemporary Art* (see p.78) to Circular Quay West. It's a long time since the crowds waved their hankies regularly, but you may still see a liner docked here; even if there's no ship, climb up the steps for good views of the water.

## The Opera House and Harbour Bridge

The **Sydney Opera House**, such an icon of Australiana that it almost seems kitsch, is just a short stroll from Circular Quay, by the water's edge on Bennelong Point. It's best seen in profile, when its high white roofs, at the same time evocative of full sails and white shells, give the building an almost ethereal quality. Despite its familiarity, or perhaps precisely because you already feel you know it so well, it's quite breathtaking at first sight. Now almost universally loved and admired, it's hard to believe quite how controversial a project this was during its long haul from plan, as a result of an interna tional competition in the late 1950s, to completion in 1973. For sixteen years, construction was plagued by quarrels and scandal, so much so that the Danish architect, Jørn Utzon, threw in the towel halfway through. The final price tag was $102 million – well over ten times the original estimate. Inside the shell are an opera and concert hall, two theatres, restaurants, bars, a cinema, an Aboriginal artists' gallery and a library. Locals have discovered other uses for it besides all this arty-farty culture: its sloping sides, easy to crawl up before they slant off precariously, make a fine slippery dip after a beery picnic and cricket match in the facing Botanic Gardens; more determined outdoor types have attempted to abseil it.

If you're not content with gazing at the outside – much the building's best feature – and can't attend a performance, there are **guided tours** available (daily 9.15am–4pm, every half hour, depending on availability of theatres; $9; tickets from the Lower Concourse; ☎250 7250). On Sunday afternoons there are always free outdoor concerts on one of the forecourts, ranging through jazz, classical, folk and rock (☎250 7111 for details, or pick up the *Sydney Opera House Diary*); Sundays are further enlivened by the **Tarpeian Markets** (forecourt; 10am–4pm), with an emphasis on crafts. During the winter months there are sometimes free weekday classical or jazz **lunchtime concerts** in the northern foyer, usually on Wednesdays. Best of all, attend an evening performance: the building is particularly stunning when floodlit and, once you're inside, the huge windows come into their own as the dark harbour waters reflect a shimmering image of the night-time city – interval drinks certainly aren't like this anywhere else.

The charismatic **Harbour Bridge**, in the opposite direction from Circular Quay, has straddled the channel dividing North and South Sydney since 1932; today it makes the view from Circular Quay complete. The largest arch bridge in the world when it was built, the cost of its construction wasn't paid off until 1988. It still costs to drive across, though, with a $2 toll paid only when heading south; you can walk or cycle it for free. Pedestrians should head up the steps from Cumberland Street in the Rocks, and walk on the eastern side (the western side is the preserve of cyclists). One of Australia's most well-known comedians, Paul Hogan of *Crocodile Dundee* fame, worked as a rigger on "the coathanger" before being rescued by a New Faces talent quest in the 1970s. To check out Hoge's vista, there's a **lookout point** (daily 10am–5pm; $2; access near intersection of Cumberland and Argyle streets) actually inside the bridge's southern pylon where, as well as gazing out across the harbour, you can study a photo exhibition on the bridge's history. The ever-increasing volume of traffic in recent years proved too much for the bridge to bear, and a harbour **tunnel** (also $2 heading south) has been built, starting south of the Opera House.

Beside the Bridge at Milsons Point, you can't miss the huge laughing clown's face that belongs to **Luna Park** (daily 10am–10pm, Fri & Sat to 11pm; free entry; ride tickets from $2.50, cheaper in bundles from $10 up; ☎922 6644 or info line ☎0055 60 266). A feature of Sydney since the 1930s at the height of the amusement park era, it was closed down for several years from the late Eighties until the grand re-opening in January 1995. The new clown's face is the eighth since Luna Park began, with the present visage closely resembling the Fifties model. Many local artists worked on the restoration of Coney Island, a sort of funfair within a funfair, repainting murals and creating slide shows. One great ride dating from the 1960s and specially designed for the park is the Wildmouse, which whizzes out over the water's edge; also recommended is the Big Dipper, a full-on modern roller-coaster with great harbour views – if you dare open your eyes. If rides don't interest, there's a boardwalk right around to Lavender Bay, or good grazing at cafés and fast-food stalls. To get here, hop on a ferry from Circular Quay or Darling Harbour to the park's own wharf or catch a train from Circular Quay to Milsons Point. There is no car park, and you'd be lucky to find a spot on the street.

# The Rocks

**The Rocks**, immediately beneath the bridge, is the heart of historic Sydney. On this rocky outcrop between Sydney Cove and Walsh Bay, Captain Arthur Phillip proclaimed the establishment of Sydney Town in 1788, the first permanent European settlement in Australia. Within decades, the area had become little more than a slum of dingy dwellings and dubious taverns. The Rocks "pushes" of the 1870s and 1880s were gangs of "larrikins" (louts) who mugged passers-by and beat up on each other. In 1900 whole streetfronts were torn down to contain an outbreak of the bubonic plague, but it remained a run-down, depressed and depressing quarter until the 1970s, when there were plans to raze the historic cottages, terraces and warehouses to make way for the spreading office towers. Thanks to the foresight of a radical building workers' union which opposed the demolition, however, the restored and renovated historical quarter of The Rocks is now one of Sydney's major tourist attractions and, despite a passing resemblance to a historic theme park, it's worth exploring.

There are times, in fact, when the old atmosphere still seems to prevail: Friday and Saturday nights in The Rocks can be thoroughly drunken, and there's frequently **trouble** – so much so that one of the old pubs was converted into a police station. New Year's Eve is also riotously celebrated here, while fireworks explode over the harbour.

**The Rocks Heritage & Information Centre**, 106 George Street (daily 9am–5pm, Dec & Jan to 7pm; ☎255 1788, free call ☎1800 067 676 or recorded info on ☎11606), in the old Sailors' Home, is an excellent source of information about the history and sights of The Rocks, and is also the starting point for guided walking tours (Mon–Fri 10.30am, 12.30 & 2.30pm, Sat & Sun 11.30am & 2pm; 1hr 15min; $9). They also sell the *Rocks Ticket* ($36), which buys you a guided tour of the area, a meal (in the *Lowenbrau Keller*), entry to either the MCA or the Earth Exchange (see below), and a harbour cruise with *Captain Cook Cruises*. The small sandstone house next to the information centre is **Cadman's Cottage**, the oldest private house still standing in Sydney, built in 1816 for John Cadman. Nowadays it's the *National Parks and Wildlife Service of NSW* bookshop and information centre (Mon 10am–3pm, Tues–Fri 9am–4.30pm, Sat & Sun 11am–4pm). At weekends, the end of George Street is taken over by the **Rocks Market** (Sat & Sun 10am–5pm), with more than a hundred stalls selling bric-a-brac, jewellery, antiques and arts and crafts, sheltered from the sun or driving rain by huge sails; there's usually some live entertainment too. If that doesn't satisfy your shopping urge, head for the **Argyle Centre** on the corner of Argyle and Playfair streets, a complex of upmarket boutiques in a beautifully restored historic building.

## Museum of Contemporary Art

The **Museum of Contemporary Art** (MCA; daily 11am–6pm; $8 all-day ticket, $5 for YHA, VIP & ISIC holders; tours Mon–Sat noon & 2pm, Sun 2pm; 24hr recorded info ☎241 5892), on the western side of Circular Quay with another entrance on George Street, is one of Sydney's most exciting museums. Opened in December 1991 in the former Maritime Services Building, it's a temple to international twentieth-century art, with an eclectic approach encompassing lithographs, sculpture, film, video, drawings and paintings ranging from Warhol to Aboriginal art. The MCA also has an inventive line in themed exhibitions, taking topics such as contemporary Japanese art, popular culture in the Fifties, or simply Television. Sunday morning readings (11.30am; $8) are often given by leading Australian authors, and there's a well-stocked bookshop and a superbly sited, if expensive, café with outdoor tables overlooking the waterfront.

## Earth Exchange and Museum for Children

Further down towards the Harbour Bridge, at the end of George Street, the revamped Geological and Mining Museum, housed in an old power station at 18 Hickson Road, is now known as the **Earth Exchange** (daily 10am–5pm; $7.50; kids $5.50). The hands-on, experience-orientated exhibits make a great place for kids, or anyone who enjoys exploding volcanoes, simulated earthquakes and the like. The displays manage to painlessly convey information about the geological make-up of Australia in general and the Sydney region in particular; the inevitable mining section glosses over ecological problems, most notably the environmental costs of uranium mining. Mining can, however, claim credit for the highlight of the museum – a dazzling collection of minerals, semi-precious and precious stones on the third floor, among them the Jubilee Gold Nugget, Australia's biggest lump of gold.

The Merchant's House at 43 George Street is a historic home built in 1848, and now houses a **Museum for Children** (Wed–Sun 10am–4pm; nominal charge for some activities; ☎241 5099 for details); it has a collection of books, prints and toys from 1850 to the present that make up the National Trust's Australian childhood collection. Best of all, there are weekend activities laid on for children which might include readings, theatre and music, or even making damper in the kitchen of the old house.

## The old wharves

At the end of George Street, under the Harbour Bridge, **Dawes Point** separates Sydney Cove, on the Circular Quay side, from Walsh Bay and the old piers; the park here is a favourite spot for photographers. Looking out past the Opera House, you can see **Fort Denison** on a small island in the harbour: "Pinchgut", as the island is still known, was originally used as a special prison for the tough nuts the penal colony couldn't crack. During the Crimean Wars in the mid-nineteenth century, however, old fears of a Russian invasion were rekindled and a defence ring was built around the harbour, of which this fort was part. There are tours for those interested in Australian history from Jetty 6 at Circular Quay (run by *Captain Cook Cruises* ☎206 1111; daily 10am, noon & 2pm; $8.50). **Pier One**, immediately west of the point, is a converted wharf now awash with touristy "market" stalls (Mon–Fri 9am–5pm, Sat & Sun 9am–6pm or later), fast-food counters, restaurants, souvenir shops and a noisy amusement arcade; a discount bookstall usually has plenty of reading on Sydney and other parts of Australia.

If you want to rest your legs in more genteel surroundings, head down the road to the café-restaurant at the **Wharf Theatre** (Pier 4/5), where you can revel in the fantastic view across Sydney Harbour to Balmain, Goat Island and the North Shore – not to mention some welcome peace and quiet. The photo exhibition in the hallway to the theatre restaurant might even tempt you to come back for a performance by the *Sydney Theatre Company* (see p.113).

## Millers Point

Beyond the wharves, looking towards Darling Harbour, **Millers Point** is a reminder of how The Rocks used to be – though it too is very much on its way up in the world. For the moment, however, the traditional street-corner pubs and shabby terraced houses on the hill are reminiscent of the raffish atmosphere once typical of the whole area. Wander up Lower Fort Street to **Windmill Hill** in Observatory Park, and as well as a marvellous view over the harbour, you can see a few original, convict-built, sandstone buildings. The **Observatory** from which the park takes its name started operating in 1858 and has been a museum of astronomy since 1982 (Mon–Fri 2–5pm, Sat & Sun 10am–5pm; free). Every evening (except Wednesdays) you can view the southern sky through telescopes and learn about the Southern Cross and other southern constellations (times vary with season; 2hr tours include a lecture, film, a look at the exhibition, guided view of the telescopes and a look at the sky, weather permitting; booking essential on ☎217 0485; $5). The **National Trust Centre** (Mon–Fri 9.30am–4.30pm, Sat–Sun 11am–5pm) is also within Observatory Hill Park in the former military hospital south of the Observatory; it houses the *S H Ervin Gallery* with a collection of Australian art, as well as a café and a specialist bookshop where you can pick up information leaflets about other historic buildings and settlements in New South Wales.

# Downtown

From Circular Quay south as far as King Street is Sydney's **Central Business District**, with **Martin Place** as its commercial nerve centre. A pedestrian mall lined with banks and investment companies, Martin Place has its less serious moments during summer lunchtimes when street performances are held at the little amphitheatre. The imposing **General Post Office** broods over the George Street end of Martin Place, while the other end emerges opposite the old civic buildings on lower Macquarie Street. The cramped streets of the CBD itself, overshadowed by office buildings, have little to offer as you stroll through. For some impression of the commerce going on here, a great spectator sport is to watch the brokers whipping themselves into a trading frenzy from the viewing gallery of the **Australian Stock Exchange** (Mon–Fri 9am–5pm), opposite Australia Square at 20 Bond Street.

On the corner of Bridge and Phillip streets, the **Museum of Sydney** is a brand new museum devoted to the city. The site itself is the reason for the museum's existence, for here in 1983 an archeological dig unearthed the foundations of the first Government House built by Governor Phillip in 1788, where the first nine governors of NSW lived until it was demolished in 1846. A modern interactive approach tells the history of Sydney through exhibition, film, interactive multimedia and events (daily 10am–5pm; $6, $12 family ticket; ☎251 4611).

### King Street to Park Street

Further south, the streets get a little more interesting. The rectangle between Elizabeth, King, George and Park streets is Sydney's prime shopping area, with a number of beautifully restored **Victorian arcades** (the Imperial Arcade, Strand Arcade and Queen Victoria Building are all worth a look) and big **department stores** like *David Jones* and *Grace Bros*. **Sydney Tower** (daily 9.30am–9.30pm, Sat until 11.30pm; $6 admission to viewing gallery), a giant golden gearstick thrusting up from Market Street, is the tallest poppy in the Sydney skyline – and, indeed, the entire southern hemisphere. The 360-degree panoramic view from the top is especially fine at sunset, and at times you can even see the Blue Mountains, a hundred kilometres away. On the floor below, there's the inevitable revolving restaurant (☎233 3722).

Nearby, at the corner of Market and George streets, a couple of fine old buildings provide a pointed contrast. If heaven has a hallway, it surely must resemble that of the restored **State Theatre** on Market Street. Step inside and take a look at the ornate and glorious interior – a lavishly painted, gilded and sculpted corridor leads to the lush, red and wood-panelled foyer. The stately **Queen Victoria Building**, opposite, is another of Sydney's finest – which hasn't stopped the populace, with characteristic disrespect, from abbreviating it to the QVB. Originally built as a market hall in 1898, the restored QVB was reopened as an upmarket shopping arcade in 1986. The interior is magnificent, with its beautiful woodwork, elevated walkways and antique lifts; Charles I is beheaded on the hour, every hour, by figurines on the ground-floor mechanical clock.

In the realm of architectural excess, however, the **Town Hall** is king – you'll find it a block further up George Street, at the corner of Druitt Street. Built during the boom years of the 1870s and 1880s as a homage to Victorian England, its huge organ gives it the air of a secular cathedral. Inside, different styles of ornamentation compete for attention in a riot of colour and detail, and the splendidly dignified toilets are a must-see. Concerts and theatre performances (details on ☎265 9230) set off the splendiferous interior perfectly.

## THE SYDNEY FILM FESTIVAL

The Sydney Film Festival is a fortnight-long line-up of features, shorts, documentaries and retrospective screenings from Australia and around the world, held annually in mid-June: some seventy features and over a hundred shorts and documentaries in all. Founded in 1954 by a group of film enthusiasts at Sydney University, the festival struggled with prudish censors and parochial attitudes until freedom from censorship for festival films was introduced in 1971. From the early, relaxed atmosphere of picnics on the lawns betweeen screenings and hardy film-lovers crouching under blankets in freezing prefabricated sheds, over the years it gradually moved off-campus, to find a home since 1974 in the magnificent State Theatre (see above).

The festival is sold on a subscription basis – no single tickets available, though there are day passes. One- or two-week passes are available in varying forms; the Blue Pass, for example, gives you access to one week of the Festival in the evenings from 6pm and weekends from 10am (around $110). For more information, drop into the Festival office at 405 Glebe Point Road, Glebe (Mon–Fri 10am–5pm) or call ☎660 3102.

### Spanish corner and Chinatown

From Town Hall to Central Station George Street moves rapidly downmarket, starting with a cluster of multi-screen cinemas. Slightly further on, the half-hearted **Spanish corner** consists basically of Spanish restaurants (see p.101 for recommendations) on Liverpool Street, and the Spanish Club on the corner of Kent Street. Sydney's **Chinatown**, in the area known as Haymarket, is a more full-blooded affair – through the Chinese gates, Dixon Street Mall is the main drag, abuzz day and night as people crowd into numerous restaurants, pubs, cafés, cinemas, food stalls and Asian grocery stores. Towards the end of January or in the first weeks of February, Chinese New Year is celebrated here with gusto; dragon and lion dances, food festivals and musical entertainment compete with the noise and smoke from strings of Chinese crackers. The **Chinese Garden** (daily 9.30am–sunset; $2), just on the edge of Chinatown at the southern fringes of Darling Harbour, was completed for the Bicentenary Festival in 1988 as a gift from Sydney's sister city Guangdong. Built on a mere acre, it feels remarkably spacious – a serene pocket of calm and a great place to take a book. The balcony of the tearoom offers a bird's-eye view of the dragon wall, waterfalls, a pagoda on a hill and carp swimming in winding lakes.

The area immediately south of Chinatown is enlivened every Saturday by the frenetic **Paddy's Markets** (8am–4.30pm), back in its undercover home at the corner of Hay and Quay streets, next door to the Entertainment Centre. It's a good place to buy cheap vegetables, plants, clothes and bric-a-brac.

### Macquarie Street

Lachlan Macquarie, reformist governor of New South Wales between 1809 and 1821, gave the early settlement its first imposing public buildings. He had a vision of an elegant, prosperous city – although the Imperial Office in London didn't share his enthusiasm for expensive civic projects. Refused both money and expertise, Macquarie was forced to be resourceful: many of the the city's finest buildings were designed by ex-convict architect Francis Greenway and paid for with rum-money, the proceeds of a monopoly on liquor sales. Today, the southern end of his namesake street is lined with the grand edifices that were the result of the governor's dreams: Hyde Park Barracks, Parliament House, the State Library and the hospital he and his wife designed. Macquarie Street also neatly divides business from pleasure, separating the office towers and cramped streets of the CBD from the open spaces of the Domain and the Royal Botanic Gardens (see below).

Sandstone **Sydney Hospital**, the so-called "Rum Hospital", was Macquarie's first enterprise, commissioned in 1814 and therefore one of the oldest buildings in Australia – apart from the central section, which collapsed and was rebuilt at the end of the century. One of the original wings is now **NSW Parliament House** (Mon–Fri 9am–4pm; free guided tours anytime Dec–Feb, at 10am, 11am & 2pm when Parliament is sitting; ☎230 2111), where as early as 1829 local councils called by the governor started to meet, making it by some way the oldest parliament building in Australia. The thick-skinned can listen in on question time (Tues–Thurs, 2.15pm). The other wing is now the **Old Mint Museum** (Mon–Tues & Thurs–Sun 10am–5pm, Wed noon–5pm; $4), having been converted into a branch of the Royal Mint in response to the first Australian goldrush, and now serving as a museum of decorative arts, stamps and coins. Next door, the **Hyde Park Barracks** (daily 10am–5pm; $5) was built in 1819, again without permission from London; the building is now a museum of the social and architectural history of Sydney, giving an insight into convict life during the early years of the colony and the lives of nineteenth-century immigrant women.

The **State Library of New South Wales** (Mon–Fri 9am–9pm, Sat & Sun 11am–5pm; Mitchell Library closed Sun; free) completes the row of public buildings on the eastern side of Macquarie Street. This complex of old and new buildings also includes the **Mitchell** and **Dixson Libraries** with their archives of old maps, illustrations and records relating to the early days of white settlement in Australia. Lectures, film and video shows take place regularly in the **Metcalfe Auditorium** (☎230 414 for details).

## Hyde Park, the Domain and the Botanic Gardens

**Hyde Park**, at the top of Macquarie Street, was fenced by Governor Macquarie in 1810 to mark the outskirts of his township, and with its war memorials and church is still very much the formal city park. From Queens Square, **St James Church** marks the entry to the park – the Anglican church, completed in 1824, was another of Macquarie's schemes built to ex-convict Greenway's design; the Catholic **St Mary's Cathedral** also overlooks this section. Behind St James, the **Archibald Fountain** commemorates the association of Australia and France during World War I. The Sandringham Memorial Gardens also remember Australia's war dead, but the most potent of these monuments is the famous **Anzac Memorial** at the southern end of the park. Just outside the park, at the junction of William and College streets, is the **Australian Museum** (daily 9.30am–5pm; $5, $3 concessionary rate includes YHA members and students; special exhibitions extra). Basically a museum of natural history, with lots on Australian wildlife, it also has a good section on Aboriginal and Pacific Islander history and culture with a couple of good films to watch, one the satirical *Babakiueria* (see *Contexts*, p.839).

### The Domain

The small Cook and Phillip parks plug the gap between Hyde Park and **The Domain**, a much larger, plainer open space that stretches right to the waterfront. In the early days of the settlement, the Domain was the governor's private park; now it's a popular place for a stroll or a picnic, with the Art Gallery of NSW, Andrew "Boy" Charlton Pool and Mrs Macquaries's Chair to provide distraction. On Sundays, assorted cranks and revolutionaries assemble here for Speakers' Corner, and every January thousands of people gather on the lawns here, spread blankets, open picnic baskets and enjoy the free open-air opera and concerts of the Festival of Sydney (see p.114).

The **Art Gallery of New South Wales** (Mon–Sat 10am–5pm, Sun noon–5pm; free except for special exhibitions, free guided tours; ☎225 1790) has a large collection of European art dating from the eleventh to the twentieth century, an extensive collection of Australian works – including some by Aboriginal Australians, and examples of arts and crafts from Papua New Guinea. The auditorium is used for art lectures, and there's an excellent bookshop and a coffeeshop.

A strip of the Domain beyond the gallery occupies a promontory sticking into the harbour between Farm Cove and Woolloomooloo Bay. At the end is the celebrated lookout point known as **Mrs Macquarie's Chair**. Here the governor's wife, Elizabeth Macquarie, had a seat fashioned out of the rock from which she could survey the harbour; the panorama may have changed dramatically since 1810, but the throne survives – and is still an excellent vantage point. On the Woolloomooloo side of the promontory, the **Andrew "Boy" Charlton Pool** is an open-air, saltwater swimming pool, safely isolated from the harbour waters (Sept–April only, Mon–Fri 6am–8pm, Sat & Sun 6.30am–7pm; $2); "the Boy", as the locals fondly call it, is a popular hangout for groovy Darlinghurst types and sun-worshipping gays.

## The Royal Botanic Gardens
The **Royal Botanic Gardens** (daily 7am–sunset, visitors' centre 9.30am–4.30pm; free) occupy the area between this strip of the Domain and the Opera House, around the headland on Farm Cove where the first white settlers struggled to grow vegetables for the hungry colony. Today's gardeners are much more successful, judging by the well-tended flower beds, lawns and ponds. With examples of trees and plants from around the world, it's still the huge native Moreton Bay Figs in all their gnarled beauty, that stand out. The gardens are always crowded with workers chewing lunchtime sandwiches, picknickers on fine weekends, people lolling about reading and lovers entwined beneath trees or squeezed into the popular café/restaurant that overlooks them. At dusk, just as you have to leave, fruit bats fly overhead in noisy groups and the possums begin to riot. More structured attractions include an Aboriginal plant trail and an impressive selection of tropical plants housed in two glass pyramids (daily 10am–4pm; $5). Free guided tours start from the visitors' centre (Wed & Fri 10am, Sun 1.30pm; 45min; ☎231 8125). Just inside the gardens at the end of Bridge Street, the **Conservatorium of Music**, housed in a lovely old mansion, has free lunchtime concerts every Wednesday during term-time (☎230 1222 for details).

# Darling Harbour and around

**Darling Harbour** is, in some ways, a thoroughly stylish redevelopment of the old wharves around Cockle Bay – the glistening water channels that run along Palm Avenue are a great piece of modern design – and if in other ways it's equally tacky and touristy, that's perhaps the inevitable result of its popularity. The **Harbourside Festival Marketplace**, with its souvenir shops and burger bars, is perhaps the biggest attraction and the worst offender, while the funfair on the other side of the bay now plays second fiddle to Luna Park and is something of an eyesore. Still, Darling Harbour and the surrounding areas of Haymarket and Ultimo have plenty else to offer: museums, an aquarium, entertainment areas, parks, gardens, a convention and exhibition centre.

**Getting here** you could quite simply walk – it's only ten minutes on foot from the Town Hall – from the QVB, walk down Market Street and across Pyrmont Bridge. Further south you can cut through on Liverpool Street to Tumbalong Park, on the far side of which is the Exhibition Centre. Car spaces are available from $4 per day. Alternatively, the **monorail** (operating Mon–Sat 7am–midnight, Sun 9am–8pm) runs from the city centre to one of three stops around Darling Harbour, and has the views to recommend it; or there's always the *Darling Harbour Tramway Bus* (a tourist bus dressed up as a Melbourne tram; single $2, day ticket $3), which runs between the Rocks and Darling Harbour every twenty minutes on weekends. Getting there by **ferry**

from Circular Quay gives you a chance to see a bit of the harbour, and to stop over in Balmain en route: State Transit ferries leave from wharf 4, Circular Quay (about every 45min weekdays, 8am–7.30pm, less often at weekends; $2.60 single) calling at McMahons Point, Darling Street Jetty in Balmain and Sydney Aquarium in Darling Harbour; or there's the *Rocket Express Ferry*, which runs from Darling Harbour via the Aquarium Wharf and The Rocks to Circular Quay, outside the MCA (every 20min, 9.40am–5.40pm; $3 single). The **Darling Harbour Super Ticket** ($36) includes rides on the monorail, a two-hour cruise with *Matilda Bay Discovery Cruises*, entry to the Aquarium and the Chinese Garden, a barbecue meal and discounts in the Harbourside shops.

For **information** about what's on, phone the *Darling Harbour Information Hotline* (☎0055 2026).

## Around the water

Having completed the obligatory trudge round the Marketplace, take a walk down to the harbourfront, where a number of fine old sailing craft are usually moored at the **Sydney seaport**, among them the **James Craig** (built in 1874). Just beyond, the new **National Maritime Museum** (daily 10am–5pm; $9) highlights the history of Australia as a seafaring nation; there's also a library, auditorium, restaurant and shop.

**Pyrmont Bridge**, between the museum and the marketplace, was "the world's first electrically operated swing span bridge", and is now a pedestrian walkway across Cockle Bay, linking the two sides of the harbour – it's also the best place to watch the periodic firework displays. Across the bridge is the **Sydney Aquarium** (daily 9.30am–9pm; $14, family ticket $34): if you're not going to get the chance to explore the Barrier Reef, this makes a surprisingly passable substitute. Head straight for the underwater walkway (two clear plastic tunnels) where you can wander in complete safety among sharks, wobbegongs, sting-rays and eely things – the safety-conscious sensation-seeker's idea of heaven. Upstairs are freshwater fish from the Murray–Darling basin, Australia's biggest river system, while another area features exotic species from the warmer waters further north, and the colourful and bizarre world of the Great Barrier Reef. Sadly though, some of the aquarium's tanks seem rather small and you can't blame the seals for looking bored with their unstimulating pool.

## Ultimo – The Powerhouse and around

**Tumbalong Park**, inland between the Exhibition Centre and the Chinese Garden (p.81), is the "village green" of Darling Harbour, and serves as a venue for open-air concerts and free public entertainment. From the park, a signposted walkway leads to **Ultimo** and its **Powerhouse Museum** (daily 10am–5pm; $5, free first Sat every month; monorail to Haymarket). Located, as the name suggests, in a former power station, this is arguably the best museum in Sydney, a young and exciting place with fresh ideas. Unusually, it combines arts and sciences, sociology and technology under the same roof: the displays are so varied they're impossible to define, but there's something of everything here, with an emphasis on an interactive approach that means you'll need hours, or several trips, to investigate the museum properly. Judging by the tears at closing time, the special kids' areas have proved a great success. The souvenir shop is also worth a look, and is a good place for unusual gifts.

Three blocks north, at 320 Harris Street in Ultimo, the **Australian Motor Vehicle Museum** (daily 10am–5pm; $8; monorail to Convention) houses more than two hundred vehicles on three levels. The usual mix of vintage cars and 1950s American style-cruisers, it also has a comprehensive collection of Australian automobilia. Elsewhere, Ultimo is fast becoming Sydney's media headquarters, with the new *ABC* offices in Harris Street and the *Sydney Morning Herald* on Broadway, next to the seventeen-storey tower of the University of Technology, with its high-profile media courses.

# Inner Western Suburbs

**West** of the centre, immediately beyond Darling Harbour, the inner-city areas of **Glebe** and **Newtown** surround Sydney University, their vibrant cultural mix enlivened by large student populations. On a peninsula north of Glebe and west of The Rocks, **Balmain** is a gentrified working-class dock area popular for its village atmosphere.

## Glebe

Just west of the centre beyond Darling Harbour and Ultimo, and right by Australia's oldest university, **Glebe** is gradually changing from a café-oriented student quarter to more upmarket thirtysomething territory with a New Age slant. The sidestreets are fringed with renovated two-storey terrace houses with white iron lacework verandas: pretty, but not (yet) as posh as Paddington, the area retains its laid-back village atmosphere. Glebe Point Road, the focal point of the area, is filled with an eclectic mix of cafés, restaurants, bookshops and speciality shops. Not surprisingly, Glebe is popular with backpackers: there are two good YHA hostels among others (see "Accommodation" listings, p.70); for **longer stays**, check the many café noticeboards for flatshares.

The place is at its best at weekends, when **Glebe Market** (which takes place on the primary school playground near Broadway) is in full swing. A heady and enthralling mixture of cheap ethnic eats, psychotic Chinese masseurs and secondhand books, the market is much better territory for bargain-hunters than its better known rival in Paddington. Opposite, at number 49, you'll find the excellent *Gleebooks* – one of Sydney's best-loved bookshops and the focus of Glebe's literary and academic aspirations, with readings and talks upstairs on a regular basis (call ☎660 2333 for details). The original *Gleebooks*, now selling secondhand and childrens books only, is worth the trek farther up at 191 Glebe Point Road, past St Johns Road and Glebe's pretty park. Across the street and a couple of blocks further on, is the groovy *Valhalla* cinema, established in 1976. You can study its programme of cult favourites while devouring a tasty snack at the *Craven Café* next door. Glebe Point Road trails off past here into a more residential area, petering out at Jubilee Park opposite Rozelle Bay's container terminal. **Buses** #431 and #434 run to Glebe via Millers Point, George Street and Central Station; #433 takes the same route, but doesn't run the full length of Glebe Point Road. Otherwise it's a ten- to fifteen-minute **walk** from Central up Broadway.

## Newtown and Enmore

**Newtown**, quite a bit further to the southwest, is another up-and-coming inner-city suburbs. What was once a working-class suburb, a hotchpotch of derelict factories, junkyards and cheap accommodation, has been transformed into a slightly off-beat and alternative area. Newtown is characterized by its large gay and lesbian population, its rich cultural mix and a healthy dose of students and lecturers from nearby Sydney University. The main drag, **King Street**, is filled with unusual secondhand and speciality shops: check out the *Greed Sisters Emporium* at number 178; the *Cornstalk* bookshop at number 262; or *Gould's Book Arcade*, the vast and chaotic secondhand book warehouse that is a beloved Sydney insitution, at number 32. Fashion is also well represented, with consistently interesting designer clothes and jewellery at *La Luna* at number 156; for something far wilder, try *Pretty Dog Recycled Clothing* in Brown Street for a good range of secondhand gear with some stunningly decked out glam/punk dummies and a great display of severed dolls' heads in the window. Newtown also has an enviable number of great cafés and diverse restaurants, especially Thai. King Street quietens down on the **St Peters** side of the train station, but it's well worth strolling down to look at the furniture shops catering to all budgets (designer, collector, secondhand and junk) and the more unusual speciality shops (buttons, ribbons, train memorabilia, cowboy high-style).

So far **Enmore**, 100m down the Enmore Road, opposite Newtown station and heading in the direction of Marrickville, has escaped gentrification, with the result that the migrant population hasn't been squeezed out by higher rents and more expensive leases. Thai grocery stores share the road with the Turkish belly-dancing school, Chinese laundry, Fijian grocer and Italian deli, while the Greek nation is well represented by a barber, a bakery and a darkly lit men's club from whence drifts the sound of clicking dominoes. It's generally much quieter than Newtown, except when Midnight Oil or a Hindi film is playing at the **Enmore Theatre**.

Numerous **buses** run to Newtown via Castlereagh Street and City Road: #422, #423, #426 and #428. They all go down King Street as far as the station, where some turn off to Enmore. You can also get here by **train** from Central Station.

## Balmain and Goat Island

**Balmain**, directly north of Glebe, is less than two kilometres from the Opera House, by ferry from Circular Quay. But, stuck out on a spur in the harbour, separated from the centre by Darling Harbour and Johnston's Bay, it is almost an hour from The Rocks by bus, via **Leichhardt**, Sydney's "Little Italy" and along Darling Street, which runs from **Rozelle** right down to Balmain's waterfront. Perhaps it's this degree of separation that has helped Balmain retain its slow, villagey atmosphere and made it the favoured abode of many writers and filmmakers. Like better-known Paddington, Balmain was once a working-class quarter of terraced houses that has gradually been gentrified. The docks are still important, though, and Balmain hasn't completely forsaken its roots. Darling Street rewards a leisurely stroll and a bit of browsing in its speciality shops, grazing in its restaurants and cafés, and is blessed with enough watering holes to warrant a pub crawl. The best time to come is on Saturday, when a lively flea market, together with some wonderfully exotic food stalls, occupies the grounds of St Andrews Church (7.30am–4pm). Further back towards Rozelle, Elkington Park has the quaint **Dawn Fraser Swimming Pool**, an old-fashioned harbour pool named after the famous Australian Olympic swimmer. Bus #433 runs out to Balmain via George Street, Central Station and Glebe Point Road, or a **ferry** from Circular Quay can take you to Darling Street jetty in less than fifteen minutes.

Just across the water from Balmain east, **Goat Island** is the site of a well-preserved gunpowder magazine complex. The sandstone buildings, including a barracks, were built by two hundred convicts between 1833 and 1839. Treatment of the convicts was harsh: eighteen-year-old Charles Anderson received over 1200 lashes in 1835 and if that wasn't enough, he was sentenced to be chained to a rock for two years, a cruel punish-

---

### HABERFIELD, FEDERATION SUBURB

Immediately west of Leichhardt, between Parramatta Road and Iron Cove on the Parramatta River, **Haberfield** was an entirely planned suburb. "Slum-less, Lane-less, and Pub-less" was the vision of the post-Federation developers; the new nation was to have the ultimate urban environment. The style of the 1500 homes, all designed by the architect J. Spencer-Stanfield, is a classic Australian confection called **Federation Style** which spread around the country from 1901. Eminently suited to the climate, the houses are a pleasing combination of the functional, such as wide verandahs to allow cooling breezes to circulate, with the fanciful, such as attics and turrets. Stained glass is an important decorative element, often with very Australian motifs of kookaburras and native flowers or flowing art-nouveau designs. Decorative barge boarding, elaborate chimneys, fretted woodwork, gables and eaves are other key features. Every Spencer-Stanfield house in Haberfield is different, so you can easily spend a fascinating afternoon wandering its tranquil, leafy streets. And you still won't find a pub.

Catch **bus** #461 from Town Hall or Circular Quay.

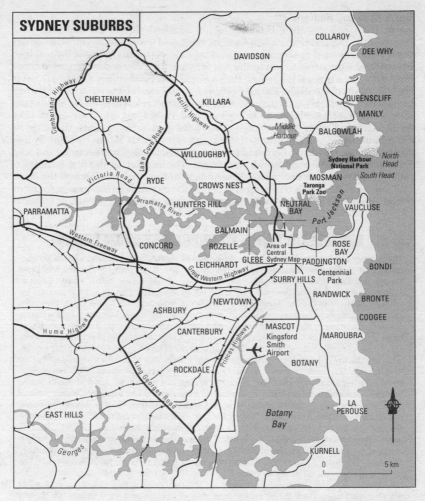

ment even by the standards of the day; you can still see the sandstone "couch". In 1994, the island was handed over to the NPWS, which runs tours at weekends (*Darling Harbour Rocket* from Circular Quay, outside the MCA, at 10.25am and 1.25pm, or from Darling Harbour at 10.40am & 1.45pm; 2hr–2hr 40min; $12; book on ☎555 9844).

## Inner Eastern Suburbs

To the east, **Surry Hills**, **Darlinghurst** and **Paddington** were once rather scruffy working-class suburbs, but have been taken over and revamped by the young, arty and upwardly mobile. **Kings Cross** is home to Sydney's red-light district as well as many of its tourists, while in adjacent **Woolloomooloo** the container ships tie up at the docks. Further east, the "Cross" fades into the more elegant suburbs of **Potts Point** and **Elizabeth Bay**, which trade on their harbour views.

## Surry Hills and Redfern

**Surry Hills**, south of Hyde Park and east of Elizabeth Street, was traditionally the centre of the rag trade, which still finds its focus on Devonshire Street. Rows of tiny terraces once housed its original poor, working-class population, many of them of Irish background. Considered a slum by the rest of Sydney, the dire and overcrowded conditions were given fictional life in Ruth Park's *Harp in the South* trilogy (see p.847), set in the Surry Hills of the 1940s. The area retains a strong local character, with the current grungy muso, studenty and ethnically varied population refusing to let the slickly fashionable scene of neighbouring Darlinghurst and Paddington take over. Surry Hills' focus is leafy **Crown Street**, filled with cafés and funky clothes shops, while **Cleveland Street**, running west to Redfern and east towards Moore Park, the Sydney Cricket Ground and the showground (see box below), is noisy, traffic-snarled and lined with cheap Lebanese and Turkish restaurants. The **market** on the first Saturday of every month, in the small Shannon Reserve next to the *Clock Hotel*, brings the black-clad doyens of Surry Hills out in force, to peruse the mothballed retro gear and feast on felafel. Surry Hills is a short **walk** along Devonshire and Crown streets, or a shorter

### THE SYDNEY SHOWGROUND AND THE SCG

The Sydney Showground is host to the huge **Royal Agricultural Show,** when the country comes to the city. Running for twelve consecutive days with the second weekend always the Easter weekend, it's familiarly known as the Easter Show (daily 9.30am–9.30pm, first Sun and last Tues until 7pm; $13 adults, $7 kids). The occasion is marked by a frantic array of amusement-park rides, parades of prize animals, show bags, fireworks and wood-chopping displays, all usually accompanied by a good dose of rain – and a dramatic increase in the number of moleskin pants and akubra hats in evidence. **Show bags** have their origins in free samples from food manufacturers in the 1930s, but have since been commercialized beyond all recognition. Kids love the whole razzamatazz, especially the **farmyard nursery**. Events in the main arena are usually horse-related during the day; at night, there's a fireworks display and other spectacles which might range from a rodeo to a giant robotic dinosaur display. Parking is a nightmare and the use of public transport is encouraged, with free buses laid on from Central and Circular Quay.

The venerated institution of the **Sydney Cricket Ground,** next to the showground, has earned its place in cricketing history for Don Bradman's score of 452 not-out in 1929, and for the controversy over England's bodyline bowling techniques in 1932. Ideally, proceedings are observed from the lovely 1886 members stand, while sipping an icy gin and tonic – but unless you're invited by a member, you'll end up elsewhere, probably drinking beer from a plastic cup. Cricket spectators aren't a sedate lot in Sydney, and the noisiest barrackers will probably come from "the Hill", or the Doug Walters stand, as it's officially known: still the cheapest spot to sit, the concreted area was once a grassy hill where rowdy supporters threw empty beercans at players and each other, but there's now strictly rationed beer served in plastic cups. The Bill O'Reilly Stand gives comfortable viewing until the afternoon, when you'll be blinded by the sun, whereas the Brewongle Stand provides consistently good viewing. Best of all is the Bradman Stand, with a view directly behind the bowler's arm, and adjacent to the exclusive stand occupied by members, commentators and ex-players. The test to see here is, of course, **The Ashes**; the Sydney leg of the five tests, each for five days, begins on New Year's Day. For information, scores, prices and times, call *Match Information* on ☎0055 63132. You can buy tickets at the gates on the day, or purchase them in advance from *Ticketek* (☎266 4800).

Die-hard cricket fans can actually go on a tour of the SCG on non-match days (10am, 1pm & 3pm; 2hr; $18; ☎380 0383); the tour also takes in the **Sydney Football Stadium** next door, where **State of Origin** Rugby League is played, coverage of which consistently produces the highest ratings on Australian television.

ride (**buses** #341, #372, #393 or #395), from Central Station; buses #303, #306, #308, #309 and #310 from Circular Quay run via Elizabeth Street, while #304 starts at the QVB and goes via Crown Street.

Just beyond Surry Hills, and only two kilometres from the glitter and sparkle of Darling Harbour, **Redfern** is Sydney's underbelly. Around the **Everleigh Street** area, Australia's biggest urban Aboriginal community lives in "the Block", a squalid street-scape of derelict terraced houses and rubbish-strewn streets – the closest Sydney has to a no-go zone. The Aboriginal Housing Company has been unable to pay for repairs and renovation work, in shocking contrast to Paddington's cutesy restored terraces and the harbour-view mansions of Sydney's rich and beautiful.

## Darlinghurst, Paddington and Woollahra

**Oxford Street**, from Hyde Park to Paddington and beyond, is a major amusement strip. Waiting to be discovered, here and in the side streets, are an array of nightclubs, interesting restaurants, cafés and pubs. Around **Darlinghurst**, Oxford Street is the focus of Sydney's very active gay and lesbian movement. Hip and bohemian, Darlinghurst mingles seediness with a certain hedonistic style: some art students and pale and wasted clubbers never leave the district – save for a coffee at the Cross or a swim (in black cossies and cats-eye sunnies, of course) at "the Boy" in the Domain (see p.83). There's another concentration of cafés, restaurants and fashion on Liverpool Street, while Victoria Street is a classic pose strip with the legendary, street-smart *Coluzzi Bar*. At 148 Darlinghurst Road, the **Sydney Jewish Museum** (Mon–Thurs 10am–4pm, Fri 10am–3pm, Sun 11am–5pm; $5), is housed in the old Maccabean Hall, which has been a Jewish meeting point for over seventy years. Sixteen Jews were among the convicts who arrived with the First Fleet, and the museum explores over two hundred years of Australian Jewish experience.

**Paddington** itself, a slum at the turn of the century, became a popular hangout for hipsters during the late Sixties and Seventies. Since then, yuppies have taken over and turned Paddington into the smart and fashionable suburb it is today: the Victorian-era terraced houses, with their iron-lace verandas reminiscent of New Orleans, have been beautifully restored. Many of the terraces were originally built to house the artisans who worked on the graceful sandstone **Victoria Barracks** on Oxford Street; it's still used by the army but there are free guided tours (Thurs 9am & Sun 10am). On the other side of Oxford Street, the small, winding, tree-lined streets are a pleasant place for a stroll and offer tantalizing glimpses of the sparkling waters of the harbour – and a chance to wander into the many small galleries or to take in some liquid refreshment. Head via Underwood and Heeley streets to **Five Ways** where you'll find cafés, speciality shops and a typically gracious old boozer, the *Royal Hotel*. But the main action is, of course, on Oxford Street, most lively on Saturdays when the crowds descend on **Paddington Market** (or Paddington Village Bazaar, as it is more properly but rarely called, every Saturday from 10am to around 4pm) on the church grounds at 395 Oxford Street. As well as being a prime spot to show off and hang out, it's a surefire source of great presents with leathergoods, jewellery and clothes – old and new – at the top of the list. Even if you're hard up, it's worth a visit just to browse – the atmosphere, music and buskers come free and the food is cheap and tasty.

**Woollahra**, along Oxford Street from Paddington, is even more monied but contrastingly staid, with severely expensive **antique shops** along Queen Street replacing the wackier style of Paddington. South of Paddington and Woollahra lies the green expanse of **Centennial Park**, opened to the citizens of Sydney at the Centennial Festival in 1888 (the bicentennial version was opened at Homebush in 1988). With its vast lawns, rose gardens and extensive network of ponds it resembles an English country park, but is reclaimed at dawn and dusk by distinctly Antipodean residents, including possums and flying foxes. The park is crisscrossed by walking paths and tracks for cycling, jogging and horse riding: you can rent a bike or hire a horse (see "Listings", p.115 for details), and then recover from your exertions in the café. Adjoining **Moore Park** has facilities for tennis, golf, grass skiing, bowling, cricket and hockey.

Transport heading in this direction includes **bus** #280 (from the corner of Young and Alfred streets, Circular Quay) and #378 (from Central Station), both of which run along Oxford Street. #389 from Circular Quay runs via Elizabeth and William streets.

### Kings Cross, Woolloomooloo, Potts Point

The preserve of Sydney's bohemians in the 1950s, **Kings Cross** is now Sydney's red-light district, its streets prowled by prostitutes, junkies, drunks, strippers and homeless teenagers. Also a bustling centre for backpackers and travellers, especially around leafy and quieter Victoria Street, the two sides of the Cross co-exist with little trouble, though some of the tourists seem a little surprised at where they've ended up, and it can be rather initimidating for lone women.

The Cross can *seem* heavy but the constant flow of people makes it relatively safe, and it's always lively, with places to eat and drink open all hours. Climbing up William Street from Hyde Park, leggy and scantily clad transvestite prostitutes shiver, pressed up against car salesrooms, as Darlinghurst Road beckons with its giant neon Coca-Cola sign; on weekends, an endless stream of ice-cream-licking suburban voyeurs trawl along the Darlinghurst Road strip past the El Alamein fountain in Fitzroy Gardens to Macleay Street, as touts try their best to haul them into tacky strip-joints and sleazy nightclubs. Kings Cross is much more subdued during the day, with a slightly hung-over feel to it: local residents emerge and it's a good time to hang out in the cafés. Every Sunday, there's a small art and crafts market in the Fitzroy Gardens by the fountain.

All around, and indeed very close by, are quieter, more upmarket places. Towards the harbour, **Potts Point** becomes more peaceful and more expensive the closer you get to exclusive Elizabeth Bay (see below). **Woolloomooloo** occupies the old harbourside quarter back towards the city, between the docks and William Street. Once a narrow-streeted slum, it's slowly being spruced up. There are some rowdy pubs here, as well as the legendary *Harry's Cafe de Wheels* on Cowper Wharf Road, a 24-hour pie-cart operating since 1945. Famous for Pea and Pie floaters, *Harry's* has become a gathering place for Sydney cabbies and hungry clubbers in the early hours of the morning.

You can get to Kings Cross by **train** (Eastern suburbs line) or **bus** (#311, #324, #325 or #327 from Circular Quay, many others from the city to Darlinghurst Road), or it's not too far to walk: straight up William Street. For a quieter route, you could head up from the Domain via Cowper Wharf Road in Woolloomooloo, and then up the McElhone Stairs to Victoria Street.

# The Harbour

Loftily flanking the mouth of Sydney Harbour are the rugged sandstone cliffs of North Head and South Head, providing spectacular viewing points across the calm water to the city eleven kilometres away, where the Harbour Bridge spans the sunken valley at its deepest point. The many coves, bays, points and headlands of Sydney Harbour, and their parks, bushland and swimmable beaches, are rewarding to explore. Finding your way by ferry is the most pleasurable method: services run to much of the **north shore** and, via Taronga Zoo, to Darling Point, Double Bay, Rose Bay and Watsons Bay in the harbourfront areas of the **eastern suburbs**. The eastern shores are characterized by a certain glitziness, the haunt of the nouveau riche, while the leafy north shore is very much old money. Both sides of the harbour, but the north shore in particular, contain pockets of bushland (and three islands) which have been incorporated into the **Sydney Harbour National Park**; walking tracks abound (☎337 5511 for general information).

# Elizabeth Bay to South Head

The suburbs on the hilly southeastern shores of the harbour are rich and exclusive. A couple of early-nineteenth-century mansions, Elizabeth Bay House and Vaucluse House, are open to visitors, giving an insight into the lifestyle of the pioneering upper crust. Bus #324 and #325 from Circular Quay via Pitt Street and Kings Cross cover the places listed below, heading to Watsons Bay via New South Head Road; #325 detours at Vaucluse for Nielson Park.

## Elizabeth Bay and Rushcutters Bay

Barely five minutes' walk northwest of Kings Cross, **Elizabeth Bay** is nevertheless a well-heeled residential area, centred around **Elizabeth Bay House**, at 7 Onslow Avenue (Tues–Sun 10am–4.30pm; $5; bus #311 from either Railway Square or Circular Quay, or walk from Kings Cross Station), a grand Regency residence with fine harbour views, built in 1832. Heading southeast, you're only a few minutes' walk from **Rushcutters Bay Park**, a wonderful setting for a game of tennis against a backdrop of the yacht- and cruiser-packed marina in the bay. Gangs of picnickers book out the courts at *Rushcutters Bay Tennis Centre* (☎357 1675 for bookings; daily 8am–11pm; courts $14 per hour, rising to $16 after 4pm; racket rental $3), feasting in between sets. If you don't have anyone to play with, the friendly managers promise a hitting partner thrown in with the court; there's a nice little coffee bar too.

## Double Bay and Rose Bay

Continuing northeast to **Darling Point**, McKell Park provides a wonderful view across to **Clarke Island** and **Bradleys Head**, both part of the Sydney Harbour National Park; follow Darling Point Road (or take bus #327 from Edgecliff Station). The next port of call is **Double Bay**, dubbed "Double Pay" for obvious reasons. The noise and traffic of New South Head Road are redeemed by several excellent antiquarian and secondhand bookshops (see p.115), while in the quieter "village" are some of the most exclusive shops in Sydney, full of imported designer labels and expensive jewellery. The eastern suburbs socialites meet on Cross Street, where the swanky pavement cafes are filled with well-groomed women in Armani outfits sipping coffee, their Mercedes and Rolls Royces illegally parked outside. If all this sounds like a turn-off, Double Bay's real delight is **Redleaf Pool** (Sept–May, dawn–dusk; free), a peaceful, shady harbour beach enclosed by a wooden pier you can wander around, dive off or just laze on; there's also an excellent café famed for its fruit salad and cappuccino. A ferry from the Quay (Wharf 2) stops at both Darling Point and Double Bay; otherwise catch bus #324 or #325 also from Circular Quay.

The ferry to **Rose Bay** (Circular Quay, Wharf 2) gives you a chance to check out the waterfront mansions of **Point Piper** as you skim past. Rose Bay itself is quite a haven of exclusivity, with the verdant expanse of the members-only Royal Sydney Golf Course. Directly across New South Head Road from the course, waterfront **Lyne Park** provides welcome distraction, in the form of a **seaplane** service: based here since the 1930s, the planes are quite a sight as they take off and land on the water (see "Listings", p.118, for details).

## Nielson Park and Vaucluse

Sydney Harbour National Park emerges onto the waterfront at Bay View Hill, where the 1.5km **Hermitage walking track** to Nielson Park begins; to get to the starting point, continue about a kilometre up New South Head Road from Rose Bay (on bus routes #324 or #325). **Nielson Park**, on Shark Bay, is one of Sydney's delights – don't worry about Shark Beach's ominous name, it's netted – providing a great place for a night-time skinny dip. Vaucluse Bay shelters the magnificent **Vaucluse House** and its

27-acre estate (Tues–Sun 10am–4.30pm; $5), with tearooms in the grounds for refreshment. The house's original owner was the explorer and reformer William Wentworth, who was a member of the first party to cross the Blue Mountains. In 1831 he invited four thousand guests to Vaucluse House to celebrate the departure of the hated Governor Darling – the climax of the evening was a fireworks display which burned "Down with the Tyrant" into the night sky. Bus #325 from Edgecliff Station will bring you right to the door.

### Watsons Bay to South Head

Narrow Parsley Bay and its finger-shaped reserve follow Vaucluse Bay to **Watsons Bay**, accessible by ferry from Wharf 4 at Circular Quay. Once a fishing village, the suburb has retained a villagey feel with old fishermen's cottages still found on the narrow streets. These associations make an appropriate location for one of Sydney's most highly regarded fish restaurants, *Doyle's*, right out on the beach by the old Fishermans Wharf, with superb views and food (see p.105). For less expensive views, settle in at the seafront beer garden of the adjacent *Watson's Bay Hotel*. You can swim in the saltwater baths at Watsons Bay or head next door to **Camp Cove**, a tiny palm-fronted beach popular with families. If you'd prefer to swim *au naturel*, Sydney's best known **nude beach**, Lady Jane (officially "Lady Bay" on maps), is a walk around to the next bay just on the harbour side of South Head. Unfortunately tour boats cruise past all weekend – Cobblers Beach is a better bet for privacy (see "Middle Harbour", opposite).

From Camp Cove, you can walk right around **South Head**, the lower jaw of the harbour mouth and part of Sydney Harbour National Park; the walking tracks here afford fantastic views of Port Jackson and the city. The cliffs of **The Gap** on the ocean side just south of the Head offer more great hiking in another large chunk of the Sydney Harbour National Park – but less happily, this is a well-known place to commit suicide. To get to South Head, take a train to Edgecliff, and then bus #325.

## The North Shore

The **North Shore** is generally more affluent than the South. **Mosman** and **Neutral Bay** in particular have some stunning, waterfront real estate, priced to match. It's surprising just how much harbourside bushland remains intact here: "leafy" just doesn't do it justice. A ride on any ferry lets you gaze at beaches, bush, yachts and stunning harbourfront houses and is one of the chief joys of this area – even if the lucky people who live "on the other side of the bridge" and use the ferry to routinely commute keep their eyes firmly glued to their newspapers.

Just east of the Harbour Bridge and immediately opposite the Opera House, **Kirribilli** and adjacent **Neutral Bay** are mainly residential areas, although Kirribilli hosts a great **market** on the last Saturday of the month in Bradfield Park, and the highlight of North Shore drinking is the shady **beer garden** at Neutral Bay's *Oaks* hotel. Bush-covered **Cremorne Point**, which juts into the harbour here, is also worth a jaunt. Catch the ferry from Circular Quay and you'll find a quaint sea pool to swim in by the wharf; from here, you can walk right around the point to Mosman Bay (just under 2km).

### Mosman: Taronga Zoo and Bradleys Head

**Mosman** **Bay**'s seclusion was first recognized as a virtue during its early days as a whaling station, since it kept the stench of rotting whale flesh from the Sydney Cove settlement. Now the seclusion is a corollary of wealth. The ferry ride into the narrow yacht-filled bay is a choice one – get off at Mosman Wharf, not Musgrave Street – and is fittingly finished off with a beer at the unpretentious *Mosman Rowers' Club* (visitors welcome).

What Mosman is most famous for, though, is **Taronga Zoological Park** on Bradleys Head Road (daily 9am–5pm; $14, $17 *Zoo Pass* from Circular Quay includes return ferry, entry and chairlift), whose occupants enjoy a dazzling location, surrounded by native bush. From its hilltop position, the zoo overlooks the harbour, city skyline and the Opera House. Fifty-eight hectares house bounding Australian marsupials, native birds including kookaburras, galahs and cockatoos, and sea lions and seals from the sub-antarctic region. You'll also find all the expected exotic beasts from around the world, including a rare snow leopard.

Beyond the zoo, **Bradleys Head**, at the point of a finger extending into the harbour, is marked by an enormous mast that towers over the rocky point. The mast once belonged to *HMS Sydney*, a victorious World War II battleship, long since gone to the wrecker's yard. It's a peaceful spot with a dinky lighthouse and, of course, a fabulous view back over the south shore. The headland comprises another large chunk of the Sydney Harbour National Park: the six-kilometre Ashton Park **walking track** starts near the ferry wharf, opposite the zoo entrance, and continues round Chowder Head to **Clifton Gardens**, where there's a jetty and sea baths on Chowder Bay.

## Middle Harbour

**Middle Harbour** is the largest inlet of Port Jackson, its two sides joined across the narrowest point at **The Spit**. The Spit Bridge opens regularly to let tall-masted yachts through – much the best way to explore its pretty, quiet coves and bays. The area also hides some architectural gems: the bridge leading to **Northbridge**, built in 1889, which Jan Morris, (see p.842), described rather fancifully, in her tribute to *Sydney*, as "an enormously castellated mock-Gothic bridge, with hefty towers, arches, crests and arrow-slits, such as might have been thrown across a river in Saxe-Coburg by some quixotic nineteenth-century princeling"; and the idyllic enclave of **Castlecrag**. The latter was designed in 1924 by **Walter Burley Griffin**, fresh from planning Canberra and intent on building an environmentally friendly suburb – free of the fences and the red-tiled roofs he hated – that would be "for ever part of the bush".

Between Clifton Gardens and Balmoral Beach, a military reserve and a naval depot block coastal access to both **Georges Head** and the more spectacular **Middle Head**, although they can be reached by road. On the Hunters Bay side of Middle Head, tiny **Cobblers Beach** (ferry to Cremorne, then bus #204) is officially nude, and is a much more peaceful, secluded option than the more famous Lady Jane at South Head.

The bush setting provided by Middle Head helps lend **Balmoral**, on Hunters Bay, the peaceful secluded air that makes it so popular with families (it's netted too, which helps). There's something very Edwardian and genteel about palm-filled, grassy Hunters Park and its bandstand, which is still used for Sunday jazz concerts or even Shakespeare recitals in summer. The antediluvian air is added to by the pretty white-painted **Bathers Pavilion** at the northern end, now converted into a scrummy restaurant serving three-course champagne breakfasts. There are really two beaches at Balmoral, separated by **Rocky Point**, a noted picnicking spot reached by a decorative footbridge. The low-key esplanade has some takeaway shops, a quiet café, an excellent fish 'n' chip shop, and a fine bottle shop. South of Rocky Point, the "baths" – actually a netted bit of beach with a boardwalk and lanes for swimming laps – have been here in one form or another since 1899; the neighbouring boatshed rents out sailboards (from $15 per hour, tuition extra; ☎938 2442).

The hillside houses overlooking Balmoral have some of the highest price tags in Sydney: for a stroll through some prime real estate, head for **Chinamans Beach**, via Hopetoun Avenue and Rosherville Road. Famous residents include Ken Done, the artist who found fame with colourful impressionistic harbour scenes that now adorn duvet covers and wine bottles – and every souvenir shop in town.

Crossing the Spit Bridge, you can walk all the way to Manly Beach along the 10km Manly Scenic Walkway (see p.96), or bus #144 goes from Spit Road to Manly Wharf, taking in a scenic route uphill overlooking the Spit marina.

# Ocean Beaches

*In Australia people always run to the coast. Maybe the myth of the bush is a myth.*

Robert Drewe, *The Picador Book of the Beach*

Sydney's **beaches** are among its great natural joys, key elements in the equation that makes this city special. The water and sand seem remarkably clean – people actually fish in the harbour, and don't just catch old condoms and plimsolls – and at Long Reef, just north of Manly, you can find rock pools teeming with starfish, anemones, sea-snails and crabs, and even a few shy Moray Eels.

Don't be lulled into a false sense of security, however: the beaches do have **perils** as well as pleasures. Some beaches are protected by special shark nets, but they don't keep out stingers like Blue Bottles (and ominous sounding Purple People Eaters...), which can suddenly swamp an entire beach; listen out for loudspeaker announcements that will summon you from the water in the event of shark sightings or other dangers. Pacific **currents** can be very strong indeed – inexperienced swimmers and those with small children would do better sticking to the sheltered **harbour beaches** or **sea pools** at the ocean beaches. Ocean beaches are generally patrolled by **surf lifesavers** during the day betweeen October and April (all year at Bondi): red and yellow flags (generally up from 6am until 6 or 7pm) indicate the safe areas to swim, avoiding dangerous rips and undertows. If you do get into difficulty, stay calm and raise one arm above your head as a signal to be rescued. It's hard not to be impressed as **surfers** paddle out on a seething ocean that you wouldn't dip your big toe in, but don't follow them unless you're confident you know what you're doing. Surf schools can teach you the basic skills and enlighten you on surfing etiquette and lingo; call the *Surf Report* to track down the best waves (☎0055 22995).

It's easy to underestimate the strength of the southern **sun**: follow the local slogan, and Slip (on a shirt), Slop (on the sunblock), Slap (on a hat). The final hazard, despite the apparent cleanliness, is **pollution**. After storms, currents and onshore breezes wash up sewage and other rubbish onto certain beaches, making them (as signs will indicate) unsuitable for swimming and surfing; Bondi is one of the worst affected. To check pollution levels before donning beach towel and "cossies", call the *Beachwatch Information Line* on ☎9901 7996.

A final note. Topless bathing is allowed on many beaches but frowned on in others, so if in doubt, do as the locals do. There are several official nude beaches around the harbour (see pp.92 and 93).

## Bondi and the eastern beaches

**Bondi Beach** is synonymous with Australian beach culture, and indeed must be one of the best known beaches in the world. The closest ocean beach to the city centre, you can take a train to Bondi Junction and then a ten-minute bus ride, or drive there in twenty minutes (parking is another story). Big, brash and action-packed, it's probably not the best place for a quiet sunbathe and swim, but the sprawling sandy crescent really is spectacular. Red-tiled houses and apartment blocks crowd in to catch the view, many of them erected in the 1920s when Bondi was a working-class suburb. Still residential, it's now a popular gathering place for backpackers from around the world –

especially on Christmas Day when the beach is transformed into a drunken party scene, as those from colder climes live out their fantasy of a scorching Christmas on the beach. This has been getting out of control over the years, and the local council are acting to discourage the whole performance. The beachfront, Campbell Parade, is both cosmopolitan and highly commercialized, lined with cafés and shops (including a *McDonalds*, to the outrage of those who saw Bondi as pure Australiana). For a gentler experience, explore some of the side streets, like Hall Street, where you'll find an assortment of kosher bakeries and delis that serve the area's Jewish community.

**Surfing** is part of the Bondi legend, its big waves ensuring that there's always a pack of damp young things hanging around, bristling with surfboards. However, the beach is carefully delineated so you shouldn't have to fear catapulting surfboards. There are two sets of flags for swimmers and boogie-boarders, with families congregating at the northern end near the sheltered saltwater pool, and everybody else using the middle flags. The beach is netted and there hasn't been a shark attack for over forty years.

**Topless bathing** is allowed at Bondi – a long way from conditions right up to the late 1960s when stern beach inspectors were constantly on the lookout for indecent exposure. If you want to join in the sun and splash but don't have the gear, *Beached at Bondi* (☎389 5836), below the lifeguard lookout tower, rent out everything from cossies and towels to boogie boards; they also sell hats and sunblock and have lockers for valuables.

Between Campbell Parade and the beach, Bondi Park slopes down to the promenade, and is always full of sprawling bodies. Along the promenade, there are two board ramps for **roller-blading** and **skateboarding**; if you want to join in, you can rent the gear from *Bondi Boards and Blades*, 148 Curlewis Street (☎365 6555; rollerblades $20 for 2hr, boards $15 for 2hr, both inclusive of protective gear). The focus of the promenade is the arcaded Spanish-style **Bondi Pavilion**, built in 1928 as a deluxe changing room complex, and now given a new lease of life as a **community centre** hosting an array of events from drama and comedy in the Seagull Room (the former ballroom) to Latin days and outdoor film festivals in the courtyard (programme details on ☎30 3325, ☎368 1253 weekends). Downstairs in the foyer, photos of Bondi's past are worth checking out, with some classic beach images of men in 1930s one-piece bathing suits, and there's a brilliant souvenir shop which utilizes lots of old-fashioned Bondi imagery.

Another Bondi institution is the four-storeyed, clock-towered **Bondi Hotel**, which has retained many of its classic 1920s features including original fireplaces with art-deco tiles. The blue-painted building of the **Bondi Icebergs Club**, at the southern end

---

## BONDI'S SURF LIFESAVERS

**Surf lifesavers** are what made Bondi famous; there's a bronze sculpture of one outside the **Bondi Pavilion**. The surf lifesaving movement began in 1906 with the founding of the Bondi Surf Life Bathers' Lifesaving Club in response to the drownings that accompanied the increasing popularity of swimming. From the beginning of the colony, swimming was harshly discouraged as an unsuitable bare-fleshed activity. However, by the 1890s swimming in the ocean had become the new thing, and a Pacific Islander introduced the concept of catching waves or **bodysurfing** that was to become an enduring national craze. Although "wowsers" (teetotal puritanical types) attempted to put a stop to it, by 1903 all-day swimming was every Sydneysider's right.

The distinctive red and yellow caps of the bronzed and muscled surf lifesavers are a famous, highly-photographed Australian image around the world. Surf livesavers are volunteers working the beach on weekends, so come then to watch their exploits – or look out for a surf carnival; lifeguards, on the other hand, are employed by the council and work all week during swimming season (year-round at Bondi).

of the beach, has been part of the Bondi legend since 1929. Traditionally the preserve of old men (although the council is currently battling to allow women to join), members swim throughout the winter, and media coverage of their icy plunge heralds the first day of winter.

From December onwards, Bondi is festival city, culminating in the Festival of the Winds, Australia's largest **kite festival**. On Sundays, the **Bondi Beach markets** on Campbell Parade (10am–5pm) place a big emphasis on groovy fashion and jewellery.

You can reach Bondi on **bus** #380 (from Circular Quay), or take the train (Eastern suburbs line) to Bondi Junction, then transfer to bus #380 or #381.

## Tamarama to Coogee

Many people find the smaller, quieter beaches to the south of Bondi more enticing. Walk round Mackenzies Point from Bondi and you'll reach the modest and secluded **Mackenzies Bay**, with convenient large slabs of rock to leave your towel on. Next up is **Tamarama Bay**, a deep, narrow beach favoured by the smart set; you can easily walk from Bondi, or hop on bus #391. The next beach around, Bronte Beach on **Nelson Bay** is more of a family affair – easily reached on bus #378 from Central Station, via Bondi. From here, it's a pleasant walk past the baths to **Waverly Cemetery**, a fantastic spot to spend eternity. Established in 1877, it contains the graves of many famous Australians, with the bush poet contingent well represented. **Henry Lawson**, described on his headstone as poet, journalist and patriot, languishes in section 3G 516, while **Dorothea Mackeller**, who penned the famous poem "I love a sunburnt country" is in section 6 832–833. Beyond here, on the other side of the ominously named Shark Point, are **Clovelly Bay** and **Gordon's Bay**, two more narrow, sheltered beaches.

Next door is **Coogee**, currently the scene of much construction, which threatens to destroy its laidback character. The medium-sized beach is still popular with families (there's an excellent children's playground at the southern end), and there's no doubt that its imaginatively modernized promenade is a great place to stroll and hang out. One of Coogee's chief pleasures are its baths: **Wylie's Baths**, a saltwater pool on the edge of the sea, is at the end of Neptune Street, while around the corner, **Coogee Women's Pool** is a secluded pool with plenty of rocks for sunbathing.

Get to Coogee on bus #373 from Circular Quay, or #372 from Central Station.

# Manly and the northern beaches

**Manly**, just above North Head at the northern mouth of the harbour, is doubly blessed with both ocean and harbour beaches. When Captain Cook passed here he saw a group of well-built Aboriginal men onshore, proclaimed them to be "manly" and named the cove in the process. During the Edwardian era it became fashionable as a recreational retreat from the city, and the promotional slogan of the time "Manly – seven miles from Sydney, but a thousand miles from care" still holds true today. A day-trip to Manly, rounded off with a fish 'n' chip dinner, offers a classic taste of Sydney life.

Ferries from Circular Quay (the ride itself is part of the fun) terminate near a small section of harbour beach. Many visitors mistake this for the ocean beach, which in fact lies on the other side of the isthmus, 500m down The Corso, Manly's busy pedestrianized main drag. Right by the jetty is **Ocean World** (daily 10am–5.30pm; $12.50, family ticket $31), where clear acrylic walls hold back the water while you saunter along the harbour floor, gazing at sharks and stingrays. **Manly Visitors' Centre** (daily 10am–4pm; ☎977 1088) is by the ocean beach, on South Steyne.

A couple of good seaside walks start at Manly. The **Manly Scenic Walkway** follows the harbour shore inland from Manly Cove all the way back to Spit Bridge on Middle

Harbour, where you can catch bus #182 or #241 back to the city centre. The eight-kilometre walk takes you through parkland with great harbour views, past a number of lovely small beaches and coves, Aboriginal middens and some sub-tropical rainforest; pick up a walking map from the Manly Visitors Centre. In the other direction, Manly is also the launch pad for trips to the **North Head**, the harbour mouth's upper jaw, with walking trails up to Fairfax Lookout and, for the less energetic, a scenic drive and car park from which you can enjoy the magnificent harbour views. The old **Quarantine Station**, on the harbour side of North Head, was used from 1828 right up until 1984: passengers with contagious diseases arriving on ships were set down at Spring Cove to serve a spell at the station. The NPWS offers guided tours, including history tours (daily 1.10pm; $6) and nightly ghost tours (Wed & Fri–Sun; 3hr; $15, including tea and damper); advance booking essential (☎977 6229).

**Ferries** leave wharves 2 and 3 at Circular Quay for Manly every half-hour or so, taking around thirty minutes ($3.60); they sail until 11.30pm, after which nightbus #150 runs from Wynyard Terminal. The *JetCat* ($4.60) goes twice as fast as a regular ferry, and is about half as much fun. Day-trippers can buy an *Oceanpass* ($16), which includes return ferry rides, entry to *Ocean World* and the local art gallery.

## North to Palm Beach

Beyond Manly, the **northern beaches** continue for thirty kilometres up to Barrenjoey Heads and Palm Beach. Sitting snugly between two rocky headlands, **Freshwater** is one of the most picturesque, immediately on from the long stretch of North Steyne Beach at Manly. The curve of **Dee Why** provides consistently good surf, while its sheltered lagoon makes it popular with families. Further north, windsurfers gather around **Long Reef**, where the headland is surrounded by a wide rock shelf creviced with rock pools – well worth a wander to peek at the creatures within. The long, beautiful sweep of **Collaroy Beach** blends into **Narrabeen**, an idyllic spot backed by the extensive, swimmable and fishable **Narrabeen Lakes** and a good campground (see p.72), popular with anglers and families. Beyond Narrabeen, **Mona Vale** is a long straight stretch of beach with a large park behind and a sea pool between it and sheltered **Bongin Bongin Bay** next door with a headland reserve and rocks to clamber on, making it ideal for kids.

**Newport**, on the Barrenjoey peninsula, boasts a fine stretch of ocean beach between two rocky headlands; crowds gather on Sundays to listen to live jazz in the beer garden of the *Newport Arms* on Kalinya Street, overlooking Heron Cove on Pittwater. Unassuming **Bilgola Beach**, next door to Newport, is one of the prettiest of the northern beaches. From here, a trio of Sydney's best beaches, both for surf and for scenery, run up the eastern fringe of the mushroom-shaped peninsula: Whale Beach, Avalon and Palm Beach. **Whale Beach** and **Avalon** are less fashionable than Palm Beach, but rather cleaner; popular surfie territory. **Palm Beach**, living up to its name, is a hang-out for the rich and famous. It also leads a double life as "Summer Bay" in the famous Aussie soap *Home and Away*, with the Barrenjoey Lighthouse and headland regularly in shot. The bush-covered headland is actually an outpost of Ku-Ring-Gai Chase National Park (see pp.120–121), the bulk of which is across Pittwater, but can be visited courtesy of *Palm Beach Ferries* (☎918 2747; $20 return, leaving Palm Beach at 11am, back at 3.30pm).

Without a car, the best way to explore the northern beaches is by the open-sided *Boomerang Beach Bus* (☎913 8402), which you can either take as a three-hour tour, or use as a hop-on, hop-off service between Manly and Palm Beach (9.15am–4.15pm; $20). The peninsula beaches can also be reached by regular **bus** from the city in about 45 minutes on an express service: #190 runs here from Wynyard Station, and there are also buses from Manly.

# Botany Bay

The southern suburbs of Sydney, arranged around huge **Botany Bay**, are seen as the heartland of red-tiled-roof suburbia, a terracotta sea spied from above as the planes land at **Mascot**. The area's most famous son, Clive James, hails from Kogarah – described as a 1950s suburban wasteland in his tongue-in-cheek *Unreliable Memoirs*, (see p.843). Further south, across the **Georges River**, fodder for social scientists was found at **Sylvania Waters**, a sort of waterfront version of a suburban cul-de-sac with boats instead of cars, which found fame as the backdrop for the BBC's fly-on-the-wall documentary focussing on the exploits of nouveau riche Noelene Donahue and her dysfunctional family. The popular perception of Botany Bay is coloured by its proximity to an airport, a high-security prison (Long Bay), an oil refinery and a container terminal. But in fact, the surprisingly clean water is fringed by quiet sandy beaches and the marshlands shelter a profusion of birdlife. Whole areas of the waterfront are designated as part of the **Botany Bay National Park** and large stretches on either side of the Georges River form a State Recreation Area.

## La Perouse

**La Perouse**, tucked into the northern shore of Botany Bay as it goes out to meet the Pacific Ocean, contains Sydney's oldest Aboriginal settlement, the legacy of a mission. Here, on January 26th every year, an all-day outdoor rock concert, *Survival*, celebrates Aboriginal culture and acts as an antidote to the mainstream white Australia Day festivities. The suburb got its name from **Laperouse**, the eighteenth-century French explorer, who set up camp here for six weeks, briefly and cordially meeting Captain Phillip, who was making his historic decision to forgo swampy Botany Bay and move on to Port Jackson; after leaving Botany Bay, the Laperouse expedition was never seen again.

Parts of the headland have been incorporated into the Botany Bay National Park, and there's a fine walk past Congwong Bay Beach to Henry Head and its lighthouse (3km return). The verandah of the *Boatshed Cafe*, on the small headland between Congwong and Frenchmans bays, sits right over the water; it's an idyllic spot for cappuccino, great cakes and Italian biscuits, sandwiches and more substantial dishes of yummy seafood, including grilled baby octopus – enhanced by the lapping of the waves below, and **pelicans** bobbing on the water. La Perouse is at its most lively on **Sunday** when, following a tradition established at the turn of the century, Aborigines come down to sell boomerangs and other goods, and snake-handling skills are on display from 1.30pm. There are also tours (Sunday 1pm & 3pm) of the nineteenth-century fortifications on **Bare Island**, joined to La Perouse by a walkway.

To get to La Perouse, catch the #394 from Circular Quay, the #393 from Railway Square (Sunday only) or the L94 express from Circular Quay.

### The Laperouse Museum

"At least, is there any news of Monsieur de Laperouse?"

Louis XVI, about to be guillotined, 1793

The **Laperouse Museum** (daily 10am–4.30pm; $2; tours in French or English, 1hr 30min; $5; booking essential on ☎311 3379 or 311 2765), run by the NWPS, sits on a grassy headland between the pretty beaches of Congwong Bay and Frenchmans Bay. The large burgundy-coloured building was converted into a museum in 1988 as a bicentennial project. Tracing Laperouse's voyage in great detail, the displays are enlivened by relics from the wrecks, exhibits of antique French maps and copies of etchings by naturalists on board. The voyage was commissioned by the French king Louis XVI in 1785 as a purely scientific exploration of the Pacific to rival Cook's voyages, and strict instructions were given for Laperouse to "act with great gentleness and humanity towards the different people whom he will visit". After an astonishing three-and-a-half-year journey through South Amercia, the Easter Islands, Hawaii, the northwest coast of America, past China and Japan, to Russia, the *Astrolobe* and the *Boussole* struck disaster – first encountering hostility in the Solomon Islands and then in their doomed sailing from Botany Bay, on March 10, 1788. Their disappearance remained a mystery until 1828, when relics were discovered on Vanikoro in the Solomon Islands; the wrecks themselves were only found in 1958 and 1964.

There is also an Aboriginal museum within the Laperouse Museum building, but it was closed indefinitely at the time of writing.

## The Kurnell Peninsula

From La Perouse, you can see across Botany Bay to Kurnell and the red buoy marking the spot where Captain Cook and the crew of the *Endeavour* anchored on April 29, 1770. During their eight-day exploration here, they recorded many Australian plants and animals for the first time; back in England, many refused to believe that such creatures existed – the kangaroo in particular was thought to be a hoax. **Captain Cook's Landing Place** is now the south head of Botany Bay National Park with an informative **Discovery Centre** (Mon–Fri 9am–4pm, Sat & Sun 10am–4.45pm; free, but $7.50 fee per car; ☎666 9111). Set aside as a public recreation area in 1899, the heath and woodland is unspoilt and there are some secluded beaches for swimming; you may even spot parrots, honeyeaters and other colourful birds if you keep your eyes peeled.

On the ocean side of the **Kurnell Peninsula** sits Sydney's longest beach: the ten-kilometre length of beach begins at **Cronulla** and continues as deserted, dune-backed **Wanda Beach**. This is prime surfing territory – and is the only Sydney beach accessible by train (Sutherland line from Bondi Junction; surfboards carried free). From Cronulla, you can catch a ferry to Bundeena in the Royal National Park (see p.144).

# Eating and drinking

Sydney boasts an extraordinary number of food stalls, cafés, takeaways, restaurants and pubs serving food as well as drink, only a fraction of which are listed here. Check out the "Pubs and bars" listings on p.107 for more casual eats. Be adventurous, as quality is uniformly high, with fresh ingredients and imaginative cuisine. If you're planning a longer stay, consider investing in the latest edition of *Cheap Eats in Sydney,* a mine of information about good, inexpensive eating places all over Sydney or the *Sydney Morning Herald Good Food Guide*, reviewing all the best restaurants.

Most of the inner suburbs are just a few minutes' bus, train, ferry or taxi ride away, and you'll generally find better, less expensive and more enjoyable places to eat and drink there. All places listed below are open daily for lunch and dinner, unless otherwise stated.

## City Centre and The Rocks

The cafés and foodstalls in the business and shopping districts of the city centre cater mainly for lunchtime crowds, and there are lots of **food courts** and stalls serving fast food and snacks. Check out the selection in the basement of the **MLC Centre** near Martin Place and in the **QVB**, or the more touristy crowd around the jetties of Circular Quay, as well as the huge food hall in the Darling Harbour Festival Marketplace. The classiest of them is probably the foodie's paradise in the basement of **David Jones** store on Market Street, where a number of counters serve rather expensive snacks and titbits. A number of museums and tourist attractions also have surprisingly good **cafés** – notably the Museum of Contemporary Art, the Earth Exchange, the Australian Museum, the Hyde Park Barracks and the Art Gallery of NSW.

There are several good **pubs** in The Rocks (see p.107), many of which serve some kind of food, but for the most part the area around the harbour has a choice of expensive restaurants or average fast food.

## Restaurants

**Bilsons**, Overseas Passsenger Terminal, Circular Quay West (☎251 5600). The cruise ships still pull in here, but half of the terminal has been given over to a couple of slap-up restaurants. Fabulous views, especially from tables in the converted lookout tower. Posh, pricey and licensed; bookings essential. Closed Sat lunch.

**Capitan Torres**, 73 Liverpool St (☎264 5574). Atmospheric Spanish, specializing in seafood: a fresh display aids your choice. Sit downstairs at the bar, or upstairs in the restaurant. Licensed.

**Chinese Dumpling Restaurant**, 372 Pitt St (☎267 4855). At the downmarket end of Pitt Street, but worth a detour. Wonderful dumpling and noodle selection. BYO; inexpensive; daily 11am–late.

**Doyles on the Quay**, Overseas Passenger Terminal, Circular Quay West (☎252 3400). Downtown branch of a Sydney seafood institution, pricey but excellent, with great harbour views. You'll probably need to book. Licensed.

**Kables**, *The Regent*, 199 George St (☎238 0000). World-class hotel restaurant with wonderful service and opulent surroundings, placing an emphasis on fresh Australian produce. Expensive, but the $40 three-course set lunch is a good deal. Lunch Mon–Fri, dinner Tues–Sat; licensed.

**Rockpool Oyster Bar**, 109 George St, The Rocks (☎252 1888). Excellent seafood, and not as expensive as it sounds, especially when you take into account the view of the water and celebrities filing into the *Rockpool Restaurant* out the back – itself worth a splurge, if your budget will run to it.

**Waterfront Restaurant**, 27 Circular Quay West (☎247 3666). Seafood on the waterfront under The Rocks, in a charming restored stone wharehouse. This is probably the best of the four restaurants sharing this prime location; touristy and expensive, but the sort of place you should go once.

**Wharf Restaurant**, Pier 4, Hickson Rd, The Rocks, next to the *Wharf Theatre* (☎250 1761). Enterprising modern food, including vegetarian dishes, is served up in a spacious old dock building with heaps of raw charm and harbour views. Expensive. Closed Sun.

## Cafés

**Bar Paradiso**, Shop 1, 7 Macquarie Place. Stylish outdoor café close to Circular Quay attracts a working crowd who plunge in for great coffee, *pizzetta* and *focaccia*. Mon–Fri, from 7.30am.

**Le Chifley**, Chifley Arcade, 6 Castlereagh St. Down-to-earth, friendly French brasserie. Generous, good-value meals, and French wines too. Mon–Fri 7am–8pm.

**Glass House Café**, Level 7, State Library, Macquarie St. Airy and with masses of plants, a relaxing place for lunch (daily); the inexpensive menu changes often.

**Pier One**, Millers Point, The Rocks. An array of fast-food stalls as well as the *Harbourside Brasserie* (☎252 3000), for good cheap eats and often live entertainment.

**Rossini's Rosticceria**, between wharves 5 & 6, Circular Quay. Inexpensive Italian fast food al fresco while you're waiting for a ferry – big round ricotta-filled doughnuts are a speciality.

# Chinatown, Darling Harbour and around

The southern end of George Street has plenty of very cheap restaurants, of variable quality. Chinatown around the corner is a better bet: many places here specialize in *yum cha* (or *dim sum*), lots of little tidbits like steamed buns and dumplings served from trolleys, and steamboat, an Asian version of fondue; both are tasty and extremely good value for money, especially for a group. There are inexpensive **food courts** in the basements of the **Chinatown Centre**, the **Sussex Centre** and the **Dixon Gourmet**, but they close around 9pm. Another food court is on the first floor of the **Prince**

**Centre**, at the corner of Quay and Thomas streets, while close by in Darling Harbour there's a huge food hall in the Festival Marketplace.

**Bali Bagoes**, 1st floor, Prince Centre, 169 Thomas St, Haymarket (☎281 3017). East Javanese food: *rijstaffel*, *gado gado* and the like – easy on the budget. Licensed and BYO. Daily until late.

**BBQ King**, 18–20 Goulburn St, Haymarket (☎267 2586). Unprepossessing but perpetually crowded Chinese specializing in barbecued meat; quick service. Licensed; takeaways. Daily 11.30am–2am.

**Grand Taverna**, the *Sir John Young Hotel*, corner of Liverpool and George streets, Haymarket (☎267 3608). Spanish food, including tapas, at the heart of Spanish corner. Authentically lively atmosphere and the best paella and sangria in town. Closed Sun.

**Lam's**, 3rd Floor, 35 Goulburn St, Haymarket (☎281 2881). Chinatown institution that's a great place for seafood steamboats as dawn approaches. Daily noon–4am.

**The Malaya**, 761 George St, Haymarket (☎211 0946). Popular, veteran Chinese–Malaysian place serving the best *laksa* in town. Licensed.

**Restaurant Manfredi**, 88 Hackett St, Ultimo (☎211 5895). Northern Italian-style cuisine, given an edge by creativity and homemade pasta. Licensed; expensive. Lunch Wed–Fri, dinner Tues–Sat.

**Mekong**, 711 George St, Haymarket. Inexpensive Cambodian fast food; BYO.

**Sun City**, 321–325 Sussex St, Haymarket (☎261 1833). The strong flavours of *Chiu Chou* cuisine dominate this glitzy place with impeccable waiters; ask them to translate the daily specials.

**TTT-E-Sarn**, 704a George St, Haymarket (☎281 5683). Authentic northeastern Thai food; choose from a huge menu. Licensed. Daily, until 3am at weekends.

**Wattle Seed Deli**, basement level, 37 Ultimo Rd, Ultimo (☎281 9532). Unusual selection of health food and bush tucker (emu, kangaroo and crocodile meat), tucked away in a basement surrounded by Chinese herbalists and butcher shops. BYO. Daily 8am–6pm, Thurs–Sat until 10pm.

**Zorro**, Shop 297, Harbourside, Darling Harbour (☎281 4383). Lots to recommend this place: views, seafood, *sangria*, *tapas* and live South American music Fri & Sat nights. Licensed. Daily until late.

## Glebe

In Glebe you'll find both cheap and upmarket restaurants, ethnic takeaways, delis, and a string of good cafés. **Glebe Point Road** is dominated by bookshops and cafés – with a cluster of particularly good cafés at the Broadway end. No particular cuisine dominates: café fare is eclectic, and Vietnamese, Lebanese and Thai eateries rub shoulders.

**Badde Manors**, 37 Glebe Point Rd. Vegetarian corner café with a wonderful ambience, always packed, especially for weekend brunch. Inexpensive. Daily until midnight, Fri & Sat till 4am.

**Café Troppo**, 175 Glebe Point Rd. Not cheap, but worth it for the wacky "tropical" decoration, as well as the mouth-watering cakes, light meals and breakfasts. Open daily until 1am.

**Le Chocoreve**, 219 Glebe Point Rd. Patisserie and café with a decadent selection of cakes, and the standard Italian/European-inspired menu of *focaccia* and soups. BYO.

**Craven Café**, 166b Glebe Point Rd. Popular place to cruise and devour tasty tidbits.

**Darling Mills**, 134 Glebe Point Rd (☎660 5666). Innovative modern Australian cuisine with fresh herbs and floral ingredients, served in an old sandstone building in a leafy garden; open fireplaces in winter. An expensive treat. Licensed and BYO.

**Excelsior Pub**, 101 Bridge Rd (☎660 7479). Restaurant serving unusual, good-value dishes like gnocchi with a walnut–gorgonzola sauce, or homemade crab ravioli.

**Iku**, 25a Glebe Point Rd. Healthy macrobiotic meals and snacks. Meditative interior, and outdoor dining area – all non-smoking, naturally. Takeaway menu. Daily noon–9.30pm.

**Lien**, 331 Glebe Point Rd, (☎566 4385). Reasonably priced Vietnamese and Malaysian meals; great view of the city from upstairs.

**Niki's**, 91 Glebe Point Rd. Not only cheap, but downright delicious: the *focaccia*, pancakes and smoothies simply must be sampled. Tues–Sun, 10am–10pm.

**No Names**, 58 Cowper St. Excellent, inexpensive Italian restaurant hidden at the back of the *Friend in Hand Hotel*.

**Rose Blues**, 23 Glebe Point Rd. Substantial meals, with spicy Italian sausages or trout, plus coffee and cakes, and all-day breakfast. Leafy garden to eat in. Daily 9am–11.30pm, later at weekends.

## Newtown and Enmore

On the other side of Sydney University from Glebe, **King Street** in **Newtown** is lined with cafés, takeaways and restaurants of every ethnic persuasion; Thai places abound.

**Akaash**, 198 Enmore Rd, Enmore (☎516 1938). A real dining experience, not only because of the authentic Indian–Fijian cooking, but also the decor. BYO. Dinner nightly.

**Bank Hotel**, 324 King St, next to Newtown Station (☎557 1280). Great Thai restaurant in a pub; eat in the leafy beer garden.

**Café Blue**, 313 King St. Stylish, relaxed café with tasty, if slightly pricey, food – *focaccia* and the like. Great coffee, and newspapers to go with it.

**Caffe Latte**, 153a King St. Specializes in excellent coffee and cakes; give the meals a miss. Good atmosphere and noticeboard.

**El Bahsa Sweets**, King St. Lebanese coffee lounge with some of the best coffee on King Street. Try it with some Lebanese sweets, all made on the premises. Daily to 11pm, later at weekends.

**Feel Cafe**, 165 King St, (☎565 1948). Tasty, filling "modern Australian" food, upbeat colourful atmosphere and friendly staff.

**Green Tea**, 171 King St, (☎557 3030). Good, cheap Japanese restaurant; sushi, sashimi, teriyaki chicken and buckwheat noodles in broth are all on the menu; BYO. Closed Mon.

**Kilimanjaro Fast Food Eatery**, 280 King St, (☎557 4565). Authentic and simple African dishes in a casual and friendly atmosphere. BYO. Dinner nightly.

**Maurice's**, 69 King St. Unassuming Lebanese restaurant and takeaway. The best (and most generous) falafel rolls in town. BYO. Closed Sun.

**North Indian Diner**, 236 King St, just past the *Commonwealth Bank*. Very cheap, absolutely delicious meals to eat in or take away. Licensed.

**Old Saigon**, 107 King St, (☎519 5931). The Vietnamese food here mixes French, Thai and Japanese influences; Saigon memorabilia covers the walls. Licensed and BYO. Closed Mon.

**Selera Malaysian Restaurant**, upstairs at 264 King Street (☎557 5186). Delicious range of authentic Malay and Indian hawker-stall dishes, including murtabak and laksa. Inexpensive.

**Steki Taverna**, 2 O'Connell St, off King St (☎516 2191). Greek taverna, with live music and dancing at weekends – when you'll need to book. Licensed. Dinner Wed–Sun.

**Stromboli**, 134–140 King St, near Bucknell St. Courtyard café has all-day breakfast and stylish Italian-influenced cuisine.

**Thai Land**, 74–78 King St, (☎516 1127). Really excellent, more expensive Thai where you can eat at low tables on cushions if you prefer; booking advised. Dinner nightly; BYO.

## Balmain, Rozelle and Leichhardt

Further west, **Leichhardt** is Sydney's "Little Italy" with a concentration of cafés and restaurants on **Norton Street**, while the **Darling Street** strip of restaurants runs from run-down **Rozelle** to more upmarket **Balmain**.

**Bar Baba**, 1a Norton St, Leichhardt. A gleaming *pasticceria* just like you'd find in Italy. *Gelato*, coffee, *focaccia*, *tramezzini*, cakes and of course, *baba al rhum*. Relaxed atmosphere.

**Bar Italia**, 169 Norton St, Leichhardt. *Focaccia* comes big and tasty, coffee is spot on. Try to squeeze into the courtyard out back.

**Le Botte d'Oro**, 137 Marion St, Leichhardt (☎560 1349). One of the best Italian restaurants in "Little Italy". Closed Sun lunch; BYO.

**Café Berlin**, 249 Darling St, Balmain (☎810 2336). A taste of Berlin in Balmain – *sauerkraut*, *aufschnitt* and *strudel*. Pricey, but BYO. Daily 11am–10pm.

**Caffe Sport**, 2a Norton St. One of the original Norton Street cafés. Very Italian and very friendly. Good prices and generous helpings of *focaccia*. Daily from 7am (8am Sun) to early evening.

**456 Darling Street**, *Cat and Fiddle Hotel*, 456 Darling St, Balmain (☎810 7931). Contemporary Australian dishes, with an open fireplace in winter and the opportunity to catch some very decent blues and jazz bands next door. BYO. Dinner daily except Mon; lunch Sun only.

**Tetsuya's**, 729 Darling St, Rozelle (☎555 1017). Creatively presented Japanese/French-style fare. There's a six-course *dégustation* menu at $75 which is an experience in itself. BYO; best to book.

## Surry Hills and Redfern

Just east of Central Station, Elizabeth and Cleveland streets in Surry Hills, running down to Redfern, are traditionally the domain of Turkish and Lebanese restaurants, which are among the cheapest in Sydney, and almost all BYO. Several Indian restaurants have recently made an appearance too. Crown Street in Surry Hills harbours several interesting cafés.

**Abdul's**, corner of Cleveland and Elizabeth streets, Surry Hills. Good-value somewhat grungy Lebanese; a late night after-pub institution, eat in or take away.

**Café Roma**, 202–210 Elizabeth St, Surry Hills (☎211 0439). Fabulous coffee, great breakfast, wicked Italian biscuits and sweets and simple blackboard food. Mon–Fri 8am–5.30pm.

**Dolphin Hotel**, 412 Crown St, Surry Hills (☎331 4800). With a multi-level beer garden and a hard-to-choose-from bistro and legendary salad bar. Busy on weekends.

**Erciyes**, 409 Cleveland St, Redfern (☎319 1309). Turkish *pide* – a bit like pizza – is delicious and comes with a range of toppings, many vegetarian. Daily 11am–midnight.

**Gazals**, 286 Cleveland St, Surry Hills (☎318 1982). Above-average Lebanese at below-average prices. Daily.

**La Passion du Fruit**, 633 Bourke St, Surry Hills (☎690 1894). The best brunch in town is served at this friendly place with interesting salads, sandwiches and light meals. Closed Mon.

**Leli and Jenny's Maltese Cafe**, 310 Crown St, Surry Hills. Café specializing in *pastizzi* – flaky pastry pockets of ricotta cheese, plain and with meat, spinach, or peas; an economical choice.

**Mohr Fish**, 202 Devonshire St, Surry Hills. Tiny but stylish fish'n'chip bar with tiled walls and stools to sit on; generally crowded with folk after the freshly cooked fish. BYO. Daily 7am–10pm.

## Darlinghurst and East Sydney

Oxford Street is lined with restaurants and cafés from one end to the other. Around **Taylor Square** is a particularly busy area, with lots of ethnic restaurants and several pubs. East Sydney, where Crown Street heads downhill from Oxford Street towards William Street, has some excellent Italian restaurants and coffee bars – particularly in Stanley Street.

### Restaurants

**Atlas Bistro & Bar**, 95 Riley St, East Sydney (☎360 3811). Smart-set Modern Australian restaurant; spacious, airy and hip. Licensed. Lunch Wed–Fri, dinner Mon–Sat.

**Balkan Seafood Restaurant**, 215 Oxford St, Darlinghurst (☎331 7670). Croatian/Italian cuisine. Fish and seafood is the best choice but you can also get huge schnitzels and other continental meat dishes. Bustling atmosphere, moderate prices. BYO. Dinner nightly.

**Bill and Toni**, 72–74 Stanley St, East Sydney. Atmospheric, cheap Italian restaurant upstairs with balcony tables. Queue to get in. The café downstairs is a great daytime hangout. BYO.

**Burdekin Dining Room**, upstairs at the *Burdekin Hotel*, 2–4 Oxford St, Darlinghurst (☎331 1046). Gourmet-edged home cooking and attentive service with views over Hyde Park. Expensive; booking recommended. Closed Sun.

**Chu Bay**, 312a Bourke St, Darlinghurst (☎331 3386). Tiny Vietnamese restaurant that's authentic, popular and inexpensive. BYO. Dinner nightly.

**fu-manchu**, 249 Victoria St, Darlinghurst. Bright, clean Chinese and Malaysian noodle bar (noodles $8–9). Perch on red stools at stainless-steel counters and pick your chopsticks from metal tins. Non-smoking. Mon–Sat noon–10.30pm, Sun noon–5.30pm.

**Forbes Ristorante**, 155 Forbes St, near William St, East Sydney (☎357 3652). Extremely good value – pleasant atmosphere, courtyard tables, good Italian food, coffee and cakes. Licensed.

**Geronimo's**, 294 Crown St, Darlinghurst. Very cheap, much-praised Indian–Pakistani food; bottomless thalis. BYO. Closed Sun.

**Govindas**, 112 Darlinghurst Rd, Darlinghurst. Excellent, cheap Indian vegetarian restaurant, in the Hare Krishna centre but no hassles. Dinner nightly.

**Metro Cafe**, 26 Burton St, Darlinghurst. Probably the best vegetarian place in Sydney, evidenced by the crowds queuing to get into the tiny eclectically decorated space and its cosy booths. Food is always imaginative and substantial. Dinner Wed–Fri & Sun.

**No Names**, 81 Stanley St, East Sydney. Above the *Arch Coffee Lounge*. Queue for traditional, plain Italian food at plain prices. Notoriously surly service is part of the fun. BYO. Daily lunch and dinner.

**Ribberies "Taste Australia"**, 411 Bourke St, Darlinghurst (☎361 4929). Creative use of native produce by French chef. Highly recommended. Expensive, but BYO. Fixed-price menus. Dinner Mon–Sat, lunch Thurs & Fri for bookings only.

**Taylor Square**, 191–195 Oxford St, Darlinghurst (☎360 5828). Smart modern restaurant, looking down on the crowds from the first floor, and specializing in contemporary Australian cuisine; expensive. Licensed; dinner daily.

## Cafés

**Bagel Coffee House**, 7 Flinders St, Taylor Sq, Darlinghurst. Divine bagels, newspapers to read; furnished with old train seats. Daily 8am–8pm.

**Bar Coluzzi**, 322 Victoria St, Darlinghurst. Famous Italian café run by a genial former boxer – tiny and always packed, with patrons spilling out onto stools on the pavement. Daily 5am–7.30pm.

**Betty's Soup Kitchen**, 269 Crown St, Darlinghurst. Soup is the speciality, and makes for a cheap meal, served with damper. Salads, pies and desserts too. Daily except Sat & Sun lunch; BYO.

**Java Bar**, 216 Crown St, Darlinghurst. Breakfast, imaginative salads, sandwiches and snacks.

**Laurie's**, corner of Victoria and Burton streets, Darlinghurst. Noisy, popular, crowded vegetarian place opposite Green Park. Takeaways too.

**Tropicana**, 227b Victoria St, Darlinghurst (☎360 9809). Italian café with old jukebox and simple food, including great *focaccia*; the place to hang out and pose, at weekends especially.

# Kings Cross and Woolloomooloo

Many of the coffee shops and eateries in the Cross cater for the tastes (and wallets) of the area's backpackers, though there are also several stylish alternatives. Most are also open late.

**Akasaka-Tei**, 22 Darlinghurst Rd, Kings Cross. Cheap noodle bar: home-from-home for the young Japanese who live in the area. Best of all, there's Japanese TV! BYO.

**Bayswater Brasserie**, 32 Bayswater Rd, Kings Cross (☎357 2794). Busy, buzzy, upmarket brasserie with interesting modern food; expensive. Licensed.

**Cafe Pralinka**, 4b Roslyn St, Kings Cross. Modest Czech café with hearty soups and a blackboard menu of filling authentic dishes. Mon–Sat 11am–10pm.

**Dean's Cafe**, 5 Kellett St, Kings Cross. A haven after a night out in the Cross. Food and coffee until 3am Mon–Fri and until 5am Saturday.

**Kelletts**, 13–15 Kellett Way, Kings Cross. Good-value pasta and vegetarian food. Daily till late.

**Piccolo Bar**, 6 Roslyn St, Kings Cross. Here forty years, so it must be doing something right: arty hangout for great cappuccino, huge breakfasts and cheap pasta specials. BYO; open very late.

**Tilbury Hotel**, corner of Forbes and Nicholson streets, Woolloomooloo. Great pub with traditional pub grub plus some much more exotic dishes, often accompanied by live entertainment.

**The Woolloomooloo Woodshed**, 132 Forbes St, Woolloomooloo (☎357 1978). All-Australian restaurant – grilled lamb chops or juicy steaks with chips and salad.

# Paddington

Oxford Street continues through Paddington, becoming more upmarket as it goes. The food you'll find here is some of the best "contemporary Australian" with fresh ingredients and diverse influences; the majority of restaurants are attached to pubs.

**Bellevue Hotel**, 159 Hargrave St (☎363 2293). Sunny courtyard dining on delicious gourmet meals. Expensive. Lunch daily, dinner Mon–Sat.

**Grand National Hotel**, 161 Underwood St. Good-value bistro with an imaginative menu, and old fashioned puddings for dessert.

**Micky's**, 268 Oxford St. Café with good breakfasts and interesting snacks.

**New Edition Tearooms**, 328a Oxford St. Attached to the bookshop of the same name. Particularly good for breakfast, and on Saturdays during the Paddington Market when there's a jazz band.

**Paddington Inn Bistro**, 388 Oxford St (☎361 4402). Award-winning upmarket pub bistro is always busy; the menu is extensive and eclectic. Expensive.

**Royal Hotel**, Five Ways (☎331 2684). Pub restaurant serving meaty modern Australian fare. Smart interior, gorgeous staff, groovy clientele.

**Sloane Rangers**, 312 Oxford St. Good, unusual vegetarian food, moderately priced. The green courtyard out back is a treat. BYO. Daily 8am–6pm.

## Bondi and eastern suburbs

Bondi is a cosmopolitan centre with the many Eastern European and Jewish people giving its cafés a continental flair and there's some fantastic kosher restaurants, delis and cake shops. Bondi Beach area is full of cheap takeaways, fish 'n' chip shops and beer gardens, as well as some seriously trendy cafés and restaurants. Other eastern suburbs – Coogee and Watson's Bay in particular – are also worth a look.

**Bondi Tratt Cafe Restaurant**, 34b Campbell Parade, Bondi Beach (☎365 4303). Considering the setting overlooking the beach, not at all expensive. Italian food, and breakfast from 7.30am daily. Invariably buzzing and crowded. Licensed.

**Bronte Café**, 467 Bronte Road, Bronte. Enjoy the view across Bronte Beach and kick back. Good café food, particularly the homemade cakes. Busy at weekends. Closed Mon & Tues.

**Burgerman**, 249 Bondi Rd, Bondi. This new burger bar sure beats *McDonalds*; gourmet burgers to slaver over. Busy takeaway service, small eat-in area. Dinner only, closed Tues.

**China Bowl Seafood Restaurant**, Level 3, 169 Dolphin St, Coogee (☎665 3308). Better and cheaper seafood than in Chinatown – and ocean views. Licensed.

**Le Crepe Cafe**, corner of Lamrock Ave and Campbell Parade. French-run so the buckwheat crepes are authentically good. Always crowded, colourful interior, with shopfront open to the beach.

**Doyles on the Beach**, 11 Marine Parade, Watson's Bay (☎337 1350); also **Doyles Wharf Restaurant** (☎337 1572). The original of the great Sydney institution is the first of these, but both serve great seafood and have views of the city across the water. The Doyles Water Taxi can transport you from Circular Quay to Watson's Bay; ask when you book. Daily lunch and dinner; licensed.

**The Fairy Grotto**, 95 Roscoe St. Funky vegetarian café just back from Campbell Parade. Jukebox with indie selections, fresh imaginative food and freshly squeezed juices. Daily 10am–10pm.

**Hall Street Cafe**, 51 Hall St, Bondi Beach. Fine daytime haunt. Newspapers, good noticeboard, great croissants and *focaccia*, interesting pasta dishes. Mon–Fri 8am–4pm, weekends until 6pm.

**India on Bondi Road**, 292 Bondi Road. Takeaway (with a small BYO eat-in section) serving generous portions of fresh and delicious North Indian food. Tues–Sat 5–10pm, Sun until 9.30pm.

**Isabella La Bella**, 114 Glenayr Ave, North Bondi. Run by a friendly Mexican/Italian couple who dish up authentic Mexican food and good pizzas at great prices.

**Jackies**, 132 Warners Ave, North Bondi. Airy cruisy café with big windows providing watery views. Good coffee and the usual Italian sandwiches and pasta. Daily 7.30am–midnight.

**Ravesi's**, corner of Hall St and Campbell Parade, Bondi Beach (☎365 4422). Stunning beach views, slightly snooty service – and contemporary cuisine from breakfast through dinner and in between. Daily 7.30am–10pm.

**Sari Rasa**, 186 Arden St, Coogee Beach, above *McDonalds* (☎665 5649). Delicious southeast Asian specialities; inexpensive, BYO. Daily noon to 3pm & 6pm to late.

**The Sports Bar**, 32 Campbell Parade, Bondi Beach (☎30 4582). Fun young brasserie decorated with sporting memorabilia. Provides a vast blackboard menu of Asian- and Italian-influenced food at moderate prices. Licensed. Mon 6pm–midnight, Tues–Fri noon–midnight, Sat & Sun 10am–midnight.

## North Shore and Manly

Military Road, running from Neutral Bay to Mosman, rivals and perhaps outdoes all the gourmet streets south of the harbour. The string of excellent restaurants tends to be expensive, but there are a number of bakeries, tempting pastry shops and well-stocked delis. Crows Nest, just north of North Sydney along the Pacific Highway, also has a heavy concentration of restaurants in a very small area. Manly offers something for every taste and budget, though cheap and cheerful is its forte.

**Brazil Café**, 29 Belgrave St, Manly. More Italian than Brazilian, in fact. Daily 9am–midnight.

**Cinema Cinema**, 1 Spit Rd, Mosman (☎968 1330). Indian restaurant where you can watch Hindi films as you eat.

**Eric's Fish Café**, 316 Pacific Highway, Crows Nest. Long-established place for plain Sydney seafood, but only till 9pm. BYO.

**Gourmet Pizza Kitchen**, 199–207 Military Rd, Neutral Bay. The name says it all.

**Indian Empire**, 5 Walker St, North Sydney (☎923 2909). Spectacular view of the city across Lavender Bay, plus everything you'd expect from a good Indian. BYO. Closed Sat & Sun lunch.

**Mum's Bento**, 236 Military Rd, Neutral Bay. The closest you're going to get to a Tokyo *bento* shop in Sydney. Takeaway, of course. Closed Sun.

**Ocean Foods**, The Corso, Manly. Best takeaway for traditional fish 'n' chips.

**Red Centre**, 70 Alexander St, Crows Nest. Pizza place; weird and wonderful toppings.

**Sentosa**, 10 Clarke St, Crows Nest (☎438 5526). Malaysian/Singaporean restaurant serving appetizing curries and seafood. Licensed. Closed Sun.

**Supermex**, 48 North Steyne, Manly (☎977 6307). Well-presented Mexican food. BYO.

**Tawan**, 672 Military Rd, Mosman (☎969 9407). Slightly pricey Thai food, but good. BYO.

**Yeado**, 193 Military Road, Neutral Bay (☎953 8979). Popular Japanese dishes like *gyoza* and *yakitori* – also Korean food. Expensive, licensed; booking recommended. Closed Sat & Sun lunch.

# Entertainment, nightlife and culture

There's an awful lot going on in Sydney, especially at the level of bands in sweaty pubs and club nights in upstairs rooms. It's easy enough to find out exactly **what's on**: in addition to the rather bland monthly programmes distributed by various tourist organizations, you'll find comprehensive listings of film, theatre and music events in *Metro*, a supplement in Friday's *Sydney Morning Herald*, or *Time Out*, a *Telegraph-Mirror* pull-out every Thursday. For more alternative goings-on – clubbing, bands, fashion, music and the like – pick up one of the many **free listings magazines**, such as *3D World* or *On the Street* with its weekly band listings and reviews. Best of all is *Beat*, a highly portable, highly hip booklet that comes out every Wednesday: it covers every base in Sydney including food, theatre, comedy and music, and can be found lying around in the cafés and boutiques of Paddington, Glebe and Kings Cross.

Sydney's **arts scene** is vibrant and extensive. **Prices** for mainstream theatre and music performances are fairly high – from $20 upwards – but are still very reasonable by international standards, while smaller fringe venues can be an extremely good deal. Pub bands and clubs are often free, especially if you get there early; where they do make a charge, it's usually less than $10. The venues for major events are the **Entertainment Centre** at Haymarket near Darling Harbour (24hr recorded info ☎11582; enquiries and credit-card sales ☎266 4800); the *Hordern Pavilion* at the showgrounds just up from Surry Hills (☎361 3769); the *Enmore Theatre*, 130 Enmore Road, just up from Newtown (☎550 3666); and the *Metro Theatre*, 624 George St (☎264 2666). *Ticketek* is the main **booking agency**, with branches located at 195 Elizabeth Street, inside *Grace Bros* at the corner of George and Market streets and within the Entertainment Centre. You can always try for cheap, same-day tickets at the **Halftix** kiosk in Martin Place (Mon–Sat noon–6pm; ☎235 1437 or 0055/20 580); they also sell regular tickets.

# Pubs and bars

The differences between a restaurant, bar, pub and nightclub are often blurred in Sydney, and one establishment may be a combination of all these under one roof. The list below consists mainly of traditional old **hotels**, though even at most of these there'll be some kind of food available, and they may even occasionally lay on entertainment. You can get a drink at any time of the day in Sydney: some pubs, known as **"early openers"**, start serving at 6am: generally fairly rough and seedy, although they can be fun places to end up after a wild night. For a guaranteed drink anytime, head for Kings Cross. On Christmas Day and Good Friday, all hotels and bottle shops are closed and it's very difficult to find a drink unless you head for a restaurant.

## City centre

**Bar Luca**, 52 Phillip St, near the Intercontinental Hotel, Circular Quay. Trendy city bar.

**Century Tavern**, corner of George and Liverpool streets, above *Hungry Jacks*. Good meeting point before or after the pictures.

**Craig Brewery and Bar**, Festival Market Place, Darling Harbour. After-work happy hour with cheap beer on weeknights between 5.30 and 8pm. Bands Fri nights and Sun afternoons.

**Forbes Hotel**, corner of King and York streets. Atmospheric turn-of-the-century hotel.

**Hero of Waterloo**, 81 Lower Fort St, Miller Pt, The Rocks. Ancient, but still packed out every night.

**Lord Nelson Brewery Hotel**, corner of Argyle and Kent Streets, Miller's Point, The Rocks. Very old pub serving beer brewed on the premises.

**The Marble Bar**, *Hilton Hotel*, 259 Pitt St. Victorian indulgence of a bar, made from Italian marble. Free jazz Fri & Sat nights 10pm–2am.

**Mercantile Hotel**, 25 George St, The Rocks. High-spirited Irish pub where you can get Sydney's best-poured Guinness.

**Orient Hotel**, corner of George and Argyle streets, The Rocks. Perennially popular, but heavy at weekends.

**Pumphouse Tavern**, 17 Little Pier St, Darling Harbour. Pleasant, restored pub with a beer garden at the edge of Darling Harbour – counter meals available.

## Kings Cross and Darlinghurst

**Bourbon and Beefsteak Bar**, 24 Darlinghurst Rd, Kings Cross. Legendary 24hr Kings Cross drinking hole; come here for a steak breakfast and a Bloody Mary after a night out.

**Darlo Bar**, corner of Darlinghurst Rd and Liverpool St, Darlinghurst. Traditional Cross meeting place; loud and crushed.

**The Dug Out Bar**, *Burdekin Hotel*, 2 Oxford St, Darlinghurst. Tiny, trendy basement bar favoured by "resting" graphic arts professionals.

**Gilligans**, above the *Oxford Hotel*, 134 Oxford St, Darlinghurst. Arrive early for a window seat and views of the crowd below over a cocktail.

**Green Park Hotel**, 360 Victoria St, Darlinghurst. Gay-friendly pub, with a relaxed atmosphere – great for a quiet daytime drink; lively and packed at night. Comfortable for solo women.

## Paddington and Surry Hills

**Bentley Bar**, 320 Crown St, Surry Hills. Popular pre- and post-clubbing venue.

**Cricketers Arms**, 106 Fitzroy St, Surry Hills. Good cross-section of people frequent this pub: old fellas watching sport on TV and young fellas (and sheilas) playing pool, plus a groovy jukebox.

**Dolphin Hotel**, 412 Crown St, Surry Hills. Cosy pub with a beer garden and good counter meals.

**Hopetoun Hotel**, 416 Bourke St, Surry Hills. Once hub of the indie band scene, and still a fine watering hole with three bars, a good pool table and occasional bands (usually free).

**Paddington Inn Hotel**, 338 Oxford St, Paddington. Slick, crowded and expensive; huge on Saturdays as it's opposite the market. The bistro is also recommended (see p.105).

**Palace**, corner of Flinders and South Dowling streets, Surry Hills. Tastefully distressed decor in the smart-set hangout downstairs, with a tiny eating area for the well-recommended kitchen. The music's so loud you can hardly talk, but several rooms of pool tables upstairs provide respite.

**Royal**, 237 Glenmore Rd, Paddington. The original renovated Paddington pub.

## Bondi

**B.B's**, 157 Curlewis St, Bondi Beach. Laid-back, unpretentious wine bar popular with local thirty-somethings; good-value meals too and sometimes live music.

**Bondi Hotel**, 178 Campbell Parade, Bondi. Huge pub dating from the 1920s with many of its original features intact. Can be quite sedate during the day but at night becomes an over-the-top, late-night backpacker (and Kiwi) hangout.

**Cock 'n' Bull Tavern**, 89 Ebley St, Bondi Junction. Long-time haunt of Brits on working visas; rowdy and in your face. Irish bands Sun night, usually free.

**Dogs Diner**, 70b Campbell Parade, Bondi. Slick, open-fronted wine bar.

## Glebe and Newtown

**Bank Hotel**, 324 King St, next to Newtown Station. Recently redesigned, stylish pub is always packed. Pool table, cocktail bar and a spacious beer garden (with Thai restaurant, see p.102).

**Marlborough Hotel**, 145 King St, Newtown. Spacious pub popular with students often has bands, but there's always somewhere quiet to talk out back on comfy lounges, or sit in the great beer garden. Good Italian restaurant attached.

**Nag's Head Hotel**, 162 St Johns Rd, Forest Lodge. Lively brew-pub with British beers.

# Live music: jazz, blues and rock

There's always a tremendous **range of music** on offer at the venues listed below, and there's often an **Africa Night** at one of the big trade clubs around town: look out for posters. For the latest info on **gigs** around town, tune in to "The Buzz" on *2SER* (107.3FM) at 6.30pm, or "Homebrew" on *Radio Skid Row* (88.9FM), weekdays 9–10pm, for a more anarchic and multicultural bent.

**Annandale Hotel**, corner of Nelson St and Parramatta Rd, Annandale (☎550 1078). Good local indie bands; cocktail bar next door.

**The Basement**, 29 Reiby Place, Circular Quay (☎51 2797). Underground venue, mainstream jazz.

**Friend in Hand Pub**, 58 Cowper St, Glebe (☎660 2326). Occasional Irish folk music.

**Harbourside Brasserie**, Pier One, Miller's Point (☎252 3000). Great location near the water with rock, jazz, blues or cabaret from 10pm; mellow atmosphere.

**Lansdowne Hotel**, 2 City Rd, Broadway (☎211 2325). Regular late venue for indie bands.

**Real Ale Tavern**, 66 King St (☎262 3277). Lives up to its name – there are more than 180 beers available. Jazz and blues bands every night.

**Rose, Shamrock & Thistle**, 193 Evans St, Rozelle (☎555 7755). Popularly known as the "Three Weeds", mainly a folk venue with local and international soul/blues acts.

**Round Midnight**, 2 Roslyn St, Kings Cross (☎356 4045). Cooking late-night jazz and blues venue.

**Sandringham Hotel**, 387 King St, Newtown (☎557 1254). Resolutely unreconstructed and grungy pub. Every night local bands (free) play squeezed behind the bar.

**Selina's**, *Coogee Bay Hotel*, 212 Arden St, Coogee Bay (☎665 0000). Huge place for big-name touring bands, usually at correspondingly big prices.

**Soup Plus**, 383 George St, in a basement near Strand Arcade (☎299 7728). Simple restaurant and live jazz. Very MOR.

**Hotel Steyne**, 75 The Corso, Manly (☎977 4977). Huge, lively hotel with loads of different bars; live band or disco most nights till late. Hugely popular with the young Manly set Sat nights.

**Strawberry Hills Hotel**, 453 Elizabeth St, Surry Hills (☎698 2997). Pub with traditional and contemporary jazz Tues–Sun nights (usually $6 cover charge, sometimes free).

**Vulcan Hotel**, 500 Wattle St, Ultimo (☎211 3283). Traditional trash thrash venue; Fri & Sat nights; around $4 cover.

# Clubs

Many of Sydney's best clubs are at gay or lesbian venues: although these are listed separately, starting below, the divisions are not always that clear – many are **theme places**, and may have a gay night one day, lesbian the next and straight the following night. The best source of **information** on the rapidly changing club scene is *Beat* (see p.106), while **rave** info is provided on the techno radio programme *MDA* on Saturday nights 10pm–2pm. If you're interested in Koori music and culture, *Radio Skid Row* is taken over by *Koori Radio* 11am–2pm Mon–Fri and 6am–6pm Thurs, with lots of music and what's on around town.

**Bar Luna**, at *Jackson's on George*, 176 George St, Circular Quay (☎217 2727). Multi-floor club nights popular with after-work office crowd.

**Blackmarket**, 111 Regent St (☎698 8863). Futuristic decor with Gothic overtones suits the mixed crowd of gay and straight on various clubnights; Thursday's *Hellfire Club* dabbles in S&M and is wildly popular, while sweaty clubbers keep dancing beyond dawn at Sunday's *Dayclub* (4am–6pm). There's a café and pool room to cool down in.

**The Cauldron**, 207 Darlinghurst Rd, Darlinghurst (☎331 1523). One of the oldest clubs (with restaurant) in Sydney, popular with young professionals.

**Club Rio**, 508 Parramatta Rd, Leichhardt (☎550 9800). Latin American music to dance to Fri–Sun nights 6pm–6am; dinner and show, set menu around $12.

**Dalleys**, *Manly Pacific Park Royal*, 55 North Steyne Rd, Manly (☎977 7666). Cheap club nights.

**Exchange Hotel**, 34 Oxford St, Darlinghurst (☎331 1936). An enduring Oxford Street institution has always been a happy mix of gay and straight, packed most nights. No cover charge. Downstairs is the Phoenix Bar (men only Sun nights); upstairs is the Lizard Lounge.

**Kings Cross Hotel**, corner of William St and Darlinghurst Rd, Kings Cross (☎358 3377). Three floors, all open 24hr, with the *Rooftop Nightclub* on top. Popular with travellers; no cover charge.

**Kinsela's**, 383 Bourke St, Darlinghurst (☎331 2699). One-time fabulous funeral parlour has been transformed into a stylish club with the art deco intact. Spread across three levels (first two usually free), each with a bar: street level is laid-back with pool to play, the middle bar is claustrophobically crowded, while upstairs is the main dance floor. Door bitches vet your style. Wed–Sat 11pm–3am.

**Mr Goodbar**, 11 Oxford St, Paddington (☎360 6759). Intimate club which plays eclectic urban grooves is a favourite model- and celeb-spotting haunt, especially Sun nights.

**Powercuts Reggae Club**, 150 Elizabeth St, City (mobile ☎0414/260 270). DJs play "the smoothest reggae known to man" Fri & Sat nights 10pm–4.30am.

**Rogues**, The Laneway off 165 Riley St, East Sydney (☎332 1718). Favoured funk-down of well-heeled North Shore belles; hefty $10 door charge.

**Sight/Soho Bar**, 171 Victoria St, Potts Point (☎358 4221). Bar and club with slick decor and DJ every night. A bit posey; mixed crowd.

**Sugareef**, 20 Bayswater Road, Kings Cross (☎357 7250). Hip club with dancing Tues, Fri & Sat nights; other nights are more mellow. Play pool or eat in the Italian restaurant.

**Taxi Club**, 40–42 Flinders St, just off Taylor Square, Darlinghurst (☎331 4256). Legendary late-night bar frequented by transvestites. Wed–Sun midnight to dawn.

**Zoom**, 163–169 Oxford St, Darlinghurst (☎360 2528). Big-name DJs and visiting European techno legends play the latest dance tracks in this big club on two levels, the closest thing to a rave atmosphere in Sydney; come down over a game of pool. $10 cover charge.

## Gay nightspots

**Albury Hotel**, 6 Oxford St, Paddington (☎361 6555). The heart of the throbbing Oxford Street scene, the Albury is popular with all ages and both sexes. Good drag shows most nights. Daily until 1am (Sun midnight).

**Blackmarket**, 111 Regent St, City (☎698 8544). Second and third Fridays of the month are big gay nights. Some S&M shows.

**Bottoms Up Bar**, *Rex Hotel*, 48 Macleay St, Potts Point (☎358 3344). Sydney's oldest gay pub is also the only one in Kings Cross. The crowd is older and mixed, but that doesn't stop it getting a little rough at times. Daily until late.

## GAY AND LESBIAN SYDNEY

Sydney is undisputably one of the world's great gay cities – indeed, many people think it capable of snatching San Francisco's crown as the Queen of them all. The importance of the lesbian and gay community to the city is indicated by the New South Wales Police Force's community policing programme, which aims to reduce harassment and bashings: special Gay and Lesbian Liaison Officers have been appointed to most of the inner-city suburbs, so you should be guaranteed a sympathetic ear – and possibly a pair of broad shoulders too.

### MARDI GRAS AND SLEAZE

From a Queer perspective the best time of year to visit Sydney is February, when the **Sydney Gay & Lesbian Mardi Gras** takes over the city and the already huge gay population is flooded by pilgrims from within and without Australia. Four weeks of exhibitions, performances and other events (including a film festival) pave the way for an exuberant night-time **parade** down Oxford Street, when up to 500,000 gays and straights jostle for the best positions. Participants devote months to the preparation of outlandish floats and outrageous costumes at the Mardi Gras workshops. Even longer is devoted to the preparation of beautiful bodies in Sydney's packed gyms. Vanity apart, fitness is a necessity for the all-night dance party which follows the parade (about $60 per ticket).

The *Mardi Gras Guide*, available from around the beginning of January, can be picked up in all the usual places or at the **Mardi Gras office** at 21–23 Erskinville Road, Erskinville. The purchase of **party** tickets is restricted to "Mardi Gras members" in order to keep out troublemakers and "to guard the gay and lesbian nature of the parties". Membership costs $35 a year or $10 associate/international membership for those who live outside Sydney. To be sure of a **ticket** (restricted to one only for associate/international members), it's best to write to Sydney Gay and Lesbian Mardi Gras Ltd (see below for details), sending a copy of your passport and the equivalent $10 membership, or order one over the phone by credit card, quoting your passport number while you're at it. They'll post it to you, or hold it for collection – again, you'll need to show your passport. Full members can buy several tickets so, if all else fails, ask around and you may find someone with a spare ticket.

Sydney just can't wait all year for Mardi Gras and the **The Sleaze Ball** is a very welcome stop-gap in September/October. Similar to the Mardi Gras party, it is held in the three halls at the Showground (see p.88), and goes on through the night. Tickets are organized by Mardi Gras Ltd and are likewise restricted to members.

### LISTINGS

**Gay** life is concentrated in Paddington, Surry Hills, Newtown, Darlinghurst and Kings Cross, but every newcomer's first stop has to be Oxford Street (or the Golden Mile as it is mock-reverentially known) – make like the locals and cruise. Sydney's self-assured **lesbians** rival the influence and visibility of the male scene and, more importantly, never take prisoners where a game of pool is concerned. The scene is heavily concentrated in a few inner-city suburbs: Newtown, Glebe, Leichhardt (or "Dyke-heart") and Annandale, in addition to the more gay suburbs of Paddington, Darlinghurst and Surry Hills. Although the listings below have been split into separate gay and lesbian listings, the scene thankfully doesn't split so neatly into them and us.

### Groups and info

**Press** *Sydney Star Observer*, 2nd Floor, 94 Oxford St, Darlinghurst (☎02/380 5577), fortnightly gay and lesbian newspaper free from venues, $1 from newsagents; *Capital Q*, Suite 5, Level 5, 15–19 Boundary St, Rushcutters Bay (☎02/332 4988); weekly (Fri) gay and lesbian newspaper free from venues; *LOTL* (*Lesbians on the Loose*), PO Box 798, Newtown (☎02/380 6529), free, non-glossy monthly magazine available in the bookshops and cafés of Newtown and Glebe; *Wicked Women*, PO Box 305, Redfern (☎02/319 7128), magazine of S&M erotica produced by the organization of the same name.

**Radio** *2SER* (107.3FM) has two good programmes: "Gaywaves", Thurs 8–10.30pm and "Out and Out", Tues 9.30–10pm.

**Support Networks** *Gay & Lesbian Counselling Service of New South Wales*, GLCS Centre, 197 Albion St, Surry Hills (postal address PO Box 334, Darlinghurst, NSW 2010); counselling line ☎02/360 2211 (daily 4pm–midnight); What's On ☎02/361 3655 (24hr recorded message). *Lesbian Line* ☎02/550 0910 Fridays 6–10pm or recorded 24hr information. *ACON: AIDS Council of NSW*, 188 Goulburn St, Darlinghurst (☎02/206 2000). *Bobby Goldsmith Foundation for AIDS and AIDS Related Diseases*, Level 4, 16 Victoria St, Darlinghurst (☎02/860 9755). *Sydney AIDS Hotline/NSW AIDS line*, ☎02/332 4000 or toll free on ☎1800/451 600. *Positive Women*, PO Box 350, Darlinghurst (☎02/283 3222), HIV-positive women's group. *ANKALI*, ☎02/332 1090, support for people with HIV; *Albion Street Centre*, 150–154 Albion St, Surry Hills (☎02/332 1090), counselling, testing clinic, information and library.

**Sydney Gay and Lesbian Mardi Gras Ltd** PO Box 557, Newtown, NSW 2042 (☎02/557 4332, fax 02/516 4446).

**Travel agents** *Silke's Travel*, 263 Oxford St, Darlinghurst NSW 2010 (☎02/380 6244, fax ☎02/361 3729) offers advice and bookings for domestic and international travel and accommodation from a gay perspective; it also produces a handy "gay map" which comes out every three months and is packed with information.

### Lesbian cafés and meeting places

**Bagel House**, Flinders St, Taylor Sq (☎360 7892). Divine bagels cooked downstairs; the café upstairs is used as a forum (for feminist discussions) during Mardi Gras. Daily 8am–8pm.

**Café Latte**, 153a King St, Newtown (☎519 9317). Any good café in Newtown has been adopted by the area's ever growing dyke population. This is one, and it serves pretty good coffee.

**Café Cinquecento**, 88 King St, Newtown (☎557 1418). Lesbian-run café that's gay-friendly.

**Clover Women's Business Club**, 122 Victoria Rd, Drummoyne (☎81 2964). Coffee-shop every second Tues 7.30pm–11.30pm.

**Craven Café**, 166b Glebe Point Rd, Glebe (☎552 2656). Popular place to cruise and devour tasty tidbits. Open daily.

**Green Iguana Cafe**, just after Forbes St on King St, Newtown (☎516 3118). Small, friendly café that does a very tasty hot chocolate with marshmallows.

### Gay cafés and meeting places

**Baby Enzo's**, 242 Oxford St, Paddington (☎331 7440). Stylish café/bar/brasserie, the place to be seen if you can afford it. Courtyard bookings recommended. Tues–Sun 11am–midnight.

**Dean's Cafe**, 5 Kellett St, Kings Cross (☎356 4569). Not a strictly gay venue, but a haven after a night out in the Cross. Food and coffee until 3am Mon–Fri and until 5am Sat.

**Downtown**, 84 Oxford St, Darlinghurst (☎361 5282) Gay-owned and -run café-restaurant.

**Oddy's Cafe**, 263 Oxford St, Darlinghurst (☎360 3947). Stays open almost around the clock, making it a very popular meeting point and the place to refuel after a hard night's clubbing. Daily 6am–2am.

**Rex Hotel**, 52 Macleay St, Kings Cross (☎358 3155). Bar, club and restaurant serving steak meals.

*See also p.71 for gay- and lesbian-friendly places to stay, pp.109 & 112 for a lowdown on the club scene and listings of specifically gay and lesbian venues.*

**DCM (Don't Cry Mama)**, 33 Oxford St, Darlinghurst (☎267 7380). Young, fast and mainly gay, *DCM* is open late Mon–Sat. $10 cover some nights.

**Lizard Lounge**, upstairs at the *Exchange Hotel*, 34 Oxford St, Darlinghurst. There's usually a crowd of beautiful young things at the bar.

**Flinders Hotel**, 63–65 Flinders St, Surry Hills (☎360 4929). A mainstay of the Oxford Street scene. Thurs drag show and Sat night strippers. Daily to 5am (Sun midnight).

**Imperial Hotel**, Erskinville Rd, Erskinville (☎519 9899). Mixed gay, lesbian and straight venue. Plenty of special nights, including regular gay and lesbian bootscoots (US-style line dancing).

**Midnight Shift**, 85 Oxford St, Darlinghurst (☎360 4319). Hosts a variety of different club nights Tues–Sat, all hot and sweaty. Cover charge up to $10. The bar downstairs is open daily.

**Newtown Hotel**, 174 King St, Newtown (☎51 1329). Something for everyone – pool tables, drag shows, "Golden Girls" screenings and a small dance floor, even a restaurant. Mixed crowd. Daily until midnight.

**Oxford Hotel**, 134 Oxford St, Darlinghurst (☎331 3467). Macho pillar of the Sydney community. Daily until 2am (Sun midnight).

## Lesbian nightspots

**Bank Hotel**, 324 King St, next to Newtown Station (☎557 1280). This stylish bar has become a dyke favourite; the Wed night women's pool competition draws large crowds.

**Blackmarket,** 111 Regent St (☎698 8544). Club venue with pool tables, café and reasonable cover charges: best dyke night is *Oblivion*, first Friday of the month.

**Divas**, 12–14 Enmore Road, Newtown (☎519 4270). Lesbian-only nightclub running Thurs–Sun with a 3am license.

**I.D.s**, corner of Botany and McEvoy roads, Alexandria (☎319 3204). Formerly the *Iron Duke Hotel*, this women-only pub with a bistro, beer garden and pool room (comps Tues) has live entertainment and disco Thurs–Sun.

**Imperial Hotel**, Erskinville Rd, Erskinville (☎519 1899). Some of the Newtown/Enmore dykes come here to drink. Gay and lesbian bootscooting is taking off in a big way in Sydney and this is one of the places to hoe down. Pool comps every Sat arvo with big prize money.

**Kinsela's**, Taylor Square, Darlinghurst (☎331 3299). Lesbian venues come and go, but *The Other Side* on Sun nights (7pm–midnight) is a real girlie dyke dance club night with staying power.

**Leichhardt Hotel**, corner of Short and Balmain roads, Leichhardt (☎569 1217). Popular lesbian watering hole, daily 10am–midnight.

# Classical music, theatre and dance

The Opera House is of course *the* place for the most prestigious performances in Sydney, hosting not just opera and classical music but also theatre and dance in its many auditoriums. Forget quibbles about acoustics or ticket prices – it's worth going just to say you've been. The free outdoor performances in the Domain, under the auspices of the Sydney Festival, are a highlight of the year, as crowds gather to enjoy the music and their picnics. Check *Metro* or *Time Out* to find out what's on at the venues below.

## Concert halls

**Conservatorium of Music**, Royal Botanic Gardens (☎230 1222). Concert hall in a delightful setting, with free lunchtime recitals every Wed during term time.

**Sydney Opera House**, Bennelong Point (☎250 7777; box office Mon–Sat 9am–8.30pm, Sun 9am–4pm) Ballet, opera etc.

**Town Hall**, corner of Druitt and George streets (☎265 9230). Centrally located concert hall.

## Theatre and dance

**Aboriginal and Islander Dance Theatre** (☎660 2312). Highly successful company offering professionally produced contemporary Aboriginal dance theatre at various venues.

**Belvoir St Theatre**, 25 Belvoir St, Surry Hills (☎699 3444). Highly regarded venue for a wide range of contemporary Australian and international theatre; Theatresports seasons plus occasional comedy festivals.

**Ensemble Theatre**, 78 McDougall St, Milsons Point (☎929 0644). Australian contemporary and classic plays.

**The Footbridge Theatre**, Parramatta Rd, Glebe (☎692 9955). Rich and varied repertoire: from *Elvis the Musical* to Shakespeare.

**Her Majesty's Theatre**, Quay St, near Central Station (☎266 4820). The place to see those big musical extravaganzas.

**The Playhouse** and **Drama Theatre**, both at the Sydney Opera House, Bennelong Point (☎250 7777; box office Mon–Sat 9am–8.30pm, Sun 9am–4pm). Modern and traditional plays, and dance.

**Theatre Royal**, MLC Centre, King St (☎231 6111 or 202 2200). Musicals and plays.

**Wharf Theatre**, Pier 4, Hickson Rd, The Rocks (☎250 1700). Home to the *Sydney Theatre Company* which produces Shakespeare and contemporary pieces by international playwrights, and also to the *Sydney* (modern) *Dance Company*.

## Fringe venues, comedy and cabaret

**Comedy Store**, 450 Parramatta Rd, Leichhardt (☎564 3900). Stand-up comics and meals.

**Harold Park Hotel**, 115 Wigram Rd, Glebe (☎692 0564). Almost a mini arts centre, with comedy, drama, readings and cabaret throughout the week. Excellent bistro and beer garden; Sun boot-scooting (country-style line dancing).

**New Theatre**, 542 King St, Newtown (☎519 3403). Professional actors (working without pay) perform contemporary pieces with socialist subtexts.

**NIDA Theatre**, 215 Anzac Parade, Kensington (☎697 7613). Australia's premier dramatic training ground – the National Institute of Dramatic Art – where the likes of Mel Gibson, Judy Davis and Colin Friels started out; student productions are often open to the general public.

**The Performance Space**, 199 Cleveland St, edge of Redfern (☎698 7235). Experimental performances.

**Stables Theatre**, 10 Nimrod St, Darlinghurst (☎361 3817). Has a mission to develop and foster new Australian playwrights.

# Film

The commercial movie centre of Sydney is on George Street, south of the Town Hall, where you'll find *Hoyt's*, *Village* and *Greater Union*; nearby, at 232 Pitt Street, is the *Pitt Centre*. Tuesday nights are half-price at *Greater Union*, *Hoyts* and *Village*. More adventurous programming can be found at the following.

**Academy Twin**, 3a Oxford St, Paddington (☎361 4453). Art-house and prestige new releases; half-price Mon $6.50.

**AFI (Australian Film Institute)**, Paddington Town Hall, corner of Oatley Rd and Oxford St (☎361 5398). Varied programme of Australian and foreign films.

**The Dendy**, MLC Centre, Martin Place (☎233 8166); plus new branch at 624 George St (☎264 1577). Cinema, bistro, bar and bookstore complex, where you can watch short films while you nosh and guzzle. Prestige new-release films; half-price Tues.

**Encore**, 64 Devonshire St, near Central Station, Surry Hills (☎281 1788). Retro; 3-D films on Fri.

**Govinda's Movie Room**, 112 Darlinghurst Rd (☎360 7853; ring for programme information with mini-reviews). Cinema run by the Hare Krishnas, and showing a range of classics and contemporary releases; kick off your shoes, lie back on cushions and gaze up at the screen.

**Mandolin**, 150 Elizabeth St, just south of Hyde Park (☎267 1968). New release arthouse/independent American and foreign films – and the best choc tops. Half-price Mon and Tues.

**Valhalla**, 166 Glebe Point Rd, Glebe (☎660 8050). Retro double-bills, new-release independents.

**Walker Street Cinema**, 121 Walker St, North Sydney (☎959 4222). Arthouse and prestige new releases. Half-price Mon.

# Galleries and exhibitions

*Metro* has comprehensive listings of all the art galleries and current exhibitions – which tend to be concentrated in Paddington. A novel way to take in some art is to catch the free **Sydney Art Bus** from *Artspace* (see below; ☎319 5091 for bookings) which visits six challenging galleries, with tours led by performance artists.

**Aboriginal Art Gallery**, Argyle Centre, The Rocks (☎247 1380). Also a branch at the Opera House.

**Artspace**, The Gunnery Arts Centre, 43–51 Cowper Wharf Rd, Woolloomooloo (☎368 1899). Wonderful location, provocative young artists. Tues–Sat 11am–6pm.

**Australian Centre for Photography**, 257 Oxford St, Paddington (☎331 6253). Photographic exhibitions. Wed–Sat 11am–5pm.

**Hogarth Galleries Aboriginal Art Centre**, 7 Walker Lane, Paddington (☎360 6839). Exhibitions of work by contemporary Aboriginal artists. Tues–Sat 11am–5pm.

**Hogarth Galleries Aboriginal and Tribal Art Centre**, 1st floor, 117 George St (☎247 9625). Huge collection of traditional Aboriginal art from around Australia. Daily 10am–5pm.

**Ivan Dougherty Gallery**, corner of Albion Ave and Selwyn streets, Paddington (☎385 0726). National and international contemporary art; forums and performances sponsored by the College of Fine Arts, University of NSW. Mon–Fri 10am–5pm, Sat 1–5pm.

**Josef Lebovic**, 34 Paddington St, Paddington (☎332 1840). Renowned print and graphic gallery specializing in Australian and international prints from the nineteenth and twentieth centuries. Tues–Fri 1–6pm, Sat 11am–5pm.

**The Performance Space**, 199 Cleveland St, edge of Redfern (☎698 7235). Experimental multimedia and plastic arts: installations and sculpture. Wed–Sun noon–8pm.

**Ray Hughes Gallery**, 270 Devonshire St, Surry Hills (☎698 3200). Stable of high-profile contemporary Australian artists; openings monthly, with two artists per show. Tues–Sat 10am–6pm.

**Roslyn Oxley**, Soudan Lane, Paddington (☎331 1919). "Avant-garde" videos and installations.

# Festivals and events

The Sydney year is interspersed with festivals of various sorts. The daddy of them all is the annual **Festival of Sydney**, an arts event that lasts the entire month of January, and comprises an exhaustive and exhausting array of events including opera, concerts, plays, "writers' week", exhibitions, and circus performances. Some events are free for all in the Domain; other venues include Circular Quay, Darling Harbour and the amphitheatre in Martin Place, and there's also a "fringe festival" based at the Bondi Pavilion. From Boxing Day to the end of January, Darling Harbour hosts its own festival, linked in with the Festival of Sydney. Most of the attractions are aimed at kids, but there's also a free promenade jazz festival, and Australia Day celebrations and fireworks on January 26. Every alternate (even-numbered) year, the *Sydney Biennale* also takes place in January, with extensive contemporary art exhibitions at various venues around town, focussing on the Art Gallery of New South Wales and the Bond Store in The Rocks. An entirely different side of Sydney life is on view at the impressive summer **Surf Carnivals**, staged regularly by local surf life-saving clubs; check the newspapers for details.

In February, the city is engulfed by the **Sydney Gay and Lesbian Mardi Gras** (see p.110). Other biggies are the **Royal Easter Show**, an agricultural and garden show in April (see box on p.88 for more); the **International Film Festival**, which takes over many of the city's screens in June (see box on p.81); the **City to Surf Race**, an eight-kilometre fun run from the city to Bondi every August; and the **Manly Jazz Festival** on Labour Day weekend in late September or early October.

The year is brought to a close by the **Sydney to Hobart Yacht Race**, when it seems that half of Sydney turns up at or on the harbour on December 26 to cheer the start of this classic regatta and watch the colourful spectacle of four hundred or so yachts setting sail for a 630-nautical-mile slog. The toughest bit is the crossing of the Bass

Strait, swept by the Roaring Forties; some years, the going is so rough that up to two thirds of the fleet drop out at this stage. Good watching spots include South Head and Nielson Park or Georges Head and Bradleys Head on the North Shore.

# Listings

**Airlines, Domestic** *Aeropelican*, 864 Pacific Highway, Pelican (☎268 1111), to Newcastle; *Ansett Australia*, corner of Oxford and Riley streets (☎13 1300); *Eastern Australia Airlines*, Qantas Airways domestic terminal, Mascot (☎13 1313), also to Lord Howe and Norfolk Island; *Hazelton Airlines*, Ansett Terminal, Mascot (☎235 1411), to country towns and outback NSW and Queensland; *Impulse Airlines*, 11th St, Mascot (☎13 1381), to Newcastle, Port Macquarie and Kempsey on the north coast, to Inverell and Glen Innes on the New England Plateau, north coast of NSW, and Norfolk and Lord Howe islands; *Lord Howe Island Airlines*, 191 Clarence St (☎290 2266);*Qantas*, 70 Hunter St, cnr Phillip St (☎13 1313).

**Airlines, International** *Aeroflot*, 388 George St (☎233 7911); *Air Caledonia*, 64 York St (☎321 9211); *Air Canada*, Level 8, 92 Pitt St (☎232 5222); *Air France*, 12 Castlereagh St (☎321 1030); *Air Lanka*, 64 York St (☎321 9234); *Air New Zealand*, 5 Elizabeth St (☎223 4666); *Air Niugini*, 100 Clarence St (☎131 1380); *Alitalia*, 32 Bridge St (☎247 9133); *British Airways*, 64 Castlereagh St (☎258 3300); *Canadian Airlines*, 30 Clarence St (☎299 7843 or free call ☎1800/251 321); *Cathay Pacific*, 28 O'Connell St (☎13 1747); *Continental*, 64 York St (☎299 1255); *Delta*, 45 Clarence St (☎262 1777); *Finnair*, 20 Bay St, Double Bay (☎326 2999); *Garuda*, 55 Hunter St (☎334 9900);*Japan Airlines*, 14th floor, 201 Sussex St (☎283 1111); *KLM*, 5 Elizabeth St (☎231 6333); *Luthansa/Lauda Air*, 143 Macquarie St (☎367 3800); *MAS-Malaysian Airlines System*, 11th floor, 388 George St (☎13 2627); *Olympic*, 37 Pitt St (☎251 1047); *Philippine Airlines*, 49 York St (☎262 3131); *Qantas*, 70 Hunter St, corner of Phillip St (24hr booking ☎957 0111); *Sabena*, 64 York St (☎321 9135); *Scandinavian Airlines*, 350 Kent St (☎299 6688); *Singapore Airlines*, 17 Bridge St (☎236 0111 or Australia-wide ☎13 1011); *Swissair*, 33 Pitt St (☎232 1744); *Thai International*, 75 Pitt St (☎251 1922); *Turkish Airlines*, 16th floor, 388 George St (☎221 1711); *United*, 5th floor, 10 Barrack St (☎237 8888).

**American Express**, 92 Pitt St (☎239 0666). Lost or stolen traveller cheques ☎886 0689, after hours ☎886 0688, outside Sydney ☎1800/25 1902.

**Banks** Main branches are mostly in the CBD, around Martin Place; hours are Mon–Thurs 9am–4pm, Fri 9am–5pm, with some suburban branches open later and on Saturdays. *ANZ*, 20 Martin Place (☎227 1911); *Commonwealth Bank*, 48 Martin Place (☎227 7111); *National Australia Bank*, 300 Elizabeth St (☎215 6789); *Westpac*, 50 Bridge Rd (☎220 1222); *Mastercard International* (lost/stolen cards, contact *Thomas Cook*, 175 Pitt St ☎229 6600); *Visa International* (lost/stolen cards free call ☎008 801 256; lost/stolen travellers' cheques ☎0014 800/125 440).

**Bike rental** *Centennial Park Cycles*, 26 Clovelly Rd, Randwick (☎398 5027); *Inner City Cycles*, 31 Glebe Point Rd, Glebe (☎660 6605).

**Bookshops** *Abbey's*, 131 York St (☎264 3111) and *Dymocks*, 424 George St (☎235 0155), are both open daily; the former is best for relaxed browsing, with more of a literary feel. *Gleebooks*, 49 Glebe Point Rd (☎660 2333), specializes in alternative books, contemporary Australian and international literature, and is open daily until 9pm. *Ariel Bookshop*, 42 Oxford St, Paddington (☎332 4581) is large, lively and very hip, and is open daily until midnight; *New Edition Bookshop*, further up at 328 Oxford St (☎360 6913), is also worth a browse. A specialist art bookshop, *Lamella* is just off Oxford St at 249 Darlinghurst Rd (☎331 4501), and there's a *Feminist Bookshop* tucked away in Orange Grove Plaza on Balmain Rd, Lilyfield (☎810 2666). For bargains, check the bookstall at *Pier One*, The Rocks, and the discount bookshop *Colorcode*, 15 Hunter St. The *Travel Bookshop* at 20 Bridge St (☎241 3554) is the place to head for maps, guides and travel journals plus a good selection of Australiana. Secondhand books at Glebe and Paddington Markets, at *Gleebooks Second Hand Books*, 191 Glebe Point Rd, until 9pm; *Lesley McKays Bookshop*, 346 New South Head Rd, Double Bay (☎327 1354), until midnight; and in the secondhand bookshops on King St, Newtown. Book collectors should head for *Berkelouw Bookdealers*, 19 Oxford St, Paddington (☎360 3200), antiquarian bookdealers since 1812 and open until midnight; *Louella Kerr*, 30 Glenmore Rd, Paddington (☎361 4664), Mon–Sat 11am–6pm; and for modern first editions in particular, *Nicholas Pounder Bookseller*, 346 New South Head Rd, Double Bay (☎328 7410).

**Boomerangs** Boomerang shop at 200 William St (☎358 2370); boomerangs sold here are mostly authentic, made by Aboriginal artisans around Australia. The owner gives free boomerang-throwing lessons every Sun between 10am and noon, in Yarranabbe Park near Rushcutters Bay.

**Bus companies** *Border Coaches*, daily to Brisbane via New England Plateau, headquarters in Armidale (☎067/72 5677 or free call ☎1800/028 937); *Bus Australia*, corner of Oxford and Riley streets, Darlinghurst (☎13 2323); *Firefly Express*, 482 Pitt St (☎211 1644), to Melbourne and Adelaide; *Great Lakes Coaches*, (☎049/97 4287 or ☎049/83 1560), daily to Forster via Newcastle; *Greyhound*, corner of Oxford and Riley Streets, Darlinghurst (☎13 1238); *Kirklands*, 488 Pitt St (☎281 2233), to the NSW north coast; *Lindsays* (☎1800/027 944), to north coast NSW and the Gold Coast; *McCafferty's*, 179 Darlinghurst Rd, Kings Cross (☎361 5125) to Melbourne and Adelaide, Brisbane and Queensland; *Murray's*, 30 Mandible St, Alexandria (☎312 1266) to Canberra; *Pioneer*, corner of Oxford and Riley Streets, Darlinghurst (☎13 2030); *Port Stephens Buses* (☎281 9366 or free call ☎1800/045 949), once daily to Port Stephens (Nelsons Bay/Fingal Bay) via Newcastle.

**Bus terminals** *Sydney Coach Terminal*, corner of Eddy Ave and Pitt St, beside Central Station; *Australian Coachlines Depot* (for *Bus Australia*, *Greyhound* and *Pioneer*), corner of Oxford and Riley streets. *McCaffertys* operate out of 179 Darlinghurst Road in Kings Cross.

**Bus tickets** can be booked at the *Traveller's Information Service* at the coach terminal (☎281 9366), at one of the *Bus Booking Centres* with locations at the corner of Springfield and Orwell streets, Kings Cross (☎368 1174) and Shop 526, below the Hilton Hotel, 255 Pitt St (☎264 3691) or direct from the bus company.

**Campervans and 4WD hire** *Access Four Wheel Drive rentals*, 220 Pacific Highway, Crows Nest (☎922 6833); *All Hours Campervan hire*, 1b Hughes St, Potts Point (☎368 1028), inexpensive; *Aussie Campervan Hire*, Epping Rd, Epping (☎868 4316, fax 868 4336), package deals for overseas visitors; *Australian Outback 4 Wheel Drive Hire Co.*, 184 Elizabeth St, next to the *Southern Cross Hotel* (☎281 9676); *Brits Australia*, 182 O'Riordan St, Mascot (☎667 0402 or 1800/331 454), campervans, 4WDs and camping gear, one-way to Melbourne, Adelaide, Perth, Brisbane, Cairns; *Daytona Rentals*, 170 Parramatta Rd, Ashfield (☎797 0166), 4WD from $70 per day; *Jay & Jay Campervan Rentals*, 94 Bryant St, Padstow (☎773 4349), campervans and motor-homes; *Koala Camper Rentals*, 16–18 Princes Highway, Arncliffe (☎599 3533 or 1800/99 8029), campervans and 4WDs, one-way deals; *Sunseeker Campervans*, 9 Wollongong Rd, Arncliffe (☎597 6155), one-way rental available to Adelaide, Alice Springs, Brisbane, Cairns, Darwin, Melbourne and Perth; *Sven Nilsson* (☎369 1988), fairly new campervans, cheap deals including insurance.

**Camping equipment** Kent Street in the city behind the Town Hall is nicknamed "adventure alley" for its preponderance of outdoor equipment stores; the most well known is *Paddy Pallin* at no. 507 (☎264 2685). Cheaper options include disposal shops such as *Boss Disposals*, 708 George St (☎211 1991) and *Mitchell King Disposals*, 323 & 327 Pitt (☎264 5440); *K-Mart* and hostel noticeboards.

**Canoeing** *Sydney Harbour Canoe Tours* (☎327 3628), sea kayaking in the harbour, lessons for beginners.

**Car rental** There are scores of car-rental firms in Sydney, and most of them seem to have a branch in Wiliam St, Darlinghurst, just below the Cross; the bigger ones are also at the airport. *Abel Rent-a-car* (☎008/777 656) one-way to Queensland available; *Airport Rent a Car*, 12 Princes Highway, Arncliffe (☎599 3000); *Ansa International*, 280 Pacific Highway, Lindfield (☎416 9054); *Avis*, branches include all airport terminals and 214 William St, Kings Cross (☎357 2000); *Bayswater*, 120 Darlinghurst Rd, Kings Cross (☎360 3622), low rates include insurance but limited km; *Budget*, several branches (☎13 2727) and at 93 William St, Kings Cross (☎339 8888); *CutPrice*, 16–18 Poplar St, Darlinghurst (☎281 3003), cheap; *Hertz*, airport and elsewhere (☎13 1918); *Kings Cross Rent-A-Car*, 169 William St, Kings Cross (☎361 0637), open daily, low rates but insurance extra; *Network*, many branches offering good value one-way rentals (free call ☎1800/077 977); *Omega*, 10 Paisley Rd, Croydon (☎747 4022), will deliver anywhere for rentals of more than a week, all brand new cars from $35 day at the airport; *Rent a Ruffy*, 48 Pittwater Rd, Manly (☎977 5777), cheap, older model cars; *Thrifty*, airport (☎669 6677) and elsewhere, including 75 William St, Kings Cross (☎380 5399).

**Cars – buying and selling** Before you start looking for wheels, pick up the NRMA's *Worry Free Guide to Buying a Car* from the NRMA Arcade, 161 Clarence St (☎13 2132). If you're a member of a motoring association overseas, you'll have reciprocal membership of the NRMA ($72 to join otherwise), which entitles you to a $98 inspection and appraisal of a potential purchase. The *Backpackers Car Market*, Kings Cross car park, Level 2, Ward Ave (☎358 5000 or fax 358 5811) is the only place where it's legal to resell your car. Dealers are barred, fees for sellers are set at $5 per day or $35 per week, and you have to show a pink slip (certificate of roadworthiness); inspections cost around $20 – call the car market for recommended mechanics. Many of the vehicles ready equipped with camping gear and other extras at good prices: get here early for the best choice. The guys will advise you and help with the paperwork, and they'll even oversee the exchanging of the contract to make sure everything's done properly, and arrange third-party property **insurance** (around $160 for 3 months, $315 for 12 months) – the NRMA is increasingly refusing to provide cover for overseas travellers. Another car market is held on Sundays (9.30am–4pm) at Flemington Market opposite Flemington Station, but is better for buying than selling: if you're trying to sell a vehicle that's travelled around Australia, particularly if the clock is past 200,000km, local buyers won't be interested; besides, fees for sellers are steep at $60 per day. There are also plenty of dealers around aimed at travellers, many of whom will buy back the vehicle at the end of your trip (see "Getting Around" in *Basics* for general advice). The best of these is *Travellers Auto Barn*, 177 William St, Kings Cross (☎360 1500, fax ☎360 1977), run by a widely travelled young Australian who employs a friendly bunch of mechanics. You can buy a car, drive it around for a few days, and if you find there's a problem you can bring it back and they'll fix it or give you your money back. Six- or twelve-month warranties ($180/$300) are available, and you can arrange a 40–50 per cent buy-back. Other reliable dealers include: *Auto Becker*, 16–20 Oxford St, Paddington (☎360 721, fax 337 4202); *Kiwi Car Company*, 774 Parramatta Rd, Lewisham 2049 (☎560 7000, fax 560 6331); and *TCC Travel Car*, Centre C, 1/ 573 Pittwater Rd, Brookvale 2100 (☎938 1129), for higher-range cars starting around the $7000 mark. Finally, if you know a fair bit about cars and want to go it alone, the *Weekly Trading Post* ($1.50), out every Thursday, has a big secondhand car section.

**Consulates** Embassies are all in Canberra (see p.166), and it's usually easier to call them, rather than going to the consulate. *British Consulate General*, Level 16, Gateway Building, 1 Macquarie St (☎247 7521 or 247 9731); *US Consulate*, corner Park and Castlereagh (☎261 9200).

**Cycling** The narrow maze of streets in Sydney's CBD and its traffic congestion plus the fair amount of hills about town mean that cycling has never been as popular here as in Melbourne or Adelaide with their flat wide streets, although more and more cycle lanes are beginning to appear. The *Roads and Traffic Authority* (☎923 7282) and *Bicycle NSW* (☎283 5200) have brochures listing routes in all suburbs, while the *Bicycle Institute of NSW* (☎212 5628) provides more general info.

**Disabled travellers** *Para Quad Association of NSW*, 33–35 Burlington Rd, Homebush (☎764 4166, fax 764 2391). *Barrier Free Travel*, 36 Wheatley St, North Bellingen, NSW 2452 (☎066/551 733) is a travel consultant service that can plan trips and give advice for a $50 fee; they also publish a useful guide to Sydney, available direct or from the NSW Tourism Commission. For taxis, try *Wheelchair Accessible Taxis* (☎339 0200) or *ABC* (☎897 4000).

**Diving** The waters around Sydney aren't the best, but there are opportunities: contact *Prodive Coogee*, Alfreda St, Coogee Bay (☎665 6334), or *Prodive Manly*, 17 Belgrave St, Manly (☎977 4355).

**Flat hunting and sharing** The best place to look for both rentals and flat-shares is Saturday's real-estate section of the *Sydney Morning Herald* or café noticeboards, especially in Newtown, Glebe and Bondi. It's difficult to get a room for less than $80 a week; most go for about $100 (rent is usually two weeks in advance, plus a bond of four weeks' rent). The best areas for good cheap flats are Bondi and around the universities in Glebe, Newtown and Randwick: check out the noticeboards at Sydney University and the University of NSW – particularly in November when overseas and country students going home for the summer might need temporary tenants. *Home Share Flatmates*, Suite 604, 6th Floor, 127 York St (☎261 3146) is a reliable agency that can help you find a flat-share; $50 gets you registration for eight weeks.

**Horse riding** *Centennial Park Horse Hire*, Showgrounds, Driver Ave, Moore Park (☎361 4513); *Glenworth Valley Pleasure Riding*, Peats Ridge (☎043/75 1120), 90km north of Sydney near Gosford – half- or whole-day rides, lessons available, free camping for customers.

**Hospitals** *Sydney Hospital*, Macquarie St (☎228 2111); *Royal North Shore Hospital*, Pacific Highway, St Leonards (☎438 7111).

**Immigration** *Department of Immigration, Local Government and Ethnic Affairs*, 190 George St (☎258 4555).

**Left luggage** The cloakroom at Town Hall Station is open Mon–Sat 9am–4.40pm, $1.50 per 24hr; lockers at the airport and *Sydney Coach Terminal*, both $4 per 24hr.

**Markets** The two best are the Paddington Market on Saturdays and the more downbeat weekend market on Glebe Point Rd (see p.89 and p.85, respectively). The Balmain Markets (Sat 7.30am–4pm) at St Andrews Church, Darling St, Balmain is similar to Glebe in atmosphere. The Rocks Market (Sat & Sun 10am–4pm), George St behind the *Earth Exchange*, is more touristy but worth a look, while Paddy's Markets (Sat & Sun 9am–4pm) sell large quantities of bargain-basement clothes and toys, plus fruit and veg.

**Medical centres** *Mediservice Clinic*, 822 George St, Broadway (☎212 2733), general practitioners open daily, appointment not necessary; *Skin Cancer Clinic*, 3rd floor, 468 George St (☎264 2155); *Sydney Sexual Health Centre*, Nightingale Wing, Sydney Hospital, Macquarie St (☎223 7066), free tests, counselling and condoms; *Travellers Medical and Vaccination Centre*, 7th floor, 428 George St (☎221 7133; recorded info ☎221 4799).

**Motorbikes** *Maverick Motorcycles*, 133 Parramatta Rd, Homebush (☎746 2005) specialize in selling and exchanging travellers' motorbikes – free helmet with every one; also swaps for cars.

**Newspapers** There are two local daily papers: the very readable morning broadsheet *Sydney Morning Herald* (Mon–Sat) and the tabloid *Telegraph Mirror* (four editions daily). Sunday papers are limited to tabloids: the decent *Sun Herald* or the less appealing *Sunday Telegraph*.

**NRMA** 151 Clarence St (☎260 9222). Road maps of NSW and other states, a useful map of Sydney and other cities, comprehensive accommodation directories and lots more information, much of it free to members of associated organizations. There's also a handy free accommodation booking service (Mon–Fri 9am–5pm; ☎1800/13 1122).

**Parks and wildlife info** *NPWS*, Cadman's Cottage, 110 George St, The Rocks (☎247 8861) has details on all National Parks in NSW and arranges camping permits; *Wilderness Society*, shop at 92 Liverpool St (☎267 7525), headquarters at 1a James Lane (☎267 7929) organizes bushwalks near Sydney; *Department of Conservation and Land Management*, 33 Bridge St (☎228 6111) provides information and detailed bushwalking maps of NSW.

**Pharmacy** *Blake's Pharmacy*, 28 Darlinghurst Rd, Kings Cross (☎358 6712) Daily 9am–midnight.

**Police** Headquarters at 14 College St (☎2 0966); emergency ☎000.

**Post office** General Post Office, 159–171 Pitt St; poste restante (c/- Sydney GPO, Sydney 2000, NSW), counter open Mon–Fri 8.15am–5.30pm, Sat 8.30am–noon (☎230 7033).

**Public holidays** Sydneysiders like days off, and in addition to the Australia-wide public holidays, the following are celebrated only in NSW: *Bank Holiday* – first Mon in Aug; *Labour Day* – first Mon in Oct; *Queen's Birthday* – first Mon in June.

**Rape Crisis Centre** ☎819 6565 or 819 7842, outside Sydney area, free call ☎1800/424 017.

**Sailing** *Aristocrat* (☎018/22 4310) catamaran trips; *Northside Sailing School*, Spit Bridge (☎369 3972), boats to rent and courses; *Scotland Island Sailing School* (☎9999 3954), sailing lessons on Pittwater from $80 per day.

**Seaplanes** *Sydney Harbour Seaplanes* (☎1800 803 558) provide a Hollywood-style service, with flights to Berowra (Fri–Sun; $50 one-way, $100 return) and other haunts of the rich and famous. For a group, a fifteen-minute scenic flight becomes more affordable at $150 for the whole plane, which seats seven.

**Shopping** Most stores are open Mon–Sat from 8.30am–5.30pm with Thurs and Fri late-night shopping until 9pm. Many of the larger shops and department stores in the city are open on Sun 10am–5pm as are shopping centres at tourist spots like Darling Harbour. Large supermarkets such as *Coles* stay open daily until about 10pm and there are plenty of 24hr *7-Eleven* convenience stores in the inner city and suburbs. Apart from its old arcades and department stores (see p.80), Sydney also has plenty of sparkling new shopping complexes where you can hunt down bargains without raising a sweat, among them the *Skygarden* (between Pitt and Castlereagh streets) and *Centrepoint*. For fashion, Oxford St in Paddington is the place, along with the Strand Arcade in the city, and some one-off finds in Crown St in Surry Hills/Darlinghurst; for cheaper styles and interesting junk, try King St in Newtown. See also *Markets*.

**Swimming pools** Most pools are outdoors and unheated, so the swimming season generally runs from the long weekend in October until Easter. The best, and open all year (covered in winter), is the heated *Sydney Olympic Pool,* 200 Miller St, North Sydney (Mon–Fri 6am–9pm Sat & Sun 7am–7pm; $2.60; ☎929 2309), an outdoor pool near the water's edge and almost under the harbour bridge, an easy walk from Milson's Point train station. Inner-city outdoor pools are at Victoria Park, City Rd (6am–7.15pm; $2; ☎660 4181), at Prince Alfred Park, Chalmers St, Surry Hills (Mon–Fri 6am–7pm, Sat–Sun 9am–5pm; $2; ☎319 7045) and the Andrew "Boy" Charlton in the Domain (see p.83). Consult the *Yellow Pages* for more in your area.

**Taxis** *ABC Radio Taxi* (☎897 4000); *De-Luxe Red and Yellow Cabs* (☎332 8888); *Legion Cabs* (☎289 9000); *Premier Radio Cabs* (☎897 4000); *RSL Radio Cabs* (☎581 1111);*Taxis Afloat* (harbour water taxis ☎955 3222); *Taxis Combined* (☎361 8222). The three major cab ranks are outside the *Regent Hotel*, George St, The Rocks; on Park St outside *Woolworths*, opposite the Town Hall; and at the Pitt St entrance to Central Station.

**Trains** All out-of-town trains depart from the country trains terminal of Central Station. Information and booking 6.30am–10pm (☎217 8812, free call within NSW ☎1800/04 3126). There are *Countrylink Travel Centres* in the city at Transport House, 11 York St (Mon–Fri 8.30am–5.30pm), in the Queen Victoria Building Arcade at Town Hall Station on George St (Mon–Sat 8.30am–8.30pm) and at Circular Quay (Mon–Sat 8.30am–8.30pm). Interstate trains should be booked as early as possible, especially the *Indian Pacific* and Brisbane–Cairns trains. City Rail information line open until 10pm on ☎13 1500.

**Travel agencies** *Backpackers Travel Centre*, Shop 33, Imperial Arcade, Pitt St (☎232 5166); *Flight Centre*, several locations including 52 Martin Place (☎235 0166) and 82 Elizabeth St (☎235 3522), cheap domestic and international air tickets; *STA*, many branches, including 732 Harris St, Ultimo (☎281 9866) and 9 Oxford St, Paddington (☎360 1822), international and domestic flights, transport, tours and accommodation within Australia; *YHA Travel*, 422 Kent St, behind the Town Hall (☎261 1111) comprehensive domestic and international travel: flight, bus and train tickets, tours and accommodation, travel guides and YHA membership – also good noticeboard; *Let's Travel Australia*, 165 Victoria St, Kings Cross (☎358 2295). For details of tours from Sydney, see p.122.

**Water sports** *Rose Bay Windsurfer School* at 1 Vickery Ave (☎371 7036) rents out catamarans ($25 first hour, $15 thereafter), windsurfers ($15 per hour), and motorboats ($40 for the first two hours, $10 for each subsequent hour, plus charge for petrol; no boat licence required, but you must be over 16).

**Wine** *Australian Wine Centre*, at the junction of George and Alfred streets in Circular Quay (☎247 2755), sells more than 1000 wines from over 300 wineries around Australia – a great opportunity to taste a few. Mon–Sat 9.30am–6pm, Sun 10am–4pm.

**Women** The big event is the *Reclaim the Night* march in late November (☎557 1461 for details). *NSW Women's Information and Referral Service* Mon–Fri 9am–5pm (☎1800/817 227); contact for info on women's organizations and referrals. *The Women's Library*, 73 Garden St, Alexandria (☎319 0529). *Women's Healing Centre Glebe*, 263 Pyrmont Bridge Rd, Glebe (☎660 4316). *Everywoman's Health Centre*, 164 Flood St, Leichhardt (☎569 9266 or 569 9522) – all doctors and staff are women; general consultations, contraceptive and pregnancy counselling, abortion access and advice.

**Work** If you have a working holiday visa, you shouldn't have too much trouble finding some sort of work in Sydney, especially in the hospitality industry over the busy summer months, and in shops during the lead-up to Christmas. The *Commonwealth Employment Service (CES)* has a hospitality, retail and travel staffing office on the first floor of 303 Pitt St (☎267 5099), or try *Troy's*, a private agency (☎389 0155). Otherwise, scour hostel noticeboards and the *Sydney Morning Herald*: Saturday's issue is the best, followed by Monday's and Wednesday's; copies are available from about 11pm the night before outside the *Oxford Hotel* on Oxford St, Darlinghurst or on Darlinghurst Rd, Kings Cross. If you have some office or professional skills, there are plenty of temp agencies that are more than keen to take on travellers: flick through the *Yellow Pages*. For a whole range of work, *Manpower* is a good bet (☎231 4844); you could also try the casual work agency of the *CES* at 10 Quay St, Ultimo (☎201 1166).

**YHA New South Wales**, 422 Kent St, behind the Town Hall (☎261 1111). Membership and travel centre; Mon–Fri 9am–5pm, Thurs until 6pm, Sat 9am–noon.

# AROUND SYDNEY

If life in the fast lane is taking its toll, Sydney's residents can easily get away from it all. Right on their doorstep, golden beaches and magnificent National Parks beckon, interwoven with intricate waterways. Everything below can be done as a day-trip from the city, although some deserve an overnight stay to explore more fully. See the box on pp.122–123 for some of the huge variety of tours on offer.

   **North** of Sydney the Hawkesbury River flows into the jagged jaws of the aptly named **Broken Bay**, which streaks across the map like a bolt of lightning. The entire area is surrounded by bush, with the huge spaces of the **Ku-Ring-Gai Chase National Park** in the south and the **Brisbane Waters National Park** in the north.

Unless otherwise specified, all phone numbers in this chapter are in the ☎02 code region.

Beyond Broken Bay, the **Central Coast** between Gosford and Newcastle is an ideal spot for a bit of fishing, sailing and lazing around. **Newcastle** is more attractive than its reputation as a coal and steel city might suggest, but not somewhere you'd go out of your way to visit. Immediately beyond, however, are the bountiful vineyards of the **Hunter Valley**, which make a great day out, with visits to wineries interspersed with some gentle driving on country roads.

To the **West**, you escape suburbia to emerge at the foot of the beautiful **Blue Mountains**, where the scenic Hawkesbury-Nepean river valley is home to historic rural towns like **Richmond** and **Windsor**.

Heading **south**, the **Royal National Park** is an hour's drive away, while on the coast beyond are a string of laidback small towns – Waterfall, Stanwell Park, Wombarra – with beautiful, unspoilt beaches. The industrial city of **Wollongong** and neighbouring **Port Kembla** are impressively located between the Illawarra Escarpment and the sea, but of paltry interest to visitors, although more interesting spots cluster around. Inland, the **Southern Highlands** are covered with yet more national parks, punctuated by pleasing little towns like **Bundanoon** and **Berrima**.

# North

The **Hawkesbury River** widens and slows as it approaches the South Pacific, joining Berowra Creek, Cowan Creek, Pittwater and Brisbane Water in the system of flooded valleys that form **Broken Bay**. The bay and its surrounding inlets are a haven for anglers, sailors and windsurfers, while the surrounding bushland is virtually untouched. Three major national parks surround the Hawkesbury River: **Ku-Ring-Gai Chase** in the south, **Brisbane Waters** facing it across the bay, and **Dharug**, inland to the west.

The **Pacific Highway** up here, partly supplanted by the Sydney–Newcastle Freeway, is fast and efficient, though not particularly attractive until you're approaching Ku-Ring-Gai Chase; if you want to detour into the park or towards Brooklyn, don't take the Freeway. The **rail** lines follow the road almost as far as Broken Bay, before they take a scenic diversion through Brooklyn and Brisbane Waters to Woy Woy and Gosford.

## Ku-Ring-Gai Chase National Park

**Ku-Ring-Gai Chase** is much the best known of the national parks and, with the Pacific Highway running all the way up one side, also the easiest to get to. The bushland scenery is crisscrossed by walking tracks, which you can explore to seek out Aboriginal rock paintings, or just to get away from it all and see the forest and its wildlife. Only 24km from the city centre, the huge park's unspoilt beauty is enhanced by the presence of water on three sides: the Hawkesbury, its inlet Cowan Creek, and the expanse of **Pittwater**, an inlet of Broken Bay. From Palm Beach, you can take a boat cruise (see p.97) through all these waters to the park's most popular picnic spot at **Bobbin Head**. There are four road entrances to the park ($7.50 entrance fee for cars); without your own transport, the best way to get here are the ferries to the Pittwater side, or by train to Turramurra Station and then a private *Hornsby Bus* #577 (☎457 8888) to the Bobbin Head road entrance; some buses continue down to Bobbin Head itself.

At the **Kalkari Visitor Centre** (daily 9am–5pm), on the Ku-Ring-Gai Chase Road, you can watch videos about the area's Aboriginal heritage, and wildlife you might encounter, pick up information about walks in the park, or take a volunteer-guided walk.

## Waratah Park and Skippy

One of Sydney's oldest wildlife reserves, **Waratah Park** (daily 9am–5pm; $11.90, children $5.90; koala petting hourly 11am–4pm & 4.30pm), sits in the middle of this stunning scenery on Namba Road, off Mona Vale Road. Waratah is famous above all as home of *Skippy, the Bush Kangaroo*, television's first marsupial star: you can still see Skippy (or at least his fifth- or sixth-generation descendant) and visit the Ranger Station where most of the filming was done. You can get here by train to Chatswood (North Shore Line), and then *Forest Coachlines* bus #284 (☎450 1236 for times).

## Pittwater

From West Head at the northeastern corner of Ku-Ring-Gai Chase, there are superb views across Pittwater to the Barrenjoey Lighthouse at Palm Beach (see p.97). The Garigal Aboriginal Heritage Walk (3.5-km circuit) heads from West Head Road to the Aboriginal rock engravings and hand art, the most accessible Aboriginal art site in the park. The only place to camp is *The Basin* (☎451 8124 for bookings) on Pittwater, reached via the *Palm Beach Ferry Service* from Palm Beach (☎918 2747 or 974 5235). Facilities at the site are minimal, with no hot showers or shops – you can buy milk and bread from the morning ferry, but bring everything else.

If you want to **stay** here in rather more comfort, the *YHA Hostel Pittwater* (☎9999 2196; ①, weekends ②; booking advised), at Halls Wharf, is one of NSW's most scenically sited: in a rambling old house surrounded by bush and with a verandah looking down onto the water, you can sit here and feed rainbow lorrikeets; sailing lessons can also be arranged. You must bring everything with you – the last food (and bottle) shop

---

### MORE CUDDLY KOALAS

If meeting Skippy and cuddling the koalas at Waratah is your kind of thing – and who could resist – there are several other hands-on wildlife experiences around Sydney you might like to try.

The **Koala Park Sanctuary** (daily 9am–5pm; adults $8.50, kids 4–14 $4.50, under 4s free; ☎875 2777 for information) was established as a safe haven for koalas in 1935, and has since opened its gates to many other Australian natives – wombats, possums, kangaroos and birds of all kinds. It's around 25km north of Sydney, not far from the Pacific Highway on Castle Hill Rd, West Pennant Hills; to get here on public transport take the train from Central Station to Pennant Hills and then bus #651 or #655 towards Glenorie (no service Sun), a journey of about an hour.

At **Featherdale Wildlife Park** (daily 9am–5pm; $8.50, kids 4–14 $4.25, under 4s free; ☎622 1705), cuddly koalas are the special attraction. Although they're generally placid, koalas have claws like Edward Scissorhands, so don't forget that wild koalas can turn nasty. Featherdale is at 217 Kildare Rd, Doonside, 30km west of Sydney off the Western Highway between Parramatta and Penrith; train to Blacktown Station (Emu Plains line) and then bus #725.

**Australia's Wonderland** is not far away, a huge family entertainment complex encompassing shows, giant waterslides, roller-coasters and the **Australian Wildlife Park**, whose "meet the animals" experience includes emus, goannas, saltwater crocodiles (from a discreet distance) and forest birds in simulated natural habitats, and is wildly popular with children. The complex is open daily 10am–5pm during school holidays, otherwise on weekends and public holidays only from; entry to the wildlife park costs $9.95 ($6.50 for kids), or $29.95 ($21.95 for kids) for the whole complex, including all rides and events (☎830 9100 for details). *Australia's Wonderland* is on Wallgrove Rd, Rooty Hill, again not far off the Western Highway approaching Penrith; take a train to Rooty Hill Station (on the Emu Plains line) and get a special *Busways* service (☎625 8900 for times) from outside the Commonwealth Bank. Alternatively, *Clipper Tours* (☎241 3983) offer a coach transfer and admission package for $39.95, kids $26.95.

is Church Point. There are two ways of getting here: take **bus** #186 from Wynyard Station to Church Point, and then a ferry across to the hostel (last at 6.30pm, earlier in winter; 24-hr service with *Pink Water Taxi* ☎018/23 8190). Alternatively, bus #190 from Wynyard runs up the coast to Newport, where a water taxi goes from the *Newport Hotel*.

# The Hawkesbury River

One of New South Wales' prettiest rivers, with much of its banks covered in bush and some interesting old settlements alongside, the **Hawkesbury River** begins in the Great Dividing Range and flows out to sea at Broken Bay. For information about the many National Parks along the river, contact the the NPWS in Sydney (☎247 8861) or at 370 Windsor Road in Richmond (☎045/88 5247). Short of chartering your own boat, the best way to explore the river system is to take a cruise (see box overleaf).

## Upstream: Wisemans Ferry

The first ferry across the Hawkesbury River was opened by Solomon Wiseman in 1827, some way inland at the spot now known as **WISEMANS FERRY**. The crossing forged an inland connection between Sydney and the Hunter Valley via the convict-built Great North Road. Unfortunately, travellers on this isolated route were easy prey for marauding bushrangers and it was largely abandoned for the longer but safer coastal route.

---

### TOURS FROM SYDNEY

**Tours** from Sydney span the range from a day spent staring out the window of a bus to a week's climbing in the mountains. We've listed a couple of regular bus-tour operators, but you'll almost certainly have a better time with one of the outfits who specialize in small-group tours, quite often with an emphasis on physical activities such as bushwalking, horse riding, white-water rafting or abseiling. In the summer and other school holidays, the NPWS organizes **activities for children**, such as guided walks and lectures, in some of the National Parks. Many hostels also organize their own trips – most often to the beach – which are usually fun and tremendously good value.

One-way tours can be the next best thing to driving yourself: small groups in minibuses travel from Sydney to Melbourne (for example), taking detours to attractions along the way that you'd never be able to reach on public transport.

**AAT Kings** (☎252 2788). One of the biggest operators, its bus tours cover city sights, wildlife parks, the Blue Mountains, Hawkesbury River and the Hunter Valley.

**Aussie Bush Discoveries** (☎637 6005, after hours ☎622 1557). Off-the-beaten-track four-wheel drive tours in the Blue Mountains, guided by an environmentalist; the idea is to go bush and avoid the crowds. Max 6 people per group, $79 per person.

**Australian Pacific** (☎252 2988). Commercial bus tours, visiting the main sights.

**CityRail** (☎217 8812, or free call ☎1800/04 3126). Day-trips by rail can be very good value, generally covering all transport and entry fees – the Hawkesbury River trip includes a cruise. Details and tickets from any *Countrylink* office or station.

**Manly In-Sight Tours** (☎9905 1350), or book through *Quayside Travel*, Manly Wharf (☎977 5296). Departing from Manly, $50 full-day tours (9am–7pm) on 16-seater minibuses to the Blue Mountains (includes a bushwalk and a visit to the Megalong Valley Farm) and the Hunter Valley (visiting five wineries); 10 percent discount for YHA/VIP members.

**Motorcycle Tours** (☎545 4321). Trips to anywhere you fancy around Sydney on Harley Davidsons; 2hr $100; full day $295.

Today it's a popular recreational spot for day-trippers – just a little over an hour from Sydney by car, and with access to the **Dharug National Park** over the river by a free 24-hour car ferry. Dharug's rugged sandstone cliffs and gullies shelter Aboriginal rock engravings which can only be visited on ranger-led trips during school holidays (☎043/244 911 for details); there's a **camping** area at Mill Creek (bookings essential for weekends and holiday periods, via Gosford NWPS ☎043/244 911). Open to walkers, cyclists and horse-riders but not fume-belching vehicles, the **Old Great North Road** was literally carved out of the rock by hundreds of convicts from 1829; you can camp en route at Ten Mile Hollow camping area. **Settlers Road**, another convict-built route, can be followed by car north of Wisemans Ferry to St Albans where you can partake of a cooling brew (or stay a while) at a pub built in 1836, the hewn sandstone *Settlers Arms Inn* (☎045/68 2111; rooms ⑥).

Other **accommodation** for a river retreat includes the blue-painted *Wisemans Ferry Inn* on the Old Northern Road (☎045/66 4301; ⑤), an old inn some of which dates from 1817, although the rooms are actually motel-style out the back; *Del Rio Riverside Resort* (☎045/66 4330; vans ⑤), in Webbs Creek across the Webbs Creek ferry, 3km south of Wisemans Ferry, is a campground with a bistro, swimming pool, tennis court and golf course – they also arrange cruises on the Hawkesbury. Better still, across the orginal ferry is *Rosevale Farm Resort*, 2km along Wisemans Ferry Road enroute to Gosford (☎045/66 4207; vans ③), with inexpensive camping in extensive bushland close to Dharug National Park. For considerably more luxury, check out houseboat rentals (see box overpage)

**Mount 'n Beach Safaris** (☎958 6451). South coast tours around Jervis Bay and Seven Mile Beach – swimming, visiting Aboriginal sites and horse riding, staying overnight at the *Berri Pub*. Also Blue Mountains 4WD day tours. Prices around $95 one day, $225 two days.

**Oz-Trek** (☎360 3444). Active full-day tours to the Blue Mountains (8am–7pm; $43), with a choice of three bushwalks (30min–1hr 30min); also abseiling and Jenolan Caves trips.

**Wonderbus** (bookings at YHA office ☎261 1111, or via YHA hostels). Good-value tours to the Blue Mountains, including dusk wildlife-watching and a satisfying bushwalk. Day-tour about $38; you can also opt to stay in Katoomba for a few days and return on another service. **White Water Connections** (☎9905 9314 or 9989 8400). Day-trips include whitewater rafting on the Shoalhaven River, abseiling at Diamond Bay in Vaucluse, canyoning in the Blue Mountains; all around $119.

**One-way tours**

**Ando's Outback Adventures** (☎02/559 2901). Seven-day tour from Sydney to Byron Bay, with a detour via Lightning Ridge in northwest NSW. Visits along the way include the Warrumbungles National Park, sheep stations, cotton farms and old mine workings. About $400, everything included; tours run two or three times a month; book well in advance.

**North Coast Safaris** (☎1800/63 4951). Sydney to Byron Bay five-day surfing trip includes gear, lessons, camping, meals and return trip to Sydney any Sunday. Departs Mondays; $249.

**Straycat** (☎1800/80 0840 or 03/48 1299). The recommended *High Country Adventure Tour* runs once or twice weekly between Sydney and Melbourne – via Yarrangobilly Caves, Canberra, Namagdi National Park, Corryong, Beechworth, Mansfield, Alexandra and the magnificent forest of the Black Spur near Healesville. The bus seats 20 people, and the trip costs about $139 including meals and entrace fees but excluding accommodation.

**True Blue Tours** (☎03/9650 4108). Sydney to Melbourne (and vice versa) in three days along the coastal Princes Highway, with detours to beaches and wineries. Departures from Sydney every Thursday, $130. Accommodation in hostels and country pubs extra.

## EXPLORING THE HAWKESBURY RIVER SYSTEM

### CRUISES

**Brooklyn**, just above the western mass of Ku-Ring-Gai Chase National Park, is the home of *Brooklyn Ferries* (☎9985 7566). Their *River Boat Mail Run* still takes letters as well as tourists up and down the river, departing from Ferry Wharf on Dangan Road (Mon–Fri 9.30am, connecting with 8.16am train from Sydney and 8.17am from Gosford; Wed & Fri 1.30pm; 4hr; around $20, or good-value combined train-boat ticket; booking essential). *Brooklyn Ferries* also run down Berowra Creek to Berowra Waters during school holidays (Mon, Tues, Thurs & Sun 11am; 5hr; $20) and operate a daily ferry service to Patonga at the edge of Brisbane Waters National Park (Mon–Thurs 1.30pm & Sun 11am & 1.30pm, additional services Jan–March Sat 11am & 1.30pm; $5 one-way, $10 return, bikes $1).

**Gosford** Public Wharf is the starting point for the *MV Lady Kendall* (☎043/23 2974 for details; bookings essential), which cruises both Brisbane Water and Broken Bay (Sat–Wed, daily during school and public holidays, 10.15am & 1pm).

**Windsor** Cruises on the *Windsor Princess* (☎045/33 3822).

**Woy Woy** is also a port of call for the *MV Lady Kendall* (see above) at 10.35am and 12.10pm.

### HOUSEBOAT RENTALS

The **NSW Travel Centre** in Sydney (☎231 4444) has details of operators such as: *Ripples Houseboat Hire*, 31 Brooklyn Rd, **BROOKLYN** (☎9985 7333), whose houseboats sleep up to six people from around $300 a day or $900 a week, and *Able Hawkesbury River Houseboats*, in **WISEMANS FERRY**, on River Road (☎045/66 4299), with prices starting around $600 per week for six to ten people; BYO linen. Bargain rates are sometimes on offer at quieter times.

## The Upper Hawkesbury: Windsor and Richmond

Just a few kilometres apart, and some 50km inland from Sydney, Windsor and Richmond are two of five towns founded by Governor Macquarie in the early nineteenth century to capitalize on the fertile, well-watered soil of the upper Hawkesbury River area. **WINDSOR** is probably the best preserved of all the historical towns in the riverlands, with a lively centre of narrow streets, big old pubs and numerous old colonial buildings. The **Hawkesbury River Museum and Tourist Information Centre** on Thompson Square (daily 10am–4pm; ☎045/77 2310; museum $2.50) is a good place to start exploring, and the **Macquarie Arms Hotel**, claimed to be the oldest in Australia, is a good place to end with a cool beer. From Windsor, Putty Road (route 69) heads north through beautiful forest country, along the eastern edge of the Wollemi National Park, to Singleton in the Hunter Valley.

**RICHMOND**'s attractions include an old graveyard and settlers' dwellings, plus its unspoilt riverside setting. Cinema buffs could take in a film at *The Regent*, a classic, beautifully decorated old theatre that's still operating. Heading on, the Bells Line of Road (route 40), from Richmond to the Blue Mountains via Kurrajong, the route lined with fruit stalls, is a great scenic drive. There's a wonderful view of the Upper Hawkesbury Valley from the lookout point at Kurrajong Heights, on the edge of the Blue Mountains, and you can take it all in from the *Balcony View Café*.

You can take a **train** to Windsor and Richmond from Central via Blacktown.

## The Central Coast

The shoreline between Broken Bay and Newcastle is characterized by large "coastal lakes" – saltwater lagoons almost entirely enclosed, but connected to the ocean by small waterways. The northernmost, **Lake Macquarie**, is the biggest saltwater lake in

New South Wales. People in a hurry can bypass the Central Coast altogether on the Sydney–Newcastle Freeway, which runs some way inland, but to see a bit more of the coastal scenery and the lakes stick to the old Pacific Highway. A further detour would take you from Gosford to **Terrigal** and then right along the narrow coastal strip via **The Entrance** and **Budgewoi** to rejoin the Pacific Highway at **Elizabeth Bay**. The fit and intrepid can get here by bike: from Manly, head up the northern beaches, hop on the *Palm Beach Ferry Service* (☎918 2747) to Patonga, then continue up through Woy Woy and Gosford to the coast. Otherwise you can take a train to Gosford and from there *Peninsula Bus Lines* (☎043/24 1255 or 62 1188) can get you to Terrigal, Avoca and Old Sydney Town.

## Gosford and around

To get anywhere on the central coast, you need to go through **GOSFORD**, perched on the north shore of Brisbane Water, and just about in commuting distance of Sydney; the latter has resulted in uncontrolled residential sprawl along much of the Central Coast, which has put a great strain on the once unspoilt lakes. Although there's plenty of accommodation in and around Gosford – details from the **Gosford City Tourist Association**, near the railway station at 200 Mann Street (☎043/25 2835) – there's not much incentive to stay. The main reason to come is that it's the gateway to two excellent national parks and a re-invention of Sydney's past at *Old Sydney Town*.

**Brisbane Waters National Park**, immediately south, holds the **Bulgandry Aboriginal engravings**, which are of a style unique to the Sydney region, with figurative outlines scratched boldly into sandstone. The site, no longer frequented by the Guringgai people whose territory ranged south as far as Sydney Harbour and north to Lake Macquarie, is 7km southwest of Gosford off the Woy Woy Road. Tiny **Bouddi National Park** is 20km southeast along the coast, at the northern mouth of Broken Bay and is a great spot for bushwalking with camping facilities at Putty Beach, Little Beach and Tallow Beach: book through the NPWS office at 207 Albury Street, Gosford (☎043/244 9110), which also has information on both parks.

**Old Sydney Town** (Wed–Sun and public holidays 10am–4pm, daily during school holidays; $15), southwest of Gosford just off the Pacific Highway, is a reconstruction of Sydney in the early years of the penal settlement. "Everyday" scenes, such as a convict's escape or a flogging, are acted out – quite good fun, if you like that sort of thing – and a token gesture towards Aboriginal culture has been made in the form of *Koorie Trading Post*, selling arts, crafts and souvenirs. Most tour buses include Old Sydney Town in their itineraries, or there's a package deal by train from Sydney Central Station ($26 buys you a ticket on the 8.15am from Central Station via Gosford and entry to the park). The place has also struck a chord with its evening **Woolshed Dances**; the Saturday-night events include three-course Aussie tucker meals and a bush band with a bar from 6.30pm (bookings essential on ☎043/40 1016). Catch *Peninsula Bus Lines* #33 or #38 to Old Sydney Town from Gosford.

## Terrigal, Avoca Beach and The Entrance

Southeast of Gosford, **TERRIGAL** is one of the most enjoyable spots on the central coast, a family-orientated beach resort with foodie and New Age inclinations. **Terrigal Visitors Centre** on Terrigal Way (daily 9am–5pm; ☎043/85 4430) is a good source of information on the whole region, and does free **accommodation** bookings. If you're after a holiday unit (around $350–950 weekly, depending on season and number of rooms), contact *Hunters Real Estate*, 104 Terrigal Esplanade (☎043/84 1444). The deluxe *Terrigal Beach Backpackers Lodge*, at 10 Campbell Crescent (☎043/85 3330; rooms ③, dorms ①), is only one minute's walk from the beach. Run by a friendly, well-travelled Canadian, it has a pleasant dining room with wooden tables and floors which opens onto the garden and barbecue area with outside tables with umbrellas; there's also a big modern kitchen, handicapped facilities, and bright clean bathrooms. There are lots of good **cafés**: *Aromas on Church Street* has excellent espresso and cakes; while on the Esplanade *Cafe Skillion* does vegetarian dishes, rock oysters and grills from $7, and the *Terrigal Hotel* bistro serves very good value meals daily. Potential activities include messing around on catamarans and **sailboards** rented from *Haven Sailing* (☎015/258 727), in front of the sailing club, or contacting *Yvonne's Learn to Surf* (☎043/85 3138) for board rental and lessons at local beaches.

Six kilometres to the south, and altogether quieter, **AVOCA BEACH** is popular with surfers, a large, crescent-shaped and sandy beach between two headlands with its own surf lifesaving club – and a safe children's rock pool. Its pleasant smalltown atmosphere is helped by the cute *Avoca Beach Theatre* on Avoca Drive (☎043/82 2156; bargain tickets Tues all day and Wed matinee), a surviving early-Fifties cinema that has changed little, with old movie stills in the foyer. **Accommodation** is limited to a couple of motels and one caravan park, *The Palms* on 160 The Round Drive (☎043/82 1227; cabins ⑥); the thing here is to rent holiday units – call *George Brand Real Estate* (☎043/821 311) for stacks of listings; weekly rental rates start at $350. A good place to hang out on the beachfront is the slightly alternative *Beachfront Café* (daily 10am–late; ☎043/82 1622), with suitably fishy dishes for around $9 at lunchtime and a more expensive evening menu, including Tuesday-night pasta specials, or just coffee and cake anytime. The café also lays on weekend entertainment, ranging from bands to poetry readings.

*Peninsula Bus Lines* serve these resorts: take #80, #81 or #82 from Gosford for Terrigal, and #79 for Avoca; the #81 also links Terrigal and Avoca Beach.

Further north, Tuggerah Lake and Munmorah Lake meet the sea at **THE ENTRANCE**, a beautiful spot with water, water everywhere as far as the eye can see. Naturally it's a favourite fishing spot, both with anglers – and swarms of **pelicans** hopeful of dusk fish-feeds. The beaches and lakes along the coast from here to Newcastle are crowded with caravan parks and motels, and with places offering the opportunity to fish, windsurf, sail or water-ski: although less attractive than places furher north, they make a great day-trip or weekend escape from Sydney. The **Entrance Visitors Centre**, Marine Parade (daily 9am–5pm; ☎043/32 9282) can help with accommodation.

## Newcastle

**NEWCASTLE** is a blue-collar town enlivened by its waterside location, and with an alternative feel provided by a big dose of surf culture and a large student community. New South Wales' second city, with a population of around a quarter of a million, it suffers from comparison with nearby Sydney and from denigration by Sydneysiders who may never have set foot here, when in fact it has plenty going for it in its own right. It is also basking in the glow of a much-needed facelift: years of accumulated soot has been scraped off its stately buildings, riverside gardens have been created in front of the city centre, and an old wharf has been converted into a waterside entertainment venue. The BHP steelworks, the docks and the slag heaps still loom in the background but, for a major industrial and port city, Newcastle is surprisingly attractive. You might not choose to spend your entire holiday here, but it can be a good base for excursions, particularly to the nearby Hunter Valley (see p.131); the surf beaches are wonderful, and there are some more sheltered sandy beaches around the rocky promontory at the mouth of the Hunter.

Newcastle was founded in 1804 for convicts too hard even for Sydney to cope with, but the river is the real reason for the city's existence. Down it came coal from the fields of the Hunter Valley, to be exported around the country and indeed around the world; coal exports are still one of the main sources of income, and the proximity of the mines encouraged the establishment of other heavy industries. In recent years,

Newcastle made world headlines two days after Christmas in 1989 when Australia's worst earthquake struck the area, killing twelve people and destroying several buildings; rebuilding has been imaginative, including colourful mosaics in the pavement at Beaumont Street in Hamilton, one of the hardest-hit areas.

## Arrival and information

If you're not driving, you'll arrive by rail or bus at Newcastle **train station**, right in the heart of the city on Scott Street. Heading west, Scott Street becomes Hunter Street after Market Street. Hunter is the city's main street, and its hub is the pedestrianized Hunter Street Mall, between Newcomen and Perkins streets, with its large department stores and shops. The extremely helpful **Newcastle Tourist Information** (Mon–Fri 9am–5pm, Sat & Sun 10am–3.30pm; ☎049/29 9299 or free call ☎1800/654 558) is at 92 Scott St, east of the station towards the beach; it also functions as a travel agency and you can buy tickets for all buses going up the coast from here. Disabled travellers can pick up a useful *Newcastle Mobility Map*.

## Accommodation

**Crown and Anchor Hotel**, corner of Hunter and Perkins streets (☎049/29 1027). Inexpensive and central hotel. ③.

**Irene Hall**, 27 Pacific St (☎049/29 3324). A combined YHA and nurses' home whose prime position close to the railway station – and, more importantly, the beach, compensates for the slightly institutional feel. Cafeteria for breakfasts and cheap meals. Rooms ③, dorms ①.

**Kent Hotel**, 59 Beaumont St, Hamilton (☎049/61 3303). A beautiful old hotel with basic singles and doubles – good value, if you don't mind the noise of the jazz downstairs. ③.

**Newcastle Backpackers**, 42 Denison St, 3km from city centre, bus #260 (☎049/69 3436). Homey place run by a friendly young family. Although it's some distance from the beach, the owner runs people down most days for free surfing lessons; surfboard rental $3. Rooms ③, dorms ①.

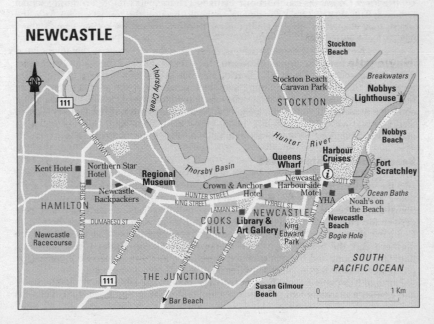

**Newcastle Harbourside Motel**, 107 Scott St (☎049/26 3244). Convenient motel near the train station. ④.

**Noah's on the Beach**, corner of Shortland Esplanade and Zaara St (☎049/29 5181). Most rooms in this upmarket, modern motel have sea views, and there's room service. ⑦.

**Northern Star Hotel**, 112 Beaumont St, Hamilton (☎049/61 1087). With a great position on this restaurant- and café-lined street northwest of the centre, all rooms here are en suite, spacious, clean and have fridges, TV, tea and coffee, and ceiling fans. ⑤.

**Stockton Beach Caravan Park**, Stockton Beach (☎049/28 1393). Picturesquely sited on an extensive beach, and only a ferry ride from the centre (but a much longer car ride). Vans ④–⑤.

**Travellers Motor Village**, 295 Maitland Road, Mayfield West (☎049/68 1394). Campsite with units for rent, about 7km northwest of the centre. Cabins ④, on-site vans ③.

## The city

Newcastle has whole streetscapes of beautiful **Victorian terraces** that would put Sydney's to shame – pick up a free *Newcastle City of Heritage and Enterprise* map from the tourist office to guide you around some of the old buildings. Close to Newcastle Beach, some handsome terraces are located on Stevenson Place: check out the 1900 Pembridge Terrace and the 1906 Belmore Terrace, which can be enjoyably viewed from the picnic area in **Newcastle Harbour Foreshore Park**. A couple of buildings here show the trend for Newcastle's wealth of disused public architecture: on one corner of the park stands the beautiful Italianate brick **Customs House**, crowned by its watchtower which now gazes upon the wooden two-storey **Paymasters House**, where you can contemplate the water over a coffee on its fine verandah.

The recently restored **Queens Wharf** sits on the Hunter River, a landmark with its distinctive observation tower. Linked to the city centre by an elevated walkway from Hunter Street Mall. The wharf boasts *The Brewery*, a popular, stylish waterfront drinking spot. A **ferry** goes from here to Stockton, with its caravan park and beach (Mon–Sat 5.15am–11pm or midnight, Sun 8.30am–8.30pm; $1.30 one-way, $2.60 return), while *Hunter River Cruises* operate **harbour cruises** (Thurs, plus Mon & Fri during school holidays; $12; ☎049/82 8352 for details, or book through the tourist office) from the wharf; they also cruise up the Hunter River to Morpeth and back (Sun 9am–5.30pm; $32.50, lunch included).

Besides Newcastle's watery attractions, there are a few other places that might interest. The **Newcastle Regional Museum**, 787 Hunter Street (Tues–Sun 10am–5pm; daily during school holidays; $3), housed in what began as a brewery in the 1870s, focuses on the history of the mining and steel industries of the area; it's appropriate then that the *Supernova* hands-on science centre is attached, much the best thing about the museum. If you're at a loose end, **Newcastle Regional Art Gallery**, Laman Street near Civic Park (Mon–Fri 10am–5pm, Sat 1.30pm–5pm, Sun 2–5pm; free) usually has an interesting temporary exhibition besides its permanent display.

## Beaches and wildlife reserves

The city centre sits on a narrow length of land between the Hunter River to the west and the Pacific Ocean to the east, so Newcastle's pleasantly low-key beaches are a major attraction. **Newcastle Beach**, only a few hundred metres from the city on Shortland Esplanade, has patrolled swimming between flags, a sandy saltwater pool perfect for children, shaded picnic tables, and good surfing at its southern end. Container ships on the horizon manage to look interesting, rather than unlovely. At the northern end, the beautifully painted art-deco style **Ocean Baths** (daily 6am–2pm, until 6pm in spring and 10pm in summer; closed in winter; free, supervised) houses the changing pavilions for the huge saltwater pool, with its own diving board.

North of Newcastle Beach, **Fort Scratchley**, built in the 1880s, overlooks the water and houses a maritime and military museum (Mon, Sat & Sun noon–4pm, Tues–Fri

9am–5pm but check on ☎049/29 2588 as it's volunteer-run; free). Beyond the fort is the long, uncrowded stretch of **Nobbys Beach**, with another lovely old beach pavilion. A walkway leads to Nobbys Head, with its nineteenth-century lighthouse and views over the river to the port and the city. You can continue your walk or cycle along the convict-built southern breakwater, from where you can watch the manoeuvrings of big ships being guided out to sea by red and yellow pilot boats; sometimes you'll even see people snorkelling and spearfishing off the rocks here.

Following Shortland Esplanade south from Newcastle Beach, the huge expanse of King Edward Park gives a nice feel to this rocky stretch of waterfront with good walking and cliff views. One section of the rock ledge holds Australia's first manmade ocean pool, the **Bogey Hole**. Chiselled out of the rock by convicts in the early nineteenth century for the Military Commandant's personal bathing pleasure, it's still a fine spot for a swim. The cliffs are momentarily intercepted by **Susan Gilmore Beach** – secluded enough to indulge in some **nude bathing**. **Bar Beach** follows around the rocks, and it's a popular surfing spot, floodlit at night. More rocks separate it from the longer **Merewether Beach** next door, the southern end of which has a fabulous ocean baths, great for salty laps, and a separate children's pool. The *Merewether Hotel*, overlooking the beach, is especially good for a drink on a summer Sunday.

**Blackbutt Reserve** is a large slab of bushland – 182 hectares – in the middle of Newcastle suburbia southwest of the city (daily 9am–5pm; free; train to Kotara or bus #261 via Kotara) with four valleys, including a remnant of rainforest, and several walking tracks to explore them. Northeast of the city, the **Wetlands Centre**, Sandgate Road, Shortland (daily 9am–5pm; $2 donation; train from Newcaste to Sandgate, then a 10-min walk) is situated on the wetlands of Hexham Swamp by Ironbark Creek, and is home to a mass of birdlife; there are walking and cycling trails, and the more intrepid can hire canoes from the visitors' centre.

## Cafés and restaurants

The two streets to head for are: **Darby Street**, close to the city centre with a multicultural restaurant mix and some fairly hip cafés, and **Beaumont Street** in Hamilton, northeast of the city centre (take the train to Hamilton station or bus #260), with a concentration of Italian places, as well as Turkish, Lebanese, Dutch and Indian.

**Al Metro**, Darby St (☎049/264 798). French chef creates authentic and reasonably priced Gallic dishes – plus there's a great upstairs balcony to dine *al fresco*. Licensed.

**Al-Oi-Thai**, 1 Bolton St. Inexpensive Thai restaurant with $6 lunch specials. BYO.

**The Brewery**, 150 Wharf Road. Popular waterfront drinking hole with crowded bistro.

**Café Northern Star**, 106 Beaumont St, Hamilton. Basic surroundings, but good inexpensive pasta.

**Food Fare**, upstairs in the Hunter St Mall. Best place in the city centre, with a good range of food bars from Italian, Chinese, hot potatoes, kebabs – and mightily generous salad sandwiches at the *Oak Dairy Bar*.

**Gelato Dolomiti**, Beaumont St, Hamilton. Great homemade *gelati*, plus pasta and *focaccia* in this typically casual Italian café.

**Goldberg's**, opposite *Delany's*, Darby St. Airy café with burnt orange ceilings and polished wooden floors; the emphasis is on coffee, supplemented by snacks and inexpensive rolls. 8am–midnight.

**Italian Centre Restaurant**, 46 Beaumont St, Hamilton (☎049/61 4656). Upstairs in the Italian community centre, the food has to be good and authentic in this homey restaurant. Dinner only; licensed.

**Karltons**, 19 Scott St (☎049/29 2989). Close to Newcastle Beach, this casual BYO restaurant has a lunch blackboard menu from $7 and good coffee. Daily lunch and dinner.

**Little Swallows Cafe**, 54 Beaumont St, Hamilton (☎049/69 2135). Captures the earthy feel of a traditional trattoria, with suitably generous portions. The Abruzzese owner is adventurous with his recipes and has a free hand with the chilli. Closed Mon; BYO.

**Scusi**, 44 Beaumont St, Hamilton. Great little espresso bar well stocked with fashion mags to plunge into. Divine coffee – the best in town – and wonderful cakes.

**Splash**, Darby St. Freshly cooked takeaway seafood; tempura prawns and crumbed calamari are among the offerings; yummy combinations from $4.90.

**Taj Takeaway**, 19 Darby St. Quick and tasty Indian takeaway – and grocery.

**Taters**, 78 Darby St. Stuffed baked potatoes, with a variety of fillings from seafood to chilli con carne with nachos. Great salads too – and nothing over $5. Daily to 8pm.

**View Factory**, corner of Scott and Telford streets (☎049/29 4580). This brasserie/gallery near the waterfront is arty, airy and slick. The menu makes creative use of seafood and fine ingredients. Lunch Tues–Sun, dinner Tues–Sat; licensed.

**Vega Cafe**, 131 Darby St (☎049/26 3779). Ventures beyond the usual vegetarian clichés of veggie burgers to produce eclectic dishes.

## Drinking and nightlife

For listings, check out the **Gig Guide** in Wednesday's *Post*. During term time, the students of Newcastle University add a lot of life to the city, but at any time there is a thriving band scene. On Friday and Saturday nights, the city pubs on Hunter Street, parallel King Street and perpendicular Watt Street all have bands, many of them free.

**The Bar on the Hill**, Newcastle University campus at Callaghan (☎049/215 000). Hosts live bands; all welcome. Take bus #260.

**Beaches Hotel**, opposite Merewether Beach (☎049/63 1574). The only place to go on a Sunday night, with live bands.

**Delany Hotel**, 134 Darby St (☎049/29 1627). Stylish renovated pub popular with suits; piano player Tues–Thurs and Sat from 6pm.

**The Kent**, corner of Cleary and Beaumont streets, Hamilton (☎049/61 6597). Beautifully renovated old pub and jazz venue (Wed, Sat & Sun) with leadlighting. Busy every night, but with several refuges, including a wonderful plant-filled beer garden and a great bistro.

**Newcastle Workers Club,** corner of King and Union streets (☎049/26 2700). Big gigs by touring bands.

**Tattersalls Club**, Watt St near the train station (☎049/29 2367). Grunge favourite.

## Entertainment and culture

The area known as "the cultural precinct", near Civic Park on King, Hunter and Auckland streets, is the location for three refurbished art-deco venues; pick up a monthly *Calendar of Events* from the tourist office for details of what's on. The **Civic Theatre** (☎049/29 1977) hosts mainly big-budget musicals, complemented by drama at the intimate **Civic Playhouse** (☎049/26 2755) attached. At the **University Conservatorium of Music** in Auckland Street (☎049/29 4133), there are often free lunchtime concerts as well as evening performances, while the grand **City Hall** (☎049/29 9370) has occasional classical music events. *Poetry at the Pub* is held Monday nights at *Newcastle City Bowling Club*, Ordance St (☎049/67 5972 for details). Film buffs should head for the small *Lyrique Cinema*, Wolfe St, off Hunter St Mall (☎049/29 5019; bargain days Mon & Tues, $6), where there's usually a choice of three films showing in repertory – one arthouse and two mainstream.

## Listings

**Banking** *Commonwealth Bank*, Hunter St Mall has foreign exchange.

**Books** *Collected Works*, 29 Hunter St (☎049/29 5688) buys and sells secondhand books with an excellent range, particularly Australiana.

**Bike rental** *Newcastle Foreshore Bike Hire*, Harbourside Markets, corner of Wharf Rd and Merewether St (☎049/57 3676); weekends and school holidays 11am—4pm; $14 per hour.

**Car rental** *Ara* (☎049/62 2488); *Thrifty* (☎049/42 2266).

**Environment** *The Wilderness Society*, 59 Hunter St, opposite the post office.

**Post office** Newcastle GPO, Hunter St, NSW 2300; Mon–Fri 8am–5pm.

**Left luggage** The railway station has a cloak and luggage room; $1.50 per article. Mon–Fri 6am–8pm, Sat 8.30am–3.30pm, Sun 8am–7pm.

**Public transport** All bus timetables, information and tickets can be got from the tourist information centre on Scott St (☎049/29 9299). *Newcastle Bus and Ferry Services* (☎049/61 8933) has an information booth at the west end of Hunter Street Mall on the corner of Perkins St; single tickets can be bought on board (from $1.20). There is only one ferry service to Stockton. Two passenger train lines have several suburban stops, one heading southwest (towards Sydney), the other northeast (towards Maitland).

**Tours** *Hunter Vineyard Tours* (☎049/91 1659) are excellent and good value; see below for details.

**Train** Countrylink office at Newcastle Station, Mon–Fri 8.30am–5.30pm, Sat 8am–3pm.

# The Lower Hunter Valley

In Australia (and, increasingly, worldwide), the **Hunter Valley** is synonymous with fine wine. The first vines were planted 150 years ago, and are mainly of the two classic white-wine varieties of Semillon and Chardonnay, with Pinot Noir and Shiraz dominating the reds. In what seems a bizarre juxtaposition, this is also a very important coal-mining region: in the upper part of the valley especially (see p.210), the two often go hand-in-hand. By far the best-known area, however, is in the Lower Hunter Valley around the old country town of Cessnock. Even the town's gaol has its own vineyard and the prisoners produce wine and manage to win prizes. One of the appeals of the Hunter wine country is bush and farming feel of the place with the vast plantings of vineyards seemingly lost amongst bushland, forested ridges, red-soiled dirt tracks and paddocks with grazing cattle.

CESSNOCK itself is much the best place to base yourself if you plan to stay overnight, while most of the vineyards are clustered around nearby **POKOLBIN**. An excellent free fold-out map and brochure to pick up is *Hunter Valley Wine Country* which contains a complete list of the lower Hunter valley's wineries, accommodation and restaurants; confusingly, another booklet of the same name has lots of small detailed maps and more in-depth winery information. Pick them both up, together with maps and other advice, from the *NSW Travel Centre* in Sydney or the **Cessnock Visitors' Centre**, on Abedare Road (Mon–Fri 9am–5pm, Sat 9.30am–5pm, Sun 9.30am–3.30pm; ☎049/90 4477); they can also book accommodation. If you're going to tour the wineries, try and do so during the week; at weekends both the number of visitors and the prices go up. In February, when the place is flooded with wine-lovers enjoying the Dionysian delights of the **Hunter Valley Vintage Festival**, accommodation is impossible to find.

### Getting there and around

To get to Cessnock, catch a train to Maitland or Newcastle and then a bus to Cessnock with *Rover Motors* (☎049/90 1699); or *Batterhams Express* (☎049/90 5000 or free call 1800/04 3339) goes direct from Sydney via the Hunter Valley to Tamworth.

If you're without transport (there's no public transport to the wineries) – or don't want to unintentionally meander off-road after excessive wine-tasting – **vineyard tours** are a good option. *Hunter Vineyard Tours* (☎049/91 1659) have small-group bus tours visiting six well-chosen wineries over six hours, all offering tastings ($29, including pick-up from Newcastle, Maitland or Cessnock; YHA and VIP discounts). Pedal power is also popular: either **rent bikes** from *Grapemobile*, on the corner of McDonalds and Gilliards roads, Pokolbin (☎049/91 2339 or 98 7639; $25 per day, $15 half-day), or go on their **bicycle tour**, also taking in six wineries ($89, including mountain bikes, support bus, tour guide, morning tea and a restaurant lunch). Alternatively, *Hertz* **car rental** is at the NRMA Centre, 191 Wollombi Road, Cessnock (☎049/91 2500).

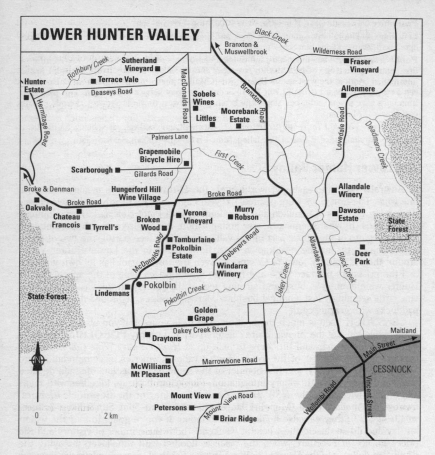

**LOWER HUNTER VALLEY**

Branxton & Muswellbrook

Black Creek

Wilderness Road

Fraser Vineyard

Rothbury Creek

Sutherland Vineyard

Terrace Vale

Hunter Estate

Deaseys Road

Hermitage Road

MacDonalds Road

Branxton Road

Allenmere

Lovedale Road

Deadmans Creek

Sobels Wines

Littles

Moorebank Estate

Palmers Lane

Grapemobile Bicycle Hire

First Creek

Scarborough

Gillards Road

Broke & Denman

Hungerford Hill Wine Village

Broke Road

Broke Road

Allandale Winery

Oakvale

Broke Road

Chateau Francois

Tyrrell's

Broken Wood

Verona Vineyard

Murry Robson

Dawson Estate

State Forest

McDonalds Road

Tamburlaine

Pokolbin Estate

Debeyers Road

Deer Park

Tullochs

Windarra Winery

Allandale Road

Black Creek

State Forest

Lindemans

● Pokolbin

Pokolbin Creek

Oakey Creek

Golden Grape

Oakey Creek Road

Maitland

Draytons

Marrowbone Road

Main Street

CESSNOCK

McWilliams Mt Pleasant

Mount View ■

Mount View Road

Petersons ■

Wollombi Road

Vincent Street

Briar Ridge

0          2 km

## Around Cessnock

Cessnock lies more or less due west of Newcastle, in an area of small creeks and tributaries of the Hunter. But even in the main valley of the Hunter, followed by the New England Highway as it heads up towards the mountains of the Great Dividing Range and the New England Plateau, the impression is overwhelmingly rural, with green meadows and pastures interspersed with cornfields, vegetable patches and, of course, vineyards. Old mansions and sleepy hamlets, dating back to colonial times, complete the seemingly idyllic pastoral scene. Yet nearby, coal is extracted from several enormous open-cast mines to feed Newcastle's power stations.

The area is dotted with interesting old country towns where even **MAITLAND** and Singleton, two of the main centres of the coal industry, boast historical buildings that help retain a beguilingly colonial flavour. Maitland, 25km northwest of Cessnock, is in fact a throughly historic place – an early convict foundation that in the nineteenth century became one of the most important towns in early Australia. There's a tourist information centre in King Edward Park right on the highway (☎049/33 2611), and in both towns, the old gaols have been converted into local history museums. Only six kilometres from Maitland, **Morpeth** is a picturesque river town that was an important Hunter Valley river port 150 years ago; today the old buildings house art galleries and craft shops.

**WOLLOMBI**, a historic homesteading settlement some 30km south of Cessnock, is the gateway to the Hunter Valley on the scenic inland route from Sydney, which involves leaving the freeway at Calga and heading north via Mangrove and Bucketty. The **Wollombi Tavern**, home of *Dr Jurd's Jungle Juice* (have a free taste and find out), makes a fine refreshment stop – sitting out on the wooden verandah looking over the creek to trees, fields and hills beyond is a real pleasure. Wollombi was once a ceremonial meeting place, and there are **Aboriginal rock carvings** and cave painting throughout the area, some of which can be visited on horseback through the *Wollombi Horse Riding Centre*, 4km past the *Wollombi Tavern* on the Singleton Road (☎049/98 3221; 1hr 30min–2hr; $30). Something quite different, halfway between Cessnock and Wollombi on the Wollombi Road is the **New Gokula Farm** (☎049/981 800), a Hare Krishna farming community which has a free Sunday vegetarian feast at noon; ask about staying in their guesthouse – a very peaceful spot flanked by bush-covered hills.

**Moving on** from the valley, it's an easy detour to **Barrington Tops National Park** (see p.184), north from Singleton or Maitland, or the **Chichester Dam**, slightly closer at hand in the same direction, surrounded by beautiful mountain and forest scenery, and inhabited by melodic bellbirds.

## Accommodation

Accommodation **prices** invariably rise on Friday and Saturday nights, as the Hunter is a popular weekender from Sydney. If you're going to be here at a weekend, or during the February vintage festival, advance **booking** is essential.

**Belford Country Cabins**, Hermitage Rd, Belford–Pokolbin (☎049/91 2777). Family-run, fully equipped wooden bungalows for up to 8 people. Great bushland location, small pool and playground. ⑤–⑥.

**Bellbird Hotel**, 388 Wollombi Rd, 5km from centre of Cessnock (☎049/90 1094). Great classic country pub circa 1908 with wide iron-lace verandah, onto which some rooms open. ④/Fri & Sat ⑤.

**Black Opal Hotel**, 216 Vincent St, Cessnock (☎049/90 1070). Pub accommodation that feels upmarket but is actually inexpensive. ③/Fri & Sat ④.

**Cessnock Valley View Caravan Park**, Mount View Rd, Cessnock, 2km northwest (☎049/90 2573). Site with barbecues and pool. On-site vans ②, cabins ④.

**The Convent**, Halls Road, Pokolbin (☎049/98 7330). The swankiest place to stay in the Hunter, with heaps of cosy cachet, fireplaces and low beams – at a price. ⑧+ (from $200 per night).

**Elfin Hill Lodge**, Marrowbone Rd, Pokolbin (☎049/98 7543). Family-run air-con motel units in timber cabins, with saltwater pool, and breakfast available. ⑤/⑥.

**Neath Hotel**, Cessnock Rd, Neath, 6km from Cessnock (☎049/30 4270). B&B in nicely furnished historical pub, listed by the National Trust. ④/Fri & Sat ⑤.

**Pokolbin Cabins**, Palmers Lane, Pokolbin (☎049/98 7611). In the midst of the wineries, this extensive complex has 2- and 3-bedroom log cabins and 5-bedroom homesteads, fully equipped with everything from linen to firewood. Swimming pool and tennis court in the shady grounds. ⑤.

**Sussex Ridge**, off Deaseys Rd, Pokolbin (☎949/98 7753). Guesthouse in a classic two-storey tin-roofed homestead among bushland, with great views from the balcony. En suite rooms, communal lounge and cooking facilities. B& B ⑤/Fri & Sat ⑦.

**Tallawanta Resort**, Broke Rd, Pokolbin (☎049/98 7854). Motel-style complex overlooking vineyards with pool, spa and tennis courts. One disabled-accessible room. B&B ⑤/Fri & Sat ⑧.

**Wentworth Hotel**, 36 Vincent St, Cessnock (☎049/90 1364). Big old country pub with original circa 1914 wooden features. Rooms are clean and spacious with washbasin, fan and heating, and rates include a generous cooked breakfast. ④.

**Wollombi Horse Riding Centre**, Singleton Road, 4km past *Wollombi Tavern* (☎049/98 3221). Barnstay accommodation in bunks, with kitchen, lounge area, fuel stove, verandah and barbecue, plus riverside camping area. ①–⑤.

## HUNTER VALLEY WINERIES

More than sixty wineries cluster around the Hunter Valley, and almost all of them offer tastings and are interesting to visit. The most-visited are in the lower part of the valley, near Pokolbin, but there are also a few gems in the upper valley, around Wybong and Denman, west of Muswellbrook. See the box on p.594 for some wine-tasting tips . . .

**Alandale Winery**, Lovedale Rd, Pokolbin (☎049/90 4526). Very picturesque small winery on a hill, with great views overlooking their vineyard, the Lower Hunter and the Brokenback Range. They're happy for you to visit during vintage time, when you can see the small operation in action; try their prize-winning Chardonnay. Mon–Sat 9am–5pm, Sun 10am–5pm.

**Cruikshank Callatoota Estate**, Wybong Road, Wybong (☎065/47 8149) Worth a visit for the winemaker Andrew Cruikshank – a real character who unapologetically makes only red wine, which he loves. Barbecue facilities and winery tours. Daily 9am–5pm.

**Draytons**, Oakey Creek Rd, Pokolbin (☎049/98 7513). A very friendly, down-to-earth family winery, established for over 130 years. In that time they've become well known for their ports; you might be lucky and get a taste of Old Decanter Port, aged 21 years. Mon–Fri 8am–5pm, Sat 9am–5pm, Sun 10am–5pm.

**Hungerford Hill Wine Village**, Broke Rd, Pokolbin (☎049/98 7666). Touristy complex with huge cellars, restaurant, kiosk and shops, plus tastings and sales of all the Hunter Valley wines. Expensive food and slow service means you'd do better to bring a picnic, and wash it down with your purchases. Mon–Fri 9am–5pm, weekends and public holidays 10am–4pm.

**Hunter Estate**, Hermitage Road, Pokolbin (☎049/98 7777). Largest commercial winery, lacking in atmosphere but offering informative wine tours. Open daily 10am–5pm; tour 9.30am.

**Lindemans**, McDonalds Rd, Pokolbin (☎049/98 7684). One of the best-known names in the valley; Dr Lindeman first planted vines in the valley in 1842. Boasts a museum with a collection of winemaking paraphernalia. Mon–Fri 8.30am–4.30pm, Sat & Sun 10am–4.30pm.

**Reynolds Yarraman**, Yarraman Road, Wybong (☎065/47 8127). Tucked away in the upper valley, but worth seeking out for the best location of all the wineries, historical buildings and excellent, prize-winning wines. Mon–Sat 10am–4pm, Sun 11am–4pm.

**Rosemount Estate**, Rosemount Road, Denman (☎065/42 2467). Produces some of Australia's best known, award-winning wines, and has an excellent vineyard bistro attached. Mon–Sat 10am–4pm, Sun noon–4pm; bistro open Fri–Sun only.

**Scarborough Wine Co**, Gilliards Rd, Pokolbin (☎049/98 7563). Small, friendly family winery in one of the prettiest spots; pleasantly relaxed tastings are held in a small cottage on Hungerford Hill with wonderful valley views. Daily 9am–5pm.

**Tamburlaine**, McDonalds Rd, Pokolbin (☎049/98 7570). The fragrant garden outside gives a hint of the flowery elegant wines within. Only a small range of wines – too small even for the domestic market, so you must buy here – but tastings are well orchestrated and delivered with a lot of wit. One of the best. Daily 9.30am–5pm.

**Tyrrell's Family Vineyard**, Broke Road, Pokolbin (☎049/98 7509). The oldest independent family vineyards, producing consistently good wines. The tiny ironbark slab hut, where Edward Tyrrell lived when he began the winery in 1858, is still in the grounds, and the old winery with its cool earth floor is much as it was. Set against the Brokenback Range, part of the Great Dividing Range, the setting is as spectacular as the wines. Mon–Sat 8am–5pm, with tour at 1.30pm.

**Verona Vineyard & Small Winemakers Centre**, McDonalds Rd, Pokolbin (☎049/98 7668). Sells wines produced by other small vineyards; the $2 tasting charge levied on some wines is refunded on purchase. Excellent bistro-restaurant. Daily 10am–6pm.

## Eating and drinking

Most of the many excellent Hunter Valley restaurants are attached to the various wineries or are among the vineyards, rather than in the towns, although some of the Hunter's large old hotels dish out some good food.

**Ali Baba's**, Vincent St, Cessnock. Inexpensive curry joint. Mon–Thurs 11.30am–9pm, Fri & Sat 11.30am–10pm, Sun 5–9pm. BYO.

**Baron's Restaurant**, at the *Neath Hotel*, Cessnock Rd, Neath, 6km from Cessnock (☎049/30 4270). Antique-filled restaurant in historical pub. Fri & Sat nights only.

**Bellbird Hotel**, 388 Wollombi Rd, 5km from centre of Cessnock . Beautiful vine-covered courtyard with reasonably priced bistro, and an intimate cocktail bar, the *Sample Bar*.

**Black Opal Hotel**, 216 Vincent St, Cessnock (☎049/90 1070). Excellent bistro has nothing over $12 – and plenty of fresh seafood. The pub is one of the most relaxed places in town for a drink.

**Blaxlands Restaurant**, Broke Rd, Pokolbin (☎049/98 7550). More than 100 wines from the Hunter Valley on the menu in this well-regarded restaurant in a sandstone cottage; you can eat outside on the verandah; expensive and bookings are advised. Open daily. Licensed.

**Il Cacciatore**, Hermitage Lodge, corner of McDonalds and Gilliards roads, Pokolbin. (☎049/98 7639). Excellent Italian restaurant with a wide choice, including fish dishes; deserts like chocolate pasta ensure the place is packed; licensed and BYO.

**Cafe Max**, McDonalds Rd, Pokolbin (☎049/98 7899). Above the *Small Winemakers' Centre* (see above), with views over vineyards from the balcony to far-off hills. Eclectic menu ranges from Creole through to solid British fare. Lunch daily; BYO.

**Hermitage Restaurant**, Hunter Estate, Hermitage Rd, Pokolbin (☎049/98 7777). All-day dining (10.30am–5pm). Rather expensive but pleasant; BYO and licensed.

**The Hoot Cafe**, 115 Vincent St, Cessnock (☎049/91 2856). Sydney style and prices in this bright and airy café with ceiling fans whirring and soul music playing. Gourmet sandwiches, croissants, yummy cakes, good coffee, and delicious stuffed potatoes. Mon–Fri 9am–5pm, Sat 9am–1pm.

**Roberts at Pepper Tree**, Halls Road, Pokolbin (☎049/98 7330). Attached to *The Convent* (see "Accommodation"), this is the place to head for a treat in a beautiful old farmhouse filled with flowers. French rustic-style food emerges from wood-fired ovens. Expensive, licensed.

**Rothbury Cafe**, Rothbury Estate, Broke Rd, Pokolbin (☎049/98 7363). Good unpretentious lunch spot overlooking the vineyards of this winery. Reasonably priced pizza and pasta of the day plus interesting modern Australian dishes; wine at cellar-door prices.

# West

For fifty years, Sydney has been sliding ever westwards, inland, in a monotonous sprawl of shopping centres, brick-veneer homes and fast-food chains, in the process swallowing up towns and villages some of which date back to colonial times. The first settlers to explore inland found well-watered, fertile river flats, and quickly established agricultural outposts to support the fledgling colony with food. **Parramatta**, **Liverpool**, **Penrith** and **Campbelltown**, once separate communities, have become satellite towns inside Sydney's commuter belt. Only more distant settlements like **Windsor** and **Richmond**, tucked away on the Hawkesbury River, have managed to retain their smalltown feel and historical atmosphere. Yet, despite Sydney's advance, bushwalkers will find there's still plenty of wild west to explore. Three wildlife parks keep suburbia at bay, fending off modernity from the beauty of the **Blue Mountains**.

## Parramatta and Penrith

Situated on the Parramatta River, a little over 20km upstream from the harbour mouth, **PARRAMATTA** was the first of Sydney's rural satellites – the first farm settlement in Australia, in fact. The fertile soil of "Rosehill", as it was originally called, saved the fledgling colony from starvation with its first wheat crop of 1789. Today, that's hard to believe, but dotted here and there among the malls and busy roads, are eighteenth-century public buildings and original settlers' dwellings, which warrant a visit if you're interested in Australian history.

You can call in to Parramatta on your way out of the city – a rather depressing drive along ugly and congested Parramatta Road – or endure the dreary half-hour suburban train ride from Central Station. But much the most enjoyable way to get here is on the sleek *RiverCat* ferry from Circular Quay up the Parramatta River (9–15 daily; last return to Sydney 5.30pm weekdays, 5.50pm weekends; 1hr; $4 one-way). The wharf at Parramatta is on Phillip Street, a couple of blocks away from the helpful **Parramatta Visitors Centre** on the corner of Church and Market streets (Mon–Fri 10am–4pm, Sat 9am–1pm, Sun 10.30am–3.30pm; ☎630 3703), a recommended first stop in tracing Parramatta's historical roots, with free walking route maps available. If you don't feel like walking, the *Parramatta Explorer* is a daily hop-on, hop-off bus service which covers the main sights and meets the *RiverCats* ($8 per day; purchase on board or at the tourist office).

Parramatta's most important historical feature is the National Trust-owned **Old Government House** (Tues–Fri 10am–4pm, Sat & Sun 11am–4pm; last admission 3.30pm; $5) in Parramatta Park by the river. Turn left onto Marsden Street from the tourist office, crossing the river, then right onto George Street. Entered through the 1885 gatehouse on O'Connell Street, the park, filled with native trees, rises up to the gracious old Georgian-style building which is the oldest remaining public edifice in Australia, built between 1799 and 1816 and used as the Vice Regal residence until 1855; one wing has been converted into a pleasant teahouse. The three other main historical attractions are close together: follow Macquarie Street from Parramatta Park and turn right at its end onto Harris Street. Running off here is Ruse Street, where the aptly named **Experiment Farm Cottage** (Tues–Thurs 10am–4pm, Sun 11am–4pm; $4, free for National Trust members) was built on the site of the first land grant, given in 1790 to reformed convict James Ruse. On parallel Alice Street, at no. 70, **Elizabeth Farm** (Tues–Sun 10am–4.30pm; $5) dates from 1793, and claims to be the oldest surviving home in the country, built and run by the Macarthurs, who bred the first of the merino sheep that made Australian wealth "ride on a sheep's back"; a small café here serves refreshments. Nearby **Hambledon Cottage** on Hassel Street (Wed & Thurs, Sat & Sun 11am–4pm; $2.50), built in 1824, was part of the Macarthur estate.

If you're continuing west, the Western Highway and the rail lines head on to **PENRITH**, the most westerly of Sydney's satellite towns, in a curve of the Nepean River at the foot of the Blue Mountains (on the way out here you pass a couple of wild-life parks, see p.121). Penrith has an old-fashioned Aussie feel about it – a tight community who are immensely proud of their boisterous rugby league team, the Panthers. From town you can take in the splendour of the spectacular **Nepean Gorge** from the decks of the paddle steamer *Nepean Belle* (bookings ☎047/331 274 or 331 888) or head 24km south to the **Warragamba Dam**. The dam has created the huge reservoir of **Lake Burragorang**, a popular picnic spot with barbecues and a kiosk, and some easy walking trails through the bush.

## The Blue Mountains region

The section of the Great Dividing Range nearest Sydney gets its name from the blue mist that rises from millions of eucalyptus trees and hangs on the mountain air, tinting the sky and the mountain alike. In the early days of the colony, the **Blue Mountains** were believed to be an insurmountable barrier in the west. The first expeditions followed the streams in the valleys until they were defeated by cliff faces rising vertically above them. Only in 1813, when explorers Wentworth, Blaxland and Lawson followed the ridges instead of the valleys, were the mountains finally conquered, allowing the western plains to be opened up for settlement. The range is surmounted by a plateau at an altitude of more than 1000m where, over millions of years, rivers have carved deep valleys into the sandstone, and winds and driving rain have helped to deepen the ravines, creating a spectacular scenery of sheer precipices and walled canyons. Occasional landslides are a reminder that the process of erosion is still under way. Before white settlement, the Daruk Aborigines lived here, dressed in animal-skin cloaks to ward off the cold. An early coalmining industry, based in Katoomba, was followed by tourism which snowballed after the arrival of the railway in 1868. By 1900, the first three mountain stations of Wentworth Falls, Katoomba and Mount Victoria had been established as fashionable resorts, extolling the health benefits of eucalyptus-tinged mountain air.

All the villages and towns of the romantically dubbed "**City of the Blue Mountains**" – Glenbrook, Springwood, Wentworth Falls, Katoomba and Blackheath – lie on a ridge, connected by the Great Western Highway. Around them is the **Blue Mountains National Park**, the fourth-largest national park in the state and to many minds the best. The region makes a great weekend break from the city, with stunning views and clean air complemented by a wide range of accommodation, cafés and restaurants, a few good shops and even some entertainment – but be warned: at weekends and during the summer holidays, Katoomba is thronged with escapees from the city, and prices escalate accordingly. Even at their most crowded, though, the Blue Mountains always offer somewhere where you can find peace and quiet, even solitude – the deep gorges and high rocks make much of the terrain inaccessible except to bushwalkers and mountaineers. Climbing schools offer weekend courses in rock-climbing and abseiling for beginners and experienced climbers.

## Getting there and around

**Public transport** is quite good but your own vehicle will give you much greater flexibility, allowing you to take detours to old mansions, cottage gardens and the lookout points scattered along the ridge. **Trains** leave from Central Station to Katoomba (frequent departures until about midnight, no booking required; 2hr; $8 one-way), and follow the highway, stopping in all the major towns en route. If you're dependent on public transport, Katoomba makes the best base: facilities and services are concentrated here, and there are **local buses** to attractions in the vicinity and to other centres (details from *Katoomba–Woodford Bus Co* ☎047/82 4213 and *Katoomba–Leura Bus Service* ☎047/82 3333). Another way to get around is with the hop-on, hop-off *Blue Mountains Explorer Bus* (weekends & public holidays, approximately hourly 9.30am–4.45pm; $15 day-ticket; ☎047/82 1866), which links the main tourist spots around Katoomba and Leura.

## Glenbrook to Wentworth Falls

The gateway to the Blue Mountains, **GLENBROOK** is a compulsory stop for the **Blue Mountains Information Centre**, on the Great Western Highway (daily 9am–5pm; ☎047/39 6266). Here you can pick up a huge amount of information about the area, including the very useful *Blue Mountains Wonderland Visitors Guide*. **SPRINGWOOD** lies 11km further west, and is home to many of the artists who have settled in the mountains, and there are numerous arty-crafty and antique shops to browse in. The *Norman Lindsay Gallery*, at 14 Norman Lindsay Crescent in **Faulconbridge** (daily during school holidays, otherwise Fri–Sun 11am–5pm; $5), has an exhibition of paintings and drawings by the controversial artist and poet, who spent the last part of his life here. The small settlement of **Hazelbrook**, 13km southwest, has a **permaculture garden** worth visiting: the *Earth Repair Foundation Gardens* on 36 Mount View Avenue (daily 9am–4pm; $3; ☎047/58 6393) concentrate on techniques for sustainable agriculture.

**WENTWORTH FALLS**, named after the explorer William Wentworth, is a small village – and home to the restored nineteenth-century **Yester Grange** (Mon–Fri 10am–4pm, Sat & Sun 10am–5pm; $5), filled with antiques and a fine watercolour collection, its neat gardens set off by their rugged backdrop. Nearby a signposted road leads from the Great Western Highway to the **Wentworth Falls Reserve**, with superb views of the waterfall tumbling down into the Jamison Valley. You can reach this picnic area from Wentworth train station by following **Darwin's Walk** – the route followed by the famous naturalist in 1836. Of the view, which has changed little, Charles Darwin wrote, "If we imagine a winding harbour, with its deep water surrounded by bold cliff-like shores, laid dry, and a forest sprung up on its sandy bottom, we should then have the appearance and structure here exhibited. This kind of view was to me quite novel, and extremely magnificent." Most of the other bushwalks in the area start from the **Valley of the Waters Conservation Hut**, about 3km from the station at the end of Fletcher Street. Bus services are infrequent; a taxi from the station costs $4.70, or you can walk – turn right onto the Great Western Highway and eventually left into Valley Road. The NPWS Hut (daily 9am–5pm; ranger-led discovery walks daily at 9.30am; 2hr 30min, $10) inhabits a fantastic location overlooking the Jamison Valley. From its wonderful tea rooms,you can take full advantage of the stupendous views through the big windows or from the deck outside. In winter the open fire crackles in the grate, and every Sunday morning there's live classical music. A wide selection of bushwalks, detailed on boards outside, range from the two-hour **Valley of the Waters track**, which descends into the valley, to an extended two-day walk to Mount Solitary. One of the most rewarding is the quite strenuous, six-kilometre **National Pass**, a one-way walk which will conveniently get you back to the train station and takes in Wentworth Falls.

## Katoomba and Leura

**KATOOMBA**, the biggest town in the Blue Mountains, is also the best located, although the town, for all its surrounding charms and café culture, can seem a little raw and characterless. When the town was discovered by fashionable city dwellers in the late nineteenth century, the grandiose *Carrington Hotel*, in its prominent position near the railway station and set in landscaped gardens, was the height of elegance, with its leadlighting and wood panelling. However, it's been sitting empty for years, as has the *Savoy Cinema* opposite, giving the town a slightly neglected air on arrival.

About a 25-minute walk from the train station, **Echo Point** is the location of the information centre (daily 9am–5pm; ☎047/82 0756), and also enjoys breathtaking vistas that take in the Blue Mountains' most famous landmark, the **Three Sisters**. These three gnarled rocky points take their name from an Aboriginal Dreamtime story which relates how the Katoomba people were losing a battle against the rival Nepean people: the Katoomba leader, fearing that his three beautiful daughters would be carried off by the enemy, turned them to stone, but was tragically killed before he could reverse his spell. So here they have stood ever since, subjected to the indignities of thousands of tourist cameras and kept awake at night by spectacular floodlighting. The Three Sisters are at the top of the **Giant Stairway**, the beginning of the very steep stairs into the valley below, where there are several walking tracks to places with such intriguing names as Orphan Rock and Ruined Castle.

If you want to spare yourself the trek down into the 300-metre-deep Jamison Valley – or the walk back up – take the **Scenic Railway** at the end of Violet Street (daily 9am–5pm; last train up leaves at 4.50pm; $2 one-way, $4 return). Originally built to carry coal, this funicular railway glides down an impossibly steep gorge to the valley floor. Even more vertiginous is the **Skyway** (daily 9am–5pm; $4), a rickety-looking cable-car contraption that starts next to the railway and travels 350m across to the other side of the gorge, giving those who can bear to look a bird's-eye view of Orphan Rock, Katoomba Falls and the Jamison Valley.

Just two kilometres east of Katoomba, **LEURA** retains its own distinct identity with a real village atmosphere. The main street – The Mall – feels quite secluded from the highway; even the station manages to looks pretty. Leura is packed with great cafés, art galleries and small boutiques, and is renowned for its beautiful **gardens**, some of which are open to the public during the **Leura Gardens Festival** (early to mid-October; $8; details on ☎047/84 1258). Open all year round, though, is the beautiful **Everglades Gardens**, 37 Everglades Avenue (daily 9am–sunset; $3), situated in the grounds of an elegant mansion with views from its formal terraces, with a colourful display of azaleas and rhododendrons, an aboretum, and peacocks strutting among it all. Less tame scenery, such as **Leura Cascades,** can be viewed from the picnic area on Cliff Drive; to see it at closer quarters, take the two- to three-hour walk to the base and back. Other waterfalls in the area include the much-photographed **Bridal Veil Falls**, accessible from the Cascades picnic area, and Gordon Falls, with a walk commencing from Lone Pine Avenue. To the east of Gordon Falls, Sublime Point Road leads to the aptly named **Sublime Point** lookout, with panoramic views of the Jamison Valley.

## Blackheath

North of Katoomba, there are more lookout points at **BLACKHEATH** – just as impressive as Echo Point and much less busy. One of the best is **Govett's Leap**, near the NPWS **Blackheath Heritage Centre** (Mon–Fri 9am–4.15pm, Sat & Sun 9am–noon & 12.45–4.15pm; ☎047/87 8877). The centre has good interpretive material on history, flora and fauna, as well as practical information (with plenty on adjacent Wollemi and Kanangra Boyd parks too). The two-kilometre **Fairfax Heritage Track** at the NPWS Centre is wheelchair and pram accessible, and takes in the Govett's Leap Lookout with its marvellous panorama of the Grose Valley – although damage from the January 1994 bushfires is still evident – and Bridal Veil Falls. Although many walks start from the centre, one of the most popular Blackheath tramps, **The Grand Canyon**, begins from Evans Lookout Road at the south end of town west of the Great Western Highway.

The village of Blackheath itself is quiet and unspoilt, with *Blue Mountains Antiques* (daily 10am–6pm), on Govett's Leap Road, a rambling junk- and antique-filled space worth exploring; the renovated theatre also displays and sells the work of local artists, and there's a very funky, relaxed coffee shop out back – you can even get dinner (Asian-influenced) here on Friday and Saturday nights (☎047/87 7439 for bookings).

Beyond Blackheath, drivers can circle back towards Sydney via the scenic **Bells Line of Road**, which heads back east through the fruit- and vegetable-growing areas of Bilpin and Kurrajong to Richmond, with growers selling their produce at roadside stalls. On the way you'll pass **Mount Tomah Garden** (Oct–Feb daily 10am–5pm; March–Sept 10am–4pm; $5 per vehicle; $2 per bicycle or pedestrian; guided tours available, ☎047/67 2154 for details), an outpost of Sydney's Royal Botanic Gardens since 1987. There's a rhododendron collection, a display of conifers, and a collection of southern hemisphere cool-climate species. If you continue west along the Bells Line of Road, the Zig Zag Railway at Clarence is just over 35km away (see below).

From Blackheath you can also take the **Megalong Valley** Road southwest into this beautiful valley, calling in to visit the marsupials and emus at *Megalong Valley Farm*.

## Mount Victoria and around

Secluded and homey **MOUNT VICTORIA**, 6km from Blackheath and the last mountain settlement proper, is the only one with an authentic, unspoilt village feel. There are several antique shops and a cluttered antiquarian and secondhand bookshop – *J. Cameron* – worth a browse. Some short **walks** start from the Fairy Bower Picnic area, twelve minutes' walk from the Great Western Highway via Mt Piddington Road: get details from any Blue Mountains tourist office, or ask at the *Victoria and Albert*

*Guesthouse* (see "Accommodation" listings below for details of this and the restorec *Hotel Imperial*).

At the foot of the scenic Victoria Pass in the small valley of the River Lett and 11km from Mount Victoria, is the **Hartley Historic Site** (daily 10am–1pm & 2pm–5pm; ☎063/55 2117 for details; courthouse tour 10am–1pm & 2–4pm, 20min; site tour hourly 10am–noon, 2.15pm & 3.30pm, 1hr), a well-preserved nineteenth-century village developed as settlers headed west and forged roads through the mountains. The need for a police centre led to the building of a Court House here in 1837, and the village of Hartley developed around it until it was bypassed by the Great Western Highway in 1887.

## Blue Mountains Accommodation

Accommodation rates hike up on Friday and Saturday nights, so you should aim to visit on weekdays when it's quieter and cheaper. **Katoomba** is the obvious choice for those arriving by bus or train, but with your own transport, you can indulge in some of the more unusual and characterful guesthouses in **Blackheath** and **Mount Victoria**.

**The Cecil Guesthouse**, 108 Katoomba St, Katoomba (☎047/82 1411). Very central choice, but back from the main drag, which makes it peaceful. Has an old fashioned 1940s atmosphere, with a wood-burning stove and tennis courts. Meals served. B&B ⑤–⑧.

**The Clarendon**, corner of Lurline and Waratah streets, Katoomba (☎047/82 1322). Old-style guesthouse with own bar and restaurant, cabaret weekends (six months of the year it's Reg Livermore, the classic Australian drag act); nice firm beds. Rooms in the guesthouse are best – avoid the fairly unattractive Seventies-style motel rooms. ④–⑦.

**Cleopatra Guesthouse**, Cleopatra St (☎047/878 456). A highly salubrious, gay-friendly guesthouse – worth it for a treat, and the price includes luscious meals at breakfast and dinner. ⑧.

**Glenella**, Govett's Leap Rd, Blackheath. Guesthouse in a charming 1905 homestead; rooms furnished with antiques. B&B ⑦ weeknights, ⑨ weekends.

**Hydro-Majestic Hotel**, Medlow Bath, 7km west of Katoomba (☎047/88 1002). Luxurious, art-deco hotel, rather tattered now, but relatively good value and still stylish. ⑧.

**Hotel Imperial**, Great Western Highway, Mount Victoria (☎047/87 1461). Nicely restored country inn with beautiful leadlighting. B&B ③–④, dorms ②.

**Jemby-Rinjah Lodge**, 336 Evans Lookout Road, Blackheath (☎047/87 7622) Timber cabins in bushland near the Grose Valley for up to six people; BYO linen. ⑦.

**Kanangra Mountain Lodge**, 9 Belvedere Avenue, Blackheath (☎047/87 8715). Gay-friendly B&B with open fireplaces in its cosy lounges and a large garden. ⑥.

**Katoomba Falls Caravan Park**, Katoomba Falls Rd, Katoomba (☎047/82 1835). Near the falls. On-site vans. ③.

**Katoomba Mountain Lodge**, Church Lane, off Katoomba St, Katoomba (☎047/82 3933). Central B&B with dorms too; free tea and coffee. Great views over the town. Rooms ②, dorms ①.

**Katoomba YHA Hostel**, 66 Waratah St, Katoomba (☎047/82 1416). Large pleasant hostel in a charming old guesthouse with open fireplaces. Very convenient for both town centre and Echo Point walks. Dorms ①, rooms ③.

**Leura Village Caravan Park**, Great Western Highway at The Mall, Leura (☎047/84 1552). Heated indoor pool, TV lounge. Cabins ⑤, on-site vans ④.

**North Springwood YHA Hostel**, Hawkesbury Rd, near the Hawkesbury Lookout, North Springwood. This simple bush hostel off the beaten track was extensively damaged by the January 1994 bushfires and is being rebuilt; call the *YHA* head office in Sydney (☎02/261 1111) for updates.

**Three Explorers Motel**, 197 Lurline St, Katoomba (☎047/82 1733). Well run three-star place a cut above the usual charmless motel, on two levels with tastefully decorated units. Spa rooms plus more practical large family suites available. ⑤–⑥.

**Three Sisters Motel**, 348 Katoomba St, heading towards Echo Point (☎047/82 2911). Old-style red-brick motel units are fairly basic with dinousaur-era decor, but the position is great. ⑤.

**Victoria and Albert Guesthouse**, Mount Victoria (☎047/87 1241). Friendly and unfussy place with art-deco features. Rooms are large and there's a pool, spa and sauna. Sun–Thurs B&B ⑥–⑦.

**Walkabout Backpackers**, 190 Bathurst Rd, Katoomba (☎047/82 4226). Old building near the station; free tea and coffee. Lifts to bushwalks. Dorms ①, rooms ③.

## Blue Mountains food, drink and entertainment

Cuisine in the Blue Mountains has gone way beyond the ubiquitous Devonshire Teas, with some of the state's best restaurants now in the area, and a real café culture developing in Katoomba. The best place for a civilized drink is the *Carrington Bar* on Katoomba Street, or you could try your luck at the salubrious little bar of *The Clarendon*, mostly reserved for guests, there's cabaret acts on here too; the *Katoomba Hotel* can get quite rough, but it's a popular place for a game of pool and there's sometimes live heavy-rock bands. Across the other side of the railway line, *Gearins Hotel* is pretty low-key, hosting the occasional poetry reading.

**Arjuna**, 16 Valley Rd, just off the Great Western Highway, Katoomba (☎047/82 4662). Excellent Indian restaurant, a bit out of the way, but with good veggie choices and spectacular sunset views. Evenings from 6pm, except Tues & Wed; BYO and non-smoking.

**Aroney's**, Katoomba St, Katoomba, opposite the *Carrington Hotel*. Typical no-frills milk bar good for breakfast, affordable salad sandwiches and snacks throughout the day, or more substantial hamburgers and steaks. Smoke-free.

**Avalon Cafe**, 98 Main St, Katoomba (☎047/82 5532). Spacious warehouse-style upstairs café that has a good ambience and sometimes live music and events. Italian-inspired menu is moderately expensive, but servings are generous. Dinner daily, plus Sun lunch; BYO and non-smoking.

**The Bakers Cafe**, 179 The Mall, Leura. A tiny fantastic little place consisting of a counter with a few stools – and heavenly bakery products to consume with coffee.

**Bay Tree Tea Shop**, Mount Victoria. The best place in the mountains for scones. Open 10.30am–5pm except Wed & Thurs.

**Glenella**, Govett's Leap Rd, Blackheath. An award-winning restaurant good for a splurge – you can eat on the terrace, surrounded by a beautiful garden.

**Hydro-Majestic Hotel**, Great Western Highway, opposite Medlow Bath station (☎047/88 1002). Turn-of-the-century spa atmosphere, and views of the Megalong Valley especially from the bar and beer garden. Café open daily 9.30am–5pm, longer hours at the bar.

**Hotel Imperial**, Great Western Highway, Mount Victoria. Good-value bistro meals can be eaten in the foyer, ballroom or garden.

**Landseers**, Shop 1, 178 The Mall, Leura. Tiny café with very striking, cosily dark interior; delicious homemade cakes. Substantial sandwiches and lasagne too. Daily 7.30am–6pm.

**The Paragon Café**, 65 Katoomba Street, Katoomba. Wonderful original art-deco interior complete with cocktail bar. They do meals but you're better off having a coffee and a gawk; known for its great handmade chocolates and sweets. Tues –Sun 10am–5pm.

**Parakeet Café**, 195b Katoomba St, Katoomba. Eclectic, colourful café, its walls covered with paintings by local artists. Smoking is practically compulsory, but you can get some air in the garden courtyard. Simple inexpensive food. Daily 7am–9.30pm.

**Patisserie Schwarz**, Renae Arcade on Station St, Wentworth Falls. German-style pastries to eat in or take away. Ideal to replenish your energies after a bushwalk. Closed Tues.

**Pins and Needles**, 189 Katoomba St, Katoomba. An original idea – a Japanese and a Italian restaurant in one. The cuisines haven't intermarried, though, each sticking to their respective Udon noodles and pasta, at excellent prices. Closed Sun.

**Siam Cuisine,** Katoomba St, Katoomba (☎047/82 5671). Crowded, inexpensive Thai with $6 lunchtime specials. BYO. Tues–Sun 11.30am–2.30pm & 5.30–10pm.

**Table Manners**, 54 Waratah St, Katoomba (☎047/82 4465). Upmarket, modern Australian restaurant with mainly French influences, very genteel and expensive. Evenings daily, lunch Fri–Sun only.

**Victoria and Albert**, Mount Victoria (☎047/87 1241). Civilized verandah café (Wed–Sun 10am–5pm), plus a highly recommended restaurant in a wonderful old dining room, open nightly, with set menus; bookings preferred for non-residents.

**Woodstack Cafe**, 6 Katoomba St, Katoomba, opposite the station. Eco-friendly cafe attracts a young alternative crowd. Free-range chicken and eggs, real beef hamburgers and affordable prices. Live music Thurs–Sun when it's open until 3am.

## Listings

**Abseiling** *High 'n Wild Australian Adventures*, 3/72 Main St, Katoomba (☎047/82 6224 or 82 5524), abseiling courses for beginners ($59 including lunch); *Rockcraft*, 182 Katoomba St (☎947/82 2014), Katoomba's original abseiling outfit with similiarly priced courses; see also *Blue Mountains Adventure Company* below.

**Adventure activities** *Blue Mountains Adventure Company*, 190 Katoomba St (☎047/82 1271), for abseiling (weekends $165 – learn to abseil the first day, tackle the Three Sisters the second), rock-climbing, canyoning, mountaineering, mountain biking, caving and bush-survival skills.

**Bookshops** *Megalong Books*, 183 The Mall, Leura, is the best in the mountains; *Angus and Robertsons*, 195 Katoomba St, Katoomba, has an excellent selection of local guides and maps.

**Camping equipment** If you haven't got your own gear, rent it in Sydney. *Rockcraft* sell all camping gear and a good range of topographic maps and bushwalking guides.

**Car rental** *B & S M Cullen*, 60 Wilson St, Katoomba (☎047/82 5535); *Cales Rentals*, corner of Parke St and Bathurst Rd (☎047/82 2917).

**Horse riding** *The Packsaddlers*, Green Gully, Megalong Rd, Megalong Valley (☎047/87 9150), rides of one day or longer in the Megalong Valley, accommodation in well-equipped cabins; *Werriberri Trail Rides*, Megalong Rd, Blackheath (☎047/87 9171), horse riding for all abilities, pony rides for children and two-day camp outs; *Mountain River Riders*, Oberon (☎063/36 1890), horse-riding into otherwise inaccessible parts of Kanangra with pick-ups from Blackheath or Katoomba.

**Hospital** *Blue Mountains District Anzac Memorial Hospital*, Katoomba (☎047/82 2111).

**Laundromat** *The Wishing Well*, K Mart car park, Katoomba. Daily 7am–7pm.

**Pharmacies** *B & H Smith Chemist*, 159 Macquarie Rd, Springwood (☎047/51 2963), Mon–Fri 8.30am–9pm, Sat & Sun 9am–7pm; *Greenwell & Thomas*, 145 Katoomba St, Katoomba (☎047/82 1066), Mon–Fri 8.30am–6.30pm, Sat & Sun 8.30am–5pm.

**Readings and literary events** *Varuna Writers Centre*, 141 Cascade St, Katoomba, based in the rambling old home of the late Australian writer Eleanor Dark (famous for the *Timeless Land* trilogy).

**Scenic Flights** *Mountain Aviation*, Alex Macarthur, Katoomba Airfield (☎047/82 2892), flights over the mountains for a minimum of two passengers; *Blue Mountains Helicopters* (☎047/88 1109) from $49 for Grose Valley flight; *Blue Mountains Flights* (☎063/55 2299) from Katoomba, Lithgow or Hartley – best is the $129 trip to the ghost town of Yerranderie in a remote, inaccessible area of the mountains.

**Supermarket** *K-Mart*, off Katoomba St, Katoomba. Mon–Sat 9am–midnight, Sun 9am–9pm.

**Taxi** Taxis wait outside the main Blue Mountains train stations to meet arrivals; otherwise call *Katoomba Leura Radio Cabs* (☎047/82 1311) or *Blackheath Radio Cabs* (☎047/82 1311).

**Tours** *Blue Mountains Walking Tours* (☎047/82 3762), guided bushwalks; *Great Australian Walks* (☎02/555 7580), guided walks in the Jenolan Caves area and along the Six Foot Track; *Nalara Adventure Treks* (☎02/747 3223 or ☎047/57 3149, small groups for bushwalking, mountain biking and canyoning.

## Lithgow and the Zig Zag Railway

Back on the Great Western Highway, 11km northwest of Hartley, **LITHGOW** is still a coalmining town and not without charm, nestled under bush-clad hills with wide leafy streets and some imposing old buildings. The reason most people come to Lithgow, though, is for the **Zig Zag Railway** situated about 13km east of the town on the Bells Line of Road, Clarence (weekends & holidays 10.30am–5.30pm, but subject to seasonal variations; details on ☎063/53 1795; $10 adults, $5 kids). In the 1860s, engineers were faced with the problem of how to get the main western railway line from the top of the Blue Mountains down the steep drop to the Lithgow Valley and they came up with a series of zig zag ramps. These fell into disuse in the early twentieth century, but tracks were relaid by rail enthusiasts in the 1970s. Served by old steam trains, the picturesque line passes through two tunnels and over three viaducts. You can stop at points along the way and catch a later train; regular services between Sydney and Lithgow (via Katoomba and Mount Victoria) will stop at a Zig Zag platform on request. If you want to stay in Lithgow, there's hostel **accommodation** at *Bentbacks Backpackers*, 45 Roy Street, off Railway Parade (☎063/53 1685, ①–③ about five minutes' walk from the station. For other options – there are plenty of motels in the vicinity – head for the **Tourist Visitors Centre**, 184 Mort Street (☎063/531 859).

## Kanangra Boyd National Park and the Jenolan Caves

**Kanangra Boyd National Park** shares a boundary with the Blue Mountains National Park. Further south than the latter, much of it is inaccessible and surrounds Warragamba Dam, a protected water source, but you can explore the rugged beauty of **Kanangra Walls** where the Boyd Plateau falls sheerly away, to reveal a wilderness area of creeks, rivers, deep gorges and rivers below. Reached via Jenolan Caves, there are three walks from the car park at Kanangra Walls, a short lookout walk, a waterfall stroll and a longer plateau walk; contact the Oberon NPWS for details (☎063/361 972). You can get to **Oberon**, a timber milling town and closest settlement to Kanangra, by *CountryLink* coach from Mount Victoria (3 weekly).

The **Jenolan Caves** (daily, guided tours every half-hour 9.30am–5pm; $5–10, depending on route) lie 30km southwest across the mountains from Katoomba on the far edge of the Kanangra Boyd National Park – or over 80km by road – and contain New South Wales' most spectacular limestone formations. Visitors are treated to stalactites and stalagmites that have tortured themselves into extraordinary agglomerations, and have been given names, such as the "Sword of Michael" and "Gabriel's Wing" (in the Temple of Baal Cave) and the "Minaret" (in the River Cave), which require the usual feat of the imagination. The system of nine limestone caves is surrounded by the **Jenolan Caves Reserve**, a fauna and flora sanctuary with picnic facilities and walking trails to small waterfalls and lookout points. There's no public transport to the caves, but many Blue Mountain tours include them on their itinerary.

You can actually **walk** from Katoomba to the Jenolan Caves; the 42km-long Six Foot Track through the bush begins at the Explorers Tree next to the Great Western Highway about 2.5km west of Katoomba Railway Station; you'll need to allow two to three days for the one-way walk, and you're advised to carry plenty of water. The track, which finishes near Jenolan Caves House, was originally cut as a bridle path in 1884 to provide access to the caves from Katoomba, and was described in an 1894 tourist guide as "steep in places, but the romantic beauty of the surroundings amply compensates for the roughness of the ground". There are four basic campsites along the way plus cabins at Binda Flats – book through *Jenolan Caves Trust* (☎063/69 3311), which will also supply details and information on guided walks. *Blue Mountains Sightseeing*, 283 Main Street, Katoomba (☎047/82 1866), provide a daily transfer service ($30) for bushwalkers on the Six Foot Track; you can leave your car in their depot.

The focus of the area, apart from the caves themselves, is the rather romantic **Jenolan Caves House**, a beautiful old hotel (☎063/59 3304; ⑧), including good, generous meals) which found fame as a honeymoon destination in the 1920s. If you decide to indulge, make sure you get one of the older rooms – the new annexe is characterless; food in the restaurant is good and plentiful. Other **places to stay** in the area include the peaceful and pleasant *Forest Lodge*, Caves Road, Oberon Plateau, 7km southeast of the caves (☎063/35 6267; ⑤), and *Porcupine Hill Jenolan Cabins*, Oberon Road, Jenolan Caves (☎063/35 6239; ⑤), where timber cabins with log fires accommodate six – bring your own linen; the outdoor deck has views over the Blue Mountains National Park, Kanangra Boyd National Park and Jenolan Caves Reserve.

# South

Once you escape Sydney's uninspiring outer suburbs, the journey south is very enjoyable. Beyond Botany Bay and Port Hacking, the Princes Highway and the Illawarra railway hug the edge of the **Royal National Park** for more than twenty kilometres. South of the park, the railway and the scenic Lawrence Hargrave Drive (route 68) follow the coast to Wollongong. There's impressive cliff scenery as you pass through **Scarborough**, **Wombarra** and **Thirroul**, tiny seaside villages with a station and not much else, except lovely local beaches. Just south of **Otford**, hang-gliders swoop down from the top of Lawrence Hargrave Lookout to **Stanwell Park**'s sandy beach. Between **Wollongong** and **Nowra**, the ocean beaches of the Leisure Coast are popular with local holidaymakers, while fishermen, windsurfers and yachtsmen gather at **Lake Illawarra**, a huge coastal lake near **Port Kembla**. A few kilometres further down the coast is the famous, and often lethal, blowhole at **Kiama**.

Inland, west of Wollongong, Sydney's drinking water is stored in Cataract and Cordeaux **reservoirs**, surrounded by picnic and leisure areas. Further southwest, past **Kangaroo Valley**, the softly rolling hills of the **Southern Highlands** are dotted with old country towns like **Berrima** and **Bundanoon**, the latter overlooking the wild and windswept crags of the **Morton National Park**.

## Royal National Park

The **Royal National Park** is a huge nature reserve right at Sydney's doorstep, only 36km south of the city. Established in 1879, it was the second national park in the world (after Yellowstone in the USA). The railway between Sydney and Wollongong marks its western border, and from the train the scenery is fantastic – streams, waterfalls, rock formations and rainforest flora fly past the window. If you want to explore more closely, get off at one of the stations along the way – Loftus, Engadine, Heathcote, Waterfall or Otford – from all of which walking trails disappear into the park. On the eastern side, the park falls away abruptly to the ocean, creating a spectacular thirty-kilometre coastline of steep cliffs broken here and there by little coves with fine sandy beaches. The terrible **bushfires** of January 1994 destroyed 98 per cent of the 15,000-hectare park, closing many of the park's tracks, but the real tragedy was the decimation of native animals. Eucalypts actually thrive on bushfires and the bush is regenerating like crazy, already looking very lush with fresh green tips, among charred and blackened tree trunks; full recovery is expected to take another five to ten years. Many of the tracks have already been reopened, including the old favourite of Otford to secluded beachfront **Burning Palms**. Others are being entirely rerouted to cause less damage to the environment: be careful to get the latest information from the visitor centre (see below).

You can also drive in ($7.50 entry; gates open 24hr except at Garie Beach, where they shut at 8.30pm) at the northern end and spend some time at the **NPWS Visitor Centre** (Mon–Fri 9am–4pm, Sat & Sun 9am–1pm & 2–4pm; ☎542 0648) near the Royal National Park Station, which is served by a limited **rail** service via Loftus. The easy one-kilometre track from here to the Bungoona Lookout boasts panoramic views, and is wheelchair-accessible. Bushwalking and camping require a permit from the centre; cars are allowed right through the park, exiting at **Waterfall** on the Princes Highway or **Stanwell Park** on Laurence Hargrave Drive. Not far south of the NPWS centre, **Audley** is a picturesque picnic ground on the Hacking River, where you can rent a boat or canoe for a leisurely paddle. Deeper into the park, on the ocean shore, **Wattamolla** and **Garie** beaches have good surfing waves; the two beaches are connected by a walking track. A stroll along Jibbon Beach leads to some rock engravings of the Dharawal people, one of about eighty **Aboriginal art sites** around Port Hacking.

There's a small, very basic YHA **youth hostel** inside the park 1km from Garie Beach (book in advance at the YHA office, 422 Kent St, Sydney, ☎21 1111, or at any YHA hostel; ②), and there are also a number of **bushcamps**; contact the NPWS for a permit. There are **kiosks** at Audley, Wattamolla and Garie Beach. An interesting alternative way to get here is by **ferry** (☎523 2990) from Cronulla Railway Station, across Port Hacking to the small town of Bundeena at the park's northeastern tip where there's a good **campsite** (☎523 9520; on-site vans ③, cabins ④).

## Heathcote National Park

Across the Princes Highway from the Royal, **Heathcote National Park** is much smaller – and quieter – than its neighbour. This is a serious bushwalkers' park with no roads and a ban on trail bikes. The best **train** station for the park is Waterfall, from where you can follow a twelve-kilometre trail through the park, before catching a train back from Heathcote. On the way you pass through quite a few different types of vegetation and by several swimmable pools, the carved sandstone of the **Kingfisher Pool** the most ravishingly picturesque. By **car**, you can reach the picnic area at Woronora Dam on the western edge of the park: turn east off the Princes Highway onto Woronora Road. **Camping** permits are available from the Royal National Park Visitor Centre (see above).

# Wollongong

Although it's New South Wales' third largest city, **WOLLONGONG** has more of a country town feel, with the students of Wollongong University giving it a bit more life in term time. Eighty kilometres south of Sydney, it's essentially an industrial centre – Australia's largest **steel works** is at nearby **Port Kembla** – but with a few natural attractions to make it worth visiting. The **Illawarra Escarpment**, rising dramatically beyond, provides a beautiful lush backdrop to the city – and tremendous views over it: if you're driving to Wollongong from Sydney on the Princes Highway, stop at appropriately named Sublime Point on the **Bulli Pass**. If you want to explore the escarpment – and have your own transport – there are walking tracks on Mount Kembla and Mount Keira around 10km from the centre.

The highlight of the city itself is **Wollongong Harbour**, with its maritime feel enhanced by a **fishing fleet** in Belmore Basin, a fish market, a few seafood restaurants, and a picturesque nineteenth-century **lighthouse** on the breakwater. On either side are Wollongong's central **surf beaches**: choose North Beach for the best surf – or the harbour beaches for more gentle swimming. There's not really much to see in the town **centre**, which has been swallowed up by a giant shopping mall on Crown Street, but if you want to kill a few hours, the **City Gallery**, on the corner of Kembla and Burelli streets (Tues–Fri 10am–5pm, Sat & Sun noon–4pm; free), is a regional art centre with changing exhibitions plus a permanent collection with an emphasis on contemporary Aboriginal and colonial Illawarra artists. Wollongong is also home to the largest **Buddhist temple** in Australia; for details contact the International Buddhist Association (☎042/72 4204).

The more usual – and quickest – route to Wollongong is to take the Princes Highway from Sydney past Heathcote and the Royal National Park, avoiding the coast. However, a more scenic coastal and bush route involves driving through the Royal National Park emerging above the cliffs at **Otford**. A few kilometres on, the lookout on **Bald Hill** above Stanwell Park provides an impressive clifftop viewing spot – you'll see not only the vista, but the breathtaking sight of **hang-gliders** taking off and soaring down. You can join in with the *Sydney Hang Gliding Centre* (☎042/94 2545 or ☎018/41 9914): tandem flights with an instructor are $120, available daily depending on the weather; they also run courses. At **Coalcliff** the *Imperial Hotel* is a must for an en route drink, sitting right on the cliff edge. By **Austinmer**, you're     at the base of the stunning cliffs and into some heavy surf territory; another drinking hole here is the legendary *Headlands Hotel*, which also offers budget accommodation (see below). A few kilometres further on, **Thirroul** is the spot where the English novelist D H Lawrence wrote *Kangaroo* during his short Australian interlude.

## Practicalities

The best and cheapest way to get here from Sydney is by **train**, which hugs the coast stopping at most of the small coastal towns on route, departing Sydney Central or Redfern every half-hour for most of the day; Wollongong Station is right in the centre just off Crown Street. *Greyhound Pioneer* has one daily bus service to and from Sydney, which departs Sydney at noon, returning from Wollongong at 11.30am, while *Pioneer Motor Service* (☎044/21 7722) has a more intermittent service which continues on to Nowra and Eden.

  **Tourism Wollongong**, near the mall at 93 Crown Street (Mon–Fri 9am–5pm, Sat & Sun 10am–4pm; ☎042/28 0300), provides information and can advise on **accommodation**. The *Boat Harbour Motel,* on the corner of Campbell and Wilson streets (☎042/28 9166; ⑤), has comfortable and spacious rooms with sea views, while even more upmarket is Wollongong's five-star *Novotel Northbeach*, at 2–14 Cliff Road, North Wollongong (☎042/26 3555; ⑧, including full breakfast). Central dorm rooms are available at *Keiraleagh House*, 60 Kembla Street, a few blocks back from the beach (☎042/28 6765; ①), an old mansion converted to provide student and backpacker accommodation. Back in Austinmer, the *Headlands Hotel*, Headlands Avenue (☎042/67 1146; ①–②) has inexpensive – dilapidated but clean – rooms which look right over the water; food is available from the cheap pub bistro or from *Pirates Restaurant* attached to the hotel. There's nowhere central to **camp** but the two caravan parks to the north are right on the beach: *Corrimal Caravan Park*, Lake Parade, Corrimal, 6km north (☎042/85 5688; cabins ⑤) at the mouth of Towradgi Lagoon, and *Bulli Beach Caravan Park,* 1 Farrell Road, Bulli (☎042/85 5677; cabins ⑤).

  Wollongong isn't really renowned for its **food**. There are a concentration of cafés on Kembla Street just down from *Keiraleagh House*: *Frenchies Cafe* is a good all-round choice. *Tannous* on Crown Street serves cheap and generous Lebanese food including falafel rolls and plenty of Lebanese sweets (daily 8am–noon). The *Boat Harbour Motel* on the corner of Campbell and Wilson streets has chintzy seventies decor in its restaurant and cocktail bar: its stunning views of the old lighthouse make it a great spot on a wild and windswept Wollongong afternoon. If you're after some **nightlife**, pick up a copy of *Drum Media*, the free weekly listings magazine, from Sydney or from Wollongong record stores and bookshops. A good bet is the *North Wollongong Hotel* (☎042/29 4177) which hosts live local and Sydney bands from Thursday to Saturday spanning a range of music from punk and rock to heavy metal.

# Kiama and around

Of the coastal resorts south of Sydney, **KIAMA** is probably the most attractive – though if you want more than a day- or overnight-trip to the beach, you'd be better off continuing down to Nowra and beyond (see p.175). A small resort and fishing town, Kiama is famous for its star attraction, the **Blowhole**. Stemming from a natural fault in the cliffs, the blowhole explodes into a water spout when a wave hits with sufficient force. Impressive, but also potentially dangerous: freak waves can be thrown over 60m into the air and have swept a good few over-curious bystanders into the raging sea – so stand well back. **Kiama Visitor Information Centre,** nearby on Blowhole Point Rd (daily 9am–5pm; ☎042/32 3322) supplies details of other local attractions like **Cathedral Rocks**, a few kilometres to the north, whose rocky outcrops drop abruptly to the ocean.

Between the rocks there are some good sandy beaches, one of the best of which is **Seven Mile Beach**, with its own small oceanfront national park, about 15km south of Kiama. The **Wild Country Park** at Fox Ground (daily 10am–5pm; $5), off the Princes Highway some 10km further south, is a rather different attraction – an open-range zoo where kangaroos, emus and other native animals roam.

West of Kiama, a steep road leads to **Mount Saddleback Lookout**, from where on clear days you get an incredible view of the entire coast – from the Royal National Park in the north to Jervis Bay in the south. Further west, about 14km from Kiama, is the **Jamberoo Recreation Park** (weekends and holidays only; $18 or $14, with a discount voucher from the tourist office in Kiama) – a mixed bag of offerings including tennis courts, giant waterslides and grass ski slopes (the last costs an extra $10). Beyond Jamberoo you can head north to join the Illawarra Highway, and follow that inland to **Macquarie Pass**, the gateway to the Southern Highlands. The **Macquarie Pass National Park** is one of the southernmost stands of Australia's sub-tropical rainforest; there's a car park on the road from where the Cascades Walk takes you on a brief loop through the forest. Alternatively, the partly surfaced Jamberoo Pass Road heads to Robertson on the Illawarra Highway via the **Budderoo National Park**. Here, the **Minnamurra Rainforest Area** has a walk through the forest with wheelchair access, picnic grounds, a kiosk and an information centre (☎042/36 0469). **Carrington Falls**, 8km east of Robertson, are also worth a detour: a turn-off from the Jamberoo Pass Road leads to lookout points over the waterfalls.

If you want to **stay** in this area you'll find plenty of motels strung out along the highway. Alternatives include *Easts Van Park*, on Easts Beach a couple of kilometres south of Kiama (☎042/32 2124; on-site vans ③, cabins ④ and units ⑤, mainly rented weekly), handy for the beach and with safe, sheltered swimming. *Chittick Lodge Conference Centre* on Bridges Road in Gerringong has a YHA hostel attached (☎042/34 1249; ①) with great location just 500m from Seven Mile Beach. *Ourie Park Caravan Park*, Werri Beach, Gerringong (☎042/34 1285; on-site vans ③–⑤), is also near the beach, while *Seven Mile Beach Caravan Park* (☎042/34 1340; on-site vans ③–⑤), benefits from a great location at the northern end of Seven Mile Beach, between Crooked River and the sand, and offers canoeing and horse-riding.

## Inland: the road to Canberra

If you want to take your time getting to Canberra, there are a number of worthwhile diversions from the speedy South Western Freeway (route 31), the main road inland which eventually joins up with the Hume Highway. Camden Valley Way heads west from here to **Camden** on the Nepean River, where John Macarthur pioneered the breeding of Merino sheep in 1805, and the town still has a rural feel and several preserved nineteenth-century buildings, the oldest dating from 1816. En route, you'll pass **Mount Annan Botanical Garden** (April–Sept daily 10am–4pm, Oct–March daily 10am–6pm; $5 per car, $2.50 per cyclist or pedestrian): actually the native-plant section of the Royal Botanic Gardens in Sydney, this outstanding collection of native flora is the largest of its kind in Australia. The garden is 57km southwest of Sydney, and can be reached by a combination of *CityRail* train to Campbelltown, followed by *Macarthur Coaches* (☎046/66 7501).

From Camden, Remembrance Drive heads to **PICTON**, a small farming town cradled by hills; you can get here by train from Sydney or with *Picton Coaches* (☎046/ 77 1564) from Campbelltown or Wollongong, via Bargo, Tahmoor and Thirlmere. Picton is a good spot for a drink in the 1839 sandstone *George IV Inn* which brews its own beer by a traditional German method; you can imbibe in the shady beergarden and indulge in one of their legendary seafood platters. Eleven kilometres south of Picton, the five connected freshwater lakes that make up **Thirlmere Lakes National**

**Park**, are named in the language of the Gandangarra Aborigines. Lake Couridjah is best for swimming, surrounded by unspoilt bushland and plenty of birdlife. En route at Thirlmere, trainspotters will appreciate the **Thirlmere Railway Museum** (Mon–Fri 10am–3pm, Sat & Sun 9am–5pm; $6). Continuing along Rembrance Drive, it's 8km to the **Wirrimbirra Sanctuary** at Bargo (daily 8am–5pm; free), a peaceful bushland spot run by the National Trust, with a native nursery, bushwalking trails, pools to swim in and engage in a bit of platypus-spotting at dawn or dusk. You might also see wallabies, kangaroos, wombats and goannas, along with 150 different species of birds. There are basic **cabins** to stay in (☎046/84 1112; ②) and outside, there's a big open fireplace to sit around, which comes into its own in April when local musicians gather for the annual *Brush with the Bush* weekend. Without your own transport, you can get here by train from Sydney to Bargo or Tahmoor and walk a couple of kilometres. Also in Bargo, on Arina Road, is the **Merigal Dingo Education Centre** (open to visitors first Sun of month, 10.30am–3pm; $3; ☎046/84 1156), which aims to increase awareness of what it considers to be a maligned native dog – you can also buy dingophernalia.

## The Southern Highlands

From Bargo, there are a couple of detours worth taking on the old road south, the Hume Highway, through the picturesque Southern Highlands which have been a favourite weekend retreat for Sydneysiders since the 1920s. Marking the beginning of the Highlands is **MITTAGONG**, a small agricultural and tourist town, 110km south of Sydney. Mostly visited on the way to the limestone **Wombeyan Caves** (daily 10am–4pm; $8) in the nearby hills, the route to the five caves begins 4km south of the town off the highway and winds upwards for 65km. Fairly special high-country scenery helps to distract you from the bumpiness of the partly unsealed road. There's a **campsite** near the caves (☎048/53 5976; on-site vans ④, cottages ⑤). For more on accommodation in the area – and free booking service – contact the **Southern Highlands Visitor Information Centre** (daily 9am–4.30pm; ☎048/71 2888) in Winifred West Park on the Hume Highway; they also have masses of information on bushwalks of varying lengths.

Mittagong and neighboring **BOWRAL**, 8km southwest, while less pretty than other Highland bases such as Berrima and Bundanoon, share a stash of impressive **restaurants**. At Mittagong, *Thonburl's*, 60 Bowral Road (☎048/72 1511), serves delicious traditional Thai meals in an elegant setting, while *The Blue Cockerel*, 95 Hume Highway (dinner Wed–Sun, lunch Sun; BYO and licensed; ☎048/72 1677) is a busy bistro with generous, home-style cooking at moderate prices. In Bowral, *The Catch*, 250 Bong Bong Street (closed Mon; licensed; ☎048/62 2677) is a city-style brasserie focussing on fish, plus wood-fired gourmet pizzas. Also on Bong Bong Street is *Epicure*, an airy stylish café which does a stunning lemon tart and excellent coffee. Also worth checking out in Bowral is *Cucina Bar Ristorante*, Bowral Motel, Kangaloon Rd (☎048/61 2027) for rustic Italian cooking. After scoffing in Bowral, cricket fans might like to check out the **Bradman Museum** in Jude Street (daily 10am–4pm; $3) which details the career of the famous Australian cricketer and the history of The Ashes.

Next on from Mittagong comes the picturesque village of **BERRIMA**, 123km southwest of Sydney, with an excellent complement of well-preserved and restored old buildings. The *Surveyor General Inn* here has been serving beer since 1835 – a good enough reason to indulge. Suitably refreshed, you can check out some of the other sights: within the sandstone **Court House** on the corner of Argyle and Wiltshire streets (daily 10am–4pm; $2), built in 1838, is the Visitor Centre, while across the road is the old **Berrima Gaol**, which once held the infamous bushranger Thunderbolt behind its bars – and also has the dubious distinction of being the first place in Australia where a woman was executed. Continue up Wiltshire Street from the courthouse to get to the **River Walk**, the end of which is marked by a fine reserve with picnic tables – and camping too. Other **accommodation** includes a slather of bed and breakfasts in pretty old stone cottages like *Parsley Cottage* (☎048/77 1427; ⑤) and *Waldon Wood* (☎048/77 1164; ⑥). Motels here are also fairly salubrious: the *Berrima Bakehouse Motel* (☎048/77 1381; ⑤–⑥), on the highway at the corner of Wingecarribee Street, is a modern brick building but with the bonus of a peaceful pleasant garden leading down to the river and a saltwater pool; the *White Horse Inn* in Market Place (☎048/77 1204; ⑤–⑥) is a large old 1832 sandstone hotel with accommodation in modern motel units in the garden. The old building is a **restaurant** with various eating areas, ranging from small fireplaced rooms overlooked by dour portraits to the cool cellar or the green gazebo out back.

Five kilometres from Moss Vale on the Hume Highway is the turn off south to **BUNDANOON**, famous for its annual April celebration of its Scottish heritage. Exploiting the autumnal atmosphere of mist and turning leaves, Bundanoon becomes Brigadoon for a day, overtaken by Highland Games – Aussie-style. Even if you miss the frivolity, it's an attractive spot set in hilly countryside scarred by deep gullies and with splendid views over the gorges and mountains of the huge **Morton National Park**. The park, and Bundanoon, have traditionally been a mecca for cyclists, with the long-established *Ye Olde Bicycle Shop* renting out bikes at very reasonable rates (daily to 4.30pm except Wed; $4 per hour, $12 half day, $15 full day; ☎048/83 6043). It also must be one of the few bike shops in the world with its own espresso machine. A recommended evening activity is a visit to **Glow Worm Glen**; after dark the small sandstone grotto is transformed by the naturally flickering lights of these creatures. It's a 25-minute walk from town via the end of William Street, or an easy forty-minute sign-posted trek from Riverview Road in the park. Set off at sunset, armed with a torch.

Bundanoon has a classic, well preserved **train** station which is a pleasure to arrive at from Sydney or Goulburn. Otherwise, *Berrima Coaches* (☎048/71 3211) have a daily service from Wollongong. *Bundanoon YHA* **hostel**, Railway Avenue (☎048/83 6010; dorms ①, rooms ③) is a spacious Edwardian-era guesthouse with wide verandahs to hang out on, as well as a large common room with an open fireplace; the enthusiastic manager dishes out loads of information and organizes activities. If you're after **B&B**, the central *Gasthof Old Heidleberg*, corner of Penrose Road and Anzac Parade (☎048/83 6242; ④) is the best value. *Bundanoon Pizzeria and Pasta*, on Railway Terrace opposite the station, is open for **meals** from 5pm daily. *Gambles on the Park*, near the entrance to the national park is more expensive and open only on weekends for generous, home-cooked meals. The *Bundanoon Hotel*, on Erith Street (☎048/83 6005) near the train station, is a quaint little country pub with open fireplaces that serves up plain affordable food and is a friendly spot for a drink. There's a supermarket on Railway Terrace open daily to 9pm.

## Kangaroo Valley

Between Nowra on the coast and Moss Vale on the inland road, **Kangaroo Valley** is a popular spot for gay weekenders from Sydney – a lovely, hidden valley situated between the lush dairy country of Nowra and the Southern Highlands. Coming from the coastal end, a narrow, winding country road climbs 700m up Cambewarra Mountain, with suberb coastal panoramas along the way. **KANGAROO VALLEY** village has tearooms and a **Pioneer Settlement Museum** (daily 9.30am–4.30pm; $2.50) with a **market** held in the grounds on the last Sunday of the month. From here the drive continues across the old sandstone Hampden Suspension Bridge over the Kangaroo River to the **Barrengarry** plateau. Allow yourself to be waylaid at **Fitzroy Falls**, at the northeastern edge of the Morton National Park, where a short walk from the car park takes you to a waterfall plunging 80m into the valley below. There's an architect-designed **NPWS Visitors Centre** here (daily 9am–3pm; ☎048/87 7270), based on a sandstone and water theme with a deck built around existing trees. An excellent café is also part of the complex, and there's disabled access to the falls.

Detailed information about walking tracks in the surrounding area is available, and the office issues **camping** permits for the nearby bushcamp at **Yarrunga Creek**. If you want to stay in rather more comfort, the **Hampden Bridge Tourist Park**, Moss Vale Road (☎044/65 1310; on-site vans ③, cabins ④) is on the banks of the Kangaroo River about a kilometre from the village centre, with canoes to get you on the water. *Kangaroo Valley Country Club* (☎044/65 1131; ⑤), on Tallowa Dam Road 4km west of Kangaroo Valley village, is an upmarket country resort with wooden cabins, as well as swimming, spa, tennis and golf facilities. *Tall Trees Bed and Breakfast*, 8 Nugents Creek Road, 1km from the village (☎044/651 208; ⑥) boasts a guest lounge with log fires, full country breakfast in the dining area, and a patio with views across the valley. *Yarrunga Park Country House*, 199 Jacks Corner Road (☎044/65 1593; ⑦) is an upmarket country house in farm- and bushland adjacent to the Morton National Park; guests get their own wing and the usual log fires and cooked breakfast feature. Near **BERRY**, the *Tara Country Retreat*, 219 Wattamolla Road (☎044/64 1472; rooms ④–⑦, camping available) is a gay and lesbian guesthouse set in farmland and rainforest with a swimming pool, spa, games room and video library; *Woodhill Mountain Lodge*, 50 Formans Road (☎044/64 2013; ⑤), also near Berry, is another recommended **gay-friendly** place.

## travel details

Sydney is very much the centre of the Australian transport network, and you can get to virtually anywhere in the country from here on a variety of competing services. The following list is at best a **minimum**; as well as the dedicated services listed below, many places will also be served by long-distance services stopping en route.

### Trains

**Sydney** to: Adelaide (2 weekly, Mon & Thurs 1.30pm; 27hr 30min); Brisbane (1 daily, 4.15pm; 16hr); Canberra (2 daily; 5hr); Dubbo (1 daily, 7am; 6hr 40min); Goulburn (5–8 daily; 3hr); Katoomba, Blue Mountains (22–30 daily; 2hr); Maitland, Hunter Valley (1 daily, 7.05am; 3hr); Melbourne (1 daily, 8.43pm; 10hr 20min; plus daily bus/train Speedlink via Albury, 3.45pm; 12–13hr); Newcastle (20–25 daily; 2hr); Perth (2 weekly, Mon & Thurs 1.30pm; 60hr); Richmond (18–25 daily; 1hr 15min); Windsor (18–25 daily; 1hr 15min); Wollongong (15–25 daily; 1hr 40min).

### Buses

**Sydney** to: Adelaide (2–3 daily; 20hr); Albury (2 daily; 8hr 30min); Armidale (2 daily; 8hr 30min); Batemans Bay (3 daily; 5hr 20min); Bathurst (2–3 daily; 4hr); Brisbane (8–12 daily; 15–17hr, with connections to Cairns and Darwin); Broken Hill (2–3 daily; 15hr 30min); Byron Bay (8 daily; 12hr 30min); Canberra (2 daily; 5hr); Coffs Harbour (8 daily; 8hr 30min); Eden (3 daily; 8hr 30min); Glen Innes (2 daily; 10hr); Grafton (2 daily; 10hr); Melbourne (5 daily; 12–18hr); Mildura (2–3 daily; 16hr); Newcastle (8 daily; 3hr); Nowra (3 daily; 3hr); Perth (2–3 daily; 52–56hr); Port Macquarie (8 daily; 7hr); Tamworth (2 daily; 7hr); Tenterfield (2 daily; 11hr 30min).

### Flights

Sydney is the main international point of entry into Australia with flights from all around the world. It is also the centre of the **domestic** network, and you can fly to virtually anywhere in the country from here. Major services include:

**Sydney** to: Adelaide (20 daily; 2hr 30min); Alice Springs (4 daily; 2hr 40min); Ayers Rock Resort (2 daily; 3hr); Brisbane (20 daily; 1hr 15min); Cairns (15 daily; 2hr 40min); Darwin (3 daily; 4hr); Hobart (8 daily; 1hr 30min); Melbourne (20 daily; 1hr 10min); Perth (10 daily; 4hr).

# CHAPTER TWO

# NEW SOUTH WALES AND ACT

**N**ew South Wales is Australia's premier state in more ways than one: not only the oldest of the five states, but the most densely populated too. Including Sydney, New South Wales covers an area about twice the size of Britain, with roughly a tenth of its population; not a very big state by antipodean standards, but its 5.5 million residents constitute one third of the country's population. Their distribution is wildly uneven: few live in the Outback or the rural regions, and the vast majority are absorbed by the urban and suburban sprawl on the coast. The state's Aboriginal population is about 40,000, approximately one fifth of the total living in Australia. This chapter also covers the Australian Capital Territory (ACT), which was carved out of NSW at the beginning of this century as an independent base for the new national capital, **Canberra**.

When Lieutenant James Cook claimed New South Wales for King and Country in 1770, naming it after a land that he'd apparently never visited – and to which it bears strikingly little resemblance – he could have hardly foreseen what would become of it. And indeed the early years, of penal settlement and timid encroachment into the fringes of the coastal area around Sydney, were hardly a promising start. But with the discovery of a passage through the Blue Mountains in 1813 (see p.136), the rolling plains of the west were opened up. Free (non-convict) settlers – **squatters** – appropriated vast areas of this rich pastureland, making immense fortunes off the backs of sheep. When **gold** was discovered near Bathurst in 1851, and the first goldrush began, New South Wales' fortunes were assured. Although penal transportation ceased the following year, the population continued to increase rapidly and the economy boomed as fortune seekers arrived in droves. At much the same time, Victoria broke off to form a separate colony, followed by Queensland in 1859. The much reduced borders that New South Wales has today were defined in 1863.

There are over a thousand kilometres of **Pacific coastline** in New South Wales, from subtropical **Tweed Heads** in the north to temperate **Eden** in the south. The year-round mild climate, together with the ocean and the **beaches**, draw visitors pretty much all the time – though it's the summer holiday season that brings Australians in their thousands. There are great surf beaches all the way up the coast, and there are also plenty of more sheltered waters, in bays, river mouths and inlets, and in a series of salt lagoons or "coastal lakes", protected behind a narrow spit from the force of the ocean waves. **South of Sydney** the coast is relatively undeveloped, and there's a string of low-key family resorts and fishing ports, great for watersports and fishing. To the **north** the climate gradually becomes warmer, and the coastline more popular – the series of big resorts up here includes **Port Macquarie** and **Coffs Harbour**, but there are also plenty of much less developed places where you can escape it all. One of the most enjoyable beach resorts in Australia is **Byron Bay**, which, despite increasing popularity, has managed to retain its slightly offbeat, alternative appeal that radiates from the still thriving hippy communes of the lush, hilly north coast **Hinterland**.

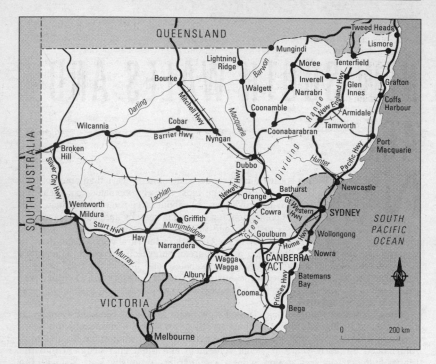

The **Great Dividing Range** runs parallel to the coastline, often very close, dividing the state in two. In the north, the gentle **New England** stretch of the range comprises tablelands ideal for sheep and cattle farming; where this plateau falls away steeply towards the coast are some of the few remaining pockets of dense, at times impenetrable, primeval **forest** – the Big Scrub that drove the early settlers to despair. To the south is the Australian Capital Territory where **Canberra**, the nation's capital and a city struggling to shed its dull image, is the gateway to the **Snowy Mountains**. Here the range builds to a crescendo as **Mount Kosciusko** (Australia's highest) marks the peak of the Australian Alps. In winter there's skiing here, but the mountains are perhaps even better in summer, when the national park that covers most of them offers some unbeatable hiking. Unsurprisingly, it's not so warm up in the mountains of the Great Dividing Range: in summer the cooler days and the drop in temperature at night offer a welcome respite from the coastal heat and humidity. In winter, however, it can be genuinely freezing, with snow even falling near the Queensland border in Tenterfield.

**West** of the range, rich agricultural country gradually fades into desert-like Outback regions where the mercury can climb well above the 40°C mark in summer, while mild winter days are followed by very cold, frosty nights. West of Canberra, between the three rivers of the Murrumbidgee, the Darling and the Murray (the latter dividing NSW from Victoria), is the fertile **Riverina**. Beyond New England, the flat black-soiled plains of the **northwest** head through cotton country to the opal-mining town of **Lightning Ridge**. It's a uniquely Australian experience to leave Sydney, cross the extraordinarily scenic Blue Mountains and be gradually sucked into this vast emptiness, where the "back o' **Bourke**" is synonymous with the Outback. The mining settlement of **Broken Hill**, almost at the South Australian border, is the obvious destination, a gracious city surrounded by the desert landscape of *Mad Max* and home to the classic Outback institutions of the School of the Air and the Flying Doctor Service.

New South Wales still has a fairly extensive **rail** network, although *Countrylink*, as it's called, have replaced many services with buses. A one-month $249 unlimited *Discovery Pass* will get you just about anywhere in the state on this system (☎13 2232 for reservations).

## Parks and wildlife

Throughout the state there are magnificent **national parks** and wilderness areas. Before European settlement, the **northeastern** corner of New South Wales was covered by dense subtropical rainforest. It's this that you can visit along the escarpment of the Great Dividing Range, though often only the very edge of these national parks or forests can be reached by road or track, while the interior is accessible only to hardy bushwalkers. These forests are inhabited by many types of parrots, occasionally by bell birds and bower birds, brush turkeys, and marsupials such as ringtail possums, bandicoots and padimelons. **Further south**, the slightly higher altitudes and the plateaus are dominated by eucalypt forest with a more open canopy, and by less dense eucalypt woodland – the preferred habitat of wombats, wallabies, other types of possum, koalas and a few small marsupials, as well as echidnas and platypuses, kookaburras, magpies and parrots. The **Snowy Mountains** are covered by snow gums, a slow-growing, cold-resistant eucalypt, although in the summer clusters of delicate wild flowers cover the mountain hillsides and meadows. Where the forest is not protected, lumber is still big business in NSW, and the source of fierce clashes between environmentalists and the towns that make their living from the timber trade. To the **west**, kangaroos, wallabies and emus roam the wide plains, and with a bit of luck a wedge-tailed eagle can be sighted. Parks here tend to encompass vast areas of desert or places marked out by extraordinary geological formations. The far southwest corner is part of the Mallee – a sandy, semi-arid area covered by the eucalypt shrubs that lend the area its name. Here the mallee fowl build the incubation mounds for their eggs in the sand.

The National Parks and Wildlife Service (NWPS) has introduced **entrance fees** – usually around $7.50 per car, $4 for motorcyles – to most of its parks. If you intend to go bush often in NSW you can buy an annual pass for $50 ($30 for motorbikes) which includes all parks except Kosciusko. Because of its skiing, entrance to Kosciusko is a steep $12 per car per day, perversely levied in summer too – so if you plan spending any length of time here, or are visiting other parks as well, consider the $60 annual pass which includes entry to it. Permits are sold at NWPS offices and some park entry stations, or by mail (include your vehicle type and its registration number), from The Cashier, NSW National Parks and Wildlife Service, PO Box 1967, Hurstville, NSW 2220.

---

## ACCOMMODATION PRICES

All the accommodation listed in this book has been categorized into one of eight price bands, as set out below. The rates quoted represent the cheapest available double or twin room in high season – except for category ①, which are per-person rates for a dorm bed, and the prices given for units, cabins and vans, which are the daily charge for the whole unit.

| | | | |
|---|---|---|---|
| ① Under $16 | ② $16–26 | ③ $27–36 | ④ $37–54 |
| ⑤ $55–74 | ⑥ $75–94 | ⑦ $95–124 | ⑧ $125 upwards |

For more accommodation details, see pp.31–34

You can **camp** in most national parks. Bushcamping is generally free, but where there is a ranger station and a designated campsite with facilities, fees are charged. If the amenities are of a high standard including hot showers and the like, or if the spot is just plain popular, fees can be as high as $15 per tent. Open fires are banned in most parks and forbidden everywhere on high fire danger days, and while there are often electric or gas barbecues in picnic areas, you'll need a fuel stove for bushcamping.

# AUSTRALIAN CAPITAL TERRITORY

In the 1820s the first European squatters settled in the valleys and plains north of the Snowy Mountains and established family dynasties on their prosperous grazing properties. Until the turn of the century, however, this remained a remote rural area. When the Australian colonies united in the **Commonwealth of Australia** in 1901, a capital city had to be chosen, with Melbourne and Sydney the two obvious and eager rivals. After much wrangling, and partly in order to avoid having to decide on one of the two, it was agreed to establish a brand new capital instead: Melbourne was to be the seat of the provisional government until the new capital was completed and the government departments had moved there. A provision in the Constitution Act decreed that the seat of government was to be in the state of New South Wales and not less than 100 miles from Sydney. In 1909, Limestone Plains, a plain south of Yass, surrounded by mountain ranges, was chosen out of several possible sites as the future seat of the Australian government. An area of 2368 square kilometres was excised from the state of New South Wales and named the **Australian Capital Territory** (ACT). The ACT officially included an adjunct at Jervis Bay, on the coast south of Nowra, to give Australia's capital its own access to the sea and a naval base. The name for the future capital was supposedly taken from the language of local Aborigines: **Canberra** – the meeting place.

Canberra is situated on a high plain (600m above sea level) and, unlike the coastal cities, experiences four distinct seasons. In summer, the average temperatures are 27°C maximum during the day and 12°C minimum at night; in winter they drop from an average of 12°C maximum during the day to freezing point (and below) at night. Spring and autumn can be really delightful, though. The mountain ranges to the west and south of the city rise up to 1900m and are snow-covered in winter.

# Canberra

In 1912, the American landscape architect Walter Burley Griffin, hailing from Chicago, won the international competition for the design of the future Australian capital: his plan envisaged a garden city for about 25,000 people which took into account the natural features of the landscape. There were to be five main centres, each with separate city functions, located on three axes: land, water and municipal. Roads were to be in concentric circles, with arcs linking the radiating design. Construction started in 1913, but political squabbling and the effects of World War I prevented any real progress being made. Little building had been done, in fact, by the time Griffin left the site in 1920, and only in 1927 was the provisional parliament building officially opened. By 1930 some 1,000 families had settled in the capital. Then the Depression set in, World War II broke out and development slowed again. After more years of stagnation, the National Capital Development Commission (NCDC) was finally established in 1958, and at last growth began in earnest.

The **telephone code** for the Canberra area is ☎06.

In 1963, the Molonglo River was dammed to form a lake eleven kilometres wide, the artificial **Lake Burley Griffin** that is the centrepiece of modern **CANBERRA**. Numerous open spaces and public buildings came into existence as a real city started to emerge. Slowly, the **Civic Centre** near London Circuit began to live up to its name. The **population** grew rapidly, from 15,000 in 1947 to over 100,000 in 1967, and now more than 300,000 people live in Canberra. This population growth has been accommodated in satellite towns with their own centres: **Woden**, 12km south of the Civic Centre, was built in the mid-1960s; five years later **Belconnen** was added in the north-west; and in the mid-1970s **Tuggeranong** in the south. It was this sprawl that fostered Canberra's image as "a cluster of suburbs in search of a centre".

Inevitably, modern Canberra is mainly a city of civil servants and administrators. There are plenty of service industries – especially ones aimed at feeding and watering all those politicians and visitors – but little real industrial activity. Canberra recently gained self-government, with only the Parliamentary Triangle remaining under federal control; the self-financing responsibilities that this entails have placed a premium on tourism revenues. The new **parliament building**, finally opened in 1988, is certainly a contributing factor to increased tourism, with its original architecture intended to blend into the landscape. Canberra is also trying very hard to present an image that escapes from its reputation as the domain of dull bureaucrats. They haven't succeeded yet: most Australians still regard Canberra as "pollie city" – a frosty, boring place where politicians (the lowest form of human life) and public servants (only marginally higher on the evolutionary scale) live it up at the expense of the hard-done-by Australian taxpayer. They also complain about its concentric circular streets which can make driving here seem like a Kafkaesque nightmare, and about the contrived, neat-as-a-pin, nature of the place.

But the image-makers have a point, and Canberra is a far more pleasant place than it's usually given credit for. As well as some impressive architecture in astonishingly well-groomed surroundings, the city has wide open spaces and many **parks** and gardens (Griffin's "garden city"), while right on its doorstep are forests and **bushland**, with unspoilt wilderness just a bit further afield in the Brindabella Ranges and the Namagdi National Park; skiing in the Snowy Mountains or surfing on the coast are only a few hours away. To appreciate it you really need a vehicle of some kind – things are very spread out, and at the weekend especially (when many residents leave and the city is pretty dead) public transport is extremely limited. Renting a car, or at least a bike – and taking advantage of the excellent network of bike paths – is strongly recommended (see "Listings").

Canberra's **nightlife** is also a great deal better than you might expect, considering its reputation. The two universities here (and the Duntroon Military Academy for officer material) means there's a large and lively student population. The city is said to have more restaurants per capita than any other in Australia – which is saying something – and there are plenty of pubs and nightclubs to choose from too. Many of them, though, are tucked away in hidden corners of the city or in the satellite towns.

## Arrival and information

Canberra's **airport**, some 7km east of the city, handles only domestic flights. *ACT Mini Buses* run between the airport and the city for around $5 (☎291 4592), or there are plenty of taxis, charging roughly twice as much. The main Canberra **train station** is located southeast of the centre, on Wentworth Avenue in Kingston, from where taxis are again the easiest way to get where you're going; trains also stop at the suburb of

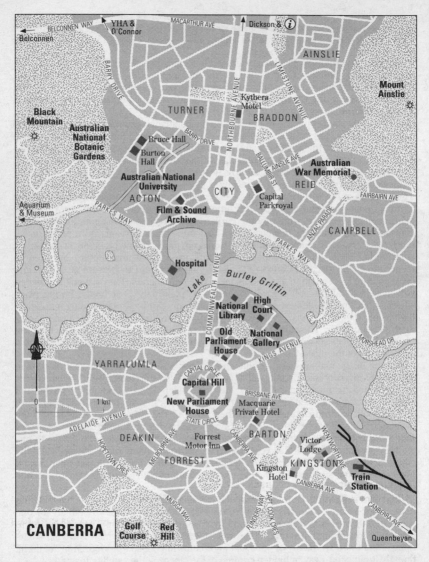

CANBERRA

Queanbeyan, in NSW, where there's some cheap accommodation. Most interstate **buses** drop and pick up at the **Jolimont Centre** right at the heart of downtown, at 67 Northbourne Avenue; the recently modernized centre has showers, lockers ($3) a TV room, snack bar and an excellent travel bookshop which may also have tourist information leaflets available.

The main **tourist office**, which can book tours, transport and accommodation, is unfortunately about 2km north of the centre, reached on the #380 bus: the *Canberra Visitor Information Centre*, on Northbourne Avenue in Dickson (Mon–Fri 9am–5pm,

Sat–Sun 8.30am–5pm; ☎205 0044, free call ☎1800/026 166). The more central **tourist information booth** on the lower ground floor of the Canberra Centre, a shopping mall on Bunda Street (Mon–Thurs & Sat 9am–5pm, Fri 9am–7.30pm), provides maps and information but doesn't make bookings.

## City transport

The handy *Murray's* **Canberra Explorer Bus** (☎295 3611; hourly 10.15am–4.15pm; one-day ticket $18, one-hour tour $7; YHA discounts) does a circuit, starting from the Jolimont Centre, covering all the main sights; the driver provides a running commentary on the places you pass as well as background information on the city.

**Municipal buses** are run by *Action*, and useful routes include service #901 (9am–3pm), which covers the same route as the *Explorer* bus, but without the commentary, and the #904, which runs daily (10.25am–3.25pm) to the Botanic Gardens, Black Mountain and Telecom Tower, and the Aquarium. Other **buses** cover all of Canberra, including the satellite towns: for details, phone *Action* **timetable information** (☎207 7611, Mon–Sat 6am–11pm, Sun 8am–5.30pm).

The City Bus Interchange, where most buses start their journeys, is at 11 East Row; you can buy **tickets** at the information kiosk here, or at most newsagents. The best option for most visitors is probably the day-trip ticket ($5), valid all day for as many journeys as you like. Other prices are $2 for a single flat-rate fare (which can also be purchased on board), $11 for a ten-trip ticket, or $18.50 for a weekly ticket. Note that bus services are severely curtailed at the weekend.

The free *Canberra City Tram*, the *Downtowner* (#301), actually a bus dolled up as a tram, runs through the shopping streets of the city centre and is a convenient way to get about – it starts from East Row and runs via Alinga Street and Marcus Clarke Street, around London Circuit along Bunda Street, crossing Akuna Street and Petrie Plaza (Mon–Fri 9am–4.30pm, every 10min).

## Accommodation

Staying in Canberra, on the whole, is not cheap, but on the other hand most places are modern and clean. **Hotels** and **motels** rarely charge less than $70 double although guesthouses often have more reasonable rates. Canberra has an excellent, modern youth **hostel**, and out-of-term inexpensive B&B is available in several student halls of residence. Accommodation in the neighbouring city of Queanbeyan, 14km away, costs on average $10–20 less, so we've listed a couple of suggestions here, too.

### Hotels, motels and guesthouses

**Acacia Motor Lodge**, 65 Ainslie Ave, Braddon (☎249 6955). Very central motel in a leafy street near the war memorial. Light breakfast included. ⑤–⑥.

**Blue & White Lodge**, 524 Northbourne Ave, Downer, 5km north (☎248 0498 or 248 8277). B&B with well-equipped rooms – TV, fridge, heating, tea-making facilities – but shared bathrooms. ④–⑤.

**Capital Parkroyal**, 1 Binara St, Civic (☎247 8999). Central four-star hotel with all the conveniences you'd expect: room service, swimming pool, sauna, gym etc. ⑧.

**Chelsea Lodge**, 526 Northbourne Ave, Downer, 4km north (☎248 0655). Recommended non-smoking B&B; rooms with TV, fridge, heating and tea-making facilities. ④–⑤.

**Forrest Motor Inn**, 30 National Circuit, Forrest (☎295 3433). Modern motel in the embassy area next to the pretty Serbian Church. Well set up units with air-con. ⑥.

**Kingston Hotel**, Canberra Ave, Kingston, 6km southwest (☎295 0123). Lively pub with backpacker accommodation, B&B, cheap counter meals. Rooms ③, dorms ①.

**Kythera Motel**, 98 Northbourne Ave, Braddon (☎248 7611). Well-equipped rooms with heating and air-con. Swimming pool. ⑤–⑥.

**Macquarie Private Hotel**, 18 National Circuit, Barton, 6km southeast of the centre (☎273 2325). Comfy place with heating; all share bathroom. Rates – weekly available – include a cooked breakfast, dinner available. ⑤.

**Sunrise Motel**, 9 Uriarra Rd, Queanbeyan (☎297 2822). Value-for-money motel with lots of extras: air-con, videos and swimming pool. ④.

**Tall Trees Motel**, 21 Ainslie St, Ainslie (☎247 9200). Pleasant upmarket motel in quiet shady grounds. Good facilities, including room service and guest laundry. Bus #350. ⑤.

## Hostels and college accommodation

**ANU student accommodation**: *Bruce Hall* (☎267 4000), *Burton & Garran Hall* (☎267 4333), *Fenner Hall* (☎279 9000), *Ursula College* (☎279 4300). Located around the ANU campus in Acton, just west of the city centre; most rooms are singles (②), but there are also a few twins (④).

**Canberra YHA Hostel**, 191 Dryandra St, O'Connor (☎248 9155). One of the YHA's best: this very modern, very friendly hostel backs onto extensive bushland – a peaceful setting – and there's an outdoor terrace to enjoy it from. Reception open daily 7am–10pm with a small shop for supplies; bike rental. Ten minutes from the centre on bus #380 – signposted from the Scrivener St bus stop in Millers Street (five-minute walk). Rooms ④, dorms ①.

**Victor Lodge**, 29 Dawes St, Kingston, 4km southwest of the centre (☎295 7777). Small backpackers hostel with a guesthouse feel. Rooms have TV, heating, washbasin and tea-making facilities, and rates include linen and a light breakfast. Rooms ④, dorms ①.

## Camping and caravan parks

**Canberra Carotel**, Federal Highway, Watson, 6km north of the centre (☎241 1377). Park with swimming pool and café. Tent sites, holiday flats (max. 6 people, ⑦), chalets ⑤, and on-site vans ④.

**Crestview Tourist Park**, 81 Donald Rd, Queanbeyan (☎297 2443). Facilities include swimming pool and shop. Camping space, plus cabins ③–④.

**Federal Highway Tourist Park**, Federal Highway, 12km northeast in Sutton, NSW (☎241 6411). Good facilities – swimming pool, tennis courts, licensed bistro and supermarket. Cabins ⑤.

**White Ibis Tourist Village and Caravan Park**, Bidges Rd, off the Federal Highway, 12km northeast in Sutton, NSW (☎230 3433). Good site with pool, tennis court and kiosk. Cabins ④.

# The City

Strictly planned as it is, Canberra is a straightforward place to find your way around – though distances are such that only in the very centre will you want to do much walking, and even there it can be something of a test of fitness. The eleven-kilometre-wide **Lake Burley Griffin** marks pretty much the heart of the city. North of the lake is the city centre proper, the **Civic Centre** or "Civic" for short, which houses shops, restaurants, cafés, pubs, cinemas and theatres, as well as the GPO and the tourist information office. The campus of the **Australian National University** (ANU) is just to the west of the centre in the suburb of Acton, beyond which rises the **Black Mountain** (806m), topped by the distinctive Telecom Tower. The **Commonwealth Avenue Bridge** links the city centre with the the political quarter south of the lake, home of government offices and the parliament buildings, and where much of the architectural interest lies. The Prime Minister himself resides at *The Lodge* in Yarralumla, at the foot of Capital Hill, while most of the foreign embassies – intended to resemble the vernacular architecture of their home country – cluster around Yarralumla and Forrest.

## National Library, museums and galleries

Crossing the Commonwealth Avenue Bridge, a left turn takes you into King Edward Terrace, the base of the **Parliamentary Triangle** whose apex is the new Parliament House on Capital Hill (see below). On the other side of King Edward Terrace, fronting the lake, are four impressive modern public buildings. First of these is the **National**

**Library** (Mon & Wed 9am–9pm, Tues & Thurs–Sat 9am–4.45pm; Reading Room Mon–Thurs 9am–9pm, Fri & Sat 9am–4.45pm, Sun 1.30pm–4.45pm; free guided tours Tues, Wed & Thurs 2pm; enquiries ☎262 1111), whose Reading Room has a comprehensive selection of overseas newspapers and magazines. There are also exhibitions in the foyer of rare books, and usually some kind of interesting temporary display including items from the 40,000-strong pictorial collection; you can view any of those not on display via an interactive touch-screen system in the foyer. The library's *Brindabella Bistro* is a good place to stop for a cappuccino and a snack – open until half an hour before the library closes.

Next to the library is **Questacon – the National Science and Technology Centre** (daily 10am–5pm; $6, kids $3), a "hands-on" museum opened in 1988 as a joint Australian/Japanese bicentennial project. The centre's six galleries are arranged around a 27m-high drum at the core of the building, and linked by a continuous spiral walkway. There are some free interactive exhibits in the foyer if you just want a taste, but it's a good place to keep kids occupied, and there's another fine café.

The **National Gallery** (daily 10am–5pm; $3, special exhibitions extra; free guided tours 11am & 2pm), is on Parkes Place, just the other side of the High Court (see below); if you're only going to see a couple of sights in Canberra, make this one of them. Occupying fourteen galleries spread over three floors, there are regular special exhibitions, including international touring shows, and the permanent displays include a major collection of Australian art, with the 25 paintings of Sidney Nolan's *Ned Kelly* series painted in the 1940s, as well as works by Russell Drysdale (including *The Drover's Wife*, probably his most famous), John Perceval, Arthur Boyd and Albert Tucker. There's also a fairly good collection of modern European and North American art: Monet, de Chirico, Magritte and Tanguy among them. For most visitors, though, the highlight is the extensive Aboriginal art collection, which ranges through politically aware contemporary work in many mediums, touching naive-style nineteenth-century drawings, and traditional pieces including some stunning bark paintings. Outside, the Sculpture Garden overlooks Lake Burley Griffin and the Carillon; on summer evenings, concerts and other events are sometimes arranged out here. There's also an excellent bookshop and two restaurants.

The rest of the city's museums are more scattered, but it's worth a slight detour to take in the **National Film and Sound Archive** on McCoy Circuit, just west of the city in Acton. Housed here is the most comprehensive collection of Australian sound and screen recordings in existence, dating back to the 1890s. An interactive exhibition (daily 9am–5pm; $1) is a real experience: via infra-red lights, special headphones tune in to the frequency of each display as you pass. A highlight of the exhibits is the yellow car that split in two in the 1986 film *Malcolm*; the scene's replayed on a video screen too. Past eras come alive at the press of a button, providing historical footage of various towns in Australia. A wildcard display of Australian TV ads feature some real humdingers from the 1970s, and you can watch fascinating snippets from old newsreels in a small projection room. The green, spacious ANU campus nearby is a pleasant place to wander: the two small **anthropological museums** at the Hope Building in Ellery Crescent are open to the public (Mon–Fri 9am–4pm; free), and there are also the usual student activities, concerts and plays: for information about current and forthcoming events phone the recorded weekly diary on ☎249 0742.

The **National Museum of Australia** is still searching for a home, but you can see a small selection of the museum's collection at the Visitor Centre (Mon–Fri 10am–4pm, Sat & Sun 1–4pm; free), Lady Denman Drive, on the northwestern shore of the lake opposite the Weston Park peninsula. The centre also shows a short film on the ambitious project that will attempt to tell the story of Australia in three integrated themes: Aboriginal Australia, Australia since 1788 and the Australian environment; the museum itself should be completed sometime next century.

Further round Lady Denman Drive, at the western end of the lake by the Scrivener Dam, is the **National Aquarium**, opened in 1989 (daily 9am–5.30pm; $10). Visitors walk through tunnels of acrylic glass underneath an Oceanarium while sharks, sting rays and other creatures glide past, only an arm's length away. Other tanks and exhibits present the ecosystem of the Great Barrier Reef, freshwater fish, sea snakes, marine turtles and saltwater crocodiles.

## The High Court

The **High Court of Australia** (daily 9.45am–4.30pm), west of the National Gallery and linked to it by a footbridge, is the highest authority in the Australian judicial system, set in an appropriately grandiose glass-fronted edifice with a stylized waterfall running alongside the walkway up to the entrance. Its functions are to uphold and interpret the constitution and to hear cases referred from the lower courts, delivering about seventy judgements a year. Visitors can watch a short video that explains the court's function and looks at two of its landmark cases: its 1983 ruling that saved Tasmania's wild Franklin River from damming as part of a hydroelectric scheme; and its finding on the 1992 landrights case, Mabo versus Queensland – a momentous decision that overturned the British legal concept of *terra nullius* whereby Australia had been decreed uninhabited prior to white settlement in 1788. The Great Hall and three court rooms are also worth a peek – and there's a licensed café upstairs.

## Parliament houses

Away from the lake, on King George Terrace at the foot of Capital Hill, is the **Old Parliament House**, whose grounds became the site of a live-in Aboriginal protest dubbed the **Tent Embassy** for over six months in 1972, and has seen sporadic landrights demonstrations since. Aboriginal activists, led by Charles Perkins, set up camp and flew a flag specially designed by Harold Thomas, of the Arrente people, in three bold colours: half black (for the people), half red (for the land), with a circle of yellow in the centre (representing the sun); this was adopted as the Aboriginal flag. The media circus that ensued provided welcome publicity for the Aboriginal landrights campaign – and the cameras were there when the police moved in to enforce a hastily passed by-law prohibiting camping on public land. The building itself, a simple white building in Neoclassical style, was the seat of government from 1927 until 1988, but now houses the **National Portrait Gallery** (daily 9am–4pm; $2; ☎273 4723).

Behind, the **New Parliament House** (daily 9am–5pm, free guided tours every half hour 9am–4.30pm; Question Time 3pm most days; public gallery bookings on ☎277 4889, information line ☎277 5399), with its grass-covered contours, merges into the hill itself. The stunning angular design of the exterior, topped by a sputnik-like flagpole, is nearly matched by the interior. Its impressive entrance hall is dominated by grand marble staircases and columns, and other chambers are adorned with paintings by famous Australian artists (Albert Tucker, Sidney Nolan and Ian Fairweather are represented) and portraits of political and regal figures as well as tapestries, photographs and ceramics. For studious types a display outlines the Australian political system. You can sit in the public gallery and watch the goings on in the House of Representatives or the Senate; Question Time at the House of Representatives makes for good viewing, though it's also the most popular time.

## The diplomatic quarters and the mint

After the visit to the parliament building, a trip through Canberra's diplomatic quarters among upmarket suburban homes – in **Yarralumla** and **Forrest** – completes the political sightseeing tour. The consuls and high commissions were asked to construct buildings that deployed the typical architecture of the countries they represent. The result is an international compendium of architectural styles. Some of the eye-catching national designs worth looking out for include the American Embassy's plantation-style mansion, and the embassies of Thailand, Indonesia (with a small cultural centre), the People's Republic of China and Papua New Guinea.

At the **Royal Australian Mint**, to the southwest in Denison Street, Deakin (Mon–Fri 9am–4pm, Sat & Sun 10am–3pm; free), you can watch money being "made" on weekdays and acquire a few items for your coin collection at the Collectors' Shop.

## The Australian War Memorial and Mount Ainslie

To the east of the city, the massive, domed building perched at the base of Mount Ainslie, at the far end of Anzac Parade – looking out towards the lake and the parliament – is the **Australian War Memorial** (daily 9am–4.45pm; free guided tours at 10.30am & 1.30pm). At the same time as commemorating the 102,000 Australian soldiers who have lost their lives in seven wars in the last hundred years, most movingly in the Hall of Memory, this is also a military museum, depicting war through miniature battle dioramas and old aircraft. Although it's the most visited museum in Australia, with an average of about a million visitors a year – many of them motivated by patriotism – this mixture makes for slightly uneasy viewing: it's an unquestioningly heroic past that's constructed here, with the Anzac legend as its most illustrious episode (see box below). For something more life-affirming, the picnic grounds in bushland behind the memorial yield the beginning of a walk to the summit of Mount

---

### THE ANZACS

Almost every small Australian town has a war memorial dedicated to the memory of the Anzacs, the **Australia and New Zealand Army Corps**.

When war erupted in Europe in 1914, Australia was overwhelmed by a wave of pro-British sentiment. On August 5, 1914, one day after Great Britain had declared war against the German empire, the Australian Prime Minister summed up the feelings of his compatriots: "When the Empire is at war so Australia is at war". On November 1, 1914, a contingent of 20,000 enthusiastic volunteers – the **Anzacs** – left from the port of Albany in Western Australia to assist the mother country in her struggle.

In Europe, Turkey had entered the war on the German side in October 1914. At the beginning of 1915, military planners in London (Winston Churchill prominent among them) came up with a plan to capture the strategically important Turkish peninsula of the Dardanelles with a surprise attack near **Gallipoli**, thus opening the way to the Black Sea. On April 25, 1915, 16,000 Australian soldiers landed at dawn in a small bay flanked by steep cliffs: by nightfall, 2000 men had died in the hail of Turkish bullets from above. The plan, whose one chance of success was surprise, had been signalled by troop and ship movements long in advance; by the time it was carried out, it was already doomed to failure. Nonetheless, Allied soldiers continued to lose their lives for another eight months without ever gaining more than a feeble foothold.

In December, London finally issued the order to withdraw; 11,000 Australians and New Zealanders had been killed, along with as many French and three times as many British troops. The Turks lost 86,000 men.

Official Australian historiography continues to mythologize the battle for Gallipoli, elevating it to the level of a national legend on which Australian identity is founded. From this point of view, in the war's baptism of fire, the Anzac soldiers proved themselves heroes who did the new nation proud, their loyalty and bravery evidence of how far Australia had developed. It was "the birth of a nation", and at the same time a loss of innocence, a national rite of passage – never again would Australians so unquestioningly involve themselves in foreign ventures.

April 25, **Anzac Day**, is a national holiday, and the legend is as fiercely defended as ever, the focal point of Australian national pride. The question of why a futile battle in someone else's interests occupies such a central place is one it may be better not to ask.

Ainslie – really a large round hill and part of Canberra Nature Park – the lookout of which provides a perfect view over the city and the Parliamentary Triangle.

## Back to the lake

On the northeastern shore of the lake is one of few historic buildings in the city: **Blundells Cottage**, on Wendouree Drive in Kings Park (daily 10am–4pm; $2), serves as a reminder of the farming industry that flourished here before Canberra became the capital; the simple farmhouse once housed workers from a sheep station, and has been preserved as a small museum. Almost due south of here, stranded on Aspen Island in the lake, is the **Carillon** (recitals Wed 12.30–1.30pm & Sun 2.45–3.30pm), whose three belltowers with 53 bells were a gift from the British government to mark Canberra's fiftieth birthday.

Heading towards the Commonwealth Avenue Bridge, you'll pass the **National Capital Exhibition** at Regatta Point (daily 9am–5pm; free); the exhibition comprises a small theatre, displays and models depicting Canberra's development from the cattle and sheep pastures of the nineteenth century to its modern incarnation as capital city. There's a great view from the terrace, though on windy days you have to beware of the spray from the **Captain Cook Memorial Jet** (10am–noon & 2–4pm; also 7–9pm during daylight saving), which spurts a column of water 140m into the air. The jet, built in 1970 to mark the bicentenary of Captain Cook's "discovery" of Australia, costs $125 an hour to run – hence the limited operating times.

## Black Mountain and around

The **National Botanic Gardens** (daily 9am–5pm; free guided tours Wed, Fri & Sun 11am, Sat & Sun 2pm), on the flanks of Black Mountain, are well worth a diversion from the city centre – beautiful in themselves and an excellent introduction to Australian flora. About 6000 species of native flora have been planted here in ecological niches including an example of Sydney Basin flora, some mallee shrubland, and rainforest species growing in a shady, watered gully. There are hundreds of different types of eucalypts, banksias and proteaceas as well as tree ferns and even an Aboriginal trail. The main entrance is located at Clunies Ross Street, beyond the university area: there's a Visitor Information Centre (daily 9.30am–4.30pm; ☎250 9450), with leaflets for self-guided tours, displays and videos, and a small bookshop; nearby there's a pleasant coffee shop (same hours).

While you're here, you should take the opportunity to drive up to Black Mountain, which rises about 200m above Canberra. On clear days, the panoramic view of Canberra and across the ACT from the 58m-high viewing platform at the **Black Mountain Telecom Tower** (daily 9am–10pm; $3) is magnificent. The tower also houses a cafeteria and a revolving restaurant (advance booking recommended on ☎248 6162). Both the gardens and tower are on the route of *Action* bus #904, which also goes to the aquarium (see below).

North of Black Mountain, the **Australian Insitute of Sport**, on Leverrier Crescent, in Bruce (☎252 1301; tours daily 11am & 2pm; $2.50) is a manifestation of Australia's craze for sport. The ultra-modern multimillion-dollar complex was established in 1981 with the aim of churning out world-class sportsmen and women. There's also a shop selling souvenirs and sports clothing – just in case you decide to take advantage of the facilities: a heated pool ($3.50), spa and sauna ($6), and indoor and outdoor tennis courts ($8–10 per hour).

## Canberra Nature Park

The bush hills and ridges which intersperse Canberra's suburbs make up the **Canberra Nature Park** with many walking tracks to explore. You can pick up maps and guides from the *ACT Government Information Shop Front*, Saraton Building, East

Row, Civic or call the park headquarters for more information on ☎207 2090. The park is actually comprised of many sites: one of the most accessible is the Bruce/O'Connor Ridge section, across Belconnen Way from the Black Mountain area of the park; from here, several walking tracks head through bushland, including one that runs right behind the well-positioned youth hostel.

# Eating and drinking

All cuisines imaginable are represented somewhere in Canberra and the surrounding suburbs, and if you've got the time it's well worth getting out of the centre to explore some of them. Woolley Street in **Dickson** is the best suburban street to head for, crammed as it is with a variety of Asian restaurants and supermarkets. The well-off areas of **Manuka** and **Kingston**, near New Parliament House, harbour gourmet delis and fine restaurants. **Civic** itself is well served with places to eat, especially in the pedestrian mall around Garema Place. In addition to the restaurants listed here, Canberra's many clubs (see "Entertainment", below) also serve very inexpensive meals in a typical Aussie atmosphere – the food is designed to keep you there, playing the pokies and other gambling machines. **Cafés** are plentiful around the centre, with a particular concentration on Bunda Street, near the cinemas.

## Restaurants

**Alaa Dean**, corner of Garema Place and Bunda Street. A simple Lebanese restaurant with eat-in booths – and takeaway service. Sticky sweets to finish with. Daily 9.30am–9.30pm; BYO.

**ANU Union**, Union Crescent in Acton. The students' union has a restaurant, a café and a super-cheap bistro specializing in Asian food; lunch and dinner Mon–Fri, BYO.

**Australian Pizza Kitchen & Brewery**, Lower Ground Floor, Bailey's Corner, London Circuit. Good, cheap pizzas plus Canberra's only "boutique brewery", where beer is brewed on the premises. Pleasant beer garden.

**Delicateating**, Macpherson St, O'Connor Shopping Centre. Trendy delicatessen-style place tending towards Italian cuisine, and conveniently located near the youth hostel. Mellow yellow walls and tables outside. Mon–Fri 10am–10pm, Sat & Sun 9am–10pm. BYO.

**Dorette's Bistro**, 17 Garema Place. Australian and international dishes, from 5pm. Jazz from 9pm most evenings. Licensed.

**Fringe Benefits Brasserie**, 54 Marcus Clarke St, Civic (☎247 4042). Stylish restaurant with an extensive wine cellar. Closed Sun; licensed.

**Glebe Park**, 15 Coranderrk St, a few minutes from the centre. A choice of inexpensive restaurants, a café and a pub under one roof. Open daily from early until late.

**Gundaroo Pub**, Cork St, Gundaroo. Features "typical Outback Aussie atmosphere" with dishes like kangaroo-tail soup, roast and three veg, or damper and billy tea.

**Karuna House**, 32 Archibald St, Lyneham. Oriental-style vegetarian restaurant at the Sakyamuni Buddhist Centre; $10 buffet dinner Tues–Sun, or $7 lunch at weekends only.

**Madam Yip**, 54 Woolley St, Dickson (☎247 1741). Modern Asian restaurant with a contemporary approach, and an emphasis on fresh seafood. Moderately priced. Daily; licensed and BYO.

**Mama's Trattoria**, 7 Garema Place (☎248 0936). Decent, usually crowded, Italian restaurant.

**Montezuma's Mexican**, FAI House, 197 London Circuit, Civic (☎248 0062). Loud and popular, with live entertainment Fri–Sun.

**New Shanghai**, 23 Woolley St, Dickson. Fabulous *dim sum* at agreeable prices. Daily; licensed.

**The Oak Room**, Hyatt Hotel, 1 Commonwealth Ave, Yarralumla (☎270 1234). Expense-account territory: suitably refined old-school dining. Blokes need a tie at dinner. Closed Sun & Mon; licensed.

**Ottoman Cuisine**, first floor, Shop 8, Franklin St, Manuka (☎239 6754). Excellent Turkish restaurant that is a little more expensive than you might pay in Sydney, but worth it. Closed Sun; licensed.

**Red Sea Restaurant**, 128 Bunda St (☎257 6633). African restaurant serving Eritrean and Moroccan cuisine – stews, couscous and the like. A club here gets kicking after 9pm, sometimes with live African music. Lunch Tues–Fri, dinner Tues–Sun; licensed and BYO.

**Tummy's Kitchen**, Manuka Shopping Centre, Furneaux St, Manuka. Popular casual Chinese and Malaysian; delicious *laksa*. Daily; BYO.

**University House Boffins**, corner of Balmain Crescent and Liversidge St, on the ANU campus in Acton (☎249 5285). Very good food daily at lunchtime and 6–9pm; advance booking recommended.

## Cafés

**The Café**, Barrine Drive, west of the Commonwealth Avenue Bridge, next to *Mr Spokes Bike Hire*. Lovely spot by the lake, open daily from 9am.

**Caffe della Piazza**, 19 Garema Place. Enjoyable place with arty pretensions spills out into the square with sidewalk tables. Great Italian coffee, *focaccia*, pizza and pasta.

**Garema Terrace Coffee Lounge**, 70 Bunda St. Lengthy opening hours, from 9am to midnight daily, later at weekends.

**Gus's Coffee Lounge**, Bunda St, next to *Cinema Center*. Canberra's best café serves inexpensive continental meals and fresh soups with a German/Eastern European bent; lots of choice for vegetarians. Tables outside under a huge tree; magazines and newspapers to read plus chess, scrabble and cards to play. Popular with students.

**The Lunch Bunch**, 7 Mort St (extension of East Row, round the corner from Bunda St). Healthy homemade spinach rolls, gourmet sandwiches, *focaccia* and savoury croissants. Open from 7am.

**Pancake Parlor**, corner of East Row and Alinga St. Open 24 hours Thurs–Sun, which is its main attraction. Mon–Wed 7am–late.

**Waffles Coffee Shop**, 46 Northbourne Ave. Open early for breakfast.

# Entertainment and nightlife

There's plenty happening in Canberra, and if it all sometimes seems rather "worthy", that's made up for by the liveliness of the student scene and by liberal licensing laws. For current events, the daily *Canberra Times* is your best bet: the most extensive **listings** are published every Thursday in a cultural and entertainment supplement, *Good Times*. For details of goings-on of bands and at clubs, pick up a copy of *BMA*, a free monthly music magazine. The Visitor Information Centre and most hotels also distribute the quarterly booklet *Canberra What's On*, with listings of major cultural events.

## Music

The *ANU Bar*, entertaining 6000 or so students, is invariably a good place for bands of all sorts, with live performances at least a couple of times a week in term (☎249 5010 for details), while the *Canberra Workers Club* (☎248 0399) hosts big touring bands. Otherwise, **rock bands** mainly play the pubs: *Moosehead's Pub*, 105 London Circuit (☎257 6496), the *Rose and Crown Tavern*, 36 Brierley Street, Weston (☎288 8428), *Matilda's Tavern* at the Cooleman Shopping Centre, Weston (☎288 4854), *The Stockade Tavern*, 17 Lonsdale Street, Braddon (☎247 0848), and the *Terminus Tavern*, East Row, Civic (☎249 6990) for indy bands. The *School of the Arts Café*, 108 Monaro Street in Queanbeyan (☎297 6857), is also worth checking out: as well as featuring new bands, it often has new plays by fringe theatre groups and comedy acts.

**Jazz** can be heard at *The Contented Soul*, Woden Town Square, Woden (☎282 1263) on Thursdays, or Sunday afternoons at the *Canberra Yacht Club*, Lotus Bay, Coronation Drive, Yarralumla (☎273 1784). *Dorette's Bistro* at Garema Place in the city (☎247 4946) is also a regular jazz venue. Sunday nights at *Tilleys*, an ambient café/bar/gallery in Lyneham at 96 Wattle St (☎249 1543), features jazz from 7pm. On Mondays, **folk** and **blues** fans head for the front bar of the *Kingston Hotel*, 73 Canberra Avenue (☎295 6844), and on Sunday evenings to the *Pot Belly Bar*, Weedon Close, Belconnen (☎251 4530). **Classical music** performances are staged sporadically at the *Canberra Theatre Centre* in Civic Square (☎257 1077), and regularly at the *Canberra School of Music*, Llewellyn Hall (☎249 5700).

## Theatre and cinema

The main **drama** venue in the capital is the impressive *Canberra Theatre Centre* in Civic Square (☎257 1077). In addition to a broad range of plays, its several theatres also host concerts, dance performances and readings – it's always worth finding out what's going on here. In addition there are a number of active independent theatre groups based at the *Gorman House Community Arts Centre* in Ainslie Avenue, Braddon: *Interact Theatre* (☎249 8092), *Jigsaw Theatre* (☎247 2133), *Human Veins Dance Theatre* (☎247 5152) and *Reid House Theatre Workshop* (☎247 2133). The *Skylark Puppet & Mask Theatre* is based at Strickland Crescent, Deakin (☎285 1121).

As for **cinemas**, the *Cinema Center* in Bunda Street (☎249 7979; half-price Tues and after 6pm Sun) is probably the best of the regular commercial choices with Saturday late shows at 11pm. For more interesting movies, try the *Electric Shadows Cinema*, Akuna Street (☎247 5060).

## Clubs

Numerous **clubs**, most of which admit visitors, are one of the features of Canberra life. They often serve cheap meals, and may also organize live music, film evenings, parties or comedy shows: the catch is that while you're here you're expected to gamble your money away on the one-armed bandits. One of the biggest is the *Canberra Workers Club* on Childers Street (☎248 0399): it boasts a bistro serving meals every day, regular discos, and darts and pool as well as the pokies. The *Canberra Tradesmen's Union Club*, 2 Badham Street, Dickson (☎248 0999), has a sauna, gym and squash courts, an observatory with an astronomical officer on duty (dusk until about 12.30am), and a Bicycle Museum (daily 9am–midnight); you can even dine in a restored tram, or have your hair cut in a 1920s-style barber shop. The attractions are all free, but children have to leave by 8pm, when the sinful poker machines rev up. The *Canberra Labor Club*, Chandler Street, Belconnen (☎251 5522), serves meals daily and offers bingo as well as occasional disco or rock nights.

More conventional **nightclubs** include *Pandora's*, corner of Mort and Alinga streets (Mon–Sat; ☎248 7405), with two floors of dance music, disco and rock; *Jagger's*, in the basement of 2 Mort Street, City Walk Arcade (Mon–Sat till late; ☎257 4249); and *The Firehouse*, 79 Garema Street (☎257 3631). When they're not hanging out at the ANU bar, students often head for *The Asylum* on 23 East Row (☎257 7311), opposite the bus interchange, a hip bar with free pool table, and a dance floor upstairs – DJs play underground dance music. Also worth checking out is *Club Asmara*, 128 Bunda St (☎257 6633), an African-run joint with live African music and Latin nights.

## Listings

**Airlines** *Ansett*, Jolimont Centre, Northbourne Ave (☎245 1111 or 13 1300); *Qantas*, Jolimont Centre, Northbourne Ave (☎13 1313). For airport transport call *ACT Minibuses* (☎250 8211).

**American Express** 185 City Walk, corner of Petrie Plaza, City (☎247 2333 or 008/230 100).

**Banks** The city branches of the bigger banks are open Mon–Thurs 9.30am–4pm, Fri until 5pm: *ANZ*, 19 London Circuit; *Commonwealth Bank*, corner of London Circuit and Ainslie Ave; *National Australia Bank*, corner of London Circuit and Ainslie Ave; *Westpac*, corner of Alinga and Mort streets.

**Bike rental** *Dial-a-Bicycle* (☎286 5463); *Canberra Bike Rental* (☎241 2216, 24hr telephone booking); *The Gecko Gang*, Glebe Park, Reid (☎257 2609); *Mr Spokes Bike Hire*, Barrine Drive at Lake Burley Griffin, Acton (☎257 1188); *Wombat Mountain Bikes*, Lyons Clatex, Devonport St (☎285 4058, after hours ☎288 2753).

**Buses** For public bus information phone *Action timetable information* (Mon–Sat 6am–11pm, Sun 8am–5.30pm, ☎251 6566), or call at the kiosk at the City Bus Interchange, 11 East Row. Long-distance services are based at the Jolimont Centre, 65 Northbourne Ave: *Greyhound.Pioneer* (☎257

4424 or central reservations ☎13 1300); *Murrays Coaches* (☎295 3611; Sydney, Wollongong, Batemans Bay & the Snowy Mountains); *Capital Coaches* (☎238 3334; west and northwest to Orange, Dubbo & Bathurst); *Cooma Buslines* (☎064/52 1250; to Cooma).

**Car rental** Cheapies include *Network Rent a Car* (☎231 5095); *Rent-a-dent* (☎257 5947, also camper vans); *Rick's Rent a Car* (☎285 1053); and *Rumbles Rent a Car* (☎280 7444). Others, mostly clustered on Lonsdale St in Braddon, with additional locations at the airport, are *Avis* (☎249 6088, airport ☎249 1601); *Budget*, airport (☎13 2727 or 13 2848); *Hertz* (☎257 4877, airport ☎249 6211); *Thrifty* (☎247 7422, airport ☎248 9081).

**Embassies and High Commissions** (all in Yarralumla, unless otherwise stated) *Canada*, Commonwealth Ave (☎273 3844); *Germany*, 119 Empire Court (☎270 1911); *Indonesia*, 8 Darwin Ave (☎250 8600); *Ireland*, 20 Arkana St (☎273 3022); *Malaysia*, 7 Perth Ave (☎273 1543); *Netherlands*, 120 Empire Circuit (☎273 3111); *New Zealand*, Commonwealth Ave (☎273 3611); *Norway*, 17 Hunter St (☎273 3444); *Papua New Guinea*, Forster Crescent (☎273 3322); *Singapore*, Forster St (☎273 3944); *Sweden*, Turrana St (☎273 3033); *Switzerland*, 7 Melbourne Ave, Forrest (☎273 3977); *Thailand*, 111 Empire Circuit (☎273 1149); *UK*, Commonwealth Ave (☎270 6666); *USA*, 21 Moonah Place (☎270 5000).

**Environment Centre** Kingsley St, Acton (☎247 3064), library and archive on environmental topics as well as a book and gift shop (Mon–Fri 9am–5pm); the *Wilderness Society*, Griffin Centre, Bunda St (☎257 5122), also has a book and gift shop and information about the local environment.

**Festivals** The big event of the year is the *Canberra Festival* – the anniversary of the city's foundation – celebrated with concerts, theatre, exhibitions, street parades and fireworks for ten days from the beginning of March. It's followed in late March by *Word Fest*, a writers' festival held at ANU (programme available from Jan; details on ☎249 7068). The *Royal Canberra Show* is an agricultural fair lasting three days over the last weekend in February, while the *Floriade* is a spring festival marked by floral displays, theatre, music and the like, from mid-September to mid-October.

**Galleries** Good private galleries include the *Chapman Gallery*, 31 Captain Cook Drive, Manuka (Wed–Sun 11am–6pm; ☎295 2550), specializing in Aboriginal art; the *Beaver Galleries*, 81 Denison St, Deakin (Wed–Sun 10.30am–5pm; ☎282 5294), for paintings, sculpture, jewellery and furniture.

**Gay and lesbian** *Gayline* ☎247 2726 (nightly 6–10pm); *Gay contact* ☎257 2855 (same hours).

**Horse-riding** *Brindabella Valley Trails*, 19 Sabine Close, Garran (☎281 6682), riding in the beautiful Brindabella Ranges close to Kosciusko National Park.

**Hospital** *Royal Canberra Hospital*, Lennox Crossing, Acton (☎243 2111); *John James Memorial Hospital*, Strickland Crescent, Deakin (☎281 8100).

**Markets** *Canberra Arts and Crafts Market*, Gorman House Arts Centre, Ainslie Ave, Braddon (Sat 10am–4pm), community market where items like pottery, handpainted T-shirts, bric-a-brac and secondhand clothes are sold; *Fyshwick Markets*, Dalby St (Thurs–Sun 8am–5.30pm), large market for fruit, vegetables, meat, fish, cheeses, deli articles and flowers.

**Nature reserves** Information on ACT parks and reserves from *Canberra Nature Park* (☎207 2090) and *ACT Parks and Conservation Service* (☎237 5120). For Namadgi National Park, which takes up virtually the whole southern half of the ACT, and nearby national parks in NSW, contact the *Australian National Parks and Wildlife Service*, 153 Emu Bank, Belconnen (☎250 0200).

**NRMA** 92 Northbourne Ave, Braddon, or Belconnen Mall, Belconnen (☎13 2132). The NRMA hands out a very useful map of Canberra and the ACT, free for members. Touring and accommodation enquiries ☎243 8844.

**Police** ☎249 7444; emergency ☎000.

**Post office** Alinga St, Canberra, ACT 2600 (Mon–Fri 9am–5pm; ☎209 1370).

**Rape Crisis Centre** ☎247 8071 or 247 2525.

**Scenic flights** *Vee H Aviation* (☎248 6766), from about $35 per person for 35–40min.

**Shopping** Shopping hours are Mon–Thurs 9am–5.30pm, Fri 9am–9pm, Sat 9am–noon. Late opening supermarkets in the shopping centres of the satellite towns. Shops at the new *Canberra Centre*, between City Walk and Bunda St in the city, are open every day.

**Taxis** *Aerial Taxis* (☎285 9222); *Diamond Radio Taxis*, Queanbeyan (☎297 3000).

**Tours and cruises** *Murrays* (☎295 3611), half- or full-day coach tours around Canberra and to the Snowy Mountains; *Mudmaps Australia* (☎257 4796), full-day 4WD wilderness tours to the surrounding mountain ranges; *Bunyip Bush Safaris* (☎255 1472), trips for small groups to the Snowy

Mountains and further afield to the national parks of southeast Australia; *Ultimate Tours* (☎291 8117), sightseeing in and around Canberra from the back of a Harley Davidson. *Canberra Cruises* (☎295 3544) offer 90-minute cruises twice daily ($11) in the Central Basin of Lake Burley Griffin, with additional evening cruises in summer.

**Trains** Ticket sales and information at the *Countrylink Travel Centre*, Jolimont Centre, 65 Northbourne Ave (☎257 1576), and at the train station in Kingston (☎239 0133). For information on trains and *Countrylink* buses in NSW, ☎1800/04 3126.

**Travel agents** *Canberra Flight Centre*, City Walk Arcade, 2 Mort St, Civic (☎247 8199); *STA Travel*, 13–15 Garema Place, Civic (☎247 8633; Mon–Sat 9am–5pm).

**Women** *Women's Information and Referral Centre*, North Building, London Circuit, City (☎205 1076; Mon–Fri 9am–5pm).

# Around Canberra

The residents of Canberra live with nature right on their doorstep: the numerous picnic grounds and bushwalking trails in the **state reserves and national parks** are only about half an hour's drive from the city centre. At the height of summer, when there is a high risk of bushfires, a total fire ban is declared and all the nature reserves and national parks are closed (call ☎06/207 8600 to check).

Bushland aside, the environs of the capital can also lay claim to historic homesteads and villages, private zoos, a former goldmining town and a few wineries, some of them across the border into New South Wales.

## Heading south

Heading south from Canberra, the private, open-range **Mugga Lane Zoo** (daily 9am–5pm, last entry 4pm; $7.50, $3.50 kids; ☎06/295 3610) is barely outside the city at all, just 4km from the New Parliament House at Mugga Lane, off Hindmarsh Drive, Symonston. Here, in nine hectares of bushland, you can see kangaroos, wallabies and wombats, as well as dingoes and emus.

Leaving the city further behind, the Tharwa Road follows the course of the **Murrumbidgee River** as it approaches Tharwa. Thirty-two kilometres from the city, at the southern end of the Tuggeranong Valley, the historic, convict-built **Lanyon Homestead** (Tues–Sat 10am–4pm, grounds open to 5pm; admission to grounds free, $3 for house, $4 including gallery; ☎237 5136) dates back to the earliest European settlement of the region. Thoroughly refurbished by the National Trust, it now houses a small display outlining the history of the area before Canberra existed, but the real reasons to come are the house itself and the **Sidney Nolan Gallery** next door, where works by the famous Australian painter are on permanent display alongside changing exhibitions of contemporary Australian art. There's no public transport out here.

Beyond the Lanyon Homestead and Tharwa, old cottages overlooking the river on the Naas Road house the galleries and antique shops of the **Cuppacumbalong Craft Centre** (Wed–Sun & holidays 11am–5pm; ☎06/237 5116); the small, licensed café serves hearty meals and local cider, and there's a spot nearby where you can swim in the river.

### Namadgi National Park

**Namadgi National Park** occupies almost half of the ACT, largely made up of wilderness areas in the west and southwest. Its mountain ranges and high plains, rising to 1900m, have a far more severe climate than low-lying Canberra; among them rise the Cotter River and many smaller streams. In the northwest, the Corin Road leads to Corin Dam, while in the south the partly surfaced Bobyan Road cuts right through the national park, emerging beneath the Snowy Mountains in the south (the park abuts the Kosciusko National Park along the state border). There are picnic grounds and bush campsites by the Orroral River and near Mount Clear in the south.

The **Namadgi Visitors' Information Centre**, 3km south of Tharwa on the Naas Road (daily 9am–4pm; ☎06/237 5222; in emergency call ranger ☎06/288 6325), has displays and videos about the park as well as detailed information on bushwalking tracks and emergency shelters in remote areas, and maps.

## West: Tidbinbilla Nature Reserve

The small **Tidbinbilla Nature Reserve** lies to the southwest of the city – an enjoyable place with relatively easy walks, and some wheelchair-accessible paths. In the area around the park entrance and visitors' centre (daily 8.30am–5.30pm; ☎06/237 5120) kangaroos and wallabies roam in spacious bush enclosures, and you can also see koalas and lots of birds. Picnic grounds are dotted all along the sealed road that leads through the reserve, and on long weekends and during the school holidays it's a busy place, especially popular with families. The **Tidbinbilla Deep Space Tracking Station** (visitors' centre open daily 9am–5pm; free) sounds like every kid's dream, though in fact the displays of spacecraft and highly sensitive communications equipment are not as exciting as you might have hoped. Operated in conjunction with NASA, the purpose of the station is to pick up even the most obscure signals from outer space; there are only two others in the world with the same range as Tidbinbilla – one near Madrid, the other in Goldstone, California.

Southwest of here, Corin Road turns off the Tidbinbilla Road towards the **Corin Forest** (winter daily 8am–10pm; otherwise Wed, Sun & holidays 10am–6pm; ☎06/247 2250) and reservoir, a popular recreation spot in the hills, with many walking trails, picnic grounds and barbecue facilities. In winter you can ski on artificial snow and during school holidays special activities are organized for children.

### Cotter Reserve

The **Cotter Reserve**, near the Cotter Dam, 22km west of the city, is another popular spot for short weekend outings. Here, around an artificial lake that was the original reservoir built to serve the new capital, you'll find picnic grounds, a restaurant and a **campsite** (☎06/271 2888); the Murrumbidgee River nearby is suitable for swimming. On the way to the Cotter Reserve you pass the **Mount Stromlo Observatory** (visitors' gallery open daily, 9am–4.30pm; free; ☎06/249 5111), some 16km from Canberra. The giant silver dome houses the telescopes of the ANU's Department of Astronomy; inside the complex, there are photographic displays and textual information on various aspects of astronomy, and you can see some of the viewing equipment. Once again, there's no public transport out here.

## North: arts, wines and mines

Leaving Canberra by the Barton Highway to the north, the first place of interest is **GINNINDERA**, some 9km out. It's a rather consciously touristy village with a few arts and crafts shops and a restaurant in a log hut, *The Green Herring*. Just before Ginnindera, on Gold Creek Road, is the **National Dinosaur Museum** (daily 10am–5pm; $7.50) – not a big government-run museum as the name might suggest, but rather a private collection of replica skeletons and some bones and fossils. Other local tourist attractions include **Cockington Green** (daily 9.30am–4.30pm; $6), a miniature model English village, and the **Artgems Gallery** (daily 10am–5pm) in the village, with exhibits of paintings, gems (especially opals and crystals), and local arts and crafts.

**HALL**, 3km north of Ginninedra, is a similar historical village with a few shops and a restaurant, and another *Artgems Gallery*.

More or less opposite the turn-off for Hall, the Wallaroo Road heads west towards the New South Wales border. Not far down the road, at Woodgrove Close, is **Brindabella Hill Wines** (☎06/230 2583), where you can sample some of the local "cool climate" vintages. There are more wineries around **MURRUMBATEMAN**, north along the Barton Highway into NSW between Canberra and the large country town of Yass (see p.228); full lists are available from the tourist office.

### The Federal Highway

Northeast of Canberra, the Federal Highway crosses into NSW shortly after leaving the city. The first of the sights out this way is **Rehwinkel's Animal Farm** (daily 10am–5pm; $6), on Mack's Reef Road, 23km from Canberra. Koalas, kangaroos, wombats and emus live in the enclosures of this private bushland zoo, ducks and black swans enjoy the ponds, and parrots, lorikeets and other native birds can be seen in the aviaries.

Not much further on is **Bywong Town Mining Village** (daily 10am–4pm; $7; tours 11am, 1pm & 3pm) where a brief goldrush at the end of the nineteenth century has left shafts and some old mine workings. The gold-diggers' camp has been reconstructed with some serious attention to historical detail, and it's well worth stopping in if you're passing by; you can also try your hand at panning, and there are picnic and barbecue areas. The historic town is on Bungendore Road, further down which lies the attractive village of **BUNGENDORE**, with a pottery, woodturner, café and shops arranged around the village green. Heading on, you can circle back round to Canberra via Queanbeyan, or strike east, a scenic drive through **BRAIDWOOD** – with more antiques and crafts shops, and a fine old hotel – towards the coast at Batemans Bay (see p.177).

# SOUTHERN NSW

There are two quite separate parts to the southern half of New South Wales, just as there are to the state as a whole: the coast, and the mountains and hinterland beyond them. The **south coast** is delightful in a quiet sort of way, green dairy country, an area for fishing or surfing or relaxing on the beaches, with no huge resorts or commercial developments. Inland the **Snowy Mountains** constitute the Dividing Range's highest peaks, the home of Australia's best skiing and, in summer, of some fine bushwalking; beyond the mountains, the southwest is dull, farming country – you're better off crossing to the riverlands of Victoria, or driving straight through.

The direct route from Sydney to Melbourne is via the inland **Hume Highway**, from which you can easily detour to Canberra or the Snowy Mountains. From Sydney to Moss Vale it's a four-lane freeway, the rest of the way a normal two-lane road with occasional overtaking lanes, very winding between Yass and Albury. It is also very busy, with heavy truck traffic, and most of the time quite boring – a potentially lethal combination. It takes roughly twelve hours to drive straight through from Sydney to Melbourne, fine if you're sharing driving, but otherwise allow two days.

The coastal route, the **Princes Highway**, is slightly longer, but much more attractive in terms of scenery. Take two or more days if you want to appreciate the surf, the sandy beaches, and the mountains, valleys and forests behind this beautiful stretch of the coast.

Most **buses** run via the Hume Highway, usually with a detour to Canberra; and the **train** follows largely the same route.

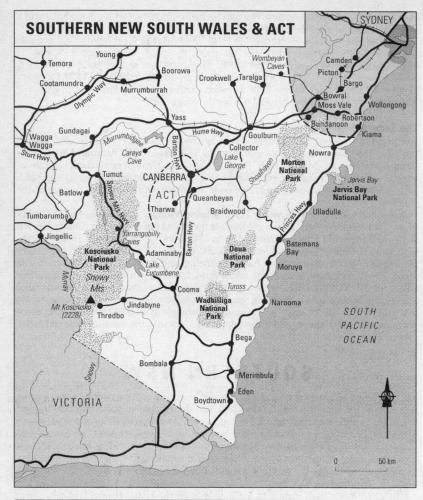

# The Snowy Mountains

The **Snowy Mountains** are just one section of the alpine highlands that spread across the southeastern corner of the Australian continent. The Australian Alps sprawl from Mount Buller, Mount Bogong and Mount Beauty in northeast Victoria via the Crackenback Range in NSW to the township of Cooma; though it's a continuous massif, only the New South Wales section is strictly known as the Snowy Mountains. **Mount Kosciusko**, at 2228m the highest mountain in Australia, is located close to the Victorian border in the far southeast; the **Kosciusko National Park** which surrounds it includes most of the Snowy Mountains region, and almost everything of interest. To the north and east of **Cooma** – the main approach to the range – the treeless, brownish-yellow **Monaro High Plain** is sheep country which is famous for the quality of its merino wool.

Compared to the high mountain ranges of other continents, the "roof of Australia" is relatively low, and despite the name, the flattened mountain tops lie below the line of permanent snow. After heavy snowfalls in winter however (roughly from the end of June to the beginning of October, but never totally reliable), winter sports fans from all over southeast Australia congregate at the **ski resorts** in the Mount Kosciusko area – Perisher, Thredbo, Blue Cow Mountain, Mount Selwyn and Charlotte Pass. It's not the most exciting skiing in the world, with few terribly challenging runs, and prices are hiked up to ridiculous levels as the resorts attempt to make their living during a very short season. Only the most fanatical European winter-sports enthusiast would come here especially to ski, but if you're in the country anyway it can be an enjoyable aside. This is also an ideal area for cross-country skiing, an increasingly popular pursuit. In summer it's a different story: price levels return to normal, the towns and resorts are not quite so crowded, and there are fabulous walks and mountain scenery to be enjoyed. Most of the skilifts still operate, transporting hikers to mountain tops from where they can embark on short or extended bushwalks across the wildflower-covered high country. There are plenty of opportunities for horse-riding, too, and trout fishing in the crystal-clear mountain streams.

The system of roads which made possible the existence of the townships and ski resorts was established by the **Snowy Mountains Hydroelectric Scheme**. This gigantic engineering project to harness the waters of the Snowy Mountains for hydroelectric power and irrigation was begun in the 1950s. Tunnels were dug under the mountains, rivers redirected and dams built. Many post-war immigrants from middle and southern Europe found their first job on the "Snowy"; some lost their lives. Twenty-five years and about 800 million dollars later, the project was completed: seven power stations now utilize the waters of the Upper Murrumbidgee, Tumut and Snowy rivers to generate electricity and provide New South Wales, the ACT and Victoria with power. The scheme's generating capacity is about 18 percent of the total for southeast Australia, while the water of the redirected rivers is used for irrigation right across New South Wales, Victoria and South Australia.

### Getting around

The most important of the area's roads is the **Snowy Mountains Highway** which leads straight across the mountain ranges and through the national park from Cooma to Tumut and Gundagai. If you want to see more of the alpine scenery, the **Alpine Way** offers a spectacular circuit, turning off the highway at Kiandra in the heart of the park, and heading via Khancoban and Geehi to Thredbo. Forty-two kilometres of the route –

---

### SKIING IN THE SNOWY MOUNTAINS

The easiest option is to arrange a **ski package** from Sydney – always check exactly what's included in the price. Recommended operators include *Alpine Accommodation* at *Snowy River Travel* (free call ☎1800/026 385) who can put together a low-season basic weekend package including coach transport, national park entry, one night's accommodation, dinner and two breakfasts for $159; similar deals can be arranged through *Alpine Tours International* (☎02/9901 4499).

A one-day **ski-lift pass** starts from about $54, and beginners' one-day group lessons cost another $54 or so. Resorts are generally pretty child-friendly, particularly at Charlotte Pass where the homey and old-fashioned *Kosciusko Chalet* (free call ☎1800/026 369) offers free childcare throughout the ski season; *Paddy Pallin* at Jindabyne (☎064/56 2922) have several cross-country skiing sessions, including an easy three-hour introduction aimed at family groups (adults $32, kids $22).

Another good source of information on the latest deals is *Inski*, a popular ski shop at 46 York St, Sydney (☎02/233 3200, 02/9233 3200 from July 1996).

around Geehi – consists of rutted gravel road: you don't need 4WD, but you will need lots of time. In winter, check road conditions before driving anywhere, even on the Snowy Mountains Highway; on the Alpine Way and on Kosciusko Road (after Sawpit Creek) **snow chains** must be used between June and October, and the roads can be closed altogether.

**Bus** services are far more frequent in winter than in summer – a **rental car** is strongly recommended for summer sojourns. *Greyhound.Pioneer* do run a shuttle service between Perisher and other ski resorts, and additional winter-only bus services include *Snowliner Coaches* (☎064/52 2312 or 52 1422), *Murrays Coaches* (☎06/295 3611) and *Cooma Coaches* (☎064/52 1259).

# Cooma

Thanks to its location at the intersection of two highways – the Monaro Highway south from Canberra and the Snowy Mountains Highway from the coast to the high peaks – **COOMA** is the obvious base for trips into the Snowy Mountains. Although it functions mainly as a service centre for skiers, it's also an attractive place in its own right, with a number of fine old buildings.

The town has really come into its own since the 1950s when it took on the mantle of administrative centre for the hydroelectric scheme. Many of the migrants who worked on the "Snowy", as it's known – particularly those who arrived from central Europe – ended up settling here, making it a fairly cosmopolitan small town. If you're interested in the history of the project and the technical details, check out the **Visitors Centre** of the Snowy Mountains Authority, in North Cooma, on the Monaro Highway (Mon–Fri 8am–4.30pm, plus weekends during school holidays; explanatory film shows Mon–Fri 11am & 3pm; free). That's about all there is to Cooma, although there's the **Llama Farm**, 19km out of town on the Adaminaby Road (Fri–Sun 10am–4pm, daily during school holidays; $7), where llamas, alpacas and guanacos are bred, to occupy a few idle moments. Llamas aside, the Snowy Mountains are traditionally regarded as prime **horse-riding** country. *Yarramba Trail Riding* at Berridale, 34km southwest of Cooma (☎064/56 3150), has escorted rides at $15 per hour or day-trips following the Murrumbidgee River, as well as extended camping safaris.

## Practicalities

The helpful **Cooma Visitors Centre**, at 119 Sharp Street (daily summer 9am–5pm, winter 7.30am–6pm; ☎064/50 1740 or free call 1800/636 525), has detailed information on Kosciusko National Park plus farmstays, horse-rides and fishing safaris, and offers a free accommodation-booking service. Pick up a copy of the free monthly *Snowy Times*, which has detailed resort information and maps, plus listings of skiing prices and packages. *Harvey World Travel*, 96 Sharp Street, is a helpful **travel agency** which can book flights out, provide details of bus services and arrange local tours (☎064/52 4677), and **car rental** is available from *Thrifty Car Rental*, 1/30 Baron St (☎064/52 5300).

**Accommodation** can be hard to come by in the ski season, when everything, especially the motels, is booked up pretty early, but the rest of the year you shouldn't have too many problems. Good options include the inexpensive and central *Royal Hotel*, on the corner of Lambie and Sharp streets (☎065/52 2132; ③); built in 1858, it's got loads of character – many of the rooms have French windows opening onto the huge balcony; or the family-run *Cooma Backpackers*, 28–30 Soho Street (☎064/52 2983; rooms ④, dorms ①) which is actually more like a guesthouse. The *Swiss Motel*, 34 Massie Street (☎064/52 1950; ④) also has holiday flats on offer – and there are plenty of other motels nearby. *Snowtels Caravan Park*, Snowy Mountains Highway (☎064/52 1828; cabins ③–⑤, apartments ⑤, on-site vans ③), with tennis court and communal kitchen, is probably the best of the campsites. Out of town, you can get away from it all with **farmstay** accommodation at *Rose Valley Station*, 8km along the unsealed Rose Valley Road, after heading 14km northeast along the Monaro Highway, which has cottages sleeping up to six (☎064/52 2885; ⑨); at *Warreen Farm Holidays*, 37km east (☎064/53 3272; ③), with accommodation in a self-catering cabin on a sheep and cattle property; or at *Litchfield Holiday Farm*, Carlaminda Road, 21km east (☎064/53 3231; ⑥) on a riverfront sheep and horse property – rates include all meals and horse-riding.

Cooma's not really a foodie sort of town. The best place to **eat** is *Cafe Upstairs*, 121 Sharp Street, next door to the tourist office: a cross between a café and a licensed brasserie, it serves everything from hamburgers to trout and good-value pasta dishes – plus decent espresso coffee – and is open daily from noon to midnight, and until 2am on weekends. Inexpensive **pub meals** can be had at the bistro of the *Australian Hotel*, 137 Sharp Street.

# Kosciusko National Park and around

New South Wales's largest national park, **Kosciusko National Park**, stretches 200km north to south, from Tumut to the Victorian border, encompassing an area of some 650,000 hectares. The scenery includes almost all of the high country, with ten peaks above 2100m, forested valleys and a treeless plateau with glacial lakes, as well as the headwaters of Australia's biggest river system, the Murray–Murrumbidgee. The main centres are the lakeside resort of Jindabyne, just outside the eastern boundary of the park, and the ski resort of Thredbo, 30km further west along the scenic Alpine Way, actually in the national park; while Perisher and Mount Blue Cow can be reached via the *Skitube* from Bullocks Flat, roughly midway between Jindabyne and Thredbo.

If you're driving through, there's a **fee** of $12 per car per day, $3.50 per motorbike – so if you plan to stay more than a day or two and/or other national parks are on your itinerary, the annual national park pass ($60) may be a good investment (see p.153 for details). Arriving by bus you'll still have to fork out a one-off payment of $4. Note that **parking** can be a problem: it's heavily restricted throughout the park, and can reach crisis-point in Thredbo – if you have a car it might be worth paying extra for accommodation with space to park.

The **National Parks and Wildlife Service** headquarters (daily 8.30am–4.30pm; ☎064/56 2102) is located in Sawpit Creek, a few kilometres northwest of Jindabyne. It offers a comprehensive service, with leaflets about walking trails in the national park, activities such as ranger-guided tours, details of campsites, as well as maps for sale and a display on the natural features of the park. There are also NPWS **ranger stations** at Perisher Valley (☎064/57 5214; winter only), Khancoban (☎060/76 9373), Tumut (☎069/47 0264) and Jindabyne (☎064/47 0264).

## Bushwalking in the park

Some of the country's most interesting and beautiful **bushwalking tracks** pass through the area. One of the most accessible of these is the walking trail around **Mount Kosciusko**. The **chairlift** from Thredbo (see below) will take you up to Crackenback station on the edge of the plateau; the actual summit is about 6km from here, though it seems barely higher than the surrounding country, or you can walk two kilometres to Mount Kosciusko **Lookout**, and panoramic views. Another good way up to the high country is the **Skitube** from Bullocks Flat on the Alpine Way (see below), a funicular railway that leads uphill and through a tunnel to Perisher Valley and Mount Blue Cow, where more fine trails await. Even if you only plan a brief walk of an hour or so, bear in mind that the weather up here is very fickle, and pack a jumper and some rain protection.

## Jindabyne and Thredbo

A resort town at the manmade lake of the same name, **JINDABYNE**, 63km west of Cooma, is the jumping-off point for the ski resorts of Thredbo, a further 30km west, and Guthega, or up the Kosciusko Road to Smiggin Holes and Perisher Valley (these two are also accessible by the **Skitube** – ☎064/56 2010 to check times and fares, which vary). Jindabyne itself is entirely new, having been relocated when the Snowy Mountains Scheme dammed the Snowy River and drowned the first settlement, and the lake is now its main attraction: there's good fishing, and in summer you can also swim and sail – most equipment is available to rent in the town. The **Snowy River Information Centre** is on Petamin Plaza (daily 9am–5pm; ☎064/56 2444).

From Jindabyne, the Alpine Way continues into the national park and up to **THREDBO**, a compact and attractive village, squeezed into a narrow valley beside the road and the Crackenback River, with alpine-style houses huddled against the mountainside. In winter it offers the best and most expensive skiing in Australia; but unlike the other resorts, it is also reasonably lively in summer and – with its **chairlift** (daily 8.30am–4pm; $15) giving easy access to the high country – makes a good base for bushwalking and other explorations.

There are several annual events in the Thredbo calendar. The two musical highlights are the three-day Thredbo **Country and Blues Festival** in mid-January and, in early May, the four-day **Jazz festival** with gigs all over the village. **Mountain bike** enthusiasts can come up for the national championships, also in May (☎1800/020 589 for details; good-value accommodation packages available).

## Yarrangobilly Caves and Kiandra

The **Yarrangobilly Caves**, a system of about sixty limestone caves at the edge of a rocky plateau surrounded by unspoiled bushland, are one of the few specific sights in the park; they're right by the Snowy Mountains Highway near Kiandra, 113km north of Cooma and 70km south of Tumut. There are several guided tours daily to the **North Glory**, **Jersey** and **Jillabenan Caves** (the latter is wheelchair-accessible; $8; ☎064/49 5334 for tour times). A fourth cave, the **Glory Hole Cave** (daily 10am–4pm; $4), can be explored on a self-guided tour. From walking trails along the edge of the rock plateau there are panoramic views of the Yarrangobilly Gorge, and a steep trail leads from the Glory Hole car park to a thermal pool at the bottom of the gorge near the Yarrangobilly River. The spring-fed pool has a year-round constant water temperature of 27°C.

**KIANDRA** itself is a ghost town and a detailed Heritage Trail walks you through the remaining ruins on this desolate windswept spot – a feature of the northern part of the park is its extensive plains, too cold for any trees to survive. It's hard to believe that the goldrush of 1860 saw 15,000 prospectors camped here; the short-term rush left a town of about 300 people who eked out a living mining and grazing.

## Kosciusko area accommodation

In winter, **rooms** are at a premium – despite the plethora of holiday flats and motels, accommodation is almost impossible to come by without a reservation. In summer, the situation is less dire, and you should have little difficulty finding somewhere in one of the resorts, or at motels on the fringes of the park – such as at Tumut in the north or even back in Cooma (see above). Most Thredbo accommodation can be **booked** through the *Thredbo Resort Centre* (☎064/57 6360); the *Snowy River Information Centre* in Jindabyne (☎064/56 2444) also handles accommodation bookings.

**Alpine Accommodation Complex**, Sawpit Creek, near the park HQ (☎064/56 2224). Tent sites and cabins. Advance booking is recommended, especially in winter when, inevitably, prices rise. Cabins ④.

**Alpine Inn**, Khancoban (☎060/76 9498), has lovely timber cottages attached to a great pub and restaurant. ⑤.

**Backpackers' & Fishermen's Lodge**, Khancoban (☎060/76 9471). Next door to the Alpine Inn, and under the same management, this lodge has a communal kitchen, TV lounge and barbecue, plus activities such as horse-riding and whitewater rafting; they also rent out fishing gear, boats and canoes. Rooms ②, dorms ①; BYO linen.

**Kasees Lodge**, Banjo Drive, Thredbo (☎064/57 6370). One of several lodges and motels along Banjo Drive, this one boasts a pool, sauna – and bargain summer rates. ④.

**Nettin Chalet**, 24 Nettin Circuit, Jindabyne (☎064/56 2692). Holiday units – complete with sauna and spa. ⑥.

**Riverglade Caravan Park**, Snowy Mountains Highway, Tumut (☎069/47 2528). Caravan park right by the river, with swimming pool, kiosk and barbecue. On-site vans ③, cabins ④.

**Snowline Caravan Park**, junction of Alpine Way and Kosciusko Rd, Jindabyne (☎064/56 2099). Good facilities, including sauna, café-restaurant and boat rental. Cabins ⑥.

**Snowy Valley Motel**, Kosciusko Rd, 9km east of Jindabyne (☎064/56 7138 or 56 7180). Motel with indoor swimming pool and sauna, as well as meals for residents and non-residents – ask about backpackers specials. Rooms ⑤, dorms ①.

**YHA Lodge**, 8 Jack Adams Pass, Thredbo (☎064/57 6376). Excellent, modern no-smoking hostel; reception open 7–10am & 4.30–9pm; between June and September, bookings must be made in writing through YHA head office in Sydney. Summer ②, winter ③–④.

# The South Coast

The southern coast of New South Wales is relatively quiet, its numerous bays, coastal lakes and inlets interspersed with unspoiled, sandy beaches and small fishing villages and seaside resorts. During the summer months, especially from Christmas to the end of January, a lot of holidaymakers escape here from the "big smoke" up north, or come up from Victoria: the towns can get busy then, especially the **Shoalhaven area** around Nowra, and **Batemans Bay** and **Merimbula**. But don't expect glamorous resort hotels and entertainment Queensland-style – it's all very low-key and family-orientated. There are a few wildlife and amusement parks to keep the kids happy, and plenty of opportunities for traditional outdoor pursuits. Exposed parts of the coast are battered by powerful waves that are a **surfer**'s delight, while the calmer waters of the numerous coastal lakes, bays and inlets are suited for **swimming**, windsurfing, sailing or paddling your own canoe. There's great **fishing** too, in the rivers and lakes, as well as the inevitable deep-sea season, when game-fishers set out to tussle with marlin. Away from the ocean there's some superb, rugged scenery and great bushwalking in the forest-clad, mountainous hinterland; also a popular area for horse-riding. When the summer holidays are over, even the bigger towns revert back to an unassuming, laidback lifestyle, and it's mild enough to enjoy them pretty much year round.

Most of the way down the coast, the **Princes Highway** runs a few kilometres inland. Away from the towns, apparently obscure turn-offs from the highway often lead to beautiful and secluded beaches – it's worth taking some time to make your own discoveries. If you're **heading for Canberra** there are three main routes from the coast: through Kangaroo Valley (see p.149), continuing via Moss Vale (or Bundanoon) and Goulburn; the Capital Highway from Batemans Bay; or the Snowy Mountains Highway from Bega via Cooma.

## Nowra–Bomaderry

Straddling the Shoalhaven River, the twin town of **NOWRA–BOMADERRY** (population about 19,500) is the centre of the Shoalhaven holiday region: Bomaderry is situated north of the river, Nowra south. The wide river around town is great for sailing, windsurfing and boating in general, while the coast, 13km away, is dotted with popular holiday settlements and numerous beaches. **Shoalhaven Heads** north of the river mouth, **Greenwell Point** in the south, **Huskisson** at Jervis Bay and **Sussex Inlet** are all easily accessible on good roads.

For further information on the beaches and how to get to them, and on local accommodation, stop first at the **Shoalhaven Tourist Centre**, 245 Princes Highway, in Bomaderry just north of the river (daily 9am–5pm; ☎044/21 6011). **Accommodation** includes an abundance of motels, plus *The Barracks YHA Hostel*, Meroo Street, Bomaderry (☎044/23 0495; doubles ③, dorms ①), a charming 1920s railway workers' lodge converted into a hostel which offers free pick-up from the bus terminal on demand and organizes 4WD tours into the mountains. *Armstrong's White House*, 30 Junction Street (☎044/21 2084; ④), is a reasonably priced guesthouse, or there's camping at *Shoalhaven Caravillage*, Terrara Road, Nowra (☎044/23 0770; cabins ③–⑤), by the river with facilities including canoe and bike rental, a pool, tennis court and kiosk.

## Jervis Bay

Just southeast of Nowra, the sheltered waters of **Jervis Bay**, by a political quirk, are technically part of the ACT, granted to provide Canberra with access to the sea. The beautiful coast of the **Jervis Bay National Park**, at the southeastern arm of the bay, is very popular, with its rugged cliffs facing the pounding ocean and tranquil beaches of dazzling white sand and clear water within the confines of the bay, while inland heaths, wetlands and forests offer strolls and bushwalks. There are a couple of **campsites** (bookings essential in summer ☎044/43 0977): the more secluded and small *Cave Beach* on Wreck Bay is the most sought-after site despite its cold showers; the larger, more expensive *Greenpatch*, on a creek by Jervis Bay, has the benefit of hot showers and car parking at each tent site. Holiday-unit accommodation, sleeping up to six, is available on Ellmoos Road, at *Kullindi* (☎044/41 2897; ⑤) and *Lumeah* (☎044/412 018; ⑦).

The **Wreck Bay Aboriginal community**, which has land in the middle section of the park, organizes a summer cultural interpretation programme, *Wreck Bay Walkabouts* (bookings and information ☎044/42 1166), covering bush tucker and medicines, archeology and wildlife. On Cave Beach Road, **Jervis Bay Botanic Gardens** (Mon–Fri 8am–4pm, Sun 10am–5pm, closed Sat except Dec–April 10am–5pm; free) is an annexe of Canberra's Australian National Botanic Gardens, and has specimens of plants from around Australia, including a pleasantly cool rainforest gully.

On the western shores of Jervis Bay, 21km southeast of Nowra, **HUSKISSON** is an old town that's a popular tourist spot, with several beachside campsites: *Huskisson Beach Tourist Park*, Beach Street (☎044/41 5142; cabins ④) has a playground and tennis courts; or try *Huskisson White Sands Tourist Park*, corner of Nowra and Beach streets (☎044/41 6025; cabins ③). The focus of the town is the beachfront *Huskisson Hotel*, or the "Huskie Pub" as it's more usually known, with a good bistro and plenty of pool-playing opportunities.

## Ulladulla

In the 1930s, many Italian fishermen settled in the small fishing village of **ULLADULLA**, and they're still a strong influence on the atmosphere of this tranquil outpost: the traditional Blessing of the Fleet is still celebrated every Easter at the harbour breakwater. It's a beautiful area, dominated by the sandstone plateau of the **Morton National Park**, rising steeply to the west of town. Mostly this is an inaccessible barrier, but there's a good bushwalk to the top of 719m **Pigeon House Mountain**. Along the coast in both directions, meanwhile, are attractive river mouths, beaches and lakes: among those worth visiting are pretty **Lake Conjola**, 10km to the north; **Lake Burill**, 5km to the south; and **Lake Tabourie**, 13km to the south – all are popular with fishermen, canoeists and campers.

**Accommodation** includes the *Quiet Garden Motel* on a rocky promontory at 2 Burrill Street (☎044/55 1757; ④–⑦); *Ulladulla Guesthouse*, 39 Burill Street (☎044/55 1796; ④–⑤) which has the luxury of a spa and sauna; the *South Coast Backpackers*, 63 Princes Highway (☎044/54 0500; ①), a family-run hostel providing lifts up to Pigeon House Mountain or Murramarang National Park (see below). The *Beach Haven Tourist Resort*, on Princes Highway in Ulladulla South (☎044/55 2110 or 55 1712; on-site vans ②–③, cabins ④, holiday flats ④–⑥), boasts a beachfront location, complete with swimming pools, spa and tennis courts. **Tourist information** can be had from the *Civic Centre* on the highway (daily 10am–5pm; ☎044/55 1269).

# Batemans Bay and around

**BATEMANS BAY**, at the mouth of the Clyde River and the end of the highway from Canberra, is a favourite escape for the landlocked residents of the capital, just 152km away. It's not the most exciting place on the coast, but since it's a fair-sized resort, there's plenty to do. Around Batemans Bay itself you can take a cruise on the **Clyde River**, or you can board one of the little trains that run through the woodlands of the **Birdland Sanctuary** (55 Beach Road; daily 9am–5pm; $8) for a closer look at the birds and native animals.

At **Murramarang National Park**, a small coastal strip just north of town, there are campsites at **Pretty Beach**, **Pebbly Beach** and **Durras Beach** – popular not only with campers, but also with kangaroos which come here at dawn or dusk to frolic on the beach. Rumour has it that they even enjoy body surfing.

From **MOGO**, 10km to the south, you can visit the open-air **Old Mogo Town** museum (daily 9am–5pm in school holidays, otherwise Fri–Sun 10am–4pm; $6), a reconstruction of a mid-nineteenth-century goldrush town near an old gold mine. Twenty-five kilometres south of Batemans Bay, just before Moruya, a small, unsealed road turns off the highway to the west, heading for more reminders of the goldrush era. It leads through a pretty valley and then winds up over hills at the edge of the remote **Deua National Park** to the former goldrush town of **ARALUEN** where, between 1868 and 1872, about 15,000 prospectors congegrated in the hope of striking it lucky.

**Batemans Bay Tourist Information** is on Princes Highway, at the corner of Beach Road (daily 9am–5pm; ☎044/72 6900). As you'd expect of a resort, **accommodation** consists of motels and a wide range of holiday units. Try *Bay Surfside*, 662 Beach Road (☎044/71 1275; ④), whose units sleep up to six and have all mod cons, including a video; or *Coachhouse Tourist Van Park*, by the beach on Beach Road, 1km south of town (☎044/72 4392; on-site vans ②–④, cabins ④–⑥), with pool and tennis court. The cottages at *Morgendoura Farm*, Hawdons Road, 8km west of Moruya on the Moruya River (☎044/74 2057; minimum booking two nights, linen included, ⑤), offer farmstays with horse-riding, canoeing and bushwalks laid on.

# Narooma and around

A small fishing village surrounded by yet more beautiful beaches, bays and coastal lakes, **NAROOMA** lies at the heart of an area famous for its succulent mud oysters. You can canoe and windsurf on the **Wagonga Inlet** or sail to **Montague Island** – an offshore sanctuary for sea birds, seals and **penguins**. If you actually want to disembark at the island, you'll have to join a tour organized by the NPWS in Narooma (☎044/76 2888; tours daily, 3hr 30min; $40), since it's a protected wildlife reserve. Southern right and humpback **whales** have begun to reappear in the bay between September and November, and the NWPS also organize whale-watching tours in the event of any sightings.

The **visitors' centre** is right on the highway (☎044/76 2881). Good **motels** and resorts include *Forsters Bay Lodge Motel*, Forsters Bay Road (☎044/76 2319; ④); *Tree Motel*, 213 Princes Highway (☎044/76 4233; ④–⑤), with pool and barbecue; and *Island View Beach Resort*, on the highway 5km south of town (☎044/76 2903; cabins ⑥), with a beachside location and tennis court. *Pub Hill Farm*, Scenic Drive, 8km west of Narooma (☎064/76 3177; ⑤), has just a couple of rooms offering farm-style B&B – and babysitting. *Lynch's Hotel* on Princes Highway (☎044/76 2001; ④) also serves counter **meals** during the holiday season, daily except Sundays.

## Tilba Tilba

Continuing southwards, take a break in the picturesque mountain villages of **TILBA TILBA** and **CENTRAL TILBA**, 17km south of Narooma, where time seems to have stood still – and various crafts shops and workshops are ready and willing to exploit the historical ambience. It's an area famous for its cheeses, and also a little-known wine-growing region: Central Tilba's hundred-year-old *ABC Cheese Factory* is open for visits (daily 9am–5pm; ☎044/73 7387), and you can follow this up with some wine-tasting at *Tilba Valley Wines and Vineyard*, signposted off the Princes Highway, 5km north of town (Mon–Sat 10am–5pm, Sun 11am–5pm; ☎044/73 7308).

The *Dromedary Hotel* on Bates Street in Central Tilba (☎044/73 7223; ⑤) is a quaint, historical pub with open fires; counter **meals** are served and there's **B&B** accommodation. The nearby *Tilba Teapot* offers Devonshire teas and light meals and is as self-consciously cute as it sounds. If you're feeling energetic you can follow the walking trail which starts from *Pam's Store* in Tilba Tilba and leads through a forest to the summit of **Mount Dromedary**, at almost 800m. The hike covers about 11km (return), and you should allow five to six hours – or go for the lazy option, with a horse from *Mt Dromedary Trail Rides* (☎044/76 3376; 3hr, $40).

## Bermagui

There's also a delightful scenic detour along the coast, turning off the highway towards **BERMAGUI** just after Tilba Tilba – although the road is partly unsealed and can be in bad condition after rain. Bermagui attracts quite a few game fishing fanatics, thanks to its associations with Zane Grey, Western writer and legendary marlin fisherman. In addition to a number of **motels**, there's the *Blue Pacific Hostel* at 73 Murrah Street (☎064/93 4921; ①) with a great verandah from which to enjoy the ocean and mountain views; pleasant old *Bermagui Hotel*, Lamont Street (☎064/93 4206; ④); *Elite Holiday Flats*, 84 Murrah Street (☎064/93 4274; ④); or the *Zane Grey Caravan Park* in Lamont Street (☎064/93 4382; cabins ③–⑤). The **Bermagui Information Centre** lies inside the *BP Service Station* at 8 Coluga Street (daily 7am–7pm; ☎064/93 4174).

Further south, unsealed tracks branch off the coast road to **Mimosa Rocks**, a coastal national park where there are opportunities for bushwalking and swimming. There are NPWS **campsites** at Middle Beach, Picnic Point and Argannu Beach (☎064/76 2888 for details and bookings).

# Bega and around

Lush green meadows, Friesian cows, wide valleys and mountains in the background – you could almost mistake this for pastoral scenery somewhere in the foothills of the Swiss Alps. Certainly the area around **BEGA** is prime dairy country: at the **Bega Cheese factory**, Lagoon Street, North Bega (Mon–Fri 9am–3pm, Sat & Sun 10am–2pm) you can watch the famous local cheese being made, and try a few samples. Scenery and cheese apart, there's no great reason to come here, but it's a convenient stopover, handy for the junction of the Princes Highway with the Snowy Mountains Highway. In town, the **Historical Museum**, on the corner of Bega and Auckland streets (Mon–Fri 10.30am–4pm, holidays also Sat 10am–noon), has regional memorabilia and photos. For more on local attractions, check out the **Bega Tourist Information Centre**, 91 Gipps Street (Mon–Fri 10am–5pm, Sat & Sun 9am–noon; ☎064/92 2045).

Bega's small, pleasant *YHA* (Kirkland Crescent, ☎064/92 3103; reception hours 8am–10am & 5–10pm; ①) is built from mud bricks. The *Grand Hotel*, 236 Carp Street (☎064/92 1122; ④), has both pub accommodation and motel-style units, as well as counter **meals** during the week. Campers can head for *Bega Caravan Park*, Princes Highway (☎064/92 2303; on-site vans & cabins ④, holiday units ⑤).

As at Tilba, the local cheese is happily partnered by local wine, and there are two **wineries** open for visits. *Grevillea Estate*, on Buckajo Road (Mon–Fri & Sun 9am–3pm, Sat & school holidays 9am–5pm; ☎064/92 3006), has a cheese shop and restaurant as well; coming from the north, turn right into West Street before the Bega River and follow the road for about 2km. *Kameruka Estate*, 18km southwest of Bega on the Candelo Road (daily 9am–4pm; ☎064/93 2335), is a stately old country residence where visitors can take a look around the property and watch the farm work being done – and every evening except Monday you can also dine in high style.

## Candelo and Tathra

**CANDELO** itself is reached by a country road which turns off the highway 11km south of Bega, a pretty village where you can browse in the galleries and craftshops and indulge in a Devonshire tea at one of the tearooms, or a drink in the old pub. The *Candelo Hotel* in Sharp Street (☎064/93 2214; ④) is a historic pub with **rooms** and good counter meals. There are also self-contained units at *Bumblebrook Farm*, Kemps Lane, 4km northwest of Candelo (☎064/93 2238; B&B ⑤), although you can take advantage of room service or dine in the homestead.

Heading on from Bega, an alternative route to Merimbula takes you along the coast road via the small holiday and fishing village of **TATHRA**. Accommodation ranges from the *Tathra Hotel* on Bega Street (☎064/94 1101; ④), with motel-style units, to the *Tathra Beach Tourist Park*, right by the beach on Andy Poole Drive, 2km from the centre (☎064/94 1302; on-site vans & cabins ③) – or try the timber cottages at *Kianinny Park Cabins* on the Snowy Mountains Highway, 2km west of the town (☎064/94 1990; ⑤), a good family place with a saltwater pool. **Tourist information** is dispensed at the helpful *Tathra Wharf Trading Post* right on the wharf (☎064/94 4062; long hours, usually 7.30am–8pm), an all-purpose place which also rents out fishing, diving and surfing gear, with a decent café; there's a **maritime museum** upstairs (daily 8am–5pm; $1.50), as befits the 150-year-old waterfront building.

Just to the south, coastal **Bournda National Park** features stunning beaches, brackish lagoons and freshwater lakes: there are NPWS **campsites** at Hobart Beach on the southern end of Wallagoot Lake (book well ahead from December to Easter; ☎064/94 1209 or 96 1434).

# Merimbula

The pretty township of **MERIMBULA** attracts a lot of holidaymakers from Victoria because of its accessibility and year-round temperate climate, plus good beaches. Between tanning sessions, you can cruise Merimbula Lake (actually the wide mouth of Merimbula River) and Pambula Lake with several different companies for around $12–15 an hour; *Sinbad Cruises* are recommended for their interesting commentary on Aboriginal history and oyster cultivation. All cruises, and boat rental too, can be arranged at the **Merimbula Tourist Information Centre**, Beach Street (Mon–Fri 9am–4pm, Sat, Sun & public holidays 9am–noon; ☎064/95 1129); they also have info on lots of other activities in the area, including 4WD forest tours and horse-riding. If the

*Sinbad* cruise kindles an interest in the Aboriginal culture of the area, look up *Umburra Cultural Tours* (☎044/73 7288) run by the local land council and led by Koorie guides.

## Accommodation

Though there are dozens of **motels** (⑤–⑦, depending on the season) and **holiday flats**, all of them can be heavily booked during the summer holidays, when many holiday flats only accept weekly bookings with rates starting around $200. The places listed below may have space at short notice.

**Kalorama Caravan Park**, Millingandi Rd, Pambula (☎064/95 6366). Swimming pool and toddlers pool. On-site vans from ②; cabins from ③.

**Mandeni Cabins**, Sapphire Coast Drive (☎064/95 9644). Fully equipped timber cottages in a bushland setting, sleeping a maximum of five. Tennis courts, two swimming pools and toddlers pool, golf course and many walking trails. ⑤–⑧.

**South Haven Caravan Park**, Elizabeth St, between Merimbula Lake and the beach (☎064/95 1304). Sauna, heated pool, tennis and squash courts. Cabins from ②; units weekly from $250.

**Wandarrah YHA Lodge**, 18 Marine Parade (☎064/95 3503). A sparkling new, purpose-built youth hostel close to both the beach and lake. Lots of organized activities and outings; free pick-up from bus or plane. Rooms ③–④, dorms ①.

**Woodbine Park Cabins**, Widgeram Rd, off Sapphire Coast Drive (☎064/95 9333). Wooden cabins in a bushland setting 8km outside town, sleeping a maximum of six. Swimming pool, tennis court and golf course. Weekly from $200.

# Eden

**EDEN**, on Twofold Bay, is pretty much the last seaside stop before the Princes Highway heads inland towards Victoria. The first whaling station on the Australian mainland was established at Eden in 1818, and whaling remained a major industry until the 1920s. For **information** on the local area, call in at the Eden Information Centre on the highway (Jan & Feb daily 9am–5pm, rest of the year Mon–Fri 9am–4pm, Sat & Sun 9am–noon; ☎064/96 1953).

Today Eden is touristy in a quiet sort of way, and there are plenty of reminders of the old days, the best of which is the **Killer Whale Museum** on Imlay Street (daily 11am–4pm, school holidays 10am–5pm; $3); as well as whaling, it looks at the fishing and timber industries which still contribute to Eden's livelihood. At the museum you can also book **cruises** on Twofold Bay and further out to sea – with luck, penguins, dolphins and, in winter, even whales might be sighted. There's more on the important and controversial timber industry at the **Harris Daishowa Chipmill**, which gobbles up thousands of eucalypts from the surrounding forests and transforms them into wood chips for export to Japan. The **Visitors Centre** at Edrom Road (daily 8am–5pm; guided mill tour Thurs 10.30am, book in advance on ☎064/96 1953) presents an exhibition and slide show about the local timber industry, past and present – no prizes for guessing whose side they're on in the forestry debate.

The forests themselves may seem a more attractive option, and as you head south you become increasingly surrounded by the vast temperate rainforests that characterize southeastern Australia. In both directions there are turn-offs from the highway into the magnificent **Ben Boyd National Park**, which hugs the coast to the north and south of Eden, offering good camping, walking and beaches. Inland, the summit of **Mount Imlay** can be reached by a 3km walking track which starts at the picnic grounds at Burrawang Forest Road, 14km south of Eden. The steep, strenuous ascent is rewarded by a panoramic view over the coast and across the dense forests of the hinterland onto the Monaro plain. At Boydtown, 9km south of Eden, take a look at the mock-Tudor, **Seahorse Inn**, which nowadays houses a small museum of local history as well as tearooms, restaurant and a hotel (see below).

## Accommodation

**Hotel Australasia**, Imlay St (☎064/96 1600). Budget accommodation in an old pub; counter meals available. Rooms ③, dorms ①.

**Bayview Motor Inn**, Princes Highway (☎064/96 1242). Deluxe motel with room service, swimming pool and spa. ⑤–⑥.

**Fountain Caravan Park**, Princes Highway (☎064/96 1798). Decent site with swimming pool and camp kitchen. On-site vans ③, cabins ④.

**Fulligans Wilderness Farm**, 50km west of Eden, via Towamba (☎064/96 7156). Farmstay accommodation in pioneer cottages or mudbrick cabins in a bush setting. Ideal for families and small groups; may pick up from Merimbula or Eden. Horse-riding $10 per hour; free fishing in trout- and perch-stocked waters. Backpacker accommodation ①, cabins ⑤.

**Seahorse Inn**, just off the Princes Highway, 9km south of Eden in Boydtown (☎064/96 1361). Mock-Tudor inn with tennis court, tearooms and restaurant. B&B ⑥.

**Shadrack Resort**, Princes Highway, Legges Beach, 4km south of Eden (☎064/96 1651). Lovely complex in bushland beachfront setting. Cabins ⑤.

**Twofold Beach Caravan Park**, Princes Highway, 7km south of Eden (☎064/96 1572). Beachside location with pool. On-site vans & cabins ③.

**Wonboyn Lake Resort**, 40km south of Eden (☎064/96 9162). Very scenic location off the beaten track at Lake Wonboyn: swimming pool, spa, shop, boat-ramp, canoe and boat rental; beach nearby. Cottages ⑤.

# NORTHERN NSW

Northern New South Wales may have nothing to match the majesty of the Snowy Mountains, as the Dividing Range falls away to the lower slopes that protect the **New England Plateau**, but the World Heritage-listed temperate and subtropical areas of the range's northeast end harbour sixteen pockets of rainforest which more than compete in terms of natural beauty. In many ways the north is more varied than the south, offering a taste of everything: big resorts and empty beaches on the coast and alternative lifestyle villages and communes in the Hinterland beyond; lovely parks and forests on the steep slopes behind the coast; and further inland quietly attractive agricultural country, dotted with interesting old towns.

The roads are generally in fairly good condition, but the busy **Pacific Highway** is not the best of them. Though it's gradually being upgraded and widened, with much-needed overtaking lanes being added, sections of this winding coastal road are still alarmingly narrow considering the weight of traffic and the big trucks that use it; bus services on the highway almost invariably run late. The inland route on the **New England Highway** via Muswellbrook, Tamworth and Armidale is a faster alternative if you're heading straight for Brisbane – plenty of buses go this way too.

# The North Coast

The coast from Sydney north to the Queensland border is more densely populated and much more touristy than the southern coast. North from Newcastle (see p.126), popular holiday destinations are strung up the coast. **Port Stephens**, **Port Macquarie**, **Coffs Harbour** and the twin city of **Tweed Heads**/Coolangatta, straddling the state line, attract local tourists as well as visitors from overseas. The subtropical part of the coast, from Coffs Harbour northward, is much the most attractive: since the Seventies the area around **Lismore**, **Byron Bay** and **Murwillumbah** has been a favoured destination for people from the southern cities seeking an "alternative" lifestyle. This movement has left in its wake not only disillusioned hippy farmers (as well as a few who've survived with their illusions intact), but also a firmly established artistic and alternative scene.

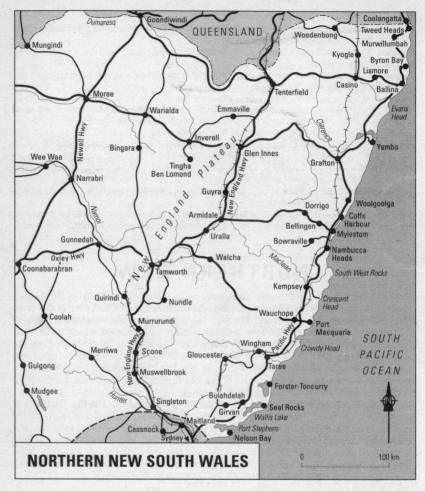

## NORTHERN NEW SOUTH WALES

As in the south, the **coastline** consists of a myriad of inlets, bays and coastal lakes, interspersed by white, sandy beaches and rocky promontories. Parallel to the coast, the rocky plateaus of the **Great Dividing Range** rise steeply from the plain; so steep is the eastern edge of this range, indeed, that it denied even the efforts of the early forest-ers, so that to this day the hills remain densely wooded. A handful of townships still depend on the timber industry, but most **forest** areas are now protected as either national parks or state forests. From the highlands, numerous streams tumble down from the escarpment in mighty waterfalls, and once on the coastal plain they flow together to form short, very wide and fast-flowing rivers. In the fertile river valleys the predominant agricultural activity is cattle breeding, while in the north subtropical and tropical agriculture takes over, especially the cultivation of bananas.

In essence, the further you go, the better this coast gets – the northeastern corner is one of the most scenic areas in the state, worth taking off to explore along remote country roads. If the bigger coastal resorts are too touristy for your liking, there's no shortage of quiet, even lonely beaches as you head further up, along with small fishing villages and sleepy hamlets inland that are virtually undiscovered. For bushwalkers there are vast areas of totally remote, rugged, wild terrain in the national parks of the Great Dividing Range.

## Port Stephens and the Lakes

Just north of Newcastle, the wide bay of **Port Stephens**, which extends inland for some 25km, offers calm waters and numerous coves ideal for swimming, watersports and popular for fishing, while the ocean side has good surf and wide, sandy beaches. In January, thousands of families pour in to take their annual holiday in the "Blue Water Paradise", as the area has been dubbed by its advertising agency. For information on the area and hotel bookings, the **Port Stephens Visitors Centre** (Mon–Fri 9am–5pm, Sat & Sun 9am–4.30pm; ☎049/81 1579 or free call ☎1800/04 5920) is at Victoria Parade in Nelson Bay. Port Stephens is actually the collective name for the main township of **NELSON BAY**, perched at the tip of the southern arm of the bay, together with the quieter settlements of Shoal Bay, Soldiers Point, Fingal Bay, Boat Harbour and Anna Bay. The highly developed, high-rise feel of Nelson Bay is contrasted with the simple pleasure of **dolphin** watching in the quiet waters here. Most dolphin cruises, which give you the opportunity to swim with the dolphins, leave from **TEA GARDENS** on the northern arm of the bay.

### Myall Lakes National Park and around

Just after **BULAHDELAH**, a small town surrounded by bush-covered hills and rocky outcrops, on the Pacific Highway, the Lakes Highway runs east towards the coast, past Myall Lake and Lake Wallis to the holiday town of Forster–Toncurry. At Bungwahl a turn-off leads, on mostly unsealed roads, to **SEAL ROCKS**, a remote fishing village and the only settlement in the **Myall Lakes National Park**. Its national park status means it's unspoilt and the small beach is truly beautiful with crystal-clear waters marooned between two headlands. Built in 1875, **Sugar Loaf Point lighthouse** (Tues & Thurs 10am–noon & 1–3pm), a rewarding ten-minute stroll away, offers a fantastic view along the coast, and the lookout below leads down to a fetching deserted beach and rocks with a view of the 4WD track that extends through the national park.

From Bulahdelah itself, a road called Myall Way heads via a toll ferry (daily 8am–6pm) to more deserted spots along the lake shore, the most popular being **Mungo Brush**, where an easy walking track (30min return) heads through the littoral rainforest – a variant adapted to salty and harsh seafront conditions, with a low canopy. A more challenging 21km walking track leads from here to **Hawks Nest**, on Port Stephens Bay.

North of the national park, a bridge connects the twin cities **FORSTER–TUNCURRY** on the spit of land that separates **Lake Wallis** from the ocean. The lake is very pretty, surrounded by trees and with bush-covered **Corrie Island** at its centre. Forster is famous for its oysters, and for its playful resident dolphins. The lake itself is superb for fishing and swimming – you can rent houseboats as well as dinghies, canoes and windsurfers.

### Practicalities

Port Stephens, Forster–Toncurry and Myall Lakes National Park are not the easiest places to reach on public **transport**: long-distance buses tend to stop only at Raymond Terrace on the Pacific Highway or Karuah (only a few even call at Bulahdelah), but there are reasonably good connections to Newcastle and Sydney with *Port Stephens Bus* (☎049/81 1207) and *Great Lakes Coaches* (☎049/83 1560). The well-organized

**Great Lakes Vistors Centre** at Little Street in Forster (daily 9am–5pm; ☎065/54 541) can provide you with stacks of information and can book accommodation and tours. A good place to **eat** is the *Lakeside Tavern*, near the K-Mart shopping village in Forster–Toncurry, for fresh good-value **seafood**. As for **accommodation**, there are scores of motels and even more holiday flats to choose from: all prefer weekly bookings during the holiday season, and many insist. If you want to stay within the national park itself, **camping** is the way to go. Houseboats are also an option (see "Listings").

**Halifax Caravan Park**, Beach Rd, Little Beach, Nelson Bay (☎049/81 1522). Well set up beachside park with camp kitchen, barbecues and kiosk. Cabins ③.

**Karen Court Holiday Flats**, 27 Townsend St , Forster (☎065/54 6856). Self-contained apartments for up to five people, sharing a swimming pool and garden. Minimum stay of two nights. ③–⑤.

**Myall Shores**, Bombah Point, 16km east of Bulahdelah in the Myall Lakes National Park (☎049/97 4495). Campsite with restaurant, shop and boat ramp, plus bushwalks, 4WD tours and cruises on offer. Bungalows ④, cabins ⑤.

**Samurai Beach Bungalows**, Frost Rd, corner Robert Connell Close, Anna Bay (☎049/82 1921). Two cabins with a bathroom and two four-bed dorms each. Undercover "bush" kitchen, idyllic and quiet bushland setting, but a bit remote if you don't have your own vehicle. ①.

**Seal Rocks Camping Reserve**, Seal Rocks (☎049/97 6164). Small site just across from the beach. Bookings during school holidays only. On-site vans ③.

**Smuggler's Cove Holiday Village**, 45 Lakes Way, 2km south of Forster (☎065/54 6666). Lakeside campsite with pool and children's playground. Cabins ②–⑤.

**Thurlow Lodge**, Thurlow Ave, Nelson Bay (☎049/81 1577). Central self-catering units sleeping up to six with communal swimming pool. From $150–600 per week.

**YHA Forster**, 43 Head St, Forster (☎065/55 8155). Just two minutes walk from the beach and the ocean baths, this hostel has plenty of nicely decorated doubles (including one with a waterbed), as well as dorms. Other perks are a great balcony and free use of bikes, fishing gear and surf- and boogie-boards. Rooms ③, dorms ①.

**YHA Shoal Bay/Shoal Bay Motel**, 61 Shoal Bay Rd, Shoal Bay (☎049/81 1744). A motel that also runs a small YHA section – non-members welcome. Sauna and spa; advance booking recommended. YHA rooms ③, dorms ①; motel rooms ⑤–⑦.

## Listings

**Cruises** Dolphin-watching jaunts are put on by *Dawson's Scenic Cruises* (☎049/84 3288; 2hr; $12), *Dolphin Watch Cruises* (2hr 30min; $25; ☎065/54 7478) and *Myall Lakes Charter Cruises* (☎049/97 1084; 3hr; $16).

**Houseboats** *Myall Lakes Houseboats*, 90 Crawford St, Bulahdelah (☎049/97 4221); *Tea Gardens Houseboats*, Marine Drive, Tea Gardens (☎049/97 0555). Weekly rates from $300 to more than $2000.

**NPWS** Lot 5, Bourke Street, Raymond Terrace (☎049/87 3108).

**Taxis** *Forster–Tuncurry Radio Taxis* (☎065/54 6555); *Nelson Bay Taxi Services* (☎049/81 1210); *Raymond Terrace Taxis* (mobile phone ☎018/68 6541).

**Tours** *Aboriginal Ranger Heritage Tours* (☎065/55 5274) depart from the Great Lakes Visitor's Centre in Forster (Fri 9am–4pm to Port Macquarie, $30; Mon–Thurs 9am–2pm to Toowabba Reserve, Cape Hawke, and Whoota Lookout, $20).

# A detour inland: Barrington Tops

Heading inland is equally attractive, and the drive from Forster via Nabiac, Krambach and Gloucester to the **Barrington Tops National Park**, for example, makes an enjoyable day trip. On the way up to the country town of Gloucester it's gently hilly farming country; from here, unsealed roads lead to various scenic spots in the national park – the Barrington Road towards Scone, or the Gloucester Tops road to the park's southwestern section. You can also approach it via the Hunter Valley from Maitland via Dungog.

The Barrington Tops themselves are two high, cliff-ringed plateaus, Barrington and Gloucester, that rise steeply from the surrounding valleys. The World Heritage-listed national park was declared in 1969 and protects the catchment areas of six streams that feed the Manning and the Hunter rivers. The altitude changes are so great – highest points are Mount Barrington (1555m) and Polblue Mountain (1577m) – that within a few minutes you can pass from areas of subtropical rainforest to warm and cool temperate rainforest, and then to high, windswept plateaus covered with snow gums, meadows and sub-alpine bog. Up on the plateau, snow is common from the end of April to early October, while heavy fogs and rains are possible at virtually any time.

The **information office** in Forster (see above) can help with specific routes or organized 4WD tours into the national park, one of which is *Bush Ranging 4WD Tours* (☎049/92 1614; $65 includes morning tea and barbecue lunch). There are plenty of picnic grounds and scenic lookouts in the park, and there's a **campsite** in the Gloucester River area. If camping isn't your thing, the closest **accommodation** is *Barrington House* (☎049/95 3212; ⑤, including dinner), a large guesthouse around 40km from Dungog – or try the cabins at *Bellbird Valley Farm*, Chichester Road, 23km north of Dungog (☎049/95 9266; ⑦) in a pleasant location near forest and waterfalls, and with a pool, spa and horse-riding on offer; meals or self-catering available.

## The Manning Valley: Taree and around

Back on the Pacific Highway north of Forster–Toncurry, **TAREE** is a quiet riverside town and the main centre of the fertile, scenic Manning Valley – and is served by trains and buses from Sydney. A pleasant alternative to the touristy hustle and bustle of Port Macquarie, the next stop north (see below), it's especially good as a base for some gentle exploration of the hills and forests. Taree was very much in the media eye for several weeks in late 1994 when a whale was stranded in the river, bringing heaps of sightseers and would-be rescuers to the town.

The very helpful **tourist office** on the Pacific Highway in Taree North (daily 9am–5pm; ☎065/52 1900) has detailed leaflets describing forest drives, most of which lead to the high plateau where waterfalls abound. **Places to stay** include *Fotheringham's Hotel*, 236 Victoria St (☎065/52 1153; ③–④), a pleasant old pub and restaurant; the *Twilight Caravan Park*, Pacific Highway, 3km north of town (☎065/52 2857; on-site vans ②, cabins ③), with a saltwater pool, barbecues, playground and kiosk.

Heading from Taree to Port Macquarie, there are a number of worthwhile detours. One of the most impressive waterfalls on the whole coast is the 160m-high **Ellenborough Falls**, about an hour's drive northwest of Taree beyond Wingham on the Bulga Forest Drive – unsealed much of the way. From the main Pacific Highway just before Coopernook, a road turns off the small **Crowdy Bay National Park**, situated between Crowdy Head and the lofty Diamond Head, whose landscape includes heathlands, swamp, lagoons, woodlands, forests and sand dunes, all enlivened by prolific birdlife. From Kew, halfway between Taree and Port Macquarie, turn right at the *Kew Hotel* for the much more interesting route that hugs the coast.

## Port Macquarie

**PORT MACQUARIE**, at the mouth of the Hastings River, was established in 1821 as a place of secondary punishment for convicts who had committed offences after arrival in New South Wales, as well as for hardened criminals from Britain. By the late 1820s, however, the spread of population meant that this was no longer an isolated outpost, so the penal settlement was closed and the area was opened up to free settlers. The convicts who were still considered incorrigible were sent off to either Moreton Bay in the Brisbane area, or to remote Norfolk Island.

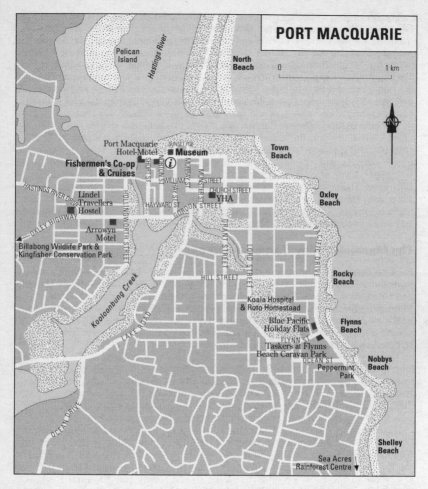

**PORT MACQUARIE**

Like many other northern coastal ports, the **harbour** was unreliable and its approaches difficult, so for more than a century the town failed to live up to its early promise of commercial success. Prosperity and expansion finally came only with the tourism boom, which started in the early 1970s and shows no signs of abating; with a population of about 26,000, Port Macquarie is now one of the fastest-growing towns on the north coast of New South Wales, particularly popular with older people from the southern cities who want to spend their retirement years in a sunny place with a moderate climate. The result is that much of "The Port" has the featureless look of just another Australian suburb; more accurately, you might say it's a series of **suburbs** sprawling along the beaches, forever encroaching further on the bush.

For visitors, in addition to the obvious scenic attractions – long, sandy beaches that start right in town and stretch way along the coast, forests and mountains in the hinterland – there's also plenty laid on in and around the town itself: amusement parks, mini zoos, nature parks, cruises on the Hastings River and connecting waterways, horse-riding, and, above all, watersports and fishing.

## Arrival and information

As a popular resort, Port Macquarie is well served by transport, although not all **buses** make the detour from the Pacific Highway, so check carefully. **Trains** stop in Wauchope, 22km west, from where there's a bus connection with *Port Macquarie Bus* (☎065/83 2161). Horton Street is the main downtown street, and the **tourist information office** (Mon–Fri 9am–5pm, Sat, Sun & holidays 9am–4pm; ☎065/83 1293) is on the corner of Clarence and Hay streets, right on the waterfront.

## Accommodation

**Arrowyn Motel**, 170 Gordon St (☎065/83 1633). Simple, inexpensive motel. ④.

**Beachside Backpackers**, 40 Church St (☎065/83 5512). Central family-run, friendly YHA-affiliated hostel, but small dorms only partly partioned off from the kitchen-cum-TV room. Small gym; free pick-up from the bus terminal; bike rental. Dorms with fan ①.

**Blue Pacific Holiday Flats**, 37 Pacific Drive, Flynns Beach (☎065/83 1686). Apartments near the beach, sleeping up to six. ③–④.

**Lindel Travellers Hostel**, Hastings River Drive, corner Gordon St (☎065/83 1791). Converted former guesthouse, family-run, clean and friendly; barbecue and small pool, free use of bikes and surfboards, free trips by shuttle bus to the koala hospital and beaches. It's further out than the YHA; book in advance for free pick-up service from the bus terminal. Rooms ②; dorms with fan ①.

**Ocean Beach Flats** 2 Bundella Ave, Lake Cathie, about 15km south (☎065/85 5292). Flats for max 5 people. ③–④.

**Port Macquarie Hotel-Motel**, Clarence St, opposite the post office (☎065/83 1011). Good value rooms. Counter meals; swimming pool. ⑤.

**Rainbow Beach Holiday Village**, Beach St, Bonny Hills, about 23km south. Spacious, beachside complex in bushland setting, with heated pool, playground, barbecue and shop. On-site vans, cabins and cottages. ③–⑤.

**Taskers at Flynns Beach Caravan Park**, 14 Flynn St, opposite Flynns Beach (☎065/83 1520). Nice, shady complex with pool, children's playground and barbecue. Cabins ④–⑤.

## The Town and around

Port Macquarie has a history of destroying reminders of its past. The only surviving remnants are **St Thomas Church**, the **Court House** (1869) in Clarence Street and the **Historical Museum** opposite (Mon–Sat 9.30am–4.30pm, Sun 1.30–4.30pm; $4) – the latter has an extensive and well-presented collection of documents and memorabilia dealing with the history of the Hastings River area.

Perhaps the best of the attractions is the **Kooloonbung Creek Nature Park**, a 50-hectare bushland reserve remarkably close to the town centre. From the entrance at the corner of Horton and Gordon streets, you step onto trails among casuarinas, mangroves and eucalypts, or sweat through a small patch of rainforest, and it's amazingly easy to believe that you're lost in the wilderness of the Australian bush, rather than minutes from the main road. The eastern part of the nature reserve is accessible to wheelchairs, and at the **Historic Cemetery** near the main entrance a few graves of pioneer settlers have been preserved.

On the ocean-facing side of town, Port Macquarie's three flagged, patrolled **beaches** are Town Beach, right near the centre, Flynn's and Lighthouse. Heading south on Pacific Drive, the **Sea Acres Rainforest Centre** (daily 9am–5.30pm; $8.50; ☎065/82 3355) is impressive, conveying an urgent environmental message about the fast-disappearing coastal rainforest of New South Wales. The centre comprises three different types of rainforest, which can be inspected at close quarters from a boardwalk a little over a kilometre long (again wheelchair-accessible).

Back towards the town centre, on Lord Street, **Roto** is a fine nineteenth-century homestead, with Australia's only **Koala Hospital** in its grounds (both open daily 9am–5pm; free, donations welcome; check feeding time on ☎065/84 1522). Volunteer-run and financed, the hospital takes in road casualties – a sad consequence of Port Macquarie's suburban sprawl – as well as disease-stricken koalas.

If you've not had your fill of cuddly animals, the **Billabong Koala & Wildlife Park**, 233 Oxley Highway (daily 9.30am–4.30pm; $6), advertises, as most of these zoos do, cute kangaroos that can be hand-fed and koalas that can be patted and embraced. There's also the **Kingfisher Conservation Park**, in Kingfisher Road (daily 9am–5pm; $6.50), with slightly more serious intentions, home to over 400 animals, some of which are threatened by extinction. **Peppermint Park** (Tues–Sun 10am–5pm, daily during school holidays; $9.80 adult or child, $36 family), heavily hyped, is a typical amusement park – giant waterslides, a mini-golf course and roller-skating are among its diversions.

## Eating and drinking

As you'd expect in a resort of this size, there are plenty of places to **eat**, and particularly fast-food outlets: not surprisingly, seafood and fish predominate. The fish and chips from the fish shop on the corner of Clarence and Short streets are especially tasty. You can also buy fish from the **Fishermen's Co-op** at the end of Clarence Street in the town wharf area and cook it yourself. The *Whalebone Wharf Restaurant* at Hastings River Drive (☎065/83 2334; closed Mon) is one of the most enjoyable of a number of more upmarket seafood restaurants, with a great location overlooking the Hastings River. *Café Margo*, on the corner of Hay and Clarence streets, is a decent sidewalk café with very inexpensive meals, including the ubiquitous fish and chips and a few vegetarian options.

## Listings

**Bike rental** *Port Push Bikes*, 155 Horton Street (☎065/83 4540).

**Camels** Rides on the beach near lighthouse (bookings via tourist office or ☎065/83 7650; $9 for 20min, $18 per hour).

**Car rental** *Economical Rent-A-Car*, 190 Oxley St (☎065/81 1020); *Budget*, William Street (☎065/83 5144); *Hertz*, 73 Hastings River Drive (☎065/83 6599); or *Thrifty* at the airport (☎065/84 2122).

**Cruises** *MV Port Venture* cruises from Clarence St Wharf up the Hastings River (1–2 daily; 2hr); *Pelican River Cruises* set sail from the Fishermen's Co-op Wharf to the everglades in Limeburners Creek National Park and an oyster farm for tastings (Mon–Fri 10am, Sat & Sun 2pm; 2hr 30min–5hr; $15–25); *Waterbus Everglade Tours* offers an Explorer Cruise (daily 2pm; 2hr 30min; $15) among others.

**Taxis** *Port Macquarie Taxicabs* (☎065/81 0081); *Wauchope Radio Taxicabs* (☎065/85 2100).

**Tours** *Port Explorer Bus* (Thurs only, hourly 10am–4pm; day-ticket $6; book at tourist information office) takes in Flynns Beach, Peppermint Park, Sea Acres Rainforest Centre, the lighthouse, camel rides, Transit Hill and the koala hospital. Operators of day tours inland include *Port Explorer* (from $22; ☎065/83 1293 or 82 1235), *Southern Cross Tours* (☎065/82 1235; $26 upwards).

**Travel agent** *Harvey World Travel*, 13 Short St (☎065/84 9766).

# Heading inland: Wauchope

**WAUCHOPE** (pronounced War-hope), 22km west of Port Macquarie, is a pretty little village surrounded by forest, and makes an enjoyable contrast to the coast. **Timbertown** (daily 9am–5pm; $12.50; ☎065/85 2322), an open-air museum 13km from the village, is a working exhibit designed to depict life as it must have been in the isolated timber settlements 150 years ago. Timber logs are pulled over muddy roads to saw-pits, where they are cut and shaped, the bakery bakes and sells bread fresh from the oven, and many other aspects of Victorian life are re-enacted. North of Wauchope, the **Wilson River Rainforest Reserve**'s picnic grounds are a popular destination for day-trips from Port Macquarie. Another feature of Wauchope is the large separatist lesbian community that lives in the vicinity – something strangely absent from the tourist literature.

The *Hastings Hotel*, on the corner of High and Cameron streets (☎065/85 2003; ④), offers pub **accommodation** and counter meals. *Mount Seaview Resort*, on Oxley Highway towards Tamworth (☎065/87 7155 or free call ☎1800/81 8804; resort ⑤, lodge ③) is a cattle station on the Hastings River offering farmstays and campsites as well as rooms; there's a bar and restaurant, tennis court, pool, horse-riding and 4WD tours.

## Port Macquarie to Nambucca Heads

The coastline between Port Macquarie and Nambucca Heads, 115km north, holds some magic spots. From Kempsey, a large service town on the Macleay River, 49km from Port Macquarie, a good sealed road runs 21km northeast to **CRESCENT HEAD**. There's some wonderful waterfront **campsites** here: *Crescent Head Tourist Park* (☎065/66 0261) which also has some very pleasant, verandah-fronted wooden chalets (④–⑤); *Delicate Nobby Camping Ground* (☎065/66 0144), in an extensive bushland setting, is more secluded, ten minutes' drive from the township. Meandering back and then away from the Pacific Highway, you come to the coastal **Hat Head National Park** and the small town of **SOUTH WEST ROCKS**, perched on a picturesque headland. Three kilometres east on **Trial Bay**, the **Arakoon State Recreation Area** has as its centrepiece **Trial Bay Gaol** (daily 9am–5pm; $3): classified as a public works prison in which prisoners could learn a trade, the gaol was considered progressive when it was established in 1886. It's certainly an impressive construction built from local granite – the massive outer walls surrounding two acres of building and supported by high buttresses with four watchtowers. The prison was closed in 1903, but reopened during World War I when it was used as an internment camp for over 500 internees, including some Buddhist monks from Ceylon, but most were German.

### Nambucca Heads

About 100km away, via the Pacific Highway, the casual resort town of **NAMBUCCA HEADS** makes a good base for trips to the rivers, mountains and forests of the hinterland; it's also a great place to break the long haul from Sydney to Brisbane – whether you're travelling by car, bus or train. From the headlands near the town centre there are fantastic views of the mouth of Nambucca River, and of the seemingly endless sweep of sandy beaches that stretch both north and south from here. There's fishing, windsurfing and canoeing available to take advantage of the gentler waters at the river mouth, and some excellent surf on the ocean beaches.

For information on these and other activities around town (including whitewater rafting and horse-riding), make for the **tourist information centre** on Ridge Street (☎065/68 6954). **Motels** and apartments are generally better value here than in Port Macquarie or Coffs Harbour: try the *Nirvana Village Motel*, Riverside Drive (☎065/68 6620; ④–⑤), with pool and barbecue; *The Ranch Guesthouse*, 4 Wellington Drive (☎065/68 6386; B&B ④); or the *White Albatross Holiday Centre*, Wellington Drive (☎065/68 6468; on-site vans ②, cabins ③), in a nice location and with facilities including tennis court and children's playground. The best of the budget options is *Nambucca Backpackers*, 3 Newman Street (☎065/68 6360; rooms ③, dorms ①), a small, cosy, family-run hostel with free use of boogie-boards and pick-up from the bus terminal or train station. A good place to **eat** is *Johnny's Pizza*, near the tourist office, with great gourmet hot dogs and salad sandwiches as well as pizza, while *Nirvana Sawasdee* at the *Nirvana Motel*, Riverside Drive (☎066/68 9622; BYO) is a traditional Thai place that makes good use of fresh local seafood. Singapore-Malay and Chinese dishes are on offer at *Ken Leong's* at the Nambucca League's Club by Coronation Park (☎066/68 7415). Local **transport** is with *Newman's Coaches* (☎065/68 1296), who run between Nambucca Heads and Coffs Harbour via Bowraville, Mon–Fri only.

Heading inland from Nambucca, it's about half an hour's drive to the picturesque former timber town of **BOWRAVILLE**, where you can rest up in the historic pub and browse in a few arts-and-crafts shops. From here, unsealed forest roads can lead you to the small, alternative town of Bellingen (see below) although it's more easily reached on the sealed road which turns off the Pacific Highway after Urunga.

# The Bellingen River and around

**URUNGA**, 20km north from Nambucca Heads, is a pleasant beachside spot where the Bellingen and Kalang rivers meet the sea. Seven kilometres further along the Pacific Highway is the turn-off to **MYLESTOM**, which occupies a stunningly beautiful spot on the wide Bellingen River. You can take advantage of its riverside setting at the Alma Doepel Reserve's sheltered, sandy river beach with changing rooms and showers. Two minutes' walk to the east a gorgeous sweep of surf beach, often gloriously deserted, stretches off into the distance, patrolled summer weekends and school holidays.

There's a great **place to stay** here, reason enough in itself to come here: the *"Caipera" Riverside Lodge*, on River Street, facing Tuckers Island (☎066/55 4245; rooms ③, dorm ①) has the comfortable, relaxed feel of an Indonesian guesthouse. All the rooms, mostly twins and doubles, are well furnished with desks, lamps and armchairs; there is one dorm. Other **facilities** here are limited: a post office with supplies and EFTPOS, a decent Chinese **restaurant**, and a swanky brasserie called *Beaches* (☎066/55 4097; with handy bottle shop).

## Bellingen

Just after Urunga, the turn-off west heads through the verdant Bellingen River valley for 12km to **BELLINGEN**, a relaxed little town with a strong alternative bent, full of arts and crafts outlets and workshops, cafés and thriving small businesses. Bellingen also has an interesting monthly market, on the third Saturday of the month (7am–2pm) in Bellingen Park with buskers, crafts and organic food stalls – and an annual jazz festival held over the long weekend in August – but really one of the best things here is the swimming in the waterholes of the Bellingen and Never Never rivers.

For more **information** on the town and surrounding area, try *The Yellow Shed* on Hyde Street (☎066/55 1189) or *Bellingen Travel*, Shop 1, 44 Hyde St (☎066/55 2055) has details of rafting, bushwalking and other tours. The *Belfry Lodge Belligen Backpackers*, at 2 Short Street (☎066/55 1116; rooms ③, dorms ①) is one of the best **hostels** around, a beautiful two-storey building with a huge balcony facing a rainforest island full of jacaranda trees that come alive at dusk with the stirrings of fruit bats. The managers will give lifts to Dorrigo for $5 and have bicycles you can ride to local swimming holes. Otherwise, there's the *Rivendell Bed and Breakfast*, centrally located at 10 Hyde Street (☎066/55 0060; ⑤); the more secluded and quite luxurious *Fernridge Cottage* which you get all to yourself, just over 4km out of Bellingen on the Dorrigo Road (☎066/55 2142; ⑤, minimum 2 nights). The *Bellingen Valley Motor Inn* (☎066/55 1599; ⑥) is also in a green expanse on the way to Dorrigo, but just 1km out of town, with room service, a swimming pool, spa, playground and barbecue. You can **camp** at the *Bellingen Caravan Park* on Dowle Street, North Bellingen (☎066/55 1338).

The town is full of great **cafés**. The light and airy *Carriageway Cafe*, at 75 Hyde Street, serves simple city fare – melts, burgers, gourmet sandwiches, bagels and croissants – all very affordable; at the back, a polished wooden staircase heads upstairs to an art gallery. The spacious *Cool Creek Cafe* on Church Street has a folksy ambience and an extensive veggie menu, as well as lasagne, and bacon and eggs for breakfast. Next door, *The Good Food Shop* is a real find for wholefood supplies; it also does a good lunch. The *Flying Fox Cafe*, on Wheatley St, North Bellingen (☎066/55 1991) has folk bands on a Friday night. The town has only one pub: the animated *Federal Hotel*, with live music, usually free, from Thursday to Sunday.

### Heading for Dorrigo

The Dorrigo Road from Bellingen follows the beautiful Bellingen River with bewitching green hills in the distance and fat cows grazing in lush riverside fields, passing through **THORA**, and its roadhouse with the pleasant *River Bend Cafe* attached. Next door, *Bellingen Canoe Hire* rents out **canoes** to explore the river (☎066/55 8510; $30 half day, $45 full day), delivering you and the canoe to your starting point upstream.

Beyond Thora, the road winds ever more steeply, a scenic route with great views from various lookout points, through the **Dorrigo National Park**, a startlingly beautiful rainforest remnant of an area that was once similiarly heavily forested but the lure of the valuable Australian cedar – "red gold" – left most of the plateau cleared by the 1920s. The ultra-modern **National Park Visitor Centre** (daily 9am–5pm) has a detailed interpretative display that goes through this sorry saga, with some insights into the life of north coast Aborigines, and some examples of red cedar furniture. The *Canopy Cafe* here, with wonderful views, light lunches and afternoon teas, is open until 4pm. Easily the most spectacular of the walks, and the least strenuous, the **Skywalk**, leaves from the visitor centre – a wooden walkway stretches out high over the rainforest canopy enabling you to look down on the forest and providing panoramic views of the surrounding landscape and distant hills. The walkway is open 24 hours, to allow observance of the forest's nocturnal creatures. Other park trails will take you to some of its best features, including a number of beautiful waterfalls – there are detailed information boards at the centre, or pick up some leaflets for details.

**DORRIGO** itself is an old settlement on the eastern edge of the New England Plateau, a classic small country town with its own newspaper, which you can peruse in *Nick's Cafe* on Hickory Street, surrounded by 1950s formica fittings and consuming scones and a pot of tea. *Oliver's Books and Blues*, 47A Hickory St (☎066/57 2300) strikes a more modern note with secondhand books, good coffee, BYO and live music. There's plenty of **accommodation** if the area appeals: the *Hotel Dorrigo* (☎066/57 2016; ④) has motel-style rooms, while *Dorrigo Mountain Resort*, 1 Bellingen Road (☎066/57 2564), close to the national park, has the full range from camping to on-site vans (③) and log cabins (④). You can get tourist information from the **Dorrigo Community Centre** on Hickory Street (☎066/57 2787).

The road west from Dorrigo cuts cross-country, past several more national parks, towards Armidale (see p.213).

## Coffs Harbour

Back on the main coastal highway, **COFFS HARBOUR** – or "Coffs" – divides neatly into two separate parts. One half is a picturesque town snuggled close to the hills near the Pacific Highway – this is the centre of town with the shopping mall, post office and all other facilities. The other part is the Jetty area around the train station and the man-made harbour. Although Coffs Harbour depends (almost) as much on tourism as Port Macquarie further south, the suburban sprawl of retirement homes and holiday flats, hotels and motels is somehow not so noticeable here; instead the dramatic coastal landscape manages to hold sway. At this point the mountains and hills of the Great Dividing Range fall almost directly into the South Pacific Ocean, and glorious white, sandy beaches stretch for miles along the coast, from the town beaches of **Boambee** and **Jetty Beach** through **Park Beach** and **Diggers Beach**, up to northern strands like **Emerald** (see below). Offshore are several small islands with fringing coral reefs designated as marine reserves; the plethora of fish around these make diving a popular activity. In summer, the cool, rainforest-clad mountains with crystal-clear creeks and tumbling torrents offer a welcome respite from the heat and humidity of the coast.

## Arrival and information

Most **buses** stop in Moonee Street, just off the other side of Grafton Street, while the **train** station (☎066/52 2312) is down by the harbour. Given the split of Coffs into two halves, the distances you have to cover are considerable; the **local bus service**, which runs between the town centre, the Jetty and Park Beach (*Coffs Harbour Bus Lines*, ☎066/52 2686; timetables from the tourist office) is barely adequate, so you may find yourself having to take taxis, or you might want to rent a bike or car – see "Listings" below for details. To get to the beaches north of Coffs, *Ryan's Bus Service* goes to Woolgoolga via Sapphire, Moonee Beach and Emerald Beach (☎066/52 3201; Mon–Fri 5 daily, Sat 2 daily).

The **Visitor Information Centre** (daily 9am–5pm, 24hr information outside; ☎066/ 52 1522) is not exactly centrally situated, positioned as it is for drivers' convenience on the corner of Marcia Street and the Pacific Highway on the north side of town. For a more alternative viewpoint on Coffs and the surrounding beaches, head for the **Coffs Harbour Environment Centre**, in The Mall (☎066/52 3940), where you can pick up a free copy of the interesting *Rave Magazine*, which focuses on environmental issues, surfing and music. The High Street Mall right in the town centre, off Grafton Street (as the Pacific Highway is called in town) is very much the heart of town, and most facilities and much of the accommodation are nearby.

## Accommodation

Coffs has everything from international resort hotels through an enormous number of motels and holiday flats to hostels and caravan parks. During the summer and Easter holidays the place is packed, and weekly **bookings** are preferred or even compulsory. As trains and buses from Sydney arrive in the late evening, it's wise to book in advance in any case, especially as the **hostels** will do pick-ups if notified. The cheapest **motels** are on the southern side of town; **resorts** sometimes have bargain off-season rates, too. The tourist office has a free-call reservations line ☎1800/02 5650.

**Aussitel Backpackers**, 312 High St, between the town centre and harbour (☎066/51 1871). Medium-sized, very well-equipped hostel with big, clean communal kitchen, kiosk with basic food-stuffs, heated pool, free use of surf- and boogie-boards and canoes (Coffs Creek is across the street), and lots of activities including an inexpensive diving course. Free pick-up from bus terminal and train station. Rooms ③, dorms ①.

**The Breakers**, 6 Vincent St (☎066/52 3714). Flats for up to five people with linen supplied; swimming pool, playground and barbecue facilities. ④–⑦.

**Country Comfort Inn**, Pacific Highway, 4km north (☎066/52 8222). One of Coffs' most popular resorts right next to the Big Banana. Not exactly cheap, but good value for money, with tennis courts, pool, sauna, restaurant and bar, all set in landscaped gardens. All rooms air-con. ⑥–⑦.

**The Dunes at Park Beach**, 28 Fitzgerald St, 23km north (☎066/52 4522). Another much fancier complex with everything from heated pool, spa and sauna, to tennis courts and barbies. ⑦.

**Park Beach Hotel-Motel**, Ocean Parade (☎066/52 3833). Inexpensive motel accommodation at the "Hoey-Moey"; prepare yourself for some noise at this rather rowdy hotel. ③–④.

**Park Beach Caravan Park**, Ocean Parade (☎066/52 3204). Huge, beachfront campground with barbecue facilities and children's playground. On-site vans ②, cabins ③.

**Sapphire Gardens Holiday Resort**, Pacific Highway, 8km north (☎066/53 6282). Camping and apartment complex with pool, barbecue and restaurant. On-site vans ③.

**Surf Beach Motor Inn**, 25 Ocean Parade, Park Beach, 2km north (☎066/52 1872). Good value motel with pool. ④–⑤.

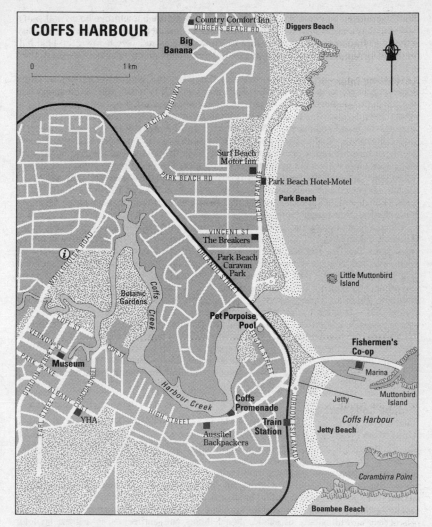

**YHA Hostel**, 110 Albany St (☎066/52 6462). Friendly, active hostel, handy for town centre with lifts every morning to the beach and the Big Banana. Garden with barbecue, spa, bike rental, free surf- and boogie-boards and fishing gear. Surf lessons and water-skiing arranged. Free pick-up from bus terminal, train station and airport. Rooms ③, dorms ①.

## The Town

In the centre of town, the small **Historical Museum**, at 191a High St (Tues–Thurs & Sun 1.30–4pm; $1), has a collection of the relics and tools of early pioneers and cedar-getters, as well as local Aboriginal artefacts, but the magnificent **North Coast Botanic Gardens**, Hardacre Street, just off the High Street (daily 9am–5pm), are far more worthwhile. These delightfully tranquil subtropical gardens are located on a triangle of land surrounded on two sides by **Coffs Creek** and feature a mangrove boardwalk and a slice of rainforest. A pleasant **creek walk** begins just near the town centre at Rotary Park in Coffs Street and heads 5.4km to Muttonbird Island (see below), the final half hour along the northern breakwater – detailed maps are available from the tourist office.

Heading alongside the creek towards the Jetty, the new development of **Coffs Promenade** contains craft and speciality shops as well as a café and ice-creamery. On the northern breakwater of the harbour, the **Fishermens Co-op** sells fresh fish; the wharf here is also the departure point for most of Coffs' cruises (see "Listings"). Beyond the boat-filled marina is **Muttonbird Island Nature Reserve**, high enough to give fantastic views of Coffs Harbour and the southern and northern beaches. There's plenty of bird life too, with an interpretative walk describing the lifestyle of the oily, migratory birds who come here to nest in summer. The best time to come is at sunset, when you can watch the muttonbirds return to their nests. Between the jetty and Parks Beach, porpoises and seals perform two shows daily at the **Pet Porpoise Pool** ($9.50, kids $4.50, family ticket $29.50; ☎066/52 2164 for times); there's also a small aquarium with sharks, other marine animals and a reef tank.

Banana plantations indicate that at Coffs you're entering a subtropical climate zone. The cultural influence of not-too-far-away Queensland becomes apparent, too, in tourist attractions like **The Big Banana** (daily 9am–5pm), a huge, bright-yellow and impossible-to-overlook concrete banana 3km north of Coffs on the Pacific Highway, advertising a "horticultural theme park". It's free to walk through the banana and look at displays covering early pioneer life in the district and Coffs Harbour's $70-million-a-year banana industry. There are various tours of the plantation (bus 30min–1hr, $3–5; monorail 1hr 30min, $9) – besides bananas and packing sheds and hydroponics glasshouses, you can see a space station and an Aboriginal Dreamtime Cave. The newest, most improbable attraction is a toboggan ride ($4), whizzing 720m down through the steep hillside plantations. For the complete banana experience, drop by the milk bar, which serves bananas in every imaginable way. The souvenir shop next door is a kitsch-lover's delight, crammed with lurid yellow objects, running the gamut from banana pencil sharpeners to "Bananas in Pajamas".

## Around Coffs Harbour

Inland from Coffs, on Bushmans Range Road at Lowanna, 42km northwest, **George's Gold Mine** (Wed–Sun 10.30am–3.30pm, daily during school holidays; $7.50), an hour's drive through tall, ancient forest, you can can tour the old Bayfield gold mine and have a look at the old stamper battery that used to crush the ore. There are also picnic grounds, barbecues and walking trails through the rainforest.

To the north of Coffs is a string of fantastic sandy beaches. **Moonee Beach Reserve**, 6km away, is in beautiful bush surrounds with a creek weaving its way gently to the ocean, providing safe swimming – but beware of strong currents at its mouth. The reserve, with plenty of shade, picnic tables and barbecues, is a great spot for picnics. Besides a caravan park, all there is here is a small shop which sells good fish 'n' chips, hamburgers and supplies. About 8km further on, relatively unspoilt **Emerald Beach** is popular with sufers; it's very picturesque, with a small island offshore.

At **WOOLGOOLGA**, another 10km or so north on the Pacific Highway, a gleaming white **temple** is evidence of the large Sikh population which settled here in the early 1970s. There's also the **Raj Mahal**, an emporium selling crafts, clothes and jewellery, plus a pricey Indian **restaurant**, although the *Temple View* (☎066/54 1122), oppposite the temple, is much better. Woolgoolga is also a popular seaside holiday resort, with excellent surfing on the ocean beach and **Woolgoolga Lake** to the north offering opportunities for swimming, boating and other calmer-water activities.

## Eating, drinking and nightlife

Places to **eat** are concentrated on High Street, and particularly at the two ends – around The Mall and the junction with Grafton Street, and down in the block or so before the Jetty. At the latter end, the *Pier Hotel* at no. 386 has good, inexpensive counter meals and *Fisherman's Katch*, on the corner of Camperdown Street, serves excellent seafood. Also in the harbour area of town, *Barhn Thai*, 23 Orlando Street, is an excellent Thai with plenty of choice for vegetarians.

**Nightlife** in Coffs is lively in summer but very mainstream. There are generally live bands playing cover versions at some venue around town from Wednesday through to Sunday, usually with free entry. On Friday and Saturday nights the *RSL Club*, on the corner of Vernon Street and the Pacific Highway, has two bands and a disco, free entry and very cheap drinks until 2am. The *Plantation Hotel* has live bands three nights a week, and the "*Hoey-Moey*", Ocean Parade, has bands on Sunday afternoons. For a more sedate drink, the *Greenhouse Tavern*, on the corner of Bray Street and the Pacific Highway, lets you sip in a reasonable approximation of tropical rainforest surrounds in its gazebo. There are two nightclubs, *High Street 66* and *Penguins*, both on The Mall; both stay open six nights a week in summer until 5am.

## Listings

**Bike rental** *Promenade Leisure Hire* Coffs Promenade, Coffs Creek, 321 High St (☎066/51 1032), $6 per hour, $15 half-day, $30 full day; also canoe rental.

**Cinema** *Coffs Harbour Cinema Centre*, Vernon St (☎066/52 2233; half price Mon–Fri before 6pm and all day Tues).

**Buses** *Lindsays Coach Service* (☎066/51 3022) to Nambucca Heads, Grafton and Dorrigo; *Jessup's Bus Service* (☎066/53 4551) to Bellingen, Nambucca Heads and Sawtell.

**Car rental** *All-Ways*, 34 Marcia St (☎066/52 1811); *Coffs Harbour Rent-A-Wreck* (☎066/56 2042); *Hertz*, 45 Grafton St (☎066/51 1899); *JR's Car & Truck Rental*, 30 Orlando St (☎066/52 8480); *Thrifty*, Pacific Highway corner of Pacific Highway and Marcia St (☎066/52 8622).

**Diving** *Aussitel Hostel* arranges inexpensive scuba courses; *Jetty Dive Centre*, 398 High St, at the harbour (☎066/51 1611), offers dives for beginners and advanced divers at the coral reefs around South Solitary Island.

**Horse-riding** *Bonville Forest Stables*, Butlers Rd, Bonville, about 16km south of Coffs (☎066/53 4537); *Valery Trails*, 20km south west of Coffs, turn off the Pacific Highway at Bonville (☎066/53 4301).

**Hospital** ☎066/52 2866

**Markets** Sunday-morning markets are held at *Treasure Island Markets* (Jetty Village Shopping Centre, Sundays 8am–2pm), and in the *Big W* car park on the corner of Castle and Vernon streets.

**Scenic flights** *Fly Scenic* (☎066/51 3244), from $45 per person.

**Surfing** *East Coast Surf School* based at Diggers Beach (☎066/51 5515) is a brilliant place to learn to surf in small groups. Introductory 2hr lesson $22 ($17 for YHA/VIP cardholders); 3-day course $68 ($46 YHA/VIP); includes surfboard and wetsuit. Write for details of their excellent-value 3-day surf camps: PO Box 6336, Coffs Harbour NSW 2450.

**Taxis** ☎066/51 3944.

**Tours** *Bushwhacker Expeditions*, Darkwood Rd, Thora (☎066/55 8607), runs expeditions into the rainforest, and canoeing and rafting in the rivers of the hinterland; *4WD Adventure Safaris* (☎066/ 58 1871 or mobile ☎018/66 5790), half- and full-day tours including George's Gold Mine, plus canoeing and horse-riding; *Mountain Trails 4WD Tours* (☎066/55 7117), well-recommended half- and full-day 4WD adventures along remote tracks to banana plantations, waterfalls and the rainforest, weekend trips to Dorrigo and mountain country, or wildlife tours at night.

**Water-skiing** All day water-skiing trips from the YHA hostel; $35 includes lunch.

**White-water rafting** Coffs Harbour is one of the few places on the east coast where you can go rafting, though after a dry winter the rivers can be low. The best outfit is *White Water Rafting Professionals* (☎066/51 4066; around $115 per day).

# Grafton

**GRAFTON** is a peaceful district capital on a bend of the wide Clarence River, which almost encircles the city and occasionally floods it. The "Big River" is the largest river system on the north coast and, with its tributaries, drains a vast area of northern NSW. An afternoon sitting on the balcony of the *Crown Hotel*, sipping a beer and watching the majestic river roll by is truly well spent. Northeast of Grafton, the river widens as it approaches the ocean and branches out into a web of waterways and channels. There are more than a hundred river islands, on many of which sugar cane is grown.

Grafton is proud of its wide, tree-lined streets and maintains itself as a very genteel, old-fashioned town. In spring, when the jacaranda and flame trees are ablaze with purple, mauve and red blossoms, they even have a **Jacaranda Festival** to celebrate them (last week Oct, first week Nov). Out of festival time it's a quiet place, where the main attraction is cruising on the river, or visiting some of the historical buildings preserved by the National Trust: **Schaeffer House** at 192 Fitzroy Street (Tues–Thurs 1–4pm, Sun 2–4pm; admission by donation), for example, which now houses a small regional museum; or the **Regional Art Gallery** at **Prentice House**, 158 Fitzroy Street (Wed–Sun 10am–4pm; admission by donation), with a fine *Courtyard Cafe* attached.

For more details, call in at the **Clarence River Tourist Association** (daily 9am–5pm; ☎066/42 4677), on the Pacific Highway at the corner of Spring Street, which can fill you in on the houses, the cruises and the national parks that surround Grafton; there's also an NPWS office at 50 Victoria Street (☎066/42 0613) opposite the courthouse. Local **bus** services are provided by *Grafton–Yamba Bus Service* (Grafton ☎066/42 2779, Yamba ☎066/46 2019): bookings and information from *Harvey World Travel*, 54 Prince Street (☎066/42 6655). There's plenty of **accommodation** should you wish to stay: try the *Grafton Hotel*, 97 Fitzroy Street (☎066/42 2000; ③), a good pub offering B&B and counter meals; *Roches Family Hotel*, 85 Victoria Street (☎066/42 2866; ③), which does the same for similar prices; the *Crown Hotel-Motel*, 1 Prince Street (☎066/42 4000; ③–④) for rooms with a river view; or the well-equipped *Glenwood Tourist Park*, Heber Street in South Grafton (☎066/42 3466; on-site vans ③, holiday units & cabins ④). A good place to **eat** is *Crabba Jack's Takeaway* at 70 Fitzroy Street for fresh fish and chips, seafood and very generously stuffed potatoes; there are a few tables to eat in. Across the street at no. 100, *Big River Pizza* is also recommended and it's usually open when most places have closed. *Stornelli's* at the *Parkview Hotel*, 93 Prince Street, is a decent Italian restaurant with a cheaper bistro attached; both are closed Mon & Sun.

## Around Grafton

Much of the coast near Grafton on either side of the mouth of the Clarence River has been declared national parkland. The twin towns of **YAMBA** and **ILUKA** – increasingly popular holiday spots – face each other across the river, with *Clarence River Ferries* shuttling between them (four daily; $3; also cruises to river islands; ☎018/66 4556). In Yamba, *Backpackers at the Pacific Hotel*, 1 Pilot Street (☎066/46 2466; ③), is in a great old pub right on the beach, and offers very cheap singles as well as larger rooms, and free use of bikes and boogie boards; ask about lifts to Byron Bay.

South of Yamba is **Yuragir National Park**, with several lovely, simple NPWS campsites where you can get away from it all ($5 per site, details from Grafton NPWS – see above), surrounded by isolated beaches and quiet lake systems. North of Iluka, between the town and **Bundjalong National Park**, the Iluka Nature Reserve protects a World Heritage-listed **rainforest remnant**, one of 16 such areas in northern NSW. The national park itself enjoys both coastline and the sheltered inland waterways of the Esk River; **camping** is at *Woody Head*, a site which is very popular with anglers (bookings advised; ☎066/46 6134). Just north of Bundjalong, **EVANS HEAD** has a range of accommodation and shops as well as boat rental; the tropics are beginning to make their presence felt here, with sugar cane growing by the roadside.

Inland, the Gwydir Highway turns off the Pacific Highway at Grafton, heading towards Glen Innes, 160km away on the New England Plateau. En route it passes the rugged and densely forested adjoining national parks of **Gibraltar Range** and **Walshpool**. Gibraltar Range is an elevated plateau 1200m above sea level, scattered with huge granite outcrops and intersected by deep gorges and famous for its wild-flower displays of Christmas bells and waratahs in late summer. There's a **Visitor Centre** on the highway at Dandahra Picnic Area and a gravel road leads from here into the park, where Mulligans Hut serves as a base for walks and camping. Walshpool National Park is very remote and barely accessible, a wilderness park on the eastern escarpment of the New England Tableland. Its **rainforest** is worth visiting, with picnic facilities, walks and camping at Coombadjha Creek – via Coombadjha Road off the Gwydir Highway 88km from Grafton.

# Ballina

At the mouth of the Richmond River, the old port of **BALLINA** experienced a short-lived goldrush in the 1880s, but it has few reminders of this era, and is now mostly a holi-day town, with a few good places to drink and some nice beaches, as well as river trips to Lismore (see p.205) and other destinations. Neither has it escaped the clutches of the "big things", with the **giant prawn** marking the entrance to town, just off the highway from Grafton. The fact that you're entering New Age territory is apparent around Ballina, where the **Thursday Plantation**, 4km north on Gallans Road east of the Pacific Highway (daily 8.30am–4.30pm; free; patio café & giftshop) was the first commercial plantation of **tea tree**, producing the all-healing tea tree oil and its products.

There's a cycling and walking track (20min walk) from the centre of the town along the sea wall to the beach. In **Las Balsas Plaza**, on River Street (daily 9am–4pm; free), is a small **maritime museum**, whose exhibits include the *Atzlan*, a balsa raft that made it across the Pacific from Ecuador in 1973 as part of the Thor Heyerdahl-like *Las Balsas* expedition. Ballina **Tourist Information Centre** (daily 9am–5pm; ☎066/86 3484; free local **accommodation** booking) is in the same plaza. The *Ballina Travellers Lodge*, 36–38 Tamar Street (☎066/86 6737; rooms ③–④, dorms ①), is a YHA-affiliated place, friendly, family-run and modern, with a swimming pool. *Ballina Gardens Caravan Park*, 3km north on the Pacific Highway (☎066/86 2475; cabins ②–④), also has a pool and is one of the better places to **camp**. If you have a car, though, the prime spot to pitch a tent is *Flat Rock Camping Ground* (☎066/86 4848) on the Coast Road 5km east of Ballina: right on the beach, this unspoilt site is for tents only and there's no power, so it's very peaceful – hot showers add a touch of comfort.

Ballina has quite a lively summer **nightlife**: the *Henry Rous Tavern*, on River Street, hosts Seventies disco nights, while the *Australian Hotel*, on the corner of Cherry and River streets, is more sedate, with jazz, piano music and a pleasant beer garden. Both pubs have recommended **bistros**, while *Something Different* at the *El Rancho Motor Inn*, on the corner of Fox and Cherry streets (☎066/86 3333; licensed, closed Sun) serves up *real* Australian food, meaning crocodile and other native critters. There's also *Mexican del Rio* on River Street (licensed, open daily from 6.30pm), or the Thai *Palm Garden* on the same street (BYO, closed Mon).

Local **bus** services include *Blanch's* (☎066/86 2144) for service to the airport and Byron Bay, and *Kirklands* (☎066/86 6566), who run to Lismore, Sydney and Brisbane. To get around, you can rent a **bike** from *Jack Ransom Cycles*, 16 Cherry St (☎066/86 3485); rental **cars** are available from *Ballina Car Rentals*, Ballina Motel (☎066/86 2208), or *Sunray Car Rentals*, 286 River St (☎066/86 7315).

# Lennox Head

The best of the surf beaches are those around the little town of **LENNOX HEAD**,
11km north, a relaxed resort with a small shopping centre, some good cafés and restaurants and a lively pub. Lennox rates among the top ten surfing spots of the world and
professionals congregate here for the big waves in May, June and July. Adding to
Lennox Head's appeal is the calm, fresh water of **Lake Ainsworth** close to the beach:
stained dark by the tea trees around its banks, it's a popular swimming spot for families
seeking refuge from the crashing surf. *Lennox Head Sailing* (☎066/876 010), on the
lake, rents out sailboards and you can arrange lessons.

Ideally situated between the lake and the beach, the *Lennox Beachhouse* **hostel**, 2–3
Ross Street (☎066/87 7636; rooms ③, dorms ①), is a relaxed place with free board-use
and fishing gear, as well as bargain rental of windsurfers and catamarans. Also in a
prime position is the *Lake Ainsworth Caravan Park* (☎066/87 7249; cabins ④). The
Mexican **food** at *Pancho Villa*, Ballina Street (dinner Sun–Thurs; BYO) is popular with
surfies; *Lennox Head Chinese*, 63 Ballina St (daily from 5pm; BYO) also gets a look in.

# Byron Bay and around

Situated at the end of a long sweeping bay, the township of **BYRON BAY** boasts 30km
of almost unbroken sandy beaches. Formerly a working-class coastal town of dilapidated weatherboard cottages, best known for its abattoir, it's now a thriving resort, first
discovered by the surfies, then the hippies and more recently by better-heeled travellers. The New Age legacy lives on, and Byron Bay's charms have not gone unnoticed in
backpacker circles either, while in summer it can seem like Sydney-by-the-sea, as half
of Paddington and Darlinghurst arrive en masse to escape the city. For the moment,
however, it remains a special and enjoyable place – small, picturesque, with an oddball
but equable local community and a splendidly scenic setting. The locals, despite being
permanently outnumbered, seem far from overwhelmed, though whether they will
survive the controversial Club Med development, planned near unspoilt Belongil
Creek, remains to be seen.

## Arrival and information

If you arrive here by **train**, you'll be right in the heart of town. Not all north coast **buses**
stop at Byron Bay; those that do will drop you very centrally, just by the train station or a
little way north near the junction of Jonson and Lawson streets (see "Listings" for details
of bus companies and travel agents that deal with bookings). The closest **airports** are at
Ballina, 39km south, or Coolangatta, 109km north in Queensland.

Check out the moderately helpful **Byron Bay Tourist Information Centre**, at 80
Jonson Street, next to the train station (daily 9am–4pm; ☎066/85 8050; no accommodation bookings), where they have information about national parks, scenic drives,
sights, activities and tours; a *Disabled Access Guide* is also available.

## Accommodation

There are plenty of places to stay in Byron Bay, but that doesn't mean it's easy to find a
bed. During December and January especially, demand for accommodation in all categories far exceeds supply, and it's essential to **book well in advance**. *A1
Accommodation*, 69 Jonson Street (☎066/85 7523; Mon–Fri 9am–5pm, Sat 9am–3pm,
Sun 10am–3pm), will make bookings for all accommodation free of charge. The
**hostels** in Byron Bay are among the best in Australia, but prices rise dramatically in
summer when everywhere is packed out; if there's a group of you, **holiday apartments** (bookable through *A1* and real estate agents in town) might be a better deal. If

everywhere in town is full, you may strike lucky in the surrounding area – either towards Brunswick Heads, about 18km further up the coast, or in the quiet town of Mullumbimby, just inland.

## MOTELS, HOTELS, GUESTHOUSES AND APARTMENTS

**Brunswick Hotel**, Mullumbimby St, Brunswick Heads (☎066/85 1236). Bargain accommodation in restored historic pub; counter meals and live music. ④.

**Byron Links Holiday Village**, 64 Broken Head Rd, 6km south (☎066/85 8105). Wooden holiday units with swimming pool, barbecue, children's playground. Next to a golf course. ⑦.

**Byron Bay Sunseeker Cabins**, 100 Bangalow Rd, 2km south (☎066/85 7369). Timber chalets sleeping a maximum of 6 people. Luxury items like videos, but limited cooking facilities. ⑦.

**Byron Bay Beach Resort**, Bayshore Drive, 3km north (☎066/85 8000). Lovely complex of wooden chalets with all facilities: pool, bar, restaurant, tennis courts, golf course. Horse and camel rides are organized from here. ⑤–⑧.

**Great Northern Hotel**, Jonson St (☎066/85 6454). No-frills pub rooms in a great position on the main street with a huge balcony from which to observe the action. The noise from the bands below make this one for confirmed night owls. Cheap single rates, particularly off-season. ④.

**Lord Byron Resort Motel**, 120–130 Jonson St (☎066/85 7444). Central position, with amenities including swimming pool, spa, sauna and tennis court. All units air-con. ⑤–⑧.

**River Oaks**, Broken Head Road, Suffolk Park, 3.5km from Byron (☎066/85 8679). Gay guesthouse, catering for men only, just a ten-minute walk through gorgeous rainforest to Tallow Beach or a short drive to secluded Kings Beach. Pick-ups from Ballina airport or from bus and train in town. Bunk rooms ②, regular rooms ⑤, studio apartments ⑦; all rates include a light breakfast.

**Sunseeker Motel**, 100 Bangalow Rd (☎066/85 7369). Motel with pool and barbecue. ⑤–⑥.

**The Wheel Resort**, Broken Head Road, 3.5km from Byron, opposite the golf course (☎066/85 6139). Designed by its wheelchair-bound owner to be totally accessible and comfortable for people like herself, this resort has won several prizes; not only disabled people stay, however. Private one- or two-roomed cabins, fully equipped (linen is provided), with verandah and TV, are set in rainforest with easy access to the beach. Cabins from ⑤, cheaper weekly rates.

## HOSTELS

**Arts Factory Lodge**, Skinners Shoot Rd (☎066/85 7709). Nice location ten minutes' walk out of town in a bushland creek setting, but with free bikes. Two-storey wooden building with balconies set around an inner courtyard with a pool have pleasant 4- or 6-share dorm rooms; alternative accommodation includes dorm beds in teepees, canvas huts for couples by the creek, a camping area and a self-contained cottage. A New Age atmosphere prevails: lots of music events and food nights plus two yoga classes a day. Reception open 8.30am–1pm & 3–6pm. Pick-up service from train and bus if booked in advance. No children allowed. Dorms ①, rooms ③, self-contained cottage ⑦.

**Backpackers Holiday Village**, 116 Jonson St (☎066/85 7660). One of the most central and long established hostels, this place is clean, friendly and well equipped, with a swimming pool, spa and barbecues. Free bikes, boards and luggage storage. Dorms ①, rooms ④.

**Backpackers Inn**, 29 Shirley St (☎066/85 8231). Motel-style complex around a central courtyard; communal kitchen, terrace, small shop. Swimming pool, barbecue and volleyball court in garden. Free bikes and boards. Out of town, but only 70m from Belongil Beach. Dorms ①, rooms ④.

**Belongil Beach House**, Childe St (☎066/85 7868). Beautiful complex in the style of a Balinese resort, with spacious, cool, high-ceilinged timber cottages around a landscaped garden; out of town, but with a prime beachside location. Parking and free bikes available. Reception open 8am–1pm & 3–6.30pm. Dorms ②, rooms ④, furnished apartments for 4 people ⑤.

**Cape Byron Lodge**, 78 Bangalow Rd (☎066/85 6445). About fifteen minutes' walk from town but they operate a shuttle bus; swimming pool and nice garden areas. Reception open 8.30am–12.30pm & 3.30–9.30pm. Dorms ①, rooms ④.

**Cape Byron YHA Hostel**, corner of Middleton and Byron streets (☎066/85 8788). Big, brand-new hostel which feels more like a resort hotel. Large courtyard with pool; dining room, kitchen and terrace. Small fee for bike ($5 plus $20 deposit) covers entire stay. Dorms ①, rooms ③.

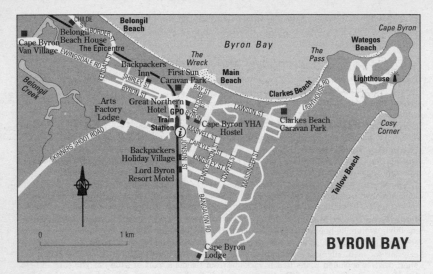

**BYRON BAY**

*CAMPSITES*

**Cape Byron Van Village**, Ewingsdale Rd (☎066/85 7378). Pool and tennis court. Cabins ③–⑤.

**Clarkes Beach Caravan Park**, off Lighthouse Rd (☎066/85 6496). Only a kilometre from the centre of town, and right on the beach. Shady, natural surrounds. Cabins ③–④.

**Ferry Reserve Caravan Park**, Pacific Highway, Brunswick Heads (☎066/85 1872). Pleasant campsite near the river, with kiosk and barbecue. Cabins ③–⑤.

**First Sun Caravan Park**, Lawson St (☎066/85 6544). Very central, overlooking Main Beach. Cabins ③–⑤.

**Maca's Camping Ground**, Main Arm Rd, near Mullumbimby (☎066/84 5211). Campsite in the bush; communal kitchen and dining room, laundry; tents for rent.

**Suffolk Park Caravan Park**, Alcorn St, Suffolk Park, 5km south (☎066/85 3353). Good location on Tallow Beach, shady, natural setting. Cabins ②–⑤.

**Terrace Caravan Park**, The Terrace, Brunswick Heads (☎066/85 1233). Shady spot by the river, near the beach. Cabins ③–⑤.

## The Town and around

There's plenty of opportunity to soak up local atmosphere, and the often bizarre mix of countercultures as surfie meets soap starlet meets hippie, simply by wandering the streets – but probably the best place to take it all in at once is the **market**, on the first Sunday of every month in Butler Street, behind the train station. One of the first places to head if you want to explore is out to the **lighthouse** on the rocky promontory of **Cape Byron**, where there's a small nature reserve (8am–5.30pm). The cape includes the easternmost point of the Australian mainland and is a popular spot to greet the dawn, but don't worry if you're not an early riser – the views from the cape and the lighthouse reserve are fabulous anytime, and there's an excellent circular walking track from the lighthouse. With a bit of luck you'll see **dolphins**, who like to sport in the surf off the headland, **humpback whales**, which pass this way heading north to warmer waters in June/July and again on their return leg south in September/October, and maybe some **sharks** too.

The main town beach – known, uninspiringly, as **Main Beach** – is as good as any to swim from, and usually relatively gentle as far as the surf goes; one reason Byron Bay is so popular with surf freaks is that it has beaches facing in all directions, so that there's almost always one with a good swell – conversely, you can usually find somewhere for a calmer swim.

East of the Main Beach, you can always find a spot to yourself on the less sheltered, long straight stretch of **Belongil Beach**, from where it's beach virtually all the way to **BRUNSWICK HEADS**, a quieter, more family-oriented little resort located between the mouth of the Brunswick River and Simpson's Creek, with a long crescent of beach on the ocean side. The grassy riverfront area is a good spot for kids with a playgrounds and picnic area in several spots. The attractive 1930s-style *Brunswick Hotel* has a popular shady beer garden facing the river, packed on Sunday afternoons when there's free live music outside.

Back in the other direction, as Main Beach curves round towards Cape Byron, it becomes **Clarkes Beach**. This and neighbouring **Wategos Beach** near the point – beautifully framed between two rocky spurs – face north, and they're usually catching the best of the big surf. On the far side of the cape, **Tallow Beach** stretches down towards the **Broken Head Nature Reserve**, 6km south of the town centre at Suffolk Park; there's good surf at Tallow just around the Cape at Cosy Corner, and also at Broken Head. From the car park here, a short stroll through rainforest leads to secluded, nudist **Kings Beach**, one of several isolated stretches of sand out this way.

When you tire of lazing on the beach and admiring the sea from above, you can take your explorations one step further and head underwater. The diversity of marine life in the waters of Byron Bay make it second only to the Great Barrier Reef as a place to **dive** on the east coast. Tropical marine life and creatures from warm temperate seas mingle at the granite outcrop of **Julian Rocks Aquatic Reserve**, a weather-protected 80-hectare area; by far the most popular spot here is the **Cod Hole**, an extensive underwater cave, and the favoured hang-out of big moray eels and huge fish. Between April and June is the best time to dive, before the plankton bloom (see "Listings" below for a rundown of dive schools).

## Cafés and restaurants

There's a multitude of places selling food in Byron Bay, and the standard is generally pretty high. Lots of more or less alternative cafés offer great health and vegetarian food, and there are plenty of takeaways and fish 'n' chip shops, as well as restaurants offering anything from Chinese to pizza.

**Athena Taverna**, Lawson St (☎066/856 810). Very popular Greek restaurant, with casual atmosphere and tables outside. Prices are moderate. Tues–Sat 6.30–10pm; BYO.

**Bay Kebabs**, corner of Jonson and Lawson streets. Scrummy marinated chicken kebabs are the thing to have here. Squeeze onto a couple of stools or take out.

**The Beach Café**, Clarkes Beach (☎066/857 598). *The* place for breakfast, from 7.30am. Great views and a globetrotting range of set breakfasts; now serving dinner in the summer.

**Belongil Beach House Café**, Childe Street, next to *Belongil Beach House*. Another great oceanfront place for breakfast, lunch and dinner though the sea view is behind beachfront bush. Outside tables, occasionally serenaded by free music. BYO.

**Byron Thai**, 32 Lawson St (☎066/858 453). Excellent Thai restaurant with a palm-garden dining area. Loads of choice for vegetarians; prices are moderate. Licensed.

**The Byronian**, Jonson St. This café, frequented by locals, has a lively atmosphere with lots of chat over good coffee. Sit outside in the front courtyard under umbrellas and palms. Delicious food served from separate breakfast, lunch and dinner menus. Good value breakfasts and lunch daily; dinner Wed–Sat; BYO.

**Caddies Coffee Company**, Jonson St. This place roasts its own coffee. Outdoor courtyard tables. Open 8am–8pm daily, except Mon to 6.30pm and Sun to 4pm. Licensed.

**Earth 'n' Sea Pizzas**, corner of Lawson and Jonson streets (☎066/856 029). An old favourite with imaginative, unusual toppings: try their Mullumbimby Madness. Generous and affordable pasta too. BYO & licensed.

## ALTERNATIVE BYRON BAY

Byron Bay offers a truly wide variety of alternative therapies, extensive browsing in New Age bookshops, a wealth of crystals, and a future foretold through palmistry and tarot readings – all underlaid with a good dose of capitalism as prices for massages and tarot readings hike up during the lucrative summer months.

The **Community Centre**, at 69 Jonson Street, is hard to miss with its bright figurative mural, and has great noticeboards packed with information on everything from Celtic Shamanism to Tibetan healing; workshops are also held here. Out on Skinners Shoot Road, the **Arts Factory** has several artists' workshops, which you can visit (Tues–Sun 10am–3pm), and the **Byron Craft Market** is held here every Saturday (8.30am–3pm) with a courtesy bus (9.30am–3.30pm) from the community centre on Jonson Street. The **Epicentre**, on Kendall Street, near Belongil Beach, has artists and crafts people in residence with several outlets, plus a large art gallery showing the work of local artists ($1 donation). Not far from here, the *Belongil Beach House* is the location for the **Relax Haven** with a float tank ($40 for 2hr) and massage available ($35 per hour).

Back in the town centre, the **Crystal Temple**, at 87 Jonson Street, has a range of therapies on offer, plus crystals, books, tapes and jewellery. One of the best alternative shops is **Cat's Recycled Emporium**, Shop 1/3 Lawson Street, which sells a mixture of clothes and art: groovy dresses for the beach made of old towels hang beside sandals created from recycled conveyor belts and leather off-cuts, next to mobiles made of cutlery and robots constructed from bits of cars.

**Epicentre Cafe**, The Epicentre, Border St (☎066/855 629). Sophisticated vegetarian menu dips into many cuisines, with an emphasis on freshness and organic produce. The outdoor courtyard, surrounded by native plants, is a real treat, particularly when it's candle-lit at night. Live entertainment every Thurs from 6pm. Closed Tues & Wed in winter; BYO.

**McMahons Cafe Restaurant**, corner of Jonson and Marvel streets (☎066/85 7320). One of the best – and most expensive – places to eat with varied imaginative cuisine using quality fresh ingredients. Save room for the delicious deserts. Mon–Sat 8.30am–9pm. Licensed.

**Misaki Byron**, 11 Fletcher St (☎066/85 7966). Excellent Japanese restaurant serves everything from sushi to noodles, in a pleasant brick courtyard. Expensive, but BYO; bookings required. Tues–Sat 6.30–10pm

**Oh! Deli Tandoori**, Bay Centre Arcade, 6 Lawson St (☎066/856 251). Byron's best Indian restaurant and takeaway. Dinner nightly except Sun; BYO and licensed.

**The Piggery**, Arts Factory, Skinners Shoot Road (☎066/85 7177). "Modern Australian" menu by a top chef. The setting is spacious, retaining the old open rafters of the building's early days as a meatworks, now painted colourfully, and with equally bright blue formica tables in booths. Dinner daily, lunch weekends only; expensive but BYO.

**Ringo's**, 29 Jonson St. One of Byron's most popular cafés, not least for the full stash of recent glossy mags to read. A large and airy place, its food is probably the cheapest in town, with a choice ranging from a simple salad sandwich to lasagne or curry, with lots of vegetarian options.

**River Oaks**, Broken Head Road, Suffolk Park, 3.5km from Byron (☎066/85 8679). This small BYO bistro – attached to a guesthouse but open to non-residents – is a gay meeting spot.

**Soul Kitchen**, 9 Fletcher St (☎066/855 895). Ocean views, good music and tasty modern Australian cuisine. Licensed with cocktail bar; open late.

### Nightlife and entertainment

The weekly free community newspaper, *The Byron Shire Echo*, has a comprehensive gig guide. There's plenty of music in summer, including the huge outdoor **Annual Byron Bay Arts and Music Festival** which, for three days in early January, takes over Belongil Fields with several stages, a rave field, an all-night cinema, food fair, market stalls and workshops; tickets available from the Tourist Information Centre (see p.198) or in advance from independent record outlets around Australia.

**Beach Hotel**, corner of Jonson and Bay streets (☎066/85 6402). Owned by John Cornell who played Paul Hogan's sidekick in a Seventies Australian comedy series, this pub is superbly sited right opposite Main Beach with a huge terrace beer garden, and attracts a cross-section of locals. Often free live music, including jazz sessions on Sunday afternoons.

**Catalina Tapas Bar**, 32 Jonson St (☎066/85 8493). Tapas from around $4, with eclectic live music, cabaret or DJ. Usually a cover charge. Tues–Sat from 6pm, with a club to 3am.

**The Car Park**, The Plaza, Jonson St (☎066/85 6170). Groovy, late-night dance club, plus a restaurant dishing up Mediterranean food.

**Chincogan Tavern**, Burringbar St, Mullumbimby (☎066/84 1550). Bands on Friday nights.

**The Epicentre**, Border St, Belongil Beach (☎066/85 6789). A multi-purpose performance space, and the centre of culture in Byron Bay: hosts everything from dance parties, comedy festivals and Aboriginal dance troupes to international and Australian musicians and singers, and visiting gurus. This is a non-smoking venue and many, though not all, of the gigs are alcohol-free.

**Great Northern Hotel**, Jonson St (☎066/85 6454). Something for everyone: a front room with pool tables, a typically blokish public bar and "The Backroom", a large stylish venue that doubles as a restaurant and a music venue with big-name Australian bands playing three or four times a week.

**Railway Friendly Bar**, next to the train station, Jonson St (☎066/85 7662). A small pub that's a popular and noisy haunt of locals and travellers alike: it has quaint train carriage decor, great counter meals, a beer garden, and free live music nightly from 6.30–9.30pm.

## Listings

**Bike rental** *Byron Bay Bicycles*, Shop 5, The Plaza, Jonson St (☎066/85 6315); *Go Bikes*, 93 Jonson St, opposite Woolworth's (☎066/85 6067).

**Buses** *McCafferty's* and *Greyhound.Pioneer* bookings through *Byron Bay Travel Centre*, 52 Jonson St (☎066/85 6733); *Kirklands* bookings at *Cape Byron Travel*, 6 Lawson St (☎066/85 6262), which is where these buses stop. *Blanch's Coaches* (☎066/86 2144) run to Ballina via Suffolk Park, Bangalow and Lennox Head. Very cheap buses to Sydney are arranged by *Backpacker Central* (free call ☎1800 634 951), next to the tourist office.

**Car rental** *Byron Bay Motor Rentals*, corner of Bayshore and Ewingsdale roads (☎066/85 8140); *Hertz*, 11–21 Butler St (☎066/85 6522).

**Diving** Most dive schools offer complete scuba diving courses, together with more affordable one-day courses and daily snorkelling trips (around $30). *Byron Bay Dive Centre*, 9 Lawson St (☎066/85 7149) also does a good-value one-day course for $110 including all equipment and a night's accommodation; *Sundive*, Middleton St (☎066/85 7755), is a small, friendly outfit. If you're already trained, one dive at Julian Rocks, with gear, costs $60, with two dives adding an extra $30.

**Gay info** *Tropical Fruits* is a social group for gays and lesbians, holding dance parties every few weeks in halls around the area; the *Fruitline* (☎066/22 4353) is a recorded telephone service that details upcoming events.

**Horse-riding** *Tyagarah Riding Ranch*, Gray's Lane, Tyagarah, 11km north (☎066/84 7499), has rides along the beach or through rainforest, suitable for beginners and experienced riders; *Seahorse Riding Ranch*, Broken Head (☎066/87 6211) has lessons available, and rides include a sunset tour.

**Left luggage** *Backpackers Central*, next to the tourist office will mind bags until 6pm for $1, $2 after 6pm, plus an extra $1 every time you want access to your bags.

**Laundry** Most accommodation has a laundry you can use; otherwise try *Byron Dry Cleaners and Laundrette*, 42 Jonson St (daily 7am–8pm) with service washes available, or the unattended self-serve one on Marvel St (Mon–Fri 6am–7pm, Sat & Sun 6am–6pm).

**Medical** *Bay Centre Medical Clinic* (☎066/856 206 all hours), Mon–Fri 8.30am–5pm.

**Surfing** Surf lessons always include loan of board and wetsuit which makes them very good value. The best outfits are the highly professional *East Coast Surf School* (☎066/85 5989; mobile ☎015/25 7243; $20 for 2hrs, discounts for YHA & VIP cardholders, pick-up from accommodation), with safety-conscious sports science graduates teaching not just technique but how to read the surf; *Girls Go Surfing* gets women of all ages and stages on board (☎066/85 5883). *Byron Surf*, corner of Lawson and Fletcher streets (☎066/857 536) rents out surf gear.

**Taxi** *Byron Bay Taxis* (☎066/85 6290).

**Tours** The following all offer tours to the rainforest, waterfalls and national parks around Byron Bay: *Mick's Bay to Bush Tours* (☎066/85 8363 or mobile ☎018/66 2684); *Big Scrub Rainforest Tours*

(☎066/85 6554); *Jim's Alternative Tours* (☎066/85 7720). More specialist and unusual tour operators include: *Backcountry Cycling* (☎066/85 5362), with 40km mountain bike expeditions from Minyon Falls to Byron; *Byron Bay Harley Tours* (☎066/85 5900), offering motorcycle tours that whizz around the beaches and hinterland; and *Rapid Action* (☎075/30 4088), who offer rafting on the Nymboida River during summer only. Most tours and activities can be booked at *Backpacker Central*, next to the tourist office (free call ☎1800/63 4951; 7am–10pm daily); they operate their own *Nimbin Tours*, that can also be used as transport to Nimbin.

**Travel agents** *Byron Bay Flight Centre*, corner of Lawson and Fletcher streets (☎066/85 5440). *Byron Bay Travel Centre*, Shop 4, 52 Jonson St (☎066/85 6733). General travel agent and STA agent, deals with bus bookings and passes, and sells YHA and VIP membership.

# Tweed Heads

From Brunswick Heads, the Pacific Highway heads around 30km inland to Murwillumbah (see p.208) and then a further 30km to the coast at **TWEED HEADS**. Although officially still part of New South Wales, Tweed Heads – the twin city of Coolangatta in Queensland (see p.278) – is for all practical purposes part of the **Gold Coast**. It certainly looks the part: high-rise buildings, concrete apartment blocks and shopping centres vie for space with grandiose club buildings and a roadscape of advertising billboards in gaudy colours. From the shore the jagged skyline of Surfers Paradise can be seen in the distance.

In its favour, it does have lots of places to stay (motels are cheaper here than further north), and even more opportunities to eat and drink – not to mention the opportunity to **gamble**, an activity that was once banned in Queensland. **Clubs** and casinos opened up just across the border to cash in: one of the biggest, brightest and longest-established of these is the *Twin Towns RSL Club* (☎07/5536 2277) on Wharf Street, whose special offers on cheap food and drink can be a good deal, so long as you don't lose too much in the machines along the way.

One of the few alternative attractions is the **Minjungbal Aboriginal Cultural Museum**, on Kirkwood Road in South Tweed Heads (daily 10am–4pm; $6), whose detailed exhibits and videos illustrate how Aborigines lived off this stretch of the coast; near the museum, a signposted boardwalk leads past an old bora ring – a sacred site used in initiation ceremonies. Ironically, the **Captain Cook Memorial** on **Point Danger** celebrates the very event that signalled the demise of Aboriginal culture in these parts: right at the state border, it was erected for the Cook bicentenary celebrations in 1970. Cook named Point Danger after nearly running aground on it, and **Mount Warning** (see below) got its name at the same time, as a landmark to help sailors navigate around the point.

## Practicalities

The **Tweed Tourist Information Centre** is at 4 Wharf Street (daily 9am–5pm; ☎07/5536 4244); they also carry information on the rest of the Gold Coast. The **transport** situation merely serves to emphasize Tweed Heads' functional integration into the Gold Coast: arriving at Coolangatta airport, buses generally make a beeline for the resort strip in Queenland, though *Kirklands* do stop on Boundary Street in Tweed Heads (☎07/5536 1063 for bookings and info). *Tweed Heads Bus* (☎07/5536 2500) runs local services up and down the Gold Coast. Should you want to **stay**, there are dozens of motels, caravan parks and holiday flats strung out along the highway, though there's even more choice over the border and you're probably better off continuing to Surfers Paradise (see p.281), for the full Gold Coast experience if that's what you're after. It's not hard to find something to **eat**, either: if the clubs don't appeal, head for oceanfront Marine Parade, where there's everything from takeaway pizza to *Doyles on the Beach*, an outpost of the famous Sydney-based seafood chain.

# Far North Coast Hinterland

The beautiful area inland from the far north coast, between artist-filled **Lismore** in the fertile Richmond River valley to the south, and staid **Murwillumbah** in the even lusher valley of the Tweed River near the Queensland border, is known as the **Far North Coast Hinterland**. But pioneers dubbed the region – once covered in **rainforest** that included species of flora extant from the era of the ancient supercontinent of **Gondwanaland** – the Big Scrub. The hinterland's three national parks, plus several reserves, are **World Heritage listed**, protecting pockets of rainforest which the settlers never managed to log, and which protesters helped to save in the first successful anti-logging demonstration in Australia, in 1979.

**Mount Warning** – Wollumbin or "cloud catcher" to the Bandjalung Aborigines – is what remains of the central magma chamber of a 4,000-square-kilometre, shield-shaped volcano; from this 1,157-metre peak, where the sun's rays first strike Australia, dazzling views reveal the area's geography. Mount Warning National Park rises in the middle of a massive **caldera** eroded on the eastern side into a huge bowl, where the Tweed River flows to the sea through the mostly agricultural patchwork of the valley floor. The northwest rim section consists of the McPherson and Tweed ranges found in the **Border Ranges National Park**; the southern section is within the **Nightcap Range National Park** near counter-culture Nimbin and **The Channon**, one of many villages in "the hills", this one famous for hosting the largest, most colourful **market** in the area.

*Fultons Bus Service* (☎066/79 5267) traverses the whole hinterland area, plying between Murwillumbah and Lismore, and stopping at Uki and Nimbin; other local bus services are mentioned in the town accounts.

## Lismore

Inland 65km from Ballina, **LISMORE** is the principal town of northeast New South Wales and the commercial focus of the fertile Richmond River valley, surrounded by prosperous dairying and farming country. This is one of the most densely populated rural areas in Australia, and has been since the early days of the colony. In the nineteenth century Lismore was an important river port for the **timber** trade as lumberjacks cut their way through the dense forest of the valley – the so-called Big Scrub – before moving up to the steep slopes of the McPherson Ranges near the Queensland border. Local red cedar, especially, was much sought-after. There's still a fair amount of forestry in the region, but these days the economic mainstay is dairy farming and cattle breeding, along with a rapidly growing tropical agriculture sector: bananas, sugar cane, avocados, tropical fruits and macadamia nuts.

For all the intense agriculture, however, this is not your typical Ocker backwater. Since the alternative-lifestyle seekers discovered the northeast in the Seventies, **cultural life** has flourished and jewellers, potters, painters, graphic artists, sculptors and other arts-and-crafts people who have settled here have brought with them a whole network of shops and galleries where they can sell their work. Once a year in October, they all come together for Lismore's **Art and Craft Expo**; at other times of the year the **Regional Art Gallery**, 131 Molesworth Street (Tues–Sat 10am–5pm; ☎066/22 2209), has a varied programme, a mixture of travelling exhibitions on the downstairs level and a selection of local artworks for sale upstairs. What's on show is normally totally contemporary, but from time to time the permanent collection is trundled out, reflecting Australian art from the 1950s and 1960s. The **Historical Museum**, next door (Tues–Fri 10am–4pm), houses an interesting, if somewhat motley, collection of pioneer relics and photographic records of the regional history. For somewhere to browse trash and treasure on a Sunday (the first and third of the month), Lismore has a car boot **market** in the *K-Mart* car park.

## Practicalities

If you're travelling by **bus**, you'll arrive at the *Kirklands Bus Terminal*, 4 Magellan Street; but since Lismore is not on the Pacific Highway, not all of the coastal services call here. As far as **trains** go, Lismore is on the Murwillumbah branch line: Murwillumbah trains will take you right here, while Brisbane ones call at Casino (see below), from where there's a connecting bus. There are several **car rental** agencies on Dawson Street, including *Lismore Rent a Car* at no. 100 (☎066/21 4118). For details of what's going on locally, head for the **Tourist Information and Heritage Centre**, at the corner of Molesworth and Ballina streets (daily 9am–5pm; ☎066/22 0122). The **NPWS** also have an office here, in the Colonial Arcade on Main Street (☎066/28 1177).

The friendliest **place to stay** is *Currendina Lodge*, 14 Ewing Street (☎066/21 6118; rooms ③, dorms ①), a pleasant B&B which will pick you up from the bus terminal or train station by arrangement – they also organize occasional tours to the surrounding national parks. The *Metropole Hotel*, 98 Keen Street (☎066/21 4910; ③), has simple pub accommodation and serves counter meals. A couple of kilometres south of town, the *Lismore Lake Caravan Park*, Bruxner Highway (☎066/21 2585; cabins ④) has inexpensive campsites, a pool, barbecue, children's playground and small shop.

Lismore isn't a bad place to **eat**, with a couple of excellent cafés. The favoured haunt of artists (and everyone else) is *Caddies Coffee Company*, at 20–24 Carrington Street, with a cool, modern interior, or you can sit outside under umbrellas; as well as damn fine coffee, they have bagels, panini and salads. *Butlers Deli-Bistro*, Nesbitt Lane, although tiny, is crammed with delicious things to eat. The *Rous Hotel*, 44 Keen Street (☎066/21 5044), is home to *Indian Dhaba* on Thursday to Saturday nights, when you can have curries to order – as mild or as hot as you like.

## Around Lismore

To explore the **country around Lismore** you really need your own vehicle. Most Sundays there's a **market** in at least one of the villages – the big ones are in the hilltop village of The Channon on the second Sunday of the month, and in Nimbin on the last. The halls of the various towns, particularly Nimbin, have dances and live music, and you may be lucky enough to be invited to a legendary hill party – there's usually one happening somewhere every weekend.

Thirteen kilometres west of Lismore, **CASINO** is a small country town on the Richmond River from where route 91 follows the rail lines south towards Grafton, or north through **KYOGLE**, with its Buddhist temple and retreat, into Queensland. One of the most scenic drives in New South Wales is the short round trip over the mountainous, winding country roads north and northeast of Lismore to Nimbin (see below), **THE CHANNON** and **CLUNES**, and then via **ELTHAM** and **BEXHILL**, with superb views from the ridges and hilltops. Accessible via Nimbin, with the 800-metre peak of Mount Nardi visible twelve kilometres beyond the town, is **Nightcap Range National Park**. The World Heritage-listed park has several walking trails from the summit.

## Nimbin

**NIMBIN** especially seems slower than most to move from a Seventies time warp, still clinging to its house facades and shopfronts painted in lurid, psychedelic designs, and small stores selling health food, incense sticks and patchouli oil. Some of the locals seem to have stuck to their Seventies dress code too. But Nimbin has caught up with the Nineties, or the Nineties have caught up with it. The range of Nimbin's cafés and restaurants has certainly expanded and, conversely, some of the area's more legendary cosmic-cake places have closed down. Getting out may rank highly in most visitors' priorities – you'll invariably be hit up for a dope deal or something stronger once you set foot in the street, and some find this threatening, while for others it's the ulterior motive for coming here.

Something akin to a "hippy hall of fame", the **Nimbin Museum** (62 Cullen Street; hours as they please; admission by donation), is certainly worth a visit. A weird and wonderful living museum run by hippies, there's plenty of local history relating to the Aquarius Festival, which set the ball rolling in 1973, Aboriginal culture, spiritual aphorisms to make you laugh or think, and a huge stone phallus in the centre of one room. Ask here about The Headpickers Ball, part of the Marijuana Harvest Festival in March. If you have affinities with the green movement, the **Nimbin Environment Centre**, also on Cullen Street, might interest you: they publicize and campaign on environmental issues, and can also arrange visits to the **Permaculture Village**, a showcase for a system of sustainable agriculture that is gaining ground worldwide but especially in developing countries.

Nearby **Terania Creek**, accessible by road from The Channon, is perhaps the area's most famous environmental attraction, saved by a 1979 protest that was dubbed a "hippy guerrilla struggle" by a *Rolling Stone* article of the period. The first successful anti-logging campaign in Australia saved this rainforest valley with its ancient brush box trees. **Protestors Falls**, named after the dispute, is a 700-metre walk from the picnic area, and the waterhole underneath is perfect for swimming. The creek is near the western edge of **Whian Whian State Forest**. On the forest's southeastern edge (reached via Mullumbimby or Dunoon), further watery delights are provided by the one-hundred-metre cascade of **Minyon Falls**.

## Practicalities

There are a number of **places to stay** in and near Nimbin. *Nimbin Backpackers Granny's Farm* hostel (☎066/89 1333; YHA dorms ①, rooms ②), very close to town but in a peaceful farm setting, is an easy-going place with log fires in winter and a swimming pool for chilling out in summer; cows graze in paddocks outside your window – or you can choose to stay in the farm's own teepee or camp. The other hostel option is the equally good but different *Rainbow Retreat* (☎066/89 1262; ②) in a bush setting by Goolmanger Creek with a swimming hole nearby; it's more intimate and you end up feeling like a personal guest of the friendly owner. The very comfortable, nicely decorated *Grey Gum Lodge*, 2 High St (☎066/89 1713; ④) is a guesthouse right in the town, with its own excellent restaurant – quality, fresh ingredients cooked superbly – and a saltwater swimming pool. The *Nimbin Motel*, 413 Croften Road (☎066/89 1420; ③), 4km north of town, near Nightcap National Park, has a small pool. Also near the park is *Turkey Creek Farm Bed & Breakfast* at Rosebank (☎066/88 2175; ⑤), a farmstay for women on an organic permaculture property in a century-old homestead; rates include a generous cooked breakfast. *Nimbin Cabins* (☎066/89 1493; ⑤), 6km north of town, offer B&B in fully equipped units with a view of the valley.

Nimbin's main strip, Cullen Street, is full of great **places to eat**. *Choices*, at no. 42, is the main place where locals gather: there's outdoor seating, vegetarian meals – great tofu and vego burgers – plus more meaty "Australian" fare. *Nimbin Pizza and Trattoria* at at no. 70 (☎066/89 1427) doles out generous servings of pizza, pasta and salad from 5pm nightly. The intriguingly named *Dancing Dervish* at no. 46 (☎066/89 1119; lunch daily, dinner Tues–Sat) is a pricey gourmet vegetarian and seafood restaurant – dishes range eclectically through Australian, Greek and Thai influences – with a comfortable, airy feel. Out of town, about 12km north, the *Calurla Tea Gardens* (☎066/89 7297; daily 10am–6pm, plus dinner Fri–Sun), on Lillian Rock Road in Lillian Rock, is a farmhouse-style café-restaurant in a delightful garden setting with views of the surrounding mountain ranges. You can pitch your tent on the property or stay in a wooden cottage (④), and watch the wild lorikeets that come to feed here.

In terms of **nightlife and entertainment**, Nimbin's only drinking hole is the *Freemason's Hotel* on Cullen Street, which sees plenty of action (the bistro also serves good counter meals) but the cultural heart of town is the *Bush Theatre* (☎066/89 1111), over the bridge opposite *Granny's Farm* hostel. A wonderful small theatre, they also run movies at the weekends: call or check town noticeboards for details. During intermission everyone heads next door to the *Mulgum Cafe* and eats fruit salad and ice-cream from china bowls on the grass.

*Gouldings Bus Services* (☎066/89 5144) runs between Lismore and Nimbin twice daily during the week.

## Murwillumbah and around

The next major stop on the Pacific Highway is **MURWILLUMBAH**, a quiet, inland town on a bend of the Tweed River, a little over 30km north of Byron Bay, that makes a good base for exploring some of the beautiful Tweed Valley and the mountains that strecth up to the Queensland border.

Murwillumbah is very well connected: it's the terminus of the coastal branch line from Sydney (one train a day in each direction), and almost all buses on the north coast route pull in. The **tourist information** office on Alma Street (daily 9am–5pm; ☎066/72 1340), has information about the immediate area, and about several other magnificent national parks and state forests in the vicinity. Cruises on the Tweed, through a remnant of coastal rainforest, are offered by *Stotts Island Rainforest Cruise* (Tues–Sat 10am–3pm; $6; ☎066/72 1138), departing from the Environment Centre on Stotts Island, off the Pacific Highway north of Murwillumbah. In the town itself, it's worth dropping by the **Tweed River Regional Art Gallery** on Tumbulgum Road, by Nicholls Park on the river (Wed–Sun 10am–5pm; free). It displays the winners of the Doug Moran National Portrait Prize, which originated here, as well as local artists and travelling exhibitions.

The Tweed Valley and the surrounding area close to the Queensland border is among the most beautiful in New South Wales, ringed by mountain ranges that are actually the remains of an extinct volcano. Some twenty million years ago a huge shield **volcano** (a flat, shield-shaped landform rather than a cone-shaped peak) spewed lava through a central vent onto the surrounding plain. Erosion carved out an enormous bowl around the centre of the resultant mass of lava, while the more resistant rocks around the edges stood firm – these are now the **Nightcap**, **Border** and **McPherson ranges**, the outer rim of a vast bowl. Right at its heart is **Mount Warning** (1150m), the original vent of the volcano, whose unmistakable, twisted profile rises like a sentinel from the Tweed Valley. A well-marked bushwalking track leads to the top from a car park just off the national park access road, itself a turn-off from the road to Uki, south-west of town. The path is extremely steep in the final stages (allow at least four hours return) but you're rewarded by a sweeping view over the ranges of the volcanic rim and across the Tweed Valley to the Pacific.

Less strenuously, there's a signposted scenic drive of 64km through the **Tweed Valley**, which takes in some of its best features. A patchwork of sugarcane fields and tropical fruit plantations is testimony to the fertility of the volcanic soil; there's even a tea plantation. Between the villages of Tumbulgum and Duranbah, the **Big Avocado** lures the wild-at-heart towards *Avocado Adventureland* on Duranbah Road (daily 10am–5pm; free admission, but train and bus rides extra), a plantation that grows avocados, macadamia nuts and many kinds of tropical fruit, and has been turned into a miniature theme park: you can ride through the plantation in open-air buses and miniature trains, or cruise around on man-made "tropical canals"; there are canoes and aqua-bikes for rent, an animal park and playground, a restaurant and café, as well as a fruit market selling plantation produce. A slightly less commercial experience awaits you during the cane-harvesting season at **Condong Sugar Mill**, on the Tweed River about 5km north of Murwillumbah (guided tours July–Nov 9am–3pm; $4; booking required; ☎066/72 2244). The turn off for the **Tree Tops Environment Centre** (daily 10am–5pm) is opposite the sugar mill; the centre is the home of *Griffith Furniture*, which creates beautiful designs from salvaged native timber like red cedar, using traditional timber-working techniques that you can observe in the workshop. Halfway between Nimbin and Murwillumbah, **UKI** is a pretty little village with views of Mount Warning; there's a small relaxed market on the third Sunday of every month in the grounds of the Community Centre. A stall sells locally grown organic coffee, or you can sample some at the *Uki Trading Post* (daily 9am–5pm).

## Practicalities

**Places to sta**y in town include the *Tweed River Motel* (☎066/72 3933; ⑤), on the Pacific Highway not far from the station, and *Mount Warning Murwillumbah Backpackers*, 1 Tumbulgum Road (☎066/72 3763; rooms ④, dorms ①), a small YHA hostel in an old house by the Tweed River with free use of canoes. There are also plenty of opportunities to make the most of the countryside by staying there: rural or farmstay accommodation includes *Midginbil Hill Holiday Farm* (☎066/79 7158; camping, plus bunkhouses ①, lodges ⑨ including all meals and most activities), a cattle station 30km west near Mount Warning, with masses of distractions including a pool, horse-riding, canoeing and archery. The *Uki Village Guesthouse*, 1 Kyogle Road, right in the centre of Uki (☎066/79 5345; ⑤), is a lovely, relaxed guesthouse in a 1920s-era building with views of Mount Warning, serving fine meals. *Forest Hideaway Units*, Byrill Creek Road, near Uki (☎066/79 7139; ④), are small motel-style units each with a double bed and bunks, fridge and cooking facilities, and there's a swimming pool, while *Bushwalker Cabins* near Doon Doon, Nightcap Pass, 30km from Uki (☎066/79 9133; ②), are simpler cabins with bunks and cooking facilities. If the lure of the coast is irresistible, *Emu Park Backpackers Resort* at Carbarita Beach (77 Coast Rd; ☎066/76 1190; rooms ③–④, dorms ①) is a good hostel on the coast road near Bogangar, with free use of bikes and boards.

Places to eat in Murwillumbah include the big old-fashioned *Austral Cafe*, an eat-in bakery on Main Street. Nearby at no. 91, *Govinda's Natural Foods* is run by Hare Krishna devotees and serves exclusively vegetarian food but with Italian, Chinese and other influences besides the predominantly Indian flavour. The *Riverview Hotel*, 267 Pacific Highway (☎066/72 1006), has a passable, inexpensive bistro serving hamburgers, steaks and pasta, and a relaxing verandah overlooking the Tweed. In terms of **entertainment**, check out the *Regent Cinema* (☎066/72 2199; closed Mon), an old gem on the corner of Brisbane and Wollumbin streets.

# The New England Plateau

The **New England Plateau** rises parallel to the coast in the northeast of New South Wales, from the northern end of the Hunter Valley to the Queensland border. At the top it's between 1000 and 1400 metres above sea level, and on the eastern edge an escarpment falls away steeply towards the coast. This eastern rim consists of steep slopes and precipitous cliff faces, deep gorges and thickly forested valleys, because of its inaccessiblity, it has remained a largely undisturbed wilderness. Streams and rivers from the highland tumble over the rocks, and in numerous mighty waterfalls pour into narrow gorges. On the plateau itself the scene is far more peaceful, as sheep and cattle graze on the undulating highland. Because of the altitude, the **climate** up here is fundamentally different from the subtropical coast, a mere 150km or so away: winters are cold and frosty, with occasional snowfalls, while in summer the fresh, dry air can offer welcome relief after the heat and humidity of the coast. Even during a summer heatwave, when the daytime temperature might reach 30°C, the nights will be pleasantly cool. Perhaps it was this that attracted the mainly Scottish immigrants who – despite the name – transformed the New England highland into pastures in the last century.

The **New England Highway**, one of the main links between Brisbane and Sydney, runs north through New England, passing all the major towns – Tamworth, Armidale, Glen Innes and Tenterfield. From any of these, good, sealed roads branch off towards the coast, and it's these minor roads that are especially worth exploring, with turn-offs leading to gorges, waterfalls and scenic lookout-points. The area around Glen Innes and Inverell is rich in gemstones, yielding industrial diamonds, zircons and, above all, sapphires. Farms and stations all over the highlands offer farmstay accommodation, with horse riding and other activities.

## The Upper Hunter Valley

The upper end of Hunter Valley is Australia's main horse-breeding and thoroughbred area – indeed it claims to deal in as much horseflesh as anywhere in the world, with at least thirty studs. There are cattle- and sheep-breeding stations up here too, while the fertile soils of the Upper Hunter also yield a harvest of cereals and fruits including, of course, grapes – see box on p.134 for a sampling of Hunter Valley wineries.

The pretty township of **SCONE** is at the centre of the Hunter Valley horse trade, and you can get further details of the business from the **Tourist Information Centre** on the corner of Susan and Kelly streets (daily 9am–5pm; ☎065/45 1526). Horse freaks can get personalized, though expensive, tours of the studs through *Scone Stud Tours* (☎065/45 3337), or, for less, you can approach *Seganoe* stud direct (☎065/43 7029). The best time to visit, when everything's open, is **Scone Horse Week** – ten days in the middle of May – which features local prize specimens in horse shows, rodeos and races, along with more general cultural and artistic events.

**Glenbawn Dam**, 15km east of Scone, makes a pleasant excursion. The dam holds back the waters of the Upper Hunter, storing up to 750,000 million litres for irrigation purposes. Recreation facilities at the reserve here include accommodation and boat rental: the lake is great for water-skiing, canoeing, sailing and fishing. Despite all the emphasis on horses, this is one of the few places where horse-riding is actually offered, on Sundays only from *Lake Glenbawn Resort Village* (☎065/43 7752). Next to the kiosk, a small **museum** (Sunday and holidays only) exhibits relics from early pioneering days in the Hunter Valley. Continue past the dam and you'll climb to the plateau of the Barrington Tops (see p.184), where the national park of the same name makes a fine day-trip, or you can continue towards the coast via Gloucester (about 150km from Scone).

To the northeast of Scone is polo country, the haunt of mega-rich Australians like media mogul Kerry Packer. If you fancy watching the elitist sport in action, there are polo grounds at **GUNDY** and at **ELLISTON**. At Gundy, you can settle for a drink at the classic green-tin-roofed *Linga Longa Hotel*. In between Gundy and Elliston, **Belltrees** is the family estate of the White family, who gave the world the Nobel prize-winning novelist **Patrick White**. Belltrees Station is a collection of buildings including 1832 Semphill Cottage, among pepper trees; there's even a small school established in 1879. Further along is the White mansion where the family still live, and if you can afford it you can stay at the country house next door or in the mountain retreat where Patrick White used to escape to in later life when he returned home to visit (☎065/45 1688 for bookings); polo tuition can be arranged as part of your stay.

Heading on towards the heart of the New England Plateau, you pass the **Burning Mountain** about 20km north of Scone, near the village of **WINGEN**. Its smoking vents indicate not volcanic activity but a coal seam burning 30m under the surface: the fire was ignited naturally, perhaps by a lightning strike or spontaneous combustion, over a thousand years ago. The area, protected as a nature reserve, can be reached via a signposted walking trail that starts at picnic grounds at the foot of the hill, just off the New England Highway; pick up the informative NPWS guide to the area's walking tracks from any NPWS office. Fourteen kilometres north of Wingen, **MURRURUNDI** marks the end of the Upper Hunter Valley: it's a really pretty spot, enclosed by the Liverpool Ranges, and the *Cafe Telegraph* here makes a good refreshment stop, with the creek flowing past the garden where you can sit.

### Practicalities

**Trains** from Sydney (four daily) and Newcastle stop at Scone. *Greyhound.Pioneer* and *Mcafferty's* pass through Scone, while a *Countrylink* **bus** runs daily to Moree.

**Places to stay** in this area are widely scattered. Right in Scone the *Royal Hotel-Motel*, 119 Kelly Street (☎065/45 1722; ③–④), offers simple pub accommodation or fancier motel units – they also serve good counter meals. About halfway to Glenbawn Dam is a delightful *YHA hostel* (☎065/45 2072; rooms ④, dorms ①) set in a former school on Segenhoe Road; you can rent bikes here to explore the countryside. Right at the lake, the *Lake Glenbawn Resort Village* (☎065/43 7752; ⑤) has three-bedroom cottages. Heading north, *Ethel Cottage* in Wingen offers farmstay-style B&B in a self-contained heritage cottage (☎065/45 2907 or 45 1526; ⑥). In Murrurundi, the colourful *Creative Escapes* (☎065/46 6541; B&B ⑤) is an artist-run guesthouse in a former bank on the New England Highway, where you can make pottery or paint in studios set in the big garden with views of the Liverpool Ranges, and the rooms are all painted in beautiful colours and decked with works of art; there's also the *Murrurundi Motel* right on the highway in Murrurundi (☎065/46 6082; ④). For something to **eat** in Scone, head for *The Station Gallery and Cafe* in the old station waiting room, where Italian-style food is served; best of all are the chunky cakes with lashings of cream. For entertainment, Scone's **Civic Theatre** (☎065/41 1569; films shown Thurs–Mon) is an Art Deco movie palace with displays of memorabilia in the foyer.

## Tamworth and around

**TAMWORTH** is the first city on the New England Plateau proper, a substantial town that's proud of its public buildings, parks and gardens. It also like to refer to itself as the "City of Lights", having been the first in Australia to be fitted with electric street lighting, in 1888. To most Australians, however, Tamworth means **country music** – a sort of antipodean Nashville. The twelve-metre-high Golden Guitar in front of the **Tamworth Country Centre** (daily 9am–5pm; $4), on the southern edge of town, sums up the town's role as the C&W capital of Australasia. Inside the centre, you'll find waxwork figures of the great Australian country stars like Chad Morgan, Buddy Williams, Smoky Dawson and his horse Flash, Slim Dusty, Reg Lindsay and Tex Morton. The girls aren't forgotten, and their outfits are even more over the top when country meets disco with Jean Stafford, "the glamorous Tasmanian", and the McKeen sisters in red corduroy A-line skirts with matching waistcoats. Take your camera in and snap some hilarious pictures with the stars. There's also a slightly incongruous collection of gems and minerals from the region – no rhinestones though. Afterwards, the *Longyard Hotel* is a handy place to weep in your beer for a while and, once a year, for a week at the end of January, it becomes the focus of the **Tamworth Country Music Festival** when fans from all over the country descend, packing out camping spots. The town is given over to starry-eyed buskers, Akubra hats, cowboy boots and rhinestones, and every pub, club and hall in town hosts music gigs, record launches and bush poetry, culminating in the presentation of the Australian country music awards. Further information and bookings from *BAL Marketing* (☎067/65 7055). The final piece of the country puzzle is found at the corner of Brisbane Street and Kable Avenue, where the **Hands of Fame** cornerstone bears the palm-prints of more country greats. A glorious spoof, the Noses of Fame memorial, can be savoured over a beer at the *Tattersalls Hotel* on Peel Street.

Don't give up on Tamworth entirely if country music isn't your thing. The new **Powerstation Museum** at 216 Peel Street (Tues–Fri 9am–1pm, weekends by arrangement; free), celebrates those pioneering street lights, and there are numerous art galleries and craft studios around town; the **Tamworth City Gallery**, housed in the Guy Kable Building on Marius Street (Mon–Fri 10am–5pm, Sat 9–11.30am, Sun 1–4pm), has a surprisingly good permanent exhibition. Natural attractions include the **Oxley Lookout and Nature Reserve** at the end of White Street, with panoramic views of the city and the Peel River Valley, and **Lake Keepit**, 56km northwest of the city, where you can rent boats and mess about on the water.

The historic gold-mining township of **NUNDLE** lies some 60km southeast of town in the "hills of gold" – people still visit with picks, shovels and sieves in the hope of striking it lucky, and you can join them for a day. You no longer need to buy a fossicking licence but it's still worth dropping by the General Store on Jenkins Street; they'll point you in the right direction to start digging.

## Practicalities

The big new **Tamworth Visitors Centre** (Mon–Fri 8.30am–4.30pm, Sat & Sun 9am–3pm; ☎067/68 4461) is on the corner of Peel Street and Scots Road. **Local buses** can get you to Nundle (*Peel Valley Coaches* ☎067/66 4418) and Gunnedah (*McPhersons Coaches* ☎067/67 7190) while *Countrylink* coaches serve Narrabri, Moree, Armidale, Walcha, Inverell and Dubbo.

As you drive into Tamworth you'll pass a string of **motels** on the New England Highway – the only time you might have trouble finding a room is during the festival, when everything's booked out. Right in the centre of town the *Tamworth Hotel* on Marius Street offers simple pub accommodation and good counter meals (☎067/66 2923; ④). The closest place for **campers and caravanners** is the *Paradise Caravan Park*, Peel St (☎067/66 3120; on-site vans ③–④), about five minutes' walk from the main part of town and fronting the river. Further out, you could try the *Thunderbird Caravan Park*, 6km north (☎067/67 9356; on-site vans ②, cabins ③) or the bigger *City Lights Caravan Park*, 6km south (☎067/65 7664; on-site vans ③, cabins ④) with a swimming pool. In Nundle there are rooms and meals at the historic *Peel Inn* on Jenkins Street (☎067/69 3377; ④), where they also organize horse-riding and gold-panning. If you want a taste of life on a sheep and cattle station, there's *Echo Hills Station*, 45km east of Tamworth at Mulla Creek (free call ☎1800/81 0243; dorms ①; pick-ups for stays of over two days, if arranged in advance). It has a kitchen you can cook in, or meals are available at $25 a day; activities also cost $25 per day, for as much horse-riding as you can take, 4WD tours and mustering cattle and sheep.

There are a couple of recommended **cafés** in Tamworth: the *Old Vic Cafe* at 261 Peel Street (Mon–Sat 9am–5pm & Sun 9am–2.30pm) and the *Weswal Gallery*, 192 Brisbane Street (daily 10am–4.30pm). Out of festival time, you'll be disappointed if you think the town's **clubs and pubs** constantly resound to C&W twangings, but you can catch some acts and atmosphere in the evenings at the *Tamworth RSL Club* on Kable Avenue (☎067/66 4661; Thurs), the *West Tamworth Leagues Club*, Phillip Street (☎067/65 7588; Sun), while on Sunday afternoons the *Longyard Hotel* (☎067/65 3411) has free country music and line dancing.

# Armidale

The small university city of **ARMIDALE**, halfway between Sydney and Brisbane, is something of a rarity in Australia, where most universities are based in the state capitals. About 3000 students are enrolled at the **New England University**, which, together with two further education colleges and a couple of famous boarding schools, provides an unexpected academic aspect in a place so far "up country". It tries hard to play up this collegiate feel, and at times it works – especially in autumn, when the city, with its church spires and many parks, is embedded in a sea of red and golden leaves. At around 1000m, the climate is unpredictable and can be decidedly brisk in winter.

Beardy Street, the town centre's pedestrian mall, is flanked by quaint Australian country pubs with wide, iron-lace verandahs, and is an excellent place to start exploring. One of the best ways to get around town is by **bike** (see below for rental places): there's a signposted city tour, as well as a bike path to the **university campus**, 5km northwest of the city, where there are a few small specialized museums, a kangaroo and deer park, and the historic Booloominbah homestead. Back in the city centre, the **New England Regional Art Museum** in Kentucky Street (Mon–Sat 10am–5pm, Sun 1pm–4pm; $5) is worth a visit, containing two important collections of Australian art. Foremost is the *Hinton Collection* of paintings spanning the 1880s to the 1940s, including some beautiful, light-filled 1890s renderings of Sydney Harbour: Arthur Streeton's evocations of Cremorne and Balmoral, and Tom Robert's capturing of Mosman. Focusing on the second half of the twentieth century, the *Coventry Collection* also has some important works, among them a wild self-portrait of the late and troubled Brett Whitely. Next door, an arresting modern building bearing a distinctive ochre-coloured tin roof heralds the Aboriginal-run **Aboriginal Centre and Keeping Place** (Mon–Fri 9am–4pm, Sat & Sun 2–4pm; free; small charge for special exhibitions; ☎067/71 1249), an educational, visual and performing arts centre that aims to foster the renewal and continuity of Aboriginal culture. Artefacts and interpretative material are on display, and there are crafts, Aboriginal-designed clothes and other items for sale in the gift shop. You might also want to take a brief look at the exhibits of the Armidale **Folk Museum**, at the corner of Rusden and Faulkner streets (daily 1–4pm; free), a collection of artefacts from the New England region and a brief overview of local history.

## Practicalities

Armidale has a helpful **Visitors Information Centre**, 82 Marsh Street (Mon–Fri 9am–5pm, Sat 9am–4pm, Sun 10am–4pm, touch-screen information available after hours; ☎067/73 8527). For details of the area's national parks (see below), head for the NPWS in the McCarthy Building, 87 Faulkner Street (☎067/73 7211). The **bus** terminal is just by the visitors information centre. Plenty of places offer **car rental** if you plan to explore the country around Armidale: among them are *Hertz* (☎067/72 5872), *Realistic Car Rentals* (☎067/72 8078), and *Refts* (☎067/71 1535), who also offer 4WD vehicles. **Bikes** can be rented from *Armidale Bicycle Centre*, 248 Beardy Street; ☎067/72 3718. For **taxis**, call *Armidale Radio Taxis* (☎067/71 1455).

The *Wicklow Hotel*, or "Pink Pub" as it's more familiarly known, on the corner of Marsh and Dumaresq streets (☎067/72 2421; dorms ①, rooms ②–③) caters for weary travellers with a full bar open from 7am for those in need of a kick-start, showers and **accommodation**. Other places include *Tatersalls Hotel*, 174 Beardy Street (☎067/72 2247; ④) and the *Royal Hotel* on the corner of Marsh Street (☎067/72 2259; B&B ④). Further out, try *Pembroke Caravan and Leisure Park*, Grafton Street, on the corner of Cooks Road, 2km east of town (☎067/72 6470; on-site vans & cabins ③, YHA dorms ①), which has a swimming pool and tennis court; or *Highlander Van Village*, 76 Glen Innes Road, 2km north of town (☎067/72 4768; on-site vans ②, cabins & units ④), with similar facilities.

Good, inexpensive **counter meals** are served at many of the grand old Beardy Street pubs, including the *New England Hotel*, and *Tattersalls Hotel*, where the steak house serves amazingly cheap slabs of beef. *Spices Indian Restaurant*, 113–115 Rusden Street, has not just Indian but Thai curries too, with plenty of choice for vegetarians; dinner nightly 6pm to late. The light and airy *Cafe Midalé*, 173 Beardy Street Mall (Mon–Fri 8.30am–5.30pm, Sat until 2pm) serves up Italian-style food – *focaccia, panini* and pasta of the day. *Rumours*, further down the mall, offers good inexpensive meals and sandwiches, plus a decent breakfast served until noon.

### Around Armidale

Surrounded by national parks and wild mountain scenery, Armidale makes a good base to stop over for a few days and explore, or perhaps try your hand at a spot of fossicking. The **New England National Park** and the several patchwork sections of the **Oxley Wild Rivers National Park** exploit the beauty of the eastern edge of the plateau; gorges and spectacular waterfalls abound, although the falls may diminish to a trickle during prolonged dry spells. The most impressive of them are the **Wollomombi Falls**, just over 40km east of Armidale, off the road to Dorrigo; the highest in Australia, they plunge 457m into a gorge. Nearby are the **Chandler Falls**, while **Ebor Falls**, a stunning double drop of the Guy Fawkes River, can be viewed from platforms just off the Dorrigo Road, another 40km beyond Wollomombi. Between Wollomombi and Ebor, **Point Lookout** in the New England National Park offers a truly wonderful panoramic view across the forested ranges. The road to the lookout is unsealed gravel, but usually in reasonable condition, and there are simple **cabins** and bush **campsites** where you can stay the night: phone the NPWS in Dorrigo for bookings (☎066/57 2309). The rest of the park is a virtually inaccessible wilderness.

On the way back to Armidale, you could detour through the gold-rush ghost town of **HILLGROVE**, where the old school has been converted into a **museum** (Wed 2–5pm, Sat & Sun 10am–5pm) displaying old mining equipment and trying to recreate the lifestyle of the once prosperous settlement. **URALLA**, 22km south of Armidale, is another old gold town, though in this case it has managed to hang on, with a population of a couple of thousand. The historic building walk will take you past the town's highlights, including **McCrossin's Mill Museum** (daily 1pm–5pm; $2), an old three-storey flour mill in Salisbury Street. Fossicking is still possible at the old Rocky River diggings: enquire at the **Tourist Information Centre**, 84 Bridge Street (☎067/78 4496). Gold apart, Uralla's other claim to fame is that **Captain Thunderbolt**, the bushranger who terrorized the New England region in the nineteenth century, was shot dead here in 1870, after a furious battle in the swampy country southeast of Uralla – an event commemorated by the bronze statue of Thunderbolt and his horse on the corner of Bridge and Salisbury streets.

Southeast of Armidale, towards Walcha, **Dangars Lagoon** is a wetland region visited by more than a hundred kinds of bird; a hide is provided for spotters. **Dangars Falls** and a network of twenty walking tracks and lookouts around **Dangars Gorge** are only 22km from Armidale on a minor road. Beyond these, about 20km east of Walcha, a turn-off from the Oxley highway leads to **Apsley Gorge** and two more waterfalls in another section of the Oxley Rivers park.

## Glen Innes and around

**GLEN INNES** is the next major stop north on the highway, another pleasant town in a beautiful setting, about 100km from Armidale. Although agriculture is still important up here, you begin to see more and more evidence of the gemfields – sapphires are big business as, to a lesser extent, is tin mining. In the centre, on Grey Street especially, numerous century-old public buildings and parks have been renovated and spruced up.

There's some fine country architecture including a couple of large corner pubs, their verandahs decorated with iron lace. The **Land of the Beardies Museum** (Mon–Fri 10–11am & 2–5pm, Sat & Sun 2–5pm; $4), in the town's first hospital on Ferguson Street, takes this feeling for the past further, displaying pioneer relics, period room settings and a reconstructed slab hut. The name alludes to the two hairy men who settled the area in the last century, and it's a title the town's proud of, along with the Scotish connections reflected in the name of the town itself and in many of its streets, which are rendered in both English and Gaelic. The local granite **Australian Standing Stones** at Martins Lookout, Watsons Drive, are based on the Ring of Brodgar, and are intended to honour the "contribution of the Celtic races to Australia's development"; there's a great picnic and barbecue area with granite seats and tables, echoing the stones themselves. The strongly Celtic nature of Glen Innes is counterbalanced by the town's department store, *Kwong Sing & Co*, which has been run by the same family of Chinese origin since 1886.

In early November, Glen Innes celebrates the **Land of the Beardies Bushfestival**, with everything from a beard-growing contest and shopping-trolley derby to dances, street parades and arts-and-crafts exhibitions. More details from **Glen Innes & District Tourism**, 152 Church Street, as the New England Highway is called when it goes through town (daily 9am–5pm; ☎067/32 2397); the 24-hour **bus terminal** is attached to this office, and they can also help with **rooms**. Good options are the *Central Motel*, Meade Street, opposite the post office (☎067/32 2826; ④); *New Tatersalls Motel*, Grey Street (☎067/32 3011; ⑤), which is slightly fancier with air-conditioning and sauna; the well-equipped *Poplar Caravan Park*, 15 Church Street (☎067/32 1514; on-site vans ②, cabins ④); or *Blue Sapphire Caravan Park*, corner of Church and Grafton streets (☎067/32 1590; on-site vans ②, cabins ③). For sustenance, try the unimaginatively named *Tea and Coffee Shop* on Grey Street, a cosy **tea room** with loads of choice including Dutch pancakes, an array of interesting sandwiches, savoury croissants and hot breakfasts, or scones and continental cakes. The *One Eighty Nine Coffee Lounge*, at 189 Grey Street, has a more down-to-earth menu of hamburgers and their ilk. The best Chinese **restaurant** is *Dragon Court*, at no. 173 (lunch and dinner daily; licensed).

### Inverell

The area between Glen Innes and **INVERELL**, 67km to the west, is one huge gemfield. Industrial diamonds, garnets, topaz, zircons and three quarters of the world's sapphires are mined in the area. Inverell is also known as "Sapphire City", and at the **Dejon Sapphire Centre**, on the Gwydir Highway, 18km east of town, you can watch the gems being mined, washed, sorted, cut and finally set (daily 9am–5pm; mine tours 10.30am & 3pm; ☎067/23 2222). The showroom has a display of sapphires in 155 colours, from pale blue and green, to gold, lemon and pink. If you want to try your luck, you'll need to contact the **tourist office**, in Campbell Street (Mon–Fri 9am–4pm, Sat 9am–noon; ☎067/22 1693), which can point you in the direction of designated areas. If you want to **stay** over and wait for that big strike, try the *Royal Motel-Hotel*, 260 Byron Street (☎067/22 2811; ④), where you can also get counter meals, or *Sapphire City Caravan Park* in Moore Street (☎067/22 1830; on-site vans ②, cabins ③).

## Tenterfield and around

Less than 20km from the Queensland border, **TENTERFIELD** marks the northern end of the New England Plateau. Although only a small town, it has a confirmed place in Australian history, being the birthplace of the Australian Federation. This title was earned when, in 1889, the Prime Minister of New South Wales, Sir Henry Parkes, made his famous Federation speech here, advocating the union of the Australian colonies; twelve years later the Commonwealth of Australia was inaugurated. A small

## THE MYALL CREEK MASSACRE

In the first decades of the nineteenth century, when European settlers started to move up to the highlands and to use Aboriginal-occupied land on the plateau as sheep and cattle pasture, many of the local Aborigines fought back. Time and again bloody skirmishes flared up. The **Myall Creek massacre** is one of the few that has found a place in the history of White Australia, while innumerable others were not mentioned in genteel pioneer circles, and have subsequently been erased from public memory.

For Aboriginal people, expulsion from the lands of their ancestors amounted to spiritual as well as physical dispossession, and they resisted as best they could: white stockmen staying in huts far away from pioneer townships or homesteads feared for their lives. In 1837 and 1838, Aborigines repeatedly ambushed and killed stockmen near the Gwydir and Namoi rivers. Then, during the absence of the overseer at Myall Creek Station, near present-day Inverell, twelve farm-hands organized a raid in retribution, killing 28 Aborigines. In court, the farm-hands were acquitted – public opinion saw nothing wrong with their deed, and neither did the jury. The case was later taken up again, however, and seven of the participants in the massacre were sentenced to death on the gallows.

**museum** (Sat & Sun 3–5pm) in Centenary Cottage recalls the occasion and displays other items of local historical interest.

As throughout the region, however, the real attractions of Tenterfield lie outside town – undulating pastures and orchards, remnants of stands of eucalypt and rainforests, and rugged granite hills. **Bald Rock**, in a national park of the same name near the Queensland border, about 30km northeast of Tenterfield, is a grey, somewhat smaller version of Ayers Rock: a solid granite monolith, 213m high. It can be climbed from its northeast side, and from the summit there are all-round views taking in both states. The excursion to Bald Rock fits in nicely with a visit to 210m-high **Boonoo Boonoo Falls**, set in another national park 32km north of Tenterfield. Access is via a gravel road which can be a bit rough, but it's worth it, and there's a beautiful picnic area. The NPWS occasionally offers tours to both national parks: details from the **Tenterfield Visitors Centre**, New England Highway (Mon–Sat 9.30am–5pm, Sun 9.30am–4pm; ☎067/36 1082).

**Accommodation** in Tenterfield includes the *Commercial Hotel*, 288 Rouse Street (☎067/36 1027; B&B ③), where you can also get counter meals. *Arnolds Tenterfield Lodge Accommodation Centre*, 2 Manners Street (☎067/36 1477; dorms ①, rooms ④, on-site vans ②, cabins ④), is an old country hotel surrounded by parklands, incorporating a caravan park and a small YHA hostel.

# WEST OF THE GREAT DIVIDING RANGE

Western New South Wales is a very different proposition from the other parts of the state. For a start, there's hardly anyone living here. Beyond the Great Dividing Range are a few towns with pioneer heritage, like **Bathurst** and **Dubbo**, where there are still small agricultural communities and green fields; beyond them it begins to get increasingly desolate and arid, and even apparently large towns turn out to be tiny communities.

Out beyond the Blue Mountains, the **Great Western Highway** takes you as far as Bathurst; from there the **Mid-Western Highway** continues to join the **Sturt Highway**, which heads via Mildura on the Victorian border to Adelaide. Any route west is eventually obliged to cross the **Newell Highway**, the direct route between Melbourne and

Brisbane that cuts straight across the heart of central New South Wales. The most exciting Outback routes head north and west, though, passing through Dubbo, at the junction of the Newell and **Mitchell** highways, and on from there dive into real isolation: north to **Lightning Ridge** or **Bourke** and western Queensland, or west on the **Barrier Highway**, right across the state to **Broken Hill**, almost at the South Australian border.

# Bathurst, Dubbo and the central west

The gracious city of **BATHURST**, elegantly situated on the western slopes of the Great Dividing Range 209km west of Sydney, is Australia's oldest inland settlement. The settlement was proclaimed by Governor Macquarie 1815, but Bathurst remained nothing more than a small convict and military settlement for years, only slowly developing into the main supply centre for the surrounding rich pastoral area. It was the discovery of **gold** at the nearby Lewis Ponds Creek at Ophir (see p.220) in 1851, and more later the same year on the Turon River, however, that caused a goldrush which changed the life of the town and the colony for ever. Soon rich fields of alluvial gold were discovered in every direction and, as the first town over the mountains for those on the way to the goldfields, Bathurst prospered and grew. The population increased dramatically: in 1885 Bathurst was proclaimed a city, and in the late 1890s it was even proposing itself (unsuccessfully) as the site of the capital of the new Commonwealth of Australia.

Although there's still the odd speck of gold and and a few gemstones (especially sapphires) in the surrounding area, modern Bathurst has reverted to the role of the centre of some of the richest agricultural land in New South Wales, a pastoral and fruit- and grain-growing district. It's also a tertiary education centre, with many students at Mitchell College. For anyone heading west, it's still the first stop beyond the mountains, the gateway to the Outback. In October, visitors are also drawn to the big annual motor-racing meeting – centred around the famous **Bathurst 1000** endurance race – at the Mount Panorama Racing Circuit.

## The Town

Thanks to its cool climate – Bathurst is still near the mountains and can be cold at night, sometimes snowy in winter – and a scattering of historic buildings, the town has a very different feel to anywhere on the coast or on the baking plains further west. The old **Court House** in Russell Street, built in 1880, makes a good place to start exploring, not just because it's one of the finest old buildings, but also as home of the local **Tourist Information Centre**, in the East Wing (daily 9am–5pm; ☎063/33 6288). There's also an interesting little **historical museum** here (Mon–Fri 9am–4.30pm, Sat 9.30am–4.30pm, Sun 10am–4pm; $1), tucked away behind the tourist office, which displays artefacts and relics of regional pioneer history along with some good Aboriginal art.

Pick up a map from the tourist office and you can start to seek out some of the stately mansions scattered around that bear testimony to Bathurst's former wealth; one of their pamphlets outlines an entertaining self-guided walk through the historic city centre. The **Regional Gallery**, 70 Keppel Street (Mon–Fri 10am–4pm, Sat 11am–4pm, Sun 1–4pm; free), is a fine provincial art gallery with a very good ceramic collection and paintings by the Australian artist Lloyd Rees, as well as regular special and travelling exhibitions. Nearby **Machattie Park** offers a chance to relax amid landscaped gardens with duck ponds and spreading shade trees; there's also a Fern House, and a Begonia House which has an impressive display from mid-February to Easter. Look out too for **Ben Chifley's Cottage** at 10 Busby Street, once the residence of Bathurst's most famous son, who was born to a blacksmith and his wife in south Bathurst in 1885, and went on to become Prime Minister of Australia between 1945 and 1949.

Further afield, a drive up to **Mount Panorama** and its famous racing circuit provides, as you might expect, panoramic views of the city: there's the **Motor-Racing Hall of Fame** on Pit Straight (daily 9am–4.30pm; $4), at the beginning of the racing circuit, featuring famous racing cars and bikes, along with photographs and memorabilia from the races. **Sir Joseph Banks's Nature Reserve** (daily 9am–4pm; free) occupies the summit of the hill, enabling native birds and animals, including wallabies, kangaroos and koalas, to enjoy the vistas from a large area of bushland; the visitors' centre houses an aquarium and a reptile collection. Not far away, the **Bathurst Gold Diggings** on Conrod Straight (daily except Sat 10am–4pm; self-guided tour $6, guided tour $10), a reconstruction of a former gold-mining area, are worth a visit if you're not going to make it to one of the actual gold towns further out. Goldrush mining methods are demonstrated and explained, and you can even take individual lessons in gold-panning. A bit further out, the **Bathurst Sheep and Cattle Drome** on Limekilns Road, 8km northeast of the city, has an educational and entertaining show (daily at 11.30am, extra shows during school holidays; $10; ☎063/37 3634 for details) covering everything you always wanted to know about sheep- and cattle-breeding, sheep-shearing and milking cows.

**Accommodation** is relatively expensive here, but try the *Park Hotel* at the corner of George and Keppel streets (☎063/31 3399; ⑤) for comfortable B&B and motel-style units. There are a dozen or more motels along the highway, as well as holiday units at *Rossmore Park Farm Holidays*, at the Bathurst Sheep and Cattle Drome (see below) on Limekilns Road (☎063/37 3634; B&B ⑤), or **camping** at the *Bathurst Caravan Park*, on the highway in Kelso, 5km east (☎063/31 8286; on-site vans & cabins ③).

## Around Bathurst

The area **around Bathurst**, heading towards the wine country around Mudgee, is dotted with semi-derelict villages and ghost towns dating back to the goldrushes of the last century. A scenic drive to the north via Peel and Wattle Flat leads to the tiny, picturesque village of **SOFALA**, 35km north of Bathurst on the Turon River en route to Mudgee. Gold was found in the river here in 1851, just three weeks after the very first gold strikes in Australia, and today the narrow, winding main street still follows the course of the river. A good spot for a drink is the *Sofala Royal Hotel*, a classic wooden pub with a big balcony; they also offer meals, and **rooms** (☎063/37 8261; ④) with a period flavour. There's simple tent space at the *Village Camping Area*, Clarke Street (☎063/37 8206).

From Sofala, a very narrow bone-rattling unsealed road traces the stream, 38km northeast, towards **HILL END**, an even more important goldrush site located on a plateau above the Turon valley, 86km from Bathurst. In 1870, Hill End was the largest inland centre in New South Wales, a booming gold-mining town with a population of about 20,000, with 53 hotels, and all the accoutrements of a wealthy settlement. Within ten years, however, gold production had faltered and it had already become a virtual ghost town. It stayed that way until 1967, when the area was proclaimed a historic site and huge efforts were made to restore and preserve the town. You can pick up a leaflet at the NPWS **visitors' centre** in the old hospital (daily 9.30am–12.30pm & 1.30–4.30pm; ☎063/37 8206; guided tours available) and take yourself off on a self-guided walk around the village, or rent some equipment and try your hand at panning or fossicking.

Another enjoyable excursion, this time to the south, takes in the former gold-mining towns of Rockley, 35km south of Bathurst, and Trunkey Creek, and then continues to the spectacular **Abercrombie Caves**, 72km south of Bathurst in the middle of a large nature reserve. The main and most impressive cavern, the **Grand Arch** (self-guided tours daily 9am–4pm, $8; guided tours daily 2pm, more on weekends, $10), is 221m long, about 39m wide at the north and south entrances, and in some places over 30m high – it's said to be the largest natural limestone arch in the Southern Hemisphere.

More than eighty other caves are dotted around the reserve. In one of them, miners constructed a dance floor more than a century ago, and concerts or church services are still held there occasionally. Also within the reserve are old gold mines, and swimming holes in Gove Creek. The creek runs right through the reserve, plunging more than 70m over the Gove Creek Falls at the southern edge. There's a **camping area** on the shore (☎063/68 8603; cabins ④), complete with a public fossicking ground.

## Mudgee: wine country

The large old country town of **MUDGEE**, Aboriginal for "the nest in the hills", is the centre for an often overlooked wine region about 120km north of Bathurst. The town is set along the lush banks of the Cugewong River, and the countryside appears more full of grazing cows and sheep than vineyards. The wines, once referred to as "Mudgee mud", have improved in the past few years: the reds such as Cabernet Sauvignon and Shiraz are the tastiest, although the area's Chardonnays are gaining a good reputation. You can reach Mudgee via Hill End, but it's along a bumpy unsealed road, and it's better to come via Sofala, an 88km drive, with the road sealed except for a small section – but watch out for sheep.

On arrival, head for the **Tourist Information Centre** at 84 Market Street (Mon–Fri 9am–5pm, Sat 9am–3.30pm, Sun 9.30am–2pm; ☎063/72 5875) to pick up a copy of the *Mudgee Region Visitors' Guide*, which has detailed winery information and maps. Mudgee's proximity to Sydney means that **accommodation** is booked out at weekends, so if you're coming then, call in advance. Some suggestions are the central *Woolpack Hotel* at 67 Market Street (☎063/72 1908; ④), with average share-bathroom pub rooms; the more upmarket but equally central *Wanderlight Motor Inn*, 107 Market

---

### MUDGEE WINERIES: SIX OF THE BEST

**Botolabar,** Botolabar Lane (daily 10am–5pm; ☎063/73 3840). Organic winery with self-guided tours (40min). Tasting with shady terrace and view; picnic area and barbecues.

**Craigmoor Winery**, Craigmoor Road (Mon–Sat 10am–4.30pm, Sun 10am–4pm; ☎063/72 2208). Dating back to 1859, the original cellar has a tin roof held up by tree-trunk beams, a vast space with a huge open fireplace. Upstairs is an equally characterful, expensive restaurant while outside, views of hills and vineyards are fronted by peaceful lawns fragrant with flowers and a perfect cricket pitch.

**Lawson Hill Estate**, Lawson Hill Drive (daily 9.30am–5pm; ☎063/73 3953). A small family-owned winery above the Henry Lawson memorial, on the site of the Australian poet's boyhood home. Friendly, low-key tasting is in the hilltop tin shed where the wine is made.

**Miramar Wines**, Henry Lawson Drive (daily 9am–5pm; ☎063/73 3874). Atmospheric tastings among old

cobwebbed casks. The well-respected winemaker here, Ian MacRae, established the winery in 1977; he's serious about his wines, and specializes in delicious whites.

**Montrose Winery**, Henry Lawson Drive (Mon–Fri 9am–4.30pm, Sat & Sun 10am–4.30pm; ☎063/73 3883). The largest and most well known of Mudgee's wineries: particularly for its *Poets Corner,* a good table red, and its prize-winning Chardonnays, Cabernets and Shiraz. The modern white brick building covered in ivy has picnic tables outside and beautiful views.

**Pieter Van Gent**, Black Springs Road (Mon–Sat 9am–5pm, Sun 11am–4pm; ☎063/73 3807). Tastings in a delightful setting: beautiful nineteenth-century choir stalls on cool earth floors, overshadowed by huge old barrels salvaged from Penfolds. Try their *Pipeclay Port*, a tawny port aged in wood, a blend of various vintages. The winemaker is Dutch, and the herbs he uses in his traditional vermouth are specially imported from Holland.

Street (☎063/72 1088; ⑤) has a pool and spa. The gay-friendly *Parkview Guest House*, 99 Market Street (☎063/72 4477; ⑥), is a quiet bed and breakfast with a wide wooden verandah. **Campers** should make for *Cooinda Caravan Village*, corner of Bell Street and Gulgong Road, 1.5km west of the centre (☎063/72 1236), with a pool, kiosk and barbecues. Mudgee isn't really an eating-out town, and your best bet for a meal is **pub food**: try the *Lawson Park Hotel*, a great old country pub with $6 pasta nights, or lunch outdoors at *Tiernay House*, on Tiernay Lane (☎063/73 3877; Wed–Sun 10am–3pm; BYO) with its $7 salad bar and good-value blackboard menu, plus cream teas.

## Orange, Forbes and Parkes

En route to Dubbo from Bathurst on the Mitchell Highway is **ORANGE**, a small city on the eastern slopes of Mount Canabolas; coming from Bathurst the drive is a pleasant one through undulating countryside, with the valley opening up before you. Orange is a pretty place full of trees, including many European varieties; it claims to have four distinct seasons, and the chilly winter one always includes a fall or two of snow. Its major industry is **apple growing**, with apple orchards southwest of the town. You can pick up **apple-picking work** here from late February/early March for about six weeks; with cherry picking from late November to early January; contact the *Commonwealth Employment Service* (CES) at 189 Anson Street (☎063/61 4144); many growers have rough accommodation on their properties but supply often outstrips demand, so bring a tent. The **Orange Visitors Centre** on Byng Street (Mon–Fri 9am–5pm, Sat & Sun 9am–4pm; ☎063/61 5226) has information on local attractions, which include the **Ophir diggings**. The first gold field in Australia, established in 1851 and only 30km north of Orange, the site is still much as the diggers left it – with open shafts to watch out for.

Orange prides itself on being a cosmopolition sort of place, and it has quite a café society. Try the *Bookshop Cafe* on Kite Street, *Scottys* at 202a Summer Street with outdoor tables and gourmet sandwiches, *Union Bank Cafe* at 84 Byng Street, which has a good range of vegetarian dishes, or *The Pet Shop Cafe* at 145a Lords Place, for great coffee and cakes. A recommended place to both stay and eat is the *Metropolitan Hotel*, built in 1872, just up from the tourist office at 107 Byng Street (☎063/62 1353; B&B ④); a huge old-fashioned country pub with an enviable wooden verandah, where you can eat barbecued everything, hot potatoes, damper and salad. Rooms are clean, nicely decorated and all have TV, but not en suite facilities. Pickers could consider the two caravan parks, both a couple of kilometres from the centre; to the north, the *Showground Caravan Park*, Margaret Street (☎063/62 7254; on-site vans ③, cabins ③–④) or, to the east, the *Canabolas Caravan Park*, 166 Bathurst Road (☎063/62 7279; cabins ③).

Forming a triangle with Orange at the apex, Forbes and Parkes to the west are also important regional towns. **FORBES**, on the Lachlan River, is a graceful old town famous as the stomping ground of the nineteenth-century bushranger **Ben Hall**, who is buried in the Forbes Cemetery. **PARKES**, 33km to the northwest along the Newell Highway is well known for its **Observatory** with a 64m radio telescope. The **visitors centre** (daily 8.30am–4.15pm; free) has a half-hour audio-visual presentation, *The Invisible Universe* (every 30min 8.30am–3.30pm; $3).

## Cowra

**COWRA**, on the banks of the Lachlan River, 107km southwest of Bathurst along the Mid-Western Highway, is famous as the location of the **Cowra Breakout** during World War II. The breakout of August 5, 1944 saw the escape of 378 Japanese prisoners of war armed with baseball bats, staves, homemade clubs and sharpened kitchen knifes – those who were sick and stayed behind hung or disembowelled themselves, unable to endure the disgrace of capture. It took nine day to recapture all the prisoners, with the death of four Australian soldiers and 231 Japanese. The breakout was little known until the publication of Harry Gordon's excellent 1970s account *Die Like the Carp* (recently republished as *Voyage of Shame*; see "Books" in *Contexts*, p.844).

You can see the site of the prisoner-of-war camp, now just fields, on the northeastern fringes of the town on Sakura Avenue, with a memorial cairn at the site of the breakout on Farm Road. The graves of the Japanese, who were buried in Cowra, were well cared for by members of the local Returned Servicemen's League, a humanitarian gesture which touched Japanese embassy officials who then broached the idea of an official **Japanese War Cemetery**. Designed by Shigeru Yura, the tranquil burial ground is further north, on Doncaster Drive. The theme of Japanese–Australian friendship and reconciliation continued in Cowra with the establishment of the **Japanese Garden** (daily 8.30am–5pm; $5) in 1979 with funding from Japanese and Australian governments and companies. The five-hectare garden, designed by the internationally known Ken Nakajima, to represent the landscape of Japan, is set on a hill overlooking the town on a scenic drive running north off Kendal Street, the main strip. The design takes advantage of the hill's large boulders and stones and is planted with native and exotic trees. Cherry and other flowering trees blossom and their leaves change colour with the autumn, mirroring a northern hemisphere change of seasons. It's very peaceful and idyllic here: cooling on a hot day, with the shade and the sound of the stream burbling through the garden. A further anti-war symbol in Cowra is the **World Peace Bell** in the Civic Square; and the planting of an avenue of cherry trees connecting the war cemeteries, the POW campsite and the Japanese garden has begun.

For more information on the town, and accommodation options if you want to stay, head for the very helpful **Cowra Visitors' Centre**, at the corner of Grenfell and Borowa roads on the Midwestern Highway (daily 9am–5pm; ☎063/42 4333), near the large riverside park. There are lots of vineyards in the Cowra area, actually more than in Mudgee, but no wineries – instead, grapes are sent off to big wineries where they're made into wine. Their origin is often revealed in the names, such as *Richmond Grove Cowra Wine*. The region is best known for Chardonnay: to taste the product of the local grapes, head for the *Quarry Cellar*, 5km from Cowra on the Boorowa Road; the attached restaurant does Devonshire teas and inexpensive light lunches of tasty pasta and good salads. It might also be possible to get some **grape-picking** work, via the CES, 41 Kendall Street (☎063/82 3366).

# Young

Seventy kilometres southwest of Cowra along the Olympic Way, the hilly town of **YOUNG** is a good spot to pick up some **cherry-picking** work, during the season (approximately six weeks from the first week of November). Being continuous rather than hard, the work attracts a genteel crowd, and is popular with retired Queenslanders. If you just want to pick your own and have a look at some orchards and packing sheds, visit *Cherry Hill South* (☎063/82 2513) on the way into town from Cowra; you could also call here about work, or better still, contact the *CES* on Boorowa Street (☎063/82 3366). The long weekend in October generally coincides with the time when the **cherry blossoms** are in full bloom – a glorious sight. There are also several vineyards on the slopes of the undulating area, which is becoming known as the Hilltops wine region; one worth visiting is the small, family-run **Wodonga Hill Winery**, 10km north of Young on the Olympic Way (daily 9am–5pm; ☎063/82 2972).

Cherries and grapes aside, Young has some historical significance too, as the site of the notorious **Lambing Flat Riots**, detailed in every Australian history book. A former gold-mining centre known then as Lambing Flats, the town was the site of racist riots against Chinese miners in June 1861. As the gold ran out, European miners resented what they saw as the greater success of the more industrious Chinese. Troops had to be called in when the Chinese were chased violently from the diggings, beaten, their pigtails cut off, their property destroyed. Carried at the head of the mob was a flag, painted on a tent flysheet with the southern cross in the centre, lettered with "Roll Up, Roll Up, No Chinese", in the manner of a circus flyer. You can see the original flag, and other exhibits relating to the riots, in the **Lambing Flat Folk Museum** (daily 10am–4pm; $2) located on the Olympic Way, just south of Boorowa Street. For more information, contact the **Young Tourist Centre**, 2 Short Street (Mon–Fri 9am–5pm, Sat & Sun 10am–4pm; ☎063/82 3394). A recommended **farmstay** outside of the town is *Old Nubba School House* (☎069/43 2513; ⑤–⑥), half way between Young and Cootamundra on the Olympic Way; the peaceful self-contained accommodation, a former schoolhouse in the grounds of the friendly family farm, sleeps up to six and breakfast provisions are included. *Gabriella's Place* on Rialto Square, Lovell Street (☎063/82 3741) is an authentic Italian **restaurant** with meals from 5.30pm nightly.

# Dubbo

**DUBBO** is a pleasant if unremarkable city on the banks of the Macquarie River, 420km northwest of Sydney, 200km or so from Bathurst. The regional capital for the west of the state, it supports many agricultural industries and is located at a vital crossroads where the Melbourne–Brisbane Newell Highway meets the Mitchell Highway and routes west to Bourke or Broken Hill.

As such, it's well used to people passing through, but not staying long. If you do stop, drop by the **Western Plains Zoo** on Obley Road, 5km south of town (daily 9am–5pm; $14; keeper talks weekends and school holidays at 10.30am, 11.30am, 1.30pm, 2pm & 3pm; ☎068/82 5888 for details). A vast open-range zoo, it features expansive landscaped habitats, through which many Australian animals are free to roam; other animals from all continents are kept in natural surroundings, separated from the public by moats or creeks rather than fences wherever possible. The zoo is criss-crossed by walking and cycling paths: especially during the hot months, the best idea is to get up early in the morning, and set off early – by noon, the temperatures can become unbearable. The youth hostel rents out bikes, as does *Wheeler Cycles*, 193 Brisbane Street, ☎068/82 9899; bikes and mini-mokes can also be rented at the zoo itself. *Langley's Dubbo Day Tours* (☎068/84 5333) do escorted coach tours (Sun & Wed 9.30am–1.30pm; $40, $8 pick-up fee), but a town bus stops one kilometre from the zoo and you could walk the rest; alternatively, take a taxi (*Radio Cabs* ☎068/82 1911).

If you have another hour to spare, head for the **Old Dubbo Gaol** in Macquarie Street, right in the centre of town (daily 9am–4.30pm; $3). A hundred years ago this fortress-style building housed some of the most notorious criminals of the west, and today it glories in the details of nineteenth-century prison life, with loving attention to the macabre: the gallows, the hangman's kit and the careers of some of those who were executed here. In the cells, life-size (and convincingly life-like) animatronic models of convicted criminals tell the stories of their lives at the push of a button.

The **Dubbo Museum** (daily 9am–4.30pm; $3), in an old sandstone building nearby on Macquarie Street, has an extensive and somewhat chequered collection of items of regional history. There are agricultural and transport exhibits, a colonial kitchen, musical instruments, a dentist's surgery and the recreation of a village square complete with drapery store, bootmaker, barber and blacksmith.

## Practicalities

The **bus** terminal is on the corner of Erskine and Darling streets. The helpful **Dubbo Visitors' Centre** (daily 9am–5pm; ☎068/84 1422) is at the corner of Erskine and Macquarie streets, just off the Newell Highway. As well as giving out good free maps and information, the centre sells zoo tickets and does free accommodation bookings.

As you'd expect, there are plenty of **motels**. A couple of the better value ones are the *Merino Motel*, 65 Church Street, 200m south of the city centre (☎068/82 4133; ④) and *Across Country Motor Inn*, on the corner of the Newell Highway and Baird Street (☎068/82 0877; ④). Two old **hotels** downtown offer a bit more character: the *Civic Hotel*, on the corner of Tabralgar and Darling streets (☎068/82 3688; ③), has simple accommodation and counter meals; the *Castlereagh Hotel*, on the corner of Brisbane and Tabralgar streets (☎068/82 4877; ④), is slightly more upmarket, and also serves meals during the week. *Dubbo Bed & Breakfast*, 10 Baird Street (☎068/82 5226; ⑥), is a friendly choice with a separate guest wing and use of a pool. *Dubbo YHA Hostel* at 87 Brisbane Street (☎068/82 0922; rooms ②, dorms ①) is a small, family-run hostel within walking distance of the train station and the city centre; they also have rental bikes and sell discounted tickets to the zoo. **Campsites** include *Dubbo City Caravan Park*, Whylandra Street in Dubbo West (☎068/82 4820; on-site vans ③, cabins ④), and *Poplars Caravan Park*, Lower Bultje Street, overlooking the river near the city centre (☎068/82 4067; on-site vans ②, cabins ④).

# The Northwest

From Dubbo, the main route from Melbourne to Brisbane, the **Newell Highway**, continues through the wheat plains of the northwest, the relentless flatness relieved by the ancient eroded mountain ranges of the **Warrumbungles**, near Coonabarabran, and **Mount Kaputar**, near Narrabri, with the **Pillaga Scrub** between the two towns. Clear skies and the lack of large towns with their attendant lights make the area ideal for the **telescopes** that stare into space at both Coonabarabran and Narrabri. The thinly populated northwest has a relatively large percentage of Aborigines, peaking in the largest town of **Moree**. In 1971 Charles Perkins, an Aboriginal acitivist, led the **Freedom Ride**, a group of thirty people, mostly university students, who bussed through New South Wales on a mission to root out racism in the state. The biggest victory was in Moree itself when the riders, facing hostile townsfolk, broke the race bar by escorting Aboriginal children into the public swimming pool. The **Namoi Valley** – stretching from Gunnedah, just west of Tamworth, to Walgett – with its rich black soil, is **cotton country**. Beyond Walgett, just off the sealed Castlereagh Highway that runs from Dubbo, **Lightning Ridge** is a scorching hot opal-mining town, relieved by the hot **artesian bore baths** which are a feature of the northwest.

## Coonabarabran and the Warrumbungles

**COONABARABRAN** is a touristy little town on the Castlereagh River, 160km north of Dubbo via the Newell Highway, 465km northwest of Sydney. People come here for bushwalking and climbing in the spectacular Warrumbungles, an ancient mountain range 35km to the west, to gaze at stars in the clear skies, and to bring their dinosaur-fixated children to look at giant tacky models of the prehistoric beasts.

By virtue of its proximity to the **Siding Spring Observatory Complex** (daily 9am–4pm; $5), perched high above the township on the edge of the Warrumbungles national park, Coonabarabran considers itself the astronomy capital of Australia. And the skies *are* exceptionally clear out here, with the dry climate and a lack of pollution and population. The giant 3.9m optical telescope (one of the largest in the world) can be viewed close up from an observation gallery, and there's an astronomy exhibition, complemented by hands-on exhibits and a video show. There's no public transport here, but the school bus does pass by – ask at the tourist office. You can't actually view the stars at Siding Spring, but the recently opened **Skywatch Observatory** (daily 2pm–10pm; book before dusk on ☎068/42 2506) on Timor Road, 2km from town on the way to the Warrumbungles, has night viewing through its modern telescope, plus a planetarium and computer space-simulation programs.

More down-to-earth attractions are on offer at **Crystal Kingdom** on Newell Highway (daily 9am–6pm; $1), where there's a display of Warrumbungle minerals including a sparkling crystal cave, and at **Miniland** theme park (daily 8.30am–5.30pm; $6), on the way to the Warrumbungles. The main attractions at the latter are the life-size animated **dinosaurs**, but there are also birds and animals, a playground with paddle boats and bumper cars, a mural of the Warrumbungles, and a fantasy Stone-Age trail through the complex.

## The Warrumbungle National Park

The rugged **Warrumbungles** are ancient mountains of volcanic origin whose jagged cliffs, rocky skyscrapers and crags jut from the western horizon. The dry western plains and the moister east coast environment meet at these ranges, with plant and animal species from both habitats co-existing in the park. Warrumbungle means "crooked mountains" in an Aboriginal language, and the park was in fact bordered by three different language groups – the Kamilaroi, the Weilwan and Kawambarai – all now extinct. Evidence of Aborigines' past visits is common, with stone flakes used to make tools indicating old campsites. The **Warrumbungle National Park** is spectacular, especially in spring when the wild flowers in the sandstone areas are in bloom. The most popular months with visitors are April, September and October: it's really just too hot for walking here in summer, and the cold winters often bring snow. If you do come in the hot months, remember to take plenty of water when you go walking, and something warm for the nights, which actually get quite cool.

The **visitors' centre** (daily 8.30am–4pm; ☎068/25 4364) has hands-on displays and detailed maps of walking tracks. The wheelchair-accessible bitumen **Gurianawa Track** makes a short circuit around the centre and overlooks the flats where eastern grey kangaroos gather at dusk. Another good introduction to the park is the short **White Gum Lookout Walk** (1km return), with panoramic views over the ranges that are particularly dramatic at sunset. However the ultimate, for the reasonably fit only, is the **Grand High Tops Trail**, 14.5km return along the main ridge. The walk begins at kangaroo-filled Camp Pincham, and follows the flat floor of Spirey Creek through open forests full of colourful rosellas and lorikeets, and lizards basking on rocks. As the trail climbs, there are views of the 300m-high Belougery Spire, and more scrambling gets you to the foot of the **Breadknife**, thrusting 90m up into the sky, and the park's most famous feature. From here the main track heads on to the rocky slabs of the Grand High Tops, with tremendous views of most of the surrounding peaks and perhaps a wedge-tailed eagle soaring above. Experienced walkers could carry on to climb Bluff Mountain and then head west for the park's highest peak of Mount Exmouth (1205m), both great spots from which to watch the sunrise. The Warrumbungles are very popular with **rock climbers** who can climb anywhere except the Breadknife; permits are required. There isn't any public transport to the Warrumbungles.

## Practicalities

The **Visitors' Centre** on John Street (daily 9am–5pm; ☎068/42 1441) has tourist information and details of **scenic flights** over the Warrumbungles (☎068/42 1560; $45 for 30min).

**Accommodation** actually in the national park is limited to **campsites**, some of which have hot showers, electric barbecues and fireplaces (note that wood is not supplied, and there's a fine for collecting it in the park), while others are more basic. Bookings aren't necessssary for any of the sites, but you will need to bring provisions. Between the park and Coonabarabran, the *Warrumbungles Mountain Motel* on Timor Road, 19km from town (☎068/42 1832; rooms ④, dorms in YHA section ①), is set in a wonderful bushland on the Castlereagh River. Rooms have extra bunks and kitchens, so are good for families or small groups; there's also a small saltwater pool and a playing field. Also along Timor Road (16km from town), nestled under Bulleamble Mountain, is *Tibuc* (✆068/42 1740; self-contained cabins ②–⑤), a mixed farm, unusually tilled with draught horses, that makes a relaxing place to stay. There are plenty of alternatives in town: on John Street there are the *All Travellers Motor Inn* (✆068/42 1133; ⑤–⑥) with air-conditioning, swimming pool, in-house films and disabled-accessible rooms, the *Imperial Hotel* (✆068/42 1023; B&B ④) and the *Royal Hotel* (✆068/42 1816; B&B ④); along the Oxley Highway, you'll find the *Wayfarer Caravan Park* (✆068/42 1773; on-site vans ②, cabins ③) and the shady *John Oxley Caravan Park* (✆068/42 1635; on-site vans & cabins ③).

Good **places to eat** in town are all on John Street. The bright and airy *Jolly Cauli*, at no. 30, has a wide choice of vegetarian dishes, lovely coffee and homemade cakes. *The Lunch Box* does inexpensive midday meals, the *Imperial Hotel* has the best counter meals, and the *Golden Sea Dragon* is a reliable Chinese restaurant.

## The Namoi Valley: cotton country

On the Oxley Highway, 76km west of the New England town of Tamworth, **GUNNEDAH**, with a population of over 8000, is one of the largest towns of the northwest. The town's claim to fame is as the inspiration for the local poet Dorothy MacKellar (1885–1968) and her patriotic verse *My Country*, in which she pledged her undying love for what was then – and still is now – a drought-stricken land. The opening stanza is familiar to most Australians, who learnt it by rote at school:

> *I love a sunburnt country*
> *A land of sweeping plains*
> *Of rugged mountain ranges*
> *Of drought and flooding rains...*

Gunnedah also has one of the healthiest **koala populations** in the state: your best chance of spotting one, wedged high in the trees, is from the Bindea Walking Track that leaves from the **Information Centre** in Anzac Park (Mon–Fri 9am–5pm; ✆067/42 1564). The *Billabong* **motel** on Conadilly Street, by the main shopping centre (✆067/42 2033; ④) is handy and economical, with well-equipped air-conditioned rooms and a swimming pool. The nearest **caravan park** is 2km east of town on the Oxley Highway (✆067/42 1372; cabins & on-site vans ②). Besides the usual pub bistros you can eat in more style at *Trelawney's Restaurant*, a shady verandahed homestead in the centre of town.

While Gunnedah does have some cotton crops, **NARRABRI**, 97km northwest via the curiously named Boggabri and Baan Baa, is recognized as the commercial centre of cotton growing. A little smaller than Gunnedah, the town has a prosperous feel. The **Tourist Information Centre**, on Tibbereena Street (Mon–Fri 9am–1pm & 2–5pm, Sat & Sun 9am–noon; ✆067/92 3583), can give you the times to go and see the five linked dishes of the **Australia Telescope** complex, 24km west on the Yarrie Lake Road. Opening times depend on what they're tracking, but the centre is staffed Mon–Fri 8am–4pm, entry is free and there are lots of computer models you can play with. The other main attraction around Narrabri is **Mount Kaputar National Park**. The drive into the park to the 1524m **lookout** – with its panoramic views encompassing the vast Pillaga Scrub, the Warrumbungles and the New England Tablelands – is steep, narrow and unsealed (call ✆067/92 1147 for road conditions). There are eleven marked bushwalking trails in the park, with brochures available from the **NWPS office** in Narrabri at 165 Maitland Street (✆067/92 4724), or the **visitors' centre** at **Dawsons Spring** campsite and picnic area, although the latter is not permanently staffed. The **camping** facilities at Dawsons Spring include hot showers, and there are a couple of cabins with bathroom, kitchen and wood-combustion stove (reservations via NPWS on ✆067/92

4724; ④). The most striking geological feature of the park is **Sawn Rocks**, a basalt formation which looks like a series of organ pipes; it's reached via the northern end of the park on the unsealed road heading to Bingara.

If you want to **stay** in the town itself, or **eat** something, the *Club House Hotel*, 87 Maitland Street (☎067/92 2027; rooms ③) fits the bill on both counts. It has attractive turn-of-the-century lead lighting and a beautiful old wooden staircase leading upstairs to a decent Italian restaurant (dinner only, Tues–Sat); there are also plain pub meals downstairs. For a snack, *Watson's Bakery* on Maitland Street serves good-quality pies and sandwiches to take away.

The drive from Narrabri to **WEE WAA**, roughly 40km west, warns of your entry into redneck territory – the roadside glitters with shattered bottles thrown from speeding cars. Wee Waa was where the Namoi cotton industry began in the 1960s, and the large cotton "gins" or processing plants are located here. During the picking and growing season (April–July) free guided tours leave Namoi Co-op (daily 10.30am & 2.30pm, 1hr 30min–3hr 30min), but you'll need your car to get around the various areas. If you can stand the rather raw, dispirited town and the blazing sumer heat, there's **cotton-chipping** work here in abundance in December and January; ask at one of the two pubs on Rose Street, the main drag, and someone will send you in the right direction. From Wee Waa you can head west to Walgett and on to Lightning Ridge.

# Lightning Ridge

The population of **LIGHTNING RIDGE**, 74km north of Walgett on the Castlereagh Highway (the road is fully sealed, but note that there's no fuel between the two), is barely more than a thousand. The reason for its existence, and the reason why people come here in some numbers, is the **opal**. Amid this harsh landscape scarred by holes and slag heaps, Lightning Ridge's opal fields are the only place in the world where the extremely valuable black opal can consistently be found. This one attraction is heavily exploited by opal galleries and **mines** you can visit, among them the *Big Opal*, 3 Mile Road (daily 9am–5pm; free entry, tour 10am daily, $6) with demonstrations of opal cutting and guided tours of an underground mine; *Spectrum Opal Mines*, Bald Hill Road (daily 9am–5pm; free), a centre displaying solid opals in an underground show-room with a film about opal mining shown on the hour; and the *Walk-in Mine*, 1 Bald Hill Road (daily 9am–5pm; tour daily 9am, $5), with tours to an underground mine and a mining display. There are also clearly demarcated fossicking areas where you can try your luck at finding opals – but don't do it anywhere else, or you may stray onto others' concessions. Recover afterwards in the 52°C water of the **Hot Artesian Bore Baths** in Pandora Street (☎068/29 0429; open 24hr; free). For something much cooler, the new Olympic Pool on Gem Street (end-Sept to Easter, daily 10am–8pm) is particularly appealing in the scorching heat, with shade areas over the pool.

### Practicalities

Lightning Ridge **Tourist Information Centre** is in the new Miners Associated building on Morilla Street (☎068/29 1466), and has opal-buying rooms attached – ask for the useful booklet *Walgett Shire and the Lightning Ridge Opal Fields*, which has a handy guide to buying opals. The tourist office can also fill you in on **accommodation** possibilities, including the *Black Opal Motel*, on Opal Street (☎068/29 0518; air-con rooms ⑤), the *Wallangulla Motel*, on the corner of Morella and Agate streets (☎068/29 0542; not all rooms air-con ⑤), and *Lightning Ridge Motor Village*, Onyx Street (☎068/29 0304; air-con rooms ⑤), which also has tent sites. The best place to **camp**, though, is *Crocodile Caravan and Camping Park*, Morilla Street (☎068/29 0437; air-con cabins ④) with a welcome pool and spa. Full **banking** facilities are available at *Westpac* in Morilla Street.

# The Hume Highway and the Riverina

The rolling plains of southwestern New South Wales, speading west from the Great Dividing Range, are bounded by two great rivers: the Murrumbidgee to the north and the Murray to the south, the latter forming the Victorian border. Known as the **Riverina**, the name conjures up a certain rural romance, a country Australia little visited by tourists – except those on route to Melbourne along the **Hume Highway**, which cuts a fume-filled swathe through the southwest. If you're looking for work on the land, you've a reasonable chance of finding it here. The land the explorer John Oxley described as "uninhabitable and useless to civilized man" began its transformation to fertile fruit bowl when the ambitious **Murrumbidgee Irrigation Scheme** was launched in 1907 and the area, around **Griffith** and **Leeton**, now produces ninety per cent of Australia's rice, most of its citrus fruits and twenty per cent of its wine grapes. The capital of the central Riverina is **Wagga Wagga**, Australia's largest inland city. Along the Upper Murray, the main towns are on the Victorian side of the river (and are covered in the *Victoria* chapter), but you may drop into **Albury** en route to Melbourne on the Hume, or into **Wentworth** as a day-trip from Mildura or heading to or from Broken Hill on the Silver City Highway.

## The Hume Highway: Goulburn to Albury

If you want a quick route to Melbourne from Sydney, or vice versa, you'll inevitably end up on the rather tedious Hume Highway which passes through the Southern Highlands, the Riverina and crosses the Murray River. Over the years the highway has been improved, but one of Australia's main arteries between its two largest cities still narrows to one lane either way in parts. Choked with trucks, particularly at night, accidents are not infrequent, so keep your wits about you. Below are the main stopping points along the way in New South Wales (for Sydney to Goulburn, see p.147) and some suggestions for food, accommodation and breaks.

### Goulburn and around

Now bypassed by the Hume Highway, **GOULBURN** is still the traditional stop-off point en route to Canberra. It's a large regional centre for the surrounding area, and for a quality **wool industry** which was established in the 1820s. With a wide-streeted conservative country feel, the town boasts a department store (*Grace Bros* on the main drag of Auburn Street) and some large impressive public buildings. Goulburn's connection to sheep, and one kind in particular, is made hugely public with the **Big Merino** (daily 8am–8pm). Another of Australia's unashamedly tacky "big things", the 15m-high sheep proudly stands next to the *Ampol* petrol station on the Old Hume Highway; the first floor has a wool industry display and on the third level you can look out over the town through the sheep's eyes. To get closer to the real thing, head for the long-established **Pelican Sheep Station** on Braidwood Road, 10km out of town (☎048/21 4668; booking essential for tours, price dependent on number of people; accommodation in bunkhouses ③, plus camping), which has been in the same family since 1827, so they must know something about these woolly animals. Tours include a shearing demonstration and seeing some sheep dogs put through their paces.

Besides sheep, there are several old places to visit in Goulburn, including the National Trust property **Riversdale**, an 1840 coaching inn on Maud Street (Fri–Sun 10am–4.30pm; $4), but by far the most interesting is the **Old Goulburn Brewery** (tastings from 11am daily) on Bungonia Road which, since 1836, has been brewing traditional ales and stouts. Details of other old properties can be gleaned from the **Goulburn Visitors' Centre**, next to the very impressive 1887 courthouse and opposite

## THE HUME AND HOVELL WALKING TRACK

This long-distance walk starts at **Gunning**, on the Hume Highway 50km east of Goulburn, and runs over 400km southwest **to Albury**, retracing as closely as possible the route taken on foot by the two eponymous explorers in the spring and summer of 1824 on their expedition from Sydney to Port Phillip, the site of what was to become Melbourne. The walk takes about fifteen to twenty days but the design – a Bicentenary project – allows for half-day, full-day and weekend walks. There are several free leaflets detailing different chunks, available from the Department of Conservation and Land Management in Sydney (☎02/228 6111, 02/9228 6111 from July 1996), Goulburn (☎048/ 23 0665), and Wagga Wagga (☎069/21 2503); the *Hume and Hovell Walking Track Guidebook* by Harry Hill (Crawford House Press, Bathurst, $19.95) is also useful.

shady, flower-filled Belmore Park, on Montague Street (Mon–Fri 9am–5pm, Sat & Sun 9.30am–3.30pm; ☎048/21 5343); they also have a list of accommodation.

The classic place to **eat** in Goulburn, obligatory on a trip to Canberra, is the *Paragon Cafe*, at 174 Auburn Street. A bastion of good, filling food – inexpensive breakfasts, great hamburgers, steaks, fish, veal, pasta and pizza – it's been here for around fifty years and retains its Forties-era fittings; it's also licensed.

The area's most intriguing place to stay – as a helper – is the **Yurt Farm**, 20km out of town on Grabben Gullen Road (☎048/29 2114; ① – four hours' work per day required, but all meals included). A yurt, in its original form, is a Mongolian round leather tent, an idea enthusiastically adopted and adapted by Californian New Agers. Those here are mostly wood, portable prefab buildings in the Californian mould – solar-powered, naturally lit and wood-heated. Essentially a sheep property, the "yurt village" has several yurts, each with a different function, providing an educational centre for groups of children to help them become more self-sufficient and environmentally aware. If you want to stay, you must call in advance; if you don't have your own transport, someone can pick you up.

Twenty-five kilometres east of Goulburn, the **Bungonia State Recreation Area** covers a rugged strip of the Southern Tablelands containing some of the deepest caves in Australia. The spectacular limestone Bungonia Gorge and the Shoalhaven River are two of its physical attractions. *Outdoor Challenges*, based at 7 Benlin Court, Goulburn (☎048/21 9354) offer guided adventure activities, and there's a well-equipped **camp-site** (☎048/48 4277, 048/44 4277 from June 1996) with hot showers.

### Yass and around

On the outskirts of **YASS** as you enter from Goulburn (87km away) sits National Trust-owned **Cooma Cottage** (daily except Tues 10am–4pm; $4) the former home of the famous explorer **Hamilton Hume**. Set in rolling countryside stocked with sheep, the well preserved nineteenth-century homestead's architectural interest is outweighed by the excellent interpretative material on Hume and his expeditions. Hume was different from many of his contemporaries in that he was born in Australia – in Parramatta to free settlers in 1797. Hume's explorations relied on his knowledge of the bush: he befriended Aborigines who taught him their skills and language, which made him infinitely better prepared than those equipped only with romantic notions. His first expedition was at the tender age of 17, accompanied by his brother and his Aboriginal friend Doual, and the trio discovered prime grazing lands in the Southern Highlands. Three years later he led the Goulburn Plains expedition, and pushing further afield in 1821 he discovered the rich and productive Yass Plains, where he settled in later life. Hume's best known exploration was when he paired with Hovell, an English sea captain, to head for Port Phillip Bay; you can follow in their footsteps on the *Hume and Hovell*

*Walking Track* (see box opposite). He also assisted Sturt in tracing the Murray and Darling rivers. The old coach house in the grounds has become the *Cooma Cottage Tea Rooms*, serving inexpensive sandwiches and great coffee. In the town itself, *Hamilton's Teahouse and Restaurant*, on 262 Cooma Street, is a snug inn that serves cappuccino, homemade soups, *focaccia*, fresh cakes and scones.

Continuing along the Hume Highway, the turn-off to the **Burrinjuck State Recreation Area** is reached after 27km, and from here it's a 25km drive on a sealed road to the bushland park set around Burrinjuck Dam, with camping and picnic areas colourful with chirping rosellas and grazed by kangaroos (☎06/227 8114; on-site vans & units ③, cottages ⑤). There are **riverboat cruises** on the *Lady BJ* (☎06/227 7270; 2–4hr) across the main basin into the narrow gorges of the Murrumbidgee River and to **Carey's Caves** at the Wee Jasper Reserve. You can also reach these caves by car, turning off the Barton Highway south of Yass (weekends and public holidays 1–4pm; $6), and there's a basic **campsite** too (☎06/227 9626 for bookings.)

## Gundagai and Holbrook

One hundred and four kilometres from Yass, **GUNDAGAI** sits on the southern banks of the Murrumbidgee, at the foot of the rounded bump of Mount Parnassus. The town was once situated on the alluvial flats north of the river, despite warnings from local Aborigines that the area suffered major flooding, and old Gundagai was the scene of Australia's worst flood disaster in 1852 when 89 people drowned. The relocated Gundagai, on the main route betweeen Sydney and Melbourne (until bypassed by the Hume Highway), became a favoured overnight stopping point, with the bullock waggons which took the pioneers into the interior favouring a camping spot out of town at Five Mile Creek. A large punt was the only means of crossing the Murrumbidgee from 1849 until the Prince Alfred Bridge was erected in 1867; now disused, the pretty wooden bridge is still open to pedestrians. Gold was eventually discovered here, and by 1864 it had become a boom town, preyed upon by the romantically dubbed bushranger **Captain Moonlight** who was eventually captured and tried at the Gundagai Courthouse in 1879.

Perhaps this colourful history and the road-much-travelled appeal of Gundagai explains why the town features so often in Australian verse and folk song, finding immortality through a Jack Moses poem, in which "the dog sat on the tuckerbox, nine miles from Gundagai" – and stubbornly refused to help its master pull the bogged bullock team from the creek. Somehow the whole image became elevated from that of a disobedient hound and a fed-up, cursing teamster to a symbol of the pioneer with a faithful hound at his side. As a consequence, a statue of the dog was erected at the original five-mile point: it's actually a very pleasant place to take a break from the rigours of the road with a shady picnic area and undulating fields with hills beyond. Inside the tourist centre, there's a range of cheerfully tacky souvenirs plus the rare opportunity to send a postcard with a special "dog on the tuckerbox" postmark.

In the town itself, the **Gundagai Tourist Information Centre** (Mon–Fri 8am–5pm, Sat & Sun 9am–noon & 1–5pm; ☎069/44 1341) can help you find somewhere to stay if need be – and also sells a tape of several folk songs featuring Gundagai, including: *Along the Road to Gundagai*, from which every Australian remembers only the tuneful snatch "There's a track winding back, to an old-fashioned shack, along the road to Gundagai". Another masterpiece from the creator of the noble dog sculpture can be tracked down at the information centre: fork out a dollar to see Frank Rusconi's **miniature Baroque cathedral**, made from thousands of pieces of twenty different kinds of NSW marble with no plans of any sort. An endeavour requiring complete patience and precision, it took 28 years to build. Satisfying more mundane appetites, *Bidgee Cakes* at 198 Sheridan Street bake traditional tarts using free-range eggs, their sausage rolls are filled with fresh lamb, and the divine honey roll is made from local honey.

Sixty-eight kilometres north of Gundagai, **HOLBROOK** is a recommended food break on the drive to Melbourne (or Sydney), with two excellent bakeries on the Hume as it heads through town. The *Holbrook Bakery* dishes out delicious beef and curry pies, and the *Scrummy Buns Bakery* across the road sells more unorthodox pies filled with crocodile, emu, kangaroo and rabbit – plus cappuccino and continental cakes. Perhaps these great bakeries are a legacy of a German past: the town, settled by Germans in the 1860s, was called Germantown right up until World War I when anti-German feeling warranted a name change.

## Albury and around

On the Murray River the small city of **ALBURY** is a major stopover point on the route between Sydney and Melbourne, being roughly halfway. The town is twinned with Wodonga across the river in Victoria, and although Albury is the major centre, the principal information centre is on the Wodonga side – **Gateway Tourist Information Centre** on the Hume Highway (daily 9am–5pm; ☎060/41 3875). You can also pick up tourist information from the **Albury Regional Museum** (daily 10.30am–4.30pm; ☎060/21 4550; free) on the Hume Highway in what was once the *Turks' Head Hotel* – opportunistically sited here when the river was crossed by punt; changing exhibitions now focus on the social history of the region. The museum is set in **Noreuil Park**, a peaceful spot looking across to a bush-covered Victorian riverbank. People lie about under the large gum trees – one of which is marked by the explorer Hovell at the point where he and Hume crossed the Murray – and swim in the river. You can also take to the water with a **cruise** on a replica paddle steamer (mid-September to mid-April only; Wed, Sat & Sun, daily during school holidays; 10am, noon & 2pm; $8–9.50; ☎060/21 1113). Another pleasant place to stretch your legs is the **Albury Botanical Gardens** at the Dean Street end of Wodonga Place: established in 1877, there are some impressive old trees here, including a huge 41-metre Queensland Kauri Pine; palm trees and flower beds fill the small grassy park and the short fern walk is pleasantly cooling.

The **Albury Regional Art Centre** is on the main street, Dean Street, at no. 546 (daily 10.30am–5pm; free; ☎060/23 8187), in the decorative old town hall. The gallery's speciality is photography but it also has a sizeable collection of Russel Drysdale's sketches and studies for paintings; the Australian artist (1912–1981) lived in the area in the 1920s and married into an Albury family. The town has its own extraordinary troupe of performers: **The Flying Fruit Circus** (☎060/21 7044 to find out when they're performing locally), which began in 1979 as a local circus project for school-children teaching them acrobatics, and went on to become a national success.

Albury is a convenient place to **stay** for the night. There's a good range of places from the comfortable activity-focused *Murray River Lodge* on Hume Street (☎060/41 1822; rooms ③, dorms ①), with cheap bike rental, to the upmarket *Carlton Albury Hotel* on the corner of Dean and Elizabeth streets (☎060/21 5366; ⑤) with swimming pool, sauna, gym, spa and room service. One of the best-value motels is the *Albury Viscount Motor Inn*, on the Hume 1km south of the centre (☎060/21 2444; ④; air-con, swimming pool), while campers are catered for at *Trek-31 Tourist Park*, 8km north on the highway (☎060/25 4355).

Dean Street is the main **food** street: a good lunchtime spot is *Bon Vivanti* (next to *Sportsgirl*) with inexpensive and healthy fast food including a self-serve salad bar. *Cafe Victor* serves up wood-fired pizzas while the *Pancake Parlour*, with its outdoor tables, is a satisfying and inexpensive place with *focaccia* and pancakes. If you're into hot and spicy food, *Rama's Curry Kitchen* at the *Globe Hotel*, 586 Dean Street, is an authentic, affordable Indian with a good range of vegetarian dishes on offer. Less conventional ways of getting a feed include a visit to the **Hume Weir Trout Farm**, off the Riverina Highway (daily 9am–dusk; $5), a pleasant spot with landscaped gardens and waterfalls where you can catch freshwater trout; there are barbecues here to cook your fish.

Albury is positioned in prime dairy country and you can try some of its produce at the **Haberfield Dairy**, 470–482 Hovell Street (Mon–Fri 9am–5.30pm, Sat 9am–1pm), renowned for its Swiss-style cheeses.

Around 10km north of Albury on the Hume, the larger-than-life **Ettomogah Pub** is a send up of an Outback pub, straight out of a sketch by the Aussie cartoonist Maynard, although the precariously skew-whiff hotel really does serve drinks. Walk up the slanting staircase to the veering verandah where there are great views of the surrounding countryside. A touristy tin shack round the back flogs souvenirs.

# Murrumbidgee Irrigation Area: MIA

Irrigation has transformed the area northwest of Albury, between the Lachlan and the Murrumbidgee rivers, into a fertile valley full of orchards, vineyards and rice paddies, cut through with irrigation canals. The **Murrumbidgee Irrigation Area** (or MIA) extends over 200,000 hectares, a mostly flat and – from ground level at least – featureless landscape that nonetheless is responsible for producing most of Australia's rice, eighty per cent of NSW's grapes (mostly sent off for wine production elsewhere), and sixty per cent of its citrus fruits. The water for the irrigation area is stored in Burrinjuck and Blowering Dams and flows over 400km down the Murrumbidgee River to Berembed Weir, before being diverted into the main canal, which is 155km long and feeds a network of 1450km of supply canals.

Probably the main reason you'll visit this off-the-beaten-track area is to find **work**, which there is in abundance for the intensive picking season from December to April – plus a considerable picking of Valencia oranges throughout the year as the largest citrus growing area in Australia. At the peak season, there are about 2500–3000 jobs going begging. The season starts in August with oranges, which are picked right through to March, joined in November by onions, then stonefruit, prunes and melons from December to March, overlapping with the grape harvest from February to March. Pay is calculated according to the amount picked and, basing yourself in Griffith or Leeton, you'll need your own transport, if only a bicycle, since the orchards are up to 10km out of the two towns. To avoid the possibility of a wasted trip, due to a late season or a poor crop, it's essential to check with the Griffith *CES* (☎069/69 1100, 069/60 1100 from May 1996) before turning up.

## Griffith

Citrus orchards line the way into the small town of **GRIFFITH**, with low hills in the background. The major centre of the MIA, it's known for its large **Italian population** and their enduring cultural life, despite the fact that some of the families got here before World War I. Most arrived in the 1920s, many already having tried mining in Broken Hill, and the area attracted post-World War II Italian immigrants too. Needless to say, a string of excellent Italian cafés and restaurants line tree-filled Banna Avenue, the main street, and the majority of wineries are run by Italian families. Designed by Walter Burley Griffin, the landscape architect from Chicago who was responsible for Canberra, the city has since grown beyond his plan.

For free maps and information, head for the **Griffith Visitors' Centre**, on the corner of Jondaryn and Banna avenues (Mon–Fri 9am–5pm, Sat 9am–3pm, Sun 10am–2pm; ☎069/62 4145). During the week, they can arrange for you to hop on a school bus-run (7am–9am & 3.30pm–5pm) to see the surrounding district, its rice paddies, citrus- and stone-fruit orchards and vineyards, for around a dollar. An even better way to get an overview of the area is to head for **Scenic Hill**, the escarpment that forms the northern boundary of the city. The **Sir Dudley de Chair's Lookout** here gives a panoramic view of the horticultural enterprises below. Immediately beneath this rocky outcrop, it's a short walk to the **Hermit's Cave** where Valerio Recetti, an Italian immigrant, lived alone and quite unsuspected for ten years until an accident in 1935. Working only at night and early in the morning, he made a home in the caves he found in the cliff, and created cliffside gardens. One cave contained a small shrine where you can still see a painted cross. Eventually, during World War II, like most of the local Italians, he was interned in Hay (around 100km to the west of Griffith), and returned to Italy to die in 1952. One and a half kilometres west of the lookout and 2km from the city centre, **Pioneer Park** (daily 8.30am–5pm; $5), in an extensive bushland setting, has 36 buildings recreating the era of the early MIA. The most interesting facet is "Bagtown", a reconstruction of an early temporary town built in 1910 to meet the needs of the Murrumbidgee Irrigation Area canal workers and pioneer farmers, and so-called because the homes were made of flour bags with corrugated iron roofs.

There are sixteen **wineries**, mainly Italian-run, in the area surrounding Griffith. Nine are open to the public, detailed in the *Griffith Visitors' Guide* booklet available from the tourist office. The very first winery, *McWilliam's*, was established in 1915 and is open for tastings in a building resembling a wine barrel (Mon–Sat 9am–5.30pm, Sun 10am–4pm; ☎069/63 0001); there are barbecues in the grounds. Several other wineries have been around for more than fifty years, dating from the influx of Italian immigrants after World War II. One of these is *Rosetto Wines* on Rossetto Road, off Leeton Road (Mon–Fri 8.30am–5.30pm). Still run by the same family, it's a down-to-earth, friendly concern known for its muscats and ports.

The *Pioneer Park* has bunkhouse **accommodation** for backpackers and fruit-pickers (☎069/62 4196; ①), but it's some way out of town and an uphill walk too, with no public transport. Most pickers camp or stay in caravans, with a choice between the *Griffith Tourist Caravan Park*, at 919 Willandra Avenue, 2km south of the centre (☎069/64 2144; on-site vans ③, cabins ④), the *Griffith Caravan Park* on the Leeton Road, 3km east (☎069/62 3785), or the basic campsite at the showground with very cheap sites. For a bit more comfort, the *Victoria Hotel*, 384 Banna Street (☎069/62 1299; ③, with bargain weekly rates), has rather basic rooms, but there's a cool covered courtyard and weekly counter lunches downstairs; or you could try the central *Griffith Motel Hotel* on Kooyoo Street (☎069/62 1011; ④, with air-con).

There's no shortage of good Italian places to **eat and drink** lining Banna Avenue, with the pavement tables of the *Pasticceria Bassano* (Mon–Thurs 8am–6pm, Fri–Sun 8am–10pm) a good place to sample excellent coffee and delicious *focaccia*; you can also get pasta, homemade *gelati*, pastries and biscuits. The much cheaper cafeteria-style *Bertoldo's Pasticerria* has filling pasta plates from $3. A casual meal can be had at *Belvedere Restaurant and Pizza*, 494 Banna Avenue, while *La Scala*, at no. 455 (☎069/62 4322; Tues–Sun 6pm–midnight; licensed) is a more upmarket and expensive choice. On Mackay Avenue, at no. 40, *La Villa Bianca* uses a wood-fired oven for its pizzas.

## Around Griffith

Fifty-nine kilometres southeast of Griffith, **LEETON** is the third largest town in the MIA, with a quarter of its population of Italian extraction; like Griffith, it was designed by Walter Burley Griffin. For information on the area, head for the **Leeton Visitor Information Centre** on Chelmsford Place (Mon–Fri 9am–5pm, Sat & Sun 9.30am–12.30pm; ☎069/53 2832). There are two **caravan parks**, both 2km southeast: the *Leeton Caravan Park* on Yanco Avenue (☎069/53 3323; on-site vans ②, cabins ③), and the *Gilgal Family Holiday Centre* on Corbie Hill Road (☎069/53 3882; cabins ③, cottage ④), with a better range of facilities. Despite the Italian population, the town feels less cosmopolitan than Griffith, but you can consume an Italian **meal** at the *MIA Social Club* on Racecourse Road (daily from 3pm; ☎069/53 4357).

Only 25km northeast of Griffith is the **Cocoparra National Park** in the woodland-covered Cocoparra Range. After heavy rains in winter, wildflowers cover the park; enquire about camping and bushwalking at the **NPWS office**, 105 Banna Avenue,

Griffith (☎069/67 8159). Much further away, on the flat plains 185km northwest of Griffith, is **Willandra National Park** reached via Hillston (64km from Griffith), on the unsealed Hillston to Mossgiel Road. The park was created in 1971 from a section of the vast Big Willandra pastoral station, a famous stud merino property which had operated from the 1860s, and now has several temporary wetland areas; as well as enabling you to experience the semi-arid riverine plains country at close quarters, a visit to the 1918 **homestead** gives an insight into station life and the wool industry. Wet weather makes all the roads to Willandra impassable, so check with the **park office** first in Hillston (☎069/67 9159; this is also the number for **accommodation bookings**, with share rooms available in shearers' quarters ①) – and take extra supplies in case you get rained in.

### Narrandera

Thirty kilometres southeast of Leeton, at the junction of the Sturt and Newell highways, **NARRANDERA** is a popular overnight stop en route from Adelaide to Sydney or Melbourne to Brisbane. It's actually a very pleasant place to take a break, set on the Murrumbidgee River with streets lined with tall native and deciduous trees owing to the foresight of the pioneer settlers; its white cedars, which blossom in November, are particularly beautiful.

A good place to cool down is **Lake Talbot**, a willow-surrounded expanse of water flowing from the Murrumbidgee River. Right next to the lake, with just a grassy bank between them, is the splendidly sited **Lake Talbot swimming complex** (third weekend in October to third weekend in April, daily 9am–9pm; adults $1.70, children 80c). The complex is very family-friendly, with picnic areas and barbecues, various watery rides, children's pools and an olympic-sized pool. Nearby, a reserve along the river has been declared a **koala regeneration area** for a disease-free colony of koalas; follow the **Bundidgerry Walking Track** around Lake Talbot and the Murrumbidgee River. Maps of the track are available at the **Narrandera Tourist Information Centre**, in Narrandera Park on the Newell Highway (☎069/59 1766; Mon–Fri 9am–5pm, Sat & Sun 10am–4pm). Fishing fanatics could try out the lake or river for some Murray Cod, Yellowbelly or Silverbeam; fish abound in the river, and 5km east of Narrandera, off the Sturt Highway, is the **John Lake Centre** at the Inland Fisheries Research Station (daily 9am–4pm; guided tours 9am, 11am, 1.30pm & 3pm; $2; ☎069/59 1488) which carries out research into the fish species of the Murray, Murrumbidgee and Darling rivers.

The best place to stay in Narrandera is the *Star Lodge*, on the corner of Whitton and Arthur streets (☎069/59 1768; rooms ④, dorms in YHA section ①): classified by the National Trust, the building retains many of its original 1916 features, and is now a fine **B&B** run by a friendly couple. East Street is the main street for **hotels** and **motels**, with several classic iron-lace-verandahed country hotels, all offering accommodation. The real bargain is the *Royal Mail Hotel* on East Street (☎069/59 2007; ②), or try the *Mid Town Motor Inn*, with its central position on the corner of East and Larmer streets (☎069/59 2122; ④) and swimming pool. Another good spot is the shady *Lake Talbot Caravan Park*, well positioned above the lake and pool (☎069/59 1302; cabins ④, on-site vans ③). Finally, the best place for a **meal** is the big old *Narrandera Hotel*, the last pub on East Street.

## Wagga Wagga

**WAGGA WAGGA**, known simply as "Wagga" to the locals, is the most populated inland city in New South Wales with around 55,000 inhabitants, but it still has the appearance of a slow and solid country town. Its curious name comes from the Widadjuri, the most populous of the New South Wales Aborigines: Wagga means crow and its repetition signifies the plural – here crows gathered in large numbers. Set on the Murrumbidgee River just under 100km east of Narrandera, with a beautiful sandy river beach to swim in close to the main street, it is the capital of the Riverina region.

Wagga's main attractions fringe the city. On its southern edges are the impressive **Botanic Gardens** at the base of Willans Hill, a huge place with a walk-through bird aviary where over 300 species flit about, a children's petting zoo, a tree chapel, specialist gardens of cacti and succulents, rainforest species, camellias, plus a Chinese-style garden, streams and ponds, and bush trails, as well as picnic areas with electric barbecues and the pleasant *Park Cafe*. Further to the south, the artificial **Lake Albert** is a popular spot for water-skiing. On weekends and during the Christmas holidays there are **boats** for rent: aquabikes, paddle boats, sailing boats or canoes located on the waterfront at the kiosk (☎069/22 5784) at Apex Park. Eight kilometres east of Wagga, the **Murray Cod Hatcheries and Fauna Park** (daily 9am–5pm; $5) is on the Sturt Highway. The huge Murray Cod is just one of the native fish (and crustaceans) from the Murray–Darling basin on display in the aquarium.

Back in the centre, the **City Art Gallery**, 40 Gurwood Street (Tues–Fri 11am–5pm, Sat 10am–5pm, Sun 2am–5pm; free) is home to the National Art Glass collection, a stunning array of contemporary glass pieces, and the Carnegie Print Collection, with over 500 originals from innovative Australian printmakers from 1940 onwards; if you're lucky, Sally Robinson's vivid *Kakadu* series might be on display.

A bit of life on Sunday mornings is sparked by the **markets** (7.30am–noon) in *Woolworths* car park; with secondhand clothes and books, crafts, local produce and cakes on sale. The *Ngungilanna Culture Centre*, 11 Gurwood Street (☎069/21 8982; Mon–Sat 9am–5.30pm) is also worth checking out: run by the Wagga Advancement Aboriginal Corporation, it sells locally made boomerangs, paintings and clothes as well as books, cards, paintings and crafts.

## Practicalities

Roughly half way between Sydney and Melbourne (470km from Sydney and 435km from Melbourne), Wagga is just off the Sturt Highway, the main route between Adelaide and Sydney. Interstate buses heading to and from Brisbane, Sydney, Adelaide, Melbourne and Canberra all pass through Wagga stopping at the **Greyhound.Pioneer Interstate Terminal**, on the corner of Gurwood and Trail streets (☎069/21 1977). To **get around**, you can rent bikes from *Kidson's Cycles* at 107 Fitzmaurice Street (☎069/21 4474), or a car from *Avis*, on the corner of Edwards and Fitzharding streets (☎069/21 9977).

**Wagga Wagga Visitors' Centre**, on Tarcutta Street (daily 9am–5pm; ☎069/23 5402) doesn't book **accommodation**, but does have information about **farmstays** in the area. Places in town include *Romano's Hotel* on the corner of Sturt and Fitzmaurice streets (☎069/21 2013; ④–⑤), a beautifully renovated old hotel that manages to be clean, stylish and inexpensive; rooms are done out in heritage style, and some have showers. *The Tourist Hotel*, 91 Fitzmaurice Street (☎069/21 2264; ③), has no-frills pub doubles, while *The Manor Guesthouse*, 38 Morrow Street (☎069/21 5962; ⑤) is a good B&B right next to the beautiful riverfront park. The best-situated caravan park is *Wagga Wagga Tourist Park*, Johnston Street (☎069/21 2540), right near the town beach and five minutes' walk from the main shops, but still shady and peaceful.

Places to eat include the *Bahn Thai* **restaurant** at the *Club Motel*, 73 Morgan Street (☎069/21 4177; BYO), for authentic Thai cuisine with a good selection for vegetarians, and the *Kebak Place Restaurant*, 152 Fitzmaurice Street (☎069/21 6307; Tues–Sat 11am–midnight; BYO) for really tasty Lebanese food. *Gingers* **café** at 35A Gurwood Street, opposite the City Art Gallery, is cosy and serves good coffee, while *Romano's Hotel* (see above) has a modern and very stylish café/bar that serves a decent espresso and is open for breakfast right though. Head for the popular *Cafe Europa* on 44 Johnston Street for affordable pasta and pizza with plenty of choice for vegetarians.

Wagga also has several huge **clubs** which offer free courtesy buses: *Wagga RSL*, on the corner of Dobbs and Kincaid streets (☎069/21 3624), includes a Chinese restaurant and Friday night piano bar, while the *Wagga Leagues Club*, Gurwood Street (☎069/21 4248) has live entertainment every Saturday and a good brasserie.

# The Lower Murray: Albury to Wentworth

Following the **lower Murray River** between Albury (see p.230) and the South Australian border, there's little of interest on the New South Wales side until the old port town of **Wentworth** and its surrounding storehouse of ancient Aboriginal history around **Lake Victoria** and in the remote **Mungo National Park**. The main centres are on the Victorian side of the river, Mildura (see p.725) and Echuca (see p.730) chief among them, although the NSW riverside towns of **Corowa** and **Tocumwal**, not far from Albury, are pleasant enough.

## Corowa and Tocumwal

Following the line of the river, it's 56km northwest to **COROWA**, across the Murray from Victoria's **Rutherglen wine region** (see p.743). Blue flags flying all over town proclaim it to be the birthplace of federation, since the Federation Conference of 1893 was held at Corowa's courthouse. **Corowa Tourist Information Centre** is in the cream-painted former train station on John Street (Mon–Sat 9.45am–4.30pm), and can fill you in on river cruises on the *MV Lynne Maree* (Sat, Sun & holidays 10am–2pm; 1hr, $9; ☎060/332 846). There are stacks of **motels** in town offering very reasonable accommodation, such as the *Corowa Murray View* at 193 River Street (☎060/33 2144; ④–⑤), with a swimming pool, spa and barbecues. Campers could try the *Ball Park Caravan Park*, by the Murray on Bridge Road (☎060/33 1426; cabins & vans ②). The main street harbours several places for a **meal**, including the *Star Hotel*, with its good-value roast of the day, the decent Italian restaurant (*Vaccari's*) at the *Royal Hotel*, and the *Old Corowa Bakehouse*, a popular café/bakery that opens early.

On the way to **TOCUMWAL**, which is just under 80km from Corowa, there's a **boomerang factory** at Barooga called the *Binghi Boomerang* (daily 10am–4pm), where you can watch boomerangs being made and test drive them. Tocumwal itself, ("Toc" to locals) is a small pleasant river town: its **Foreshore Park**, just behind the main street, is peaceful and shaded by large gum trees; a sandy river beach is a mere ten minutes' walk further along. In front of the park, there's a rather tacky fibreglass model of a huge Murray Cod, beside which the **Tocumwal Tourist Centre** (daily 9am–5pm; ☎058/74 2131) dispenses local information and can book ultralight instructional flights or rides in a glider, flying over the Murray.

Tocumwal has some classic old **country hotels**, most notably the *Tocumwal Hotel* on Deniliquin Street (☎058/74 2025; ④), a single-storey hotel built in 1861, fronted by palms and an iron-laced verandah with tables to laze at. Next door is *Central Store Antiques*, with good tea rooms at the back for scones, jam and cream or well-priced sandwiches and light meals. The best place to **camp** is the riverfront *Bushlands on the Murray* (☎058/74 2752; on-site vans ③, cabins ④), right on the swimming beach.

## Wentworth and Lake Victoria

Once a thriving river port, **WENTWORTH** is now a sleepy historic town overshadowed by nearby Mildura, 31km back along the Sturt Highway and across the Murray River in Victoria. Located at the junction of the Murray and the Darling, the "two

In March 1997, the **phone code** for **Tocumwal** will change from ☎058 to ☎03/58, and that for the **Wentworth** area will change from ☎050 to ☎03/50.

rivers" town was for seventy years the centre of river trade between New South Wales, Victoria and South Australia. The extension of the railway at the turn of the century by-passed Wentworth, however, and at the same time killed off much of the river trade. Nowadays it makes a pleasant stopover en route to or from Broken Hill, 261km north on the sealed **Silver City Highway**, or a brief excursion from Mildura (in Victoria). Enquire at the **Tourist Information Centre**, Shop 4, Wentworth Place, Adams Street (daily 9am–5pm; ☎050/27 3624), about river cruises on the circa 1914 *MV Loyalty* (or direct on ☎050/27 3330). There's the **Wentworth Gaol** in Beverly Street to visit (daily 10am–5pm; $4.50), built of handmade bricks in 1879, but the interpretative displays consist of bits of curling cardboard and dejected dummies, making it hardly worth the entrance fee. Opposite, **Pioneer World** (daily 10am–5pm; $3.50) is a folk museum exhibiting items related to Aboriginal and European history of the area, and very tacky models of megafauna. You can also take a tour through citrus groves at **Orange World** in Mourquong, back towards Mildura (daily except Fri, 9am–4pm, guided tractor tours 10.30am & 2.30pm, 1hr, $5; ☎050/23 5197).

The Aboriginal land council in Wentworth organizes visits to significant **Aboriginal sites** around Lake Victoria to the west, and Mungo National Park (see below) among the dry salt lakes to the northeast. The tours are run by *Harry Nanya Tours* at Shop 10, Wentworth Place, Sandych Street (☎050/27 2076), and are accompanied by accredited Barkindji guides. Ancient Aboriginal graves were recently discovered at **Lake Victoria** – the Barkindji had always spoken of their existence. In April 1994, the partial draining of the 11,193-hectare lake revealed skeletons buried side by side and in deep layers; some of the estimated ten thousand graves date back six thousand years, in what is believed to be Australia's largest pre-industrial burial site – surpassing any such finds in Europe, Asia or North and South America. The site also challenges the premise that all Aboriginal lifestyles were nomadic, suggesting that here at least they lived in semi-permanent dwellings around the lake.

If you want to stay in Wentworth itself, a wonderful place is *Red Gum Lagoon*, 210 Adams Street (☎050/27 2063; ⑤) whose luxury **apartments** front a gum-lined lagoon, and there's free use of canoes and row boats. Another good waterfront choice is the *Willow Bend Caravan Park* on Darling Street (☎050/27 3213; on-site vans ②, cabins ③), right near the shops but also at the confluence of the Darling and Murray rivers with plenty of trees – watch out for ferocious possums, though. You can get right on the water by hiring a **houseboat** from *Twin Rivers Houseboats* at 1 William Street (☎050/27 3626; $620–1200 per week, sleeping up to 6).

## Mungo National Park

**Mungo National Park**, in the far southwest of New Souths Wales, is most easily reached from the river townships of Wentworth (see above) or Mildura (over the Victorian border, about 110km away – see p.726); organized tours run from both towns. If you want to tackle it on your own, you'll need four-wheel drive. The park is part of the dried-out **Willandra Lakes System**, a UNESCO World Heritage area in recogni-tion of its Aboriginal legacy and record of past climates preserved in the landscape. The Willandra Lakes contain the longest continuous record of Aboriginal life in Australia, dating back more than 40,000 years. During the Ice Ages, between 40,000 and 15,000 years ago, they formed a vast chain of freshwater lakes strung along Willandra Creek, then the main channel of the Lachlan River, flowing into the Murrumbidgee. The waters teemed with fish, attracting waterbirds and mammals to its shores; Aborigines camped at the lake shores, fished and hunted, and buried their dead in the sand dunes. When the lakes started drying out 15,000 years ago, Aborigines continued to live near soaks along the old river channel. The park covers most of one of these dry lake beds, and its dominant feature is a great, crescent-shaped dune (a "lunette"), at the eastern edge of the lake, commonly referred to as the **Walls**

**of China**. Elsewhere, the vegetation consists of saltbush on the lake floors and mallee (a low-growing scrubby type of eucalypt) on the dune fields. Casuarinas grow on the sand plains, and western grey and red kangaroos can sometimes be seen.

The **visitors' centre** by the southwestern entrance to the park (☎050/23 1278) has a very informative display about the geological and Aboriginal history of the national park, and nearby the impressive old **Mungo Woolshed** is open for inspection. From there it's a short drive to the lookout point on the rim of the lake, the former shore, from where you can look across the dry lake bed to the Walls of China. A signposted track takes you on a round trip across the lake floor to the Walls of China, then over the dune and to the northwestern part of the park. At sunset or on nights with a full moon, the scenery takes on an eerie, other-worldly quality.

If you want to **stay** nearby, beds in the former shearers' quarters or at NPWS campsites in the park can be booked in advance through the visitor centre, or *Mungo Lodge* on Arumpo Road (☎050/29 7297; ⑤) has motel units or self-contained cottages as well as a licensed restaurant.

# Back o' Bourke: the Outback

Once you're past Dubbo you're really getting away from the populated coast and towards the red plains that make western New South Wales the quintessential Australian Outback. The searing summer heat makes touring uncomfortable from December to February, and you'd be well advised to visit at a cooler time of year. Bourke, about 370km along the sealed **Mitchell Highway**, is generally considered the turning point; venture further and you're into the the land known as "Back o' Bourke" – the back of beyond. The Mitchell passes through **NYNGAN**, at the geographical centre of New South Wales and 133km from Dubbo, where there's the choice of heading west along the sealed **Barrier Highway** for 584 sweltering kilometres, through Cobar and Wilcannia, to Broken Hill. Flood-prone Nyngan, on the eastern bank of the Bogan River, is a sizeable (compared to what you'll find beyond), old-fashioned country town where you can refuel and freshen up. There's a small shady park on Main Street where you can slump at picnic tables provided, or *Arnold's Take Away*, 133 Main Street, is a spacious café where generous pots of tea help to quench thirst and a ceiling fan manages to circulate a bit of air.

## Bourke

**BOURKE** is mainly known for its very remoteness and this alone is enough to attract tourists; certainly the endless, barely populated plains all around are convincingly desolate. However, the town is also a historic port on the Darling River, the chief means of transport before the roads, and the commercial centre for a vast sheep- and cattle-breeding area. Thanks to irrigation with Darling River water, crops as diverse as cotton, lucerne, citrus and sorghum are successfully grown here despite the 40°C summer heat, while to the north there are rich grazing lands across the Queensland border around Cunnamulla and Charleville. Chiefly, though, the local business is sheep.

The **information centre** is on Anson Street within the train station (☎068/72 2280). **Accommodation** in town includes the pleasant, renovated *Old Royal Hotel* on Mitchell Street (☎068/72 2544; ③–⑤), the *Bourke Riverside Motel*, 3 Mitchell Street (☎068/72 2539; ④) with swimming pool, and the *Back o' Bourke Backpackers*, on the corner of Oxley and Sturt streets (☎068/72 3009; ①) with small dorms and plenty of local information. A better way to see how life is lived out here is to stay on an **Outback station**, such as **Urisino Station**, a mere 230km west of Bourke (☎068/74 7639). If there's work around and it's what you want, you can stay for virtually nothing and get stuck in; otherwise, there's backpacker accommodation in self-contained mudbrick cottages (①) per person) or B&B in the rambling homestead (⑤, or ⑦ including all meals and activities) – and heaps of things to do, such as camel rides, sheep-shearing and guided bushwalks. Four-wheel drive is only essential after rain; if you lack transport, a twice-weekly mail truck heads from Bourke to Wanaaring, 40km east – ask Urisino to arrange a lift and collect you from Wanaaring. The information centre in Bourke has details of other stations that take visitors.

## Cobar

Since copper was discovered in 1869, **COBAR**, just under 160km south of Bourke and the first real stop on the Barrier Highway between Nyngan and Broken Hill, has experienced three mining booms. Today, it's home to the vast **CSA Mine**, said to be the most highly mechanized in Australia, extracting about 850,000 tonnes of copper every year. Earlier booms have left their mark too, in the form of a number of impressive public buildings, among them the 1882 **Court House**, the Police Station and the *Great Western Hotel* in Marshall Street, whose lacework verandahs are said to be the longest in the state. None of which adds up to a very compelling reason to visit – you're here, if at all, to refuel before the long stretch to Wilcannia.

For more about the town, head for the **Cobar Regional Museum** (Mon–Fri 8am–5pm, Sat & Sun 10am–5pm; $3) in Marshall Street, which has interesting exhibits about the history of mining and the people in the area and is also the local **tourist office** (☎068/36 2448). They can tell you about above-ground tours of the CSA mine (Friday afternoons, or by arrangement ☎068/36 2001), and about the region's other claims to fame: an important silver-lead-zinc mine which opened in 1983, a big wool industry, and the channelled water supply that has made Cobar a green oasis in the surrounding semi-arid landscape. Forty kilometres northwest of Cobar (via the Barrier Highway and then a turn-off to the north), near the **Mount Grenfell Homestead**, **Aboriginal cave paintings** of human and animal figures cover the walls of a series of rock shelters. Permission to inspect these should be obtained at the homestead (☎068/36 2692); there are picnic and barbecue areas with a swimming pool nearby.

There are a number of **motels** along the highway in Cobar – two to try, both with air-conditioning and pools, are the *Hiway Motel* (☎068/36 2000; ⑤) and the *Cross Roads Motel*, at the corner of Bourke and Louth roads (☎068/36 2711; ④); alternatively there's the *Cobar Caravan Park* (☎068/36 2425; on-site vans ②, cabins ③).

## Wilcannia and White Cliffs

Two hundred and sixty kilometres west of Cobar, the next major town on the Barrier Highway is **WILCANNIA** (current population about 1000). The former "queen city of the west" was founded in 1864 and towards the end of the nineteenth century was a major port on the Darling River, from where produce was transported by paddle-steamers and barges down the Darling–Murray river system to Adelaide. Droughts, the advent of the railways and the motor car killed the river trade, and today the ruins of the docks and the old lift-up bridge, along with a few impressive public buildings – the post office, courthouse and the Athenaeum Chambers which house the **tourist centre** (☎080/91 5909) – are reminders of the once properous era. Nowadays what's left of Wilcannia survives as a service centre for a far-flung Outback population, and

From March 1997, the **phone code** for the **Broken Hill area** (which includes all phone numbers from here to the end of this chapter) will change from ☎080 to ☎08/80.

includes a *Westpac* **bank** and a **filling station**. You are welcomed into town by the black, red and yellow Aboriginal flag, and there's a sporadically-open Aboriginal arts and crafts shop on the same street as the imposing sandstone police station and courthouse, recognizable by a colourful mural outside.

If you need **somewhere to stay**, try the *Wilcannia Motel* (☎080/91 5802; ⑤) or *Grahams Motel* (☎080/91 5040; B&B ⑤), both on the Barrier Highway. But if you want to experience Outback life, head 85km southeast of Wilcannia along the gravel Cobb Highway to **Yelta Station** (☎080/91 9467) a sheep and cattle property run by Bill and Chris Elliot. There are three kinds of accommodation: camping, fully equipped shearers' quarters (④), or the full works in the house with the family (⑧, including all meals, drinks at night, tours, sheep mustering and other farm activities). Two-wheel drive is fine to get you out here, unless it's been raining when the road is generally closed; they'll also arrange for you to be picked up from Wilcannia, for a small charge.

From Wilcannia, an unsealed road leads north to the opal fields at **WHITE CLIFFS**, about 100km away. White Cliffs is famous largely for the extraordinary summer heat, and for the way in which the miners escape it – many of the 150 or so residents live underground in so-called "dug-outs", where it's cool in summer and warm in winter. There are all sorts of underground attractions, including a motel and an art gallery, as well as a high-tech attempt to exploit the climate in the form of an experimental solar power station. For the authentic local experience, the only place to stay is the *White Cliffs Dug-Out Motel* (free call ☎1800/02 1154; ⑤), which comes complete with licensed restaurant, swimming pool and opal shop. A more straightforward, cheaper option is the *White Cliffs Hotel* (☎080/91 6606; ③).

The only fuel stop between Wilcannia and Broken Hill is the *Little Topar Hotel*, roughly halfway along the 195km.

# Broken Hill

The ghosts of mining towns that died when the precious minerals ran out are scattered all over Australia. **BROKEN HILL**, on the other hand, celebrated its centenary in 1988, and its famous "**Line of Lode**", one of the world's major lead-silver-zinc ore bodies and the city's raison d'être, still has a little life left in it after being mined continuously for 110 years. Inevitably, Broken Hill revolves around the mines, but in the last decade it has also evolved into a thriving arts centre, thanks to the initiative of the **Brushmen of the Bush**, a painting school founded by local artists Pro Hart, Hugh Schulz, Jack Absalom, Eric Minchin and John Pickup. Diverse talents have been attracted to Broken Hill, and their works displayed in galleries scattered all over town. Some may be a bit on the tacky side, but others are interesting, unique, even excellent, and it's well worth devoting some time to gallery-browsing.

Almost 1200km west of Sydney, and with about 500km still to go to Adelaide, this surprisingly gracious Outback mining town, with a feel and architecture reminiscent of the South Australian capital, and a population of around 24,000, manages to create a welcome splash of **green** in the harsh desert landscape that surrounds it. Extensive revegetation schemes around Broken Hill have created grass- and park-lands that, apart from being visually pleasing, contain the dust that used to make the residents' lives miserable. It's helped by a reliable water supply – secured for the first time only in 1953 – via a 100km-long pipeline from the Darling River at Menindee.

Remember to change your watch: Broken Hill operates on South Australian **Central Standard Time**, half an hour behind the rest of NSW. When it's noon in Sydney, it's 11.30am in Broken Hill and Adelaide. All local transport schedules are in CST, but you should always check.

# The Town

Green it may be, but the huge slag heap towering over the city centre leaves you in no doubt that, above all, this is still a mining town. Even the streets – laid out in a grid – are mostly named after minerals: Argent Street (from the Latin for silver) is Broken Hill's main drag, with the highest concentration of historic buildings and interest; parallel to either side are Crystal Street, with the train station, and Blende Street, while at right angles across the centre run Bromide, Sulphide, Chloride and Oxide streets. The **Tourist Information Centre** is at the corner of Bromide and Blende streets (daily 8.30am–5pm; ☎080/87 6077) and it's very useful, with a interesting historical interpretative section too. Their self-guided Heritage Walk ($2 for map) along Argent and Blende streets or historic walking tour you can join (Wed, Fri & Sun 10am; 1hr 30min) will give you an idea of what there is to see in the centre. An unexpected sight is the **Afghan Mosque** on the corner of William and Buck streets, on the site of the former camel camp where Afghan and Indian camel drivers loaded and unloaded their camel teams; you can inspect it Sundays at 2.30pm.

## Mines and minerals

One thing you shouldn't miss in Broken Hill is an underground mine tour. You can do it right in town at **Delprat's mine**, or further out at the **Daydream Mine**. At Delprat's (tours Mon–Fri 10.30am, Sat 2pm, more on holidays; 2hr; $18), you don a miner's hat, boots and a heavy belt with batteries for your helmet light, before descending, jammed with thirty or so others in the miners' cage, 130m below the surface. Here, ex-miners working as guides will take you on a tour through the system of tunnels ("stopes") while describing and demonstrating how miners used to work in the bad old days, and how the work is done now. It's a good tour, and the guides, as their colourful miners' lingo betrays, are mostly the real thing, with stories to tell about life in "The Hill" and down the mines. The Daydream Mine (10am–3pm, tours on demand; 1hr; $10) is 20km out of Broken Hill on the Silverton Road – turn right at the sign and follow the 13km dirt road; tours here are similar, but half as long and a little tamer. Both tours can be booked through the tourist office, who can also arrange transport.

If you can't face going underground, a visit to the bizarre but wonderful **White's Mineral Art Gallery and Mining Museum**, 1 Allendale Street (off Silverton Rd; daily 9am–6pm; $5), is the next best thing. The art section is pretty extraordinary, consisting mainly of collages of crushed minerals depicting Broken Hill scenes – mining, historical buildings and the Outback. And at the back there's a walk-in underground mine, recreated so convincingly that it genuinely looks and feels like the real thing: inside, you're given an entertaining lecture, with videos and models, on the history of Broken Hill and its mines. Back at the front, a shop sells minerals, opals, jewellery and pottery.

Another mine-related exhibit is the **Railway, Mineral and Train Museum** opposite the tourist centre (daily 10am–3pm; $2), which features an extensive mineral collection as well as old railway machinery and memorabilia. Finally, the **Geocentre** on the corner of Bromide and Crystal streets (daily 1–5pm; $3), in a nineteenth-century bond store, looks at Broken Hill's geology, minerology and metallurgy; unless you're a real geology freak, the most exciting exhibit is the one entitled "The Mineral Streets of Broken Hill" with a street map which lights up as you press buttons set underneath bits of different minerals – so you can highlight Uranium, Beryl, Chloride, Slag and Boron Street, to name a few. Out the back is an example of a tin miner's shed – you can just imagine what the heat must have been like in summer.

## Art and the Outback

There's not only indoor art in galleries in Broken Hill; the town is full of public murals and outdoor sculpture. Pick up a *Broken Hill Art Trail* fold-out poster ($2) from the tourist office, with colour photgraphs and maps.

## MINING AND UNIONISM IN BROKEN HILL

The story of Broken Hill began in 1883 when a German-born boundary rider from Mount Gipps station, Charles Rasp, pegged out a forty-acre lease of a "broken hill" that he believed was tin. A syndicate of seven was formed and the **Broken Hill Proprietary** (BHP) was founded to work what turned out to be rich silver, lead and zinc deposits. Since then, the Broken Hill mines have contributed greatly to the wealth of Australia: the deposit, more than seven kilometres long and up to 250 metres wide, is thought originally to have contained more than 300 million tonnes of sulphide-rich ore. Even now there's said to be fifteen to twenty years left in the "Line of Lode", though only one mine is currently working it.

In the early years, living and working **conditions** for the miners were atrocious. The climate was harsh, housing was poor and diseases such as typhoid, scarlet fever and dysentery – to say nothing of work-related illnesses like lead poisoning, and mine accidents – caused a death rate almost twice as high as the NSW average. The mine and the growing town rapidly stripped the landscape of timber, leaving the settlement surrounded by a vast, bleak plain. Dust storms were common. Not surprisingly, perhaps, Broken Hill was at the forefront of **trade union** development in Australia, as the miners, many of them recent immigrants, fought to improve their living and working conditions. It was their ability to unite that ultimately won them their battles, above all in the Big Strike of 1919–20, when after eighteen months of holding out against the police and strikebreakers, major concessions were won from BHP. Not that the trade union movement at Broken Hill should be viewed through too rosy glasses. The union, which, once accepted, effectively ran the town in conjunction with the mine companies, was also a bastion of racism and male supremacy. Non-white persons were not tolerated in town, nor were working women who happened to be married. Even now, these attitudes have not altogether disappeared.

Despite the life left in Broken Hill's mineral deposits, the future is none too certain. With modern mining technology the ore is removed faster, and the numbers employed are lower. Between 1970 and 1975, about 4000 people were employed in the mines. By the early 1980s this number had been reduced to 2500, and in 1993 the workforce consisted of a mere 800. The spectre of permanent unemployment haunts the city, and many people are leaving in search of work opportunities elsewhere.

Broken Hill's artistic side is perhaps best expressed at the **Broken Hill City Art Gallery** (Mon–Fri 10am–5pm, Sat & Sun 1–5pm; $2; guided tours Mon–Fri 11am), in the Entertainment Centre in Chloride Street, where there's an excellent representative collection of Broken Hill artists. Established in 1904, it's the second oldest gallery in the state – after the Art Gallery of New South Wales in Sydney – and therefore has a small collection of nineteenth- and early twentieth-century paintings. It's the recent work that's interesting, though, including a Sidney Nolan and a John Olsen, as well as the works of the "Brushmen of the Bush". Look out, too, for the spectacular **Silver Tree**, a 68cm-high figurine, wrought of pure silver from the Broken Hill Mines, depicting five Aborigines, a drover on horseback, kangaroos, emus and sheep gathered under a tree.

**Pro Hart's Gallery**, at 108 Wyman Street (Mon–Sat 9am–12.30pm & 1.30–5pm, Sun 1.30–5pm; $2), should be next on your list. Pro Hart is a former Broken Hill miner turned artist and national celebrity who claims the only artistic influence he had was studying the colours and subjects of his family's sheep station as a child, and illustrating his correspondence lessons. His trademark humorous Outback scenes – race meetings, backyard barbecues – of lively figures in a caricature style make him into a sort of Australian Brueghel, with all sorts of antics going on in a large scene. His gallery is said to hold the largest private art collection in Australia. The three cramped levels are certainly packed, with a truly astounding collection of the artist's own work as well as works by other Australian painters – Tom Roberts, Sidney Nolan, William Dobell, Donald Friend, Fred Williams, Charles Blackman and Albert Namatjira among them – not necessarily their best works, though. A collection of his sculpture pieces are in a lot across the road – you can check them out for free. Also in the city centre are the **Ant Hill Gallery**, at 24 Bromide Street (Mon–Fri 9am–5pm, Sun 1.30–5pm), and the **Art of Broken Hill Gallery**, at 219 Argent Street (Mon–Fri 10am–6pm, Sat 10am–1pm, Sun 1–5pm); both display a variety of local artists' works, and the *Ant Hill Gallery* is the only place in Broken Hill where you can buy Pro Hart's paintings.

One of the most worthwhile craft places to visit is **Wimpatja Wana Aboriginal Crafts**, 84 Oxide St (Mon–Fri 9am–5pm; ☎080/87 7413), with a workshop out the back where you can watch the artists at work between 9am and 3.30pm making traditional wooden tools, weapons and musical instruments. Wood is gathered (not felled) from as far afield as Wilcannia, and each type has a specific purpose: didgeridoos are made from sections of mallee gums eaten hollow by termites, clapping sticks and nulla nullas are made from mulga, bowls from burls of river red gums, small mulga roots from riverbanks make good carved snakes, and prickly wattle or "purple wood" is used in brooches.

But the most stunning and original art exhibit is in the desert itself, 6km out of town in **The Living Desert**, a reserve in the eroded Barrier Ranges desert region that is the location for an arrangement of sculptures carved from Wilcannia sandstone boulders. The twelve artists involved in its creation were drawn from diverse cultures – two from Mexico including one Aztec Indian, two from Syria, three from Georgia (in the Caucasus), and five Australians including two Bathurst Islanders – and this is reflected in the variety of their works. The pieces from the Georgian artists are particularly fine: Badri Sulushia has created an Outback Madonna and Child, with beautifully flowing lines, an achingly graceful hand and a face reminiscent of a Botticelli; Jumber Jikiya has hewn a horse's head as a tribute to the rare breed of Georgian horses which were slaughtered on Stalin's orders; and a cubist interpretation by Valerian Jiiya. The Aboriginal artist Badger Bates, from Broken Hill, was inspired by the stone carvings of his ancestors, and his piece shows two rainbow serpents travelling north. Eduardo Nastra Luna of Mexico badly injured his hands and his work became a collective effort, depicting a soaring eagle and with the hands of the sculptors who helped him imprinted in the rock. The best time to come is at sunset when the light is magical and you can really soak up the atmosphere.

On a very different note, Broken Hill also offers an excellent opportunity to visit two Australian Outback institutions, the **Royal Flying Doctor Service** (RFDS) and the **School of the Air**. The RFDS, at Broken Hill Airport, offer guided tours of their operation (Mon–Fri 10.30am & 3.30pm, Sat & Sun 10.30am, with extra sessions during school holidays; bookings at the tourist office or direct on ☎080/88 0777; $3). You're shown a video on the history and work of the Flying Doctors, followed by a tour through the headquarters, past the radio room where calls from remote places in New South Wales, South Australia and Queensland are handled, to the hangar to see the aircraft. The increasing popularity of the tours is due to the Australian television series *The Flying Doctors* which is shown worldwide. At the **School of the Air**, lessons are conducted via two-way radio for children in the Outback in a transmission area of 1.8 million square kilometres. The service was established in 1956 to improve education for isolated Outback kids: if you want to listen to the first hour's transmission in a schoolroom surrounded by the kids' artwork, plus watch an informative 15min video, you have to be there and seated by 8.30am (Mon–Fri, termtime only; book in advance at the tourist office; $2). It's frighteningly like being back at school yourself, with jolly primary school teachers hosting singalongs; what comes out of the radio is a static squawk, but the far-flung kids seem to enjoy it.

# Practicalities

Arriving in Broken Hill by bus or train, you'll be pretty centrally placed. The **bus terminal** (☎080/88 4040, or for 24-hr reservations ☎13 2030) is behind the **tourist office** at the corner of Bromide and Blende streets. The **train station** is on Crystal Street, just a block below Argent Street – though unless you're travelling in style on the Sydney–Perth *Indian Pacific*, you'll actually pull in on a *CountryLink* bus. In addition to what's on offer at the tourist office, you can pick up advice on nearby attractions from the district **NPWS** office at 5 Oxide Street (Mon–Fri 8am–4.30pm; ☎080/88 5933).

## Accommodation

**Astra House Backpackers**, 393 Argent St (☎080/87 7788). Friendly rambling hostel in an old pub; rooms are a much better bet than the spartan dorms. Small kitchen and TV room, plus a large balcony where you can sit and stare down onto the main street. Trips to the Sculpture Site, Silverton, Mundi Mundi, and longer trips to Outback stations organized. Rooms ②–③, dorms ①.

**Grand Hotel**, 317 Argent St (☎080/87 5305). Upmarket pub accommodation, with air-con and breakfast. ⑤.

**Lake View Caravan Park**, 1 Mann St, 3km northeast (☎080/88 2250). Big site with swimming pool. On-site vans ②, cabins ③–④.

**Old Vic Guesthouse**, 230 Oxide St (☎080/87 1169). Comfortable and central guesthouse in a great old homestead with wide verandahs. ⑤.

**Royal Exchange Hotel**, 320 Argent St (☎080/87 2308). Old pub, some rooms with en-suite facilities, but mostly normal pub accommodation. B&B ④.

**Silver Spade**, 151 Argent St (☎080/87 7021). Motel with swimming pool and air-con. ⑤.

**Theatre Royal Hotel**, 347 Argent St (☎080/87 3318). Historic pub with simple rooms, most air-conditioned. ③.

**Tourist Lodge**, 100 Argent St (☎080/88 2086). Friendly clean guesthouse and YHA-affiliated hostel near the tourist office and bus terminal with the added bonus of a solar-heated swimming pool and bike rental at bargain rates. Rooms ③, dorms ①.

**Wompinie Station**, 80km west, in South Australia (☎080/87 6956). A great way to experience the Outback on this sheep property: you can stay with the family in the homestead or in shearers' quarters. Room rates, including all meals and tour of station ⑦, share accommodation ②.

## Food, drink and nightlife

Broken Hill still has the proverbial **pub** on every corner – most of them serve inexpensive counter meals as well as having icy-cold beer on tap. Broken Hill has always been a legendary drinking hole with over seventy hotels having operated in the town. Many have been converted to other uses, but at the time of writing there were still 34 hotels licensed to operate and a pub crawl is highly recommended. Some places to include might be the *West Darling Historic Hotel* on the corner of Argent and Oxide streets with funk on Fridays from midnight; the *Black Lion Inn* on the corner of Blende and Bromide streets, good anytime; the *Royal Exchange Hotel* on the corner of Thomas Street and Horsington Avenue is open until after midnight every night; and the *Theatre Royal Hotel* is also a lively boozer.

Another option is to sample the local culture at one of the numerous **clubs**. These make most of their money out of gambling – with snooker tables, darts and endless parades of one-armed bandits – and they're happy to draw their customers in and keep them playing by tempting them with cheap food, and quite often live entertainment too. Best known of them is the *Demo Club* (the *Barrier Social Democratic Club*) at 218 Argent Street (counter lunches Mon–Fri, bistro meals daily; great inexpensive breakfasts 6am–9am; ☎080/88 4477), which now has Broken Hill's famous **Two Up School**, once an illegal back-lane gambling operation. You could also try the *Broken Hill Legion Club*, 166–170 Crystal Street (counter meals daily, dinner at *J.J.'s* restaurant Mon–Sat;

☎080/87 4064), the *RSL Club*, 2 Chloride Street (☎080/87 2653), and the *Broken Hill Musicians Club*, 276 Crystal Street (bistro meals daily; ☎080/88 1777).

Apart from the pubs and clubs, there are several good **cafés and bakeries** on Argent Street where you can get something to eat and drink – restaurants aren't really Broken Hill's style. *Food Affair* at no. 360 is a friendly sit-in bakery; the *Heritage Coffee Shop* at no. 295 Argent Street, with a gallery upstairs; and both *Ruby's Coffee Lounge*, on the corner of Oxide Street and *Charlotte's* at no. 317, opposite the post office, are recommended.

## Listings

**Airlines** *Hazelton Airlines* (Sydney daily and to other NSW and Queensland destinations) and *Kendell Airlines* (Melbourne and Adelaide) through *Traveland* at 350 Argent Street (☎080/87 1969); *Southern Australia Airlines* to Melbourne, Adelaide and Mildura (☎050/22 2444).

**Bike rental** ☎080/88 5110.

**Books** *ABC Centre*, 309 Argent St (☎080/88 1177), specialists in local history and the Outback. *Blue Duck Books*, 51 Oxide St, for secondhand tapes and books with exchange possible. There's a good literary choice as well as the fat popular paperbacks and a small Australiana section; Mon–Fri 9am–4pm, Sat 9am–1pm.

**Car rental** *Budget*, corner of Argent and Bromide streets, ☎080/87 2210; *Hertz*, at the visitor centre, ☎1800/87 2719; *Holmes' Hire*, 475 Argent St, ☎080/87 2210; or *SCV 4 Wheel Hire*, 320 Beryl St, ☎080/87 3266, for landcruisers with UHF radio, ice box, water bottle and shovel.

**Cinema** *Village Silver City Cinema*, 41 Oxide St (☎080/87 4569).

**Hospital** Broken Hill Base Hospital and Health Services, 174 Thomas St (☎080/88 0333).

**Late night grocery** *International Store*, 71 Oxide St (daily 7am–midnight).

**Laundry** *Oxide Street Laundromat*, 241 Oxide St (☎080/88 2022), service washes available, with free pick-up and delivery; *Coin Operated Laundromat*, 400a Argent St (daily 7am–10pm).

**Pharmacy** *Amcal Chemist*, Galena St (☎080/88 4800, after-hours emergency ☎080/88 5639).

**Phone numbers** From March 1997, the phone code for the Broken Hill area will change from ☎080 to ☎08/80.

**Taxis** *City Radio Cabs*, 20 Oxide St (☎080/88 1144); or *Radio Taxis*, 337 Crystal Lane (☎080/13 1008).

> From March 1997, the **phone code** for the **Broken Hill area** (which includes all phone numbers up to the end of this chapter) will change from ☎080 to ☎08/80.

# Excursions from Broken Hill: Silverton

The ghost town of **SILVERTON**, just 25km northwest of Broken Hill on a good road, makes a great day out. Take note that there is no fuel available at Silverton. If the scene looks vaguely familiar, you probably have seen it before: parts of *Mad Max II* were shot around here, and the **Silverton Hotel** (daily 8.30am–9.30pm, though they often close early) has appeared as the "Gamulla Hotel" in *Razorback,* the "Hotel Australia" in *A Town Like Alice*, and the latest addition, "Juanita's Diner" in *Fiddlers Green* with Don Johnson. It also seems to star in just about every commercial that features an Outback scene. The stark impact of the pub, with barren, red earth stretching forever to the horizon, has been somewhat diminished by the greening of the desert, but it's still the ultimate Outback image and a must for every photo collection. The pub has its own collection, the lower walls covered with snapshots from the various film shoots; the upper walls piled high with an assortment of beer cans and old bottles. In some ways it feels like a milk bar, with a fridge full of cold soft drinks, a tea urn, and the only food available some limp sandwiches, pies and pasties.

## TOURS FROM BROKEN HILL

### Air charters and scenic flights

If you have a bit of cash to spare, small aircraft are an excellent way of getting around, covering the enormous distances quickly and in relative comfort.

**Crittenden Air**, Airport Terminal (☎080/88 5702). Tour flights to Tibooburra ($265), Outback stations ($160), White Cliffs ($190) as well as several more local scenic tours. Bush mail-run including lunch and tour of White Cliffs leaves 6.30am Sat ($220).

### Bus tours

These tend to be overpriced, given that they merely provide transport to places that could well be more enjoyably visited with a rental car or bike, or even by taxi. Departures are generally once a week, or are dependent on demand.

**Arnolds Tourist Bus Service** (☎080/87 7701 or via tourist office). Half-day tours to Silverton, History of Broken Hill, Daydream Mine; day-tours to Kinchega National Park and White Cliffs.

**Silver City Tours** (☎080/87 6956 or via tourist office). Half-day tours of city mines, Delprat's Underground Tour, RFDS, School of the Air, Silverton, Daydream Mine; day tours to White Cliffs, Mootwingee National Park, Menindee Lakes and Tandou Irrigation Farm.

### Four-wheel-drive tours

**Alf's Outback Tours**, enquiries and booking at the tourist office (☎080/87 6077, after hours 87 8108). Overnight camping tours to national parks including Kinchega and Mootwingee ($220) and extended three-day to Tibooburra and around ($330).

**Broken Hill Outback Tours and Corner Country Adventures** (☎080/87 5305). $45 day-tours Tues & Fri to Silverton, through the Mundi Mundi Plains and past sheep and cattle stations, with most of the time spent in the vehicle. Also longer 4WD trips including a four-day/three-night trip to all four national parks for $615.

**Goanna Safari** (*Astra House Backpackers* ☎080/87 7788 or *Westward Downs* ☎080/91 2518). Three-day tours to Westward Downs, a remote sheep station 180km north of Broken Hill on demand ($350); one night at Westward Downs, second day exploring the area and camping overnight, third day return to Broken Hill via the Dog Fence and Silverton. Short trips to the Sculpture Site ($5), Silverton and Mundi Mundi ($15) and day-trips to White Cliffs ($80) and Mutawintji ($60).

Taking the **Silverton Heritage Trail**, a two-hour stroll around town marked by white arrows, is a good way to work up a thirst. But really it's far too hot to attempt it in the summer, and best undertaken during the cooler months. Along the way it'll take you past the tourist information centre in the old **Silverton School Craft Centre**, and the 1889 vintage **Silverton Gaol Museum** (daily 9.30am–4.30pm; $2), with the usual collection of relics from pioneer days and Outback stations, plus mining equipment. There's a burgeoning art scene here too, with four galleries to browse through. **Peter Browne's Gallery** (9am–5pm daily) in a 1884 house on a hill, is worth a look for its uniquely original decoration and the humorous paintings of bush scenes, shearing koalas, kookaburras boiling the billy, and his trademark emus with huge, saucer-shaped eyes. Also interesting is Albert Woodcroffe's and Bronwen Standley's **Horizon Gallery** (daily 9am–5.30pm), opposite the pub. The husband and wife team paint in a similiar style, creating trademark lengthy, finely detailed horizon paintings, mainly in acrylics, that really capture the sense of space and the seemingly endless skyline.

One of the best things to do while in Silverton is to go on a camel tour. The Cannard brothers, Harold and Grahame, who run **Silverton Camel Farm** (☎080/88 5316), are an essential ingredient in Silverton's unique atmosphere. With forty working camels, the pair of real Aussie characters come from a long line of camel trainers. The Cannards do everything for the camels including making the leather saddles, breaking them in, and pegging their noses. You can't miss the camel farm on the way into Silverton, with the shapes of camels looming like desert mirages. You can exercise a whim and hop on for 15 minutes ($5), or trot for an hour along the nearby creek ($20), but the best experience is the $40 sunset trek; a two-hour ride to watch the sun drop over the Mundi Mundi Plain and travel back under the night stars with entertaining company and a pack of lively dogs.

Beyond Silverton, the road continues a further 14km to the **Umberumberka reservoir**, Broken Hill's only source of water until the Menindee Lakes Scheme came on stream. There's a signposted lookout area which makes a nice spot for a picnic. A few kilometres further on you reach the **Mundi Mundi Plains Lookout**. Here, the undulating plateau you have been driving across descends gradually to a vast plain, and on clear days you can see the blurred outline of the northern Flinders Ranges in South Australia in the distance. This is where, at the end of *Mad Max II*, Mel Gibson tipped the semi-trailer.

If you want to stay in Silverton, your only choice is to **camp** at Penrose Park, where there's a shower, toilets and barbecue; rates are nominal – ask at the house there.

## Kinchega National Park and Menindee Lakes

Flat **Kinchega National Park** is situated among the **Menindee Lakes** near the township of **MENINDEE**, southeast of Broken Hill. There's sealed road for the 110km from Broken Hill to Menindee and the park entrance, gravel roads thereafter; the park ranger's number is ☎080/91 4214. The Menindee Lakes are a widespread, natural oasis, feeding the Darling and Murray rivers and, most importantly, supplying water to Broken Hill; they're also a big recreation area, with facilities for for camping, power-boating, water-skiing, sailing, swimming and fishing. The waters protected in the Kinchega National Park, **Menindee Lake** and **Cawndilla Lake**, are a haven for water-birds. There's a visitor **information** centre about 15km into the park, and an information shelter 10km before that: river campsites are scattered through the river-red-gum woodland along the river, and also on the shores of Lake Cawndilla. Burke and Wills stayed at the *Maidens Hotel* (☎080/91 4880; ④–⑤) in Menindee on their ill-fated trip north in 1860 (see box on p.389); it still operates, or you can stay at the *Burke & Wills Motel*, Yartla Street, Menindee (☎080/91 4313; ④), or camp in more comfort than is on offer in the park at *Menindee Lakes Caravan Park* on Lakes Shore Road, 5km northwest of Menindee (☎080/91 4315; on-site vans ②), with a kiosk and grocery shop.

## Mootwingee National Park

**Mootwingee National Park**, 130km northeast of Broken Hill in the Bynguano Ranges, has totally different and perhaps even more fascinating scenery to offer: secluded gorges and quiet waterholes that attract a lot of wildlife. The main attractions of the park are the ancient galleries of **Aboriginal rock art** in the caves and overhangs; you can only visit these accompanied by an an Aboriginal tour guide or ranger (☎080/91 2587 for details and costs) – note there are no tours in the hot summer months. While on the tour you get to visit the **Mootwingee Cultural Resource Centre**, with brightly painted murals depicting Aboriginal myths. There's a **camping** area at *Homestead Creek* among river red gums at the entrance to Homestead Gorge and a number of **walking trails** (including the short wheelchair-accessible Thakaaltjika Mingkana Walk). Access to and within the park is via unsealed gravel roads, and make sure you bring extra fuel as none is available here. It's normally fine for two-wheel-drive vehicles, but check locally, as the roads can quickly become impassable after even light rain; bring extra food just in case. The NPWS office in Broken Hill should know the latest, and they can also provide camping **permits** and other information.

## Tibooburra and the Sturt National Park

A remote Outback settlement in the far northwestern corner of New South Wales, 337km from Broken Hill, **TIBOOBURRA** can be reached by normal vehicle on a well-maintained dirt road from Broken Hill – the Silver City Highway. You can also reach it from Bourke, 454km southwest along various unsealed and mostly deserted roads. After rain, roads may become impassable, and although it's important to find out about road conditions and weather conditions before you set out, it's also crucial to take extra food, water, fuel and vehicle spares in case you get stranded later on. Refer to the the tourist information offices in either town for advice. It's been settled for over a hundred years, with stone buildings from the 1880s giving it some charm. The nearby granite outcrops, worthy of a sunset stroll, gave the town its former name of The Granites. In the nearby **Sturt National Park**, a network of roads and tracks is also maintained by the NPWS to two-wheel-drive standard, but check with the rangers at Tibooburra before setting out (☎080/91 3308; also for camping permits). The park's 3500 square kilometres are cut in two by the Grey Range: to the west are the rolling red sand dunes of the Strezlecki Desert, to the east the stone-covered, so-called gibber plains extend for hundreds of miles. The area supports a number of red and grey kangaroos, emus and lizards.

At the edge of the park, the border between Queensland, New South Wales and South Australia is delineated by the **Great Dingo Fence**. This, the world's longest fence, was originally constructed by the Queensland government to stop the invasion of rabbits from the south; it's now maintained to keep dingoes out of sheep-grazing land. The point where the three states meet is known as **Cameron's Corner**, and is marked by a post: it's a popular target for travellers, so much so that there's even a shop here, the *Corner Store*, of course. As well as dishing up the ubiquitous meat pie and other typical Aussie fillers, they dispense fuel and useful road advice.

There are a couple of pleasant **hotels**, with welcome air-conditioning, on Briscoe Street in Tibooburra: the *Family Hotel* (☎080/91 3314; ④) is marginally the fancier with a wall mural by Australian artist Clifton Pugh, and some en suite rooms, while the *Tibooburra Hotel* (☎080/91 3310; ③–④) vies for attention with its wall full of old hats. Both also serve decent counter meals. *The Granites Caravan Park*, at the corner of Brown and King streets (☎080/91 3305; on-site vans ②, cabins ③), has a refreshing pool.

## travel details

Most public transport in NSW originates in Sydney, and the main services are outlined in the "Travel Details" at the end of *Chapter One*.

### Trains

There are nine main train routes departing from Sydney that pass through the region covered in this chapter; all trains connect with *Countrylink* buses run by the state rail system to fill in the gaps. Destinations within the area of this chapter are printed in bold type below.

- Sydney–**Albury** (1 daily; 7hr 20min), via **Cootamundra** (5hr) and **Wagga Wagga** (6hr).

- Sydney–**Armidale** (1 daily; 7hr 45min), via **Tamworth** (5hr 40min).

- Sydney–**Brisbane** (1 daily; 13hr 30min), with stops at **Taree**, **Coffs Harbour** and **Grafton**.

- Sydney–**Canberra** (1 daily; 4hr), via **Goulburn** (2hr 30min).

- Sydney–**Dubbo** (1 daily; 6hr 30min), via **Bathurst** (3hr 30min).

- Sydney–Melbourne (1 daily; 12hr), with stops at **Cootamundra** and **Wagga Wagga.**

- Sydney–**Moree** (1 daily; 8hr 40min), via **Scone** (2hr 55min), **Gunnedah** (6hr 5min) and **Narrabri** (7hr 15min).

- Sydney–**Murwillumbah** (1 daily; 13hr 30min), via **Taree**, **Coffs Harbour**, **Grafton**, **Lismore** and **Byron Bay**.

● The NSW leg of the *Indian Pacific* linking
Sydney and Perth takes in **Condoblin** (10hr
35min from Sydney), **Ivanhoe** (13hr 50min),
**Menindee** (16hr 10min) and **Broken Hill** (18hr
20min).

## Buses

**Albury** to: Corowa (3 a week; 1hr); Cowra (1
daily; 4hr); Echuca (3 a week; 4hr 15min).

**Armidale** to: Brisbane (6 daily; 7hr 45min);
Melbourne (2 daily; 18hr 45min); Sydney (4 daily;
8hr); Tenterfield (2 daily; 2hr 20min); Tamworth (3
daily; 1hr 45min).

**Broken Hill** to: Adelaide (2 daily; 7hr); Cobar (3
daily; 5hr 30min); Dubbo (5 daily; 8hr 30min);
Mildura (3 a week; 4hr); Sydney (2 daily; 16hr).

**Bourke** to: Dubbo (3 a week; 4hr 45min).

**Byron Bay** to: Ballina (3–8 daily; 25min);
Brisbane (10–11 daily; 2hr 20min); Coffs Harbour
(6 daily; 5hr); Surfers Paradise (6–7 daily; 1hr
5min); Sydney (6 daily; 12hr 15min).

**Canberra** to: Bairnsdale (3 a week; 7hr);
Batemans Bay (1–2 daily; 2hr 40min); Bega (1
daily; 3hr 30min); Bombala (3 a week; 3hr 30min);
Cooma (1–2 daily; 1hr 50min); Eden (1 daily; 4hr
20min); Melbourne (6 daily; 8hr 30min); Narooma
(1–2 daily; 4hr 30min); Nowra (1 daily; 4hr
45min); Wagga Wagga (1 daily; 4hr); Wollongong
(1 daily; 4hr 45min).

**Coffs Harbour** to: Byron Bay (6 daily; 3hr 40min);
Grafton (5 daily; 1hr 10min); Nambucca Heads (6
daily; 50min); Tweed Heads (1 daily; 6hr 10min).

**Coonabarabran** to: Adelaide (3 daily; 12hr);
Brisbane (4 daily; 19hr); Canberra (3 daily; 5hr
40min); Melbourne (5 daily; 7hr 30min); Sydney
(5–6 daily; 8hr 30min–10hr).

**Cootamundra** to: Dubbo (3 a week; 4hr 15min);
Gundagai (6 a week; 45min); Tumbarumba (6 a
week; 2hr 45min).

**Dubbo** to: Bathurst (2 daily; 2hr 45min); Bourke (3
a week; 4hr 45min); Brewarrina (3 a week; 5hr
45min); Broken Hill (5 daily; 8hr 30min); Canberra
(4 a week; 6hr 10min); Cobar (3 daily; 3hr 30min);
Coonabarabran (3–5 daily; 1hr 50min);
Cootamundra (3 a week; 4hr 15min); Cowra (1–2
daily; 3hr 20min); Griffith (2 daily; 4hr 45min);
Lightning Ridge (1 daily; 4hr 50min); Moree (3
daily; 4hr 20min); Orange (2 daily; 2hr 40min);
Tamworth (3–5 daily; 4hr); Wagga Wagga (2
daily; 6hr).

**Griffith** to: Canberra (1 daily; 6hr 15min);
Cootamundra (1 daily; 2hr 35min); Hay (1 daily;
3hr 50min); Leeton (1–2 daily; 50min); Narrandera
(1–2 daily; 1hr 15min); Wagga Wagga (1–2 daily;
2hr 40min).

**Lismore** to: Ballina (1–3 daily; 45min); Brisbane
(3–5 daily; 3hr); Byron Bay (4–6 daily; 1hr 15min);
Casino (2 daily; 25min); Murwillumbah (3–5 daily;
2hr); Nimbin (2–3 daily; 25min); Tweed Heads (3–
5 daily; 2hr 45min).

**Lithgow** to: Bathurst (3–6 daily; 1hr);
Coonabarabran (6 a week; 5hr 30min); Cowra (6 a
week; 2hr 40min); Dubbo (6 a week; 4hr 30min);
Mudgee (1 daily; 2hr 30min); Orange (2–5 daily;
1hr 45min–2hr).

**Newcastle** to: Cessnock (3–6 daily; 45min);
Forster–Toncurry (1–2 daily; 2hr 30min); Port
Stephens (10 daily; 1hr).

**Port Macquarie** to: Armidale (3 a week; 6hr
10min); Ballina (5 daily; 6hr); Bellingen (3 a week;
3hr 15min); Brisbane (5 daily; 10hr 30min); Coffs
Harbour (5–6 daily; 2hr 40min); Dorrigo (3 a week;
3hr 50min); Grafton (5 daily; 4hr 10min); Surfers
Paradise (5 daily; 9hr).

**Tamworth** to: Cessnock (1 daily; 4hr); Dorrigo (3
a week; 4hr 10min); Gunnedah (2 daily; 1hr);
Inverell (1 daily; 3hr 40min); Port Macquarie (3 a
week; 8hr 30min); Scone (2 daily; 2hr 15min);
Tenterfield (2 daily; 4hr 30min).

## Flights

**Armidale** to: Brisbane (1–2 daily; 1hr 10min);
Coolangatta (3 a week; 50min); Sydney (1–3
daily; 1hr 10min).

**Ballina** to: Brisbane (1–3 daily; 45min); Sydney
(3 daily; 1hr 10min).

**Broken Hill** to: Adelaide (1–4 daily; 1hr 40min);
Dubbo (6 a week; 2hr); Sydney (2–4 daily; 3hr
45min); Mildura (6 a week; 1hr 30min).

**Canberra** to: Ballina (2–3 daily; 4hr 40min); Coffs
Harbour (4–6 daily; 3hr 20min); Dubbo (1–2 daily;
2hr 15min); Grafton (1–2 daily; 2hr 30min);
Lismore (1–4 daily; 4hr 10min); Moree (1–2 daily;
3hr 55min); Narrabri (1–2 daily; 3hr 15min);
Newcastle (3–4 daily; 2hr 10min); Port Macquarie
(3–9 daily; 2hr 25min); Sydney (6–25 daily; 2hr
35min); Tamworth (4–8 daily; 2hr 25min).

**Coffs Harbour** to: Brisbane (2 daily; 45min);
Sydney (3–5 daily; 55min).

**Lismore** to: Brisbane (2–3 daily; 25min); Sydney (5–8 daily; 1hr 50min).

**Port Macquarie** to: Brisbane (3–6 daily; 1hr); Coffs Harbour (2–3 daily; 25min); Sydney (6 daily; 55min).

**Tamworth** to: Brisbane (4–12 daily; 2hr 20min); Cobar (8 weekly; 1hr); Melbourne (2–3 daily; 3hr 20min); Mildura (6 a week; 1hr 30min); Sydney (3–8 daily; 1hr).

# CHAPTER THREE

# SOUTHEAST QUEENSLAND

T he **coast** of south Queensland consists of an eight-hundred-kilometre stretch between the New South Wales border and Fraser Island containing many of the classic features that lure visitors to Australia's second largest state. Surf rolls in to long, sandy beaches, backed by vibrant towns in exotic settings; behind them, the land rises a thousand metres or more to lush, rainforest-clad plateaux. It's one of Australia's busiest tourist venues, a factor which will be central to your impressions of the region: some love the hype and pace, others loathe it for the same reasons and despair of ever finding an untramped corner.

However, although the **Gold Coast** undoubtedly lives up to this image, it occupies a mere fraction of the region and there are plenty of places to escape the glitz. An hour away, the **Scenic Rim's** green heights may be crowded at times but provide the perfect antidote to the concrete coast; remoter sections of this chain of **national parks** offer a challenge for even experienced bushwalkers. Heading north, fruit and vegetable plantations behind the gentle **Sunshine Coast** benefit from rich volcanic soils and a sub-tropical climate; while offshore looms **Fraser Island** where huge forested dunes, freshwater lakes and sculpted coloured sands form the backdrop to exciting, self-drive (4WD) safaris.

**Brisbane**, Queensland's capital, is in the state's southeastern extremity, between the Gold and Sunshine coasts, but seems curiously unaffected by either. Attracting controversy ever since Queensland separated from New South Wales in 1859, Brisbane was an unpopular choice for a capital with northern pioneers, who felt the government to be too far away to understand, or even care about, their needs. These needs centred around the north's sugar plantations and the use of Solomon Islanders for labour, a practice the south equated with **slavery** and finally banned. This resulted in demands for further separation, this time between tropical and southern Queensland, and although this never happened, there's a definite division between the two which is felt in more than just the climate: the remoteness of northern settlements from the capital has led to local self-sufficiency and made Queensland far less centralized than other states.

After World War II, when General MacArthur used Brisbane as his headquarters to co-ordinate attacks on Japanese forces based throughout the Pacific, Brisbane stagnated, earning – along with the rest of Queensland – a reputation as a dull, underdeveloped backwater. During the 1970s and early 1980s, the stranglehold of a strongly conservative National Party government, led by the charismatic **Johannes Bjelke-Petersen** (always known simply as "Joh"), did nothing to enhance the city's image. Citing law and order issues to justify granting the police sweeping powers, he created a repressive and domineering government, characterized by his own peculiar, slippery oratory. He was finally hoisted by his own petard after initiating the Fitzgerald Inquiry – an investigation into government corruption – which implicated his cabinet in a variety of offences and forced him from office. As if to remove all trace of his rule, Brisbane underwent a thorough facelift before hosting the 1988 **World Expo**, when eighteen million visitors came to experience "Leisure in the Age of Technology". Not least for locals, who treated it as something of a coming-out party, the Expo provided a real boost after years of tedium and today the city is still busy and optimistic.

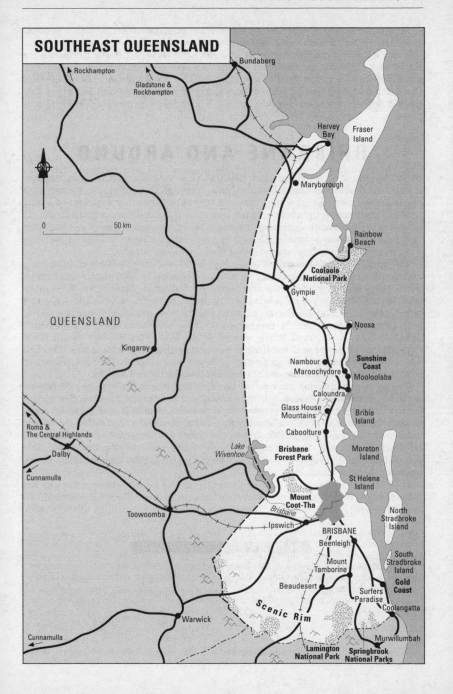

**SOUTHEAST QUEENSLAND**

Rockhampton

Gladstone &
Rockhampton

Bundaberg

Hervey
Bay

Fraser
Island

Maryborough

Rainbow
Beach

0        50 km

**Cooloola
National Park**

Gympie

QUEENSLAND

Noosa

Kingaroy

Nambour          **Sunshine
Maroochydore      Coast**
                  Mooloolaba

Caloundra

Glass House
Mountains              Bribie
                       Island

Roma &
The Central Highlands

Caboolture

Lake          **Brisbane          Moreton
Wivenhoe      Forest Park         Island**

Dalby

St Helena
Island

Cunnamulla

**Mount
Coot-Tha**

Brisbane           North
                   Stradbroke
Toowoomba          Island

Ipswich            BRISBANE
                   Beenleigh

                   Mount              South
                   Tamborine          Stradbroke
                                      Island

Beaudesert

                   Surfers       **Gold
                   Paradise      Coast**

                                 Coolangatta

Warwick

Cunnamulla                       Murwillumbah

                   *Scenic Rim*

**Lamington      Springbrook
National Park    National Parks**

As a major tourist destination, travel and accommodation are seldom a problem along Queensland's south coast, and in many places the only trouble is making some sort of choice between the vast array of alternatives. However, **busy periods** – the Easter and Christmas holidays, and weekends – see room shortages and staggering price hikes in all accommodation except hostels. This is most pronounced on the Gold Coast, though you'll find a degree of seasonal price rises as far north as Hervey Bay. Book in advance whenever possible, and don't be afraid to bargain outside of the peak times.

# BRISBANE AND AROUND

By far the largest city in Queensland, **BRISBANE** is not quite what you'd expect from a state capital with over one million residents. Although there are urban sprawl, high-rise buildings, slow-moving traffic, crowded streets and the other trappings of a business and trade centre, there's little of the pushiness that usually accompanies them. To urbanites used to a more aggressive approach, the atmosphere is slow, even backward (a reputation the city would be pleased to lose) but to others the languid pace is a welcome change, reflecting relaxed rather than regressive attitudes.

The origins of most Queensland cities are a blend of chance and design; Brisbane is no exception. In 1823, responding to political pressure to shift the "worst type of felons" away from Sydney and the southeast – the further the better – the government sent **John Oxley**, Surveyor General, sailing north to find a suitable site for a new prison colony. At Moreton Bay he encountered three shipwrecked convicts who had been living with Aborigines for several months; they introduced Oxley to a previously unknown river. He explored briefly, named it "Brisbane" after the New South Wales Governor, and the next year established a convict settlement at coastal Redcliffe. This was immediately abandoned in favour of better anchorage further upstream, and today's city centre became the site of Brisbane Town by the end of 1824.

Twenty years on, events came full circle. With land scarce in the south, the government was persuaded to move out the convicts and free up the Moreton Bay area to settlers. Immigrants on government-assisted passages poured in and Brisbane began to shape up as a busy **port** – an unattractive, awkward settlement of rutted streets and wooden shacks. Only after fire destroyed the centre in 1864 were the first substantial buildings constructed. Development was slow and uneven: new townships were founded around the centre at Fortitude Valley, Kangaroo Point and Breakfast Creek, gradually merging into a city.

Brisbane's character arises largely from this lack of formal planning: the city has made the best of circumstances rather than anticipated them. There's a confused blur of old and new, crammed in side by side rather than split into distinct districts, while

## ACCOMMODATION PRICES

All the accommodation listed in this book has been categorized into one of eight price bands, as set out below. The rates quoted represent the cheapest available double or twin room in high season – except for category ①, which are per-person rates for a dorm bed, and the prices given for units, cabins and vans, which are the daily charge for the whole unit.

| ① Under $16 | ② $16–26 | ③ $ 27–36 | ④ $ 37–54 |
|---|---|---|---|
| ⑤ $55–74 | ⑥ $75–94 | ⑦ $95–124 | ⑧ $ 125 upwards |

For more accommodation details, see pp.31–34

## ABORIGINAL BRISBANE

Oxley recorded the Brisbane Aboriginals as friendly; they had looked after the shipwrecked convicts and, in the early days, even rounded up and returned runaways from the settlement. In his orders to Oxley on how to the indigenous peoples, Governor Brisbane admitted, though in a roundabout way, that the land belonged to them: "All uncivilized people have wants...when treated justly they acquire many comforts by their union with the more civilized. This justifies our occupation of their lands".

But future governors were not so liberal in their views, and things had soured long before the first squatters moved into the Brisbane area and began leaving out "gifts" of poisoned flour and calling in the Native Mounted Police to **disperse** local Aborigines – a euphemism for exterminating them. Bill Rosser's grim account in *Up Rode the Troopers – The Black Police in Queensland*, tells the story through dialogues with the grandson of one of the last tribal members in the Brisbane area, and gives a good idea of how communities were split up and scattered by Queensland's Protection Act, which remained in force until the 1970s.

A trace of Brisbane's Aboriginal past is found at the **Nudgee Bora Ring** about 12km north of the centre at Nudgee Waterhole Reserve, at the junction of Nudgee and Childs roads. Last used in 1860, two low mounds where boys were initiated form little more than an icon today, and you'll probably feel that it's not worth the trip. More rewarding are the several recently constructed **Aboriginal walking trails** at Mount Coot-tha; the City Hall information desk has leaflets on these which explain traditional uses of the area.

new suburbs are blithely added to the shapeless edges as required. The people, too, are spontaneous, partly because many are new to the area. Economic malaise in the southern states has seen a steady migration north of people seeking **work** – or at least finding Queensland a better place to be unemployed – and Brisbane is the obvious first stop.

Seen from the river or the top of Mount Coot-tha, Brisbane is pretty enough, but there's nothing that you won't find in most Australian places of a comparable age – a historic precinct, museums, botanic gardens – and few visitors stay long enough to appreciate its strongest point; a healthy, unpredictable **social scene**. Meeting people is easy here, and whether you enjoy yarning over a beer in a downtown hotel or tracking down an ever-changing nightlife, you've missed out if you don't make a few local contacts. As far as exploring further afield goes, you'll find empty beaches and surf on **North Stradbroke Island** and **Moreton Island** – both easy to reach from the city – as well as sub-tropical woods in **Brisbane Forest Park**, a twenty-minute drive from the centre.

# Arrival and information

**Brisbane Airport** is located 9km northwest of the centre, at the end of Kingsford Smith Drive. You'll find banks (including autotellers) and luggage lockers at both domestic and international terminals. **Taxi** prices into the city can vary considerably depending on your time of arrival – during the morning rush hour the journey can take forever and you're better off hanging around at the airport until after 9am. Expect to pay at least $15 to reach central Brisbane. The *SkyTrans* bus ($5.40 per person) to the Transit Centre (see below), meets incoming flights and takes about forty minutes. This also runs the other way roughly twice an hour between 5am and 8.30pm; check with the *Coachtrans* desk (☎3236 1000), on the top floor of the Transit Centre, for the exact times. There's also a bus link to the **Gold Coast Airport** at Coolangatta (*Baxway Coaches*; ☎3236 4163 for details).

The **telephone code** for Brisbane is ☎07.
Unless otherwise specified, all phone numbers in this chapter are in the ☎07 code region.

Arrival by **rail** or **bus** lands you at Brisbane's grubby, functional **Transit Centre**, located in the heart of the city on Roma Street. Up top of the three levels are the bus offices, luggage lockers and a 24-hour **hostel information** desk; the middle floor has an information booth, fast-food joints, a bar, **medical centre** and autotellers; while the ground floor is the arrival and departure point for local and interstate **trains**.

During the day, reaching your accommodation seldom poses any problems as the local buses and taxis leave from just outside the Transit Centre, on Roma Street, and the majority of hostels either meet coaches or will pick you up if you call them. However, if you're arriving **late at night** you'd be advised to take a taxi. While Brisbane is still behind most European or American cities of its size in terms of violence, you don't really want to go wandering around after midnight with your luggage in tow; some areas – particularly Fortitude Valley – are best avoided altogether. If you simply must get somewhere and don't have the cab fare, it's worth considering leaving your luggage in the lockers.

### Tourist information

City information is available from council-run **booths** (Mon–Fri 8.30am–5pm, Sat 9am–noon) located at the airport; on the second floor of the Transit Centre (☎3236 2020); and in the City Hall foyer. For the rest of Queensland, the **Government Travel Centre**, on the corner of Adelaide and Edward streets (Mon–Fri 8.30am–5pm, Sat 9.30am–12.30pm; ☎3221 6111) has a stock of brochures covering the most popular trails, and is also helpful on out of the way places.

# City transport

Brisbane's centre is small and possible to cover **on foot**, though since it's the only city in Queensland with anything like a decent **transit system**, you might consider taking advantage of this luxury. Anywhere further afield is relatively easy to reach with private or public transport.

### Buses, trains and ferries

All fares are calculated on a zonal basis – the more zones you cross, the more you pay: for example, a single fare in the central zone is $1.20, while a train out to the suburbs costs around $2.10. One-way tickets can be bought on your journey (bus drivers give change); for multiple journeys and long stays it's cheaper to buy a book of tickets or a **pass** of some kind from the **Administration Centre** (69 Ann Street, Mon–Fri 8.15am–4.45pm), or agencies around the city – look for flags outside shops. Some passes discount day travel (for example, the *Day Rover* gives unlimited bus travel for $5.50), others give weekly or monthly discounts, or are valid on all buses, trains and ferries (*Roverlink*, unlimited day travel for $8). For bus, train or ferry **information** call ☎13 1230.

**Buses** come in several types: you'll make suburban trips on *Cityxpress*, while the *Citybus* serves central destinations. Services operate roughly between 7am and midnight, with most buses travelling via **Queen Street Bus Station** (below the Myer Centre), where platforms are named after native animals (platypus, koala, etc) and there's an **information office** (Mon–Fri 8.30am–5pm, Sat 8.15am–4.45pm). Central Brisbane's historic attractions are toured by the *Citysights* open-top **tram** (daily except Tues 9am–4pm; $9), which you hail from the clearly signposted special stops.

The electric **Citytrain** network provides a faster service than the buses, but it's not as frequent or comprehensive. Lines from as far afield as Caboolture and Beenleigh converge on downtown Brisbane, with trains every few minutes, but individual routes to the suburbs may operate only once an hour. Last trains leave **Central Station** in Ann Street at about 11.45pm – timetables are available from ticket offices. Buy **tickets and passes** at most stations – a *Day Rover* ($8.50) gives unlimited travel after 9am.

**Ferries** operate across the river at several points, useful for short cuts. **Fares** start around $1.20 for a direct crossing, and some bus passes are also valid. The two main departure points in the city are Waterfront Place and the Riverside Centre, both in Eagle Street.

## Taxis, cars and bikes

The public transport system closes down by midnight, so you may well need a **taxi** if you're out on the town. After dark they tend to cruise round the clubs and hotels; during the day Roma Street is a good place to find one. To call a cab, try *B&W Cabs* (☎3238 1000) or *Yellow Cabs* (☎3391 0191).

**Driving** is not much fun until you get your bearings. Unfortunately, signs *at* rather than before junctions are typical not just of Brisbane but of the whole state, and you'd be well advised to lay your hands on some sort of street directory as soon as possible. Once familiar with the city, there are no great problems, although **parking** spaces tend to be in short supply in the centre. For details of car rental agencies, see "Listings", p.270.

However, **cyclists** are well catered for with a number of bike routes throughout the city. Maps are available from libraries and Council offices. Some hostels loan bikes or they're easily rented, too – again, see "Listings".

# Accommodation

Beds are usually only hard to find during major Rugby League events and the Brisbane Show (the "Ekka") in August. The most expensive places are in the city; cheaper hotel rooms and hostels are clustered around Petrie Terrace, Fortitude Valley and over the river in South Brisbane. If you're staying for a while, ask about **weekly rates**, which might amount to a free night in seven.

**Backpackers' hostels**, here as elsewhere along the Sydney–Cairns route, are tremendously variable in quality, though most have polished up their act in response to local laws aimed at ensuring that they meet certain safety standards. All have dormitory beds, though you'll often find good-value doubles available, too. Other benefits at many hostels are entertainment and work connections, bikes for rent or loan, pools and courtesy buses on arrival (and sometimes departure).

## City centre

Prices here reflect location rather than exceptional quality, although good-value rooms can be found. Rates often drop at weekends and outside peak season, due to the scarcity of business customers and the competition from the Gold Coast.

**Annie's Shandon Inn**, 405 Upper Edward St (☎3831 8684). Twee, but a rather nice, family-run bed & breakfast. ④–⑤.

**Beaufort Heritage**, Edward St (☎3221 1999). Topnotch hotel overlooking the river and Botanic Gardens. ⑧.

**Hotel Majestic**, 382 George St (☎3236 2848). Hardly lives up to its name but as central as they come; breakfast available. ⑤.

**Mayfair Crest**, corner of Roma and Ann Streets (☎3229 9111). Standard business hotel with all the usual facilities. ⑦.

**Sportsmans Hotel**, 130 Leichhardt St, Spring Hill (☎3831 2892). Gay-friendly pub with rooms; predominantly male clientele but both sexes welcome. ④.

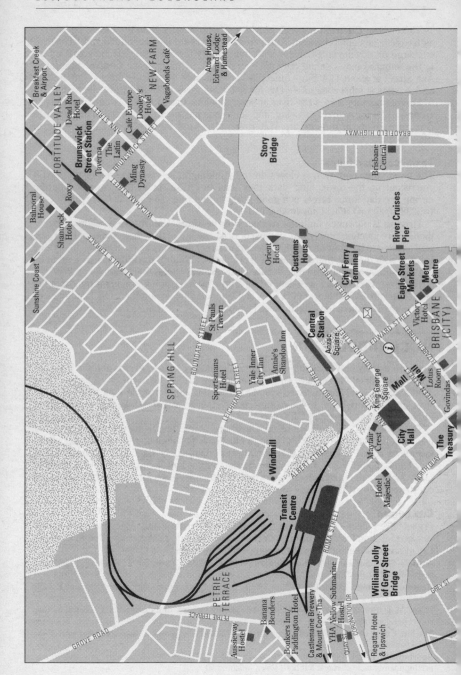

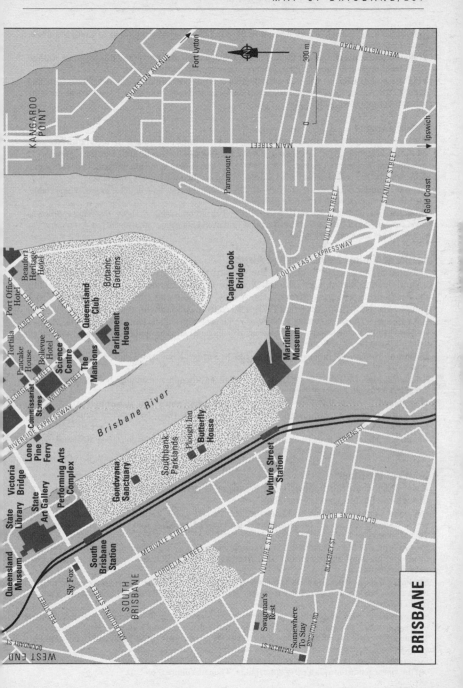

BRISBANE

WEST END

BOUNDARY ST

Queensland Museum

State Library

State Art Gallery

Sly Fox

PEEL STREET

MELBOURNE STREET

South Brisbane Station

SOUTH BRISBANE

MERIVALE STREET

CORDELIA STREET

Performing Arts Complex

Victoria Bridge

Lone Pine Ferry

RIVERSIDE EXPRESSWAY

Commissariat Stores

WILLIAM STREET

GEORGE STREET

Pancake House

Tortilla

ALICE ST

MARGARET ST

ELIZABETH ST

ALBERT STREET

Bellevue Hotel

Science Centre

The Mansions

Port Office Hotel

Beaufort Heritage Hotel

Queensland Club

Parliament House

Botanic Gardens

Brisbane River

Gondwana Sanctuary

Southbank Parklands

Plough Inn

Butterfly House

Maritime Museum

Captain Cook Bridge

Vulture Street Station

VULTURE STREET

GLADSTONE ROAD

STEPHENS ST

BLAENEY ST

Swagman's Rest

Somewhere To Stay

FRANKLIN ST

BRIGHTON RD

KANGAROO POINT

SHAFSTON AVENUE

Fort Lytton

N

500 m

0

MAIN STREET

Paramount

Ipswich

VULTURE STREET

SOUTH EAST EXPRESSWAY

STANLEY STREET

Gold Coast

WELLINGTON ROAD

**Yale Inner City Inn,** 413 Upper Edward St (☎3832 1663). Ordinary but pleasant enough and very central bed & breakfast. ④–⑤.

**Yellow Submarine,** 66 Quay St (☎3211 3424). Small hostel, with rooms and dorms, in refurbished 1860s building. Full kitchen facilities, laundry, barbeque and garden. ①–③.

**YHA Brisbane City,** 53 Quay St (☎3236 1004). Sterile but with excellent facilities, including limited parking, an inexpensive restaurant, dorms and double rooms. A $3 surcharge for non-members covers three nights. ②.

## Petrie Terrace

This area has the best of the city's budget accommmodation, and is a ten-minute walk from the Transit Centre – or take bus #144 from opposite the Transit Centre to stop 5.

**Aussie Way Hostel,** 34 Cricket St (☎3369 0711). Former dive being totally renovated with verandahs, balcony and period decor added in 1994. When finished will be very smart. ①.

**Banana Benders,** 118 Petrie Terrace (☎3367 1157). Dorms and double rooms; comfortable, friendly and quiet, though becoming threadbare. ①.

**Bonkers Inn,** 60 Petrie Terrace (☎3367 0558). Pub accommodation above *Paddington Barracks Hotel* converted to a backpacker hostel; spend Friday and Saturday nights at the bar downstairs 'cos you won't get any sleep anyway. ①.

## Fortitude Valley, New Farm and Airport

Because of the number of clubs in the vicinity, the Valley's streets can be either seedy or intimidating late at night, though New Farm is quiet enough. Most buses travelling up Adelaide Street pass through the Valley, or take the train to Brunswick Street station. For New Farm, take bus #177 or #178 from Adelaide Street.

**Atoa House,** 95 Annie St (☎3358 4507). Well-run hostel, with slightly higher rates than usual offset by good facilities, free laundry, and long-stay discounts. There's camping out the back, and if they can't meet you they'll pay your taxi fare. ①–②.

**Balmoral House,** 33 Amelia St (☎3252 1397). Secure, clean and handy for Chinatown and Brunswick St. ①.

**Edward Lodge,** 75 Sydney St (☎3254 1078). Small, gay-friendly guesthouse, both sexes welcome. Breakfast included. Bunks ②, rooms ⑤.

**Homestead,** 57 Annie St (☎3358 3538). Purpose-built hostel with a party atmosphere. ①.

**Mitchells' Budget Accommodation,** 114 Kingsford-Smith Drive (☎1800/777 590). Convenient for the airport. ②.

**Shamrock Hotel,** 186 Brunswick St (☎3252 2421). Basic hotel rooms and noisy weekend nights above one of the Valley's busiest pubs. ①.

## South of the River

Less sleazy than the Valley, South Brisbane is generally a pleasanter place to stay, though the hostels are very variable.

**Brisbane Central,** 200 Main St, Kangaroo Point (☎3891 1434). Close to the *Storey Bridge Hotel*, where backpackers can get budget meals. Take bus #120 or #130 from the corner of Wharf and Turbot streets. ①.

**Paramount,** 649 Main St (☎3393 1855). Motel-style rooms and good facilities, with two free pub meals and breakfast at the *Pineapple Hotel* across the road if you stay for a week. Buses as for Brisbane Central. ③.

**Sly Fox,** corner of Melbourne and Hope streets (☎3846 5930). Popular hostel in a restored, turn-of-the-century, brick hotel; inexpensive meals for guests and close to the South Bank and city. Train to South Brisbane. ①.

**Somewhere to Stay,** 45 Brighton Rd (☎3846 2858). Should be good, but is gradually falling apart under a couldn't-care-less approach. Pay the extra and get a room with a view over Brisbane's skyline rather than one of the basic dorms. Bus #177 from corner of Adelaide and George streets, or a 15-minute walk from South Brisbane or Vulture Street stations. ①–④.

**Swagman's Rest,** 145 Vulture St (☎3844 9956). A handy alternative to *Somewhere to Stay*, but without the views; tends towards a party atmosphere. Train to Vulture Street. ①.

## Camping

The places listed below are the most central, and at least have a regular bus service.

**Alpha Motel/Caravan Park**, 1434 Gympie Rd, Aspley (☎3263 4011). Bus #55 or #182 from the corner of Queen and Creek streets, or from Adelaide Street outside City Hall. About 10km north on the main highway; if full, try *Acres* next door or *Caravan Village*, 763 Zillmere Rd, about 500m further on.

**Carinya**, 1497 Creek Rd (☎3398 9550). Bus #505 from Platypus G platform at Queen Street Bus Station, or #8A–D from Ann Street near King George Sq. East of the city and slightly closer.

# The City

The city finds its focus around the meandering loops of the **Brisbane River**, with the triangular wedge of the business centre on the north bank surrounded by community-orientated suburbs. At its heart are the busy, upmarket commercial and administrative precincts around **Queen Street**, a mix of glass spires and century-old sandstone facades terminating in riverside **Botanic Gardens**. Radiating **north**, the polish fades with the cheaper shops, accommodation and eateries around Spring Hill, Fortitude Valley, New Farm and the aspiring suburbs of Petrie Terrace and Paddington. To the **west** is a blaze of riverside homes at Milton and Toowong and the fringes of Mount Coot-tha and Brisbane Forest Park. **Across the river**, the major landmarks are the Cultural Centre and newly created Conference Centre, and South Bank Parklands, which stretch to Kangaroo Point. Beyond are the open, bustling streets of **South Brisbane** and the **West End**, more relaxed than their northern counterparts.

The central area is easily manageable on foot: try following the **Tourist Trail**, marked by brass arrows in the pavement, or there's even a central **Tree Trail**; **maps** of both are available from tourist information booths. Refer back to "City Transport", p.254, for details of the *Citysights* tram tour.

## Downtown

**Queen Street** is Brisbane's oldest thoroughfare, its southern section between George and Edward streets now a pedestrian mall with the **Myer Centre** as its focus: a multi-storey shopping complex capped by an indoor roller-coaster on the fifth floor. Most of the stores inside are on the chic side but you can, for kicks, ride the glass elevators or buy designer Outback accessories and fluffy koalas. One aspect worth investigating are the food centres on the Queen Street level, crammed at midday with office workers grabbing lunch. There's a huge variety of classy fast foods, from Asian takeaways to Greek kebabs, at slightly higher prices than the local hotel nosh. Outside, the **mall** is always busy with people running errands, window shopping or just socializing. There's usually some kind of entertainment, too: either informal efforts – acrobats, buskers and the occasional soap-box orator – or more organized events, like Aboriginal and Islander dancing or jazz sessions, on the small stage about halfway down the street.

### City Hall and the Observatory

Escaping the mall and heading north along Albert Street, you come upon **City Hall**, across from King George Square: look out for the bronze sculptures based on silicon chips in front of the fountains. A stately building ruined by an ugly clock tower, there's sad irony – and a reflection of former policies – in the triangular sculpture over the portico. A figure representing the state faces out from the centre, arms spread to protect all citizens, while to the left the Aboriginal way of life is depicted "dying out before the approach of the white man". The **City Art Gallery** (daily 10am–5pm; free) inside has a rather staid smattering of paintings, pottery and glassware, though it's worth checking to see if there are any temporary exhibitions of work by Australian artists, or if there are any screenings at the tiny cinema. The clock tower is sometimes open, too, if you want a view of the city centre.

Moving further up Albert Street is Wickham Park and the grey cone of Brisbane's oldest building, a convict-built **windmill** known locally as the Observatory. Built in 1829 to grind corn for the early settlement, the original wooden sails were too heavy to turn and grinding was done for years by a treadmill: severe punishment for the convicts who had to work it. Describing the scene in 1836, Quaker missionary George Walker was quietly appalled: "They work from sunrise to sunset, with a rest of three hours in the middle of the day...the exertion requisite to keep this up is excessive. I am told the steps of the wheel are sometimes literally wet with the perspiration." The sails, useless for catching the wind, were put to work as gallows before being pulled off in 1850 and, with the convicts gone, the building subsequently became a signal station. For now it stands empty, held together with a cement glaze and firmly locked.

## Eagle Street

Turning west towards **Eagle Street**, you enter the business district. Heavily developed in the 1980s and left with a legacy of glassy high-rises, the few surviving old buildings are hidden away. The copper-domed **Customs House** at the north end of Queen Street is currently home to the University of Queensland Press, publisher of Peter Carey's surrealistic novels, while rustic **All Saint's Church** on the corner of Wickham Terrace, and neo-Gothic **St John's Cathedral** in Ann Street, sport some elegant stained glass. Sunday morning is enlivened by the **Eagle Street Markets** between the river and the road – too trendy for bargains, but not bad for jewellery and leatherwork, clothing and $10 massages.

You might even join the crowds for a **river cruise** from the pier at Waterfront Place. *The Kookaburra Queen*, a three-tier Mississippi-style paddleboat decked out in timber and brass, is *the* way to see the city from the river. The ninety-minute jaunt is a popular Sunday excursion (daily 10am & 12.45pm, additional Sunday departure 3.30pm; from $10.90 to $30, depending on level of refreshments), and there's an evening cruise during the week (Mon–Sat 7.30pm, Sun 6.30pm; $25 2-course meal, up to $49.90 for seafood); book on ☎1800 77 7102.

# The historic precinct

The area between Queen Street and the Botanic Gardens contains some of Brisbane's finest architecture, dating from the earliest days of settlement until the turn of the century, and looking sprightly after extensive cleaning in 1988. The **Commissariat Store** in William Street, contemporary with the windmill but in considerably better shape, is currently a museum (Tues–Fri 11am–2pm, Sun 11am–4pm; $1; ☎3221 5198) and the headquarters of the Royal Historical Society of Queensland. Originally a granary, there have been a few changes but it still looks reasonably authentic from the outside. The museum itself – with its dusty collection of relics dating back to convict times – is less worthy, but is redeemed by its staff, who are very knowledgeable about Brisbane's past.

**Parliament House**, at the southern end of Alice Street, was built following a design by Charles Tiffin in 1864 and illustrates an appealing architectural compromise between French Renaissance style and adaptations to the tropical climate such as shuttered north windows, shaded colonnades and a high, arched roof. You can see the grand interior on an hour-long **guided tour** (Mon–Fri 10am & 2pm; free) and there's access to the chambers when there's no debate in progress. Opposite, on the corner of George Street, the **Queensland Club** was founded in 1859, just four days prior to the separation of Queensland from New South Wales. Heavy walls, columns and spacious balconies evoke a tropical version of a traditional London club; entrance and membership – still barred to women – is by invitation only.

Further north along George Street you pass **The Mansions**, one of Brisbane's last surviving terraced house blocks, built in 1890 and guarded by stone cats on the parapet corners. Between Elizabeth and Queen streets, occupying an entire block, is the classical facade of the former **Treasury**. Built in the 1890s, it reflects the wealth of Queensland's gold mines (though by this point most were on the decline) and was a slap in the face to New South Wales, which had spitefully withdrawn all financial support from the fledgling state on separation, leaving it bankrupt. With a twist typical of a state torn between conservatism and tourism, the building is now Queensland's third casino.

One block down from the Treasury, Brisbane's **Science Centre** (Mon–Fri 9.30am–4pm, Sat 1–5pm, Sun 9.30am–5pm; $5) is definitely worth a look. A hands-on approach makes it great fun and very therapeutic if you like to prod and dismantle exhibits instead of peering at them through a protective glass case. Favourites include the various optical illusions – a spinning spiral right out of the 1960s, guaranteed to hypnotize, and the egocentric paradise of a giant kaleidoscope – and the "Thongophone", a set of giant pan pipes played by whacking the top with a flip-flop. Good rainy-day material.

## The Botanic Gardens

Bordered by Alice Street and the river, Brisbane's **Botanic Gardens** overlook the cliffs of Kangaroo Point and, while more of a park than a botanic garden, bamboo thickets and greenery do provide an escape from city claustrophobia. Legend has it that the area was once a vegetable patch cultivated by convicts. Formal gardens were laid out in 1855 by Walter Hill, who experimented with local and imported plants to see which would grow well in the North's untried climate. Some of his more successful efforts are the oversized **bunya pines** around the Edward Street entrance, planted in 1860, and a residual patch of the **rainforest** that once blanketed the area, at the southern end of the park. Mangroves along the river, accessible via a boardwalk, are another native species more recently protected. You can spend summer evenings here at the open-air **stage** listening to classical music recitals. During the day, cyclists flock to the park, as it's at one end of a popular cycling and jogging track that follows the north bank of the river south to St Lucia and Queensland University.

## The northern suburbs

**North of the river**, just beyond Brisbane's business district, are several former suburbs which have been absorbed by the city sprawl: Paddington and Petrie Terrace to the west, Spring Hill and Fortitude Valley in the north, and New Farm to the east. Houses in the area are popular with Brisbane's aspiring professional class, and while office blocks and one-way streets are beginning to encroach, there's also an older character reflected in the **Queenslander**-style houses (see box overpage) still standing around Spring Hill and Petrie Terrace.

### XXXX – The local brew

Just down the hill from Petrie Terrace in Milton, the **Castlemaine Perkins Brewery** (Milton Rd; ☎3361 7322) has been making Queensland's own beer since 1878, and had no real competition until *Powers* came on the scene in the 1980s. Their famous yellow-and-red XXXX emblem is almost part of the Queensland landscape: splashed across T-shirts and the roofs of Outback hotels, or on labels on countless discarded bottles and cans littering everywhere from roadsides to the depths of the Barrier Reef. For enthusiasts, the brewery opens its gates for a **free tour** (Mon–Wed at 1pm & 3.30pm), which incorporates a brief rundown on the brewing process and then about thirty minutes

---

## QUEENSLAND HOUSES

There can hardly be a more typical image of rural Queensland than a high-set "Queenslander" surrounded by green fields of sugar cane. A response to the northern climate, these houses come in all shapes and styles but the basic design is a wooden box on piles with a verandah or balcony – the idea being to have a cool flow of air underneath the house to reduce the humidity inside. Traditional colours, now more commonly seen in cities where it's becoming popular to renovate them, are cream, red or green, while older buildings may have corrugated iron awnings, red "bull-nosed" roofs and wooden latticework on porches and eaves. In Brisbane they're generally low-set, but tend to be raised further off the ground as you move up into the tropics – the exception to prove the rule is at Redcliffe, just 12km north of Brisbane, where the pole houses have supports ten metres high to compensate for a steep hill.

---

watching filmed eulogies and swilling beer. Booking ahead is essential, because you won't get past the security guards unless your name is on the list.

### Fortitude Valley

While the other areas are mainly residential, **FORTITUDE VALLEY**'s tangled ethnic mix of shops, restaurants and bars makes it one of the more interesting places in Brisbane to wander at random. Grubby, and definitely on the sleazy side – grotty revue bars haven't disappeared entirely – in less than a kilometre the main thoroughfare of **Brunswick Street** passes two Irish pubs, a compact **Chinatown** complete with the usual busy restaurants, stores and martial arts centres, and an embryonic European **street-café scene**. It's best at the weekends; on Saturday morning there's a downbeat secondhand market in Brunswick Street and the cafés are buzzing. After dark the Valley's streets can be menacing at times, although early on there are plenty of people around; if you've any distance to go on your own after the pubs close, call a taxi.

### Breakfast Creek

Named by John Oxley, who tucked into a morning meal here in 1823 on his voyage of exploration upstream, **BREAKFAST CREEK**'s shops and hotel mark an acute traffic bottleneck where the road bridges the creek between the upper reaches of Fortitude Valley and the way to the airport. A pretty, if noisy, spot, looking out over usually placid water to inactive wharves, the real estate in nearby Hamilton and Ascot is becoming quite exclusive. If you're out this way – perhaps en route to the airport or heading north – consider looking around **Newstead House**, Brisbane's oldest residence. A low, solid brick and stone building with a slate roof, it was constructed as a private home in 1845 by convict labour, and became the Government House twelve years later. Enlarged by the governor, the house formed the social focus of the day, protected from Aboriginal onslaught during ball nights by armed police. Restored and now open as a **museum** (Mon–Fri 10am–4pm, Sun 1pm–5pm; $3), the house and grounds are remarkably quiet. Taking in the views across the creek from one of the elegant windows, and surrounded by turn-of-the-century furniture, it's easy to forget how close you are to the city. The house is off Breakfast Creek Road just south of the bridge; to get here by public transport, take the train to Bowen Hills and walk for one kilometre.

## South Brisbane

Across the river from the city centre, the **Cultural Centre** and its environs – comprising state museum, library, gallery, performing arts complex, conference centre and parkland – is Brisbane's most obvious tourist attraction. Immediately south of Victoria

Bridge (itself a continuation of Queen Street), it's easily reached by train to South Brisbane station, while plenty of buses from all over the city stop right outside in Melbourne Street.

Beyond here, the **West End** is South Brisbane's answer to Fortitude Valley, with a similar ethnic mix – Asian, Greek and Italian – but accompanied by less sleaze and a decidedly more relaxed atmosphere. There are no sights here as such, but it's worth a visit for the knot of Asian stores and continental delicatessens, and for a number of inexpensive restaurants and cafés around the hub at Boundary Road and Vulture Street, popular with students from Queensland University across the river at St Lucia; see p.266 for details.

## Queensland Museum

**The Queensland Museum** (daily 9am–5pm, Wed until 8pm; free, except for special exhibitions) is essentially a natural history musuem, but it benefits from a bias toward unorthodox methods of presentation. Wedge-tailed eagles hover overhead, koalas climb the walls and, in the foyer, there's the unsettling experience of walking underneath full-scale models of a family of humpbacked whales suspended from the ceiling. There's a rundown on western Queensland's fossil beds, including a reconstruction of Queensland's own *Muttaburrasaurus* and a section of the Lark Quarry **dinosaur trackways**, while above swings a furry pterodactyl, reflecting recent ideas that Australia was subject to a cold climate during the era of the dinosaurs. Upstairs, more recently extinct **megafauna** from the Darling Downs, just west of Brisbane, unexpectedly return to life – a breathing, twitching model of a marsupial lion lounging on a rock at the top of the escalators catches everyone by surprise. Rock hounds and prospective gem hunters will also be interested in the museum's **mineral collection** – dozens of multi-coloured rocks from around the state and pointers on how to identify them in the field.

**Ethnographic displays** mostly relate to traditional life in New Guinea and Melanesia, with the glaring omission – apart from a handful of tools and a small section on the rainforest tribes from the north – of anything on Queensland's Aboriginal and Torres Strait Islander history. The collection is rounded off by miscellaneous items including an eclectic collection of period furniture.

## State Art Gallery and Library

Queensland's **State Art Gallery** (daily 10am–5pm, Wed until 8pm; free, except for special exhibitions) provides a large, airy space for its wide-ranging collection, which includes a sizeable collection of twentieth-century painters. As well as works by visionaries like Brett Whitely, Arthur Boyd and Sidney Nolan, there are some unusual (and very European) landscape watercolours by **Aboriginal artists** Walter Ebataringa and Albert Namatjira (for more on the latter, see p.473), alongside a few functional tribal items – dilly bags, headwear and shields – labelled as "art" but somehow out of place here. One of the most interesting pieces in the gallery is a nineteenth-century stained-glass window depicting a kangaroo hunt – a quintessentailly Australian theme in an unlikely medium; other Australian works include the romantic paintings of Tom Roberts and Frederick McGubbin's impressionistic canvases. Sculpture is scattered throughout the gallery in a somewhat offhand manner, and there's a small collection of high-quality **glasswork** hidden away at the back.

Probably as rewarding is a visit to the **State Library** (Mon–Thurs 10am–8pm, Fri–Sun 10am–5pm), best known for its *John Oxley Library* on level 4 which records every aspect of Queensland's past in endless books, journals and photographs. Level 3 is devoted to music and art; they lend scores and there's even a piano room available for practice. Film buffs should head to level 2 to sample the video collection and check out the cinema's programme.

## The South Bank Parklands

The **South Bank Parklands** are a resoundingly successful contrivance, brought into being with little rhyme or reason other than that *something* had to be done with the 1988 Expo site. The weekend crowds come to stroll along the river, watch street performers and stuff their faces full of candy floss and hot dogs – blissfully unconcerned that everything, from the sand around the pool to the Nepalese pagoda and rainforest plants at **Gondwana Sanctuary**, is imported and artificial. Bands play most Saturday nights on the outdoor stage, and other attractions range from a guided tour through the **Butterfly House** (daily 10am–4pm; $7) to viewing the frigate in the dry dock at the **Maritime Museum** (daily 9.30am–4.30pm; $5).

# Along the River

The sluggish, meandering **Brisbane River** is 400 million years old, one of the world's most ancient waterways. It flows from above Lake Wivenhoe – 55km inland as the crow flies – past farmland, into quiet suburbs and through the city before emptying 150km downstream into Moreton Bay, behind Fisherman Island. Once an essential trade and transport link with the rest of Australia and the world, it now seems to do little but separate the City from South Brisbane, and residents are strangely oblivious to its potential as a waterway. Although it's superficially active around the city centre, with pleasure craft and dredgers keeping it navigable, most of the old wharves and shipyards now lie derelict or buried under parkland.

If the locals seem to have forgotten the river, it has a habit of reasserting its presence through **flood**. February 1893 saw cyclonic rains swell the flow through downtown Brisbane, carrying off the Victoria Bridge and scores of buildings: eyewitness accounts stated that "Debris of all descriptions – whole houses, trees, cattle and homes – went floating past". This has since been repeated many times, notably in January 1974 when rain from **Cyclone Wanda** completely swamped the centre, swelling the river to 3km wide at one stage. Despite the grim reminder of the brass plaques marking the depths of the worst floods at *Naldham House Polo Club* (1 Eagle St, near the markets), some of Brisbane's poshest real estate flanks the river, with waterfront mansions at Yeerongpilly, Graceville and Chelmer. They're all banking on protection from artificial Lake Wivenhoe, completed in 1984, which should act as a buffer against future floods. You can explore the river's upper reaches by **kayak** on one- or two-day expeditions with *Wilderness Escapes* (☎3359 3486).

### Fort Lytton

Surrounded by the pipes and chimneys of the *Ampol Oil* refinery at Wynnum, **Fort Lytton** (Mon–Fri & Sun 10am–4pm, museum open Sun only; $3 covers fort and museum) is a product of the colonial struggles around the Pacific rim at the end of last century. Only a few days away from French forces on Noumea, Queensland felt threatened by competing European empires and developed a string of coastal defences during the 1880s. Brisbane received the best of these: by the turn of the century, the river mouth at Fort Lytton bristled with artillery and a barrage of floating mines. However, the defences were never put to the test and modern warfare made them obsolete. The fort was downgraded to a secondary line of defence after World War I and abandoned altogether in 1945.

As a piece of military history, the buildings look the part: austere concrete bunkers dug into slopes and capped in grass, gun ports trained on the river and an underground tunnel for checking the mines running down to the water. The best time to visit is the first Sunday of each month when the historical museum is open and **Brisbane Garrison Battery** adds a bit of human activity to the grounds, dressing up in period costume and firing the 64-pound gun at 11am, 2pm and 3pm. The fort is at the end of Lytton Road, west of Wynnum at the mouth of Brisbane River; there's no public transport.

## Lone Pine Sanctuary

**Lone Pine Sanctuary** at Jesmond Road, Fig Tree Pocket (daily 8.45am–4.45pm; $12), has been a popular day-trip upstream since first opening its gates in 1927. Here you can see a large number of native fauna in their natural state which, in the case of the sanctuary's hundred-odd **koalas**, means asleep for 18 out of every 24 hours. At close quarters they're revealed as grey cushions wedged into convenient forks in the trees, occasionally waking up for long enough to chew eucalyptus leaves and blink myopically at the crowds. In nearby cages you'll find other slumbering fauna: Tasmanian devils, fruit bats, blue-tongued lizards, dingoes. Indeed, about the only activity is provided by the bird cages and a colony of hyperactive sugar gliders in the nocturnal house – or head for the outdoor paddock where tolerant wallabies and kangaroos allow themselves to be petted, fed and occasionally roughed up by visitors.

The best way to reach Lone Pine is on a leisurely **river cruise** past Brisbane's waterfront suburbs. Ferries leave from Wharf Road below Victoria Bridge: *Mirimar Cruises* (☎3221 0300) depart daily at 11.30am, arriving back at 4.30pm (90min each way; $15).

# Eating

Brisbane has no gastronomic tradition to exploit, but there's a good variety of bars and restaurants all over the city, with a current trend towards "Mediterranean" cuisine, and café society making inroads in Fortitude Valley and the West End.

Counter meals and unlimited buffets at hotels are the cheapest route to a full stomach in Brisbane – aim for lunch at around noon and dinner between 5pm and 6pm – or try one of the scores of **cafés** in the centre catering to office workers. For something more adventurous, the city's **restaurants** open around 11am–2pm for lunch, 6–10pm or later for evening meals; many are closed for one day a week (often Monday).

## City centre

**Café the Hague**, Myer Centre Level A (next to cinema complex). Dutch-style coffee house, way above the fast-food joints opposite. Try the *poffertjes* – sweet pancakes – and a gourmet coffee for breakfast.

**The Council Club**, Floor 21 BAC Building, 69 Ann St, behind City Hall (☎3225 4164). Good-value Oz-style buffet at $4.50 per head; not for vegetarians. Open Fri 5–8pm only; club membership unnecessary.

**Govindas**, Elizabeth St. Krishna-run vegetarian food bar, with a $5 all-you-can-eat menu. Open lunch Mon–Fri 11.30am–2.30pm; dinner Fri 5.30–7.30pm, Sun 5pm onwards.

**Lotus Room**, 203 Elizabeth St (☎3221 8546). Food way outclasses the tatty red decor, and if you can muster a group of at least ten, they have a $35-per-person banquet, which includes ten courses with unlimited beer and wine. Closed Sun.

**Myer Centre**, Queen Street Mall. Heaps of fast food from kebabs to Chinese, all reasonably priced and freshly prepared, but it can be tough finding somewhere to sit at lunchtime.

**Pancake House**, 18 Charlotte St. Open 24 hours, this restored church with high-beamed roof and stone floor is an unlikely setting for the consumption of fast food. Portions are on the small side for the $8–10 tag, though the food's not bad and there are vegetarian options.

**Port Office Hotel**, corner of Edward St and Margaret St. Flagstones and heavy wooden furniture at one of the city's oldest watering holes, with bargain counter-lunch specials on Tuesday and Thursday, and a free beer with steak or fish meals. Beer garden out the back.

**Readheads Café**, Metro Arts Building, 109 Edward St. Tasty vegetarian and wholefood – salads, *focaccia*, sandwiches – served in a basement setting; live music at weekends.

**Tortilla**, 26 Elizabeth Arcade, off Charlotte St (☎3221 4416). Café meals, Spanish and Mexican à la carte restaurant with live Flamenco guitar on Saturday nights; Mon–Fri lunchtime *tapas* from $12.50 per person (minimum of two). Closed Sat & Sun lunch.

**Transcontinental Hotel**, Roma St, opposite the Transit Centre. Recommended both for its good-value lunchtime *smorgasbord* during the week and live music on Friday night.

**Victory Hotel**, 127 Edward St. Nice beer garden with braziers taking the chill off in winter. The bistro meals are popular with the local business folk.

## Petrie Terrace

**Café Phoenecia**, 23 Caxton St, (☎3368 2084). Greek and Italian home cooking stands out from more upmarket restaurants in the locality; seafood salads and pasta dishes are the pick of the menu from around $11. Closed Mon.

**Casablanca**, 52 Petrie Terrace (☎3368 1899). Inexpensive brasserie and café serving the young and pretentious while taped Brazilian music or live bands provide atmosphere. *Tapas* are served at the bar for around $8.50, and the food is excellent and mouthwateringly spicy, with genuine leanings towards North African cuisine.

**Mediterraneo**, 25 Caxton St (☎3368 1933). Spearheading the recent proliferation of Mediterranean-style restaurants, the food – specialities include "wood-fired" pizzas, char-grilled baby octopus and *fettuccini carbonara* – is very good, but there's atmosphere wanting on a quiet night. A main course and salad will be around $20, and it's enough to satisfy. Closed Sun & Mon.

## Fortitude Valley

**Café Europe**, 360 Brunswick St (☎3252 2424). Café/BYO restaurant with classic cooking and a well-deserved reputation as one of Brisbane's finest restaurants. Stick to the French items; some vegetarian dishes. Main courses from around $15. Closed Mon.

**Chinatown**. Chinese bakeries and roast meat shops in Wickham St and Duncan St Mall are worth checking out for inexpensive snacks.

**Cosmopolitan Coffee**, 332 Brunswick St. Next to *The Latin* but noticeably more relaxed and down-market. Something of an institution with Brisbane's café society, and better than the surrounding competition.

**The Latin**, corner of Brunswick and Ann Streets. Established upmarket café with street tables outside; marble, tubular aluminium furniture and plenty of space inside.

**Ming Dynasty**, 185 Wickham St (☎3252 1181). Although billed as a seafood restaurant, the thing to do is join the crowds of Chinese who come for *dim sum* between 11am and 3pm.

**Taverna**, 27 Warner St (☎3257 1660). Good atmosphere at weekends, with live music and plate smashing in the corniest of Greek style; lunches start at $12.

**Vagabonds Café**, 454 Brunswick St (☎3358 5906). The aroma of eggplant, squid, ricotta, artichokes, peppers, pesto and spices makes up for the name and cold decor – the food tastes good, too. Open Fri & Sun for lunch, Tues–Sun for dinner.

## West End

**Caffé Tempo**, 181 Boundary St (☎3846 3161). Not sophisticated cuisine, but the best in Italian-style home cooking in Brisbane, with fresh salads and fine seafood pasta among its virtues. Most expensive dish is $10.50, and they stay open until the last customer leaves.

**Franco's Coffee Bazaar**, West End Markets, corner of Melbourne and Boundary streets (☎3844 8513). Strong coffee and mild cruising. Open with the market, until 5.30pm.

**King Ahiram**, 88 Vulture St. A decent Lebanese takeaway, not worth crossing town for but good if you are in the area.

**New Asia**, 153 Boundary St (☎3846 3569). Forget flashier Vietnamese restaurants in the neighbourhood: this is the best – prawns grilled on sugar cane, deep-fried quail, rice-noodle dishes – all for less than $4.50 a dish.

**Three Monkeys Coffee Shop**, 58 Mollison St, West End (☎3844 6045). Rapidly acquiring a distinctly lesbian flavour.

# Nightlife, entertainment and culture

The city's entertainment horizons are gradually being expanded by an ever-increasing range of clubs, and a sound, if unadventurous, arts scene. The best cross-section of attractions are central, with Petrie Terrace more upmarket, Fortitude Valley, the West End and South Brisbane less pretentious, if sometimes seedy.

## Pubs, clubs and live music

Brisbane nights were once a byword for boredom. The few places that offered after-dark entertainment were either illegal or lifeless and closed early; locals tended to head to the coast for their weekends. But things are changing. On Friday and Saturday evenings the centre is crowded, and you could, should you want to, see a pub band every night of the week. Hotels are the mainstay, with competition encouraging free passes and happy hours, while the club situation is slowly consolidating a few regular venues. The places listed below might be here to stay, but check with music stores and the weekly **free magazines** *Rave*, *Time Off*, *The Bug* and *The Scene* for up-to-the-minute reviews and listings. Although some international bands make it as far north as Brisbane, most acts you'll see are Australian – for information and tickets, try *Rocking Horse*, 101 Adelaide Street. The **Brisbane Biennial**, held at the end of May in alternate (odd-numbered) years, is a showcase of jazz and other music – check with the tourist offices for details.

### City centre

**Arizona's**, Wintergarden Tavern, Queen St Mall. Pretty trendy at present, with cheap drinks on selected nights; open late on Sun.

**Big Kahuna Inshore Beach Club**, near corner of Turbot and George streets (☎3236 2848). Has a reputation as a bit of a meat market – redeemed by irregular *Club Afro-Carib* (see below) meetings.

**City Rowers**, Waterfront Place, 1 Eagle St. Very much a yuppie hangout and you'll need to be smartly dressed to gain entry and enjoy the evening views over the river.

**Club Afro-Carib**. More a state of mind than a venue, this outfit hosts frenetic dancing to the likes of *Toots and the Maytals* and *Angelique Kidjo* at varying locations (*Big Kahuna* is the current favourite), depending on circumstances and performers.

**Disorient Club**, at the *Orient Hotel*, 560 Queen St. Dance club/disco with occasional live music, tending towards covers of Oz-rock classics; a mix of people end up here after midnight. 9pm–5am.

**Ruby's**, at the *Waterloo Hotel*, corner of Ann St and Commercial Rd (☎3852 1101). Light and friendly lesbian evenings every first and third Saturday night of the month.

**St Pauls Tavern**, corner of Leichhardt and Wharf streets. Brisbane's most established independent music venue, but avoid the dreary hotel bar by having a few somewhere else first. Variable, though most of the bands here are worth checking out.

**Story Bridge Hotel**, 200 Main St, Kangaroo Point. Live bands most nights downstairs at *The Bomb Shelter*. Also hosts the five-day National Beer Festival in July when around 60 of Australia's finest ales are on offer.

---

### DRINKS FOR WOMEN: THE REGATTA HOTEL

Though Australian pubs tend towards being all-male enclaves, women were once legally barred to "protect" them from the corrupting influence of foul language. On 1 April, 1965, Merle Thornton (mother of actress Sigrid) and her friend Rosalie Bogner chained themselves to the footrail of the **Regatta Hotel** bar at Toowong in protest; the movement they inspired led to the granting of "the right to drink alongside men" in the mid-1970s. The pink-and-white colonial hotel which once saw such activity is now a trendy place for a drink after work on Friday; it's on the west bank of the river along Coronation Drive, about 2km from the city centre towards St Lucia.

## GAY AND LESBIAN BRISBANE

Despite its name, Queensland has long had a reputation for repressive attitudes towards gays and lesbians. However, whereas in 1985 you could virtually be arrested on suspicion of being gay, public attitudes have relaxed considerably in the last few years: homosexuality has been **decriminalized** and anti-discrimination legislation is in force. Today, Brisbane's gays and lesbians are reveiling in a loud and energetic scene which gets better every year. In June, the Pride Collective hosts the annual **Pride Festival**, a diverse event, with a street march, fair, art exhibitions, a film festival, sports events, general exhibitionism and a dance party too – the **Queen's Birthday Ball**. April offers another opportunity to wallow in sin, at the **Sleaze Ball**.

The gay scene is largely clustered around the suburbs of Spring Hill, Fortitude Valley, New Valley, New Farm and Paddington. For up-to-the-moment **information**, listen to *Queer Radio*, station *ZZZ* 102.1FM (Wed 6–9pm) or pick up a copy of *Queensland Pride* from gay nightclubs, street distributors and some coffee shops.

### Support groups and information

**AIDS** *Brunswick Building Medical Centre*, 720 Brunswick St, New Farm (☎3358 3333); *Gladstone Road Medical Centre*, 38 Gladstone Rd, Highgate Hill (☎3844 6806), medical services and counselling; *Queensland AIDS Council*, 32 Peel St, South Brisbane (☎3844 1990); *QUIVAA*, 93 Brunswick St, Fortitude Valley (☎3252 5390), needle exchange and safe-sex gear.

**Books** *Women's Bookshop*, 15 Gladstone Rd, Highgate Hill (☎3844 6650) stocks the latest lesbian titles.

**Counselling and information** Gay (7–10pm; ☎3844 2967); lesbian (Tues & Sun 7–10pm; ☎3844 2967).

**OWLS** PO Box 90, Red Hill, QLD 4059. Older, Wiser Lesbian Social Group; for the over 35s.

**The Pride Collective** PO Box 5159, West End 4101. Organizers of the Pride Festival – write for details.

**Queensland Pride** PO Box 591, Mt Gravatt, QLD 4122 (☎3849 7184). Free monthly publication covering Brisbane and the rest of the state.

**Travel** *Triangle Vacations/World Express*, 355 Queen St (☎3221 7527). Specialists in gay and lesbian accommodation, bookings and travel.

*Note: For gay-friendly accommodation, try* Edward Lodge *or the* Sportsmans Hotel *(see* Accommodation *listings, pp.255 & 258); happening cafés include* Franco's *and* Three Monkeys*, both reviewed on p.266, while nightlife focuses on* The Beat, Options, Ruby's, Suzannas*, the* Sportsmans Hotel *(again), and* The Terminus *– all listed on p.267 & below.*

**Suzannas**, at the *Riverside Lounge*, 471 Adelaide St. Women-only on Fri nights; $5 cover.

**Treasury Tavern**, George St. Cheap beer and loud music Wed, Fri & Sat; alternative live bands at weekends – organizes riotous boat cruises from time to time.

## Petrie Terrace

**Café Neon**, 183 Given Terrace. Happy hours Sat 9–11pm, live bands and cheap drinks Friday in the upstairs *Alchemy Bar*.

**Crazies**, corner of Caxton and Judge streets (☎3369 0555). Cabaret restaurant employing professional actors, where the tone is set by the dress regulations – "Wear what you bloody like, it doesn't worry me" – and the floor show can only be described as original. Go in a group and book well in advance. Prices vary with the season; basic charge is $40 per person.

**Paddington Hotel**, 186 Given Terrace. Band and disco on Friday night with a crowded beer garden early on in the evening.

**Underground**, 61 Petrie Terrace. Predictable nightclub and disco – loud pop, coloured lights, expensive drinks, the works.

## Spring Hill

**Options**, at the *Spring Hill Hotel*, corner of Leichhardt and Little Edward streets (☎3831 2210). Two-level gay and lesbian nightclub with bar, dancefloor, coffee-shop and cabaret stage. Events include drag shows, karaoke, strip nights and sausage sizzles. Young crowd, with women's nights on the second and last Friday of each month – *Options* hosts the Ms Wicked Queensland competition. Closed Mon & Tues.

**Sportsmans Hotel**, 130 Leichhardt St. Gay, lesbian and straight crowd filling two floors; pool tables, pinball, bottleshop and bistro.

**The Terminus**, Tues–Sun at the *Actress and Bishop Tavern*, corner of Boundary and Leichhardt streets. Cruisey gay cabaret dance-bar.

## Fortitude Valley

**The Beat**, 677 Ann St. Gay and lesbian pub: small, crowded and sweaty inside; beer garden outside where you can recharge your batteries on bar food.

**Dead Rat Hotel**, Ann St. One of those places which has been totally revamped, but the old crowd still come...sometimes-rough nightclub/disco with weekend bands.

**Roxy**, 201 Brunswick St. Touring bands like *Hunters and Collectors* have been known to play at this long-established venue.

**Shamrock Hotel**, 186 Brunswick St. Huge, rowdy Irish hotel, rated as the best in the Valley for drinking, so other entertainment is only background atmosphere.

**Wickham Hotel**, 308 Wickham St. Acid-Jazz and booze every Sat, with free beer 2–3pm.

**Zoo**, 711 Ann St. A hard-core night out with jazz, local bands and reggae plus $5 meals; Wed–Sun 5pm–late.

## Suburbs

**Brisbane Entertainment Centre**, Melaleuca Drive, Boondall (☎3223 0444). This is where the big commercial acts play, 10km or so north of the centre, but you'll need your own transport.

**Van Gogh's Earlobe**, 588 Stanley St, Wooloongabba (☎3217 2111). A fair way out but offers a wide variety of independent, international talent; Ted Hawkins and *Junkhouse* were recent performers.

# Film and theatre

Compared with the rest of the state, which tends to get only mainstream commercial successes, Brisbane has some very good **cinemas** and a varied programme of films. *The Classic* (963 Stanley St, East Brisbane; ☎3393 1066), *Schonell* (University of Queensland, St Lucia; ☎3371 1879) and *Metro* (109 Edward St; ☎3221 3505) all show contemporary and vintage foreign-language and "offbeat" films. Even the multi-screen *Hoyts* cinema (☎3229 2133), in the Myer Centre, and the luxurious, grand *Regent* (☎3229 5250) further down the mall, are worth checking for unexpected offerings, as is the *State Library* (☎3840 7811). August sees the **Brisbane International Film Festival** in town with a bundle of goodies from around the world shown over a week – contact one of the cinemas for details. Big **theatrical productions** are staged at the *Suncorp Theatre* (179 Turbot St; ☎3221 5177) and the **Performing Arts Complex** (☎3846 4444) on the South Bank in the *Concert Hall*, *Cremorne* or *Lyric* theatres; look out for lower-key lunchtime performances, workshops and foyer exhibitions. Over on Petrie Terrace, *La Boite* (57 Hale St; ☎3369 1622) offers more down-to-earth repertory fare, as do the West End's *Rialto* (59 Hardgrave Rd; ☎3844 3274) and Queensland University's *Cement Box Theatre* (St Lucia; ☎3377 2240).

# Art galleries

Besides the State Art Gallery (see p.263), the most accessible of Brisbane's art showrooms is the *Queensland Aboriginal Creations Gallery* at 35 George Street (☎3224

5370), whose collectable artefacts – made for the tourist trade but as good as you'll find anywhere – include crafts from the Torres Straits, prints, paintings and books. The gallery behind contains sculpture, watercolours and batiks, some "conventional", others personal and stylized.

Moving to more familiar ground, Brisbane's other galleries tend to be somewhat serious. *The Institute of Modern Art* (4th floor, 106 Edward St, opposite the Metro Centre; Tues–Fri 10am–5pm, Sat 11am–4pm; free; ☎3229 5666) is typical, with a severe decor enlivened only by various local artists' experiments and travelling exhibitions; take the rickety lift – the staircase is blocked off at the gallery. Equally rigid are the *Museum of Contemporary Art* at 8 Petrie Terrace (☎3368 3228), and *Fire-Works Gallery* at 336 George Street (☎3221 1069), who display "Aboriginal Art & Other Burning Issues" – too heavy-handed to be enjoyable.

# Listings

**Airlines** *Air New Zealand*, 288 Edward St (☎3229 2799; reservations ☎13 2467); *Air Niugini*, 12 Creek St (☎13 1380); *Air Vanuatu*, 247 Adelaide St (☎3221 2566); *Ansett*, 733 Ann St, Fortitude Valley (☎3854 2828; 24hr reservations ☎13 1300); *British Airways*, Level 17, 241 Adelaide St (☎3223 3123); *Cathay Pacific*, 400 Queen St (☎3221 6747; reservations ☎13 1747); *Flight West*, 333 Adelaide St (☎13 2392); *Garuda*, 288 Edward St (☎3210 0688); *Japan Airlines*, 400 Queen St (☎3229 9916); *Lufthansa*, 380 Queen St (☎3229 2666); *Malaysian Air*, 17th Floor, 80 Albert St (☎3221 5800); *Olympic*, 141 Queen St (☎3221 7747); *Philippine Air*, 141 Queen St Mall (☎3229 6022); *Polynesian Airlines*, corner of George and Queen streets (☎3867 6969); *Qantas*, 214 Adelaide St (International ☎1800 177 767; domestic ☎13 1313); *Singapore*, 344 Queen St (☎3237 7700); *Swissair*, 217 George St (☎3236 2298); *Thai International*, 145 Eagle St (☎3832 2778).

**Banks** Queensland banking hours are Mon–Fri 9.30am–4pm; major branches in the centre are around Queen and Edward streets.

**Bikes** Rental and repairs: *Brisbane Bike Sales*, 87 Albert St (☎3229 2433); open daily (and late Fri night). Bike tours: *Bush Biker Tours* (☎3848 7009): 600cc off-road fun for between one day and two weeks (around $200 per day for trips longer than a day – fully inclusive; cheaper for day-trips). You must be over 21 and have a motorbike licence.

**Books** *American Book Store*, 197 Elizabeth St (☎3229 4677), has a broad selection; *Billabong Books* (☎3229 2801), corner of Queen and North Quay streets centres on environmental concerns; *Dymocks*, 117 Queen St Mall (☎3229 4266), is a good standard bookshop; *Travel Books*, 66 Boundary St, West End (☎3846 5432), has a small but comprehensive range of guides and travel literature; *Women's Bookshop*, 15 Gladstone Rd, Highgate Hill (☎3844 6650) stocks the latest lesbian titles; *UQP*, Customs House, Queen St (☎3365 8926) for academic works and Queensland authors.

**Buses** All ticket desks are on the third floor of the Transit Centre, Roma St. For Queensland and Interstate: *Border Coaches*, (☎3236 4189); *Brisbane Bus Lines* (☎3355 0034); *Bus Australia* (☎13 2323); *Greyhound* (☎13 1238); *Kirklands* (☎3236 4444); *McCafferty's* (☎3236 3033); *Pioneer* (☎13 2030). For Gold Coast and Southeast: *Australia Pacific* (☎13 1304); *Baxway Tours* (☎3236 4163); *Coachtrans* (☎3236 1000); *Sunstate* (☎3236 3355); *Sunshine Coast Coaches* (☎3236 1901).

**Bushwalking** *Brisbane Bushwalkers Club*, 2 Alderley Ave, Alderley (☎3856 4050), 8km west of the centre by train.

**Camping supplies** *Scout Outdoor Centre*, 132 Wickham St, Fortitude Valley (☎3252 4744) and *K2*, 140 Wickham St, Fortitude Valley (☎3854 1340) for top-quality camping gear and information; *Wilderness Shop*, 97 Albert St (☎3229 4178) for more general needs.

**Canoes** There's a good Canoe Trail on Bulimba Creek, out east from the city at Wynnum, which includes riverine forest and mangrove habitats. The City Hall has details on the trail and canoe hire, or call the coucil on ☎3225 6757. You can also explore the upper reaches of the Brisbane River by kayak on one- or two-day expeditions with *Wilderness Escapes* (☎3359 3486).

**Car rental** You'll pay at least $40 for a single day's rental; longer terms work out from $30 a day. Shop around and read rental conditions before signing. Most places will deliver; minimum age is 21. *AA Bargain*, 151 Brunswick St, Fortitude Valley (☎3252 3803); *Ace*, 23 Taylor St, Bowen Hills

(☎3252 1088); *Aircond*, 2/25 Montpelier Rd, Bowen Hills (☎3216 033); *Compass*, 683 Main St, Kangaroo Point (☎3891 2614); *National*, corner of Wickham and Bridge streets, Fortitude Valley (☎3854 1499); *Network Rent A Car*, 398 St Pauls Terrace, Fortitude Valley (☎3252 1599, free call ☎1800 077 977); *Rent-A-Car*, 339 Wickham St, Fortitude Valley (☎3854 1809); *Rent 1 Convertibles* (☎3808 6433, free call ☎1800 773 433);*Roadway*, 238 Nudgee Rd, Hendra (☎3868 1500).

**Consulates** *Austria*, 30 Argyle St, Breakfast Creek (☎3262 8955); *Belgium*, 92a Macarthur Ave (☎3268 7955); *Bolivia*, 210 Queen St (☎3221 1606); *Britain*, BP House 193 North Quay (☎3236 2575; passport/visa info ☎0055/2 0273); *Chile*, 204 Baroona Rd, Rosalie (☎3368 4073); *Cyprus*, 280 Sir Fred Schonell Dve, St Lucia (☎3371 5105); *Denmark*, 180 Queen St (☎3221 8641); *France*, 10 Market St (☎3229 8201); *Germany*, 10 Eagle St (☎3221 7819); *Greece*, 215 Adelaide St (☎3228 5677); *Italy*, 133 Leichhardt St, Spring Hill (☎3832 0099); *Japan*, 12 Creek St (☎3221 5188); *Netherlands*, 101 Wickham Tce (☎3839 9644); *New Zealand*, 288 Edward St (☎3221 9933); *Norway*, 301 Wickham St, Fortitude Valley (☎3854 1855); *Papua New Guinea*, 307 Queen St (☎3221 7915; visas ☎3221 8067); *Phillipines*, 482 Kingsford Smith Dve (☎3268 7212); *Solomon Islands*, 255 Adelaide St (☎3221 7899); *Spain*, 131 Elizabeth St (☎3221 8571); *Sri Lanka*, 139 Roghan Rd (☎3265 3693); *Sweden*, 60 Edward St (☎3221 9797); *Switzerland*, 15 Corowa St, Wavell Heights (☎3266 9782); *Thailand*, 101 Wickham Tce (☎3832 1999); *USA*, 383 Wickham Tce (☎3831 3340).

**Disabled visitors** For information on facilities for disabled visitors, call ☎3225 4416 or ☎3225 6795. The *Disabled Persons Service* maintains a database of accessible accommodation and other facitilites throughout Queensland (☎3224 8031, or outside Brisbane free call ☎1800/177 120).

**Diving** Nearest dive sites to Brisbane are off North Stradbroke and Moreton islands; details on pp.275–277. *South Bank Dive & Hire*, Stanley St (☎3844 7160), is well connected; or contact *Redland Scuba*, Unit 12, 100 Redland Bay Rd, Capella Bar (☎3245 1005).

**Emergencies** Dial 000 and ask for Fire, Ambulance or Police. Queensland Police Headquarters is opposite the Transit Centre in Roma St (☎3364 6464).

**Flights** *Biggles Over Brisbane*, Archerfield Airport (☎3275 3331) provides biplane thrills; free pick-up for two or more people. More stately are *Balloon Flights*, Davies Park, PO Box 12, West End (☎3844 6671).

**Gay and lesbian Brisbane** See box on p.268.

**Hospitals/medical centres** *Roma St Medical Centre*, Level 2, Transit Centre (☎3236 2988); *Royal Brisbane*, Herston Rd, Herston (☎3253 8111; buses #126, #144, or #172 from outside City Hall); *Travellers' Medical Service*, Floor 5, Coles Building, 210 Queen Street (☎3221 8083, after hours ☎3831 9999), Mon–Fri 8am–6pm, Sat 9am–noon, for general services, inoculations, and women's health.

**Left luggage** At the airport, Transit Centre and in basement of Myer Centre.

**Markets** Eagle St (Sun until 3pm) and Brunswick St Mall (Sat until 3pm) for bits and pieces; *Paddy's Markets*, corner of Macquarie and Florence streets, New Farm (daily 9am–4pm) for everything.

**Maps** *Hema*, 239 George St (☎3221 4330), has a wide range of travel literature and maps, from bushwalking guides to road atlases; *Royal Automobile Club of Queensland*'s series (free to members from all RACQ centres) goes down to 4WD-only tracks; *Sunmap*, the state mapping department, sells general-purpose and detailed survey maps, Floor 5, Land Service Centre, Anzac Sq.

**National Parks and Wildlife Service (NPWS)** 160 Ann St (☎3227 7111). Officially the *Department of Environment and Heritage* in Queensland; plenty of fluffy toys and general information about the state's national parks.

**Pharmacies** *Transit Centre Pharmacy*, open from 7am (☎3236 3055); *Day & Night Pharmacy*, Queen St Mall (Mon–Sat 8am–9pm, Sun 10am–5pm).

**Post office** GPO, 261 Queen St (☎3405 1202 or 3405 1448); bring photo ID to collect poste restante.

**RACQ** 300 St Pauls Terrace, Fortitude Valley (☎3361 2468, breakdown service ☎3340 1122).

**Sailing** The *Sail Training Association of Queensland*'s rigged schooner *South Passage* makes 4–10-day voyages around Moreton Bay, with vacancies for 28 trainee crew. Contact the association at P.O. Box 114, Manly 4179 (☎3808 7767 or free call ☎1800 651 271).

**Sheep shearing** The *Australian Woolshed*'s highly polished performance includes a parade of trained sheep (a rarity in itself) and shearing demo, morning tea and sheepdogs putting startled flocks through their paces. They're west of town at 148 Samford Rd, Ferny Hills (☎3351 5366); doors open at 9.00am, shows start 11am and 2pm; $10 per person. Take the train to Ferny Grove, turn right out of the station past Ferny Grove Tavern and it's about an 800-metre walk.

**Sport** Queensland's sport is Rugby League, and the QEII Jubilee Sport Centre at Nathan is the new home of the Brisbane Broncos, though their traditional stomping ground is Lang Park, near the XXXX brewery in Milton. The event of the year is the State of Origin series in May/June. Cricket matches are played at "The Gabba", Vulture St (☎3391 6280).

**Telephones** International pay phones are located in the arcade beside the GPO at 261 Queen St.

**Tours** *Australian Bush Tours*, PO Box 614, South Brisbane 4101 (☎3891 5544), 4WD through the southeast; *Downunder Tours* (PO Box 149, Maryborough 4650; free call ☎1800 072 535) have various all-inclusive, luxury coach packages from Brisbane – from a four-day excursion to Carnarvon Gorge ($386 camping/$755 motel accommodation) to a 22-day Gulf Savannah, Reef and Outback tour ($2478 camping only); *Far Horizons* (☎3284 5475), day-trips to Lamington; *Great Value Tours* (☎3818 0686), Gold and Sunshine coasts, Scenic Rim and whale watching; *Safari O'Neil*, 5 Photinia Place, Bellbowrie 4070 (☎3202 6166), southeast day-trips.

**Trains** Taking the train – comfortable, fabulously slow and inevitably booked out months in advance – is only marginally more expensive than a standard bus fare. Advantages are a bar, restaurant, people to talk to and – a luxury after bus travel – room to move. Unless you book early the best you can hope for is a last-minute cancellation; trains leave from the Transit Centre's ground floor.

**Travel agents** Discounted air fares and other travel arrangements from: *Aardvark Flight Centre*, 181 George St (☎3229 0105); *Flight Centre*, 180 Adelaide St (☎3221 8900); *Jetset Travel*, Floor 18, 288 Edward St (☎3227 1777); *STA*, 111 Adelaide St (☎3221 9388); *World Express Travel*, 355 Queen St (☎3221 7527). There's also the *Backpackers Travel Centre* in room 12, Balcony Level, Brisbane Arcade, off Queen St Mall (☎3221 2225), and a *YHA* office at 154 Roma St (☎3236 1680).

**Women's Brisbane** Contact *Women's Infolink*, 2nd Floor, Pavilion Building, corner of Albert and Queen streets (☎3229 1264 or 3229 1580).

**Working** Popular with job-hunters, Brisbane seems to offer fairly good employment prospects, if you're not too choosy. However, the *CES* seems to actively discourage travellers and your best chance is through a newspaper advert or word of mouth; hostels might need staff, or may be able to arrange bar work, handing out leaflets and the like. There also seems to be a fair amount of casual labour needed to prepare the Exhibition Grounds about eight weeks before the "Ekka" in August.

# Outer Brisbane and Moreton Bay

With the grossly hyped Gold Coast and Hinterland for competition, it's not surprising that few people bother with the country touching Brisbane's fringes. Only 5km to the west, the city is hemmed in by **Mount Coot-tha**'s botanic gardens and the foothills of **Brisbane Forest Park**, which covers the green, wet heights of the D'Aguilar Range and stretches to the edge of **Lake Wivenhoe**.

In the opposite direction, coastal suburbs provide access to the shallow waters of **Moreton Bay**, famed Australia-wide as the home of the unfortunately named Moreton Bay Bug, which is actually a small, delicious lobster-like crustacean. While Brisbane is hardly famous for its beach life, with muddy shorelines attracting mangroves rather than sun worshippers, the largest of the bay's islands, **Moreton** and **North Stradbroke**, are just the right distance from the city to make their sandy beaches accessible but seldom crowded. The island of **St Helena** is not somewhere you'd visit for sun and surf, but its prison ruins recall the convict era and make for an interesting day-trip. In the bay itself, look for dolphins, **dugong** (sea cows), and humpbacked **whales**, which pass by in winter en route to their calving grounds up north – *Great Value Tours* (☎3818 0686) run seasonal whale-watching cruises.

## Mount Coot-tha

The lower slopes of **Mount Coot-tha** are the setting for Brisbane's second **Botanic Gardens**, located on Sir Samuel Griffith Drive (daily 8am–5pm; free; bus #37A from Ann St). A popular place for a Sunday excursion, careful landscaping and the use of enclosures creates varying climates – dry pine and eucalypt groves, a cool sub-tropical rainforest complete with waterfalls and streams, and the elegant **Japanese Gardens**. In summer, the **tropical plant dome** seems an unnecessary feature in an already sweltering climate; inside, the floor is almost completely occupied by a pond – stocked with fish – and is overshadowed by towering tropical greenery, dripping with moisture. Worth hunting out are the vanilla orchid's extraordinary flowers and the lotus lilly's flat pads, usually found only a thousand kilometres to the north.

The other dome in the gardens does duty as a **planetarium** (show times: Wed–Fri 3.30pm & 7.30pm, Sat 1.30pm, 3.30pm & 7.30pm, Sun 1.30pm & 3.30pm; $8). While the foyer display is somewhat dry and dated, the show itself, which you view lying back under the dome's ceiling, is an interesting – if not wildly exciting – look at the key features of Brisbane's night sky.

After the Botanic Gardens most people head up the road to the **summit** for panoramas of the city and, on a good day, the Moreton Bay islands. **Walking tracks** from here make for moderate hikes of an hour or two through dry gum woodland, and include several **Aboriginal trails** – the best of which branches off the Slaughter Falls track and points out plants and their uses as food, artefacts and hunting poisons. Pamphlets on the tracks are available from the Botanic Gardens library (Tues–Fri 9.30am–4.30pm, Sat 10am–noon) and the City Hall information desk.

## Brisbane Forest Park

If your plans don't include seeing any other forests in the southeast, take advantage of **Brisbane Forest Park**'s proximity to the city. While lacking the sustained beauty of Lamington and the Scenic Rim, it contains the area's last tracts of virgin forest, well-stocked with wildlife, pretty lookouts and easy walking tracks. A day is ample time to look around, or you could make the park the first stage of a scenic circuit from Brisbane via Lake Wivenhoe and Toowoomba.

There are a dozen or more places to head for within the park's 28,000-odd hectare boundaries. The pick of these include **Bellbird Grove** (4km from Park Headquarters), containing another of the city's Aboriginal trails with an outdoor museum of bark huts housing more information on traditional plant uses; **Boombana**'s one-kilometre rainforest circuit, complete with moss-covered logs, towering, buttressed trees, and optimistic signs identifying birds you should encounter; and **Maiala National Park** (30km into the park), a fascinating tract of sub-tropical forest similar to Lamington's, where palms, figs and other giant trees compete for light, vines tangle up the forest floor and gullies guide fast-flowing creeks. Between these enclaves are the townships of Mount Nebo and Mount Glorious, as well as **Manorina Bush Camp**, the park's sole tent site (see "Practicalities" below).

There's plenty of **wildlife** to be encountered along the park's many kilometres of **walking tracks**. Catbirds snarl at each other in rainforest, while male satin bowerbirds woo females with an elaborate tunnel made from grass and decorated with blue objects (Queensland dairies changed the colour of their plastic bottle lids when it was suggested that bowerbirds were throttling themselves on them). At night, you'll see wallabies on verges, glider possums around flowering trees in open woodland, echidnas scraping through leaf litter for ants, and possibly the bandy-bandy, a timid snake boldly striped in black and white, which forms a spiral with its body when frightened.

**Lake Wivenhoe** was created in the late-1970s to stop the Brisbane River flooding the city again; its southern end is just visible from the outlook about 10km west of Maiala. The outlook sits on the western edge of the **D'Aguilar Range** and the view drops off wooded hills down to the drier country of the southwest. A road links the park with the Brisbane Valley highway and if you're westward-bound, Toowoomba (see p.380) is 140km away via the Wivenhoe Dam – a slower-paced route than the alternative Warrego highway.

## Practicalities

While you can come within 500m of the park gates via **The Gap**, 5km west of the city, by **bus** (*Cityexpress* #506 from Albert Street), you really need your own **car** to get around – or you could take a **guided tour**. The **Park Headquarters** (Mon–Fri 9am–4.30pm, Sat & Sun 10am–4.30pm; ☎3300 4855) makes a good first stop, for maps, information, details of tours and, if you want to **camp out**, a permit. The only **accommodation** in the park is the rather rudimentary Manorina Bush Camp, whose facilities run to barbecues, pit toilets and water; note that the nearest source of supplies is 3km away, at Mount Nebo. Ask at the desk about the *Go Bush* series of films, lectures and tours which introduce the environment and show you what to expect. In general, spring is the best time to visit; animals are active, many plants are in flower and rain infrequent. It can be cold at night in winter, with low cloud.

Below the headquarters is the **Freshwater Study Centre** (Mon–Fri 9am–4.30pm, Sat & Sun 10am–4.30pm; $3.50), an idealized creek system where lungfish, turtles, snakes and frogs co-exist with few of the stresses they'd encounter living this close together in the wild. Everything is well labelled and it's unlikely you'll ever get better views of crayfish mincing over the gravel at the bottom of the stream or water dragons sunning themselves on rocks.

# St Helena

Small, low and triangular, **St Helena Island** sits 8km from the mouth of the Brisbane River. Managed by the National Parks (local office ☎3396 5113), you can get there on a day-trip with *St Helena Island Tours* (from BP Marina, 101 Kingsford Smith Drive, Breakfast Creek – reached by bus #190 or #160, taxi at weekends; Mon–Fri $23, Sat & Sun $29 including barbecue lunch; ☎3260 7944) or *Cat-o'-Nine-Tails* (from Manly Jetty, best reached by train from the city; $23; ☎3393 3726) – departures vary according to season, so phone tour operators for details.

Once the hunting grounds of local tribes, St Helena took its name from a parallel drawn with the exile of Napoleon Bonaparte to St Helena in the South Atlantic – in 1828 an Aborigine known as Napoleon was dumped here after he became too troublesome for the Dunwich jail. Forty years later, the spectre of overcrowding in mainland prisons prompted the government to turn the island into a penal settlement, and after clearing rainforest for timber and to prevent escapes, gardens were planted and houses built from coral blocks and clay. In some respects it was a model system: prisoners were taught a trade and even paid for their labour, and there were only three escapes in 65 years. The government found it particularly useful for political troublemakers, such as leaders of the 1891 shearers' strike and, with more justice, a couple of Blackbirders.

A **tour** of the prison island, endearingly tagged the "Hell Hole of the South Pacific" during its working life, leaves you thankful you missed out on the "good old days". A clue to why there were so few escapes is provided by the rusty swimming enclosure at the jetty, which was constructed to protect warders from the sharks whose presence was actively encouraged around the island. Evidence of the prisoners' industry and self-sufficiency are still to be seen in the stone houses, as well as in the remains of a sugar mill, paddocks, wells and an ingenious lime kiln built into the shoreline (and fed seashells). The Deputy Superintendent's house has been turned into a bare museum, displaying a ball and chain lying in a corner, and photographs from the prison era. Outside, the gardens that once produced prize-winning olive oil are now sparse, and the two cemeteries have been desecrated: many headstones were carried off as souvenir coffee-tables, the corpses dug up and sold as medical specimens. The remaining stones comprise simple concrete crosses stamped with a number for the prisoners, or inscribed marble tablets for the warders and their children. The last inmate left in 1933.

# Moreton Island

A narrow band of stabilized sand dunes 38km long, **Moreton Island's** faultless beaches are distinctly underpopulated for much of the year – perfect for surfing, fishing or camping. The island can be reached by resort **ferry** to Tangalooma (☎3268 6333); the *Moreton Venture* (☎3895 1000) to Tangalooma or Kooringal, or the *Coombie Trader* **barge** (and vehicle transport) to Bulwer (☎3203 6399). However you decide to go, the trip takes up to two hours, costs around $20 and you'll need to check timetables and book in advance. The worst times to visit are at Christmas and Easter, when up to a thousand vehicles crowd onto the island at once.

Taking your own **vehicle** to the island, whose sand tracks are 4WD-only, will cost at least $130 return. **Tours** organized by *Combie Trader* and *Sunrover Expeditions* (1 Eversleigh St, Scarborough; ☎3203 4241 or free call ☎1800 07 7353), last from one to three days. The **rules of the road** are the same as on the mainland; check tide times before driving on the beach, and be aware that pedestrians may not hear you above the sound of the surf. **Supplies** on the island are expensive and limited to Bulwer and Kooringal, so you need to be self-sufficient – including in water if you camp. There are no banks. And before you go in the water, remember that the beaches aren't patrolled and there are no shark nets.

## Bulwer, Tangalooma and Kooringal

The island's northernmost landing is at **BULWER**, a cluster of weatherboard "weekenders" and a **store** (☎3408 2202; fuel, beer, plus basic **accommodation** in 6-person units, ⑤). The barge offloads next to the Bulwer Wrecks, rusty skeletons grounded on the beach forming a useful perch for anglers. An expensive 4WD **minibus** ($45 return; ☎3408 2661) is usually waiting if you want transport to anywhere on the northern end or across to the island's eastern side. Halfway down the island, **TANGALOOMA's** barge lands at another set of wrecks: deliberately sunk to create an artificial harbour, but gradually swamped by sand, they've become a **snorkelling** site at high tide. A National Parks **campsite** here (with water, showers and toilets) gets as crowded as anywhere on the island. The resort ferry lands just south at *Tangalooma Resort* (PO Box 1102, Eagle Farm; ☎3268 6333; ⑥), which has parts of a former whaling station incorporated into its buildings. Shady but busy over weekends and holidays, it has the only cold drinks and restaurant on the island – neat dress required to indulge. Right at the tail end of the island, **KOORINGAL** is a sleepy version of Bulwer with another store (fuel and units; ☎5549 7170; ⑤) that only opens for two hours, two days a week – opinion is divided as to which two.

You can **camp** anywhere along beaches where there aren't signs asking you not to, with designated areas at Tangalooma and Ben-Ewa (3km towards Bulwer) on the west coast and Blue Lagoon and Eagers Creek on the east side. Permits are available from barge operators or on site at $3 per person per night.

## Around the rest of the island

The **northern** end of Moreton is about 9km wide, covered in ferns, grasstrees, paperbark and banksias around the shore, and dense scrub inland. North Point is just that: dunes nearby form near-vertical cliffs, while fresh water, brown with tannin, seeps out into lagoons. The island is anchored around rocky **Cape Moreton**, which is capped by a red-and-white lighthouse, built between 1857 and 1928 and still operating. There's a museum in the house below and fine views down the east coast from adjacent cliffs.

The island's **eastern** side is more attractive than the west – always less crowded, the campsites are nicer and the beach has good surf. Dolphins come in close to shore here – something the Aborigines turned to their advantage by using the dolphins to chase fish into the shallows. Writing in the 1870s about his life in Brisbane, Tom Petrie reported that the Ngugi men would beat the surf with their spears, and:

> By and by, as in response, porpoises would be seen as they rose to the surface making for the shore and in front of them schools of tailor fish. It may seem wonderful, but they were apparently driving the fish towards the land. When they came near, [they] would run out into the surf, and with their spears would jab down here and there at the fish, at times even getting two on one spear, so plentiful were they.

**Blue Lagoon** is the largest and most accessible of the island's freshwater lakes, only 500m from the beach and adjacent to the smaller, picturesque **Honeyeater Lake**. The beach makes an ideal place to camp: 13km from Bulwer by road, it is blessed with shady trees, and the site is supplied with water, showers and toilets. Another campsite at Eagers Creek is joined to Tangalooma by a ten-kilometre road, which may be slightly too convenient for the landing point at busy times.

The central and **southern** inland parts of the island mainly consist of exposed dunes, some covered in scrub, others forming white "blows": destabilized, shifting hills that slowly roll over forests. From Kooringal, diversions include **Mount Tempest's** 280-metre peak, sand-tobogganing in the **Desert**, and the twelve-kilometre return trip to **Big and Little Sandhills** via Toompani beach and eerie, long-dead stands of trees in the wake of the dunes. Take plenty of water.

There's decent **diving** around the deepest points of Tangalooma's wrecks, but Curtain Reef is superior – an artificial conglomeration of barges, tugs, cars and tyres encrusted with shells, it attracts all types of marine life including sharks, dolphins, groupers and huge rays. Contact the resort for seasonal details, transport and rental gear or look under "Diving" in the Brisbane "Listings", p.271.

# North Stradbroke Island

**North Stradbroke Island** is, at 40km long, the largest and most established of the bay's islands, with sealed roads and the fully serviced townships of Dunwich, Amity and Point Lookout. Ninety percent of "Straddie" is given over to rutile (titanium oxide) mining and the majority of the 3200 residents are employees of *Consolidated Rutile Ltd.* The mine sites south of Amity, and in the central west and south, are far from exhausted but their future is precarious, thanks to oversupply of the world market. Other industries focus on timber, a by-product of preparing land for mining and, increasingly, tourism.

**Transport to the island** leaves from Toondah Harbour at Cleveland, with *Stradbroke Water Taxis* crossing to Dunwich at least ten times daily (return fares $9 per person, $63 per car; ☎3286 2666). There's also a daily **bus** ($24 return includes water taxi; ☎3287 1275) from Brisbane's Transit Centre to Amity and Dunwich, which also collects en route at Cleveland train station. Some island accommodation will arrange **transport** for their guests – see below.

Some roads on Stradbroke are open to mining vehicles only, so drivers should look out for the signs. Off-roading through the centre is ill-advised: quite apart from the damage caused to the dune systems, the sand is very soft and being pulled out can be ruinously expensive.

## Dunwich to Main Beach

Unless you need to fuel up or visit the bank, there's little to keep you at **DUNWICH**. Two sealed roads head out of town, east through the island's centre towards **Main Beach**, or north to Amity and Point Lookout. The road through the centre passes two **lakes**, the second and smaller of which, Blue Lake, is a national park and source of fresh water for the island's wildlife, which is most plentiful early on in the day. Beyond

Blue Lake you have to cross the **Eighteen Mile Swamp** to reach Main Beach and, though there's a causeway, it's 4WD from there on. You can **camp** behind the beach anywhere south of this causeway (north is mining company land), but come prepared for the mosquitoes that swarm around the mangroves; the southernmost point, looking over to South Stradbroke Island (see p.286), is an angling and wildlife mecca, with bird life and kangaroos lounging around on the beaches.

## The Top End

Heading north from Dunwich, it's 10km to where the road forks left to Amity and right to Point Lookout: **AMITY** is a very sleepy place based around a jetty, while **POINT LOOKOUT** is where most visitors end up if they don't want to camp. Nineteen kilometres from Dunwich, Point Lookout spreads out around Stradbroke's single rock headland, overlooking a string of beaches. Stretched out along the road are a pub, takeaway pizza place, a store, some cafés and various **accommodation** establishments. Top of the range is *Anchorage Village Resort* (☎3409 8266; ⑥), a comfortable, if unimaginative, place to stay. At the other end of the scale, *Stradbroke Island Guesthouse* (☎3409 8888; ①) and *Straddie Hostel* (☎3409 8679; ①) both have dorm beds, free loans of surfboards, bikes and fishing gear and **cheap bus deals** from Brisbane's Roma Street Transit Centre; call the hostels for details. Other distractions are offered by *Stradbroke Riding and Canoes* (☎3409 8279): riding costs $20 for one hour, or $35 for two hours; half-day canoe trips on Stradbroke's freshwater lakes let you get close to waterlilies, wildfowl and pretty scenery – all for $35. Outside of Point Lookout's two **caravan parks**, you can camp on the foreshore west of Rocky Point's beach access road.

The **beaches** here are good. **Flinders** runs west of Amity; **Home** and **Cylinder** between here and Cylinder Headland are both patrolled and, therefore, crowded during holiday weekends. If you don't mind risking unwatched waters, make for **Deadman's Beach** or **Frenchman's Bay**. Above on the headland, there are fine views and the chance to see loggerhead turtles, dolphins and – with binoculars – maybe whales from the walking track around North Gorge down to Main Beach. Offshore, Stradbroke's **dive sites** around Flat and Shag rocks are renowned for groups of grey nurse sharks, moray eels and butterfly cod. *ProDive North Stradbroke* (☎3409 8074) discount their five-day dive course through the hostels.

# THE GOLD COAST

Beneath a jagged skyline shaped by countless high-rise beachfront apartments, the **Gold Coast** is Australia's Miami Beach or Costa del Sol, a striking contrast to Brisbane, only an hour away. As a point of entry into Queensland it could hardly provide a less typical picture of the rest of the state. Aggressively superficial, it's not the place to go if you're seeking peace and quiet: the endless succession of nightclubs, bars and theme parks provide raucous, relentless entertainment. It can be enjoyable for a couple of days – perhaps as a weekend break from Brisbane – but there's little variation on the beach/ nightclub scene and if you're concerned that this will leave you jaded, bored or broke you might well be better off avoiding this corner of the state altogether.

The coast forms a virtually unbroken beach 40km long, from **South Stradbroke Island** past **Surfers Paradise** and **Burleigh Heads** to the New South Wales border at **Coolangatta**. Surfers Paradise has the highest concentration of people and skyscrapers; as you head south through the strip of motels and shops the pace slows (relatively) and it's easier to find some unoccupied sand. The beaches are still touted as the main attraction, though they've become a backdrop to more commercial interests, and they swarm with bathers and board-riders all year round. **Surfing** bloomed along the coast in the 1930s and still pulls in veterans and novices; learning is as easy as renting a board and trying. Coolangatta, Burleigh Heads and South Stradbroke have the best waves and definitely the more serious surfies, but you'll find gentler swell all the way along the coast.

With around three hundred days of sunshine each year there's little "off-season" as such. **Rain** can fall at any time during the year, including mid-winter – usually dry in the rest of the state – but it's the possibility of cyclones between January and Easter that tends to thin out the crowds, who reappear in time for the Gold Coast **Indy car race** in March and their numbers gradually swell over the year, peaking at Christmas.

## Getting there and around

A **bus** from Brisbane's Transit Centre costs $12 – less with a student or hostel card – and takes an hour to Surfers, slightly more to Coolangatta. If you're **driving**, there's a detour at Beenleigh to Queensland's oldest rum distillery at the *Beenleigh Tavern* (tours at 11am, noon, 1pm & 2pm; ☎3287 2488); it started in 1860 as a pirate business on the Albert River.

The coastal highway from New South Wales enters Queensland at Coolangatta, where you'll also find the **Gold Coast Airport**. *Airport Transit* **shuttle buses** run to Coolangatta and Surfers Paradise (☎5536 6841 for information).

The Gold Coast highway is covered by a 24-hour **local bus** service (*Surfside Buses*) running between Coolangatta and Southport. The whole journey costs $4; you'll save money with a **day rover** pass for multiple trips. Otherwise you'll need to take a **taxi** or **rent** a vehicle; more details in individual resort accounts.

# Coolangatta

**COOLANGATTA** merges seamlessly with Tweed Heads (in New South Wales; see p.204) along Boundary Road. With only a few pointers to tell them apart – a sign welcoming you to the sunshine state, a sudden absence of "Adult Shops" in Queensland – you'll probably make the crossing between states without realizing it. Unless it's New Year, when everyone takes advantage of the one-hour time difference between the states to celebrate twice, most travellers bypass Coolangatta completely in favour of Surfers Paradise. In doing so, they miss some of the best surf, least crowded beaches and the only place along the coast which can boast a real "local" community.

## Arrival and information

The **bus station** (Mon–Fri 7.30am–5.30pm, Sat 8am–4pm, Sun 8am–noon; ☎5536 6600) is in downtown Coolangatta, on the corner of Warner and Griffith streets, the latter an extension of the Gold Coast highway which terminates on the border, one kilometre south at Point Danger. In the other direction, the road jinks sharply around Kirra Point before joining the highway 3km north, outside the Gold Coast Airport: *Airport Transit* (☎5536 6841; $4) shuttle buses serve Coolangatta. The helpful **information centre** (Mon–Fri 8am–4pm, Sat 8am–1pm; ☎5536 7765) is located at Beach House, Marine Parade, around the corner from the bus station.

## Accommodation

Budget **accommodation** is strung out along the highway in Bilinga and Kirra, while the more expensive places occupy the tower blocks overlooking the sea on Marine Parade and Point Danger: the list below details some of the options. For **camping**, try *Border Van Park*, Boundary Street, Tweed Heads (☎5536 3134).

**Coolangatta Sands Hotel**, Griffith St (☎5536 3066). Decent hotel rooms with shared bathrooms and the usual sleepless Friday nights. ④.

**On the Beach**, 118 Marine Parade, Greenmount Beach (☎5536 3624). Single or double rooms in self-contained flats. Tidy and well placed for town and surf. ⑤.

## SURFING THE GOLD COAST

As locals will tell you, the Gold Coast has some of the best surfing beaches in the world. And in terms of consistency this might be true – on any given day there will be rideable surf somewhere along the coast – with 200-metre-long sand bottom point breaks and rideable waves peaking at about four metres in prime conditions. The area is known for its barrels, particularly during the summer cyclone season when the winds shift around to the north; in winter the swell is smaller but more reliable – good learning conditions. A rule of thumb for finding the best surf is to follow the wind: north when the wind blows from the north, south when it comes from the south. Generally, you'll find the best swell along the south coast (Surfers Paradise doesn't really live up to the name) and on South Stradbroke. While sharks might worry you, more commonplace hostility is likely to come from the local surfies who form tight-knit cliques with very protective attitudes towards their beaches.

On the subject of sharks and general safety, all beaches as far north as Surfers are patrolled; look for the signs. Sea temperatures range between 26°C in summer and 17°C in winter so a 2–3mm wet suit is adequate. Hard-core surfies come for Christmas and the cyclone season, though spring is really the busiest time. You'll find competitions or events most weekends, advertised through local surf shops.

**Queensland Hotel**, Boundary St (☎5536 2600). Bed above the bar, with breakfast; very noisy weekends. ④.

**YHA**, 3km up the coast at 230 Coolangatta Rd/Gold Coast Highway, Bilinga, next to the airport (☎5536 7644). Threadbare and unwelcoming; reports suggest that they won't open the door if you arrive after the 10pm lockup. ②.

## The town and the beaches

Coolangatta is set out along **Griffith Street**, one block back from the beach, where you'll find banks, shops, and pleasantly little in the way of high-density development. Even the motel towers on Point Danger are well spaced, and the black-and-white chequered paving harks back pleasingly to smalltown seaside life in the early 1960s. **Marine Parade** fronts the shore, the view north over sand and sea ending with the jagged teeth of the skyscrapers on the horizon at Surfers Paradise.

Straddling the border at Point Danger, the **Captain Cook Memorial Lighthouse** forms a shrine where pillars enclose a large bronze globe detailing Cook's peregrinations around the southern hemisphere. Erratic flashes of colour among the waves 25m below are surfers making the most of Flagstaff Beach's swell – at weekends the water is very crowded.

Coolangatta's daytime action is in the **surf**, the best being between Point Danger and Kirra Point (or Flagstaff, across the state border in Tweed Heads) – exactly where depends on the wind. Greenmount is fairly reliable and a good beach for beginners; Snapper Rocks round to Point Danger is for the more dedicated. For sun worshippers, Coolangatta beach is fine if you're staying nearby, but the six-kilometre stretch of sand north of Kirra Point is wider and less crowded. **Surfing supplies and rentals** can be had from either *Pipedream* (Griffith St; ☎5599 1164), the best for gear and information about local conditions and competitions, or *Mount Woodgee* (122 Griffith St; ☎5536 5937). Board/ski hire is around $20 a day plus a $40 deposit, wetsuits start at $7.50 plus $20 deposit. All shops have decent secondhand boards for sale, though local boards tend to be rather thin and refined if you plan to use them elsewhere. Or you could look for a bargain in the pawnbroker's shop in Griffith Street. For personal **tuition**, try *Beachcomber Bill* (Greenmount Beach, near *Oskars Restaurant*; ☎5536 7084). He's been living here for thirty years and has taught several champions in his time.

Cook Island and Nine Mile Reef are the main **diving sites**, with two shipwrecks nearby. Of interest are nurse sharks, turtles, canyons and scattered groups of reef fish. *Kirra Dive Centre* (corner of Creek and South streets, Kirra; ☎5536 6622) charge around $55 plus equipment for two local dives.

### Eating, drinking and nightlife

If you're doing your own cooking, there's a small **supermarket** opposite the cinema in Griffith Street, or cross the border and seek out the main shopping complex on Wharf Street, in Tweed Heads. There are plenty of **snack bars** along Griffith Street, and you should definitely check out *Orbansen's Milk Bar* (23 Griffith St) – not for the food, but for the original 1950s decor, complete with jukebox selectors at each table. The *Queensland Hotel* on Boundary Street has cheap lunches and early breakfasts for a post-surf refill. More upmarket is *Oskars Restaurant* on Greenmount Beach (☎5536 4621), with cheap breakfasts, pricier main meals, and a nice view of the surf; *Thai Star* (☎5536 6202) in Griffith Street is the pick of the Asian restaurants.

Coolangatta's **nightlife** centres around the pubs – you'll have to rely on posters to find out what's on since the coast's weekly magazines concentrate on Surfers Paradise and ignore the south. Best are sessions at the *Coolangatta Sands Hotel*'s fairly relaxed bar (corner of Griffith and McLean streets; ☎5536 3066) and the *Coolangatta Hotel*'s nightclub (corner of Griffith and Warner streets), which has good live music and pool competitions. *The Patch* at the *Queensland Hotel* has very live bands and "high-energy rock 'n' roll" Friday and Saturday nights, audible on the other side of town.

### Listings

**Airlines** *Ansett* ☎5536 0600; *Qantas* ☎5599 0199 (flight information only).

**Camping Supplies** *Sherry's Disposals*, 27–31 Wharf St, Tweed Heads (☎5536 3700).

**Car rental** *Cheap Wheels* (112 Griffith St; ☎5536 6261) charges $20 per day (plus insurance) for unlimited kilometres; *Car-Azy Rentals* (41 Gold Coast Highway; ☎5536 8388) starts at $25 inclusive; *Surfers Rent-a-Car* (☎5572 0600) charges $15 plus insurance. *Economy* (57 Golden Four Drive, opposite airport; ☎5536 8104) and *Kelly's* 101 Golden Four Drive (☎5599 1122), start at $25 a day.

**Flights** *Paradise Helicopters* (☎5536 9422) charge $35 per person for a 10-min "scenic" flight up the coast; they can also take you out to Mount Warning, Moreton Island or Brisbane.

**Skydiving** With 30min of training you're ready for a free-fall parachute jump with *Tandem Skydive* (☎5599 1920), jumping with an instructor from 2800m. Considering the length of time in the air it's far better value ($270) than a bungee jump and for pure terror the experience can't be beaten.

**Taxi** ☎5536 1144.

# Currumbin to Surfers Paradise

The central section of the Gold Coast lacks any real focus. Haphazardly developed and visually unattractive, it exists very much in the shadow of Surfers Paradise, but can't match its intensity. The highway is just a continuous maze of crowded, multi-lane traffic systems and drab buildings which gain momentum the further north you drive, but leave the road and there are beaches, two **wildlife sanctuaries** and – unbelievable amid all the commotion and noise – Burleigh Head's tiny **national park** which preserves the coast's original environment.

### Currumbin Beach and Sanctuary

Seven kilometres from Coolangatta, **CURRUMBIN BEACH** is a nice, relatively undeveloped stretch between Elephant Rock and Currumbin Point, and with a breeze there are usually some decent rollers to ride. **Accommodation** prospects include *Ronian Caravan Park* (11 Cooinda Ave; ☎5534 2367) and a few boarding houses facing the beach along Pacific Parade.

Just to the north, **PALM BEACH** is more sheltered and *Le Beach Club* (953 Gold Coast Highway; ☎5598 3816; ②) has dorm beds and loans out surf gear and canoes – try heading up Currumbin creek. For **meals**, *Vikings* in the Surf Club building below Elephant Rock is open for lunch Friday to Sunday noon–2pm, for dinner from Wednesday to Sunday 6–9.30pm and breakfast from around 8am on Sunday. The $8 all-you-can-eat pasta plates and dessert will replace energy lost to the surf.

**Currumbin Sanctuary** in Tomewin Street (daily 8am–5pm; $15) was started in 1946 by Alex Griffiths, who foresaw the decline of the coastal environment and developed the seventy-acre park as a wildlife refuge. Forest, lake and grassland fairly bustle with native fauna. There are the usual feeding times and tame kangaroos but the park's strongest point is the apparently natural surroundings, best experienced from the **elevated walkways** through the forest, where you'll see koalas, tree kangaroos and birds at eye-level.

### Burleigh Heads: the Last Rainforest

The Gold Coast's bitumen and paving was, less than fifty years ago, dense eucalypt and vine forest. The last fraction is preserved in a tiny, fragile **national park** halfway between Coolangatta and Surfers Paradise at **BURLEIGH HEADS**. Entrance is on foot from the car park on the Esplanade, or turn sharply at the lights below the hill just south of the headland for the **visitors information centre** (daily 9am–4pm; ☎5535 3032).

**Geologically**, Burleigh's headland stems from the prehistoric eruptions of the Mount Warning volcano, 30km to the southwest. Lava surfaced through vents, cooling to hard basalt which was extruded into tall hexagonal columns, now mostly tumbled and covered in vines. Rainforest colonizes the richer volcanic soils, while stands of red gum grow in weaker sandy loam; along the eastern seafront there's a patch of exposed heathland bordered by groups of pandanus and a beach along the mouth of Tallebudgera Creek. This diversity is amazing considering the minimal space, but urban encroachment has seriously affected the wildlife. Butterflies and **birds** are the most obvious inhabitants – look out for the fairy wren's telltale black and red pattern on the heathland – but the gums also support a small koala population (though, notoriously sensitive to disturbance, they often make themselves scarce). Natural resources once attracted Aborigines; there are a few mounds of half-buried shells up on the headland to mark their passing.

These subjects come to life two kilometres inland at **Fleays Fauna Centre** (West Burleigh Rd; daily 9am–5pm; $10; ☎5576 2411, bus service ☎5592 4166). David Fleay was the first person to persuade platypus to breed in captivity and the park has a special section devoted to this curious animal. The **free guided tours** are good; take advantage of their night **spotlight** and daily **Aboriginal** talk. Outside the parks, Burleigh's main attraction is **surf** around the headland, but the rocks make it rough for novices. There are no campsites nearby, so you'll have to make it a day-trip unless you fancy one of the local hotels – the *Burleigh Hotel* (☎5535 1000; ④), on the Esplanade, is a good as any, and offers $10 meals.

## Surfers Paradise

Spiritually, if not geographically, **SURFERS PARADISE** is at the heart of the Gold Coast, the place where its aims and aspirations are most evident. For the residents, this involves making money by providing services and entertainment for tourists; visitors reciprocate by parting with their cash. All around and irrespective of what you're doing – shopping for clothes, sitting on the beach, partying in one of the frenetic nightclubs or even finding a bed – the pace is brash and glib. Don't come here expecting to be allowed to relax; subtlety is non-existent and you'll find enjoying Surfers depends largely on how much it bothers you having the party mood rammed down your throat.

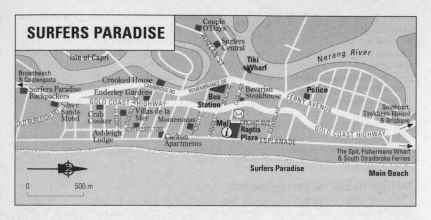

Surfers' beaches have been attracting tourists since late last century, though the town only started developing along commercial lines during the 1950s when the first multi-storey beachfront apartments were built. The demand for views over the ocean led to ever higher towers which began to encroach on the dunes; together with the sheer volume of people attracted here, this soon caused serious **erosion** problems along the entire coast. Attempts to stabilize the foreshore with retaining walls, groynes and sand pumping from offshore have had little long-term success. But this hardly seems to matter. Although Surfers Paradise is a firm tribute to Australia's skill in advertising its lifestyle overseas as an eternal beach party, most people would probably say that they come here not for the beaches but simply because everyone else does.

### Arrival, information and security

Surfers' **bus station** (☎5531 6400) is in Beach Road on the corner of the highway, one street down from Cavill Avenue. Here you'll find **luggage lockers**, **coach company desks**, and an **accommodation information** counter. From the Gold Coast **airport**, hop on an *Airport Transit* bus ($8 one-way, $14 return). If the hostel of your choice isn't present, phone them for a **free pick-up**, and don't be surprised if, while walking around with your luggage, hostel minibuses hail you as they pass. The **tourist information office** is on Cavill Avenue (Mon–Fri 8am–5.30pm, Sat 9am–5.30pm, Sun 9am–4pm; ☎5538 4419).

**Security** is worth bearing in mind. Many people migrate to Surfers in search of an easier life, only to find themselves homeless and hard up. Don't leave vehicles unlocked at any time, don't take valuables down the beach, and don't wander alone at night; muggings are common, especially around nightclubs – so take advantage of the courtesy buses run by hostels. The situation definitely deteriorates around the peak times of Christmas and Easter.

### Accommodation

You need to **book** all **accommodation** in advance. Typically quiet early on, the **hostels** come to life late in the day and you won't be left in peace until you've signed up for trips to nightclubs, parties and beach events. They've all struck deals with various clubs for cheap entry and drinks, and all have much the same facilities, too – pool, dormitories, kitchen, TV, and loans of surfboards. Many places don't encourage long stays, but it may be worth asking about weekly rates. **Motels**, on the other hand, sometimes insist on a minimum three-day stay – during quieter times they might acquiesce and bargaining may get you a reduced rate. Peak-season rates range from $45 to a few hundred dollars a night; off-season and mid-week, rooms are considerably cheaper. Expect to pay more for ocean views. There are simply too many possibilities to give a comprehensive list; those below are central and relatively inexpensive.

**Ashleigh Lodge**, 19 Vista St (☎5539 8541). Not the most modern place, but the self-contained units, arranged around the pool, are clean and comfortable. ④.

**Carlton Apartments**, corner of Northcliffe Terrace and Clifford St (☎5538 5877). Fully self-contained units in a seven-storey block on the beach. Price is per unit (2 people) per night for a minimum of five nights. ⑤.

**Couple O' Days**, 18 Whelan St (☎5592 4200). Faded and quiet hostel with little pressure laid on; budget meals and off-street parking. ①.

**Enderley Gardens**, 38 Enderley Ave (☎5570 1511). Self-contained units, one block away from the beach, 10min from the heart of Surfers; facilities include pool, spa and tennis court. ⑤.

**Main Beach Caravan Park**, Main Beach Parade (☎5581 7722). No camping, but on-site vans available. Very crowded. ②.

**Silver Sands Motel**, 2985 Gold Coast Highway (☎5538 6041). Low-rise and pleasant, despite a location on the main highway. 100m from the beach; there's a pool, too. ⑤.

**Surf and Sun**, 3323 Gold Coast Highway (☎5538 7305). Small, helpful hostel with a happy-go-lucky attitude and some self-contained rooms. Free bike loans and good connections if you're looking for work. ①.

**Surfers Central**, 40 Whelan St (☎5538 4344). Close to the bus station and with its own squash court; tatty but good-humoured and less hyped than most. ①.

**Surfers Paradise Backpackers**, 2835 Gold Coast Highway (☎5538 7250). Purpose-built, sparklingly clean and efficient, the bed price covers everything, including use of washing machines; it's a large place and rooms are spacious. They also organize tours to Scenic Rim national parks. ①.

**Surfers Tradewinds**, 42 Beach Parade (☎5592 1149). Large and impersonal but otherwise excellent, both in terms of facilities and value for long group stays. Price is per person, based on four sharing a two-bedroom unit for seven nights. ②–③.

**Trekkers**, 22 White St, Southport (☎5591 5616). Beautifully restored old house 3km from the centre; comfortable and with heaps of deals, offers and trips. Very hard-sell though, and there's no escape from continuous piped music. ①.

**Villas de la Mer**, corner of Markwell Ave and Northcliffe Tce (☎5592 6324). Security-conscious apartments in three-storey complex, with ocean views from upper levels. Rooms simple but modern and well furnished. Price is per person, based on four sharing a two-bedroom flat. ④.

## The town – and theme parks

Downtown Surfers Paradise is a thin ribbon of partially reclaimed land between the ocean and the **Nerang River** which – as the Broadwater – flows north, parallel with the beach, past **the Spit** and South Stradbroke Island into the choked channels at the bottom end of Moreton Bay. Reclaimed land in the river forms islands whose names reflect the fantasies of their founders – Isle of Capri, Sorrento, Miami Keys – and which have become much-sought-after real estate.

From the dingiest club to its best restaurant, Surfers exudes entertainment, and at times – most notoriously New Year and Christmas – you can spend twenty-four hours a day out on the town. Another thing you'll spend is money; the only free venue is the beach and with such a variety of distractions it can be financial suicide venturing out too early on in the day. The city is full of tourists staggering around at noon, with terrible hangovers and empty wallets, complaining how expensive their holiday has become. The area around **Cavill Avenue** is a bustle of activity from early morning – when the first surfers head through to the beach and the shops open – to after midnight, when there's a constant exchange of bodies between **Orchid Avenue**'s bars and nightclubs. If you spend any length of time in town, you'll get to know the district intimately. The block between the sea and Orchid Avenue is a **mall**, given over to snack bars, coffee houses and shopping arcades; you can pick up a cheap T-shirt or play a game of chess at one of the outdoor tables. **Raptis Plaza** here is a collection of exotic eateries overlooked by a replica of Michelangelo's *David*.

Across the Esplanade, the **beach** is all you could want as a place to recover from your night out. In early afternoon, the sun moves behind the tower blocks, but you can escape the shadows by moving up to Main Beach. If you're feeling energetic, seek out a game of volleyball or head for the surf: the swell here isn't bad in a northerly wind, but most of the time it's better for boogie boards. Beyond Main Beach, **the Spit**'s attractions are **Fisherman's Wharf** – an upmarket version of Raptis Plaza – and **Seaworld** (daily 10am–5pm; $35, family rates; access on the *Surfside Bus* from the highway), on the Spit, the longest running of the Gold Coast's theme parks. Besides various stomach-churning rides, the park features immaculately trained dolphins and killer whales, and was recently criticized by environmental groups for taking animals from the wild instead of other aquaria. Your stomach can be churned some more at the **bungee jump**, next to *Sea World* on the west bank of the Spit (☎5531 1103), though this is a dismal way to do it – from a wire cage hauled to the required height by a crane.

The other theme parks are out of town. **Dreamworld** (daily 10am–5pm; $35, family rates; bus service ☎5573 1133), on the Pacific Highway at Coomera, 17km north of Surfers Paradise, has a violent double-loop roller-coaster and a fairground atmosphere, while **Movie World** (daily 10am–5pm; $35, family rates; bus ☎5573 3999), also on the Pacific Highway, 14km north of Surfers, is a slice of Hollywood featuring studio tours, and Western and stunt shows. Near *Movie World*, **Wet 'n' Wild** (daily 10am–4.30pm or later; $17) has a series of pools linked by vicious water slides – the back-breaking "twister" and the 25-metre-tall, high-speed slide alone are worth the entrance fee.

## Eating

Some of the beachfront resorts offer bargain all-you-can-eat **breakfasts**, while during the rest of the day there's always something to eat at the **cafés** and **snack bars** along Cavill Avenue and the Esplanade. **Restaurants** are geared towards the exotic, although some offer early-bird specials in the evening before a certain time. For supplies, there's a **supermarket** downstairs in the *Paradise Centre* (on Cavill Avenue mall) and a late-opening *Night Owl* store on the highway near Elkhorn Avenue.

**Bavarian Steakhouse**, corner of the highway and Cavill Ave (☎5531 7150). Multi-floor theme restaurant with counter-meal prices; about $8 for steak, salad and fries.

**Beachside Café**, 18 Elkhorn Ave (☎5592 2368). 24hr snack bar specializing in cappuccini and sandwiches; a between-clubs meeting point.

**The Crab Cooker**, corner of Gold Coast Highway and Thornton St (☎5538 6884). Good, Australian-style fresh seafood restaurant where a plate of prawns, bugs and fish will set you back around $18, and their famous mud crabs start at $40. Lunch from noon, dinner from 5.30pm.

**Crooked House**, corner of Markwell Ave and Gold Coast Highway (☎5570 1766). In a crooked building, you eat surrounded by Aussie icons like Don Bradman's bat. Menu is "authentically Australian" – from witchetty grubs and camel steak to the more traditional bucket of prawns served with a stubbie of beer. Expensive.

**Fawlty Taco's**, corner of Tedder St and Woodroffe Ave, Main Beach (☎5571 0091). Not in *Montezuma's* class, but fun Mexican fast food. Evenings only.

**Green Garden Chinese**, Centre Arcade, Gold Coast Highway (☎5592 6789). Pick your own fish or exotic seafood – including abalone – from the tank, and have it served with spring onions and oyster sauce, or choose from the standard menu of less exotic dishes. Open 11am–late daily.

**Montezuma's**, 8 Trickett St, under the Aloha Tower (☎5538 4748). A cramped Mexican restaurant, but the food's fresh and spicy. $15 will fill you up; open for lunch and dinner.

**Rusty Pelican**, Orchid Avenue (☎5539 8699). Great name. Good-value $10, 4-course lunch specials which might include chowder, grilled red snapper, or lobster; otherwise expensive.

**Sumo**, Raptis Plaza. Japanese takeaway known for its fair prices and large portions, from sashimi ($8.50) down to humble buckwheat noodle soup ($5).

**Tandoori Place**, 7–9 Trickett St (☎5592 1004). Fast-food ambience, but actually better than first impressions would suggest; their sweet curries are engagingly different. Nothing over $15, most main dishes around $12.

## Entertainment

Find out **what's on** through the hostels or by word of mouth; the free weekly magazines, *Point Out* and *Wot's On*, are essentially business directories. If you are desperate
for an injection of culture amid all the brash goings-on, check out the programme at the
**Arts Centre**, 135 Bundall Road (☎5581 6900), where there's a theatre, gallery, restaurant and bar; and the **cinema**, on the corner of Clifford Street and Gold Coast Highway
(☎5570 3355).

Realistically, though, it's Surfers' **clubs** that provide most of the nightlife. Initially,
particularly if you're staying at a hostel or have picked up a **free pass** somewhere, your
choice will most likely be influenced by the various deals on entry and drinks. The
places listed below have been around for a while and have a dependable reputation;
none are especially chauvinistic, though places do change. Opening times are from
around 6pm until 3am or later.

**Benson's**, 22 Orchid Ave (☎5538 7600). Boasts one of the few surviving dance floors that lights up,
*Saturday Night Fever*-style.

**Cocktails and Dreams**, Orchid Ave (☎5592 1955). Rhythm and Blues nights from time to time,
extended happy hours.

**The Party**, *The Mark*, Orchid Ave (☎5538 2848). Seventies nights Tues, 8pm onwards.

**Rose and Crown**, Raptis Plaza, Cavill Ave (☎5531 5425). Hosts "Rear of the Year" every Friday.

**Shooters Bar**, at *The Mark*, Orchid Ave. Cheap drinks and filling $3.50 suppers.

**Surfers Beergarden**, Cavill Ave, opposite Orchid Ave. Live music with local and interstate band
talent Thurs–Sat nights.

**Tunnel Cabaret**, Orchid Ave (☎5592 2717). *Club Survival* reggae dance meet Wed.

## Listings

**Airlines Offices** are near Cavill Ave: *Ansett*, 3232 Gold Coast Highway (☎5592 1511); *Japan
Airlines*, Orchid Ave (☎5592 0443); *Qantas*, 3047 Gold Coast Highway (☎5570 0530).

**Banks and exchange** *American Express*, 21 Cavill Ave (☎5538 7588); *ANZ*, 3232 Gold Coast
Highway (☎5531 6444); *Commonwealth*, 3206 Gold Coast Highway (☎5579 3588); *Thomas Cook*,
Paradise Centre, Cavill Ave (☎5531 7770).

**Boat and jet ski rental** *Sunbird Watersports*, next to the bungee crane on the Spit (☎018/76 6800);
*Tiki Village Boat Hire*, river end of Cavill Ave (☎5538 0022), and *Captain Barb-E*, Ferny Ave, 50m
from *Tiki* (☎5531 6176) – the latter with self-drive launches from $10 per hour (based on daily
rental).

**Books** *Hooked on Books*, Paradise Centre, Cavill Ave.

**Buses** *Coachtrans* (☎5538 9944); *Greyhound Pioneer* (☎5531 6677); *McCafferty's* (☎5538 2700).

**Car rental** Competition keeps prices low, but advertised prices are often for long rentals, and
exclude insurance and mileage charges: *East Coast Car Rentals*, 25 Elkhorn Ave (☎5592 0444) from

### THE GOLD COAST INDY

Despite financial and sponsorship problems, the **Gold Coast Indy** car race every March
is Surfers' premier "event" of the year. The biggest fans of the race – first held in 1990
and boosted by Nigel Mansell's 1993 Indy debut – are the businesses that benefit from
the longer tourist season it creates; other locals are somewhat ambivalent about the
disturbance it causes to everyday life. The track takes in a section of the Pacific highway
between Breakers Street and View Avenue and completes the circuit along the
Esplanade. Trackside passes start at $150 but one way around this is to find a room over-
looking the race. While you pay top prices for booking in advance, if you start looking
about a week before the race, prices are far lower; with only days to go, it's not unknown
for motels on the track to charge as little as $45, but you run the risk of ending up with-
out accommodation. The only way you'll get this kind of deal (they won't be advertised)
is by walking around to motels along the circuit and bargaining hard.

$40 a day; *Red Back Rentals*, opposite the bus station, Beach Rd (☎5592 1655) from $25 per day; *Rent-a-Bomb*, 8 Beach Road (☎5538 8222) from $1 per hour.

**Flights** *Ken Keane's Air Adventure* (☎5598 2643). Brief $45 flights (minimum 2 people) in an open-cockpit bi-plane; *Skyworx Aviation* have less adventurous 30-min flights in a light aircraft for $45 (☎018/92 4089 for pick-up).

**Hospitals and clinics** *Gold Coast Hospital*, Nerang St, Southport (☎5571 8211); *Sexual Health Clinic*, 2019 Gold Coast Highway, Miami (☎5576 9033).

**Pharmacy** Galleria Shopping Plaza, corner of Elkhorn Ave and Gold Coast Highway (☎5592 1321); open 24hr.

**Post office** Main post office at 25 Cavill Ave (☎5538 4144).

**Surf rental** *Surfworld*, Paradise Centre, off Cavill Ave (☎5538 4825) Typical prices are $5 per hour/ $15 a day for board rental, plus ID deposit (passport or drivers' licence).

**Taxis** ☎5588 1234.

**Tours** Some hostels organize tours of the Scenic Rim, or try the following for day-trips to the Hinterland (Lamington, Natural Bridge, Mount Tamborine and Binna Burra), Sunshine Coast (Noosa, The Big Pineapple or Mooloolaba) and Brisbane (most offer free pick-ups): *Coachliner* (☎5536 8990); *Currumbin Palm Tours* (☎5598 5544); *Coachtrans* (☎5592 3488). *Mountain Trek Adventures* (☎5536 1700) and *Camp Trek Australia* (☎018/76 2696) run 4WD day tours around the Hinterland; the latter also has extended, all-inclusive camping safaris lasting 3 days for $300. See below for trips to South Stradbroke Island.

## South Stradbroke Island

**South Stradbroke Island** is a twenty-kilometre-long, narrow strip of sand, separated from its northern neighbour by the 1896 cyclone and, as tower blocks edge closer, doomed to become an extension of the Gold Coast. For now, though, Stradbroke's relatively isolated and quiet beaches offer something of an escape from the mainland, though most day-trippers come over simply to get plastered at the bar at **South Stradbroke Island Resort** (☎5577 3311; cabins ⑤). Alternatives are to enjoy the fine **surf** along the southeast shore (though local surfies are notoriously protective) or to **fish** in the Jumpinpin channel between here and North Stradbroke.

**Day cruises** to the resort cost around $50 including lunch, with evening booze cruises about $30; operators include *Island Queen* (departures from Appel Park Wharf, off the river end of Cavill Avenue; ☎5592 2332) and *Shangri-La* (departures from Fishermen's Wharf, The Spit;☎5591 1800). Cheaper alternatives ($25 or less) are the **resort ferry** (10.30am–2.30pm; Runaway Bay Marina, 5km north of Surfers on Bayview Street, but no public transport), or *Aqua Taxi* (☎018/756 335).

# THE HINTERLAND AND SCENIC RIM

One hundred and twenty kilometres inland from the coast's jangling excesses, the **Scenic Rim** forms a barrier between the coastal flat and the pastoral Darling Downs, encompassing a series of mountainous **national parks**. Here you'll find Queensland's largest expanse of sub-tropical rainforest and – the main attraction – the **Lamington Plateau**, packed with powerfully beautiful scenery, animals and birds. Whether you're a day-tripper, veteran hiker or just fancy camping in the same spot for a few days it's not to be missed. Closest to the coast, **Springbrook**'s waterfalls and undeveloped pockets at **Mount Tamborine** make easy day-trips and so are the most-visited destinations, while tough tracks at the region's extremes in the **Main Range** remain the prerogative of experienced bushwalkers.

# The Eastern and Central Rim

The **Mount Tamborine–Lamington** area is covered in a network of graded, well-trodden paths, so you don't have to be particularly skilled at **bushwalking** to enjoy the experience. Come prepared though – to tackle the longer or steeper routes requires some degree of **fitness**; test your condition on shorter walks first. **Paths** are often well marked but sometimes narrow and slippery with little fencing along cliffs and water-falls, so **footwear** should have a good grip and, ideally, be waterproof. Rain is a year-round possibility; the most comfortable weather conditions occur between June and November, though everything looks its best in the middle of the wet season with water-falls in full flood and the greenery shockingly intense. If you do visit during the wet (Jan–March), you'll have to endure high **humidity**, deep and fast-flowing rivers, occasionally closed paths and an unwelcome abundance of insects.

**Accommodation** is limited to resorts and campsites, so if you're on a tight budget you'll need a tent. Winter (July–Sept) nights are cool enough to warrant a sleeping bag and pullover. Campsites have water and **stores** nearby, but you'll save money by bringing your own supplies. A **fuel stove** is a good idea – although there are often barbecues, finding dry wood can be difficult. **Access** to the area is easy enough in itself but because of local geography there are few interconnecting roads, making backtracking unavoidable if you want to visit more than one place. If you can, get hold of a vehicle; only Lamington and Tamborine Mountain have a regular bus service, though **tours** visit most locations – see "Listings" for Brisbane (p.272) and Surfers Paradise opposite.

## Tamborine Mountain

**Tamborine Mountain**'s nine fragmentary national parks offer a pleasant introduction to many of the key features of the Hinterland. If you're **driving**, consult a map and aim for North Tamborine township: from Brisbane (75km), leave the Pacific highway at Beenleigh; from the coast (45km), turn inland at Nerang or Oxenford. There's a daily **bus** service from Surfers Paradise (*Coachliner*, $25; ☎5536 8990), but nothing from Brisbane.

The mountain top is moderately cleared and settled with remaining patches of forest concentrated around the adjoining compact settlements of **NORTH TAMBORINE** and **EAGLE HEIGHTS** – quiet, upmarket escapes from lowland suburbia. North Tamborine's services include a general store, garage and information centre (more reliable than the frequently unattended National Parks office on the Knoll road); Eagle Heights has a post office, but no banks. From North Tamborine, it's between four and six kilometres to the most distant **parks**: Cedar Creek in the north and Macrozamia Grove southwards.

Once the haunt of the Wangeriburra Aborigines, Mount Tamborine's forests were targeted by the timber industry late last century until locals succeeded in getting the area declared as Queensland's first national park in 1908. This event is commemorated by a roadside monument one kilometre south of North Tamborine, where a three-kilometre track slaloms down to **Witches Falls** through open scrub and rainforest. It's an easy walk, but is more rewarding for the views from the mountain than the falls themselves – a trickle disappearing over a narrow ledge below the lookout.

The strongest feature of Mount Tamborine's parks is the diversity of native forest types they contain. At opposite ends of the scale, there's a stand of primitive, slow-growing cycads (see box on p.386) at **Macrozamia Grove**, and the limpid, eerie gloom created by a piccabean palm forest at **Palm Grove**, near Eagle Heights. Hidden twenty metres up in the canopy are elusive **wompoo pigeons**, often heard but seldom seen –

despite their vivid purple and green plumage and onomatopoeic call. Closer to North Tamborine, about a kilometre north, walking tracks at **Joalah** follow Cedar Creek downstream through woodland to a rock pool; look out for giant epiphytic ferns in the canopy and the **Albert lyrebird**, with its incredibly shaped tail and liquid song. For a break from the heat, **Cedar Creek Falls**, to the north, tumble refreshingly cold water into a wide pool – take your swimming gear. Of the other parks, **MacDonald** at Eagle Heights has a very short walk through typical sub-tropical rainforest; there's a stand of **flooded gum** at North Tamborine's environmental park; and views northwest from **the Knoll**'s picnic tables.

## Thunder Eggs

Four kilometres from North Tamborine on the Brisbane road, the privately owned **Thunderbird Park** (store, campsite, units; ☎5545 1468; ②–⑤) exploits the area's volcanic origin. **Thunder eggs** – or geodes – are to be found here in quantity and an hour or more digging for them in the sun is sufficient to satisfy the average curiosity. Formed when volcanic liquids were drawn into nodules, they appear to be rather unprepossessing lumpy white spheres, but when cut in half and polished the centres are revealed as banded **agates**. Stones from different sites vary in colour and it usually takes a bucketful to find a couple of good examples. As they're not valuable, the real satisfaction comes from digging them out yourself and the thrill of being the first person to see inside. Mining permits cost $10 per session (from *Thunderbird Park*) and if you don't happen to be carrying a pick and bucket you can rent these, too; they'll also cut and polish your finds for you.

# Springbrook National Parks

Close to the coast along the New South Wales border, **Springbrook**'s three parks feature abundant waterfalls and swimming holes; though grouped together, access to each section is by a different road. **Mount Cougal** is 21km west of Currumbin: you're there when the road runs out. Rainforest flanks the upper reaches of Currumbin creek with a path following the stream to an abandoned sawmill, past pools and pretty cascades. For higher drama and a short, moderately demanding walk, head for **Purling Brook Falls**, 30km from Burleigh Heads via Mudgeeraba. There's a campsite outside the forest, near the top of the falls, with a store about 4km back along the main road. The 109-metre falls look best after rain when the river shoots over the edge of the plateau; a four-kilometre track zig-zags down the escarpment and into the rainforest at the base of the falls before curving underneath the waterfall – expect a soaking from the spray – and back up the other side. In the plunge pool at the foot of the falls, the force of the water is enough to push you under; **swimming** is more relaxed in a couple of pools downstream, picturesquely encircled by lianas and red cedar. A ten kilometre drive beyond the falls takes you to **Best of All Lookout** and a broad vista south to Mount Warning from the very edge of the Rim.

At **Natural Bridge** a collapsed cave ceiling beneath the riverbed has created a subterranean waterfall. An exciting but very dangerous leap down the falls will take you into the cave – or beyond: several people have been killed trying it, and the recommended mode of entry is simply to walk in through the mouth, fifty metres downstream. From the back of the cave the forest outside frames the waterfall and blue plunge pool, surreally lit from above; **glow worms** illuminate the ceiling at night. The park is 49km from Burleigh Heads or Southport via Nerang and about 27km from Purling Brook. *Numinbah Valley Adventure Trails* (half-day rides $35, pick-up from accommodation in Surfers $5; ☎5533 4137) heads out on **horseback** from their base near Nerang to otherwise inaccessible volcanic caves near Natural Bridge.

# Lamington National Park

The McPherson Range and Lamington Plateau occupy the northwestern rim of a vast caldera centred on Mount Warning, 15km away in New South Wales. This is **Lamington National Park**, an enthralling world of rainforest-flanked rivers, open heathland and ancient eucalypt woods, and its position on a **crossover zone** between sub-tropical and temperate climes have made it home to a staggering variety of plants, animals and birds, some forming isolated populations of species found nowhere else.

There are two possible **bases**: Binna Burra on the drier northern edge and *O'Reilly's Guesthouse* at Green Mountain, in the thick of the forest. Routes come in from Canungra to Green Mountain (37km) and Beechmont for Binna Burra (10km); narrow, twisting roads cutting through patches of forest and cleared grazing land. From the Gold Coast, turn off at Nerang – roads to both Binna Burra and Green Mountain diverge from here; from Brisbane, leave the highway at Beenleigh – you pass through Canungra to reach Beechmont this way.

**Buses** from the Gold Coast or Brisbane to either base cost $35 return; good value for long stays but as the journey takes between ninety minutes and three hours (depending on where you start) it's best to rent a car for day-trips. When you buy your ticket, make it clear whether you want to return the same day or another day; it's also possible to walk between Binna Burra and Green Mountain (see below for details), so you might want to arrange to be dropped at one and collected at the other. Green Mountain can be reached from Surfers' bus station with *Mountain Coaches* (who also rent out tents and camping gear; ☎1800/077 423) and from Brisbane's Transit Centre with *Allstate Scenic Tours* (☎3285 1777). Binna Burra's only bus is the *Mountain Lodge*'s Gold Coast service (☎1800/074 260 for details).

Lamington has to be explored **on foot**: most of the tracks described below are clearly signposted and **free maps** are available from local NPWS ranger stations. If you're experienced and want to head off along less-defined paths, contact the rangers first for advice.

## Binna Burra

It's some time since guests had to walk the last few kilometres through the steep forest to **BINNA BURRA** with their luggage on a horse, and nowadays the cosy wooden cabins and log fires place *Mountain Lodge* (☎1800/074 260; ⑦) firmly upmarket. The only alternative is the **campsite** (☎5533 3622) up the road, either using your own gear or renting one of their on-site tents (②). Facilities include hot showers and a tea room aimed at day-trippers, but which also sells bread and some basic provisions; otherwise, the nearest shops are wherever you've just arrived from. Don't leave food unguarded at the campsite – it's infested with bold scrub turkeys.

Hikers can bush camp between February and November; contact the **park ranger** (8am–3pm; ☎5533 3584) at the station, 1.5km before the lodge, for details.

Both lodge and campsite overlook the Numinbah Valley from woodland on the crown of Mount Roberts, and **walking** anywhere always leaves you with an uphill return journey. The lethargic can simply wander 500m between the campsite and the lodge at **night** with a torch to be rewarded by the sight of groups of wallabies grazing on the verges; commotion in the trees betrays the presence of brushtail possums foraging for flowers and leaves. Try the lodge's unique **senses trail**: blindfolded and following a rope you become aware that there's more to the forest than a blaze of green – a drop in temperature under the canopy, textures of bark and leaves, wafts of scent from the forest floor.

Of the longer walks, try the easy five-kilometre **Caves Circuit**, which follows the edge of the Coomera valley past the white, wind-sculpted **Talangai Caves** to remains of Aboriginal camps, strands of *psilotum nudum*, a rootless precursor of the ferns, and a hillside of strangler figs and red cedar. Plunging into another forest below the camp-site, the harder **Ballunji Falls** track is a typical compromise between access and terrain, with occasional vertical drops to test sure-footedness. Features on the way include views of **Egg Rock** from Bellbird Lookout, at its most mysterious when shrouded in dawn mists, and a stand of majestic forty-metre-tall box brush trees. Dedicated walkers can extend the track out to **Ships Stern**, an arduous and very dry 21-kilometre return (allow a minimum of 8hr) with some wonderful views off the escarpment. **Dave's Creek Circuit** is similar but about half as long, crossing bands of rainforest and sclerophyll before emerging onto heathland. Look for tiny clumps of red sundew plants along the track, which supplement their nitrogen intake by trapping insects in sticky globules of nectar.

Other longer tracks can be joined together, allowing you to spend days hiking without ever returning to base. Most popular of these is the **Border Track**; a relatively easy 21-kilometre/nine-hour (one-way) path linking Binna Burra with Green Mountain. If you need road transport between the two, *Dwyer's Taxis* (☎5545 1577) charges $66, reason-able split between four passengers. Or you might try your luck at the lodge – they've been known to take people to *O'Reilly's* at Green Mountain on Thursdays for a fee.

## O'Reilly's and Green Mountain

For many, Green Mountain's forests are the best of the entire Scenic Rim. With so much to dazzle the senses here the initial experience is confused, but gradually the various types of plants and trees become familiar, as do the distinct layers between the rainforest floor and canopy. Random rustles and trills resolve into wallabies thumping around tree roots, scrub turkeys scratching up leaf litter and a whipbird's cracking call; it's easy to become lost in the environment's complex structure.

The road from Canungra to **Green Mountain** ends at *O'Reilly's Guesthouse* (☎5544 0644; ⑦), a splendidly comfortable place opened in 1926 – bookings advised at week-ends and during holiday periods. The guesthouse has a limited store (with EFTPOS facilities) and moderately priced restaurant for meals and snacks throughout the day. There's also an exposed NPWS **campsite** with showers; call the **ranger's office** (1–3pm only; ☎5544 0634) for (essential) advance booking.

The **bird life** near the guesthouse is prolific and distracting: you can't miss the chat-tering swarms of crimson rosellas mingling with visitors on the lawn, and determined twitchers can clock up over fifty species without even reaching the forest – most spec-tacular is the black-and-gold **regent bowerbird**. But it's worth pushing on to the **tree-top walk** just beyond the clearing, where a suspended walkway swings 15m above ground level. At the halfway anchor point you scale a narrow ladder to vertigo-inducing mesh platforms 30m up the trunk of a strangler fig to see the canopy at eye level. Soaking up the increased sunlight at this height above the forest floor, tree branches become miniature gardens of mosses, ferns and orchids. By night the walkway is the preserve of possums and weird stalking insects.

If you only manage one day-walk at Lamington, make it the exceptional **Blue Pool/Canungra Creek track** (15km/5hr), which features all the jungle trimmings: fantastic trees, river crossings, waterfalls, swimming holes and countless opportunities to fall off slippery rocks and get soaked. The first hour is dry enough as you tramp downhill past some huge red cedars to Blue Pool, a deep, placid waterhole where **platypus** are some-times seen on winter mornings; this makes a good walk in itself. After a dip, head upstream along Canungra Creek; the path traverses the river a few times (there are no bridges, but occasionally a fallen tree conveniently spans the water) – look for **stone cairns** that indicate where to cross. Seasonally the water can be almost absent; if more than knee-deep, you shouldn't attempt a crossing and will need to retrace your steps. Follow the creek as far as Elabana Falls and another swimming hole, or bypass the falls; either way, the path climbs back to the guesthouse.

Other trails to the eastern escarpment are lengthy day-walks and join the Border Track to Binna Burra. Rewards are views into New South Wales and encounters with clumps of **antarctic beech** trees, a strange Gondwanan relict also found in South America. For seasoned, well-equipped walkers, there's a chance to delve into local history by way of an overnight hike to the **Stinson Wreck**. In February 1937, a plane bound for Sydney crashed into dense forest and the survivors were only located thanks to the incredible efforts of Bernard O'Reilly who, on his own, hiked to the plane from Green Mountain and returned with a rescue party. **Westray's grave**, where one of the survivors who died looking for help is buried, is nearby but very difficult to reach from Green Mountain. Today most of the wreck has been carted off by souvenir hunters or covered by jungle, but the guesthouse and park rangers can give you advice on the walk and may be able to put you in touch with bushwalkers who've been there.

### Beaudesert

At the right time of year, and if you have your own wheels, you can take a 40-kilometre **shortcut** from *O'Reilly's* to **BEAUDESERT** along Duck Creek road: turn left into the forest 3km from the guesthouse on the Canungra road and negotiate 20km of rough, hairpin tracks followed by a smoother section of bitumen. Depending on the conditions, you may need 4WD and the track's closed after heavy rain; ask around before you start. Beaudesert is a straightforward place; stay at the *Beaudesert Caravan Park*, Albert Street (☎5541 1368), drink at the *Beaudesert Hotel* and eat at the *Beaudesert Café*.

# The Western Rim

In contrast to the obvious charms of the Eastern Rim, the drier **Western Rim** is mainly given over to open eucalypt woods, with the steep peaks covered in heath. With few facilities, it's a place for serious bushwalkers; on weekends you're likely to meet other hikers at the campsites, but the best way to explore is with a **bushwalking club** (see Brisbane "Listings", p.270). Even "easy" routes are fairly demanding, with few neat paths or signposts, so come equipped, don't walk alone and carry plenty of water. Access is along the Cunningham and Mount Lindesay highways from Boonah or Beaudesert in the east and **Warwick** from the west; there's no public transport.

### Mount Barney, Main Range and Mount Mistake

**Mount Barney**'s multiple peaks form an extremely rough region along the New South Wales border, 45km southwest of Beaudesert. Wherever you're approaching from, aim for Rathdowney then take Barney View Road past Bigriggen to **Yellowpinch** campground. Nearest supplies and alternative camping are at Rathdowney and Bigriggen.

There's a distinct, hour-long track to the **Lower Portals**, a pool on Barney creek flanked by vertical cliffs, from the car park some 5km from Yellowpinch. The only other marked hike (though even for this you might need a topographic map), is the misleadingly named "tourist trail" along the south ridge to the saddle between **Mount Barney**'s peaks: be prepared for an exhausting seven-hour return trip from Yellowpinch. Experienced walkers, with permits and advice from the NPWS about current conditions (PO Box 121, Boonah; ☎074/63 1579), could camp in the saddle at **Rum Jungle** and climb the peaks in the morning; the eastern peak is the easier of the two and has the better views across to Mount Lindesay's tor, poking above wooded slopes.

**Main Range**'s precipitous terrain and sharp, progressively higher peaks are most directly accessible along the Cunningham highway at **Cunningham's Gap**, between Brisbane and Warwick, about 90km from Boonah. Here you'll find some of the easier trails: through rainforest along West Gap Creek and ascents of Bare Rock and Mount Mitchell. There's an NPWS **campsite** at the Gap (☎074/63 1579); phone in advance to check on conditions. **Mount Mistake** is an undeveloped park on the junction of three mountain ranges which form the northernmost extent of the Scenic Rim. Walking is said to be tricky but well worth the effort; if you're tempted, contact the national park manager on ☎076/39 4599.

# THE SUNSHINE COAST

The **Sunshine Coast**, stretching north of Brisbane to **Noosa**, is a more pedestrian version of the Gold Coast, where largely domestic tourist development is tempered by, and sometimes combined with, agriculture. Much local character is due to the lack of death taxes in Queensland – something which, together with the pleasant climate, attracts retirees from all over Australia. The towns tend to be bland places, lively enough at Christmas, but out of season you may be hard pushed to find much to do after dark. Even so, the beaches and surf are good, improving in character as you progress north and providing an excuse to linger for a few days. And though you'll find the Hinterland far tamer than down south, it still sports some arresting landscapes and scattered hamlets rife with Devonshire cream teas and weekend markets.

Without your own **transport**, the easiest way through the area is by **bus** – *Sunshine Coast Coaches* (☎074/43 1011) is the local alternative to the national operators – or on a **tour** from Brisbane or the Gold Coast; Brisbane's *Citytrain* network can get you into the region at Caboolture. For the intrepid, Hal Conway of *Adventures Sunshine Coast* organizes day-trips **climbing** in the Glasshouse Mountains, **bushwalking** the Obi Obi gorge in the Blackall range, or **canoeing** the Mooloolah River south of Maroochydore ($55 per person, including lunch and pick-up from lodgings along the coast; ☎074/44 8824).

# Caboolture to Mooloolaba

**CABOOLTURE** marks the start of the Sunshine Coast, 40km north of Brisbane. There's no reason to stop here besides the *Abbey Museum of Art and Archaeology* (Old Toorbul Point Rd, via Bribie Island exit from the highway; Tues, Thurs & Sat 10am–4pm; $4; ☎95 1652), whose staff can direct you to a couple of local **Aboriginal sites** and which, curiously, has a wide-ranging exhibition on European and Mediterranean civilization.

### The Glasshouse Mountains

It's worth conquering at least one of the **Glasshouse Mountains'** nine peaks; the views are superb and the mountains are one of the few really special places on the Sunshine Coast – dramatic, isolated pinnacles, visible as far away as Brisbane. Catching sight of them from the sea, Cook named them after their shape and "elevation", a resemblance obscure today. You can reach them along the old highway 16km north from Caboolture or off the new one 10km north of Beerburrum; *Sunshine Coast Coaches* stop at the Glasshouse Mountains turn-off. **Accommodation** and camping in

The Sunshine Coast **telephone code** is ☎074; in April 1997, this will change to ☎07/54. *(For more on changes to phone numbers Australia-wide, see p.40.)*

the area is at *Log Cabin Caravan Park*, south of **GLASS HOUSE MOUNTAINS** township (☎96 9338; cabins ③).

To the Kabi Aborigines, the mountains are the petrified forms of a family fleeing the incoming tide; their names for the peaks are more evocative than Cook's – Tibrogargan, Tibberoowuccum and Beerwah, to name just three. The peaks themselves vary enormously: some are rounded and fairly easy to scale, while a couple have vertical faces and sharp spires requiring competent climbing skills. **Beerburrum**, overlooking the township of the same name, and **Ngungun**, near Glass House Mountains township, are two of the gentlest to climb, with well-used tracks; the latter's views and scenery are better than some of the harder peaks and you'll need only two hours for the return trip. **Tibberoowoccum** must be climbed from the northwest, and the only special equipment you'll need is a map; ask at *Log Cabin Caravan Park* for directions. The taller mountains – Tibrogargan, Coonowrin and Beerwah (the highest at 556m) – are at best tricky, and Coonowrin should only be attempted by experienced climbers. Contact the NPWS, Roys Road, Beerwah 4519 (☎94 6630), for more information.

## Caloundra

**CALOUNDRA** sits diagonally opposite suburban Bribie Island, and there's little going on beyond the **beaches**. Bulcock Beach is central, and so tends to collect the crowds; if you don't mind a walk, Golden Beach, overlooking Bribie's narrow tip, or Shelly Beach, on the other side of Caloundra Headland, are just as good. The closest **campsite** to the centre is at the tiny council-run caravan park (☎91 3428), five minutes' walk along Burgess Street, a continuation of Bulcock Street where *Sunshine Coast Coaches* pull up, or there's another at Shelly Beach if this is full. For **rooms**, try *Palm Breeze Motel*, 105 Bulcock Street (☎91 5566; ④).

## Around Mooloolaba

Twenty kilometres north, **MAROOCHYDORE**, **ALEXANDRA HEADLAND** and **MOOLOOLABA** are gradually filling the foreshore between the Mooloolah and Maroochy rivers with an amoeba-like blob of housing. But for once there are things to do to fill in time between sunbathing sessions.

**Mooloolaba Wharf**, a kitsch tourist attraction with trendy shops and restaurants, is the area's focus. Around the corner, **Underwater World** (Parkyn Parade, Mooloolaba; daily 9am–5pm; $14.50, students $9) has superb freshwater tanks where barramundi – fish revered by Queensland anglers for their taste and legendary fighting spirit – and inoffensive freshwater crocodiles stare blankly at you through huge windows. For the real thing, *Scuba World* (Parkyn Parade; ☎44 8595) can train you or take you **diving** to local sandstone terrain where you'll find occasional giant grouper, nudibranch and bottom-dwelling sharks. Numerous places nearby hire out **surfboards** at around $15 a day.

If you're tempted to stay in the area, try *Suncoast Backpackers* at 50 Parker Street, Maroochydore (☎43 7544; ①), a well-organized **hostel**; in the same price bracket, but otherwise a poor alternative, *Zord's* (Cotton Tree Parade; ☎43 1755; ①) is very run-down. There's a **campsite** opposite *Zord's* and a *YHA* close to the Maroochy River on Schirrmann Drive (☎43 3151; ①) – out of the way but with free loans of surfboards, bikes and fishing gear. **Eating** options are clustered along the Esplanade, including *Mooloolaba Surf Club*'s smart restaurant (daily 11am–1pm, 5.30–7pm, plus Sun 8am for breakfast) near the Wharf, and *Karakas* at no 59, for fiery Mexican cooking and **live music** through the week. *Mooloolaba Hotel*, also on the Esplanade, has the inexpensive *Spagalini's* restaurant and hosts non-stop rock nights; the *Alexandra Hotel*, on the highway at Alexandra Headland, is the venue for big-name bands.

# Nambour to Noosa

Bisected by tramways from surrounding sugar plantations, **NAMBOUR** sits inland from Maroochydore in the centre of the Sunshine Coast's farming community. Five kilometres south at **WOOMBYE** lurks the *Sunshine Plantation* (daily 9am–5pm; free except rides; ☎42 1333) overshadowed by its renowned, ridiculous **Big Pineapple**; activities include trips around the plantation on a cane train and, of course, climbing the fibreglass fruit. *Sunshine Coast Coaches* can bring you here from Nambour.

A two-hour circuit drive from Nambour into the **Hinterland** along the Blackall range takes you into a rural English-like idyll quite unexpected in sub-tropical Queensland. Fields are dotted with herds of pied dairy cattle, and "villages" like **MALENY** – with its annual **folk festival** over Christmas and New Year – **MONTVILLE** and **MAPLETON**, are thick with potteries and tearooms, and occasional long views over rolling green hills to the coast. After rain it's worth stretching your legs to reach a couple of respectably sized **waterfalls** up here: **Kondalilla**, 3km from Montville, with swimming holes along **Obi Obi Creek**; and **Mapleton Falls**, just west of Mapleton, where the river plunges over basalt cliffs.

Approached from Nambour along the highway, you reach Noosa either by turning coastwards at **EUMUNDI** – known for its **weekend markets** and its beer, once brewed at the *Imperial Hotel* but now made elsewhere – or **COOROY**; this sees you entering town along the river via **TEWANTIN**. From Maroochydore, the journey is half as long, following the coast past unevenly spaced townships and neglected beaches.

## Noosa

The exclusive end of the Sunshine Coast, **NOOSA** is dominated by an enviably beautiful headland, defined by the mouth of the placid Noosa River and a strip of beach to the south. Popular since surfers first came in the '60s to ride fierce waves around the headland, the setting makes up for any neon and concrete in town. It's also a starting point for trips to Cooloola National Park and Fraser Island in the Great Sandy Region directly north (see p.295). These tend to overshadow Noosa's own national park on the headland (see opposite page) and unless you're a beach addict or board rider you'll probably find that you only stay around long enough to plan your next move.

"Noosa" is a loose term covering three merging satellite settlements: **NOOSAVILLE** and the town centre at **NOOSA HEADS**, which between them stretch 7km west along the river from the headland to Tewantin – a distinct township in its own right with access to the wilds of Cooloola – and the discreet suburb of **SUNSHINE BEACH** on the headland's south side. The best beaches are those at **Noosa Beach**, which runs parallel to chic **Hastings Street** at Noosa Heads, and the longer, less crowded **Sunshine Beach**; both are patrolled. During the week there's an hourly bus service (7am–6.30pm) connecting the three suburbs. **Sunshine Beach Road** at Noosa Heads is the main street, where you'll find the purely mercenary **Noosa Tourist Centre**, banks, restaurants, shops and a supermarket; Noosaville has plenty of stores along the river and there's another shopping centre at Sunshine Beach.

More natural attractions can be found around the Noosa River and in a modest national park. The **Noosa River** deposits low, muddy islands as it passes Tewantin and Noosaville, emptying into the sea at Laguna Bay. In the late afternoon, half of Noosa promenades along Gympie Street as the sinking sun colours a gentle tableau: mangroves on the opposite shore, pelicans eyeing anglers for scraps and landing clumsily midstream, and everything from cruise boats to windsurfers and kayaks out on the water. With a spare day you can **cruise** or **canoe** (if you're energetic and start early enough) upstream to shallow lakes **Cooroibah** and **Cootharaba** (see p.299), or just paddle around, fish at the river mouth or hire a **jet ski** and have fun getting soaked (see "Listings" below for rental outlets).

Noosa's small **national park** is worth a look for its mix of mature rainforest, coastal heath and fine beaches – **Granite Bay** and **Alexandria Bay** have good sand pounded by unpatrolled surf – all reached along graded paths. These start from the picnic area at the end of Park Road (a continuation of Hastings St), where you'll probably see **koalas** in gum trees above the car park.

## Accommodation

**Hostels** have courtesy buses for beach, town and nightclubs, and all accommodation will help organize tours. **Motels** are concentrated along the river between Noosa Heads and Noosaville; some offer weekly rates which might add up to a free night, but prices double during school holidays. Monolithic upmarket accommodation is as close to the river as possible along Hastings Street.

**Backpackers on the Beach**, 26 Stevens St, Sunshine Beach (☎47 4739). Very clean, quiet hostel – no pool, but it's just two minutes from the beach. ②.

**Barry's Beachouse**, William St, Noosaville (☎49 8151). Slowly receiving the repairs it desparately needs, a small hostel with pool, canoe-, bike- and board-rental. If open, their tiny *Bratpacker's Café* offers budget meals every night. ①.

**Halse Lodge**, 17 Noosa Drive, Noosa Heads (☎47 3254). Giant, sprawling, immaculate 1888 Queenslander aimed at scout-style groups and definitely not for partying. Bed & breakfast; single, double and family rooms. ②.

**Koala**, 44 Noosa Drive, Noosa Heads (☎47 3355). Central budget accommodation in dorms and motel units; a noisy, party atmosphere with pool, restaurant and bar. ①.

**Melaluka**, 7 Selene Street, Sunshine Beach (☎47 3663). Somewhat small brick self-contained units in sight of the sea. ①.

**Munna Point Caravan Park**, Noosa Parade, Noosaville (☎49 7050). Basic campsite and van park; no cabins.

**Noosa Court**, 55 Hastings St, Noosa Heads (☎47 4455). Private motel-style rooms hidden among more pretentious establishments. ⑦.

**Noosa River Resort**, 275 Gympie Terrace, Noosaville (☎49 7040). Very pleasant, low-key place with basic, neat furnishings and river views. ③–④.

**Tingirana Motel**, 25 Hastings St (☎47 3274). Few frills but clean budget rooms; good value for the location. ⑤.

## Eating, drinking and nightlife

Noosa's three communities – surfers, retirees and tourists – seldom share the same enthusiasms; evenings tend to be spent with your own crowd. This doesn't seem to affect the **nightlife** though, and there are plenty of places to **eat and drink**, too.

**Beach Chalet**, Tingira Crescent, Sunshine Beach (☎47 3944). Trendy spot, where you need to be "intending to dine" to watch the bands.

**Café le Monde**, Hastings St, Noosa Heads (☎49 2366). Slightly snobbish street atmosphere and a menu which touches on most continents – try the spinach and pumpkin charlotte or hickory-smoked pork at around $15. Opens 7.30am for cappuccini; Fri happy hours 4.30–6.30pm; live evening music through the week.

**Laguna Bay Beach Club**, Hastings St (☎49 4793). Ocean views, and a mix of Greek and Italian grills. Mains around $15.

**Noosa Heads Surf Club**, on the beach, Hastings St. Evening bistros for under $10 and great views over the beach and bay.

**Rolling Rock**, Hastings St, Noosa Heads (☎47 2255). A busy, sweaty club featuring discos and bands every night.

**Roma Pizza**, 36 David Low Way. Good-value takeaway pizzeria, plus a trattoria-style restaurant featuring red-checked tablecloths and inexpensive pizza and pasta meals.

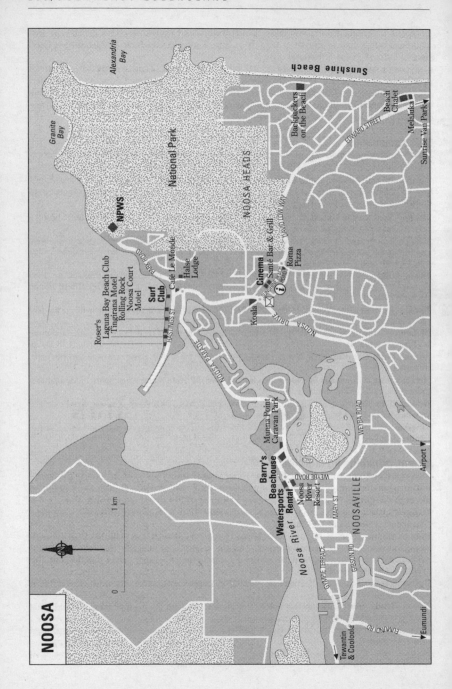

**Roser's**, 1 Hastings St (☎47 3880). Best of the local upmarket seafood restaurants, with original dishes like "Mango Bugs" – clawless lobster in a mango and peppercorn sauce. Main dishes from $16.50.

**Royal Mail Hotel**, Tewantin. Live rock 'n' roll at weekends, late happy hours and dress regulations.

**Sante Bar and Grill**, Sunshine Beach Rd, Noosa Heads. Eclectic range of central European and Mediterranean cooking. Main courses cost upwards of $15, but are worth it; for the terminally indecisive, there's a $14.50 nine-course menu "sampler" served only on Sundays 11am–2pm.

## Listings

**Bike hire** *Koala Bike Hire* (☎48 0599) mountain bikes for $10 a day, including delivery to accommodation.

**Camping supplies and rental** *Outdoor Store*, 28 Sunshine Beach Rd, Noosa Heads (☎47 2688). All you'll need for Fraser Island and Cooloola national parks.

**Car rental** *Allterrain*, Commercial Court, Noosaville (☎49 0877), and *Sunshine 4WD*, next to the Noosa post office (☎47 3702), have 5-seater 4WDs from $150 per day plus deposit. For a conventional runaround, try *Noosa Car Rentals*, 13 Noosa Drive (☎47 3777).

**Cinema**, Sunshine Beach Rd, Noosa Heads (☎47 5300).

**Cruises** *Everglades Waterbus*, Harbour Town Complex, Tewantin (☎47 1838) have half-day cruises upriver for $43; $70 full-day tours add a 4WD run along Rainbow Beach. *Noosa River Tours*, Gympie Terrace, Noosaville (☎49 7362) also have day-tours on the river for around $50.

**Diving** *Dive Boatique*, Sunshine Beach Rd (☎47 4300). Exciting encounters with deep-sea life off Wolf Rocks.

**NPWS** Park Rd, at Noosa National Park's picnic area (☎47 3243).

**Surf gear** *Surf World*, Sunshine Beach Rd, Noosa Heads (☎47 3538).

**Watersports rental** *Pelican Boat Hire*, on the river bank at Gympie Terrace (☎49 7239), for canoes and surf skis at $7 per hour, $28 per day; *Pro Ski* (☎49 7740), in the same place, for water skiing at $45 for 30min, $80 an hour, including instruction for novices and jet skis at $30 per 30min. The *Great Australian Fishing Skiff Co* (☎49 9353), at the Harbour Town Complex in Tewantin, rents out fishing boats with fuel, rods, bait pumps, crab pots, ice boxes and the rest, for $10 an hour.

# THE GREAT SANDY REGION

Halfway between Brisbane and the tropics, the **Great Sandy Region – Cooloola National Park** and **Fraser Island** – sports giant dunes, forests, coloured sands and freshwater lakes where fishing and four-wheel driving take precedence over more usual beach activities. But it doesn't have to be a macho tangle with the elements: for once it's relatively easy and inexpensive to hire tents and a 4WD and set off to explore in some comfort. You can venture in for a day, or circuit the region in a week, driving through Fraser and Cooloola and then back along the highway to return your vehicle.

Europeans were initially unimpressed with this part of the coast, but abundant fresh water, seafood and plants must have supported a very healthy **Aboriginal population**; camp fires along the beach allowed Matthew Flinders to navigate Fraser Island at night in 1802. Flinders also coined the region's name by labelling Fraser Island and the Cooloola coast as "the Great Sandy Peninsula" on his maps, though he suspected that Fraser Island was in fact separated from the mainland. The Queensland government declared the area an Aboriginal reserve in the early 1860s but, with the discovery of **gold** at Gympie in 1867, Europeans flocked into the region in their thousands. This influx, and the economic boom that went with it, saved the infant Queensland from bankruptcy, but brought the usual conflicts, and the reserve gradually became little more than a holding pen for tribal survivors from all over the state. Decimated by disease, the last few were relocated to other reserves around Queensland at the turn of the century so the area could be opened up for recreation.

> The **phone code** for Cooloola is ☎074, but will change to ☎07/54 from April 1997;
> Hervey Bay and Fraser Island is ☎071.

**Sand mining** and **logging** are other incendiary topics here and there's a predictable split between conservationists and those people who count on local industries for their livelihood. Forestry is a particularly bitter issue; the inland town of Maryborough was built on timber felling, and logging bans have aroused fury at what is seen as a sell-out to the Green movement. Locals too, once drawn to the area for its natural appeal, now feel crowded out by regulations made to protect the coast from over-use by 4WDs and drunken campers leaving piles of garbage behind them. While it's unlikely that any of this will have a negative impact on a brief visit, a balance between protection and "development" – a word with almost religious connotations in Queensland – is far from being established.

### Getting there

**Cooloola National Park** is immediately north of Noosa, across the river at Tewantin. Surfaced roads from Tewantin and Gympie are the main routes in to the lakes and **Rainbow Beach** township respectively; beach access is via Tewantin's river ferry at the end of Moorindil Street (daily 6am–9pm or later; cars $4.50 one-way, $7 return; pedestrians $2 each way). Barges cross daily to **Fraser Island** from Hervey Bay and Rainbow Beach. **Tours** run from Noosa and Hervey Bay, though given the grand scale of the Great Sandy region – 190km from Tewantin to the tip of Fraser Island – they're inevitably rushed. The wildlife and overall serenity of the area is elusive, to say the least, unless you get away from the more popular places, camp for the night and explore early on in the day. Assembling a group and hiring a 4WD is one way to do this. Another is simply **walking**, an alternative ignored by almost all visitors, but one which allows unequalled access and intimacy with the region.

Unless on a tour, you'll definitely need **maps**. *Cooloola Coast*, covering Noosa to Tin Can Bay, is available at local newsagents and garages for $9, as are the *Sunmap* series of the region. Relevant sheets on national parks, from the NPWS, supplement these. **Drivers** need **tide timetables**, as most beaches are only reliably negotiable at low tide. Rain won't ruin your stay – in fact it makes driving on sand far easier and enhances the colours – though in rough conditions services to Fraser might be cancelled, leaving you stranded.

# Cooloola National Park

Often overlooked in the stampede to reach Hervey Bay and Fraser Island, the **Cooloola Coast** appears, at first glance, to be a poorer version of its northern neighbour. But, while less spectacular, there's plenty to see if you take the time: the south is dominated by features of the Noosa River which pools into lakes **Cootharaba** and **Cooroibah** as it nears Tewantin, while stands of commercial timber and dry sclerophyll woodland cover the interior, rising to dunes along the beach stabilized by scrubby heath. The beach runs straight north to **Double Island Point** and then bows west to Rainbow Beach township, backed by vertical, coloured-sand cliffs whose weathered contours and tones constantly change with the shifting sun. Below, the windswept strip of sand separating land from sea becomes a 4WD highway at low tide and you'll see bright-coloured flashes of canvas hidden in places where the cliffs are low enough to form a protective foreshore suitable for camping. Most of the beach and interior north of Cootharaba is **national park**, as is the lake's shoreline.

## Practicalities

Cooloola's 27km of river is best explored by tour or **canoe** from Noosaville (see Noosa "Listings", p.297) or, for less money, Boreen Point and Elanda Point townships on Lake Coothoraba. **Outboards** – $55 a day at the lake – increase your range if you want to fish. **Four-wheel drive** is essential for the beach, access roads leading to it, and inland tracks after rain – again, see Noosa "Listings" for operators. Conventional vehicles can reach Boreen and Elanda points.

**Hiking**, you'll find the easiest path along the beach, but it makes things more interesting if you head inland at some stage. Walking tracks for the well-equipped head upstream from Elanda Point, past the top of Lake Coothoraba and along the **Cooloola Wilderness Trail**, or towards the coast – contact the NPWS first.

**Accommodation** on the southern lake is at *Lake Cooroibah Holiday Park* (PO Box 220, Tewantin; ☎47 1706; ①–③), 2km after the Tewantin ferry, on a good gravel road. They provide coin-operated laundry and showers; you supply your own bedding for four-berth cabins or tents – or you can pitch your own tent. At **Lake Coothoraba** there are campsites at Boreen Point and Elanda Point; both rent canoes and boats. **Rainbow Beach** has *Rainbow Waters Holiday Park* (☎86 3200; ③) and *Rainbow Beach Caravan Park* (☎86 3222; ③), both with tents and cabins; *Rainbow Beach Hotel* (☎86 3125; ④) has motel rooms. You can **bush camp** throughout the park. Sites are located along the upper reaches of the Noosa River and wilderness trail, while on the beach you can pitch a tent anywhere south of Little Freshwater Creek and at Freshwater and Double Island Point campgrounds, run by the NPWS. Permits and details on conditions in the park can be obtained from *Rainbow Beach Information Centre* (daily 7am–4pm; camping gear rental; ☎86 3227) or from the ranger at Elanda (daily 9am–3pm; ☎86 3160).

**Provisions** are available at Boreen Point (fuel, general store, hotel, telephones), Elanda Point (small general store) and Rainbow Beach (post office, petrol, hotel, shops). A hotel just down the road from *Cooroibah Holiday Park* serves good counter meals.

## The lakes, river and inland

**Cooroibah** and northerly, larger, **Coothoraba** are joined by a six-kilometre twist of the Noosa River. Placid, and fringed with paperbarks and reedbeds, they look their best at dawn before there's any traffic about; they're saltwater and average just one metre in depth, subject to tides. At Coothoraba's top end, Kin Kin Creek and the Noosa River spill lazily into the lake through thickets of mangroves, hibiscus and ti-trees – the so-called **Everglades**. A boardwalk from Kinaba's **information centre** leads to a hide where you can spy on birdlife, and there's more on nearby **Fig Tree Lake**. The picnic area here is a former corroboree ground.

As you head upstream, the river freshens as it winds through the **Narrows** to **Harry Springs Hut** – an easy enough paddle in a canoe, though submerged obstacles require care with an outboard. A campground on the edge of the rainforest at Harry Springs Hut is a convenient gateway to the park's interior; from here another 8km of river is navigable by canoe and walking tracks lead off into the bush. The longest of these tracks is the **Cooloola Wilderness Trail**, a three-day, 46-kilometre hike out to the Rainbow Beach Road; clearly marked and not too strenuous, it can become swampy after rain. Best conditions are in September: relatively cool with heathland scattered with wildflowers. Highlights are the first day's trekking through rainforest and mangroves, and the chance of spotting birdlife around the waterholes at Wandi and Neebs. A good **day walk** (20km return) follows the river upstream from Harry Springs Hut and then climbs across dunes to Cooloola Sandpatch – a "blow" caused by winds stripping vegetation off a sandhill and destabilizing it. The track starts on the opposite bank from Harry Springs Hut – but come prepared: you'll have to swim 50m with your clothes in a plastic bag.

You can also **drive** via a forestry plantation and native woodland to Rainbow Beach Road; although bumpy and treacherous when wet, at other times you shouldn't have much trouble.

## The coast

With over forty kilometres of uninterrupted beach at Cooloola you'd think that crowds would hardly be a problem, but there are times when you seem to be constantly dodging oncoming traffic. Tewantin is the most direct **point of entry**; the ferry drops you five minutes' drive from the sea. The powdery foredunes at the end of the road look too small to worry about, but you wouldn't be the first to get stuck driving through them; a **campsite** here has fine views of Noosa, but this close to town things can get busy. From Rainbow Beach township you can drive (or walk) directly on to the northern beach or take the vehicle track to **Freshwater Creek** campsite which starts 4km south along Rainbow Beach Road – a rough ride through rainforest with the road scarred and rutted from wheel spins in the soft sand. Just keep going. There's a similar track to **King's Bore** (about halfway along the coast) off the Lock's Pinch road, with a memorable descent down the side of a blow onto the beach. The east and north beaches are joined by two tracks below Double Island Point. Drivers should take care to avoid a patch of **quicksand** about one kilometre south of Freshwater Creek – and remember that there are no exits off the beach between the Tewantin access and Freshwater Creek (30km), so make sure that you have enough time before the tide comes in – the King's Bore track is too steep to use.

**Coloured sands** are a feature of the region, caused by minerals leaching down the cliffs from above leaving broad bands of orange, red and white. This is impressive at a distance; the colours seem less vivid close up but you'll find some curious rounded sculptures formed by the weather. There's also the **shipwreck** of the *Cherry Venture*, grounded between Double Island Point and Freshwater Creek in 1973. It looks the part, with sand piling up on its leewards side and slowly engulfing its rusting frame and funnel.

**Heading on,** the **Fraser Island ferry** leaves Inskip Point, 10km north of Rainbow Beach, for Hook Point on the island's south (daily 7am–5pm; $45 return per vehicle, $5 for foot passengers; ☎86 3120); you'll need a **permit** from the NPWS on the Rainbow Beach road (7am–4pm daily; ☎86 3160). For **Gympie** there's a bus from Rainbow Beach Road at 7.20am on schooldays for $10; miss that and you're looking at $90 for *Rainbow Beach Taxi* (☎86 3235) to cover the eighty-kilometre run.

# Hervey Bay

Back on the highway and heading north from Tewantin, it's a couple of hours to Hervey Bay past **GYMPIE** and **MARYBOROUGH**, historic relics of gold and timber industries, now healthy market towns with handsome stone and wooden period buildings in their centres testifying to their wealthy past. **HERVEY BAY**, a collection of coastal suburbs, has no such pretentions, and the only reason to visit is to join the throng crossing to Fraser Island – or perhaps to venture into the bay to spot **whales** in the spring. **Pialba** is the centre, with shops strung along the **Esplanade** as it runs 7km from here west through **Scarness** and **Torquay** to **Urangan** harbour; barges to Fraser Island leave from here and from River Heads, 17km south. **Approaching** Hervey Bay from the south, turn off at Maryborough; from the north, leave the highway at Howard. The **bus**

The **phone code** for Hervey Bay and Fraser Island is ☎071.

**station** is on the main road into town about a kilometre from Pialba, and the **Tourist and Visitor Centre** is at 63 Old Maryborough Road, Pialba (☎28 2603), but most activities can be booked through your accommodation.

Watersports enthusiasts with time to kill might want to take advantage of *Torquay Beach Hire* (on the Esplanade; ☎25 5528), which has it all – from surf skis to windsurfers and outboard-driven tinnies for a day's **fishing**. More sedentary folk could indulge in a beach bonfire, while nature lovers can search out **echidna**, which have been spotted snuffling around in the strip of vegetation between the Esplanade and beach.

## Whale watching

**Humpbacked whales** are among the most exciting of marine creatures to encounter: growing to 16m long and 36 tonnes, they make their presence known from a distance by their habit of "breaching" – making spectacular, crashing leaps out of the water – and expelling jets of spray as they exhale. Prior to 1952 an estimated 10,000 whales made the annual journey between the Antarctic and tropics to breed and give birth in shallow coastal waters; a decade later whaling had reduced the population to just 200 animals.

Now protected, their numbers are increasing and you're fairly likely to see one if you put out to sea between Brisbane and the Whitsundays during the whale-watching season of May to October. The whales' migration brings them close to Hervey Bay between July and September, and the town is particularly well attuned: there's an August **Whale Festival**, and operators are always searching for new gimmicks to promote **day cruises** and **flights**. In perfect conditions you'll see whales breach, swim directly under the boat and raise their heads out of the water, close enough to touch. You might also, of course, see nothing at all. Whether all this voyeurism disturbs the animals is unclear; but they seem at least tolerant of the attention paid to them.

For **flights**, try *Harry's Air Charter* (☎28 9056) or *Hervey Aviation* (☎25 5888); costing from $45 per person, minimum of three for a half-hour buzz. **Cruises** last for a morning or full day, cost around $50, and are booked through an agent; some get very crowded – check the boat size and how many will be going. *Matilda II*, *Safari Princess*, *Princess II*, *Golden Phoenix*, *Bay Runner*, and *Islander* all come recommended, while *Spirit of Hervey Bay* has the bonus of being a **glass-bottomed** vessel. For the added pleasure of **sailing** out to the whales, look for the yachts *Madison* and *Stefanie*.

## Accommodation

Accommodation is packed during the whale-watching season (July–Sept), and at Christmas and Easter (when motel prices double). Hostel buses will pick you up from the bus station.

**Beaches**, 195 Torquay Rd, Torquay (☎24 1322). Standard, busy party hostel, one street back from the Esplanade. ①.

**Colonial Backpacker Resort**, Pulgul St, Urangan (☎25 1844). Untidy self-contained wooden cabins for five, and dormitory beds. Close to the harbour. ②.

**Harbour Views Caravan Park**, end of Miller St, Urangan (☎28 9374). Right next to the harbour, ideal for catching the early ferry.

**Koala Backpackers**, 408 Esplanade, Torquay (☎25 3601). Tatty rooms and large hostel grounds; close to shops. ①.

**Midway Terraces**, 335 Esplanade, Scarness (☎28 4119). Quiet, tidy rooms, nothing fancy but good value. Rooms ④; ① per person per night, based on four sharing a two-bedroom unit for a week.

**Olympus**, 184 Torquay Rd (☎24 3488). Excellent purpose-built hostel, so far tidy and untarnished; units complete with kitchen and TV. Staff are helpful and the price includes a basic breakfast. ①.

**Pialba Caravan Park**, corner of Main St and the Esplanade, Pialba (☎28 1399). On the foreshore, close to the centre.

**Playa Concha**, 475 Esplanade, Torquay (☎25 1544). Beachfront motel accommodation with palm and fern surroundings, comfortable if nothing special. ⑥.

## Eating

Apart from snack bars and fast-food joints in Pialba, most of the places to eat and spend the evening are down the Esplanade at Torquay.

**Dolly's**, 410 Esplanade, Torquay (☎25 5633). Adorned with 50s iconography, there's a DJ or live music every night and a range of smorgasbord and all-you-can-eat deals.

**Gringo's**, 449 Esplanade (☎25 1644). Usual Mexican menu of enchiladas, chilli con carne and nachos, spiced to individual tolerances and with bean fillings as an alternative to meat. Main courses $8–10.

**Ivey's**, 355 Esplanade, Scarness (☎24 5466). Burgers, barbecued chicken and chips. Open late.

**O'Reileys**, 446 Esplanade (☎25 3100). Safe and savoury pizza, pasta and crepes, but best for fruit pancakes and cream.

**Sails Brasserie**, 433 Esplanade (☎25 5170). Very upmarket Mediterranean-style menu, with fresh oysters and some unusual specialities – try Moreton Bay bugs in a *Pernod* sauce.

## Listings

**Bus tours** Full-day tours to Fraser start around $50, overnight camping trips about $130. *Top Tours* (☎25 3933) concentrate on the island's north (Eli Creek, Maheno, Lake Allom and Waddy Point); *Fraser Venture Tours* (☎24 1900) head through Central Station to Lake Birrabeen and along the beach as far as the Pinnacles.

**Camping and fishing gear** *Camping and Leisure*, 68 Boat Harbour Drive, Pialba (☎24 2511).

**Car and scooter rental** *Hervey Bay Car Rentals* (☎25 5534), non-4WD vehicles from $25 a day plus extras; *Bayside*, 4 Fraser St, Torquay (☎25 3733) for scooters at $12 an hour. See box on p.304 for 4WD rentals.

**Diving** *Diver's Mecca* (472 Esplanade; ☎25 1626) and *Dive Connection* (382 Esplanade; ☎24 1133), for shallow wreck diving and grouper, sea snakes and other pelagic creatures.

**Fishing** Out of season, whale cruise boats take to fishing, charging around $40 for a dawn start with all gear included. *Fighting Whiting* (☎24 1300) stays closer to shore for $25.

**Flights** *Air Fraser Island* (☎24 3549), $35 per person (group of 6) for day flights to Fraser.

**Four-wheel-drive rental** *Bay 4WD Centre*, 54 Boat Harbour Drive, Pialba (☎28 2981), two-seaters $80 a day, four-seaters $100 a day, 5–8-seaters $115 a day; *Aussie Trax*, 56 Boat Harbour Drive, Pialba (☎24 4433), 8-seaters from $77 a day, plus insurance. (See box on p.304 for more on Fraser Island trips.)

**Laundry** Corner of Esplanade and Frank St, Scarness (behind *Dot's Food Bar*); 7am–7pm.

**NPWS** City Council Office, Torquay (☎25 0222). Open Mon–Fri 9am–5pm, for camping permits and island information.

**Pharmacy** *Day and Night Pharmacy*, 418 Esplanade, Torquay (☎25 2733); daily 8.30am–8pm.

# Fraser Island

At 123km long, **Fraser Island** is the world's largest sand island, but the dry facts do little to prepare you for the experience. Accumulated from sediments swept north from New South Wales over the last two million years, the scenery ranges from silent forests and beaches sculpted by wind and surf, to crystal-clear streams and dark, tannin-stained lakes. The east coast forms a ninety-kilometre razor-edge from which Fraser's tremendous scale can be absorbed as you travel; with the sea as a constant, the dunes along the edge seem to evolve before your eyes – low and soft in places, hard and worn into intriguing canyons elsewhere. By contrast, slow progress through the forests of the island's interior creates more subtle impressions of age and permanence – a primal world predating European settlement – brought into question only when the view opens suddenly at a lake or a bald blow.

This idyll, however, is sobered by a number of factors. Most alarming is the volume of traffic tearing along the beach and main tracks, which you necessarily increase by visiting. The foredunes are trampled and littered with camping detritus too, and the island has become the epitome of Queensland's environmental conflicts, with conservationists, tour operators, foresters and Aboriginal groups vying for control of resources.

To the Kabi Aborigines, Fraser Island is **Gurri**, a beautiful woman so taken with the earth that she stayed behind after creation, her eyes becoming lakes that mirrored the sky and teemed with wildlife so that she wouldn't be lonely. The story behind the European name is far less enchanting. In 1836, survivors of the wreck of the *Stirling Castle*, including Captain Fraser and his wife Eliza, landed at Waddy Point. Though runaway convicts had already been welcomed into Kabi life, the castaways suffered "dreadful slavery, cruel toil and excruciating tortures", and after the captain's death Eliza was presented as a prize during a corroboree at Lake Cootharaba two months later. She was rescued at this dramatic point by former convict John Graham, who had lived with the Kabi and was part of a search party alerted by three other survivors from the *Stirling Castle*. The exact details of Eliza's captivity remain obscure as she produced several conflicting accounts, but her role as an "anti-Crusoe" inspired the work of both novelist Patrick White and artist Sidney Nolan.

## Practicalities

It's best to sort out your **crossing to Fraser Island** in advance. Unless on an organized tour, you need a **barge ticket, vehicle permit** for the island ($15), plus **camping fees** for NPWS sites ($7.50 a night). All these can be obtained where you rent your vehicle – and are usually covered in package deals – or from barge offices at Urangan and River Heads. Note that you can only use return tickets on the same barge; if you're planning a different exit from the island, you'll have to buy two singles. Pack insect repellent.

The **Urangan Harbour to Moon Point** (central west coast) barge leaves at 8am and 3.30pm, returning at 9am and 4pm. Returns are $50 for vehicle and driver plus $3 for passengers; pedestrians pay $10 each way. The Moon Point landing is difficult so if you're unsure of your driving abilities, leave from River Heads. **River Heads to Wanggoolba Creek** (access to **Central Station**), leaves daily at 9am, 10.15am and 3.30pm, returning 9.30am, 2.30pm and 4pm; the **Kingfisher Bay** barge leaves River Heads at 7am, 11am and 2pm, returning 9.45am, 12.45pm and 4.30pm; fares are the same as Urangan's. **Pedestrians** are also served by **hovercraft** from Urangan to various points around Fraser ($20 return), and a **high-speed catamaran** from Urangan to *Kingfisher Bay* resort ($25).

### Getting around
**Driving** requires a **four-wheel drive vehicle**; the east beach serves as the main highway, with roads running inland to popular spots. Other tracks, always slower than the beach, criss-cross the interior; main tracks are often rough from heavy use, and minor roads tend to be in better shape. Rain and high tides harden sand surfaces, making everything easier. Most **accidents** involve collisions on blind corners, rolling in soft sand, and trying to cross apparently insignificant creeks on the beach at 60kph – 4WDs are not invincible. Pedestrians can't hear vehicles on the beach and won't be aware of your presence until you barrel through from behind, so give them a wide berth. Road rules follow the mainland.

**Walking** is the best way to see the island. There's only one **established circuit**, and even that is very under-used, running from Central Station south past lakes Birrabeen and Boomanjin, then up the coast and back to Central Station via lakes Wabby and McKenzie; highlights are circumnavigating the lakes, chance encounters with goannas and dingoes and the energetic burst up **Wongi Blow** for sweeping views seawards. A good three-day hike that renders you unconscious by sundown after all that walking across sand, it requires no special skills beyond endurance.

## Essentials and accommodation

**Beds** need to be pre-booked. Top of the range is the plush *Kingfisher Bay Resort* (free call ☎008 072 555; ⑨) on the west coast; the more down-to-earth *Happy Valley Resort* (☎27 9144; ②) provides comfortable cabins and good food, plus basic self-contained, three-bedroom apartments aimed at fishing groups renting on a weekly basis, as does *Yidney Rocks Cabins* (☎27 9167; ②), just to the south. *Eurong Beach Resort* (☎27 9122; ⑤) has average motel-style rooms, while *Dilli Village* (☎27 9130; ③) has self-contained four-bed bunkhouses.

With a permit, you can camp anywhere along the eastern foreshore, or if you need facilities, use the NPWS **campsites** at **Lake Allom**, **Dundubara** and **Waddy Point** on the east coast, **Wathumba** on the west, or **Central Station**, **Lake Boomanjin** and **Lake McKenzie** elsewhere. There are privately run campsites at the unfriendly *Cathedral Beach Resort* (☎27 9177) or nicer *Dilli Village* (☎27 9130).

For **supplies**, **HAPPY VALLEY** and **EURONG** have stores, telephones, bars and fuel; there's another store at *Cathedral Beach Resort* but no shops or restaurant at Dilli. You'll save money by bringing whatever you need with you – take the empties home.

# Around Central Station

Most people get their bearings by making their first stop at **Central Station**, an old logging depot with campsite, telephone and information hut under some monstrous bunya pines. You'll certainly see **dingoes** here; *don't* feed them, as the expectation of hand-outs makes them aggressive. As there are no domestic dogs on the island, Fraser's dingoes are held to be Australia's purest strain.

From the station, take a stroll along **Wanggoolba creek**, a magical stream so clear that it's hard at first to see the water as it runs across the forest floor. Apart from encounters with swimming dingoes or slender pythons drowsing on a branch, it's a botanic walk past some prehistoric *angiopteris* ferns to **Pile Valley** where **satinay trees** humble you to insignificance as they reach sixty metres skyward. They produce a very dense timber, durable enough to be used as sidings on the Suez Canal – and consequently in such demand that the trees have almost been logged out on Fraser.

There are several **lakes** around Central Station, all close enough to walk to and all along main roads. Nine kilometres north (track distance), **McKenzie** is the most popular on the island: ringed by white sand with clear, tea-coloured water reflecting a blue sky, it's a wonderful place to spend the day. To the south, **Birrabeen** (8km) is mostly hemmed in by trees, while **Boomanjin** (16km) is open and geologically "perched" in a basin above the island's water table. There's a fine campsite and communal fireplace here, attended by tame goannas.

# East Beach

**Seventy-Five Mile Beach** on the east coast is one of the busiest strips of sand you'll ever encounter. Vehicles hurtle along, pedestrians and anglers hug the surf, tents dot the foredunes; this is what beckons the crowds over from the mainland. Sights along the way include **sand** in all its different forms: **Hammerstone Blow**, six kilometres north of Eurong, is slowly engulfing **Lake Wabby**, a small but deep patch of blue below the dunes – another century and it will be gone. At **Rainbow Gorge**, about five kilometres south of Happy Valley, a short trail runs between two blows, through a hot, silent desert landscape where sandblasted trees emerge denuded from their ordeal by sand. Incredibly, a dismal spring seeps water into the valley where the sand swallows it up; "upstream" are the gorge's stubby, eroded red fingers. A path leads in, but you'd only be contributing to the vandalization of the brittle structure.

Six kilometres north of Happy Valley you cross picturesque **Eli Creek**, where water splashes briskly between briefly verdant banks before spilling hopelessly into the sea. Sand-filtered, it's the nicest swimming spot on the island. Back on the beach, another four kilometres brings you to the *Maheno*, shipwrecked in 1935 and now a skeleton almost consumed by the elements. More striking are the coloured cliffs known as the **Cathedrals**, which run from the wreck north to Indian Heads.

## The Interior, west coast and far north

Fraser's **wooded centre**, a real contrast to the busy coast and popular southern lakes, gets relatively few visitors. It encloses **Yidney Scrub**, the only major stand of **rainforest** left on the island, and although the name doesn't conjure up a very appealing image, the trees are majestic and include towering **Kauri pines**. There's a circuit through Yidney from Happy Valley, taking in **Boomerang** and **Allom** lakes on the long way back to the beach near the *Maheno*. You can camp at Allom, a small lake surrounded by pines and cycads, and completely different in character from its flashy southern cousins. Further north, another road heads in from Dundabara township to **Bowarrady**, a not particularly exciting body of water famed for turtles who pester you for bread – if you can't imagine being pestered by a turtle, try refusing to hand it over.

The island's **west coast** is largely inaccessible to vehicles, though you can cross either to **Moon Point**, then take some rough roads through the interior Lake Bowaraddy and Happy Valley, or to *Kingfisher Bay Resort*, with routes to the east coast via the Central Station area. With time to spare, it's worth visiting the top end of the island beyond **Indian Heads**, which for the most part is complete wilderness. A vehicle ban has been suggested for the area, sparking a row between residents and the NPWS, so you need to check the latest position on access before setting off. If you make it this far, the bubbling saltwater pools just north of Indian Head at the **Aquarium** are great fun, and there are some good views from the head itself.

## travel details

**Trains**

**Brisbane** to: Beenleigh (8 daily; 55min); Bundaberg (7 weekly; 6hr); Caboolture (8 daily; 1hr); Cairns (6 weekly; 31hr); Charleville (2 weekly; 16hr 25min); Cleveland, for Stradbroke Island (8 daily; 50min); Emerald (2 weekly; 15hr 15min); Longreach (2 weekly; 24hr); Mackay (7 weekly; 16hr 30min); Maryborough (7 weekly; 3hr 45min–5hr); Nambour (7 weekly; 1hr); Proserpine (7 weekly; 19hr); Rockhampton (7 weekly; 11hr); Roma (2 weekly; 3hr 30min); Sydney (1 daily; 14hr); Toowoomba (2 weekly; 3hr 30min); Townsville (6 weekly; 23hr); Tully (6 weekly; 27hr 30min).

## Buses

**Brisbane** to: Airlie Beach (6 daily; 18hr); Beenleigh (8 daily; 40min); Bundaberg (9 daily; 6hr); Burleigh Heads (8 daily; 1hr 50min); Caboolture (4 daily; 45min); Cairns (9 daily; 27hr); Caloundra (9 daily; 1hr 10min); Charleville (2 daily; 10hr 35min); Coolangatta (8 daily; 2hr 10min); Hervey Bay/Pialba (8 daily; 4hr 40min); Lamington National Park (1 daily; 3hr); Longreach (2 daily; 16hr); Mackay (9 daily; 15hr 30min); Maroochydore (1 daily; 2hr 5min); Maryborough (11 daily; 4hr); Mount Isa (2 daily; 25hr); Nambour (9 daily; 1hr 30min); Noosa (1 daily; 2hr 50min); Roma (3 daily; 7hr 20min); Surfers Paradise (9 daily; 1hr 30min); Sydney (8 daily; 15hr 30min); Toowoomba (8 daily; 2hr 15min); Townsville (9 daily; 21hr 30min); Tully (8 daily; 25hr 30min); Winton (2 daily; 18hr).

**Hervey Bay** to: Brisbane (8 daily; 4hr 30min); Caboolture (3 daily; 4hr 10min); Caloundra (8 daily; 3hr 20min); Maroochydore (1 daily; 4hr); Maryborough (8 daily; 30min); Nambour (8 daily; 3hr); Noosa (1 daily; 3hr 15min).

**Noosa** to: Brisbane (1 daily; 2hr 15min); Caloundra (1 daily; 1 hr); Hervey Bay (1 daily; 3hr 10min); Maroochydore (1 daily; 35min); Maryborough (1 daily; 2hr 35min).

**Surfers Paradise** to: Brisbane (9 daily; 1hr 30min); Burleigh Heads (1 hourly; 30min); Coolangatta (1 hourly; 1hr); Lamington National Park (2 daily; 1hr 30min); Sydney (8 daily; 15hr 30min); Tamborine Mountain (1 daily; 1hr); Toowoomba (2 daily; 3hr 30min).

## Ferries

**Brisbane** to: Moreton Island (1 daily; 2hr); North Stradbroke Island (8 daily; 30min); St Helena (3 or more weekly; 2hr).

**Hervey Bay** to: Fraser Island (10 daily; 30min–1hr).

**Rainbow Beach/Inskip Point** to: Fraser Island (daily, on demand; 45min).

**Surfers Paradise** to: South Stradbroke Island (3 or more daily; 30min).

## Flights

**Brisbane** to: Adelaide (8 daily; 3hr 30min); Alice Springs (5 daily; 4hr 30min); Cairns (12 daily; 2hr 10min); Canberra (at least 5 daily; 2hr); Darwin (at least 4 daily; 3hr 40min); Gold Coast/Coolangatta (at least 4 daily; 25min); Hervey Bay (3 daily; 1hr 15min); Hobart (at least 9 daily; 3hr 50min); Melbourne (14 daily; 2hr 25min); Perth (12 daily; 5hr); Sydney (29 daily; 1hr 35min); Townsville (6 daily, 1 hr 50min).

**Gold Coast/Coolangatta** to: Adelaide (10 daily; 3hr 35min); Brisbane (at least 4 daily; 25min); Cairns (3 daily; 3hr 40min); Canberra (10 daily; 2hr 40min); Darwin (2 daily; 7hr 25min); Hobart (7 daily; 6hr 10min); Melbourne (14 daily; 3hr 35min); Perth (8 daily; 6hr); Sydney (21 daily; 1hr 15min); Townsville (2 daily; 3hr 10min).

**Hervey Bay** to: Brisbane (3 daily; 1hr 15min); Cairns (at least 2 daily; 4hr); Townsville (at least 1 daily; 4hr).

# CHAPTER FOUR

# TROPICAL QUEENSLAND AND THE REEF

The move towards, and into, Queensland's **tropical coast** is far more obvious than simply passing the Tropic of Capricorn marker at Rockhampton. North of Hervey Bay the landscape browns as the temperature rises, and though there's still an ever narrowing farming strip hugging the coast, the Great Dividing Range edges coastwards as it progresses north, dry at first but gradually acquiring a green sward which culminates in the steamy, rainforest-draped scenery around **Cairns**. Along the way are scores of beaches, vivid archipelagoes of **islands**, and regularly spaced cities, including **Townsville**, north Queensland's largest. There is also a wealth of **national parks**, some – like **Hinchinbrook Island** – with superb walking trails, and others where you might encounter rare or unusual wildlife. Moving north of Cairns, rainforested ranges ultimately cede to the savannah of the huge, triangular **Cape York Peninsula**, a sparsely populated setting for what is widely regarded as the most rugged 4WD adventure in the country.

The transition between Queensland's southeast (see *Chapter 3*) and tropics is also reflected offshore, with the appearance of the **Great Barrier Reef**, among the most beautiful and extensive coral complexes in the world. The structure, which begins to make its presence felt round the level of Bundaberg, drastically changes the nature of the coastline by blocking incoming surf and producing currents that deflect ocean-borne sand far out to sea. As a result, most **islands** north of Fraser are **continental**, formed when the peaks of ranges were drowned by rising waters at the end of the last Ice Age, creating abrupt coastlines and coral rubble beaches entirely different in character from the southeast's sandy formations. On the reef's outer edge, however, small isolated islands (**cays**) form, which tend to become encircled by fringing coral reef. These are particularly a feature of the southern reef, many close enough to ports for a day-trip, but for a real change of pace, try camping on one for a week or splashing out on a comfortable resort. Further north, the cays thin out, while the main body of the reef thickens into thousands of individual shoals as it ventures nearer the coast. **Divers**

## ACCOMMODATION PRICES

All the accommodation listed in this book has been categorized into one of eight price bands, as set out below. The rates quoted represent the cheapest available double or twin room in high season – except for category ①, which are per-person rates for a dorm bed, and the prices given for units, cabins and vans, which are the daily charge for the whole unit.

| | | | |
|---|---|---|---|
| ① Under $16 | ② $16–26 | ③ $ 27–36 | ④ $ 37–54 |
| ⑤ $55–74 | ⑥ $75–94 | ⑦ $95–124 | ⑧ $ 125 upwards |

For more accommodation details, see pp.31–34

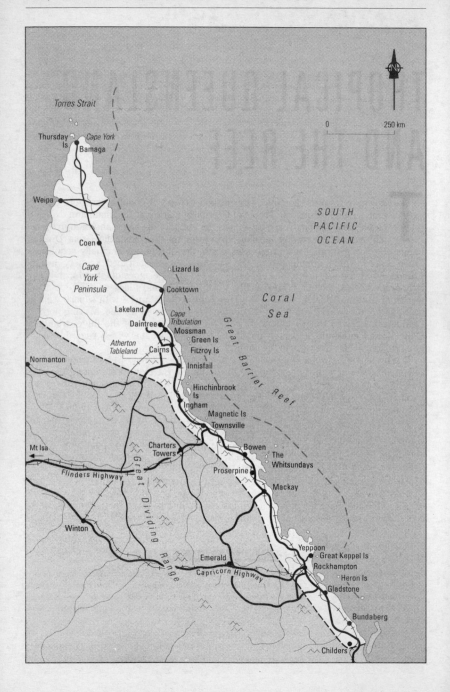

are well catered for, but novices needn't miss out on the best of the coral, which is within snorkelling range of the surface.

**Access** is along the **Bruce Highway** to Cairns, which is then briefly replaced by the **Cook Highway**, until notions of "main roads" begin to fall apart north of Mossman. Beyond here lie the jungles of the **Daintree**, the outpost of **Cooktown** and the beginnings of seasonal roads, humble tracks and the savannah wilderness of the Cape York Peninsula. Frequent **bus** and **train** services stop at all centres between Bundaberg and Cairns, but ideally you'll either be **driving** or willing to hitch to those places that the travel brochures have overlooked. One hazard peculiar to the region is the slow, endless **sugar cane trains** that regularly cross roads during the crushing season (roughly June–Dec); crossings are often (but not always) marked by flashing red lights.

Winters are dry and pleasant, but the summer climate (Dec–April) can be oppressively humid, with unpredictable **cyclones** bringing torrential rain and devastating storms, severing the coastal highway at times and making roads on Cape York impassable. To avoid the worst of the **crowds** at key places (the Cairns region and the Whitsunday Islands), come as soon as the wet season is over (around May).

# THE SOUTHERN REEF

Outside the tropics, the Barrier Reef is represented by the **Capricorn** and **Bunker** groups, a string of cays about 80km offshore from the ports of **Bundaberg** and **Gladstone**. Fundamentally different in character from towns further south in Queensland, these places are primarily farming and residential centres; you'll notice a change in the climate, which dries out as you get near the tropics. Bundaberg lies 50km off the Bruce Highway from Childers (south) or Gin Gin (north); Gladstone is 20km off the highway about 100km south of Rockhampton. Both are on the train line.

Approaching through **CHILDERS**, the down-to-earth *Palace Hostel* (72 Churchill St; ☎071/26 2244; ①) is becoming a popular alternative to Bundaberg for **farm work**; managed by locals, they've good connections and will do their best to find you a job.

# Bundaberg and offshore

Despite being surrounded by canefields and tomato farms, **BUNDABERG** has the atmosphere of a town somewhere in Outback Queensland rather than on the coast; even the **Burnett River** doesn't really manage to add much colour or relieve the heat. Famous throughout Australia for its **rum**, the town is otherwise a pretty humdrum sort of place and its value as a jumping-off point for trips to Lady Elliot and Lady Musgrave islands is hardly advertised. Apart from the reef, the most likely reason to stay over is the chance of finding seasonal (year-round except Dec–Jan) **work**, picking mandarins, tomatoes, snow peas and zucchini. During the summer, biologists come to watch **turtles** laying their eggs at the beaches.

## The Town and around

"Bundie" is synonymous with dark rum throughout Australia and if you believe their advertising pitch, Bundaberg's **rum distillery** on Whittered Street, about 2km east of the town centre along Bourbong Street (tours Mon–Fri 10am, 11am, 1pm, 2pm & 3pm, Sat & Sun 10am, 11am, noon & 1pm; $3), accounts for half the rum consumed in Australia each year. Fans will relish the opportunity to wallow in the overpowering pungency of raw molasses on a tour of the distilling process. Molasses – cane syrup after the sugar is removed – is diluted and heated in huge settling tanks to kill any rogue microbes and to separate out any impurities; yeast is then added to metabolize alcohol. After being distilled twice, raw rum with a spirit content of 78 percent is left to mature to full flavour for two years in white oak vats before being coloured, diluted and bottled. The tour ends, of course, with a **free sample**, but you probably won't need to drink much after inhaling the fumes in the vat sheds where – no kidding – cameras are prohibited in case a flash ignites the vapour. This isn't just paranoia: the distillery was gutted by fire back in 1936.

### Hinkler House and the Mystery Craters

Flying 1,270km from Sydney to Bundaberg in 1921, **Bert Hinkler** set a world record for continuous flight in a light aircraft, demonstrating its potential as transport for remote areas and leading to the formation of *Qantas* the following year. It was quite an achievement in his *Baby Arvo* – all flimsy wires and canvas; there's a replica inside the tourist office on Bourbong Street. In 1983, the house where Hinkler lived at the time of his death in Southampton, England, was rescued from demolition and transported to Bundaberg as a shrine to his feats. **Hinkler House** (daily 10am–4pm; $2) now stands in the Botanic Gardens, 4km from the centre over the Burnett Bridge towards Gin Gin. Outside, landscaped gardens surround ponds where Hinkler was supposedly inspired to design aircraft by watching ibises in flight.

The **Mystery Craters** on the Gin Gin road, 27km from Bundaberg (daily 8am–5pm; $3.50) are 35 pits ("craters" is more evocative than accurate) that have baffled geologists since their discovery on a pineapple plantation in 1971. Between two and three metres wide and excavated only to a depth of about one metre, you may feel the journey wasted to look at what are, essentially, holes in someone's backyard.

### Mon Repos Beach and Turtle Rookery

**Mon Repos Beach** is 15km east of Bundaberg, near Bargara; your accommodation may arrange transport or there's a **bus** from outside the council offices in Barolin Street (Mon–Fri 9am, noon, 2.40pm & 3.55pm, Sat 9am, noon & 2.40pm). Once the site of a French telegraph link to New Caledonia, today its reputation rests on being Australia's most accessible **loggerhead turtle rookery**. From October to January, females clamber laboriously up the beaches after dark, excavate a pit with their hind flippers in the sand above the high-tide mark, and lay about a hundred parchment-shelled eggs. During the eight-week incubation period, the ambient temperature will determine the sex of the entire clutch. The endearing, rubbery brown young hatch at night and head for the sea; normally they'd run a gauntlet of predators, but at Mon Repos human intervention raises their chances. Even so, only a handful reach maturity at fifty years old and return to lay on the beach where they hatched. About a dozen turtles lay each night in season, and watching the young leave the nest and race towards the water is both comical and touching – your chances of seeing both in one evening are best during January.

## Practicalities

Bundaberg lies south of the Burnett River, with the port at **Burnett Heads** and satellite suburbs – Bargara, Innes Park, Elliot Heads – spreading about 15km east along the coast. **Bourbong** is the main street, parallel with the river; the **bus terminal** is in **Targo Street**, and the **train station** is half a kilometre west in **McLean Street**, each of which crosses Bourbong. The **tourist office** is on the corner of Bourbong and Mulgrave streets, about a kilometre west of the centre (daily 9am–5pm; ☎071/52 2333). Cafés and hotels along Bourbong Street provide all the **food** and after-dark entertainment there is; try the grill-dominated counter meals at the *Grand Hotel*.

Central **accommodation** options include the *Grand Hotel* (89 Bourbong St; ☎071/ 51 2441; ③), which has basic beds and inexpensive meals, but makes you feel like

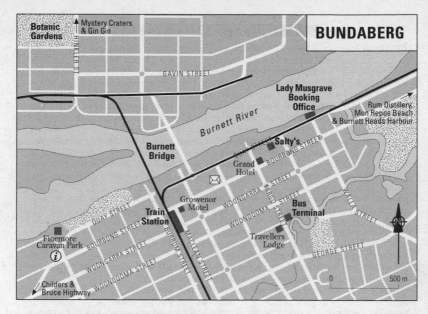

royalty, and the *Travellers Lodge*, opposite the bus terminal in Targo Street (☎071/52 2080; ①), a clean but usually full hostel. Near the train station, both the *Grosvenor Motel* (216 Bourbong St; ☎071/51 3501; ①) and *Federal Guest House* (221 Bourbong St; ☎071/53 3711; ①) specialize in finding seasonal farm work for travellers, but are pretty rough and ready. The closest **campsite** is *Finemore Caravan Park* (☎071/51 3663), behind the tourist office in Quay Street. At Bargara, try the beachfront *Turtle Sands Caravan Park* (Mon Repos Beach, Bargara; ☎071/59 2340), complete with an aspiring **restaurant**, or *Kelly's Beach Resort* (6 Trevors Rd, Bargara; ☎071/59 1222; six-share cabins ⑦), whose self-contained units are a good deal for a group. Both will be full over Christmas.

### Listings

**Airport** On the Bundaberg–Childers road, about 4km from the city centre. *Ansett* (☎071/51 2644); *Sunstate* (☎13 1313).

**Banks** Scattered along Bourbong St.

**Buses** *Greyhound/Pioneer* (☎071/13 2030); *McCafferty's* (☎071/52 9700).

**Camping gear** *Smith's Camping Centre*, 15 Takalvan St (☎071/51 5436).

**Diving** Sites include Nudibranch Park, the encrusted wreck of a *Beaufort* bomber, and Evan's Patch; inhabitants include a large grouper, pelagics, and sea snakes. Competition makes Bundaberg a very cheap place to learn: best is *Salty's* (Salty's Arcade, 22 Quay St; ☎071/53 4747), with their own boat; *Anglo Diving* (200 Bourbong St; ☎071/51 6422) and *Kelly's Beach Resort* (6 Trevors Rd, Bargara; ☎071/59 1222) are good alternatives.

**NPWS** Government Office Building, Quay St, near the bridge (☎071/53 8620). All camping on southern reef islands must be booked through the Gladstone office.

**Post office** 157b Bourbong St (☎071/53 2700).

**Shopping centre** Maryborough St.

**Taxi** ☎071/51 2345.

**Train station** McLean St (☎071/53 9711; bookings ☎071/13 2232).

## THE GREAT BARRIER REEF

The **Great Barrier Reef** is to Australia what rolling savannahs and game parks are to Africa, and is equally subject to the corniest of representations. "Another World" is the commonest cliché, which, while being completely true, doesn't begin to describe the feeling of donning mask and fins and coming face to face with extraordinary animals, shapes and colours. There's so little relationship to life above the surface that distinctions normally taken for granted – such as that between animal, plant and plain rock – seem blurred, while the respective roles of observer and observed are constantly challenged by shoals of curious fish following you about.

Beginning with Lady Elliot Island, off the coast from Bundaberg, and extending 2300km north to New Guinea, the Barrier Reef follows the outer edge of Australia's continental plate, running closer to land as it moves north: while it's 300km to the main body from Gladstone, Cairns is barely 50km distant from the reef. Far from being a continuous, unified structure, the nature of the reef also changes along its length, forming long **ribbons** north of Cairns, concentrated groups of low sand islands (**cays**) further south, and **fringing reef** around islands. All of it, however, was built by one animal: the tiny coral **polyp**. Simple organisms, related to sea anemones, polyps huddle together like building blocks into modular colonies – corals – which form the framework of the reef's ecology by providing food, shelter and hunting grounds for larger, more mobile species. Around their walls and canyons flow a bewildering assortment of creatures: large rays and turtles "fly" effortlessly by, fish dodge between caves and coral branches, snails sift the sand for edibles, and brightly coloured nudibranches dance above rocks.

The reef is administered by the **Marine Parks Authority**, which gamely tries to battle against – or at least gauge – the effects of over-fishing, industrial and agricultural pollution, and tourism. Underfunding, and the lengthy study time required to find practical long-term solutions for the reef's protection, mean that little has been achieved to date. The most obvious signs of damage – broken and dead coral – are probably due to the sheer volume of visitors, with divers bumping against outcrops and boats dropping anchors. A popular villain, the **crown of thorns starfish**, undoubtedly causes severe destruction during cyclic plagues, but not enough to account for the level of damage you'll see. Don't let this put you off going – major damage is restricted to only a handful of sites, and overall the reef is still healthy. But it's clear that the reef needs to be treated with respect if it is to retain its natural wonder. In order to minimize damage, visitors should take care not to stand on shallow reefs when snorkelling, and always avoid touching coral; even if you don't break off branches, you'll certainly crush the delicate polyps.

DIVING AND OTHER WAYS OF SEEING THE REEF

If you have the money, **scuba** diving is the best way to come to grips with the reef, and **dive courses** are on offer right along the coast. **Five days** is the absolute minimum needed to safely cover the course work – three days' pool and theory, two days at sea – and secure you the all-important C-card. The quality of training and the price you pay vary enormously: cheaper courses tend to have a higher student-to-instructor ratio, which means that problems can go unnoticed for longer; less importatantly, they often

## Lady Elliot Island

The reef's southern outpost, **Lady Elliot Island** has suffered over the years from phosphate mining and the effects of feral goats. In their wake, vegetation is returning, with soft-leaved *pisonia* trees asserting themselves over a bed of pulverized coral rubble and sand. The elegant **lighthouse** was built in 1866 after an extraordinary number of wrecks on the reef; on average, one vessel a year still manages to come to grief. Wailing shearwaters and the occasional suicide of lighthouse staff didn't endear the island to early visitors, but it has since become a popular escape with those who value the very remoteness that once haunted those stationed here.

use island reefs rather than the main reef. The best deals are to be had where the tourists go – Airlie Beach or Cairns – but you'll also find a higher proportion of more dubious courses in these places. With adequate funds and time, you're better off learning away from these centres and then diving them once you're qualified. Another consideration is whether you ever plan to go diving again: if this seems unlikely, **resort dives** (a single dive with an instructor) will only set you back $50 or so, and they're usually available on day trips to the reef and island resorts.

While the extra weight will be a drag between dives, **qualified divers** can save on rental costs by bringing some gear along; tanks and weightbelts are normally covered in dive packages but anything else is extra. You need an alternative air source, timer, C-card and log book to dive in Queensland (the last is often ignored but some places insist).

**Snorkelling** is a good alternative to diving: you can pick up the basics in about five minutes and with a little practice the only thing you sacrifice is the extended dive time that a tank allows. If you think you'll do a fair amount, buy your own mask and snorkel – they're not dramatically expensive – as rental gear nearly always leaks. Look for a silicone rubber and toughened glass mask and ask the shop staff to show you how to find a good fit. If getting wet just isn't for you, try glass-bottomed "subs", which can still turn up everything from sharks to oysters.

## REEF HAZARDS

Shark attacks, savage octopuses and giant clam legends all make good press, but are best shrugged off as lurid exaggerations. However, there are a few things at the reef capable of putting a dampener on your holiday, and it makes sense to be careful.

**Coral and shell cuts** are the commonest of mishaps, and easily become infected if not treated immediately by removing any fragments and dousing with antiseptic. **Tropical ear** is a fungal infection of the ear canal and can be very painful in its advanced stage. Treatment is with ear drops and if you think you might be susceptible, use them anyway after getting wet. **Animals** to avoid tend to be on the small side. Shore divers might encounter the dangerous **box jellyfish** (see warning on p.20); jellyfish found at the reef can cause nausea and raise a painful weal, but they're not life-threatening. Some **corals** can also give you a nasty sting, but it's more of a warning not to touch than something to worry about. Brightly patterned, conical **cone shells** are home to a fish-eating snail armed with a poisonous barb which has caused fatalities in people who've picked them up. Don't: there is no "safe" end to hold them. Similarly, the shy, small, **blue-ringed octopus** has a fatal bite and should never be handled. **Stonefish** are nightmare creations camouflaged to look like a rock. They spend their days immobile, sucking in anything small and edible that floats past, and protected from reprisals by a series of poisonous spines along their back. If you tread on one, you'll end up in hospital – an excellent argument against reef-walking. Of the larger animals, **rays** are timid, flattened fish with a sharp spine capable of causing deep wounds – don't swim close over sandy floors where they hide. **Sharks** are rarely encountered and the only ones you're likely to see are inoffensive varieties.

Finally, while this list sounds daunting, the truth is that nothing is out to get you: leave everything alone and you shouldn't have any problems.

The island can only be reached **by air** on daily flights with *Sunstate* (day return $105, period return $145; ☎13 1313). Accommodation at **Lady Elliot Island Resort** (reservations ☎1800/07 2200; information ☎071/53 2485; ⑦) is in comfortable but basic cabins, and meals are included in the rates; packages including airfare are better value.

**Diving** around Lady Elliot certainly has its moments, with optimum visibility around 40m, reduced to 20m on a bad day; this is where to come if you want to see graceful, gigantic **manta rays** and **loggerhead turtles** heading shoreward to lay their eggs. Shore dives cost $25 for the first two, then $10 for each dive on the same day; boat and night dives are $35, or $30 at dawn. The dive shop has an underwater video too, so pick up a compact VHS tape before you go and have yourself filmed with the mantas.

## Lady Musgrave Island

**Lady Musgrave Island** is a pretty place, where encircling coral forms a large turquoise lagoon scattered with trawlers, its trees home to nesting colonies of **black noddies** between November and February. **Diving** the shallow coral outcrops is unexciting, but it *is* worthwhile **snorkelling** and, while light sleepers will want to avoid a stay during the tern nesting season, Lady Musgrave is the best of the southern cays to **camp** on.

Day **cruises** on *MV Lady Musgrave* depart from Burnett Heads boat harbour (Tues, Thurs, Sat & Sun, 8.30am; $92), about half an hour's drive from Bundaberg; the booking office is at 1 Quay Street (☎071/52 9011) and they can arrange a **bus pick-up** from your accommodation ($6). **Campers** need permits from the Gladstone NPWS (see below) and ferry tickets well in advance; the return fare is $180. The island has no facilities: if you're camping, take everything including **water**, although you can arrange for the *Lady Musgrave* to bring fresh provisions if you're staying for a while. There's a limit of fifty campers at a time but it only gets this busy over Christmas and Easter.

# Gladstone and nearby islands

**GLADSTONE** is a busy port, and also the site of a processing plant which refines aluminium from ore mined at Weipa on the Cape York Peninsula. Glaringly hot, it's not an unfriendly place, but there's no reason to stop here unless you're trying to reach the reef. In fact, if you're planning to camp on any of the southern cays, it's here that you need to make arrangements – through the **NPWS office** at Parklane Plaza, Tank St, PO Box 315 Gladstone (☎079/76 0766).

The main strip is **Goondoon Street**, where there's a "mall" – just the usual high-street shops, post office and banks – and a couple of hotels and motels. A cool, casual **hostel** is hidden away at 12 Rollo Street (☎079/72 5744; ①): go to the marina end of Goondoon Street, turn left and it's three streets down past a small supermarket, or give them a call and they'll pick you up from transit terminals. *Gladstone Reef Hotel* (38 Goondoon St; 079/72 1000; ⑤) has good views from a rooftop pool and ordinary **motel** rooms. **Cafés** in the mall range from *Munchies* (46 Goondoon St; ☎079/72 5052), a cheap and cheerful Mexican with $5 lunches during the week, to *Swaggy's* (52 Goondoon St), where you can spoil yourself with native cuisine – emu, crocodile, kangaroo – at gourmet prices. Hotel **entertainment** is patchy: mud wrestling and live bands (probably not at the same time) seem to be standard fare.

**Diving** is easy to arrange through the sole dive shop, *CQ Fishing and Diving Supplies* (16 Goondoon St; ☎079/72 4658). They take qualified divers out for the weekend (Fri–Sun; $250), and offer a seven-day dive course for $400 all-inclusive – good value given that this is the only way you'll get to see Heron reef. Unless you're venturing to one of the islands (see below), the only distraction around Gladstone is a trip to **Quoin Island**, whose ferry ($6 return) leaves from O'Connel Wharf on Friday, Saturday and Sunday mornings. While not on a par with the reef islands (mangrove beaches leave much to be desired for sunbathing), the **resort** (☎079/72 2255; ⑦) is pleasant and day-trippers can use their facilities.

## Tryon and Masthead islands

Remote both in feel and location, **Tryon** and **Masthead** islands remain virtually undisturbed, with limited numbers of campers permitted at any one time. Masthead takes about an hour to walk around, Tryon is even smaller. Both are valuable nesting sites for burrowing brown shearwaters (muttonbirds), tree-roosting black noddies, and mixed colonies of black-naped, roseate and crested terns nesting in the open. The ruckus generated can be quite disturbing, but in the right frame of mind this all becomes part of the experience. Don't overlook the reef's **snorkelling** or **fishing** if you have the gear, though bear in mind that certain sections of reef are protected zones where fishing is prohibited – check with the NPWS in Gladstone first.

The only way to reach Tryon and Masthead is by **charter boat** from Gladstone: at $1300–1500 you need a party of at least ten for it to be financially viable, but split ten ways, it's good value for a long stay. Try *Gladstone Star* (☎079/79 2506), Robert Poulson (☎079/72 5166), *Voyager* & *Hyland C* (☎079/72 2191) for boats. **Camping arrangements** for all the southern cays must be made through the Gladstone NPWS (see above), and you need to take everything: food, at least five litres of water per person per day, waterproof tents and sand pegs, shovels, first aid kit, radio (for weather forecasts), garbage bags and emergency rations.

# Heron Island

Famous for its diving, **Heron Island** escaped the depredations of goats and guano hunters earlier this century and, though a turtle-canning factory operated on the island for several years, it has survived more or less intact. Small enough to walk around in a relaxed thirty minutes, about half the cay is occupied by a comfortable **resort** and **research station**, the rest covered in groves of shady *pisonias*, screw pine and coconuts; patches of long grass hide ground-dwelling **rails** (moorhen-like birds) which rocket from underfoot. And **herons** *do* stalk around the coral tops at low tide, fishing the pools – they're typically white, but a black form also frequents the island. Where the trees peg out, sand takes over, ringing the island.

Progressing into the water, coral starts growing immediately below the tide line and you can literally walk off the beach and onto the reef, or swim along the shallow walls looking for action. The eastern edges of the lagoon are good for snorkelling at any time, but **diving** must be arranged through the resort (see "Practicalities" below; $30 for a standard dive, $85 for two "adventure" dives, $45 to venture out at night; equipment extra). Dive **packages** save a few dollars if you're staying long enough to take advantage of them. Best time to visit is during the November **dive festival** when there's a chance to rub shoulders with visiting veterans and pick up workshop hints on equipment use and photography.

A drift along the wall facing Wistari reef to The Bommie covers about everything you're likely to encounter. The coral itself is poor (explanations range from cyclones to over-use), but the amount of life is astonishing: tiny boxfish hiding under ledges; turtles, cowries, wobbegong, moray eels, scorpion fish and octopuses hiding in the rubble; larger reef fish gaping vacantly as you drift past. The Bommie itself makes first-rate **snorkelling**, with an interesting swim-through if your lungs are up to it, while the Tenements along the reef's northern edge are good for bigger game – including sharks.

## Practicalities

There is a price to pay for all this natural wonder, namely no day-trips and no camping. The *P&O*-owned resort (reservations ☎02/364 8300; island reception ☎079/78 1488; ⑨) is excellent but its rates, coupled with the $130 ferry cost, place it well outside the budget bracket. **Standby fares** offered by travel agents in Gladstone are worth looking into – try *Traveland*, 124 Goondoon Street (☎079/72 2288) – but don't expect miracles. Ferries leave from Gladstone Marina at 11am, daily except at Christmas; there's a **car lockup** here ($5 a day) operated by the tackle shop (8am–5pm). The alternative is to fly in by helicopter, at a whopping $335.

# THE TROPICS: ROCKHAMPTON TO CAPE YORK

**Rockhampton** marks the start of the tropics, but with the exception of the Mackay region, it's not until you're well past the line and north of **Townsville** that the tropical greenery associated with north Queensland finally appears. Then it comes in a rush, and by the time you've reached **Cairns** there's no doubt that the area deserves its reputation: coastal ranges covered in rainforest and cloud descend right to the sea. **Islands** along the way lure you with good beaches, hiking tracks and opportunities for snorkelling and diving: the **Keppels** near Rockhampton, the **Whitsundays** off Airlie Beach, **Magnetic Island** opposite Townsville, **Hinchinbrook** and **Dunk** further north. Cairns itself serves as a base for exploring highland rainforest on the **Atherton Tablelands**, the **Daintree**'s coastal jungles, trips onto the **Cape York Peninsula** and, of course, to the most accessible sections of the **Great Barrier Reef**.

# Rockhampton and around

**ROCKHAMPTON**, which straddles the Tropic of Capricorn, an hour north of Gladstone, was founded by accident. A false goldrush in 1858 left hundreds of miners stranded at a depot forty kilometres inland, on the banks of the sluggish **Fitzroy River**; their rough camp below **Mount Archer** was soon put to use by local stockmen as a convenient port. The iron trelliswork and sandstone buildings along the river stand as a testament to the balmy 1890s, when money was pouring into the city from central Queensland's prosperous cattle industry and the gold and copper mines at nearby **Mount Morgan**. Today, Rockhampton depends on a depressed beef market, with gun and leather shops adding their distinctive scent to quiet streets. Appallingly humid summers convince most visitors to use the city simply as a springboard for the adjacent Capricorn Coast (see below), but there are a few unusual diversions: an Aboriginal version of history at the **Dreamtime Centre**; a group of **limestone caves** which you can explore without a guide; and the mining town of **Mount Morgan** itself.

### The Town and surroundings

It doesn't take long to look around. The **Tropic Marker** at the southern entrance of town is just a spire informing you of your position at 23° 26' 30" S. And that's it, apart from the pleasant **botanic gardens** behind the marker in Spencer Street, or the brown-stained boulders in the river that gave the city its name.

About 5km north on the highway, and served by *Rothery's Coaches* (see below), is the **Dreamtime Cultural Centre** (daily 10am–5.30pm; tours with an Aboriginal guide at 11am & 2pm; $9, including tour if times coincide with your visit), built in 1988 both to educate visitors and as a cultural focus for Torres Strait Islanders and central Queensland Aborigines. Inside, chronological and dreamtime histories are intermingled, ranging from unusual exhibits such as the suspended carving of Wangard and the Goon Goon Bird to archeological dissections of Carnarvon Gorge and other central highlands sites. Outside, surrounded by woodland, modern gunyahs and stencil art, you'll find the original stone rings of a **bora ground**; these once marked the main camp of the Darumbal whose territory reached from the Keppel Bay coastline inland to Mount Morgan. The tour also introduces boomerang and didgeridoo skills – audience participation is definitely encouraged. Rockhampton also sports a couple of staid settlers' museums. **Glenmore Homestead** (daily except Sat 11am–3pm; $6, includes guided tour) is about 5km out – look for the turning left. The homestead was founded in

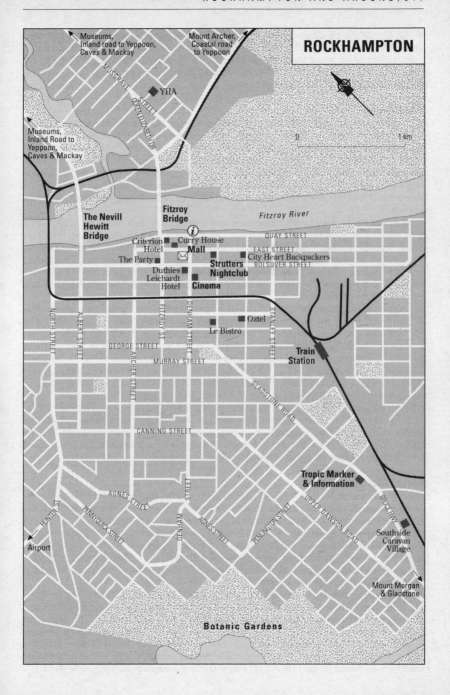

ROCKHAMPTON

Museums,
Inland road to Yeppoon,
Caves & Mackay

Mount Archer,
Coastal road
to Yeppoon

YHA

Museums,
Inland Road to
Yeppoon,
Caves & Mackay

0          1 km

The Nevill
Hewitt
Bridge

Fitzroy
Bridge

Fitzroy River

QUAY STREET

Criterion
Hotel

Curry House

Mall

EAST STREET

City Heart Backpackers

BOLSOVER STREET

The Party

Strutters
Nightclub

Duthies
Leichardt
Hotel

Cinema

Oztel

Le Bistro

MUSGRAVE STREET

QUEEN ELIZABETH DR

NORTH STREET

ALBERT STREET

FITZROY ST

DENHAM STREET

STANLEY STREET

ARCHER STREET

GEORGE STREET

MURRAY STREET

Train
Station

GLADSTONE ROAD

CANNING STREET

AGNES STREET

DENHAM STREET

Tropic Marker
& Information

HUNTER ST

PENNYQUICK STREET

AGNES STREET

PENLINGTON STREET

UPPER DAWSON ROAD

BRUCE HWY

Airport

Southside
Caravan
Village

Mount Morgan
& Gladstone

**Botanic Gardens**

the 1850s and the buildings remain rare period pieces, from the original beam hut, with gun ports to fend off Aboriginal attacks, to the more substantial homestead. Right out of town (23km north along the highway then follow the signs), **Heritage Village** (daily 9am–4pm; $5) is an eccentric collection of everything, including vintage cars, whaling cannons and a New Guinea outrigger canoe.

## The Caves

The limestone hills 25km north of Rockhampton are riddled with an interesting **cave** system discovered in the 1880s. Turn off the Bruce Highway at **THE CAVES** township, cross the rail line and turn left. Johansson's (see below) is straight on past a council depot and around to the right; for **Cammoo** (daily 8.30am–4pm; $9; ☎079/34 2774) and **Olsen's** (daily from 8.30am; $9; ☎079/34 2883) turn right after the hotel and follow the billboards. Johansson's are undeveloped, but there are **tours** of Cammoo and Olsen's – the latter is more interesting; *Rothery's Coaches* visit both during the week (see box opposite).

The caves have few classic stalagmites and stalactites, which need continuous dripping water to form: in their place are tree roots, encased in stone after forcing their way down through rocks, "cave corals" and "frozen waterfalls" – minerals deposited by evaporation after annual floods. Two endangered species, the **ghost bat** (Australia's only carnivorous bat) and **little bent-winged bat**, use the caves for roosts. The former breeds at Johansson's Cave, and you might catch the odd group huddled together on a cave roof, eyes peering down at you over leaf-shaped noses.

Exploring **Johansson's Cave** (Feb–June 6am–8pm; closed when bats are in residence) is mildly adventurous, as there are no signs or markers. Take a torch and suitable footwear, and check with the NPWS first for an update on conditions; it's best to go in a group – while you're unlikely to get seriously lost, there's comfort in having others to blame when you start wandering around in circles. At the entrance the air becomes cool and all noise is deadened as the path heads down into a large cavern, inadequately illuminated by a natural window. Occasional squeaks come from high up on the ceiling, and silver beads of light reflected in the torch beam reveal a surprising number of moths and spiders. Bear right into a low passage and out into a smaller cave lit by another skylight. Wooden trestles here are left over from the extraction of **guano**, which was used in the manufacture of explosives around the time of World War II. **Rhino Cavern**, a bit further on, is named after a spiky rock and the track continues from here to another cave, but this may well be flooded out.

## Mount Morgan

Gold was found at **MOUNT MORGAN** in 1880 and became one of the richest prospects in Queensland; from the lookout hill across the Dee River, you can still see the 342-metre-deep mine terraces. While gold petered out in the first years of the twentieth century, enough **copper** was found to keep the mine active until 1981. Apart from its deposits, Mount Morgan is famous for its instrumental role in the formation of the *BP* company, which was founded by one William Knox D'Arcy after he had made his money through shares in the mine. The township is 40km south of Rockhampton along Highway 17; see box for **bus** details.

Though reprocessing of old tailings began in 1994 the town itself seems to be basking, and it's easy to feel as if you've stepped back fifty years among the dated pubs and houses; the only recent intrusion is the crumbling tarmac on the road. The **museum** (open when the curator is in), on the corner of Morgan and East streets, has a geology display which includes some plesiosaur fossils, minerals and local history exhibits. **Mine tours** (weekdays at 1pm from outside the museum) include a visit to a nearby cave with **dinosaur footprints** in the ceiling; contact *Young's* buses for further details.

## TOURS AROUND ROCKHAMPTON

**Rothery's Coaches** (☎079/22 4320) pick up from accommodation or outside *Duthie's Leichardt Hotel*. Tours visit Koorana Crocodile Farm near Yeppoon (Mon 9.30am); Olsen's Caves (Mon, Wed & Fri 9am); Cammoo Caves, Heritage Village and Glenmore Homestead (Tues 9am); Rockhampton and sites surrounding (Wed & Fri 9.30am); The Dreamtime Centre (Mon, Wed & Fri 12.15pm); Capricorn Coast (Thurs 9.30am); they also run a daily service to Rosslyn Bay ferry terminal for the Keppel islands.

**Young's** (☎079/22 3813) run a bus to Yeppoon and all points along the Capricorn Coast from the corner of Denham and Bolsover streets (Mon–Fri 9 services daily, tour connection at 10am; Sat & Sun 3 daily); and to Mount Morgan from outside the Capricornia Credit Union, corner of East and William streets (Mon–Fri at 6.15am, 10am & 4.30pm, Sat 7.30am & 12.15pm).

## Practicalities

Rockhampton is divided by the river, with all services clustered directly south of the **Fitzroy Bridge** along **Quay Street** and **East Street Mall**. *McCafferty's* **buses** stop just north of the bridge, and also at the *Mobil* service station on the south side; *Greyhound/ Pioneer* halt across from *Duthies Leichardt Hotel*. The **train** station is east of the centre at the end of George Street. Driving in, the highway runs right through town past two pairs of fibreglass bulls (often painfully disfigured). **Information** is from the booth on the highway at the Tropic Marker, or the more comprehensive and central *Riverside Information Centre* in Quay Street (9am–5pm; ☎079/22 5339).

The pick of the **accommodation** choices are the good-value suites overlooking the river at the historic *Criterion Hotel* in Quay Street (☎079/22 1225; ④), which occupies the site of Rockhampton's first pub, the *Bush Inn*, built in 1857. Motel-style units are available at *Duthies Leichardt Hotel* in the centre on Bolsover Street (☎079/27 6733; ⑤), where they sometimes rent spare units to backpackers for ①); Other budget options include the *YHA*'s isolated compound north of the river (60 MacFarlane St; ☎079/27 5288; ②); the sleepy, basic *Oztel* (212 Kent St; ☎079/22 5343; ①); thin mattresses and makeshift rooms at *City Heart Backpackers* (170 East St; ☎079/22 2414; ①); or *Southside Caravan Village* (on the highway 2km south; ☎079/27 3013; ①–③), with **campsites**, cramped on-site vans, shop, pool, and pick-up from town.

A **steak** of some kind is the obvious choice in Australia's "Beef Capital", and any of the hotels can oblige. There's a smattering of cafés around the mall, where you'll also find the *Indian Tandoori & Curry House* (☎079/27 4182), featuring totally un-Indian decor, anonymous curry lunches from under $7 and excellent evening dishes at $12 or less. Gastronomes should prepare themselves for *Le Bistro* (William St; Mon–Sat 6.30pm–late; ☎079/22 2019), where dishes such as pork fillets in coffee and tahini sauce, or fish in cumin and gin, test the tastebuds; mains are about $18. For **nightlife**, there's the cinema on Denham Street, and clubs at *Strutters* on the Mall, and *The Party*, on the corner of Fitzroy and Bolsover streets – both are open Wednesday to Sunday from 8pm to late for disco and host frequent **live bands**.

**Moving on**, the Capricorn Highway heads towards Emerald and points west (see *Outback Queensland*), while the Bruce Highway continues north. The Capricorn Coast is serviced by local **buses** to Emu Park, Rosslyn Bay and Yeppoon – see box for details.

### Listings

**Airlines** *Ansett*, 137 East St (☎079/31 0741); *Qantas*, 107 East St (☎079/22 1033).
**Banks** Branches around the Mall.

**Buses** *Greyhound/Pioneer*, at *Duthies Leichardt Hotel* (☎079/27 6288); *McCafferty's*, corner of Brown and Linnett streets (☎079/27 2844); *Rothery's*, 13 Power St, North Rockhampton (☎079/22 4320); *Young's*, 274 George St (☎079/22 3813).

**Bushwalking club** (☎079/38 1818)

**Camping gear** *Campco*, 121 William St (☎079/27 2050).

**Car rental** *Network*, corner of George and Archer streets (☎079/22 2990); *Rockhampton Car Rentals*, on the highway south (☎079/22 7802); *Thrifty*, 43 Fitzroy St (☎079/27 8755).

**Chemist** *CQ Pharmacy*, 150 Alma St, next to the cinema (☎079/22 1621); daily 8am–10pm.

**Diving** *Capricorn Reef Diving*, 189 Musgrave St, North Rockhampton (☎079/22 7720). Certification courses from around $380, diving around the Keppels. Qualified divers can organize trips to the Bunker and Capricorn groups.

**Farm Stays** *Myella Farm*, The Eather Familly, Myella, Barabala, Qld 4702 (☎079/98 1290) and *Cooper Downs Station*, Dennis Stevenson, Banana, Qld 4702 (☎079/96 5276) are a couple of hours out of town and offer accommodation, meals and participation in farm life from ⑦ upwards.

**Hospital** Base Hospital, Canning St, South Rockhampton (☎079/31 6211).

**NPWS** A helpful crowd, but 5km out of town on the Yeppoon–Rockhampton Road (☎079/36 0511).

**Post office** 80 East St Mall (☎079/27 6566).

**RACQ** 134 William St (☎079/27 2255).

**State Forestry Department** 209 Bolsover St (☎079/31 9815); permits for access to Byfield National Park (see p.323).

**Supplies** *City Centre Plaza Shoppingtown* in Bolsover St.

**Taxi** (☎079/22 7111).

**Trail rides** *The Oaks* on the Rockhampton–Yeppoon Road (☎079/39 4255).

**Trains** Murray St (☎079/32 0211).

# The Capricorn Coast

Views from volcanic outcrops overlooking the **Capricorn Coast**, east of Rockhampton, stretch across graziers' estates and pineapple plantations to exposed headlands, estuarine mudflats and the **Keppel Islands** 20km offshore. The coastal townships of **Yeppoon** and **Emu Park**, settled by cattle barons in the 1860s, were soon adopted by Rockhampton's elite as places to beat the summer heat. Despite some modern development, the coast retains a pleasantly dated holiday atmosphere and it's a great place for independent travel. Everyone goes to **Great Keppel Island**, but other places – **Byfield** for one – are only just being discovered by visitors and remain largely untouched.

## Rockhampton to Yeppoon: coast and inland

There are two routes to Yeppoon from Rockhampton: the coastal **Lakes Creek Road** (immediately north of the Fitzroy Bridge) past Emu Park and Rosslyn Bay, or the inland **Yeppoon Road**, off the Bruce Highway, 5km from town (opposite the Dreamtime Centre).

First stop on the **coastal road**, about 25km from Rockhampton, is **Koorana Crocodile Farm** (tours daily at 1pm; $9; ☎079/34 4749), where they breed estuarine crocs (*koorana* means "giving birth") to supply the leather industry and restaurants. If the reptiles' ultimate fate doesn't bother you, the tours are interesting – despite a certain amount of showmanship involved in feeding and meeting Koorana's "stars". With luck you might see babies hatching, bleating as they squeeze themselves out of tiny eggs. The **sea** appears suddenly at **EMU PARK**, a breezy hillside covered by scattered "Queenslander" houses, a store, hotel and van park. From the cliffs at the **Singing Ship** the wind howls mournful tunes through the wires of this peculiar monument to Captain Cook. There's little to do between here and Yeppoon except take in the seascape; the road runs a gauntlet of units, van parks and campsites as it alternates between twisting headlands and flat beachfront. Possible stops might be at **KINKA BEACH**, where stir-crazy hawksbill turtles endlessly circle the motley aquarium, or **ROSSLYN BAY** where the cliffs have been weathered into hexagonal columns behind the **island ferry terminal** – views from the windswept top are good, but take some lunch to make it worthwhile. Further on, **COOEE BAY** is virtually a suburb of Yeppoon, with an annual "Cooee Competition" when competitors give their tonsils a good airing from Wreck Point.

Following the **inland road**, you'll find the plains dotted with **volcanic plugs**, some of which can be climbed. **Mount Jim Crow** is to the left of the highway, about 15km along the Yeppoon Road; look out for the well-hidden sign to the national park. From the car park, a rough track leads to a small quarry on the left side of the mountain, then follows shallow gullies and water run-offs uphill through some fairly dense scrub. What really takes up time are the huge, tough webs of the **golden orb weaver spider**; the giant female spiders are timid, but still an unwelcome sight as you plough into their webs. A good hour should see you safely at the top admiring the scenery; on the way down don't be tempted to take short-cuts as the rocks are unstable.

## Yeppoon

Built around the sheltering hills of Spring Head, **YEPPOON** faces North Keppel over a blustery expanse of sand and sea. Though busy at Easter and Christmas, it generally keeps a low profile, and residents seem to cherish this tranquillity – to the extent that the *Capricorn International Resort* just along the coast was **bombed** when construction plans overruled local wishes; for $25 you can spend a day here with brunch, use of all facilities and the chance to birdwatch through melaleuca swamps thrown in.

All services are in **James Street**, at right angles to **Anzac Parade** and seafront **accommodation** – *Tropical Nights Motel*, 34 Anzac Parade (☎079/39 1914; ④) has small self-contained rooms, but for views, you're better off at *Hacienda Holiday Units*, 18 Anzac Parade (☎079/39 1403; ③–④), a tidy and quiet guesthouse. *Barrier Reef Backpackers*, 30 Queen Street (☎079/39 4702; ①), can collect you from Rockhampton if you call in advance, and has airy, wraparound verandahs, while the *Blue Dolphin Caravan Park* (☎079/39 3140), at 74 Whitman Street, is relatively sheltered.

The *Flaming Steer*, at *Tropical Nights Motel*, has little competition for their claim to serve the best steaks in town, while the **Yacht Club** opposite may let you in for cheap beer, average **food** and the best views across to the islands. There's a nightclub at the *Strand Hotel* on Anzac Parade and another one road back in Hill Street; both come to life only at weekends.

## The Keppel Islands

The eighteen **Keppel Islands** boast white sand so fine that it squeaks when you walk through it, and the sea is an invitingly clear blue – just right for a few days of indolence. Most of the islands are national parks and, with the exception of North and Great Keppel, very small. The resort and facilities on **Great Keppel** make it the most popular, but there are also reefs to snorkel and isolated camping on the other islands. Good-value package deals are sometimes on offer at the resorts outside of the Easter and Christmas holidays, with discounts of around ten percent on accommodation or offering seven nights for the price of five.

There's free parking at Rosslyn Bay harbour's **ferry terminal** (see above); for protection from salt spray, leave your car undercover at *Kempsea Car Park* ($8 a day). *Reefseeker* (☎079/33 6744) runs ferries to Great Keppel (daily 9.15am, 11.30am, 3.30pm; $25 return) and twice weekly day-trips to **Barren Island** for snorkelling ($70). *Keppel*

*Island Taxis* (☎079/39 5095) run from Rosslyn Bay and Emu Park on demand to any of the Keppel group; costs are at least $40 return (minimum of two). Finally, *Keppel Isles Yacht Charters* (☎079/39 4949) offer fishing, snorkelling or just cruising day-trips for $40 per person, for a minimum of three people; the price includes lunch.

## Great Keppel

Arriving on **Great Keppel**, the ferry leaves you on a spit directly in front of the budget **accommodation** and, if you haven't booked in advance, your priority should be to head for the relevant reception. *Wapparaburra Haven* (☎079/33 6744) occupies sheltered, sandy woodland behind Putney Beach with tent sites in the dunes, beds in their pre-fab *Tent Village* (③) or self-contained cabins for up to six (⑧). The adjacent *YHA* (☎079/39 4341; ②) is a cramped bunkhouse in the same pleasant surroundings, but is frequently full. Along the beach, the modern and comfortable *Great Keppel Island Resort* (☎079/39 5044; ⑥), or rather its *Shipwreck Bar*, is the island's after-dark social focus; by day, the resort cultivates a family atmosphere and there's a pool available for day-trippers. *Wapparaburra* has a **restaurant**, occasional barbecues, and a store specializing in tooth-paste. There's also a late-opening **pizza shack** near the youth hostel – much frequented after the bar – and a tearoom at the *Shell House* on Fisherman's Beach.

The main **beaches**, Putney and Fisherman's, are remarkably pleasant considering the number of people that you find lounging on them at any one time, but the effort of a half-hour walk will reward you with some more secluded spots. **Leakes Beach** seldom hosts more than a handful of people; the quickest way there is over the point at the rocky end of Putney, where there's a steep path. Reached on a woodland path past the resort, **Long Beach** attracts a few more sun-worshippers, while snorkellers make the short haul over sand dunes at the western end to shallow coral on **Monkey Beach**; shell mounds here were left by Woppaburra Aborigines, who were enslaved and forci-bly removed to Fraser Island by early settlers.

**Inland** is dry, and the paths double as 4WD tracks for the island's few vehicles. For views, take the road behind the resort up a short and steep hill to the lookout. The best walk is the hour-long return trip up **Mount Wyndham**, ending on a cliff with the coast at your feet. Longer excursions to Butterfish Bay, Wreck Beach or Bald Rock Point lighthouse will take at least four hours return.

## Other Keppels

The only way of getting to these islands is with *Keppel Island Taxis* (see above); once you're there, there are no **provisions**, and (unreliable) **drinking water** only on Humpy and North Keppel. NPWS camping **permits** can be picked up at the Rockhampton (see p.320) or Rosslyn Bay offices.

**North Keppel** is an undeveloped version of Great Keppel. There's an NPWS camp-site on the west side of the island, behind the dunes at Considine Bay, with a sporadic supply of tank water, showers, toilets and a ban on wood fires; take precautions against sandflies, which are abundant in sheltered spots here. A walking track from the group of cabins at the southern end of Considine Beach leads to the reef at Maisy Bay.

**Pumpkin Island**, off North Keppel, is a privately owned fifteen acres of beach, mangroves and coral with four basic cabins (☎079/39 2431; ②).

**Middle Island** is lightly wooded with an NPWS camping area and underwater observatory complete with scenic Taiwanese junk; only a short hop from Great Keppel, you might be able to pick up a day-trip from there to the observatory. Olive Head Point is famous for sea snakes, if you plan to dive. **Humpy Island**, also off Great Keppel, is locally popular for fishing and has the best snorkelling reef of all the islands. The hump doesn't do much to protect it from the southeasterlies, which are the main problem with camping here; facilities are similar to those on North Keppel.

## The Byfield Coast

Cape York aside, the top of the Capricorn Coast is the wildest area in eastern Australia. The biggest attraction is the scenery and wildlife at **BYFIELD NATIONAL PARK**, a massive system of tropical and sub-tropical forests, multicoloured parabolic sand dunes, rivers and swamps fed by underground reservoirs – one of the most unusual stretches of coast in the country. Even so, until disputes over **sand mining** erupted in the 1990s, few people had even heard of it. The lack of public transport which means you really need your own vehicle to explore.

Twenty kilometres from Yeppoon along the Byfield Road you come across a massive forestry plantation: neatly planted rows of Caribbean Pines make for monotonous scenery, though there are two riverside **campsites** among the trees, both with self-registration, toilets, barbecues and tables – **Upper Stoney Creek** is the better. Pick up a free **permit** to use the track in to the national park at the **Forestry Office** on the main road; shortly afterwards you reach a crossroads on the edge of the forest. **Nob Creek Pottery**, with its Anagama kiln and fruit trees, is to the left, minuscule **BYFIELD** township and the Shoalwater Bay Military Zone are straight ahead, right is the coast road to the national park. This twenty-kilometre drive to the coast takes about forty minutes and is really **4WD only**; the road comes out at **Stockyard Point**, opposite Five Rocks Island's fish beds; if you camp here note that the dunes are sensitive to erosion and clearing new sites doesn't help. Access along the beaches may be restricted by tides, so check current conditions with the NPWS in Rockhampton.

# Roads to Mackay

Both routes between Rockhampton and Mackay are tedious; apart from emus bolting out of the scrub the only relief on the longer **inland road** is at **LOTUS CREEK** where you can pick up fuel and leather stock whips. The **coastal route** is faster but not much more interesting, unless you take advantage of the mudflats and mangroves to go fishing. The roads rejoin at **SARINA**, a small town 35km from Mackay, built on a visible border between dry plains to the south and the damper Pioneer Valley. The coastal scenery here is dominated by the loading facility at **Hay Point** which protrudes nearly a kilometre out to sea; surrounded by a swarm of ships, it serves as the terminal for the millions of tonnes mined annually from the **Bowen Basin coalfields**, bound for Japan's steel industry.

# Mackay and around

**MACKAY** makes a pleasant break from the otherwise dry country between Rockhampton and Townsville. Despite encounters with aggressive Juipera Aborigines, John Mackay was impressed enough to settle on the **Pioneer River** in 1861. Today the city radiates a confidence built on sugar and mining, and reflected in tidy and busy streets, which belie its origins as a place where "brute force, savage debauchery and disgusting language" held sway. Migrant communities common to the north rub shoulders in town and it's not unusual to hear English, Pidgin and Maltese spoken within earshot of each other. As Australia's sugar capital, the city and its surroundings are a fine place to tour a mill or photograph a cane fire. Away from the fields there's rainforest and beach at **Eungella** and **Cape Hillsborough national parks**, while offshore **Brampton Island** and local **reefs** offer much the same attractions as the Whitsundays (see p.332) – but without the volume of tourists.

You can get to grips with Mackay's **sugar industry** at **Polstone Cane Farm** (tours May–Dec Mon–Fri 1.30pm; $12.50; ☎079/59 7359), where you get a rundown from a tractor-towed wagon; it's off the Peak Downs Highway past the Eungella turn-off, or contact them to arrange a pick-up. **Racecourse Mill**, also on the Peak Downs Highway, is open for tours during the crushing season (June–Nov; ☎079/53 8200 for times).

## Practicalities

Mackay's centre is the crossroads of **Victoria Street** and **Sydney Street**, with the **bus station** a short walk distant in **Milton Street**. Both **train** and **plane** arrive south of town and you'll need to take a taxi (around $7.50 to town, $25 to the northern beaches area). The **tourist information centre** (☎079/52 2677) is inconveniently pitched 3km south of town along the **Nebo Road** (Bruce Highway), but your accommodation or the bus station will generally help with bookings.

### Accommodation

There's a range of accommodation **in town**, but for sun and sand, take the highway towards Townsville and then turn off and follow the signs for the **northern beaches**.

**Backpackers Retreat**, 21 Peel St (☎079/51 1115). Bright pink and right behind the bus station; neat self-contained dorms. ①.

**Bucasia Caravan Park**, at Bucasia, northern beaches (☎079/54 6375). Beachfront camping.

**Ko Huna Resort**, at Bucasia, northern beaches (free pick-up; ☎079/54 8555). Very casual, comfortable place with self-contained cabins, restaurant, bar and pool; excellent value for groups. ④.

**Larrikin Lodge/YHA**, 32 Peel St (☎079/51 3728). A friendly, low-set Queenslander house with wooden furnishings and laid-back atmosphere, two minutes down the road from the bus station. ①.

**Pioneer Villa**, 30 Nebo Rd (☎079/51 1288). Small motel with good restaurant and pool. ④.

**White Lace Motor Inn**, 73 Nebo Rd (☎079/51 4466). Elegant iron tracery and wraparound balconies hide tidy, modern rooms with TV; pool out the front. ④.

---

### SUGAR

**Sugar cane**, grown in an almost continuous belt between Bundaberg and Mossman, north of Cairns, is the tropical coast's economic pillar of strength. Introduced in the 1860s, the crop subtly undermined the racial ideals of British colonialists when farmers, planning a system along the lines of the southern United States, employed **Solomon Islanders** – Kanakas – to work the plantations. Though only indentured for a few years, and theoretically given wages and passage home when their term expired, Kanakas on plantations suffered greatly from unfamiliar diseases, while the recruiting methods used by "**Blackbirder**" traders were at best dubious and often slipped into wholesale kidnapping. Growing white unemployment and nationalism through the 1880s, rather than any humanitarian considerations, eventually forced the government to ban blackbirding and repatriate the islanders. Those allowed to stay were joined over the next fifty years by immigrants from Italy and Malta, who mostly settled in the far north and today form large communities scattered between Mackay and Cairns.

After cane has been planted in November, the land is quickly covered by a blanket of dusky green; before cutting, seven months later, the fields are **fired** to burn off leaves and maximize sugar content. Cane fires often take place at dusk and are as photogenic as they are brief; the best way to be at the right place at the right time is to ask at a mill. Cut cane is then transported to the mills along a rambling rail network.

The **mills** are incredible buildings, abandoned for half the year, with giant pipes and machinery looming out of makeshift walls. Cane is juiced for raw sugar or molasses, as the market dictates; crushed fibre becomes fuel for the boilers that sustain the process; and ash is returned to the fields as fertilizer. During operations the mills belch out steam around the clock and acquire a strange organic quality when they're lit up at night.

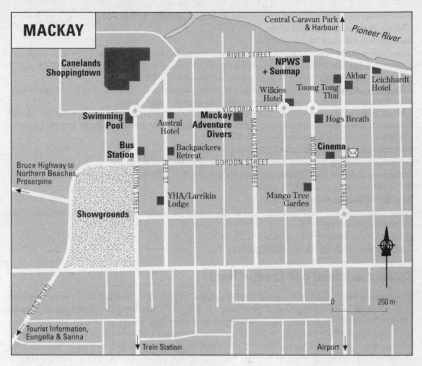

**MACKAY**

Central Caravan Park & Harbour
*Pioneer River*

RIVER STREET

Canelands Shoppingtown

NPWS + Sunmap

Akbar

Leichhardt Hotel

Wilkies Hotel

Toong Tong Thai

VICTORIA STREET

Swimming Pool

Austral Hotel

Mackay Adventure Divers

Hogs Breath

Bus Station

Backpackers Retreat

Cinema

GORDON STREET

Bruce Highway to Northern Beaches, Proserpine

MACALISTER STREET

WOOD STREET

SYDNEY STREET

MILTON STREET

PEEL ST

YHA/Larrikin Lodge

Mango Tree Garden

Showgrounds

0          250 m

NEBO ROAD

Tourist Information, Eungella & Sarina

Train Station

Airport

## Eating

Mackay has plenty of good, cheap **places to eat**. There are snack bars all around the centre, or try one of the places below for a restaurant meal. Fruit and vegetables are available at the mart on the corner of Gordon and Wood streets.

**Akbar**, 27 Sydney St (☎079/53 5111). Inoffensive Indian cooking with some unusual offerings; under $20 a head.

**Austral Hotel**, Victoria St (bus station end). A carnivore's dream, with marinated grilled steaks in 600g, 800g and 1kg servings for around $15.

**Hog's Breath**, corner of Wood and Victoria streets. Tex-Mex food; superb rib roasts from $13, but "vegetarian menu" (salad) was designed by a rabbit. Fully licensed bar and late opening.

**Leichhardt Hotel**, River St. A ten-metre crocodile is said to have been shot from the hotel during a flood in the 1890s, and they serve tail steaks from its descendants today.

**Mango Tree Garden**, 136 Wood St (☎079/57 7266). Cosy restaurant with grills and genuinely imaginative vegetarian options. Mains at around $15.

**Toong Tong Thai**, 10 Sydney St (☎079/57 8051). Perpetually busy Thai restaurant and takeaway with impeccable food, authentically hot and spicy if requested; best is their mussaman curry. Under $25 for a full meal.

**Wilkies Hotel**, Victoria St. Bargain $2.50 counter lunches and regular $4 pasta nights.

## Listings

**Abseiling** *Action Challange*, ☎079/56 4334. Half-day excursions from $55.

**Airlines** *Ansett*, 99 Victoria St (☎079/57 1571), airport (☎079/57 1542); *Qantas*, 105 Victoria St (☎079/57 4999).

**Banks** Branches of all major banks are around the Sydney/Victoria St crossroads.

**Bike rental** *Rock n Road Cycles*, 164 Victoria St; $10 per day plus deposit.

**Bushwalking club** (☎079/53 4661).

**Bus station** Milton St (☎079/51 3088).

**Camping gear** *Great Outdoors Centre*, corner of Victoria and Endeavour streets (☎079/57 2000).

**Car rental** *Cut Rate Rentals*, 105 Alfred St (☎079/53 1616) are best, with 200km free for each day of rental – almost enough to get you to Eungella National Park and back.

**Cinemas** In Gordon Street and a drive-in behind Racecourse Mill. The latter has the bonus of fruit bats flying around the screen, giving some films an edge of (sur)realism.

**Diving** *Mackay Adventure Divers*, 153 Victoria St (☎079/51 1472). An excellent crew for untouched and untouristed sites; offer regular certification courses, trips to local islands and the famous Hardline – the very edge of the Barrier Reef.

**Hospital** *Base Hospital*, Bridge Rd (☎079/51 5211).

**NPWS** and *Sunmap* Corner of Wood and River streets (☎079/51 8788).

**Pharmacy** *Day and Night Pharmacy*, 65 Sydney St (☎079/57 3360); daily 8am–9pm.

**Post office** Sydney St (☎079/53 1615).

**RACQ** 214 Victoria St (☎079/57 2918).

**Shopping** Caneland Shoppingtown, across the road from the bus terminal, has everything from camping equipment to food.

**Taxi** (☎079/51 4999).

**Train station** Boddington St (☎079/51 7211).

## Brampton Island and Credlin Reef

**Brampton** and adjacent, uninhabited **Carlisle**, are thickly wooded, their rocky shorelines dotted with pretty coral beaches. Brampton's unobtrusive beachfront **resort** (☎079/51 4499; ⑨) boasts a wonderfully dated train that meets guests at the jetty, and you can sunbathe, snorkel, surf-ski or use the pool – conveniently within spitting distance of the bar. There's decent **snorkelling** in the channel between the islands, despite dead coral covered in weeds. Away from the resort, paths lead to **Turtle Bay**, a beautiful shallow beach with crisp, clear water, while other tracks cut through pine forests and up Brampton's peak.

  **Credlin reef** is the most touristed local dive site, complete with pontoon, but there's a fair amount to see, including shallow coral outcrops and a one-metre-wide sea anemone with resident clownfish and harlequin tuskfish. Divers should ask about access to the nearby **Catacombs** for something more adventurous.

  Boats leave from the **harbour** in North Mackay, about 5km from the centre. *Roylens Cruises* (☎079/555 1303) run to **Brampton Island** daily at 8.30am ($40 includes lunch at resort; cheaper tickets available through *Mackay Adventure Divers*), continuing four times a week to **Credlin Reef** ($85).

## Cape Hillsborough and Newry Island

**Cape Hillsborough** is about an hour's drive north of Mackay, based around a pretty beachfront national park with tame wildlife; offshore from here are the **Newry Islands**, home to the area's last remaining koalas. *Brigitte's Tropical Tours* ($35; ☎015/ 63 2521) run twice weekly from Mackay to the national park; see below for access to the islands. Driving, head towards Townsville and take the signposted Seaforth Road from **The Leap**. This takes its name from the events of 1866, when a settler was killed by Aborigines and the police drove an Aboriginal woman over the cliff during reprisals. The woman turned out to be holding a baby in her arms which miraculously survived and was adopted by a local family. One of Mackay's oldest hotels is right underneath and you can contest the details of the story over a cold beer if you're interested. From here the road passes the inevitable canefields on the way to Mount Jukes, before

## CANE TOADS

Native to South America, the huge, charismatically ugly **cane toad** was recruited in 1932 to combat a plague of greyback beetles, whose larvae were wreaking havoc with Queensland's sugar cane. The industry was desperate – beetles cut production by ninety percent in plague years – and resorted to seeding tadpoles in waterholes across the north. They thrived, but it soon became clear that toads couldn't reach the adult insects (who never landed on the ground), and didn't burrow after the grubs. Instead they bred whenever possible, ate anything they could swallow, and killed predators with their poisonous neck glands. Native wildlife suffered: birds learned to eat non-toxic parts, but snake populations have been seriously affected. From the quantity of flattened carcasses on summer roads (running them over is an unofficial sport), there must be millions of them lurking in the canefields, and they're gradually spreading into the Northern Territory and New South Wales. Given enough time they seem certain to infiltrate most of the country.

The toad's outlaw character has generated a cult following, with its warty features and nature the subject of songs, toad races, T-shirt designs, a brand of beer and the award-winning film *Cane Toads: An Unnatural History* – worth seeing if you come across it on video. The record for the largest specimen goes to a 1.8kg monster found in Mackay in 1988.

descending to coastal flats. The road to **Cape Hillsborough** starts a couple of kilometres before **Seaforth** township and branches before the park, the right fork heading to the main area, the left terminating at undeveloped **Smalleys Beach**.

### The national park

The main area of the national park is set around a flat, two-kilometre beach bounded by the wooded cliffs of Cape Hillsborough to the north and Andrews Point to the south; the shallow bay is good for swimming outside the stinger season. Local fauna includes bush turkeys and some butch **kangaroos** – they're often on the beach in the early morning, males flexing muscles and chasing does in a parody of the stereotype Aussie male. Pitch your tent past the **ranger's office** at the sheltered council **campsite** (with water, showers, toilets). *Cape Hillsborough Resort* (☎079/59 0152; ④) has cabins but is really just a glorified van park, and if you venture beyond the **store** (which closes at 5.30pm) and restaurant they'll sting you for a "$5 visitor's permit". There's also an NPWS campsite over at Smalley's Beach (not directly accessible from the main area), with tank water and toilets but no shop.

Trails head out to **Hidden Valley**, a palm forest on a rocky beach where you'll find middens and the outline of an **Aboriginal fish trap**. Dolphins and turtles are often seen from here and from the top of Andrew's Point. Another fine walk is to a **swimming hole** at the foot of the cape, reached either along the beach or via a formed track from the picnic area – see the park ranger for details.

### Seaforth and Newry

**SEAFORTH** is a pleasant township with a store, caravan park and enclosure on the beach to ward off jellyfish. After Seaforth, the road runs up to **Port Newry** for access to **Newry** and **Rabbit islands**, quiet, untouristed locations with eucalypt woodland supporting a koala population introduced in the 1920s. Newry Island's friendly **resort** (call in advance to arrange a ferry and, possibly, a lift from Mackay; ☎079/59 0214; ②–④) dates from the 1930s and looks like it; but while the island lacks great beaches, it's nicely unhyped and you can always **camp** and use the resort's facilities, which include a bar. Rabbit is uninhabited, but the resort can take you over there; to stay, you'll need to arrange a camping permit through the NPWS in Mackay (☎079/51 8788) or Seaforth (☎079/59 0410).

# Eungella National Park

At the end of the bitumen, 80km west of Mackay, magical rainforest, mountains and rivers would make **EUNGELLA NATIONAL PARK** worth the journey even if you weren't almost guaranteed to see **platypuses**. There are two sections: swimming holes at **Finch Hatton Gorge** and highland forest at **Broken River**. Finch Hatton's rainforest is authentically tropical, while Broken River's plants are more closely allied with sub-tropical forests; isolation has produced several unique species, including the Mackay tulip oak, the Eungella honeyeater and the much discussed **gastric brooding frog**, discovered in 1985 but not seen since 1987.

**Day-trips** to both sections of the park can be arranged – either with unreliable *Reeforest Tours* ($45; ☎079/55 4100), or twice weekly with chirpy *Brigitte's Tropical Tours* ($37; ☎015/63 2521). Otherwise, rent a car from Mackay (see "Listings"), head south down the Nebo Road (Bruce Highway) to the city limits and follow the signs.

## Along the Pioneer Valley

The road passes through prime cane country as it runs the length of the **Pioneer Valley**. Some 60km from Mackay, **FINCH HATTON** marks the turn-off to **Finch Hatton Gorge**, 15km off the main road; continuing towards Eungella township, it's not long before you approach the range road, infamous as a nightmare track with crumbling edges until cyclone Aivu dropped 120cm of rain in one afternoon in 1989 and the hillside collapsed into the valley. Repair works have widened the road, and though still steep it is now well surfaced. Take an immediate left at the top of the slope and have a drink at *Eungella Chalet* (☎079/58 4509), which has taken advantage of its 705-metre altitude by installing a hang-glider ramp next to the swimming pool; their accommodation (③) is somewhat worse for wear. During the September **North Queensland Hang-gliding Championships** you can sit out on the terrace sipping a drink and watching the action. The general store, post office and other buildings which lie scattered around the top of the road form the rest of **EUNGELLA** township, while 5km along the main road, through patches of forest and dairy pasture, is Broken River (see below).

## Finch Hatton Gorge

To reach **Finch Hatton Gorge** from the main road, you make your way down tracks of varying quality until you reach the first ford. From here access depends on the season, though generally it's open to all vehicles; you pass a small tearoom before the track ends at a picnic area, with walking tracks leading off into the forest. The gorge winds down the side of Mount Dalrymple as a rocky creek pocked with swimming holes and overshadowed by a hot jungle of palms, vines and creepers – the sort of scenery Hollywood dreams about. This is where to spend a summer's day in icy water; pluck up courage for the five-metre jump from **Araluen Falls** or, if the track has been repaired, slide and swim at the **Wheel of Fire Falls**.

*Platypus Bush Camp* (☎079/58 3204; cabins ③, camping also available), just over a kilometre from the park boundary, provides the sole **accommodation**: mattress, pillow, amenities and kitchen are supplied; the rest (including food) is up to you.

## Broken River

**Broken River** is often crowded during holidays and weekends, but visit at other times and the forest is truly memorable, its quiet, cool interior a naturalist's paradise. **Accommodation** is at *Broken River Mountain Retreat* (☎079/58 4528; 4-person cabins with fireplaces ⑥), with an excellent NPWS **campsite** (hot showers and barbecues) as the alternative. Book in advance and pick up **free maps** at the ranger's office (☎079/58 4255). Next door is a **kiosk** with meals and minimal supplies. Be prepared for **rain** – Eungella translates as "Land of Cloud".

The swimming hole downstream is good for a dip during the day and, in winter, becomes a picturesque stage for **platypus watching**; the best vantage points are upstream from the road bridge or on the purpose-built platform. Normally fairly timid creatures, here they've become quite tolerant, and you're most likely to see them at dawn or dusk. To spot other **wildlife**, wander around the picnic area after dark with a torch to see feathertail gliders, bettong, possums, grey kangaroos and owlet nightjars; down by the river, frogs, cane toads and platypuses stay up late. Squirrel gliders are sometimes seen in the huge gum trees up along the main road, and pythons use the warm verges to energize before a night's hunting.

The real star of Broken River, though, is the **forest** itself, where ancient trees with buttressed roots and immensely high canopies conceal a floor of rich rotting timber, ferns, palms and vines. It can be hard to see animals in the undergrowth but the sun-splashed paths along riverbanks attract reptiles, especially goannas and snakes. The best walks are through the forest to the *Eungella Chalet* (see above) on the **Palm Lookout** track, or along the river towards Crediton; both are about 18km return, though there's an excellent half-hour circuit from the picnic grounds to **Crystal Cascades**.

# On to Whitsunday

**PROSERPINE**, 123 km north of Mackay, is an everyday sugar town on the turn-off from the Bruce Highway to Whitsunday, strangely unaffected by the surge in tourism along the coast. The major transit point for the Whitsunday region, **trains** are met by *Sampson's Buses* (☎079/45 2377), who run about seven times a day to Airlie Beach; the main **bus** lines also have services which detour daily to Airlie. The airport is 10km south of town; call ☎079/46 6289 for a taxi. *Proserpine Motor Lodge* (184 Main St, ☎079/ 45 1588; ⑤) or the van park in Jupp Street can put up late arrivals.

Twenty kilometres off the highway, **WHITSUNDAY** is the cover-all name for **Cannonvale**, **Airlie Beach** and **Shutehaven**, sprawling communities that twenty years ago were known only to a handful of weekend campers and yachties. Mass tourism discovered the **Whitsunday Islands** (see p.332) in the 1980s and the area boomed, but even now nobody comes to Whitsunday to spend time in town; it's just something you do while deciding which island to visit. Airlie Beach and Cannonvale are the service centres; Shutehaven (Shute Harbour), where island ferries generally leave from, is 10km on from Airlie, past Cape Conway National Park. Other cruise and dive boats leave from Abel Point Marina in Airlie. *Sampson's Tours* run a bus from Cannonvale to Shutehaven roughly once an hour from around 6am to 5pm.

## Airlie Beach, Cannonvale and Shutehaven

**AIRLIE BEACH** – where most people stay – occupies a beautiful position between the sea and the Conway Range's pine forests, but despite the name there are only a couple of gritty stretches of sand, covered at high tide. Everything is crammed into one short street, **Shute Harbour Road**; the **bus terminal** is at the Cannonvale end, and **local buses** stop halfway down on the bridge. **CANNONVALE** is on the other side of the hill, towards Proserpine, and has no centre at all, just buildings scattered along the highway over a kilometre or so.

The main preoccupation in Whitsunday is organizing a cruise, so there's not much else laid on. You can rent gear from the **watersports** kiosk on the beach, or hop on the courtesy bus to the **Wildlife Park** (daily 9am–5pm; $14; ☎079/46 1354), a small zoo 7km towards Proserpine, which has an excellent reptile collection. Next door is *Barrier Reef Bungy* (☎079/46 1540; $65), though jumping from a crane is no way to do this, even if it is Australia's highest. Better are the **hills behind Cannonvale**, explored on horseback with *Brandy Creek Trail Rides* (pick-up from accommodation; ☎079/46 6665), 2km past Eden Park; a half-day in the saddle costs $35 and they sometimes stage overnight trips.

**Conway National Park** covers much of the coast facing the islands: most of it is inaccessible mountains and mangroves but there's a small campsite (NPWS fees apply) on the roadside about 7km from Airlie on Shute Harbour Road. You'll need padding on cold winter nights and your attention may be sought by hordes of possums which infest the area. An easy walking track climbs **Mount Rooper** to an observation platform, from where the islands appear as white peaks jutting out of the unbelievably blue sea.

**SHUTEHAVEN** is a cluster of houses overlooking the islands – and one of Australia's busiest harbours – from wooded hills above Coral Point; a new yachting complex and booking office hopes to win back business lost to Airlie. There's very limited **parking space** here; undercover facilities are available behind the *Shell* garage ($5 a day), which also rents tinnies for fishing, and there's an open-air grid at the harbour itself ($7.50 a day).

## The Reef

The Barrier Reef starts about 50km northeast of Airlie; further out than at Cairns but not so heavily touristed, this section has many fair dive locations regularly visited by dive boats (see "Listings" below). Both **Fairey Reefs** and **Black Reef** are good, with a variety of marine life and dive sites, but the best diving is at **Bait Reef**, with patchy coral gardens, shells, maori wrasse and morays. Bommies on the outer edge make for good drift diving, and manta rays are often seen at dawn. Other sites include **Hardy**, where there's a pontoon for day-trippers, and fringing reefs around the islands themselves – see island accounts below for details of these.

# Practicalities

Unless you arrive during the September **Whitsunday Fun Race** you'll have little trouble finding **accommodation**, but the emphasis is very much on choice rather than quality. All places act as tour agents, some offering reductions or free nights if you book through them, and some hostels might trade lodgings for housework. Hostels are usually cramped, but pool, kitchen and room fridges come as standard.

Airlie's **food** outclasses the accommodation, with a string of places along the Esplanade or Shute Harbour Road. For self-caterers, there's a supermarket near the bridge. **Nightclubs** can legally only serve drinks to those "intending" to eat – but you can intend to eat until you leave.

## Accommodation

**Airlie Cove Van Park**, Shute Harbour Rd, 3km towards Shutehaven (☎46 6727). Tidy, green and comfortable van park.

**Backpackers by the Bay**, Hermitage Drive, Airlie; 400m towards Shutehaven (☎46 7267). Cramped and sticky rooms with somewhat spartan furnishings but nice views. ①.

**Beaches**, Airlie, 362 Shute Harbour Road (☎46 6244). Brash, full-on party backpackers' hostel, which has been known to eject guests found making bookings through other agents. ①.

**Bush Village**, St Martin's Rd, Cannonvale (☎46 6177). Steamy cabins; but somewhere to go if Airlie is full. Pick-up from the bus terminal. ①.

The Whitsunday **telephone code** is ☎079

**Club Crocodile**, Shute Harbour Rd, Cannonvale (☎46 7155). Good-value standby resort rooms and pool; fairly modern place but a little threadbare. ④.

**Club Habitat/YHA**, 394 Shute Harbour Rd, Airlie (☎46 6312). Tidy dorms, characteristically busy and somewhat crowded. ①.

**Reef Oceania**, Shute Harbour Rd, Cannonvale (☎46 6137). Hostel and family units with throbbing video bar; free pick-up service. ①–③.

**Shute Harbour Motel**, Shute Harbour Rd, Shutehaven (☎46 9131). Unpretentious old motel over-looking Shute harbour. ④.

**13 Begley Street**, 13 Begley Street, on the hill towards Cannonvale (☎46 7376). Time-share flats converted to a backpacker hostel; very small rooms but well organized. ①.

**Whitehaven Holiday Units**, 285 Shute Harbour Road, Airlie (☎46 5710). Extraordinarily quiet, given central location; simply furnished rooms facing out to sea. ④.

**Whitsunday Village Resort**, Shute Harbour Rd, Airlie, by the bridge (☎46 6266). Shoddy self-contained cabins, pleasantly sheltered lawns, comprehensive booking service and loud club next door. ①.

## Food and entertainment

**Airlie Beach Hotel**, on the Esplanade. Seedy dive; about the only place you'll find more locals than tourists. Hosts toad races and *Faces Nightclub* with live rock bands at the weekends.

**Airlies Own**, on the Esplanade. Sandwich and coffee bar, offering $3.95 breakfasts (egg, sausage, tomato, chips and toast) and $4.95 dinners.

**Charlies Round The Bend**, Shute Harbour Road, last on the left heading for Shutehaven (☎46 6250). Grilled and deep-fried steak and fish dishes for $10–20; most people come for the bar and disco, which is mainly a pick-up joint.

**Hog's Breath Café**, Shute Harbour Rd, near the bus terminal. The original of this chain of Tex-Mex grill restaurants, still serving good grub with main courses around $15. A recent renovation swapped the old encrusted decor for polished heavy wood furnishings.

**KC's**, 50 Shute Harbour Rd. Blow-out on chargrilled steak and seafood in noisy comfort. Around $20–30 for a full meal.

**Magnums**, next door to *Whitsunday Village Resort*, Shute Harbour Rd. Cheap meals between 5 and 6pm; otherwise serves standard bar and bistro dishes.

**Marinos**, Shute Harbour Rd, next to the bottle shop. Newly opened Italian restaurant; for $12–15, try mussels in white wine or *carpaccio* (marinated air-dried beef) served in a salad with mushrooms.

**Spice Island Bistro**, Shute Harbour Rd, opposite the bottle shop. Exceptional Asian menu, with Indian, Malaysian and Thai dishes; hard to go wrong whatever you choose here, but the curries are something else. Moderate prices; closed Mon.

## Listings

**Airlines** *Ansett*, 40 Main St, Proserpine (☎45 1433); Hamilton Island (☎46 9390).

**Boat charters** *Australian Bareboat Charters* (☎1800/075 000); *Charter 20° South* (☎46 5100), bare-boat charters, but with skippers provided; *Mandalay*, 384 Shute Harbour Rd (☎46 6298), Mandalay Point (☎46 6722). Five-person yachts start around $350 a day; *Whitsunday Tourism* (on the Esplanade at Airlie; ☎46 6673) publishes a full list of charter operators.

**Bus** *Greyhound/Pioneer* and *McCafferty's* through *Jilly's*, on the bridge at Airlie (☎46 5255); *Sampson's* head office is at 8 Nicoll St, Proserpine (☎45 2377; after-hours info ☎46 1296).

**Camping gear** Rental available through *Mandy's Mine of Information*; see below.

**Car and scooter rental** *Airlie Beach Rentals*, Begley St, Airlie (☎46 6110).

**Dive boats** Best value are three-day trips on the *Reef Enterprise* (☎46 7228) to Fairey Reef at $290, all-inclusive; for some real comforts and excellent diving, *Pacific Star* (48 Coral Esplanade; ☎079/46 6338) run week-long explorations of Coral Sea sites for around $2000. *Whitsunday Diver* (☎46 5366) goes daily to Bait reef (2 all-inclusive dives for $115; snorkellers $70); *Scuba Sport* (☎46 6204) charge $150 for two all-inclusive dives (snorkellers $80) and visit Bait Reef, Manta Ray Bay (Hook Island) and Blue Pearl Bay (Hayman Island); *Fantasea Cruises* (☎46 5111) run a high-speed catamaran daily to the pontoon at Hardy Reef (divers $125, snorkellers $99). Some dive shops have their own boats too, and island cruises can often accommodate divers; check with them for details.

**Dive schools** Beware of bargain courses; Airlie doesn't have a good safety record. Try *Oceania Diving* (near the bus terminal; ☎46 6032) and *Barrier Reef Diving Services* (The Esplanade; ☎46 6204).

**Fishing** A day deep-sea fishing ranges from $40 to $150. Try *MV Jillian* (☎015 575 029), *MV Moura* (☎46 6665), *MV Jane* (☎46 5999) or *Invader* (☎46 6848).

**Flea market** Sat 8am–noon, by the creek, for local produce and souvenirs.

**Information** *Mandy's Mine of Information* (top of the Esplanade; ☎46 6848) will unravel complex options and make bookings.

**NPWS** Shute Harbour Rd, 3km out towards Shute on the left of the road (☎46 7022). Island camping permits and a small environmental display.

**Pharmacy** *Airlie Pharmacy*, next to the supermarket; daily 8am–6pm (☎46 6156).

**Post office** On the sea side of the road, at the edge of Airlie Beach, heading towards Cannonvale (☎46 6515).

**Sea Kayaking** $48 for a day, $130 for an overnight trip along the coast (☎018 318 354).

**Tours** *Fawlty Tours* (☎46 6848). Half-day excursions to the local countryside include a short rainforest walk and barbecue lunch for $35.

**Work** *Whitsunday Personnel* (☎46 5539) and *Work Connection* (☎46 7630), both in the *Beach Plaza* on the Esplanade, do their best to find you a job; while the region has a high turnover there's also heavy competition so bring relevant documents. Without Queensland qualifications, you're unlikely to find boat work except as a Divemaster, but island jobs can *sometimes* be picked up by walking into the resort and asking.

# The Whitsundays

The **Whitsunday Islands** look just like the mountain peaks they once were before rising sea levels cut them off from the mainland six thousand years ago. They were seasonally inhabited by the Ngaro Aborigines when Cook sailed through in 1770; he proceeded to name the area after the day he arrived, and various locations after expedition sponsors. Today, dense green pine forests and roughly contoured coastlines give the islands instant appeal, and the surrounding seas bustle with yachts and cruisers. Resorts first opened in the 1930s, but the majority of islands are still undeveloped and controlled by the NPWS, who maintain campsites on thirteen and resorts on four. The few islands left in private hands house another three resorts, while the rest are mainly uninhabited and largely the domain of local yachties; those covered below all have regular connections to the mainland.

There are two basic options for exploring the Whitsundays – staying on the islands or cruising around them. **Staying** allows you to choose between camping and resort facilities, with snorkelling, bushwalks and beach sports to pass the time; **cruises** spend one or more days around the islands, perhaps putting ashore at times (check this if it's the islands themselves you want to see) for diving or snorkelling. If you're **camping**, you first need to arrange transport, then obtain **permits** from the NPWS office on the Shutehaven Road; take everything you'll need with you, especially insect repellent, fuel stove and **drinking water** – ferrying supplies for long stays can be arranged with cruise boats. **Resorts** sometimes have a higher profile than the islands they're built on; though staying is often beyond budget means, standby deals can slash prices and polite bargaining is always worth a try. Most, in any case, allow day-trippers the use of their facilities. **Swimming** around the islands is fairly safe: the waters are free from box jellyfish and only one shark attack has ever been recorded (it happened in 1992) – and this was provoked by divers cornering the animal.

Simple **ferry transfers** from one island to another are relatively expensive (see individual island accounts for connections), though campers should check out *Whitehaven Adventurer's* **Camperpass** – details of this and **cruises**, which are generally a better deal, are covered in the box oposite.

## CRUISES

**Day cruises** usually take in two or more islands, and offer the chance to experience the thrills of boomnetting* and do some snorkelling; others may concentrate on a single theme, such as whale watching, fishing or lazing on Whitehaven Beach. **Long cruises** cover much the same territory but at a slower pace, and may give sailing lessons. Lastly, experienced groups might consider **chartering a boat** (see "Listings" above for operators).

The list below is not exhaustive; word of mouth is the best method of finding out about who is still in business, current deals and if operators live up to their advertisements. Things to check out include: how long is actually spent cruising and at the destination, whether food is provided on the last day, how many others will be coming along, and the size of the vessel. **Bookings** are best made through an agent, bearing in mind that some may promote specific cruises, and that weather conditions can affect destinations offered.

*Day Trips – Sailing*
Cost $45–52.
**Apollo** (☎079/46 6922) Record-holding maxi and veteran of three Sydney–Hobart yacht races; Whitehaven Beach (Mon, Wed, Fri) and Langford Reef (Tues, Thurs, Sat, Sun). Can drop off campers en route.
**Gretel** (☎079/46 7529) America's Cup challenger, still flying the green and gold boxing kangaroo mainsail. Daily to Langford Reef and around.
**Jade** (☎079/46 6848) Large yacht sails to South Molle and Daydream islands Tues, Thurs & Sun; Langord Reef Mon, Wed, Fri & Sat; usual complement of watersports.
**Tri Tingira** (☎079/46 6848) Trimaran recommended for sailing, snorkelling and boom-netting around Langford Reef. Might drop off campers at Stonehaven Beach (Hook Island).

*Day Trips – Powered vessels*
Cost $20–45.
**Island Gypsy** (☎079/46 5255) Day transfers to Hook, South Molle and Daydream islands.
**Whitehaven Adventurer** (☎079/46 6848) Daily to Whitehaven Beach, Border and Daydream islands; their *Camperpass* ticket ($20 extra) is valid for drop-offs at Whitsunday, Hook, Border, Henning and North Molle – one after the other, if you want. Currently the only such deal available.
**Whitsunday All Over** (☎079/46 6900) Twelve options ranging from simple island transfers to multi-island cruises.
**Whitsunday Wanderer** (☎079/46 6224) Slow, leisurely outings to South Molle, Long and Daydream islands for use of resort facilities and snorkelling.

*Longer Trips*
Cost $210–300-plus for two-night, three-day outings; departure time is around 9am from Abel Point Marina, returning on day three about 4pm. The basic itinerary is to visit Hook Island via Nara Inlet, then move round to Whitehaven Beach on Whitsunday.
**Mollo** (☎018/77 6032) This sail-catamaran is smaller and less of a party boat than most (Tues & Fri).
**Prince Regent II** (☎079/46 6848) Dive-oriented ketch trips (Wed & Sat).
**Ragamuffin II** (☎079/46 6922) Mono-hull yacht offering sailing lessons and snorkelling (Wed & Sat).
**Southern Cross** (☎079/46 7619) High-speed 68-foot America's Cup challenger (Wed & Sun).

*Boomnetting: sitting in a large rope hammock stretched above the water at the front of the boat so that you catch the full soaking force of the waves – great fun.

## Whitsunday Island

The largest island in the group, NPWS-run **Whitsunday Island**, is also one of the most enjoyable, with tropical forests, short walking tracks and the brilliant **Whitehaven Beach**. On the west side, **Cid Harbour** has three **campsites** above coral and pebble beaches. Dugong Beach is the nicest, sheltered under the protective arms and buttressed roots of rainforest trees, and reached by a twenty-minute walk along narrow hill paths from Sawmill Beach, where you'll probably be dropped off if you arrive on a cruise boat; there are no regular ferry services.

On the east side, isolated **Whitehaven** is easily the finest beach in the islands. Long, white and still clean despite the numbers of day-trippers and campers, it's a beautiful spot as long as you can handle the lack of distractions. The campsite is above the tide line, with minimal shelter provided by whispering casuarinas. Snorkellers should head down to the far end of the beach facing **Hazelwood Island**.

## Hook Island

Directly north of Whitsunday and pretty similar in appearance, **Hook Island** is the second largest in the group. A daily **ferry** ($18) runs to the very low-key **resort** – really just a set of cabins – and **campsite** at the island's southern end; there are also two NPWS sites.

Cruises often pull into **Nara Inlet** for a look at the Aboriginal paintings, on the roof of a small cave above a tiny shingle beach. Visually unarresting, the art is significant for the net patterns incorporated in its designs, which are otherwise found only at central highland sites. On the rocks below the cave are some more recent graffiti, left by boat crews over the last thirty years.

NPWS **campsites** are at **Curlew Beach** and **Stonehaven Beach**, both sheltered, pretty and only accessible with your own vessel. The **resort** has few frills but offers share-cabin accommodation (☎079/45 2165; ②–③) with fine views over the channel to Whitsunday, a bar, free gas barbecues, small store and a cafeteria serving meals and snacks. **Campers** utilizing their beachfront sites can use resort facilities.

**Snorkelling** on the reef directly in front of the resort is a must; snorkelling gear and surf skis are free (with deposit) to guests. The water is cloudy on large tides, but coral outcrops are all in fairly good condition and there's plenty of life around, from flatworms to morays and parrotfish. Other opportunities to spy on marine life can be had at the **underwater observatory** ($8) near the resort, or on day cruises to Hook that visit the top-rate fringing coral at **Manta Ray Bay**, **Langford Reef** and **Butterfly Bay**.

## Molle, Planton and Denman islands

**South Molle Island** was a source of **stone** for Ngaro Aborigines, and tools made from a type unique to Molle have been found on other islands and may help in mapping their trade routes. The relaxed **resort** (☎1800/07 5080; ⑦–⑧) in the north of the island languishes in comfortable surroundings; rates include guided walks, all sports and facilities, and the ferry from the mainland – but not reef trips. Walking tracks from behind the golf course lead to gum trees and rainforest, encompassing vistas of the islands from the top of Spion Kop and Mount Jeffreys, and some quiet beaches at the south end. There's a daily **ferry** from Shute Harbour ($25 return).

*Whitehaven Adventurer* (see box above) can organize a lift to the campsite on uninhabited **North Molle Island**, only 2km from the resort; the beach here is made up of rough coral fragments, but the snorkelling is fairly good. There are another couple of campsites on **Middle Molle Island**, joined to South Molle by a low-tide causeway about half a kiometre from the resort.

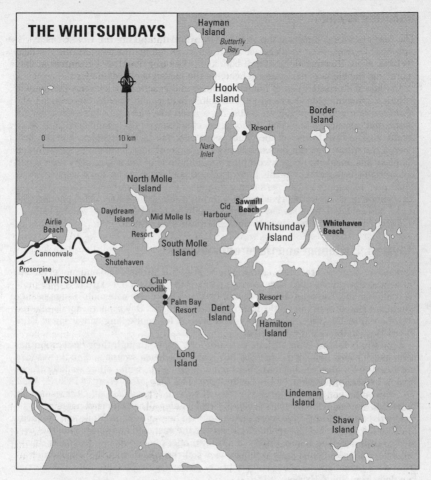

**THE WHITSUNDAYS**

Hayman Island

*Butterfly Bay*

Hook Island

Border Island

Resort

0    10 km

*Nara Inlet*

North Molle Island

Daydream Island

Mid Molle Is

Cid Harbour

**Sawmill Beach**

Airlie Beach

Resort

Whitsunday Island

**Whitehaven Beach**

Cannonvale

South Molle Island

Proserpine

Shutehaven

WHITSUNDAY

Club Crocodile

Palm Bay Resort

Resort

Dent Island

Hamilton Island

Long Island

Lindeman Island

Shaw Island

Tiny **Planton** and **Denman islands** are just offshore from South Molle with no facilities and limited camping at NPWS sites – about as isolated as you'll get in the Whitsundays. Both are surrounded by reef, but be careful of strong currents. Cruise boats bound for Whitsunday Island will sometimes drop you off here.

## Long Island

**Long Island** is exactly that, being not much more than a narrow ten-kilometre ribbon almost within reach of the mainland forests. There are a few worthwhile hikes through the rainforest to **Sandy Bay** or up **Humpy Point**, and two low-profile **resorts** at the north end of the island. *Club Crocodile Long Island* (☎1800/07 5125; ⑤) at **Happy Bay**, and *Palm Bay Hideaway* (☎079/46 9233; units or canvas cabins ④–⑤) half a kilometre south at the island's waist, have a similar range of entertainment (disco, parasailing, water-skiing and a dozen other sports), but the latter's emphasis is more on peace and quiet. Ferries run daily from Shute Harbour to both ($18 return).

## Hamilton Island

The tower blocks dominating the view on **Hamilton Island** are the Gold Coast revisited, and it's interesting to speculate about what will happen to them during the next cyclone. An enormous colony of fruit bats live in the trees behind the waterfront and, apart from the flocks of cockatoos, seem to be the only native wildlife here.

The island is privately owned, and its businesses operate under a lease: development includes a quaint colonial waterfront with hotel, bakery and various other stores, the *Hamilton Island Resort* (☎1800/075 110; ⑦), a small zoo, and so many restaurants, gift shops and sports facilities that the original character of the island has long since vanished. The twin towers of the resort loom over the beach complex, and the best view of the whole area can be had by travelling to penthouse level in one of the external glass lifts. Inside the **beach complex** you'll find one of the pricier places to eat and lots of signs in Japanese; outside, there's a huge pool for humans and a conspicuously small one for a glum pair of performing dolphins. One of Hamilton's saving graces is the chance of work, in theory advertised through job agencies in Airlie; phoning the resort and asking if there are any openings usually just lands you on a "waiting list".

There's a daily ferry service from Shute Harbour ($32 return).

## Hayman, Lindeman and Daydream islands

Expensive as they are, with extravagantly Baroque furnishings and underground tunnels so that guests don't have to cross paths with the staff, the extremely high price of rooms at the **Hayman Island** resort (☎079/469100; ⑧) pales into insignificance when compared with the $300 million building costs. Day-trippers aren't allowed anywhere near the place, but cruises might stop off for snorkelling and diving at **Blue Pearl Bay**, on the island's west coast.

**Lindeman Island** is an obvious victim of feral goats, though their eradication has seen native plants making a comeback in a small melaleuca swamp and on the wooded northeast side. **Mount Oldfield** offers panoramic views, while other walking tracks lead to swimming beaches on the north shore. The *Club Med* resort (☎1800/80 1823; ⑧), Australia's first, has all the services you'd expect; *Whitsunday All Over* visits daily to take advantage of the former's facilities ($98 includes all activities but not meals).

**Daydream Island** is little more than a tiny rise between South Molle and the mainland, with a narrow beach running the length of the east side and coral to snorkel over at the north end. The **resort** (☎079/48 8488; ⑧) offers fine food and hospitality, but to onlookers, its regimental lines dominate views of the island from the sea and detract from what must once have been a very pretty place; day-trippers are tolerated. Ferries run daily from Shute Harbour ($18).

# Bowen and the route to Townsville

**BOWEN**, a quiet settlement an hour north of Proserpine, was once under consideration as the site of the state capital, but it floundered after Townsville's foundation. Today, first impressions created by the sterile bulk of the saltworks on the highway are compounded by a uniform grid of wide, drab, treeless streets that dwarf people and buildings alike, and it's only the clean beaches on Bowen's northern shore that begin to compensate. The other attraction is the prospect of seasonal **farm work**: Bowen's mangoes and tomatoes are spoken of in reverential tones, and each April the town's population is swelled by an influx of itinerant pickers. Both backpacker hostels (see below) can help with finding work, but don't expect miracles. There's no public transport in the Bowen area.

The town centre overlooks **Edgecumbe Bay**, at the harbour end of **Herbert Street**, where you'll find the usual range of services and a couple of old colonial exteriors on the **Grand View Hotel** and the Harbour Office. **Accommodation** consists of the claustrophobic but clean *Bowen Backpackers* (☎077/86 3433; ②) in Herbert Street and the more spacious *Barnacles* (☎077/86 1254; ①), around the corner in Gordon Street; the only mid-range place is the *Mango Tree Motel*, 3km south on the highway (☎077/86 2499; ④). Find **food** at the *Club Hotel* across from the post office, the late-night **pizza shop** down by the harbour, or stock up at *Magees Supermarket* in Williams Street and at numerous fruit and vegetable stalls.

Bowen's attractive **beaches** are a couple of kilometres north of the town centre. The nicest is **Horseshoe Bay**: small, and hemmed in by some sizeable boulders, its waters are home to a variety of reef fish. *Horseshoe Bay Caravan Park* (☎077/86 2564) makes an excellent base, two minutes' walk from the sea, or you could simply rent snorkelling gear and a bicycle from one of the hostels and make a day of it.

## The Burdekin River and Mount Elliot

Further on up the highway from Bowen, about 115km past Bowen, are the towns of Home Hill and Ayr, separated by a mill, a few kilometres of canefields and the iron framework of the **Burdekin River Bridge**. One of the north's most famous landmarks, the river is still liable to flood during severe wet seasons, despite having to fight its way across three weirs and a dam.

North of Ayr, **Mount Elliot** looms on the horizon, the only accessible section of the fragmented **Bowling Green Bay National Park**. The turn-off from the highway is at **ALLIGATOR CREEK** township, about 55km from Ayr; supplies and fuel are available at the general store here, otherwise press on to the NPWS **ranger station** and **campsite** (☎077/78 8203) in a valley at the end of the road (open 6am–6pm only). Huge-eyed geckos in the shower blocks have yet to make an impression on the camp's **cicadas**, whose high-pitched chirp is equally likely to drive you mad or lull you to sleep.

Along the valley, the creek widens into a chain of rock pools and deeper channels. The ponds become more private the further you get from camp and though swimmers might attract cruising eels and nibbles from freshwater shrimp, it's pretty idyllic. A couple of **hikes** add variety: you could spend the day rockhopping up **Cockatoo Creek**, or follow **Alligator Creek** to waterfalls that plunge down the mountain. About halfway there, a giant mango tree marks an abandoned farm; after this, the track cuts through and along the creek before ending in forest below the falls. A couple of deep pools are a short distance up the side, but the rocks above them are too hot to climb during the day.

# Townsville

Hot and stuffy, **TOWNSVILLE**, sprawling around Castle Hill and Ross Creek, is north Queensland's "capital". The city's detractors unflatteringly describe its two biggest attractions as Magnetic Island and Cairns, but Townsville does have its moments – above all the muggy, salty evening air and old pile houses on the surrounding hills that distinguish it as the coast's first really *tropical* city.

Townsville was founded in 1864 by John Melton Black and **Robert Towns**, entrepreneurs who felt that a settlement was needed for northern stockmen who couldn't reach Bowen when the Burdekin River was in flood. Despite an inferior harbour, the settlement soon outstripped Bowen in terms of both size and prosperity, its development accelerated by **gold** finds at Ravenswood and Charters Towers. Today, it's the gateway to the far north, an important military centre and seat of a university, with substantial Asian and Islander communities.

Townsville's **telephone code** is ☎077.

## Arrival and information

The **airport** is 5km north, and a **shuttle** bus meets most flights, stopping at points around town for $5–8. Buses stop at the **Transit Centre** on the south side of Ross Creek in Palmer Street, while the **train station** is across the other side of the creek on Flinders Street. **Driving** into Townsville, you'll encounter a lack of signposts combined with confusing one-way systems – even with a map it's easy to end up travelling the wrong way down the highway.

Public **transport** serves the suburbs rather than the sights, so you'll need to rent a vehicle to get around; some hostels have bikes available. **Information** booths are located at the Transit Centre, *Great Barrier Reef Wonderland*, and the mall (both Mon–Fri 9am–5pm, Sat & Sun 9am–noon; ☎21 3660).

## Accommodation

Lodgings are concentrated around the centre and near the Transit Centre, but hostels might collect you from further afield for the price of a phone call.

**Adventurers Resort/YHA**, Palmer St (☎21 1522). A huge, impersonal complex with dorms for between three and eight people; guests can use the undercover parking while they're on Magnetic Island. ①.

**Backpackers International**, 205 Flinders St (☎72 4340). Ramshackle old place in a central location, and with good views from the balcony. ③.

**Civic House**, 262 Walker St (☎71 5381). Clean and helpful, if not wonderfully modern; noticeboard advertises jobs and lifts. Free accommodation with dive courses at *Mike Ball* (next door) booked through hostel. ①.

**Globetrotters**, Palmer St, just down from the bus station (☎71 3242). Small hostel with pool and simple rooms; almost always full. ①.

**Reef Lodge**, 4–6 Wickham St (☎21 1112). Tidy, well-connected hostel near *Barrier Reef Wonderland*; somewhat cramped. ①.

**Rowes Bay Caravan Park**, Heatleys Parade (☎71 3576). Off the Strand, 3km north of the centre towards Pallarenda, overlooking Magnetic Island.

**Sheraton Breakwater Casino**, Sir Leslie Thiess Drive (☎22 2333). Townsville's top-notch accommodation, the casino was famous as an enclave of liberality during conservative years. ⑦.

**Townsville Travelodge**, Flinders Mall (☎72 2477). Resembles a giant sugar-shaker; comfortable and bland business venue. ⑥.

**Transit Centre Hostel**, Palmer St, above the bus station (☎21 2322). Minimum space, comfort and security; only worth it if you arrive late at night. ①.

**Yongala Motel**, 11 Fryer St (☎72 4633). A welcoming place, named after the city's most famous shipwreck, with modern motel rooms joined to a historic old Queenslander with original furnishings. ⑤.

## The Town and around

Townsville's scanty attractions are best picked up as you wander around. Central **Flinders Street Mall**, for instance, is an unimaginative assortment of pharmacies, newsagents and banks with bizarre bronze sculptures stranded in the fountains, but has fine colonial facades, some of which retain their balconies. The *Percy Tucker Art Gallery* (Tues–Thurs 10am–5pm, Fri 2–9pm, Sat 10am–5pm, Sun 10am–1pm; free) here displays some fine exhibitions, though they're often upstaged by the stylish Victorian exterior. Also worth a look is the offbeat work by local artists at the *Umbrella Gallery*, 222 Sturt Street (Mon–Wed noon–6pm, Fri 2–9pm, Sat & Sun 10am–12.30pm). On Sundays the mall hosts **Cotters Market** (8.30am–12.30pm), which is good for local produce.

Castle Hill looms over the city centre. There's a road to the top from Stanley Street, but on foot head along Gregory Street to Stanton Terrace; a walking path of sorts climbs to the lookout with vistas over the city to the distant Hervey Range and Magnetic Island.

The Strand runs along Townsville's seafront, boasting views of old houses, fig trees and coastal scenery. About half an hour's walk away, Kissing Point, at the far end, is a grassy headland, with an unattractive concrete saltwater pool below and military museum (Mon, Wed & Fri 9am–12.30pm & 1.30–3pm, Sat & Sun 2–4pm) above, built into an underground gun emplacement.

More of the city's tropical architecture is on show at the National Trust site in Castling Street (Wed 10am–2pm, Sat & Sun 1–4pm; $3), just off Ingham Road, where two 1880s houses have been relocated and fully restored. The wide verandahs and exteriors are painted in their original greens, reds and browns – not whitewashed, as they're always (erroneously) imagined to have been.

## Great Barrier Reef Wonderland

The Great Barrier Reef Wonderland, in Flinders Street East (daily 9.30am–5pm; aquarium $12, Omnimax Theatre $9.80, museum $3; combined ticket $21) is – without question – Townsville's premier attraction, a blend of illusion and reality that carries you to the outer reef or outer space within moments. The Aquarium is terrific, with colossal live tanks housing immaculate re-creations of the reef – built out into the harbour and largely self-sustaining. You can spend hours watching schools of fish drifting over coral, clown fish hiding inside anemones' tentacles and myopic turtles cruising past. Equally absorbing is a stroll along the glass tunnel through a tank patrolled by sharks and other solitary fish. Between the main tanks are smaller ones for oddities: sea snakes, deep-sea nautiluses, baby turtles and lobster. Upstairs, videos about the reef are shown, and you can handle some inoffensive invertebrates – tiny clams, sea slugs and starfish.

In the Omnimax Theatre (hourly shows) the film is projected onto a domed ceiling, to create an overwhwelming, wraparound image. While you're waiting for the next show, spend some time in the museum, which concentrates solely on northern Queensland. Walking in, you're confronted by a variety of fossils from out west and a furry pterodactyl; unusually, there's also some regional anthropology, with a section on Torres Strait Islanders, and a few relics from the sad story of Mary Watson of Lizard Island (see p.370).

## The Maritime Museum

The Maritime Museum (Mon–Fri 10am–4pm; $3) is on Palmer Street, near the Transit Centre. The focus of the exhibition is the story of Queensland's most notorious shipwreck, the Yongala, which went down with all hands during a cyclone in 1911, and was finally located intact in shallow waters in 1958. Other wrecks covered include the Blackbirder vessel Foam and the Gothenburg, a gold transport which sank near Bowen in 1875; ghoulish salvagers recovered the captain's safe and, assuming that corpses loaded with bullion had been eaten by sharks, began to fish for them, spurred on by the prospect of recovering gold from the carcases.

## Townsville Common Environmental Park

The Townsville Common Environmental Park (daily 6.30am–6.30pm; free) is 6.5km north of the centre, on the coast at Pallarenda. The Bohle River pools into wetlands below the Many Peaks Range, a habitat perfect for wildfowl including the brolga, stately symbol of northern marshes. Less popular – with rice farmers anyway – are huge flocks of magpie geese that visit after rains, and are a familiar sight over the city.

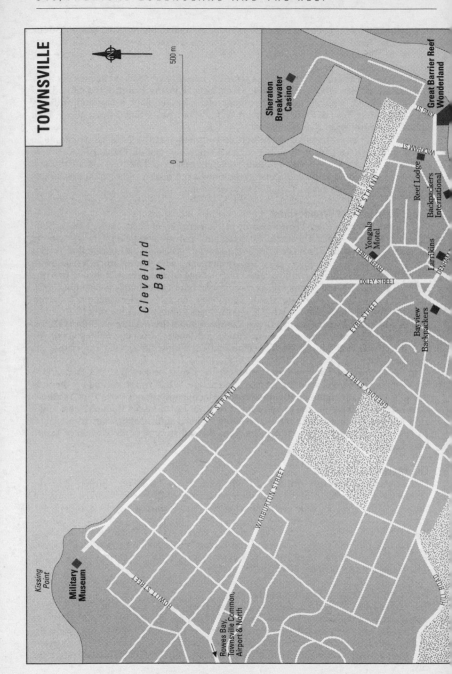

## TOWNSVILLE

500 m

0

Great Barrier Reef
Wonderland

Sheraton
Breakwater
Casino

KING ST

WICKHAM ST

THE STRAND

Reef Lodge

Backpackers
International

DENHAM

Yongala
Motel

FRYER STREET

Larrikins

OXLEY STREET

EYRE STREET

Bayview
Backpackers

GREGORY STREET

*Cleveland
Bay*

THE STRAND

WARBURTON STREET

HILL ROAD

*Kissing
Point*

**Military
Museum**

EBBIS BLVD

Rowes Bay,
Townsville Common,
Airport & North

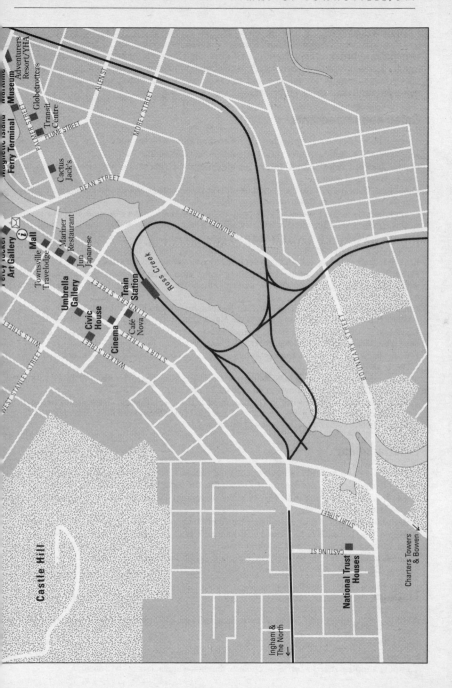

Castle Hill

Ingham &
The North

National Trust
Houses

CASTLING ST

Charters Towers
& Bowen

STURT STREET

WEST STANLEY STREET

WILLS STREET

Umbrella
Gallery

Civic
House

Cinema

WALKER STREET

FLINDERS STREET

STURT STREET

Café
Nova

Train
Station

Ross Creek

SAUNDERS STREET

Townsville
Travelodge

Mall

Perc Tucker
Art Gallery

Mariner
Restaurant

Jun
Japanese

Cactus
Jack's

DEAN STREET

PLUME STREET

PALMER STREET

Transit
Centre

Globetrotters

MOREY STREET

ALLEN ST

Adventurers
Resort/YHA

Maritime
Museum

Magnetic Island
Ferry Terminal

You need a vehicle, at least to reach the park; once there you could get about on foot, but a car or bike makes short work of the less interesting tracks between lagoons. Camouflaged **hides** at Long Swamp and Pink Lily Lagoon let you clock up a few of the hundred or more bird species: egrets stalk frogs around waterlilies, ibises and spoonbills strain the water for edibles and geese honk at each other, undisturbed by low-flying airport traffic. Bring binoculars.

## Cafés and restaurants

Townsville's diversity is reflected in its restaurants, which range from Mexican too Japanese; reasonable counter meals are available at most hotels.

**Cactus Jack's**, Palmer St (☎21 1478). Tex-Mex burgers, chimichangas and tacos, served amid plenty of noise and neon.

**Café Nova**, Flinders St, near the station. A student venue, with occasional bands and walls hung with work by local artists; meals from around $10.

**Covers**, upstairs at 209 Flinders St East (☎21 4630). A cocktail bar and restaurant that's primarily somewhere to be seen; the menu is ordinary grills and salad ($20). Open Tues–Sun from 6pm.

**Dynasty**, 225 Flinders St East (☎72 7099). Chinese seafood joint, where you pick your own fish from the tank; $15–20 a head.

**East Side Café**, Flinders St East. Stays open late for sandwiches and hot drinks.

**Fisherman's Wharf**, by the bridge, Flinders Street (☎21 1838). Riverside restaurant and bar strung along embankment; good-value seafood and steaks (around $15); happy hours Mon–Fri noon–2pm, daily 5pm–6pm.

**Jun Japanese**, 436 Flinders St (☎72 3394). Inexpensive restaurant with decent-sized portions of standards like miso soup, sashimi and teriyaki. Mains from $12.50; open Mon–Sat 6.30pm–late.

**Larrikins**, 95 Denham St (☎72 5900). Your chance to eat native animals in considerable comfort: emu, crocodile, barramundi, all simply served. Mains from $15.

**Luvits**, Flinders St, below *Backpackers International*. Open from 6am for pancakes, croissants and coffee; from 6pm for dinner.

**Mariner Seafood Restaurant**, 428 Flinders St, near the Stanley St crossroads (☎72 7477). All-you-can-eat crumbed squid, bugs, prawns and scallops for $25.

**Yongala Restaurant**, 11 Fryer St (☎72 4633), next to the motel. Historic, authentically furnished surroundings where you can enjoy live music and good Greek-influenced food. Appropriately, the building's architect was on the *Yongala* when it sank.

## Entertainment

Many of Townsville's hotels have occasional music, for which you might have to pay a cover charge. Check *This Month in Townsville*, the local free magazine, for listings.

**Bank**, Flinders St East. Sometimes heavy nightclub sporting Corinthian columns, spiked iron railings and bars on the windows.

**Bullwinkles**, Flinders St East. A venue for hard-core clubbers.

**Criterion Hotel**, corner of the Strand and King St. Cheap pasta bar, $1.50 drinks Fri–Sat 8pm–10pm; garden barbecue and band Sun 5pm–7pm.

**Shamrock Hotel**, Palmer Street. Very busy hotel opposite Transit Centre, with a happy hour 6.30pm–7.30pm; perfect if you're waiting for the 8pm bus to Mt Isa.

## Listings

**Airlines** *Ansett*, airport (☎27 3666); *Garuda*, Suncorp Plaza, 61–77 Sturt St (☎21 4699); *Qantas*, 320 Flinders Mall (☎53 3311).

**Books** *Mary Who?*, 155 Stanley St (☎71 3824).

**Buses** *Campbell's Coaches* (☎74 5099); *McCafferty's* (☎72 5100); *Greyhound/Pioneer* (☎71 2134).

**Camping supplies** *Askerns Disposals*, opposite the station in Flinders St (☎72 3088).

**Car rental** *Allcar Rentals*, 12 Somer St (☎72 3311) and *Meteor*, 333 Ingham Rd (☎79 4422) offer deals on one-way rental to Cairns; *Rent-a-Rocket*, 14 Dean St (☎72 6880) and *Townsville Rentals*, 12 Palmer St (☎72 1093) start around $40 a day.

**Cruises** *Pure Pleasure Cruises*, desk at *Great Barrier Reef Wonderland* (☎21 3555), have a high-speed catamaran which leaves Tues–Thurs, Sat & Sun and whiles away the day at the Kelso Reef pontoon for $120; *Worripa* (☎21 1913 or ☎78 5937) is a 51ft catamaran which spends the day sailing around Magnetic Island ($35 for circular cruise from Magnetic Island; $58 package from Townsville includes return ferry crossing, the bus on the island, and a cruise on *Worripa*).

**Diving** Main sites are Kelso Reef and the fascinating *Yongala*, an intact wreck 15–30m underwater and one of Australia's best, with unforgettable night diving. *Mike Ball Dive Expeditions* (252–256 Walker St; ☎72 3022) and *Pro-Dive Townsville* (*Great Barrier Reef Wonderland*; ☎21 1760) are both very well organized and run qualification courses, day-trips and longer tours. AIMS – the *Australian Institute of Marine Science*, 35km south of Townsville (☎78 9211) – sometimes needs volunteers with at least 15 hours experience for scientific trips to the reef; you might dive or help with paper-work for the duration.

**Fishing** If you've a hundred dollars to spare for a day's game fishing, contact *Challenger Charters* (☎72 4857) or *Hyperspace* (☎79 6370).

**Hospital**, Eyre St (☎81 9211).

**Left luggage** Transit Centre and airport.

**Maps** *Sunmap*, 37 Tully St (☎21 3622).

**Motorbike rental** *Townsville Rentals*, 12 Palmer St (☎72 1093) rents out scooters for $10 a day.

**NPWS** Display and info at *Great Barrier Reef Wonderland*, otherwise call ☎74 1588.

**Pharmacy** *Amcal*, Flinders Mall (☎71 6088).

**RACQ** 202 Ross River Rd, Aitkenvale (☎75 3999).

**Taxi** Stand at the mall; ☎72 1555.

**Tours** *Detours* (☎21 5977) run day-trips to Charters Towers, Magnetic Island, Paluma and Ravenswood; *Ringtail*, PO Box 319, Aitkinvale, Qld 4814 (☎75 5719), 3-day minibus excursions to Cairns via coastal rainforest; *Sullivan's*, 25 Mandalay Ave, Nelly Bay, Qld 4819 (☎1800/648 036), 2-day 4WD trips to Cairns via coast and inland.

**Travel agents** *STA Travel*, 100 Stanley St (☎72 7382).

# Magnetic Island

Another island named by Cook in 1770 – this time after his compass played up as he sailed past – **Magnetic Island** is a beautiful triangular granite core about 12km from Townsville. There's a lot to be said for a trip: lounging on a beach, swimming over coral or bouncing around in a moke from one roadside lookout to another; enjoying the sea breeze and the island's vivid colours. And if you've ever wanted to spot a **koala** in the wild, this could be your chance: they're often seen wedged into the fork of a tree in the northeast corner.

From the sea, **Mount Cook** hovers above eucalypt woods variegated with patches of darker green vine forest. The north and east coasts are pinched into shallow sandy bays punctuated by eroded headlands and coral reefs; the western part of the island is flatter and edged with mangroves. A little under half the island is designated **national park**, with the settlements of **Picnic Bay**, **Nelly Bay**, **Arcadia** and **Horseshoe Bay** – idyllic suburbs of Townsville – dotted here and there along the east coast. Although prices are higher than on the mainland, there's no need to bring any supplies with you.

## Arrival and getting around

**Ferries** leave from *Great Barrier Reef Wonderland* and the *Sheraton Breakwater* termi-nal for Picnic Bay at least ten times daily, with extra journeys at weekends (☎077/72 7122; $17 return); pick up a **timetable** from any information booth. There's no need to book, just buy a ticket on board. Some island hostels offer discounts: usually a deal for the ferry and one night's accommodation.

The island has 35km of road, including a dirt track to West Point and a sealed stretch between Picnic and Horseshoe bays. *Magnetic Island Bus Service* (☎077/78 5130) meets all ferries and runs from Picnic Bay to Horseshoe Bay; their **day pass** ($7) allows unlimited travel. The alternatives are to ring hostels in advance for a pick-up, or make use of *Moke Magnetic* (Picnic Bay mall; ☎077/78 5377), who rent out **bikes, scooters** and **mini-mokes**. Mokes are great fun, for around $28 a day (plus mileage); rental conditions stipulate a minimum driver age of 21 and that you stick to sealed roads. You can, of course, simply **walk** your way around the network of trails.

# Accommodation

Magnetic Island's busiest location is **Picnic Bay**, though that's not saying very much; **Nelly Bay** and **Arcadia** are even more relaxed, but the nicest beaches are to be found up around **Horseshoe Bay**. Most lodgings rent out snorkelling gear, bikes, beach gear and watersports equipment.

### Picnic Bay and Nelly Bay

**Dunoon**, The Esplanade, Picnic Bay (☎1800/079 540). Pleasant modern motel units with extensive landscaped grounds and pool. ⑥.

**Hideaway Hostel**, 32 Picnic St, Picnic Bay (☎077/78 5110). Crowded party hostel next to Picnic Bay's hotel, and with a small pool. ①.

**Latitude 19 Resort**, Mandalay Ave, Nelly Bay (☎1800/079 902). Smart motel rooms; the vast range of facilities may lead you to forget that the sea is so close. ⑤.

**Palm View Chalets**, 114 Sooning St, Nelly Bay (☎077/78 5596). Totally self-contained and very private A-frame units surrounded by palms and views; advance booking essential. ⑥.

**Picnic Bay Hotel**, The Esplanade, Picnic Bay (☎077/78 5166). Comfortable units with a beer garden, but not as noisy as you'd expect. ④.

### Arcadia and Horseshoe Bay

**Arcadia Hotel Resort**, 7 Marine Parade, Arcadia (☎077/78 5177). Neat motel-style units around a pool, enabling you to ignore the rest of the island. ⑥.

**Centaur House**, 27 Marine Parade, Arcadia (☎077/78 5668). Run down in an appealing tropical way, this is the island's pleasantest hostel. Clean, quiet, close to shops and the best snorkelling. ①.

**Foresthaven Backpackers**, 11 Cook Rd, Arcadia (☎077/78 5153). The multilingual owners maintain tidy, variously sized cabins sleeping 2–3 per room in this quiet location just two minutes' walk from the beach. ①.

**Geoff's Place**, 40 Horseshoe Bay Rd, Horseshoe Bay (☎077/78 5577). Shaded, busy and well organized. Gives refunds if it rains for more than three consecutive hours during the day; pool, bar, restaurant and dive shop. ①.

**Magnetic North Apartments**, 2 Endeavour Rd, Arcadia (☎077/78 5647). Large apartments sleeping up to six; nothing flash but good value. ⑤.

# Around the Island

After the thirty-minute crossing, the first thing to strike you as you step ashore at **PICNIC BAY** is the shade, a welcome contrast to Townsville's parched environment. Picnic Bay is quiet, and an unnecessary pedestrian mall decked out in trendy paving and lighting fortunately fails to dispel the languid atmosphere. Services include an unhelpful **information** booth (Mon–Fri 8am–4pm, Sat & Sun 8am–3pm), a **bank, post office**, and *Dee Jay's* **store** (with EFTPOS facilities). Places to **eat** include *Troppo's Garden Bar* and the popular *Crusoe's Restaurant*; both serve grills and salads.

The beach has a swimming enclosure and is pretty enough, but it's certainly not the best on the island, so most people head off after sorting out transportation. If you want to hang around and fish, you can get tackle from *Magnetic Sports* on the mall. The island's often-unattended NPWS office is at the end of Granite Street (☎077/78 5378), where you'll also find the start of an eight-kilometre-return **walking track** out to **WEST POINT**, a small, assertively private community. The "main" road is closed to rental cars as it ends in a blaze of loose, powdery sand, and the only reason to head out this way is to birdwatch around dry-season lagoons.

## Nelly Bay, Arcadia, The Forts and Koalas

**NELLY BAY** is simply a sprawl of houses fronted by a fair beach with a little reef some way out; two streets back is a shopping complex with supermarket, Mexican restaurant and coffee shop. Bushwalkers can follow the difficult trail up **Mount Cook** from the end of Mandalay Avenue; forest blocks the view, but take a pen and you can add your name to the list in the metal cylinder left there for the purpose.

**ARCADIA** surrounds **Geoffrey Bay** and counts *Blue Waters Café* (☎077/78 5645) and its $11.95 set menu, with a choice of grill, soup and coffee, among its attractions. **Alma Bay** is a perfect swimming beach hemmed in by cliffs and boulders, and there's good snorkelling over the coral, just offshore. **Diving** here (through *Arcadia Hotel Resort*), is marred by low visibility, but there's plenty of fish and brain coral, and a disintegrating **shipwreck**. A walking track from the end of Cook Road leads towards Mount Cook and the track to Nelly Bay, or up to Sphinx Lookout for sea views. At dawn or dusk, you might see the diminutive island **rock wallaby** on an outcrop or boulder near Arcadia's jetty.

North of Arcadia the road forks, with the right branch leading to Radical Bay, the main road carrying on to Horseshoe. Leave your car at the junction and continue on foot to **the Forts**, built during World War II to protect Townsville from attack from the Pacific. The walking track climbs gently for about 1.5km through gum-tree scenery to three gun emplacements, now just deserted blockhouses, set one above the other among granite boulders and pine trees. Best views are from the slit windows at the command centre, right at the pinnacle of the hill.

Locals rate the woods between here and Horseshoe Bay as the best place to see **koalas**, introduced in 1930; you'll find them wherever there are eucalypt trees. They sleep during the day, so tracking them down involves plenty of wandering around, tripping over tree roots and cricking your neck.

## Horseshoe Bay and Radical Bay

The road ends at **HORSESHOE BAY** on the island's longest beach. The focal point are shops along the eastern end, with **jet skis**, **paragliding**, **surf skis** and **boats** available through *Water World* (☎077/78 5169). **Koala Park Oasis** (daily 9am–4pm; $8) offers a chance to see and pet this elusive creature and demonstrates why they're so hard to spot in the wild: the comatose grey bundles are perfectly camouflaged against eucalypt bark. Other diversions include tours of the **Magnetic Mango** fruit plantation or trail rides at **Bluey's Horseshoe Ranch** (☎077/78 5109) – $35 for two hours, including a beach ride, or $65 for an all-day trip across the north of the island to West Point.

Walking tracks lead over the headland to Radical Bay via tiny **Balding Bay**, arguably the nicest on the island; a day spent here snorkelling the coral gardens just offshore and cooking on the hotplate provided is perfection. **Radical Bay** itself is small but pretty, half a kilometre of sandy beach sandwiched between two huge, pine-swathed granite fists.

# Townsville to Cairns

The character of the coast gradually begins to change beyond Townsville: the arid landscape that has prevailed from Bundaberg is transformed just an hour north into dark green plateaux shrouded in cloud. There's superlative scenery at **Wallaman Falls**, inland from Ingham, and near Cairns as the slopes of the coastal mountains rear to front the **Bellenden Ker Range**. Forests here once formed a continuous belt almost to Cooktown but logging has thinned them to a disjointed necklace of plantations and national parks. Even so, it seems that almost every side-track off the highway leads to a waterhole or falls surrounded by natural jungle – this is where having your own vehicle pays off. There are also a handful of **islands** including the wilds of **Hinchinbrook**, as well as the **Mission Beach** area between Tully and Innisfail, where you might find regular work on fruit plantations or further opportunities to slump on the sand.

## Paluma Range and Jourama National Park

The change in climate starts some 60km from Townsville, in the **Paluma Range**. The Mount Spec road turns off the highway and climbs a crooked 18km to Paluma township; halfway there, a solid stone bridge spans **Little Crystal Creek**, which you might want to follow as it burbles over cascades into swimming holes overshadowed by rainforest. Look for large, metallic-blue Ulysses butterflies bobbing around the canopy; the gorgeous black and blue Victoria riflebird is also resident, but you'd be lucky to see one. **PALUMA**, a cluster of tearooms and shops, marks the top of the range and the start of trails into the forest; **accommodation** is in the self-contained cabins of *Misthaven Units* (☎077/70 8536; ④), or (by turning right 4km further on) lakeside camping at Paluma Dam.

Past the dam turn-off, the range descends westwards, leaving the dark, wet coastal forest for open gum woodland. *Hidden Valley Cabins* (☎077/70 8088; ④), 24km past Paluma on a dirt road, provides everything you'll need: spa, pool, beer, meals and packed lunches. Nearby is **the Gorge**, a lively section of river with falls, rapids and pools – drive down in a 4WD or walk the last kilometre.

There's more aquatic fun at **Jourama Falls**, off the highway, 20km north of the Crystal Creek junction. The unsurfaced road (closed after heavy rain) ends at a very pleasant, open NPWS **campsite**; an hour-long walking track beyond follows chains across the rocky river bed to more swimming holes and the falls themselves – fairly insignificant by the end of the dry season but impressive in full flood.

## Around Ingham

**INGHAM** is well placed for trips inland to three national parks or for access to the port of Lucinda. The highway through the centre has everything you'll need: the NPWS office (11 Lannercost St, PO Box 1293, Ingham; ☎077/76 1700), which issues **permits** and information about local parks and Hinchinbrook Island, is hidden away in the arcade next to the post office. There's a **caravan park** (☎077/76 2403) and **motel** (☎077/76 2355; ④) at the southern entrance to town. For the national parks, turn west to Trebonne (lucidly marked "This road is not Route 1"); for Lucinda, follow signs for Forest Beach and Halifax.

### Mount Fox, Wallaman Falls and Herbert River

The road divides at Trebonne, the northern branch running 50km to the borders of Lumholtz National Park, the southern route splitting again to Wallaman Falls or Mount

Fox. For **MOUNT FOX NATIONAL PARK**, stay on the sealed road for 55km as it crosses cattle country to the base of this extinct volcano cone. A rocky, loose path climbs to the crater rim through scanty forest; it's hot work, so start early.

The **Wallaman Falls** track initially follows the same road, but soon leaves the bitumen, on a signposted turning to the right, for a dusty forty-kilometre run up the tight and twisting range; heavy rain makes it impassable. Tunnelling through thick rainforest along the ridge, the road emerges at an NPWS **campsite** before reaching the falls lookout. The falls – Australia's highest at 305m – really are spectacular, leaping over the sheer cliffs of the plateau opposite in a thin ribbon, and appearing to vaporize by the time they reach the gorge floor. A walk down to the base dispels this impression as the mist turns out to be from the force of water hitting the plunge pool; platypuses are sometimes seen further downstream on Stony Creek.

Set around the **Herbert River**, the dense rainforest-clad interior of **Lumholtz National Park** shields rare tree kangaroos and Herbert River Ringtail possums. The park is the domain of determined bushwalkers only, and 4WD is needed to reach the **Yamanie Falls** track's trailhead at the end of the road from Trebonne. Contact the NPWS first – you need to know the latest on a huge **saltwater crocodile** resident in the river – and come fully equipped for a two-day hike.

### Lucinda and the Palm islands

**LUCINDA** is simply a store and a few homes scattered around a sugar loading terminal's immense jetty. Most people find themselves here as they return from the hike along Hinchinbrook Island's east coast (see below), but there are a couple of other islands that reward the effort required to get to them. While **Great Palm Island** is an off-limits Aboriginal reserve, both **Orpheus** and **Pelorus** are undeveloped strips of forest and beach surrounded by reef – perfect places for a few days of quiet snorkelling. There are basic NPWS **campsites** on Orpheus and free camping on Pelorus' central beach, but you'll need to take everything with you – especially water. A **boat charter** (Jim Judge, PO Box 84, Halifax, Qld 4850, ☎077/77 8220; Bill Pearce, 48 Patterson Parade, Lucinda, ☎077/77 8307) will cost at least $120 – not unrealistic spread over several days.

# Cardwell

There's very little to **CARDWELL** – a quiet string of shops on one side of the highway, the sea on the other – but it's somehow attractive, not least because Hinchinbrook Island hovers just offshore, so close that it almost seems to be part of the mainland. Caldwell has recently been in the news as property developers and the government wrestle over the building of a huge resort and marina to the south of town, in a "protected" mangrove zone. The aim is to double regional tourism, but the resulting increase in marine traffic and the uncontrolled access to Hinchinbrook could be disastrous for this fragile area; already the once common dugong has all but vanished, along with the sea-grass beds it feeds on.

Back in town, **accommodation** is in *Kookaburra Caravan Park* (☎070/66 8648; ①– ④), which has everything from motel rooms to tent sites and a self-contained hostel block, or at *Cardwell Backpackers* (178 Bowen St, ☎070/668014; ①), closer to the sea with neat dorms and facilities. Back towards Ingham the **jetty** faces banks, post office, supermarket, hotel and *Seaview Café*. The NPWS office (PO Box 74, Cardwell 4816; ☎070/66 8601) is in the arcade next door, but the café will issue island permits when the office is closed. Around Christmas time, you can buy lychees very cheaply from local growers – look for signs along the road north of town.

# Hinchinbrook Island

Across the channel from Cardwell, **Hinchinbrook Island** looms huge and green, with mangroves rising to forest along the mountain range that runs along the island's spine and peaks at **Mount Bowen**. The drier east side, hidden behind the mountains, has long beaches separated by headlands and the occasional sluggish creek. This was Giramay Aboriginal land, and though early Europeans reported the people as friendly, attitudes changed with white settlement and "dispersals" had the same effect here as elsewhere. The island was never subsequently occupied; apart from an insular resort, Hinchinbrook remains much as it was two hundred years ago.

Bushwalkers explored as best they could until the NPWS were prompted to form two vague paths along the east coast into a thirty-kilometre track: if you are moderately fit and have the slightest interest in hiking, this **East Coast Trail** is a must. More adventurous, unmarked routes scale Mount Straloch – site of a USAF B24 **plane wreck** from World War II – and Mount Bowen from the east coast; you'll need permission and advice from the NPWS in Cardwell (see above) to tackle these.

## The East Coast Trail

The thirty-kilometre **East Coast Trail** is manageable in two days, though at that pace you wouldn't see much. **Trailheads** are at Ramsay Bay in the north and George Point in the south; the route is marked with orange triangles.

First landing is at the island's northern tip at **Cape Richards** in front of a luxurious resort (☎1800/77 7021; ⑨), whose charming tree-top units are connected by walkways – a real treat, if your budget will stretch to it. An hour's stroll along the track through the forest leads to **Macushla**, a pretty beach with tent sites but no water. The trail proper starts when the boat which brought you over picks you up again from Macushla and ferries you through the mangroves to a boardwalk across to the eastern side of the island at **Ramsay Bay**. The couple of hours from here to **Nina Bay** takes you along a fantastic stretch of coast with rainforest sweeping right down to the sand and Mount Bowen and Nina Peak as a backdrop. If long bushwalks don't appeal, spend a few days here instead; a drinkable creek spills out onto the end of the beach. There's a small cliff to negotiate at the southern end of Nina, followed by a pine forest walk to **Little Ramsay Bay** (drinking water from Warrawilla Creek), which is about as far as you're likely to get on the first day.

Moving on, you rock-hop over boulders at the far end of the beach before crossing another creek (at low tide, as it gets fairly deep) and entering the forest beyond. From here to the next camp at **Zoe Bay** takes about five hours, following creekbeds through lowland casuarina woods and rainforest, before exiting onto the beach near Cypress Pine waterhole. A clearing at the southern end of Zoe Bay beside South Zoe Creek marks the campsite and water bottles can be filled just beyond, but heed the crocodile warnings. This is one of those places in which you'll be very glad you brought insect repellent.

Next day the path goes first to the base of **Zoe Falls**, then struggles straight up them, emerging to great vistas from the cliff top. Across the river, forest and heathland alternate: the hardest part is crossing **Diamantina Creek** – fun during the dry season with huge, slippery boulders and a fast-flowing river. **Mulligan Falls**, not much further on, is the last source of fresh water, with several rock ledges for sunbathing above a pool full of curious fish. Zoe to Mulligan takes around four hours, and from here to George Point is only a couple more if you push it, but the falls are a better place to camp and give you the chance to backtrack a little to take a look at **Sunken Reef Bay**.

The last leg to **George Point** is the least interesting: rainforest replaces the highland trees around the falls as the path crosses a final creek before unattractive

**Mulligan Bay**. The campsite at George Point has a table and fireplace in the shelter of a coconut grove but there's nothing to see except Lucinda's sugar terminal, and little to do except wait for your ferry.

## Practicalities

The usual procedure for the East Coast Trail is to start in the north and walk to George's Point opposite Lucinda. Either *Hinchinbrook Travel* (PO Box 128, Cardwell, QLD 4816; ☎070/66 8539) or *Hinchinbrook Adventures* (135 Victoria St, Cardwell, QLD 4816; ☎070/66 8270) can organize transport to and from the island ($50 return), and arrange for transport back from Lucinda; you'll also need to get NPWS **camping permits** ($5 per site per night) in advance. As the number of bushwalkers allowed on the island at any one time is limited to forty, the trail is often booked solid: to be sure of getting a place during Christmas and Easter holidays, aim to book three or four months in advance; otherwise, a month should be enough. **Bookings** can be made through NPWS offices in Cardwell, Ingham, and at the *Great Barrier Reef Wonderland* in Townsville.

Optimum conditions are during winter (June–Oct) but it rains frequently all year. Essentials include water-resistant footgear, pack and tent, a lightweight raincoat and insect repellent. Although streams with **drinking water** are fairly evenly distributed, they might be dry by the end of winter – take care to collect from flowing sources only. Wood fires are prohibited, so bring a fuel stove; accommodation and booking agents in Cardwell rent out limited camping gear. Mice sometimes gnaw through tents to reach food – hanging stores from a branch might prevent damage; snakes are also common, if seldom encountered, and you should beware of crocodiles in lowland creek systems.

If you'd prefer to spend your time **cruising**, there are a number of options from Cardwell. Both *Travel/Adventures* run **day-trips** to Hinchinbrook or the reef around **Brook** and **Goold islands** ($35; you can camp on the latter); **bareboats** from *Hinchinbrook Rent a Yacht* (PO Box 150, Cardwell, QLD 4816; ☎070/66 8007) work out around $75 per person per day (in a group).

# Edmund Kennedy National Park and Murray Falls

The **Edmund Kennedy expedition** landed north of Cardwell in 1848, complete with one hundred sheep and three carts, and set off to walk to Cape York. Slowed by dense vegetation and harassed by local tribes, the party gradually ran out of food and by December Kennedy had left the others while he raced the last 100km with his Aboriginal companion, **Jackey-Jackey Galmarra**. Kennedy was killed by Jadhaigana Aborigines while negotiating a river within sight of the cape; Jackey managed to reach the waiting schooner *Ariel*, which set off down the coast to find only two of the other expedition members still alive. **Edmund Kennedy National Park**, off the highway 22km from Cardwell, marks the spot where the expedition struck inland, and you have to ponder the wisdom of trying to manoeuvre carts through the paperbark and mangrove thickets – romantically described by Kennedy's informant as "wooded hills and green valleys". There's an NPWS **campsite** here, and views across to Dunk and Hinchinbrook from the beach.

The road to **Murray Falls**, roughly opposite, heads past banana plantations to the edge of the Cardwell Range and Murray Falls. There are two **camping areas** here and tracks through the forest to permanent swimming holes and lookouts across the bowl of the valley. The nearest source of supplies is the store on the approach road, some distance from the falls. Alternative **accommodation** is at *Bilyana Hostel* (phone in advance for free pick-up from the highway; ☎070/66 5562; ①), where **fruit-picking work** may be available.

# Tully, Mission Beach and around

Two hundred kilometres north of Townsville, **TULLY** lies to the left of the highway on Mount Tyson's foothills, its 450-centimetre annual rainfall the highest in Australia. Settled by Chinese, who pioneered banana plantations here at the turn of the century, it's nothing special today: cultivated lawns and flowerbeds back onto roaring jungle at the end of Brannigan Street, a constant reminder of the colonists' struggle to keep chaos at bay. *Tully Backpackers* (19 Richardson St; ☎070/68 2820; ①) has **work** connections, but most people drive the extra twenty minutes to Mission Beach (see below).

The Mission Beach area is named after the **Hull River Mission**, destroyed by the savage 1918 cyclone and thence relocated to safer surroundings on Palm Island; a monument stands at the original site in South Mission, signposted on Mission Drive, above the beaches area (see below). At the end of the South Mission road, the **Kennedy Track** weaves through coastal forest for a couple of hours to where Kennedy landed near the Hull River. Other rainforest trails include **Lacey Creek**, about 6km out of Mission Beach towards the highway, and **Licuala Palm forest** near South Mission; look for **cassowaries**, a rainforest version of the emu, whose strange bony crest is believed to facilitate movement through vine thickets.

## Mission Beach

A dozen peaceful kilometres of beach and forest with access to Dunk Island, **MISSION BEACH** also refers more mundanely to the cluster of shops, restaurants, banks and post office where buses set down. Either side of Mission are even smaller residential townships; 6km north past **Clump Point Jetty** is **BINGIL BAY**, pleasantly isolated from Mission's pretensions, while in the opposite direction is **WONGALING BEACH** and shopping centre (5km) and **SOUTH MISSION BEACH** (8km). **Bikes** can be rented from the complex opposite Mission's post office, **mini mokes** from *Island Coast Moke Hire* at Wongaling (☎070/68 8668). Hostel buses pick up from outside Mission Beach's post office, and a **local bus** plies between the end points roughly eight times a day Monday to Friday, with restricted services Saturday and Sunday (☎070/68 7400).

**Accommodation** options include *Watersedge*, 32 Reid Road, Wongaling (☎070/68 8479; ④), whose self-contained flats are good value for a group; and beachfront *Castaways Resort*, Pacific Parade, Mission Beach (☎070/68 7444; ⑤), a comfortable, more upmarket place right on the beach, with large balconied rooms looking out to sea. The best in the budget range is the *YHA/Treehouse Hostel* at Bingil Bay (☎070/68 7137; ①), a splendid pole-frame house surrounded by forest, though some distance to the beach; closer waterfront options are *Scotty's Beachhouse*, 164 Reid Road, Wongaling (☎070/68 8676; ②), an excellent, busy place with bunkhouses around the pool, and *Mission Beach Backpackers*, 28 Wongaling Beach Road (☎070/68 8317; ②), whose large dorms are also close to shops and the area's only pub. All the hostels provide you with a pool, kitchen, cheap meals, barbeque nights, guided **rainforest walks** with Giramay Aborigines, **white-water rafting** on the Tully River, and bike rental. **Campsites** include *Coconut Village*, South Mission Beach (☎070/68 8129), which also has tidy twin-share units (①); and *Hideaway*, Mission Beach (☎070/68 7104).

## Dunk Island

In 1898, Edmund Banfield, a Townsville journalist who had been given only weeks to live, waded ashore on **Dunk Island**. He spent his remaining years – twenty-five of them – as Dunk's first European resident, crediting his unanticipated longevity to relaxed island life. A smaller version of Hinchinbrook, Dunk attracts far more visitors to its resort and camping grounds. While there is a reasonably satisfying track over and around the island, it's more the kind of place to make the most of the beach – as Banfield discovered.

### DUNK ISLAND FERRIES

*All the ferries detailed below run daily, and all cost $22 return.*

**Dowd's Water Taxi**, Wongaling Beach (☎070/68 8310). Departs 8am, 9am, 10am, 11am, 12.30pm, 2pm & 4.45pm; free car lock-up available.

**Dunk Island Cruises**, Clump Point (☎070/68 7211). Depart 8.45am & 10.30am; also act as agents for day-trips ($70) on *One & All*, a square-rigged brigantine cruising local waters.

**Dunk Island Water Taxi**, 120 Kennedy Esplanade, South Mission (☎070/68 8333). Departs 9am, 10am, 11am, 2pm & 4.30pm.

**Quick Cat**, Clump Point (☎070/68 7289). Departs 10am; also offers "Uninhabited Island Cruise" ($38), daily except Sun and Wed.

You put ashore on or near the jetty, next to a beach rental shop and **canteen** selling sandwiches and hot meals; there's no store on the island. On the far side is the shady NPWS **campsite** (permits from the rental shop or the Cardwell office; see p.347), with toilets, showers and drinking water; five minutes along the track is the **resort** (☎070/68 8199; ⑨), a low-key affair well hidden by vegetation. The best places to relax are either on **Brammo Bay**, in front of the resort, or **Pallon Beach**, behind the campsite. Note that the beaches are narrow at high tide and the island is close enough to the coast to attract box jellyfish in season, but you can always retreat to the resort pool.

Before falling victim to incipient lethargy, head into the interior past the resort and Banfield's grave (still carefully tended) for a circuit of the island's west. The full nine kilometres up **Mount Cootaloo**, down to **Palm Valley** and back along the coast is a three-hour rainforest trek, best tackled clockwise from the resort. You'll see green pigeons and yellow-footed scrubfowl foraging in leaf litter, vines, trunkless palms and, from the peak, a vivid blue sea dotted with hunchbacked islands.

**Ferries** to Dunk cost $22 (see box for details of operators), and you can book direct or through your accommodation in Mission Beach. The island is barely fifteen minutes offshore, but even so the tiny water taxis are not really suitable if you have much luggage. **Camping gear** can be rented from the complex next to the post office in Mission Beach; you can also leave surplus equipment with them.

## Innisfail and the Bellenden Ker Range

Back on the highway, the next major town is **INNISFAIL**, a busy place on the Johnstone River which has clearly seen better times, but is still a good spot to look for **work** picking bananas in season: *Backpackers Innisfail*, 73 Rankin Street, near the bright pink church (☎070/61 2284; ①), can help if you stay with them.

Just beyond town, the Palmerston Highway turns off across the bottom end of the Atherton Tablelands, and at about the same time you begin to see the **Bellenden Ker Range**, which dominates the remaining 80km to Cairns. This coastal aspect of the Tablelands includes Queensland's highest mountain, **Bartle Frere**. While the two-day return climb to the 1600-metre summit is within the reach of any well-prepared bushwalker, the path is unformed and you should contact the Cairns NPWS in advance for accurate information about the route. To reach the start of the track, leave the highway 19km north of Ingham at one-house Pawngilly, past Bartle Frere township to **Josephine Falls**. Even without going any further, the falls – wonderfully enclosed jungle waterslides – are worth the trip. The climb to the peak is through rainforest and large granite boulders, out onto moorland with wind-stunted vegetation. Unfortunately the summit is blinded by scrub and is usually rainy, but there are great views during the ascent.

Further along the highway, there's a detour at **Babinda** to another waterhole at **the Boulders**, where an arm of Babinda Creek forms a wide pool before spilling down a collection of house-sized granite slabs. Cool and relatively shallow, the waterhole makes for excellent swimming and acrobatics from a rope swing, but hides a sinister reputation. Legend has it that an Aboriginal girl was raped here and cursed the pool against men – several deaths have been caused by subtle undertows dragging people over the falls. Take care.

Nearing the end of the range at Gordonvale, the tortuous **Gillies Highway** climbs from the coast to lakes Barrine and Eacham on the tableland. Marking the turn-off is **Walsh's Pyramid**, a natural formation which really does look like an overgrown version of its Egyptian counterpart. From here, the last section of the Bruce Highway carries you – in half an hour – through the suburbs of **Edmonton** and **White Rock** to Cairns.

# Cairns

**CAIRNS** was pegged out over the site of a sea-slug fishing camp when gold was found to the north in 1876, though it was the Atherton Tablelands' tin and timber resources that really established the town and kept it ahead of rival Port Douglas. The harbour is the focus of the north's fish and prawn concerns, and tourism began modestly when **marlin fishing** became popular after World War II. But with the "discovery" of the **reef** in the 1980s and the appeal of the local climate, tourism snowballed, and Cairns today seems to be little more than a tropical version of the Gold Coast. High-profile development seeks to capitalize on tourism at the expense of what everyone originally came to Cairns to enjoy: a beautiful, unspoiled, lazy tropical atmosphere. Wild stories about plans for the city's future abound, and crazy as they sound (a tunnel to Kuranda, for one), some may be more than rumour; the truth is that nobody can keep up with the pace of change, and based on what *has* happened in the last few years, anything is possible.

For many visitors primed by hype, the city falls far short of expectations. However, if you can accept the tourist industry's shocking glibness and the fact that you're unlikely to escape the crowds, you'll find a great deal on offer and easy access to the surrounding area – the Atherton Tablelands, Cape York and, naturally, the Great Barrier Reef and islands. Used as a base to explore these regions, Cairns can be fun, so long as you accept its limitations as a city.

## Arrival and accommodation

**Downtown Cairns** is the grid of streets behind the **Esplanade**, overlooking the harbour and Trinity Bay. **Buses** pull in at the end of the Esplanade at Trinity Wharf **coach station** and **trains** stop 500m away in **McLeod Street**, although plans are under way for a huge transit centre combining train and bus station in Bunda Street, on the far side of the tracks from the current train station. The **airport** is about 4km north, along the Cook Highway; a **taxi** into town costs $6, or a **shuttle** ($4) connects with most flights and delivers to the city. **Local buses** leave from the mall at the intersection of Lake and Shields streets; hostels meet buses and might pick up from the train and airport if forewarned. Accommodation may also **rent bikes** for getting about, or check out the vehicle rental outfits in "Listings' on p.360. For **tourist information**,

The Cairns **telephone code** is ☎070.
*(For details of impending changes to phone numbers Australia-wide, see p.40.)*

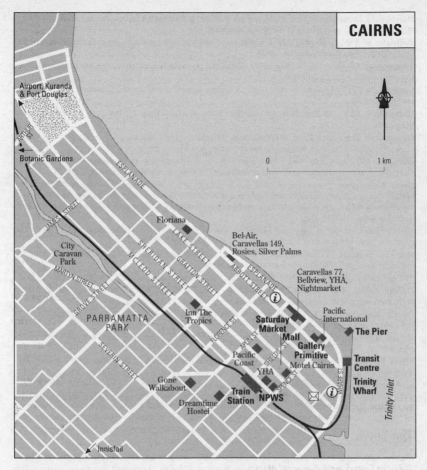

head for 99 Esplanade (Mon–Fri 9am–4pm), or *Far North Queensland Promotion Bureau* (Mon–Fri 9am–5pm, Sat 9am–1pm; ☎51 3588) on Grafton Street near Trinity Wharf.

## Accommodation

The bulk of lodgings are along the Esplanade, with luxury high-rises overlooking the bay and much of the city's **budget accommodation** between Shield and Aplin streets. If you don't want to party, however, avoid hostels in this area. Expect seasonal **price fluctuations** at motels and resorts; there also tends to be something of a shortfall despite the quantity of rooms, so **book ahead**. All hostels have kitchens, most have a courtesy bus service and a pool, and many give deals on long stays – it's worth haggling over this – but may become mysteriously full if you try to rebook; competition means slim profits are made on beds, and you're only of value while you're still booking tours through the hostel. The nearest **campsite** to the centre is the **City Caravan Park**, at 14 Little Street (☎51 1467).

**Bel-Air**, 157 Esplanade (☎31 4790). A newish venture, and though some rooms are stuffy it's generally more relaxed than others in the neighbourhood. ①.

**Bellview**, 85 Esplanade (☎31 4377). Clean and comfortable hostel with good facilities, one of the best organized on the Esplanade. ②–③.

**Castaways**, 207 Sheridan St (☎51 1238). Small but sociable hostel, about ten minutes' walk from the centre with good facilities. ①.

**Caravella's 77**, 77 Esplanade (☎51 2159). A warren of dark corridors and passages; very busy with small dorms. ①.

**Caravella's 149**, 149 Esplanade (☎51 2431). More spacious than 77, but then it crams in more people. ①.

**Dreamtime Travellers Rest**, 4 Terminus St, behind the train station (☎31 6753). Another small, clean, friendly hostel attracting good reports; ten minutes from the centre. ①.

**Floriana**, 183 Esplanade (☎51 7886). Pleasant, small guesthouse overlooking the sea, with Art Deco decor in the reception and small shared units or self-contained rooms and cabins. ⑤.

**Gone Walkabout**, 274 Draper St (☎51 6160). All the better for being a 15-minute walk from the centre, this is Cairns's nicest hostel, and even runs to air-conditioning in the dorms; small, welcoming and tidy with a spa pool. Stay here and get free transport to their sister hostel in the Atherton Tablelands (see p.361). ①.

**Hides Hotel**, corner of Lake and Shield streets (☎51 1266). One of the oldest and formerly the roughest hotel in town, now totally revamped under the *Flag* banner. ⑤–⑥.

**Inn The Tropics**, 141 Sheridan St (☎31 1088). Comfortable, upmarket hostel with pool, kitchen, barbecue area and self-contained accommodation. ③.

**Motel Cairns**, 48 Spence St (☎51 2271). Definitely nothing elaborate, but close to everything. ④.

**Pacific Coast**, 100 Sheridan St (☎51 1264). Clean and tidy rooms in an old-style pub, now converted to a guesthouse, with wooden balcony, small pool and garden. ④.

**Pacific International**, 43 Esplanade (☎51 7888). Plush high-rise hotel in a prime location close to the casino, restaurants and shops. ⑧.

**Rosies**, 155 Esplanade (☎51 0235). Secure, informed hostel; rooms are small but otherwise pretty pleasant. ①.

**Silver Palms**, 153 Esplanade (☎31 6099). Guesthouse with shared facilities and simple rooms. ④.

**YHA**, 20–24 McLeod St (☎51 0772). Two tiers around an open courtyard with pool and competent booking office. Can be noisy this close to the train station. ①.

**YHA on the Esplanade**, 93 Esplanade (☎31 1919). Crowded, animated hostel, very pushy with tour bookings. ①.

## The Town

Cairns' strength is in doing, not seeing: there are few monuments, natural or otherwise. This is partly because the Cape York goldfields were too far away and profits were channelled through Cooktown, and partly because Cairns was remote, lacking a rail link with Townsville until 1924; people came here to exploit resources, not to settle. Your best introduction to the region's heritage is at the **Cairns Historical Museum** (Shields and Lake streets; Mon–Sat 10am–3pm; $1), which covers maritime history, the Tjapukai and Bama Aborigines from the tablelands, Chinese relics from the Palmer goldfields, and chunks of beautiful deep blue Chillagoe marble.

The **pedestrian mall** around the museum is Cairns' souvenir-shopping centre, where you'll find limitless quantities of cafés, T-shirts, boomerangs, paintings and cuddly koalas. Local orators and performers do their best (or worst) at the small **sound shell** here throughout the day, and there's often more professional offerings in the evening. One block over behind **Spence Street**, the **Saturday morning markets** sell a great range of local produce from crafts to herbs, coffee and fish. Moving from the mall area down towards Trinity Wharf, the shops become more upmarket but they're still selling essentially the same things; increasingly, signs are directed at the huge number of Japanese visitors. While its motives are purely commercial, *House of*

*10,000 Shells* (32 Abbott St) has an incredible display of molluscs from around the world; *Gallery Primitive* (26 Abbott St) is likewise almost a museum of Pacific crafts, and the two are well worth a visit. **Trinity Wharf** itself is a lacklustre collection of shops and **cruise terminals**, but the bar above the bus station overlooks Trinity Inlet. *Osborne's Hotel*, opposite, is the last of the original rough and ready bars; if you're after local colour, this is where you'll find it.

The new **casino** faces *The Pier*, a flashy shopping complex, where many tour and cruise operators have booking offices ready to tempt you with brochures and videos of their activities. **Wonambi Wildlife Display** (daily 9.30am–5.30pm; donation) here has a fine collection of reptiles, including sea snakes and taipans, rated as Australia's most toxic animals; Jabiru **Aboriginal dancers** (Mon–Fri 5.30pm; free) add to the atmosphere, and encourage onlookers to try didgeridoo playing.

In the evenings, the **Esplanade** is packed with people cruising between accommodation and restaurants, but grabbing an early-morning coffee here you'll witness a quintessentially Australian scene: fig trees frame the waterfront, a couple of trawlers and seaplanes bob at anchor in the harbour, and drunks languish on the benches. Joggers jog, others promenade along the edge at low tide and look for birds feeding on the mud flats – there's an identification chart in the park. Sand actually covered the seafront until Trinity Inlet was dredged during the last war, and while conservationists are happy with the mangroves, others with plans to restore the beaches are busy pulling them out.

Heading out of the centre, the city's other natural attractions include the pretty **botanic gardens** and adjacent **Mount Whitfield Environmental Park** in Collins Avenue, off the highway near the airport (bus #8 from the Mall). Ringed by suburbia, the rainforest is dense enough for cassowaries and wallabies, and the longer of two walking tracks is surprisingly good – a fine escape from Cairns. Also worth a look are the **mangrove walks** on the airport road, which offer a chance to see the different varieties of mangrove trees, mudskippers and red clawed, asymmetric fiddler crabs from boardwalks and hides; take some repellant or else give the flies a free lunch.

## Around Cairns

Cairns' variously developed **beaches** start 10km north (there's a beach bus from the Mall): **Palm Cove** has a full-scale resort, while **Trinity** and **Yorkeys Knob** attract campers and day-tripper crowds with a van park, shops and watersports gear for rent. If you want to escape for a few days however, get out to **Ellis Beach**, half an hour north on the Port Douglas road (contact *Coral Coaches* on ☎98 2600 to arrange transport) – you couldn't ask for a finer place to camp.

West off the highway, past Redlynch, **Crystal Cascades** (Wongalee Falls) is a narrow forest gorge gushing with rapids, small waterfalls and swimming opportunities. Somewhere to picnic rather than explore, you should heed warnings about the large, pale-green, heart-shaped leaves of **stinging trees**; the stories may seem apocryphal but once stung you'll believe them all. Backtracking through Kamerunga, you can drive into the **Barron Gorge** as far as the **power station** (free tours; bookings ☎51 2213) and then walk through the forests to Kuranda. The gorge is also used for **Rap Jumping**, which is basically head-first abseiling; if doing this from the road seems a little tame, descents are sometimes made down the 83-metre falls themselves. *Macka Mackail* (☎018/45 0120) was the original operator but seems to be experiencing tough times, so ask around for the latest.

If you must **bungee jump** in Queensland, then this is the one: a purpose-built platform surrounded by rainforest in the hills 15km north of Cairns. With airborne time, including rebounds – only a matter of seconds – it's the climb up to the tower and steeling yourself to take the plunge into what looks like a fish pond that gets the adrenalin going. Contact *AJ Hackett* (☎31 1119); it costs $85 for the first jump, cheaper thereafter. For those with an aversion to heights, there's **white-water rafting** in the Barron Gorge – wild fun despite being a conveyor-belt business: as you pick yourself out of the river, the raft is dragged back for the next busload. Serious thrill-seekers should look for combination deals which include bungee jumping and rafting for around $85; agents include *Raging Thunder* (☎31 1466) and *RnR* (☎51 7777).

For something different, *Foaming Fury* (☎32 1460) go **sea kayaking** ($89) to **Yarrabah Aboriginal community**, 6km across the inlet at Cape Grafton. The fitness grading is "easy", and the full-day trip includes a tour of Yarrabah's craft workshops, where many of the souvenirs sold in Cairns are made.

# The Reef and diving

Seeing the **Great Barrier Reef**, either on a cruise or as a diver, is what attracts many visitors to Cairns, and there are so many ways to do this that making a choice can be almost impossible. Broadly speaking, the reef can be classified into three **regions** – inner, outer and island – each somewhat different in character. The **inner reef**, a sheltered section between the outer walls and Cairns, is flat and fairly shallow, a good place for novices. The **outer reef** borders the open sea, so has more dramatic appeal, in the shape of walls, canyons, deeper water and bigger fish. **Island reefs** are generally a blend of inner and outer sites, but have very easy access; again, ideal if you're unsure of your limits.

---

### REEF TRIPS AND DIVE SCHOOLS

The **Reef Cruises** and **Diving** categories below are not mutually exclusive – most outfits offer diving, snorkelling, or just plain sailing – but are based on main interests. **Prices** can come down by as much as thirty percent during the low seasons (Feb–April & Nov), depending on how busy operators are. On trips longer than a day, you generally sleep on board.

**Reef Cruises**

*Yachts*

Day-trips $39–100; 2 nights/3 days $300

**Ocean Free** (*Silver Sails Cruises Ltd*, PO Box 1045; ☎070/31 6601). Day-trips to the reef around Green Island aboard a 61ft rigged schooner.

**Ocean Spirit** (143 Lake St; ☎070/31 2920). Day-trips to Michaelmas and nearby cays on a luxury sail-catamaran.

**Vagabond/Investigator** (*New Image Cruises*; ☎070/33 2664). 57ft luxury yachts for 1–3 days' sailing to Moore and Sudbury reefs, Fitzroy and Frankland islands.

*Power Boats*

$88–128 (day-trips only)

**Frankland Islands Cruises** (☎1800/079 039). To the Frankland Islands, a group of sand cays, for underwater pursuits; coral here is said to be all right though unexceptional.

**Quicksilver** (Pier Marketplace; ☎070/31 4299). A lightning-fast service from Port Douglas to Agincourt Reef and the Low Isles, with a connecting shuttle to and from Cairns.

**Sunlover Cruises** (Trinity Wharf; ☎1800/ 810 512). High-speed catamaran to Moore and Arlington reefs and Fitzroy Island.

**Diving**

*Day Trips*

$40–132

**Down Under** (*Down Under Aquatics*, 27 Shields St; ☎070/31 3318). Roving permit to many reefs; small, powered, catamaran gets you there quickly.

**Falla** (mobile phone ☎018/18 7201). Old pearling lugger from the Torres Straits; top-value package including snorkelling, diving and storytelling.

**GBR Diving Centre** (☎070/31 2599). Flights to Cod Hole ($585) and Pixie

All regions are visited on **day cruises**, with vessels ranging from old trawlers to racing yachts and high-speed cruisers; if you want to stay longer, check into an island **resort** or take an extended **dive trip**. One way to choose the right boat is simply the **price**: small, cramped tubs are cheapest while roomy, faster catamarans are the most expensive. To narrow things down further, find out which serves the best food. Generally, if you've seen the reef or dived before, consider going cheaply; if this is going to be your only visit, pay the extra. Before going, catch the two-hour **Reef Teach** slide show at the City Library in Lake Street (☎51 6882; $10), which gives more background than the dive schools and tour operators have time to impart.

You might be a little taken aback by the state of the coral: the sheer number of visitors has largely wrecked Cairn's inner reef; further afield, the outer reaches are in better condition, though popular sites are beginning to suffer. From a wider perspective, things are not as bleak as they may first appear: since only a limited number of sites are open to the public, these are inevitably going to be sacrificed in order to minimize the impact on the entire structure. In any case, you'll still see abundant wildlife, ranging from squid to sharks, and only seasoned divers are likely to be disappointed.

## Dive sites

The dozen or more **inner reef** sites are much of a muchness. Concentrated day-tripping means that you'll probably be sharing the experience with several other boat-loads of people, with scores of divers in the water at once. On a good day, snorkelling

Pinnacle ($605 combined), but the increased risk of decompression sickness must be taken into consideration.

**Noah's Ark** (☎070/35 4054). Real budget diving at Michaelmas Cay and Hastings Reef; good value but don't expect any comforts.

**Seastar II** (262 Aumuller St; ☎070/31 2336). No-frills budget tub to Hastings and Michaelmas; another good deal if you don't care about arriving in style.

**Tusa Dive** (*TUSA*, corner of Aplin St and Esplanade; ☎070/31 1248). A roving permit to ten separate reefs; the best in its category.

### Longer

Overnight $175–220; 2 nights/3 days $275–345; longer as stated.

**Atlantic Clipper** (*Down Under Diving*, 155 Sheridan St; ☎070/31 1288). 140ft brigantine cruising around Norman, Saxon and Hastings reefs and Michaelmas Cay.

**Coral Reeftel** (*CDC*, 135 Abbott St; ☎070/51 0249). Purpose-built 85ft catamaran to Norman and Arlington complexes.

**Nimrod III** (46 Spence St; ☎070/31 5566). Motorized catamaran with basic or plush cabins; 4–7-day Cod Hole trips $800–1850.

**Rum Runner** (☎1800/803 183). Two schooners spending 4 days at Coral Sea locations or the Cod Hole and Ribbons reefs for around $745; well organized and low-pressure.

**Taka II** (*Underwater Camera Centre*, 131 Lake St; ☎070/51 8722). Refurbished trawler with fair facilities, including photographic equipment rental and E-6 processing on board. Four days at the Cod Hole and Ribbon reefs $650–850.

### Dive Schools

As always, ask around and beware rock-bottom dealers; prices vary seasonally but you'll be looking around the $400 mark for a 5-day Open Water Certification course. The following are long-established and have a sound reputation:

**CDC**, 135 Abbott St (☎070/51 0294).

**Deep Sea Divers Den**, 319 Draper St (☎070/31 2223).

**Down Under Aquatics**, Shop 27, Shield St (☎070/31 3318).

**Downunder Diving**, 155 Sheridan St (☎070/31 1288).

**Pro Dive**, Marlin Parade, near Hilton (☎070/31 5255).

**Tusa Dive**, corner of the Esplanade and Aplin St (☎070/31 1248).

over shallow outcrops is enjoyable; going deeper, coral shows more damage but there's plenty of marine life, albeit patchily distributed. **Michaelmas Cay**, a small sand island, is worth a visit: sooty terns roost on the island, while giant clams, sweetlips, reef sharks and tunnels feature underwater. Nearby **Hastings Reef** has better coral, an artificial **wreck** in the making, resident moray eel and maori wrasse, and plenty of starfish and snails in the sand beneath. The two are often part of dive packages.

One of the cheaper options for diving the **outer reef** is to take an **overnight trip** to nearby sections such as **Holmes**, **Moore** or **Arlington reefs** – rather generalized terrain, but the advantages over a simple day excursion are that you get longer in the water plus the opportunity for night dives. **Longer trips** venture further from Cairns into two areas; a circuit north to the Cod Hole and Ribbon Reefs, or straight out into the Coral Sea. The **Cod Hole**, near Lizard Island (see p.370) is justifiably famous for mobs of giant potato cod which rise from the depths to meet you; large sharks, including hammerheads and tigers, have also been encountered. **The Ribbons** are a 200-km string with some relatively pristine locations and good visibility, as are **Coral Sea** sites; where you'll go on the latter depends on weather, but seasonally you'll find mantas, whales and sharks, along with varied pelagic species.

### Green Island and Fitzroy Island

Heart-shaped, tiny and sandy, **Green Island** is the easiest of any of the Barrier Reef's coral cays to reach, making it a near-essential day-trip from Cairns. This, combined with the island's size, means that it can be difficult to escape other visitors, but the forested interior is surprisingly varied and you only need to put on some fins, visit the **underwater observatory**, or go for a cruise in a glass-bottomed boat to see plentiful coral, fish and turtles. Daily **ferries** include *The Big Cat* (☎070/51 0444; $32) and *Reef Jet* (☎070/31 5559; $60 includes lunch and selected activities), both from the Pier Marketplace; and *Great Adventures* ($27–$74 depending on vessel; ☎1800/079 080) from Trinity Wharf. All run **courtesy buses** which will collect you from your accommodation. The recent overhaul of **Green Island Resort** (☎070/31 3300; ⑨) fuelled much controversy, but in fact the new buildings are carefully hidden and infinitely better than the previous operation, whose leaking sewerage pipes and squalid kitchens were quietly ignored for years. Vegetation removed during construction was restored immediately afterwards and the shifting beaches are typical of all coral cays, not a symptom of disturbance. Now five-star rooms beckon long-term guests, there's a restaurant and pool open to day-trippers, plus plenty of sand to laze on.

**Fitzroy Island** is a continental island, not a cay like Green Island, and has a low-key, good-value **resort** (☎070/51 9588; 4-bed budget units ⑥–⑦) set in forest near the shore, from where you can dive on the island's reef. Fitzroy is actually quite large and, away from the resort, there are some good walks through highland greenery where you can escape the sunbathing hordes. *Sunlover* (☎070/31 1055; $22) and *Great Adventures* ($22) operate daily **ferries** to the island from Cairns.

## Eating and nightlife

Cairns has no shortage of places to **eat**. Least expensive are takeaways between the Esplanade's hostels: Chinese food, felafel, kebabs and pasta. Some open early while others, like *La Pizza* on the corner of Aplin Street, never close, switching from fast food to coffee and croissants at dawn. Otherwise, any of the restaurants listed below are good value; alternatively, you can stock up at the **supermarkets** in Lake and Sheridan streets.

**Clubs** open around 6pm; most charge $5 entry for bar and disco entertainment, more if there's a band playing. Many **pubs** also get **live music** in once a week –

reviews and details are in Cairns' free weekly **listings magazine**, *Son of Barfly*. One way to have an unforgettably bad night out is to binge-drink, as **pickpockets** and bag-snatchers work the nightclubs. More worrying is the increase in reported rapes in recent years – make sure you arrange some form of **safe transport** back to your accommodation.

## Cafés and restaurants

**Barnacle Bill**, 65 Esplanade (☎51 2241). Get in early or book for this popular seafood restaurant, where you choose your lobster and Moreton Bay bugs from the live tank. Mains around $20.

**Casa Mia**, 82 Sheridan St (☎51 5871). Mediterranean-style restaurant with the accent on Spain; $15 upwards for main courses.

**Cock & Bull**, 6 Grove St, junction with Grafton St (☎31 1160). Keg *Guinness*, good quality and huge counter meals ($7–12), and a nice garden atmosphere.

**Dundee's**, 40 Aplin St (☎51 0399). Characterless restaurant, but with excellent steak and seafood, as well as "local tucker" – crocodile, emu and buffalo. Expensive at around $20–35 for a meal.

**Fawlty Toms**, 82 Lake St (☎51 8676). Three-course specials for $10 include soup, steak or seafood with salad, and dessert.

**La Fettuccine**, 43 Shields St (☎31 5959). Excellent homemade pasta from $8.

**Gypsy Dees**, 41a Shields St (☎51 5530). A mixture of Oriental and European main courses from $14, accompanied by live music.

**Manohra**, 55 Spence St (☎31 6208). Thai red curries, *tom yam* soup and a complete vegetarian menu; $20 per head banquets for a minimum of four.

**Mediterranean Café**, 92 Lake St. Best of the mall's snack bars, with good spinach and feta rolls.

**Mozart Pastry**, corner of Spence and Grafton streets. Top-notch patisserie with crisp strudels, rich cakes and fine coffee.

**Samuels** at the *Playpen*, corner of Lake and Hartley streets. Budget restaurant and salad bar attached to club.

**Taj**, 61 Spence St, at the corner of Sheridan St (☎51 2228). Curries ranging from mild to incendiary and including vegetarian options; a $16 thali is served on Wednesday. Open from 6pm.

**Woolshed**, 22 Shields St (☎31 6304 for free pickup). Latest in a long line of budget/backpacker diners in this location; cheap meals and free beer (with vouchers) are the main attractions.

**Workers Club**, 124 Spence St (☎31 7476). Best crocodile steaks and witchetty grubs in Queensland.

## Nightlife

**Cape York Hotel**, corner of Spence and Bunda streets, west of rail line. Live music and very cheap, huge feeds.

**End of the World**, corner of Abbott and Aplin Streets. Traditional backpackers' haunt, with a huge video screen and a youngish clientele.

**Johno's Blues Bar**, below *McDonald's* on Shield St (☎31 5008). Cairns's live music mainstay, but fairly rough at times. Even if it's only the house band – and they're not bad – someone plays every night.

**Playpen**, corner of Lake and Hartley streets. Trashy nightclub/disco, with lingerie evenings and "free drinks for ladies" nights.

# Listings

**Airlines** *Air New Zealand*, airport (☎35 9366); *Air Niugini*, 4 Shield St (☎13 1380); *Ansett*, 84 Lake St (☎50 2211); *Cape York Air Services*, airport (☎35 9399); *Cathay Pacific*, airport (☎13 1747); *Flight West*, corner of Grafton and Spence streets (☎13 2392); *Garuda*, Hilton Hotel, Wharf St (☎31 2288); *JAL*, 15 Lake St (☎31 2700); *Qantas*, corner of Lake St and Shield St (☎50 4000).

**Barges to Cape York** May take payment or let you work a passage; check "General Notices" in the *Cairns Post* for openings (see also "Tours" below).

**Bike and motorbike rental** *2 Wheel Adventures*, 148 Sheridan St (☎31 5707); *Mountain Bike Adventures* (☎51 0108) for guided bike tours; *Cairns Dial a Bike*, 171 Sheridan St (☎31 2322) for pedal- and motorbikes delivered to the door; *Jolly Frog*, 101 Esplanade (☎31 2322).

**Books and maps** *Walkers Bookshop*, 96 Lake St (☎51 2410) for general needs; *Cairns Book and Ecology Centre*, 27 Shields St (☎51 0888) for tomes on environmental issues. Maps from bookshops, Department of Lands (Sunmap), 15 Lake St, and *Croc Shop*, Shields St Mall.

**Buses** *Coral Coaches* (☎98 2600); *Greyhound/Pioneer* (☎51 3388); *McCafferty's* (☎51 5899); *White Car Coaches/Cape York Coaches* (☎51 9533).

**Bushwalking** *Jungle Tours* (☎32 2111) come highly recommended for their 2–6-day treks through the Daintree and Cape York.

**Camping gear** *Adventure Equipment*, 69 Grafton St (☎31 2669).

**Car rental** *Aus Drive* 26 Abbott St (☎31 2000); *Brits 4WD*, 411 Sheridan St (☎1800/331 454); *Delta*, 78 Spence St (☎1800/67 0031); *Jolly Frog*, 101 Esplanade (☎31 2379); *Rent A Rek*, 60 Abbott St (☎31 3995); *Sams*, 101 McLeod St (☎31 2556); *Mini Car Rentals*, 150 Sheridan St (☎51 6288); *Reef Rent-a-Car*, 142 Sheridan St (☎31 5500); *Sugarland*, 134 Sheridan St (☎52 1300); *Tropical*, 60 Abbott St (☎31 3995); *Leisure Wheels*, 196 Sheridan St (☎51 8988).

**Cinema** *Multi-Screen*, 108 Grafton St (☎51 1222) and *Coral Twin Drive-In*, Bruce Highway, about 5km out ($10 all-night sessions; ☎54 1005).

**Cruises** *Kangaroo Explorer* (79 Wattle St, Yorkeys Knob; ☎1800/079 141). Week-long return cruises to Thursday Island via Cooktown and Lizard; economy berths from $1655; cruise up/fly back from $1000. (For the lowdown on reef cruises, see box on p.333.)

**Diving** See boxes on p.312 and p.357.

**Farmstays** *Mount Mulligan Station* (☎94 8360). Budget accommodation west of the Tablelands; $69 for two nights, including courtesy bus from Cairns.

**Fishing** Estuarine: *Dolphin Boat Hire*, near Hilton Hotel, Esplanade (☎51 4139); *All Tackle* (☎53 3599); *Calm Waters* (☎53 5230). Heavy tackle and reef: *Cairns Reef Charters Service* (☎31 4728); *Lady* (☎31 3528). For fishing tackle you'll need the services of *Erskine's*, 51 Mulgrave Rd (☎51 6099).

**Hospital** Base Hospital, northern end of Esplanade (☎50 6333); *Shield Street Medical Centre*, 29b Shield St (☎31 3717), open Mon–Fri 8am–5.30pm.

**Left luggage** At the airport, train and bus stations; also *Tropical Paradise Travel*, 29 Spence St ($2 a day).

**NPWS** 10–12 McLeod St (☎52 3096), open Mon–Fri 8.30am–4.30pm.

**Parachuting** *Paul's* (☎35 9666) for free-fall thrills.

**Pharmacy** Base Hospital, northern end of Esplanade (☎51 2466) open daily 8am–9pm.

**Police** 55 Esplanade (☎51 2000).

**Post office and telephones** 13 Grafton St (☎51 4200).

**RACQ** 112 Sheridan St (☎51 4788).

**Taxis** ☎51 5333.

**Tours** *OZtours*, PO Box 6464 Cairns 4871 (☎1800/079 006) and *Kamp-Out Safaris*, PO Box 1894, 4870 (☎31 4862) organize trips to Cape York by 4WD, boat and plane, and enjoy reliable reputations. *Zebra*, 89 Esplanade 4870 (☎31 7477), to Cape Trib and Bloomfield; and *True Blue Tours*, 108 Digger St (☎31 6922), to the Atherton Tablelands, also get good reports. Otherwise, for Cape Trib, Daintree and Cooktown: *Australian Wilderness Safaris*, PO Box 396, Mossman 4873 (☎98 1766); *QLD Adventure Safaris*, PO Box 264, Trinity Beach 4879 (☎57 6299); *Trek North Safaris*; 23 Nolan St, Whitfield (☎51 4328); *Tropics Explorer* (☎50 0659); *Ventry's* (☎51 9533); *Wildtrack*, PO Box 2397, 4870 (☎55 2247). Atherton Tablelands: *Jungle Tours* (☎1800/817 234); *Ringtail Tours*, PO Box 490, 4870 (☎51 4055). Chillagoe, Undara and the Gulf: *Ventry's* (☎51 9533). Cape York: *Kuranda Safaris* (☎93 7175). Check under "Barges" and "Cruises" above for other Cape York travel options.

**Train** McLeod St (☎52 6249).

**Travel agents** For budget travel and tours, try *Adventure Travel Company*, 105 Lake St (☎51 8177); *Cairns Flight Centre*, Central Court, Lake St (☎52 1077); *STA*, Central Court, Lake St (☎31 4199); or *Tropical Paradise Travel*, 25 Spence St (☎51 9533).

**Yacht club** 4 Esplanade (☎31 2750). Worth contacting for hitching/crewing onwards.

# The Atherton Tablelands and Chillagoe

The **Atherton Tablelands**, the highlands behind Cairns, are named after **John Atherton**, who made the tin deposits at **Herberton** accessible by opening a route to the coast in 1877. Dense forest once covered these highlands before the majority was cleared and given over to dairy cattle, tobacco and grain. The remaining pockets of forest are magnificent, but it's the understated beauty that draws most visitors today, and though **Kuranda** and its markets pull in bus-loads from the coast, there are also a handful of quieter **national parks** brimming with rare species. You could spend days here, driving or hiking through rainforest to crater lakes and endless small waterfalls, or simply camp out one night and spotlight for wildlife. For a contrast, consider a side trip west to the mining town of **Chillagoe**, whose dust, limestone caves and Aboriginal art place it firmly in the outback.

Drivers can reach the tablelands on the **Palmerston Highway** from Innisfail, the **Gillies Highway** from Gordonvale, and the **Kennedy Highway** from Cairns to Kuranda. The unforgettable **train ride** from Cairns to Kuranda, through gorges and rainforest, is the stylish way onto the tablelands; due to open in late 1995, the **Skyrail Cablecar** was designed to lessen the number of tour buses on the roads and promises a seven-kilometre aerial view of the forest canopy between Smithfield and Kuranda. Numerous **tours** run from Cairns to Kuranda and tableland highlights; look for bus and train packages. *White Car Coaches* (from *Tropical Paradise Travel*; ☎070/51 9533) run **buses** to tableland towns and Chillagoe, but you really need your own transport to explore at leisure.

## Kuranda

At first glance, the constant stream of buses crawling up the steep range from Cairns has turned **KURANDA** into a stereotypical resort – something this once atavistic community was keen to escape. But despite expanding development and heavy market-day tourism, it's hard not to like the place. **Buses**, and the highway, stop at the top of town, **trains** at the overgrown station 500m down the hill, with essential services – post office, store (EFTPOS), bank, cafés – laid out between them along Coondoo Street.

Opposite the station you'll find the old, quiet *Kuranda Hostel* (6 Arra St; ☎070/93 7355; ①), with a plentiful supply of bunks, large grounds (where you can camp), kitchen and laundry. Around the corner is *The Bottom Pub*, the best place in town for meals and lively Friday nights. Out on the highway, *Kuranda Rainforest Resort* (☎070/93 7555; ⑤) has a spa and gym (and access by private buses from the coast).

---

### WET TROPICS AND WORLD HERITAGE

Queensland's **wet tropics** – the coastal belt from the Paluma range, near Townsville, to the Daintree north of Cairns – has been nominated under **World Heritage** listing as containing one of the oldest surviving tracts of rainforest anywhere on earth. Whether this listing has benefitted the region is questionable however; logging has slowed, but the tourist industry has vigorously exploited the area's status as an untouched wilderness, constantly pushing for more development so that a greater number of visitors can be accommodated. The clearing of mangroves for a marina and resort at Cardwell is a worst-case example; Kuranda's *Skyrail* project one of the few cases designed to lessen the ultimate impact (another highway was the alternative). Given the profits to be made, development is inevitable, but it's ironic that a scheme designed to promote the region's unique beauty may accelerate its destruction.

The **markets** that attract so many tourists open at 9am on Sunday, Wednesday and Friday; the first buses arrive an hour later. Don't expect bargains – the market is a commercial affair with craft, fruit and clothes stalls, a fake plane wreck and a bungee jump over a "rainforest pool". Nearby, forest fauna can be seen close up at the **Butterfly Sanctuary** (daily 10am–3pm; $9), where guides point out the dozen local species protected by their breeding programme, and in the **Noctarium**'s (daily 10am–4pm; $8) collection of possums, wallabies and bats. Further down Coondoo Street, the hour-long show at **Tjapukai Dance Theatre** (daily 11am & 1.30pm; $16) is a good humoured, but hardly eye-opening, session of didgeridoo playing and storytelling.

### Walks around Kuranda

Kuranda sits at the top of the **Barron Gorge**, spectacular in the wet season when the river rages down the falls, but otherwise tamed by a hydroelectric dam upstream. A dubious **walking track** descends to cold swimming spots along the river from the lookout at the end of Barron Falls Road, 2km from town; safer trails follow the road beyond the falls to **Wright's Lookout**, then continue to dense forest along **Surprise Creek** and the **Power Station**. Closer to town, there's another forest walk from the Noctarium to Jumrum Creek, about an hour's worth – and a huge colony of **flying foxes** to see, hear and smell opposite the *BP* garage at the top of Coondoo Street.

# Mareeba

West of Kuranda, rainforest quickly gives way to dry woodland and tobacco plantations, quite a change from the coast's greenery. **Davies Creek** is down a track 25km on; paths lead from a campsite to where falls pour over a granite rockface to a pool surrounded by boulders and scrub. The main road continues past a memorial to **James Venture Mulligan**, the veteran prospector who discovered the Palmer River Goldfields (see p.371).

MAREEBA has little going for it, despite being the tablelands' oldest settlement. Byrnes Street has all the shops and banks; **motels** and the pleasant *Tropical Tablelands Caravan Park* (☎070/92 1158) are on the highway as you enter town. After dark you can tangle with the farming fraternity in one of the hotels, or at the **Apollo Night Club** (Thurs–Sat 7pm–3am) on Byrnes Street. **Leaving**, Atherton is 30km south; the **Peninsula Developmental Road** heads north to Mount Molloy; and **Granite Gorge**, another swimming spot, is 12km along Chewko Road (west off Byrnes St, down Rankin, fifth on the left). The *AMPOL* service station at the north end of town marks the start of the Chillagoe road.

# West to Chillagoe

The 150-kilometre road to Chillagoe mysteriously alternates between corrugated gravel and isolated sections of bitumen, but poses no real problem during the dry season. Look for graffiti on boulders (**Top Cat Pass** is a gem) and enticing adverts for the *Almaden Hotel*, whose cool, mirrored, well-supplied bar and beer garden is an incredible oasis in ramshackle, dilapidated **ALMADEN**. From here until Chillagoe's inactive smelter chimney appears from behind an outcrop of rock, the road passes blocks of cut marble awaiting shipment to Italy.

CHILLAGOE dates from 1887, when enough copper ore was found to keep a smelter running until the 1950s; now a gold mine 16km west at **Mungana** seems to keep the place ticking over. Red dust, a service station, oversized hotels and general store complete the picture. Arrange **camping** and **cave tours** (daily 9am & 1.30pm) through the post office/NPWS (☎070/94 7163) down the street, but note that numbers on the tours are limited. There are two campsites (tank water and pit toilets), one close to town, the other 7km out near the caves themselves; if you need more luxury, the *Chillagoe Lodge Motel* (7 King St; ☎070/94 7106; ⑤) has a pool, meals, TV and sheltered garden.

## The Caves

Chillagoe's **caves** are ancient coral reefs, hollowed out by rain and broken up into fluted masses half-buried in the scrub. Guides can take you through some, others are open to solo exploration with instructions from the ranger. The caverns are varied by limestone sculptures deposited by evaporation and, unusually for the location, some large stalagmites; the best formations are at **Royal Arch**, **Donna** and **Trezkinn**. Wildlife here includes grey swiftlets and agile pythons which somehow manage to catch bats on the wing. A **footpath** leads through grassland between the caves, where you'll find echidnas, kangaroos, black cockatoos and frogmouths, odd birds which perfectly fit their name; given that this is perfect snake country, solid shoes and trousers would be wise. **Balancing Rock** offers panoramic views, with the town hidden by low trees, while obscure **Aboriginal paintings and engravings** have been found near **the Arches**, west at Mungana. Past here, the road continues 500km to Normanton, Karumba and tracks up western Cape York – but it doesn't improve and there's no fuel or help along the way.

# Atherton and around

Centrally placed for fôrays to most of the tablelands' attractions, **ATHERTON** is the only active highlands town. **Buses** stop at the junction of Main and Vernon streets; the post office is in Vernon Street, and banks and cafés are along Main Street, with a supermarket right at the top end where the highway comes in from Mareeba. **Accommodation** includes the heavily tiled and hospitable *Atherton Backpackers Hostel* (37 Alice St, off Vernon St at the fire station; ☎070/91 3552; ①), green and spacious tent sites at *Woodlands Tourist Park* (141 Herberton Rd; ☎070/91 1407), and *Hinterland Motel* (44 Cook St; ☎070/91 1885; ⑤). The *Fu Wah Chinese Restaurant* and the pizza shop in Main Street are worth a visit, and cafés open very early for breakfast. From town, roads head north to Mareeba, south to Ravenshoe and Herberton, and east to lakes and Yungaburra.

## Tinaroo, Barrine, Eacham and Yungaburra

Heading east from Atherton towards Yungaburra, turn left to **Lake Tinaroo**, a convoluted reservoir formed by pooling the Barron River's headwaters. An unsurfaced, dry-weather road runs around from the dam to the Gillies Highway, passing **campsites** on the north shore before cutting deep into native forests. It's worth stopping along the way for the short walks to bright green **Mobo Crater** and **Cathedral Fig**, an enormous parasitic strangler fig tree. While common enough in rainforest, one this size – 50m tall and 43m around the base – is extraordinary, with the thick mass of tendrils supporting the crown all fused together like melted wax.

Barrine and Eacham are **maars**, or crater lakes: blue, still circles surrounded by thick rainforest. **Barrine** is the most developed, enough for you to want to escape the crowds around the kiosk and cruise boat (daily at 10.15am, 2pm, 3.15pm; $7) by following a six-kilometre track around the lake past two enormous **kauri pines**, more commonly found in New Zealand and Western Australia. **Eacham**'s circuit is just 4km but otherwise similar, with birds and insects foraging on the forest floor, frogs and water dragons at the water's edge. Both lakes are fine to swim in but spooky; **amethystine pythons** are often seen sunning themselves around the shore.

Heading back towards Atherton, **YUNGABURRA** makes another good base, consisting of an old hotel, a café/store, and pine-and-slate comforts at *On the Wallaby*

*Hostel* (37 Eacham Rd, ☎070/95 3686; ①–③), run by *Gone Walkabout* in Cairns. They loan canoes for Lake Eacham, and can direct you to local **platypus** watching sites and another giant **Curtain Fig** on the Atherton road.

## The Crater and Southern Tablelands

Heading towards Ravenshoe and the **southern tablelands**, from where you can circle back to Cairns via Innisfail, it's worth detouring to **the Crater** at Mount Hypipamee, a 56-metre vertical rift formed by steam blowing its way through molten granite, now filled with pale green water. There are picnic tables with ridiculously tame Lewins Honeyeaters and the forest is a fantastic place to **spotlight**: rare possums and tree kangaroos are resident, and with patience you'll find the amazing leaf-tail gecko on tree trunks.

**HERBERTON**, west of the Crater, is a quaint, one-time timber town, whose **Historic Village** (daily 10am–4pm; $10) is a meticulous but lifeless collection of about thirty pioneer buildings relocated from elsewhere: a schoolroom, bishop's residence, hotel, Chinese relics, bottle dump, you name it.

**RAVENSHOE**, apart from endless explanations for its name, is only notable for the *Tully Falls Hotel*, Queensland's highest pub, and broad **Millstream Falls**, 5km away. Southwest, the road continues past steamy upwellings at **Innot Hot Springs** and **MOUNT GARNET** to the start of the Gulf Developmental Road (see p.410); east is **MILLAA MILLA** at the top of the **Palmerston Highway**. There's a **waterfall circuit** here, where a 15-kilometre road passes three small tumbles and swimming holes; best is **Elinjaa**, with a curtain cave. The highway itself was named after **Christie Palmerston**, a fugitive who hid with Aborigines on the tablelands in the 1870s. Later, appreciation for his trail to Port Douglas bought him a pardon, but he stayed in the bush. **PALMERSTON NATIONAL PARK** is worth a stopover for free camping and the best of Atherton's rainforest, though you'll need some protection from summer flies. A local oddity is the **musky rat kangaroo**, a small, black, uniquely diurnal marsupial common in leaf litter on the forest floor. The pick of the walking tracks lead to mossy **Tchupala Falls** and the impressive **Nandroya Falls**, while the highway descends past the park to Innisfail.

# Heading North: Cairns to Cape Tribulation

The **Cook Highway** makes the Daintree and Cape Tribulation, tamed fringes of the Cape York Peninsula, only a couple of hours' drive north of Cairns. The highway initially runs in sight of the sea to **Port Douglas** and **Mossman**, a beautiful drive past isolated beaches where hang-gliders patrol the headlands. North of Mossman is the road to **the Daintree**: Australia's largest surviving stretch of tropical rainforest. World Heritage listing hasn't saved it from development: roads are being surfaced, land has been subdivided, and there's an ever increasing number of services in place, undermining the wild and remote brochure image. While this disappoints some visitors, the majestic forest still descends thick and dark right to the sea, and there's all the time in the world to explore paths through the jungle, watch for wildlife, or rest on the beach.

Day **tours** from Cairns will show you the sights, but you really need longer to come to grips with the rich scenery and atmosphere. For once it's not essential to have a vehicle: *Coral Coaches* (☎070/98 2600) run a daily **bus** between Cairns, Cape Trib and (weather permitting) Cooktown, which allows multiple stopovers; some hostels along the way also operate services for guests. If you want to arrive in style, *Quicksilver's* (☎070/31 4299) high-speed **catamaran** plies between Cairns and Port Douglas, and also zooms to the outer reef (see below).

# Port Douglas and Mossman

The turning to **PORT DOUGLAS**, an hour north of Cairns, is signalled by an ostentatious colonnade of West African palm trees. This once pretty fishing village has become a quaint, upmarket tourist attraction, as manifest by the huge **Mirage Resort** on the way in – project of troubled media tycoon Peter Skase – and a multitude of trendy boutiques. Even so, it's more relaxed than Cairns, and an alternative base for exploring the area: less flamboyant lodgings include *4 Mile Beach Caravan Park* on Reef Street (✆070/98 5281); the pleasant *Port O'Call Lodge/YHA* (Port St; ✆070/99 5422; ①), with its *Shoestrings Restaurant*; and *Mango Tree Apartments* (91 Davidson St; ✆070/99 5677; ⑤), for self-contained units just back from Four Mile Beach.

All services are on **Macrossan Street**, which runs between **Four Mile Beach** and **Anzac Park**; the **tourist information** (no. 23; daily 8.30am–5.30pm; ✆070/99 5599) can sort out everything from Aboriginal-guided tours of Mossman Gorge to sailing trips and buses to the Daintree. *Port Douglas Bike Hire* (no. 40; ✆070/99 5799) rents mountain **bikes** from $10 a day. **Cafés** and restaurants also congregate around Macrossan Street: *Court House Hotel* has boozers and dogs sprawled across the verandah, with lunch specials and a barbecue menu in the garden; the excellent, if expensive *Catalina* (Wharf St; ✆070/99 5287; closed Mon) specializes in seafood, with dishes such as Chilli Crab and Barramundi Duxelle; while *Rusty's Bar and Bistro* (123 Davidson St; ✆070/99 5266) goes Mediterranean with pasta, crumbed prawns and baby octopus, and ventures further afield with such exotica as grilled coral trout and Thai red curries.

Anzac Park is scene of a Sunday morning **produce market**, good for fruit, vegetables and souvenirs. Near the park's jetty you'll find the whitewashed timber of **St Mary's by the Sea**, built after the 1911 cyclone carried off the previous structure. Behind at **Ben Cropp's Shipwreck Museum** (daily 9am–5pm; $5) bronze cannon, teapots and the results of twenty years salvaging are piled around a continuously playing video of Ben's exploits. On the other side of the church, *Port Douglas Dive Centre* (✆070/99 5327) visits the **Low Isles**, **Chinaman**, **Tongue** and **Opal reefs**, all decent sites though in much the same condition as those off Cairns – prices are steeper, too. *Quicksilver*, based at Marina Mirage (✆070/99 5500), also runs a sailing boat to the Low Isles ($82), while its high-speed catamaran will whisk you to the **Agincourt Reef** for the day ($118).

## Mossman

**MOSSMAN**, 14km past Port Douglas, is a quiet town which can hardly have changed in the last thirty years; rail lines between the canefields and mill still run along the main street. Ten minutes inland, **Mossman Gorge** looks like all rainforest rivers should, the boulder-strewn flow good for messing around in on a quiet day but subject to streams of tour buses in peak season. *Bamanga Bubu Ngadimunku* (✆070/98 1046), the local community, put together the Aboriginal **walking trail** here and conduct tours of the gorge explaining history and plant usage.

**Heading on**, the road continues to Daintree township or via Daintree Ferry to Cape Tribulation; backtracking south lets you leave the highway and climb to Mount Molloy and the Peninsula Developmental Road – the easier, inland route to Cooktown.

# The Daintree

If you detour off the Mossman–Cape Trib road to take in **DAINTREE** township, you'll find that the former timber camp is little more than a place to organize a half-day **crocodile tour** with *Daintree Wildlife Safaris* (✆1800/079 102; $26), while 4WDs test their mettle on the **CREB Track** to Cooktown. Instead, most people follow the road to the **Daintree River Ferry** (continuously 6am–midnight; pedestrians $1, vehicles $5) and the start of the partially sealed 35-kilometre Cape Tribulation road.

Across the river, you can detour to quiet **lodgings** at **Cape Kimberley** (cabins, campsite, basic store; ☎070/90 7500; ②–⑤) or continue 8km through rainforest over the convoluted range to **FLORAVILLE** and **Cow Bay**. Floraville's café hands out local advice and doubles as a *Commonwealth Bank* agent; the *Environmental Centre* here explains forest subtleties and local background. Hostels don't get better than the jungle-clad cabins of *Crocodylus Village/YHA* at Cow Bay (Buchannan Creek Rd, turn at airstrip; ☎070/98 9166; ①–②); bikes, forest walks and snorkelling/dive trips around Cape Trib and local reefs can be arranged.

Back on the main track, at **Thornton Beach** you'll find sand, a licensed kiosk, rock-bottom prices for camping and a creek said to be "loaded with crocodiles". If this sounds worrying, *Inn the Rainforest* (cabins, camping, supplies; ☎070/98 9162; ②–④), *Lync Haven* (camping, supplies, night walks; ☎070/98 9155; ②–④) and *Heritage Lodge* (cabins, restaurant, tours; ☎070/98 9138; ⑤) are all further inland – look for signs on the road.

Plants close in on the **Marrdja Botanical Walk** at **Noah Beach**, where concrete paths and boardwalks follow the creek through a mixture of forest to mangroves at the river mouth. Look for spiky lawyer cane, lianas twisted into corkscrew shapes where they once surrounded a tree, and the spherical pods of the **cannonball mangrove** – dried and dismembered, they were used as puzzles by Aboriginal peoples, the object being to fit the irregular segments back together. The NPWS has a **campsite** here. Just up the road is *Coconut Beach Resort* (bar, all facilities; ☎070/98 0033; ⑦), with a huge A-frame restaurant requiring "smart tropical dress". Fringing coral comes right up to the shore about 1km to the south.

## Cape Tribulation

**Cape Tribulation** – a forty-minute drive from the ferry crossing – was named when Captain Cook's vessel hit a reef offshore in June 1770. The cleared area below **Mount Sorrow** sports a café, store, boardwalk onto the beach and the **Bat House**, worth a visit to handle tame orphaned flying foxes. **Beds** are available at the noisy, officious *PK's* **hostel** (☎070/31 5650; ①) where they organize **horse riding** and **sea kayaking**, but you're better off at *Pilgrim Sands* **campsite** (☎070/90 0030), about 2km along the road; at least here you'll go to sleep with the sound of surf, not a disco, in your ears.

The area is best explored on foot – for the simple pleasure of walking through the forest with the sea breaking on a beach not five minutes distant. A **path** runs out to the cape, where you may see brilliantly coloured pittas (small, tail-less birds with a buff chest, green back, and black and rust heads) bouncing around in the leaf litter, or even a crocodile sunning itself on the beach. One way to penetrate the undergrowth away from the paths is to follow small creeks: **Emmagen**, about 6km north, runs halfway up Mount Sorrow and comes recommended for its safe swimming holes. Persistence and luck may expose a tree kangaroo, given away during the day by its long tail hanging down like a vine while the animal slouches in the tree tops, asleep.

## The Bloomfield Track

Scene of vicious confrontations in 1984 between construction crews and environmentalists who tried unsuccessfully to stop this alternative road to Cooktown being built through virgin forest, the **Bloomfield Track** is completely impassable after rain and otherwise needs 4WD. Spanning 80km from Cape Trib to where the track joins the Cooktown Road at **Black Mountain**, the fun section with drastic gradients lies before the halfway mark of the tidal **Bloomfield River**, which has to be crossed at low water. After **WUJAL WUJAL** community the road flattens out past *Home Rule Rainforest Lodge* at **ROSSVILLE** (inexpensive meals, kitchen, horse riding; ☎070/60 3925; ③), before reaching *The Lions Den* at **Helenvale** near Black Mountain (see opposite), about half an hour from Cooktown.

# THE CAPE YORK PENINSULA AND TORRES STRAIT ISLANDS

The **Cape York Peninsula** points north towards the **Torres Strait** and New Guinea, and tackling the rugged tracks and hectic river crossings on the "Trip To The Tip" is an adventure in itself – as well as a means to reach Australia's northernmost point and the communities at **Bamaga** and **Thursday Island**, so far removed from southern attitudes that they could easily be in another country. But it's not all four-wheel driving across the savannah: during the dry season the historic settlement of **Cooktown**, wetlands at **Lakefield National Park** and **Laura**'s Aboriginal heritage are only a day's journey from Cairns in any decent vehicle. Given longer you might get as far as **Weipa**, but don't go further than this without off-road transport; while some *have* reached the Tip in family sedans, most who try fail miserably.

With thousands making the journey between May and October, a **breakdown** won't leave you stranded, but the cost of repairs will make you regret it. **Bikers** should travel in groups and have some off-roading experience. Those without their own vehicle can take **buses** from Cairns to Cape Trib or Cooktown and overland **tours** beyond that. There's also a twice-weekly bus to Weipa (when the roads are open), and **flights** or **cruises** up the coast, often calling in at islands on the way; see "Travel Details" at the end of this chapter for regular services, and "Listings", p.360, for tour operators.

You'll find a few roadhouses and motels along the way, but **accommodation** on the cape is largely a matter of camping, and it's inevitable if you head right to the Tip that one night at least will be spent in the bush. Settlements also supply meals and provisions, but there won't be much on offer so take all you can carry. On this note, don't turn bush campsites into rubbish dumps: take a pack of bin liners and remove all your garbage. **Estuarine crocodiles** are present throughout the Cape; read the warning under "Wildlife" in *Contexts*. There are few **banks**, so take enough cash to carry you between points – some roadhouses accept plastic. In Cairns, the Department of Lands and *RACQ* can help with advice on road conditions and **maps**; other maps from *Pinevale Publications* (try bookshops), *Croc Shop* (10 Shield St) and NPWS fill in local and historical information. Vehicles should carry a **first-aid kit**, a comprehensive tool-kit and spares, extra fuel, and a tarpaulin for creek crossings. A winch and equipment for removing, patching and inflating tyres might also be sensible.

## Mossman to Cape York

Not as pretty as the coastal tracks but considerably easier, the 260-kilometre road to Cooktown and points north leaves the Cook Highway just before Mossman and climbs to the drier scrub at **MOUNT CARBINE**, a former tungsten mine whose *Wolfram Hotel* and roadhouse fulfil all functions. The descent of the far side of the range an hour later is rough, a foretaste of the Cape's incredibly dusty byways. **LAKELAND**'s hotel and fuel stop marks the junction for routes north along the **Peninsula Developmental Road** to Laura, but the way to Cooktown lies east, past **Annan River gorge** and the mysterious **Black Mountain**, two huge piles of algae-covered granite boulders near the road. Aborigines reckon the formation to be the result of a building competition between two rivals fighting over a girl, and tell stories of people wandering into the eerie, whistling caverns, never to return.

At this point it's worth a 4-kilometre detour south along the **Bloomfield Track** to the *Lions Den* at **Helenvale**. The *Den* is an old-style pub playing up for tourists during the day but damagingly authentic at night, from the iron sheeting and beam decor to those nasty exhibits in glass bottles on the piano.

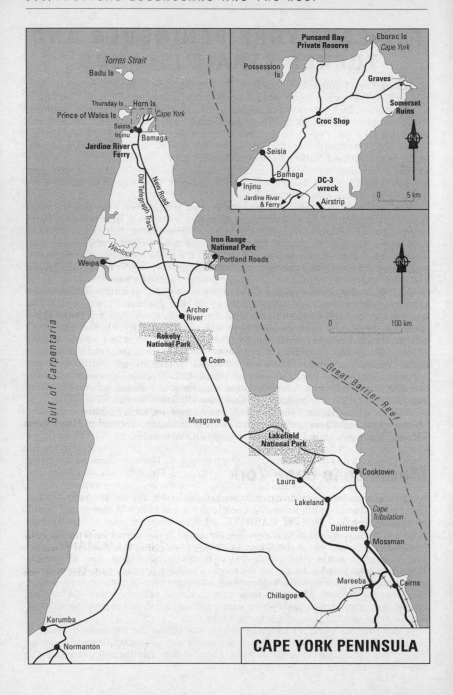

**CAPE YORK PENINSULA**

# Cooktown

After the *Endeavour* nearly sank at Cape Tribulation in 1770, Captain Cook landed at a natural harbour to the north, where he spent two months repairing the vessel, observing the "Genius, Temper, Disposition and Number of the Natives" and – legend has it – naming the kangaroo after an Aboriginal word for "I don't know". Tempers wore thin on occasion, as when the crew refused to share a catch of turtles with Aborigines, and Cook commented: "They seem'd to set no value upon any thing we gave them".

The site lay dormant until gold was discovered southwest on the **Palmer River** in 1873: within months a harbour was being surveyed at the mouth of the Endeavour River for a tented camp known as **COOKTOWN**. A wild success while gold lasted, the settlement once boasted a main street alive with hotels and a busy port doing brisk trade with Asia through thousands of **Chinese** prospectors and merchants. But the reserves were soon exhausted and by 1910 Cooktown was on the decline. Today, Cooktown's main drag, Charlotte Street, is good for random wandering past the old wharves and **Endeavour Park**, site of Cook's landing. A kiosk on the waterfront organizes two-hour **cruises** through the mangroves, and among monuments on the lawn are the remains of defences sent from Brisbane last century to ward off a threatened Russian invasion: one cannon, three cannonballs and two rifles (accompanied at the time by just one officer). At the far end of town, on the Endeavour Valley Road, is a **cemetery**, whose most famous resident is Mary Watson of Lizard Island (see below), and a Chinese shrine.

The best views of the town and river are from the top floor of the old Sisters of Mercy Convent, now a regional **museum** (daily 9.30am–4pm; $5) with a bit of everything: artefacts jettisoned from the *Endeavour*, exhaustive local history, a reconstructed joss house, a rundown on pearling around Thursday Island, and the history of the "hopelessly insolvent" Cooktown–Laura railway. By comparison, the **Marine Museum**, on the corner of Helen and Walker streets (daily 8.30am–5.30pm; $5), is a thin jumble of flotsam and details of the 1899 cyclones Mahina and Nachon, which collided north of Cooktown sinking 76 vessels and killing 350 people.

There are more views of the district from the red-and-white corrugated iron cone of **Grassy Hill Lighthouse**, reached on a concrete track from the end of Hope Street. **Mount Cook** is a rather tougher proposition, a two-hour return hike through very thick forest on meagre paths – follow orange triangles from the nondescript starting point that you'll find beyond Ida Street. Down below, the **Botanic Gardens** merge into original paperbark woodland, with a track running to **Finch Beach** on Cherry Tree Bay. It's rated as a safe swimming beach, but heed the homemade warning signs in pidgin: "Dispela Stap Hia" and a picture of a croc.

## Practicalities

The June **Discovery Festival** is a predictably thorough piss-up, but even then **accommodation** shouldn't be too difficult to find. If you're **camping**, the *Tropical Breeze* site is handy for town, but the *Peninsula Van Park* has the nicer location, in forest below Mount Cook. *Cooktown Backpackers*, Charlotte Street, has cheap beds and little else (☎070/69 5166; ①); *Motor Inn Motel* (Charlotte St, 4WD rentals for local use; ☎070/69 5357; ⑤), *Sovereign Hotel* (Charlotte St, beer garden and pool; ☎070/69 5400; ⑤) and *River of Gold Motel* (corner of Hope and Walker streets; ☎070/69 5222; ⑤) are good alternatives. Numerous cafés and hotels supply **food and drink**; a **supermarket** and grocer are the last source of fresh provisions before Weipa.

**Moving on**, conventional vehicles have to head back to Lakeland for Laura and the north; stronger sets of wheels have the option of reaching Lakefield National Park

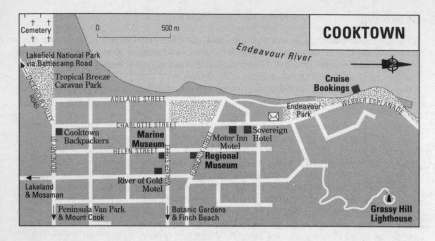

more directly by heading towards Hope Vale community and then taking the Battlecamp Road. The last fuel this way is found about 33km from Cooktown at *Endeavour Falls Tourist Park*.

## Lizard Island

A granite rise covered in stunted trees and heath, **Lizard Island** is one of the most isolated resorts in Australia, 90km north of Cooktown, and within sight of the outer reef. Divers rave about the fringing coral reefs here but even so, reaching Lizard is an expensive business: options are limited to a daily **flight** on *Qantas* from Cairns, trying your luck at hitching through *Cairns Yacht Club* (see "Listings", p.360), or large groups might contact Brad Palmer in Cooktown (☎070/69 5519) for a charter boat. Those unable to afford the **lodge** (☎070/60 3999; ⑧) can use the NPWS **camping area** (permits from Cairns; see p.360) down on Watson Beach. The lodge won't help out with *anything* except in real emergencies, and, as gas cylinders can't be carried on the plane, charcoal beads are the recommended fuel for fires.

Shell middens show that Lizard was regularly visited by Aboriginal peoples, but the island was uninhabited when **Robert Watson** built a cottage and started a sea-slug processing operation here in the 1870s, accompanied by his wife **Mary** and two Chinese servants. Aborigines attacked the house while Robert was at sea in October 1881, killing one of the Chinese and forcing Mary, her baby and Ah Sam to flee in a water tank; they paddled west for five days before dying of thirst. Her painfully matter-of-fact diary is kept at Brisbane's John Oxley Library, while the tank is on display at the Queensland Museum in Townsville.

## Quinkan Country: Laura and The Palmer

Back on the Peninsula Road, 60km north of Lakeland, **LAURA**'s store/post office, road-house and *Quinkan Hotel* (☎070/60 3236; ⑦) support the two-day **Aboriginal Dance Festival**, an electrifying assertion of Aboriginal identity, held in June of odd-numbered years. At other times, visit the sandstone caves and ridges at **Split Rock**, 13km south of town, where a steep track leads to a two-hour gallery circuit. Paintings depict animals and startling spirit figures associated with sorcery: spidery, frightening

Quinkan with pendulous earlobes, and dumpy Anurra, often with their legs twisted upwards. Other sites show scenes from post-contact life, depicting horses, rifles and clothed figures; some caves were probably in use until the 1930s. You can find out more through the *Ang-Gnarra Aboriginal Corporation Caravan Park* (☎070/60 3214) or *Trezise Bush Service* (☎070/55 1865), which has a camp at Jowalbinna (4WD only; ask directions at Laura's *Quinkan Hotel* – see above) .

Sites along the **Palmer River**, southwest of Laura on a terrible 4WD track, recall the gigantic 1873 goldrush. Mining life was volatile: Aborigines waged guerrilla warfare, and race riots erupted between whites and the Chinese – who at one time outnumbered the entire European population of Queensland and infuriated whites by doggedly extracting gold from "exhausted" claims. The settlements at Maytown and German Bar were abandoned once the gold had gone and today there's virtually nothing left except atmosphere; the Cairns NPWS (see p.360) stocks **maps** and permits.

## Lakefield National Park

Ideally you'd take a week to absorb **LAKEFIELD NATIONAL PARK's** half a million hectares of savannah and riverine flats, drifting between the 21 **campsites**; but even a single night spent here will give you a feel for the Cape's most accessible wilderness area. Apart from the **Old Laura Homestead** – built between 1892 and 1940 and standing abandoned in the scrub on the Laura River – the park's pleasures revolve around outdoor pursuits, fishing and exploring lagoons for wildlife. Lakefield's **crocodile-conservation programme** means you might see both fresh- and saltwater types; bird-life is plentiful and mammals put in an appearance. **Magnetic anthills** are a common landmark: flattened towers aligned north–south to prevent overheating in the noon sun.

Conventional vehicles can sometimes manage the rough 170-kilometre track through the park between Laura township and Musgrave Roadhouse. High clearance is needed for other routes, including the Battle Camp road to Cooktown. **Ranger stations** are located along the road at New Laura (southern park, 50km from Laura township), Lakefield (central, 80km) and Bizant (north, 100km). Popular places to camp and watch wildlife are **Horseshoe Lagoon** past Old Laura, **12 Mile Hole** near New Laura (4WD only), **Kalpowar Crossing** (near Lakefield, with showers and toilets) and **Hann Crossing**, in the north of the park.

## Laura to Iron Range and Weipa

Following the main road, the 300km that stretches between Laura and Archer River passes in a haze of dust, jolts and roadhouses supplying fuel, food, beds and drink. First on the list is **MUSGRAVE** (135km), a converted homestead where the track from the Lakefield joins the road, followed by a two-hour roller-coaster ride down to **COEN's** *(S)Exchange Hotel* (107km). Coen's service station handles **camping**, provisions, post office business and banking; the *Homestead Guest House*, on Regent Street, has beds (☎070/60 1157; ②) and can provide meals, while *Clark's* workshop can fix the car. The 4WD track into **ROKEBY NATIONAL PARK** is a further 25km; the ranger station lies 75km west, with camping at undeveloped bush sites. Past the park turn-off, **ARCHER RIVER ROADHOUSE** (70km from Coen; ☎070/60 3266) has accommodation and the **last reliable fuel** on the main road before Bamaga, 400km away; beyond are routes east to Iron Range (155km) and west to Weipa (190km) – more on these overpage.

## Iron Range

You may have seen rainforest before, but you'll have experienced nothing like the magnificent jungle at **Iron Range**, a leftover from the Ice Age link to New Guinea, which hides fauna found nowhere else on the continent – the nocturnal **green python** and brilliant blue-and red-**eclectus parrot** are best known. Four hours' bouncing along a 4WD track from the main road should see you at a clearing where the army simulated a nuclear strike in the 1960s – fortunately using tons of conventional explosives instead of the real thing. Turning right at the junction here takes you past the **ranger station** (☎070/60 7170) to **LOCKHART RIVER**, an Aboriginal mission and fishing beach; there's fuel here during weekday trading hours, but don't just turn up unannounced – phone the garage on ☎070/60 751. The road left leads to **PORTLAND ROADS'** few houses and public telephones, overlooking a monument to Edmund Kennedy and the remains of a harbour used by US forces in World War II. **Bush camping** is a few kilometres before Portland at **Chilli Beach**, a blustery, tropical setting.

Next day, you have the chance to experience something unique on the mainland – sunrise and sunset over different seas – by taking the roller-coaster **Frenchman's Road** to Weipa. This starts 30km back from the Lockhart/Portland junction, crosses the difficult **Pascoe** and **Wenlock** rivers, and emerges on the Peninsula Developmental Road, 2km north of **Batavia Downs**. Head through Batavia and cross more creeks, which look worse than they are, to the main Weipa road; coast to coast might take six to eight hours.

## Weipa

Those without 4WD have to give Iron Range a miss, but can still reach **WEIPA**, a town of red clay and yellow mining trucks dealing in kaolin and **bauxite**. The area was one of the first in Australia to be described by Europeans: **William Janz** encountered "savage, cruel blacks" here in 1606, a report later reiterated by **Jan Cartenz** who found nothing of interest and sailed off to chart the Gulf of Carpentaria. Apart from a mission built at **Mappoon** last century, little changed until aluminium ore was recognized in the 1950s and *Comalco* built the town and began mining.

All the traffic in Weipa gives way to the gargantuan mine vehicles and stays out of the restricted areas. The town comprises mostly company housing, but it does offer long-forgotten luxuries: you can pick up spares for your vehicle at the **auto wreckers** and service station on the way into town; and there's a **supermarket**, a post office and a branch of the *Commonwealth Bank* (with automatic cash dispensers) just in front of large **campsites**(featuring hot showers and a laundry) where you can unwind and swap tales about the rigours of the trip. The **hotel** up the road sells relaxant and looks out over the western sea; fishing trips and **mine tours** can be arranged at the campsite office. Hardened **bikers** should try to catch the August **Croc Run**, Australia's richest and most challenging endurance race which weaves its way through mangroves and creeks.

Around town, the library's **Cape York Collection** contains a unique collection of books and documents relating to the area, while the **Uningan Nature Reserve** situated on the Mission River preserves sixteen-metre-high **middens** composed entirely of shells left over from Aboriginal meals – some have been dated to 1600 years ago. Driving is the only way to get here, and guidebooks are available from the campsite. Keep an eye out for crocs while walking around the reserve.

**Leaving**, there's a barge to Normanton in the Gulf once a week, and occasional services to Thursday Island – contact the **travel agent** next to the bank (☎070/69 7266) or *Gulf Freight Services* (☎070/69 8619). Note that there is **no fuel** between Weipa and Bamaga (340km).

## North of The Wenlock

The fast-flowing **Wenlock River**, an hour north of the Weipa junction on the main road, marks the start of the most challenging part of the journey north, with road conditions changing every wet season. The routes divide 42km after the Wenlock: die-hards follow the old **Telegraph Track**, which has all the interesting scenery and creek crossings; those less certain of their abilities take the **New Road**, consisting of 200km of loose gravel and bulldust. The Telegraph Track's lines were dismantled in the wake of satellite communications, and many of the poles have been robbed of their ceramic caps by souvenir hunters. The first travellers of the year build simple rafts and log bridges to cross the creeks; as tracks dry and traffic increases, jarring corrugations and potholes are more likely to pose a problem, constituting a serious test of vehicle strength. There are some fine **creeks** on this route: Bertie's potholes are large enough to submerge an entire vehicle; Gunshot's four-metre vertical clay banks are a real test of skill (use low range first, and keep your foot off the brake); and the north exit at Cockatoo is deceptively sandy. Dozens wipe out on Gunshot every season, and for the cautious there's a 24-kilometre detour via open scrub at **Heathlands** to the north side.

The two routes rejoin briefly after 75km, then the New Road diverges left 54km to the **Jardine Ferry** ($80 return includes use of Injinu campsite at Bamaga), while the Telegraph Track ploughs on past beautiful clear green water and basalt **waterfalls** to Nolans Brook – often necessitating a brief submarine dip – and the hundred-metre-wide **Jardine River**. Once the main crossing, the river became impassable here in 1994 and the likelihood of crocodiles makes any attempt extremely dangerous. It *is* worth the trip to camp though (assuming you have enough fuel), before heading back to the ferry. From there, the last hour to Bamaga passes the remains of a **DC-3** that crashed just short of the airstrip in 1945.

## Bamaga

Even the distance travelled doesn't prepare you for **BAMAGA**, a community of stilt houses and banana palms founded by Saibai islanders in 1946 which owes nothing to suburban values. Around the intersection you'll find a workshop and service station selling **fuel** (Mon–Fri 9am–5pm, Sat 9am–12.30pm, Sun 1.30–3pm), a *Commonwealth Bank* (Mon–Fri 9.30am–3pm; bank books only), airline offices, a hotel and a **shopping centre** (fresh veggies, *National Australia Bank* agent, telephones, café and post office). For **accommodation**, turn left at the junction to **Injinu campsite** (Cowall Creek), or right past the shopping centre to the coast at **SEISIA** (Red Island Point). Camping here is under palms near the jetty (showers, laundry, fishing safaris; ☎070/69 3243); other services include a roadhouse, tackle shop, taxi (☎070/69 3333) and 4WD rental.

### CROSSING CREEKS

Before attempting to drive them, **walk** creek crossings, keeping alert for crocodiles, to gauge the depth and find the best route. *Never* blindly follow others across. Make sure all rescue gear – shovel, winch, rope, etc – is easy to reach, outside the vehicle. Electrics on petrol engines need to be waterproofed. On deep crossings, block off air inlets to prevent water entering the engine, slacken off the fan belt and cover the radiator grille with a tarpaulin; this diverts water around the engine as long as the vehicle is moving. Select an appropriate gear (changing it in midstream will let water into the clutch) and drive through at walking speed; clear the opposite embankment before stopping again. If you stall, switch off the ignition *immediately* and don't restart it until you've made sure that water hasn't been sucked in through the air filter – which will destroy the engine. If this happens, exit through windows and winch out.

## Cape York and Somerset

To make local contacts, stay around Bamaga; to keep with the overland crowd head north to the *Croc Shop*'s information hut, then bear left for the idyllic beach at **Punsand Bay Private Reserve**, a just reward for the trials of the journey, with pre-fab tents, camping, meals, basic provisions, and a limited repairs service but no fuel (☎070/69 1722; ②–④). The rare **palm cockatoo**, a huge, crested black parrot with a curved bill, might also be in evidence.

You could spend a day recuperating on the beach, or return to the *Croc Shop* and take the road past the Somerset fork to its end at another **campsite** (shower, water and kiosk) and the exclusive *Pajinka Lodge* (☎070/69 2100; bookings ☎1800/802 968; ⑦). Follow the footpath through vine forest onto a wild, barren headland and down to a turbulent sea opposite the lighthouse on **Eborac Island**; a sign concreted into an oil drum marks **the tip** of mainland Australia and the end of the journey.

### Somerset

Established on government orders in 1864 to balance the French naval station in New Caledonia, **Somerset** was founded by John Jardine, who was succeeded by his son Frank the following year. Frank became a legend on the Cape and tales of his exploits assume larger-than-life proportions (fearless pioneer to some, brutal colonial to others). Though envisaged as a second Singapore, Somerset never amounted to more than a military outpost under constant attack from termites and local tribes. In 1877, after the pearling trade in the Torres Strait erupted into lawlessness, the settlement was abandoned in favour of a seat of government closer to the problem at Thursday Island.

Today, Somerset is a large paddock with only a few cannon, machine parts and mango trees as signs of former habitation; the buildings succumbed to white ants or were moved long ago. Frank and his wife Sana are buried on the beach directly below, next to a Chinese cemetery and traces of a jetty into the Adolphus Channel. Exploration of the dense undergrowth above the beach to the left might uncover remains of a **sentry post** and a cave with stick-figure paintings, presumably Aboriginal. Past Somerset, a track continues onto another beach before circling back towards the *Croc Shop*.

# The Torres Strait: Islands and Islanders

Beyond Cape York, barely 200km of sea separates Australia from New Guinea: **the Torres Strait** is an obstacle-strewn stretch named after Luis Vaez de Torres, who navigated the waters in 1606. Prior to European contact, the Strait's islands had developed trade links with Australia and highland New Guinea, which supplied outrigger canoes – no suitable trees grow in the Strait – in exchange for oyster and trochus shell, and heads. Warfare between islands pervaded all aspects of life, and the eastern cult of Malo required human jaws as tribute.

The early nineteenth century saw the first trade with Europeans, who soon discovered the Strait's rich *bêche de mer* (sea cucumber) and pearl beds and occupied the islands as bases for the industry, decimating the Islanders through violence and disease. Then on 1 July, 1871, the **London Missionary Society** landed on Darnley Island: once Islanders realized that the mission protected them from the more piratical whites, they converted to Christianity at a speed that amazed even the missionaries. The advent of Christianity (known here as **the Coming of the Light**) stabilized communities but also heralded the end of traditional life, as cults were undermined and wages and stores replaced the barter network. Another influential group were **South Sea Island** teachers, who brought their own dance styles and crops, and gradually intermarried with the locals.

The church created **island councils**, but real power lay with Queensland's **segregation laws**, which prevented emigration to the mainland. The only job in the Strait was pearling (for mother of pearl), and white boat-owners would have lost their labour pool if Islanders went south. Until World War II the islands made the best of it, but army service overseas gave returning recruits a better understanding of what they deserved from the government, and pressure removed some barriers to migration. The advent of plastics led to the collapse of the mother of pearl industry, and the unemployment that followed forced the government to drop all protectionist policies, with the result that by the mid-1970s half the Strait's former population were living on the mainland. The remainder formed a movement to establish an **Islander Nation**, which bore its first fruit on 3 June 1992 when the **Mabo Decision** acknowledged the Merriam as traditional owners of Murray Island, thereby setting a precedent for mainland Aboriginal claims and sending shock waves through the establishment.

**Ferries** cross regularly between Cape York and Thursday Island, the Strait's administrative centre – which, even on a brief visit, offers a fascinating glimpse into an all but forgotten corner of Australia. In theory, travel beyond Thursday (except to neighbouring islands) is impossible for casual travellers, but the rules are occasionally stretched.

## Thursday Island

A three-square-kilometre speck within sight of the mainland, between Prince of Wales, Hammond and Horn islands, **Thursday Island** wears a few aliases: coined "Sink of the Pacific" for the variety of peoples who passed through in pearling days, the local tag is *Waiben* or (very loosely) "Thirsty Island" – once a reference to the availability of drinking water and now a laconic aside on the quantity of beer consumed. The hotel clock with no hands hints at the pace of life and it's only for events like Christmas, when wall-to-wall aluminium punts from neighbouring islands make the harbour look like a maritime supermarket car park, that things liven up. Other chances to catch Thursday in carnival spirit are during the Coming of the Light festivities on 1 July, and Island of Origin league matches later in the same month, when rugby is taken to its logical conclusion. One season saw twenty-five people hospitalized, and the spectators often play as big a part in the action as the teams.

In town there are traces of the old **Chinatown** district around Milman Street, and a reminder of Queensland's worst shipping disaster in the **Quetta Memorial Church**, way down Douglas Street, built after the ship hit an uncharted rock in the Adolphus Channel in 1890 and went down with virtually all the Europeans on board. The Aplin Road **cemetery**, where two of the victims are buried, boasts tiled Islander tombs and depressing numbers of **Japanese** graves, each marked by a short pillar and kanji inscription. All died diving for pearls. As a by-product of the industry, Japanese crews had accurately mapped the Strait before the last war and it's no coincidence that the airstrip was bombed when hostilities were declared in 1942; fortifications are still in place on Thursday's east coast. Bunkers and naval cannon at the **Old Fort** on the opposite side date from the 1890s.

### Practicalities

There are **ferries** to Thursday Island every weekday morning from Cape York (2hr), Punsand Bay (1hr 30min) and Seisia (1hr 15min); prices are around $80 return/$40 one-way. Passing **Possession Island** on the way over, you come within sight of a plaque commemorating James Cook's landing here on 22 August 1770, when he planted the flag for King and Country. Then it's into the shallow channel between Prince of Wales and Horn; Horn has an **airport** and open-cut gold mine, **Prince of Wales** is the Strait's largest island, stocked with deer and settled by an overflow population unable to afford Thursday's exorbitant land premiums.

The wharf on Thursday sits below the colonial-style **Customs House**, a minute from the town centre in **Douglas Street**. Here you'll find a post office with payphones, the *National Australia* **bank**, cafés and two of the island's hotels: the *Torres* just beats the neighbouring *Royal* as Australia's northernmost bar. Facing the water on **Victoria Parade**, the *Federal* (☎070/69 1569; ⑤) is fractionally quieter as **lodgings** on a busy night, but the one-time mainstay, the *Grand* (famous for once briefly accommodating novelist Somerset Maugham) burned down in 1993. Other facilities include a **travel agent** on the corner of Victoria and Blackall streets (☎070/69 1264), and a **pharmacy** and **laundry** in Douglas Street. *Willie Nelson's T.I. Tours* meets incoming ferries for a ninety-minute tour of the island ($15 per person).

## Travel options

Though you generally need permission from the local council, it's possible that you may be privately invited to other islands in the Strait. While some are within outboard range – "one drum trips" – you're looking at $100 or more each way to fly to anywhere more distant. Far to the east, Murray Island (Mer) is enticing for its remoteness and importance in island history; to the north are Badu, centre of the Strait's burgeoning crayfish industry, and Saibai, a low deltaic island just 16km from the New Guinea border. This is the only place in Australia where you can see another country, and there *is* regular trading between the two – but New Guinea is not the place to be caught without a visa.

## travel details

### Trains

**Bundaberg** to: Cairns (4 weekly; 25hr); Mackay (5 weekly; 11hr); Proserpine (5 weekly; 13hr 30min); Rockhampton (5 weekly; 4hr 30min); Townsville (4 weekly; 17hr).

**Cairns** to: Bundaberg (4 weekly; 25 hr); Kuranda (1–2 daily; 1hr); Mackay (4 weekly; 13hr 20min); Proserpine (4 weekly; 11hr 30min); Rockhampton (4 weekly; 19hr); Townsville (4 weekly; 4hr 40min).

**Mackay** to: Bundaberg (5 weekly; 11hr); Cairns (4 weekly; 13hr 20min); Proserpine (5 weekly; 2hr 30min); Rockhampton (5 weekly; 5hr 30min); Townsville (4 weekly; 7hr).

**Rockhampton** to: Bundaberg (5 weekly; 4hr 30min); Cairns (4 weekly; 19hr); Longreach (2 weekly; 12hr 30min); Mackay (5 weekly; 5hr 30min); Proserpine (5 weekly; 7hr 40min); Townsville (4 weekly; 12hr).

**Townsville** to: Bundaberg (4 weekly; 17hr); Cairns (4 weekly; 4hr 40min); Mackay (4 weekly; 7hr); Mount Isa (2 weekly; 19hr); Proserpine (4 weekly; 4hr 40min); Rockhampton (4 weekly; 12hr).

### Buses

For more on services to **Far North Queensland** and **Cape York**, contact *Coral Coaches* (☎070/98

2600) or *White Car Coaches/Cape York Coaches* (☎070/51 9533).

**Airlie Beach** to: Bundaberg (6 daily; 11hr 30min); Cairns (6 daily; 9hr 45min); Mission Beach (6 daily; 8hr); Townsville (6 daily; 3hr 30min).

**Bundaberg** to: Airlie Beach (6 daily; 11hr 30min); Cairns (8 daily; 21hr); Mission Beach (3 daily; 19hr); Townsville (8 daily; 14hr 30min).

**Cairns** to: Airlie Beach (6 daily; 9hr 45min); Atherton Tablelands (1 daily; 1–3hr); Bundaberg (8 daily; 21hr); Cape Tribulation (3 weekly; 3hr); Cardwell (9 daily; 3hr); Chillagoe (3 weekly; 5hr); Cooktown (3 weekly; 6hr); Laura (June–Nov only 2 weekly; 5hr); Mission Beach (3 daily; 2hr); Port Douglas (2 daily; 1hr 30min); Townsville (9 daily; 5hr 20min); Weipa (June–Nov only 2 weekly; 15hr).

**Mackay** to: Airlie Beach (6 daily; 2hr); Cairns (8 daily; 12hr 45min); Dingo (1 daily; 9hr 30min); Emerald (1 daily; 6hr); Mission Beach (4 daily; 23hr); Townsville (9 daily; 5hr 15min).

**Rockhampton** to: Airlie Beach (6 daily; 6hr 10min); Anakie (3 weekly; 4hr 30min); Cairns (9 daily; 16hr); Longreach (3 weekly; 9hr); Mount Morgan (Mon–Sat 2–3 daily; 2hr); Townsville (9 daily; 9hr 30min); Yeppoon (3–9 daily; 1hr 30min).

**Townsville** to: Airlie Beach (6 daily; 3hr 30min); Bundaberg (9 daily; 15hr); Cairns (8 daily; 5hr 20min); Cardwell (8 daily; 2hr); Charters Towers (3 daily; 1hr 30min); Mount Isa (3 daily; 11hr 30min); Rockhampton (9 daily; 9hr 30min).

## Ferries

**Airlie Beach/Shute Harbour** to: Daydream Island (1–2 daily; 45min); Hamilton Island (1–3 daily; 1hr); Hook Island (1–2 daily; 1hr 30min); Lindeman Island (2 daily; 1hr 30min); South Molle Island (2 daily; 45min); Whitsunday Island (1 daily; 2hr).

**Cape York** to: Thursday Island (Mon–Fri 3 daily; 1hr 15min–2hr).

**Cardwell** to: Hinchinbrook Island (2 daily; 1–2hr).

**Mackay** to: Brampton Island (1 daily; 1hr).

**Mission Beach** to: Dunk Island (10 or more daily; 15min).

**Rosslyn Bay** to: Great Keppel Island (3 daily; 1hr).

**Townsville** to: Magnetic Island (10 or more daily; 45min).

**Weipa** to: Normanton (1 weekly; 24hr).

## Flights

For **Cape York services**, contact: *Ansett* (☎070/ 50 2211) for Cairns–Weipa; *Sunstate/Qantas*

(☎13 1313) for Thursday Island; *Flight West* (☎13 2392) to Cooktown, Coen, Lockhart River (Iron Range), Weipa and Bamaga; and *Aussie Airways* (☎070/53 3980) for Lizard Island, Cooktown and Cape York. There's also the **Peninsula Mail Run** to these destinations and others; it leaves Cairns before dawn, arriving at Horn Island (Thursday Island) about 11.30am. Contact *Cape York Air Services* (☎070/35 9399) to see if there's room for passengers.

**Cairns** to: Bamaga (1 daily; 2hr 45min); Bundaberg (3–5 daily; 3hr 30min); Lizard Island (1 daily; 1hr); Mackay (1–2 daily; 2hr 45min); Proserpine (6 weekly; 2hr); Rockhampton (1–3 daily; 3hr); Thursday Island (1–2 daily; 2hr); Townsville (2–4 daily; 1hr).

**Mackay** to: Brampton Island (3 daily; 20min); Cairns (1–2 daily; 2hr 45min); Townsville (1–2 daily; 1hr).

**Rockhampton** to: Cairns (1–3 daily; 3hr); Great Keppel Island (3 daily; 25min); Proserpine (6 weekly; 1 hr 40min); Townsville (1–3 daily; 1hr 50min).

**Townsville** to: Bundaberg (3–4 daily; 3hr 40min); Cairns (2–4 daily; 1hr); Dunk Island (1–2 daily; 45min); Mackay (1–2 daily; 1hr 30min); Proserpine (6 weekly; 50min); Rockhampton (1–3 daily; 1hr 50min).

# CHAPTER FIVE

# OUTBACK QUEENSLAND

**O**utback Queensland, the west of the state, is thinly populated by tenacious farming communities swinging precariously between famine and survival, and seems hard to reconcile with the lushness of the wet tropics. The population is concentrated in the relatively fertile highlands along the **Great Dividing Range**, running low behind the coast; on the far side, featureless plains slide over a hot horizon into the fringes of South Australia and the Northern Territory. Almost untouched by overseas visitors, the only places attracting tourists in any numbers are the **Stockman's Hall of Fame** at Longreach, the oases of **Carnarvon Gorge** in the Central Highlands, and the Gulf of Carpentaria's **Lawn Hill Gorge**. But elsewhere, the opportunities for exploration are immense: **precious stones, fossils, waterholes** and **Aboriginal art**, all in abundance.

Choosing where to go is often determined by the most convenient starting point. **Main roads** and **trains** head west from Brisbane, Rockhampton and Townsville; interstate **bus** services from Townsville are good, but otherwise the highways are only partially covered. If you're **driving**, your vehicle must be sound and you should carry essential spares, as even main centres often lack replacements.

Unless you're very experienced and well equipped, you'll find that western **summers** (Dec–April) effectively prohibit travel, with searing temperatures and violent flash floods that can isolate regions (especially in the Channel Country on the far side of the Great Dividing Range) for days or weeks on end. On the other hand, water revives dormant seeds and fast-growing desert flowers, which cover the ground to the horizon in good years. At other times, expect hot days and cool nights, plenty of dust and spartan landscapes.

## BRISBANE TO BIRDSVILLE AND COOPER CREEK

The thousand-plus-kilometre haul from the coast's comforts to Queensland's remote southwestern corner dumps you tired and dusty on the South Australian border, with some exciting routes down the Birdsville and Strzelecki tracks or through the hostile red barrier of the Simpson Desert yet to come (see *South Australia*). There are two ultimate targets: the outpost of **Birdsville**, with its annual horse races, and the Dig Tree at Nappa Merrie on **Cooper Creek**, monument to the Burke and Wills tragedy. The highway scenery is as bleak as you'd expect: after crossing the fertile disc of the **Darling Downs**, the country withers and dries, marooning communities such as Cunnamulla, Charleville, Quilpie in isolation and hardship. Detour north through Queensland's **Central Highlands**, however, and you'll find a landscape peppered with forested sandstone gorges and **Aboriginal sites** – worth the journey even if you don't go any further.

The most practical route into the area is the **Warrego Highway**, through Toowoomba, Roma and Charleville towards Quilpie. Roma is the jumping-off point into the highlands; from Quilpie there are largely unsurfaced roads to Birdsville and the Dig Tree. The *Westlander* **train** runs in this direction to Charleville, as do buses en route from Brisbane to Mount Isa.

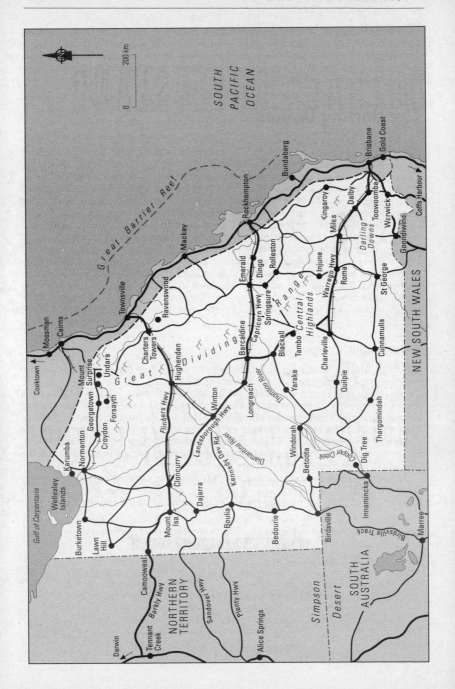

Parallel but further south, the **Cunningham Highway** crosses the Downs between Warwick and Goondiwindi (the limit of the **bus** services), then heads out to Cunnamulla. West of Cunnamulla you're heading across oil-, gas- and opal-fields towards the Dig Tree; 4WD is preferable **beyond the bitumen** and is probably essential for reaching the Dig Tree.

# The Darling Downs

The **Darling Downs** sprawl westwards from the back of the Great Dividing Range behind Brisbane down to the state's southern boundaries. The Warrego Highway climbs a steep escarpment to **Toowoomba** and the Northern Downs, while the Cunningham Highway cuts through Cunningham's Gap to **Warwick** and the south. Highway towns west of Toowoomba – Dalby, Miles and Chinchilla – are unadorned farming centres, and it's more the scenery along the Downs' fringes, particularly at the **Bunya Mountains** and **Girraween**, that warrants a visit. But even tearing across the Central Downs without stopping, the flat grasslands are clear evidence of Aboriginal custodial practices: created by controlled burning designed to clear woodland and increase grazing land for game, they perfectly suited European pastoral needs. The Downs are relatively fertile and stud farms, grazing, dairy, cotton, wool and cereals have all been successfully tried at one time or another. Even unwanted plants thrive. During the 1920s millions of acres were infested by **prickly pear**, a South American cactus finally brought to heel by the tiny *cactoblastis* moth in 1930 – a success story of biological control in Queensland to match the later failure of the introduction of the cane toad (see p.327).

## Toowoomba

**TOOWOOMBA** is a busy yet dull university city perched on the edge of a 600-metre escarpment, a promising setting it can't quite live up to. To be fair, though, Toowoomba's side streets and numerous gardens *are* pleasant, with stylish houses a reminder of the city's business wealth late last century, and there's a September **flower festival** during which the **tourist office** (Town Hall, 541 Ruthven St; Mon–Fri 8.30am–4pm; ☎076/32 1988) hands out lists of exhibition gardens to visit. At other times, the **Cobb and Co. Museum**, at 27 Lindsay Street (Mon–Fri 10am–4pm, Sat & Sun 1–4pm; $3), is the main attraction, recalling days when intrepid coaches bounced across the Outback delivering mail and passengers.

**Accommodation** prospects include the *Jolly Swagman Caravan Park* (47 Kitchener Rd; ☎076/32 8735), about 1km east of the centre; *Shannon's Range Motel*, on Tourist Road (☎076/32 3133; ④), near the plateau's edge with fine views; and the more central

*Burke and Wills Hotel*, 554 Ruthven Street (☎076/32 2433; ⑤). **Moving on** from Toowoomba, the **New England Highway** runs north to Kingaroy, plied by *Polleys Coaches* (☎074/82 2700 for times), and south to Warwick (*Crisp's*; ☎076/61 2566). Goondiwindi is three hours southwest with *McCafferty's* or *Greyhound*, and the Warrego Highway continues west across the Central Downs.

# Around Kingaroy: the Northern Downs

**KINGAROY** is a small town in the heart of peanut country, on the very fringes of the Downs, a couple of hours drive from Toowoomba and Dalby to the south or Gympie on the coast. A peanut silo towers over a mobile van specializing in peanut cuisine, and Kingaroy basks in the fame it owes to **Johannes Bjelke-Petersen**, who farmed nuts here before taking Queensland under his thumb in 1968. His wife Flo has made it on to postcards featuring her pumpkin scone recipe – but with a dam, bridge, road and sportsground named after him, not to mention his ominous catchphrase "Don't you worry about that" on everyone's lips, Joh is in no danger of obscurity. *Fairfield Caravan Park* on Walter Road (☎071/62 1808) is a friendly **place to stay**, while the *Club Hotel* (☎071/62 2204; ④) offers beds, cheapish meals and occasional live music. *Polleys* buses leave daily from Kingaroy to Gympie and Toowoomba, while drivers can take the Bunya Highway to Dalby.

## The Bunya Mountains

Southwest of Kingaroy, there's a sixty-kilometre section of twisting road along the crumpled **Bunya Mountains** before you reach Dalby (see p.383), back on the Warrego Highway. Among general greenery and clusters of unlikely flowers, you'll find enormous **bunya pines**, which once covered large tracts of southern Queensland. Every few years tribal boundaries were overlooked as clans gathered to gorge on the pine seeds; assisted by loops of vine, the Aborigines scaled the trees and threw down the cones, which gave up their thumb-sized nuts to be eaten raw or roasted. The indefatigable **Ludwig Leichhardt** (see p.826) witnessed such a feast in 1844 and persuaded the government to make the area an Aboriginal reserve, free from logging or settlement. The decree was revoked in 1860 and today the Bunya Mountains contain the last significant stand of pines.

NPWS sites (rangers' office ☎076/68 3127) along the road make for good **camping**, though in winter the mountains are generally several degrees cooler than the plains below. **Walking tracks** lead through the forest to orchid-covered lookouts and waterfalls.

# Warwick, Stanthorpe and the Southern Downs

Small and relaxed, **WARWICK** makes a fine base for exploring the Southern Downs. Services are centred around Grafton and Palmerin streets, where sandstone buildings date back to the time when Warwick graziers competed fiercely with Toowoomba's merchants to establish the Downs' premier settlement. The October **rodeo** is about the only time you might experience trouble finding **accommodation**: try *Warwick Tourist Park* (18 Palmer Ave, north of town on the highway; ☎076/61 8355; cabins ③), the *YHA* (6 Palmerin St; ☎076/61 3660; ②) or *Centre Point Motel* (32 Albion St; ☎076/61 3488; ④).

The **Condamine River**, unimpressive where it flows through town, is part of Australia's longest river system. Originating on the highlands east of Warwick, it joins the Murray/Darling before emptying into the ocean near Adelaide. At **Queen Mary Falls**, 43km from Warwick through Killarney, a tributary exits the forest in a plunge off the top of the plateau. A track climbs the cliff from the *Queen Mary Falls* **campsite** (☎076/64 7151); there's a kiosk, but no shops or transport to the falls.

Moving on, the **New England Highway** runs south to Stanthorpe then over the border to Tenterfield. *Crisp's* buses (1 daily) – and the Cunningham Highway – continue 200km west to **GOONDIWINDI** and the banks of the Macintyre River, which mark the state border. The town's **Bachelors and Spinsters Ball** in May is a night of chaos fuelled by unlimited beer, burgers and bands – you need to sport a tie and look smart; entry is $60.

## Stanthorpe and Girraween

Sixty kilometres south of Warwick, **STANTHORPE** is a quiet town known for the fruit stalls and small-scale **wineries** that throng the highway here. *Old Caves Winery* (New England Highway, just outside Stanthorpe; ☎076/81 1494), *Stone Ridge Vineyards* (Glen Aplin; ☎076/83 4211), *Sundown Valley* (Ballandean; ☎076/84 1226) and *Bungawarra* (Ballandean; ☎076/84 1128) are all making a name for themselves and are open daily – phone first to arrange a convenient time.

The surrounding hills are granite, exposed as fantastic monoliths at **GIRRAWEEN NATIONAL PARK**, 30km south down the New England Highway. There's an NPWS **campsite** here (☎076/84 5157) with showers, toilets – and the chance of seeing small, shy, active sugar gliders just after dark: listen for claws clattering over bark and then shine your torch overhead to catch a glowing set of eyes in the spotlight.

With more energy than skill, you can climb several of the giant hills with little risk, as long as rain hasn't made them dangerously slippery. **Castle Rock** (2hr return) is entertaining: initially a gentle uphill walk past lichen-covered boulders in the forest, the track follows a dotted white line into a fissure – look up and see loose rocks balanced above you – before emerging onto a thin ledge above the campsite. Follow this around to the north side and clamber to the very top for superb views of the Pyramids, Sphinx and Mount Norman poking rudely out of the woods. **The Sphinx** and **Turtle Rock** are another half an hour from the base of Castle; Sphinx is a broad pillar topped by a boulder, while Turtle's more conventional shape means a scramble, with no handholds on the final stretch. But pat yourself on the back if you make it to the top of the completely bald **South Pyramid** (2hr return) without resorting to hands and knees. Take a well-earned rest at the top and look across to unscaleable North Pyramid from below **Balancing Rock**, an oval boulder teetering so precariously on its narrow end that you can see underneath to where the support is surely only a few years away from collapse. **Mount Norman**, the park's 1267-metre apex, lies an hour beyond Castle Rock and should only be attempted by experienced climbers; check details with the ranger.

# The Central Downs and around

To break the unexciting journey west across the Downs from Toowoomba to Dalby, call in at **Jondaryan Woolshed** (daily 8.30am–4pm; $9; ☎076/92 2229), 3km south of the highway from Jondaryan and about 45km from Toowoomba, to look around the collection of old buildings – all relocated from elsewhere, with the exception of the shed itself. Exhibits worth a closer look include a document, dating from 1880, which itemizes some of the schoolmistress's tasks as splinting broken legs, wallpapering buildings to keep out snakes and being able to fight off swaggies trying to sleep in the schoolhouse. Make sure you catch one of the **tours** (10.30am, 1pm & 3pm), when the smithy is working and you can watch sheep shearers at work beneath the vast emptiness of the handcrafted woolshed roof, lit by a bare bulb – a very surreal tableau. There's also **accommodation** in shearers' quarters around the back, with a fire to cook on, hot showers, and the choice of a campsite or bitterly cold tin dorms. The next stops over the following 200km are **DALBY** and **MILES**, rural centres devoid of specific attractions but with the usual complement of van park and motel accommodation.

If you have your own transport, two undeveloped **national parks**, Expedition Range and Isla Gorge, north from Miles off the Leichhardt Highway, are worth investigating: you need to be self-sufficient, competent at orientation and bushwalking – and to contact the ranger first (PO Box 175, Taroom, QLD 4420; ☎076/ 27 3358). The massive **Expedition Range** is centred on Robinson Gorge, west of **Taroom** (itself 125km north of Miles) along a ninety-kilometre, 4WD-only track. Rock formations, Aboriginal art and waterfalls lie in tributary canyons, and a couple of the northern gorges are said to have some fine plant fossils, but, even with survey maps, navigation is tricky. Easier to reach, but with the same provisos on getting around, **Isla Gorge** is a small, triangular park right on the highway, 54km north of Taroom. Climb up to the lookout for orientation before descending down the dangerously loose slopes into a maze of offshoot gorges, where you could spend days exploring.

# Roma

**ROMA**, 140km west of Miles, was founded by settlers eager to occupy country made available by the opening up of the Darling Downs in 1862. Once considered for a rail junction to link the east coast with the Gulf of Carpentaria, the town thrives on farming, supplemented by the **oil** and **gas fields** which have been exploited intermittently since the turn of the century.

A typical inland town – tidy, with a slightly dated air lent by the iron decorations and wraparound balconies of the hotels, Roma has a reputation for cattle markets; one day-long event saw over $1.6 million change hands. And **Roma Vineyards** have been producing prize-winning wine since 1863 – if you want to buy, they're about a kilometre north of town on the Carnarvon Road, at Quintin Street (Mon–Fri 8am–5pm, Sat 9am–noon & 2–4pm; ☎076/22 1822).

**Accommodation** choices include *Motel Carnarvon* (18 Northern Rd; ☎076/22 1599; ④) and *Roma Central* (24 Bowen St; ☎076/22 1333; ④), which both offer standard motel beds, and the *Big Rig Caravan Park* (4 McDowell St; ☎076/22 2538), near the oil bore off the Bowen Road heading east, with welcome hot showers available during sub-zero winter nights. **Restaurants** in Roma are fairly basic, though *No Tie Required* (77 Quintin St) does good steaks, and the restaurant at the *School of Arts Hotel* (104 McDowall St) has decent pizzas. The **train station** is in Station Street (☎076/22 9411), and **buses** stop at the *BP* roadhouse in Bowen Street. Organize all tickets with *Maranoa Travel*, 71 Arthur Street (☎076/22 1416). Heading north, the **Carnarvon Developmental Road** (Quintin St from the town centre) has access to Mount Moffatt and Carnarvon Gorge (see below); otherwise the next stops west are Mitchell and Charleville.

# The Central Highlands

Queensland's **Central Highlands** consist of a broad band of weathered sandstone plateaux along the Great Dividing Range, with spectacularly sculpted sheer cliffs and pinnacles sectioned into a group of **national parks** around **Carnarvon Gorge**, 200km north of Roma. An extraordinarily primeval landscape, and one still visibly central to Aboriginal culture, poor pasture left the highlands relatively unscathed by European colonization. Within its boundaries, **Carnarvon National Park** includes the gorge, **Mount Moffatt** and the **Ka Ka Mundi/Salvator Rosa** regions further west; most people head for Carnarvon Gorge itself, as it's here that you'll find the main facilities, the highest concentration of Aboriginal art and arguably the best scenery. For the more adventurous, Mount Moffatt can usually be reached in a non-4WD vehicle; Ka Ka Mundi and Salvator Rosa are well off the beaten track, requiring advance preparation to explore.

Wherever you're going, expect at least 75km of dirt road – which will be closed after heavy rain (most likely Nov–May). Always carry extra rations in case you get stranded for a while and, unless you're desperately short of supplies, stay put in wet weather – you'll only churn the road up and make it harder for others to use. At all sections except Carnarvon Gorge, remember to allow for enough **fuel** to get you around the park once you've got there; it's impossible to drive directly between any of the park's four sections. Summer **temperatures** often reach 40°C, while winter nights will be below freezing; note that gathering firewood is prohibited inside the park, so stop on the way in or bring a gas stove. The **NPWS district headquarters** are in Emerald (PO Box 906, Emerald, QLD 4720; ☎079/82 4555); regional offices are detailed below.

## Mount Moffatt

**Mount Moffatt** is part of an open landscape of ridges and lightly wooded grassland to the west of Carnarvon Gorge. From Roma, it's a 248-km drive to the campsite via Injune; from Mitchell it's 220km direct (if you're approaching from the west). Although the park perimeter can often be reached in conventional vehicles, you'll need to rely on 4WD or walking to get around once there. Last fuel is at Injune (150km) or Mitchell. The access road ends at the **ranger station** (Mount Moffatt, Carnarvon National Park via Mitchell, QLD 4465; ☎076/26 3581) where you can collect your map of the area, plan any bushwalking and book a site. The only **facilities** are pit toilets, tank water (boil before drinking) and somewhere to pitch a tent; some sites are close to water-holes – handy if tanks run dry.

Mount Moffatt's attractions are spread out, and seeing them involves driving to an area and then walking around. More or less in the vicinity of the ranger station, **the Chimneys** area has some interesting pinnacles; alcoves in the rock face here once housed bark burial cylinders – look for the stencil of an entire body, arms spread-eagled. **Marlong Arch**, 6km west of the ranger station, is a sandstone arch decorated with handprints and engravings; 5km northeast, a trail leads to **Kookaburra Cave**, named after a weathered, bird-shaped hand stencil.

Elsewhere, consultation with the ranger might get you access to **Marlong Plain** (10km), a pretty expanse of blue grass surrounded by peaks, and **Kenniffs Cave** (20km), Mount Moffatt's richest site. The Kenniff brothers were cattle rustlers who used the cave as a hideout around 1900, but the cave had been used long before the Kenniffs' time; excavations in 1960 were the first to reveal that Aboriginal occupation of Australia predated the last Ice Age. Art in the cave includes stencils of feet, artefacts and a painted human figure. If you're still in doubt as to the area's significance in Highland Aboriginal culture, visit the **ochre mine** and **bora ring** at **West Branch**

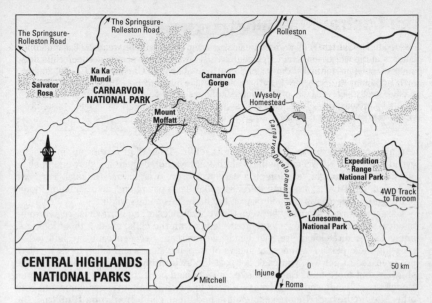

**Camp**, although in truth, there's little to see at either site today. Ochre was used ceremonially in stencilling and body-painting, and mines were a source of trade for tribes who controlled them, while a bora ground was central to male initiation ceremonies. For pure scenery, head east 15km north of the ranger station and follow the track about 7km to the **Mahogany Forest**, a stand of giant stringybark trees. **Mount Moffatt** itself and **Devils Canyon**, in the park's southeast, are more difficult to reach, requiring bushwalking skills, maps and fitness; views from the mountain are fair and the canyon's pink sandstone walls are lovely.

## Carnarvon Gorge

To reach the gorge **from Roma**, head 199km north along the Carnarvon Developmental Road, past Injune to Wyseby Homestead, then 45km west to the Lodge (see below) and campsite. During winter only, the Lodge's ration truck might be able to give you a lift from Roma for $60 (Tues, leaving Lodge at 6.30am and returning from Roma at 2pm), but this must be arranged in advance on ☎079/84 4503. Consider detouring 15km east, between Injune and Wyseby, to **LONESOME NATIONAL PARK**, where the ridges above Arcadia Valley provide grand views of both the Carnarvon and Expedition ranges.

**From Emerald**, it's 230km south along the Gregory/Dawson highways through Springsure and Rolleston; the last fuel on the way is at Injune (155km) and Rolleston. A **bus** from Emerald to Rolleston operates once weekly (Fri 7.35am; 1hr 35min), but still leaves 96km to hitch on to the gorge.

Driving in at dawn, the **Consuelo Tableland** stands out magnificently above dark forests as the road crosses the plains below, gradually rising to the foothills on the park's edge before terminating at the mouth of the gorge. Here, the **Oasis Lodge** (reservations: PO Box 475, Spring Hill, QLD 4004; ☎1800/074 260; ⑦) is surrounded by a neat lawn and respectably sized cycad palms; they've comfortable rooms, a bar

---

## CYCADS

**Cycads** are extremely slow-growing, fire-resistant plants with tough, palm-like fronds – relics of the age of dinosaurs. Female plants produce bright orange seed cones which attract emus to eat and thereby distribute the nuts within. Despite their being highly toxic to humans – almost every early explorer made themselves violently ill trying them – these seeds were a staple of highland Aborigines, who detoxified flour made from the nuts by prolonged washing. They also applied "fire-stick farming" techniques, encouraging groves to grow and seed at Carnarvon by annual burning.

---

and a **store** selling basics, fuel and LP gas refills. About 2km further on, in a wilder cycad grove, the NPWS **campsite** is almost always full, despite icy showers; book in advance. The **ranger station** (Carnarvon Gorge, Carnarvon National Park via Rolleston, QLD 4702; 7am–4pm; ☎079/84 4505) has a pay phone, an orientation model of the gorge, **free maps** and a library on the highlands and its wildlife.

Carnarvon Creek's journey between the vertical faces of the gorge has created some magical scenery, where low cloud often blends with the cliffs, making them look infinitely tall. A three-kilometre trail heads downstream between campsite and lodge, crossing the creek a few times by means of stepping stones and fallen trees; if you're not prepared to get wet, you can't get past the **swimming hole** here (as cold as the showers, but more fun). **Baloon Cave**, in woodland behind the lodge, shelters some stencil art of hands and boomerangs – easy to reach if unimpressive compared with other sites in the park. Before setting off to find them, climb **Boolimba Bluff** from the campsite for a rare chance to see the gorge system from above; a tiring climb but the views from the "Roof of Queensland" make the three-kilometre track worth the effort.

The day walk (19km return) **into the gorge** takes some beating, with intriguing side gorges: best are the **Moss Garden** (3.5km), a vibrant green carpet of liverworts and ferns lapping up a spring as it seeps through the rockface; the awesomely quiet, claustrophobic **Amphitheatre** (4km), open to the sky and reached by a long ladder from the gorge floor; and **Alijon Falls** (5km), concealing the enchanting **Wards Canyon**, where a remnant group of *angiopteris* ferns hang close to extinction in front of a second waterfall and gorge, complete with bats and blood-red river stones.

Carnarvon's two major **Aboriginal art sites** are the Gallery (5.6km) and Cathedral Cave (at the end of the trail, 9.3km from the campsite), both on the gorge track, though keep your eyes open and there's plenty more to be found. Despite containing Queensland's most documented Aboriginal art, understanding of the significance of the gorge's two galleries is limited to representational terms. A rockface covered with engravings of vulvas lends a pornographic air to **the Gallery**; other symbols include kangaroo, emu and human tracks. A long, wavy line might represent the rainbow serpent, shaper of many Aboriginal landscapes. Overlaying the engravings are hundreds of coloured stencils, made by placing an object against the wall and spraying it with a mixture of ochre and water held in the mouth. Always personal and striking, hands – including children's – form the bulk of the designs, but there are also artefacts, boomerangs and complex crosses formed by four arms. Goannas and mysterious net patterns at the near end of the wall have been painted with a stick. **Cathedral Cave** is larger with an even greater range of designs, including seashell pendant stencils – proof that trade networks reached from here to the sea – and engravings of animal tracks and nests of emu eggs.

Beyond Cathedral Cave, there's a **bush campsite** and a number of little-visited canyons to explore plus, with advice and permission from the rangers, the possibility of hiking right through to Mount Moffatt.

## Salvator Rosa and Ka Ka Mundi national parks

Trips to **Salvator Rosa** and **Ka Ka Mundi national parks** demand careful planning, 4WD and extra supplies, as they are notorious places to get stuck for a week or two after rain. Don't go without first contacting the NPWS at Emerald or PO Box 157, Springsure, QLD 4722 (☎079/84 1173 or 079/84 4086). Access is from the towns of Springsure (p.392) or Tambo, which have the last fuel. The parks are bisected by a series of north–south plateaus; east lies Ka Ka Mundi, west is Salvator Rosa. Spring water (don't rely on it) should be boiled and basic maps can be collected when you buy your camping permit from the nearest NPWS.

**Ka Ka Mundi National Park** is undeveloped and tent sites must be cleared by hand. The access road follows **Jacksons Creek** across brigalow scrub plains ringed by high sandstone escarpments to a campsite at **Bunbuncundoo Springs**, home to a dingo spirit in Aboriginal lore. Ferns suggest that rainforest once covered the area – and now lure birds and wallabies. The most interesting walking country lies west towards **Cave Hill** and the monolith of **Mount Mooloolong**, dreaded by Aborigines as the home of evil spirits; you'll need compass and topographic maps to avoid getting lost – and thick clothing to guard against getting spiked on undergrowth.

**Salvator Rosa National Park**'s two tent sites are near the banks of the **Nogoa River** and at **Belinda Springs**, an upwelling into a bed of ferns and reeds. The track ends at **Major Mitchell Springs**, overlooked by **Pyramids** and **Wubin Hill**, both recommended for walks; Wubin is riddled with tunnels, while the open woodland around the Pyramids reminded the explorer Mitchell of canvases by the Spanish painter Salvator Rosa – hence the park's name. The best walking is along the sandy bed of the Nogoa River, pocked with waterholes and with plenty of bird life along the banks.

# West to Birdsville and Cooper Creek

The last place of any size on the journey west from Roma is **CHARLEVILLE**, terminus for the **train** and a compact, busy town with broad streets, shaded pavements and some solid buildings constructed when the town was a droving centre and staging post for *Cobb & Co*. Also known for its contradictory weather, the town centre was inundated by five-metre-deep floodwaters from the **Warrego River** in 1990 – a dramatic end to years of drought. At the turn of the century, attempts were made to end another dry spell with **Stiger Vortex Guns**, giant conical contraptions supposed to seed rainclouds. During trials, two of the six guns exploded and the meteorologist who recommended them was run out of town; the only surviving one is outside the Scout Hut in Sturt Street, heading south towards Cunnamulla.

### BOOMERANGS

Curved throwing sticks are not unique to Australia – they were used in Egypt and Europe for scaring birds into nets – but Aborigines seem to be the only people to have made fully returning boomerangs, albeit only as children's toys. The non-returning types represented show how sophisticated boomerangs became as weapons. Some are massive with acute elbows, designed to cartwheel along the ground and bring down large game or break legs in fights, others are more refined for general use, including digging. Long, gently curved hunting boomerangs stencilled in pairs are not the same design repeated but portraits of two identical weapons with identical flight paths; if the first missed, the user could immediately throw the second, knowing how it would behave.

Rooms can be found at the *Charleville Motel* (☎076/54 1566; ⑤), on King Street, or head for *Cobb & Co. Caravan Park* (off Alfred St; ☎076/54 1053), a pleasant spot, with hot water, barbecues and a small shop (7am–8.30pm). All services are clustered around the Wills/Galatea junction on the Quilpie side of town; you can draw cash on bank cards at the *BP* service station opposite the post office. There's the usual coffee shops, or counter **meals** at the *Corones Hotel*, also across from the post office.

Around town, the NPWS complex and **fauna park** (Park St, on the Roma road; Mon–Fri 9am–4.30pm) sports some graceful yellow-footed rock wallabies; you'll have to head up towards Blackall in a 4WD to see them in the wild. **Anglers** can try their luck along the river where the prize catch is large Murray cod, though perch and fresh-water catfish are more likely. Get directions to prime fishing spots from the **Tourist Information Centre** (☎076/54 3057), on the corner of Wills and Edward streets. **Bus and train** bookings (Charleville lies on the Brisbane–Mount Isa bus route, with at least two services daily in each direction, and also on the Quilpie–Brisbane train line, with two trains a week) can be made with *Western Travel Service*, 37 Wills Street (☎076/54 1260).

## Around Cunnamulla and Quilpie

From Charleville, you can either continue west to Quilpie and routes to Birdsville or the Dig Tree (see below), or detour south to **CUNNAMULLA**, a nondescript handful of service stations and motels 200km south of Charleville on the Mitchell Highway. West towards Thargomindah are the **Yowah Opal Fields**, 86km away, where shallow deposits yield much-sought-after Yowah Nuts – opalized ironstone nodules. You'll need a Miner's Right ($14.50 from the Mining Office in Cunnamulla) to start your own diggings. Beware of unfenced vertical shafts, which are practically invisible until you're on your way down: always look where you're going and never step backwards. Yowah has bore water, fuel and a **caravan park** (☎076/55 4953; cabins ②).

**QUILPIE** is a dusty rail and farming community 200km west of Charleville; ameni-ties include a baker, butcher, fuel depot, caravan park and the *Imperial Hotel* (☎076/56 1300; ⑤) which can supply basic beds above the bar or quieter units out the back. The hotel serves evening meals between 6pm and 7.30pm, or there are a couple of cafés in town which close at about 5.30pm.

## Quilpie to the Dig Tree

A **map** is essential if you plan to drive from Quilpie to the Dig Tree at Nappa Merrie, 50km from Innamincka in South Australia, as there are few signposts. Last **fuel** on the 490-kilometre, largely unsealed, route lies an hour west of Quilpie at **EROMANGA**. From here you're heading across the stony plains above huge gas and oil reserves of the Cooper Basin, past the cattle stations of Durham Downs and Karmona, lonely "nodding donkeys" and unaccountably healthy-looking droughtmaster cattle, to the Dig Tree on **Cooper Creek**.

The site of Burke and Wills' stockade (see box opposite), **Depot Camp 65**, is a beautiful shaded river bank alive with pelicans and parrots, and it's hard to believe that anyone could have starved to death nearby. **The Dig Tree** is still standing and protected by a walkway, but the three original blaze marks reading "BLXV, DIG 3FT NW, DEC 6 60-APR 21 61" have been cemented over to keep the tree alive. Burke's face was carved into the tree on the right by John Dickins in 1898, and is still clearly visible.

Pressing on, you'll be relieved to know that Innamincka's pub at the top of the **Strzelecki Track** in South Australia (see p.634), is only 50km away; if you've made it this far you shouldn't have much trouble with the road.

## THE BURKE AND WILLS SAGA

In 1860, the government of Victoria, then Australia's richest state, decided to sponsor a lavish expedition to make the first south–north crossing of the continent to the Gulf of Carpentaria. Eighteen men, twenty camels (shipped, along with their handlers, from Asia) and over twenty tons of provisions started out from Melbourne in August, led by **Robert O'Hara Burke** and **William John Wills**. Problems had already begun by the time the party reached **Cooper Creek** in December: Burke had impatiently left the bulk of the expedition and supplies lagging behind and raced ahead with a handful of men to establish a base camp on Cooper Creek. Having built a stockade, Burke and Wills started north, along with two other members of their team (Gray and King), six camels, a couple of horses and food for three months. Four men remained at camp, led by William Brahe, waiting for the rest of the expedition to catch up. In fact, most of the supplies and camels were dithering halfway between Cooper Creek and Melbourne, unsure of what to do next.

As Burke and Wills failed to keep a regular diary, few details of the "rush to the Gulf" are known. They were seen by Kalkadoon Aborigines following the Corella River into the Gulf, where they found that vast salt marshes lay between them and the sea. Disappointed, they left the banks of the Bynoe (near present-day Normanton) on 11 February 1861 and headed back south. Their progress slowed by the wet season, they killed and ate the pack animals as their food ran out. Gray died after being beaten by Burke for stealing flour; remorse was heightened when they staggered into the Cooper Creek stockade on 21 April to find that, having already waited an extra month for them to return, Brahe had decamped that morning. Too weak to follow him, they found supplies buried under a tree marked "Dig", but failed to change the sign when they moved on, which meant that when the first rescue teams arrived on the scene, they assumed the explorers had never returned from the Gulf. Trying to walk south, the three reached the Innamincka area, where Aborigines fed them fish and nardoo seeds, but by the time a rescue party tracked them down in September only King was still alive.

# Quilpie to Birdsville

The long road from Quilpie to Birdsville is a relatively easy journey which you can manage without 4WD in good conditions, though depth markers along the road give an idea of how saturated this **Channel Country** becomes after rain. First stop is **WINDORAH**, a limp settlement of a dozen buildings offering fuel, a post office and an amazingly well-provisioned store; the town last made the news when an errant crocodile was dragged out of the creek and there was talk of having it mounted above the hotel bar. Even without the croc, the *Western Star* **hotel** (☎076/56 3166; rooms ⑤) is hard to pass by for a cold drink and a look at its collection of old photos; they also might let you **camp** here.

Ruins of the **John Costello hotel** lie 80km further on towards Betoota, opposite a windmill. Tired of riding 30km every morning to round up his stockmen from the bar, the manager of a nearby station had the local liquor licence transferred from the *JC* to his homestead in the 1950s. He pulled the roof off the hotel for good measure, and there's now little left beyond the foundations and some posts.

**BETOOTA**, 220km from Windorah, has fuel and a cramped, century-old adobe hotel with local ringers for company, the bar literally stocked to the roof with cobweb-covered bottles of spirits. They don't provide beds but there's plenty of room to pitch a tent along the river banks behind. Beyond Betoota the country turns into a rocky, silent plain, with circling crows and wedge-tailed eagles the only signs of life, and it's hard to see what the occasional fenceline or grid is keeping apart. Look for red sand dunes, distant outposts of the Simpson Desert. Driving can be hazardous here, and every time you pass a wreck or shredded tyre you hope you're not next; with care (and luck), however, the Diamantina River and Birdsville are three hours away.

## Birdsville and beyond

Famous for the **horse races** on the first weekend in September when thousands of beer-swilling spectators pack out the dusty little settlement, at other times **BIRDSVILLE** promises to be something of an anticlimax, a dilapidated handful of buildings where only the hotel and fuel stations seem to be doing business. But unless you've flown in, you'll probably be very glad simply to have arrived intact. The **caravan park** is just a bulldozed patch of scrub, with a new amenities block and disconcerting signs claiming no responsibility for vehicles blown away by duststorms. If you can live without facilities, camp along the creek or artesian overflow where huge flocks of raucous corellas seem to justify the township's name, although in fact it's a corruption of "Burt's Ville", after the first storekeeper. Given the lack of alternatives, don't be surprised to find the **hotel accommodation** at the *Birdsville Pub* (☎076/56 3244; ⑤) full; during race weekend, all beds are reserved for the bar staff anyway, so you have to camp. **Provisions** and snacks can be bought from the general store; if you're organizing your own food, prepare the next day's meals after dark when the flies have settled down. You owe yourself at least one drink in the pub; order by 5.30pm if you want a full **evening meal** – the "$15, seven-course takeaway" is a pie and a six-pack.

The **old hospital** across the street, now just a stone shell, operated as the original Australian Inland Mission between 1923 and 1927. On the other side of the **airstrip** (conveniently laid out next to the hotel) is the pale blue **post office** (*Commonwealth Bank*) and **police station** (☎076/56 3220), where you should check on the state of the various outback tracks if you're planning to use them. **Monuments** at the airstrip name the various expeditions that have passed through the area, including the Simpson Desert traverse by Ted Coulson and an Aborigine named Peter in 1936. See if someone (the hotel makes a good starting point) can guide you to another tree blazed by Burke and Wills across the Diamantina, otherwise hard to locate among the scrub.

**Around Birdsville** there's a stand of slow-growing, old and very rare **Waddi trees**, 9km north on the Bedourie road. They're about five metres tall and resemble sparse conifers wrapped in prickly feather boas with warped, circular seed pods, and the wind blowing through the needles makes an eerie noise like the roar of a distant fire. For something more dramatic, head out 41km to **Big Red** at the start of the Simpson Desert crossing; Simpson's largest dune may seem unimpressive from below, but your opinion will change radically if you walk up or try to plant a 4WD on the top. Conventional vehicles can often reach the base (check with the police before setting off) and it's worth it to see the dunes, flood plains and stony gibber country on the way.

North of Birdsville, Mount Isa (see p.404) is a lonely 700km distant, with fuel available every 200km or so. Expeditions heading west across the Simpson Desert to Dalhousie Springs need a **Desert Parks Pass** ($50) from the Birdsville store; the NPWS office on Graham Street (☎076/56 3249) provides general information only. Feasible in any vehicle during a dry winter, the 520-kilometre **Birdsville Track** heads from the racecourse down to Marree in South Australia; see pages 635–637 for details of this and the Simpson Desert crossing.

# ROCKHAMPTON TO WINTON

Heading west from Rockhampton, the **Capricorn Highway** provides an alternative route to Mount Isa, or simply a break from the inevitability of a trip along the coast. The main attractions in this central section of inland Queensland are the sandstone and forest scenery of the **Blackdown Tablelands**, hunting **sapphires** on the Gemfields, and the **Stockman's Hall of Fame** at Longreach; none requiring more than a couple of days' detour from Rockhampton. There's also access from Emerald to Carnarvon Gorge and the Central Highlands. **Historically**, the area is rich: *Qantas*, the Labor

Party and Waltzing Matilda originated here, and the district's fossil record includes dramatic dinosaur footprints at **Lark Quarry**. **Buses** travel as far as Winton, and the **train** connects Rockhampton to Longreach.

# Into the Northern Highlands

As you move inland the coastal humidity is left behind and the gently undulating landscape becomes baked instead of steamed. Passing the white rubble moonscape atop **Mount Hay**, where you could stay at the van park and fossick for agates, the road loops over low hills before adopting a pattern that becomes ever more familiar: straight for miles and then an unexpected bend. Bottle trees, with their bulbous, thick grey trunks and spindly, thinly leaved branches, herald the drier climate. Gradually, the deep blue platform of the **Blackdown Tablelands** emerges from the horizon, and, by the time you reach **DINGO**, dominates the landscape. Dingo is somewhere to stock up: there's a hotel, van park and a bronze monument to the town's namesake. Heading north towards Mackay, the Dingo–Mount Flora road is direct but uninteresting, skirting the eastern edge of the Bowen Basin's coal mines through fields of sunflowers and corn.

## The Blackdown Tablelands

Floating 600m above the heat haze, the **Blackdown Tablelands'** gum forests, waterfalls and escarpments are a delight, a scenic refuge from the dry, flat lands below. A corrugated, unsealed twenty-kilometre **access road** is signposted on the highway 11km from Dingo, but there's no public transport into the park. Campsite bookings are through the NPWS in Rockhampton or Emerald, or from the local **ranger** (☎079/86 1964); outside school holidays you could well have the place to yourself.

The track runs flat through open scrub to the base of the range; the climb is steep, twisting and slippery as "pea gravel" puts in an appearance. Views over a haze of eucalypt woodland are generally blocked by the thicker forest at the top of the plateau, but at **Horseshoe Lookout** there's a fabulous view north and, after rain, **Two Mile Falls** rockets over the edge of the cliffs. From here the road widens and runs past Mimosa Creek, dead-ending at the **Rainbow Falls** car park.

The **Mimosa Creek campground** is excellent, shaded by massive stringybark trees with tank water, tables, toilets, fire pits and a creek to bathe in. At night the air fills with the sharp scent of woodsmoke and the occasional dingo howls in the distance; with a torch, you might see **greater gliders** or the more active brushtail possum. Watch out for crows that raid unattended tables, tents and cars for *anything*, edible or not. Temperatures can reach 40°C on summer days, and drop below zero on winter nights.

**Walks** in the park include the short trip to **Officers Pocket**, a moist amphitheatre of ferns and palms with the facing cliffs picked out yellow and white in the late afternoon; a **circuit track** along Mimosa creek, past remains of cattle pens and stock huts, to some beautifully clear **ochre stencils** made by Gungaloo Aborigines a century ago; and the park's finest scenery at **Rainbow Falls**, 6km past the campsite. At its glorious best around dawn, this track leads from the car park through an eerie gum forest to the top of the gorge, then follows around to where the creek seeps down steps into the greenery. From the edge you can spy on birds in the rainforest beneath; explosive thumps from below signal rock wallabies tearing across ledges hardly big enough for a mouse. A long staircase descends into a cool world of spring-fed gardens, ending on a large shelf about halfway into the gorge where Rainbow Falls sprays from above into a wide, clear pool. Pretty it may be, but the water's paralysingly cold; for a warmer dip, climb back up the stairs and follow the path to the top of the falls, where the creek runs in full sun and the bed has handy, bath-sized holes to sit in.

Bushwalkers might also head to **Stoney Creek Falls**, although the ten-kilometre round trip off a track between Mimosa Creek and Rainbow Falls, through tinder dry woodland to magnificent views from the top of the falls, follows a frequently vague path, and you'll need instructions from the ranger first(☎079/86 1964).

# Emerald and around

The road west of Dingo crosses the lower reaches of the **Bowen Basin coalfields** at **BLACKWATER**, then moves into **cotton country**, signalled by fluffy white tailings along the roadside around **YAMALA**, where there's a cotton **gin** to tour during the picking season (tour times ☎079/82 3888).

**EMERALD** is a misleadingly named place. This close to the Gemfield towns of Sapphire and Rubyvale, you'd think its origins could be traced to precious stones, but in fact the area was named Emerald Downs by a surveyor who saw its rich green after heavy rains. Ironically, as you'll realize after stopping for a drink every ten minutes, a drier, hotter town would be hard to imagine. Still, as a junction for the mid-west's produce, with roads north to Mackay and south to the Central Highlands, Emerald is a busy place at the heart of a surprisingly productive district: the rich soil supports citrus trees, which attract hundreds of fruit-pickers each season.

Most essential services are in **Clermont Street**, where the main feature is the pristine station, built in 1901 and restored in 1986. One road back from this is Egerton Street, where there are **fossil tree trunks** on the lawn outside the Town Hall; thought to be over a million years old, they're preserved in great detail, right down to the texture of the bark. The **tourist information** booth (Mon–Fri 9am–4pm; ☎079/82 4142) has leaflets on local attractions. **Accommodation** is in the hotels or van parks in Opal Street, although during the April harvest there may be very little room available. Try *Motel 707* (17 Ruby St; ☎079/82 1707; ④), with air-conditioned units, a bar in reception and room meals available; *Meteor Motel* (corner of Opal and Egerton streets; ☎079/82 1166; ④), which has a pool and a good steak restaurant; or *Karinya Van Park* (6 Opal St; ☎079/82 2268; cabins ②–③), which is pretty central and often has a spare site for overnighters.

### South to Springsure

You can reach **Carnarvon Gorge** (see p.385) from Emerald, 200km or so south through the town of **SPRINGSURE**, which is set below the dramatic orange cliffs of **Mount Zamia**. From the moment this district was settled, Aborigines put up a strong resistance. At **Rainworth Fort** ($2; call first for hours on ☎079/84 1674) settlers built a squat stockade of basalt blocks and corrugated iron for protection after "**the Wills Massacre**" when, on 17 October 1861, Aboriginal forces stormed Cullin-la-ringo station and killed nineteen people in apparent retaliation for the slaughter of a dozen Aborigines by a local squatter. White response was savage, spurred on by vigilantes and a contingent of Native Troopers; newspapers reported that "a great massacre has been made among the blacks of the Nogoa". The fort and later structures of **Cairdbeign School and Homestead** are 10km southwest of Springsure and house a few relics of the period.

### The Bowen Basin

North of Emerald, the **Bowen Basin** is largely flat, rough country patterned by acres of giant sunflowers against a horizon of low hills. **Coal mining** is the mainstay, contributing coal trains and tailing mounds to the scenery. Well-equipped settlements provide shops and housing for miners, but lack character; many residents spend their spare time in Mackay or Rockhampton.

The road through the basin to Mackay (covered by a daily **bus**) runs first to **CLERMONT**, originally a gold-mining town now given over to pastoral pursuits and coal industries. There's a free **mine tour** every Tuesday (details from ☎079/83 1133). After Clermont, the highway passes **Wolf Fang Peak** – famous for its spiders, views and wallabies – on the way to **MORANBAH**, a confusing system of one-way streets lined with trees and a not-so-obvious town centre, which also acts as base for weekly tours to local mines; ☎079/41 7254 for details.

# The Gemfields

The country an hour west of Emerald is sparse and always hot, the scrub interrupted only by ugly cleared patches covered in rubble from mining operations. This wasteland masks one of the richest **sapphire fields** in the world and, with hard work, the chances of finding some are good – though you're unlikely to get rich.

## GEM MINING

Gems were first discovered in 1870 near **Anakie** but until Thai buyers came onto the scene a century later operations were low-key, and even today there are still solo fossickers making a living from their claims. The most common gems are **zircons, sapphires** and **rubies**: formed by prehistoric volcanic actions and later dispersed along waterways and covered by sediment, they lie in ancient riverbeds and can be identified by a layer of gem-bearing gravel above a clay base. This layer can be up to fifteen metres down, so gullies and dry rivers, where nature has already done some of the excavation for you, are good places to start.

Looking for surface gems, or **specking**, is best after rain, when a trained eye can see the stones sparkle in the mud. It's erratic but certainly easier than the alternative – **fossicking** – which requires a pick, shovel, sieve, washtub full of water and a canvas sack before starting (this gear can be rented at all the fields). Cut and polished, zircons are pale yellow, sapphires pale green to deep blue, and rubies are of a light pink hue here, but when they're covered in mud it's hard to tell them from gravel, which is where the washing comes in: wet gems glitter like fragments of coloured glass.

You have to be extremely enthusiastic to spend a summer on the fields; the mercury climbs steadily to 42°C, topsoil erodes and everything becomes filmed in dust. The first rains bring floods as the sunbaked ground sheds water, and if you're here then you'll be treated to the sight of locals specking in the rain, dressed in *Akubra*s and *Drizabone*s and shuffling around like mobile mushrooms. Conditions are best as soon after the wet season as possible (around May), when the ground is soft and fresh pickings have been uncovered – not surprisingly, this is also the busiest period.

If this all seems like too much hard work, try a **Gem Park** such as *Pat's* (see below), where they've done all the digging for you and supply all the necessary gear for about $5. All you have to do is sieve the wash, flip it onto the canvas and check it for stones. There's an art to sieving and flipping, but you're pretty sure to find something, since park owners lace the wash with rejects. Gem parks will also value and cut stones for you. Another break from the business end of a pick is to pay $5, take a **mine tour** and see if the professionals fare any better. In some ways they do – the chilled air five metres down is wonderful – but the main difference is one of scale rather than method or intent.

You need a **fossicker's licence**, available from shops and gem parks, which allows digging in areas set aside for the purpose or on no man's land. The $5 license is valid for two months, and gives you no rights at all other than to keep what you find and to camp at fossick grounds. To stake a claim and keep others away you need a **Miner's Right** from the field officer in Emerald (Department of Minerals and Energy, Clerana Centre, Clermont St; ☎079/82 4011); this also carries obligations to restore the land to its original state and maintain it for two years after quitting the site.

The easiest fields to reach are the **Anakie Fields**, with facilities at Anakie, Sapphire and Rubyvale. Anakie township is off the highway about 45km from Emerald; Sapphire is 9km north of Anakie, and Rubyvale a further 8km. Though well worked, the *Anakie Fields* are the best place for the newcomer to pick up tips; old hands proceed directly to **the Willows**, 27km west of Anakie.

**ANAKIE** ("permanent water") has no gemfields itself, but gave its name to those at Sapphire and Rubyvale. Unusually pretty, it comprises a van park with hot showers by the waterhole, backing onto a pub, post office and store. The **information centre** near the highway has fuel, licences, rough maps and advice.

In contrast, the country around **SAPPHIRE** looks like a war zone. You'll find a post office-cum-store and houses scattered along the road and an elbow of Retreat Creek, where the first gems were found. *Sunrise Cabins* (☎079/85 4281; ②) are across the road from the medical centre, in sight of the creek. Towards Rubyvale is *Pat's Gem Park* and opposite the *Big Spanner* mechanic is *Gemini Campsite* (☎079/85 4280) – a store, ice-cold pool, clean shower block and barbecue area all count for a lot out here, and the owner regularly feeds about fifty rainbow lorikeets.

**RUBYVALE** has several shops, fuel and a few mines to look around: tour groups tend to visit *Miners Heritage*, but cheaper and equally interesting is *Bobby Dazzler* on the hill as you approach town. The ground beneath each new development here has to be mined first; outdoor tennis courts and the surfaced road were only built after years of wrangling over whether the ground had given up all its treasures. Rubyvale also seems to be the place to pick up on apocryphal stories, like the one about the largest star sapphire ever found being used as a doorstop – and you'll hear plenty more during the annual **August Gemfest**.

The **Willows Gemfield** is still in the making, part mining camp, part township. The immaculate *Willows Caravan Park* (☎079/85 5124) is well shaded, has wangled a liquor licence and acts as a bank agent. The gemfields are just down the track from the park.

# Beyond the Range to Winton

Vistas from the rounded sandstone boulders at the top of the Great Dividing Range west of Emerald reveal terrain to test a spirit level's accuracy. Below, rivers flow to the Gulf of Carpentaria or towards the great dry lakes of South Australia, while unsealed roads run north to Clermont and south to Tambo and Charleville. You'll notice an increase in temperature; flies appear from nowhere, tumbleweeds pile up on fences and trees never seem closer than the horizon. In terms of numbers, sheep are the dominant mammal in these parts, though there are some cattle and even a few people out there.

## Barcaldine and Blackall

The only place of any size on the way to Longreach is **BARCALDINE**, 300km from Emerald, an unassuming grid of quiet streets belying an important niche in Australian history. It was near here during the 1885 drought that geologists first tapped Queensland's artesian water, revolutionizing Outback development. The town further secured its place in history during the 1891 **shearing strike** which, though a failure itself, ultimately led to the formation of the Labor Party. On the highway, outside the station which became the focus of the dispute, is a granite monument – sculpted to resemble the tips of a pair of shears – to shearers arrested during the strike. Right next to it, the sagging silver trunk of the **Tree of Knowledge** struggles gamely to improve on its 155 years; sadly, this ghost gum, where shearers rallied a century ago, looks to be on the way out. Now nearly completed, the **Workers' Heritage Museum** (daily 9am–5pm; admission by donation) is unmissable underneath a yellow and blue marquee in Ash

Street. Concentrating on the history of the workers' movement after the shearers' strike, videos, artefacts and plenty of sepia-tinted photos cover themes including Outback women and Aboriginal stockmen, the museum rounds out exhibits at Longreach's Stockman's Hall of Fame (see below).

Across the road from the Tree of Knowledge, the shaded verandahs of the *Artesian Hotel* provide a reminder of the value of a reliable watering hole. **Accommodation** options are limited to the *Barcaldine Motel* (☎076/51 1244; ④) or *Homestead Van Park* (☎076/51 1308), both in Box Street, off the highway on the Longreach side. Banks and other services are also in Box Street.

Two hours south of Barcaldine on the Landsborough Highway, a sign at **BLACKALL** welcomes you to Merino Country; it was near here in 1892 that Jackie Howe fleeced a record 321 sheep in under eight hours, using hand shears; it took decades to better his score. The town sits on the banks of the usually feeble, often dry (and occasionally 5m deep), Barcoo River; an 800-metre-deep artesian bore provides a more reliable water source. While here, you could visit the steam-driven **woolscour**, built in 1908 and operational for seventy years (contact the motel – details below – for access; $2.50) or track down the famous **black stump**, a surveying point used in pinpointing Queensland's borders last century and now the butt of many jokes. Near Blackall, **Idalia National Park** preserves Queensland's last population of yellow-footed rock wallabies in the wild; access details, and long-distance **bus** tickets, are available from *Blackall Travel* (☎076/57 4422).

At *Blackall Caravan Park* (turn at the *Caltex* garage) you can yarn with other travellers around a huge campfire and be fed pot roasts, billy tea and damper for an extra fee. **Motel** accommodation is available at the *Blackall Motel* (☎076/57 4611; ④), behind the *BP* service station at the Barcaldine end of town. **Shamrock Street** has a few places to **eat**, banks, and any supplies you'll need. Entertainment is provided by the hotels, which range from grand and comfortable (*Tattersalls*) to just plain tatty (*Barcoo*).

## Longreach and the Stockman's Hall of Fame

**LONGREACH**, 110km west of Barcaldine, is different from other western towns: it's doing more than surviving. This is mainly down to the Stockman's Hall of Fame, an ambitious museum which pulls in bus-loads of tourists, but even before this Longreach was an enterprising settlement with a firm place in history. Ever since the discovery of artesian water it has been a stronghold of cattle- and sheep-farming, but really took off as the original headquarters of *Qantas* – their first hangar still stands at the airport.

**The Stockman's Hall of Fame** (daily 9am–5pm; $15) is a masterpiece, not just in architectural design – a blend of aircraft hangar and cathedral – but in being an encyclopedia of the Outback right in its heart; since opening in 1988 its success has silenced critics who underestimated the Outback's widespread appeal. A minor complaint might be that the displays themselves are fairly ordinary, but once you're here the Hall of Fame has achieved its dual aim of bringing people out west and provid-

---

**QANTAS**

There's always been contention between Longreach and Winton as to which was the birthplace of **Qantas** – the *Queensland and Northern Territories Air Service* – but the first joy-flights and taxi service flew from Longreach in 1921, pioneered by Hudson Fysh and Paul McGuiness. Their idea – that an airline could play an important role by carrying mail and passengers, dropping supplies to remote districts and providing an emergency link into the Outback – inspired other projects like the Flying Doctor Service. *Qantas* stayed at Longreach until 1945, by which time both the company and its aeroplanes had outgrown the town.

ing background to the development of a vast portion of Australia. *Greyhound Coaches* cover the couple of kilometres to the Hall of Fame from Eagle Street, or you can walk.

Inside, the Outback is romanced through videos, slide shows, photographs and exhibits – but this is not just another local museum where anything more than five years old is shown for its own sake. History starts in the Dreamtime and moves on, via a directory of those on the First Fleet, to early explorers and pioneers (including a large section on women in the Outback), ending with personal accounts of life in the bush. Among more day-to-day features are some offbeat selections; if you thought barbed wire was just something to get stuck on, then check out the collection here, with over a hundred types – from the old hook design to modern razor wire. You'd be hard pushed not to find something of interest, be it boxing kangaroos, rodeos, bark huts or tall stories. The library and exhibitions by Outback artists (displayed in the art gallery) are also worth a browse.

Other local activities include visiting the **Longreach School of Distance Education** (tours at 9am, 9.30am & 10am on school days), a chance to see how three hundred pupils in this remote area are taught via radio; or **cruises** round waterways. **Tours** of nearby sheep stations offer an insight into Outback life, but the cost can be outrageous in relation to the time spent on the station – check how long is spent in transit. Better value are **homestead stays**, where you can participate in farm life or simply laze around: ask at Longreach's tourist office for details.

## Practicalities

Longreach is a more active version of Barcaldine, with plenty of spruce old buildings. Eagle Street, where the bus sets down, is the main drag and here you'll find hotels, cafés, **banks**, a cinema and the first well-stocked supermarket in a long while. Longreach's **tourist office** (☎076/58 3555) is in the replica *Qantas* office here on the corner of Duck Street. Of the half-dozen **hotels**, try the *Lyceum* for counter food, or *Starlight's* for nightlife. If you still have unbent tent pegs, *Gunnadoo* (☎076/58 1781), looking across to the Hall of Fame, and *Longreach Van Park* (☎076/58 1770) in Ibis Street, are the **campsites**. *Longreach Swaggies* (81 Wompoo St; ☎076/58 3777; ②) is a friendly but very run-down **hostel**; you can indulge in **motel** comforts at the *Longreach Motel* (127 Eagle St; ☎076/58 1996; ⑤).

# Winton and beyond

Scenery doesn't come blander than on the Longreach–Winton stretch: your only worry as a driver is to keep your foot down and stay awake as the car cruises the empty Mitchell Plains. After 125km there's a turn-off to **Lorraine Station** (☎076/57 1693; ②–④), a working sheep property open to guests from April to November. Get up before sunrise for an early-morning muster on horseback, or tour the station in a four-wheel drive; birdwatching, swimming and lounging at the bar are other possibilities.

**WINTON** is a real frontier town: dust devils blow tumbleweeds down the streets, and the main change over the last fifty years is that four-wheel drives have superseded the horse as a means of getting around. As an important transport junction and Queensland's largest cattle-trucking depot, there's a constant stream of road trains rumbling through – and conversations overheard in hotels tend to revolve around problems of stock management. Winton has its share of history, too: *Qantas* held its first meeting here in 1920 and **Waltzing Matilda**, that evergreen ballad, premiered at the *North Gregory Hotel* (see box for more). The surrounding countryside is an eerie world of eroded **jump-ups** – flat-topped hills layered in orange, grey and red dust – complete with **opal deposits** at Opalton and a stunning set of **dinosaur footprints** at Lark Quarry.

### WALTZING MATILDA

In April 1995, Winton celebrated the centenary of the first public performance of Banjo Patterson's ballad **Waltzing Matilda** at the *North Gregory Hotel*, and stirred a century of gossip and rumour. Legend has it that Patterson was told the tale of a sheep-rustling swagman by Christina MacPherson, while staying with her family at nearby Dagwood Station. Christina wrote the music to the ballad, a collaboration which so incensed Patterson's fiancée, Sarah Riley, that she broke off their engagement. While a straight-forward "translation" of the poem is easy enough – "Waltzing Matilda" was contemporary slang for tramping (carrying a bedroll or swag from place to place), "jumbuck" for a sheep, and "squatters" refers to landowners – there is some contention as to what the poem actually describes. The most obvious interpretation is of a poor tramp, hounded to death by the law, but first drafts of the poem suggest that Patterson – generally known as a romantic rather than social commentator – originally wrote the piece about the arrest of a union leader during the shearers' strike, and later toned it down. Either version would account for the popularity of the poem, which was once proposed as the national anthem: Australians readily identify with an underdog who dares to confront the system.

All **services** (bank, post office and fuel station with EFTPOS and cash-withdrawal facilities) are around **Elderslie Street**; the *Gift and Gem Centre* (☎076/57 1296) here doubles as an **information office** and sorts out **bus** tickets and **tours** to local sights – check with them about road conditions before visiting Opalton or Lark Quarry. The best **accommodation** prospects are at the *Matilda Caravan Park* (43 Chirnside St; ☎076/57 1607), or the nearby *Matilda Motel* (☎076/57 1433; ⑤). If there's a film on, treat yourself to a session in the outdoor **cinema** next to the *Gem Centre*; the café here stays open after dark.

Further down Elderslie Street, opposite a tepid swimming pool and bronze statue of the jolly swagman, the **Qantilda Museum** (Mon–Fri 9am–5pm, Sat & Sun 9am–noon) has some unusual items: a fine display of Aboriginal artefacts featuring an entire tree with a boomerang half-carved out of its trunk, and an unbelievable bottle collection ranging from poisons to schnapps. For some really ludicrous fun, the **Australian Crayfish Derby**, held on odd-numbered years in September, has to be worth a look. The owner of the winning crustacean nets $1500, the "loser" gets to eat all the competitors.

### Lark Quarry

It takes about two hours to drive the 120km south from Winton to **Lark Quarry**, dodging kamikaze kangaroos and patches of bulldust, and once you've arrived there's no doubt that this is the rough heart of the Outback. Nor is it surprising to find **dinosaur remains** here: the place looks prehistoric, swarming with flies and surrounded by hills where stunted trees and tufts of grass tussle with rocks for space. A hundred million years ago this was a shrinking waterhole across which a carnivorous dinosaur chased a mixed group of turkey-sized herbivores through the mud to a rockface where it caught and killed one as the others fled back past it. Over three thousand **footprints** have been found portraying these few seconds of action, excavated in the 1970s and now protected by an awning and walkway around them. Indentations left by small, amazingly sharp three-clawed feet – some very light as the prey panicked and ran on tiptoe – stream in all directions, while those left by the larger predator go only one way. Paths lead around to other, buried tracks where the chase ended.

### Opalton and Carisbrooke

The Opalton track (110km) follows the Jundah road for a short way before bearing left; 10km past Bladensburg Station turn-off is a track on the left to **Skull Waterhole**, named after the "dispersal" of the Goa Aborigines by the Native Mounted Police. Despite this sad history it's an interesting spot, as the water attracts kangaroos, budgerigars and ring-necked parrots, and there are also some **caves** to poke around in.

**OPALTON** is a multicultural area right now, with Yugoslav and Czech miners, as well as deserters from Coober Pedy, reworking century-old diggings with Chinese and Korean finance. You need to be entirely self-sufficient here: the only modern feature is a telephone and there isn't any water. During the summer there won't be any miners either – hotels in Winton are easily preferable to the 40°C-plus temperatures. Fossicking zones have been established where you can pick over old tailings for scraps.

Without your own transport, it's worth seeing the area on a **tour** to **Carisbrooke Station** ($60; book through the *Gem Centre* in Winton). The trip includes visits to an opal mine and to caves covered in Aboriginal paintings – some abstract, others recognizable outlines of boomerangs and nulla-nullas (clubs).

### Onwards

Heading **on from Winton**, the main route follows the **Landsborough Highway** to Cloncurry and Mount Isa (covered by bus) while the **Kennedy Developmental Road** runs west to Boulia. Towards Cloncurry, the **Combo Waterhole** near the low-slung *Blue Heeler Hotel* at Kynuna (165km) provided the inspiration for Banjo Patterson's classic poem "Waltzing Matilda"; it's a fairly typical muddy soak, decorated by trees and beer cans, and with some solid stone walls built at the turn of the century by Chinese labourers. The other feature on the journey is the *Walkabout Hotel* at **McKINLAY**, used as the rowdy Outback pub in the film *Crocodile Dundee*.

The journey **to Boulia** is a long (335km) continuation of the Winton landscape, with fuel available every 150km and the chance to see the enigmatic **Min Min Lights** bobbing around the bush at night. **BOULIA** consists of a hotel, van park and roadhouse (with only limited EFTPOS – unless you have a *Commonwealth Bank* passbook to withdraw money from the post office, don't rely on replenishing funds here). From here, Mount Isa is 300km north on bitumen, Birdsville is 400km south on a poor road; if you're really enjoying the ride, Alice Springs is 800km west on the unsealed Donahue/Plenty "highways"; there's little fuel or help, so all off-roading checks apply (see pp.26–28).

# THE NORTHWEST

All the major settlements in **Queensland's northwest** are mining towns, so far apart that precise names are redundant: **Mount Isa** becomes "the Isa", **Cloncurry** "the Curry", **Charters Towers**, "the Towers", as if nowhere else existed. Scattered across the vast tracts between are geological treasures waiting to be discovered, as well as traces of those who've tried before, and with a 4WD or careful manoeuvring there's plenty to see as you head interstate. Most people never stop to find out, grimly tearing along as fast as possible between Townsville and Three Ways along the **Flinders/ Barkly Highway**. This is a shame, because even with limited time and relying on public transport, the century-old ambience at Charters Towers and Mount Isa's strange setting are worth a stopover. With the freedom of your own vehicle, there's untramped bush at the **Great Basalt Wall** and **Porcupine Gorge** and the spectacular oasis of **Lawn Hill Gorge**, all a lifetime away from the coast's often banal spirit. With the highway forming the main link between Queensland and its neighbour, the major **bus lines** have at least daily services interstate, or there's the twice-weekly *Inlander* **train** between Townsville and Mount Isa.

# Gold Country

There's little scenic variation over the two-hour journey from the coast to the heights of the inland range at Mingela, but dry scrub at the top once covered seams of ore which had the streets of both Charters Towers and Ravenswood bustling with lucky-strike miners. Those times are long gone – though gold is still extracted from old tailings – and the towns survived at opposite extremes; connected by road and rail to Townsville, The Towers became a busy rural centre, while Ravenswood, half an hour south of Mingela, was just too far off the track and wasted to a shadow. *Detours* (☎077/21 5977) run day-trips from Townsville to one or the other for about $40.

## Ravenswood

As wind blows dust and dried grass around the streets between mine shafts and lonely old buildings, **RAVENSWOOD** fulfills ideas of what a ghost town should look like. Gold was discovered here in 1868 and within two years there were solid brick houses, a frenetic atmosphere and seven hundred miners on Elphinstone Creek working seams of gold, silver and lead ore: "every building in the main street was either a public house and dance house or public house and general store".

Today there's only one store, which doubles as a post office and sells fuel, and the main attraction is to wander between the restored buildings, trying to imagine how the others must have looked. Unsurprisingly, the two most complete survivals are hotels – though how they both keep going with a scattered population of barely a hundred souls is anybody's guess. You'll probably end up in one as the day heats up; the *Imperial* looks the worse for wear but has original wood panelling, mirrors and swing doors on the bar. Across the road attempts are being made to renovate a church and school, still just standing.

## Charters Towers and the Basalt Wall

Once Queensland's second largest city, and often referred to in its heyday simply as "the World", **CHARTERS TOWERS** is a showcase of colonial architecture. An Aboriginal boy named **Jupiter Mosman** found gold here in 1871 and within twelve months three thousand prospectors had stripped the landscape of trees and covered it with shafts, chimneys and crushing mills. At first, little money was reinvested – the cemetery is a sad record of cholera and typhoid outbreaks from disorganized sanitation – but by 1900, despite diminishing returns, Charters Towers had become a prosperous centre. There's been minimal change since then and the population, now mainly sustained by cattle farming, has shrunk to about a third of what it was in its prime. Good times to visit are for the May Day weekend **Country Music Festival**, and the **Rodeo** at Easter.

The main streets are Gill and Mosman, where you'll find everything from supermarkets to banks; **buses** and **trains** stop at the far end of Gill Street. For **accommodation**, the *Mexican Van Park* (corner of Church and Towers streets; ☎077/87 1161), on the site of the once busy Mexican Mine, is shaded and central. In tune with the local atmosphere is *Scotty's Outback Inn* on York Street, (10-min walk from town; ☎077/87 1028; ③), an old timber building with verandah, hammocks, and dogs. *Park Motel* (corner of Mosman and Deane streets; ☎077/87 1022; ⑤) is also close and comfortable. Hotels are the best bet for **meals**, and there's a Sunday morning market in the Stock Exchange building. The **information centre** (Mon–Fri 8.30am–5pm, plus variable hours Sat mornings) next to the post office has rough maps and advice on **gold-panning** tours in the area.

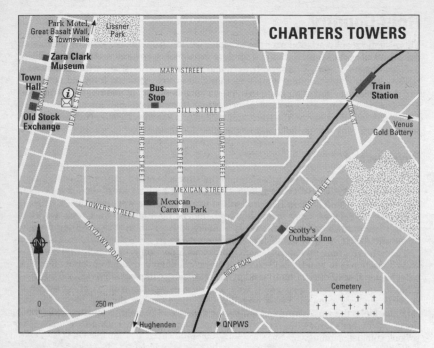

## The Old Centre and Venus Battery

Just about every building in Gill and Mosman streets catches the eye: a brightly painted police station, the *Excelsior Hotel*'s tottering wooden frame, the classical elegance of the post office, or the shaded country arcades outside the stores. The courtyard and glass roof at the former Stock Exchange and Assayer's Office now front some quiet shops and a lifeless **mining museum**; next door, the solid facade of the **Town Hall** betrays its original purpose as a bank, which stored gold bars smelted locally. Just down Mosman Street is the **Zara Clark Museum** (daily 10am–3pm; $3), housing an absorbing jumble of everything from old wagons to a set of silver tongs for eating frogs' legs. Further along the road is **Lissner Park**, whose Boer War memorial recalls stories of Breaker Morant, a local executed by the British after shooting a prisoner.

The **Venus Gold Battery**, 5km down Gill Street (tours daily 10am & 2pm; $3), is a fascinating illustration of the monumental efforts needed to separate gold from rock. Abandoned in 1972 after a century of operations, the battery is a huge gloomy temple to the past, its machinery lying silent and piecemeal around the place. The intention is to restore it to full working order, presumably without re-creating the actual conditions – it was a hideous place, a sweatbox filled with noxious fumes and noise. Ore was ground to a powder in one of the seven massive crushers, mixed with water and passed over a mercury screen. Any gold formed an amalgam and adhered to the mercury which was then heated in a crucible to leave a pitted nugget, and later remelted with flux to absorb any impurities. Sludge from the mercury screens was soaked in cyanide to leach out more gold, then the cyanide was neutralized with sulphur and piled up outside. These mounds are now being reprocessed using modern methods to extract the last vestiges of the precious metal.

## The Great Basalt Wall

About a half-hour north of Charters Towers, the Gregory Developmental Road crosses the eastern side of a 100km-long **lava flow** known with some justification as the **Great Basalt Wall**. Central sections form an impenetrable band of black boulders, riddled with gullies and caves; aerial surveys show dense vegetation weighed down beneath rubber vines, hiding colonies of fruit bats and hundreds of unconnected saline water-holes. Compasses don't work around basalt and those who've entered the maze are not short on tales about getting promptly lost and wandering around for hours.

You can get an impression of what it's like on the fringes of the wall, at Red Falls and Big Bend. At **Red Falls** (40km along the Developmental Road and then 44km west down a dry-season track) the river runs at right angles to the lava flow; water pours into an Olympic-sized swimming hole, and then down a sandy creekbed lined with paperbark trees and overlooked by a bush **campsite**. Walking about 200m further upstream to swim at Silent Hole, you'll see that the riverbed is pocked by the frozen impressions of burst bubbles where gases erupted through the solidifying rock. **Big Bend** (33km north of the Towers and then 2km east) is best reached in a 4WD, though it's not far to walk from the road. This is where the Burdekin River was diverted as lava edged into it, forming a concave cliff and swimming spot at **Echo Hole**. The flows covered an ancient coral reef and you can still pick out some shapes in the limestone rocks where the lava has worn away.

# Hughenden and around

**HUGHENDEN**, 350km west of Charters Towers, looks big next to the places you pass on the way. A dozen wide streets, a supermarket, a couple of **hotels** and banks all conspire to make you feel that you've arrived somewhere. The faceless *Grand Hotel* (☎077/41 1588; ③) offers budget beds, but the *Rest Easi Motel* (☎077/41 1633; ①–④) is quieter; you can also **camp** here. *Pete's Country Kitchen*, the **café** before the tracks at the other side of town has good burgers; opposite is the filling station/bus stop and a newsagent selling yesterday's papers.

There are two places to spend time: the **swimming pool** on Resolution Street and a free **museum** just past the hotel, dedicated to the *Muttaburrasaurus* dinosaur, a swamp-dwelling iguanadon. Bones were found at Muttaburra near Longreach in 1963 and assembled into a ten-metre-long skeleton after souvenir hunters handed over pieces to the Queensland Museum. Usually thought to be vegetarian, its needle-like teeth have prompted a rethink about this type of dinosaur's diet.

## Porcupine Gorge

**Porcupine Gorge** is 70km north of Hughenden, along the partially surfaced Kennedy Developmental Road, accessible only if you have your own vehicle (although you can usually scrape by without 4WD). A deep gash completely invisible among the drab brown scrub until you're virtually in it, it's best seen at the start of the dry season (May–July) before the river stops flowing, when the beautifully coloured cliffs and good swimming holes reward the effort of getting here. A **campsite** at the top of the gorge has limited cold water, toilets and nothing else. Look for wallabies on the walk into the gorge, which leads down steps, then on an increasingly steep, rough path carpeted in loose stones. The white riverbed has been moulded by water into soft, elongated forms, curving into a pool below the orange, yellow and white bands of **Pyramid Rock**. This is the bush at its best: sandstone glowing in the afternoon sun against a deep-blue sky, with animal calls echoing along the gorge as the shadow of the gorge wall creeps over distant woods. Walk along the road at dusk and you'll see groups of kangaroos.

# Cloncurry

**CLONCURRY**, 390km west of Hughenden, is caught between two landscapes, where the flat eastern plains rise to a rough and rocky plateau. Besides being where Australia's highest temperature (55°C) was recorded, Cloncurry offers glimpses into the mining history that permeates the whole stretch west to the larger and less personal settlement of Mount Isa. Copper was discovered here in 1867 but as the town lacked a rail link to the coast until 1908, profits were eroded by the necessity of transporting the ore by camel to Normanton. This meant that Cloncurry never reflected the quality of its mines: there are no traces of a wealthy past because there never was one.

Buildings at the **Mary Kathleen Memorial Park Museum** (Mon–Fri 9am–5pm; $4) were salvaged from Mary Kathleen, a short-lived uranium mining town between Cloncurry and Mount Isa (see below). The museum is primarily of geological interest, though Aboriginal tools and Burke's water bottle add some historical depth. The mineral collection is a comprehensive catalogue of local ores, fossils and gemstones arranged in long cases. Joy Long at the office gives out information on old mining camps and fossicking details if you feel inspired to try your luck hunting for garnets, copper and maltese crosses (hard, reddish-brown staurolite crystals paired at right angles).

A positive side to Cloncurry's isolation is that it inspired the formation of the Royal Flying Doctor Service. **John Flynn Place** on Gregory Street (Mon–Fri 7am–4pm, Sat & Sun 9am–3pm; $4) is a monument to the man who pioneered the use of radio and aeroplane to provide a "mantle of safety over the outback". The exhibition explains how ideas progressed with technology, from pedal-powered radios to assistance from the young *Qantas*, resulting in the opening in Cloncurry of the first Flying Doctor base in 1928. A different aspect of Cloncurry's past is evident in the two foreign **cemeteries**. To the left of the highway, before you cross the creek on the way to Mount Isa, a hundred overgrown plots recall a brief goldrush last century when the harsh conditions took a terrible toll on **Chinese** prospectors; equally neglected are the unnamed graves of **Afghans** at the north end of Henry Street, all aligned with Mecca. Afghans were vital to Cloncurry's survival before the coming of the railway, organizing camel trains which carried the ore to Normanton whence it was shipped to Europe – a role now largely forgotten.

### Practicalities

At times almost deserted, Cloncurry's **services** are clustered along the highway and in Scarr Street. Draw money from the bank or via *Lee's Supermarket* EFTPOS facilities. The best of Cloncurry's six bars – and serving good meals as well – is the *Wagon Wheel* **hotel** (☎077/42 1866; rooms ⑤), on the corner of Ramsay Street; a public house has occupied this same site since 1867. *Oasis Caravan Park* (☎077/42 1313) has shade, a small store, frigid swimming pool and bindi-eye thorns.

Leaving, Mount Isa is just 118km to the west, while the **Burke Developmental Road** heads north to Normanton past several historic roadhouses: **QUAMBY**'s old country hotel with races and an underwear-throwing contest in May, and the **Burke and Wills Roadhouse**, at the junction of the sealed road west towards **Gregory Downs** and Lawn Hill Gorge (see p.408).

# Cloncurry to Mount Isa

The rough country between Cloncurry and Mount Isa is evidence of ancient upheavals which shattered the landscape and created the region's extensive mineral deposits. While the highway continues safely to Mount Isa past the **Burke and Wills monument** and the **Kalkadoon tribal boundary** at Corella Creek, forays into the bush will uncover remains of less fortunate mining settlements. In any vehicle you can manage the brief detour to Mary Kathleen, while with a 4WD, tracks lead through old camps to mineral formations – ask in Cloncurry or Mount Isa about road conditions. *Campbell's* runs safaris from Mount Isa to parts of the bush drive described below – see Mount Isa "Listings".

## Mary Kathleen

About halfway to Mount Isa, the road to **MARY KATHLEEN** is still surfaced and two minutes from the turn-off you're there. By all accounts, **uranium** was found here by accident when a car broke down; while waiting for help the driver and his friends tried fossicking and found ore. The two-street town was built in 1956 and completely dismantled in 1982 when export restrictions halted mining. Since then, once manicured lawns have run riot, bougainvillaea grows unchecked, and an unkempt row of casuarinas tangle along the access road; in a few years, it will all have gone. Further on are the terraces of the open-cast mine, now reminiscent of a flooded Greek amphitheatre.

---

### GOING BUSH

There are two sections to this route: firstly 21.5km from the highway past abandoned camps at **Rosebud Dam** and **Ballara** to **Fountain Springs**, then 25km back to the highway past some working copper mines and maltese cross site. While you might cover the track to Fountain Springs in a normal vehicle, the second section is 4WD only; it's impossible, however, to predict road conditions and you'll need a **map** from Mount Isa tourist information or the Cloncurry museum, possibly combined with the *Mines Department 1:100,000 Mary Kathleen* map. Allow an hour to reach Fountain Springs from the highway, and three for the second section.

The Fountain Springs track starts south of the highway just over 60km from Cloncurry, opposite a new rest area. **Rosebud Dam**, on Corella Creek, is a good place to pick over; there are a couple of waste heaps on the north bank, visible from the creek crossing, and old tins and matchboxes are still found around the place. A bottle dump, 50m downstream, might hide an unbroken gem missed by previous collectors. Bear right at the slag heaps 2.5km past Rosebud and continue another 7km to the **Lady J** junction, where you bear left. Two kilometres further on there's an obviously cleared spot; over on a rise in the scrub to the right is a concrete platform and traces of foundations and rail line. This is **Ballara**, once a depot for ore off to the smelters at Kuridala. Again, long grass hides occasional relics. South from here the long ridge of the **Fountain Range** comes into view on the right. A cleft part way down marks the springs, reached 4km from Ballara. Water oozes into a small waterhole at the foot of perpendicular cliffs, and the mouth of the gorge is marshy and surrounded by trees. You could camp here, or just have a picnic and head back.

**Backtracking to Ballara**, find the concrete platform and head west (left coming back from the springs) along vague wheel tracks across a fenceline and onto the old railway. From here the track hugs a hill to the right over various gradients, then divides briefly after 2km; the left way passes a tubular cross marking the grave of Thomas Tame, killed while mining in 1912. Another 1.6km past anthills and you're at **Hightville**, surrounded by ridges and mostly lost in the scrub; a few concrete sidings, slag heaps and junk are all that remain. Don't try negotiating the narrow, potholed tunnel; follow the newer track through gullies and rubble to the **Wee McGregor Mine**, which is still worked intermittently for copper – rocks below are stained green with salts from the mine. Four kilometres later the hills recede, and on a small plateau between two ranges you'll find **maltese crosses** carpeting the road. Good specimens are rare and the area is picked over each year; try towards the hillside on the right. After this the track traverses sandy flats between creeks until **Guts Ache Gap**, roughly 10km from the crosses. Onwards, it's 3km to **Mount Frosty** (or **Krusty**), a source of limestone flux for Mount Isa and now a flooded quarry. The highway is two minutes distant, 9km closer to Mount Isa from where you left it.

# Mount Isa and around

As the only place of consequence for 700km in any direction, the smokestacks, concrete paving and sterile hills at **MOUNT ISA** assume oasis-like qualities on arrival, despite being undeniably ugly. While the novelty might wear thin after a cold drink, the city has a few points to savour before the next journey. There's evidence of the area's **Aboriginal heritage**, a couple of unusual **museums**, tours of the mines themselves, Australia's largest **rodeo** every August and, not least, the fascinating situation and the community it has fostered.

The largest city in the world in terms of surface area – its administrative boundaries stretch as far as Cloncurry – Mount Isa sits astride a wealth of zinc, silver, lead and copper, and owes its existence to these reserves and their need for a staging post on their way to Townsville. The city's founding father was **John Miles**, who discovered ore in 1923, established *Mount Isa Mines* the next year and began commercial mining in 1925. Originally a settlement of canvas and scrap wood, the city enjoyed a forty-year boom under the benevolent hegemony of *MIM* until the late 1980s saw a decline in profits, not yet stemmed by the opening up of Hilton Mine in 1990.

## The Town

Having passed so much mining history consigned to the scrub, there's a certain novelty value in exploring Mount Isa's still-active mines. The **surface tour** ($12) includes a stint looking at videos and pieces of machinery at the **Mining Museum** on Church Street (Mon–Fri 9am–4pm, Sat & Sun 10am–1pm; $3) and a bus ride around surface operations. **Underground tours** ($25), from which women were once barred as harbingers of bad luck, descend to see subterranean mining, crushing and the workshops. Book through the tourist office (see below) and expect a waiting list of up to a month for the underground tour, or try for a cancellation.

The **Frank Aston Museum** on Marian Street (Mon–Fri 9am–3pm; $4) is partly outdoors, and partly underground in a tunnel full of mining memorabilia of a type you'll recognize if you went bush between here and Cloncurry. A staircase rises up through a mineshaft to a walkway above the museum, graced by old cars and mining trucks which look dated in *MIM*'s shadow.

---

### MIM

The **Mount Isa Mines** complex is a land of trundling yellow mine trucks, mountains of slag, intense activity and miles of noisy vibrating pipelines. Above all this the two chimneys trail Mount Isa's signature across the sky, marking the copper mine to the south and separate silver, lead and zinc deposits. Ore is mined almost 2km down by a workforce of 1200, roughly crushed and hoisted to the surface before undergoing a second crushing, grinding and washing in flotation tanks, to separate ore from waste rock. Zinc is sold as it is, while copper and silver/lead mix are smelted into ingots before being transported to Townsville or overseas for refining. Power for the mines and the entire region comes from *MIM*'s own plant; surplus is sold to the state grid. During nocturnal power failures residents often hike up to the rotary lookout and place bets on which part of town will be reconnected first.

The scale of the process will be brought home to you if you stand under one of the mountains of tailings awaiting future treatment – next to which are humble mounds of green copper ore, bought off a local miner and representing maybe a year's effort – or look down into the depths of the open-cut mine, worked simply for rubble to fill in old shafts. At the edge of the mine, the last ridge of the original Mount Isa, and site of the first finds seventy years ago, has been left as a memorial.

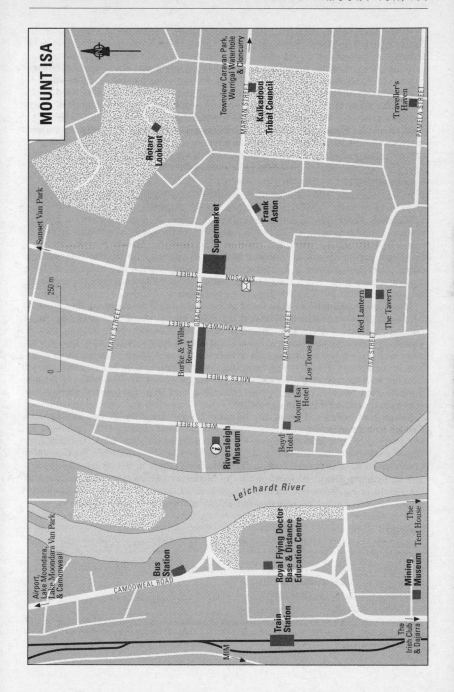

At the **Riversleigh Museum** (daily 9am–4.30pm; $3), before the bridge on the corner of Grace and West streets, is history of another kind. Paleontologists have been working at **Riversleigh fossil site** (see p.408) for a decade and have discovered an incredible record of marsupial and mammalian evolution and environmental change between ten thousand and twenty million years ago. The museum's single room is crammed with rocks, models, dense text and a continuous video loop, all of which can be more enlightening than a visit to the actual site. Over the river and left down Camooweal Road is the **Royal Flying Doctor Base** (Mon–Sat 9am–3pm; $2) and adjacent **Distance Education Centre** (schooldays 10am–noon). Ten minutes further south on the corner of Third and Fourth avenues, the *National Trust* **Tent House** is the last survivor of the city's earliest architecture – a canvas hut with a roof.

## Practicalities

Illuminated at night, and with two huge chimneys – the Rotary lookout in Hilary Street gives a good view – **MIM** is the city's major landmark, west of the often dry **Leichhardt River**. The highway runs through town and over the river to the **bus station**, **trains** stop below *MIM*, and the **airport** is to the north, where taxis meet arrivals. The city centre is along the highway (Marian/Grace Street) between Simpson and West streets; there's no public transport. At present, the **tourist information office** (daily 9am–4.30pm) is located at the *Riversleigh Museum* (see above), but there are plans for a new complex on Marian Street which will incorporate the museum, information centre, NPWS office and Aboriginal council.

**Motel accommodation** can be found at the *Burke and Wills Resort*, on the corner of Grace and Camooweal streets (☎1800/679 178; ⑥), where somewhat twee rooms decorated in "period" style cluster around a courtyard. Cheaper beds are on offer at *Traveller's Haven*, on the corner of Spence and Pamela streets (☎077/43 0313; ①), with a free pick-up from the bus station; it's sometimes crowded, though you can often negotiate a mattress on the floor. For **camping**, *Sunset Van Park*, 14 Sunset Drive, about 2km north of the centre (☎077/43 7668), has inexpensive tent sites, while *Moondara Caravan Park* (☎077/43 9780) is plain, quiet and next to a bird-infested creek some 4km from the city off the Camooweal road.

Mount Isa's hotels and clubs are the main source of **meals**, though *Red Lantern Chinese* (corner of Simpson and Isa streets) and *Los Toros Mexican* (19 Camooweal St) are pretty good, if a little expensive. Everyone goes to the *Irish Club* (Buckley Ave, 2km south of the centre) for weekend bands and inexpensive food, while the *Concordia Club*, next to the bus station, hosts an **Oktoberfest**. Closer to the centre, the upstairs grill at the bulky *Mount Isa Hotel* (corner of Marian and Miles streets) is reliable, and the *Tavern* in Isa Street has excellent-value lunches; look out for other hotel all-you-can-eat specials. For **provisions** there's a shopping complex in Simpson Street.

## Listings

**Airlines** *Ansett*, 8 Miles St (☎077/44 1753); *Flight West*, 14 Miles St (☎077/43 9333); *North Western Air* (☎077/43 7720).

**Bus station** *Campbell's* (☎077/43 2006); *Greyhound* (☎077/43 6655); *McCafferty's* (☎077/43 3685).

**Pharmacy** *Cristaudo's*, Marian St (☎077/43 3773).

**Post office** Simpson St (☎077/49 1857).

**Taxi** ☎077/43 2333.

**Tours** *Campbell's* (☎077/43 2006) run day tours to local mines and Aboriginal sites, as well as three-day safaris to Lawn Hill Gorge between May and October. Book through the bus station or your accommodation.

**Trains** ☎077/43 5077.

## Kalkadoon territory

The scrub around Mount Isa is thick with abandoned mines, waterholes and Aboriginal sites. Either take a **tour** (see above) or, if you're doing your own driving, check at the tourist office for latest news on road conditions.

The city marks the centre of the territory of the **Kalkadoons**, a tribe often compared with the Zulus for their fierce opposition to white invasion last century. After hounding squatters for ten years with guerrilla tactics, they were all but exterminated in a pitched battle with an army of local settlers and Native Mounted Police near Kajabbi in 1884. Kalkadoon bones littered the region for years, but their stand gained them respect for their organized resistance to Europeans.

Numerous sites around Mount Isa attest to the Kalkadoons' abilities as prolific tool-makers and painters, and their **Tribal Council** office (variable opening hours; $1) in Marian Street is worth the token entry fee to talk to the staff. Bear in mind that although it's against the law to alter Aboriginal sites in any way, many local sites have been vandalized and you might find the council evasive.

### Warrigal Waterhole, Poison Hole and Lake Moondara

You need high clearance or care to reach **Warrigal Waterhole**: drive 7km towards Cloncurry from the Tribal Council office in Marian Street, turn right and bear left along a very rough track to reach a parking area 3.4km later, from where you walk past "ripple rocks" to the waterhole. One red figure with strange hair outlined in yellow on the left seems to have escaped damage; not so other figures and symbols which have melted to ochre smears. The waterhole itself is hemmed in by sheltering rocks, a cool retreat from the sun.

A flooded open-cut mine, **Poison Hole**'s name comes from the surreal appearance of the water, coloured green by copper, but it's actually safe to swim in. Tracks there change each year, but the hole is about ten minutes from the highway, and the turn-off should be roughly 25km back towards Cloncurry; look for signs spray-painted on the road. **Lake Moondara** (20km, follow the signs from the highway heading towards Camooweal) is less offensively toned, and packed out at weekends with windsurfers and boats. Away from the crowds, other animals are attracted to the water – goannas, wallabies and flocks of pelicans.

# Camooweal and Lawn Hill

West of Mount Isa, the **Barkly Highway** continues to Camooweal and the Northern Territory, with routes to Gregory Downs and Lawn Hill National Park heading north off it. If you're making for Lawn Hill, ensure you have a **campsite** booked (see below for details) and check the latest **road conditions** – the routes are sometimes 4WD-only or closed. Driving anywhere, fuel up; it's 200km to Camooweal and at least twice this to Lawn Hill.

## Camooweal and the Caves

The lonely highway curves over the last edge of the ranges and on to hot plains where Mount Isa's chimneys are lampooned by anthills. A little over halfway to the state border there's the unsealed road north leading to **Gregory Downs**, Lawn Hill and Burketown; otherwise it's a monotonous journey west to Camooweal and the fringes of the black-soil **Barkly Tablelands**.

There's no way to avoid **CAMOOWEAL** but you might wish there was; the township's atmosphere of lazy aggression is exacerbated by a total lack of charm. The highway from Mount Isa forms the main street, built in 1944 by American servicemen whose names are painted on a rock at the edge of town. You'll find a roadhouse, mechanic, general store (and *Westpac* agent), post office and hotel – a risky place for a last drink in Queensland. The store's old decor is worth a peek, and murals at the **service station** (with EFTPOS facilities) should raise a chuckle; around the back are cabins and a **campsite** with thick grass to raise a tent over. Otherwise, move on.

The best features of the surrounding area are dolomite sinks known as **the Caves**; drive 8km down the Urandangie road south of Camooweal, then turn left and follow the dirt track for about thirty minutes. There's an NPWS **campsite** with toilets and a fence to keep out marauding cattle; flocks of gibbering green budgerigars congregate around the creek and if you can put up with their racket it's preferable to a night in town. The park's nine caves are intriguing terraces, spiralling down ten metres before tapering to vertical shafts. The district is riddled with them; one is a roost for **ghost bats**, another has become famous for its coolabah trees. Caused by tunnels into the water table collapsing at the surface, the shafts continue straight down for anything between 18m and 75m before levelling out into an uncharted system. Instability makes approaching the mouths dangerous, so don't even think about exploring underground.

**Heading on** from Camooweal there's another track north to Lawn Hill, while 200km south beyond the Caves is **Urandangie** and a 650-kilometre, 4WD "short cut" across to Alice Springs. West, it's a mere ten minutes' drive to the cattle grid separating Queensland from the Northern Territory's time zone and better roads. Next fuel is at the Barkly Homestead, 275km away.

# Gregory Downs and Lawn Hill National Park

Hidden from the rest of the world by the Constance Range and a hot ocean of bleached grass, the red sandstone walls and splash of tropical greenery at **Lawn Hill Gorge** seem outrageously extravagant. There's little warning: within moments a land which barely supports scattered herds of cattle is exchanged for palm forests and creeks teeming with wildlife. The **national park** covers two sections: **Riversleigh Fossil Site** and the gorge itself, about 70km from each other, with access either through Riversleigh to the gorge, or direct to the gorge via the **Gregory Downs Roadhouse**. Either way, there's going to be hours of dirt driving, which at its best will be slow going; the Riversleigh route is definitely worth it, but the Gregory Downs track is less remote.

For either, leave the Barkly Highway 116km from Mount Isa and head north on the Gregory Downs road. The Riversleigh road diverges left after another 118km; otherwise, stay on track for where routes from Burketown and Cloncurry meet at **GREGORY DOWNS**, whose pub organizes cold drinks, petrol, some mechanical repairs and a wild **canoe race** down the Gregory River on the May Day weekend. For Lawn Hill, head west across the river and follow the 110-kilometre track to the gorge.

### Riversleigh Fossil Site

The track from the Barkly Highway/Gregory Downs road to Riversleigh crosses the **Gregory River** three times around Riversleigh Station, which is why you might need 4WD on this route. The crossings are a foretaste of Lawn Hill – sudden patches of shady green and cool air in an otherwise hostile landscape – and you can **camp** at the third ford, though there are no facilities.

Like Lawn Hill, Riversleigh was once cloaked in rainforest supporting many ancestral forms of Australian fauna. The **fossil finds** here cover a period from twenty million to just ten thousand years ago, a staggering range for a single site and one which details the transitional period from Australia's climatic heyday to its current parched state. Riversleigh may ultimately produce a fossil record of evolutionary change for an entire ecosystem, but don't expect to see much *in situ* as the fossils are trapped in limestone boulders which have to be blasted out and treated with acid to release their contents. A roadside shelter houses a map of the landscape with fossil sites indicated on a rock outcrop nearby where, with some diligence, you can find bones and teeth protruding from the stones.

## Lawn Hill Gorge

When **Lawn Hill Creek** started carving its forty-metre-deep gorge, the region was still a tropical wetland but, as the climate began to dry out, vegetation retreated to a handful of moist, isolated pockets. Animals were drawn to creeks and waterholes and people followed the game – middens and art detail an Aboriginal culture at least 17,000 years old. The NPWS **campground** (tank water, showers, toilets) occupies a tamed edge of the creek at the mouth of the gorge and is booked solid between Easter and October (book in advance on ☎077/48 5572). An alternative campsite is at the pleasant **Adels Grove**, a *Savannah Guides* post (☎077/48 5502) 5km from the gorge and run by Barry Kubala, an expert on the gorge's vegetation.

**Canoes** ($3 per person per hour) let you explore the gorge from the inside. An easy hour's paddle over calm green water takes you from the NPWS campsite between the stark, vertical cliffs of the Middle Gorge to **Indari falls**, an excellent swimming spot with a ramp to carry your gear down. Beyond here the creek relaxes, alternating between calm ponds and slack channels choked with vegetation before slowing to a trickle under the rock faces of the Upper Gorge. Saltwater crocs are absent from the gorge, but you'll certainly see plenty of birds – egrets, bitterns and kites all put in an appearance. Freshwater crocodiles are unlikely to show: since visitor numbers have increased, this timid reptile has retreated to quieter spots, although you might see a "freshie" at dusk in the **Lower Gorge** – a sluggish tract edged in waterlilies and forest where goannas lounge during the day and rare **purple-crowned fairy wrens** forage in pandanus leaves.

In the creek itself are turtles, shockingly large catfish, and sharp-eyed **archer fish** who spit jets of water at insects above the surface. Just how isolated all this is becomes clear from the flat top of the **Island Stack**, a twenty-minute walk from the camp. A pre-dawn hike up the steep sides gives you a commanding view of the sun creeping into the gorge, highlighting orange walls against green palm-tops which hug the river through a flat, undernourished country. The rocks along the banks of the Lower Gorge are daubed with designs relating to the Dingo Dreaming, while fuel drums, tins and middens inside an overhang demonstrate that Lawn Hill has only recently been abandoned by **Aborigines**. This fact was rammed home when a group of fifty people from local communities staged a month-long sit-in at the park in October 1994, demanding joint management – something they'd been promised three years previously. They've since been assured of future involvement in the park, and it's possible that Aboriginal tour guides may soon be on hand to show you around.

# THE GULF OF CARPENTARIA

The great savannahs and intricate river systems of western Cape York and the **Gulf of Carpentaria** were described in 1623 by the Dutch explorer **Cartenz** as being full of hostile tribes – not surprising, since he'd already kidnapped two men and chased the rest off with musket fire. Ignored for centuries thereafter, except by Indonesians gathering sea-slugs to sell to the Chinese, interest in the Gulf's potential was stirred in 1841 by **John Lort Stokes**, a lieutenant on the *Beagle* (which had been graced by a young

Charles Darwin on an earlier voyage) who absurdly described the coast as "Plains of Promise":

> *A vast boundless plain lay before us, here and there dotted with woodland isles...I could discover the rudiments of future prosperity and ample justification of the name which I had bestowed upon them.*

It took Burke and Wills' awful 1861 trek (see box on p.389) to discover that the pastures were deficient in nutrients and that the black soil became a quagmire during the wet season. Too awkward to develop, the Gulf hung in limbo as settlements sprang up, staggered on for a while, then disappeared; even today few places could be described as thriving communities. Not that this should put you off visiting: with few real destinations but plenty to see, the Gulf is a perfect destination for those who just like to travel. On the way, and only half a day's drive from Cairns, the awesome lava tubes at **Undara** shouldn't be missed, while further afield there are **gemstones** to be fossicked, the coast's birdlife and exciting **barramundi** fishing, and the Gulf's sheer remoteness to savour.

Two mostly sealed **roads** to Normanton – the **Gulf Developmental** which starts southwest of Ravenshoe and the Atherton Tablelands, and **Burke Developmental** from Cloncurry – are covered by **buses** from Cairns and Mount Isa. In the dry season, any sound vehicle could handle these routes, although the Croydon–Normanton section includes a seventy-kilometres unsealed section that's about the roughest a conventional vehicle can handle, so take it slowly. The Mareeba to Normanton "road", via Chillagoe, is a shattering, unserviced 500-kilometre track best tackled by well-equipped off-road transport only – as are all the Gulf's remoter stretches. In the **wet season**, flying is the sole option for *any* travel. **Safaris** run from Mount Isa or Cairns (see p.406 and p.360, respectively) if you don't have the right vehicle. The Gulf also sports two rustic **railways**, from Mount Surprise to Forsayth, and Croydon to Normanton.

Most visitors to the Gulf need to be reasonably self-sufficient, as there are few banks and accommodation is largely in campsites (no hostels) or pricey hotels. The NPWS are joined by the Savannah Guides, a private organization less altruistic than the government-funded NPWS but no less informed, who run campsites with rangers to show you around. On a more alarming note, you might also come face to face with the Gulf's two **crocodile** species – take care.

## Undara

The **Undara Lava Tubes** are astounding, massive tunnels running in broken chambers for up to 35km from the side of the volcano's low cone. It wasn't until 1989 that the majority of the caves were located and mapped and Undara declared an area of scientific interest, currently run by the Savannah Guides but NPWS-owned. The volcano is on **Yarramulla Station**, ten minutes south off the Gulf Developmental Road, 130km from Ravenshoe. **Accommodation**, bar and restaurant at the *Lava Lodge* (☎070/97 1411; cabins ⑤, camping also available) are in eleven restored railway carriages brought over from Mareeba and set up amongst a thin wattle forest – an eccentric but comfortable idea.

Because the tunnels are hard to enter – and some host a virulent lung fungus – you must take a **tour**. Although not cheap ($18 for a one-hour introduction, $52 a half day, $75 full), these are good value considering that as well as the chance to explore the tubes, you get an intimate rundown on local geology, flora, fauna and history from a member of the Collins family, who've lived on the station for over a century. For an extra $55 you can **fly** over the tubes and see the collapsed tunnels' intermittent trails of green running through the brown scrub.

## Tubes and caves

When Undara erupted 190,000 years ago, lava rivers snaked northwest towards the Gulf. Away from the cone the outside surfaces hardened, forming insulating tubes which kept the lava liquid and allowed it to run until the tubes were drained; these were then covered by later accumulations, and they'd still be unexplored if hot gasses hadn't popped holes in the tube ceilings which eventually collapsed, creating a way in.

The edge of the flow is marked by darker soil and healthier vegetation; at cave mouths this becomes rampant, successfully concealing the entrances and making your first view of the tubes something of a shock – what looks like a bush at ground level turns out to be the top of a giant fig tree growing from the cave floor. The caves are decked in rubble and remnant pockets of thick prehistoric vegetation quite out of place among the dry scrub on the surface. **Tool sites** around the cave mouths show that Aborigines knew of their existence, but there's no evidence that they ventured in.

Once **inside**, the scale of the 52 tubes is overpowering. Up to 19m high and 900m long, their glazed walls bear evidence of the terrible forces that created them: coil patterns and ledges formed by cooling lava, whirlpools where lava forged its way through rock from other flows, and "stalactites" made when solidifying lava dribbled from the ceiling. Some end in lakes, others are blocked by lava plugs. Their size deadens sound and, except for twitching colonies of bats clinging to the ceilings, there's no sign of life.

## Mount Surprise and Ambo

**MOUNT SURPRISE**, 40km from Undara, takes its name from the shock of the local Aborigines when they first saw whites. Little more than a van park/gem shop/filling station (☎070/62 3153) and **hotel** (☎070/62 3118; ③), the main point of interest lies a bumpy hour's drive to the north at **O'Briens Creek Topaz Field**; you'll need a 4WD. Arthur Griffin lives on the field and, for $10 a head, will organize fossicking trips led by Jim Scott for anyone turning up by 8.30am at his home, **the Oasis**. You might find a handful of topaz in a couple of hours, and while it's not very valuable, there's pleasure in the hunt.

West of Mount Surprise the road crosses **the Wall**, where expanding gasses in a blocked subterranean lava tube forced the ground above it up 20m into a long ridge. The same gaseous expulsion also seems to have cracked open a much deeper seam at **Ambo Springs** on Tallaroo Station. Formed by water 3km down becoming heated and forcing its way to the surface, the clear blue, sulphurous pools gradually accumulate a crusty grey collar around their vent from dissolved lime, which eventually closes the outflow – until the build-up of pressure explodes through to create a new spring. The water emerges at 92˚C, but there are some cooler spas that are more comfortable for soaking in, and the station is open between Easter and October daily until 4pm ($8; ☎070/62 1221).

## Out from Georgetown

**GEORGETOWN** is a neat, faded settlement, 90km from Mount Surprise. Forty kilometres of unsealed road south, **FORSAYTH** is the terminus for one of the region's anachronistic **railways**, which runs in recently renovated splendour from Mount Surprise through Einasleigh and down to Forsayth. You spend the five-hour journey being hauled over rickety bridges in carriages sporting corrugated-iron ceilings and wooden dunnies – a pastiche of Outback iconography. The train leaves Mount Surprise on Monday and Thursday at around noon, departing from Forsayth for the return leg Tuesdays and Fridays at 7am ($35 single, $70 return); an extra $40 buys you dinner and a bed at Forsayth's *Goldfield Tavern*.

**Agate Creek gemfields** are two hours south of Forsayth through some rough 4WD scrub and sandstone scenery. There's a **camp** here (Easter–Oct; ☎070/62 5335) catering to **agate hunters** who scour the creek banks after each wet season and rate Agate Creek the best site in the world for these semi-precious stones. This may be a matter of opinion but the colours, ranging from honey through to delicate blue, justify the time spent grubbing around with a pick looking for them. Sandstone ridges flanking the creek conceal a fair amount of **Aboriginal** artefacts and paintings, as well as black veins of **fossilized palms**.

**EINASLEIGH**, 65km east of Forsayth, consists of a handful of weatherboard and iron houses – eminently forgettable apart from the huge, delicious evening meals served at its **hotel** (☎070/62 5222; rooms ④), and summer dips in Einasleigh Creek's basalt **gorge**. On from Einasleigh, the dirt runs a further 70km east to **Lynd Junction Roadhouse**, with routes north to the Atherton Tablelands (see p.361) and south to Charters Towers or Hughenden.

## Croydon

**CROYDON**, 150km west of Georgetown along the main road, was the site of Queensland's last major **goldrush** after two station hands found nuggets in a fencepost hole in 1885. For a brief period the region received the attention it had always craved: within five years the railway was built, and lucky miners whooped it up at Croydon's 36 hotels, but chaotic management brought operations to a close by 1900. Whether the rush brought any lasting benefits is doubtful: today, mining junk and vacant blocks set the scene and you wonder how close Croydon is to being completely abandoned; all buildings predate 1920, the *Club Hotel* (last of the 36) and general store both have their original fittings and offer directions to other scattered relics. There's plenty of atmosphere, though, and if you're tempted to stay, there's a **van park** on the Georgetown side.

Moving on, you could indulge in a nostalgic trip to Normanton, 154km west, on the *Gulflander* train, which takes half a day to trundle from the station in Helen Street to arrive at the faded splendour of Normanton (Thurs 8.30am, returning Wed 8.30am; $35 one-way, for an extra $110 you can load your car aboard and drive away at the far end). When the rails and sleepers were unloaded at Normanton's wharves last century they were meant to form the first stage of a line to Cloncurry, but it was redirected to Croydon when gold was found.

## Normanton and around

**NORMANTON**, founded on the banks of the Norman River in 1868, was the Gulf's main port, connected to the Croydon goldfield by rail and Cloncurry's copper mines by camel train. Set in gritty, flat country, Normanton's fortunes declined along with its mineral deposits, and today there's only a collection of stores and filling stations, a *Westpac* **bank** and **post office**, with shop awnings and a handful of trees providing scant shade. The *Gulfland Motel* (☎077/45 1290; ⑤) down towards the station has a thick lawn and pleasant **rooms**, while the van park provides access to a shower block and the choice of which bit of gravel to camp on. Normanton's **hotels** rate a mention, especially the lurid paint job on the **Purple Pub**, and the *Albion*'s corrugated iron and wooden fittings – both pretty frenetic watering holes. When you've had enough boozing, Karumba and routes onto western Cape York lie north. West is the fuelless, 220-kilometre Burketown road, with features along the way including the site of Burke and Wills' northernmost camp near the Bynoe River, and the often difficult **Leichhardt River** crossing where the pocket-sized **Leichhardt falls** contrast with the aridity of the surrounding sand dunes, deposited each year when the river is in spate.

Reached from Normanton across 70km of cracked, burning saltpan, **KARUMBA**'s tidy gardens are ridiculously suburban and camouflage the remote setting – betrayed the moment you buy a newspaper and realize that it's two days old. Once a candidate for a telegraph connection with Asia, today the single-street township survives, barely, on prawn trawling and fishing. Aborigines shun the area as many died in a battle nearby – whether in a tribal war or against settlers isn't clear. Luxuries include a **campsite**, **store**, *Westpac* **bank**, **post office** and the *Karumba Lodge* (☎077/45 9143; ⑥); stay out of the infamous *Animal Bar* unless you're extremely serious about drink and occasional bouts of hand-to-hand combat. For a more relaxing time and the chance of catching something for the pot, contact Graham Sneddon (☎077/45 9316) for **river cruises** in search of fish, crocs or birds. If you have your own tackle, *Karumba Boat Hire* (☎077/45 9393) rent out 14' tinnies from $35 for a half-day.

### Onwards: the Wellesleys and western Cape York

*Gulf Freight Services* (☎077/45 9333) run a weekly barge from Karumba to **Weipa** ($200, vehicles extra; see p.372 for more on Weipa itself). The journey takes twenty-four hours; the price is all inclusive, and you might even be able to work your passage. Erratic services also go to **Thursday Island** or the Wellesleys, depending on cargo. Domain of the Lardil Aborigines, the **Wellesley Group** comprises two dozen wind-swept islands north of Burketown with excellent fishing around fragmented coral rubble. Never settled by whites, today they are Aboriginal communities with expensive but basic **resorts** on **Mornington** and **Sweers** islands. Day flights can be booked through Burketown's post office (see below).

Off-road drivers after wildlife might be tempted by superb wetlands on the western edge of the Cape York Peninsula, accessed from the Normanton–Karumba stretch off a 4WD-only, 500-kilometre track which ultimately takes you to Chillagoe (see p.362). Detouring north from it, you'll find the coast thick with creeks, waterholes and animals; **Dorunda Station** (food, drink and limited fuel supplies; ☎077/45 3477; units ⑤), about 180km up the road, is a working cattle property which arranges **hunting safaris** with cameras or .303s – targets are pigs, fish, birds or crocodiles. There's more of the same even further north at **Mitchell and Alice Rivers National Park**, via the Aboriginal community of **Kowanyama**. You'll need all supplies, an NPWS permit and permission from the community (contact Cairns NPWS on ☎070/52 3096 for details).

## Burketown and beyond

Set on the Albert River, **BURKETOWN** balances on the dusty frontier between grass-land and the Gulf's thirty-kilometre-deep, unfriendly coastal flats. Styled Queensland's "Barramundi Capital" after the delicious sports fish, most of the population of 235 work at the huge road maintenance depot. Despite lukewarm fame for providing background to Nevil Shute's *A Town Like Alice*, there's little beyond the dodgy *Albert Hotel*, a store, a couple of **fuel pumps**, and a post office (which also acts as an agent for day-flights to the Wellesley islands; call ☎077/45 5177 for details). The store runs a **campsite** but to engage in barra fishing, you'll need your own boat and fishing gear. To rent these, head for **Escott Lodge** (☎077/48 5577; units ⑤), 16km west, where you can also go riding or mustering, or tour one of the Gulf's cattle stations that eke out a precarious living. There's a **restaurant** and **bar** at the lodge but no store.

### Onwards: The Hells Gate Track

The best road from Burketown heads south for about two hours to **Gregory Downs Hotel** and routes to Lawn Hill and Cloncurry. If you're serious about **fishing** and have a 4WD, however, head west from the Gregory Downs/Burketown road via **Tirranna Roadhouse** (food and fuel facilities) and the Aboriginal community at **Doomadgee**, to the **Hells Gate Roadhouse** (☎077/45 8258; last fuel before Borroloola), 50km from the Northern Territory. Fishing information can be obtaind here, or you could try **Massacre Inlet**, reached from **Wollogorang Station** (☎089/75 9944; camping and meals) just over the Territory border. Giant anthills, pandanus-frilled waterholes and irregular tides are the rewards – and the area is stacked with wildlife, including **saltwater crocs**.

The road on from Hells Gate improves inside the Territory and once there you shouldn't have any trouble reaching Borroloola (see p.455), 266km down the track.

## travel details

### Trains

**Charleville** to: Brisbane (2 weekly; 15hr 35min); Quilpie (2 weekly; 4hr 30min); Roma (2 weekly; 5hr); Toowoomba (2 weekly; 12hr).

**Charters Towers** to: Cloncurry (2 weekly; 11hr 30min); Hughenden (2 weekly; 5hr); Mount Isa (2 weekly; 20hr); Townsville (2 weekly; 2hr 30min).

**Croydon** to: Normanton (1 weekly; 5hr).

**Emerald** to: Barcaldine (2 weekly; 6hr); Longreach (2 weekly; 8hr); Rockhampton (2 weekly; 4hr 30min).

**Longreach** to: Barcaldine (2 weekly; 2hr); Emerald (2 weekly; 8hr); Rockhampton (2 weekly; 12hr 30min).

**Mount Isa** to: Charters Towers (2 weekly; 15hr 30min); Cloncurry (2 weekly; 4hr 15min); Hughenden (2 weekly; 11hr).

**Mount Surprise** to: Forsayth (2 weekly; 5hr).

**Roma** to: Brisbane (2 weekly; 10hr 20min); Charleville (2 weekly; 5hr 10min); Quilpie (2 weekly; 4hr 30min); Toowoomba (2 weekly; 11hr 40min).

**Toowoomba** to: Brisbane (2 weekly; 3hr 30min); Charleville (2 weekly; 12hr 30min); Quilpie (2 weekly; 18hr 15min); Roma (2 weekly; 6hr 40min).

### Buses

**Charleville** to: Barcaldine (2 daily; 4hr 40min); Blackall (2 daily; 3hr 30min); Brisbane (3 daily; 10hr 40min); Cloncurry (2 daily; 10hr 50min); Longreach (2 daily; 6hr 30min); Mount Isa (2 daily; 14hr); Quilpie (2 weekly; 4hr 30min); Roma (3 daily; 3hr 40min); Toowoomba (3 daily; 8hr 25min); Winton (2 daily; 7hr 50min).

**Charters Towers** to: Cloncurry (3 daily; 8hr); Emerald (1 weekly; 6hr 30min); Hughenden (3 daily; 3hr); Mount Isa (3 daily; 10hr); Townsville (4 daily; 1hr 40min).

**Emerald** to: Anakie (3 weekly; 35min); Barcaldine (3 weekly; 3hr 40min); Charters Towers (1 weekly; 6hr 30min); Clermont (1 daily; 1hr 20min); Dingo (3 weekly; 1hr 35min); Longreach (3 weekly; 5hr); Mackay (1 daily; 4hr 20min); Moranbah (1 daily; 2hr); Rockhampton (3 weekly; 3hr 30min); Rolleston (1 weekly; 1hr 35min); Springsure (2 weekly; 45min–1hr).

**Longreach** to: Anakie (3 weekly; 4hr); Barcaldine (2 daily; 1hr); Blackall (2 daily; 3hr 15min); Brisbane (2 daily; 16hr 10min); Charleville (2 daily; 6hr 45min); Cloncurry (2 daily; 6hr 30min); Dingo (3 weekly; 7hr 30min); Emerald (3 weekly; 5hr); Mount Isa (2 daily; 7hr 50min); Rockhampton (3 weekly; 9hr 30min); Roma (2 daily; 10hr 25min); Toowoomba (2 daily; 14hr); Winton (2 daily; 2hr).

**Mount Isa** to: Barcaldine (2 daily; 9hr); Blackall (2 daily; 11hr 10min); Brisbane (2 daily; 25hr 20min); Camooweal (1 daily; 2hr 10min); Charleville (2 daily; 14hr 40min); Charters Towers (3 daily; 9hr 50min); Cloncurry (3 daily; 2hr 35min); Hughenden (3 daily; 7hr); Karumba (1 weekly; 7hr 10min); Longreach (2 daily; 8hr); Normanton (1 weekly; 6hr 10min); Roma (2 daily; 18hr 20min); Toowoomba (2 daily; 23hr); Townsville (3 daily; 12hr); Winton (2 daily; 3hr 30min).

**Roma** to: Barcaldine (2 daily; 8hr); Blackall (2 daily; 7hr); Brisbane (3 daily; 7hr); Charleville (2 daily; 3hr 30min); Cloncurry (2 daily; 14hr 20min); Longreach (2 daily; 10hr); Mount Isa (2 daily; 18hr); Toowoomba (3 daily; 4hr 30min); Winton (2 daily; 12hr).

**Toowoomba** to: Barcaldine (2 daily; 13hr); Blackall (2 daily; 12hr); Brisbane (8 daily; 1hr 50min); Charleville (3 daily; 11hr 40min); Cloncurry (2 daily; 20hr 30min); Coolangatta (2 daily; 3hr 40min); Goondiwindi (3 daily; 2hr 30min); Kingaroy (1 daily except Fri; 3hr); Longreach (2 daily; 14hr 30min); Mount Isa (2 daily; 22hr 20min); Rockhampton (2 daily; 12hr 45min); Roma (4 daily; 5hr); Surfers Paradise (2 daily; 3hr); Warwick (Mon–Sat daily; 3hr); Winton (2 daily; 16hr 30min).

**Winton** to: Barcaldine (2 daily; 3hr); Blackall (2 daily; 5hr 15min); Brisbane (2 daily; 19hr 25min); Charleville (2 daily; 8hr 45min); Cloncurry (2 daily; 4hr 30min); Longreach (2 daily; 2hr); Mount Isa (2 daily; 6hr); Roma (2 daily; 12hr 25min); Toowoomba (2 daily; 17hr).

### Flights

**Charleville** to: Brisbane (1 daily; 2hr).

**Emerald** to: Brisbane (2 daily; 2hr); Cairns (1–2 daily; 6hr 40min); Mackay (5 weekly; 5hr); Maroochydore (1 daily; 4hr 35min); Rockhampton (1–2 daily except Sun; 4hr); Townsville (1 daily except Sat; 4hr).

**Longreach** to: Brisbane (1 daily; 2hr 25min); Roma (5 weekly; 2hr).

**Mount Isa** to: Brisbane (1–2 daily; 2hr 15min); Burketown (1 weekly; 1hr 35min); Cairns (1–2 daily; 5hr 20min); Mackay (Mon–Sat 1 daily; 8hr); Mornington Island (5 weekly; 1hr 50min); Rockhampton (1–2 daily; 4hr); Townsville (1–3 daily; 2hr). *Air Mount Isa* (☎077/43 2844) flies Wed morning on a mail run to Lorraine, Gregory Downs, Hells Gate Roadhouse, Lawn Hill and Burketown; *North Westinair* (☎077/43 7720) and *Air Mount Isa* also have three- and five-seater charter planes.

**Roma** to: Brisbane (1–2 daily; 1hr 10min); Longreach (4 weekly; 2hr).

**Winton** to: Townsville (2 weekly; 1hr 25min).

# CHAPTER SIX

# NORTHERN TERRITORY

*Far in the north of Australia lies a little-known land, a vast half-finished sort of region, wherein Nature has been apparently practising how to make better places. This is the Northern Territory of South Australia . . .The decline and fall of the British Empire will date from the day that Britannia starts to monkey with the Northern Territory.*

A.B. ("Banjo") Paterson, 1898.

T his rather ominous prophecy by the bush balladeer "Banjo" Paterson, author of *Waltzing Matilda*, is still the way many Australians view the frontier lands of the **Northern Territory**, usually known as "The Territory", or simply "NT". Even the name conjures up a distant, untamed province and to an extent, it really is like this: just one percent of Australians live here, in an area covering one sixth of the continent. This tiny population and lack of economic autonomy explain why the Territory has never achieved full statehood, only gaining self-government from Canberra (itself a territory) in 1978.

Territorians relish their tough, maverick image, as well as the extremes of climate, distance and isolation that mould their temperaments. In this utmost corner of the country, drifters get washed up, fugitives cower and failed entrepreneurs pursue another abortive venture or become politicians. That great Australian institution of the "character" is in its element here, propping up the bars and bolstering the mythology of the Territory's recent lawless frontier history in what Xavier Herbert once described as the "Land of Ratbags". His classic 1938 novel, *Capricornia*, remains a scathing allegorical saga of the early Territorian years, based on Herbert's experience in 1930s' Darwin.

Within the Territory's boundaries there's evidence of the most recent colonial presence set among the oldest-occupied Aboriginal sites in Australia. **Darwin**, the Territory's capital, is an efficient, modern tropical town – a year-round temperature in the low thirties compelling a laidback lifestyle. Travellers the world over flock here to explore the **Top End** (as tropical NT is known), primarily **Kakadu National Park**'s abundant wildlife and the Aboriginal art sites. Adjacent **Arnhemland**, to the east, is Aboriginal land, too – and effectively out of bounds to casual visitors, although some exclusive tours do visit this never-colonized wilderness of scattered communities. Heading south, you pass through various historical pioneering towns before reaching **Katherine**, where nearby gorges within the **Nitmiluk National Park** are the town's principle attraction. At Katherine, the **Victoria Highway** heads west, past the spectacular ranges of the Gregory National Park to Western Australia, while just beyond the thermal resort of **Mataranka** a road winds eastwards along the palm-fringed Roper River to the Gulf Country. Here, **Borroloola**, a briefly thriving and lawless outpost, once on the Gulf stock route from northern Queensland, has since been bypassed into oblivion.

By the time you reach the much-derided town of **Tennant Creek** you're out of the interminable light woodlands and passing pastoral tablelands on the way to the central deserts surrounding **Alice Springs**. By no means the dusty Outback town many expect, Alice makes an excellent base to explore the natural wonders of the region, of which that famous monolith, **Ayers Rock** – or **Uluru** – 450km to the southwest, is but one of many. This is one of the finest areas to begin to learn about the Aborigines of the western desert, among the last to come into contact with European settlers.

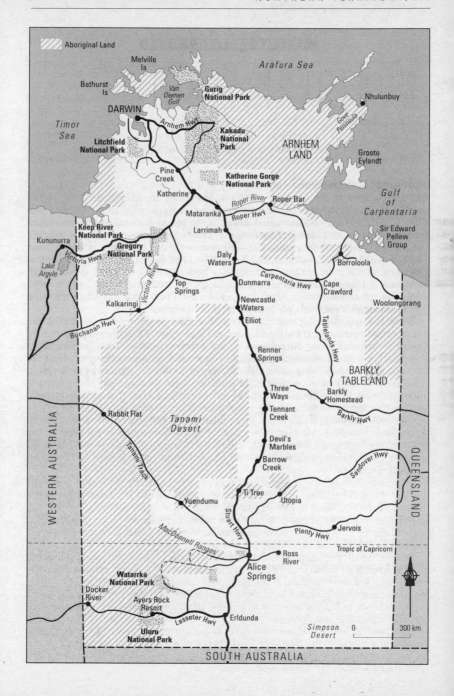

## Aborigines in the Northern Territory

Nearly a quarter of the Territory's 170,000 inhabitants are Aborigines, a far higher proportion than anywhere else in Australia. Most modern maps show that over one third of the Territory is **"Aboriginal Land"**, returned to nominal Aboriginal control following lengthy land claims. This uniquely Territorian demography is the result of the federal government's cautious co-operation with the politically powerful Land Councils within the NT, established following the Land Rights Act of 1976. Since that time, one of the most notable victories has been the return of the national park surrounding Uluru (Ayers Rock) to the Anangu, its traditional custodians, in 1986. Excepting the national parks, Aboriginal lands are out of bounds to visitors without a permit, although some roads which cross them are exempt.

While the overwhelming majority of non-Aboriginal people tend to live in the two major urban centres of Darwin and Alice Springs, most Aborigines live in remote Outback communities, or **outstations**, in self-imposed isolation from modern white society. This is worth remembering before you judge the depressing spectacle of the Aboriginal underclass living around the fringes of Katherine, Tennant Creek and in Alice's usually-dry Todd River. Ejected or estranged from their own strict communities, while at the same time alienated from the affluent white society that surrounds them, these people are the casualties of the catastrophic clash of white and Aboriginal culture which, in the Territory, is still within living memory. As Bill Harney, the first ranger at Ayers Rock, observed over thirty years ago: "The traveller only sees the ones on the roadway, for should he want to visit one of the Aboriginal Reserves he has to go through a wall of red tape. Thus is the best side of Aboriginal life hidden and the worst exposed to our view."

The chasm between the two vastly different cultures is actually far greater than most visitors realize. The failure of assimilation – the ethnocentric and naive policy of the 1950s and 1960s – added to mutual cultural (rather than racial) ignorance makes any meaningful contact for the short-term visitor unlikely. Weary suspicion of patronizing white curiosity, as well as an entirely different strategy in social dealings, renders most exchanges awkward and superficial.

Despite the all-too-conspicuous disparity in standards of living and levels of material wealth, Aboriginal **culture** is thriving in the Territory as growing political clout has encouraged self-determination. A renaissance of cultural pride in the face of formerly overwhelming white control has enabled self-expression in lifestyle, spirituality and – most obviously to the visitor – arts and crafts. Gradually, progressive outstations are inviting responsible tour operators to visit their settlements and experience something of their way of life. For those interested in getting to the heart of the enigmatic Australian wilderness, the Northern Territory offers enriching and memorable travel: an introduction to a continuously inhabited land that has sustained a fascinating and sophisticated culture for at least 40,000 years.

# DARWIN AND THE TOP END

**Darwin**, the Territory's capital, lies midway along Australia's convoluted northern coast. It's the only major town in the **Top End**, as tropical northern Australia (especially the top third of the NT) is familiarly called. Most tourists end up spending no more time here than it takes to visit nearby **Kakadu** and **Litchfield National Parks**, sell their vehicle or fly on to Indonesia. To many short-term visitors the city's appeal is elusive, but it remains the easiest place to fix up a **tour** into the surrounding area – something well worth considering if time is limited, or if you don't have your own transport.

## Darwin

Establishing a European settlement on Australia's remote northern shores was never going to be easy. It took four abortive attempts over a period of 45 years before **DARWIN** (originally called Palmerston) was surveyed in 1869 by South Australians keen to exploit their recently acquired "northern territory". The early colonists' aim was to pre-empt foreign occupation and create a trading post, a "new Singapore", for the British Empire.

Things got off to a good start with the arrival in 1872 of the **Overland Telegraph Line** (OTL), following the route pioneered by explorer **John McDouall Stuart** in 1862, that finally linked Australia with the rest of the world. **Gold** was discovered at Pine Creek while pylons were being erected for the OTL, prompting the inevitable goldrush, and the construction of a southbound railway. After the goldrush subsided, a cyclone flattened the depressed town in 1897, but by 1911, when Darwin adopted its present name, the rough-and-ready frontier outpost had grown into a small government centre, servicing the mines and properties of the Top End. In 1942, just five years after a second cyclone had razed the town, repeated **Japanese air raids** destroyed Darwin yet again – this time at a human cost of almost a thousand lives. The fear of invasion, and an urgent need to get troops to the war zone, led to the swift construction of the Stuart Highway, the first reliable link between Darwin and the rest of the country.

Three decades of guarded post-war prosperity followed until Christmas Day, 1974, when **Cyclone Tracy** devastated Darwin. For many residents this traumatic event was the last straw and, having been evacuated, they never returned. Indeed, the myth of Darwinian resilience is just that: the town has always accommodated a transient, easy-going population, happy to "give it a go" for a couple of years and then move on. The surrounding land (among the world's most lightning-prone regions) is agriculturally unviable and Top End beef (an industry recently decimated by disease-eradication programmes) is among the poorest in Australia; most is exported as live cattle to Asia.

At first glance, Darwin has the bland and incongruous appearance of a company town which, in a way, it is. More than half the workforce consists of much-reviled public servants, sitting out short contracts bolstered by associated perks; much of the remaining population services their needs. Were it not for Canberra's support in this

---

**TELEPHONE NUMBERS**

The **telephone code** for the Northern Territory is ☎089,
but this will change to ☎08 in April 1996.

Also in April 1996, **all Northern Territory phone numbers** will have the prefix 89
added; so, for example, what was ☎089/xx xxxx will become ☎08/89xx xxxx.

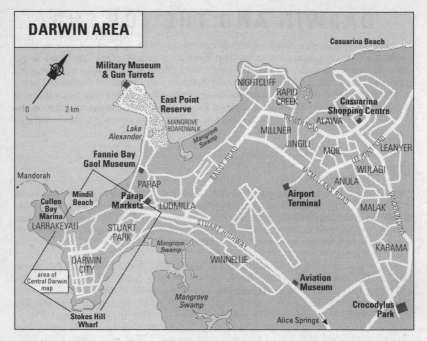

manner, Darwin would be merely a stagnating outpost on Australia's northern shore. As it is, backed by federal funds, Darwin is making a concerted effort to take itself seriously as the commercial "gateway" into Asia (or *from* Asia, as persistent flotillas of boat people see it). The town's famed reputation for excessive **drinking** is a response to utter boredom rather than a demonstration of irrepressible *joie de vivre*, and the oft-lauded multi-ethnicity is in fact a subtle Anglicization of numerous ethnic groups – it's certainly no greater a feature of life than in many other Australian cities. Darwin is clearly a colonial aberration that continues to fill a strategic gap in the vacant northern coastline, its future prosperity guaranteed by a military build-up set to increase the population by fifty percent over the next decade.

And yet, for the fraction of the 80,000 people that choose to make it their permanent home, Darwin exerts a perverse attraction that baffles outsiders. The year-round stifling heat and geographical isolation demands a casually indifferent "she'll be right, mate" attitude, unsuited to aspiring types. To live through a few mean Wets (as the torpid rainy seasons are known) with a limply-spinning fan, and not go mad, is an achievement worthy of Territorian citizenship. As the great Australian social philosopher, Dame Edna Everage, once observed, "Darwin is a virus, not a city; there is no cure".

## Arrival and information

All flights arrive at **Darwin Airport**, 12km northeast of the city centre. A **shuttle bus** service (☎45 3332; $6) meets international flights and takes you to your preferred accommodation or delivers you to the central **Transit Centre**, at 69 Mitchell Street; a **taxi** (☎81 8777) to town from the airport costs about $13. Given the proximity of Indonesia, the city is the cheapest place from which to leave Australian soil (see "Listings", p.431, for details).

By road, Darwin is a long way from anywhere in Australia – the bus journey from Cairns takes a gruelling day and a half, including changes, and coming direct from Sydney, Melbourne or Perth, you'd probably do better to fly. **Interstate buses** arrive at the Transit Centre, where you can make reservations for onward journeys (well in advance during high season); you can also buy various **passes** here, which are better value than ordinary tickets. Bus routes out of Darwin are given in "Travel Details" at the end of this chapter.

For information, the **Transit Centre Travel Desk** (daily 7am–7pm; ☎81 9733) is most convenient – offering maps and advice on the plethora of tours available in the Top End. Ten minutes' walk away, at 31 Smith Street Mall, the **Darwin Regional Tourist Association** (daily 9am–5pm; ☎81 4300) is the official tourist information outlet and has a **Conservation Commission** desk with plenty of information on national parks throughout the NT. Around town there are also several independent tourist information offices, all competing for their slice of the cake; it's worth checking out a few before you shell out a couple of hundred dollars on a tour. The free booklet *This Week In Darwin*, which can be picked up at many places around town, is mostly ads and rose-tinted descriptions, but is handy for **maps**. A half-kilometre radius around Smith Street Mall encompasses Darwin's city centre, catering for most of your needs, and there's little reason to visit the sea of suburbs spreading towards the northern beaches, apart from the beaches themselves.

## City transport

The city's inexpensive **bus service** (maximum fare $1.70; pay the driver) can deliver you to most corners of Darwin. Services operate daily from around 7am to 8pm, with some routes running until after 11pm on Friday and Saturday. The **Bus Terminus** (☎99 6540) is on Harry Chan Avenue, at the bottom of Cavenagh Street, though there's also a major interchange (☎99 8451) in the shopping centre at Casuarina, in the northern suburbs. Buses run as far out as Palmerston, Howard Springs and, on weekdays, Humpty Doo, 50km from town on the Kakadu road.

Most hostels and some hotels rent out **bicycles** for around $8–10 a day. Although Darwin is flat, it's also hot and sticky, so East Point Reserve, 8km from the centre, is about as far as you'd want to ride for fun. On the corner of Smith and McLachlan streets, several cheap **car rental** outfits do battle, with prices starting at around $25 a day. While certainly not the latest air-conditioned models, when shared by a foursome they make an inexpensive way of getting to Darwin's outlying attractions (see "Listings", p.431, for recommeded outfits). **Taxis** work out at about a dollar a kilometre and there are plenty cruising around: either hail one on the street or give them a call on ☎81 8777.

If you're looking to **buy a vehicle**, hostel noticeboards can be a good starting-point, or browse along Mitchell Street, opposite the Transit Centre, where many prospective sellers park their cars. Plenty of travellers also offer **lifts** to save on fuel bills over the long distances involved in leaving Darwin – again, check noticeboards at the bigger hostels or at the Transit Centre.

## Accommodation

Darwin has plenty of accommodation ranging from hostels to luxury hotels, most of it conveniently central. During the Wet season, when the town is deserted, prices in the upmarket establishments can take a dive, with half-price weekend packages frequently available.

### Hotels, motels and apartments
Most hotels and motels are right in the city centre, with the more prestigious and plush examples found along Mitchell Street or the Esplanade, behind it. If you're look-

ing for a self-catering place, there are several apartment-hotels in the centre, but for the most part they're further out; note that the price codes for self-catering apartments represent the daily rate for four-person units.

**Air Raid City Lodge**, 35 Cavanagh St (☎81 9214). Good-value, well-appointed rooms right in the centre. There's a communal kitchen and an attached restaurant. ⑤.

**Asti Motel**, 7 Packard Place (☎81 8200). Exemplary large motel with spa, restaurant and pool. ⑥.

**Atrium Hotel**, Esplanade (☎41 0755). Attractive and good-value hotel with all the comforts and service you'd expect at these prices. ⑧.

**Capricornia Motel**, 44 East Point Rd (☎81 4055). Small motel out near Fannie Bay, 4km from the centre (bus #4 or #6), with pool and cooking facilities. ⑤.

**Cherry Blossom Motel**, 108 Esplanade (☎81 6734). Opposite the Esplanade park, this fairly ordinary "drive-in" motel has a pool and restaurant. ⑥.

**City Gardens Apartments**, 93 Woods St (☎41 2888). Centrally located family units in a tropical setting. Two minutes' walk from a large park, five from town. ⑦.

**Frontier Darwin**, Buffalo Court, at the end of Woods St (☎81 5333). Not much to look at but boasts comfortable rooms, restaurants, bars and Corroboree-inspired entertainment. ⑦.

**Hotel Darwin**, 10 Herbert St (☎81 9211). Still going strong after fifty years, this is one of the city's oldest intact buildings, retaining vestiges of colonial charm and a few great-value rooms, alongside its more expensive options. Budget rooms ④, otherwise ⑥.

**Top End Hotel**, corner of Mitchell and Daly streets (☎81 6511). Attractively designed motel with large pool and bistro, but next to a sleazy pub/club complex. ⑥.

**Ti Tree Apartments**, 92 Woods St (☎41 0568). Small collection of comfortable holiday units close to town and Frogshollow parkland. ⑦.

## Hostels

Hostels in Darwin vary from central, but fairly grim ex-single men's quarters and former motels, to smaller and quieter converted tropical houses further down Mitchell Street. Some sport excellent facilities, including pools, as well as any number of incentives to preclude your early departure. Many hostels more than a kilometre from the Transit Centre have minibuses which offer regular rides uptown or meet incoming long-distance buses. Note that some places charge a dollar or two extra for beds in air-conditioned dorms or rooms.

**CWA Hostel**, 3 Packard Place (☎41 1536). Not a backpackers' place but a small, shady house in its own grounds for women, couples and families only. Dorms ①, rooms ②–③.

**Darwin City Lodge**, 151 Mitchell St (☎41 1295). Friendly, family-run, comfortably converted house (also with a less attractive annexe), featuring a pool, tour-booking service and regular lifts uptown. Dorms ①, rooms ③.

**Darwin Rest House**, 11 Houston St (☎81 1638). Well-hidden and amicably run hostel, one of Darwin's first, oozing genteel decay. There's a large tropical garden and pool and a free "cultural debriefing" service for those just arrived from Southeast Asia. ①.

**Gecko Lodge**, 146 Mitchell St (☎81 5569). Clean hostel with a small pool, but close to Mindil Beach. Free pick-ups and nightly lifts uptown. Dorms ①, rooms ③.

**Elke's**, 112 Mitchell St (☎81 8399). Very well-refurbished old building at the quiet end of Mitchell Street, with a pool and free pick-ups; one of Darwin's best, but charges for luggage storage unless you take their tours. Dorms ①, twins ③.

**Fawlty Towers**, 88 Mitchell Street (☎81 8363). Friendly hostel in an elevated cabin-style building with air-con rooms and a pool. ①, rooms ③.

**Frogshollow Backpackers**, 27 Lindsay St (☎41 2600). Popular, attractive tropical building opposite a large park and with a light breakfast included in its rates. Tour bookings, pick-ups and spa available, but it suffers from badly partitioned 16-bed mixed dorms. Dorms ①, rooms ④.

**Ivans Backpackers Resort**, 97 Mitchell St (☎81 5385). Converted motel popular with 18–24s on the loose, with pool, bar and tour bookings. ①.

**Larrakeyah Lodge**, 50 Mitchell St (☎81 2933). Recently refurbished concrete block opposite the Transit Centre, next to the used-car selling zone. Dorms ①, rooms ③.

**Salvation Army Red Shield Hostel**, 49 Mitchell St (☎81 8188). Well-equipped and cheap single rooms, which would suit impoverished misanthropes; 4-bed dorms, too. ①.

**YHA**, 69a Mitchell St (☎81 3995). Next to the Transit Centre and *Banyan Junction* food markets. The twin and triple rooms have all seen better days but offer fan-cooled near-privacy. ①.

**YWCA**, 119 Mitchell St (☎81 6104). Succesfully shedding its institutional image, with well-kept twin rooms as well as men's and women's dorms. Dorms ①, rooms ③–④.

## Camping and Caravan Parks

The following **camping** and **caravan parks** are all along the Stuart Highway in Winnellie, between 7km and 14km from the centre. Winnellie itself is a rather godforsaken light-industrial suburb, lying along the southern edge of the airport. Buses #5 and #8 run here from the central bus terminus.

**Leprechaun Caravan Park**, Airport Gates, Stuart Highway (☎84 3400). Behind a motel of the same name and closest to Darwin, this has a pool and shady tent sites. On-site vans ③.

**Shady Glen Caravan Park**, corner of Farrell Crescent and Stuart Highway (☎84 3330). Pool and kiosk with tent sites. On-site vans ③.

**Overlander Caravan Park**, corner of Stuart Highway and McMillans Rd, Berrimah (☎84 3025). Close to shops, and to the subterranean ironstone, making Berrimah a top spot for catching lightning shows during November's Build Up (to the Wet season). On-site vans ③.

# The Town

Present-day Darwin projects northwards from the end of a stubby peninsula where a settlement was originally established in 1869 on the lands of the Larrakeyah Aborigines. Over the years, the suburbs have spread across the flat, mangrove-fringed headland, but for the visitor, most of the points of interest lie between the city and East Point, 8km to the north. It is not by any means a good-looking city: huge tides create a sludge-filled sea devoid of waves, while repeated destruction from cyclones and Japanese bombs has left any surviving colonial architecture discreet and intermittent.

Short of renting a bike, the **Tour Tub** (daily 9am–4pm; day-ticket $14; ☎85 4779 ) is the best way to see most of the places detailed below. Departing on the hour from Smith Street Mall, opposite *Woolworth's*, the minibus trundles along its route allowing you to hop on and off as you please.

## The Wharf Precinct

Recent years have seen tentative development nudging the fishermen and skateboarders off the old wharves at the southern end of town. *Christo's* seafood restaurant (see "Eating", below) set the ball rolling by moving into the old shed at the end of **Stokes Hill Wharf**. Souvenir shops and a seasonal bungy-jumping tower have followed, as has the award-winning live coral display operated by **Indo-Pacific Marine** (daily 9am–6pm; $8). In the right frame of mind, you could spend hours observing the transposed marine envionments, and the regular informative talks will set you straight about corals – the Timor Sea north of Darwin is one of the world's richest and most diverse coral environments but is occluded by tidal silt. In the same building, the **Australian Pearling Exhibition** (Mon–Sat 10am–6pm, Sun noon–6pm; $5) is a similarily worthwhile and imaginative historical display, entertainingly describing Darwin's part in northern Australia's pearling exploits. Round the other side of the harbour, a walk up Hughes Avenue and then left down the Esplanade brings you to **Government House**, built in 1883 after the original residence was devoured by white ants. Rarely open to the public, it's a good example of an elegant, though much restored, tropical building.

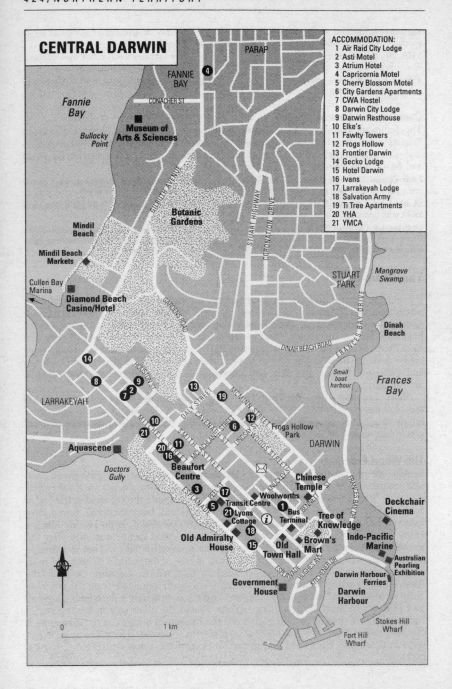

# CENTRAL DARWIN

ACCOMMODATION:
1 Air Raid City Lodge
2 Asti Motel
3 Atrium Hotel
4 Capricornia Motel
5 Cherry Blossom Motel
6 City Gardens Apartments
7 CWA Hostel
8 Darwin City Lodge
9 Darwin Resthouse
10 Elke's
11 Fawlty Towers
12 Frogs Hollow
13 Frontier Darwin
14 Gecko Lodge
15 Hotel Darwin
16 Ivans
17 Larrakeyah Lodge
18 Salvation Army
19 Ti Tree Apartments
20 YHA
21 YMCA

PARAP

FANNIE BAY

CONACHER ST

*Fannie Bay*

*Bullocky Point*

Museum of Arts & Sciences

GILRUTH AVENUE

Mindil Beach

Botanic Gardens

Mindil Beach Markets

Cullen Bay Marina

Diamond Beach Casino/Hotel

GARDENS ROAD

STUART HIGHWAY

CORONATION DRIVE

STUART PARK

*Mangrove Swamp*

*Dinah Beach*

DINAH BEACH ROAD

FRANCES BAY DRIVE

HOUSTON ST

LARRAKEYAH

Aquascene

*Doctors Gully*

DAY STREET

CAVENAGH STREET

SMITH STREET

MCLACHLAN ST

MITCHELL STREET

ESPLANADE

Beaufort Centre

Old Admiralty House

Government House

MCMINN STREET

LINDSAY ST

WOODS STREET

KNUCKEY ST

BENNETT ST

Frogs Hollow Park

DARWIN

*Small boat harbour*

*Frances Bay*

Woolworths

Transit Centre

Bus Terminal

Lyons Cottage

Old Town Hall

Chinese Temple

Tree of Knowledge

Brown's Mart

FRANCES BAY DR

HUGHES AVE

KITCHENER DR

Deckchair Cinema

Indo-Pacific Marine

Australian Pearling Exhibition

Darwin Harbour Ferries

*Darwin Harbour*

*Stokes Hill Wharf*

*Fort Hill Wharf*

N

0                 1 km

## The City Centre

There are more old buildings in nearby Smith Street. The **Old Town Hall** (1883) was practically demolished by Cyclone Tracy, but its ruins occasionally host outdoor performances by a theatre group, which is based in the stone building, **Brown's Mart**, opposite. In the park behind Brown's Mart is a huge banyan tree known as the **Tree of Knowledge**, while nearby is the ornate **Chinese Temple** (Mon–Fri 8am–4pm, Sat & Sun 8am–3pm) in Woods Street, near the corner of Bennett Street. Another postcyclone restoration, using the altar and statues from the 1887 original, this still serves Darwin's Chinese population – considerably diminished since the early days of white settlement, when Chinese labourers were responsible for building virtually everything, including the railway.

From the temple, take a walk through **Smith Street Mall** to examine the refurbished **Hotel Victoria**. As the former *Vic' Hotel*, it was once Darwin's answer to a Wild West saloon, but is now leading the city's pub-gentrification programme. From here, a left turn down Knuckey Street leads to the Esplanade, where two more buildings await inspection. On the left corner is the former **Admiralty House** (Mon–Sat 10am–5pm; free), a tropical-style house elevated on stilts which has survived two cyclones and numerous air raids. Opposite, **Lyons Cottage** (daily 10am–noon & 12.30–5pm; free) is a stone bungalow, also dating from the 1920s, with displays of early Territorian history.

A pleasant walk along the lawns of the **Esplanade** leads to Daly Street, which marks the very end of the Stuart Highway. If you've had enough, it's a straight 1500-kilometre run to Alice from here, with only about half a dozen traffic lights to hold you up on the way. Otherwise, a left turn down Doctor's Gully leads to the absurdly popular **Aquascene** (call ☎81 7837 for tide-dependent opening hours; $3.50), where at high tide scores of catfish, mullet and metre-long milkfish come in to be hand-fed on stale bread (supplied free).

## The Fannie Bay museums

From town it's a two-kilometre walk north to the **Botanic Gardens** (daily 7am–7pm; free), Darwin's main park, housing a large collection of palms as well as a separate Plant Display House (daily 7.30am–4pm). A further kilometre brings you to the **Museum of Arts and Sciences** (Mon–Fri 9am–5pm, Sat & Sun 10am–5pm; free) in Conacher Street, overlooking Fannie Bay. An excellent museum and art gallery, it's particularly notable for its Southeast Asian perspective, in pleasing contrast to the usual exclusive focus on recent white achievements. In fact, the small art gallery is let down by the drab European selection, but on the whole the museum displays are lively and absorbing, particularly the section on Tiwi culture, from the Bathurst and Melville islands. The stuffed remains of "Sweetheart", a five-metre-long rogue crocodile with a taste for outboard engines, are particularly alarming, while the massive boatshed is a mariners' paradise, with boats as diverse as pearling luggers, Indonesian *praus*, Polynesian outriggers and the simplest of bark canoes. The museum's most recent addition is an imaginatively designed exhibition commemorating Darwin's destruction by **Cyclone Tracy**. By 3am on Christmas Day, 1974, many thought the worst was over, as winds that had raged since midnight began to abate. Instead, the becalmed eye of the storm was passing over the part-ruined city, only to return with even greater fury from the opposite direction. Lamposts were bent flat along the ground, houses were ripped from their piers, and at the Yacht Club, mangled remains of boats filled the car park. Mercifully, a low tide meant that only 66 people lost their lives but Tracy marked the end of old Darwin, psychologically as well as architecturally.

**Fannie Bay Gaol Museum** (daily 10am–5pm; free; bus #4 or #6), further north along the bay, 5km from the city centre, served as Darwin's prison for nearly a hundred years until 1979. Displayed alongside the grim prisoners' quarters is an old train, a reminder of the thorny issue of Darwin's rail link with the rest of the country.

This has been promised by successive campaigning prime ministers, but Anthony Trollope's observations of 120 years ago – "I do not believe that I shall live to see a railway from Adelaide to Port Darwin, or even that younger men than I will do so" – may still be considered the last words on the subject.

## On to East Point

Right by the Gaol Museum, the main route (and buses #4 and #6 ) curves right, while East Point Road continues straight up to the **East Point Reserve**, an area of largely natural bushland that's home to around two thousand wallabies. After a kilometre you pass **Lake Alexander**, a jellyfish-free saltwater recreational lake suitable for year-round swimming and nearby, a **mangrove boardwalk** taking you into the tidal environment. The road ends 3km from the gaol at the **East Point Military Museum** (daily 9.30am–5pm; $5). Most visitors – and quite a few Australians – are unaware that Darwin was repeatedly bombed by the Japanese in 1942; at the time, news of both the air raids and the 30,000 enemy troops massed on Timor, awaiting the order to invade, was successfully supressed. The museum commemorates these events with a short video and some rather staid displays of uniforms, medals and other wartime memorabilia, while in the grounds a collection of neglected World War II guns, aircraft engines and associated hardware quietly rust away. The guns themselves were never actually used and were eventually sold ten years later as scrap to – ironically – the Japanese. East Point is also an ideal spot to watch the striking hues of Darwin's multichrome sunsets; if driving, watch out for roadside wallabies on the way back.

### The Aviation Museum and Crocodylus Park

Set in a hangar off the Stuart Highway, on the southeastern edge of the airport, the **Aviation Museum** (daily 8.30am–5pm; $6; bus #5 or #8) is easily dominated by the huge bulk of a B52 bomber on loan from the US Air Force. Despite their age, B52s saw service as high-level "carpet bombers" during the Gulf War. Next to it, all the other aircraft and engine displays look rather tame.

Continuing down the Stuart Highway and turning left at the Berrimah traffic lights leads you to **Crocodylus Park** (daily 9am–5pm; $10; ☎47 2510; bus #4 or 10 to Casuarina, then bus #9). The displays are absorbing and educational but the actual croc pens lack the variety of huge monsters presently viewable at the *Crocodile Farm* (see p.442); the usually passive crocs leap into frenzied action during the daily feeding sessions.

### Darwin's beaches

Several factors exclude Darwin from being the beach resort you might have hoped for. A high tidal range, the fierce tropical sun and the seasonal but deadly menace of stinging box jellyfish (from October to May) – which rules out swimming in the sea at the hottest time of year – mean that, despite its few beaches, you're rarely pushed for a spot to roll out your towel. Traps in the harbour regularly capture *most* of the crocodiles. **Fannie Bay's** beaches (see above; bus #4 or #6) are closest to the town centre and have a kiosk and water craft hire. However, the **Casuarina Coastal Reserve** (bus #4 or #10; 40min), capping the northern suburbs, has the city's most attractive sandy stretches, including a "free beach" for nudists. Take provisions with you as there are no facilities here.

## Eating

In Darwin, the distinct cuisines of eastern Asia are all on offer, with Mindil Beach Market(see "Markets and shopping", below) a good place to grasp their distinguishing features, and *Banyan Junction Markets* the place to blur the distinctions again. Adventurous carnivores can tackle exotic meats like **kangaroo**, buffalo, camel and **crocodile**, though they're often more entertaining in the bush than on a plate. Ironically, the climate makes it likely that seafood will have been frozen, and so might as well be from Vladivostok as from the Timor Sea. That said, anglers come here from all over Australia hoping to catch **barramundi** – a fine fighting fish, but at first taste rather bland; snapper is generally more flavoursome.

## City centre and the wharf area

**Banyan Junction Markets**, Transit Centre, Mitchell St. Various stalls selling mostly Asian food, and catering mainly to impoverished travellers. Open daily, early to late.

**Capri**, Knuckey Street. Plush city-centre coffee bar.

**Christo's**, Stokes Hill Wharf (☎81 8658). Old shed at the end of the wharf area, offering Greek and Mediterranean-style seafood with a view. Great views but fairly slack service, especially given the prices.

**Confetti's**, opposite the cinema in Mitchell Street. Cool coffee shop that attracts young guns on shiny Harleys.

**Fisherman's Eatery**, Fisherman's Wharf, Frances Bay Drive. Fish and chips kiosk which also sells fresh local seafood.

**Galleria Restaurant**, Galleria Mall, off Smith St Mall. Superior café open during shopping hours with delicious luncheon temptations.

**Hog's Breath**, 15 Smith St Mall (☎41 3333). Lively and popular American joint with ribs, burgers and Tex-Mex dishes at reasonable prices.

**Lee Dynasty**, 21 Cavenagh St (☎81 7808). Darwin's top-notch Chinese restaurant with an extensive Cantonese menu.

**Lindsay Street Café**, 2 Lindsay St (☎81 8631). Attractive garden restaurant with simple but wholesome pasta dishes.

**Magic Wok**, GPO Centre, Cavenagh St. Mongolian BBQ restaurant – choose your food and they stir-fry it before your eyes. Quick, fun and original.

**Pancake Palace**, 28 Cavenagh St. Fun venue with variations on a pancake theme.

**Peppi's**, 84 Mitchell St (☎81 3762). Established, pre-cyclone French restaurant that continues to strike the right chord with its formal decor and classy cuisine.

**Rendezvous**, Star Village Arcade, Smith St Mall. Malaysian-flavoured cheap lunch spot.

**Roma**, Cavenagh Street. This classic, Italian-inspired coffee bar serving tasty snacks and breakfasts is an old favourite.

**Siggi's**, *Beaufort Hotel*, Mitchell St (☎82 9911). Intimate silver-service restaurant, this is one of Darwin's best and most expensive.

**Sizzler's**, Cinema Complex, Mitchell St. The easily-pleased queue for steak, seafood and salad. Fast and tasty – eat all you can and get out.

**Toots**, corner of Smith and Peel streets. Minimally converted filling station that needs some foliage to soften its lines, but serves winning Malaysian dishes at bargain prices.

**Uncle John's Cabin**, 4 Gardiner St (☎81 3358). The city's most original seafood restaurant, set in a grounded Indonesian *prau* in an eccentrically landscaped front garden.

## Fannie Bay, East Point and Nightcliff

**Asian Gateway**, 58 Aralia St (☎48 1131). Tucked away in Nightcliff, a northern suburb beyond the airport, this is the best spot in Darwin for Thai food.

**Cornucopia**, Museum of Arts and Sciences Complex, Conacher St (☎81 7791). Sunset views from the terrace and a contemporary Australian menu. Moderate prices.

**Holtze Cottage**, Botanic Gardens (☎41 1299). Specializes in *à la carte* seafood and novelty crocodile, roo and buffalo dishes, plus herbaceous borders.

**Koh-I-Noor**, *Sea Breeze Motel*, 60 East Point Road (☎81 0999). Quality Indian, Thai and Malaysian cooking, licensed and with a pleasant tropical outlook.

# Drinking, nightlife and entertainment

Darwin's thirst for alcohol used to be legendary, with some statistics for beer consumption averaging out at around 230 litres per year for every man, woman and child. Eliminating the largely teetotal children and moderate women drinkers, that meant each grown man knocking back nearly a pair of "slabs" (24-can cartons) each week – fifty percent more than in the rest of Australia. In recent years, consumption has eased off considerably, as the NT government, embarrassed by this boozy image, instigated a "Lighten Up" campaign, imploring moderation and reducing the price of "lite", low-alcohol beer. However, nightlife in Darwin is much more varied than this might suggest, with a smalltime band scene, cinemas (including a seasonal outdoor one) and, of course, a striking waterfront casino at Diamond Beach. The Dry is enlivened by several festivals and associated mayhem.

## Pubs and bars

Pubs have responded to changing demands by transforming their intimidating and outdated frontier-town atmosphere into something more conducive to their new-found clientele of public servants and tourists, with the added benefit that many are no longer no-go areas for unaccompanied women. The "Lighten Up" campaign is characterized by the refurbishment and ascent upmarket of the once-rowdy *Hotel Victoria*, ideally positioned in the mall to attract tourists – it seems that the former patrons have been successfully repelled by the new decor. Sleazedom endures, in any case, at the *Sportsman's Bar*, on Mitchell Street, with twice-daily strip shows, and the "boutique" *Frontier Bar* out back: no more than a gimmick but popular with young drinkers. Even the *Beachfront Hotel* in Nightcliff (in the northern suburbs) has forsaken its raging afternoon sessions for something akin to, God forbid, a family-orientated bistro.

On the Esplanade, the *Atrium Hotel* has the pleasant *Jabiru Bar*, while further along the Esplanade, the *Beaufort Hotel* invites you to its cosy *Raffles Bar*, as frightfully English as they get up here. The ageing *Darwin Hotel*, in Herbert Street, milks its neo-colonial image with the *Pickled Parrot* piano bar and airy *Green Room*. On the corner of Bennett and Mitchell streets, *Petty Sessions* is a wine bar/bistro/nightclub appealing to the "Thank God It's Friday" crowd, and next door, the five-star *Plaza Hotel* is a surprisingly egalitarian place for a beer. And don't turn down an invitation to the "members only" *Yacht Club* in Fannie Bay, a fine place to watch the sun set over the Timor Sea. Also out this way, *Cool Spot*, on Fannie Bay Road, just near the East Point turn off, is a fashionable late-opening bar with great drinks – but give the food a miss.

## Clubs and live music

Like Darwin's transient population, things change quickly on the city's **club scene**, with the *Northern Territory News,* or the bi-monthly *Daily Plan It*, keeping abreast of developments and the odd trend. Though the streets remain oddly deserted, Wednesdays to Saturdays are the nights to cut loose in Darwin's clubs. *The Time* and *The Pit*, both in Edmunds Street, have traded their dated decor and sleazy image for wholesome rock and roll sounds, including downright Seventies' Retro on Sunday nights. Alternatively, to mix it with Uni students, try *Circles*, at the *Beaufort Hotel*, opposite the cinema in Mitchell Street. The *Diamond Beach Casino* (see below) hosts several diversions, including *Crystals*, a straightforward disco, while karaoke crooning takes off in the early hours at the enlarged *Sweethearts Bar*. The *Beachcomber* disco, behind the *Sportsman's Bar* in Mitchell Street is, if nothing else, only a brief stagger away from the hostels.

The current hot spot seems to be the *Big Country Saloon* in Cavenagh Street, the best place for **live bands** and site of *Pandora's Box*, the city's principal gay bar. Stranded on McMinn Street is the comparatively serene, rainbow-coloured *Old Workers Club*, an alternative venue for easygoing local bands out for a jam. Sunday afternoons'

"Jazz on the Lawn" behind the casino is strictly middle of the road: there's more spirited jazz on Friday nights at the *Hotel Darwin's Green Room*, in Herbert Street. Finally, at *Banyan Junction Markets* (behind the Transit Centre) during the Dry you can listen to local vocalists mutilating pop classics night after night, with the occasional angelic voice rousing the supine audience. This is also the venue for the *Elcho Island Dancers'* free weekly shows, incorporating some great didgeridoo-ing.

## Theatre, cinemas and the casino

For **theatrical performances**, see what *Brown's Mart Community Arts* (☎81 5522) are up to, or check out the programme at the *Performing Arts Centre* (☎81 1222), next to the *Beaufort Hotel* on Mitchell Street, which hosts top acts and shows from all over the country. The five-screen **cinema**, *Cinema Darwin,* just over the road, has cheap tickets on Tuesdays, but take a sweater to combat the over-zealous air-conditioning; for an alternative to mainstream films, check out the al fresco *Deckchair Cinema* down on Stokes Hill Wharf (closed in the Wet).

Only smartly dressed **gamblers** get past the watchful doormen at the *Diamond Beach Casino* (off East Point Road, near Mindil Beach; open nightly), a sawn-off pyramid designed to withstand 350km-per-hour winds – and filled with a variety of distractions designed to remove your money just as fast.

## Events and festivals

The Dry season sees an upsurge in popular activity as the city shakes off the langour of the Wet. As well as lacklustre rodeos, agricultural shows and racing, mid-June's **Bougainvillea Festival** sees bands, plays, parades and all sorts of happenings around the city, and is well worth catching. Late July is the time for the famous **Beer Can Regatta** in Fannie Bay – wacky boat races in sea craft made entirely from beer cans. A genuine manifestation of Territorian eccentricity, this inevitably involves drunken revelries, and there have been attempts by the "Lighten Up" brigade to make the event more family-orientated. In early August, there is more nuttiness during the barefoot **Mud Crab Tying Competition**, a speed event that can cost you your digits.

# Markets and shopping

Every Thursday night from 5.30pm (May–Oct only) **Mindil Beach Market** attracts thousands of locals who park, unpack their eskies and garden furniture, and settle in for the sunset. A superb array of sizzling food stalls from all corners of the earth (but mostly Asia) excite the taste buds; New Age remedies, handicrafts and teeming humanity round off Darwin's one unmissable event. The market has become so popular (with attendant parking and sanitary complications) that the council is threatening to curb the event, so go before they do. It's a three-kilometre walk from town through the Botanical Gardens, or a short ride on a #4 or #6 bus from the city centre. Alternatively, call *Tour Tub* (☎018/89 5434; $2) for a pick-up. **Parap's** Saturday morning market, on Parap Road (bus #6), or **Rapid Creek market** off Trower Road on Sundays (bus #6 or #10), are good year-round substitutes, with a smaller food selection, old books and knick-knacks.

Darwin has entire emporia filled with souvenir trash, from cute rubber crocs to didgeridoo armbands, but the shops below offer decent merchandise that you needn't be ashamed to have scrutinized by customs on the way home.

**Bookworld**, 30 Smith St Mall (Mon–Fri 9am–5pm, Thurs until 7pm, Sat 9am–noon). Excellent bookshop with a full selection of Top End literature, coffee-table souvenirs and contemporary reading.

**Blazez**, Star Village, off Smith St Mall (Mon–Fri 9am–5.30pm, Sat 9am–noon). To use their words, "ethnic and unusual collectables" with an Asian theme.

**Dusty Covers**, 1st floor, Chin Arcade, 29 Cavenagh St (Mon–Fri noon–5pm). Unusually good selection of secondhand books including Asian travel guides and rare Australian first editions.

**Framed Showcase Gallery**, corner of Geranium St and Stuart Highway (Mon–Sat 8.30am–5.30pm, Sun 11am–5pm). Spend hours regarding Darwin's best display of contemporary and traditional art. Bus #5, #8 or a 3-km walk from the centre.

**Indigenous Creations**, Smith St Mall. Good selection of Aboriginal arts and crafts at reasonable prices.

**Riji Dij**, Anthony Plaza, Smith St Mall (Mon–Fri 9am–5pm, Sat 9am–2pm). All Australian T-shirts worth framing, clothing printed with vivid Aboriginal designs, Tiwi batiks and some classy postcards.

**Shady Lady**, Shop 9, West Lane, behind *Plaza Hotel* (Mon–Fri 9am–5pm, Sat 9am–1pm). Full range of *Akubra* and other brand-name hats with knowledgeable staff.

## Listings

**Airlines** *Ansett Airlines,* 46 Smith St Mall (☎13 1300), has very cheap, one-way backpacker fares to Kununurra and Broome. *Garuda* (☎81 6422) or *Merpati* (☎41 1030) have flights to Bali and Kupang, in Timor, both departing four times a week, while *Malaysian Airlines* (☎41 2323) flies to Singapore twice a week.

**Bushwalking** *Darwin Bushwalking Club* (☎85 1484) organizes weekend walks in the Top End and welcomes visitors.

---

### TOURS FROM DARWIN TO THE TOP END

For the visitor, Darwin itself isn't a destination of enduring interest, but the surrounding countryside certainly is. Kakadu is the obvious draw, and for many is the primary reason for visiting the Top End, but Litchfield Park is nearer, croc-free and a fun day out. While Litchfield remains a popular day-trip, many Kakadu tour operators are now offering two- and three-day tours, providing a less hurried way of enjoying the park. Below are some recommended **tour operators** in the Top End not mentioned elsewhere in the text.

**All Terrain** (☎41 0070). Good value two-day minibus and three-day 4WD (includes Twin Falls, $300) eco-adventure tours in Kakadu, with knowledgeable guides. Prices include jumping croc cruise (see below), but not the park entry fee.

**Australian Kakadu Tours** (☎81 5144). Tours for the less active, ranging all over the Top End; up to ten days, costing between $80 and $200 per day. Also excellent, though expensive, tours to the unique Tiwi islands.

**Coo-ee Tours** (☎41 0070). Enjoyable twelve-hour waterfall hop through Litchfield ($75, includes Tjedeba Falls) with a dinkum Aussie family. Mama Coo-ee's cakes, yarns and songs all add to the experience. Also two-day Kakadu tours.

**Far North Safaris** (☎41 0070). A provocative guide gets you thinking while tramping about Kakadu and Litchfield for three days ($300).

**Kakadu Plus** (☎81 2560). Cheap and cheerful 19-seater minibus on two-and-a-half-day Kakadu and three-and-a-half-day Kakadu/Litchfield tours – very popular

with backpackers. Plenty of free extras to compensate for the bargain-basement food and mozzie-ridden campsite.

**Keetleys** (☎81 4422). Established tour operator for those who prefer not to rough it too much. One-day Litchfield and Katherine and two-day Kakadu tours for $300.

**Saratoga** (☎81 6473). Well-regarded two-day Kakadu tours with zoologist guide. Those genuinely keen on the park's wildlife and nature won't be disappointed.

**Southern Cross** (☎81 6473). Small, three-day Kakadu/Katherine tours in a plush, 4WD minibus; $395, including horse-riding, accommodation and decent food. Worth the extra cost.

**Wild Quest** (☎81 6473). Off-the-beaten-track two-day tours show Litchfield as more than a waterfall hop, with guides committed to quality tourism. Two-and three-day Kakadus in chunky 4WD bus.

**Willis Walkabouts** (☎85 2134). Bushwalking in the Top End, Kimberley and the Centre for committed walkers.

**Car rental** *Brits Australia*, Daly St (☎81 2081), has 4WD campers and motorhomes for rent from $100 per day, as well as saloon cars, and can arrange one-way drop-offs at major cities. *Nifty* , 10 Mclachlan St (☎81 2999), has mokes for local use from $25 a day; *Network*, 90 Mitchell St (☎81 9300) also has mokes from $25/a day, plus 4WDs. *Territory Rent-a-Car*, 64 Stuart Highway (☎81 8400) has air-con two-door runabouts from $39/day, 20c/km; and *Thrifty*, 89 Smith St (☎81 8555), offers three-day packages for around $300.

**Cars – buying and selling** Mitchell Street, opposite the Transit Centre, is where travellers park and sell their cars; also check out the hostel noticeboards.

**Car trouble** *AANT*, MLC Building, 81 Smith St (☎81 3838). Vehicle breakdown service, road maps and information. For roadside service call ☎41 0611.

**Disabled Persons Bureau** Shop 7, Ground Floor, Casurina Plaza (☎22 7213). Provides information on access and facilities for visitors to Darwin.

**Gay and Lesbian Society** Call ☎81 6812 for information and details of social activities and weekly meets at *Mississippi Queen* in Gardiner St.

**Hospital** *Royal Darwin Hospital*, Rocklands Drive, Casuarina (☎20 7211).

**Indonesian Consulate** 18 Harry Chan Ave (PO Box 1953, Darwin 0801; ☎41 0488); Mon–Fri 9am–1pm & 2–5pm.

**Pharmacy** 46 Smith St Mall (☎81 9202). Open 9am–9pm.

**Police** Main police station is at West Lane (☎81 1866).

**Post office** 48 Cavenagh St, on the corner of Edmunds St (☎80 8227).

**Secondhand stuff** *City Secondhand and Pawnbrokers*, 6 Harriet Place (where Daly crosses Smith St) has some useful used gear such as cameras, bikes, eskies, tools and hats.

**Swimming** The nearest decent-sized pool is at Ross Smith Ave, Parap (☎81 2662); take bus #6 or #10 from the city centre. Or try Lake Alexander at East Point.

**Tours** See box opposite for details of Top End tours from Darwin

**Travel agent** *Jalan Jalan*, 15a Knuckey St (☎81 0990) specializes in packages and flights to Indonesia.

**Vaccinations** Contact the *Travel and Immunization Service* (☎81 7197) for vaccination service if you're heading for Asia.

# Around Darwin

Day trips from Darwin, not counting the popular national parks (for which see below), include inexpensive visits to the resort of **Mandorah**, a ferry ride across the harbour, and to **Howard Springs**, a ninety-minute bus ride away, where there's safe swimming and a patch of rainforest. Both are agreeable locations, giving at least the impression of getting out of town, although they can both get extremely crowded with locals at the weekend. Only a thirty-minute flight from town, the Aboriginal-owned Bathurst and Melville islands – known as the **Tiwi Islands** – are Australia's largest islands after Tasmania: well worth more than just a flying visit if you can afford it.

## Mandorah

Across the harbour from Darwin is the Cox peninsula and the tiny resort of **MANDORAH**, an easy jaunt if you want to escape the city for a day. It's 140km away by road, right around the harbour, but infinitely more direct is the **jet shuttle** operated by *Darwin Harbour Ferries* (6 daily; $15 return; Mandorah ☎78 5094, Darwin ☎81 7600), which departs from Cullen Bay, taking twenty minutes to reach Mandorah.

The *Mandorah Inn* (☎78 5044; ⑤), a venue for illicit weekend liaisons and famed for its precocious frogs, is set on a lovely beach, and has a bar, pool and a restaurant – it's the only place to eat. **Camping** is not permitted near the inn, but no-one will chase you out of the nearby woods. Walking along the shore in the other direction from the jetty (there's a map in the inn's bar), passing subsided gun emplacements, the grubby shoreline soon improves and features deserted sandy beaches, but you may be sharing the water with dangerous crocs, so take extreme care. The road inland leads 6km to the town of Mandorah, which has a supermarket and service station and not much else.

## Howard Springs

A popular day out for Darwinites is the trip to the outlying suburb of **HOWARD SPRINGS** 25km southeast of Darwin. The **nature park** (daily 8am–8pm), 2km from town, has a kiosk and barbecue facilities (though no camping), and is centred on a spring where a dammed pool allows you to swim with barramundi and long-necked turtles. A two-kilometre walk leads through the monsoonal rainforest which thrives along the creek. The *Nook Caravan Park* (☎83 1048), on Morgan Road, back in town, has camping, on-site vans (③) and cabins (④).

## The Bathurst and Melville islands

Since the time, around 6000 years ago, when rising sea levels created the **Bathurst and Melville islands**, 80km north of Darwin, they have been the home of the **Tiwi** Aborigines – indeed, the islands are often known simply as the Tiwi Islands. Differing significantly from mainland Aborigines, with whom they had limited contact until the last century, the Tiwi people's hostility towards all intruders hastened the failure of **Fort Dundas**, Britain's first north Australian outpost (on Melville Island), which lasted just five years until 1829. The Tiwi word for white men, *murantani* or "hot, red face", probably originates from this time.

In just two generations, since a Belgian missionary cautiously established the present-day town of **NGUIU**, on Bathurst, the Tiwi have moved from a hunter-gatherer lifestyle to a commodity-based economy with remarkable ease. Running their own tours and manufacturing their own crafts and garments, they are now seen as an offshore model for successful Aboriginal self-determination.

The **Tiwi Land Council** (☎47 1838) issues permits for visitors to the islands, but doesn't allow individual tourism. Without an invitation, **tours** are the only way to see the islands, and even then you'll see very little. *Tiwi Tours* (☎81 5144) offers small-group tours of the islands, from $230 for a day-trip, including return flight and permit. It's a bit of a shopping trip, inspecting Tiwi art and craft outlets such as *Bima Wear*'s showroom, but lunch at Taracumbie waterfall and a visit to an overgrown burial ground, where lopsided crosses mingle with carved *pukamani* burial poles, add some flavour – as does the half-hour flight over Van Diemen Gulf. The **overnight tours**, while at least twice as expensive, are much more worthwhile. Based at the luxurious *Putjamirra* bushcamp, a twenty-kilometre jeep drive from Pularumpi airstrip on Melville Island, you get a chance to go food-gathering with local Tiwi, either offshore or through the bush. It's a refreshingly spontaneous encounter which, alongside the camp's informal hospitality, makes for a splendid tour.

# The Arnhem Highway to Kakadu

The **Arnhem Highway**, which runs east towards Kakadu, parts company with the main southbound Stuart Highway 10km after Howard Springs. Eleven kilometres from the Howard Springs turning, the small settlement of **HUMPTY DOO** (bus #19 from Palmerston) has a **pub** renowned for its Sunday sessions; adjacent is the *Hard Croc Café*. Next door to the café is **Grahame Gow's Reptile World** (daily 8.30am–5.30pm; $4; ☎88 1661) which displays an array of deadly, and deadly-looking, reptiles. Australia contains over 75 percent of the world's venomous snakes and most of them, as well as pythons and other reptiles, are represented here. Grahame Gow, a world authority on snakes, has been bitten enough times to be thought immune to snake venom.

Just down the road, 6km north of the highway, is **Fogg Dam Conservation Reserve**. Originally established as an experimental rice- and cotton-growing area, it rapidly attracted migrating birdlife in search of food, with magpie geese nabbing the aerially sown seeds even before they hit the ground. Since then the dam has had much more success as a bird sanctuary: early morning or twilight are the best times for spotting jacanas, egrets and geese, and maybe pythons, goannas and wallabies. There's also a 3.6-kilometre signposted boardwalk through the adjacent woodland. During the Dry, rangers lead night-time walks along the dam. A little further along the highway the distinctive observation platform of the **Windows on the Wetlands** overlooks the Adelaide River floodplain from the top of Beatrice Hill while describing the surrounding ecology with a number of interactive displays.

## Adelaide River Crossing: jumping crocodiles

Seeing crocodiles in their natural habitat is one of the Top End's undoubted highlights and at the **Adelaide River crossing**, 64km east of Darwin, you can sign up for the so-called **jumping crocodile cruise**. The familiar appeal, "Don't Risk Your Life", posted along northern Australia's waterways and shorelines from Broome to Rockhampton, takes on greater significance once you realize that the model by the café here is not a gargantuan replica, but supposedly half a metre *shorter* than the biggest crocodile ever seen.

---

### CROCODILES

Two distinct types of crocodile inhabit the Top End. Bashful **Johnston's** or **freshwater** crocodiles ("freshies") grow up to three metres in length, eat seafood, birds and small mammals, and live exclusively in freshwater rivers and billabongs. Unique to Australia, and distinguishable by their narrow snouts and neat rows of spiky teeth, they look relatively benign and are considered harmless to man. Some swimming areas in Kakadu are known to harbour freshies.

**Estuarine**, or **saltwater** crocodiles ("salties"), can inhabit both salt and fresh water and are the world's biggest reptiles. Once fully mature (up to six metres long and 1000kg in weight), they have no natural predators other than each other and have been known to "take" (the approved euphemism) buffaloes trapped in the mud – although fishermen and swimmers are a much less strenuously acquired snack. Their broad, powerful snouts and gnarled jawline comprise a fascinating and gruesome sight that has changed little since the time of the dinosaurs, 160 million years ago – only then salties were four times bigger than they are now. They are brilliant hunters, catching their prey in sudden, short bursts of speed and then resuming their customary inactivity for days at a time.

Aborigines have lived alongside, and eaten small crocodiles or their eggs, for thousands of years, but earlier this century crocodiles were hunted close to extinction – either for sport, as vermin, or for their skin. Legislation reversed this trend in the mid-1960s and in another thirty-odd years the thousands of post-conservation crocs in the Territory will have reached full-grown maturity – something not everyone in the Top End is happy about.

The absence of **warning signs** does not guarantee safe swimming (the signs are persistently stolen as souvenirs), nor does the *apparent* absence of salties. Hard enough to spot even when they're above water, crocodiles can lie submerged for hours. In short, unless you're sure it's safe, don't swim; if you're camping, don't prepare fresh meat by the water's edge, and don't collect water from the same place every day. Fatalities are surprisingly rare but all attacks make instant news. Grisly stories are part of every tour guide's repertoire and are firmly entrenched in Territorian folklore.

The *Adelaide River Queen* (from $18 for 90-min cruise; check times and availability of seats in advance on ☎88 8144) departs up to five times a day. The cruises involve enticing the river's numerous salties with bits of boney offal, making the business of snapping stunning photographs relatively straightforward and safe. All the crocs have individual personalities, like the sprightly Mr Reliable or the generally languid 900-kg Marrakai. Sea eagles sometimes swoop in and snatch morsels from the crocs' maw and, whatever your thoughts on the methods or wisdom of encouraging crocodiles to jump two metres out of the water, they are an amazing spectacle.

## The Mary River Wetlands

Continuing along the Arnhem Highway, 12km past the *Bark Hut Inn,* the **Old Darwin Road** (also known as the Jim Jim Road) leads southeast into Kakadu. Another 6km further on, you'll see a track turning northwards into the **Mary River Wetlands**, an opportunity for those with their own vehicle to explore a wetlands environment no less impressive for not being in Kakadu. Birdlife is abundant here, as are crocodiles, especially downstream of the barrage near **Shady Camp**, perhaps so called because of the dense clouds of mosquitoes that thrive here. *Point Stuart Wilderness Lodge* (☎78 8914; dorms ①; four-bed units ⑥) is a good bet for an overnight stay, with a pool and communal facilities. Boat **cruises** on the Mary River cost $18 – book at the lodge – and dinghies with fishing gear included are also available for hire. Nearby, the *Wildman River Wilderness Lodge* (☎78 8912; ⑧, including meals) offers slightly plusher accommodation, as well as two-day Kakadu tours, boat cruises and dinghy hire.

# Kakadu National Park

A hundred and fifty kilometres east of Darwin you reach the western boundary of **KAKADU NATIONAL PARK**, a unique area of largely unspoilt wilderness and, apart from the glories of Uluru (Ayers Rock), the most visited natural site in Australia. On UNESCO's World Heritage List, it was brought to worldwide attention when used as an Outback location in the film *Crocodile Dundee*. The park derives its name from the Gagudju language group of Aborigines, who number among the area's traditional custodians; the *Gagudju Association* now manages the park, with the assistance of the Australian National Parks and Wildlife Service. The association also claims a royalty from the **uranium** mined in Kakadu: along the eastern border with Arnhemland (see below) lies fifteen percent of the world's known reserves, and the Ranger Uranium Mine, near Jabiru, yields around $10 million a year for the association. Indeed, the environmental debate over the proposed mining in the late 1970s was instrumental in the establishment of the park.

The park's 20,000 square kilometres encompass the entire catchment area of the **South Alligator River**, misnamed by an early British explorer after the river's prolific crocodile population. In its short run to the sea the river passes through, and creates, a number of varied topographical features. Ravines in the southern sandstone escarpments shelter scattered pockets of monsoonal **rainforest**, while downstream, the more commonly seen **eucalypt woodlands** merge into the paperbark **swamps** and tidal **wetlands** of the coastal fringe.

Within these varied habitats an extraordinary diversity of flora and fauna thrives. Included are 1300 different **plants**, over 10,000 species of **insect**, half the Territory's species of **frog**, a quarter of Australia's **freshwater fish** and over 120 different **reptiles** – some, such as the freshwater (or Johnston) crocodile, unique to the Top End. A third of Australia's **birds** can also be found in Kakadu, including the elegant Jabiru stork, the similarly large brolga, with its curious courting dance, lily-hopping Jacanas, white-breasted sea eagles, which build life-long nests from heavy sticks, as well as galahs and magpie geese by the thousand. **Mammals** include kangaroos, antilopine and black walleroos, agile wallabies, 26 bat species, and dingoes – a barkless and incorrigibly wild dog introduced by Aborigines 5000 years ago.

With so many interdependent ecosystems, maintaining the park's natural balance has become a full-time job. The **water buffalo**, introduced from Timor early last century and one of ten **feral species** found in the park, proliferated so successfully that its wallowing behaviour soon turned the fragile wetlands into mudbaths. However, bovine eradication in the Top End (200,000 animals have been destroyed since 1979) has left other problems in its wake, not least the aptly named **salvinia molesta weed**. With no buffaloes to eat it, the exotic weed has invaded vast areas of the wetlands, creating a thick, sunlight- and oxygen-depleting mat that chokes all other plant and fish life.

The other ever-present danger is **fire**. Burning off has long been recognized as a technique of land management by Aborigines, who lit small, controllable fires as an aid to hunting and to stimulate new plant growth. Today, rangers imitate traditional Aboriginal practice, burning off the drying speargrass during June to preclude bush-fires at the end of the Dry, when the dessicated countryside could be devastated by an early electrical storm. Finally, the disastrous effect that Queensland's poison-army of **cane toads** (see p.327) might have on Kakadu's precious ecology doesn't even bear thinking about.

### Ancient rock art

Up to 5000 **Aboriginal art sites** cover the walls of Kakadu's caves and sheltered outcrops, ranging from thirty to over 20,000 years in age. Most of them are inaccessible to visitors, and many are still of spiritual significance to the 300 or so Gagudju and other language groups who live in the park. The paintings include a variety of styles, from the earliest handprints to detailed cross-hatched depictions of animals and fish from the rich **Estuarine period** of 6000 years ago. At this time, rising sea levels submerged the land bridge by which early Aborigines crossed into Australia. It is not unusual to see paintings from successive eras on one wall: **contact period** images of seventeeth-century Maccassan fishing *praus* and larger European sailing ships might be superimposed over depictions of ancient and bizarre spirit-beings. Though partially understood at best, Kakadu's rock art provides a fascinating record of a culture that, recent excavations reveal, has survived here for as long as 63,000 years.

## Visiting the park

It must be stressed that Australia's largest national park is a difficult place to appreciate in one short visit. Access to the park's diverse features is limited, and those expecting to find the air a-flutter with colourful birds and the bush humming with wildlife will be disappointed. Furthermore, at the most popular times of year for visitors, Kakadu is much drier than might be imagined, and most of the wildlife is active only during the early morning, in the evening or at night. The danger from crocodiles and of inadvertent desecration of sacred Aboriginal sites, as well as the harsh terrain, means that the wetlands and especially the escarpment country are best appreciated from the air, something which can be arranged in Jabiru (see below) or through the *Gagudju Lodge* in Cooinda (☎79 0145), with scenic flights for around $95 per hour.

Although Kakadu's Aborigines distinguish six **seasons** throughout the year, to most people it's either the Wet, with up to 1600mm (just over five feet) of torrential rainfall between December and March, or the Dry, an almost complete drought.

The dry-season months of **June**, **July** and **August** are the most popular times to visit the park, with acceptable humidity and fairly conspicuous wildlife. Towards the end of the Dry, birdlife congregates around the diminishing waterholes, while November's rising temperatures and epic electrical storms – known as the Build Up – herald the onset of the Wet. To see Kakadu during the **Wet** is, some say, to see it at its best: water is everywhere and, while some sights are inaccessible and the wildlife dispersed, the land demonstrates the kind of verdant splendour that people often expect, but fail to find, in the Dry.

## Getting there

The **Arnhem Highway** leaves the Stuart Highway 43km south of Darwin, following which it's a fairly dull 210-km drive to the Park HQ near Jabiru (see below). On the way you'll pass the **Park Entry Station**, where you pay the $15-per-person entrance fee; tickets are valid for two weeks, and you can leave and re-enter the park as many times as you like. From Jabiru the sealed **Kakadu Highway** heads southwest through to Pine Creek on the Stuart Highway (an alternative entry point into the park if approaching from the south), passing Cooinda, which is pretty much at the heart of the park. It is along this road that you'll encounter many of Kakadu's best features.

The **Old Darwin Road or Jim Jim Road**, unsealed, but suitable for ordinary cars in dry conditions, is a good alternative to slogging the full length of the Arnhem Highway. It starts 12km east of the **Bark Hut Inn** on the Arnhem Highway and joins the Kakadu Highway near Cooinda, 100km later. Entering the park this way, you should pay at the Cooinda resort or at the Park HQ, near Jabiru; for both, see below.

Without your own transport you'll have to rely on a **tour** (see p.430 for some recommended operators). There are **buses** into the park: *Greyhound.Pioneer* operates daily between Darwin, Jabiru and Cooinda (Jabiru office ☎79 2548). But once there, you're stuck, unless you hitch or take the Jabiru-based day tours (which also pick up from Cooinda ☎79 2411). **Car rental** can be arranged through the *Territory Rent-a-Car* office at the *Gagudju Crocodile Hotel* in Jabiru (see "Accommodation", below).

## The Park Headquarters and Bowali Visitors' Centre

At the eastern edge of the park, 250km from Darwin, near the junction of the Arnhem and Kakadu highways, you arrive at the **Park Headquarters and Bowali Visitors' Centre** (daily 8am–5pm; ☎79 2101). The multi-award-winning visitors' centre is a masterpiece of thoughtful and relevant landscaping and design and should not be missed; maximizing prevailing breezes while offering space and shade, the rustic feel and overall layout makes for a pleasant environment. Here you can get an official *Visitors' Guide* that suggests how to make the most of your visit, while for further information, *Park Notes*, covering all aspects of the park, are available at the desk. A *What's On* pamphlet has details of the informative ranger-led walks at many of the sites covered below, and the programme of evening slide shows at the caravan parks and resorts.

An innovative walk-through exhibition takes you through a condensed Kakadu habitat, passing across underfloor snakes and under a croc's belly. The 25-minute **audiovisual show** "Kakadu Through the Seasons" is shown regularly in the theatrette and there's a range of **videos**, shown on demand, near the main desk. Try and see the excellent, but ultimately gloomy, documentary, "Twilight of the Dreamtime", featuring Bill Neidje, a Gagudju elder whose philosophical poems feature in his book *Kakadu Man*. A café and gift shop round off the centre's facilities.

## Accommodation

Within Kakadu there are resorts at **South Alligator** and **Cooinda**, and a hotel and caravan park at **Jabiru**. There are also seventeen camping areas scattered all over the park, ranging from basic sites, which are free, to better-equipped caravan parks at

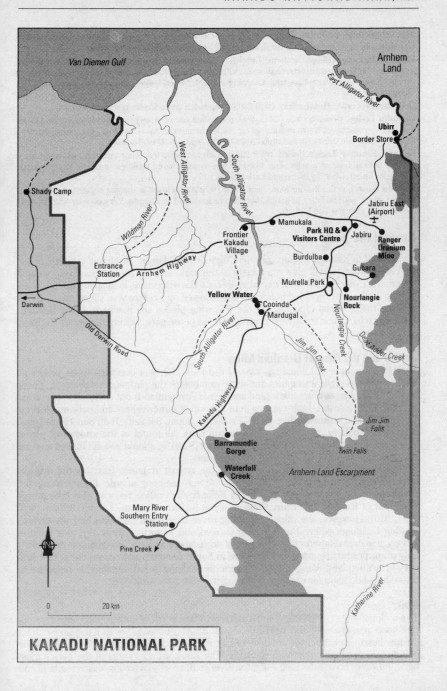

**KAKADU NATIONAL PARK**

**Mardugal** near Cooinda, **Muirella Park** near Nourlangie Rock, **Merl** at Ubirr and at **Gunlom**. In the Dry season, booking ahead at the Park HQ is advisable.

**Frontier Kakadu Village**, Arnhem Highway, 2.5km west of South Alligator Bridge (☎79 0166). Attractively landscaped resort/roadhouse (with café and restaurant), but a bit far from anything except its own Gungarre nature trail. Camping available; 4-bed lodge (air-con with shared facilities) ⑥; motel rooms ⑦.

**Gagudju Crocodile Hotel**, Jabiru (☎79 2800). Top-notch crocodile-shaped hotel. ⑧.

**Gagudju Lodge**, Cooinda (☎79 0145). Well-positioned resort near Yellow Waters with an $14 all-the-veggies-you-can-eat bistro making up for the kitchenless cabins. Camping, plus sparse but functional 2-bed air-con cabins ②, and motel units ⑦ (dry season), ⑥ (wet season).

**Kakadu Frontier Lodge**, Jabiru (☎79 2333). Caravan park (camping available) surrounding a grassed pool and bar area, with plain 4-bed air-con rooms, shared facilities and basic kitchen (extra charge for linen). Close to Jabiru and Park HQ. ⑥.

**Kakadu Hostel**, at the Border Store near Ubirr (☎79 2985; closed in the wet season). An old lodge past its prime, with facilities to match, but the cheapest bed in Kakadu. Very popular with mosquitoes from all over the Top End. ①.

# Around the park

If your visit to Kakadu is short, seeing **Ubirr** or **Nourlangie Rock** and taking a cruise on **Yellow Waters** will give you a taste of the park, and can be crammed into a day if necessary. However, the best way to appreciate the wilderness is to spend up to a week visiting all the spots detailed below, ideally followed by a return visit six months later, to observe the seasonal changes. All the following places are reached off the **Kakadu Highway** which runs southwest from Jabiru out of the park, joining the Stuart Highway at Pine Creek.

### Jabiru and the Ranger Uranium Mine

JABIRU, a couple of kilometres east of the Park HQ, is a company town, originally built to serve Kakadu's uranium-mining leases before the park was established. There are four mine leases in the park (and another in Arnhemland) but only one is operating at present. As a result, Jabiru is less than half full of mineworkers and park employees. There is a small **supermarket** (Mon–Fri 9am–5.30pm, Sat 9am–1pm, Sun 10am–2pm), a takeaway, bakery, post office and *Westpac* bank, all found in the **shopping plaza**. You'll also find a **Health and Dental Clinic** (☎79 2018), should you fall ill, and a swimming pool (9am–7pm; $2) in which to recuperate.

*Kakadu Air* (☎79 2411) operates out of the airport at Jabiru East (as the original townsite 6km east of Jabiru is known), offering one-hour **scenic flights** along the escarpment and wetlands for $95. From *Kakadu Air*'s office you can also take a one-hour tour of **Ranger Uranium Mine** (daily at 9.15am, 10.15am, 1.15pm, 2.30pm; ☎79 2411; $10). However, the mine is nothing more than a pit, pipelines and mysterious looking buildings where the ore is processed and exported, while the tour itself is largely a public-relations litany designed to assuage visitors' misgivings. Australia's only other productive uranium mines are in South Australia and across the park boundary in Arnhemland. Ranger itself is currently working at half capacity, in response to the reduced demand for uranium following the end of the Cold War.

### Ubirr

The rock-galleries at **UBIRR**, along a dirt road 43km north of the Park HQ, illustrate the rich food resources of the wetlands. Fish, lizards, marsupials and the now-extinct Tasmanian tiger or thylacine are depicted, as well as stick-like Mimi spirits, mischievous beings said to inhabit cracks in the rock. The **Lookout** offers one of the park's most beautiful views across the East Alligator River to the rocky outcrops of Arnhemland and should not be missed, while the six-kilometre **Rockholes Walk** along the East Alligator River is one of the few longish walks in the park – a good way to escape the crowds.

## Nourlangie Rock Area

**Nourlangie Rock**, Kakadu's most accessible and therefore most visited site, is 31km south of the Park HQ. It includes the **Anbangbang Rock Shelter**, where the dry ground preserves evidence of occupation stretching back 20,000 years; dimples on boulders show where ochre was ground and then mixed for painting. The **Anbangbang Gallery**, a few minutes away, depicts the dramatic figures of Nabulwinjbulwinj, Namarrgon (the Lightning Man) and his wife Barrkinj. Unusually vivid, they were in fact repainted (a traditional and sometimes ritual practice) between 1963 and 1964, over similar but faded designs. The **Lookout** over the Arnhemland escarpment, to the home of Namarrgon, is also the beginning of the twelve-kilometre **Barrk Walk** (see box below). Other places in the Nourlangie Rock area, all signposted, and marked in the *Visitors' Guide*, include **Nanguluwur**, a less popular but fascinating art site one kilometre from the Nourlangie car park, which includes images from the Contact Period when Aborigines first encountered explorers and settlers. **Nawulandja Lookout** looks onto the imposing hulk of Nourlangie Rock itself, which looms over **Anbangbang Billabong**, one of the locations used in the film *Crocodile Dundee*. During the Dry, a two-and-a-half-kilometre track circumvents the billabong. **Gubara** or Burdulba Springs, 13km off the Nourlangie road, is a nice, croc-safe spot to cool-off after a day's tramping.

## Jim Jim and Twin Falls

Although over a hundred kilometres south of Park HQ, at the end of a tricky 4WD-only track, these two falls are definitely worth visiting; allow two hours for the 60-km drive from the Kakadu Highway. **Jim Jim Falls** tip 215m straight off the edge of the escarpment and are best caught in the early Dry, as soon as the road re-opens – they often stop flowing later and will certainly look less impressive. A rocky, one-kilometre trail leads alongside the large pool to the base of the falls.

Twin Falls, a rough 10-km drive from Jim Jim, are reached by a short walk from the car park, and then a swim up the monsoon-forested gorge for another kilometre – an airbed and waterproof containers help here. This little bit of adventure is rewarded by the sight of Twin Falls cascading into a pool edged by an idyllic sandy beach, a beautiful and relatively secluded spot to while away the day. The sure-footed can scramble to the top of the falls via the overgrown gully to the right – a difficult climb capped with a view you won't forget in a hurry, but note that fatal accidents have occured here. Both falls are inaccessible in the Wet season, but are increasingly featured in the itineraries of Darwin's Kakadu tour operators.

---

### BUSHWALKING IN KAKADU

One of Kakadu's biggest disappointments is the lack of long-distance marked trails. A leaflet at the Park HQ lists twenty marked trails in the park, but most are short **nature trails**, such as the six-kilometre **Rockholes Walk** near Ubirr. Only the twelve-kilometre **Barrk Walk** – a six-hour trek through Nourlangie Rock's back country – offers any challenge; although the trail is marked and gets you into the bush without the need for skilled navigation, it still should not be undertaken lightly.

**Experienced bushwalkers** can apply to Park HQ with proposed itineraries, which need to be approved before a permit is given. *Willis Walkabouts* (☎85 2134) in Darwin organizes extended bushwalks up in the escarpment country; Russell Willis also produces an excellent "Guide to Bushwalking in North Central Australia". For something less strenuous, *The Darwin Bushwalking Club* (☎85 1484) organizes weekend walks in the Top End and welcomes visitors.

## Yellow Waters and Cooinda

As Jim Jim Creek begins meandering into the floodplains close to the Cooinda resort, 50km southwest of Jabiru, it forms the inland lagoon of **Yellow Waters**. From the car park here, a short walk leads along the edge of the billabong, while very popular **cruises** (five daily; book in advance on ☎79 0145) weave through the lushly vegetated waterways. The early-morning cruise (2hr; $22.50) catches the lagoon and wildlife at their best: heat-of-the-day tours are half an hour shorter and a few dollars cheaper. At Cooinda, there's also a new **Warradjan Aboriginal Cultural Centre** (☎38 1100 for details) with interpretative displays on Aboriginal culture, together with an arts and crafts shop.

## Barramundie Gorge and Waterfall Creek

High-clearance cars can manage the twelve-kilometre 4WD track from Kakadu Highway to **Barramundie Gorge** (also known as Maguk), the best of Kakadu's few swimming holes; it's 57km southwest of Cooinda. From the car park, a path leads along the creek to the large pool, possibly still the home of a harassed freshie; for its sake rather than yours, keep away from the left bank. The top of the waterfall and more rock pools can be reached by clambering up the tree roots to the right of the falls.

**Waterfall Creek** (known also as Gunlom or UDP – Uranium Development Project – Falls) is another *Crocodile Dundee* location, 36km off the Kakadu Highway, close to the park's southern exit. Although the falls don't flow all year, it's another paperbark-shaded, safe swimming spot and well worth the diversion if entering or leaving via Pine Creek.

# Arnhemland

Individual tourist access into Aboriginal-owned **ARNHEMLAND**, a vast wilderness east of Kakadu, is virtually impossible. By and large, the 3000 Aborigines who live in this remote region, where supplies come in by sea or air, want to be left alone – as they have been for over 40,000 years. In 1963 the Yirrkala of northwestern Arnhemland appealed against the proposed mining of bauxite on their land. It was the first such protest of its kind, and included the presentation of sacred artefacts and a petition in the form of a bark painting to the government in Canberra. Although unsuccessful on this occasion, their actions brought the issue of Aboriginal land rights to the public eye and paved the way for subsequent successful land claims.

The **Northern Land Council** (Darwin ☎20 5100; Jabiru ☎79 2410) issues expensive permits, allowing a maximum of fifteen tourist vehicles in at any one time. The only major settlement is Gove/Nhulunbuy, in the northeast corner, a mining town of no appeal to tourists, and with no facilities. Most of the visitors to Arnhemland are fishermen heading up to **Smith Point**, an approved destination for which permits are booked up months in advance. *Umorrduk Safaris* (☎79 0218), will take you to its remote bushcamp in northwestern Arnhemland but charge a stiff $600 for a day-trip (flights included) and $165 for each subsequent day (plus $30 permit per day). However, the personal service, as well as the superb rock art and other sacred sites that you'll be shown, are quite unlike anything on offer in Kakadu. *Davidson's Arnhemland Safaris* (☎27 5240) is another established operator offering tours in the Mount Borradaile area for around $300/day plus flights. Less adventurous (and far less extravagant) is a trip with *Arnhemlander* (☎79 2411), a daily eight-hour **bus tour** from Jabiru which takes a token hop over the border for $110, visiting the Aboriginal community at **Oenpelli** accompanied by a local guide.

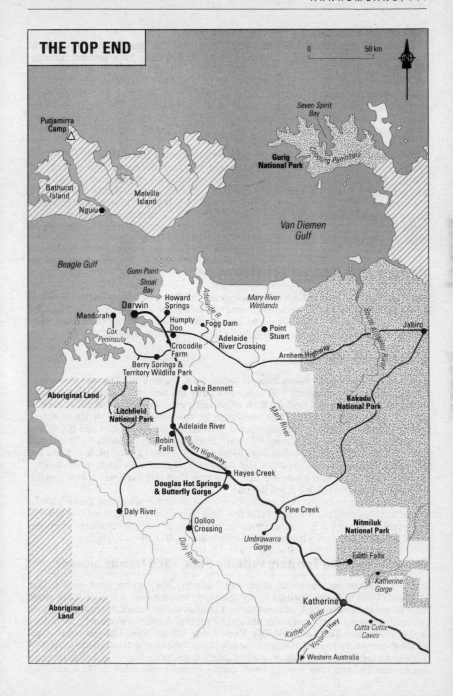

THE TOP END

0    50 km

Putjamirra Camp

Bathurst Island

Nguiu

Melville Island

Seven Spirit Bay

Gurig National Park

Cobourg Peninsula

Van Diemen Gulf

Beagle Gulf

Gunn Point
Shoal Bay

Mandorah

Darwin

Cox Peninsula

Howard Springs

Humpty Doo

Crocodile Farm

Berry Springs & Territory Wildlife Park

Adelaide R

Fogg Dam

Adelaide River Crossing

Mary River Wetlands

Point Stuart

South Alligator River

Jabiru

Arnhem Highway

Aboriginal Land

Litchfield National Park

Lake Bennett

Kakadu National Park

Adelaide River

Robin Falls

Stuart Highway

Mary River

Hayes Creek

Douglas Hot Springs & Butterfly Gorge

Daly River

Oolloo Crossing

Pine Creek

Umbrawarra Gorge

Nitmiluk National Park

Edith Falls

Daly River

Aboriginal Land

Katherine River

Katherine Gorge

Cutta Cutta Caves

Katherine

Victoria Hwy

Western Australia

**The Cobourg Peninsula**
The **Cobourg Peninsula** – also known as the **Gurig National Park** – is a largely inaccessible headland clinging to northwestern Arnhemland by a slender isthmus. With the failure of Fort Dundas on nearby Melville Island, the British tried again to establish a foothold, first at **Raffles Bay** and later at **Port Essington** (from 1838 to 1849), where the explorer Ludwig Leichhardt arrived in 1844 after his extraordinary overland trek from Moreton Bay, in Queensland. Port Essington was abandoned after eleven years due to malarial epidemics, harassment by local Aborigines and Indonesian pirates, and – more tellingly – the peninsula's severe climatic extremes, being hotter and wetter than anywhere else in the Territory.

The only place on the peninsula you can get to is **Seven Spirit Bay** (☎79 0277), an exclusive and utterly remote eco-tourist **resort**, reached by boat or light aircraft and offering five-star service and cuisine, with various activities at your disposal. At $395 per person per night for twin-share "habitats" (flights are extra), it's the place to politely ignore film stars trying to get away from it all. If you're keen to visit this area under your own steam, ask for more information at the Conservation Commission desk in the Darwin tourist office in Smith Street Mall (☎81 4300); permits for individuals ($10) are strictly limited, and you need to apply well ahead of time.

# Along the Stuart Highway

From Darwin, the **Stuart Highway** passes early mining and pastoral outposts and is bordered intermittently by overgrown airstrips dating from World War II. Along its length are a number of attractions which can be visited either as excursions from Darwin or as diversions on the journey to Katherine, 400km to the south.

## Darwin Crocodile Farm

South of the Arnhem Highway turn-off, 40km from Darwin, the **Darwin Crocodile Farm** (daily 9am–5pm; $8.50; ☎88 1450) is a farm and research facility where crocodiles are both studied and bred for their skins and meat. The lucky ones get scarred at an early age, rendering themselves unsuitable for conversion into handbags or shoes, and become breeding stock. Rogue crocs that harass local communities and the scores caught annually in the traps around Darwin Harbour are also relocated here. If you haven't been to *Crocodylus Park* in Darwin (see p.426), this is a good place to learn the difference between salties, freshies and American alligators. Besides, nowhere else could you get as close to a monster like five-metre Burt (kept behind cyclone fencing and corrugated iron)and live to tell the tale.

The usual souvenirs and croc burgers are available at the shop, and **guided tours** set off at 11am and 2pm, when some of the 7000 crocodiles and alligators also get fed. It's worth trying to catch feeding time, since it's one of the few occasions when the crocs actually move (extra feeding sessions at noon on Mon, Wed, Sat & Sun).

## Berry Springs, the Territory Wildlife Park – and termite mounds

Eight kilometres further south down the highway, the turning west to the Cox Peninsula leads to **Berry Springs** (daily 8am–7pm; no camping), a further 10km away. This picnic and swimming spot is set along a rainforest-lined creek, though the largely peaceful atmosphere is occasionally marred by yobbish drunks at weekends. Next door is the 400-hectare **Territory Wildlife Park** (daily 8.30am–6pm, last admission 4pm; $10), where you can spend a happy couple of hours wandering through the variety of Territorian habitats, which include walk-in aviaries, nocturnal houses and walk-through aquariums. The entry fee – worth every cent – includes free rides on the circulating train, which saves trudging along the four-kilometre roadway. *Darwin Day Tours* (☎81 8696) leaves daily at 7.30am for a half-day visit to the park ($30, including entry fee).

Before the Cox Peninsula road veers north over **Bulldog Pass** to Mandorah (see "Around Darwin" above), there's a turning onto the corrugated and seldom-used northern approach road to Litchfield Park (see below). Crossing the Finniss River, this track passes fields of **termite mounds**, both fluted "cathedral" mounds, up to four metres high, and so-called "magnetic" or "meridian" mounds. Not often seen in the same vicinity, both designs accomplish their aim of regulating the internal temperature. Magnetic mounds are unusual things: made of digested grass, they're always aligned along a polar axis, and were once thought to be in tune with the earth's magnetic field. In fact, they are arranged so as to present a thin edge to the midday sun, thus maintaining the habitat at a termite-preferred 30°C; you can feel the temperature difference by touching either side of the mound.

# Litchfield National Park

"Kaka-don't, Litchfield-do" is an over-simplified quip expressing many people's preference for **LITCHFIELD NATIONAL PARK** over its better known neighbour. Situated 100km south of Darwin, and roughly 16km west of the Stuart Highway, it encompasses the **Tabletop Range**, a spring-fringed plateau from which issue several permanent and easily accessible **waterfalls**. The whole park is a popular and enjoyable destination, generally free of restrictions, long drives and intangible expectations. It is also **crocodile-free** and you can swim and splash around to your heart's content – a much more attractive prospect than some of the sterile dammed lakes closer to Darwin. **Bushwalking** is encouraged: walkers planning extended hikes should contact the **Conservation Commission** in Darwin (☎81 4300) or in Batchelor (☎76 0282) for camping permits, as well as information about trails and maps. For details of organized tours, which are the only way to see the park without your own transport, see p.430.

## Batchelor

**BATCHELOR** – 8km west of the highway – is the halfway-house town you pass through en route to Litchfield National Park, which is a further 8km west. Originally built to serve the post-war rush to mine uranium at nearby Rum Jungle, the townsfolk managed to resist its closure in the early 1970s when large-scale mining ceased. The establishment of the national park in the 1980s gave the town a new lease of life, though don't expect much; just about the only sight of note is a replica of **Karlstein Castle**, next to the police station, built by a homesick Czech immigrant. There are a couple of **caravan parks** around Batchelor, but **camping** in the park is generally more appealing (some of the best sites are detailed in the text below). For those who don't want to rough it, the *Rum Jungle Motor Inn* (☎76 0123; ⑥), on Rum Jungle Road, is a comfortable **motel** with a decent restaurant – an alternative to the town's several takeaways.

## Into the Park

There's no admission fee to enter the park, and no visitors' centre either, so get all the information you need from the **Conservation Commission** in Darwin (☎81 4300) or in Batchelor (☎76 0282). Heading **into the park** from Batchelor you'll pass black soil plains dotted with grey, tombstone-like "magnetic" termite mounds (see above). **Buley Rock Holes**, down a right turn, 38km from Batchelor, are nothing more than a couple of rock pools, but a five-kilometre trail follows the creek from here to **Florence Falls**. A high lookout surveys the twenty-metre falls, which can be reached along a newly-cut path leading from the car park down to the plunge pool: there's not much room to spread out picnics, but the water is beautifully cool, and a 4WD track leads back to the Batchelor road. **Camping** is permitted at both the rock holes and the falls.

The **Lost City**, off the main road through the park, 6km after the Florence Falls turn-off, is a jumble of unusually weathered sandstone columns. These are interesting enough in themselves, but getting to them is the real highlight: they're at the end of an increasingly difficult, eight-kilometre 4WD track – and should not be visited in rented vehicles unless you know how to drive over steep rock steps without damage. The very rarely used track, which continues on to Blyth Homestead and Sandy Creek (see below for more on these – and an easier way of getting to them), gets trickier still after the Lost City. Back on the main road through the park, the pool below **Tolmer Falls** is closed to the public, to grant the rare orange horseshoe bat some seclusion. However, the long, slender falls can be appreciated from a fine lookout (signposted off the main road), from where the eagle-eyed will spot a rock arch at the top of the falls. A two-kilometre path leads from the lookout to an area of pools and minor cascades which are swimmable in the Wet, before heading back to the car park .

Unmarked on most maps, **Tjedeba Falls** is an idyllic spot visited by some tours. A twenty-minute walk and a creek crossing leads through rainforest to a series of shady cascades and pools – in the Wet, easily the most attractive of the park's falls. Back on the road, a track leads south to **Blyth Homestead** and **Sandy Creek** (or Tjaynera Falls). The abandoned homestead adds some token historical interest to the park, while Sandy Creek (accessible by 4WD only) is a series of falls and a pool surrounded by rainforest, with a **campsite** less than 2km away. From Sandy Creek, the 4WD track continues (with a steep creek crossing) to the Reynolds River – back in crocodile country – and on to Daly River or the Stuart Highway.

The park's most popular waterfall, with easy access to tree-shaded lawns and a large pool, is **Wangi Falls**, 55km east of Batchelor. There is a sun-warmed natural spa pool near the base of the left-hand cascade, once a sacred site for Aboriginal women and forbidden to men. Strangely enough, several men, including some trying to save drowning women, have perished at Wangi; tri-lingual signs now warn of the danger, and the pool closes in the Wet when abnormal **undertows** develop. A trail leads through a rainforest boardwalk (the initial section of which is wheelchair-accessible), up over the falls and down the other side via a **lookout** – a good way to work off lunch. Wangi tends to get overcrowded at weekends and in school holidays, since it has the best equipped **campsite** in the park.

A corrugated dirt road leads north from Wangi out of the park and across the Finniss River (where "Sweetheart" the crocodile once roamed before falling prey to the taxidermist at the Darwin Museum of Arts and Sciences; see p.425) and on to Berry Springs.

## Adelaide River to Hayes Creek

Established during the construction of the Overland Telegraph Line, the town of **ADELAIDE RIVER** was the supply head for Darwin's defence during World War II and consequently suffered sporadic Japanese bombing after 1942. Today the town, 110km south of Darwin, provides little more than a lunch-stop along the Stuart Highway. You may, however, want to visit the town's **war cemetery** where many of the victims of the air raids are buried. Officially, 243 people died as a result of the eighteen months of Japanese bombing, which commenced in February 1942, but it is thought that the real death toll may have been up to four times as high. At the southern end of town, **Memory Lane** (daily 9am–5pm; $3) has filled the old train station with miscellaneous memorabilia and also acts as an informal tourist office. Enquire at the *Mobil Roadhouse* for **camping** space, or try the *Adelaide River Inn* (☎76 7047; dorms ①, motel rooms ⑤), which also provides counter meals and has a **restaurant**.

Just before the train station, the old highway forks west along a rolling 75-kilometre **scenic drive** before rejoining the main road at Hayes Creek. A short drive along the scenic route leads to **Robin Falls**, 17km from town, while a further 17km marks the turn-off for Daly River.

## The Daly River region

A quiet backwater,120km southwest of Adelaide River, and a popular "barradise" for fishermen, the **Daly River region** is a great spot for a few days' relaxation – though you'll need your own vehicle to get here. It wasn't always so pleasant: in 1884, four copper miners were killed by local Aborigines. The *Northern Territory News* was apopleptic with indignation, but calmed down enough to reassure its readers that "the right class of men are now on the tracks of the Daly River natives, but we do not expect to hear many particulars of their chase; the less said the better…it is far more sensible to avoid complications by the exercise of judicious reticence". Two years of punitive "bush riding" followed until the Wilwonga Aborigines were all but wiped out.

**Accommodation** is spread out along the river, with the *Mango Farm* (☎78 2464) offering four-bed cabins (⑤), safari tents and a seven-berth gazebo for backpackers (①), as well as a pool, bistro, dinghy rental and river cruises. *Bamboo Creek Rainforest Park* (☎78 2410; ⑤) has three-bed cabins for rent, while the main attraction at the *Daly River Roadside Inn* (☎78 2418; ⑤) is a four-metre-long pet saltie called Boris. At the *Woolianna Tourist Park* (☎78 2478) there are more boats for rent, a pool and **camping**.

## Douglas Hot Springs, Butterfly Gorge and Oolloo Crossing

Back on the scenic route from Adelaide River, a turn-off leads 35km southwest to **Douglas Hot Springs**, where 40°C water bubbles out of the sandy creek bed – very agreeable, but often crowded during school holidays. **Camping** costs just $1, but you'll need to collect your firewood on the way in, as the nearby woods have been picked clean. From the springs, a 4WD track leads 17km to the secluded **Butterfly Gorge**. When you can drive no further, follow the creek upstream on foot, past massive paper-barks and over rocky outcrops to the beautiful, orange-walled gorge and sandy beach. Swimming across the pool leads to more rockpools, but there's no camping in this area.

Another 31km from the hot springs turn-off, *Lukies Farm* (☎78 2411) is just before **Oolloo Crossing** on the Daly River. Camping is available, and the Garibaldi family offers river cruises or rental boats if you want to try catching that elusive barra.

## Hayes Creek and the "Historic Hotel"

**Hayes Creek**, 178km from Darwin, is a roadhouse with camping, cabins (③) and free showers in the spotless ablution blocks. The "historic hotel" sign, tempting you 16km off the highway, leads to **Grove Hill Hotel** (☎78 2489; ①): the rather grim rooms make Fannie Bay Gaol look comfortable, but you can also camp out the back. Built in 1930, alongside the now disused railway line, the hotel is a functional corrugated-iron shed decorated with miners' relics, a survivor from the days when the area was the site of many small mining ventures. A dirt road winds south from the hotel, across the path of the old railway, to Pine Creek, while the straightened-out main highway achieves the same destination via **Emerald Springs** roadhouse.

# Pine Creek and around

Site of the Territory's first goldrush, the small town of **PINE CREEK**, 230km from Darwin, has retained its colonial appearance, making it an unusually appealing stop along the highway. Gold was discovered while digging holes for the Overland Telegraph Line pylons in 1871 and fools rushed in, hoping to pan their way to fortune. Unfortunately the gold was in the rock, not the riverbeds, requiring laborious crushing with heavy stamp batteries – which, for most prospectors, was too much like hard work for unpredictable returns. The subsequent labour shortage was solved by importing cheap Chinese labour, which kept the progressively poorer quality ore coming for a couple of years until fears of Asian dominance (the Chinese workers outnumbered Europeans six-to-one by this time) led to their being banned from the Territory in 1888, a shot in the foot for gold production. A modern gold mine now goes at it hammer and tongs, as technology has made viable the extraction of the remaining deposits. If you're lured by the prospect of easy pickings, *Back o' Beyond Tours* (☎76 1221) can take you on a two-hour historic- and gold-panning tour for $12.

Around the town, the various time-worn buildings, like the 1889 **Old Playford Hotel** and **Old Bakery**, may lead you to contemplate the crucial role of corrugated iron, or "galvo", in the pioneering colonial process. The **Miners Park**, at the northern end of town, displays the crude mining hardware of a hundred years ago and there's a **museum** in the old train station, on the other side of the tracks. In town, there's a **caravan park** (☎76 1217) with camping, or try the *Pine Creek Motel* (☎76 1288; ⑤) opposite, which is also the only place to **eat** in town. *Ah Toys* general store in Main Terrace is still run by the descendants of its original Chinese owner.

From Pine Creek it's 200km along the sealed **Kakadu Highway** to Jabiru, in the heart of Kakadu National Park, passing the majority of the park's highlights on the way (described in the Kakadu section, pp.434–440). South of town, on the way to Katherine, there are a couple of other diversions within a short drive of the Stuart Highway.

### Umbrawarra Gorge and Edith Falls

At **Umbrawarra Gorge**, 22km southwest of Pine Creek along a corrugated track with several dry creek crossings, you can camp for a dollar and walk up the shaded gorge which has pools throughout the year, but **Edith Falls**, halfway to Katherine, 20km east of the highway, is more impressive. The falls, within Nitmiluk National Park, drop to a large forest-encircled pool in three stages, around which an adventurous five-kilometre loop **walk** has been completed. There's camping at Edith Falls, for a $5 fee. It's also possible to walk to Katherine Gorge from here, along a 66-kilometre trail (see "Nitmiluk National Park", p.450).

# KATHERINE TO ALICE

An obligatory stopover (at least for a couple of days) for visitors to the Top End, **Katherine** is a small but rapidly growing regional centre on the southern banks of the Katherine River. It's just 32km from **Katherine Gorge**, the town's primary tourist attraction and itself part of the larger **Nitmiluk National Park**.

West of Katherine, the **Victoria Highway** leads for 500km west to the WA border, passing Timber Creek and the entrance to the 4WD tracks of the **Gregory National Park** on the way. South of town, a dip in **Mataranka**'s thermal pool and a couple of "bush pubs" are the highlights of the 670km to **Tennant Creek**, unless you take the former droving route via **Borroloola** and the Gulf of Carpentaria, to northern Queensland, still a rough track, but passable to sturdy cars in the Dry. South of Tennant Creek, only the rotund boulders of the **Devil's Marbles** brighten the string of road-houses along the Stuart Highway which stretches for just over 500km to Alice Springs.

# Katherine

Traditionally home of the Jawoyn Aborigines, the **Katherine River** area must have been a sight for explorer Stuart's sore eyes as he struggled north in 1862. Having reached here, he named the river after a benefactor's daughter and within ten years the completion of the Overland Telegraph Line (OTL) encouraged European settle-ment, as drovers and prospectors converged on the first reliable water north of Alice Springs. In 1926, the railway from Darwin finally spanned the river and "Kath-rhyne", as the die-hard locals still call the town of **KATHERINE**, became established on its present site. Today, the country's biggest airforce base, at Tindal, south of town, defends Australia's barely inhabited north from supposedly hostile Asian entities.

# Arrival and information

All buses arrive at the **Transit Centre**, at 6 Katherine Terrace (daily 7.30am–6.30pm; ☎72 1044), next to the 24-hour *BP Roadhouse*. Katherine is a busy interchange for buses, with at least one daily arrival or departure for Darwin, Kununurra, WA and Alice Springs. Just over the road you'll find the **Tourist Information Centre** (Mon–Fri 8.45am–5pm, Sat 8.45am–noon; ☎722 650) which produces a free guide to the region. The **airport** is 8km south of town; a taxi to Katherine will cost about $15 (call ☎72 1777 or ☎72 1999).

# Accommodation

Thanks to the immense popularity of Katherine Gorge, there's plenty of choice for places to stay in town. The tourist information centre provides a list and current prices of all the town's accommodation; the best options are detailed below.

## Motels

**Beagle Motor Inn**, 2 Fourth St (☎72 3998). The best choice for a cheap motel in town, this also has a backpackers' dormitory. Dorms ①, rooms ⑤.

**Crossways Hotel**, corner of Katherine Terrace and Warburton St (☎72 1022). Bring earplugs or join in the rowdy drinking in the hotel bar. ⑤.

**Frontier Motor Inn**, Stuart Highway, 3km south of town (☎72 1744). Spacious motel, spread out in its own grounds, with tennis courts and *Matilda's* restaurant (see below). ⑦.

**Katherine Hotel/Motel**, 14–15 Katherine Terrace (☎72 1622). Right in the town centre, and perhaps too close to the pub for comfort. ⑤.

**Paraway Motel**, corner of O'Shea and First streets (☎72 2644). The most comfortable motel in the town centre. ⑥.

**Springvale Homestead**, Shadforth Rd (☎72 1355). Motel units by the river. ⑤.

## Hostels

**Kookaburra Lodge**, corner of Lindsay and Third streets (☎71 0257). Motel units converted into 8-bed air-con dorms, which can get rather crowded, but combined accommodation, canoe- and bike-rental deals, plus other amenities, make this Katherine's most popular backpackers' haunt. Dorms ①, rooms ③.

**Palm Court Backpackers**, corner of Giles and Third streets (☎72 2722). Ineffectually converted motel offering 8-bed air-con dorms and twin rooms with bathroom, fridge and television. There's a small kitchen and pool, too. Dorms ①, rooms ③.

**Victoria Lodge**, 21 Victoria Highway (☎72 3464). Hostel with a small pool and very cheap breakfasts. 4-bed dorms ①, rooms ③.

## Caravan parks

**Katherine Gorge Caravan Park**, Nitmuluk National Park (☎72 1253). Sites close to the gorge but 32km from Katherine. Makes a good base for exploring the park on foot.

**Katherine Low Level**, Shadforth Rd (☎72 3962). Close to the Low Level Nature Reserve, with free canoes and plenty of shady, grassed sites. On-site vans ③.

**Red Gum Caravan Park**, 42 Victoria Highway (☎72 2239). Nearest to town centre (about 1km west), with licensed store and takeaway. On-site vans ③.

**Shady Lane Caravan Park**, Giles St (☎71 0491). An inexpensive site, but 4km from town, out along the gorge road. On-site vans ③.

**Springvale Homestead**, Shadforth Rd (☎72 1355). Caravan park in a pleasant riverside setting.

# The Town and around

The Stuart Highway becomes **Katherine Terrace**, the main street, as it passes through town. Along it lie most of the shops and services, including a big *Woolworth's*, giving Katherine a compact – and unexpectedly busy – feel. In the centre there's a **Railway Museum** (Mon–Fri 10am–noon & 1–3pm; $2), housed in the old station on Railway Terrace, but for the full story head 3km up Giles Street to the **Katherine Museum** (Mon–Fri 10am–4pm, Sat 10am–2pm, Sun 2pm–5pm; $4), just before the old townsite at Knotts Crossing, where a few original OTL pylons still remain upright. Inside are displays relating to Katherine's colonial history, including early medical instruments and a biplane from the time when the building did duty as a Flying Doctor base.

*Mimi Arts* in Lindsay Street is an Aboriginal-owned **gallery** selling carved wood-work, bark paintings and **didgeridoos** (made from branches hollowed-out by white ants), which are indigenous to the Katherine area. *Framed*, at 34 Katherine Terrace, is a plusher gallery with high-quality artefacts and prices to match.

Three kilometres down Victoria Highway are some decidedly **warm springs**. From here, it's just a short walk to the **Low Level Nature Park**, a pleasant spot for a stroll, swim or canoe along the pandanus-fringed river, seasonal floods permitting. Any crocs you might encounter will be bashful freshies.

**Springvale Homestead**, at the end of Shadforth Road, 8km west of the town centre, is a tourist resort based around the oldest homestead in the Territory, built in 1884. The station was at one time run by Ted Ronan, a writer of the wry and romantic school, who helped mythologize the Outback with novels such as *Vision Splendid*. There are free, half-hourly tours of the homestead (May–Oct daily 10.30am & 2.30pm) and the local Jawoyn also perform light-hearted **Corroborees** here (May–Sept Mon, Wed & Sat at 8pm; $15); you can eat here, too (see below).

**Cutta Cutta Caves**, 24km south of town, offer guided tours of two systems, Cutta Cutta and Tindal Cave (hourly 9am–11am & 1–3pm; closed at the height of the Wet; $6.25 for one cave, $11 for both; ☎72 1940). Both display extraordinary subterranean karst features as diverse as they are delicate. Cutta Cutta is the more visually impressive, but Tindal is also the home of the rare orange horseshoe bat and rather alarming stalactite-climbing brown snakes.

# Eating, drinking and nightlife

There's nothing terribly memorable about eating in Katherine, although there are some good **restaurants** concealed within the motels – which is just as well, because the pubs' front **bars** are rough and sometimes rowdy places.

### Restaurants and cafés

**Alfies**, 1km southwest down the Victoria Highway. Chicken and pizza restaurant where you can fill up for around $12.

**Buchanan's**, *Paraway Motel*, corner of O'Shea and First streets (☎72 2644). Sharing the honours, with *Matilda's*, as the best restaurant in town. Around $20 a head.

**Croc Room**, *Beagle Motor Inn*, 2 Fourth St (☎72 3998). Serves up its namesake, baked, at moderate prices.

**Georgie's Seafood**, Katherine Terrace. Fish 'n' chiperie and Chinese meals for under $15.

**Jade Cafe**, Katherine Terrace. Just about the only pleasant lunch spot in town, serving wholesome snacks.

**Matilda's**, *Frontier Motor Inn*, Stuart Highway, 3km south of town (☎72 1744). Eat your heart out from a droolsome menu of steak and seafood, for $20–25 a meal. Reserve in advance.

**Springvale Homestead**, Shadforth Rd (☎72 1044). "Bush kitchen" meals coincide with other activities, such as thrice-weekly Aboriginal didgeri-dancing shows and nightly croc-spotting cruises along the Katherine River. Both cost around $30 a head, with pick-ups from town; book in advance.

## TOURS FROM KATHERINE

**Brolga Airways** (☎71 7000). Scenic flights include Katherine Gorge and Kakadu (half-day, with Yellow Waters cruise option; $175).

**Campbell's Trail Rides**, based 14km up the gorge road (☎72 1394). Ride along the river with yarn-spinning ex-stockman Mick Campbell – from $35 for three hours. Inexperienced riders welcome.

**Jankangyina Tours** (book through *Travel North* on ☎72 1044). Two-day tours of Wardaman art sites west of Katherine, in the company of an Aboriginal guide, for around $230.

**Katherine Adventure Tours** (☎71 0246). Three-day tours in Kakadu for $270, and a five-day trip for $480, with an optional drop-off in Darwin – worth considering if heading north.

**Manyallaluk** (call *Travel North* on ☎72 1044). One-day Aboriginal culture tours for $90 ($60 self-drive) and longer guided walks through Nitmiluk and Kakadu from $385.

**Three Rivers Wilderness Tours** (book through *Travel North* on ☎72 1044). Two-day canoeing trips for around $200. Suitable for beginners and in many ways far more satisfying than the rather crowded Katherine Gorge.

## Bars and nightlife

The front bars of Katherine's two **pubs**, *Brady's*, at the *Katherine Hotel*, and *Crossways* (both on Katherine Terrace) are rough watering holes patronized by feuding locals. *RJ's*, behind the *Katherine Hotel*, and the cheerily named *Last Chance* back-bar at *Crossways Hotel* are probably the least uncomfortable places to drink in. The town's only **nightclub** is *Wings*, also at the *Crossways*, open until the early hours from Thursday to Saturday. The *Katherine Club* on the corner of Second and O'Shea streets is at the other extreme, with cosy folk/country music evenings, but you'll need to befriend a member to sign you in.

## Listings

**Airlines** *Ansett* (☎72 1344) for Australia-wide flights; *Brolga* (☎71 7000) for scenic and charter flights across the Top End.

**Banks** All major banks are situated in Katherine Terrace.

**Bike rental** Ask at *Kookaburra Lodge*, corner of Lindsay and Third streets (☎71 0257).

**Bus reservations** *Transit Centre*, 6 Katherine Terrace (☎72 1044).

**Car parts** *Katherine Wreckers*, Stuart Highway, 2km north of town (☎72 1682). Plenty of bits for ageing *Kingswoods* and the like.

**Car rental** *Avis*, c/o *Hobbitt's Auto Electrical*, 47 Victoria Highway (☎72 1482).

**Conservation Commission** Giles St; just over 1km from town, after O'Shea Terrace (☎73 8770). Detailed information on Nitmiluk, Gregory and Keep River national parks.

**Hospital** ☎72 9211.

**Police** ☎72 0111.

**Swimming pool** Stuart Highway south. Dry season 10am–6pm, wet season 1–8pm; $1.25.

# Nitmiluk National Park

The central attraction of the **Nitmiluk National Park** ($6 entry per peson) is the magnificent twelve-kilometre **Katherine Gorge**, carved by the Katherine River through the Arnhemland plateau. Often described as thirteen gorges, it is in fact one continuous cleft, turning left and right along perpendicular fault lines and separated during the dry season by rock bars. The spectacle of the river, hemmed in by orange cliffs, makes for a wonderful **cruise** or canoe trip and, unlike Kakadu, Nitmiluk also welcomes bushwalkers along its many marked **trails**.

*Kookaburra Coachlines* (☎71 0257) and *Travel North* (☎72 1253) both operate **bus** shuttles along the sealed road between Katherine and the gorge for $13 return. Buses stop at the **Park Visitors' Centre** (daily 8am–6pm; ☎72 1886), 31km east of Katherine, which has interpretive displays and videos on the park's features, and provides maps and further information on the trails including the "Guide to Nitmiluk National Park" ($4.95) with topographical walking maps.

**Bushwalks** include the 66-kilometre **hike to Edith Falls**, in the park's northwestern corner, for which you'll need at least four days, a minimum of two people and a $50 deposit, which will be returned on deregistration. Away from the gorge itself, the terrain is rough and very dry; be sure to wear sturdy footwear and a hat, and carry plenty of water. As a safety precaution, all walkers must **register** ($1; overnight stays $20 refundable deposit) with the rangers at the visitors' centre: those on day-hikes must check in again by 6pm. Behind the centre is the helipad (see below) and **caravan park** (☎72 1253), where there's **camping**, a takeaway kiosk and shop (7am–7pm).

## Exploring Katherine Gorge

A kilometre east of the visitors' centre and caravan park is the **jetty**, from where canoe trips and cruises **through the gorge** commence (and buses from Katherine terminate). Swimming is also permitted here: there's more danger from cruise boats and canoe paddles than nibbling freshies; saltwater crocs are virtually unknown in the gorge. While waiting for a cruise, you might want to take the steep, 400-metre walk leading from the jetty to a superb cliff-top **lookout** up the river (there's no need to register for this walk).

**Cruises** ply the gorge in a series of boats. *Travel North* (☎72 1253) offers two-hour cruises to the second gorge (the limit during the wet season) for around $21, a four-hour cruise to the third gorge for $37 and an eight-hour "safari" (around $63), which includes some rock-hopping that demands secure footwear. This relaxed cruise includes a barbecue lunch, refreshments, plenty of time for swimming and a peep at the sixth gorge; it gets away from the rather busy downstream sections and is highly recommended. Note that boat cruises must be pre-booked – tickets are not sold at the jetty. There are also thoroughly exhilarating **helicopter** flights up the gorge (minimum of three people required; 15min $65 per person, 30min $100).

**Canoeing** up the gorge is an option for the more energetic, but don't expect to paddle up to the "thirteenth" in a day. *Kookaburra Canoe Hire* (☎72 3604) rents solo canoes for $25 a day and two-person canoes (easier to control for beginners) for $40; waterproof containers are provided. The rental period is 8.30am–5pm; overnight trips cost an extra day's rental. Alternatively, put your own canoe on the river, for a small fee payable at the Visitors Centre. Expect long sections of canoe-carrying over boulders and successively shorter sections of water as you progress up the gorge. Those determined to reach the thirteenth gorge (which, scenically-speaking, is not really worthwhile) will find it easier to leave the canoe at the fifth and swim/walk the last couple of kilometres.

The first permissible overnight **campsite** is Smith's Rock in the fourth gorge (or anywhere upstream from there) – this is regarded as a fair day's paddling and portaging. The best time to canoe the gorge is early in the dry season, when small waterfalls run off cliff walls and the water level is still high enough to reduce the length of the walking sections.

# The Victoria Highway to Western Australia

The **Victoria Highway** stretches for 510km southwest of Katherine to Kununurra in Western Australia. After an initial, dull 125km a narrow sealed road leads south off the Highway down to a bleak roadhouse at **TOP SPRINGS** (☎75 0767; cabins ⑤), where there's camping and fuel. From here, a dirt road heads west past the legendary **Victoria River Downs** (VRD) station through to Jasper Gorge, rejoining the Victoria Highway east of Timber Creek. Once the country's biggest cattle station, the Victoria River Downs, established in the great droving days of the 1880s, is, like many "unmanageable" properties, now owned by a business consortium better able to weather the fluctuating market. It still operates over a massive, semi-arid area, with the "homestead" more like a small township, incorporating a post office and shop. The station is also the base of Australia's biggest heli-mustering outfit, which pursues the daredevil practice of mustering widely dispersed stock with helicopters. From Top Springs, the **Buchanan Highway** (in fact just a dirt road) continues south and west through Wave Hill to **HALLS CREEK** (WA), a stretch of nearly 700km that should not be undertaken lightly. Wave Hill is notable as the site of the Aboriginal stockmen's strike in 1966, which led to the first successful land claim and the birth of the Aboriginal **Land Rights Movement**.

Back on the Victoria Highway, the tarmac narrows as it enters a picturesque spur of the Gregory National Park (see below). The *Victoria River Wayside Inn* (☎75 0744), at the Victoria River crossing, boasts "the cheapest caravan park in Australia" and twin-share **motel** rooms (④). There are river cruises and 2WD access into the park during the Dry, but note that dangerous saltwater crocs inhabit the Victoria River.

## Timber Creek

Although little more than a pair of roadhouse/bars with adjacent campsites, **TIMBER CREEK** makes a welcome break on the route to Kununurra, 300km west of Katherine. Lying on the Victoria River, it was originally known as the "Depot" a century ago, when the inland port supplied the vast pastoral properties being established throughout the region. But this remote outpost was soon the scene of bitter disputes between the Aborigines and the new landowners. In 1885, a police station was set up at Timber Creek, staffed by two policemen and a black tracker whose task was to patrol an area the size of Tasmania. Diana Bell's harrowing book, *Hidden Histories*, describes the ruthless pastoral occupation of the area from an Aboriginal perspective.

The **museum** (daily 1–3pm, but check in town; $2) is housed in an early police station, west of the town. It's a familiar display of miscellaneous pioneering relics, retrieved from the surrounding undergrowth and used to illustrate a pithy historical commentary about the region. On a different note, the town sees the easternmost examples of the curious, bottle-trunked **boab trees** – according to Aboriginal mythology, a tree once thought so beautiful it was turned upside-down by envious spirits. Behind one such tree, a twin-trunked boab on the south side of the highway, 4km west of town, lies the miserable **grave** of Tom Lawler or Lander. He was not the first disillusioned inhabitant of Timber Creek to seek solace in alcohol and ultimately, in 1906, with a bullet through his brains, but is one of the few to get a marked grave. Another boab, **Gregory's Bottle Tree**, on the banks of the Victoria River, was inscribed by the explorer, Gregory, in 1856. A short distance upstream, his ship ran aground and he was forced to make repairs here, giving Timber Creek its name.

### Practicalities

**Tourist information** (☎75 0850) is dispensed by the ever-spry Max from his office situated between the two pubs. He will doubtless insist that you undertake his morning boat tour ($30) along the Victoria River, an indefatigable performance of bushcraft, legend and history straight out of vaudeville, which is interrupted at your peril.

**Accommodation** can be found at the grandly named *Timber Creek Hotel*, incorporating the *Circle 'F' Caravan Park* and *Fogarty's Store* (☎75 0772; ④–⑤), which has camping, cabins and motel rooms. The *Wayside Inn* (☎75 0732; ④) has less expensive camping and cabins, with shared ablutions. The *Shell Roadhouse* here is open 24 hours.

**Eating** entails sampling the customary frozen/microwaved roadhouse fare, while the two pubs have all the character of a gym changing room. During all-nighters at the graffiti-covered *Wayside Inn*, a chummy game of darts gives way to belly-sliding head first off the beer-oiled bar. You might as well enjoy it – it's a DT-inducing 225km to the next pub. If you fancy a bigger thrill than the pub games, ask around for Scott, who will take you up in his **helicopter** ($40 for 15min) when he's not mustering.

## Gregory National Park

The Territory's newest and second-largest park, **GREGORY NATIONAL PARK,** is entered by turning off the Victoria Highway, 11km east of Timber Creek. Carved out from various pastoral leases, the park exhibits sandstone escarpments and limestone hills covered in light woodland. Because of its remoteness and rough terrain, it's best explored in a 4WD vehicle and it's a good idea to call at the **Conservation Commission** office in Timber Creek (turn right just before Watch Creek, west of town, ☎75 0888), to study the large map and get information about conditions. A **permit** is required for the two 4WD tracks (see below), available at the office or from the Park Ranger at **Bullita Outstation** (☎75 0833). *Katherine Adventure Tours* (☎71 0246) are among the first commercial operators to explore this little-visited park in 4WDs.

Conventional cars can get as far as **Limestone Gorge**, a corrugated 60km south of the entrance. Here you find a 25-minute marked walking trail looping up onto the surrounding escarpment, and a **croc-free billabong**, the only safe swimming hole in the park. There's no point in 2WDs going on to the stockyards at **Bullita**, 6km south of the Limestone Gorge turn-off, unless you want to see the ranger. However, self-sufficient drivers in 4WDs should register here before starting the **Bullita Stockroute**, 90km of scenic limestone outcrops and river crossings, which loops back northward and involves a full day's driving. **Camping** is permitted at designated spots along the way.

Alternatively 4WDs can choose to leave the park further south, along the **Humbert River Track** – allow at least six hours for the 112km to the park boundary, from where you head east along station roads: the ranger will explain the way. The park section of this route has some very slow, rocky sections and the tricky Humbert River crossing will challenge the inexperienced even in the Dry. Both routes are **one-way** only from Bullita, require logging in and out at either end and are closed from December to March.

## Keep River National Park and the WA border

West of Timber Creek, the land flattens out into the evocatively named **Whirlwind Plains**, where the East and West Baines rivers frequently cut the Victoria Highway in the Wet. **KEEP RIVER NATIONAL PARK** lies just before the Western Australia border, 185km from Timber Creek. Accessible to all vehicles, it's an easily explored area of dissected sandstone ridges, gorges and Aboriginal art sites. Marked trails start from the two **campsites** in the park, and the **Ranger Station** (☎091/67 8827), 3km from the highway, supplies details on longer walks and other attractions.

By now you can hardly have failed to get the message that Western Australia does not want any infested Territorian **livestock, produce** or **honey**. The intensively irrigated agricultural area around Kununurra is hoping to remain free from pests found elsewhere in Australia, so eat up your fruit and veg before the border or throw it away; Note, too, that Western Australia is an hour and thirty minutes *behind* the Territory.

At the **border**, Kununurra is just 40km away.

# South to Alice

The 1100km from Katherine, south down the "Track" (as the Stuart Highway is known) to Alice Springs, are regarded as something of a no-man's-land for travellers. A flat, arid plain rolls from the Top End's big rivers to the waterholes of the Red Centre. The white population in this region is sparse, and consists largely of individuals who are either unusually tenacious, transient or slowly going "troppo". West of the Track, the vast Aboriginal lands of the Warlpiri and neighbouring groups just about occupy the entire **Tanami Desert**, while to the east are the grasslands of the **Barkly Tablelands**, a declining pastoral region extending north to the seldom-visited coast of the **Gulf of Carpentaria**. **Tennant Creek**, just over halfway, can be a rather anti-climactic break to a bus journey, and even car drivers tend to press on down the Track before something wears out or breaks. The landscape as seen from the Stuart Highway inspires a kind of agoraphobic urgency (or just plain boredom), while the mind churns repetitively over such imponderables as "just how many anthills *are* there in the Northern Territory?".

## Mataranka and the Roper River Region

MATARANKA – just over 100km from Katherine – is a small town, the capital of the "Never Never" country, so named after Jeanie Gunn's classic 1908 novel of a pioneering woman's life, *We of the Never Never*, set and filmed in the region. Site of despised Administrator John Gilruth's planned Northern Territory capital, and of failed experimental stations in the early federation years, today the town is partially eclipsed by the nearby **Mataranka Homestead** resort, which attracts most buses and passing tourists. South of town is the **Elsey National Park** leading to the often overlooked freshwater wetlands of the **Roper River**.

There's not much to the town itself. Outside the *Stockyard* (see below) you can feed a dollar into the statue of **The Fizzer** to hear the tale of the punctual postman, Henry Peckham of "Never Never" fame, who was tragically drowned in action.

All **accommodation**, along with the supermarket, roadhouses, museum, café and craftshop, is lined up along **Roper Terrace**, the main highway. The *Shell Roadhouse* (☎75 4571) has camping, on-site vans (③) and a restaurant; the *Mobil Roadhouse* has cheaper on-site vans (②–③). The town's only **pub**, the *Old Elsey Hotel* (☎75 4512) offers motel rooms (⑤), and there's also a lovely shaded beer garden here, and a small "dress rules" (effectively "white") indoor bar. The *Territory Manor*, on Martins Road (☎75 4516; ⑤), is a plush motel set in its own landscaped grounds, catering for bus tours: it also boasts a caravan park (with camping) as well as the town's only licensed **restaurant** with freshly cooked meals for $20 or so. Stave off the roadhouse meat pies while you can with the Stockyard's (daily 9am–5pm) range of snacks and enjoy a browse through their gallery for local arts and crafts. If your car needs spare parts, there's a good **wreckers** south of town, the last until you reach Elliott, 300km further south.

### Mataranka Homestead

Mataranka Homestead, 6km from town (☎75 4544), was established by Gilruth to raise sheep and horses and now is a popular holiday resort offering an array of recreational activities, including (expensive) bike- and canoe-rental, horse riding, and imbe-cilic three-hour tractor-towed "wagon safaris", to name but a few. A replica of the **Elsey Homestead**, used in the 1981 film version of *We of the Never Never*, is open for daily tours at 11am. The original "Old Elsey Homestead" site and cemetery is south of town, just past the Roper Highway turn-off – of interest only to Jeanie Gunn devotees.

The resort has a bar and bistro, and free nightly entertainment (April–Sept only) as well as a tour-booking service. **Accommodation** includes camping, a hostel (①; book in advance as it fills quickly), budget, air-conditioned, en-suite rooms that sleep three (⑤), plus self-catering cabins and motel rooms (both ⑤). Overland **buses** stop at the homestead, which is signposted to the south of Mataranka.

The **thermal pool**, in Elsey National Park (see below), but almost part of the resort, is the main attraction – it's free, always open, and the water is a pleasant 34°C. A soak in the palm-shaded, pale-blue water is divine, with early mornings or candlelit night-time dips least crowded.

### Elsey National Park and the Roper River

A twelve-kilometre road into **ELSEY NATIONAL PARK** (turn off just before the Homestead) leads to a more secluded **campsite** with less of a holiday-camp atmos-phere, offering canoe rental and swimming in the (almost croc-free) upper Roper River, as well as a small kiosk.

The **Roper River** itself is difficult to visit independently, since it's barely been devel-oped, yet it's as scenic as the wetlands of Kakadu. *Brolga Tours* (✆75 4538) are your best bet, operating **cruises** along the river from May to October. Their four-hour river tour (around $55) leads you along the river's so-called **Pandanus Avenue** and through some "African Queen"-type channels into the beautiful **Red Lily Lagoon**, the most extensive freshwater wetland in the Territory.

### The Roper Highway

A couple of kilometres south of Mataranka, the **Roper Highway** leads east for 185km (the bitumen ends at 140km) to the remote store at **ROPER BAR**. It was here in 1844, during his epic 5000-kilometre trek from Moreton Bay in Queensland, that naturalist-cum-explorer **Ludwig Leichhardt** dined on fruit bat and built a "bar" (a ford) across the Roper River. Driving across the slippery bar is good for splashing photo-opportunities, but beyond is Aboriginal Land – strictly off-limits without a permit. The store provides the local Aboriginal community and visiting barramundi fishermen with pricey fuel, food and the biggest selection of cheap toys and gobstoppers for 200km. Up behind the store are some self-catering **cabins** (②) or there's a **campsite** 2km back towards the highway. If you go boating or fishing here, take care because you're back in "saltie waters" again.

If you've got this far, you'll have seen the turn-off to Borroloola, 380km away (see below). Corrugated enough to test the calmest temperaments, this rarely used route to the Gulf and Queensland (where the dirt roads deteriorate drastically) is passable in the Dry for regular cars in good shape.

## Down the Track to Three Ways

**LARRIMAH**, 76km south of Mataranka, was where the Darwin railway terminated until 1976 when it closed for good, due to a lack of maintenance following Cyclone Tracy. Up until then Larrimah had been a World War II base and busy road-train termi-nus, bringing goods to the north from the railhead at Alice Springs. Now it's just a fuel and lunch stop on the highway, known mainly as the home of the "Irish Ashes" regional cricket trophy, and as the base of Janet the Bush Barber, who serves the area's haircutting needs.

Ray at the *Larimah Hotel/Wayside Inn* is committed to selling inexpensive fuel and will gladly join you for a drink at the Territory's "highest bar". This is a typical **bush pub**, full of eccentricity, old bottles and half-melted *Spitfire* engines; you can **camp** for free but there's a $2 charge for showers. Over the road, the *Shell Roadhouse/Green Park Caravan Site* has a pool (the five-metre-long pet saltie gets one to himself) and an aviary, as well as camping and a café/shop. At the *Top of The Town*, Angela also offers camping as well as budget **rooms** (①), cabins (③) and "the cheapest slabs in town". Although you're unlikely to spend more than a night in Larrimah, it's a friendly and mildly sozzled place to stop over.

Another 89km brings you to the **Daly Waters Pub**, situated 3km off the highway. Having held a "gallon licence" since 1893 it positively drips with memorabilia, including the only traffic light for miles. There are cheap and basic **rooms** (③). During the 1930s, when *Qantas's* Singapore flights refuelled here, world-class aviators used to pop in for a pint, and these days tourists come to marvel at the quaintness of it all and buy the famously off-beat tea towels.

Just beyond here, the **Carpentaria Highway** (technically the circumnational Highway 1) heads off east to Borroloola (414km); the turn-off is at the *Highway Inn Roadhouse* (open 24hr). There's a second turn-off, further down the Track, just before *Dunmarra Roadhouse*, where the **Buchanan Highway** heads west to *Top Springs Roadhouse* (185km; see p.451) and ultimately Halls Creek in Western Australia (see p.563), along almost 800km of unsealed road suitable for wheel vehicles only.

Back on the Track, **Newcastle Waters**, signposted west off the highway, 60km before Elliott, can't seem to make its mind up whether it's an historic droving township wanting to encourage tourists or a semi-abandoned ghost town. Right up to the 1950s, when road trains replaced the great cattle drives, it was the junction (hence the *Junction Hotel*) of the Barkly and Murranji stock routes, but excepting nostalgic drovers it's of little interest.

**ELLIOTT** is little more than a string of roadhouses with cheap **camping** at the *Mobil Roadhouse* and slightly better facilities at the *Midland Caravan Park* (also the local post office). The *BP Roadhouse* and the *Elliott Hotel* (☎69 2018) both offer simple **rooms** (③). There are a few shops serving the Jingili Aboriginl communities at either end of town, but apart from filling up with fuel or a counter meal at the pub, there's no earthly reason to stop.

Leaving town to the south, the trees which have blocked the horizon for days recede into shrubs and soon disappear altogether as you approach the deserts of Central Australia. **RENNER SPRINGS** is a roadhouse (rooms ③–④) built after World War II from bits of ex-army junk, giving it a certain worn-in charm lacking in most modern roadhouses; you can camp here, and there's the usual roadhouse food. The distinctive outcrop nearby is **Lubras Lookout**, once an Aboriginal meeting place.

On the way to the roadhouse at **THREE WAYS** (open 24hr) watch out for the turn off to a rocky profile of Churchill's Head and also the **Attack Creek Memorial** – where explorer Stuart was repelled by Aborigines on one of his expeditions. At Three Ways, the **Barkly Highway** heads east to Camooweal, Mount Isa and eventually Townsville; it's 210km on to the *Barkly Homestead* (6am–1am), a roadhouse with all the usual services. From here, Tennant Creek (see p.457) is just 26km down the road.

## Borroloola and the Gulf Country

Situated on the croc-infested **MacArthur River**, which drains the predominantly flat Gulf Savannah lands, **BORROLOOLA** has a colourful history which reads like an exaggerated version of the familiar boom, bust and dribble pattern of so many Outback towns. The explorers Leichhardt and Gregory came this way in the mid-eighteenth century, reporting good pasture, and the cattle followed in droves. By the early 1880s, when Tennant Creek and Katherine were still just shacks on the Overland Telegraph Line, the settlement was a wild outpost that even the missionaries avoided. Ships which supplied the OTL in the early 1870s now came upriver with provisions for the hard-living drovers, who were helping stock the pastoral leases right across the north of Australia.

Borroloola was proclaimed, or "gazetted", in 1885 and a new police station was established in an attempt to control the town's lawless urges. Although well-watered, the **Great Coast Route** which Borroloola serviced fell victim to the bovine disease of Red Water Fever, after which the southern stock route (today's Barkly Highway) became the favoured droving route. By the turn of the century, just a handful of whites remained in "The 'Loo" and, with their frenzied passing, the maritime Mara and land-based Karawa and Kurwani Aborigines reclaimed the town and surrounding land, which now serves their communities and outstations.

The only original building to have survived the punch-ups, white ants and cyclones is the **Old Police Station**, now a museum. The key is available from *MacArthur Caravan Park* on Robinson Road – or at least they'll know who has it – and a donation of $2 is welcome. With Borroloola's exceptional white history (see the box below), the museum couldn't fail to be fascinating. Read, for example, E Gaunt's hair-raising account of "The Birth of Borroloola", recalling the sporadic insanity of the early days; it seems the toxic home brew known as "Come Hither", whose label showed a red-eyed Lucifer beckoning malevolently, was to blame. By telling comparison, the coverage of local Aboriginal history is so lightweight as to be incredible. The old **cemetery** a couple of kilometres down the Batten Point road has a few old graves and a lot of good firewood, if you're not superstitious.

## Practicalities

Although on Aboriginal Land, no permit is required to visit the town, which sees a few intrepid tourists and fishermen. Borroloola is mainly on the itinerary of those taking the coast route from Queensland to Darwin or travelling on to Western Australia.

There's plenty of light **air traffic** to and from the town, mostly from Katherine, which otherwise is over 700km away to the northwest by sealed road. *Skyport* makes mail runs three times a week; the *Bulk Discount Store* (☎75 8775) is their agent in Borroloola. Alternatively, call *Brolga Air* (Katherine ☎71 7000, Borroloola ☎75 8791). Either way, it will cost you about $200 one-way.

By road, Borroloola is easily accessible along the **Carpentaria Highway**, via the *Heartbreak Hotel* at Cape Crawford (see "The Savannah-Gulf Country" below), set at

---

### THE CLASSICS LIBRARY AND HERMITS OF BORROLOOLA

There are a number of more or less unlikely explanations for Borroloola's improbable classics **library**, including that which starts with a bored policeman's request for reading matter to New York's Carnegie Foundation. In truth, it was a gradual acquisition of nearly 2000 literary classics by the town's MacArthur Institute at the beginning of the century. Termites tucked into the library, a cyclone destroyed the remains and only a handful of books survived, many in "private collections", gathering what must be enormous overdue fees.

In 1963 a boyish David Attenborough made a TV documentary about three **hermits** who had chosen to retreat to the 'Loo. Jack Mulholland came over as a slightly jaded recluse when pressed about "loneliness and....women", and the reputedly aristocratic "Mad Fiddler" was too deranged to face the camera, but **Roger Jose** was, and looked like, the real thing. Having devoured the library ahead of the ants, he lived in a water tank with his Aboriginal wife and was a humane if eccentric "bush philosopher" who once observed "a man's riches are the fewness of his needs". He is buried at the end of the airstrip in Borroloola.

the junction where the single-width **Tablelands Highway** comes up from the main Queensland road. Depending on who you ask, the **dirt road** to **Woologorang** (a roadhouse with access to coastal inlets) and Hells Gate (Queensland) is either terrible or not bad, but it's bound to be an adventure; the Queensland gulf towns are by no means renowned for their sobriety. The dirt road up to Roper Bar is good until Nathan River, where the corrugations will turn your brain into a froth for about 100km.

Borroloola's isolation makes it an **expensive** place to visit, with little fresh food available and prices (except for fuel) up to thirty percent higher than those you'll find in Katherine. Most facilities are on Robinson Road, where the *MacArthur River Caravan Park* charges $10 for a **campsite**. This is also the home of *Croc Spot Tours* (☎75 8734), which can run you up and down the river, or out to to islands to go fishing, for about $100 a day. *Borroloola Holiday Village* (☎75 8742) is less exposed, with budget **rooms** (③–④) around a pleasant kitchen/communal area, as well as self-contained apartments (⑦). The *Borroloola Hotel* (☎75 8766; ①) is the town pub, with "quiet" and "rowdy" bars, and a grassed pool area popular with cane toads on the march for Kakadu. The MacArthur River is renowned for its massive crocodiles, but you can camp for free by the boat ramps along the river, providing you have your own "shower and toilet facilities" and are familiar with croc-etiquette (see box on p.433).

Other facilities include the *Malandari* **supermarket**, located at the top of Robinson Road (7am–9pm); the **post office** next door (Mon & Thurs 11am–3pm, Wed 11am–4pm, Tue & Fri 9am–3pm) and, next to that, *Tony's Pizza Bar* with a range of frozen/ microwaved fast foods available from 9am–3pm-ish, depending on how they feel. Over the road is *Bulk Discount* supermarket and towards the Tank Hill lookout, there's the **police station and health centre** (Mon–Fri 8am–noon & 1–4.30pm; ☎75 8757).

### The Savannah-Gulf Country

The inviting coast and islands of the **Savannah-Gulf Country** are presently off-limits to independent tourists, hidden away on largely defunct cattle properties or on Aboriginal Land. However, because of disastrous over-grazing and a disease-eradication programme which has decimated the herds, station owners right across the North are looking towards tourism to save them, either developing "dude ranches" that take paying guests or exploiting unusual natural features.

**Nathan River Station**, 185km northeast of Borroloola (☎75 9940; camping available) is a prime example: the owners charge $35 for the key (literally) to the **Lost City of Nathan**, an eerie escarpment of bizarrely eroded columns reached along a thirty-kilometre 4WD track. Other stations in the area are beginning to offer accommodation and access to similar natural wonders for adventurous tourists. The *Heartbreak Hotel* at **Cape Crawford** (☎51 1420) – a bougainvillea-draped roadhouse 113km southwest of Borroloola – offers helicopter rides (from $60) out to another Lost City, inaccessible by public road, as well as 4WD tours with *Savannah Guides* to the waterholes of the Bukalara Ranges. Just offshore, northwest of Borroloola, are the **Sir Edward Pellew Islands,** mostly owned by the Mara Aborigines or the subject of land claims in progress. However, the Conservation Commission has acquired **North Island** and plans to develop the **BURRUNYI NATIONAL PARK** into a simple island retreat, where you can cast yourself away for a few days – providing you can get there. There is a small airstrip: contact Peter Fittock, owner of Borroloola's *Croc Spot Tours* (☎75 8734 or ☎75 8721), who will fill you in on the latest arrangements.

## Tennant Creek

People expect to be disappointed by **TENNANT CREEK**, the butt of much "nether regions of the Universe" humour. Lying 26km south of Three Ways, the town's vitality has traditionally stemmed from mining and recently things have been a bit quiet.

Certainly, its appeal to tourists is not immediately apparent, but hang around and you'll discover an unpretentious Outback town, facing stagnation but hoping for prosperity.

Stuart came through in the early 1860s, followed by the Overland Telegraph Line ten years later. Pastoralists and prospectors came from south and east, and in 1933 Tennant Creek was the site of the last major **goldrush** in Australia. This was the time of gritty "gougers", like Jack Noble and partner Bill Weaber (with one eye *between* them), who defied the Depression by pegging some of the town's most productive claims. Other finds and minerals come and go: recently, the once great Peko mine, presumed exhausted, was sold for a song; within a couple of weeks, its new owners struck payable gold.

## Arrival and information

Tennant Creek is 504km from Alice and 664km from Katherine. The **airport** is about 3km from the centre, at the end of Davidson Street; *Skyport* flies daily to Alice and Darwin; for a **taxi** into town from the airport, call ☎62 1061. The **visitors' information centre** (Mon–Fri 9am–5pm; ☎62 3388) on Paterson Street (the town's main road) is right next to the Transit Centre where interstate **buses** pull in – pick up the detailed *Visitors' Information Map* describing the town's delights.

Some buses come through at 3.30am, which doesn't exactly encourage stopovers, although the YHA (see "Accommodation", below) hangs the keys out so you can get a bed. Both air and bus tickets can be bought or changed at the newsagent in Paterson Street (☎62 2664), just up from *Goldfields Pub*.

## Accommodation

**El Dorado**, Paterson St North (☎62 2402). The town's best motel, with a licensed restaurant and nice pool area. ⑥.

**Outback Caravan Park**, Peko Rd (☎62 2523). Shady and comfortable caravan park with shop and pool. On-site vans ③, self-contained cabins ④.

**Safari Backpackers**, Davidson St (☎62 2207). Clean new block with air-con 4-bed dorms ①, and other rooms ③–④.

**Safari Lodge Motel**, Davidson St (☎62 2207). Comfortable rooms right in town with the *Dolly Pot Inn* next door. ⑤–⑥.

**TC Caravan Park**, next to *Shell Service Station*, Paterson St (☎62 2325). Recently renovated, the new owners offer good deals. Options include camping, backpackers' cabins ②, on-site vans ③ and roomy cabins ④.

**YHA**, Leichhardt St (☎62 2719). Nicely refurbished, ex-working men's quarters provide twins and triples with rattly air-con, a pool and an authentic "Tennant" feel. ①.

## The Town and around

Armed with your *Visitors' Information Map* and a free day, the limited prospects of Tennant Creek are spread before you. In town, the **museum** (daily 3.30–5.30pm; $2), close to the *YHA*, minutely details the history of Tennant Creek, using a chronological timescale starting from the year "0 AS" (After Stuart) and displaying plenty of pioneering relics. Take a look in the *Anyinginyi Aboriginal Arts and Crafts*, near the information centre in Paterson Street, where there's a small selection of local dot **paintings and crafts**, much cheaper than in Alice Springs – a place to buy as well as look.

That's about it unless you've got your own vehicle or want to **rent a bike** (see "Listings"), in which case head up Peko Road, past the gem and art displays at the Civic Centre, to the **Gold Stamp Battery** (Mon–Fri 9am–4pm, Sat & Sun tours only 9am & 4pm; $4), 1.5km from town. Have a look around the remarkably crude and still usable ore crusher, but give the perfunctory one-hour guided tour a miss. The next turning off Peko Road leads up to **One Tank Hill** lookout, where wind-blown empties rattle around and the serenely bleak panorama reddens at sunset. There's a paved cycle and walking trail out to the **Mary Ann Dam Recreation Area**, 5km north of town, with picnic space, birdlife and swimming in the rather dank reservoir.

You'd have to be keen to ride out to the various abandoned **mine sites** east of town, and careful when you get there. *Ten Ant Tours* (☎62 2358) can take you around the mines and other sites for around $10 an hour, but their sunset rides to the **Devil's Pebbles** (16km northwest of town; free camping but no facilities) – outcrops of rounded granite boulders – shouldn't be confused with trips to the much more impressive Devil's Marbles (see below) on the road to Alice Springs. *Norm's Gold and Scenic Tours* (contact the YHA) offer similar, though less expensive, tours around the mines and down to the Marbles. On the way to the Pebbles, you pass one of four surviving **Telegraph Stations**, recently restored as an historic exhibit (☎62 3388 for times). If you've come down the Track and not seen an OTL station yet, here's your chance.

## Restaurants

With the exception of the *Dolly Pot Inn*, Tennant Creek's eating opportunities mirror the surrounding landscape – an acquired taste, with the better places listed below.

**Dolly Pot Inn**, Davidson St (☎62 2824). The Territory's only squash court–restaurant, renowned for its slow service and excellent food. People come from all over for a thrash against the wall while waiting for their order.

**Rocky's Pizza**, Paterson St (☎62 2049). Between the *ANZ* bank and the bakery. Pizzas to stay or go, with a "real topping", no less. Open 4pm–midnight, closed Mon; $2 delivery charge.

**Sporting Club**, Ambrose St (☎62 3347). A decent Chinese restaurant to eat in or take away; and a quiet place for a drink afterwards.

**Tennant Creek Hotel**, Paterson St. Good restaurant attached to one of the town's pubs trying to recreate itself.

## Drinking and nightlife

Dedicated drinkers are well looked after; the town boasts thirteen licences and three **pubs** where miners and Aborigines come to get smashed as quickly and as completely as possible. Front bars can be intimidating arenas of flying bottles and vitriol, while the carpeted back bars are for games of pool and benign socializing. Pubs are generally open from 10am–midnight.

The *Goldfields*, in Paterson Street, has a cleared front bar where you can get a good swing at your neighbour without breaking any of the fittings; the back bar is the place to take your mum for a sherry. Over the road, the *Tennant Creek Hotel* has tried to revamp its old mining image with a blues-proof (punch-ups, not John Lee Hooker) front bar and a tamer back bar for a quiet drink. The *Tavern* at the north end of Paterson Street could be fairly described as the least rough, with enough room to host live bands, and doubling as venue of the town's only **disco** (Thurs–Sat 11pm–3am), enabling licensed drinking into the night.

## Listings

**Bike rental** YHA, Leichhardt St (☎62 2719); *Bridgestone Tyre Centre,* 52 Paterson St (Mon–Sat 8am–5pm; ☎62 2361).

**Book exchange** *Billy's,* opposite the swimming pool on Peko Rd (Tues, Thurs & Fri 10am–4.30pm, Sat noon–2pm).

**Car rental** *Outback Caravan Park,* Peko Rd (☎62 2459) for *Hertz;* or *Ten Ant Tours,* Transit Centre, Paterson St (☎62 2358).

**Car spares** *TC Auto Spares,* Paterson St (☎62 2066).

**Hospital** ☎62 4399.

**Pharmacy** 50 Paterson St (after hours ☎62 2093).

**Police** Paterson St, next to the post office (☎62 1211).

**Post office** Corner of Memorial Drive and Paterson St (☎62 2196).

**Supermarket** The *Food Barn,* opposite the post office (Mon–Sat 8am–6pm).
**Swimming pool** Peko Rd (Sept–Oct 11am–6pm; Nov–May 6–7.30am & 11am–7.30pm; $1).

# Towards Alice and the Centre

The 500km from Tennant Creek to Alice are no more enthralling than the 500km that's gone before, and the places en route, detailed below, are only easily visited by those with their own transport or by especially determined bus travellers.

The **Devil's Marbles**, just over 100km south of Tennant Creek are a genuine geological oddity, a scattering of huge rounded boulders, thought by the local Warumungu Aborigines to be the eggs of the Rainbow Serpent; they're well worth a look, as they're only 2km off the highway. There's a spacious camping area and car park with toilets, barbecues and shaded tables, but no water and little firewood. A **helicopter** stands by, offering ten-minute flights for $35 (☎64 1936; minimum of three people required). A short drive from the Marbles is the comfortable old roadhouse/pub of **WAUCHOPE** (pronounced "walkup"). **WYCLIFFE WELL**, a little further south, is more modern and touristy and with a foreign beer selection that can make you awfully homesick, and may have something to do with the several UFO sightings hereabouts – one such spacecraft is displayed on the roadhouse's forecourt.

**BARROW CREEK**, 60km further on, is one of the oldest roadhouses on the Track, originally a telegraph station, and remembered as the site of the **Barrow Creek Massacre**. It's never quite clear to whom the word "massacre" applied – the two dead and several wounded during an attack on the two-year-old station by the local Kaytej, or those who perished in the two months' "speedy and severe" retribution demanded by the *Northern Territory News*. The pub itself has walls covered in coarse humour, and old-fashioned rooms (④) or cheaper cabins (②–③) out back.

At **TI TREE**, an Aboriginal community close to the middle of the continent, the *Aaki Gallery* sells keenly priced artefacts and paintings produced by local Anmatjera. After another 43km, the **AILERON** roadhouse has the last fuel before Alice and also sells Aboriginal art; in a shrewd marketing ploy, the first beer in the bar is free to backpackers staying overnight (②).

## The Plenty Highway and Tanami Road

Heading towards Alice, the land finally begins to crumple into some contours as you near the MacDonnell Ranges. The **Plenty** and **Sandover Highways**, which run off the highway 66km south of Aileron, head northeast towards Queensland through the Harts and Jervois ranges. Both are passable to sound, well-equipped conventional cars – the Plenty is easier on the suspension, though there are 500km from Jervois to Boulia (Queensland) with no fuel.

Twenty kilometres north of Alice, the **Tanami Road** leads over 1000km northwest to Halls Creek in Western Australia. Again, the track is easily passable in a 2WD up to the NT/WA border, but from there things get a little rough, with patches of **bulldust** that are best assessed on foot first and then driven through fast to avoid getting bogged down. The longest section without fuel is from Yuendumu to **Rabbit Flat** (a roadhouse with expensive fuel and closed Tues–Thurs), a distance of 305km, with the following section to Carranya Station (fuel and shop) nearly as long.

Before embarking on either route, it's wise to phone **Emergency Services** in Alice Springs (☎52 3833 during office hours, or ☎52 7111 for a recorded message); you can also get a **print-out** of the latest conditions and facilities on these remote roads from the tourist office in Alice Springs. While they shouldn't be considered a time-saving short-cut, the Plenty and Tanami tracks are both perfectly feasible in a well-equipped vehicle, and certainly give a taste of the real Outback you could never get on the tarmac highway.

# ALICE AND THE CENTRE

*A land such as this, with its great loneliness, its dearth of life, and its enshrouding atmos-phere of awe and mystery, has a voice of its own, distinctly different from that of the ordinary Australian bush.*

Ernest Favenc, *Voices in the Desert*, 1905

Set in what is just about the geographical centre of the continent, **Alice Springs** has a population of just 25,000, yet is still the largest settlement of the Australian interior. A clean, modern and compact town in the midst of the MacDonnell Ranges, it makes an excellent base from which to plan trips into the surrounding countryside.

The **Red Centre**, a marketing term coined to describe the area to the south, west and east of Alice Springs, is an historically rich and scenically spectacular region. It forms a part of the lands inhabited by the Anangu, the collective name for the Aborigines of the **Western Desert**. The Anangu were fortunate in being among the last of the Aboriginal Australians to come into contact with white settlers. As a result of this and the necessary strictness of Anangu laws and traditions, they and their fascinating culture have survived relatively unscathed. Here, as much as anywhere in Australia, some Aborigines are living the life of their choice on their traditional home-lands, and dealing with the neighbouring white culture on their own terms. In recent years, the Anangu have become world-renowned for their paintings, carvings and jewellery.

**Ayers Rock** – known to the Anangu as **Uluru** – is Australia's most famous and most visited natural spectacle, and still the primary reason why most people come to the Red Centre. At first sight, even jaded "seen-it-all" cynics will find it hard to take their eyes away from its awesome bulk. But there's much more here than just the Rock, and it's rare in Outback Australia to find such a large region crammed with worthwhile and accessible places of interest. The **West MacDonnells**, a series of rugged ridges cut at intervals by slender chasms or enormous gorges, start right on Alice's doorstep. In the other direction, the **Eastern MacDonnells** are less visited but no less appealing, with the remote tracks of the **Simpson Desert** to the south attracting the intrepid. To the west, **Palm Valley** and **Kings Canyon** can add a few days to a trip which, including the Rock, makes for one of the most memorable tours in the Outback.

## When to go
The aridity of the Centre results in extremes of temperature that are best avoided, if at all possible. In the mid-winter months of July and August, **freezing nights**, especially around Uluru, are not uncommon, while there is no escaping the **summer heat**; in December and January the temperature may have already reached 40°C by 10am and not drop below 30°C all night. Autumn (April–June) and Spring (Sept & Oct) are ideal times to explore the region in comfort.

Rain is a rare and wonderful thing in the Centre. In Alice, most houses don't have gutters: they would rarely be needed and, in any case, would be unable to cope with the deluge when it came. Whenever you visit, a sudden storm may temporarily transform the desert into a garden of exquisite flowers – a blooming celebrated by normally dormant and elusive wildlife with epicurean frenzy.

Out here a **wide-brimmed hat** is not so much a fashion accessory as a life saver, keeping your head and face in permanent shadow. All but the shortest of walks will also require a **water bottle** and loose, long-sleeved clothing plus lashings of **sun block** on any exposed skin. Australia's many venomous, but rarely aggressive, snakes, and the carpet of prickly spinifex grass that covers most of the Western Desert, make a pair of **covered shoes or boots** the final elementary precaution to safe and comfortable enjoyment of the Centre.

# Alice Springs

Most visitors are surprised by the modern, even sophisticated, appearance of **ALICE SPRINGS**. The bright, clear desert air gives the Outback town a charge you don't find in the languid, tropical north. Whether it's the American influence from the satellite tracking station at Pine Gap or that, though remote, Alice is relatively accessible, allusions to Nevil Shute's dusty, flyblown *A Town Like Alice* have long been obsolete.

The area has been inhabited for at least 10,000 years by Aranda Aborigines, who moved between the waterhole of Alice Springs, or Tjanerilji, and other relatively abundant water sources in the Western MacDonnells. But, as elsewhere in the Territory, it was only the Overland Telegraph Line's arrival in the 1870s that led to a permanent settlement here. Following **John McDouall Stuart**'s exploratory journeys through the area in the early 1860s, it was the visionary **Charles Todd**, then South Australia's Superintendent of Telegraphs, who saw the need to link Australia with the rest of the Empire. The town's river and its tributary carry his names, and the spring that of his wife, Alice.

With repeater stations needed every 250km from Adelaide to Darwin to boost the OTL signal, the site just north of today's town, with its permanent "spring" (actually a billabong on the Todd River), was ideal as a place to erect the necessary buildings. When a spurious ruby rush led to the discovery of gold at Arltunga in the Eastern MacDonnells, **Stuart Town** (the town's seldom-used official name in its early years) became a jumping-off point for the long slog to the riches out east. Arltunga's goldrush fizzled out under desperate conditions, but the township of Stuart remained, a collection of shanty dwellings serving a stream of pastoralists, prospectors and missionaries.

In 1929 the **railway line** from Adelaide finally reached Stuart Town. Journeys that had once taken weeks by camel from Oodnadatta could now be undertaken in just a few days and by 1933, when the town officially took the name Alice Springs, the population had mushroomed to nearly five hundred Europeans. In 1942 the bombing and subsequent evacuation of Darwin saw Alice Springs become the Territory's administrative headquarters, and a busy military base, supplying the war zone in the north. After the hostilities ceased, some of the wartime population stayed on and Alice's fortunes continued to grow slowly. In the meantime, wealthy tourists began to visit the mysterious monolith in the desert, southwest of town – a site that had been considered sacred by the Anangu for thousands of years.

With the reconstruction of the notoriously unreliable rail link from Adelaide and a new, tar-sealed, Stuart Highway completed in the mid-80s, Alice has only recently attained its present size and unexpected modernity. A **tourist boom** at this time, helped in no small measure by the massive publicity surrounding Azaria Chamberlain's reputed canine abduction at the Rock, has waned a little in recent years, but Alice still remains the undisputed "capital" of the Outback. Even so, the population remains tiny: within a 1000-kilometre radius of "The Alice", as it's affectionately known, there are fewer than 40,000 inhabitants. The town has embraced tourism wholeheartedly and although the continuing development of the on-site Ayers Rock Resort has affected trade, Alice still seems set to succeed, primarily because both the town and surrounding area have much to offer, even without the obligatory visit to the Rock.

## Arrival, information and transport

The **airport** is 14km south of town: the airport shuttle (☎53 0310) meets incoming flights and costs $9, a taxi (☎52 1877) about twice that amount. *Greyhound.Pioneer* **buses** arrive outside *Melanka Lodge* in Todd Street, *McCafferty*'s outside their office in Gregory Terrace, which crosses the south end of Todd Mall. Some of the keener hostels send minibuses to meet incoming buses (as well as some incoming flights). The **train station** is on the west side of the Stuart Highway, just off Larapinta Drive, about a fifteen-minute walk (or $4 taxi ride) from the town centre. See "Listings", on p.470, for bus and train **departures** from Alice.

The *Central Australian Tourism Industry Association* (*CATIA*) **tourist information office** (daily 9am–6pm; ☎52 5199) is on the corner of Hartley Street and Gregory Terrace, and has assorted useful information including a free *Central Australia Visitors' Guide*. There is also a helpful *Conservation Commission* desk here (☎51 5210), providing information on their parks and other services in Central Australia.

## Transport

The centre occupies a compact area between the Stuart Highway and Leichhardt Terrace, along the dry Todd River, bordered to the north and south by Wills Terrace and Stott Terrace, respectively. Bisecting this rectangle is **Todd Mall**, once the main street, now a relaxing pedestrian thoroughfare lined with al fresco cafés, galleries and souvenir outlets.

The town's sights are scattered, but you could still get around them all in a couple of easy days on foot. An alternative is to use the **Alice Wanderer** (☎52 2111; day-ticket $15), a "hop on, hop off" bus service with commentary, visiting most of the places of interest every seventy minutes. The Yeperenye Shopping Centre, around the corner from the tourist office, in Hartley Street, is the terminus for the **suburban bus** network. This is tailored for shoppers and schoolchildren, which means you'll have to plan your ride around a timetable (available from the tourist office or the Council Offices in Gregory Terrace), rather than just turning up at a bus stop and waiting; of the four main routes, **#1 West** and **#4 South** are the most useful. Otherwise your best bet is to rent a **bicycle** from any of the hostels, for around $10 a day. There's an enjoyable seventeen-kilometre **paved cycle track** through the bush to Simpson's Gap, starting at Flynn's Grave, 7km along Larapinta Drive, west of the town centre.

# Accommodation

There's plenty of choice of accommodation in Alice, most places (except the campsites) either in the central area or along **Todd Street** and **Gap Road** and adjacent avenues. Booking ahead is advisable during the winter school holidays (June–July). Note that the price codes given for self-contained apartments are for a unit sleeping between four and six people.

## Motels

**Diplomat Motor Inn**, 15 Gregory Terrace (☎52 8977). Right in town, a large motel more popular with tour groups than with individuals. ⑥.

**Frontier Oasis Motel**, 10 Gap Rd (☎51 1444). Better than average motel with landscaped pool area, very comfortable rooms and a fine restaurant/bar. ⑥.

**Midland Motel**, 4 Treager Ave (☎52 1588). Friendly, independent motel with a pleasant pool. ⑤.

**Territory Motor Inn**, Leichhardt Terrace (☎52 7829). Large motel backing onto Todd Mall. ⑥.

**Vista Motel**, Stephens Rd (☎52 6100). Very attractive and well-equipped modern hotel tucked under the Macdonnell Ranges with a pool, tennis courts and a good restaurant. ⑧.

## Self-contained apartments

**Alice Sundown**, 39 Gap Rd (☎52 8422). Bigger rooms than most and free pick-ups. ⑤.

**Alice Tourist Apartments**, corner of Gnoilya St and Gap Rd (☎52 2788). Award-winning apartments, but with a tiny pool. ⑤.

**Desert Palms Resort**, Barrett Drive (☎52 5977). Four-bed villa with TV, pool and jungles of palms, but seriously under-equipped kitchens. ⑤.

**Outback Motor Lodge**, South Terrace (☎52 3888). Among the best deals in this category with well-equipped rooms at good value prices. ⑤.

**White Gums Holiday Inn**, 17 Gap Rd (☎52 5144). Nearest self-contained apartments to town centre. ⑤.

## Hostels

**Alice Lodge**, 4 Mueller St (☎53 1975). Converted house in a quiet, residential area on the east side of the river, with no parking problems. Long-stay deals, nice garden and pool. Four-bed dorms ①, rooms ③.

**Gapview Resort Hotel**, south end of Gap Rd (☎ 52 6611). All the facilities at this spacious complex, plus plenty of parking. The converted motel rooms have 4 beds, bathroom, TV *and* video, but the tiny kitchen is a joke. Free runs up-town plus a bar, restaurant, attractive pool area and tennis courts. ①.

**Melanka Lodge**, 94 Todd St (free call ☎1800/89 6110). Huge complex of ageing motel buildings popular with young backpackers not too fussy about cleanliness. Has a licensed bar, "Skippy's" cafeteria with cheap meals, a pool and tour-booking information. Dorms ①, rooms ③.

**Ossies Homestead**, 18 Warburton St (☎52 2308). Small and friendly hostel in quiet residential street about fifteen minutes' walk from the centre, with a pool, bikes, mixed dorms plus a few four- and twin-bed rooms. Rates include a light breakfast. ①.

**Pioneer YHA**, Todd River end of Parsons St (☎52 8855). This award-winning hostel in the centre of town is well managed, clean and spacious, with four-bed air-con dorms, a pool, bikes and a tour-booking service. ①.

**Toddy's Backpackers**, 41 Gap Rd (☎52 1322). Large resort with mixed, 8-bed dorms, smaller dorms for a few dollars more, or "deluxe" double rooms where you can indulge yourself with bath, fridge and TV. Bargain evening meals with bar, barbecues and occasional entertainment, pool, bikes, tour information and bookings. Air-con dorms ①, rooms ③.

**YWCA**, Stuart Terrace (☎52 1894). Set in a nice garden, with some parking, but works out expensive for singles. ②–③.

## Campsites and caravan parks

**All Seasons Red Centre Resort**, Stuart Highway, 3km north of town (☎52 8955). Extensive, landscaped resort with powered sites. Four-person cabins ④.

**Gapview Resort Hotel**, south end of Gap Rd (☎ 52 6611). Camping available in the resort grounds, if there's space.

**Heavitree Gap Caravan Park**, Palm Circuit, 2km south of Heavitree Gap (☎52 2370). Campsite with powered sites and good facilities. On-site vans ③.

**Stuart Tourist Park** (opposite *Araluen Centre*), Larapinta Drive (☎52 2547). Most central caravan park with regular camping and powered sites. On-site vans ③.

# The Town

Start your tour of town by nipping up to **Anzac Hill** (off Wills Terrace) for a great view over Alice to the Heavitree Ranges beyond. Next stop is the **Museum of Central Australia**, on the first floor of Alice Plaza (daily 10am–5pm; $2; children free), with a focus on regional natural history including displays of gems, fossils and local meteorites, plus a cast of the petroglyphs at Ewaninga (see p.478). Try and catch a showing of the video *The Triumph of the Nomads*, (just about all that remains of the museum's suspended Aboriginal section), based on Geoffrey Blainey's incisive book. Both recount how the Aborigines were skilful masters rather than helpless victims of their environment, contrary to commonly-held perceptions. Just down Parsons Street is the **Old Courthouse and Residency** (9am–4pm weekdays) a small bungalow that the governor of the southern NT used to call home. A few rooms are still decorated in period style, and there's a small exhibition of Aboriginal artefacts and costumes that were used in the film *We of the Never Never*.

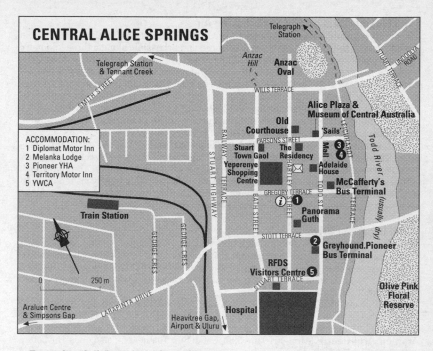

From the "Sails" awning where Parsons Street crosses Todd Mall, a short stroll down the mall will take you past **Adelaide House**, an ingenious convection-cooled building designed by the Reverend John Flynn, founder of the Royal Flying Doctor Service (RFDS). Adelaide House was the first hospital in Central Australia, and also the site of Flynn and Alf Treager's innovative radio experiments using portable, pedal-generated electricity. Although presently closed, it still houses early medical and RFDS memorabilia. If you want to learn more about the RFDS, head down Hartley Street to the **RFDS Visitors' Centre** (Mon–Sat 9am–3.30pm; $2) in Stuart Terrace, which has half-hourly tours including a film describing the work of this unique medical organization, still subsidized by charitable donations.

Next door to Adelaide House is the **John Flynn Memorial Church** and around the corner, at 65 Hartley Street, is **Panorama Guth** (Mon–Sat 9am–5pm; $3), a museum and art gallery displaying Henk Guth's eminently forgetable landscapes, original Albert Namatjira watercolours (see p.473 for more on Namatjira's life and the Hermannsburg school of painting he founded), and a much more curious collection of rare Aboriginal artefacts, including some sacred and totemic objects (*tjuringas*). The panorama, from which the gallery takes it name, is a novel if unremarkable painting, sixty metres in circumference, showing the area around Alice, but the gallery below is a wonderfully comfy and congenial place to snooze through the regional home movies on show.

When you've had enough of artefacts and memorabilia, pack a lunch and cycle out to the **Olive Pink Botanical Reserve** (daily 10am–6pm), just across the causeway on Tuncks Road. Olive Pink was a passionate defender of Aboriginal rights long before the issue became fashionable. She also collected native flora from the surrounding lands, all of which can be seen neatly labelled along pathways winding up through the reserve. Displays in the **Visitors' Centre** (daily 10am–4pm) explain the various strategies the plants use to survive in the desert.

## The Telegraph Station and School of the Air

The old **Telegraph Station** (daily 8am–7pm, until 9pm Oct–April; $2.50) is tucked in the hills just to the north of town. Fully restored and accessible along a three-kilometre riverside walk from Wills Terrace (or off the Stuart Highway, 4km north of town), the historical reserve – situated right by the pool from which the town derives its name – faithfully recreates the settlement's earliest years. There are free and informative twenty-minute **tours** at half past the hour, further detailing pioneering life at the telegraph station and, even disregarding the history, it's a pleasant place to while away a quiet afternoon. The station is also the starting point of the **Larapinta Trail** bushwalk to Standley Chasm in the Western MacDonnells (see below).

On the other side of the Stuart Highway is the **School of the Air** (Mon–Fri 8am–noon; $2, children free; closed during school holidays), at 80 Head Street. Explanatory sessions are offered every half-hour on this famous Outback institution, through which children living on remote stations are taught over the radio. It's mostly visited by overseas schoolchildren and teachers, though visiting British royalty have taken an interest at various times, too. From town, take bus #3 and alight at stop number 5 or 11.

## Along Larapinta Drive

**Larapinta Drive** heads out through the western suburbs past the Araluen Arts Centre, some 2km from the town, which is at the heart of a small cluster of places that could occupy a spare afternoon if you're so minded. Bus #1 winds through the back roads from the bus station, only really useful if you're heading for the Diorama Village and then walking back to Araluen.

The **Diorama Village** (Mon–Fri 10am–5pm, closed Jan; $2.50; bus #1, stop 12) boasts of being Alice's biggest souvenir supermarket, but its fabricated caves depicting sculptures of Dreamtime myths are for kids or rainy days only. Of more interest is the **Araluen Arts Centre** (Mon–Fri 9am–5pm, Sat & Sun 10am–4pm; also open 1hr before performances), Alice's performing arts and entertainment centre, incorporating a gallery, cinema and theatre. Look out for the bi-monthly "What's On" sheets available here and around town.

Next to the Arts Centre is the **Ted Strehlow Research Centre** (daily 10am–5pm; $4), which houses an absorbing exhibition dominated by the life and works of Ted Strehlow, son of a Hermannsburg missionary and Aranda initiate, who devoted his life to studying these Aborigines. Betraying their trust in later years, Strehlow disclosed his ceremonial knowledge and sacred objects to his second wife, Kathleen, and a battle now rages for the return of the material that the late Strehlow collected. Many of the *tjuringas* are locked "for safe keeping" in the centre's vault; some are so sacred that they should only ever be seen by initiated Aranda men.

Around the corner in Memorial Drive are the **Museum of Transport, Technology and Communications** and the **Central Australian Aviation Museum** (both daily 10am–4pm; donations welcome). The former has a collection of old planes, cars and motorbikes housed in the hangars of Alice's old airport, and includes several pristine Model T Fords and the original 8WD road train that used to slog up to Darwin during the 1930s at a hot and noisy 20mph. The adjacent aviation museum houses many of the aircraft that pioneered travel in the Outback. There is a special memorial to the "**Coffee Royale Incident**" of 1929, when the rescuers of missing aviator, Charles Kingsford-Smith, themselves crashed and perished in the northern Tanami desert. Kingsford-Smith, a national hero, was accused of cynically staging the crash for publicity purposes; the memorial poignantly displays the wreckage of the long-lost *Kookaburra* used in the search. Finally, **Alice Springs Memorial Cemetery**, also in Memorial Drive, includes the graves of pioneer aviator Eddie Connellan, artist Albert Namatjira and the reburied remains of the legendary, luckless prospector Harold Lasseter, after whom the town's casino is rather ironically named.

## Sights south of Alice

Through **Heavitree Gap**, a couple of kilometres south of town, is another collection of sights. The first three described below are within range of the #4 bus, which terminates at the **Old Timers Museum** (daily 2–4pm; $1; closed Dec–March), just off the Stuart Highway, yet another display of pioneering memorabilia. The remainder are easily reached by bike, or on the *Alice Wanderer* bus route.

Head first for the **Pitchi Ritchi Sanctuary** (daily 9am–2pm; $8), out on Palm Circuit, which, in addition to being a collection of fairly crude, bush-gnarled relics, is also an animal sanctuary. The work of Leo Corbett, who once staked a bogus gold-mining claim on Heavitree Gap (Pitchi Ritchi means "gap in the range") to prevent it being quarried and widened, the sanctuary also features the peculiar Aboriginal-inspired sculptures of William Ricketts, which further enhance the place's eccentric feel. While here you're offered a mug of billy tea and damper and given the opportunity to crack whips, throw boomerangs and play a didgeridoo while the resident "bushie" plies you with bush tales and Aboriginal lore.

Next door, the **Mecca Date Farm** (Mon–Sat 9am–5pm, Sun 10am–4pm) was Australia's first commercial date farm, set up in the 1950s. It now produces around 3000kg of the fruit a year from trees introduced last century by Afghan cameleers. You are offered a free sample on arrival and tours of the farm – basically rows of date palms – on the hour.

A farm of a very different sort is just a couple of kilometres down the Ross Highway. The **Frontier Camel Farm** features short rides ($6) on that other well-known Afghani introduction into Australia, plus a museum of camels and cameleering and a display of "Arid Australian Reptiles" (daily 9am–7pm; $5), a creepy round-up of the Centre's snakes and lizards. Introductory camel talks are given at 10.30am and 2pm ($6; the *Alice Wanderer* bus coincides with these), and the Camel Farm also organizes longer tours in the area.

Back on the Stuart Highway, railway enthusiasts will hope that the efforts of the *Ghan Preservation Society* have seen the train workshops at **MacDonnell Siding**, 10km south of town, re-open. Here, a troupe of enthusiastic volunteers have converted a period station into a museum of Alice Spring's early rail years and are also involved in the refurbishment of old *Ghan* locomotives and rolling stock, which are used for **train rides** (call ☎55 5047) along a short section of track.

---

### GHAN . . . BUT NOT FORGOTTEN

The legendary unreliability of the **old Ghan rail service** must have had the Afghan cameleers, whose services it replaced and in whose honour it was named, chuckling in their graves. The poorly surveyed line, which was laid directly onto the sand with little regard for contours and floodways, buckled, subsided and was frequently completely washed away by flash floods. Indeed, it was not terribly uncommon for the track to be washed out either side of the stranded train, requiring parachute drops of essential supplies to sustain the passengers while the line was relaid and bedded-in. Consequently, late arrivals were common – trains arriving up to *three months* late were recorded.

In 1980, the new line from Port Augusta, rerouted and constructed from "continous", welded rails, reached Alice ahead of schedule, with trains now carrying twice the number of passengers in half the time. With its arrival, the fifty-year-long era of the notorious *Ghan* passed into history. The millions of redundant timber sleepers from the old line have been put to a variety of uses all over central Australia, propping up bars and cattle yards or fabricated into restaurant tables. They can still be found in the bush or bought inexpensively at MacDonnell Siding, making an authentic, if cumbersome, souvenir of the Centre's first rail link.

A further 5km south, down Petrick Road, **The Winery** (formerly *Chateau Hornsby*; daily 11am–4pm) is central Australia's only winery, with a restaurant (see "Eating" below) and evening entertainment most nights. While it's a pleasant enough place for a meal, the wines are more memorable for their novelty than their quality.

# Eating

As elsewhere in the Territory, Alice provides the staples of "steak 'n' seafood", with the accent strongly on the former – and not necessarily of bovine origin, either. But it's **where you eat**, as much as what you eat, that can make dining out in Alice a special occasion. Some places that turn a meal into an event include dinners on the old *Ghan* train once or twice a week (☎55 5047); evenings at *The Winery* (☎55 5133), accompanied by Ted Egan's Outback wit; or a ride out into the bush to crack whips and throw boomerangs while the damper bakes, with the *Camp Oven Kitchen* (☎53 1411; $45). Alternatively, start the day with a gourmet **champagne breakfast** having just watched the sunrise from three thousand feet up in a hot air balloon (see "Tours", below).

Otherwise, Todd Mall is lined with cafés providing outdoor seating, and the pubs (see "Drinking, nightlife and entertainment") provide counter meals for well under $10. Besides the places listed below, many hotels offer decent food; a queue of chattering locals is always a good sign.

### Cafés and snack bars

**Alice Plaza**, Todd Mall. Food halls with Asian- and Italian-inspired lunches.

**Bar Doppio Mediterranean**, Fan Arcade, Todd Mall. Good-value Italian and Greek dishes.

**Boomerang Café**, Yeperenye Shopping Centre, Hartley St. Adequately revives exhausted shoppers with capuccinos and snacks.

**Joanne's**, off Todd Mall in Reg Harris Lane. Wholesome homemade tucker.

**Swingers**, Gregory Terrace, opposite the Environment Centre. Popular snazzy café, the place to show-off your new haircut and gossip.

### Restaurants

**Al Fresco**, Todd Mall, next to the cinema (☎53 4944). Delicious pasta and salad concoctions, with movie-and-meal deals on Monday nights.

**Camels Crossing**, Fan Arcade, off Todd Mall (☎52 5522). Cheap and surprisingly fine Mexican food.

**Chopsticks**, 42 Hartley St (☎52 3873). A predictable name, but the best Chinese food in town.

**Matilda's**, *Frontier Oasis Motel*, 10 Gap Rd (☎52·1444). Surprisingly good venue for seafood given the distance from the sea. Around $20 per person.

**Overlander Steakhouse**, 72 Hartley St (☎52 2159). For the spirit *and* taste of the Outback, the croc *vol-au-vents* are a dream; all your favourite Aussie fauna on a plate.

**Plaza Hotel**, Barrett Drive. Sunday brunch, an Alice institution, served from 11.30am. All-you-can-eat quality food for around $30.

**Puccini's**, Undoolya Rd (☎53 0935). Alice's best Italian restaurant, pricey but worth it.

**Scotty's Tavern** and **Alice's Restaurant**, Todd Mall. Bar and restaurant serving Territorian food (including emu) amid a rogues' gallery of photographs of local identities.

**Sri Devi**, Shop 2, Gregory Terrace (☎52 3188). Alice's only Indian restaurant seems to have scared all the competition away with its delicious and varied menu.

# Drinking, nightlife and entertainment

Like the surrounding desert, night-time Alice initially appears lifeless. However, with careful scrutiny, something can be found going on somewhere most nights, particularly in the latter half of the week.

The *Todd Tavern*, at the top of Todd Mall, is the town's premier **drinking** spot, with a jam session until the early hours on Monday night. Thursday nights at *Bojangles* in Todd Street are upbeat and *AJ's Tavern*, out on the Ross Highway, also features **live bands** most nights. There's **jazz** at *Scotty's* on Friday nights and at *The Winery* on Sunday afternoons. If nothing else tempts you, there's always the **cinema** at the top of Todd Mall, with cheap nights on Tuesdays. Check the programme at the **Araluen Arts Centre** (☎52 5022) on Larapinta Drive: you'll usually find a worthwhile play, film or concert. And if you're feeling lucky, *Lasseters Casino* on Barrett Drive can accommodate you – but not in thongs and a tatty singlet.

## Events

More energetic activities tend to have to wait for the cooler months, starting with the **Bangtail Muster** on the first Monday in May, a colourful and tongue-in-cheek parade and celebration of silliness. The **Camel Cup races** in mid-July is Australia's biggest camel race meeting, followed by a **Food and Wine Festival** the next day. The string of **rodeos** along the Track hits Alice in late-August, while the town's most famous event, the wacky **Henley-on-Todd Regatta** kicks off in early October. Bottomless boats are run down the dry river bed; needless to say, the event is heavily insured against the Todd actually flowing, and there's a **Beerfest** the following week. Christmas sees the **Corkwood Festival**, a celebration of art, music and dance, with

## TOURS FROM ALICE

A large number of professional **tour operators** offer adventurous, cultural, or historical tours throughout the area – some recommended operators are listed below. Many hostels and hotels offer a tour-booking service, but if you feel you need more advice, ask , at the tourist office on Hartley Street (see "Arrival, information and transport", p.463).

**AAT Kings** (☎52 5266) and **Holidays NT** (☎53 2897). Day-trips to Uluru for just over $100 – but you'll regret such a short visit. AAT also offer Eastern MacDonnell tours on demand.

**Cookies** (☎53 4888). Popular one-day runs through the West MacDonnells with a thought-provoking guide.

**Frontier Camel Farm** (☎53 0444). Short camel rides down the Todd River, two-and-a-half-day West MacDonnells jaunts from *Glen Helen Lodge*, and five-day Simpson Desert treks.

**Ossie's Outback Trail Rides** (☎52 2308). Day, sunset and overnight rides up the Todd River's east bank from $60. Beginners welcome; discounts or YHA/VIP members.

**Noel Fullerton Camel Safaris** (☎56 0925). Based at Stuarts Well, 90km down the Track, Noel Fullerton, Australia's leading camel expert, organizes tours out to Rainbow Valley and beyond, lasting from half a day to several weeks.

**Outback Experience** (☎53 2666). The best operator currently running trips to Chambers Pillar and other places deep in the Simpson Desert.

**Skyport** (☎52 3977) or **Alice Springs Air Charter** (☎55 5200). Flights to the Rock and back in a day for around $300.

**Spinifex** (☎53 4800), **Outback Ballooning** (☎52 8723) or **Aussie Balloons** (☎53 0544). Alice is Australia's ballooning capital and any of these will take you up, up and away and back down to a champagne breakfast (*Spinifex*'s is held at *The Winery*, the others are in the bush). Don't wear your best clothes as all hands are needed to pack up the dusty balloon.

**Rod Steinert** (☎55 5000). Several Aboriginal culture tours in the Alice area, including the excellent, half-day *Dreamtime* tour. While certainly a show, it's also educational, very (some say *too*) informative and is highly recommended.

**Trek-About** (☎53 0714) or the slightly upmarket **Sahara** (☎53 0881) offer two-, three- and five-day camping tours through the West MacDonnells, to Kings Canyon and Uluru. As is often the case, the longer tours are much the best value.

food and craft stalls in Todd Mall. There's also a rather uninspiring **market** every other Sunday in the Mall.

## Shopping for Aboriginal art

Alice has become a centre for the art and crafts produced by the Anangu Aborigines, and Todd Mall is full of galleries selling a vast range of high-quality work. Most unusual are the **dot paintings**, canvas depictions of the temporary sand paintings used to pass on sacred knowledge during ceremonies, each being someone's sole property and responsibility. This school of art originated in the early 1970s at Papunya, northwest of Alice, under the encouragement of a local teacher, Geoff Bardon; what was intended as a kind of constructive graffiti for youngsters was taken up by the elders. Clifford Possum and Billy Stockman were among the earliest of the Papunya artists to find fame, and their paintings are free of the clumsy flashiness of some contemporary work.

While it's difficult to recommended a single **gallery**, you'd do well starting your search at the *Original Dreamtime Gallery*, 63 Todd Mall, or the *Aboriginal Art and Culture Centre*, 86 Todd Street; both are attractive galleries full of good-quality work. Less fancy in appearance but loaded with excellent unframed canvases is the Aboriginal-owned *Papunya Tula Artists*, at 78 Todd Street, and there are a couple of similar Aboriginal-owned places round the corner in Gregory Terrace: you won't necessarily save money by buying direct – usually the opposite – but you might feel happier about who benefits from the proceeds. Another recommended place, with good paintings and crafts at keen prices, is *Awenthe's Art & Artifacts*, 113 Todd St, nearly opposite *Melanka Lodge,* but in the end it's just a matter of spending half a day or more looking for what you want at a price that you find acceptable. The more you spend, the more chance there is of making a deal, with free overseas postage and insurance usually offered at the bigger places.

If you're heading north, the galleries in Aileron and Ti Tree (see p.460) and Tennant Creek (p.457) have a much smaller range of Aboriginal art on sale, but often at less than half the price of that in Alice's galleries. And finally, if you're concerned with authenticity, it's useful to know that didgeridoos and bark paintings are indigenous to the Top End (where they can also be cheaper to buy), not the Western Desert.

## Listings

**Airlines** *Ansett* (☎50 4100); *Qantas* (☎50 5222).

**Bike rental** From most hostels for around $10 a day.

**Bookshops** *Arunta Bookshop*, Todd St, and *Arid Lands Environment Centre* (*ALEC*), around the corner in Gregory Terrace, are both good for local history and Aboriginal culture. *Bookworm*, Colacag Plaza (in the block between Gregory and Scott terraces), sells secondhand books.

**Buses** *Greyhound.Pioneer* depart up to twice daily for Adelaide and Darwin; change at Three Ways Roadhouse for Queensland and at Katherine for WA. Their office is situated next to *Melanka Lodge* in Todd St (☎13 2303). Queensland-based *McCafferty's* are gradually encroaching westward, with daily runs from Alice north to Darwin, east to Townsville and Cairns via Threeways, and south to Adelaide with a connecting service at Erldunda on to Uluru. Their office is at Shop 3, 91 Gregory Terrace (☎52 3952). The Alice-based *Territory Coachlines*, at the corner of Stott Terrace and Hartley St (☎008 806 491) undercut both the above operators on their daily Adelaide run ($90), and the *Wayward Bus* (☎1800/882 823) returns home to Adelaide every Saturday (with an overnight stop in Coober Pedy included) for just $60.

**Camping supplies** *Alice Springs Disposals*, Reg Harris Lane, off Todd St Mall.

**Car parts** *Centrewreck*, 25 Stuart Highway (☎52 3525), sells secondhand spare parts: other mechanical services are found off Smith St and Elder St in the light-industrial northwest part of town.

**Car rental** *CC Rentals* (☎52 1495) at the *Mobil* service station at the top of Todd Mall has mopeds, mokes and Suzuki jeeps, and frequently offers special deals, as does *Territory/Cheapa Rent-a-Car* (☎52 9999).

**Central Lands Council** 31–33 Stuart Highway (☎51 6249). Issues permits to enter Aboriginal lands in central NT: note that in most cases, simply "wanting to go there" won't be a good enough reason; even if your application is accepted, expect several weeks' wait.

**Fuel** 24-hour service at the *BP Roadhouse* on the North Stuart Highway.

**Gay Life** *Centre Network* (☎53 2844) will be glad to hear from any gay or lesbian visitors; a good meeting place is the *Galah Bar* at the *Frontier Oasis Motel* in Gap Rd on Friday evenings from 5.30pm.

**Hospital** Gap Rd (☎50 2221).

**Maps** *The Map Shop*, 21 Gregory Terrace (☎51 5393), for detailed maps of the Centre.

**Police** Parsons St (☎51 8888).

**Post office** Hartley St (☎52 1020).

**Trains** The *Ghan* leaves Alice Springs each Tuesday and Friday at 5.10pm, and arrives in Adelaide at 4pm the next day, with the return leg to Alice departing Adelaide on Monday and Thursday at 2pm, and arriving at 11am. In coach class (no bed or meals) it costs $139, the same price and duration as the bus journey; first class costs nearly three times as much with a sleeper and meals included, and the holiday class gives you a four-berth sleeper for around $229 but no meals. Change at Port Augusta to connect with the *Indian Pacific* line.

# The MacDonnell Ranges

The **MacDonnell Ranges** are among the longest of the parallel ridge systems that corrugate the Centre's landscape. Their east-west axis, passing right through Alice Springs, is broken in many places by gaps carved through the ranges during better-watered epochs. It is these striking ruptures, along with the grandeur and colours of the rugged landscape – particularly west of Alice – which make a few days spent in the MacDonnells so worthwhile. The expansive **West MacDonnells National Park** is best appreciated with at least one overnight stay at *Glen Helen Lodge*, or any of the campsites mentioned below, while the often overlooked **Eastern MacDonnells** have a more compact, intimate feel and are a better bet if your time is limited. Both ranges can be visited as part of a tour (see the box on p.469) or with your own vehicle.

**Larapinta Trail** is an arduous walk along the West MacDonnell ridge, starting at the Telegraph Station north of town (see p.466) and ending 220km west of Alice at Mount Sonder. So far, only some sections of the trail, laid by local prisoners, have been completed; call or visit the Conservation Commission in Alice (☎51 5210) for latest details and maps.

## The West MacDonnells and Finke Gorge national parks

The **route** described below follows an anticlockwise loop out along Larapinta Drive and then Namatjira Drive to *Glen Helen Lodge*, from where a 140-kilometre dirt road brings you round to Palm Valley (which is accessible to 4WD vehicles only), Hermannsburg and back to Alice – a total distance of nearly 400km. The track passes through **Aboriginal Land** on its return section, but no permit is required (unless stated), providing you keep to the road and camp at designated sites.

Leaving Alice along Larapinta Drive, you reach **Flynn's Grave**, 7km from town. Situated beneath Mount Gillen, a granite boulder set on a plinth marks the spot where John Flynn, founder of the RFDS, had his ashes interred in 1951. A little further is a turning to **Simpsons Gap** (gates open daily 8am–8pm), the nearest and most popular of the West Macs' gaps, where a white sandy riverbed lined with red and ghost gums leads up to a small pool. Agile rock wallabies live on the cliffs and there's an excellent **visitors' centre** and barbecues, as well as a seventeen-kilometre cycle track leading back to town. The first stage of the **Larapinta Trail** ends here – a tough day's walk from the Telegraph Station.

A turning south off Larapinta Drive leads to **White Gums Wildlife Park** (daily 8am–dusk; $3), once Alice's dairy, and now a sanctuary for emus, kangaroos and wallabies. There's a café, shop and camping here, plus walks leading through the park's 500-year-old gums or, more strenuously, up on to the Heavitree Range to Mount Brown. Further along Larapinta Drive are the **Twin Ghost Gums**, immortalized in **Albert Namatjira**'s definitive painting of the Centralian landscape.

Just after the famed gums is a turn-off north to **Standley Chasm** (daily 7.30am–5pm; $2.50), 50km from Alice. Situated on Iwupataka Aboriginal Land, this is another popular spot, where a walk up the cycad palm-lined riverbed leads to a narrow chasm formed by the erosion of softer rock that once lay between the red quartzite walls. Around noon the shutters click, as both the eighty-metre-high walls are briefly lit by the overhead sun. There is also a café with a terrace and a souvenir shop; black-footed rock-wallabies are fed here daily at 9.30am.

## Along Namatjira Drive

Another 6km along Larapinta Drive, **Namatjira Drive** turns north amid the West MacDonnell Ranges; keeping straight on would bring you to Hermannsburg and Palm Valley (see below). Along Namatjira Drive, a scenic 42km ahead is **Ellery Big Hole** (barbecues, toilets and camping; $1), the deepest – and thus most permanent – waterhole in the area, and certainly the coldest. Nevertheless, caught between the brief ebb and flow of visiting bus tours, it's a pleasant spot, and your stealth may be rewarded by glimpses of thirst-quenching wildlife. Eleven kilometres to the west is **Serpentine Gorge** (toilets but no camping): the only way to truly appreciate this gorge is to swim across the small pool or climb over the ridge to the right. Few bother to exert themselves, and consequently the secluded inner gorge has become popular with hardy nudists. For the wildlife's sake, keep out of the upstream pools.

The **Ochre Pits** signposted off Namatjira Drive are just that – pits of maroon and bright yellow ochre still used by the Aranda for ceremonial purposes, but not really worth the stop. However, fourteen kilometres further west, **Ormiston Gorge** and **Pound National Park** (barbecues and camping) are definitely worth the effort. One of the most scenically spectacular spots in the West MacDonnells, the short ascent up to **Gum Tree Lookout** (the walk continues down into the gorge) gives a great view over the 250-metre-high gorge walls rising from the pools below – home to ducks and even the odd black swan. The three-hour **Pound Walk** includes some rock-hopping and longer, overnight walks can be undertaken by those who are properly prepared – ask the rangers at the Park Information Centre, who also organize occasional free slide show evenings for campers.

Just west of Ormiston is **GLEN HELEN**, another perennial waterhole along the bed of the ancient **Finke River**, which – on the rare occasions when it flows – can reach Lake Eyre in South Australia. **Accommodation** and refreshment is available at *Glen Helen Lodge* (☎56 7489; motel rooms ⑥, backbackers bunkhouse ①), which also has camping, fuel, and counter meals; the *Yapalpa* restaurant here is one of the loveliest spots in the West MacDonnells with a very cosy bar and terrace out back, while indoors the antique furniture, classy crockery and superbly cooked food make for a memorable indulgence. Helicopter flights over the nearby Ormiston Gorge can also be arranged; ask at the bar ($55 for 15min; minimum of three people required). If you're heading towards Kings Canyon along the **Mereenie Loop Track**, get your free permit here and make sure you have enough fuel for the entire journey.

## On to Redbank Gorge, Gosses Bluff and Ipolera

Beyond Glen Helen the bitumen ends, but the natural spectacles continue. If you intend to complete the loop, it's about 110km of dirt to the Hermannsburg/Palm Valley turn-off, and another 30km east along Larapinta Drive back to the bitumen leading to Alice. Providing you stay on the road, it's easily done by 2WD vehicles at a sensible pace in dry conditions, but most regular cars turn back after visiting Redbank Gorge.

Keeping the distinctive outline of **Mount Sonder** in view to the north, the turn-off for **Redbank Gorge** is 20km from Glen Helen, with a further 10km to the car park, passing the rather exposed **campsite** on the way. Redbank is the longest and narrowest cleft along the MacDonnells, its slippery walls no more than a metre apart in places and rarely warmed by direct sunlight. To get a full impression of the gorge you'll need an airbed and a pair of sports shoes to swim the 400m to the other end, which involves crossing seventeen freezing pools and some awkward scrambling.

Seventeen kilometres from the Redbank turn-off, you keep straight on for Tylers Pass, passing the Haasts Bluff and Papunya turn-off to your right. The road becomes fairly rough until you're over the pass, from where a steep ascent to the radio mast gives a superb view of **Gosses Bluff**. Day visits to the interior of this huge crater, five kilometres in diameter, are now possible although much of the Bluff, known to the Western Aranda as *Tnorula*, is out of bounds. Scientific theory suggests that the crater was formed when a comet struck the earth about 130 million years ago, with a force one million times greater than the atomic explosion at Hiroshima. The best way to appreciate the crater's size is to scramble to its rim; from this vantage point, the impact which created the 200-metre-high circular ridge is made a little more comprehensible.

South of the Bluff, along a perfectly smooth and sandy track, you reach the Hermannsburg–Kings Canyon road: the Mereenie Loop. Turning west leads to the Aboriginal community of **IPOLERA**, set up by the visionary Hermann Malbunka as a Utopian outstation away from the deteriorating Hermannsburg of the early 1980s. This

### ALBERT NAMATJIRA: 1902–1959

Born on the Hermannsburg Lutheran mission in 1902, Albert, who added his father's name to appease Eurocentric propriety, was the first of that mission's much-copied school of landscape watercolourists. Although without previous painting experience, Namatjira assisted Rex Battarbee on his painting expeditions through the Central Australian deserts in the 1930s. His talent soon became obvious to Battarbee, who later became Namatjira's agent. Like all NT Aborigines at that time, Namatjira was forbidden to buy alcohol, stay overnight in Alice Springs or leave the Territory without permission, but at the insistence of southern do-gooders – and against his wishes – he was the first Aborigine to be awarded Australian **citizenship**, in 1956. This meant he could travel without limitations, but needed a permit to visit his own family on Aboriginal reserves, while the house in Alice he longed for was denied him for fear of the "entourage" he might have attracted. He became a reluctant celebrity, compelled to pay taxes on his earnings and further drained of his wealth by the "share-it-all" kinship laws that still hamper successful Aboriginal artists today. A shy and modest man, much respected for his earnestness and generosity, he died in 1959 following a sordid conviction and short imprisonment for supplying alcohol to fellow Aborigines.

Critics could never make up their minds about his work, but his popular appeal was undoubted: exhibitions in the southern cities, which he rarely attended, persistently sold-out within hours of opening, and today his paintings remain among the most valuable examples of Australia's artistic pre-occupation with its landscape. If you'd like to buy prints of Albert Namatjira's work, the cheapest place in Alice is the *Museum of Central Australia*'s shop in Alice Plaza.

model community offers camping as well as occasional **tours** (☎56 7466; closed Dec–Jan) focusing on local Aboriginal culture and including a visit to a massive, authentic sand painting. You are requested to respect the privacy of Ipolera's residents and also not to bring or consume alcohol here.

## Finke Gorge National Park

The popularity of **FINKE GORGE NATIONAL PARK** is founded on its prehistoric cycads and unique red cabbage palms which have survived in the park's sheltered **Palm Valley** for over 10,000 years. Despite the difficult 4WD road leading to the valley, there are almost always large tour groups here, but it doesn't quite live up to expectations. The pleasant forty-minute loop walk is the valley's highlight; visiting the rest of the park requires a 4WD vehicle, as does the route along the Finke River bed from Hermannsburg (see box below). On the way in or out of the gorge, you can climb up to the once sacred **Initiation Rock**, giving a fine view over the **Amphitheatre**, a cirque of sandstone cliffs. The park has barbecues, toilets, solar-heated showers and camping.

**HERMANNSBURG**, until recently a Lutheran Mission, is the oldest Aboriginal community in the Centre, dating from the 1870s. Unusually, visitors are able to visit the town, or more particularly the **Historic Precinct** (daily 9.30am–3pm; $2.50) which features the original mission buildings converted into tea rooms and an art gallery. Bob will give you a tour of the gallery and fill you in on the history of the mission and the life and work of Albert Namatjira who was born here (see box on p.473). There is also a supermarket and fuel (cash only) but no accommodation.

Back towards Alice Springs, passing the **Albert Namatjira Memorial**, you reach the small community of **WALLACE ROCKHOLE**, offering one-hour tours (☎56 7415; $5) of the nearby Aboriginal petroglyphs as well as a shop, fuel and camping. The same rules and courtesies apply as for Ipolera – see above. From here, it's 117km of bitumen back to Alice Springs.

### FINKE RIVER ROUTE

With a day to spare and some experience with a 4WD, following the Finke River bed from **Hermannsburg** down to the **Ernest Giles Road** makes a wonderful antidote to the hypnotically dull highway scenery; rewards include stark gorge scenery, encounters with dingoes, wallabies and other wildlife, and the likelihood that you'll have it all to yourself.

The 93.5km track starts immediately south of Hermannsburg, and along the way are unevenly spaced signs for Kings Canyon (confusing as the track isn't a direct route there), otherwise you're on your own. After about 10km of just rough road, you descend into the **river bed**, and from here on it's pretty demanding four-wheel-driving through sand – you might need to deflate your tyres to around 20psi to minimize the risk of getting stuck. The sole designated **campsite** is at Boggy Hole, around three hours (28.5km) from Hermannsburg and generally the only source of fresh water on the journey. The campsite looks out from beneath river red gums to permanent reed-fringed water holes, best seen at dawn as the first sunlight creeps across the gorge and the ponds are alive with birdlife. Beyond Boggy Hole, there's a slow patch of gibber country before the roller-coaster ride to the Giles Road across some low, blood-red dunes thinly wooded with desert oaks – beware of oncoming traffic in blind crests. Boggy Hole to the Giles Road takes another three hours to cover 65km.

You don't need a permit for this track, but it's advisable to check on **conditions** and pick up a **map** from the *Conservation Commission* in Alice (see p.463) first.

# The Eastern MacDonnells

Heading out of Alice through the **Heavitree Gap** and along the Ross Highway, you soon reach **Emily Gap**, Alice's nearest waterhole, 10km from town. This is one of the most significant Anangu sites in Central Australia, the start of the Caterpillar Dreaming trail. There are engravings on the far side of the soupy pool, and plenty of darting birds and irksome flies; camping or open fires are not permitted. **Jessie Gap**, a little further east, is similar in appearance, but usually dry and of limited appeal. **Corroborree Rock** (camping), 45km east of Alice, is an unusual, fin-like outcrop of limestone with an altar-like platform and a crevice whose polished appearance suggests that, if not Aranda initiates, then plenty of tourists have squeezed through in a rite of passage. Known as *Antanangantana* to the Aranda, it was once a repository for sacred *tjuringa* stones.

## John Hayes Rockhole and Trephina Gorge

The John Hayes Rockhole and the Trephina Gorge, by far the most satisfying of the accessible destinations in the Eastern MacDonnells, are just 80km from Alice. Both offer superb scenery and a selection of enjoyable walks, and there's a four-hour ridge walk linking the two. **John Hayes Rockhole** (limited camping space), reached along a four-kilometre track requiring a high-clearance vehicle, is a series of pools linked by (usually dry) waterfalls along a canyon. The ninety-minute "Chain of Pools" walk takes you to the top of the gorge and down through the pools: an ideal way to get hot, but happily with plenty of opportunities to cool off. Alternatively, the lower pools are accessible from the car park.

**Trephina Gorge**, perhaps the most impressive spot in the eastern part of the range, is a beautiful, wide, sandy gorge whose rich red walls shelter a rather sick-looking pool, but this doen't seem to deter the local fauna. There is a pleasant **campsite** and the "Gorge" and "Panorama" walks (both taking about fifty minutes) are well worth the effort. The *Conservation Commission* in Alice (see p.463) produces an attractive colour brochure for this area.

## Ross River Homestead and Arltunga Historical Reserve

Five kilometres beyond Trephina Gorge, the Ross Highway peters out into two tracks: eight kilometres to the southeast (90km east of Alice Springs) is the **Ross River Homestead**, an Outback resort (☎56 9711; cabins ⑦, bunkhouse ①, camping also available), which offers "dude ranch" bush activities such as camel, horse and wagon rides, boomerang throwing, whip cracking and billy tea with damper. It's a comfortable, if relatively busy, base for a few days' stay in the Eastern MacDonnells, and has a popular bar, pool and restaurant.

The other track, a 35-kilometre corrugated dirt road heading east, leads to **ARLTUNGA**, the site of central Australia's first goldrush. The road here may be long overdue for a grading, but a whole heap of money has been spent in the last few years on restoring the ghost town, which spreads over six kilometres, and providing it with a fancy **Visitors' Centre** (daily 8am–5pm; ☎56 9797). All the place needs now is some visitors. Arltunga's story began in the 1890s, in the midst of the country's first economic depression, when gold was discovered by the miners originally drawn to the garnets at Ruby Gorge (see below). Over the next fifteen years, they pushed barrows the 600km from Oodnadatta railhead to grope for their fortunes in desperate conditions for pitiful returns. Arltunga was never a particularly rich field and remains an abandoned testament to pioneering optimism.

## Ruby and Glen Annie gorges

From Arltunga it's a fairly rough but scenic two-hour drive in your 4WD out to Ruby and Glen Annie gorges, beautiful and wild places both. Back in 1885 the explorer

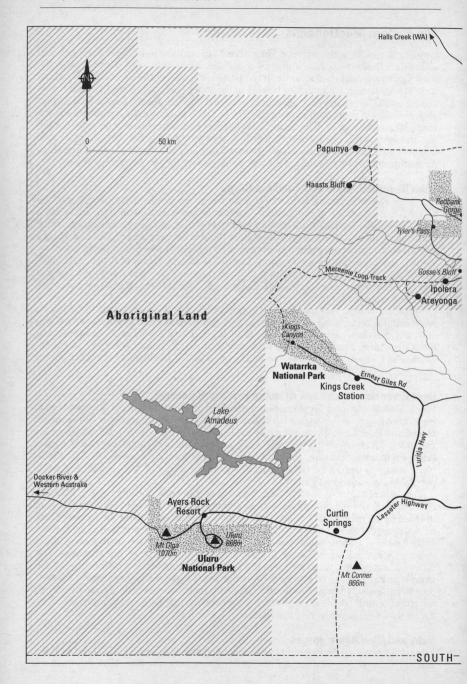

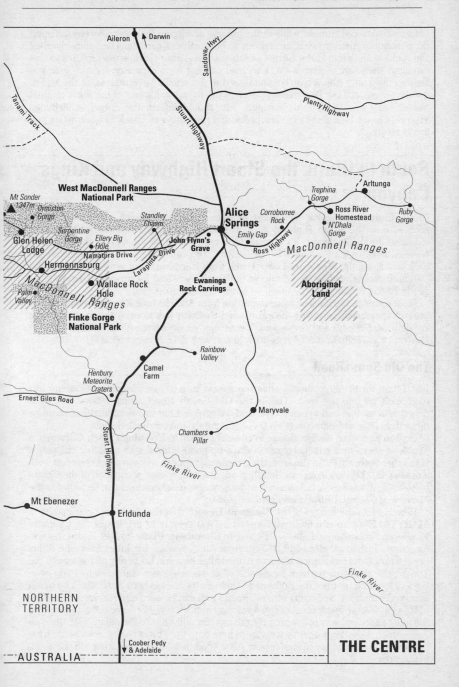

Aileron • ↑ Darwin

Sandover Hwy

Tanami Track

Plenty Highway

Stuart Highway

**West MacDonnell Ranges National Park**

Arltunga

Mt Sonder
▲ 1347m
Ormiston Gorge

Trephina Gorge

**Alice Springs**

Corroborree Rock

Ross River Homestead

Ruby Gorge

Standley Chasm

Serpentine Gorge

Ellery Big Hole

Glen Helen Lodge

Emily Gap

N'Dhala Gorge

John Flynn's Grave

Namatjira Drive

Larapinta Drive

Ross Highway

*MacDonnell Ranges*

Hermannsburg

*MacDonnell Ranges*

**Wallace Rock Hole**

Palm Valley

**Ewaninga Rock Carvings**

**Aboriginal Land**

**Finke Gorge National Park**

Rainbow Valley

Camel Farm

Henbury Meteorite Craters

Ernest Giles Road

Maryvale

Stuart Highway

Chambers Pillar

*Finke River*

• Mt Ebenezer

Erldunda

*Finke River*

**NORTHERN TERRITORY**

↓ Coober Pedy & Adelaide

—AUSTRALIA—

**THE CENTRE**

Lindsay discovered "rubies" while in the process of digging for water, thereby initiating the customary rush for what turned out to be worthless garnets. The sandy riverbed and rocks leading into **Ruby Gorge** and then **Glen Annie Gorges** (no facilities except camping) definitely require a 4WD vehicle, not just high clearance – make sure you keep in the sandy ruts or you're guaranteed to get stuck. Nevertheless, at the end of the day, even with the flies handing over to the mozzies, it's one of the most tranquil places you'll find in Central Australia. You should inform the ranger at Arltunga Visitors' Centre (see above) of your plans, and remember to check in again when you finally return.

# South to Uluru: the Stuart Highway and Kings Canyon

**Kings Canyon** is 320km southwest of Alice Springs, of which the 100-kilometre section from the Stuart Highway turn-off towards Stockyard Homestead/Wallara is unsealed. From Stockyard, it's single-width sealed road all the way to the Watarrka National Park which envelopes Kings Canyon. You can also get to Kings Canyon the back way along the **Mereenie Loop Track** from Hermannsburg, a distance of around 260km. If you're heading straight down the Track there's an increasingly barren run of nearly 700km to Coober Pedy (itself no oasis) in South Australia.

Most **tours** of two days or more departing from Alice include Kings Canyon on their see-it-all itineraries, providing the easiest and cheapest way to enjoy the canyon. There are daily *McCafferty's* and *Greyhound.Pioneer* bus services from Alice Springs to Kings Canyon (☎52 7888), or from Ayers Rock Resort with *AAT Kings* (☎56 2171).

## The Old South Road

Just 14km out of Alice, shortly after the airport turn-off, an insignificant-looking dirt road leads off into the bush. This is the **Old South Road**, which follows the abandoned railway line and original Overland Telegraph Line to Adelaide, 1550km away; these days only adventuresome 4WDs ply the sandy and corrugated route.

Ordinary cars can easily manage to cover the 35km to **Ewaninga Rock Carvings**, a jumble of rocks by a small claypan (a dried up pool) littered with neolithic chippings. Like other petroglyphs in the area, their meaning remains unknown but their age, estimated at 35,000 years, suggests that they might even pre-date occupation of the Centre by today's Aborigines; a full-size cast of the mysterious engravings can be found at the *Museum of Central Australia* in Alice (see p.464).

Heading into the fringes of the **Simpson Desert**, past the windswept community at **MARYVALE** (shop and fuel), you'll need a 4WD vehicle to get across the Charlotte Ranges and subsequent dunes on the way to **Chambers Pillar** (toilets, barbecues and camping), an historic dead-end, 165km from Alice. Named by Stuart after one of his benefactors (who has natural features named after him and his family all the way to the Timor Sea), the 80-metre-high sandstone pillar was used as a landmark by early overlanders heading up from the railhead at Oodnadatta, in Southern Australia. The plinth is carved with their, and many others', names and can be seen after scrambling up the pillar's base. After many dire but futile warning notices, a visitors' book was found to be the most expedient way of averting illegal, modern additions to the pillar. Note that you cannot take a short cut directly west from here onto the Stuart Highway without crossing private land. *Outback Experience* in Alice (☎53 2666) has interesting full-day tours to this area.

# The Stuart Highway to Kings Canyon

Around 76km from Alice, the left turn off the Stuart Highway to **Rainbow Valley** (toilet, barbecues and camping, but no water or firewood) is easy to miss – look out for the sign "Jim's Place 14km". A twenty-kilometre dirt track, the very last bit of which may be sandy, leads to the "valley", actually a dramatic outcrop set behind claypans which are said to produce rainbows following rain. More commonly, sunset catches the red-stained walls spectacularly and it's a wild place to spend the night, best followed in the morning by a climb up the crag.

**Noel Fullerton's Camel Farm**, (daily 7am–5pm; ☎56 0925) lies another few kilometres down the main highway. One of Australia's most experienced cameleers, Fullerton exports some of the Centre's huge population of feral camels back to their Arabian homelands, where a fit racer is worth about $5000. Popular photo-opportunity rides cost $3, and longer camel safaris are also offered; see p.469.

Beyond the Camel Farm you reach the Ernest Giles Road, where you turn off for Kings Canyon. Not far along this road there's another turn-off, to **Henbury Meteorite Craters**. The extra-terrestrial shower that caused these twelve depressions, 2m to 180m in diameter, may have occurred in the last 20,000 years, given that the Anangu have several names for the place, one of which translates as "sun walk fire devil rock". A walk with interpretive signs winds among the faintly visible craters, long since picked clean of any unearthly fragments. It's a rather bleak, treeless area for camping, but there are barbecues and toilets.

The Ernest Giles Road heads west, sandy at times but a lot of fun if you're in the mood, ending at the former Stockyard Homestead from where the sealed Luritja Highway leads down to Ayers Rock Resort and a single-width bitumen road continues west, past **Kings Creek Station**, 35km from the Canyon, where there's fuel, a shop and grassed campsites.

## Watarrka National Park (Kings Canyon)

As you cross the boundary of the **WATARRKA NATIONAL PARK**, you'll see the **ranger station** (☎56 7460), which has a relief model of **Kings Canyon** and its environs, but is not really a visitors' centre and you may well have to coax the rangers into imparting their knowledge. What attracts visitors here is the superb three-hour walk from the car park up and around the canyon's rim: undertaken in a clockwise direction, it starts with a steep ascent as the well-marked trail leads through the **Lost City**, a maze of domes resembling giant petrified cowpats stacked at random. Don't miss the exposed **lookouts** over the 200-metre-high southern wall before you cross the **Garden of Eden**, a palm-filled cleft bridged by an impressive array of staircases and a bridge. On the far side there's an easily missed detour downstream to the waterhole and a dramatic lookout from the very throat of the canyon. From the car park another less strenuous and less impressive walk leads into the canyon itself, while a new, twelve-kilometre trail east to Kathleen Springs is planned in the near future.

There are all the usual facilities but no **camping** at Kings Canyon itself, although you can camp elsewhere in the park with a ranger's permit. Ten kilometres past the canyon, the *Frontier Kings Canyon* (☎56 7442) is an eco-designed **resort** with a neat, new campsite, a bunkhouse with four-bed rooms (②) and a bare kitchen. Away from the rabble, the more expensive *Lodge* has immaculate rooms (⑦), a pool and great views. The café (6am–9pm), by the service station and **shop** (daily 7am–7pm), serves **meals** for about $10, or $25 will get you a feed at *Carmichaels Restaurant* by the lodge. Ask at the resort's reception (daily 7am–9pm; ☎56 7442) about *Kurkara Tours'* daily outings with Aboriginal guides, as well as helicopter **flights** and Mereenie Loop permits. A **shuttle bus** ($10) operates from the resort reception to the canyon.

# Uluru–Kata Tjuta National Park and Ayers Rock Resort

Uluru–Kata Tjuta National Park encompasses **Uluru** (the Anangu name for **Ayers Rock**) and **Kata Tjuta** (or the **Olgas**). The park is the most visited single site in Australia and if you're wondering whether all the commotion is worth it, then the answer is, emphatically, yes – here is a place that justifies all the hype. The Rock, its textures, colours and not least its elemental presence, is without question one of the world's natural wonders. Overt commercialization has been controlled and other tourists can be avoided, especially if you choose not to undertake the climb.

Kata Tjuta (meaning "many heads") lies 45km west from the park entry station. A cluster of rounded domes divided by narrow chasms and valleys, it is geologically quite distinct from Uluru. Public access is largely limited to the "Valley of the Winds" walk, partly because the eastern area is of great significance to the present-day Anangu. None of the domes, including Mount Olga, actually 200m higher than Uluru, is safe to climb.

### Getting there

It is 210km from Alice to **ERLDUNDA**, a busy roadhouse on Stuart Highway, from where **Lasseter Highway** heads to Ayers Rock Resort, 247km to the west. That said, *Mount Ebenezer Roadhouse* (☎56 2904), another 56km along the Lasseter, is a more pleasant place to break the long drive to the Rock, with its shaded picnic area, restaurant and art gallery, not to mention its famous kangaroo pies. The inexpensive **accommodation** offered includes camping and motel rooms (④). After *Mount Ebenezer* you'll pass the sealed **Luritja Highway** which leads up to the Kings Canyon road.

The next thing to catch your eye will be the flat-topped mesa of **Mount Connor**, sometimes mistaken for Uluru by the myopically over-keen. *Curtin Springs Station* (☎56 2906), 11km west of Mount Connor, is a roadhouse and bar offering the last cheap accommodation (camping free with $1 charge for showers; rooms ④–⑤) before Ayers Rock Resort. There's also a shop, fuel and a vaguely intimidating locals' bar. You-know-what is now only 80km away.

## Ayers Rock Resort (Yulara)

Like any purpose-built settlement, **AYERS ROCK RESORT** (or Yulara), built at a cost of $250 million and presently being further extended, possesses a certain prefabricated sterility, but it's not the eyesore it could have been. A couple of years ago a private company took over the management of the resort from the NT government, which somehow managed to keep losing money at a place just about everyone *has* to visit on the way to the Rock. Liberal renaming and more relevant improvements have succeeded in burying Yulara's notorious reputation once and for all.

### Arrival and information

**Buses** will either drop you off at your chosen accommodation, where you'll be given a town map, or at the Shopping Square which is the hub of the resort. All incoming **flights** to Connellan Airport, 6km from town, are met by a free shuttle bus – **taxis** (☎55 2152) cost about $5. The **Visitors' Centre** (daily 8am–9pm; ☎56 2240) is a couple of minutes from the Shopping Square. Besides all the information you might need about the resort and its services and activities, it has excellent visual displays on the geology, nature and Anangu connections with Uluru – well worth an hour's browse. Note that there is also a **Park Visitors' Centre** within the national park, on the access road to the Rock (see p.482).

## Accommodation

With the new management have come long-overdue improvements, including some price reductions, although it's still pretty expensive. Wherever you stay, **book ahead** during the winter school holiday period (June/July), unless camping. All these places are situated off Yulara Drive, no more than ten minutes' walk from the Shopping Square.

**Ayers Rock Campground** (☎56 2055). Electric barbecues, small shop, swimming pool and well kept grassy sites for tents. On-site vans ⑤.

**Desert Gardens Hotel** (☎56 2100). Three-star hotel with pool; rooms from $210. ⑧.

**Emu Walk Apartments** (check in at *Desert Gardens Hotel*, ☎56 2100). Good value for groups, and close to shops and pub. Fully self-contained 1- and 2-bedroom units (sleeping 4–6). ⑧.

**Outback Pioneer Hotel** (☎56 2170). Positive changes for backpackers and self-caterers with new kitchen facilities, a takeaway kiosk and the pricier *Rocks Bistro* by the grassy pool area. 20-bed dorms, ② first night and ① thereafter; cabins (sleeping up to 4, with fridge, tea/coffee making facilities), ⑤–⑥; motel rooms with en-suite bathrooms ⑧.

**Sails in the Desert Hotel** (☎56 2200). Luxury-class hotel with rates starting around $260. ⑧.

**Spinifex Lodge** (☎56 2131). One-bedroom units (sleeping up to 4), with a basic kitchenette but shared ablutions, near the Shopping Square. ⑥.

## The Town

All the town's facilities branch off a central ring road called Yulara Drive around which a **free bus** circulates between 10.30am–2.30pm and 6.30–11.30pm. Within this ring is a duned area criss-crossed with tracks and the Imalung Lookout, scanning the Rock, 15km away as the spangled drongo flies. In the **Shopping Square**, off Yulara Drive, you'll find the *Tavern* (10am–midnight; with EFTPOS facilities) and bottle shop, post office, supermarket (daily 9am–9pm), newsagent, takeaway and an *ANZ* bank (Mon–Thurs 9.30am–4.30pm, Fri 9.30am–5pm). The pub and adjacent ampitheatre host the occasional evening's entertainment (with a resident Aboriginal band) during the busier, winter months.

Alternatively you can join in a tour of the *Sails in the Desert Hotel*'s expertly cultivated **gardens** (Mon–Sat 7.30am–8.30am; free) while if you're really awestruck by the resort's splendour, there's a free, hour-long tour from the **Visitors' Centre** (see above) every weekday at 10am. Finally, the **Observatory** (☎56 2282), near the Imalung Lookout, takes advantage of the exceptionally clear skies in the desert to scan the sun by day and stars by night. Tours, costing $15, include pick-ups and drop-offs and start at 8.30pm and 10.15pm.

## Eating and drinking

**Kunia Room**, *Sails in the Desert Hotel* (☎089/56 2200). Exclusive and excellent à la carte restaurant – perfect for a splurge, or if someone else is paying.

**Outback Pioneer Hotel**, Yulara Drive. The kiosk (6.30am–9pm) here has various offerings, including fish and chips for $7, but the best deal is the hotel's cook-your-own barbecue for around $6–10 including salad. The *Rocks Bistro* also has a mouthwatering buffet for $25 a head.

**The Tavern**, Shopping Square. The only pub in town, and probably the resort's most popular place to eat. $10 gets you something substantial, and it's open till 2am on Wednesdays and Saturdays.

**Yulara Take Away**, Shopping Square. Dispenses the cheapest fast food around (7.30am–9.30pm).

## Listings

**Bicycle rental** Ask at the *Mobil Service Station* on Yulara Drive.

**Car rental** The major companies are here, but they're not cheap; enquire at the visitors' centre (☎56 2240) in the first instance.

**Childcare centre** Near the *Sails in the Desert Hotel* (daily 7.30am–5.30pm).

**Medical centre/ambulance** ☎56 2286.

**Police** ☎56 2166.

---

## ULURU NATIONAL PARK TOURS FROM AYERS ROCK RESORT

**AAT Kings** (☎56 2171). Shuttle service and bus tours to the park. Sunrise or the climb for $28; five-hour Rock/Olgas tours for $45 and sunset viewing for $16.

**Harley Davidson Tours** (☎56 2423). The original back-seat posing around the Rock which started a countrywide trend, from around $60; also self-ride accompanied tours, costing $250 for a half day.

**Rockayer** (☎56 2345) and **Jayrow** (☎56 2093). Thirty-minute scenic flights and 15-minute helicopter flights around the Rock, both from $65, with longer options as far as Kings Canyon available.

**Sunworth Taxis** (☎56 2152). Reasonable prices for tours without the crowds.

**Uluru Experience** (free call ☎1800/80 3174). Personalized walking tours around Uluru and Kata Tjuta with local experts from $35. See their free one-hour slide show at the auditorium, next to the visitors' centre, daily at 2pm.

---

**Taxis** *Sunworth Taxi Service* 24-hour service (☎56 2152).

**Travel agent** *Yulara Travel Agency*, Emu Walk, off the Shopping Square (Mon–Fri 9am–5pm, Sat & Sun 10am–4pm; ☎56 2075), act as agents for the major bus companies and airlines.

# Uluru–Kata Tjuta National Park

> *"Even with our bus tours and our fully automatic cameras and our cries of "Oh, wow!",*
> *we still couldn't belittle it. I had come expecting nothing much, but by the power of the*
> *thing itself I had, like some ancient tribesman wandering through the desert and*
> *confronting the phenomenon* [sunset on Uluru]*, been turned into a worshipper. Nobody*
> *was more surprised than I."*
>
> Geoff Nicholson, *Day Trips to the Desert*

The entry fee for **ULURU–KATA TJUTA NATIONAL PARK** (daily 6am–7.30pm; $10, under 16s free) permits unlimited access for up to five days. Besides the two major sites of Uluru and Kata Tjuta, the park also protects over 500 species of plants, 24 native mammals and no less than 72 species of reptiles – for this reason access off the sealed roads, away from the two sites, is forbidden.

The **Park Visitors' Centre** (daily 8am–5pm; ☎56 2299), situated on the access road one kilometre before the Rock, houses a much-improved display and is next to the splendid new Aboriginal-designed **Cultural Centre** which opened in 1995, on the tenth anniversary of the handback of Uluru to its traditinal owners. Leaflets are available on the park's geology, flora and fauna, as well as informative "Park Notes" on various topics and issues. The *Tour Operator's Workbook* ($35) is the definitive handbook to the park, with as comprehensible an explanation of Anangu culture as you'll find anywhere. Around the back of the centre is a kiosk, souvenir shop and the outdoor *Maruku Gallery* (daily 8.30am–5.30pm), displaying arts and crafts from local artisans.

Free ranger-guided walks are organized from the visitors' centre. The **Mala Walk** (daily 10am, starting at the base of the climb; 90 mins), is a good introduction to Anangu perceptions and beliefs; the recommended **Liru Walk** (Tues, Thurs & Sat, 9.30am from the visitors' centre, booking required; one hour) is led by an Anangu guide, and concentrates on Aboriginal bush tucker and their relationship with the environment; or there's the ninety-minute **Kuniya Walk** daily at 4.30pm from Mutitjulu car park. The visitors' centre sells a guide to the above walks for $1, written from an Anangu perspective.

## Uluru

The first European to set eyes on the Rock was the explorer Ernest Giles, in 1872, but it was another explorer, William Gosse – and his guides – who completed the first recorded ascent a year later, naming it **Ayers Rock** after a South Australian politician. With white settlement of the Centre came relocation of the Anangu from their tradi-

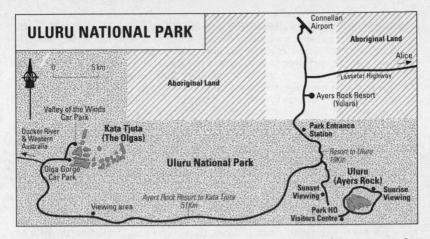

tional lands around Uluru, merely to make way for pastoralists' stock to overgraze the sensitive desert environment.

In 1958 the national park was excised from what was then the Petermann Aboriginal Reserve but subsequently returned, with much flourish, to the Anangu in 1985, following a ten-year battle for this pan-culturally significant site. Reclaimed as Uluru, the site was initially not much changed under Aboriginal ownership, since the park was immediately leased back to the Australian Nature Conservation Agency and tourism continued unaffected. But since that time the traditional owners' influence has manifested itself with characteristic subtlety, gently guiding the park's development.

## ANANGU MYTHOLOGY

Uluru, Kata Tjuta and the surrounding desert are bound to a living culture whose holistic cosmology sees the People (or "Anangu"), the Land and the Law as comprising their central tenet – known as the *Tjukurpa* or "Dreamtime". The Anangu are thought to have occupied this area for around 20,000 years and *Uluru* is the name of a waterhole near the summit.

While Uluru is a key intersection along many "dreaming trails" (or *Songlines,* as Bruce Chatwin's excellent book of that title described them) – principally those of the **Mala** (hare wallaby), **Liru** (poisonous snake) and **Kuniya** (python) – it is not the Mecca-like shrine some imagine; a muddy waterhole 200km away may be as significant. Uluru is important to the Anangu as a reliable source of water and food and as one of many landmarks along the trails created by the Anangu's Dreamtime ancestors.

## GEOLOGY

The reason Uluru rises so dramatically from the surrounding land is because it is a **monolith**, that is, a single piece of rock. With few cracks to be exploited by weathering, and the layers of very hard, coarse-grained **sandstone** tilted to a near-vertical plane, the Rock successfully resists the denudation of the landscape surrounding it. In places, the surface of the monolith has peeled or worn away, producing bizarre features and many caves, while over the years the less resistant layers of sandstone have been worn down, producing the pronounced fluting effect along the Rock's southeast and northwest flanks. Brief, but spectacular, waterfalls stream down these channels following storms. The striking orangey-red hue, enhanced by the rising and setting sun, is merely skin deep, the result of oxidation ("rusting") of iron in the normally grey rock.

## UP AND AROUND THE ROCK

It takes less than an hour to **climb** to the summit of Uluru, but make no mistake, it will probably be the greatest exertion you undertake during your visit to Australia. Although an Anangu sign at the base requests you not to undertake the climb (only Mala men used to do so), seventy percent of visitors to the Rock come to conquer the summit. Probably a third give up (as a consolation, the view from halfway up is as good as that from the top) and on average, one climber a year dies, either from a heart attack or by chasing windborne lens caps into oblivion. Gasping up the 45-degree chained section you'll see why – for around fifteen minutes it's a very hard slog and if you slip or collapse you'll roll straight back down to the car park. But with a firmly attached hat, some water, secure footwear and frequent rests, you'll safely attain the summit, often a windy spot. After the climb you can catch your breath while queuing to sign the book. If you're at all unfit or nervous about heights and exposed places, *do not* attempt the climb.

Far less strenuous is the nine-kilometre **walk around the Rock**, which takes an easy three hours. It offers a closer look at Uluru's cultural sites (though note that some of the sacred sites are closed to "uninitiates" – heed any warning notices) and the extraordinary textural variations. While the walk may not be such a triumphant achievement, it can be more rewarding and is certainly more in keeping with the spirit of the place. For incorrigible coach potatoes, the twenty-minute walk from the base of the climb to **Mutitjulu**, a secluded spring, art site and scene of epic ancestral clashes marked by gashes in the rock, is recommended.

## Kata Tjuta

The "many heads", as **Kata Tjuta** – or the **Olgas** – translates from the local Aboriginal dialect, are situated 46km from the park entry station. This remarkable formation may have once been a monolith ten times the size of Uluru, but has since been carved by eons of weathering into 36 "monstrous domes", to use Giles's words, each smooth, rounded mass divided by slender chasms or broader valleys. The different composition from Uluru's fine-grained rock can be clearly seen in the massive, sometimes sheared, boulders set in a conglomerate of sandstone cement which makes up Kata Tjuta. Access to this fascinating maze is limited to just two walks, in part because of earlier problems with overambitious tourists: dehydration is a real danger here because of the intense heat that can be radiated by the valley walls. Furthermore, the east of Kata Tjuta is a site sacred to Anangu men and is not accessible to the public.

The first of the permitted walks, the **Olga Gorge Walk** is a rather unsatisfying one-kilometre stroll into the chasm flanking Mount Olga (which, at 546m, is the highest point in the massif). Better and more challenging is the **Valley of the Winds Walk**, a six-kilometre loop trail which takes about three hours and, undertaken in a clockwise direction, becomes less of a procession. This is as much as you can see of Kata Tjuta's interior without a permit. It's worth knowing that the large tour buses tend to visit the Rock in the early morning and Kata Tjuta in the afternoon. By reversing this trend you can avoid the worst of the crowds and enjoy this magical place in reasonable solitude.

## travel details

### Trains

**Alice Springs** to: Adelaide (Tues & Fri; 20hr); Port Augusta (Tues & Fri; 17hr; change for Sydney or Perth).

### Buses

**Alice Springs** to: Adelaide (3–4 daily; 27hr); Darwin (2–3 daily; 19hr); Katherine (2–3 daily; 15hr; change here for WA); Tennant Creek/Three

Ways Roadhouse (2–3 daily; 6hr/6hr 30min; change at Three Ways for Queensland destinations).

**Darwin** to Alice Springs (2–3 daily; 19hr); Katherine (2–3 daily; 4hr; change for WA); Tennant Creek/Three Ways Roadhouse (2–3 daily; 13hr/13hr 30min).

**Katherine** to Alice Springs (2–3 daily; 15hr); Darwin (2–3 daily; 4hr); Kununurra (2 daily; 6hr 30min); Tennant Creek/Three Ways Roadhouse (2–3 daily; 9hr 30min).

**Tennant Creek/Three Ways** to Alice Springs (2–3 daily; 6hr); Darwin (2 daily; 13hr); Katherine (2–3 daily; 13hr); Townsville (2 daily; 12hr).

**Domestic Flights**
**Darwin** to Alice Springs (1–2 daily; 2hr); Brisbane (1–2 daily; 4hr); Broome (1 daily; 2hr); Cairns (1 daily; 3hr); Perth (1 daily; 4hr 30min).

**International Flights**
**Darwin** to Denpasar, Bali (3 times a week); Kuala Lumpur, Malaysia (1 direct flight a week, or change at Singapore); Kupang, East Timor (4 a week); Singapore (5–6 a week).

# CHAPTER SEVEN

# WESTERN AUSTRALIA

**W**estern Australia (WA) covers a third of the Australian continent; nearly the size of India, yet with less than half a percent of that country's population. Always revelling in its isolation from the more populous eastern states, recent years have seen this privacy increasingly invaded as more and more national and worldwide attention is focussed in this direction. Mirroring the rest of the country, WA is primarily a suburban state: one in four of its 1.7 million inhabitants live within 100km of Perth and almost all the rest are strung along the coastline.

**Perth** itself, long neglected or rather unconsidered, boomed in the 1980s and retains the leisure-orientated vitality of a young city, while oceanside **Fremantle** resonates with a largely European charm. South of Perth, the **Margaret River region**'s low, wooded hills and trickling streams support the state's foremost wine-growing and holiday making area. To the southeast, the giant **eucalypt forests** around Pemberton further soften a land fed by heavy winter rains; the intensively farmed wheat belt stretches to the east, an interminable manmade prairie. Along the Southern Ocean's storm-washed coastline, **Albany** is the primary settlement, a rejuvenated resort with the dramatic granite peaks of the **Stirling Ranges** just visible from its hilltop lookouts. To the east, past Esperance on the edge of the Great Australian Bight, the deserted monotony of the **Nullarbor Plain** extends to South Australia, while the time-warped curiosity of **Kalgoorlie**, sole survivor of the Eastern Goldfield's century-old boom, lies inland.

While the temperate southwest of WA has been relatively tamed by colonization, the north of the state, above the 26th parallel, is where you'll discover the raw appeal of WA's **wilderness**. The spinifex-carpeted aridity of the state's virtually unpopulated eastern deserts is best known to the few Aborigines who live there, while the west coast's winds only abate once you venture into the tropics just north of **Shark Bay**, home of the amicable dolphins at **Monkey Mia**. From here, the mineral-rich **Pilbara** region fills the state's northwest shoulder with the often overlooked gorges of the **Hamersley Ranges** at its core. The **Ningaloo Reef**, just off the North West Cape's beaches, offers a submarine spectacle nearly equal to that of Queensland's Barrier Reef.

Northeast of the Pilbara, **Broome**, once the world's pearling capital, is a welcome jewel in the cyclone-swept coastline of the rugged Northwest, and an ideal preliminary to the **Kimberley**'s wilderness and hard-won cattle country. Generally cut-off by floods in the wet season, it is regarded as Australia's last frontier, its convoluted and inaccessible coasts washed by enormous tides, and only inhabited by isolated Aboriginal communities and crocodiles. On the way to the Northern Territory border, the surreal enigma of the **Bungle Bungle** massif is one of WA's greatest natural wonders, carefully protected by cautious and minimal "eco-development".

If you hope to explore any significant part of the state's million and a half square kilometres, and in particular the remote and fascinating Northwest, your own vehicle is all but essential, although combining buses with local **tours** will also get you to the most interesting places. Either way, WA offers an essential mix of Outback grandeur, albeit more dispersed than elsewhere, and urban sophistication that should not be overlooked on the way to the "Eastern States", as the rest of Australia is known in these parts.

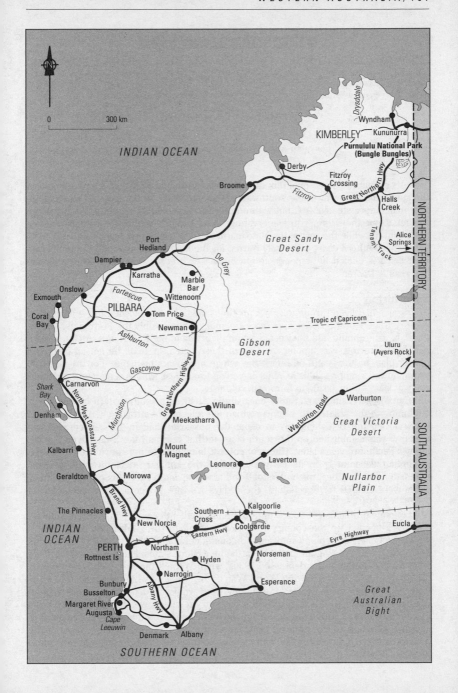

0  300 km

INDIAN OCEAN

Drysdale

Wyndham

KIMBERLEY  Kununurra

Purnululu National Park
(Bungle Bungles)

Derby

Fitzroy
Crossing

Broome

Fitzroy

Great Northern Hwy

Halls
Creek

NORTHERN TERRITORY

Alice
Springs

Tanami Track

Great Sandy
Desert

Port
Hedland

De Grey

Dampier

Karratha

Marble
Bar

Onslow

Fortescue

Wittenoom

Exmouth

PILBARA

Tom Price

Coral
Bay

Newman

Ashburton

Tropic of Capricorn

Gibson
Desert

Uluru
(Ayers Rock)

Gascoyne

Shark
Bay

Carnarvon

Great Northern Highway

Denham

Murchison

Wiluna

Warburton

Warburton Road

Great Victoria
Desert

North West Coastal Hwy

Meekatharra

Kalbarri

Mount
Magnet

Leonora

Laverton

Geraldton

Morowa

Nullarbor
Plain

The Pinnacles

Brand Hwy

New Norcia

Southern
Cross

Kalgoorlie

Coolgardie

Eucla

INDIAN
OCEAN

Eastern Hwy

Eyre Highway

PERTH

Northam

Rottnest Is

Hyden

Norseman

Bunbury

Narrogin

Esperance

Great
Australian
Bight

Busselton

Albany Hwy

Margaret River

Augusta

Cape
Leeuwin

Denmark

Albany

SOUTH AUSTRALIA

SOUTHERN OCEAN

## ACCOMMODATION PRICES

All the accommodation listed in this book has been categorized into one of eight price bands, as set out below. The rates quoted represent the cheapest available double or twin room in high season – except for category ①, which are per-person rates for a dorm bed, and the prices given for units, cabins and vans, which are the daily charge for the whole unit.

| ① Under $16 | ② $16–26 | ③ $ 27–36 | ④ $ 37–54 |
|---|---|---|---|
| ⑤ $55–74 | ⑥ $75–94 | ⑦ $95–124 | ⑧ $ 125 upwards |

For more accommodation details, see pp.31–34.

WA's **climate** is a seasonal mix of temperate, arid and tropical. Winters are cool in the south and very wet in the southwestern corner, while in the tropics the temperature maintains a steady 30°C but with no rain and acceptable humidity: this is the dry season. Come the summer, the enervating "Wet" (from December to March) washes out the north while the rest of the state, particularly inland areas, crackles in mid-40°C heat. The southern coast is the only retreat for the heatstruck, although the temperate west coast is cooled by dependable afternoon sea breezes – in Perth known as the "Fremantle Doctor".

## Some history

Aborigines had lived throughout WA for thousands of years by the time seventeenth-century traders of the *Dutch East India Company*, and possibly the Portuguese before them, began running into the west coast on their way to the East Indies. A Dutch mariner, **Dirk Hartog**, was among the first of these when, in 1616, he left an inscribed pewter plate on the island off Shark Bay which now bears his name. For the next 200 years, however, impressions of WA's barren and waterless fringes remained – commercially at least – uninspiring to European colonists.

France's increasing exploratory curiosity in Australia's southwestern corner at the beginning of the nineteenth century, which left a legacy of attractively named coastal features, led the British hastily to claim the unknown land in 1826. Fredrickstown (Albany) was established on the south coast in that year and the Swan River Colony, today's Perth, two years later. The **new colony**, initially rejecting convict labour and so struggling desperately in its early years, had the familiar effect on an Aboriginal population that it at best misunderstood and at worst, annihilated. Aborigines and their lands were cleared for agriculture: these days it's rare to see a black face south of Perth.

Economic problems continued until the mid-nineteenth-century marches of stalwart explorers opened up the country's interior, leading to the goldrushes of the 1890s which propelled the colony into autonomous statehood in less than a decade. This **autonomy**, and growing antipathy towards the eastern states, led to a move to secede from the federation in the depressed 1930s, when WA felt the rest of the country was dragging it down. But following World War II, the whole of white Australia, and especially WA, began to thrive, making money from wool and, later, from huge mineral discoveries which, to this day, form the basis of the state's wealth. Meanwhile, WA's 40,000 Aborigines continue to live in squalid and remote communities, as if in another country, although in the wake of the Mabo Decision (see p.830) huge tracts of the Northwest have been subject to land claims, destined to struggle through the courts for years to come.

# PERTH AND THE SOUTH

South of the **Great Eastern Highway**, which joins Perth to Kalgoorlie, is the most climatically benign portion of Western Australia, supporting intensive agriculture and seaside towns, and with all points well connected to **Perth**, the modern face of the state's wealth. East of the state capital, the **Darling Ranges** offer a number of appealing day destinations, while south of Perth, the **Margaret River region**'s uniquely mellow landscape rests easily on the eye, supporting orchards, wineries and numerous small holiday hideaways in the giant karri forests around **Pemberton**. Both **Albany** and **Esperance** are attractive resort towns on the Southern Ocean's rugged coastline, where sea breezes take the edge off the summertime heat. They make ideal bases for exploration of their adjacent national parks, while the dreary **Wheatlands**, north of the coast, are a region to pass through rather than head for. **Kalgoorlie**, at the heart of the once-thriving **Eastern Goldfields**, is a colourful caricature of an Outback mining town and certainly deserves a stop off on the way east.

# Perth

Try as you might, and contrary to expectations, it's hard to get excited about **PERTH**, although its lack of urban grime can create a favourable impression. Western Australia's modern capital of nearly one and a half million – most of the state's population – has a reputation for sunshine, youthfulness and an easygoing lifestyle. Perhaps because of this complacency Perth lacks the substance and charisma, the tension of diverse wealth and ethnicity, that make a really great city more than just a clutch of shiny skyscrapers.

In the 1980s, mineral prosperity and a spate of cocky, self-made wheeler-dealers (now largely bankrupt, disgraced or in prison) created a mini-boom for Perth. Wealth begat growth, recognition and an exciting, "upwardly mobile" tag; suddenly Perth, stranded by thousands of kilometres of desert or ocean, was the place to be. But the banks of glass towers which erupted in the 1980s are still only half full, mocking the callow values of that era's transient prosperity. Despite upbeat campaigns to attract visitors into the city centre, it remains a functional CBD, bustling during office hours but otherwise deserted. Other than shopping and some excellent museums and galleries, it has little to offer, although the thriving café and club district of **Northbridge** becomes increasingly energized as the week draws to a close. The riverside Foreshore, along the **Swan River**'s north shore, remains a highway corridor, visited only by joggers and seagulls, and even **Kings Park**, the city's showpiece patch of untamed bushland is isolated by knots of freeway interchanges. If you're looking for action, imitate the locals and head for the hills, the beaches or cruise on down to Fremantle, by the ocean, 20km from Perth.

## Arrival and information

Perth's **international airport** is 16km east of the city centre and the **domestic** one a few kilometres closer. **Shuttle buses** (international $7, domestic $6; ☎250 2838) meet arrivals at both airports and ferry you to your chosen accommodation in the city; from the domestic terminal, you can also catch a green *Transperth* bus to the city ($2). Otherwise, allow thirty minutes and $20 to or from the international airport in a **taxi** (call ☎333 3333 or 444 4444). Interstate **trains, buses** and *Westrail* country buses arrive at the **East Perth Rail and Bus Terminal**, three train stops from the central *Transperth* suburban rail and bus station on Wellington Street.

## TELEPHONE NUMBERS

The **telephone code** for Perth is ☎09, but this will change to ☎08 in September 1997.

Also in September 1997, all **Perth numbers** will have the prefix 9 added; so, for example, what was ☎09/xxx xxx will become ☎08/9xxx xxxx.

*(For more on changes to phone numbers Australia-wide, see p.40.)*

The main **tourist office** (Mon–Fri 8.30am–5.30pm, Sat 9am–1pm; ☎483 1111) is just over the road from the *Transperth* station, in Forrest Chase precinct, with numerous free city guides and maps, tour information and state-wide promotional videos. The *Pinnacles Tourist Centre* (☎221 5411), on the corner of Hay and Pier streets, stays open on Saturday afternoons and Sundays.

## City transport

*Transperth* is the city's excellent, under-used and inexpensive **suburban transport** network, with frequent trains to Fremantle and the northern, eastern and southern suburbs of Joondalup, Midland and Armadale, and a fleet of buses filling the gaps in between. The city centre has two **bus stations**, one at Wellington Street, next to the central **train station**, and, for services south of the river, the City Busport at the bottom of Mill Street. There are *Transperth* **information offices** with tireless staff at both bus stations (Mon–Fri 7am–6pm, Sat 7.30am–3pm; ☎13 2213) and also in the city centre at Plaza Arcade, Hay Street Level. Both bus stations, as well as the local train stations one stop either side of Perth train station, are within the **Free Transit Zone**, or FTZ. Most buses passing through the FTZ offer free travel within it, as do any of the four blue, red, green and yellow "**Clipper**" buses serving the zone (Mon–Fri 7.30am–5.30pm, Sat 9–11.30am; timetables available from *Transperth* offices).

Outside the FTZ, Perth is divided into eight concentric zones – zones 1 and 2 ($2) are the most useful to visitors, incorporating Fremantle, the northern beaches and Midland. **Tickets** (from $1.40–5.50, depending on the number of zones) are available from bus conductors or vending machines at all (often unstaffed) stations; they are valid for two hours' unlimited travel within the specified zones on *Transperth* buses, trains and the ferry to South Perth from Barrack Street jetty. If you plan to do a lot of suburban travel, **Multi Rider Tickets** can be bought in batches of ten (each valid for two hours) from kiosks, newsagents and at the main bus stations, saving you 20 percent and avoiding the need for change or queueing.

The tourist-orientated **Perth Tram** (daily 9.30am–5pm, every 90mins; day-ticket $12; ☎367 9204), most conveniently caught at Barrack Street jetty, can relieve you of the unlikely agony of thinking that you've missed something really gripping, allowing you to jump off at points of interest and reboard a later tram.

For **taxis** call ☎333 3333 or 444 4444.

## Accommodation

There's a full range of **accommodation** around the centre of Perth, all of it – from backpackers' hostels to hotels and apartments – inexpensive, presentable and conveniently close to, or even right in, the city centre. The nearest campsites are 7km from the city. Booking ahead for motels and apartments is advisable in summer.

### Hotels and motels

**Airways City Hotel**, 195 Adelaide Terrace (☎323 7799). Better than average motel, excellent value and right in the centre. ⑨.

**Bailey Parkside Motor Lodge**, 150 Bennett St (☎325 3788). Good-quality and fairly central motel with pool and parkland nearby. ⑤.

**Chateau Commodore**, corner of Victoria Ave and Hay St (☎325 0461). Right in the centre of town, with parking, restaurant, bar and pool. ⑥.

**Court Hotel**, 50 Beaufort St (☎328 5292). Very central and very friendly gay and lesbian accommodation and bar. ④.

**Hotel Regatta**, 560 Hay St (☎325 5155). A little past its prime, but great value and couldn't be more central. ⑤.

**Miss Maud European Hotel**, 97 Murray St (☎325 3900). Pleasingly varied rooms, an interior with a Swedish/Alpine flavour and a popular *smorgasbord* served downstairs in the restaurant. ⑦.

**Pacific Motel**, 111 Harold St (☎328 5599). Inexpensive motel with pool, a 20-minute walk north of the centre. ⑤.

**Sullivans Hotel**, 166 Mounts Bay Rd (☎321 8022). Excellent, family-run hotel with pool, free bikes and fine restaurant. ⑥.

**Wentworth Plaza/Royal Hotels**, William St, between Murray and Wellington (☎481 1000). Refurbished grand hotels, with non-en suite bargains in the less fancy *Royal*. ④–⑤.

## Self-contained apartments

**Brownlea Holiday Units**, 166 Palmerstone St (☎328 4840). Just north of the centre with a pool and bargain rates. ④.

**537 William St** (☎221 1112). High rise ten minutes' walk north of Northbridge with bargain-priced apartments. ③–④.

**Mount Street Inn**, 24 Mount St (☎481 0866). Luxury apartments overlooking the river. ⑦.

**Mountway Holiday Units**, 36 Mount St (☎321 8307). Excellent-value units between the city centre and Kings Park. ④.

## Hostels

Most of Perth's hostels, chiefly located around Northbridge, just north of the central train and bus stations, aren't much to look at. The selection below includes the more popular and reliable establishments, most of which provide bike rental, tour-booking service and contacts for casual employment; all three YHAs are chore- and curfew-free. Note that on-street parking is a hassle in the very centre of Northbridge.

**Backpackers International**, corner of Aberdeen and Lake streets (☎227 9977). Bright, clean hostel rather lacking in atmosphere. ①.

**City Backpackers HQ** (*Lone Star Tavern*), corner of Beaufort and Newcastle streets (☎328 7566). Converted Tardis-like hotel over a pub with two- or four-bed rooms, balconies and "Big Wednesday" backpackers' nights. ①.

**Cheviot Lodge**, 30 Bulwer St (☎227 6817). Modern, clean and roomy lodge with parking, in a central position but away from Northbridge's hubbub. Five-bed dorms ①, rooms ②.

**North Lodge**, 225 Beaufort St (☎227 7588). Small, quiet family-run hostel with clean and modern bath and kitchen areas and free pick-ups. Rooms ②–③, dorms ①.

**Perth Travellers Lodge**, 158 Aberdeen St (☎328 6667). A spacious, laid back place with the odd few permanent residents and off-street parking. Rooms ②, dorms ①.

**Rory's Backpackers**, 194 Brisbane St (☎328 9958). Very popular small hostel in good shape and away from the noise and hubbub. Keen owners encourage responsible partying. Mixed, six-bed dorms ①.

**12:01 Central**, corner of Aberdeen and Fitzgerald streets (☎227 1202). Popular place with hard-working, responsible-partying staff, café and small four-bed rooms. ①.

**YHA Britannia**, 253 William St (☎328 6121). Biggest of the three YHAs, this one is in the heart of Northbridge, a stone's throw from the clubs and cafés and with some recent renovations, but still a warren of rooms and corridors. 24-hour reception. No smoking. ①.

**YHA**, 46 Francis St (☎328 7794). Enthusiastically-run pair of old guesthouses with a nice courtyard and a homey feel.The best all-round YHA. Rooms ③, dorms ①.

**YHA**, 60 Newcastle St (☎328 1135). A little out of the way but recently refurbished and with a light breakfast included in the rates. Pick-ups, plus plenty of off-street parking. Six-bed dorms, ①.

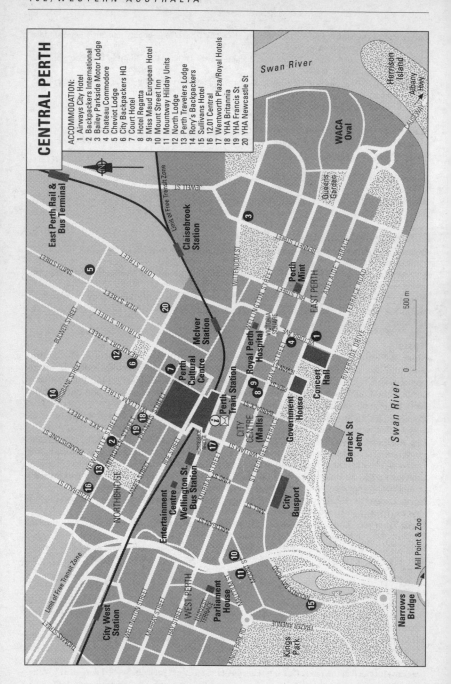

# CENTRAL PERTH

ACCOMMODATION:
1 Airways City Hotel
2 Backpackers International
3 Bailey Parkside Motor Lodge
4 Chateau Commodore
5 Cheviot Lodge
6 City Backpackers HQ
7 Court Hotel
8 Hotel Regatta
9 Miss Maud European Hotel
10 Mount Street Inn
11 Mountway Hiliday Units
12 North Lodge
13 Perth Travelers Lodge
14 Rory's Backpackers
15 Sullivans Hotel
16 12.01 Central
17 Wentworth Plaza/Royal Hotels
18 YHA Britannia
19 YHA Francis St
20 YHA Newcastle St

Swan River

Herrison Island

Albany Hwy

Causeway

WACA Oval

East Perth Rail & Bus Terminal

Claisebrook Station

Queens Garden

Limit of Free Transit Zone

Perth Mint

EAST PERTH

McIver Station

Perth Cultural Centre

Royal Perth Hospital

VICTORIA SQUARE

Perth Train Station

CITY CENTRE (Malls)

Concert Hall

Government House

Barrack St Jetty

Swan River

500 m
0

Entertainment Centre

Wellington St Bus Station

NORTHBRIDGE

City West Station

WEST PERTH

Parliament House

City Busport

Mill Point & Zoo

Kings Park

Narrows Bridge

Mill Point & Zoo

## Caravan parks

**Central**, 38 Central Ave, 7km east of Perth (☎277 5696). Closest good park to city centre, located in Redcliffe, by the domestic airport. Cabins ④.

**Coogee Beach**, Cockburn Rd, Coogee (☎418 1810). Large resort on the beach, 7km south of Fremantle. Cabins ③–④.

**Scarborough Starhaven**, 18 Pearl Parade (☎341 1770). Situated in a popular beach suburb, a half-hour bus ride from the centre. On-site vans ③.

# The City

The compact and walkable central area of Perth, from Wellington Street down to St George's Terrace, and bounded vaguely by Hill Street to the east and Milligan Street to the west, is an easily understood grid – much of your time will be spent exploring new ways of cutting between **Hay Street** and **Murray Street**. Both are pedestrianized between William and Barrack streets and linked by numerous, glittering arcades: the mock Tudor **London Court** and its idealized, "Olde English" iconography is much admired and photographed. To the north, William Street hops over the railway at **Horseshoe Bridge** and into lively Northbridge, while southwards Barrack Street runs down to the ferry **jetty** on Perth Water, a lagoon on the **Swan River** formed by the bridged **Narrows** and popularly used by windsurfers, sailors and thrill-seeking para-scenders. From the jetty a *Transperth* ferry regularly crosses the Narrows to Mends Street jetty on the south shore, while commercial ferries ply the river upstream to the Swan Valley wineries and downstream to Fremantle and Rottnest Island (see box below). **Sightseeing** in Perth is something best done between idle wandering and window shopping.

## The Perth Cultural Centre

Situated just over the tracks in Northbridge, at the end of James Street, the **Perth Cultural Centre** comprises the **West Australian Art Gallery** (daily 9am–5pm; free) and **Museum** (Mon–Fri 10.30am–5pm, Sat & Sun 1–5pm; free), as well as the state library. The gallery's constantly changing displays include Aboriginal art, other contemporary and classic works of Western Australian artists, as well as some exqui-site ceramics, textiles and sculptures. There's always something worth seeing, and free guided tours (Tues–Fri 12.15pm, Sat & Sun 3pm) expand informatively on the work displayed. The museum, part of the same complex, is housed in a collection of buildings, old and new, and has a slightly drab, worthy feel to it. It includes a floor devoted to Aboriginal culture, plus exhibitions of vintage cars, stuffed marsupials, a 25-metre whale skeleton, meteorites, a swamp diorama and the inevitable old gaol.

## Old buildings

Perth's old buildings, the staple of many sightseeing itineraries, are a generally dull bunch of colonial survivors dwarfed by the city's soaring skyscrapers. In a westward sweep from the manicured perfection of **Queens Gardens** (a delight when the flower-beds are in bloom), at the east end of Hay Street, they start with the **Perth Mint** (Mon–Fri 9am–4pm, Sat 10am–1pm), on the corner of Hill Street. Operating from its original 1899 base, Australia's principal specialist mint still trades in precious metals in bar or coin form and displays some huge replicas of gold nuggets and alluring 400-ounce ingots. Visitors can also take a tour ($3) and observe minting operations in the refurbished foundry.

Moving down onto St Georges Terrace, south of Hay Street, you arrive at **Stirling Gardens**, on the corner of Pier Street, with its "Ore Obelisk" sculpture symbolizing WA's mineral diversity, and the ornate Gothic extravagance of the 1860s' **Government House**. The **Old Courthouse** (Tues & Thurs 10am–2pm; free), the colony's oldest surviving building, is also in the gardens, housing the dreary *Francis Burt Law Museum*, while Other relics in the area include the **Deanery** on the corner of Pier Street, the **Cloisters** – now an *Ansett* office – and the **Old Perth Boys' School**, at 139 St Georges Terrace (Mon–Fri 9am–5pm; free), restored and now run by the National Trust. At the far end of the terrace you can just make out the **Barracks Archway**, the remains of an 1860s' structure not really worth closer inspection unless you are heading up that way, while the easily missed Jacobean-style facade of the **Town Hall**, dating from the 1870s, sits on the corner of Hay and Barrack streets.

One old building that has managed to retain its charm is the **Old Mill** (Mon, Wed & Thurs 1–5pm, Sat noon–4pm, Sun 1–5pm; admission by donation; *Transperth* ferry from Barrack Street jetty), situated at Mill Point, south of the Narrows and in the shadow of the Kwinana Freeway bridge. A quaint, fairytale relic, this mill ground the colony's first flour and now houses a collection of pioneering bull-carts and period artefacts in its own pretty grounds. **Perth Zoo** is a short walk from here (see "Perth for kids" below).

## Kings Park

Perhaps the city's best attraction is the part-uncultivated, five-square-kilometre expanse of **Kings Park**, a two-kilometre walk west of the centre down Mount Street, turning off at the end of St Georges Terrace (or take bus #33 from Wellington Street). Created with great foresight in 1872, the park remains Perth's premier recreational area (other than the river), and no visit would be complete without a wander around, enlivened by various flora and fauna. Although the park is small enough to enjoy on foot, you can rent **bicycles** from *Koala Cycle Hire* (Mon–Fri 9.30am–4pm, Sat & Sun 9.30am–6pm; ☎321 3061) in the main car park on the park's east side, where a fine, tree-framed view overlooks the city. There's a trail leading through the native bushland, a botanic and an aromatic garden, playgrounds, picnic areas and free guided tours from the **information centre** (daily 9.30am–3.30pm) by the car park, which also provides maps of the park.

## Perth for kids

Besides the obvious appeal of the beaches (see p.505), river cruises (see box on p.499) and bicycle rental (the riverside tracks to Fremantle are now marked all the way), there are a number of attractions in and around the city, some specifically designed to amuse children. See "Around Perth", starting on p.499, for other diversions.

**Adventure World**, 17 Progress Drive, Bibra Lake, 18km south of centre (daily 10am–5pm; closed May–Sept; adults $19.50, children $16, family of four $64; ☎417 9666; bus #105 then #196). Perth's main amusement park, and an expensive jaunt, although the magic castle, zoo, rides and slides are free once you're in. Next door, on Bibra Lake, is the 40m-high *Bungee One* tower (☎417 2500).

**Caversham Wildlife Park and Zoo**, Arthur St, West Swan, 20km northeast of centre (daily 9am–5pm; adults $5, children $1.50; ☎274 2202; train to Guildford then taxi). Small park which lets young ones get close to, and even feed, indigenous marsupials, introduced mammals, monkeys and exotic birds.

**Cohunu Wildlife Park**, Mills Rd, Gosnells, 24km southeast of centre (daily 10am–5pm; adults $9, children $4; ☎390 6090; train to Gosnells and walk). Definitive Australian wildlife – 'roos, emus and koalas – roams around this small park with a huge walk-through aviary. Good for photography and a "nature break" on the way down to *Pioneer Village* (see below).

**It's a Small World**, 12 Parliament Place, West Perth, 2km west of centre (Sun–Fri 10am–5pm, Sat 2pm–5pm; adults $5, children $4, family of four $14; ☎322 2020; FTZ Green Clipper from Bus Station). Amusing collection of undersized miscellany and dioramas for younger kids and model-making adults.

**Perth Zoo**, Labouchere Rd, South Perth, 2km south of centre (daily 10am–5pm; adults $6, children $2; ☎3474 3551; bus #108 or #110 from Busport, or ferry from Barrack St to Mends St jetty and 500-metre walk). Hundred-year-old zoo moving with the anti-zoo trend. Pushchairs, wheelchairs and video cameras for rent and enough exotic wildlife to make a good afternoon out. The train ride around the zoo is really only worth it if it's too hot to walk.

**Pioneer Village**, corner of Albany and South West highways, Armadale, 30km southeast of centre (daily 10am–5pm; free; ☎399 5322; train to Armadale). Nineteenth-century era recreated with period performances, carriage rides and an animal park.

**Scitech Discovery Centre**, *City West Complex*, corner of Sutherland St and Railway Parade, West Perth, 2km west of centre (daily 10am–5pm; adults $10, children $7, family of four $25; ☎481 6295; train to City West). Inquisitive ten-year-olds will be barely controllable at this innovative and fun hands-on collection of elementary scitechnic displays. Not to be missed.

**Underwater World**, Hillarys Boat Harbour, West Coast Drive, Hillarys, 25km northwest of centre (daily 9am–5pm; adults $13.50, children $6.50, family of four $33.50; ☎447 7500; train to Sterling then bus #423). Excellent, but limited marine life display includes a transparent tunnel through a giant aquarium with shark- and fish-feeding by scuba divers, as well as captive dolphins in the harbour. A bit overpriced but a day out at adjacent Sorrento Quay and beach makes up for it.

**Whiteman Park**, Lord St, West Swan (daily 9am–6pm; $4 per car; ☎249 2446). Bush theme park with train, tram and bicycle rides, crafts village (Wed–Sun only), playgrounds and the Mussel Pool picnic area. Fits in well with a parental wine tour of the Swan Valley (see "Around Perth").

# Eating and drinking

To eat well and inexpensively in Perth, stick to **Italian** and **Asian** places. Both are frequently represented in the **food courts**, where you can easily get a decent meal for as little as $6. In Northbridge there are the *Shang Hai* and *Pavilion* on James Street, while in the city you'll find the *Down Under* and fancier *Carillon* off Hay Street Mall. At the other end of the scale, some of the snazzy seafood restaurants may set you back $30 per head. **Northbridge**, especially around James and Lake streets, is the heart of Perth's café and restaurant scene, with over forty establishments crammed into a square kilometre. Every evening, except Sunday and Monday, is busy here, with people wandering from place to place, eating, drinking and enjoying themselves; if you want to be sure of getting into a particular place towards the end of the week, book in advance.

## Cafés and cheap eats

**Aberdinos**, corner of Aberdeen and William streets. Jazzy coffee bar for the image-conscious.

**L'Alba Café**, 100 Lake St. Serves smooth cappuccinos and cheap, tasty pasta seven days a week

**Café Sport**, William St, north of Francis St. Unpretentious coffee and newspaper rendezvous with Italian snacks and meals.

**Café Universal**, William St, south of Francis St. Cappuccino and street life, with food when you need it.

**Dim Sim House**, 309 William St. High-speed dumplings with mysterious fillings. Daily 8am–3pm.

**Hare Krishna Food Centre**, 232 William St. Vegetarian dishes at rock-bottom prices.

**Hawkers Paradise**, 19 Lake St. Cheap MSG-free Malay food – go for the chicken rice. Daily from lunchtime.

**Iguana Cafe Bar**, 397 Murray St, on Shafto Lane. City-side pizza and tapas lunchspot and evening bar. Closed Sun.

**Seoul Korean**, 253a William St. Two-course lunches for around $6 and evening meals for twice that in a low-key oriental setting. Daily lunchtimes and 6pm till late.

**Sri Melaka Nyonya**, 313 William St. Best of the budget Malay places, with "home-style" cooked food. Daily (except Mon), from noon.

**Teds**, corner of Lake St and Aberdeen St. Popular corner café-diner, with inexpensive cakes, steaks and Kiwi ice cream. Daily 9am–late.

## Restaurants

**Botticelli's**, corner of Lake St and James St (☎328 3422). Top "see-and-be-seen" position, rustic Mediterranean decor, classic and classy Italian dishes. Lunch Mon–Fri, dinner Mon–Sat.

**Dusit Thai**, 233 James St. Least expensive of the authentic Thai places in Northbridge, with main courses for around $7. Closed Mon.

**Emperor's Court**, 66 Lake St (☎328 3881). Sumptuous decor and fine Szechuan, Beijing and Cantonese dishes. Nightly karaoke in the cocktail bar. Lunches Mon–Fri, dinners nightly.

**Fishy Affair**, 132 James St (☎328 6636). Reasonably priced seafood if you keep off the crayfish. Open Mon–Fri lunch and every evening.

**The Gardens/Ord St Café**, 27 Ord St, West Perth (☎321 6021). Sophisticated restaurant overlooking Kings Park with a café next door serving steak, salads and seafood.

**Harry's Seafood Grill**, 94 Aberdeen St (☎328 2822). Seafood garden restaurant with top prices and good service. Open Mon–Fri lunch and daily for dinner.

**Lee Gardens**, 18 Plain St (☎325 8906). Large and reputable Chinese restaurant opposite the *Hyatt Hotel*.

**Mamma Maria's**, corner of Lake and Aberdeen streets (☎328 4532). Long-established and sometimes hectic pasta house; try the grilled chicken. Open Mon–Fri lunch and every evening.

**Oyster Bar**, 20 Roe St (☎328 7888). Upmarket seafood delicacies served Mon–Fri lunch and every evening.

**Il Padrino**, 198 William St. Huge wood-fired pizzas and lunchtime specials. Closed Wed and weekend lunchtimes.

**Planes & Trains & Automobiles**, 46 Lake St. Novelty Australiana interior with all-you-can-eat deals from around $13.

**The Plum**, 47 Lake St (☎328 5920). Cosy, cottage interior with a pricey French-influenced menu. Closed Sun.

**Royal India**, 1134 Hay St West (☎324 1368). Elegant, upmarket restaurant specializing in tandoori dishes. Open daily for dinner, Mon–Fri only for lunch.

**Vino Vino**, 157 James St (☎328 5403). Authentic Italian and seafood dishes, with half-price deals on Mon and Tues evenings. Dinner daily, otherwise lunch Wed–Fri.

# Entertainment and nightlife

As with food, **Northbridge**, just north of the city centre, is the focal point of after-dark action, with plenty of **pubs**, **bars** and teeming **dance clubs** concealed in improbable buildings. In view of Perth's famed isolation, a night in Northbridge is the hottest spot for thousands of kilometres in any direction; there's also the odd lively bar in the city and inner suburbs. Many pubs and bars in this area feature **free beer**, happy hours and other value-added incentives to get loaded and let the good times roll. The free weekly music and gig guide, *X-Press Magazine*, has **listings** for all the places detailed below, and plenty more besides; alternatively, check out the entertainment section of Thursday's *West Australian* newspaper. For the lowdown on the **gay scene**, see the box below.

## Bars, live music venues and clubs

**Aberdeen Hotel**, 84 Aberdeen St. Popular meeting place for Northbridge's backpacking crowd, with live bands most nights.

**Aqua**, 230 William St. Seriously trendy dance club and late-night bar.

**Brannigans**, *Mercuer Hotel*, 10 Irwin St. Great club with free entry and hip music; very popular with Perth's West Indian and African community.

**Brass Monkey**, corner of William St and James St. Good-looking pub in the heart of Northbridge with live bands at the end of the week.

**Connections**, 81 James St. Perth's most established gay and lesbian night spot. Solid dance music and floorshows. Closed Mon.

**DC's (Dual Control)**, 105 Francis St. Gay club attracting a young crowd. Men only on Wed, live shows at the weekend. Closed Mon and Tues.

**Exit**, 187 Stirling Rd. Dance yourself into the the early hours. This place gets packed on Fridays and Saturdays.

**Fenians**, corner of Hill St and Adelaide Terrace. Irish-theme pub serving Guinness and hosting Irish bands most nights.

**Gobbles**, 613 Wellington St. Casual, relaxed dance club with its own in-house band.

## GAY AND LESBIAN PERTH

Perth has a robust, self-sufficient and extremely friendly gay and lesbian scene. The heart of the action is **Northbridge**, but neighbouring North Perth, Highgate and Mt Lawley all have more than their share of gay residents, while lesbians seem to opt for a relaxed lifestyle down in Freo. As usual, the quickest way to plug into the scene is to pick up the community paper: in Perth it's the *Westside Observer* (*WSO*); free at gigs and available for a dollar at the *Arcane Bookshop*, 212 William St, Northbridge (Mon–Fri 10am–5.30pm, Sat 10am–5pm; ☎328 5073), along with plenty of other gay, lesbian and feminist literature.

The *Lumiere Cinema* has screens for queens when the **Gay and Lesbian Film Week**, still smouldering from the Sydney Mardi Gras, arrives in March. October heats up with **Perth Pride**, celebrated with the usual array of fun and games, including a night march and dance party. Legions of right-thinking women march to **Reclaim The Night** in the same month and every November competitors get set and go for glory at the **Western Australia Gay Olympics**. At other times of year, outdoor organizations such as *GAGS* and *Team Perth* (see below) can put you in touch with other pink athletes.

**Community Organizations**
**AIDS groups** *Aids Help Line* (☎227 8619 or free call 1800/19 9287; Mon–Fri 9am–10pm); *ACTUP Perth*, PO Box 231, Northbridge (☎344 5751); *Western Australia AIDS Council*, 107 Brisbane St, PO Box T1872, Perth (☎227 8355).
**Other organizations** *Gay Activities Group Services* (*GAGS*), PO Box 8234, Perth 6000, is responsible for the Gay Olympics and other sporting events; and contact the *Gay Outdoor Group*, PO Box 263, Cottesloe, Perth 6011 (☎270 7181); *Team Perth*, PO Box 3234, Stirling St, Perth 6849; or *Wednesday Women* (☎328 9044), a lesbian social group.

*For gay- and lesbian-friendly accommodation, try the* Court Hotel *(see p.491) or the beach-side* Swanbourne Guest House *(see p.507); night-time venues include* Connections, DC's *and the* Northbridge Hotel *(see "Bars, live music and clubs" listings opposite and below).*

**Hip-E-Club**, corner of Anzac Rd and Oxford St, Leederville. Retro-psychedelia with Sixties' and Seventies' music and backpackers' nights on Tuesday.2**James Street Club**, 193 James St. Hardcore techno dance club.

**Lone Star Saloon**, corner of William and Aberdeen streets. This is the place to break in your cowboy boots to the sound of country and dixie.

**Northbridge Hotel**, 198 Brisbane St. Attracts a mixed gays and lesbian crowd, with three bars, pool tables and live music on Wed and Sun.

**Pockets**, 44 Lake St. Pool and cocktail lounge with evening gigs and comedy sessions.

**Rosie O'Grady's**, west end of Lake St. This Irish theme pub is among Northbridge's best.

## Cinemas and theatres

Most of Perth's mainstream movie **cinemas** are located in arcades off Hay and Murray streets in the city centre. Tuesday nights are cheap, with matinees also discounted at some places. The *Lumiere Cinema*, part of the *Perth Entertainment Centre* (☎321 1575) in Wellington Street, has a programme of arthouse re-releases and bargain double bills on Sunday afternoons and midweek matinees. Other like-minded cinemas close to the centre include *Cinema Paradiso*, in James Street's *Galleria* complex; the lovely, deco-style *Astor*, on the corner of Beaufort and Walcott streets; and the *Luna* in Oxford Street, Leederville, fifteen minutes' walk west of Northbridge. One cinematic experience that shouldn't be missed, especially if you've never seen an IMAX film before, is a visit to the *Omni Theatre* in the *City West Complex* on Sutherland Street, West Perth. A huge, wraparound screen turns what would otherwise be fairly ordinary documentaries into sensory roller-coaster rides.

Any out-of-the-ordinary **shows** that visit Perth tend to set the city astir and are advertised and patronized heavily. The *Burswood Resort and Casino* (☎362 7777) just over the Causeway, southeast of the centre, is a do-it-all leisure complex comprising a five-star hotel, numerous restaurants and a huge dome hosting all sorts of sporting and showbiz events. Otherwise the *Perth Concert Hall* on St Georges Terrace (☎325 9944), *Her Majesty's Theatre* (☎322 2929) on the corner of King and Hay streets, or the *Perth Entertaiment Centre* (see above) are likely venues for the city's main concerts and plays.

# Listings

**Airlines (International)** *British Airways* (☎483 7711); *Garuda* (☎481 0963); *Malaysian Airlines* (☎325 4499); *Qantas* (☎225 2222); *Singapore Airlines* (☎483 5777); *United Airlines* (☎1800/23 0322).

**Airlines (Domestic)** *Ansett* (☎13 1300); *Rottnest Airbus* (☎478 1322); *Skywest* (☎334 2288).

**Airport shuttle buses** *Perth Airport Bus* (☎250 2838); *Airport–City Shuttle* (☎479 4131).

**Bookshops** *Arcane Bookshop*, 212 William St, Northbridge, has an eclectic, alternative selection, with good gay, lesbian and women's sections. *Book Bonanza Book Exchange*, 81 Barrack St; secondhand paperbacks and car manuals. *New Editions*, South Terrace, Fremantle, is almost an informal reading club, with heaps of absorbing titles and a bookworms' café.

**Bicycle rental** *About Bike Hire*, near Causeway Bridge, Riverside Drive (☎221 2665); bikes for riverside cycling from $15 a day, or try the *YHA* hostels. Secondhand bikes from *WA Bicycle Disposals*, 47 Bennett St, East Perth (☎325 1176), from around $80; also informal rental and buy-back service.

**Buses** *Greyhound.Pioneer* (☎13 2323) for interstate services; *South West Coach Lines* (☎322 5173), for daily services to the Margaret River region as far as Augusta; *Westliner* (☎250 2838) for twice-weekly services to Kalgoorlie, Leinster and Laverton; *Westrail* (☎326 2222), for daily services south and east of Perth and, less frequently, north to Kalbarri and Meekatharra. All have offices at the Wellington St Bus Station, but interstate and *Westrail* country buses come and go from the East Perth Terminal.

**CALM (Department of Conservation and Land Management)**, 50 Hayman Rd, Como (☎367 0333). State-wide information and maps of national parks.

**Car rental** Perth's car-rental companies are among the cheapest in the country and while the "$20/ day" deals should be scrutinized carefully, a week's rental is the best way of exploring relatively compact areas like the Southwest at your own pace. One operator especially tuned in to backpackers' needs is *Network U*, 254 William St, Northbridge (☎227 8810) offering new cars and 4WDs with low excesses and good-value one-way and "country" (unlimited kms) rates. Other companies include *Ace Rent-a-Car* (☎221 1333), *Perth Rent-a-Car* (☎227 9997), *ATC Rent-a-Car* (☎325 1833).

**Dentist** Contact the Dental Hospital in Goderich St (☎325 3452).

**Disabled visitors** *ACROD*, Unit 9, 189 Royal St, East Perth (☎222 2961), provides information for visitors to WA with disabilities. For information about accessible accommodation, call the *Para Quad Association* (☎381 0173), or use the fairly reliable *RACWA Touring Guide* (see below).

**Gay and lesbian life** See box on p.497.

**Hospitals** *Royal Perth*, Victoria Square (☎224 2244); *King Edward Memorial* (for women), Bagot Rd, Subiaco (☎340 2222); *Fremantle*, Alma St (☎431 3333).

**Library** *Perth Cultural Centre*, James St (☎427 3111).

**Maps** *Perth Map Centre*, 891 Hay St (☎322 5733); full range of topographic and touring maps.

**Motoring associations** *RACWA*, 228 Adelaide Terrace (☎421 4444). Offers full range of services, plus maps and the excellent, annually updated *Touring and Accommodation Guide*, with graded accommodation (including backpacker hostels), and heaps of motoring advice and information.

**Permits** Apply to the *Aboriginal Affairs Planning Authority*, 35 Havelock Street, West Perth, 6005 (☎09/483 1333), for permission to cross Aboriginal lands.

**Police** 2 Adelaide Terrace (☎222 1111).

**Post office** Forrest Chase, off Murray St (☎326 5211).

**Swimming pool** Nearest to the centre is the three-pool complex on the corner of Vincent and Charles streets, fifteen minutes' walk northwest of Northbridge; open daily, $3. For riverside and ocean beaches see "Perth's beaches", p.505.

**Tours** See box below.

## RIVER CRUISES AND TOURS FROM PERTH

Besides the commercial ferry operators, all based at Barrack Street jetty and offering cruises up and down the Swan River, bus and 4WD tours leave daily in all directions from Perth. Popular day-tours include the curious Pinnacles, near Cervantes (see p.535), Wave Rock near Hyden (see p.524), the wineries of the Upper Swan (see p.508), and the Margaret River region (see p.513). Longer excursions can be taken to see the dolphins at Monkey Mia or to make a more thorough appraisal of WA's diverse Southwest region. Booking for all tours can be made at your hostel or hotel; at *YHA Travel*, 236 William Street, Northbridge (☎227 5122); or at the tourist office in Forrest Chase (☎483 1111).

### RIVER CRUISES

**Golden Sun Cruises** (☎325 9166). A bit of a barge compared to the other two operators' sleek vessels. Cruises upriver to visit the National Trust property at Tranby House ($10), faintly historic Guildford ($20) and a day-cruise to and tour around the Swan Valley wineries ($36); also downriver to Fremantle (non-stop; $18). All with an informative and entertaining commentary.

**Captain Cook Cruises** (☎325 3341). Daily half- and full-day runs to Fremantle, with the option of a three-hour stopover, one-way from $13, return from $25.

**Boat Torque** (☎221 5844). Full range of tours on plush vessels upriver to Tranby House ($15) and Swan Valley wine-tasting ($35).

### TOURS

**Western Travel Bug** *YHA Travel* (☎227 5122). Popular bargain-priced tours of the Southwest (although not all basic costs are covered) with plenty of activities and a fun atmosphere.

**Overland 4WD Safaris** (☎354 4396). Four- and five-day Monkey Mia and ten-day Perth–Broome tours, with the dolphins taking second place to the off-road Murchison section on the five-day tour which includes eye- (and tinnie-) opening visits to some remote stations.

**Pinnacles Tours and Travel Centre**, 16 Irwin St, corner of Hay St (☎221 5411). One-day tours to the Pinnacles (4WD option), Wave Rock and Margaret River, plus longer runs as far afield as Coral Bay (5 days), together with seasonal whale-watching and wild-flower tours, all led by courteous drivers.

**Redback Safaris**, *YHA Travel* (☎227 5122). One-day Pinnacles specialist with small 4WD van to indulge in a spot of dune-riding on the way back.

**Travelabout**, *YHA Travel* (☎227 5122). One of WA's leading operators, with a full range of professionally run all-action adventure tours from four days through the Southwest to a 35-day see-it-all epic up to the Kimberley and Darwin and back via Ayers Rock to Perth. Around $75 a day.

# Around Perth

While Perth may not be all it's cracked up to be, the area around the city more than compensates. The port of **Fremantle**, at the mouth of the Swan River on the Indian Ocean, should not be overlooked, nor should a day trip to **Rottnest Island**, an eighty-minute ferry ride from the city. Perth's **beaches** lie in a near-unbroken line north of Fremantle, just a short train or bus ride from the centre, while with your own vehicle you can head to the **national parks** northeast of Perth, atop the **Darling Ranges**, which parallel the coast. Patchily forested hills, just half an hour's drive east of the city, they offer a convenient escape to a network of cool scenic drives and marked walking trails amidst jarrah woodlands. After Fremantle, Rottnest Island and the beaches, the best of the local trips are detailed below, described in a clockwise arc starting to the north of the city. CALM (☎367 0333) produce an excellent guidebook, *Perth Outdoors*

($20), a detailed and superbly illustrated guide to the national parks and other natural envionments in and around Perth.

# Fremantle

Although long since merged into the metropolitan area's suburban sprawl, Perth's port of **FREMANTLE** – "Freo" – retains an identity and charm all of its own. Much of the convict-built dock dates from the 1890s and survives today, spruced up for the 1987 Americas Cup yacht race and an eagerly anticipated tourist boom that never quite materialized. The formerly rundown port is now quite presentable, but the jazzed-up image takes a knock as an unmistakable ovine pong settles over the whole town when a continuous stream of "baa-ing" road trains load up Arabia-bound sheep freighters.

Freo's relaxed, Mediterranean ambience attracts hoards of weekenders to its famed artsy markets (worth planning your visit around) and "cappuccino strip", as café-lined South Terrace is known. It's worth noting that in the heat of summer Fremantle is often a breezy 5°C cooler than the city centre, a mere 25 minutes away by train. **Trains** leave regularly from Perth for the 19-kilometre run down to Fremantle station, located at the top end of Market Street, five minutes' walk north of the town centre. **Buses** (routes #102–#106 & #151 from Perth's City Busport) also stop here; local **taxis** can be called on ☎335 3944. For **ferries** to Perth, see box on p.499. The small **tourist office** (Mon–Fri 9am–5pm, Sat 9am–1pm, Sun 10am–3pm; ☎430 2346 or 335 2952) is behind the Town Hall on St John's Square.

## The Town

Exploring Fremantle on foot, with plenty of streetside café breaks, is the most agreeable way of visiting the town's compactly grouped sights, although the **Fremantle Tram** offers informative commentaries with its various tours (daily, on the hour, 10am–4pm; $7–10), which depart from outside the **Town Hall** in St John's Square.

By starting your appraisal of Freo on the relatively dull east side and moving down towards the ocean, you end up, worn out but satisfied, at the Fishing Boat Harbour, ready for a sunset seafood dinner. First off, there's the **Fremantle Arts Centre** (daily 10am–5pm, Wed 7–9pm; free) and **Museum** (Thurs–Sun 1–5pm; free) on the corner of Finnerty and Ord streets, though the small museum's local history displays are barely worth the effort. The Arts Centre itself, albeit in an attractive building with a gallery, is more of a rendezvous for the arty and litterati set and a venue for live performances on summer Sunday afternoons than a rewarding place to visit. The gallery's local offerings vary, but aren't a patch on the collection of the West Australian Art Gallery in Perth.

At the end of Quarry Street, half a kilometre from the Arts Centre, the **Energy Museum** (Mon–Fri 10.30am–4.30pm, Sat & Sun 1–4.30pm ; free), at 12 Parry Street, is a rather stodgy, educational display of power-generating apparatus with a few "hands-on" displays. Continuing down Parry Street brings you to the hillside enclosure of **Fremantle Prison** (entrance in The Terrace; daily 10am–6pm; $10), only decommissioned in 1991. Built by convicts in 1855, soon after the struggling colony found it

---

### TELEPHONE NUMBERS

The **telephone code** for Fremantle is ☎09, but this will change to ☎08 in September 1997.

Also in September 1997, all **Fremantle numbers** will have the prefix 9 added; so, for example, what was ☎09/xxx xxx will become ☎08/9xxx xxxx.

*(For more on changes to phone numbers Australia-wide, see p.40.)*

couldn't do without their labour, it's now one of the biggest tourist gaols in a country full of grim reminders of its origins. The high admission charge is offset by free tours of the prison buildings, guided by ex-wardens.

Things look up from here on in. If it's a Friday, Saturday or Sunday, **Fremantle Markets** (Fri 5–9pm, Sat 10am–5pm, Sun 11am–5pm), on the corner of Henderson Street and South Terrace, will be open and a hub of activity. A real local market where people actually buy things, it's well worth a browse for some fresh food, unusual souvenirs courtesy of the substantial arts and crafts contingent, or cosmic clothes and accessories. Moving down **South Terrace**, Fremantle's main drag, you can revive your aching feet with some refreshment in one of the many inviting, al fresco **cafés** that give the town its vaguely European atmosphere.

Suitably re-caffeinated, you now head into the "**West End**", as the old shipping office and freight district of Freo is known. As South Terrace curves to the right, a left turn down Bannister Street to the **Bannister Street Workshops** at no. 8 (Tues–Fri 10am–5pm, Sat & Sun 12.30–5pm) allows you to watch local wood, glass and ceramic artisans engaged in their craft. More craftsmanship (at 1:22 scale) is on display a couple of minutes' from the Workshops at the **Henry Street Station Model Railway**, 48 Henry Street (daily 10am–5pm; $5), where Thomas the Tank Engine and all his merry chums can be set chuffing around a splendid rendition of model-railway heaven. Round the corner in Croke Lane is **Timothy's Toys** (Mon–Sat 9am–5.30pm), a collection of handmade wooden toys ranged around a dark, semi-animated studio straight out of a Grimm fairy-tale.

The **West Australian Maritime Museum** in Cliff Street (Mon–Thurs 10.30am–5pm, Fri–Sun 1–5pm; free), right next door to the toy studio, is one of Fremantle's highlights. Pride of place goes to the *Batavia* display, the Dutch East Indiaman wrecked off present-day Geraldton over 360 years ago. As well as the ship's reconstructed stern, the display includes the stone portico bound for the Company's unfinished fort at Batavia (Jakarta) and numerous corroded artefacts, together with a fascinating video about the extraordinary drama and subsequent salvage of the wreck.

Just north of the museum, past **Bather's Beach**, is the **Round House** (10am–5pm; free), the state's oldest building and original gaol, with fine views across town and out to sea. From here you can take a walk to the end of **South Mole**, where the Swan River meets the ocean, or continue up to the Port Authority Building on Victoria Quay. Here there's a statue to **C Y O'Connor** who masterminded the rebuilding of the docks in the 1890s and, nearby, the **B Shed**, an intriguing historic boat museum decked out with all sorts of craft – Perth's inhabitants boast the world's highest proportion of boat-owners.

South of the Maritime Museum, passing the grassy **Esplanade** and being distracted by the aroma wafting from the numerous seafood outlets on **Fishing Boat Harbour** (see "Eating", below), you soon reach the **Fremantle Crocodile Park** on Mews Road (Mon–Fri 10am–4pm, Sat & Sun 10am–5pm; $8). It's only small and you don't get that close to the crocs, but it's definitely worth a look if you won't be heading up north to the larger, wilder outdoor parks near Broome or Darwin.

## Accommodation

Fremantle isn't over-endowed with conveniently located accommodation, and a lot of grotty, former seamen's quarters and pub rooms await refurbishment.

**Esplanade Hotel**, corner Marine Terrace and Essex St (☎430 4000). Fremantle's showcase luxury hotel, twice the price of its closest competition but with all the trimmings. ⑨.

**Fremantle Hotel**, corner of High and Cliff streets (☎430 4300). Right by the Round House, this hotel has rooms with shared and en suite facilities. ④.

**Fremantle Village Caravan Park**, corner of Cockburn and Rockingham roads, South Fremantle (☎430 4866). The nearest campsite to the centre of town. On-site vans ④.

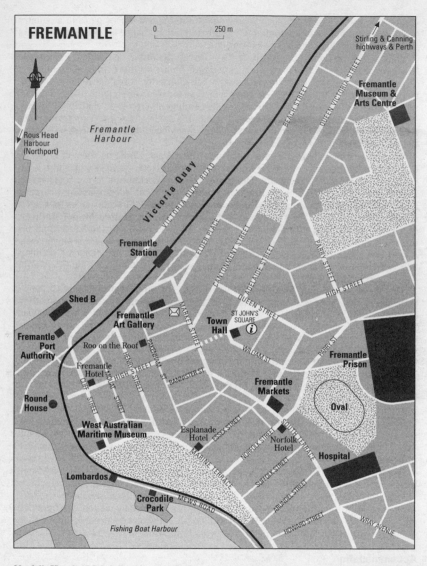

**FREMANTLE**

0        250 m

Stirling & Canning highways & Perth

Fremantle Museum & Arts Centre

Rous Head Harbour (Northport)

*Fremantle Harbour*

Victoria Quay

VICTORIA QUAY ROAD

BEACH STREET

QUEEN VICTORIA STREET

Fremantle Station

PARRY STREET

HIGH STREET

ELDER PLACE

CANTONMENT STREET

ADELAIDE STREET

QUEEN STREET

Shed B

Fremantle Art Gallery

MARKET STREET

ST JOHN'S SQUARE

Town Hall

Fremantle Port Authority

Roo on the Roof

PACKENHAM ST

WILLIAM ST

Fremantle Prison

Fremantle Hotel

HIGH STREET

HENRY STREET

CLIFF STREET

MOUAT STREET

BANNISTER ST

PARRY ST

Round House

Fremantle Markets

Oval

West Australian Maritime Museum

Esplanade Hotel

ESSEX STREET

MARINE TERRACE

NORFOLK STREET

SOUTH TERRACE

Norfolk Hotel

Hospital

Lombardos

SUFFOLK STREET

ARUNDEL STREET

Crocodile Park

MEWS ROAD

HOWARD STREET

WRAY AVENUE

*Fishing Boat Harbour*

**Norfolk Hotel**, 47 South Terrace (☎335 5405). The best bet for a short stay in Fremantle, with the pleasant outdoor bar an attraction in itself. ⑤.

**Ocean View**, 100 Hampton Rd (☎336 2962). High-rise hostel on busy road but with good facilities, including a pool. ②.

**Roo on the Roof**, 11 Packenham St (☎335 1998). This hostel has an air of neglect, with only a central location in its favour. ①.

**Sunny's Motel**, 8 Canning Highway (☎339 1888). Riverside motel with tastefully decorated, balconied rooms. ⑤.

**Tradewinds Hotel**, 59 Canning Highway (☎339 8188). Comfortable motel accommodation close to the river, 4km from the centre. ⑤.

**Woodan Point**, Lot 132, Cockburn Rd, 10km south of Fremantle (☎434 1433). Large beach resort and caravan park. On-site vans ③, cabins ④.

## Eating

Although taken seriously, dining out in Fremantle is pleasantly free of unnecessary formality. **Seafood** restaurants perch over the Swan River or jut into the Fishing Boat Harbour by the Esplanade. In town, South Terrace and its adjacent streets are lined with predominantly **Italian** or **Asian** cafés and restaurants, none of them expensive and all adding to Freo's distinctive ambience.

**Bunga Raya**, 8 Cantonment St. Drab interior, but inexpensive Indo-Malay dishes encourage experimentation. Closed Sun.

**Captain Munchies**, 2 Beach St. Bleary-eyed 24-hour establishment for those late-night appetites.

**Chunagon**, 46 Mews Rd, Fishing Boat Harbour (☎336 1000). Classy Japanese restaurant which suits those who know their sushi from their sashimi or can afford to learn. Closed Mon.

**Cicerillo's**, Fishing Boat Harbour. One of the best fish 'n' chips places in town.

**Falduzzi**, 5 Bannister St. Small, earthy pizzeria with pizzas on the light and unusual side from $8. Try the Pizza D'Enfer if you're brave, and cool down with some sweet or savoury crepes.

**George Street Café**, 73 George St, East Fremantle. Pleasant small café on the east-side alternative to the central Freo coffee "strip".

**Gino's**, 1 South Terrace. Best streetside café on the strip; popular, unpretentious, great coffee, inexpensive food and famously grim "comfort stations".

**Kailis**, Mews Rd, Fishing Boat Harbour. Fast and inexpensive seafood cafeteria and takeaway, right on the waterfront.

**Left Bank Bar & Café**, 15 Riverside Rd, East Fremantle. Trendy riverside venue with brimming "subs" (French bread rolls), or eat in the upstairs restaurant-with-a-view for around $20.

**Lombardos**, Mews Rd, Fishing Boat Harbour (☎335 1088). Along with *Cicerillos*, the best of the $5 fish 'n' chips places on the harbour – a Freo institution that's also a bistro, pub, club and restaurant.

**Mexican Kitchen**, 19 South Terrace. Wholesome Mexican classics at around $15, with half-price nachos on Tuesday nights.

**Nyonya Mas**, Manning Arcade. Indonesian "Straits" cuisine; not for conformists, but an exotic and spicy blend of Chinese–Malay origin – discuss your tastes and apprehensions with the waiter.

**Oyster Beds**, 26 Riverside Rd, East Fremantle (☎339 1611). Definitive seafood restaurant, right over the water, at around $25 a head.

**Pigeon Restaurant**, 4 Market St. Friendly Vietnamese place with no dish over $10.

**Prickles**, corner of South Terrace and Douro Rd, South Fremantle (☎336 2194). A chance to sample the tastes of the Australian bush: crocodile, emu, buffalo and kangaroo. The croc will be a tasty surprise to most.

**La Spezia**, 19c Essex St. Wood-fired pizzas to stay or go.

**Sails**, 47 Mews Rd, Fishing Boat Harbour (☎430 5050). Elegant, upmarket harbourside seafood specialities for around $23 per person.

**Thai Village**, 22 Bannister St. Best Thai in Freo with all-you-can-eat lunches on Thursday and Fridays for around $12.

**Upmarket Food Halls**, Henderson St. Array of global, but mostly Asian "pop food" next to the markets, a good place to experiment with inexpensive Japanese morsels. Thurs–Sun noon–9pm.

## Drinking and entertainment

Like the town itself, **entertainment** in Fremantle is generally a laidback, easygoing affair; a jazzy/folky scene as opposed to Northbridge's more frenetic, but no less fashion-conscious, venues. The *Sail & Anchor* in South Terrace is the town's main watering hole, serving a variety of "boutique" beers – the upmarket home-brew trend originated in Fremantle. The *Norfolk Hotel*'s outdoor bar, on the corner of Norfolk Street and South Terrace, and the *Left Bank Café & Bar*, on Riverside Drive in East Freo, are good-looking and popular spots, both packed on sunny weekends. Pubs with live music include *Clancy's*, an Irish club in Cantonment Street; the *Black Swan* at *Lombardos* on the harbour; the *Cave Bar* next to the old bridge on Queen Victoria Street; and the daggy *Orient Hotel* in the High Street. The *Metropolis*, 52 South Terrace, is Fremantle's gigantic nightclub with a choice of bars and dance floors – this is usually the venue for any big indoor gigs that hit town. The *Fly By Night*, at the prison end of Queen Street, is a musicians' co-op airing local folk talent and makes an enjoyable, smoke-free change from pub venues.

For **performing arts**, check out the *Fremantle Herald* or Thursday's *West Australian*. Local troupes, such as the innovative *Deck Chair Theatre* based at 3 Packenham Street (☎336 2372), or *Spare Parts Theatre*, 1 Short Street (☎335 5044), are worth seeing, or head for the *Arts Centre*, Ord Street, on a summer Sunday afternoon. Fremantle has three **cinemas**, in Essex Street, William Street and Adelaide Street, all with cut-price tickets on Tuesdays and some matinees.

# Rottnest Island

Eighteen kilometres offshore, west of Fremantle, **ROTTNEST ISLAND** was so named by seventeenth-century Dutch mariners who mistook its unique, indigenous **quokkas**, beaver-like marsupials, for rats. Today, following an ignominious period as a brutal Aboriginal penal colony in the nineteenth century, Rottnest is a popular holiday destination, easily accessible from Perth or Fremantle by ferry and, at the very least, makes a fun day out.

The island, colloquially abbreviated to "Rotto", is 11km long and less than half as wide, with one settlement, the main resort, stretching along the sheltered Thompson's Bay on the east side. West of the settlement, a low heathland of salt lakes meets a coastline of clear, scalloped bays, small beaches and offshore reefs ending at the "West End", as the seaward "tail" of the island is known. Although well attuned to the demands of its 400,000 annual visitors, Rotto gets packed-out during the summer school holidays, especially around New Year when accommodation can be hard to find. Motorized traffic on the island is virtually non-existent, a real treat which makes **cycling** from bay to sparkling bay, and quokka to overfed quokka, the best way to appreciate Rottnest. Besides riding around the island, you can take a train ride up to Oliver Hill (five trips daily, allow 2 hours; $9), or explore underwater with the *Dive Shop* (daily 7.30am–6pm; ☎09/292 5167), which organizes **dive trips** and rents out everything from a humble snorkel to a full scuba rig. A couple of days spent here, especially during the less busy mid-week, are well worth the excursion from Perth. Its beautiful coves, ideal for snorkelling, are unlike anything you'll find on the adjacent mainland.

## Practicalities

There are no less than four **ferry** operators servicing Rotto from a variety of destinations in Fremantle and Perth. Services are currently in a state of flux, so check the details with the tourist office (or your hostel). To cut a long story short, *Boat Torque's* plush vessel running from Barrack Street jetty is the most expensive ($50), with *White Dolphin* (*Boat Torque's* budget arm), *Oceanic Cruises* and the new *Rotto Express* cheapest if departing from Fremantle: return fares with these three operators range from $15–25; the latter two also carry bikes for free. The trip from Perth takes about eighty minutes, half as long from Fremantle. You can also **fly** to Rotto in 20 minutes from Jandakot airport (about 20km south of the city) with *Aeroscene Aviation* (☎444 2279; $130 return, including pick-ups and drop-offs), *Skyworx* (☎246 2156; free pick-ups, ask about backpacker specials) and the *Rottnest Airbus* ($80 one-way). Rottnest airport is a 15-minute walk from the settlement.

Ferries arrive at the jetty in Thompson Bay right in front of the island's **information office** (Mon–Sat 8.30am–5pm; Sun 10am–4.30; ☎09/372 9752) which has maps and bus time tables. The office is also a **post office** with *Commonwealth* and *Westpac* bank agencies. Daily two-hour **bus tours** depart from here, at 11.30am and 1.30pm ($9). The more or less hourly *Bayseeker* **bus service** (Oct–April daily 9am–5pm; $2 per trip) also visits the island's bays as far as the isthmus, Narrow Neck, 3km from the West End. The settlement has a general **store** (daily 9am–5.30pm, *R&I* and *ANZ* teller machine), bakery, takeaway and **bistro**, with **bike** rental (daily 9am–1pm & 2–5pm; $15 per day; ☎09/372 9722) behind the hotel, a couple of minutes south of the information office.

**Accommodation** is found along Thompson, Longreach and Geordie bays, all adjacent to each other at the developed northeastern end of the island and linked by an hourly bus service (daily 8am–5pm; $1). A small YHA-associate **hostel** (booking essential; ☎09/372 9780; ①) is located in Kingstown Barracks, at the southeastern end of Thompson Bay, 1km from the shops. **Camping** is available at *Tentland* (☎09/372 9737), just behind the settlement: tents and mattresses can be rented (①) or there are four- and six-bed cabins (④); note that camping is not permitted elsewhere on the island. The island authority rents out all sorts of bungalows, villas, units and cottages (book ahead on ☎09/372 9729; four-bed units ⑤–⑦); rates are substantially lower for subsequent nights, and there's a minimum stay of two nights at weekends. The *Rottnest Hotel* (☎09/292 5011; ⑧), a former governor's residence, and *All Seasons Rottnest Lodge* (☎09/292 5161; ⑨), a prison converted into first-class motel units, are upmarket alternatives close to the settlement.

# Perth's beaches

Perth's closest **beaches** stretch along the Indian Ocean's **Sunset Coast**, 30km of near-unbroken sand and coastal suburbs stretching north of the Swan River and cooled by afternoon sea breezes. There are also inshore beaches along the Swan River at Crawley, Nedlands, Peppermint Grove and Mosman Bay on the north shore, and Como, Canning Bridge and Applecross on the south, all calm and safer for bathing with young children.

**Cottesloe Beach**, 7km north of Fremantle, is the most popular city beach, with safe swimming in the lee of a groyne. There are ice-cream vendors, cafés and watercraft-rental outlets all just a short walk from Cottesloe train station. North of here **Swanbourne Free Beach,** cut off by army land in both directions but accessible from the road, has nude bathing. Further north, the surf and currents are more suited to wave riding and experienced swimmers, with fewer beachside facilities, tending to reduce crowds.

**SCARBOROUGH BEACH**, dominated by the *Radisson Observation City Hotel*, is as much a holiday resort as beachside suburb and is the best base along the Sunset Coast if you want to stay a day or two. Popular with surfers and their groupies, the suburb exhibits an easygoing Californian tan-upmanship, plus enough services, inexpensive accommodation and activity to sustain a few days out of central Perth. **Bus #400** leaves from Perth's Wellington Street Bus Station for the 40-minute journey.

## Beachside accommodation

The accommodation at **Scarborough Beach** is mostly self-catering, suited to extended stays. The *Mandarin Gardens YHA,* 20 Wheatcroft Street (☎09/341 5431; ①, units ⑤), while a little rough round the edges, is the most spacious of Scarborough's three hostels; with a decent-sized pool and plenty of grassy areas it can be quite a relief after some of Northbridge's cramped and noisy equivalents. Another good backpackers' place is the improved *Western Beach Lodge*, a converted house at 6 Westborough Street

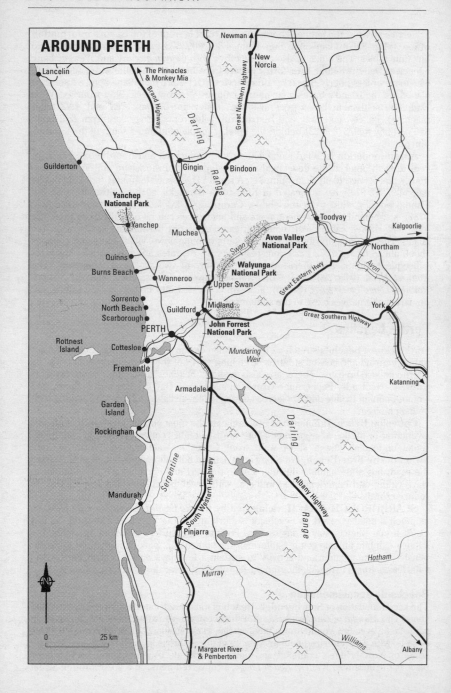

**AROUND PERTH**

Lancelin

The Pinnacles
& Monkey Mia

Guilderton

Yanchep
National Park

Yanchep

Quinns

Burns Beach

Sorrento
North Beach
Scarborough

PERTH

Rottnest
Island

Cottesloe

Fremantle

Garden
Island

Rockingham

Mandurah

Newman

New
Norcia

Gingin    Bindoon

Muchea

Avon Valley
National Park

Toodyay

Kalgoorlie

Northam

Walyunga
National Park

Upper Swan

Wanneroo

Guildford    Midland

John Forrest
National Park

Great Eastern Hwy

York

Great Southern Highway

Mundaring
Weir

Katanning

Armadale

Serpentine

South Western Highway

Pinjarra

Murray

Albany Highway

Hotham

Williams

Albany

Margaret River
& Pemberton

Darling

Range

Brand Highway

Great Northern Highway

Swan

Avon

Darling

Range

0    25 km

(☎09/245 1624; ①), while *West Coast Seas* (☎09/341 4101; ⑤), right next to *Observation City*, offers a range of self-catering units, and the *Indian Ocean Hotel*, at 23 Hastings Street (☎09/341 1122; ⑥), is a good-value hotel. Further south in **Swanbourne**, the *Swanbourne Guest House*, 5 Myers Street (☎09/349 1408; ⑤), offers gay- and lesbian-friendly lodgings.

# New Norcia

One of WA's most striking cultural sights is the nineteenth-century monastic community of **NEW NORCIA**, 130km northeast of Perth on the Great Northern Highway. This unexpected collection of Spanish-style architecture, extraordinarily out of place in the Australian bush, is part of a community founded by Benedictine monks in 1846. **Dom Rosendo Salvado** established the mission (named after St Benedict's birthplace) with the aim of converting the local Aborigines to the twin blessings of agriculture and Christianity, and to escape persecution back home. Nowadays it's a popular tourist attraction, which tends to compromise the monastic tranquillity its ageing inhabitants seek, and yet pays for the upkeep of their remarkable endowment.

The community has a roadhouse that accommodates a restaurant, **tourist office** (daily 7am–8pm; ☎096/54 8056), museum, art gallery, general store, post office and the *New Norcia Hotel* (☎096/54 8034; ④), whose **rooms** don't quite match the grand exterior but still offer an old-fashioned treat. The two-kilometre New Norcia **heritage trail** (guide leaflet from tourist office or museum) begins here, and wanders among the community's impressive buildings. The **museum and art gallery** (daily 10am–4.30pm; $3), originally an orphanage and girls' school, describe the Bendictines' motivations in coming here in the first place, with the art gallery housing a fine collection of post-Renaissance and contemporary religious art.

The two most impressive and ornate buildings, either side of the cemetery, are **St Gertrude's Residence for Girls** and **St Ildephonsus' Residence for Boys**, the latter with striking Moorish minarets. Both were built by the the mission's second abbot, Bishop Torres, at the beginning of this century. Daily tours ($10) now allow you to explore their ornate interiors and you can also visit the **Flour Mills** and the **Abbey Church** – relatively ordinary by comparison. The **monastery** is still the residence of New Norcia's few remaining monks and closed to the public, although weekend retreats (☎096/54 8022; $40 per person) can be undertaken in the adjacent guesthouse. From here an 800-metre marked trail leads down to the old wells and Bishop Torres' gazebo-like **Beehouse** by the Moore River; on the way back there are great views of St Ildephonsus' turreted roofline poking through the trees.

Several bus tour companies offer **day tours** to New Norcia, which is otherwise only served three times a week by *Westrail*'s rural bus service.

---

### WILDFLOWERS

In Springtime, much of temperate WA, but especially the better-watered southwest region around Perth, becomes carpeted in thousands of varieties of tiny **wildflowers**. This phenomenon, which usually lasts from August to November, while not unique, is promoted as one of the state's premier attractions. Varieties of banksia, grevillia, orchid and kangaroo paws (WA's floral emblem) transform the otherwise dreary, evergreen heathland into mosaics of colour which are best appreciated on foot. During the season, Perth's bus-tour operators organize trips to especially florid areas and, for the independently mobile, the WATC produces a fine brochure, "Wildflower Discovery – A Guide for the Motorist", detailing many of the recognized "wildflower ways" through the state; available at Perth tourist office in Forrest Chase (see p.490).

## Toodyay

The charming old town of **TOODYAY**, set among the wooded hills of the Avon Valley, 85km northwest of Perth, makes an agreeable diversion on the way to or from New Norcia. The town was founded in 1836, making it one of the earliest inland settlements of the Swan River Colony, and many buildings survive from that era. The unembellished bulk of **Connors Mill** in the main road, Stirling Terrace, is now an **information centre** and **museum** (Mon–Sat 9am–5pm, Sun 10am–5pm; ☎096/574 2435; museum $1), featuring, among the usual relics, the exploits of the local bushranger, known as "Moondyne Joe". The **Old Newcastle Gaol** in Clinton Street is also a local history museum (Mon–Fri 11am–3pm, Sat 1–4pm, Sun 11am–4pm; $2); other historical buildings include St Stephen's Church, opposite the Mill, and the Mechanics' Institute, also in Stirling Terrace, featuring unusual adzed-timber scissor trusses supporting the roof.

These aside, the town is a pleasant place for a stroll, with antique and country crafts outlets and pleasant parks or riverside walks. The *Wendouree Tea Rooms* are open daily (8am–late) for refreshment, while *Sisters* and *Emma's* **restaurants**, at the *Avondown Inn* and *Freemason's Hotel* respectively, are open from Friday to Sunday for lunch and dinner. The **Avon Valley** and **Walyunga national parks** follow the Avon river southwest of town and make a further scenic diversion on the road to Perth.

## Guildford and the Swan Valley

North of the town of **GUILDFORD**, just half an hour's drive from Perth, is WA's oldest wine-growing region: the **Upper Swan Valley**. Set at the foot of the Darling Ranges, it invites a pleasant day's **wine-tasting**, although the wines produced here cannot match the more recent vintages from the Margaret River region (see p.513). Guildford itself is another historic town, dating back to the earliest years of the colony, with several federation-era grand hotels to admire and the *Guildford Village Potters* in 22 Meadow Street acting as the town's **tourist office** (Mon–Fri 10am–3pm, Sat & Sun 10am–4pm; ☎09/279 9859). If you're heading up the valley, pick up the "Swan Valley Drive – Route 203" guide from here, detailing the area's attractions and its dozen or so wineries. And before you leave town (or on your way back), take a look at the **Halls Museum**, at the back of the *Rose and Crown Hotel* (WA's oldest), at 105 Swan Street (Tues–Sun 10am–4.30pm; $3). Proclaiming itself the largest private collection of **diverse memorabilia** in the southern hemisphere, it includes displays of inkwells, corkscrews and evening bags the like of which you won't find anywhere else.

### The Swan Valley Drive

Heading north from the *Guildford Village Potters*, a clearly marked thirty-kilometre drive follows the west side of the river. A turn-off left down Banera Road leads to **Pinelli Wines** in Bennet Road (Mon–Sat 9am–6pm, Sun 10am–5pm; ☎09/279 6818), offering two-litre flagons of decent table wine. Back on the West Swan Road, **Sandalford Wines** (Mon–Sat 10am–5pm, Sun 11am–4pm; ☎09/274 5922) has some of the valley's best wines, but you'll probably be more impressed by their Margaret River selection. Caversham Wildlife Park & Zoo and Whitemans Park (see "Perth for kids", p.494) make handy diversions if your children are getting restless. Further up Route 203, the **Little River Winery & Café** (daily 10am–5.30pm, café 11am–4pm; ☎09/296 4462) is a small, independent winery with some award-winning wines and a pleasant café in which to enjoy them.

Coming down the valley's east side, several more wineries tempt you: **Talijancich Wines'** (daily except Sat 11am–5pm; ☎09/296 4289) rich muscat can be bought rather than tasted, while **Houghton's**, on Dale Road (daily 10am–5pm; ☎09/274 5100), is the area's biggest and most diverse producer of wines, with an art gallery and tended lawns on which to contemplate your savourings. The route returns to Guildford and thence to Perth via Midland, passing the Toodyay Road (see above) winding up into the Ranges.

*Feature Tours* run regular **bus tours** through the valley as do some of the Swan River **boat cruises**.

## Mundaring Weir and around

At the crest of the Darling Ranges, 40km from Perth and 7km south of the town of **MUNDARING** on the Great Eastern Highway, is **Mundaring Weir**, a dam constructed in the 1890s to provide water for the Goldfields Water Scheme. It was the then innovative solution of the colony's chief engineer, C Y O'Connor, to the desperate water shortage that was hampering development of the Eastern Goldfields. O'Connor, who was also responsible for the development and construction of Fremantle Harbour and the colony's railway system, planned to raise the water the 400m up to Kalgoorlie with the aid of a series of pumping stations. Such a radical idea was ridiculed in the press and mocked in parliament – O'Connor struggled all the way to secure funds for his scheme and eventually took his own life on Fremantle Beach just ten months before water finally gushed into Kalgoorlie's Mount Charlotte Reservoir in 1903. Today, the Goldfields are still fed by an upgraded version of the pipeline and pumping stations which parallel the Great Eastern Highway to Kalgoorlie.

At the base of the dam wall is the **C Y O'Connor Museum** (Mon, Wed–Fri 10.30am–3pm, Sat 1–4pm, Sun noon–5pm; $1), housed in the primary steam pumping station. Inside are early versions of the pitch and wood pipeline, at that time the longest in the world, and details of O'Connor's other public works, as well as a biographical video on his achievements. The museum also outlines a little of Kalgoorlie's goldrush history.

Just up the road from the museum is the *Mundaring Weir Hotel* (☎09/295 1106; ⑤), used by O'Connor as an office and now a popular weekend pub, with Sundays featuring a lamb-on-a-spit and bush bands; a small pool overlooks the jarrah woodlands. Right opposite the pub, a track leads up to the similarly idyllic YHA **hostel** (☎09/295 1809; ①), a great spot for a few days' break from Perth – as long as school trips haven't over-run the place. Call in advance to ask about pick-ups from the city or from Mundaring townsite's bus stop, 6km away.

The **John Forrest National Park** lies north of the Great Eastern Highway between Mundaring and Midland, right on the edge of the Darling escarpment and just half an hour's drive from Perth. An area of natural bushland with swimming, waterfalls, walking and riding trails, as well as barbecues and a restaurant, it's one of the highlights of the nearby parks.

## York

Stranded in the Avon Valley, 97km from Perth, like a film-set for an Australian Western, **YORK** is the state's most complete pioneering settlement, its early architecture pleasingly preserved for contemporary inspection. The commercial centre of the Avon Valley until the railway, and with it the Great Eastern Highway, bypassed it 30km to the north, York is now an agricultural centre but also plays a historical role as a venerable museum of ornate nineteenth-century public buildings, coaching inns and churches.

The **York Motor Museum** (daily 9am–5pm; $6), opposite the tourist office in Avon Terrace, capitalizes on York's antiquarian charisma with a large collection of vintage and classic vehicles – from a hundred-year-old single-cylinder tricycle to Ossie Cranston's 1936 Ford V8 racer. At the north end of the Terrace are the **Sandalwood Yards** where the perfumed wood, once prolific in WA and highly prized in the Orient, was stored during York's heyday. Near here you can take a walk down to the wobbly **suspension bridge** spanning the generally sluggish Avon River and have a look at the

1854 **Holy Trinity Church**, with its modern stained-glass designs by Robert Juniper, one of WA's foremost artists. Walking south along the east side of the river to Balladong Road, you arrive at the **Residency Museum** (Tues–Thurs 1–3pm, Sat & Sun 1–5pm; $1), next to the Old Hospital in Brook Street – a perfunctory display of pioneering-era memorabilia.

Recrossing the river, passing the Shire Offices and old cemetery, a left turn down the southern end of Avon Terrace leads to **Balladong Farm** (daily 10am–5pm; $5.50), restored by the National Trust and still functioning as a tourist attraction. At a time when York was a key inland settlement and jumping-off point for treks into the interior, the farm played a pivotal role in the region and today still employs machinery and husbandry techniques from that era. An elevated view of York and the Avon Valley can be enjoyed from **Mount Brown Lookout**, signed two kilometres to the east of town.

### Practicalities

York's **tourist office** (Mon–Fri 9am–5pm, Sat & Sun 9am–5pm; ☎096/41 1301) is at 105 Avon Terrace, the main road on which most of York's fine old buildings stand. A **town map** and information sheet is available here, which locates and briefly describes all of these relics as well as places to stay and eat. York's **hotels** ooze charm, with the *Settlers' House* (☎096/41 1096; ④–⑤) offering great-value elegantly furnished rooms with breakfast, a fine restaurant and pleasant daytime café. The *Imperial Inn*, 83 Avon Terrace (☎096/41 1010; ④–⑤), is a restored, century-old hotel also full of olde-worlde charm, while the pricier *Castle York Hotel* (☎096/41 1007; ⑦) offers similar bygone-age appeal in even greater splendour. The only real budget accommodation is at the *Mount Bakewell Caravan Park* (☎096/41 1421; on-site vans ③).

Good **cafés** to seek out include *Café Bugatti* and the *Terrace Café* (both in Avon Terrace), as well as the café attached to the the *Settlers' House* hotel. **Buses** leave *Westrail*'s East Perth terminal up to three times daily (but no service on Sat), with some **tours** popping in to York on the way to or from Wave Rock at Hyden, 250km to the east. The town hosts the **York Jazz Festival** around September time, but note that in the summer months, York, like all of inland WA, often reaches 40°C and is barely visited.

# The Southwest

The region south of Perth and west of the Albany Highway is known, not unnaturally, as **The Southwest**, and is not only the corner of the state but of the very continent, where the cool Southern and warm Indian oceans meet. North of **Bunbury**, 180km from Perth, are a knot of industrial installations and satellite towns like Rockingham and Mandurah which offer little interest to the visitor compared to what's ahead.

South of Bunbury things improve greatly. The **Margaret River** area offers tasteful tourist facilities in a picturesque landscape of dairy farms and wineries – WA's most popular holiday destination; to the southeast is the **Tall Timber Country** and **Pemberton**, a logging town amid the remnants of centuries-old eucalypt forests. Finally, again to the southeast, the **Rainbow Coast**'s sheltered inlets and rocky headlands lead to the historic and fashionable town of Albany – described in the following section, starting on p.518.

*South West Coach Lines* (in Busselton, ☎097/52 1500; in Perth, at Wellington Street Bus Station, ☎09/322 5173) offer an alternative to *Westrail*'s provincial bus service as well as ten-day unlimited-travel **bus passes** for around $100, and are set to introduce a useful new circular bus service from Perth via Margaret River and Pemberton. *Geographe Bay Coachlines* (☎097/54 2026) offer good-value **day-tours** from Bunbury and Busselton of the Margaret River area. The best way to get about is with your own **car**, although the area is ideal for **cycling**, too, with many logging roads passing

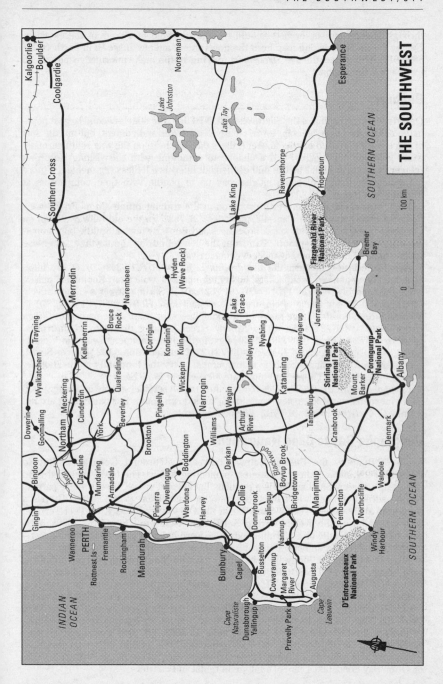

THE SOUTHWEST

through shaded forests; cyclists should try and get hold of a copy of the excellent *Cycling Down South* biking map from the government agency *Bikewest* in Perth (☎09/ 389 0611). Otherwise, the five *Streetsmart* **touring maps** make informative aids for all travellers in the region.

# Bunbury

Described as the capital of the Southwest, **BUNBURY**, the state's second-largest population centre, is a very pleasant town, clearly prosperous and content, but not the sort of place you've crossed oceans to see. A day's dallying here on the way south certainly won't give you nightmares, and a chance to commune with the visiting **dolphins** (currently found around The Cut on Leschenault Inlet) is a lot less regimented, if more unpredictable, than schlepping all the way up to paddle with their compatriots at Monkey Mia (see p.541).

Daily **bus services** from Perth drop you at the **tourist office** (Mon–Fri 8.30am–5pm, Sat 9am–5pm, Sun 9.30am–4.30pm; ☎097/21 7922) in the old railway station on Carmody Place, replete with maps, brochures and Bunbury-obelia. Shuttle buses operate from the new **train station**, 3km from the centre, during the daytime, otherwise **taxis** (☎097/21 2300) generally meet evening arrivals.

**Accommodation** includes the *Wander Inn Lodge* (☎097/21 3242; ①), at 16 Clifton Street, a young-at-heart backpackers' hostel ten minutes' walk from Koombana beach, while the superbly restored *YHA* (☎097/91 2621; ①) in Stirling Street is comparatively serene, but is under threat of closure. The elegant *Rose Hotel* (☎097/21 4533; ④) in Victoria Street, boasts a large range of boutique beers, or there's the upmarket *Clifton Beach Motel* (☎097/21 4300; ⑤) in Molloy Street. Among the many **restaurants**, *Memories of Bond Store* (☎097/91 2922), next to the Entertainment Centre in Victoria Street, is outstanding, *Eagle Towers* (☎097/21 2762; closed Mon), 192 Spencer Street, serves seafood including local blue manna crabs, or try the **foodhalls** at the *Bunbury Pavilion* (11am–9pm, Thurs–Sun), opposite *Memories of Bond Store*.

*Cheapa Rent-a-Car* (☎097/21 9669), at the *Ampol* service station in Blair Street, offers inexpensive vehicles, new and old, for trips down south. For pushbiking around town, visit *Cycletrek* (☎097/21 4216), 75 Spencer Street.

# Geographe Bay to Cape Naturaliste

South of Bunbury the Bussel Highway curves west around **Geographe Bay** to **BUSSELTON**, named after a prominent pioneering family. The town, sheltered from the ocean's currents and swells, is a popular "bucket and spade" resort where parents can be sure their kids won't be swept away or dashed on to the rocks. There's a **museum** (daily except Tues 2–5pm; $2) in the Old Butter Factory, off Peel Terrace, with an exhibit on the ill-fated **Group Settlement Scheme**. During the 1920s, overseas families with little or no farming expertise were induced to settle the Southwest – most failed miserably and ended up rotting in "humpies" like the one on display.

After Busselton, the highway turns south towards Margaret River, but continuing west brings you to **DUNSBOROUGH**, 21km from Busselton, a small holiday resort with one of the best-positioned *YHA* hostels (☎097/55 3107; ①) around. Situated 4km southeast of town, right on the beach, the modern **hostel** offers free bikes and watercraft and a happy, family atmosphere. Otherwise, try the *Green Acres Caravan Park* (☎097/55 3087; on-site vans ③) on the seafront, one of the various **resorts**, or treat yourself at the *Carramar Rural Retreat* (☎097/55 3063; ⑤), 3km from town, a smart B&B adapted for disabled access. With numerous wrecks and little tidal variation, Geographe Bay is ideal for **diving**; the *Dunsborough Bay Village Resort* (☎097/55 3397), on Dunn Bay Road, takes care of equipment rental and charters.

Cape Naturaliste, 14km northwest of the resort, is the less impressive of the two capes which define the Margaret River region. Its truncated **lighthouse** (daily except Wed 9.30am–4pm) is open for inspection, and along the way there are turn-offs to secluded beaches with the **Sugarloaf** offering particularly fine views.

# Along Caves Road to Margaret River and Cape Leeuwin

South of Dunsborough you head into the **Margaret River region** proper, characterized by caves, wineries, choice restaurants and snug hideaways all interspersed with more galleries, craft studios and potteries than in the rest of the state put together. Passing **Yallingup Cave** (see box below) and the turn-off for **YALLINGUP**, a seaside resort where surfers bob around like seals, you come to the *Gunyulgup Gallery* (daily 10am–5pm). Taking a refreshingly confident quality-not-quantity attitude to its exhibits, it displays a selection of fine furniture and art from local artisans, for sale at suitably rarefied prices.

A couple of kilometres back down Caves Road is a crossroads with the inviting *Crayfish Inn* (☎097/55 2028; ⑤) and restaurant on the corner, and a right turn leading 3km to **Canal Rocks**, where the waves relentlessly pound the pink granite outcrops into curious, scalloped forms. Continuing south are turn-offs to the **Abbey Vale Winery** and **Moonshine Brewery** (daily 10.30am–5pm; ☎097/55 2286) and, further on, **Cape Clairault Winery** (daily 10am–5pm), one of the better choices if you fancy some wine-tasting. Those intent on visiting some of the forty-five wineries within half as many kilometres should pick up the *Margaret River Regional Vineyard Guide* ($2.50) from Margaret River **tourist office** (see below).

Another turning west off Caves Road leads 4km to **Quininup Beach**, accessible only to high-clearance vehicles and so rarely crowded, and **GRACETOWN**, 12km south, on the sheltered Cowaramup Bay. Another 5km south down Caves Road sees a right turn leading to **Ellenbrook House**, a Bussell homestead from 1857, bare inside but in a lovely, quiet spot by the brook. From here a thirty-minute walk leads up to the luxuriant **Meekadarribee Falls** which, unusually, manage to spiral underneath themselves.

After Ellenbrook you come to the crossroads leading east 5km to Margaret River (see below), while a right turn takes you to the resort of **PREVELLY PARK,** on the estuary of the Margaret River. The Greek **Chapel of St John** will certainly catch your eye: a memorial to the Preveli Monastery on Crete which sheltered Allied soldiers, Australians among them, in World War II. The turning opposite leads down to the blustery beach where November's annual Margaret River Classic **surfing** championships are held, a great spot to watch surfers and acrobatic sailboarders in action. Back at the chapel, the road continues down into the **resort** and the usual chalets and caravan parks. Check out the *Café Gnarabup* (daily 8.30am–sunset), overlooking the sea and offering frothy cappuccinos wobbling in the breeze and with the mouth-watering aroma of sizzling fish.

### Margaret River
The town of **MARGARET RIVER**, like the eponymous region, has come to symbolize every stress-worn Perthian's aspiration to escape the rat race, open an aromatic candle boutique and claim their share of the good life. It's a pleasant *mélange* of partying wave-riders, floral-clad muses and the vanguard of fortunate late-Eighties "mappies" (middle-aged professionals) who moved in ahead of the real-estate boom.

Margaret River is not necessarily the best place to actually stay – prices can be high in the summer when the town is busy – but it's handy for shopping, eating out and browsing, while its **tourist office** (daily 9am–5pm; ☎097/57 2911), on the Bussell Highway, represents the whole region. *Westrail* and *South West Coach Lines* **buses** visit daily from Perth; local **taxis** (☎097/57 3444) are used to being taken along on

## GOING UNDERGROUND

A band of limestone passing through the cape has created some 300 **caves** around Margaret River, four of which are open to the public. Most involve guided tours to avoid damage and accidents, with relatively high entrance fees and shuffling crowds rather detracting from the cavernous spectacle, but a visit to the region would be incomplete without a look around at least one of the caves. All are humid, possibly causing breathlessness, and temperatures are around 17°C. Tours are less frequent from May to August – for more details ask at the Margaret River tourist office.

**Lake Cave** (4–6 tours daily 10am–3.30pm; $7; ☎097/57 7543). Impressive, overgrown entrance with a huge "1000-year-old" karri tree and, inside, a unique "suspended table" hangs over the subterranean lake.

**Jewel Cave** (4–5 tours daily 9.30am–3.30pm; $7.50; ☎097/58 4541). The best cave, featuring extraordinary and fragile formations such as 5-metre "helictites" (delicate, straw-like formations) protected by breeze-proof doors. Also includes *Moondyne Cave* (up to 3 tours daily,

approx 2hr, equipment supplied, 10 people max; $25) with some hands-and-knees crawling for the more adventurous.

**Mammoth Cave** (3–5 tours daily 9.30am–3.30pm; $7). Large cavern and easy access with some bones and fossils of now extinct creatures, but really the last choice.

**Yallingup Cave** (daily 9.30am–3.30pm; $6.50). Continuous access down steep steps avoids regimented crowds. Plenty of nooks to explore and delicate features to wonder at.

some serious wine-tasting jaunts; while *Leeuwin Car Hire* (☎097/57 2671) rents cars between Busselton and Augusta. Highly recommended are local *Bushtucker Tours* (☎097/57 2466) which take a closer look at the area's ecology.

The range of **accommodation** is vast, but booking ahead would be prudent in summer: conversely, good deals are offered during typically wet winters. The *Margaret River Lodge* (☎097/57 2532; rooms ③, dorms ①), 220 Railway Terrace, 2km west of town, takes good care of backpackers and has rental bikes, while the *Margaret River Hotel* (☎097/57 2655; ⑥) is a plush, fifty-year-old country inn right in town. *Peppermint Brook Cottages* (☎097/57 2485; ⑥), at 1 Mann Street, offer self-contained cottages sleeping six, and both the *Margaret River* (☎097/57 2180; on-site vans ③) and the *Riverview* (☎097/57 2270; on-site vans ③) **caravan parks** are just a kilometre out of town.

The whole countryside is dotted with charming **restaurants**, often attached to wineries, but in town try the *Ark of Iris*; the renowned sesame burgers at the *Country Kitchen*; or *Settlers Bistro's* homemade desserts – the latter good for drinks too, with a young crowd and live music in the summer. Alternatively, dabble in the *Margaret River Hotel's* range of boutique brews or the *1885* on Farrelly Street.

### Augusta and Cape Leeuwin

Five kilometres southwest of Margaret River, on Boodjidup Road, one of the more interesting attractions vying for your attention is **Eagles Heritage** (daily 10am–5pm; $4.50), a fascinating collection of birds of prey. Aviaries house huge wedge-tail and white-breasted sea eagles, peregrine falcons and a few owls – a rare menagerie of impressive flying hunters.

Rejoining Caves Road, having passed the turning for the **Leeuwin Winery** (daily 10am–4.30pm; ☎097/57 6253) with its art gallery and restaurant if you need a break, you head south into the silvery-barked karri forest. It's a magnificent sight, well worth taking some time to appreciate now if you're not planning to visit Pemberton. Down the road, beyond Mammoth and Lake caves, Boranup Drive takes an off-road detour through the **Boranup Forest**, a great place for **biking and riding**.

South of the forest, the Brockman Highway leads 90km east to Nannup, while continuing 3km south down Deepdene Road brings you to a turn-off to the old timber port of **HAMELIN BAY**, with a beachside **caravan park** (☎097/58 5540; on-site vans ③) offering bikes for rent. Passing **Jewel Cave**, another 8km down Deepdene Road brings you to the small town of **AUGUSTA**, on the estuary of the Blackwood River, the state's oldest settlement after Albany and Perth. Little remains of those days, although the **museum** (daily Oct–May 9am–5pm, otherwise 10am–noon; $1), in Blackwood Avenue, retains some old relics and is more absorbing than you might expect.

**Buses** visit Augusta once a day, generally in the evening, departing back north early the following morning. For **accommodation**, the *Georgina Molloy* (☎097/58 1255; ⑤) is the better of the two **motels**, while the *Augusta Backpackers* (☎097/58 1433; ①), on the corner of Bussell Highway and Blackwood Avenue, is cramped but cheap, and rents **bikes** for a spin to Cape Leeuwin. *Doonbanks Caravan Park* (☎097/58 1517; on-site vans ③) is just opposite, and there are two more caravan parks south of town. **Eat** healthily at *Squirrels Gourmet Wholefood Kitchen* or more opulently at the *Colonial Restaurant*, both on the main road.

**Cape Leeuwin**, 9km south of town, is probably why you've come this far, and it's worth the journey, giving a bleak, windswept "land's end" feel to this continental corner, especially on a mean and moody day. A Dutch captain named the cape after his ship 370 years ago, and Matthew Flinders began the onerous task of mapping Australia's coast right here in 1851. From the top of the **lighthouse** (daily 9am–3pm; $3) you can contemplate your position – about 5000km from the South Pole. Nearby, an **old waterwheel**, originally constructed for the lighthouse builders and now petrified in salt, is a popular landmark.

# Tall Timber Country

Sandwiched between the popular tourist areas of Margaret River and Albany's Rainbow Coast, the forests of the **Tall Timber Country** are sustained by high winter rainfall (1000mm) and WA's longest perennial rivers. **Logging** remains this region's primary industry and small company towns, each with their own mill, busy themselves with their controversial work, while **Pemberton**'s woodcraft galleries, surrounding attractions and scenic drives form the focus of most visitors' attentions. Excepting the sinuous **Blackwood River** (ideal for sedate canoeing adventures, especially west of Nannup), the highlight of the region is the brooding, primeval majesty of the **karri forests**. Not so much for the arboreal gimmicks – of which the "climb-if-you-dare" **Gloucester Tree** is the best-known example – but for the raw, elemental nature of this unique forest environment, well worth marvelling at for a couple of days.

**Public transport** is limited to *Westrail*'s service which leaves you stranded in the larger towns, although their proposed Margaret River–Pemberton link will do in two hours what currently takes a whole day.

## The Blackwood River Valley

The northern part of the forest country is watered by the **Blackwood River** and divided by scenic roads through jarrah woodlands linking the riverside mill towns. **NANNUP**, on the Vasse and Brockman highways, 60km southeast of Busselton, is perhaps the most picturesque town in the region, nestling quietly among wooded hills. The **tourist office** (☎097/56 1211) is located in the Old Police Station in Brockman Street, with the *Blackwood Café* nearby being an ideal lunch spot and *Crafty Creations*, a few doors down, exhibiting some gorgeous and affordable woodcraft. For a **bed**, the cosy *Black Cockatoo Hostel*, 27 Grange Road (☎097/56 1035; ①), looks after backpackers, while the upmarket *Lodge* (☎097/56 1276; no children allowed; ⑦), on

## THE CALM CHAINSAW MASSACRE

The soothing acronym of the department of Conservation and Land Management, which does such a good job in WA's national parks, disguises its true role. Park management and helpful rangers account for only a fraction of the activities of this government agency, whose primary goal is securing the interests of the Southwest's $300m logging industry.

With *CALM*'s assent (and for a substantial cut), *Bunnings*, the prominent hardware store chain and long-established timber millers, enjoys a virtual monopoly on logging the world's only stands of giant eucalypts. In the 1970s, eco-activists brought the destruction of WA's native forests to public attention and *Bunnings*, which employs 20,000 in its milling operations, has since been forced to adopt a more acceptable public face: building playgrounds and "timber parks", and issuing lustrous brochures of "pulp fiction", with such titles as "No One Wants A World Without Trees", while at the same time shedding jobs and increasing production to assuage demand and efficiency.

For the original settlers, the need for timber was understandable; jarrah is famously termite-resistant and millions of jarrah sleepers still support Australia's railways. However, the drastic practice of **clearfelling** vast tracts of native forest for **woodchips** used in paper manufacture (the fate of 85 percent of the timber), is like shooting elephants for dog food, and has profound repercussions on the entire eco-system. A strikingly cynical practice is the preservation of fringes of old growth along the tourist routes, to create an impression of deep forest while actually concealing the true extent of the devastation – hence the curious absence of scenic flights in these parts. Already half of the native forests have been cut down and only a sixth of the remainder is protected.

This sorry situation typifies the short-sightedness at which Australia has always excelled, flogging-off rich resources for a quick buck, then buying back the value-added product at a far greater price. Jobs versus a load of trees is, of course, an emotive issue, but the burgeoning tourism industry may offer a viable alternative, and would certainly be a more sustainable and constructive long-term strategy.

the hill, promises to spice up your marriage or affair in lavish but intimate comfort. Lost among the jarrah 6km northwest of town, the *Nannup Bush Cabins* (☎097/56 1170; ⑤) are enchantingly situated hideaways. *Blackwood Expeditions* (☎097/56 1209) has **canoe rental** and guided tours on the smoother sections of the lower Blackwood River.

From Nannup, a **scenic drive** winds 41km along the river, passing the craft-packed *Old Cheese Factory* (daily 9am–5pm), a few kilometres before unremarkable Balingup; the Brockman Highway, heading east 46km to **BRIDGETOWN**, is no less sylvan in its splendour. Bridgetown is a busy place, with a large **tourist centre** (daily 9am–5pm; ☎097/61 1740) on Hampton Street, but despite some token tea and craftshops, it's fundamentally a place to have your chainsaw serviced or retreads put on your ute. By the river, where some pleasant bankside walks commence, the National Trust property of *Bridgedale House* (Thurs–Mon 10am–4pm; $2 admission) rents out **canoes**.

### Towards Pemberton

Thirty-seven kilometres south of Bridgetown, **MANJIMUP** is the region's commercial centre, handy for shopping and other services but, apart from a visit to the **Timber Park** (daily 9am–5pm), behind the **tourist office** (daily 8.30am–5.30pm; ☎097/71 1831) in Rose Street (both celebrating the local timber industry), it has little appeal. Graphite Road is a picturesque if slippery forest drive heading west 22km to **One Tree Bridge** and, after another couple of kilometres, to the magnificent **Four Aces**, a quartet of huge, 350-year-old karri trees standing in line. With a detailed map it's possible to follow these logging roads to Pemberton.

## Pemberton and around

Small enough to retain its backwoods charm while maintaining the quality of accommodation, eating and creative outlets that makes the Southwest such an attractive destination, **PEMBERTON** is the best base for touring Tall Timber Country. The **tourist
information** office is in Brockman Street (daily 9am–5pm; ☎097/76 1133): pick up the
excellent "Pemberton–Northcliffe" map and guide ($1), as well as information on
**riding**, **canoe** and **bicycle rental**, local **tours** and the interactive Karri Forest
Discovery Centre ($3), which replicates the forest environment. *CALM* in Kennedy
Street (on the way to the Gloucester Tree) issues entry permits to nearby national
parks, but you can also pay on entry.

In Dickinson Street, the excellent **craft gallery**-cum-restaurant *Fine Woodcraft*
displays regional artisans' woodwork and other art, as well as a commendable dearth of
wombat tea cosies and similar tack. A fun way of seeing the surrounding forest is to
take the **tram** (☎097/76 1322) between Pemberton and Northcliffe (Tues, Thurs & Sat;
5hr 30min return, including photo stops); with less time, settle for the shorter trip to
Warren, which is the better half of the ride anyway (twice daily; 1hr 45min return). The
tram rattles along the old logging railway, over rustic timber bridges spanning tiny
creeks, and visits the local beauty spot, the **Cascades** (also accessible by road), a thoroughly enjoyable excursion.

The region's single most popular attraction is the **Gloucester Tree**, situated a clearly
signposted 3km southeast of town. At 61m high, its platform, accessible by climbing a
spiral of horizontal stakes, is the world's tallest fire-lookout tree. Only a quarter of visitors to the tree actually climb up to the platform – the climb itself is more satisfying than
the actual view – and those who do can have their efforts validated by a certificate available at the tourist office in town. The countryside all around is criss-crossed with peaceful
walking trails and enchanting forest drives cutting deep into the awesome karri woodlands. **Beedelup National Park**, on the Vasse Highway 20km west of town, has a short
walk to a single karri bridge over **Beedelup Falls**, while the drive through the native
karri forests of the **Warren National Park**, 10km southwest of town, will leave you in
awe of these huge trees flourishing in their natural environment.

The basic *YHA* at Pimelea (☎097/76 1153; ①), 10km northwest of town, is a rather
mozzie-ridden collection of timber **lodges**, offering bike and canoe rental, or there's
*Warren Lodge* (☎097/76 1105; ①), a similarly unrefined ex-mill workers' lodgings right
in town by the bus stop, but due for improvements. Otherwise, the surrounding countryside abounds in tranquil woodland retreats, such as *Pump Hill Farm Cottages*
(☎097/76 1379; ⑤), 2km west of town, or *Karri Valley Hideaway Cottages* (☎097/76
2049; ⑥), 20km west. *Forest Lodge* (☎097/76 1113; ④–⑦), with a range of accommodation, is just a couple of kilometres from town, while the *Tammeron Motor Hotel* on
Widdeson Street (☎097/76 1019; ⑤) provides conveniently situated rooms in town.
Campers can stay at the town's central **caravan park** (☎097/76 1300; on-site vans ③)
or **camp** at any of the CALM-approved sites in the surrounding forests. For fresh country **food**, including local trout and marron (freshwater crayfish), try the *Shamrock*
restaurant for a $25 splurge, or the less extravagant *Cloe's Kitchen* up the hill.

Thirty kilometres south of Pemberton is **NORTHCLIFFE**, a small, untouristed
logging town of little interest to passing visitors. Southwest of the town is the long
spread of coastal heathland and inland dunes comprising the **D'Entrecasteaux
National Park**: it's barely accessible, although *Southern Forest Adventures* (☎097/761
1222) offers 1–5 day 4WD tours which include parts of the park in their itinerary.
**Windy Harbour**, 30km south of Northcliffe, is the only point between Augusta and
Walpole, to the southeast, where non-4WD vehicles can get down to the ocean.
Limestone cliffs dip briefly here to a couple of exposed white beaches and a basic
**campsite** (free), usually occupied by fishermen.

# Albany and the Rainbow Coast

The alternating sheltered bays and rugged headlands of the **Rainbow Coast** around **Albany**, WA's original colonial settlement, have been gentrified by semi-retired pastoral yuppies with cultivated tastes and a yen for alternative lifestyles. As throughout the Southwest, the temperate climate creates a rural antipodean-English idyll unknown elsewhere in WA – and comforting to mother-country migrants.

Albany, 410km from Perth, is promoted as a mildly sophisticated holiday destination, while **Denmark**, 54km to the west, is a twee, arty hamlet with **Walpole's** bays and karri forests marking the Rainbow Coast's limit. An hour's drive north of Albany are the up-and-coming wine-making region of **Mount Barker** and the fine hiking opportunities of the **Porongurup and Stirling Range national parks**. A visit to this region from Perth is ideally included in tour of the whole of the Southwest over a pleasant and varied week.

Perth's radial **bus services** to the main centres are regular, but moving around requires careful planning to avoid inconvenient delays. *Westrail* buses depart from Perth for Albany at least twice daily, either directly down the Albany Highway (6hr) or four times a week via Bunbury and, twice weekly, via Pemberton (8hr). Car or motor-bike rental, or shared lifts, are clearly a better option and **tours**, while having a breath-less, see-it-all pace, will indeed show you it all, however briefly.

## Albany

In 1826, two years before the establishment of the Swan River Colony, the British sent Major Lockyer and a team of hopeful colonists to settle the strategic **Princess Royal Harbour**. It was a pre-emptive response to French exploration of Australia's Southwest and the small colony, originally called Fredrickstown, was allowed to grow at a natural pace – avoiding the vicissitudes of Swan River Mania that plagued Perth's early days. Prior to the building of Fremantle Harbour in the 1890s, **ALBANY** was a key port on the route from England to Botany Bay, a coaling station in the age of steamers; it was also the last of Australia many Anzacs saw on their way to Gallipoli in 1914.

Now serving the southern wheat- and sheepbelt, Albany has become the focus of intensive hype as WA's latest hot-spot: weekending proximity to Perth, moderate summer temperatures, a surfeit of natural splendour and historical kudos all combine to make an agreeable and genuine destination, largely bereft of bogus tourist traps.

### Arrival and information

*Westrail* **buses** arrive near the old train station on Lower Stirling Terrace, site of the **tourist office** (Mon–Fri 8.30am–5.30pm, Sat & Sun 9am–5pm; ☎098/41 1088) which dispenses handy local and regional sketch **maps**. *Loves Bus Service* (timetables at the tourist office, or call ☎098/41 1211) offers in-town **public transport**: the #301 route between York Street, the town's main road, and Middleton Beach/Emu Point is useful (Mon–Fri 9am–3pm, Sat 9.15–11am).

### Accommodation

Albany offers several guesthouses, as well as the customary range of along-the-highway motels and self-contained units found in the Middleton Bay area, 3km east of the centre. In the countryside, farmstays mix with classy cottages and other pastoral hideaways. The tourist office has a detailed photographic portfolio of the town's accom-modation options.

*HOSTELS AND GUESTHOUSES*

**Albany Backpackers**, corner of Stirling Terrace and Spencer St (☎098/41 8848). Lively alternative to the YHA, with plenty of activities. Rooms ③, dorms ①.

**Albany Colonial Guest House**, 136 Brunswick Rd (☎098/41 3704). Nice old house with unmatching furniture and a resident ghost. ④.

**Discovery Inn**, 9 Middleton Rd (☎098/41 3160). An especially agreeable old guesthouse and restaurant, close to Middleton Beach. ④.

**Middleton Beach Guest House**, 18 Adelaide Crescent (☎098/41 1295). The most inexpensive guesthouse in Middleton Beach area. ③.

**Norman Guest House**, 28 Stuart Terrace (☎098/41 4995). Plusher sort of guesthouse, close to town, with disabled access and bright rooms. ⑤.

**YHA**, 49 Duke St (☎098/41 3949). Traditionally-run hostel, popular with families and backpackers, offering good service and with relatively painless 5-minute chores. ①.

## SELF-CONTAINED UNITS AND MOTELS

**Albany Channel Resort**, 3 Mermaid Ave, Emu Point (☎098/44 1136). Superbly-equipped apartments with sea views from *both* sides – book well ahead. ⑦.

**Coraki Holiday Cottages**, Lower King River, 11km east of town (☎098/44 7068). Great value cottages in their own gardens by Oyster Harbour (minimim stay of 2 days). ⑤.

**Dog Rock Motel**, 303 Middleton Rd (☎098/41 4422). Good-value place with restaurant, close to town and shops. ⑤.

**Dolphin Lodge**, 1 Golf Links Rd, Middleton Beach (☎098/41 6600). Popular family units. ⑥.

**Flinders Mews**, 5–7 Flinders Parade, Middleton Beach (☎098/41 8757). Luxury two-storey units facing the beach. ⑥.

**Middleton Holiday Units**, 6 Garden St (☎098/41 4080). The least expensive units in Albany, opposite park. ④.

**Travel Inn**, 191 Albany Highway (☎098/41 4144). Albany's best motel, with large comfortable rooms. ⑥.

## CARAVAN PARKS

**Emu Beach**, Emu Point, 7km from town centre (☎098/44 1147). Not a bad spot to park up for a few days, with trampolines and mini-golf. On-site vans ③, cabins ④.

**Middleton Beach**, Flinders Parade, Middleton Beach (☎098/41 3593). Right on the weekend-posing drag and sometimes windy beach. On-site vans and cabins ③.

**Mount Melville**, 22 Wellington St (☎098/41 4616). Has a useful camp kitchen and is just 1km from town. On–site vans ③, chalets ④.

# The Town

Albany's attractions are spread between the Foreshore, where the original colonists set up camp, and the beaches around **Middleton Beach** and Emu Point on the still waters of Oyster Harbour. Driving around the harbour leads to the nature reserve at Two Peoples Bay, 40km from town, while the features and attractions on the **Torndirrup Peninsula**, 20km from town, along Frenchman's Bay Road, should not be missed.

On the **Foreshore** there's a replica of the *Amity* (daily 9am–5pm; $1.50), the brig which landed its three-score colonists here on Boxing Day, 1826, after six months at sea. Nearby is the **Old Gaol** (daily 10am–4.30pm; $3), with the usual bare cells and barred doors. The **Albany Residency Museum** (daily 10am–5pm; free) is much more interesting, with meticulous displays of the town's maritime history, a section on Aboriginal bush medicines, an annexe with an obsolete lighthouse lens too good to throw away and, upstairs, an educational see-and-touch gallery for kids.

They've gone a bit over the top with telecom-memorabilia at the **Inter Colonial Communications Museum** (Mon–Sat 10am–4pm, Sun 2–4pm; free) in the **Old Post Office** on Stirling Terrace, Albany's most striking building, wasted on displays of "dialling tones and switchboards through the ages". In Duke Street, next to the YHA, is Albany's oldest building, the **Patrick Taylor Cottage Museum** (daily 2–4.15pm; $1.50), jammed to its 1832 rafters with period knick-knacks.

## Towards Middleton Beach

The curious tower on top of **Mount Melville Lookout**, off Serpentine Road, is colloquially known as "the spark plug". One of two lookouts in Albany, this one offers the better maritime vista. From here, backtrack to York Street, turn left and head 2km down Middleton Road to **The Old Farm**, Strawberry Hill (daily 10am–5pm; $2.50; closed June), tucked behind modern houses in its own enchanting gardens. Reminiscent of an English cottage, the farm (WA's first) provided the colonists with fruit and veg, while the 1836 building here housed visiting Governor Stirling and today offers Devonshire teas and displays of domestic accoutrements.

**Middleton Beach** is dominated by Albany's pride and joy, the prestigious *Esplanade Hotel* with the **Extravaganza Gallery** (daily 9am–5pm summer; 11am–4.30pm winter; $5) round the back. Connoisseurs of all things classic and beautiful will appreciate this fine collection of art and crafts, wine and classic cars – all of it for sale.

From the gallery, head up Marine Drive and turn right towards **Mount Clarence Lookout**, with its ANZAC memorial and, on a clear day, a view as far as the Stirling Ranges, 80km to the north. On the way down you pass **The Forts** (daily 9am–5pm; $3), an impressively restored naval installation dating from the end of the last century.

## The Whale Museum and Torndirrup National Park

Southeast of town, Frenchman Bay Road curls round Princess Royal Harbour to **Whaleworld** (daily 9am–5pm, tours on the hour 10am–4pm; $5.50), site of Australia's last whaling station until operations finally ceased in 1978. The informative, hourly tours begin with a gory video and move on to the crude and sickening whale-dismembering machinery and towering *Cheyne IV* whale chaser, before an upbeat, eco-ending in the skeleton shed.

Returning along the peninsula, check out the view at **Stony Hill** but give the feeble **blowholes** a miss – they're a washout unless the wind and swell are aligned just right. **The Gap** and **Natural Bridge** are well worth a look, however; there is something mesmeric about watching the Southern Ocean pound into the Gap's boxed walls and rebound, frothing, in all directions, while the Natural Bridge satiates the "freak of nature" brigade. This area has claimed several lives, most claimed by **king waves** that well up onto the continental shelf, just 30km offshore here; play it safe, and don't walk under the bridge.

## Eating

Fortunately, Albany echoes the Southwest's laudable preoccupation with quality eating; several independent restaurants fill the gap between fast-food franchises and dreary motel dining rooms in a most appetizing way.

**Al Fornetto**, York St (☎098/42 1060). Steak and seafood *al Italiano* as well as pizzas from $10. Daily 6pm–late.

**Café Bizzare**, Sterling Terrace. Trendy interior overlooking the bay, and meals for around $15. Wed–Sun 11.30am–late.

**Cravings**, Mermaid Ave, Emu Point (☎098/44 1111). Popular *smorgasbord* place right by Emu Beach, with good-value seafood and chips next door. Daily 5.30pm–late.

**Dylan's on the Terrace**, 82 Stirling Terrace. Burger and pancake dispensary, good for early breakfast. Mon–Sat 7am–midnight, Sun 7am–10pm.

**Food Station**, Lower York St. Cafeteria with daily specials around $9. Best of the fast and fluorescent joints. Daily 8am–9pm.

**Genevieves**, *Esplanade Hotel*, Flinders Parade, Middleton Beach (☎098/42 1711). Fine dining from $25, at the hotel that changed Albany's image. Daily 8am–late.

**Kookas**, 204 Stirling Terrace (☎098/41 5889). Quaintly restored old house for gourmet dinners at around $25 a head. Tue–Sat 11.30am–late.

**Savannah's**, 14 Peels Place. Meals and snacks with African themes and flavours for around $10. Mon & Tue 8.30am–5pm, Wed–Sun 7.30am–late.

## Listings

**Banks** Most branches are along York St.

**Bus** *Westrail* (☎098/41 0464).

**CALM** 44 Serpentine Rd (☎098/41 7133). Information and pamphlets on local national parks.

**Post office** Corner of Grey and York streets (☎098/41 1811).

**Shopping centre** At the junction of Albany Hwy and Lockyer Ave.

**Taxi** ☎098/44 4444.

**Tours and cruises** *Escape Tours* (☎098/41 2865) have day and half-day minibus tours around the region; *Bushed* (☎098/42 2127) has adventure activity tours; *Silver Star Cruises* (☎098/41 3333) has cruises in King George Sound.

# Along the Rainbow Coast

**West of Albany**, West Cape Howe National Park is a coastal wilderness best suited to exploration by 4WD, while William Bay National Park, west of Denmark, has many inviting coves accessible to regular vehicles. Just before Walpole, the Valley of the Giants is a stand of huge tingle trees, marking the edge of the timber country. *Westrail* buses run between Albany and Perth (via Bunbury) four times a week (Tues, Wed, Thurs & Sat) but you won't see much this way – renting a car or arranging a lift is a better bet.

### Denmark and William Bay National Park

**DENMARK**, set on the eponymous river that leads into Wilson Inlet, has been transformed into a cute little town, a great spot to enjoy a pleasant lunch, graze your way around some galleries, and stroll or boat up the river. If you want to get to the coast, give the anemic Wilson Inlet a miss and head west to the **William Bay National Park**, through the hills along **Shadforth Scenic Drive**. Once there, you'll find **Green Pool** to be one of the prettiest spots along the coast, with Madfish Bay and Waterfall Bay also worth a visit.

Denmark's **tourist office** (daily 9am–5pm; ☎098/48 1265) in Strickland Street can advise you of the array of places to **stay** all around. The *YHA* is essentially part of *Wilson Inlet Holiday Park* (☎098/48 1267; ①), 3km southwest of town; the pristine *Edinburgh Guest House & Backpackers* (☎098/48 1477; ②–③), right in town, is a much better bet. In the surrounding hills, try *Mount Shadforth Lodge* (☎098/48 1555; ⑦), 3km north of town; on the Inlet, *The Cove* (☎098/48 1770; ⑥) or *Tree Tops* (☎098/48 1265; ⑥) are both 4km south of town. For a **meal**, the natty *Fig Tree Bistro*, off Strickland Street, or the friendly *Blue Wren* on the main road, are good alternatives to fast food.

### The Valley of the Giants, Nornalup and Walpole

About 40km west of Denmark you can turn south to **Peaceful Bay**, a pleasant lunch stop with a **caravan park**, or turn north along Valley of the Giants Road, where another turn-off leads to the secluded *YHA* (☎098/40 8073; ①), off Dingo Flats Road. Even if you're fresh from the luxuriant rainforest over east, the short loop into the forest of massive tingle and karri trees, which make up the **Valley of the Giants**, will amaze you. **NORNALUP**, back on the highway, is remarkable for this area in that it has no art and craft outlets; even more refreshing, a track 6km west of town leads to the lovely **Conspicuous Beach**.

**WALPOLE**, 10km down the road, is the hub of many scenic drives to more soaring forests, oceanic lookouts and sheltered inlets. Light **meals** are served at *Anne's Pantry*, or try the café next to the *Glassblower's Gallery*. There are a couple of **caravan parks** on Walpole and Nornalup Inlets; for more creature comforts, try *Hideaway Cottage* (☎098/40 1138; ⑤), 10km north of town, or *Che Sera Sera Chalets,* 15km north (☎098/40 8004; ⑥). Backpackers are taken care of by *Tingle Budget Accommodation* (☎098/40

1041; ①) at the west end of town. Just east out of town you'll pass the turn-off to **Nuyts Wilderness,** where a number of walking trails pass through groves of jarrah and karri to secluded coastal coves at which camping is permitted.

From Walpole, the **South Western Highway** commences its scenic run northwest through more colossal forests to Northcliffe (100km) and Pemberton (138km) at the heart of the Tall Timber Country (see p.517).

## The Porongurups, the Stirling Ranges and Mount Barker

North of Albany are the ancient granite highlands of the Porongurups and the majestic 1000-metre Stirling Ranges, 40km and 80km from town respectively – both designated as **national parks**; CALM in Albany has further information and maps. To the west are the youthful vineyards of Mount Barker, whose viticulture potential has barely been exploited and which may one day merge with Margaret River as a homogeneous wine-making region. Several small **wineries** open their cellar doors for tasting and prospective purchases; details from the tourist office in Albany.

The **Porongurups,** said to be the oldest hills in the world, feature a dozen wooded peaks with bald summits of over 600m. The 15-kilometre-long ridge catches any coastal moisture to support its isle of karri forests, thereby leaving the loftier Stirlings to the north denuded of trees.

Most people are happy to do no more than take the five-minute stroll to the **Tree in a Rock**, a natural oddity near the park's northern entrance, but if you want to get your teeth into a good walk, head up the marked trail to **Devil's Slide** (671m) and, if you're up to it, return via Nancy and Hayward Peaks; the full route needs at least half a day, stout footwear, water and a hat. **Balancing Rock**, at the eastern end of the park, can be reached in forty-five minutes from the car park, with a cage on the exposed outcrop of Castle Rock providing safe viewing. There's no camping in the park, but half a dozen establishments offer **accommodation** close to the northern entrance, among them the *Porongurup Caravan Park* (☎098/53 1057; on-site vans ③) and the nearby *Karribank Lodge* (☎098/53 1022; ④), an inexpensive guesthouse.

### The Stirling Ranges
Taking the Chester Pass Road northward towards the looming **Stirlings**, the distinctive profile of Bluff Knoll will hopefully reveal itself from the cloudbanks which often obscure its summit. Avid hillwalkers could spend a few days "peak-bagging" here and come away well satisfied – the mild weather makes the Stirlings WA's best mountain-walking area, although five peaks are over 1000m and sometimes receive winter snow. Less strenuous activities are also catered for: the unsealed 45-kilometre Stirling Range **scenic drive** winds amid the peaks to Red Gum Pass in the west, where you can turn round and reverse the drive (with superior views) or continue down to Mount Barker. **Bluff Knoll**, the park's highest and most popular ascent, has a well-built path involving a three-hour-return slog. The weather can often surprise you from the unseen, south-east side: no matter how hot you feel, take a jumper for the summit. Better views can be had looking onto the park's eastern summits from the west: **Talyuberup**, halfway along the scenic drive and around 800m high, is a short, steep ascent to magnificent views, while **Toolbrunup** (1052m) is among the harder climbs in the park, with some exposed scrambling – allow a tough half-day, there and back. Many other **trails** wander between the peaks and could link up into overnight walks. Before heading off, discuss your plans with the **ranger** (☎098/27 9230 or 9278), at his residence by the park campsite off Chester Pass Road.

There are basic facilities at the **campsite,** or much better options at the *Stirling Range Caravan Park* (☎098/27 9229; on-site vans ②, chalets ① per person or ④ sole-use), just outside the park's northern boundary, opposite the Bluff Knoll turn-off.

## Mount Barker

MOUNT BARKER is at the centre of a small wine-growing region and makes a pleasant day out from Albany, driving around the lanes sampling the fruits of the vine. There are six wineries around the town and a couple more near Porongurup. **Plantagenet Wines** (Mon–Fri 9am–5pm, Sat & Sun 10am–4pm; ☎098/51 2150) on Albany Highway, is the region's most established, and undertakes bottling for the lesser wineries in the vicinity. The atmosphere is courteous and amiable, with tastings as well as informal behind-the-scenes **tours**. Wine-tasting apart, Mount Barker, on the old mail-coach route between Albany and Perth, is just another country town, although **St Werburgh's Chapel**, built in 1873 on a hillside a few kilometres west of town (get directions from the **tourist office**, 57 Lowood Rd; ☎098/51 1163) is worth a look – an unexpected relic of Mount Barker's god-fearing pioneers.

# The Wheatlands

WA's **Wheatlands**, the Wheatbelt, is a region of intensive grain agriculture and sheep pastures extending from the southwestern coast into the arable areas north of the Great Eastern Highway. The greatest interest this area holds for the visitor is some unusual granite rock formations, of which **Wave Rock** near Hyden, 340km from Perth, is the best known. The names of the desolate farming communities often end with the letters "-in", as prolific as the ending "-up" in the Southwest: both are thought to be an Aboriginal suffix meaning "place of water".

### Narrogin and Katanning

Many visitors pass through the eastern Wheatbelt on their way down the **Albany Highway** or its parallel alternative, the **Great Southern Highway**, to Albany. The former is a direct route to the Rainbow Coast, with few notable distractions, while the latter emanates from the top of the Avon Valley and winds its way casually south to the two highways' confluence, 90km north of Albany.

There's not much to stop for along the way. In **NARROGIN**, 192km from Perth, an old school has been turned into the **Old Courthouse Museum**, a collection of rural pioneering artefacts. The **Axe Handle Factory** (☎098/83 6075 to visit) is fascinating by comparison, displaying a selection of axe handles hand-made from local wood – the only place of its kind in WA. Eleven kilometres east of town on the Harrismith Road are **Yilliminning** and **Birdwhistle Rocks**, picnic spots on the way to **Albert Facey's Homestead** (daily 9am–5pm; ☎098/82 7040), 39km from Narrogin. The late Albert Facey's autobiography (and subsequent TV mini-series) *A Fortunate Life* is a self-effacing account of his life's few ups and repeated downs, endured with the stoic fatalism of a true Aussie "battler", an appellation reserved for the likes of Facey. The homestead conveys those hard times with authentic paraphernalia, as well as a range of locally-made craftwork. **Overnight stays** in Narrogin are catered for at the *Narrogin Motel,* 56 Williams Road (☎098/81 1660; ⑤), west of the town centre, or at *Stoke Farm* (☎098/85 9018; B&B ⑥) at Highbury, 16km south of town.

You can hardly fail to notice the seven-metre-high giant merino ram as you drive through **WAGIN**, 38km south of Narrogin, reason enough to keep going. A further 56km south of Wagin, **KATANNING** is a late nineteenth-century farming centre on the mail route from Albany to Perth. The **Old Mill**, on the corner of Clive Street and Austral Terrace, houses the **tourist office** (☎098/21 2634), although the town is better known for the mosque serving its Muslim Community from Christmas Island – an Australian protectorate south of Java. Adults can regress deliriously in the **All Ages Playground** nearby, a collection of oversize playground equipment and a miniature railway. The *Katanning Motel* (☎098/21 1657; ⑤) in Albion Street offers **accommoda-**

tion and a BYO restaurant; the *Katanning Caravan Park* on Aberdeen Street (☎098/21 1066) looks after campers.

### Hyden and Wave Rock

Perhaps WA's best known natural oddity is **Wave Rock**, 3km from the tiny farming settlement of **HYDEN**, at the eastern edge of the Wheatlands. At 15m high and 110m long, the formation resembles a breaking wave, an impression enhanced by the vertical water stains running down the overhanging face. While the rock, formed by wind and rain, is certainly unusual, its spell wears off within minutes and it's not worth the commonly undertaken day-trip from Perth unless you like sitting on a bus all day. Even as a diversion south of the Great Eastern Highway (Merredin is 185km away and Southern Cross 178km), its appeal is dubious. Along the base of the rock a marked, twenty-minute trail leads to another outcrop, **Hippo's Yawn**, while 21km from Wave Rock, on the way to Southern Cross, **Bates Cave** features Aboriginal hand paintings.

Hyden offers a **tourist information** service (☎098/80 5182) and you can **spend the night** at the *Wave Rock Caravan Park* (☎098/80 5022; on-site vans ③, chalets ④). Back in Hyden, there's *Diep's B&B,* 17 Clayton Street (☎098/80 5179; ④) or the *Hyden Hotel* in Lynch Street (☎098/80 5052; ⑤).

# Esperance and the South Coast

The town of Esperance, 721km southeast of Perth, is at the western end of the **Archipelago of the Recherche**, both town and archipelago named after French ships which visited the area in the late eighteenth century and whose persistent nosing around precipitated the hasty colonization of WA by the British. The archipelago is a string of haze-softened, grey granite isles bobbing in the inky blue Southern Ocean, presenting an almost surreal seascape common to coasts washed by cold currents. The mild summer weather (rarely exceeding 30°C), fishing possibilities and surrounding national parks make the town a popular destination for heat-sensitive holidaymakers.

Southeast of Esperance are **Cape Le Grand** and the much less visited **Cape Arid National Park** on the edge of the Great Australian Bight, while 130km north of town is the undeveloped Peak Charles National Park – a hill in the middle of nowhere. Back towards Albany, the **Fitzgerald National Park** offers a wilderness of rare flora. Care should be taken all along this restless coastline, as **king waves** (unexpectedly huge waves indistinguishable in the swell) frequently sweep away fishermen and clamberers from exposed, rocky headlands.

You can get to Esperance from Kalgoorlie with *Westrail*'s **bus service** (Mon, Thurs & Sat; 5hr) or direct from Perth (four weekly; 10hr). Albany, nearly 500km to the east along the South Coast Highway, can only be reached direct on Mondays and Thursdays (change on Wed & Fri). Arranging a **lift** in Albany from fellow travellers is a feasible alternative. *Skywest Airlines* (☎09/334 2288, 08/9334 2288 from Sep 1997) flies to Esperance and back every morning and evening (1hr 50min).

## Esperance and around

The town of **ESPERANCE**, which prospered briefly as a supply port during the heyday of the Eastern Goldfields, was revived after World War II when its poor soils were made fertile with the addition of missing trace elements. Now an established farming and holiday centre, the town lacks the charm promised by its name, but makes an ideal base from which to enjoy a westward exploration of WA's often spectacular and storm-washed southern coast.

Dempster Street is the town's main road and site of the arts-and-crafts vending cabins which comprise the **Museum Village**. Nearby, the actual **museum** (daily 1.30–4.30pm; $2), on James Street, is a much better than expected repository of local memorabilia – diverse enough to momentarily engage most visitors. It's very proud of its *Skylab* display: the satellite disintegrated over Esperance in 1979 and NASA were reputedly fined $400 for littering.

Besides a walk along the Norfolk Pine-lined Esplanade and a round of mini-golf, that's your lot in Esperance, so rent a bike or a car and head out along the 36-kilometre **scenic loop** west of town. Travelling clockwise, you'll come first to the **Rotary Lookout** (following a mean climb for cyclists), which overlooks the captivating seascape. You'll spot the **windfarm**, a modest experiment in alternative energy generation, on the way to **Twilight Beach**, an idyllic and sheltered spot, much prettier than the town's exposed beaches. From here it's more windswept grandeur to **Observation Point Lookout** and a free (nudist) beach, before the road turns inland towards **Pink Lake**, sometimes luridly so-coloured by salt-tolerant algae, whose marine cousins give the coastline its enchanting turquoise hue.

The hundred or so islands of the romantically-named Archipelago of the Recherche, known as the **Bay of Isles** around Esperance, are chiefly occupied by colonies of seals, feral goats and multitudes of seabirds. Dolphins may also be seen offshore and Southern Right Whales are commonly observed migrating to the Antarctic in spring. *Mackenzies Island Cruises*, 71 Esplanade (☎090/71 1772), have got a spiffing new boat and depart on some cruise or another every day at 9am (depending on numbers), with the possibility of overnight stays on **Woody Island** (summer only), which is equipped with enough facilities to cast yourself away in comfort.

## Cape Le Grand and Cape Arid national parks

A visit to **Cape Le Grand National Park** ($5 per car) is well worth the expense of renting a car or taking a tour; it's essentially a climb up a hill and a beach-hop – but they're the sort of beaches you want to roll up and take home with you. Once in the park, the climb to the summit of **Frenchman's Peak** (262m) is not as hard as it looks, and well worth the half-hour's exertion in a sturdy pair of shoes. The secret of the distinctive, hooked summit is an unexpected hole which perfectly frames the impressive view out to sea. Just after the Frenchman's Peak turn-off, a track leads to **Hellfire Bay**; sheltered coves don't come any more perfect than this. From here you can take a tough, three-hour walk to **Le Grand Beach** (limited camping; water) to the northwest or a less demanding two-hour trek to **Thistle Cove**, from where an easier trail leads to the broad arc of **Lucky Bay** (camping and water), with more sheltered swimming and unbelievable colours. **Rossiter Bay** is distinctly scungy by comparison and not worth the corrugations.

If you're still having trouble getting away from it all, keep heading east to **Cape Arid National Park**. This is best explored in a 4WD, but ordinary cars can make it as far as **Yokinup Bay**, **Thomas River** and **Sandy Bight**, where there's camping; all visitors must carry their own **fresh water**. East of the park is **Israelite Bay**, well worth a visit if you've come this far, with another impossibly blue beach, the remains of an old telegraph station and a track up to Balladonia on the Eyre Highway, which blasts its way to South Australia (see p.533 for details of this route).

## Practicalities

*Westrail* buses stop in the town centre, with **taxis** available on ☎090/71 1782. The **tourist bureau** (Mon–Fri 8.45am–5pm, Sat & Sun 9am–5pm; ☎090/71 2330), in the Museum Village, Dempster Street, provides detailed town maps and takes care of bookings for local tours and onward travel. The **post office** is on the corner of

Dempster and Andrew streets, with a **shopping centre** up Andrew Street, over the roundabout. CALM (☎090/71 3733) at 92 Dempster Street provides information on the national parks around Esperance. **Bicycles** are rented out along the Esplanade from *Wilds Jet Ski Hire* (Dec–March daily 8.30am–5pm; $12–15 per day; jet ski $1 per min), with a rattier but cheaper selection of cycles from the *Captain Huon* motel. For inexpensive **car rental**, ask at the *YHA*. The *Diving Academy* (☎090/71 5111), along the Esplanade, takes care of **diving** charters, courses and refills, while *Vacation Country Tours* (☎090/71 2227) offer half-day **tours** to Cape Le Grand (Tue & Sun; $25, including lunch), and *Safari Wheels* (☎090/71 1564) take care of more active pursuits along the coast. Both hostels (see below) also have 4WDs to take informal runs along the coast if there's enough interest.

There's plenty of choice **places to stay** around town, although the self-contained units will almost certainly be booked out during school holiday periods. Besides the counter lunches at the *Pier* and *Esperance* hotels, there are a couple of interesting **restaurants** to match the mouth-watering seascapes.

## ACCOMMODATION

**All Seasons Holiday Units**, 73 The Esplanade (☎090/71 2137). The cheapest units in town and fully equipped; book ahead. Each unit sleeps a maximum of four. ④.

**Bayview Motel**, Dempster St (☎090/71 1533). Motel with some self-contained units, which sleep up to four. ⑥.

**Captain Huon**, 5 The Esplanade (☎090/71 2383). Excellent small motel with some self-contained units and bike rental. ⑥.

**Crockers Park Caravan Park**, Harbour Rd (☎090/71 4100). Well-tended but 3km from town. On-site vans ③, cabins ④.

**Esperance Backpackers**, 14 Emily St (☎090/714 724). Nicely converted house with 20 beds and all mod cons. ①.

**Esperance Bay Caravan Park**, corner of Esplanade and Harbour Rd (☎090 71 2237). So close to town you feel like you're camping in someone's garden. On-site vans and cabins ③, chalets ⑤.

**Esperance Shire Caravan Park**, Goldfields Rd (☎090/71 1251). The best choice for camping close to town and the beach.

**Hospitality Inn**, The Esplanade (☎090/71 1999). Rooms with air-conditioning, to ride the occasional heatwave. ⑤–⑥.

**Old Hospital Motel**, William St (☎090/71 3587). Boutique establishment which offers an antidote to motel sterility with considered and tasteful decor. ⑤.

**Orleans Bay Caravan Park**, Cape Le Grand National Park (☎090/75 0033). Located at Duke of Orleans Bay, reached along a turn-off about 88 km from Esperance, this site is ideal for those in search of seclusion. On-site vans ②, cabins ③–④.

**YHA**, Goldfields Rd (☎090/71 1040). Barrack-like hostel facing the bay that's rather unusually *too big* for comfort. Free use of bikes. ①.

## RESTAURANTS

**The Gray Starling Restaurant**, southern end of Dempster St (☎090/71 3187). Attractive and relaxing interior with tasty menu – one of the best eating spots in town. Daily except Wed from 6pm and Sun 11.30am–3pm.

**Peaches Restaurant**, *Bay of Isles Motel*, 32 The Esplanade (☎090/71 3999). Top quality à la carte cuisine for around $20 a meal and with a view to match. Daily 6–9pm.

**Savoury's Country Cuisine**, Dempster St. With a name like that what else can you expect but wholesome country tucker; good for cheap lunches.

**Spice of Life**, Andrew Street. The quest for original names for vegetarian cafés continues. Daily 9am–6pm.

**Village Café**, Museum Village. New venue to indulge one's offspring over seafood and chips. Daily 9am–5pm.

## Esperance to Albany

From Esperance, the **South Coastal Highway** leads 479km to Albany with just a couple of small farming settlements along the way; a fairly dull day's drive with only the military museum and rabbit-proof fence at Jerramungup to perk you up. If you're not in a hurry, turn south along a network of dirt roads, just after **Stokes Inlet National Park**, popular with beach fishermen and waterfowl alike, to Hopetoun on the coast. East of here is the mountainous eastern edge of the Fitzgerald River National Park which can be traversed to **Bremer Bay**, a peaceful resort a couple of hours' drive from Albany. The RAC "Bremer Bay – Hopetoun" map covers the area in excellent detail.

**RAVENSTHORPE** is a former mining (and presently farming) town, 186km along the highway west of Esperance. **Accommodation** options here include the good-value *Palace Motor Hotel* (☎098/38 1005; ④, with breakfast), right in town, or the caravan park at the east end of town. Grab a **snack** at the *Ravensthorpe Country Kitchen* (daily 9am–8pm) on the main road at the east end of town. There's a good route from here to **HOPETOUN** with a scenic diversion up Ethel Daw Drive. A picturesque holiday and fishing spot, Hopetoun is most usefully a place to get into the adjacent national park. If you need to stay overnight, the best deals are at the *CWA Cottages* (☎098/38 3128; ③) in Canning Street or the cushy **caravan park** in Spence Street (on-site vans ③). Otherwise, pamper yourself at the *Hopetoun Motel* (☎098/38 3219; ④) in Veal Street, and tuck in at the rather pleasant *Starboard Café* (BYO or takeaway; 7am–2pm & 4–8pm) right in the middle of town.

Just outside Hopetoun, a road leads east, across the causeway separating the ocean from Culham Inlet – where explorer Eyre observed Aborigines fishing in 1841 – and up towards **East Mount Barren**. This marks the eastern edge of the **Fitzgerald River National Park** ($5 entry per car), one of two parks in WA designated by UNESCO as a world heritage biosphere. Nearly two thousand species of wildflowers are protected in the park, including the curious, flame-like hakae and scores of orchids, seventy of which are found nowhere else in the world. Access is limited due to the presence of the tropical fungus known as dieback, the root-rotting spores of which are easily spread by wheels and boots. Four-wheel drives can reach the sea at **Quoin Head** and camping for all is provided at **Mylies Beach**, at the foot of East Mount Barren. In the western half of the park, **Point Ann**, 64km south of the **ranger's residence** (☎098/35 5043) along Quiss Road, is the spot to head for; the magnificent view across the sea alone is worth the corrugations. Think twice before descending the sandy track to the campsite here if you're by yourself in a 2WD.

# The Eastern Goldfields

Five hundred kilometres east of Perth, at the end of the **Great Eastern Highway**, lie the **Eastern Goldfields**. Just over a century ago, gold was found in what still remains one of the world's richest gold-producing regions. Lack of fresh water made life very hard for the early prospectors, driven by the national economic depression into miserable living conditions, disease and, very often, premature, unmarked graves. Nevertheless, boom towns of thousands, boasting grand public buildings, several hotels and a periphery of hovels, would erupt and collapse in the length of time it took to extract any payable ore.

In 1892 the railway from Perth reached **Southern Cross**, just as big finds turned the rush into a national stampede. This huge influx of people worsened the water shortage, until the visionary engineer C Y O'Connor constructed a 556-kilometre **pipeline** from Mundaring Weir (see p.509) that finally reached Kalgoorlie in 1903. By this time many of the smaller gold towns were already in decline, but the Goldfields' wealth and boost in population finally gave WA the economic autonomy it sought in its claim to statehood.

In the years preceding the goldrush, the area was briefly one of the world's richest sources of **sandalwood**, an aromatic wood greatly prized throughout Asia. Supplies in the Pacific had become exhausted so that, by 1880, the perfumed wood was WA's second-largest exportable commodity after wool. Exacerbating the inevitable over-cutting came the goldrush's demand for timber to prop up shafts or to fire the pre-pipeline water desalinators. Today the region is a pit-scarred and prematurely deserti-fied landscape, dotted with the scavenged vestiges of past settlements.

The Goldfields are centred around the rich reef of gold adjacent to the reluctantly twinned towns of **Kalgoorlie–Boulder**, with Kalgoorlie being the thriving, energetic core. This prosperous town's unexpected vitality is accentuated by stagnating or decay-ing settlements all around it: adjacent Boulder and **Coolgardie** to the west, and the semi-abandoned communities and **ghost towns** in the desert to the north.

Even if you're not expecting to pass through the Goldfields, a couple of days based in Kalgoorlie are well worth an excursion from Perth – if nothing else, for the novelty of riding on the **Prospector**, the daily rail link between Perth and Kalgoorie, which stops off at all towns along the highway. Buses depart with similar regularity and a visit to the Goldfields can be undertaken as part of a 2000-kilometre loop along WA's south-ern coast, making use of Perth's inexpensive car rental agencies. The *Streetsmart* "Goldfields Touring Map" is highly recommended, especially if you're thinking of exploring the area north of Kalgoorlie.

## The Great Eastern Highway

Heading from Perth to the Goldfields, there's precious little to detain you until you reach Coolgardie. **MECKERING**, 132km east of Perth, was destroyed by an earth-quake in 1968 and a gazebo off the main road commemorates the event. **CUNDERDIN**, 24km further east, has a pioneering **museum** (daily 10am–4pm; $2), housed in one of the eight steam pumping stations that once propelled the water to Kalgoorlie at a little over one-and-a-half kilometres per hour. **KELLERBERRIN**, not far from Cunderdin, was one of the earliest settlements along the Great Eastern Highway, and dates from 1861. It also has a **museum** (Mon–Fri 8.30am–5pm; $2), set in a historic building, and inexpensive **rooms** at the *Ampol Roadhouse Motel* (☎090/45 4007; ④) on the Highway. **MERREDIN** is a bigger wheat and wool town than most, with a **museum** (daily 9am–3pm; $2) housed in an old railway station, built from bricks of Kalgoorlie clay that are said to contain gold of mineable grade.

East of Merredin the country becomes drier and, by the time you get to **SOUTHERN CROSS**, 370km from Perth, the Wheatbelt is behind you. It was here in 1887 that small traces of gold precipitated the country's largest and most fruitful goldrush, and with the arrival of the railway in 1892, the town became a jumping-off point for the greater finds to the east. Nowadays Southern Cross has that moribund feel so familiar to rural settlements with prosperous pasts; the disproportionately wide streets, common to all the goldrush towns, allowed camel trains to turn round. Local goldrush history is described in the **Yilgarn History Museum** (Mon–Sat 9am–noon & 1.30–4pm, Sun 1.30–4pm; $1) in Antares Street, while **accommodation** is available at the *Southern Cross Motel* (☎090/49 1144; ⑤) in Canopus Street and the *Southern Cross Caravan Park* (☎090/49 1212; on-site vans ③), on the eastern edge of town.

## Coolgardie

Rather too sanitized and intact to carry the name "ghost mining town", **COOLGARDIE** is more of a museum to itself, a town which, at its peak, had twenty-three hotels, three breweries and six newspapers serving a population ten times greater than its present 1500. Arthur Bayley increased the pitch of the gold fever when he returned to Southern Cross – then the easternmost extent of the rush – in 1892 with nearly 16kg of gold. The ensuing wave of prospectors started within hours and culminated in a fourfold increase in WA's population by the end of the century.

Coolgardie is best reached from Perth by the daily *Greyhound.Pioneer* or *Westliner* **bus services**, as the train now stops at Bonnie Vale, 14km north of town. Alternatively, during school term time, you can visit the town from Kalgoorlie with *Goldenlines* (Mon–Fri departs Kalgoorlie 7.10am, returns around 4pm; $2.75; ☎090/21 2655). Kalgoorlie-based *Goldrush Tours* (☎090/21 2954; Tues & Fri mornings; $29) also offers half-day tours to Coolgardie.

## The Town and around

The imposing **Wardens Court Building** in Bayley Street is a good point from which to start an appraisal of Coolgardie's numerous gold-boom relics. The building houses the **tourist office** (daily 9am–5pm; ☎090/26 6090) and has one of the most extensive provincial **museums** (daily 9am–5pm; $2.50) in WA, filling the grand upper floors with an especially comprehensive collection of bottles. It rewards a prolonged browse, giving you a feel for the dramatic effect the goldrush had on the area.

Outside the museum is an index to the 155 **historic markers** set around the town, and right opposite you can't miss the varied miscellany and just plain old junk comprising **Ben Prior's Open Air Museum** (always open; free). Half a kilometre up Hunt Street, at the end of McKenzie Street, **Warden Finnerty's Residence** (Mon–Sat 1–4pm, Sun 10am–noon & 1–4pm, closed Tue; $2) is the finely restored 1895 residence of the man whose unenviable job it was to set the ground rules for mining at the height of the rush.

On the way back to Bayley Street, a left down Woodward Street leads to the **Railway Station Museum** (daily 9am–5pm, closed Fri afternoon; donation welcome), housed in a station used until 1971, when the railway was rerouted north of town. Featured is the drama of the 1907 Varischetti mine rescue and the story of the once-thriving sandalwood industry.

Other attractions around Coolgardie include the **cemetery**, west of town, and the **Coolgardie Camel Farm** (daily 9am–5pm; $2, yard rides $3.50, 1hr, day- and overnight treks from $20 for a minimum of two people, booking essential; ☎090/26 6159), a couple of kilometres further west, which describes the crucial role camels played in the years before the arrival of the railway.

## Practicalities

Coolgardie has no banks although there is a cash machine in the *BP* service station on Hunt Street; the **post office** is around the corner. The cheapest **accommodation** in town is the large old house run by the *YHA* (☎090/26 6051; ①), on the corner of Hunt Street and Gnarlbine Road, or try the *Goldrush Lodge* (☎090/26 6446; rooms ④, dorms ①), at 75 Bayley Street. For greater comfort, the *Caltex Roadhouse Motel* (☎090/26 6049; ⑤) and the *Coolgardie Motor Inn* (☎090/26 6002; ⑤) are at the west and east ends of Bayley Street, respectively. There are two **caravan parks** just west of town with on-site vans (②–③).

When it comes to gourmet restaurants, Coolgardie earns its ghost town appellation with ease. For light **meals**, try *Aunt Jessie's Café* opposite the *Goldrush Lodge* or the *Premier Café* (Mon–Sat 7.30am–8pm, Sun 8.30am–7pm), opposite the tourist office. For something more substantial, the *Coolgardie Motor Inn*'s restaurant (daily 6–8pm) or the outdoor one at the *Coolgardie Motel* (daily 6–8.30pm; ☎090/26 6080), opposite *Prior's Museum* in Bayley Street, are the only alternatives to foraging in the bush.

# Kalgoorlie–Boulder

**KALGOORLIE**, recently twinned (municipally, if never emotionally) with its sister town **BOULDER**, has an idiosyncratic appeal similar to places like Coober Pedy (in South Australia) or Las Vegas. All three seem to disregard their isolation and bleak surroundings, so devoted is their attention to the pursuit of earthly riches – in Kalgoorlie's case, **gold**.

In 1893 **Paddy Hannan** (then 53 years old) and his mates, Tom Flannigan and Dan O'Shea, brought renewed meaning to the expression "the luck of the Irish" when a lame horse forced them to camp by a tree which still stands at the top of Egan Street. With their instincts highly attuned after eight months prospecting around Coolgardie, they soon found gold all around them: as the first on the scene, they enjoyed the unrepresentatively easy pickings of surface gold. Ten years later, when the desperately-needed water pipeline finally gushed into the **Mount Charlotte Reservoir** (which, incidentally, affords a good viewpoint over the town), Kalgoorlie was already established as the heart of WA's rapidly growing mineral-based prosperity. Today, as sole survivor of the original rush, and revitalized by the 1960s nickel boom, Kalgoorlie has benefited from new technology that has largely dispensed with slow and dangerous underground mining. Instead, the fabulously rich "**Golden Mile**" reef east of town – which Boulder was originally built to serve – is being devoured wholesale by machinery and explosives to create the vast, open-cast "Super Pit".

Proud of its history, isolation and continued prosperity, Kalgoorlie is known as one of the most parochial towns in a country that's full of them. Sophistication in "Kal" is a fully clothed barmaid and, once the superb **architecture** and history have been appreciated, it is this crassness, in tandem with a cultural curiosity that gets only as far as the video store (or, of course, the pub), that leaves some visitors, especially single women, feeling distinctly uncomfortable.

Start your tour of the town by taking a walk up to the top of Hannan Street, where the bright red headframe cannot have failed to attract your attention. This is the impressive entrance into the **Museum of the Goldfields** (daily 10am–4.30pm; free), right next to the spot where Paddy and his crew found their first, auspicious nuggets. Inside is a modern display of Goldfields artefacts and history, with the very stuff that keeps the town going viewable in the basement vault. Aboriginal history and the sandalwood industry are also covered in this excellent introduction to the area, and there's a lookout over town from the top of the headframe. Next door is the **British Arms** pub, now a coffee shop but better known as Australia's narrowest pub.

**Hannan Street** itself is one of Kalgoorlie's finest sights, with its superbly restored turn-of-the-century architecture, imposing public buildings and the numerous flamboyant hotels. You're welcome further to appraise the grandiose interior of the **Town Hall** (Mon–Fri 9am–4pm; free), with its spendid hall and less impressive art gallery. It's only when you stop to reflect that this is a remote, hundred-year-old town in the west Australian desert that the stunning wealth of the boom years, however transient, is brought home to you. Outside, a replica of the bronze **statue** of Paddy himself invites you to drink from his chrome-nozzled waterbag – the much vandalized original is inside the Town Hall.

The **School of Mines Museum** (Mon–Fri 10am–4pm; free), on the corner of Egan and Cassidy streets, perhaps outstrips most visitors' enthusiasm, with its vast display of minerals and replicated nuggets; just over the road, in Maritana Street, is the stop for the Boulder-bound bus.

## Boulder and further afield

Boulder, 5km south of Kalgoorlie, is much quieter and smaller – a place to visit rather than stay in. One glance down **Burt Street** reveals that it's very much Kalgoorlie's poorer sister, although this is not an observation to make at the top of your voice in the dingy interiors of the local pubs. Originally set up as a separate settlement to serve the Golden Mile, Boulder's heyday passed as Kalgoorlie's suburbs seeped towards it.

Bou'.der has a similar collection of grand old buildings, with, again, the pubs, especially the *Cornwall*, *Grand* and deliciously ramshackle *Metropole*, a delight to look at if not to drink in. One thing worth coming to Boulder for is a ride on the **Golden Mile Loopline**. Departing daily (Mon–Sat 10am & 12.45pm, Sun 3pm; $8; ☎090/93 3055) from the former train station at the top of Burt Street, the "Rattler", as it is known, once delivered workers to their pits and served all shifts round the clock. Now it will take you on a one-hour circuit of the Super Pit.

Just north of town are a couple more attractions without which a visit to Kalgoorlie–Boulder would not be complete. **Hannan's North Tourist Mine** (daily 9.30am–4.30pm; $14; ☎090/91 4074) is an old mine now transformed into a mining theme park. From the gloomy interior of a tent an amusing, video-faced mannequin of the venerable Mr Hannan cheerily regales you with the details of his fortuitous "stroike", while the forty-minute, ex-miner-guided underground tours are probably as long as you'd want to spend down a mine – especially when you're given a brief demonstration of the pneumatic "air leg" drill. Allow about two and a half hours for your visit.

Back on the Menzies Road, follow the "Two Up" signs a short distance to Kalgoorlie's once-clandestine and, since 1983, the country's only legal **Two Up School**, 7km from town. Two Up is, more or less, a game of "heads or tails" played with two pennies. In the decidedly functional "galvo" arena, the deadly serious and utterly absorbed gamblers bet on how the pennies will land – each double tails (or "white cross") result punctuated by the exchange of fistfuls of notes. It sounds simple and you are welcome to join in ($10 minimum stake), but to most outsiders the proceedings are totally baffling. Gambling commences daily (except on fortnightly paydays) from 3.30pm till dusk, with no under-18s or alcohol allowed within 100m.

## Practicalities

*Westliner* (☎1800/19 9649) and *Greyhound.Pioneer* (☎090/21 7100) buses arrive outside Kalgoorlie's **tourist office** (Mon–Fri 8.30am–5pm, Sat & Sun 9am–5pm; ☎090/21 1966), 250 Hannan Street, which has informative sketch maps pinpointing and describing the town's dispersed attractions. The **post office** is at 204 Hannan Street, Kalgoorlie's main thoroughfare, where most of your needs will be met. The **train station** (*Westrail*; ☎090/21 2923) is 500m down Wilson Street from its junction with Hannan Street. Taxis (☎090/21 2177) meet incoming trains.

A local **bus service** operates between the two towns (Mon–Sat, 8am–6pm; $1.20), with timetables available from Kalgoorlie's tourist office or the Town Hall. **Car rental** (*Hertz*, 71 Maritana St; ☎090/91 2625) is expensive, but rented **bicycles** (*Johnstons Cycles*, 78 Boulder Rd; ☎090/21 1157) might be useful for exploring the sights around the Golden Mile as far as the Two Up School. *Goldrush Tours'* (☎090/21 2954) daily "Kalgoorlie–Boulder" tour is recommended, visiting many of the places mentioned above and offering discounts on *Hannan's North* underground tours.

## *ACCOMMODATION*

Although it's unlikely that Kalgoorlie will maintain your interest for more than a couple of days, the town does get busy with holidaymakers in the winter school holidays, when it's best to check availability in advance. The many splendid-looking hotels along Hannan Street deteriorate alarmingly inside, but they all offer inexpensive rooms with either shared or en suite facilities. The backpacker revolution hasn't hit Kal yet; instead guesthouses patronized by all types of thrifty travellers and itinerant workers offer twin-bed rooms, but no kitchens.

**Cornwall Hotel**, 25 Hopkins St, Boulder (☎090/93 2510). Yet another fabulous-looking old hotel with a dark history and an outdoor restaurant. Shared bathrooms. ⑤.

**Exchange Hotel**, 135 Hannan St (☎090/21 2833). Skin-deep beauty but good-value rooms. ④–⑤.

**Golden Village Caravan Park**, 406 Hay St (☎090/21 4162). Closest to town. On-site vans ②.

**Hannan's View Motel**, 430 Hannan St (☎090/91 3333). Good-value motel units with pool, cheap breakfasts and some wheelchair-accessible, self-contained units. ⑥.

**Midas Motel**, 409 Hannan St (☎090/21 3088). Top-of-the-range motel with nightclub, pool and the excellent *Amalfi* restaurant. ⑦.

**Prospector Caravan Park**, Great Eastern Highway, 3km west of town (☎090/21 2524). Excellent park with pool, playground, kitchen and grassy sites. Cabins ④.

**Surrey House**, 9 Boulder Road (☎090/21 1340). Guesthouse offering cheap breakfasts and a TV room. ②–③.

**Windsor House**, 147 Hannan St (☎090/21 5483). Better equipped guesthouse (behind the jewellers) with shared bathrooms, kitchen and TV room. ②.

**York Hotel**, 259 Hannan St (☎090/21 2337). Probably the best-looking facade in Hannan St. Shared bathrooms but rates include breakfast. ⑤.

*EATING AND DRINKING*

An unpretentious outback town hundreds of kilometres from the nearest fresh tomato isn't the place to look for gourmet delicacies. Instead, treat yourself to a good old **counter meal** for around $10 at any of the pubs, or try *Basil's*, 268 Hannan Street, for Italian homestyle cooking and something to read or the *Kalgoorlie Café* (10.30am–3pm & 6pm–1am) on the other side of the road, which has more of a family atmosphere. *Health Works*, 75 Hannan Street, caters for veggies. Next door is the *Top End Thai* (6pm–late; ☎090/91 4027), a rare, exotic treat at around $15 a meal, or there's the *Main Reef Bistro*, 32 Dwyer Street, for Italian, seafood and *smorgasbords*, and *De Benares*, 193 Hannan Street, for a $15 steak in comfortable surroundings. Topping the bill and emptying the wallet is the *Midas Motel*'s restaurant, the *Amalfi* (☎090/21 3088).

You'll need a couple of weeks if you plan to have a drink a night at every licensed establishment in Kalgoorlie–Boulder (if you're going to go for it, ask about the "Kal pub crawl" T-shirt at the tourist office). The roughest of the rough is the *Federal*, right at the top of Hannan Street, with the *De Benares' Tavern*, Hannan Street, making the brave transformation into a wine bar, with dress regulations for customers *and* staff. In between you can take your pick from the *Exchange*'s dreary interior, livened up with bands on Thursday nights; the *Palace*'s more formal atmosphere; or the *York*'s pleasant balcony overlooking the street life below.

# North of Kalgoorlie-Boulder

North of town a number of isolated communities supporting either small mining operations or rural Aboriginal communities stretch along a sealed road (bar a short section north of Leinster) to Meekatharra, 726km from Kalgoorlie and half way up the Great Northern Highway. This arid and sparsely populated region has nothing to offer visitors other than prime chunks of WA's Outback: dust, heat, flies, treacherous salt lakes, more flies, and towns in varying stages of atrophy. It's worth knowing that most **ghost towns** in this area, especially the ones closer to Kalgoorlie, are mere stumps of long-since ruined buildings, surrounded by decidedly un-ghostly rubbish. The desperate shortage and expense of building materials in the Goldfields ensured that any useful structure which fell into disuse was quickly scavenged for use elsewhere.

From **LEONORA**, a sealed road also branches northeast to Laverton where the **Warburton Road**, a corrugated but straightforward Outback track (not to be confused with the unmaintained Gunbarrel Highway) leads 1160km to Ayers Rock Resort (see p.480). The time taken to obtain **permits** to pass through Aboriginal Land in both WA and NT (usually quicker from the Alice end) is what dissuades most people from undertaking this route. Apply to the *Aboriginal Affairs Planning Authority*, 35 Havelock Street, West Perth 6005 (☎09/483 1333, 08/9483 1333 after Sep 1997) and the *Central Lands Council*, 33 Stuart Highway (PO Box 3321), Alice Springs 5750 (☎089/52 3800, 08/8952 3800 after April 1996).

*Westliner* (☎09/250 2838, 08/9250 2838 after Sep 1997; or Kalgoorlie tourist office) runs **buses** as far as **LEINSTER** and **LAVERTON** twice a week (Thurs & Sun overnight from Perth, 4hr from Kalgoorlie, returning Mon & Fri mornings), stopping on the way at **MENZIES** and Leonora.

### Broad Arrow and Ora Banda

Just north of Kalgoorlie the two ghost towns of **BROAD ARROW** and **ORA BANDA** (respectively 38km and 66km from Kalgoorlie) can make a satisfactory nibble into this area, especially if you complete the 185-kilometre loop (100km of corrugated dirt) back to Kalgoorlie via Coolgardie. Broad Arrow is just a couple of dilapidated shacks and a **pub** covered with inane graffiti (to which you are most welcome to contribute) and is popular with weekending Kal–Boulderians looking for a change of scenery. The historic *Ora Banda Hotel* (☎090/24 2059; ⑤) is built of stone rather than the more usual galvanized iron, and has recently been rebuilt. There's an old stamp battery nearby and the track continues back south to Coolgardie, passing the abandoned townsites of Kintore and Kununalling.

# The Eyre Highway to South Australia

South of Kalgoorlie, the twin-centred town of **KAMBALDA** on the shores of the salty, recreational Lake LeFroy, is experiencing its second boom, this time in nickel, after gold reserves expired in 1906. There's nothing here you haven't already seen in Kalgoorlie, so rejoin the Great Eastern Highway and continue south to Norseman, at the western end of the **Eyre Highway**. The highway is named after the explorer John Eyre, who crossed the southern edge of the continent in 1841, a gruelling five-month trek which cost his companion's life and would have cost his own but for help from Aborigines in locating water. Eyre crawled into Albany on his last legs but set the precedent for future crossings, the telegraph and, most recently, the highway.

**NORSEMAN** was named after a prospector's horse which kicked up a large nugget in 1894 – a real case of lucky horseshoes – and now a bronze statue of Norseman stands proudly on the corner of Roberts and Ramsay streets. Arrivals from South Australia may be eager to pick up their "I crossed the Eyre Highway" certificate from the **tourist office** (daily 9am–5pm; ☎090/39 1071) in Roberts Street. There are also public showers and a swimming pool next door in which to further celebrate this achievement, or perhaps a meal and an overnight stay at either the *Great Western Motel* (☎090/39 1633; ⑥), at the north end of Princep Street, or the *Norseman Eyre Motel* (☎090/39 1130; ⑤), opposite. More modest accommodation is available at the **caravan park** next to the *Great Western* (on-site vans ③), or there are basic rooms at *Lodge 101* (☎090/39 1541; ①) nearby. If you're in a quandary about which route to take **onwards to Perth**, the inland road, after a stop in Kalgoorlie–Boulder, is fast and fairly dull while the coast road can be made into an enjoyably scenic dawdle of at least a week.

Following the Eyre Highway, it's about 730km to the South Australian border and another 480km from there to Ceduna, where the bleak **Nullarbor** section ends. That still leaves 800km before you reach Adelaide – a solid two days' drive of legendary monotony. Although the road has been sealed for over twenty years and the longest fuel-less stage is only around 200km, do not underestimate the rigours of the journey in your own vehicle. Carry reserves of fuel and water, take rests every three to four hours and beware of kangaroos and other beasts, especially between dusk and dawn. There are no banks between Norseman and Ceduna, and both towns have a quarantine checkpoint for the large range of prohibited animal and vegetable goods which must be discarded there.

**BALLADONIA**, 193km from Norseman, is the first settlement on the way to the border, with the *Balladonia Motel* (☎090/39 3453; ⑤) and adjacent caravan park your choice for an overnight stop. Then, 200km further, mostly along a 145-kilometre section of dead-straight road, you reach **CAIGUNA** (motel and caravan park; ☎090/39 3459; motel units ⑤, on-site vans ②) and, after another 66km, **COCKLEBIDDY**. On the coast near here, 16km east of town and 32km south of the highway on a 4WD track, are the remains of an old telegraph station that once linked WA with the rest of Australia and which today houses the *Eyre Bird Observatory* (accommodation, with prior notice only, ⑥, plus $25 for pick-up and return; ☎090/39 3450). Overlooking **Twilight Cove** on the Great Australian Bight, this is a paradise for twitchers. **MADURA**, 92km east of Cocklebiddy, is home to the *Madura Hospitality Inn* (☎090/ 39 3464; ⑤), while **MUNDRABILLA**, 116km east of Madura, has a combined motel and campsite, the *Mundrabilla Motor Hotel* (☎090/39 3465; motel units ④, cabins ②).

**EUCLA**, just 12km from the border, was re-established up on the escarpment after sand dunes exposed by overgrazing engulfed the original settlement by the sea. Only 4km away, the old telegraph and weather station are still visible above the sands, an eerie sight well worth a stroll. From the **Eucla National Park**, the vertical cliffs can be seen extending eastwards for hundreds of kilometres along the South Australian coast. Eucla has a **caravan park** and the *Amber Motel* (☎090/39 3468; ③–⑤); right on the border, there's the inspiringly named **Border Village** (☎090/39 3474; ④).

For the South Australian section of this route, turn to p.624.

# FROM PERTH TO KUNUNURRA

The 4400-kilometre haul up Western Australia's arching coastline to Broome, across the Kimberley and on to Darwin in the Northern Territory, is one of Australia's great road journeys. Even without detours it's a huge, transcontinental trek between the country's two most isolated capitals, fringing the barely inhabited wilderness that separates them. From the **WA/NT border** 40km east of Kununurra, it's still 730km to Darwin; this final stretch, along the Victoria and Stuart highways, which meet at Katherine, is covered on pp.446–453.

If any single trip across Australia benefits from independent mobility, it's this one: a car enables to you explore intimately or linger indefinitely. While some days in WA's **Northwest** will be punctuated by nothing more than road trains and roadhouses, there are several places where the climate, scenery and ambience will collectively conspire to subdue your road fever for a few days. If you're interested in discovering the wayside attractions, allow at least four weeks for the journey right through to Darwin; otherwise a week to ten days will let you whizz through the highlights.

The route is sealed all the way, but a glance at any map clearly shows the long distances between roadhouses, let alone settlements. Your vehicle should be in sound condition with particular reference to tyres and the cooling system, both of which will be working hard in the heat and dirt-road detours of the Northwest. If you're undertaking the trip in summer, once you get north of **Exmouth** you can expect storms, flooding and even cyclones. Following damage, roads and bridges on Highway 1 are repaired amazingly quickly, but if rain persists, routes can be impassable for weeks at a time. A **radio** is an indispensable aid to keeping track of cyclones, similarly troublesome "rain-bearing depressions" and the status of roads. With forewarning, it's usually possible to gun ahead of a front or find somewhere agreeable to sit out the storm.

If you don't have a car, the rigid schedules and limb-numbing sectors of long-distance **bus** travel require a certain equanimity. *Greyhound.Pioneer* offers a range of good-value **regional passes**, including the "Western Explorer" (Perth–Darwin) and the "Pearl Diver" (Perth–Broome). It should be noted that by doing the journey *from* Perth, schedules generally match connections to places off the highway with little delay. In the opposite direction, you are travelling "against the flow" of the timetable and can expect long waits on roadhouse forecourts unless heading directly back to Perth.

# Up the Coast to Broome

Ironically, nowhere along the 2400-kilometre drive along the North West Coastal Highway to Broome will you glimpse vistas of frothing surf breaking temptingly onto golden beaches and the taste of salt in the air. The highway takes a more sheltered inland course, and even access to the ocean is limited by the existence of private land, not to mention the sheer impenetrability of some of the terrain. The myth of beach-camping your way up a deserted coast is unfortunately just that, but there are enough attractions to make up for this deficiency. High points along the route include the spooky monoliths or **Pinnacles** of the **Nambung National Park** near Cervantes, the idyllic resort of **Kalbarri**, and the amicable dolphins of **Monkey Mia**. Further north, the **Ningaloo Reef** running down the North West Cape should not be missed, while a detour into the highlands of the **Pilbara** will make **Broome's** serene charm all the more delectable.

## The Brand Highway

Travelling the **Brand Highway**, there's an all-but-obligatory detour to view the remarkable Pinnacles in **Nambung National Park**, 250km from Perth. A young crayfishing town, beaten by strong winds in summer, **CERVANTES** is the closest overnight stop: there are two caravan parks, with tent sites and on-site vans (②) or, for greater comfort, the *Cervantes Pinnacles Motel* (☎096/52 7145; ⑤). Minibus **tours** of the park leave daily (1pm plus 9.45am & 4.15pm, depending on demand; $12 plus $2 entry fee; ☎096/52 7041) from the *Pinnacle Country Café,* which is also the **tourist information centre** (daily 8am–6pm), next to the *Shell* service station.

Otherwise, entry into the park (no camping) is $5 per car. There's access to the ocean at **Kangaroo Point** and **Hangover Bay** but the **Pinnacles** are the main attraction: a forest of phallic limestone columns up to 4m high, formed by subsurface erosion and since exhumed from their sandy tombs by the perennial southwesterlies. A three-kilometre loop drive winds right among them, but even the laziest will find it hard not to park and wander around this eerie expanse, sometimes enhanced by a "mist" of fine, windblown sand. Most tours from Perth arrive around midday, missing the evening sun's long shadows which add still further to the Pinnacles' photogenic qualities. When the novelty fades, you can always repair to the vast tracts of beach hidden behind spectacular sand dunes along this stretch of coast.

After the Pinnacles there's really very little of interest until you get to the tiny coastal resort of **GREENOUGH**, 400km north of Perth. **Greenough Historical Hamlet** (daily 9.30am–4.30pm; $2.50 including guided tour; ☎099/26 1140) is an unusually well-restored nineteenth-century farming community that would make an ideal period-film location. Up the road you'll see Greenough's strange **leaning trees** – some bent almost flat against the ground by the prevailing salt-laden winds – the imposing three-storey bulk of **Clinch's Mill**, the **Pioneer Cemetery**, and the **Pioneer Museum** (daily except Friday 10am–4pm; $1.50; ☎099/26 1058), recording the area's heritage.

On the west side of the highway, more of Greenough's relics include the *Hampton Arms*, privately restored into a delightful **guesthouse** (☎099/26 1057, ⑤, with breakfast and lunch) and **restaurant** (daily noon–2pm, 7pm–late), which make a welcome rustic change from anodyne motels. The *Greenough Rivermouth Caravan Park* (☎099/21 5845) is a better-than-average facility offering tent spaces, on-site vans (③) and cheap fuel, but the nearest backpackers' **hostel** (☎099/27 1581; ①) is at 32 Waldeck Street, Dongara, 40km to the south.

# Geraldton

**GERALDTON** isn't much to look at, being larger and more industrial than you might have expected, a crayfishing, mining and pastoral centre with towering portside wheat silos. In fact it's the state's third-largest city, at the centre of the **Batavia Coast**, named after the Dutch shipwreck of 1629, and a popular winter resort as well as being a world-renowned mecca for **windsurfers**.

The **tourist office** is in the *Bill Sewell Complex* (Mon–Fri 8.30am–5pm, Sat & Sun 9am–4.30pm; ☎099/21 3999) on Chapman Road, 2km north of town. *Greyhound.Pioneer* **buses** arrive here daily and *Westrail* buses alight at the old train station, just down the road. The modern town has little of interest bar one of the two museums and the extraordinary cathedral. The **Maritime Museum** (Mon–Sat 10am–5pm, Sun 1pm–5pm; free) in Marine Terrace, by the yellow submarine (an aborted crayfishing venture), focusses on the fascinating tragedy of the *Batavia* and the many other shipwrecks off the treacherous Batavia Coast, as well as describing the contemporary "treasures" of the crayfishing industry.

The completion of the **St Francis Xavier Cathedral** in Cathedral Drive, built over a 25-year period and completed in 1938, was the crowning glory of Monsignor John Hawes' career. A qualified architect before taking up the cloth, there are half a dozen examples of his unique Romanesque-Byzantine architectural style in the vicinity, of which the cathedral is his masterpiece, just as stunning and bold inside as out. If you're sufficiently impressed, ask about the **John Hawes Heritage Trail** at the tourist office (see below) which leads you around some of his other works.

These apart, the city's **beaches** aren't particularly attractive and are often windy, like much of the west coast below the tropics. There's the obligatory **Old Gaol**, now a craft centre, next to the *Bill Sewell Complex*, and a **lighthouse** at Point Moore, while the old **Keepers' Cottage** (Thurs 10am–4pm; donation welcomed), off Chapman Road, 5km north of town, is fastidiously maintained in its original state.

## Accommodation

**Batavia Backpackers**, *Bill Sewell Complex*, Chapman Rd (☎099/64 3001). Spacious and clean ex-hospital with wards for dorms, and more rooms planned. Rooms ②, dorms ①.

**Batavia Motor Inn**, Fitzgerald Street (☎099/21 3500). Good-value motel rooms. ⑤.

**Quality Inn Motel**, Brand Highway (☎099/21 2455). Customary motel chain comforts. ⑥.

**Peninsula Guest House**, 311 Marine Terrace (☎099/21 4770). Functional old hostel somewhat overshadowed by the arrival of *Batavia Backpackers*. ①.

**Sun City Guest House**, 184 Marine Terrace (☎099/21 2205). Family-run guesthouse in the middle of town supplies bed and breakfast and takes no nonsense. ②.

**Sun City Tourist Park**, Sunset Beach, 6km north of town (☎099/38 1655). Geraldton's best caravan park but rather a long way out. On-site vans ②.

## Eating and drinking

Geraldton has a fair selection of places to eat, and may be your last chance to sample a freshly-caught **crayfish** if heading north. For drinks and live bands, the *Geraldton Hotel* in Lester Avenue is the place to go, with the refurbished *Freemasons* in Marine Terrace offering a more refined alternative.

## THE HOUTMAN ABROLHOS ISLANDS

Seventy kilometres off the Geraldton coast is the archipelago of the **Houtman Abrolhos**, over a hundred sparsely vegetated islands barely above water, surrounded by a maze of reefs and channels.

While these are "desert islands" in the scientific sense, tropical and temperate currents mingle among them to create an unusual diversity of marine flora and fauna, offering some of the best **diving and snorkelling** along the west coast.

**Access** is limited to tours of various kinds: *Force Five Charters* (☎099/21 6416) have a superbly equipped vessel for charter, at a cost of $270 per person for a fully-inclusive weekend diving trip; *Biggals Cruises* (☎099/64 4668) have day-trips for around $100, including meals; and scenic flights over the islands are operated by *Shine Aviation Services* (☎099/23 3600), for a similar price.

**Fiddlers**, 103 Marine Terrace (☎099/21 6644). The best seafood in town, with main courses for around $15.

**Golden Coins**, 198 Marine Terrace (☎099/21 7878). Best Chinese around and noted for its big portions.

**Ocean Centre Restaurant**, Foreshore Drive (☎099/21 7777). Excellent seafood at similar prices and with a better view than *Fiddlers*.

**Manchu's Mongolian BBQ**, corner of Fitzgerald St and Lester Ave (☎099/21 8546). Serves fast and inexpensive stir-fried meat and vegetables with appropriately spartan, yurt-like interior.

**Skeetas**, George Rd (☎099/64 1619). Very popular garden restaurant, ideal for sunny salad lunches.

## On to Kalbarri

North of Geraldton, the North West Coastal Highway heads through **NORTHAMPTON**, an early lead-mining and pastoral settlement with a good caravan park and budget accommodation at the *Nagel Centre* (☎099/34 1488; ①), next to the church. At Northhampton you can deviate from the highway to investigate the tiny seaside resort and crayfishing port of **HORROCKS** (25km west), or **PORT GREGORY** (46km northwest, and where the bitumen finishes), with the nearby ruins of an aborted convict-hiring depot from the 1850s. Both towns have fine beaches, reefs offering sheltered swimming, and caravan parks. The main road to Kalbarri, however, is the 70-kilometre Ajana Road, heading west to the coast, a few kilometres after the Binnu Roadhouse.

## Kalbarri

Situated at the mouth of the Murchison River, whose sandbar shelters its beach, **KALBARRI** is the best of the west coast's resorts. Without so much as a dreary old jail to shuffle through, the small town is simply a great place to do as much or as little as you like. With the dramatic scenery of the Kalbarri National Park on its doorstep, few resorts can boast such an ideal location, together with good, inexpensive accommodation, and a host of activities.

The area's history holds a few wonders of its own. In the 1920s a stockman discovered the remains of a **castaway's camp** on the clifftops north of Kalbarri and excavation revealed the wreck of the Dutch trader, *Zuytdorp*, at the base of the cliff, but no human remains. The fate of the survivors had been a 300-year-old mystery until the diagnosis of the rare Ellis van Creveld Syndrome (endemic in seventeeth-century Holland) among children of Aboriginal descent suggested that some of the *Zuytdorp's* castaways carried the gene and passed it on during liaisons with local Aborigines.

## Arrival, information and getting around

Daily *Greyhound-Pioneer* **buses** from Perth drop passengers at the **Ajana turn-off** on
the highway, to be met by a shuttle bus on Mondays, Thursdays and Saturdays only.
*Westrail* buses from Perth come right into town on Monday, Wednesday and Friday and
return on Tuesday, Wednesday and Saturday. The **tourist office** (daily 8.30am–5.30pm;
☎099/37 1104) is in the Allen Centre in Grey Street, where many of the local activities
and tours can be booked. The small **shopping centre** in Porter Street includes a
bakery, supermarket and **post office**, with bank agencies and cash machines at various
outlets around town. *Suzuki* **4WD jeeps** can be rented from either *Kalbarri Hire Cars*
(☎099/37 1277) or the *Kalbarri Auto Centre* (☎099/37 1290), both in Sutherland Street.
Mileage is unlimited in the Kalbarri and national park area and the drive up the river to
Gregory's Rock will give you a chance to fiddle with the transmission levers.

## Accommodation

In the school holidays when Kalbarri is busy, most holiday units insist on a minimum
one-week's booking. If you are coming at this time, book ahead. *Kalbarri
Accommodation Service* (☎099/37 1072) rents out privately owned holiday homes.

**Kalbarri Backpackers**, 2 Mortimer St (☎099/37 1430). One of the best-run hostels in WA with
free use of bikes, barbecues and early-morning snorkelling runs. Mixed dorms ①, rooms ②, 2-
bedroom family units. ④.

**Kalbarri Beach Resort**, off Clotsworthy St (☎099/37 1061). Large resort with a pool, sauna and
the *Zuytdorp Restaurant* offers units sleeping up to five people. ⑥.

**Kalbarri Reef Villas**, Coles St (☎099/37 1165). Best value in town, with well-cared-for units, plus
pool, and free use of rowboat and bikes. ⑤.

**Kalbarri Seafront Villas**, 37 Grey St (☎099/37 1025). Well-equipped units, some with ocean views.
⑤.

**Kalbarri Tudor**, Porter St (☎099/37 1077). Best caravan park, close to shops. On-site vans, chalets
and cabins ③–④.

**Murchison Park**, Grey St (☎099/37 1005). Well-shaded park right opposite the Foreshore. On-site
vans ③.

**Murchison View Apartments**, corner of Grey and Rushton streets (☎099/37 1096). Quality 2- and
3-bedroom units with a pool and some sea views. ⑧.

**Sunsea Villas**, 18 Grey St (☎099/37 1187). Units overlooking the ocean and river mouth. ⑤.

## The Town and around

In town, Fantasyland ($2.50) houses a collection of dolls, gems and fossils and a simu-
lated mine downstairs, which may amuse pre-*Nintendo* kids; the owners also feed visiting **pelicans** most days at 8.45am. The **Kalbarri Entertainment Centre** (☎099/37
1105) in Porter Street has mini golf, trampolines and mini carts and also rents **bicycles**
for $8 a day. **Rainbow Jungle** (Tue–Sat 9am–5pm, Sun 10am–3.30pm; $5), 4km south
of town, is just the place to visit on a bike. A minor architectural work of art, heaving
with tropical fauna, it's a superb and imaginative display of stunningly colourful parrots
which includes a new walk-through aviary.

For those not content to laze on **Chinaman's Beach** all day, there are plenty of
more active pursuits on offer. An easy way to get moving is to take a **cruise** up the
Murchison River on the *Kalbarri River Queen* (☎099/37 1104) or rent all sorts of
**watercraft** on the Foreshore from *Kalbarri Canoe Safaris* (☎099/37 1245), which can
also take you up the lower Murchison to Gregory's Rock for a morning's downstream
canoeing, and a traditional bush breakfast on the way, for $35. *Big River Ranch* (4km
inland from Kalbarri, pick-ups available; ☎099/37 1214) offers very popular **horse-
riding** for beginners and experienced alike; the three-hour sunset ride, through the
river, along the beach and back again, is the highlight ($35). **Scenic flights** with
*Kalbarri Air Charter* (enquire at the gift shop, 28 Grey St; ☎099/37 1130) start from

just $24 for the short but spectacular Coastal Cliffs run, up to $129 for the Grand Tour or a five-hour visit to Monkey Mia. *Kalbarri Sports and Dive* (☎099/37 1226) can organize **dives** and refills, while the *Reef Walker IV* (☎099/37 1356) sets off on a variety of coastal cruises with diving or fishing opportunities.

## Kalbarri National Park

**KALBARRI NATIONAL PARK** ($5 entry per car), which surrounds the town, has two popularly visited areas: the serpentine **river gorge** of the upper Murchison River, reached off the Ajana Road east of town, and the **coastal gorges** created by lesser rivers, a few kilometres south of Kalbarri, just about within cycling range. *Kalbarri Coach Tours* (☎099/37 1104) visits both areas several times a week, for around $30, and they also have a range of more adventurous options.

The **coastal gorges** are accessible by tracks and short walks off the unsealed Kalbarri–Port Gregory road, which begins just before *Red Bluff Caravan Park*. **Red Bluff** is the prominent butte overlooking Jakes Corner (good surfing) and site of some barely discernible, prehistoric crustacean fossils. **Rainbow Valley** has some intriguing features exposed by weathering and a coastal walk up to **Mushroom Rock**, the most interesting part of the coastline. Pot Alley is another lookout and Eagle Gorge has a tiny secluded beach, but the view from the cliffs above **Natural Bridge** (at 16km, the furthest from town) gives the impression that you are poised on the edge of the world.

Eleven kilometres east of Kalbarri, a corrugated road turns north for 25km to the **gorge** along the Murchison River, where a junction leads on a few kilometres to either **the Loop** or **Z Bend**. It's possible to walk round the Loop (a horseshoe-shaped meander of the Murchison River) in rather less than the six hours suggested by the noticeboard, but this may be prolonged by the abundance of swimming opportunities, birdlife and the odd, mean-looking feral pig; the walk is best undertaken early in the morning. Z Bend is the most dramatic lookout over the Murchison River far below, accessible down a steep track. *Kalbarri Coach Tours* (see details above) offer canoe trips a few kilometres downstream from here, and *Kalbarri Safari Tours* (☎099/37 1632) offer a day-trek through the Murchison canyons for $30. You can also **abseil** down Z Bend's cliff; enquire at *Kalbarri Backpackers*. Back on the Ajana Road, heading inland for 30km from the Loop turn-off, **Hawks Head** and **Ross Graham Lookout**, both a few kilometres off the road, are less impressive but worth popping into on the way out of Kalbarri if you're driving.

It is possible to **walk** from Z Bend to the Loop over a couple of days and from Ross Graham Lookout to the Loop in four days, but both are demanding walks and you should inform the **park ranger** (☎099/37 1140) of your plans and safe return.

## Eating and drinking

Don't leave Kalbarri without checking out *Finlay's Fish BBQ* (daily 5.30–8.30pm; ☎099/ 37 1260), even though it's hard to find in Magee Crescent. With fresh fish, salad and damper for under $10, and a fine outdoor setting (plus occasional fireside bush balladeer), *Finlay's* on a balmy night is a treat.

All the other **restaurants** are rather ordinary by comparison. *Echoes,* in the shopping centre, is the town's best, with meals for $15; the *Zuytdorp* (6–10pm) at the *Kalbarri Beach Resort* is a close rival with $14 *smorgasbords*. The *Lure 'n' Line* (daily 10am–8pm) in Grey Street has views and seafood lunches, or try *Rivers Café* (daily 10am–8pm), opposite the wharf, for more fresh seafood and takeaways. *Kalbarri Pizza* (Tues–Sun 5.30pm–late), behind the *Gilgai Tavern* in Porter Street, serves average pizzas from $8, and there's a good health-food café inside the shopping centre.

Of the two **pubs**, the *Kalbarri Hotel* in Grey Street suits the locals, while the livelier *Gilgai Tavern* in Porter Street is where travellers congregate.

## Shark Bay

**Shark Bay** is the name given to the two prongs of land and their corresponding lagoons which comprise Australia's westernmost point. **Denham**, the only settlement, is on the west side of the Peron Peninsula, while at **Monkey Mia Dolphin Resort**, on the sheltered side of the peninsula, dolphins come in almost daily to meet and greet people, as they've been doing for the past 30 years. The shallow and clear waters of Shark Bay have earned it a world heritage listing as a remarkable ecological habitat, a fact that tends to be overshadowed by the over-hyped dolphin visitations. These particular dolphins are in fact not especially unique nor unusual; dolphins also "interact", albeit less reliably, at Bunbury, 180km south of Perth (see p.512).

**Getting there**, *Greyhound.Pioneer* runs all the way to Monkey Mia three times a week: if you plan to visit, make sure your pass includes this excursion. Otherwise, *Shark Bay Taxi Service* (☎099/48 1331) connects with interstate buses at the notoriously hot *Overlander Roadhouse*, which marks the turning off the highway to Shark Bay, charging $20 to Denham and $30 to Monkey Mia.

### The Road to Monkey Mia

It's 150km to Monkey Mia from the *Overlander Roadhouse*, a dull drive through dense mulga scrub punctuated with some unusual sights along the way. **Hamelin Pool** is home to a uniquely accessible colony of **stromatolites**, mats of sediment-trapping algae, one of the earth's earliest lifeforms, dating back over three billion years. The examples in Hamelin Pool, flourishing because no potential predator can handle the pool's hyper-saline water, are about 3000 years old and look rather like lumps of blackened concrete. The **Old Telegraph Station** (daily 8.30am–5.30pm; $2), 2km from the pool, has a display, video and pet "stromie" in a tank; altogether more interesting than

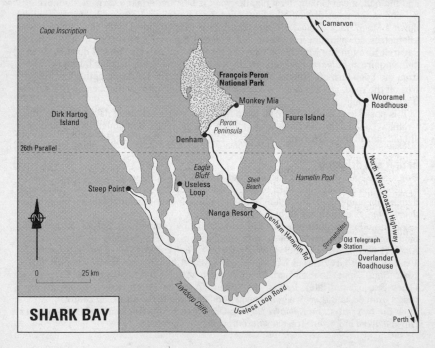

the things themselves. There are also some old telecommunications relics and a shop/ café with a small **caravan park** (☎099/42 5905; on-site vans ③).

Fourteen kilometres further along the Denham Road, a turn-off leads to the salt and gypsum workings at Useless Loop, and from there on to **Steep Point** (4WD only; $2 entry fee), Australia's most westerly mainland extremity. **Dirk Hartog Island**, off the north end of Steep Point, is where the first European is known to have set foot on what is now Australian soil, 150 years before Captain Cook; Dutch mariner Hartog left a pewter plate dated "Anno 1616" on the island. Continuing towards Denham, you'll pass *Nanga Bay Resort* (☎099/48 3992; dorms ①, cabins ④, units ⑤), a popular fishing spot but otherwise uninspiring, and **Shell Beach**, composed of millions of tiny shells several metres deep. Twenty kilometres before Denham, **Eagle Bluff** is an impressive clifftop lookout where dugongs, dolphins and manta rays may be spotted in the clear waters of Freycinet Reach below.

## Denham

A tiny prawning port and holiday resort, **DENHAM** thrives in the lee of Monkey Mia's indefatigable popularity. Between here and Monkey Mia (25km away), **François Peron National Park** is fully accessible only in a 4WD vehicle. The CALM office (☎099/48 1208) in Knight Terrace has more information about the park and other natural features in the Shark Bay area.

The **tourist office** (☎099/48 1253) is at 83 Knight Terrace, the town's main road, where there are also a couple of supermarkets and a post office. **Buses** for Monkey Mia leave daily at 8.45am and 3pm, returning half an hour later. The *MV Explorer* (☎099/48 1246; $40 upwards) operates **cruises** around Shark Bay, offering a good chance of seeing some of the clear-watered bay's submarine wildlife; private diving and fishing charters are also arranged. *Shark Bay Safari Tours* (☎099/48 1247; tours $35–100) offer 4WD **tours** around the whole Shark Bay area and also have rental cars. *Shark Bay Air Charter* (☎099/48 1284) and *Monkey Mia Air Charter* (☎099/48 1307) both offer **scenic flights**.

**Places to stay** include *Bay Lodge*, 95 Knight Terrace (☎099/48 1278; ①–③); with basic dorms, refurbished family units and a pleasant courtyard, it's the cheapest place to stay in Shark Bay. The *Tradewinds Holiday Village* (☎099/48 1222; ⑤) has units which sleep up to six people, and the *Heritage Resort* (☎099/48 1133; ⑦), on the corner of Durlacher Street, is the town's best with a very pleasant bar. Of the three **caravan parks** in town, the *Denham Seaside Caravan Park* (☎099/48 1242; cabins ③), at the top of Knight Terrace, is your best bet. Note that **water** is very precious in the Shark Bay area since rain rarely falls: salty bore water is used as widely as possible but locally desalinated, fresh drinking water is available at a tap next to the Shire Office at 42 Hughes Street.

The only notable **restaurant**, apart from the one in the *Heritage Resort,* is the *Old Pearler* opposite, built from shell block and with an attractive maritime interior; meals cost around $15. Other than that, there are a couple of cafés, a pizza bar and a bakery along Knight Terrace.

## Monkey Mia

> *One Japanese woman could not restrain herself. With a choking cry of "I love you, I love you", she leaped at a dolphin and threw her arms around it. The dolphin shrugged and slipped away.*
>
> *National Geographic*, January 1991.

After all the hype you might be pleased to find **MONKEY MIA** ($4 entry fee) nothing more than an attractive caravan park and a jetty by a pretty beach looking out over the inauspiciously named Disappointment Reach where thousands of people flock to witness the almost daily **dolphin** visits (usually between 8–10am). An interesting video and other related displays in the **Dolphin Information Centre** (daily 8am–6pm) explain how the entirely unprompted interaction began in the 1960s. Almost all that is known about dolphins has been gleaned from studies of Monkey Mia's regular troupe of visitors, each one known by name.

Unfortunately, as is so often the case, the place has become a victim of its massive popularity. Grumpy rangers bark instructions at the obediently timid crowd, select a lucky individual to pop a fish into a dolphin's mouth and keep a vigilant lookout for any breach in dolphin-watching etiquette. Furthermore, the dolphins' repeated visits and their spontaneous familiarity seem to take a toll on their wellbeing: due to diseases caught from humans, no cub has been successfully weaned for over a decade.

One of the best things to do at Monkey Mia is to take a ride on the *Shotover* catamaran around the bay: **cruises** start from just $14 for an hour, departing from the jetty at 9am, but the day-long tours are much more rewarding, with plenty of marine life (including prancing dolphins) to be observed and enjoyed.

The *Monkey Mia Dolphin Resort* **caravan park** (☎099/48 1320) is right on the beach: it has tent spaces, on-site vans (③), cabins (④) and caters for backpackers with large tents featuring bunk beds, lockable trunks and a basic kitchen (①). There is a pool and spa, a restaurant and a small shop with basic groceries and takeaways.

## Carnarvon and around

A centre for prawning fleets and the sheep stations of the Upper Gascoyne region, tropical **CARNARVON** also supports a large agricultural zone, thanks to the apparently dry Gascoyne River's retrievable subterranean water. The town is attempting to redress its heavy reputation for drink-related violence and crime by curbing anti-social behaviour and improving its appearance. Nevertheless, there is little here to interest the passing traveller: a tour of a banana plantation (try *Munro's*, 10km east of town on South River Road, daily 10am–4pm; $2), and a visit to the redundant OTC satellite dish which guided the early Gemini and Apollo space flights, is about as good as it gets.

A couple of diversions up the coast can add up to a fun day out, though. Six kilometres east of Carnarvon a ford crosses the riverbed and, passing the 65°C thermal well of **Bibbawarra Bore**, joins the sealed Blowholes Road, which leads to the **Blowholes** at Point Quobba, 65km from town. On all but the calmest days, incoming waves compress air through cavities and vents in the low cliff to erupt like geysers up to 20m into the air, a sight well worth the detour. A couple of kilometres to the south is a basic campsite (but no water) and sheltered snorkelling in the bay. Heading north past *Quobba Homestead* (camping, basic rooms ②) and occasional tracks down to shell-lined beaches, you cross the private road linking the Dampier Salt works at Lake MacLeod with the jetty at Cape Cuvier. Just north of the cape is the wreck of the *Korean Star*, beached here during a cyclone in 1988. It was here too that a "**fish feeding frenzy**" caught the world's attention in 1992 when several species of shark and whale appeared to co-operate in devouring a glut of small fry (see box on p.544). North of here is Red Bluff beach and *Gnaraloo Homestead* (camping), the domain of beach fishermen and hard-core windsurfers.

### Practicalities

The **tourist office** (daily 9am–5pm; ☎099/41 1146), at the end of Robinson Street, has information on tours into the surrounding countryside including Mount Augustus (see below). **Buses** also arrive here and the **post office** is right next door.

Recomended **accommodation** in town includes the *Gateway Hotel* in Robinson Street (☎099/41 1532; ⑤), with good-value rooms, a pool and restaurant; the *Hospitality Inn* (☎099/41 1600; ⑤) in West Street; or an attractive B&B called *The Outcamp* (☎099/41 2421; ⑤) at 16 Olivia Terrace overlooking the Fascine, as the foreshore is known. As for the **hostels,** the *Backpackers Paradise,* next to the tourist office (☎099/

41 2966; ①), has seen considerable improvements of late, and with a large kitchen, TV room, garden and ping pong, it's easily your best bet. There are no less than seven **caravan parks** within 5km of town, the *Carnarvon Tourist Centre* (☎099/41 1438; on-site vans ③), 500m up Robinson Street from the post office, being the most central.

Snacks and counter **lunches** can be found at the *Port* and *Carnarvon* hotels (the latter being the better bet for a trouble-free evening out) or at *JR's Lunch Bar*, all in Robinson Street. The *Harbourview Café* near the Small Boat Harbour south of town has good but pricey seafood and meagre milkshakes, or try the *Fascine Coffee Lounge*, next to the tourist office. If you're after an evening **meal** not based on the clichés of chicken, hamburger or pizza, check out the motels' restaurants or the *Dragon Pearl Chinese Restaurant* in Francis Street.

### Inland to Mount Augustus

East of Carnarvon, a dirt road follows the Gascoyne River inland, past the swimming hole of **Rocky Pool**, to **GASCOYNE JUNCTION**, a tiny, moribund settlement from the droving days, where the outlaw Ned Kelly (see p.741) was reputed to have once hidden out. The *Junction Hotel* (☎099/43 0504; ⑤) is a century-old relic with a small general store and fuel. Northwards, a road leads past the escarpment of the **Kennedy Ranges** whose fascinating canyons are accessible to regular cars. This is a slightly longer route to **Mount Augustus National Park** (also known as Burringurrah National Park) than continuing to the main access road another 215km away, but is well worth the detour.

**Mount Augustus**, the world's largest monadnock (a residual hill), is trumpeted as being bigger and older than Uluru (Ayers Rock) in the Northern Territory. While it hardly matches Uluru's elemental majesty, the drive there gives you a good feel for the Outback's dusty isolation and expanse. Camping and basic **accommodation** is provided at *Cobra Station Homestead* (☎099/43 0565; fuel, shop, closed Sat; cabins ④), 40km from the hill, or at the *Mount Augustus Outback Resort* (☎099/43 0527; fuel, shop; ③), right at the base, from where a day's hike to the summit can be undertaken. Mount Augustus is 450km from Carnarvon and 350km from Meekatharra on the inland highway. Whichever way you come, it's a long, hot drive on dirt roads, so be sure you and your vehicle are prepared for the trip. *West Coast Safaris* (see box on p.545) run four-day tours from Exmouth to this region on demand.

## The Northwest Cape

Six kilometres after the *Minilya Roadhouse* (dorms ①), renowned for its inhospitality to those waiting for buses, a turning splits off to the **Northwest Cape**. This hot and arid spike of land is notable for the **Ningaloo Reef** which fringes its western edge and is, in places, accessible right off the shore. Exmouth is the only settlement on the cape, but without your own transport the resort of Coral Bay is not only more convenient and more pleasant, but the easiest place from which to view the reef.

**Buses** leave from Carnarvon (Mon, Thur & Sat morning), stopping in at Coral Bay on the way to Exmouth before returning to Carnarvon each afternoon. If you're heading further north after an excursion to the cape, you might as well go all the way back to Carnarvon and catch the bus you'd otherwise wait for at *Minilya* – it's certainly more comfortable that way. It's also possible to get a seat on the nightly mail van going to *Minilya* (departs Exmouth 8.30pm; $10) to meet the southbound bus; and *Ansett* flies daily between Perth and Exmouth.

### Coral Bay

**CORAL BAY** is a tiny beach resort 14km off the Exmouth road and, school holidays excepted, is a lovely, quiet spot with a tropical-island feel to it – a good place to rest up for a couple of days. At present the resort is little more than three caravan park/motels,

## SEX AND FOOD ON THE REEF

**Sex** on the reef is a spectacular, yet strangely impersonal, affair: around the time of full moon in March/April, the **corals** off Exmouth all spawn simultaneously, releasing huge clouds of sperm and eggs, which are fertilized as they mingle in the waters above the reef. The perpetuation of life on this scale makes it an incredible event to witness – all the better at night because, lit by divers' flashlights instead of filtered sunlight, the polyps appear in their true, vivid colours. As a side-effect, the spawning creates a largesse of food that attracts marine animals, notably filter-feeding **whale sharks**, which migrate annually to the Northwest Cape region between March and May.

Another phenomenon is triggered by the spawning, as huge shoals of bait fish move in to the area in search of **easy pickings**. Similarly motivated groups of whales and sharks herd these shoals into shallow water, trapping them in dense black bands against the shore and then charging in, mouths agape. The waters are so shallow that the larger predators are often in danger of being beached, and have to turn on their sides, bodies half out of the water, to feed.

**Dive boats** from Exmouth sometimes run out to witness the spawning, and there are regular excursions while the whale sharks are around (see "Tours and Cruises from Exmouth" box, below). Witnessing the coastal feeding frenzy is pretty hit-and-miss – it was first observed as recently as 1992 – and you'll have to ask around to find out the latest; there's no need to get wet, however, as the best vantage points are the cliff tops overlooking the action north of Carnarvon (see p.542).

a couple of shops and reef cruises operating around the sheltered, sand-fringed bay. **Water** comes from a hot and salty bore, suitable for cooking and washing but not drinking; look out for freshwater taps.

Two glass-bottomed boats operate one-hour **cruises** over the reef in Coral Bay (daily, times depend on the tides): the *Sub-Sea Explorer* ($15, backpackers half price; ☎099/42 5955) is the better of the two and also provides free use of snorkelling gear for the rest of the day, a wonderful experience best at low tide. Ask them also about scenic flights over the cape.

The *Bayview Holiday Village* and *Coral Bay Lodge* **motel** (☎099/42 5932; ⑥) together form a large resort that also offers camping, on-site vans (③) and various configurations of chalets and cabins (③–⑤), as well as a cursory backpackers' dorm (①), a small **shop** (daily 7am–7pm) and a restaurant. The *Coral Bay Hotel* (☎099/42 5934; ⑥), incorporating the *Ningaloo Reef Resort,* offers similar options and prices for accommodation and camping, with slightly more accomplished backpacker accommodation (①), plus a **bar**, restaurant and takeaway and a grassed pool area with a great view over the small bay.

The **general store** (daily 8am–6pm) is the bigger and slightly cheaper of the two shops in Coral Bay; it accepts credit cards and has EFTPOS facilities – there are no bank agencies. Next door, the *Dive Shop* (☎099/42 5940) offers refills, gear rental, five-hour dive trips (scuba $50, snorkel $25; plus rental charge) and memorable scuba-diving courses for around $300.

## Exmouth

On the Exmouth road, north of Coral Bay, you pass the rough **Bullara–Giralia** road to the highway, which cuts 150km out of the journey between Exmouth and the north. Continuing towards Exmouth, two roads lead up onto the Cape Range: the **Charles Knife Road** is a masterpiece of 1950s' roadbuilding, leading precipitously to the top of the range, 311m above sea level. From here it's possible to walk to the head of **Shothole Canyon** (allow 2 hours), which is also accessible off the Exmouth road but this option makes a far less dramatic introduction to the range.

EXMOUTH was built in 1967 to serve the American Naval VLF (very low frequency) Communications Station and has since become a tourist base for visits to the Cape Range National Park and Ningaloo Marine Park (see below). The cloud-free atmosphere – so suited to VLF transmissions – and the prolific marine wildlife (including whale sharks in autumn and and giant turtles in summer) makes the town a popular winter holidaymakers' resort. The town beach is adequate, but to see the reef you need to head for **Bundegi Beach**, 14km north of Exmouth, opposite the antennae of the naval station.

**Buses** stop at the shopping centre in Thew Street, where the **tourist office** (daily 9am–5pm; ☎099/49 1176) is located. The **post office** is nearby, in Maidstone Crescent, and there's a book exchange at the *Ocean Exhibits Shell Museum* (Mon–Fri 10am–5pm, Sat 10am–1pm; free) in Pellew Street; the "musuem" is basically a souvenir shop with an unusually comprehensive selection of sheepskin slippers. *ExCape Hire* (☎099/49 1334), opposite the *Exmouth Cape Tourist Village*, rents out everything from light 4WDs and bicycles to beach umbrellas.

*Exmouth Cape Tourist Village* (☎099/49 1101; backpacker units ①, on-site vans ③, chalets ⑤) on Murat Road, one kilometre south of the town centre, is a **caravan park** with an attractive pool area, free use of bikes, plus snorkelling gear and *Suzuki* jeeps for rent; they meet all buses. The *Potshot Hotel Resort* (☎099/49 1200; **motel** rooms & units ⑥) is the town's upmarket complex with good restaurants, a pool and sporting facilities. *Exmouth Caravan Park* (☎099/49 1331; ③–⑤), in Lefroy Street, has the cheapest four-bed chalets as well as a pool with bar, bike rental, kiosk and restaurant.

When it comes to **food** there's little to get excited about: two high-cholesterol **fish 'n' chips** outlets in Maidstone Street and Pelios Street, *So and So Pizza* in the shopping centre, and the *Golden Orchid* Chinese restaurant next to the tourist office. The *Walkabout Café* near the shopping centre has a pleasant shaded terrace, while takeaways and a **baker** can also be found here, but the seasonally open *Mildura Room* in the *Potshot* is the only refuge for foodies. The resort also accommodates the town's **pub**.

## Cape Range National Park and Ningaloo Marine Park

The two parks are adjacent land- and sea-conservation areas on the western edge of the Northwest Cape: to explore them, you really need a vehicle, or you could take one of the tours offered (see box below). The proximity of the continental shelf to the shore gives the **Ningaloo Marine Park** a stunning variety of marine life: over 500 species of fish and 220 species of coral have been recorded here. **Cape Range National Park** is essentially a coastal drive past several bays, lagoons and campsites. The reef here is a couple of hundred metres off shore, which may be too far for most snorkellers except at low tide, but the shallow sandy bays, of which Turquoise Bay is the best, are perfect for swimming.

---

### TOURS AND CRUISES FROM EXMOUTH

*West Coast Safaris* (☎099/49 1625) and *Ningaloo Safari Tours* (☎099/49 1550) both offer full-day "over the range" **tours** for $80, or a shorter "round the range" half-day tour for $45. The full-day tour is a highly recommended, a 240-kilometre round trip showing you the best of the cape; *West Coast* also does day-trips to Coral Bay as well as four-day tours to Mount Augustus and the Karijini (Hamersley Range) National Park.

The *Ningaloo Coral Explorer* (☎099/49 1625) offers **reef-viewing cruises** off Bundegi Beach ($15), and the *Exmouth Dive Centre* (☎099/49 1201) in Payne Street takes care of **diving charters** and equipment rental with day-runs out to the Muiron Islands for around $120 with gear loan, or snorkelling for half that, with plenty to eat and drink. Open-water scuba courses cost around $300, and dives to watch the coral spawning (see box above) are sometimes available for around $50. *Exmouth Air Charter* (☎099/49 2492) will take you on **scenic flights** around the cape.

The **Milyering Visitors Centre** (Sun & Wed–Fri 10am–4pm), 52km from Exmouth, is a modern, solar-powered complex with videos and displays on the local ecology and enthusiastic, helpful staff. Another 30km past various bays and campsites brings you to Cape Range's most accessible highlight, **Yardie Creek**, a steep-walled canyon just a kilometre from the ocean. This is as far south as 2WDs can get in the park but the walk up along the gorge's cliffs is well worth the effort, the one-hour cruise (April–Oct; $15) up the short gorge suiting the less energetic.

## To Dampier and Karratha

Back on the North West Coastal Highway, it's over 500km from Carnarvon to the industrial twin towns of Dampier and Karratha with nothing but the occasional roadhouse along the way. At *Nanutarra Roadhouse* a road heads east to **Tom Price** and the Pilbara's highlands, and further on a road leads north 80km to the cyclone-battered **ONSLOW** (camping and motel; ⑤), an old coastal settlement bypassed by the highway and most travellers. Between Onslow and Dampier another turn-off leads to *Robe River Iron*'s mine at Pannawonica, a closed town with no facilities for tourists. However, 4WDs can take a track starting 20km west of the town, which crosses the Robe River on the way to the Millstream-Chichester National Park (see below), a distance of 127km.

The two young towns of **DAMPIER** and **KARRATHA** are a major industrial conurbation and the Northwest's largest population centre. Dampier is the port for *Hamersley Iron*'s mines at Tom Price, Paraburdoo and Marandoo, linked by a 350-kilometre railway. Karratha was established in 1968 when Dampier's boulder-strewn environs were deemed unsuitable for further expansion, growing dramatically when the **North-West Shelf Natural Gas Project** got underway in the early 1980s. The project collects gas from an offshore platform 135km northwest of Dampier, from where it's piped 1500km to Perth or liquified for export to Japan.

While being well equipped for shopping, vehicle repairs and other services, the two towns hold little of interest to the traveller apart from **cheap fuel**, tours of the industrial installations or a cruise among the islands of the **Dampier Archipelago** with *Coral Coast Tours* (☎091/83 1269; winter only) and for those keen and determined enough, exploration of the prolific **Aboriginal engraving** on the **Burrup Peninsula** (enquire at CALM, see below). Dampier's **tourist office** (daily 7am–9pm; ☎091/83 1440) is located at the reception of the *Kings Bay Holiday Village*, 138 The Esplanade (☎091/83 1440; motel rooms ⑥, cabins ③), where mopeds and bicycles can be rented. The resort doubles as the town's entertainment and sporting complex. The *Mermaid Hotel* (☎091/83 1222; ⑥), also on the Esplanade, has a **restaurant**, or try the *Captain's Galley* (☎091/83 1053) along the Esplanade for non-hotel food. Karratha's motels tend to be more expensive, but the town has the nearest **caravan park** off the highway: *Rosemary Road Caravan Park* (☎091/85 1855; cabins ③), which also provides **tourist information** (☎091/44 4600). The Northwest's regional CALM office is based in the SGIO Building, Welcome Road, Karratha (☎091/86 8288), and is a good place to pick up information and maps on all the national parks of northern WA.

## Roebourne and around

**ROEBOURNE**, established in 1864 (and once the capital of the Northwest), is the oldest surviving settlement between Port Gregory and Darwin. The renovated **Old Gaol** is perhaps the most significant survivor in the small town, nowadays housing the **tourist office** (Mon–Fri 8.30am–4.30pm, Sat 9am–4pm, Sun 10am–2pm; ☎091/82 1060) and **museum**. In 1982, the Old Gaol was the scene of the first of a spate of Aboriginal "deaths in custody" that tarnished Australia's human rights record throughout the 1980s and early 1990s. Although similarly suspicious deaths had occurred prior to this, these were the first such incidents to garner worldwide publicity and condemnation.

Other nineteenth-century institutional buildings are dotted around the town with the *Victoria Hotel* (☎091/82 1001; ⑤), in the main street, still offering refreshment and rooms and a **diner** open from 8am to 8pm. There's also a **caravan park** (☎091/82 1063; on-site vans ③) in De Grey Street, at the town's east end.

## Cossack and Point Samson

COSSACK, once simply known as "the Landing", was the small sea port which begat the town of Roebourne, and it's well worth a look. All early settlers to the Northwest came through Cossack: pastoralists, pearlers, and prospectors heading for the gold-fields of the East Pilbara. The original tin and timber buildings used to be chained to the ground so as to weather the occasional cyclones. At the turn of the century the inlet by the quay began silting up and the harbour was moved to nearby Point Samson until Port Hedland's became pre-eminent, and by the 1950s Cossack was all but abandoned, its tram lines to Roebourne long since uprooted for scrap.

In just a few years an excellent restoration job has been done on this historic "ghost port". The **Courthouse**, with its museum of the settlement, is the most impressive building, both inside and out, while the **Post and Telegraph Office** is now a small art gallery displaying some fine local work. **Settler's Beach**, past the old cemetery at the end of Perseverance Street, is a sandy and sheltered swimming spot. Basic **accommodation** is available at the *Cossack Backpackers* (☎091/82 1190; ①) housed in the old police barracks, and with pick-ups from the Wickham bus stop by arrangement.

Passing *Robe River Iron's* oddly anachronistic company town of **WICKHAM** (handy for facilities and services, and on the Perth–Darwin bus route), **POINT SAMSON** is one of the few places on the WA coast that could be compared to a British fishing village. The coastline hereabouts has that sharp, windswept, Atlantic quality, even if it does happen to be 320km inside the tropics. The port once had the ignoble distinction of receiving and shipping out the **blue asbestos** mined at Wittenoom, in the Hamersley Ranges. This may explain the inordinate abundance of **car parks** for such a tiny settlement, with the potentially cancer-causing dust in the tailings being expediently sealed under lashings of bitumen. **Honeymoon Cove** has fine swimming and is close to the town.

Gastronomes will relish the **seafood** with a view at the *Trawlers Tavern* first-floor restaurant (daily 6–8pm) or *Moby's Kitchen* fish and chips takeaway (daily 11am–2pm & 5–9pm), on the ground floor, both right by the pier. If you develop a taste for the food, **stay over** at *Samson Accommodation,* 56 Samson Road (☎091/87 1052; rooms ④, cabins ⑤), or the small *Solveig Caravan Park* (☎091/87 1414), also on Samson Road, next to the *Trawlers Tavern.*

*Snappy Gum Safaris* (☎091/85 1278) organizes **day-tours** from Karratha/Dampier to the Roebourne, Cossack and Point Samson area, and further afield to Millstream-Chichester National Park (see below).

# Millstream-Chichester National Park

Not much more than a scenic drive and an oasis of palms and pools along the Fortescue River, the **MILLSTREAM-CHICHESTER NATIONAL PARK** is worth a visit if you're coming or going from the Hamersley Ranges – note, however, that this entails a fuel-less 300km stretch. Two routes lead into the park from the north: the private road alongside the Dampier–Tom Price railway can be used with an easily-gained **permit** from *Hamersley Iron*'s security gate in Dampier (☎091/43 5364). Alternatively, the conventional route breaks off the coastal highway between Roebourne and Whim Creek, passing Pyramid Homestead soon after. Looking back northward from the climb up into the **Chichester Ranges** you'll see why the homestead is so named; the view across this ancient Pilbara landscape is stirring and timeless.

Just inside the park, **Python Pool** is a pea-green waterhole backed with black and orange cliffs, and cut by the shriek of birds, worth a picture if not a dip. From this point it's a 60-kilometre run to **MILLSTREAM**, 150km from Roebourne and 183km from Wittenoom, where an old homestead has been converted into an unusually good **visitors' centre** (daily 8am–5pm; ☎091/84 5144). A section describes the rustic bliss of the Yinjibarndi Aborigines of Ngarrari (Millstream), but unaccountably forgets to mention that they were cleared out by pastoralists and today live in the Roebourne area. **Chunderwarriner Pool**, a short walk from the homestead, is a lily-dappled pool surrounded by palm trees, recovering nicely after a lost tourist panicked and set them all on fire. The date palms, introduced by Afghan cameleers, have overrun the indigenous Millstream palm, but this does not detract from the unexpectedly luxuriant scene. Black flying foxes hang from the palms' fronds, and Millstream is also a haven for dragonflies and damselflies: 22 species have been recorded here. Walking trails up to 7km long follow the palm- and paperbark-lined Fortescue River to **Crossing** and **Deep Reach pools**, where you may **camp**.

# Port Hedland

BHP (Broken Hill Proprietary), the Australian mining giant, has its work cut out for it in its project to beautify the sprawling works at **PORT HEDLAND**, an iron and salt port of such unrefined ugliness it's strangely captivating. The town centre, set on an island surrounded by mangroves and sludge, is coated in pale-red iron dust, which prohibits the use of external cash dispensing machines among other inconveniences. South Hedland, a satellite suburb on the highway, is where most of the population choose to live, with only a shopping centre and cheap fuel of interest to the traveller. There's an array of heavy industrial grot of which the town seems inordinately proud, labelling itself rather clumsily "The Port of Big Ships". Bus travellers on the coastal route should alight here to get to Wittenoom's gorges and, if you're heading north, the good news is that Broome is only 600km away.

The staff at the tourist office (see "Practicalities" below) have no hesitations about Port Hedland's appeal, and promote the town and adjacent Pilbara with laudable zeal. One of the most popular diversions is the 90-minute tour (Mon–Fri 9.30am; $8) of the **BHP loading facility**, where ships load up with 250,000 tonnes of iron at a time. Whale- and turtle-watching tours are organized in the wet season (roughly November to March) by the tourist office, as well as fishing and diving charters and harbour cruises, as incentives to stop travellers leaving town on the next bus. You can also visit the **Royal Flying Doctor** base in Richardson Street (Mon–Fri 11.15am; free). If by now, the prospect of escape is becoming irresistible, *Design-a-Tour* (☎091/44 1460) operates **tours** to the Karijini (Hamersley Range) National Park and other parts of the Pilbara, with pick-ups from Port Hedland.

### Practicalities
Overland **buses** stop next to the **tourist office** in Wedge Street (Mon–Fri 8.30am–5pm, Sat & Sun 8.30am–1pm, 2–4.30pm; ☎091/73 1711), while **local buses** operate between South and Port Hedland (#501; $2) from 8am to 5.30pm weekdays and until 3pm on Saturdays, handy for shopping or getting to **Pretty Pool** beach, 8km away. The **post office** is opposite the tourist office in Wedge Street, where most banks are also situated.

The liveliest place to stay is at *Port Hedland Backpackers* (☎091/73 3282; ①), 20 Richardson Street. A slightly run-down **hostel**, befitting the town, it offers verandah views of the huge ore-carriers gliding up the channel to the port, and heaps of activities run by a tuned-in owner. The *Pier Hotel* (☎091/73 1488; rooms ⑤, dorms ②) on the Esplanade describes itself as "infamous", and is a safe bet for a beer, band or a punch-up. *Oceanview Budget Accommodation* (☎091/73 2418; ②–③) at 59 Kingsmill Street,

## THE STRIKE THAT NEVER ENDED

There can be little doubt that Australia's once-legendary pastoral wealth was accrued at the expense of the Aboriginal people, on whose land and cheap labour it depended. Even John Forrest, WA's turn-of-the-century premier, pastoralist and former explorer, conceded that "many of us could not be in the position we are today without native labour on our stations".

By the 1940s Australia was producing a sixth of the world's mutton and a quarter of its wool. In the Northwest, two million sheep grazed vast tracts of meagre land, a marginal enterprise made economical by the employment of black stockmen paid barely $2 a week. The archaic **Native Administration Act** protected the interests of rural industry by hampering mobility and sanctioning low or non-existant pay for black workers.

Around this time Don McLeod, a white prospector still active in Aboriginal rights campaigns today, encouraged **Clancy McKenna** and **Dooley Binbin** to defy their degrading conditions and, after several years of painstaking preparation, 800 black workers simultaneously walked off the stations in the Port Hedland/Nullagine region on May 1, 1946. Police were instructed to harass the two camps established near Port Hedland and east of Marble Bar, and arrested McKenna and Binbin for communist subversion. Post-war food coupons were withheld, so the strikers returned to traditional ways of feeding and trading among themselves. Port Hedland was at this time a small town with an "official" (white) population of just 150 and a "mob" of 400 strikers down the road. Jittery police arrested a visiting mediator, Padre Hodge, for being "within five miles of a congregation of natives", adding further support to the strike, coverage of which was largely censored from the national press.

In 1949 things came to a head, and a station-to-station march was organized calling all remaining workers to join the strike. Arrest for such defiance was certain, and the strikers cheerfully offered to fill up the jail at Marble Bar and others throughout the Northwest. Only when the Seamen's Union banned the handling of "slave station" wool did the government hastily concede to McLeod's proposals – though the government swiftly reneged on the deal. All through the 1950s McLeod employed and assisted the strikers in mining ventures around Marble Bar until the big mining companies began taking an interest in the Pilbara's mineral wealth and pushed them off their claims. The strikers never returned to the stations, demonstrating black assertion long before the 1960s' civil rights campaigning in the USA with which the movement is associated in the popular imagination.

close to town, is a good compromise between a hostel and a motel. Upmarket alternatives include the *Hospitality Inn* (☎091/73 1044; ⑦), in Webster Street, 4km from the centre, or the *Quality Inn* (☎091/72 1222; ⑦), on the highway opposite the airport. *Dixon's Caravan Park* (091/72 2525; chalets ④), also on the highway, suits those who just want to crash out, while *Cooke Point Caravan Park* (☎091/73 1271; on-site vans ③), in Athol Street, is by the ocean, 8km from town (bus #501).

Iron-ore dust can't do much for the tastebuds judging by Port Hedland's **eateries**. Good restaurants are confined to the *Hospitality* and *Quality* inns (see above), and *Katherine's Fine Dining*, Keesing St, Cooke Point. *Marg's Kitchen* is a handy snack bar in Wedge Street, or try the *Coral Trout*, at the end of the road, for all sorts of seafood to stay or fish and chips to go.

### Port Hedland to Broome

The 600-kilometre run from Port Hedland to Broome is one of the most boring sections of the coastal route, a dreary plain of spinifex and mulga, marking the northern edge of the Great Sandy Desert. Halfway to Broome, the *Sandfire Roadhouse* (6am–midnight) provides a welcome and for some essential fuel stop before the 286-kilometre stage to *Roebuck Roadhouse*.

Despite your proximity to the ocean, beach access is only possible in a few places and even 4WDs regularly get stuck along the enticingly named **Eighty Mile Beach**. *Pardoo Station* (☎091/76 4930; dorms ①), 133km from Port Hedland, offers a closer look at station life, while **Cape Keraudren**, a little further east, is a bleak, unmaintained oceanside campsite, just before *Pardoo Roadhouse*. *Eighty Mile Beach Caravan Park* (☎091/76 5941; tent spaces, backpacker bunks ① & cabins ⑤), 10km off the highway and 250km from Port Hedland, is popular with fishermen and 4WDs.

After *Sandfire Roadhouse, Port Smith Caravan Park* (☎091/92 4983), 23km off the highway and 143km from Broome, offers basic camping and also has a tropical garden and bird park ($2) near the homestead.

# Inland to the Pilbara

About a thousand kilometres north of Perth are the ancient, mineral-rich highlands of the **Pilbara**, a geographical area north of the 26th parallel and including Mount Meharry, at 1245m the highest point in WA. The world's richest surface deposits of **iron ore** were found here in the 1950s and several mining companies, including the giant BHP, are engaged in the task of reducing mountains into pits while their private railroads transport the ore to the coastal ports for shipping to Japan's steel-hungry industries. Surrounding the huge open-cast mine sites are typically vast pastoral properties, over-grazed since Australia's sheep and wool heyday following World War II. In the centre of this region is the often-overlooked rugged grandeur of the **Karijini National Park**, excised from the spectacular, water-carved gorges of the Hamersley Ranges – a worthy substitute if time or weather forbids a visit to the Kimberley (see p.560).

## The Great Northern Highway

Scenically, there's not much to commend the **Great Northern Highway**'s 1635-kilometre inland section from Perth to Port Hedland – most people shoot through in two long days and, with the honourable exception of the Hamersleys, they miss very little. *Greyhound.Pioneer* buses operate a thrice-weekly service between Perth and Port Hedland, stopping at the few places along the highway, including **Munjina** (formerly Auski) **Roadhouse**, where tour operators from Wittenoom, 42km west of the highway, will meet your bus if you call them in advance (see below).

Among the half dozen towns along this inland route, only the semi-abandoned **CUE**, 650km north of Perth, retains some character from the goldrush era of the 1890s. *Dorsett Guest House* (☎099/63 1291; ④), opposite the Rotunda in the High Street, also acts as the **tourist information** centre for the area's rich history.

**MEEKATHARRA**, 115km north of Cue, is a thriving mining and pastoral centre, with many century-old **hotels** along the main road, still looking good and competing for custom. From Meekatharra, a sealed road leads east and then south for 726km through Outback mining towns to Kalgoorlie (for a description of this route, see p.532), while in the other direction **Mount Augustus** (see p.543) lies at the end of a 350-kilometre dirt road. North of Meekatharra a roadsign marks the **26th parallel** and welcomes you to the fabled "Nor'west". As if to underline the isolation and extremes "the 26th" symbolizes, an unvarying 350km leads to Newman with only the **Collier Range National Park** – nothing more than a series of 4WD tracks – and a roadhouse or two along the way.

**NEWMAN** was built to serve what is now the world's largest open-cut iron-ore mine, and the **mine tours** (daily at 8.30am & 1pm; 1hr 30min; $3), departing from the **tourist information centre** (Mon–Sat 8am–5pm, Sun 9am–1pm; ☎091/75 2888) on Newman Drive, are the only reason you might want to stop here. The tours clearly

Newman has the odd, artificial quality of an extra-terrestrial community, built for, and guided purely by, commerce – a ghost town in the making. Unlike single men's towns, where cheap and copious beer is the only embellishment, much is done here to keep the workforce and their families contented, loyal and even grateful to the company. Industrial unrest is not tolerated, though wages for the straightforward work are not as high as you might expect. Instead, the standard of living is buoyed by subsidized education, housing and health services to ensure that morale remains at optimum levels and round-the-clock productivity is never compromised.

The idea is to supply everything you could possibly want, short of money: saving up scrupulously over five years and moving back to one of the nicer Perth suburbs may be on everyone's mind, but is not playing by the company's rules. Young families, however, welcome the benefits of these remote but socially self-sufficient communities, which make ideal environments for child-rearing, away from the cities' pernicious influences. Crime, vandalism and other forms of anti-social self-expression are low, with the surrounding countryside used as a wholesome vent for inevitable daily frustrations.

demonstrate the simplicity and scale of the operation as **Mount Whaleback** is gradually turned inside out for its iron ore, which is sent overseas only to return transmogrified into mining machinery. Local companies also run **tours** (see box on p.553) lasting between half a day and three days to local waterholes, the Karajini (Hamersley Range) National Park and the rarely visited Canning Stock Route to the east. The town has three **caravan parks** and an expensive **motel**, as well as a busy shopping centre.

### Marble Bar and Rudall River National Park

From Newman a dirt road leads northward for 300km through the scenic East Pilbara to **NULLAGINE** and **MARBLE BAR**, the latter notorious for being Australia's hottest town, once clocking up 160 days over 100°F in 1923–4. This is the sole reason many visitors come to "the Bar", misnamed after a colourful bar of jasper by the Coolingan River 5km south of town. For an overnight stay, there's a **caravan park**, a **motel** (☎091/76 1166; ⑤) and the town's famed, windowless *Ironclad Hotel* (☎091/76 1066; ⑤) – a good place to get some drinking done.

The **RUDALL RIVER NATIONAL PARK**, 300km east of Newman, is an undeveloped national park, designated more for reasons of conservation than as a recreational area, and also the site of some ultra-remote Aboriginal outstations. Accessible only to self-sufficient 4WDs from Newman, Telfer to the north, or off the Canning Stock Route, the park's protective role stands to be severely tested following the discovery of substantial **uranium** deposits just inside the park's boundaries – part of BHP's systematic combing of the WA deserts for the mineral wealth thought to exist there.

## Wittenoom and the Karijini (Hamersley Range) National Park

The Karijini (Hamersley Range) National Park remains one of WA's undiscovered pearls, offering dramatic, time-worn scenery equal to any in Australia. Hampered by its off-highway location and hesitant promotion, due to the controversy surrounding the future of Wittenoom (the park's most convenient base), its main attractions are the **gorges** cut deep into the Pilbara's highlands and the singular lack of tourist trappings.

All the points of interest can be briefly visited on a long day's drive or tour, but Wittenoom's bargain accommodation and pervasive charm make a few days' exploration and relaxation much more rewarding. All the roads in the park are unsealed but usually in good condition; indeed, barring thunderstorms, the park remains accessible throughout the year.

## Wittenoom

At each end of **WITTENOOM**, warning signs proclaim the possible health hazard incurred by entering the town as a result of the asbestos mining carried out here from 1937 to 1966, by – among others – the young Rolf Harris. It is believed that, by the end of the century, one in ten of the ex-miners and former inhabitants will have died of diseases associated with inhaling asbestos dust.

In its natural state **blue asbestos** is a harmless and unusual fibrous mineral, still evident in Yampire and Upper Wittenoom Gorge, but it is the **dust** produced during milling that can be lethal. Unfortunately, tailings from the mine were once used to grade the town's streets, leaving all those resident at the time susceptible to disease and with grounds for compensation. These days, resurfacing has been completed and, unless you're kicking about in the tailings, the air contains no more harmful particles of asbestos than most urban centres. The emotional overreaction to the "Town of Death" is neatly summed up in the bumper sticker available at the *Gem Shop* that states: "I've been to Wittenoom and lived".

Perhaps because of its tragic history, and certainly due to the intransigence of its remaining two score inhabitants, the town, which the government wanted razed long ago, possesses an intangible ambience like few other places in WA. In the 1950s it was the biggest settlement in the Northwest but today the ramshackle, deserted buildings and empty streets speak of a ghost town not prepared to die. In late 1994 the government stepped up the pace by threatening to cut off power and water in 1997, while offering derisory compensation for freeholds. These extreme tactics have led to speculation that health may not be the only issue at stake: with Wittenoom out of the way, the way would be clear for the construction of a new resort in the south of the national park or the exploitation of rich iron-ore reserves on Wittenoom's doorstep.

**Buses** stop at the *Munjina Roadhouse* on the Great Northern Highway, 42km from town. If you call in advance, *Dave's Gorge Tours* (☎091/89 7026) will pick you up for $10 one way. There are **no banks** in town and the only **shop** (daily 8am–6pm; ☎091/89 7077), which also serves as a post office and filling station, is destined for closure, so come prepared. **Tourist information** is dispensed at the *Gem Shop* in Sixth Avenue (daily 8am–6pm; ☎091/89 7096) with detailed **sketch maps** of the national park.

There's plenty of choice of **accommodation** in Wittenoom, none of it plush but all cheap. *Wittenoom Holiday Homes* (☎091/89 7096; ④; ask at the *Gem Shop* in Sixth Ave) offers complete three-bedroomed houses for rent. The *Bungarra Bivouac*, in Fifth Avenue (☎091/89 7026; ①), with its distinctive rainbow tree, is run-down but popular with backpackers. The *Wittenoom Tourist Village*, or "the Convent", in Gregory Street (☎091/89 7060; rooms ③, dorms ①), is a lovely and well-kept old building with a screened verandah and mild air-conditioning. **Campers** head for the *Gorges Caravan Park* in Second Avenue (☎091/89 7055; on-site vans ③), which also has plans to take over as the town's **shop**, though on a smaller scale. On the bright side, you can't miss *Doc Halliday's Café*, which has re-opened in a blaze of glory and, the pub being closed, is a good place to mingle.

### Exploring the gorges

The many gorges in **KARIJINI NATIONAL PARK** offer opportunities for some spectacular views, adventurous walks and, at times, exposed or slippery climbs. Deaths and several accidents have occurred but **rangers** are rarely seen, their headquarters (☎091/89 8157) being, for some absurd reason, tucked away in the corner of the park where no-one ever goes. Take heed of the clearly marked warnings and take advantage of the tours (or their guides' advice) based in Wittenoom. If you're driving through the park, note that distances can be deceptive: a full tour of all the gorges can cover over 240km.

Coming from Tom Price (see below), you'll pass **Hamersley Gorge** in the north-western corner of the park, 48km west of Wittenoom. With its spa-like pool and acutely folded beds of blue-grey and orange rock, it's unlike any of the other gorges and a bit of exploring up- and down-stream could easily fill a day here. Just east of the Hamersley Gorge turn-off, the road passes through **Rio Tinto Gorge**, which bears an extraordinary resemblance to a box-canyon film set from those 1950s' Westerns.

Just south of Wittenoom itself is **Wittenoom Gorge**, not actually in the park but with a number of pools handy for a cooling dip. At the end of the sealed road which leads up the gorge is the largely abandoned **Settlement**, 11km from town (possibly demolished by now). On the west side of the gorge are the **mine** and the mill, surrounded by the dreaded and dangerous **tailings**. From the Settlement, it's possible to walk up to the dramatic entrance to **Red Gorge** and walk/swim (including some 400m stretches) up to **Junction Pool** below Oxer's Lookout. From here, the "Miracle Mile" (see below) is a rather intrepid way of returning to the Settlement, but unless you've already been initiated, this shouldn't be tackled without a guide.

East of town, 24km towards *Munjina Roadhouse*, a turning leads south into the wooded **Yampire Gorge**, where evidence of the first hand-mining operations from the 1930s can still be seen. At the top of the gorge a right turn continues to the main "Four Gorges" area, but a little further on a left turn leads 10km to **Dales Gorge** (with camping) in which Fortescue Falls, Fern Pool and Circular Pool are found. All can be joined up in a superb half-day walk with plenty of water to cool off in along the way.

**Kalamina Gorge**, on the way to the Four Gorges area, offers good walks along its bed without too much climbing and scrambling and **Joffre Gorge** is an impressive lookout onto the tiered amphitheatre of Joffre Falls (usually dry). There is camping nearby and the road leads on to **Knox Gorge**, which ends in the exhilarating (to say the least) "Knox Slide" featured in *Dave's Gorge Tours*.

Back on the main road, a turning ends at a car park on the spur between **Hancock** and **Weano Gorges**. From here, a short walk leads to the exposed **Oxer's Lookout**, surveying a confluence of four gorges that is as impressive as any in WA. Straight ahead is **Red Gorge**, which runs on into Wittenoom Gorge and the Settlement. Also starting from the car park, the "Miracle Mile", with its somewhat shady origins as a 1960s character-building exercise for Perth schoolboys, descends over loose rock into Hancock and returns up Weano Gorge. A thrilling half-day's swimming and climbing, this should only be attempted with someone who knows where the tricky moves are – and how to accomplish them. For the less adventurous, the short walk into Weano Gorge to **Handrail Pool** is recommended. From the Four Gorges the road continues across the roof of the Pilbara to **Mount Bruce**, at 1235m WA's second-highest peak and site of the new Marandoo mine, with a sealed road leading to Tom Price. Eastwards, a 4WD track passes the Rangers HQ to Highway 95 and Newman.

## TOURS OF THE PILBARA

**Dave's Gorge Tours** (☎091/89 7026), in Wittenoom, have become a legend on the backpackers' circuit. All tours cost $50 a day (with discounts) but "Tour 3" is the one they come, and even wait days, for, incorporating the "Miracle Mile" and "Knox Slide" – a day you won't forget in a hurry.

**Design-a-Tour** (☎091/89 7059) offer a full day's run around all the gorges for $65

(with lunch) and also longer tours with pick-ups from Port Hedland.

**Newman Eco Tours** (☎091/75 2944) run 4WD tours to beauty spots around Newman and into Karijini (Hamersley Range) National Park.

**Snappy Gum Safaris** (☎091/85 1278), based in Karratha, run two- to four-day tours through the Pilbara, including Millstream-ChicesterNational Park, from $240.

## Tom Price

WA's highest town, whose many young families produce a statistical average age of just 11 years, **TOM PRICE** is an alternative, but much less convenient, base for exploring the Hamersleys while Wittenoom's future is dithered over. You can drive to the top of the 1128-metre **Mount Nameless** which overlooks the town, although the steep climb may have your radiator steaming while you gaze across the spinifex-carpeted vista. The **tourist office** (8am–5pm Mon–Fri; ☎091/88 1112), in Central Road, organizes **tours** (daily 9am; 1hr 30min; $10) of *Hamersley Iron*'s mine.

**Accommodation** is either at the *Hillview Lodge* (☎091/89 1625; ④–⑦) in Stadium Road, with the best buffet **restaurant** in town, or out at *Tom Price Caravan Park* (☎091/89 1515; on-site vans ③). The town also has a swimming pool, outdoor cinema and all the services you'd expect, including a couple of nondescript cafés and a **supermarket** (Mon–Fri 8am–6pm, Sat 8am–12.30pm, Sun 10am–1pm).

# Broome and around

"Slip into Broometime" is the well-worn local aphorism that attempts to capture the reclining tropical charm of **BROOME**, a popular and unexpectedly classy resort town of 9000, which hangs on a drip of land over Roebuck Bay. William Dampier, the English buccaneer-explorer, passed the area in 1699 while on the run from an irate Spanish flotilla, and nearly 200 years later the Djuleun Aborigines repelled an early fleet of prospective pastoralists. However, the imminent discovery of literally heaps of pearl shell soon led to the **"Pearl Rush"** of the 1880s and firmly set Broome on the colonial map of Australia.

It was actually the nacre-lined shells, or **mother-of-pearl**, rather than pearls themselves, which brought brief fortune to the town. By 1910, eighty per cent of the world's pearl shell, used in the manufacture of buttons, came from Broome, whose rich (though not always harmonious) ethnic mix developed at this time. "Chinatown" teemed with raucous and sometimes rioting Filipinos, Japanese, Arabs, Malays and Kupangers (from Timor), servicing the 400 luggers and their crews involved in the dangerous business of diving for shells. While Broome's cemeteries steadily filled, perhaps one shell in a thousand produced a perfect example of the silvery pearls unique to this area.

Stagnation followed both world wars, although the Japanese, masters in the art of culturing pearls, invested in pearl-farming ventures around Broome's ideal coastal habitat. Things improved with the sealing of the coastal highway from Perth in the early 1980s and the philanthropic interest of English peer, Alistair McAlpine, who fell for Broome and subsequently financed its renovation. Tasteful development and refurbishment have celebrated the town's oriental and pearling mystique, enhanced by the sweeping expanse of **Cable Beach**, **Gantheaume Point**'s brick-red outcrops and the **Indian Ocean**'s stunning turquoise hue. The recession and McAlpine's own financial troubles have frozen the town's development at a perfect stage, retaining its easy-going character and making the place a tropical retreat for diverse lotus-eating individuals, from New Age hippies to cappuccino-sipping yuppies.

### Arrival and information

**Buses** arrive at the depot in Hamersley Street (☎091/92 1561), where the two hostels' minibuses meet all arrivals. The **airport terminal** in McPherson Street couldn't be more central, less than a kilometre west of Chinatown, and taxis meet incoming flights. Close to the terminal, on the corner of Bagot Street and Broome Road, is the **tourist office** (Mon–Fri 8am–5pm, Sat & Sun 9am–5pm; ☎091/92 2222), which dispenses an *Information Guide* (50¢) whose maps help you find your way around the dispersed and sometimes confusing layout of Broome.

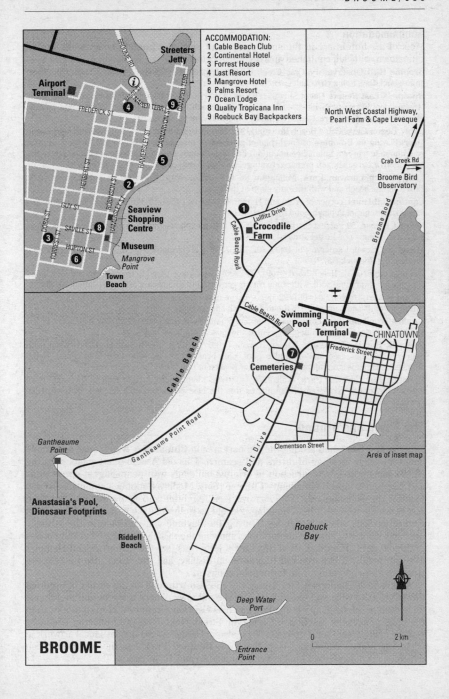

**ACCOMMODATION:**
1 Cable Beach Club
2 Continental Hotel
3 Forrest House
4 Last Resort
5 Mangrove Hotel
6 Palms Resort
7 Ocean Lodge
8 Quality Tropicana Inn
9 Roebuck Bay Backpackers

**BROOME**

## Accommodation

Most of the **hotels** are in the southern part of town, the **hostels** congregate around Chinatown, with self-contained apartments in between.

**Broome Bird Observatory**. Crab Creek Rd (☎091/93 5600). Secluded camping 18km from town on Roebuck Bay. Rooms ③, chalets ④.

**Broome's Last Resort**, Bagot St (☎091/93 5000). Very popular hostel with a sometimes too lively "18–30s" feel but great facilities – a pool, bar, free beach runs, coin-operated lockers and air-con. Also bicycle rental and great-value Kimberley tours. Rooms ③, dorms ①.

**Cable Beach Club**, Cable Beach Rd (☎091/92 0400). A large, exquisitely designed and landscaped resort playing on Broome's oriental theme; an all-expenses-paid stay here is just the sort of prize you'd hope to win in a holiday competition. For most rooms, rates are in excess of $200 per night, but if there's a group of you prepared to share, the bungalows can work out around ⑥–⑧.

**Cable Beach Caravan Park**, Millington Rd (☎091/92 2066). Cable Beach's only caravan park, 2km from the beach and with the only shop in the area.

**Continental Hotel**, corner of Weld and Hamersley streets (☎091/92 1002). Good-value rooms and excellent restaurant in plush hotel right on the bay. ⑦.

**Forrest House**, 59 Forrest St (☎091/93 5067). This guesthouse has rooms with shared facilities, but a refreshingly non-hostel atmosphere. ③–④.

**Mangrove Hotel**, Carnarvon St (☎091/92 1303). Very comfortable and well positioned on a rise overlooking Roebuck Bay. ⑦.

**Ocean Lodge**, Cable Beach Road (☎091/93 7700). Good-value motel between town and beach and opposite big swimming pool, with some rooms converted to backpacker accommodation. ①–⑤.

**Palms Resort**, Hopton St (☎091/92 1898). Large resort taking up a whole block, with three pools, two restaurants and bars; close to the town beach and shopping centre. ⑦–⑧.

**Quality Tropicana Inn**, corner of Saville and Robinson streets (☎091/92 1204). Cheapest of the good motels, right opposite shopping centre and close to the town beach. ⑥.

**Roebuck Bay Backpackers**, Napier Terrace (☎091/92 1221). Newly managed and cheap, with improved facilities, free air-con, and a pool, plus beach runs, TV room and bike rental. Being attached to Broome's raging pub can be either heaven or hell. 4-bed units ④, dorms ①.

**Roebuck Bay Caravan Park**, Walcott St (☎091/92 1366). Location right next to the small town beach and *Seaview Shopping Centre* makes this the best positioned caravan park in town. Bike rental available.

# The Town and around

Broome first flourished around the old port area in **Chinatown**, which once accommodated the lively melange of divers and seamen. This old Asiatic quarter has seen the most concentrated reconstruction of original buildings with penta-lingual street signs and payphones topped with jaunty Chinese roofs. Modern boutiques and cafés occupy most of the buildings, but *Sun Pictures* (see "Nightlife and festivals") in Carnarvon Street, which opened in 1916 (making it as old as Hollywood itself), is one of the oldest picture gardens still in use today. During the daytime you can take in the virtually unchanged interior and see photographs showing the racially segregated seating codes of the old days. The dilapidated **Streeter's jetty** runs into the mangroves off Dampier Terrace; nearby a battered old **lugger** is on display, and the street also hosts a few **pearl dealers** operating from former warehouses.

A walk down Hamersley Street, past the 1888 **Courthouse** on the corner of Fredrick Street, leads to what was the rich end of the old town, where masters and merchants once lived in splendid, airy bungalows such as **Captain Gregory's House** (not open to the public), near the junction of Carnarvon Street. Next door, the *Kimberley Creations Gallery* (daily 10am–5pm; ☎091/93 5811, also in Carnarvon St) displays local artwork in what was *Matso's Store*, and over the road, **Bedford Park** has the old train coach which once chugged the 2km between Chinatown and Town Beach.

The "orientalized" *Seaview Shopping Centre* (daily 8am–6pm) is Broome's only shopping area and the *Customs House* houses the local **museum** (April–Nov Mon–Fri 10am–4pm, Sat & Sun 10am–1pm; $2). Naturally focussing on the town's maritime traditions, and with a pleasing "junk shop" appearance, it could easily occupy a couple of hours. Round the back, the old **Pioneer Cemetery** looks over **Town Beach**, the nearest to the town centre. From the jetty, very low tides reveal the remains of Dutch **sea planes** bombed by the Japanese in 1942. This is also the best vantage point for observing the "Golden Staircase to the Moon", the over-rated lunar reflections in the mudflats, which occur for a few nights each month, around the full phase of the moon. Dates and precise times for the "Staircase" can be gained from the tourist office.

## Gantheaume Point and Cable Beach

The outskirts of Broome present a number of interesting attractions, and a full day could be spent cycling along the following route (including 9km of firm, sandy roads) ending at **Cable Beach**, 6km from town on the ocean side of the peninsula. The town's bus service (☎091/92 1068; $2, ten-ride ticket $15) runs 12 times daily between the town and Cable Beach, via most of the town's accommodation centres, and returns from the *Cable Beach Club* at 45 minutes past the hour. Timetables are available at the tourist office.

Just past the turning for Cable Beach, off Fredrick Street, is the old **cemetery** from the pearling years. The Japanese section's enigmatic headstones (recently refurbished by an anonymous philanthropic countryman) testify to the 900 lives lost in the hazardous search for mother-of-pearl. The 1908 cyclone alone cost the lives of over 150 men, five per cent of the workforce at that time. The Chinese cemetery next door is less cared for, and the Muslim and Aboriginal graveyards at the back are barely distinguishable.

Continuing down Port Drive for 5km, a right turn onto the nine-kilometre dirt road section leads to **Riddell Beach**. Walk right along the shore, past the outcrops weathered by eons of wind and water, to **Gantheaume Point** where the dark red sandstone formations contrast sharply with the dusky-white expanse of Cable Beach stretching northward. The old lighthouse is now a beacon, but the pool built by the former keeper for his crippled wife, Anastasia, remains among the tidal rocks. A cast of some 120-million-year-old **dinosaur footprints** is set in the rocks – the originals out to sea are only visible at extremely low tides. From here you can walk 7km along the beach to the resort, or ride/drive over a slightly longer distance.

Named after the nineteenth-century telegraph cable which came ashore here, **Cable Beach** extends for an immaculate 22km north of Gantheaume Point. Cars are permitted onto the beach north of the rocks, near the access ramp, at a maximum speed of 15kph. Note that several cars a year are caught by up to ten-metre **tides** around Broome's beaches: on Cable Beach's flat sands it can come in very fast. The area north of the rocks is also designated a free (nudist) beach. A **kiosk** overlooking the beach serves basic meals, as does the *Diver's Camp Tavern* and bottle shop, on Cable Beach Road. Windsurfers and sailboards are available on the beach during the season (May–Oct) from *Broome Surf Cat Hire* (☎091/93 5551).

## Crocodiles and birds

Broome is loosely regarded as the westernmost limit of the range of saltwater **crocodiles**. The *Broome Crocodile Farm* (Mon–Sat 10am–5pm, Sun 2.30–5pm; guided tours daily 3pm; feeding Wed, Fri & Sun; $9) on Cable Beach Road can show you hundreds of these fascinating beasts at close quarters.

**Roebuck Bay**, on Broome's eastern flank, is on the flight path for thousands of migratory wading birds and a third of Australia's species have been seen here. The

**Broome Bird Observatory** (☎091/93 5600; $2), 18km from town (last 9km dirt) welcomes day and overnight visitors (see "Accommodation" above). There are walks through the bushland around the observatory, with tours and courses also offered for those interested in local fauna, feathered or otherwise.

## Eating and entertainment

Not surprisingly, the food in Broome is distinctly oriental in flavour. The customary fast-food outlets and a couple of healthfood outlets are also evident, while the hotels accommodate their own very reputable **restaurants**.

*Bloom's Gourmet Deli and Café* (8.30am–late) in Carnarvon Street is the only classy coffee shop for 2000km either way, popular with the Nor'West's spangled yuppies and with an airy jarrah interior, great drinks and light snacks. The *Roebuck Hotel* has cheap counter meals from $7, and *Mango Jack's*, next to the pharmacy in Hamersley Street, is an average burger and chips joint. Down by the Town Beach, the *Stairway Takeaway* lets you do just that, and there's a small food hall in Johnny Chi Lane featuring Italian and Asian outlets.

For more substantial **meals**, the hard-to-find *Tea House*, tucked in the car park on Dora Street, opposite Saville Street, serves authentic Thai cuisine to eat in or takeaway and, at around $15 a head, it's worth the search. For Chinese food *Chin's*, opposite the *Shell* sevice station in Hamersley Street, is the least expensive of the good ones, though service and decor aren't up to much. *Tong's*, round the corner in Napier Terrace, and *Murray's*, in Dampier Terrace, are among the two best Chinese restaurants in town. Out at the *Cable Beach Club*, *Asian Affair* has more Thai delicacies for around $20 per person, or *Lord Mac's* offers a view over the ocean for less expense.

Finally, *Dampiers on the Terrace* serves light snacks by day and Mexican food by night; the *Portlight* at the *Continental Hotel* in Weld Street (☎091/92 1002) is regarded as Broome's best restaurant, a place to treat yourself; and *Charters* (☎091/92 1303) at the *Mangrove Hotel* in Carnarvon Street has seaward views and seafood menus.

### Nightlife and events

Broome's raging **pub** is the *Roebuck Bay Hotel* in Napier Terrace, with live entertainment, happy hours and $1 Monday middies. It's trying to improve its image, taking a hard line on those keen to create their own "live entertainment"; the least rough of the three bars is the "Pearlers' Rest". *The Divers' Camp Tavern* out at Cable Beach comes a close second, and usually gets the bands after the "*Roey*". Two **nightclubs** are to be found in Chinatown: the *Nippon Inn* in Dampier Terrace or *Tokyo Joes* round the corner in Napier Terrace, featuring banks of pool tables. However, for a uniquely Broometime experience, *Sun Pictures* (☎091/92 1677; $8) in Chinatown lets you watch the latest **movies** while mozzies nibble your ankles and bats flit across the screen.

The tourist office promotes various events – check exact dates with them. Early June sees the **Broome Fringe Arts Festival**, a celebration of local artiness and culture. The **Shinju Matsuri**, or Festival of the Pearl, in late August/early September is the big one, lasting over a week and bringing people from all over the country. The town celebrates its ethnic diversity, and the pearl which created it, with the crowning of the Pearl Queen and a beach concert, finishing up with a huge fireworks display. Broome gets packed out for the Shinju, so unless you want to end up camping miles away, book your accommodation in advance. The end of November sees ripening mangoes dropping from the trees, a good excuse for the **Mango Festival**. Mangoes are said to have a strange effect on people's behaviour, although the concomitant, sweltering "Build Up" probably has more to do with it. Either way things get pretty sticky, with markets, a mardi gras and juicy mangoes at every turn.

# Listings

**Airlines** *Ansett*, corner of Barker and Weld streets (☎091/93 5444).

**Bookshop** *Kimberley Bookshop*, 6 Napier Terrace (Mon–Fri 8.30am–5pm, Sat 8.30am–2.30pm, Sun 10am–1pm; ☎091/92 1944). The best bookshop between Darwin and Perth, with an excellent regional Aboriginal section and a children's bookshop two doors down.

**Bicycle rental & repair** *Broome Cycle Centre*, corner of Hamersley and Fredrick streets (☎091/92 1871), $8 for 24hrs.

**Car rental** Besides the big guys, try *ATC* at Broome Airport (☎091/937 788); *Topless Rentals*, 58 Hunter St (☎091/93 5017); or *Woody's*, Dampier Terrace (☎091/92 1791).

**Dentist** ☎091/92 1624.

**Hospital** Weld St, near Anne St (☎091/92 1401).

**Kimberley tours** *Flak Trak Tours* (☎091/92 2222), small-group 4WD tours, including 1-day Cape Leveque and 4-day West Kimberley/Gibb River Road; *Last Resort Adventure Tours* (☎091/93 5000), 2-day backpacker tours of the West Kimberley; *Pearl Coast 4WD Tours* (☎091/93 5786), West Kimberley or Cape Leveque 2-day tour; *Regional Safari* (☎091/92 1198), various 3- to 15-day, small-group 4WD tours deep into the Kimberley.

**Motorbike and scooter rental** *Roadrunner Motorcycle Hire*, 7 Farrell St (☎091/92 1971).

**Pharmacy** Next to *Shell* service station in Hamersley St (☎091/92 1399).

**Police** ☎091/92 1212.

**Post office** Hamersley St, near Barker St (☎091/92 1020).

**Taxi** ☎091/92 1133.

**Tours** *Broome Day Tours* (☎091/92 1068), for daily 3-hr historical tours $28, and trips out to Willie Creek Pearl Farm (see below); *Red Sun Camel Safaris* (☎091/93 7423) and *Ships of the Desert* (☎091/92 2222), for sunset camel rides along Cable Beach; *Broome Aviation* (☎091/92 1369) for scenic flights. Also more unusual jaunts on Harleys, helicopters and hovercrafts – enquire at the tourist office. (See also "Kimberley tours", above.)

# Cape Leveque

About 10km outside Broome, just after the *Bird Observatory* turn-off (see above), a road leads north to the Aboriginal lands of the northern Dampier Peninsula. The **Willie Creek Pearl Farm** (daily 9.30am–12.30pm & 1.30–4.30pm; closed Sun Oct–May; ☎091/92 4918; $12.50), 35km from Broome and 9km off the unsealed Cape Leveque Road, is housed in a beautiful building on Willie Creek. In the creek, racks of seeded oysters hang for two years at a time, building layers of pearlescent nacre over their implants as they feed from the tidal nutrients. The mysteries of this fascinating and normally highly secretive process are explained in informative **tours** (daily 10.30am & 2.45pm). *Broome Day Tours* (☎091/92 1068) offers daily visits, which coincide with the guided tours, for a rather steep $40, although this includes the entrance fee and a bit of an "eco-run" around the lanes on the way back.

The **Cape Leveque Road** continues unsealed to **BEAGLE BAY MISSION** (☎091/92 4913), 120km from Broome, where permission should be sought to continue your journey north on Aboriginal land (day permit required). Beagle Bay's **Sacred Heart Church**, built by German missionaries in 1917, is a beautiful building with an unusual altar decorated with mother-of-pearl. The store at **LOMBADINA MISSION** (closed Sun; ☎92 4942), further north, sells locally made shell-jewellery and artefacts. An overnight stay at the Aboriginal-run **Kooljaman Resort** (☎091/92 4970; ⑤; booking essential), on the very tip of Cape Leveque, is probably why you endured all those corrugations. Anywhere else this would be turned into an exclusive upmarket wilderness experience, but here you can camp or rent a basic four-bed cabin. There are also barbecues, a kiosk and a small café. If you've found Broome stressful, then Cape Leveque is the tonic.

# The Kimberley

*If one were to paint this country in its true colours, (he wrote), I doubt it would be believed. It would be said at least that the artist exaggerated greatly, for never have I seen such richness and variety of hue as in these ranges.*

*Kings in Grass Castles*, Mary Durack

A highland area between Derby and Kununurra, and about the size of Poland, **THE KIMBERLEY** is commonly described as Australia's last frontier. Divided by ranges and seasonally torrential rivers, it is a wilderness of huge cattle stations and small, isolated Aboriginal communities, with a ragged, tide-swept coastline inhabited chiefly by crocodiles. The extreme seasons and harsh terrain make access slow and difficult – for those who live here, light aircraft are a necessity rather than an indulgence.

With the demise of the beef industry in a region racked by floods and bushfires, some stations are opening up to adventure tourism, and there is talk of turning the whole area into a vast national park. There is little else: even the exploitation of minerals known to exist in the northwest of the region is made uneconomical by the climate and isolation; this alone says a lot about the Kimberley's remoteness. The road between Fitzroy Crossing and Halls Creek was the last section of the circumcontinental Highway 1 to be sealed, in the mid-1980s.

The region, particularly the barely accessible **Drysdale River National Park**, has many examples of the unusual Wandjina-style rock paintings, which depict rows of mouthless beings with owl-like heads as deities, rather than the widespread Rainbow Serpent figures. Otherwise, **tours** operate from Broome (see p.599), Fitzroy Crossing (see below), Halls Creeek (see p.563) and, most conveniently, from Kununurra (see box on p.566), along the **Gibb River Road** and to the popular **Bungle Bungles**. It would take a lifetime (or a heap of money, 4WDs and a helicopter) to get to know the whole of this immense wilderness, but that in itself is the very essence of the Kimberley's untameable appeal.

## Derby and Fitzroy Crossing

Situated on King Sound at the mouth of the Fitzroy River and surrounded by mudflats stirred by enormous tides, **DERBY**, 36km north of the coastal highway, is a mineral exploration base and an administrative centre for local Aboriginal communities. The **Gibb River Road** stock route, along which Kimberley beef was periodically exported, ends near Derby and is as close as most people get to this lacklustre but friendly old town.

The **tourist office** (Mon–Fri 8.30am–4.30pm, Sat 8.30–11.30am; ☎091/91 1426) is in Clarendon Street, where **buses** also arrive. **Places to stay** include the conveniently central *Kimberley Entrance Caravan Park* (☎091/93 1055, with bicycle rental), while the *Aboriginal Hostel* (☎091/91 1867; ①), 233 Villiers Street, provides good-value meals and a bed. The *West Kimberley Lodge* (☎091/91 1031; ④), in 17 Sutherland Street, is a guesthouse with shared facilities; or try the lively *Spinifex Hotel* (☎091/91 1233; dorms ①, motel units ⑤), next to the tourist office.

The Gibb River Road (see p.567) starts just out of Derby and cuts straight across the Kimberley, rejoining the tarmac near Wyndham 667km later. If you are heading east and want to see **Windjana Gorge** and **Tunnel Creek**, follow the Gibb River Road for 119km to the Windjana turn-off. From here you rejoin the Great Northern Highway after 123km. This section is no problem in dry weather in a 2WD and is more interesting (and only 30km longer) than following the highway to Fitzroy Crossing, 256km from Derby.

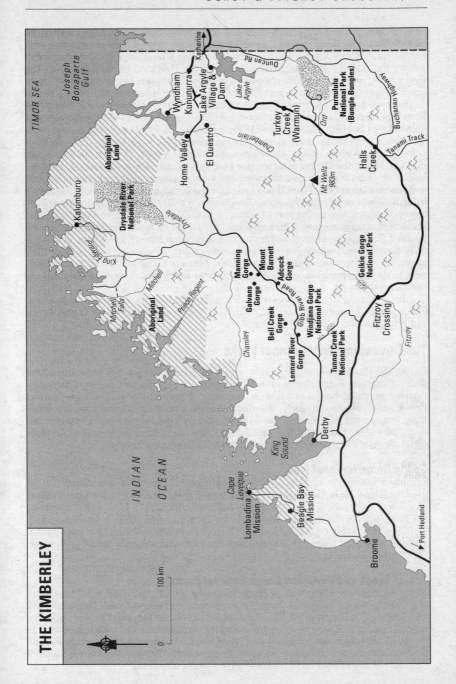

**THE KIMBERLEY**

Since the pastoral expansion into the Kimberley late last century, **FITZROY CROSSING** has been a small travellers' rest and crucial ford across the still-troublesome Fitzroy River. Today it's little more than a roadhouse and "welfare town" serving the region's Aboriginal communities. In the Dry it's a bleak, dusty place, the river a string of pools, but during a good Wet when the town is frequently cut off, water laps just under the road bridge and the land is flooded for miles around.

The town itself has nothing of any great interest, but the *Crossing Inn* in Skuthorpe Road has a century-old reputation for converting many moderate drinkers, stranded by weeks of flooding, into staggering dipsomaniacs. A Friday-evening session here will give travellers the most memorable experience the town has to offer, short of being swept away by floods. The *Fitzroy River Lodge* (☎091/91 5141; ⑤–⑦), on the highway east of the bridge, is far too good for Fitzroy, offering motel rooms, bushland lodges (or "canvas accommodation modules") and grassy campsites. It also has a pool and two **restaurants** and bars if you can't face the *Crossing Inn*, and acts as the town's **information centre**. *Darlngunaya Backpackers* (☎091/91 5140; ①) in Ross/Russ Street/Road (no one seems sure) is situated in the old post office, around which the settlement originally grew. With a pleasant, airy feel, it's a quiet place to catch up with yourself for a couple of days and if you ring in advance, they'll meet your bus in the early hours. The *Crossing Inn* (☎091/91 5080; cabins ③) also has tent sites and the obligatory counter meals, while the neglected *Tarunda Caravan Park* (☎091/91 5004) next to the **supermarket/post office** in Forrest Road, has cheap tent sites and on-site vans (③).

*Fitzroy Crossing Charter Tours* (☎091/91 5155) offer twice-daily, three-hour **tours** to Geikie Gorge (including cruise) for $20, and thrice-weekly day-tours to Tunnel Creek and Windjana Gorge for $70 – see below.

# The Devonian Reef National Parks

During the Devonian Era, 350 million years ago, a large barrier reef grew around the then submerged Kimberley plateau. The limestone remnants of this reef are today exposed north of Kununurra and in the national parks of **Geikie Gorge**, **Tunnel Creek** and, most spectacularly, **Windjana Gorge**. These three attractions are sometimes erroneously described as the "West Kimberley", but they are just a dramatic and easily accessible fraction of the west Kimberley's many natural spectacles. All three parks are closed and periodically submerged from November to April.

### Geikie Gorge National Park

Seventeen kilometres upstream from Fitzroy Crossing, the river has carved out the five-kilometre **Geikie Gorge** through the exposed reef, best seen on the **boat cruises** (April–Nov daily 9am & 3pm; 1hr 30min; $12; ☎091/91 5121). "High water" marks on the gorge's walls clearly show how high the river can rise, while below the surface harmless freshwater crocodiles jostle with freshwater-adapted stingrays and sawfish. Walking trails lead along the forested western banks, strategically dotted with picnic sites, barbecues and campsites.

### Tunnel Creek and Windjana Gorge National Parks

Along the Highway, 42km west of Fitzroy Crossing, a well-graded dirt road turns north to follow the Napier Range (as the reef is know here) to **Tunnel Creek National Park** (no camping), 105km from Fitzroy. Here Tunnel Creek has burrowed its way under the range, creating a 750-metre tunnel hung with overhead bats and who-knows-what in the pools. Although the collapsed roof illuminates the cavern halfway, the wade into progressively deeper and colder water to the other end still takes some nerve – a torch and shoes that you don't mind soaking help immeasurably.

A hundred years ago the caves were the hideout for the Bunuba Aborigine, Jandamarra (better known as **Pigeon**), and his gang of bushrangers. A police tracker for many years, one day he shot the officer at nearby Lillimoorla police station (now a ruin 2km south of Windjana Gorge) and released all the prisoners. A three-year spree of banditry followed before Pigeon was cornered and killed by fellow trackers in 1897.

The most dramatic remainders of the reef are the towering walls of **Windjana Gorge** (camping allowed), 135km from Fitzroy or 140km from Derby. A walking trail leads through a limestone crevice into a wide gorge splitting the Napier Range, lined with paperbark and Leichhardt trees. Freshwater crocs share the pools with various birds and can be seen sunning themselves in the afternoons.

# Halls Creek

**HALLS CREEK**, strung out along the highway, has a much livelier appearance than its nearest neighbour, Fitzroy Crossing, 288km to the west. In 1885 WA's first **gold-rush** took place in the hills south of town where the ruins of the **Old Town** (17km) crumble away. In less than four years the thousand prospectors succeeded in exhausting the area's potential, before stampeding off to new finds in the Eastern Goldfields.

There's precious little to see in town, but the gold-bearing hills to the southeast have a few diversions for those with their own transport. **China Wall** is a block-like vein of quartzite looming over a toxic pool, 6km from town, which appears even more impressive from the air. **Caroline Pool**, 15km from town, can be a good swimming hole early in the Dry, although **Palm Springs** and **Sawtooth Gorge**, a further 30km to the south, are scenically more appealing.

### Practicalities

There is an **information centre** (May–Sept daily 8am–5pm; ☎091/68 6262) off the main road in the middle of town. For **somewhere to stay**, the *Halls Creek Caravan Park* (☎091/68 6169; ③–④), Roberta Avenue, has tent sites, cell-like air-conditioned cabins and more spacious on-site vans. The *Shell Roadhouse* (☎091/68 6060; ④) has twin-share cabins, and the relatively salubrious *Kimberley Hotel* (☎091/68 6101), opposite the caravan park, has pokey bunkhouses (②), standard motel units (⑥) and luxury units (⑦). It's also the only pub and decent **restaurant** in town, although the **baker's** on the highway is a treat.

If you fancy flying over the **Bungle Bungles**, call *Crocodile Air* (☎091/68 6250) or *Kingfisher Aviation* (☎091/68 6218) a day or two in advance. The ninety-minute early-morning flights are the ones to go for, and even at around $110 they're well worth it. Alternatively, hire a jeep or a more spacious landcruiser from *Baz Industries*, 137

---

### SOME REMOTE SHORT-CUTS

Three long-distance Outback tracks converge near Halls Creek, each giving you a taste of remote Outback dust. The **Tanami Track** is signposted off the highway, 17km west of town, indicating 1040km to Alice Springs. The WA section can be rough and sandy, but after the NT border it's merely corrugated, and by the sealed road it's twice as far. A turning at *Carrunya Roadhouse/Station* leads to **Wolfe Creek Meteorite Crater**, the second biggest in the world, but not worth the 137-kilometre detour from the highway unless you're coming from or going to Alice.

The road south of Halls Creek to the Old Town leads on to the **Buchanan Highway**, an old stock route that joins the Stuart Highway near Dunmarra (NT) – nearly 800km long, it gets even less traffic than the Tanami. Finally, you're unlikely just to drive down the **Canning Stock Route** to Wiluna on a whim. At 1860km (4WD only) it's the world's longest stock route and the ultimate challenge for well-equipped off-roaders.

Duncan Road (☎091/68 6150). *Halls Creek and Bungle Bungle Tours* (☎091/68 6217) offer various **tours**, including an overnight fly-drive to the Bungles for around $300.

## Purnululu (Bungle Bungles) National Park

The spectacular **Bungle Bungle** massif (officially known as **Purnululu National Park**; closed Jan–April; $11) is one of Australia's greatest natural wonders and a couple of days spent exploring its chasms and gorges is well worth the effort and expense involved. Brought to prominence ten years ago by a film crew documenting the ravages of over-grazing in the area, the Bungles have quickly attracted a mystique matching that of Uluru (Ayers Rock). The delicate nature of the banded rock domes, as well as the difficulty in patrolling the remote park, means that limiting land access to 4WDs saves money, the eco-structure of the park, and tourists' lives. Following the failure of negotiations for a joint management plan (as has been successfully implemented in Kakadu and Uluru national parks in the NT), local Aborigines have staked a land claim on the Purnululu area, as others have done all over the Northwest in the wake of the Mabo Decision (see p.830).

The **fly/drive tours** available in Halls Creek (see above) and Kununurra (see box on p.566), which involve flying to the park's airstrip and then being driven around in a 4WD, offer the best of both worlds, and the half-hour **helicopter flights** ($115) available in the park get right into the gorges and will leave you grinning for hours – if you've ever wanted to fly in a chopper, save your money for the Bungles. Flights are also available from Turkey Creek (see below) and Kununurra (see p.566).

From the highway it's a rough 55-kilometre, two-hour, four-wheel-drive journey to the **ranger's residence** (☎091/68 7300), where the entry fee must be paid in return for a map. From here you can go to either of the two basic camps in the park. **Kurrajong Camp**, with a crude, solar-heated shower, is 10km to the north and gives access to **Echidna Chasm**, a one-hour-return walk into a slender chasm a thousand metres long and half as high – not the place to be caught in a flash flood. **Frog Hole** is another, wider chasm with a pool at the end, while **Mini Palms** involves squeezing into yet another narrow gorge to a cave at the end, as part of a walk that takes at least two hours and requires plenty of water and a torch. At any point on these walks you can look up and see palms clinging to the rock walls hundreds of metres above you; the scale of the clefts is underlined when you realize the palms can be up to twenty metres high.

**Wilardi Camp** (25km from the ranger's residence) is close to the **airstrip**, from where a track leads on to a cleared patch of ground used as a car park on the south flank of the plateau, site of the striped domes with which the Bungles are commonly associated. The weathered, beehive-like domes have horizontal bands of silica (orange) and lichen (grey), together forming a fragile crust over the powdery interior, and are a most unusual sight. From here a half-hour walk leads into **Cathedral Gorge**, a huge overhanging amphitheatre with the chance of a large pool early in the season.

**Piccaninny Gorge** is a hard, full-day's return walk requiring large quantities of water and a hat. The ground underfoot is soft sand and shade is negligible during the day. Although there is a pool towards the end, if you plan to walk up the gorge, leave very early in the morning and turn back long before your water runs out. There is an emergency hand-pump close to the car park.

## On to Wyndham

Halfway between Halls Creek and Kununurra is the roadhouse at **TURKEY CREEK** where a helicopter (☎091/68 1811) offers **flights into the Bungles** for $125. A faster, though less exhilarating, enclosed "Jetranger" is used, but it's still a stunning (and officially preferred) way of seeing the park.

From Turkey Creek the road continues directly northward, passing the **Argyle Diamond Mine** (no admission to the public), source of a third of the world's diamonds – although most of them end up on the tips of drills. The scenery takes a rugged turn as you pass the **Ragged** and **Carr Boyd ranges** to the junction with the Victoria Highway. Kununurra is 45km to the east and Wyndham 50km northwest.

Set on the muddy banks of the Cambridge Gulf, **WYNDHAM** was the port established to serve the brief goldrush at Halls Creek in the 1880s. The town was then well positioned to process and export beef from the east Kimberley until the meatworks closed in 1985. Now the town is just about on its last legs by regional standards with a *Crocodile Farm* (daily 9am–4pm; feeding 3pm; $5) and and the **Five Rivers Lookout** from the top of the 335-metre Bastion Ranges the only things worth checking out. There are plenty of undomesticated salties languishing hopefully near the blood and offal drain that once ran into the harbour; you may spot their gruesome silhouettes by the wharf at night. The **tourist office** (daily 8am–5pm; ☎091/61 1054) is in O'Donnell Street and you can camp at the *Three Mile Caravan Park* (☎091/61 1064) in Baker Street or enjoy a bit more luxury at the *Wyndham Community Club* (☎091/61 1130; ⑤) on the highway, 4km from town. The *Wyndham Town Hotel* (☎091/61 1003; ⑥) in O'Donnell Street has rooms, plus the town's one **restaurant** – the only choice for food besides the usual takeaways.

# Kununurra and the Ord River

**KUNUNURRA** is the Kimberley's youngest town, built in the early 1960s to serve the **Ord River Irrigation Project**, fed by Lake Kununurra. The Diversion Dam Wall, a stunning sight as you come in from the west, created this lake, essentially the bloated Ord River. Fifty kilometres upstream is the Argyle Dam Wall, built in 1971 to ensure a year-round flow to the project, creating the world's largest manmade body of water, Lake Argyle. Despite early problems, the Ord River Irrigation Project has come into its own in recent years, creating an intensive (but still barely developed) agricultural area.

Perhaps because of its youth and surrounding countryside, Kununurra escapes the resigned, rather jaded feel of the older Kimberley towns. Instead, the town has an appealingly relaxed atmosphere, enhanced by the copious amounts of fresh water nearby which have attracted recreational use. Besides being an ideal base from which to explore the adjacent Kimberley, the town is also a good place to seek out casual **farming work** during the dry season – some of the hostels may be able to help in this respect.

A couple of kilometres from town is Kununurra's own national park, **Hidden Valley**, where a road leads into a narrow valley of "mini-bungles" and terminates with some short trails – you couldn't ask for a better walking area so close to town. Another popular spot is **Ivanhoe Crossing**, 13km north of town on the Ord River. Officially the ford is closed to vehicles and you wouldn't want to try crossing it in anything less than a hefty 4WD. This is croc-country and, although people still fish and swim tentatively by the banks, this is inadvisable, being just the sort of habitual behaviour salties go for. If you get across the ford, **Black Rock Falls**, 4km down the road, is a safe place to swim and may still be flowing in the early Dry.

*Triple J Tours* (☎091/68 2682) offer cruises up **Lake Kununurra** to **Argyle Dam** with optional return by bus, a much more enjoyable excursion than you might expect. *Kimberly Canoeing Experience* organizes canoeing trips down the Ord River, driving you up to the dam and letting you float back over three days for $85. The *Zebra Rock Gallery* (daily 8am–6pm; ☎091/68 1114), 6km out of town on Packsaddle Road, has examples of the unusually banded rock found on an island in Lake Argyle as well as a small wildlife park, while back in town, *Warringarri Aboriginal Arts* (Mon–Fri 8.30am–noon & 1–4.30pm; ☎091/68 2212) in Speargrass Road, opposite the **Kelly's Knob** turn-off (a sunset viewing spot), has locally made arts and crafts to peruse or buy.

**REGIONAL TOURS FROM KUNUNURRA**

Kununurra is in the best position to offer a range of tours to the Bungles as well as the East Kimberley, and many operators are based here. The *Desert Inn* (☎091/68 2702)offers two-day Bungles and five-day Gibb River Road adventures (ending in Fitzroy to connect with the bus if you're heading west), and *Kununurra Backpackers* (which trades as *Kimberley Wilderness Adventure*, ☎091/68 1711) run 4WD tours throughout the region for around $100 a day. *KWA*'s three-day Bungle and comprehensive thirteen-day Kimberley tours ($1290) are especially good value. *East Kimberley Tours* (☎091/68 2213) do a fly-out, drive-back two-day Bungle tour.

*Alligator Air* (☎091/68 1575) has two-hour Bungle flights in high-wing aircraft (to give unobstructed views) for around $135 (no minimum numbers) and their five-hour Kimberley "The Works" flight ($225) includes a stop on the Mitchell Plateau. The latter is one of the best scenic flights over the Kimberley and is excellent value, but will only run with a minimum of five passengers; call in advance if you're heading for Kununurra.

## Practicalities

The **tourist bureau** (daily 8am–5pm; ☎091/68 1177) in Coolibah Drive has displays and videos on the area's many attractions, and details of all the tours which take you there. There is a perennially warm **swimming pool** ($2) next door, and the **post office** is also in Coolibah Drive. **Buses** arrive outside the *Kununurra Hotel*, passing through daily for Katherine, Darwin or Broome.

There are two **hostels** in town. The *Desert Inn* (☎091/68 2702; ①), on Konkerberry Drive, is a new building close to the pub and supermarket with a recent extension of eight-bed air-conditioned dorms and a cool spa. The popular *Kununurra Backpackers* (☎091/68 1711; ①), 111 Nutwood Crescent, has a small pool, a longer-term workers' accommodation section, TV and, like the *Desert Inn*, runs a whole range of good-value tours into the Bungles and along the Gibb River Road. Of the town's five **caravan parks**, the *Town* (☎091/68 1763) in Bloodwood Drive is the most central; the *Kona* (☎091/68 1031) is by Lake Kununurra, west of town; and *Hidden Valley* (☎091/68 1790), a kilo-metre north of town, has cheap tent sites but, like a lot of places, discourages farm work-ers. The *Quality Inn* (☎091/68 1455; ⑦), on the highway, is the town's best **motel**, with a good restaurant, or try the *Hotel Kununurra* (☎091/68 1344; ⑥) in Messmate Way.

**Places to eat** include the *Three Star Café* (daily 7am–7pm) in Banksia Street, *Valentino's* (daily 5–10pm) in Papuana Street for delicious pizzas, or *Chopsticks Restaurant* (daily 6–9.30pm) at the *Country Club Hotel*, next to the post office. *Gulliver's Tavern*, opposite the *Desert Inn*, gets the occasional band in the picking season, when the town gets fairly lively.

## Lake Argyle

When the **Argyle Dam** was completed in 1972, the Ord River (whose source is near Mount Wells, north of Halls Creek) managed to fill **Lake Argyle** in just one wet season; the lake itself, which covers an area of 700 square kilometres, holds enough water to supply the world's population with a thousand litres each. The fish population has grown over the years to support commercial fishing, as well as providing ample food for the numerous birds that flock here. When the lake was proposed, the Durack family's *Argyle Homestead* was moved to its present site, 2km from the tourist village (see below), and is now a **museum** (May–Oct daily 8.30am–4.30pm; $2) of early pioneering life in the Kimberley, as described in Mary Durack's droving classic *Kings in Grass Castles*.

Close to the dam wall, 70km from town, the old construction workers' camp has been turned into *Lake Argyle Tourist Village* (☎091/68 7360; ⑤), offering camping and cabins. *Lake Argyle Cruises* can take you right across the lake for half a day showing you wallaby caves, jabirus and other birds, freshwater crocs and **Zebra Rock Island**; *Bower Bird Cruises* offer shorter tours. Both are bookable at the *Lake Argyle Tourist Village* where a video is shown (daily 4.30pm) on the building of the dam.

# The Gibb River Road

On the way to Wyndham you pass the start of the unsealed **Gibb River Road** with its attendant warning sign. Originally built to transport beef to Wyndham and Derby, it cuts through the heart of the Kimberley, offering just a slice of this vast and rugged expanse. At around 670km to Derby, it's 230km shorter than the Great Northern Highway, but no-one uses the "Gibb River" as a short-cut; with around half a million corrugations per kilometre, it's rare to get across without something breaking or falling off, and punctures are very common. Furthermore, the attractions that make the route interesting are off the road and some are only accessible to high-clearance vehicles or 4WDs. **Tours** are available from Broome (see p.559) and Kununurra (see above).

If you seriously want to explore the interior of the Kimberley, ideally in a 4WD, seek out a copy of *The Kimberley: An Adventurer's Guide* by Ron and Viv Moon (published by *Kakirra Adventure Publications*), which is an excellent guide to the region. The two *Streetsmart* maps titled "West Kimberley" and "East Kimberley" are similarly detailed companions for driving in the area. Distances given in parentheses below are to destinations off the Gibb River Road.

## Along the Cockburn Range to the Kalumburu Road junction

The scenically impressive 250-kilometre eastern section up to the Kalumburu junction is the roughest part of the road, crossing many ranges and crossed in turn by big rivers, the first of these being the sandy **King River**, 17km from the highway.

The turn-off for the plush mini-resort at **Emma Gorge** (1km; $5 day-use; ☎091/61 4320), part of *El Questro Station*, leads to a bushcamp with an expensive restaurant and bar, a pool and small but comfortable "executive" tents (⑥) with shared facilities. There's a forty-minute walk along Emma Creek to the beautiful, fern-draped **gorge** (sunlit in the mornings), which alone is worth the entry fee.

Further down the Gibb River Road, *El Questro Station* (16km; $5 day-use; ☎091/61 4320) is a million-acre working cattle station that welcomes visitors. Part upmarket dude ranch and part pseudo-national park, the access road goes *through* the Pentecost River just before the homestead – call to ask for a pick-up if your car is too low-slung. There are all sorts of station activities (at a price), including heli-fishing, gorge cruises, horse and camel rides, dirt bikes and bullcatchers (stripped-down, armoured jeeps), but bargain **overnight deals** include some of the above, meals *and* pick-ups from Kununurra. Among the many attractions, the three-hour slog up to **El Questro Gorge** is straight out of an Indiana Jones movie and **Zebedee Springs** is a small, warm pool to soothe away the aches and pains of the day's exploits. **Accommodation** includes secluded camping with distant ablutions, or bungalows with shared kitchens (⑤).

From the *El Questro Station* turn-off, the Cockburn Range's cliffs lead you to the wide **Pentecost River** crossing (usually a dry ford at this point, but take care, crocs about). Just east of the crossing, the Karunjie Track (4WD only) leads 45km back to Wyndham. Eight kilometres after the Pentecost River crossing is *Home Valley Station* (1km, fuel; ☎091/61 4322; ⑦), another moribund cattle property easing its way into Outback tourism; as well as camping, they offer full-board lodgings. The same people also run *Jack's Waterhole* (fuel, camping, $5 entry fee; huts available ④) by the Durack River and *Karunjie* (or *Durack River*) *Station* (49km; $5 entry fee), with tours to beauty spots on their property. From here, there's nothing more than the wide open Kimberley countryside until you reach the junction with the road up to Kalumburu (see below).

## Mount Barnett to Derby

From this point the road west is smoother and, from *Mount Barnett Roadhouse* (daily 7am–6pm, May–Oct; ☎091/91 7007), which has the last fuel until Fitzroy Crossing or Derby, there are a number of watered gorges and possibly waterfalls that you'll most likely have to yourself. You can camp at the lovely **Manning Gorge** for $5, or for free at **Galvans** (700m) and **Adcock** (5km) gorges, all idyllic swimming breaks from the dusty road. **Bell Creek Gorge** (29km; 4WD only) is a long, rough drive but **Lennard River Gorge** (8km; 4WD only), on the other side of the King Leopold Ranges, is perhaps the most dramatic, carved through tilted tiers of rock.

A rock-chiselled profile of Queen Victoria's Head is evident as you pass through the gap in the **Napier Range**, and 9km later the turning leads southeast to Windjana Gorge National Park (21km; see p.562) and Fitzroy Crossing (165km; see p.560). The last 62km to Derby are tarmac.

## The Northern Kimberley

This is a remote and rarely visited part of the Kimberley with the spectacular, three-tiered **Mitchell Falls** (240km) and other sites on the **Mitchell Plateau** being the main destinations for self-sufficient visitors, and the rough road putting just about everyone else off. It's a long way to go for a swim, with a store and fuel at *Drysdale River Homestead* (59km; April–Oct daily 8am–noon & 1–5pm; ☎091/61 4236). The **Drysdale River National Park** is tantalizingly inaccessible by private vehicle but the determined should call Darwin-based *Willis Walkabouts* (☎089/85 2134, 08/8985 2134 from April 1996) which operates bushwalking tours that sometimes include the park – access is by light plane, 4WD and helicopter, so it won't be cheap. '

**Kalumburu Aboriginal Community** (267km, fuel and store Mon–Fri 7am–4pm; ☎091/61 4300 for permits), a mission set up last century by Spanish Benedictine monks (see New Norcia, p.570), welcomes visitors but requires an entry permit, which must be obtained in advance. It's one of the few places where you can get to the tide-swept and croc-ridden coast and is one of Australia's remotest corners.

## travel details

### Trains

**Perth** to: Bunbury (2–3 daily; 2hr); Kalgoorlie (1–2 daily; 7hr 30min); Port Augusta, SA (1 daily; 37hr); Sydney (2 weekly; 60hr).

### Buses

**Dampier-Karratha** to: Perth (5 weekly; 21hr); Port Hedland (5 weekly; 4hr).

**Kalgoorlie** to: Esperance (3 weekly; 5hr); Perth (2–4 daily; 8hr); Leonora (2 weekly; 11hr); Adelaide (1 daily; 36hr).

**Perth** to: Adelaide (1 daily; 35hr); Albany (3 daily; from 6hr); Augusta (6 weekly; 6hr); Broome (5 weekly; 32hr); Bunbury (1–2 daily; 2hr); Carnarvon (5 weekly; 11hr); Dampier-Karratha (5 weekly; 21hr); Darwin (3 weekly; 56hr); Denham (for Monkey Mia; 3 weekly; 12hr); Derby (3 weekly; 37 hr); Esperance (4 weekly; 10hr); Exmouth (3 weekly; 13 hr); Fitzroy Crossing (3 weekly; 40hr); Geraldton (2–4 daily; 6hr); Halls Creek (3 weekly; 44hr); Hyden (for Wave Rock; 2 weekly; 5hr); Kalbarri (3 weekly; 8hr); Kalgoorlie (1–4 daily; 8hr); Kununurra (3 weekly; 49hr); Margaret River (3 daily; 5hr); Meekatharra (4 weekly; 10hr); Newman (3 weekly; 13hr); Port Hedland (1 daily; 25hr).

### Flights

**Perth** to: Adelaide (2 daily; 4hr 15min); Alice Springs (5 weekly; 4hr); Ayers Rock Resort (3 weekly; 3hr 45min); Brisbane (3 weekly; 6hr 15min); Broome (1 daily; 2hr 30min); Darwin (1 daily; 6hr 15mins); Esperance (2 daily; 1hr); Kalgoorlie (1 daily; 1hr); Kununurra (6 weekly; 3hr 15min); Melbourne (1 daily; 5hr 15min); Sydney (1 daily; 6hr).

# CHAPTER EIGHT

# SOUTH AUSTRALIA

South Australia, the driest state of the driest continent, splits into two very distinct halves. The southern part, long settled, watered by the Murray River, and with **Adelaide** as a cosmopolitan centre, has been throughly tamed; the northern half, arid and depopulated, most definitely has not.

Most of southern – which is to say southeastern – South Australia lies within three hours' drive of Adelaide. Food and especially **wine** are among its chief pleasures: from the Adelaide Hills to the commercial hype of the Barossa Valley, and from the quiet pleasures of McLaren Vale on the Fleurieu Peninsula to the Clare Valley, this is prime grape-growing and winemaking country. As well as its wineries the **Fleurieu Peninsula**, just south of Adelaide, has a string of fine beaches along the Gulf St Vincent coastline. Cape Jervis, at the peninsula's tip, is the departure point for ferries to sparsely populated **Kangaroo Island**, a fine place to see Australian wildlife at its unfettered best. The **Yorke Peninsula**, facing Adelaide across the Investigator Strait, is primarily an agricultural area, preserving a little copper-mining history and some great fishing. The superb wineries of the **Barossa Valley**, originally settled by German immigrants in the nineteenth century, are only an hour from Adelaide on the **Sturt Highway**, the main road to Sydney. This crosses the Murray at Blanchetown and follows the fertile **Riverland** region to the New South Wales border. Following the **southeast coast** along the Princes Highway, you can head towards Melbourne via the extensive coastal lagoon system of the Coorong and enjoyable seaside towns like Robe, exiting the state at **Mount Gambier** with its crater lakes. The boring inland trawl via the **Dukes Highway** is faster, but far less interesting. Heading north from Adelaide, there are old copper-mining towns to explore at Kapunda and Burra, in the area known as the **mid-north**, which also encompasses the Clare Valley, a quieter, more down-to-earth wine centre and perhaps the southeast's most enjoyable.

In contrast with the gentle and cultured southeast, the remainder of South Australia – with the exception of the relatively refined **Eyre Peninsula** and its strikingly scenic west coast – is unremittingly harsh desert, a naked country of vast horizons, salt lakes, glazed gibber plains and ancient mountain ranges. Although it's tempting to scud over the forbidding distances, rewards from this introspective and subtle landscape develop slowly and you'll miss its essence by hurrying. For every predictable, monotonous highway there's a dirt alternative, which may be physically draining but enables you to

---

## ACCOMMODATION PRICES

All the accommodation listed in this book has been categorized into one of eight price bands, as set out below. The rates quoted represent the cheapest available double or twin room in high season – except for category ①, which are per-person rates for a dorm bed, and the prices given for units, cabins and vans, which are the daily charge for the whole unit.

| | | | |
|---|---|---|---|
| ① Under $16 | ② $16–26 | ③ $ 27–36 | ④ $ 37–54 |
| ⑤ $55–74 | ⑥ $75–94 | ⑦ $95–124 | ⑧ $ 125 upwards |

For more accommodation details, see pp.31–34.

get closer to this precarious environment. The folded red rocks of the central **Flinders Ranges** and **Coober Pedy**'s post-apocalyptic scenery are on most agendas and *could* be worked into a sizeable circuit, but overall the Outback lacks any real destinations. Making the most of the journey is what counts – the fabled routes to **Oodnadatta**, **Birdsville** and **Innamincka** are still real adventures, and not necessarily 4WD only.

**Rail** and road routes converge in Adelaide before the long cross-country hauls west to Perth via Port Augusta or north to Alice Springs and Darwin. *The Ghan* to Alice Springs is one of Australia's great train journeys; as is the *Indian Pacific* between Perth and Sydney, which passes through Adelaide – though if you hop on the eastbound train here, you'll have missed traversing the country which is really the point of the journey.

Adelaide and the surrounding gulf lands, cooled by the Gulf St Vincent, enjoy a Mediterranean **climate** that makes them tremendously fertile; as you head further north the temperature hots up to such an extreme that by Coober Pedy people live underground to escape the searing summer temperatures.

## Some history

When South Australia was first settled by Europeans in 1836, it was home to as many as fifty distinct **Aboriginal groups**, with a population estimated at 15,000. Three distinct cultural regions existed: the Western Desert, the Central Lakes, and the Murray and southeast region. It was the people of the comparatively well-watered southeast who felt the full impact of white settlement, those who survived being shunted onto missions and controlled by the government. Some Aborigines have clung tenaciously to their way of life in the Western Desert, where they have gained title to some of their land, but most Aborigines now live south of Port Augusta, many in Adelaide.

The coast of South Australia was first **explored** by Europeans in 1627 by the Dutch; in 1792 the French explorer d'Entrecasteaux sailed along the Great Australian Bight before heading for southern Tasmania; and the Englishman Matthew Flinders thoroughly charted the coast in 1802. The most important expedition though, the one which led to the foundation of a colony here, was **Captain Charles Sturt**'s 1830 navigation of the Murray River from its source in New South Wales to its mouth in South Australia.

South Australia was planned from the start: in the idealistic scheme of Edward Wakefield, there were to be no convicts – instead free settlers would be sold small units of land (rather than given large free land grants) in a state guaranteeing them civil and religious liberty. The success of the scheme was guaranteed when George Fife Angas formed the **South Australia Company** to finance it. In 1836, **Governor Hindmarsh** landed at Holdfast Bay, now the Adelaide beachside suburb of Glenelg, with the first settlers; the next year Colonel Light planned a spacious attractive city with broad streets and plenty of parks and squares, some distance inland. By 1839, Angas was assisting persecuted Lutheran communities from the eastern provinces of Prussia to settle in South Australia.

Early problems with the harsh, dry climate and financial incompetence (the colony was bankrupt in 1841) were eased by the discovery of substantial reserves of **copper** over the next decade. By 1870, Adelaide's population had almost doubled. The tradition of **libertarianism** in South Australia continued; in 1894 its women were the first in the world to be permitted to stand for parliament and the second in the world to vote (after their sisters in New Zealand). Social improvement through slum clearances began after World War I. Of all the mainland states, the depressions and recessions of the inter-war period hit South Australia the hardest. After World War II, new migrants came, boosting the output of industry and injecting new life into the state.

The 1970s was the **Don Dunstan** decade. The flamboyant Labor Premier was an enlightened reformer who had a strong sense of social justice: he abolished capital

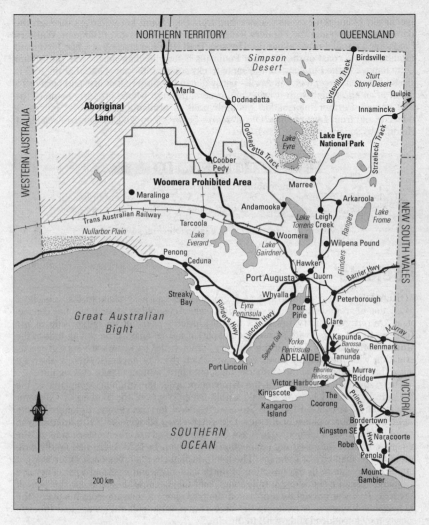

punishment, outlawed racial discrimination and decriminalized homosexuality. The state has been a duller place since his retirement in 1979, and a poorer one since the recession started to bite at the end of the Eighties.

# ADELAIDE AND THE SOUTHEAST

As far as transport goes, Adelaide is very much the heart of the state, with all routes radiating from the city. There are good **bus** connections throughout the southeast, but more rewarding alternatives are worth considering. Much of the country is flat and great for **cycling**. The principal route is the newly developed **Mawson Trail**, 800km specifically planned for cyclists, extending from the Mount Lofty Ranges through the Barossa and traversing the Flinders Ranges to the Outback town of Blinman. **Walkers** can follow a parallel route along the **Heysen Trail**, 1500km starting at Cape Jervis and running up the coast of the Fleurieu Peninsula before heading north over the Mount Lofty Ranges to the Flinders, on the same tracks some of the way. Note that the trail is closed between December and April – partly due to the high risk of fire, and partly as a result of an agreement with private landowners, through whose property some of the trail passes. Further information on both trails is available from tourist offices in Adelaide and from *Leisure Directions Resource Centre*, Shop 20, City Centre Arcade, 11 Hindmarsh Square (☎08/226 7373).

---

### TELEPHONE NUMBERS

The **telephone code** for Adelaide is ☎08.
All **Adelaide numbers** are due to be changed in August 1996: **seven-digit** numbers will have the prefix 8 added, while **six-digit** numbers will have the prefix 84 added.

*(For more on changes to phone numbers Australia-wide, see p.40.)*

---

# Adelaide

**ADELAIDE** is always thought of as a gracious city, an easy place to live: despite a population of around one million and a slick veneer of sophistication, it still has the feel of an overgrown country town. It's a pretty place – laid out on either side of the **Torrens River**, ringed with a green belt of parks, and set against the rolling hills of the **Mount Lofty Ranges**. During the hot, dry summer, the parklands are kept green by irrigation with the Murray River water on which the city depends; there's always a sense that the rawness of the Outback is just out there, waiting to take over again.

The traditional way of life of the **Kuarna people**, the original occupants of the Adelaide Plains, had been destroyed within twenty years of the landing of Governor Hindmarsh at Holdfast Bay. The Surveyor General for the colony, Colonel William Light, had visionary plans for the new city. After a long struggle with Hindmarsh, who wanted to build on a harbour, Light got his wish for a city on the western side of "the enchanted hills", with a strong connection to the river. In 1823, Light had really written of the Sicilian city of Catania: "The two principal streets cross each other at right angles in the square in the direction of north and south and east and west. They are wide and spacious and about a mile long", and this became the basis for the plan of Adelaide. Post-war immigration provided the final element missing from his plan – the human one: Italians now make up the biggest non-Anglo cultural group, and the café society they introduced adds spirit to the city.

With its Mediterranean-style hot dry summers, al fresco eating and drinking is commonplace, and lends the city a vaguely European air, with its wide, well-planned streets and squares transformed with a squint of the eye into boulevards. One of the chief delights of Adelaide is the interest its inhabitants take in **food** and **wine**, with restaurants and cafés as culturally varied as Sydney and Melbourne's but much cheaper, and South Australian wine monopolizing every cellar. Unlike a European city, though, except for a couple of lively thoroughfares, the centre is virtually deserted in the evening and on Sundays. However, culture is held in high esteem, and is brought to life by the biennial **Adelaide Arts Festival**.

Outwardly conservative, Adelaide nonetheless has the advantage of South Australia's liberal traditions, with a nudist beach, relaxed drug laws and 24-hour hotel licences. It's the free and easy **lifestyle** within an ordered framework that's so appealing; Adelaide may not be an obvious destination in itself, but it's a great place for a relaxed break on your way up to the Northern Territory or across to Western Australia, with only daunting Outback and great distances ahead.

## Arrival and information

**Buses** from out of town, including the airport bus, will drop you off at the **Central Bus Terminal**, 111 Franklin Street. The international **airport**, 8km from the centre, is small, modern and easy to handle; there's a small currency exchange and information booth. The **airport bus** ($4) will drop you off at most city accommodation on request; its set route stops at Victoria Square and North Terrace as well as the bus terminal. A taxi will cost around $13 to the city and $10 to the beachside suburb of Glenelg, 11 km from the centre. Arriving by **train** at the interstate terminal at **Keswick**, you can again take the airport bus, which stops here on its way back from the airport to the city ($2.50 to city, $4 out to airport), or walk to the suburban platform and catch a train into Adelaide Train Station on North Terrace. To book a return airport bus, call ☎381 5311.

### Information

The obvious first stop for information is the **South Australian Travel Centre**, at 1 King William Street on the corner of North Terrace (Mon, Wed, Thurs & Fri 8.45am–5pm, Tues 9am–5pm, Sat & Sun 9am–2pm; ☎212 1505). Staff are very helpful at this large modern office, where masses of general information is displayed and there are excellent touring guides and maps of Adelaide and the state, all free. You need to queue for more specific enquiries or to book tours and accommodation. The **State Information Centre**, 77 Grenfell Street (Mon, Tues, Thurs & Fri 9am–5pm, Wed 9.30am–5pm, Thurs 9am–5pm; ☎226 0000) sells the *Department of Sport and Recreation*'s maps of the Heysen Trail, Mount Lofty walks and South Australian cycle routes; there are also some free maps and brochures. The **Natural Resources Information Centre**, ground floor, 77 Grenfell Street (☎204 1910), has lots of information on national and conservation parks in and around Adelaide and the state.

## City transport

The square mile of the city centre is obviously compact to walk around, and its flatness makes that an easy option. A free bus, the **Bee Line**, is a handy alternative that cuts out a lot of the leg work – it leaves from Victoria Square (every 8min; Mon–Thurs & Sat 8am–6pm, Fri 8am–9pm) and heads up King William Street to North Terrace, then along past the train station and back to Victoria Square.

To explore further out of the city centre, you'll need to use the **State Transit Authority**'s (STA) system, which comprises mainly buses, plus suburban trains and one tramline from the city to Glenelg. Free timetables are available from the centrally located **Information Bureau Trans Adelaide** (Mon–Fri 8am–6pm, Sat 8am–2pm) on the corner of King William and Currie streets, where they also have maps of the system ($1) and staff to advise on routes and tickets; timetable information and advice is also available over the phone (Mon–Fri 8am–7.30pm, Sat 8am–4pm, Sun 9am–4.15pm; ☎210 1000). Times are often not displayed at the stops and waits can be long – buses and trains run until about 11.30pm, with reduced services on Sundays. **Tickets** come in multi-trip, single-trip and day-trip, and are interchangeable between buses, trains and the tram; they can be bought on board buses, but are marginally cheaper at train stations, post offices and selected shops. The day-trip ($4.40 on a bus or $4 from outlets) is much the easiest, and you only have to make about three journeys for it to

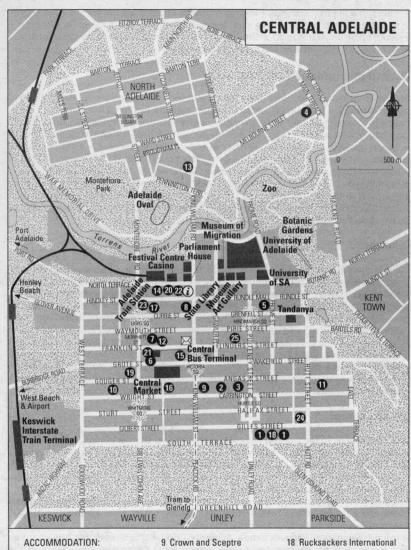

# CENTRAL ADELAIDE

ACCOMMODATION:

1 Adelaide Backpackers Hotel
2 Adelaide Backpackers Inn
3 Adelaide City Backpackers
4 Adelaide Meridien
5 Austral Hotel
6 Backpack Australia Hotel
7 Cannon Street Lodge
8 City Central Motel

9 Crown and Sceptre
10 Director's Hotel
11 East Park Lodge
12 Franklin Hotel
13 Greenways Apartments
14 Grosvenor Hotel
15 Metropolitan Hotel
16 New World International
17 Plaza Hotel

18 Rucksackers International
19 Sportsmans Hotel
20 Strathmore Hotel
21 Sunny's
22 Terrace Intercontinental
23 Wests Private Hotel
24 YHA
25 YMCA

be worthwhile. When you get on the bus or train you must validate your ticket in the machine by the door.

Four suburban **train** lines run from Adelaide Train Station, a modern complex with shops and cafés in North Terrace. **Violence** on trains does happen late at night, but the problem is being addressed by extra guards; if you're worried, buses are generally safer for night-time travel. The **tram** to seaside Glenelg (30min) leaves from Victoria Square every fifteen to twenty minutes. The **O-Bahn** is a fast-track bus which runs on concrete rails through scenic Torrens Linear Park, between the city (Grenfell Street) and Tea Tree Plaza in Modbury, 12km northeast of the city.

**Cycling** is an excellent alternative: the flat city area and its wide, multi-laned streets make riding a breeze, and there are several good cycling routes – including the **Torrens Linear Park track**, which goes from the mountains to the sea, weaving itself along the river. A map of this and other cycling routes is available from the State Information Centre (see above); for bike rental outlets, see "Listings", p.590.

## Accommodation

The only time you may have difficulty finding accommodation is during the Arts Festival, when you'd be well advised to book ahead. Most of the **hostels** are in the southwest quarter of the city or around the bus terminal in Franklin Street; there are cheap **hotel** rooms on Hindley Street but it's much less pleasant, and some women may find it threatening. The swankiest accommodation is along North Terrace.

Adelaide has loads of **hostels**, many of them dingy and unappetizing. Most are in Gilles or Carrington Street, about ten minutes' walk from the city centre, and will pick up from the bus or train station if you call them; some will even come to the airport if you call in advance. The most central **campsite** is the *Adelaide Caravan Park*, Bruton St, Hackney, 3km out (☎363 1566; on-site vans ③, cabins ④), but for a beachfront setting, head to *West Beach Caravan Park*, Military Rd, West Beach (☎356 7654; bus #272 or #273; on-site vans ③, cabins ⑤), though you'll need to be prepared for the summmertime hordes.

The seaside suburb of **Glenelg** and the nearby beach resorts (see p.583) are good alternatives to the city, and are only about half an hour away by public transport.

### Hotels

**Adelaide Meridien**, 21 Melbourne St, North Adelaide (☎267 3033). On fashionable Melbourne St, the building's an eyesore but creature comforts include sauna, spa and outdoor pool. ⑦–⑧.

**Director's Hotel**, 259 Gouger St (☎231 3572). Modern hotel aimed at executives, with studio apartments; highly perfumed and muzaky, but close to Chinatown and the Central Market. ⑦.

**Grosvenor Hotel**, 125 North Terrace (☎231 2961). Genteel establishment dating from 1918 complete with potted palms in the foyer. ⑥–⑦, including breakfast.

**Plaza Hotel**, 85 Hindley St (☎231 6371). Once a grand hotel, now very seedy; the interior courtyard with its huge palm tree compensates though. ④.

**The Strathmore**, 129 North Terrace (☎212 6911). You're really paying for the location rather than the facilities; rooms are small, viewless and rather suffocating. Car parking available. ⑥.

**The Terrace Intercontinental**, 150 North Terrace (☎217 7552). This new high-rise luxury hotel couldn't be more central, with views of the Festival Centre, but room rates are in excess of $200. ⑧.

**Wests Private Hotel**, 110B Hindley St (☎231 7575). Grotty foyer is off-putting, and rooms basic though clean; bargain rates, but not the best choice for a solo female. ③.

### Pubs, motels and self-catering

**Austral Hotel**, 205 Rundle St (☎223 4660). Basic rooms in one of Adelaide's best pubs in this "arty" street are great if you want to go out; otherwise bands nearly every night can be noisy. ③.

**City Central Motel**, 23 Hindley St (☎231 4049). Centrally located budget motel. ④.

**Colley Motel Apartments**, 22 Colley Terrace, Glenelg (☎295 7535). Excellent value, self-contained apartments with TV, fridge and kitchen, opposite the beach. Few frills but well equipped. ④–⑦.

**Crown and Sceptre**, 308 King William St (☎212 4159). Quiet, centrally located pub has inexpensive rooms. ③.

**Esplanade Hotel**, Esplanade, Brighton (☎296 7177). Basic seaside pub rooms. ④.

**Franklin Hotel**, 92 Franklin St (☎231 4703). Virtually opposite the bus station, an unrenovated working man's pub; basic rooms, but with air-conditioning and cheap meals available. ④.

**Glenelg Seaway Apartments**, 18 Durham St, Glenelg (☎295 8503). Falls into the cheap and cheerful category. Clean, spartan apartments, but with linen supplied. Friendly owner. ④.

**Greenways Apartments**, 45 King William Rd, North Adelaide (☎267 5903). One-, two- and three-bedroom self-catering units. ⑤–⑧.

**Heartsease**, 19 Colley Terrace, Glenelg (☎294 6779). Two-bedroom unit accommodating up to 6 with laundry and parking. ⑥–⑦.

**Meledon Villa**, 268 Seaview Rd, Henley Beach (☎235 0577). Seafront bed and breakfast in a lovely turn-of-the-century bungalow. B&B ④, self-contained unit ⑥.

**Metropolitan Hotel**, 46 Grote St (☎231 5471). One of the nicer pubs to stay in, full of nineteenth-century charm downstairs, and with basic but clean rooms upstairs. Breakfast available. ③.

**Sportsmans Hotel**, 185 Grote St (☎231 3250). Simple rooms in no-frills pub are clean and close to the bus station; an early-opening pub (5.30am–9pm), so noise won't keep you awake at night. ③.

**St Vincent Hotel**, 28 Jetty Rd, Glenelg (☎294 4377). Friendly, homey place popular with country folk visiting the city; one self-contained flat. ⑤.

## Hostels

**Adelaide Backpacker's Hostel**, 263 & 255 Gilles St (☎223 5680). Long-established hostel has 40 beds in two houses: dorms are large and bright, and two double rooms are also available. Women's dorms are en suite. Free tea and coffee; bike rental. Rooms ②, dorms ①.

**Adelaide Backpackers Inn**, 112 Carrington St (☎223 6635). Small and shabby, but with a good friendly ambience. Reception doubles as a travel agency (bus and train tickets). There's also annexe accommodation across the road, in a brighter, more modern building with a car park and plenty of singles and doubles. Rooms ③, dorms ①.

**Adelaide City Backpackers**, 118 Carrington St (☎232 7022). Very ugly and poky, but new owners are attempting to spruce the place up; good security and parking. Rooms ②, dorms ①.

**Albert Hall**, 16 South Esplanade, Glenelg (☎376 0488). Once an exclusive private hotel, now a hostel, with three floors of crumbling grandeur gradually being renovated. A great spot opposite the water, with an outdoor area to relax in – and good room security. Ask for the dorm on the balcony overlooking the ocean. Rooms ③, dorms ①.

**Backpack Australia Hostel**, 128 Grote St (☎231 0639). Friendly, clean and modern, with licensed bar – definitely a party hostel, this one; good-value meals and free tea and coffee. Dorms are tiny though; double and single rooms are also available. Rooms ②–③, dorms ①.

**Backpackers Glenelg Beach Headquarters**, 7 Moseley St, Glenelg (☎376 0007). Lovely heritage building; doubles and singles available. Bar and restaurant. Rooms ③, dorms ①.

**Cannon Street Lodge**, 11 Cannon St (☎410 1218). Down a lane opposite the bus station, this huge warehouse-style space has a groovy grunge feel to it. The main living areas are airy and spacious with a pool table area downstairs and murals on the walls. Bathroom privacy is a little lacking, although some en suites are available, and the kitchen's very small. However, undercover parking and lock-up garages are good for drivers and cyclists. Licensed travel agents at reception. Rooms ③, dorms ①.

**East Park Lodge**, 341 Angas St (☎223 1228). Adelaide's best hostel, in a leafy, well-heeled area, is a spacious three-storey building with views of the hills from its balconies and a peaceful atmosphere. Mainly single, double or twin rooms; good weekly rates. Rooms ③, dorms ①.

**New World International**, 29–31 Compton St (☎212 6800). Close to Central Market and Chinatown, a clean, modern hostel although a bit lacking in atmosphere. Dorms ①.

**Rucksackers International**, 257 Gilles St (☎232 0823). Low-key hostel with a young crowd, run by Americans. Pleasant courtyard area. Pay showers (20c for 5min) are a drag, but enable the hostel to undercut the going rate by a couple of dollars. Dorms ①.

**Sunnys**, 139 Franklin St (☎231 2430). Right next to the bus terminal, this place has recently been transformed into a comfortable place with an agreeable feel and much upgraded toilet and bath-room facilities. Train, bus and plane tickets sold and tours booked. Rooms ③, dorms ①.

**YHA**, 290 Gilles St (☎223 6007). Large, light and peaceful hostel; office closed 10am–1pm but 24-hour access for guests. No curfew. Only one "family room", which must be booked in advance. ①.

**YMCA**, 76 Flinders St (☎223 1611). Central location, open to both sexes. Dorm stays limited to one week (includes linen); private rooms for a maximum of three weeks. Rooms ③, dorms ①.

# The City

Adelaide's city centre, south of the river, is a strict **grid** surrounded by **parkland**: at the very centre of the grid is **Victoria Square**, and each city quarter has its own smaller square. **North Terrace** is the cultural precinct with all the major museums, the two universities and the state library. **Hindley Street** is the liveliest in town, and the focus of the city's nightlife, while **Rundle Mall**, its continuation, is the main shopping precinct, and **Rundle Street**, further east, the arty café strip. The other important area lies west of Victoria Square: between Grote and Gouger streets is the lively **Central Market** and the small **Chinatown**. North of North Terrace, the **Torrens River** flows, with the **Botanic Gardens** and the **Zoo** on the south bank. Three main roads cross the river to quiet, suburban **North Adelaide**, with **O'Connell Street** the main drag on this side.

Wandering the streets of Adelaide, one of the most striking aspects is the bourgeois solidity of the structures, a solidity enhanced by the fact that virtually every building, public or domestic, is **stone**: sandstone, bluestone, South Australian freestone and slate. The city's well preserved **Victorian architecture** is not the over-the-top style of Melbourne from money made quick in the 1850s goldrush. Rather Adelaide, with numerous economic setbacks and then a steady mining industry, built up its wealth slowly, and the buildings are as permanent and dependable as the city itself. There's really only one place to start your tour, and that's tree-lined **North Terrace**, a mile-long heritage streetscape perfect for exploring on foot.

## The Botanic Gardens and Ayers House

At the eastern extremity of North Terrace is the main entrance to the **Botanic Gardens** (Mon–Fri 7am–dusk, Sat & Sun 9am–dusk; free guided tours from the kiosk by the main lake Tues, Fri & Sun 10.30am). Although the gardens, founded in 1855, are lovely – with statues, heritage buildings, lakes and fountains – they're too enclosed to be a real haven from the city: the ugly Adelaide Royal Hospital towers over them and you never fully escape the noise of traffic. The **Palm House**, completed in 1877, was based on a similar structure in Germany. An elegant glass and wrought-iron structure, its role of displaying tropical plant species has been taken over by the new **Bicentennial Conservatory** (daily 10am–4pm, extended to 5pm in summer; $2.50). This, the largest glasshouse in Australia, is stunning, housing a complete rainforest environment with its own cloud-making system. Other attractions are a fragrant herb garden you can wander around, and **Simpson House**, a pleasantly cool thatched hut containing palms and ferns beside a stream. At the northern entrance to the gardens, **North Lodge**, once the caretaker's residence, is now a shop (daily noon–4pm) that sells books on botany and gardening, and other souvenirs.

Heading away from the gardens on North Terrace, the first building of note is National Trust-owned **Ayers House** (Tues–Fri 10am–4pm, Sat & Sun 2–4pm; $2). Home to the politician Henry Ayers, who was premier of South Australia seven times betweeen 1855 and 1897, it started life as a small brick dwelling in 1845: the fine bluestone mansion you see now is the result of thirty years of extensions. Inside, it's elaborately decorated in late-nineteenth-century style, with Ayers family portraits.

## The University and Gallery of South Australia

Between Frome Road and Kintore Avenue, a whole block of North Terrace is taken up with the two universities, and the art gallery, museum and state library. The **University of Adelaide**, the city's oldest, was established in 1874 and admitted women from day one, another example of South Australia's advanced social thinking. The grounds are pleasant to stroll through: along North Terrace are **Bonython Hall**, built in 1936 in a vaguely medieval style, and **Elder Hall**, a turn-of-the-century Gothic-Florentine design now occupied by the Conservatorium of Music (free lunchtime concerts Fri 1.10pm; ☎303 5925 for details). The highly decorative Gothic-inspired **Mitchell Building** beside it constituted the entire original university; on the first floor is the **Museum of Classical Archeology** (Mon–Fri noon–3pm, termtime only; free).

From Bonython Hall to Kintore Avenue are overbearing Victorian busts and statues of the stern and upright founders of Adelaide. But respite is at hand, in the form of the two contemporary abstract sculptures outside the **Art Gallery of South Australia** (daily 10am–5pm; free; guided tours Mon–Fri 11am & 1pm, Sat & Sun 11am & 3pm). The gallery itself has an extensive collection of **Aboriginal art** including many non-traditional works with overtly political content; major works of the Western Desert school of Aboriginal artists is permanently on display in Gallery 7. There's a good selection of **colonial art** too: it's interesting to trace the early derivation from European art and the point at which the Australian scenes and colours start coming alive. The collection of **twentieth-century Australian art** has some good stuff – Sidney Nolan, Margaret Preston, Grace-Cossington Smith – but a lot of dross too. Finally there's a large collection of twentieth-century British art, including paintings by Robert Fry and Vanessa Bell (Virginia Woolfe's sister). The gallery's other facilities are good, with a bookshop, coffee shop and a free cloakroom.

## Museums – and the State Library

Next door to the gallery, in the **South Australian Museum** (daily 10am–5pm; free; ☎207 7500 for details of special exhibitions), a huge whale skeleton can be seen through the unfortunate modern glass frontage. Two matching wings with cupolas enclose the pleasant courtyard through which you enter: with its fountain and palm-shaded it's a popular lunch spot for shoppers. First impressions are of the usual old-fashioned museum – dimly lit, with stuffed animals in glass cases and a concentration on **natural history**. Mostly it is rather staid, but travelling exhibitions and special displays add interest, and there's also a lively, hands-on **information centre** with microscopes, specimens, live animals and a scientist on hand to answer all sorts of weird and wonderful questions about natural history and anthropology. The museum is best known, though, for having the world's largest collection of **Aboriginal artefacts**. However, in recognition of their continuing significance, and the often dubious manner in which they were acquired, some of the human remains and sacred objects are now being returned to their traditional owners. Level 5 has the permanent collection as well as changing Aboriginal exhibitions: there's a fantastic large-screen **video** telling the Ngarrindjeri Dreamtime story of Ngurunderi, an ancestral hero; from here you move on to a section that cleverly uses the story as a metaphor to describe the life of the Ngarrindjeri people.

Next door to the museum, on the corner of Kintore Avenue, the 1884 **State Library** (Mon, Tues, Wed & Fri 9.30am–8pm, Thurs 9.30am–5pm, Sat & Sun noon–5pm; ☎207 7200) has everything from archives to a newspaper reading room; there's also a cosy magazine room with comfy chairs and hundreds of the latest glossies, where you can rest awhile.

Around the corner on Kintore Avenue, the **Museum of Migration** (Mon–Fri 10am–5pm, Sat & Sun 1–5pm; free) completes the mega-culture block. Surprisingly for a country populated overwhelmingly by immigrants, this is Australia's only museum of immigration history. You're taken on a journey from port to settlement, in the company of South Australia's migrant settlers, through the use of interactive displays and reconstructions. The exhibits here have a reputation for confrontation and innovation: the "White Australia Walk", for example, where a push-button questionnaire gives you the red, green or amber light for immigration under the guidelines of the White Australia policy, which was in force from 1901 to 1958. One writer called it a "museum of grief" and it does focus on the grim individual struggles of everyday lives, as well as celebrating cultural diversity. Ironically, the museum is housed in what was in the nineteenth century the **Destitute Asylum**, where the city's poor and homeless were hidden away; its story forms a part of the permanent exhibition.

## Government and art

Continuing west along North Terrace past the **War Memorial**, on the next corner is **Government House**, Adelaide's oldest public building, completed in 1855: every governor except the first has lived here. Across King William Street, two parliament houses, the old and the new, compete for space. The current **Parliament House**, begun in 1889, wasn't finished until 1939 because of a dispute over a dome: there's still no dome (and only half a coat of arms) but it's a stately building with a facade of marble columns. The modest **Old Parliament House**, built between 1855 and 1876, is now a museum (Mon–Fri 10am–5pm, Sat & Sun noon–5pm; $4; ☎207 1099) where you can see the restored House of Assembly Chamber, with its impressive wood panelling, brass chandeliers and red velvet drapes. A slide show in the auditorium is lifted from the doldrums by holographic talking heads on either side of a very wide screen; these apparitions discuss the political and economic development of South Australia as images flash past.

On the corner of North Terrace and Morphett Street, the **Lion Arts Centre** is the base for the biennial Adelaide Fringe Festival (see box on p.587) and alternative arts in general – there are theatres, bars, a cinema and galleries. The **Experimental Art Foundation** functions to educate people about contemporary art and was the first alternative art space in Australia to be government-funded; artists have studios upstairs and the gallery downstairs is always provocative. The bookshop has a noticeboard where invitations to private views are tacked up, so if you want some free wine and a peek at the (small and incestuous) Adelaide art scene, take a look. Meanwhile, the **Jam Factory Craft and Design Centre** (Mon–Fri 9am–5pm, Sat & Sun 10am–5pm) highlights the tenuous nature of the dividing line between art and craft: here beautiful objects made of leather, glass, wood and clay combine aesthetics with utility. The work is for sale and there's always an exhibition in the gallery. Amid vibrant orange walls and a pyramid-shaped skylight, a blue-metal spiral staircase leads to a viewing platform above the **glass-blowing centre** (demonstrations Mon–Fri 9–10.30am, 11am–1pm & 2–4.15pm, Sat & Sun 10am–4pm).

## Along the Torrens River: Festival Centre and Zoo

The **Torrens River** meanders between Adelaide and North Adelaide, surrounded by parklands. Between Parliament House and the river is the **Festival Centre**: two geometric constructions of concrete, steel and smoked glass, ensconced in a concrete arena littered with abstract 1970s civic sculpture. The theatre complex was built for the 1973 festival and is still its focus (see p.587 for more on the festival itself), but the theatres are open all the time. The main auditorium, the *Festival Theatre*, is the largest in Australia, hosting opera, ballet and various concerts; the smaller *Playhouse Theatre* is the home of the *State Theatre Company*; while the *Space Theatre* is often used for cabaret and stand-up comedy. Wander in to look at the various displays and the paintings of the Coorong by Fred Williams in the *Festival Theatre* foyer; there are free recitals here every Sunday in winter. **Art Space** (daily 10am–4pm) is a small commercial gallery in the *Playhouse* foyer, while the *Space Theatre* foyer has free **children's workshops**, plays and films on winter Saturdays (2–4pm). Call ☎216 8600 for details of specific events.

Outside, the **amphitheatre** has free rock concerts on summer Sundays (2–4pm), a fountain jets up from the river and black swans float leisurely by. This is **Elder Park**, in whose ornate Victorian cast-iron bandstand brass bands play on Sunday mornings. The *Popeye* cruise to the zoo leaves from here (35min return; $5 return, $3 one way; ☎295 4747), or you can rent paddle boats ($6 per 30min) from the green shed at **Jolleys Boathouse**, across King William Road. The boathouse is an Adelaide institution: there's a restaurant (see p.585), as well as a kiosk, and some seats from where you can enjoy the same river views for less.

The nicest way to get to the **Zoological Gardens**, on Frome Road (daily 9.30am–5pm; Jan also Wed & Sun until 8pm; $9; free guided tours 11.30am & 2pm; ☎267 3255 for details), is to follow the river, either by boat (see above) or a pleasant fifteen-minute stroll. Alternatively, walk from the Botanic Gardens through Botanic Park, entering through the children's zoo entrance on Plane Tree Drive, or take the #272 or #273 bus from Currie Street. Opened in 1883, the country's second-oldest zoo (after Melbourne's) is as much a botanical garden as anything. There are century-old European and native trees, including a huge Moreton Bay fig, and the grounds are full of picnic tables surrounded by gobbling families. Even the classic Victorian rotunda has tables inside where you can eat. The remaining Victorian architecture is well preserved; most of the animal houses have long since been replaced but a few classic examples like the **Elephant House**, built in 1900 in the style of an Indian temple, have survived. There are all the usual caged exotics, but Adelaide zoo is best known for its extensive collection of native birds: there are two large walk-through aviaries.

## King William Street and Victoria Square

As the city's main thoroughfare, **King William Street** is lined with imposing civic buildings and always crowded with traffic. As you walk down, look out for the **Edmund Wright House** at no. 59, whose elaborate Renaissance-style facade (designed by Wright) is one of Adelaide's most flamboyant. On the other side of the street, and a couple of blocks south, the **Town Hall** (1866), is another of Edmund Wright's designs revealing his love of the Italianate. The **General Post Office**, on the corner of Franklin Street, is another portentous Victorian edifice, this time with a central clock tower: take a look at the main hall with its decorative roof-lantern framed by opaque skylights. On the opposite Flinders Street corner, the **Old Treasury Building** has a small museum concentrating on the exploration, settlement and development of South Australia (Mon–Fri 10.30am–3.30pm; free).

Interrupting King William Street, pleasant **Victoria Square** with its fountain is a favourite Aboriginal meeting place, with people sitting on the shady ground and talking – no longer overlooked by tall gums but by the porter of the *Hilton Hotel*. Around the square are also the Catholic **Cathedral of St Francis Xavier** and the imposing **Supreme Court** on the corner of Gouger Street. Just to the west, the **Central Market** (Tues 7am–5.30pm, Thurs 11am–5.30pm, Fri 7am–9pm, Sat 7am–1pm) has been a beloved part of Adelaide for over a hundred years; under one roof there are European goodies, cheeses, meat, fish, fruit and vegetables in an orgy of smelly stalls and lively banter.

## Rundle Mall and Rundle Street

The main shopping area in the central business district is **Rundle Mall**, where several arcades radiate off a busy pedestrian mall. It manages to be bustling yet relaxed at the same time, enhanced by trees, benches to sit on, al fresco cafés, fruit and flower stalls, and usually a busker or two to draw a crowd.

Behind its Victorian facade, the futuristic **Myer Centre** is like a science-fiction invention of Jules Verne or H G Wells, with its eight levels, glass lifts and huge atrium. There's an extraordinary amusement park, **Dazzleland,** on the top two floors, and shops include the city's two best department stores, *Myer* and *David Jones*, the latter with a fabulous food department. While you're here take a look, too, at the decorative **Adelaide Arcade** and Regent Theatre. By night, Rundle Mall is eerily deserted, a strange contrast to Hindley and Rundle streets, either side, which really come to life after dark.

**Rundle Street** was the traditional home of Adelaide's wholesale fruit and vegetable market, though its lively, down-at-heel feel has long been appropriated by the alternative and arty. This is now the focus of up-and-coming Adelaide, full of outdoor cafés and restaurants, with the two best pubs in town (*The Austral* and *The Exeter*, see p.587) and some slick bars. The **East End Market** (Fri, Sat & Sun 9am–6pm) here is a 200-stall covered bazaar selling New Age trinkets, though these are increasingly outweighed by mass-produced commercial stuff. The main area has a cosmopolitan food court and an excellent fresh produce market, but it's all a bit sanitized. Sundays are busiest, when the place is packed with families, and Chinese masseurs are out in force. Head to the **flea market** (Sat–Sun 8am–5pm) in the adjacent East End Palais car park for a more alternative scene. Opposite the East End Market, the disused **Adelaide Fruit and Produce Exchange** (1903) is worth a peek. In red brick with curved archways and yellow plaster friezes above of fruit, vegetables and wheat, it's a classically Edwardian building.

## Tandanya

**Tandanya**, the *Aboriginal Cultural Institute*, is situated opposite the classic old market buildings at 253 Grenfell Street (daily 10am–5pm; $4; ☎223 2467 for details of exhibitions and events). The centre is managed and controlled by Aboriginal people, who lobbied for fifteen years for such a space: its major focus is **visual arts**, with temporary exhibitions of national significance, but there's also a performance space and workshops. The exhibition space is large and open with screens hung from the exposed rafters. Displays might cover Dreaming stories, history, or contemporary Aboriginal writing, while political paintings confront black deaths in custody and other issues, and explore Aboriginal self-expression and identity. Video screens are dotted around, and speakers play Aboriginal music, which you can buy in the **shop**. This is an excellent place to buy Aboriginal products if you want to be sure where your money is going: choose from original paintings, didgeridoos, hand-carved weapons and shields, tapes, literature and bush tucker, as well as T-shirts and other souvenirs.

# North Adelaide

**North Adelaide**, a ten-minute walk from the central area, makes for an enjoyable stroll past stately mansions and small bluestone cottages, or a good pub crawl around the many old hotels. There are three ways of getting there. The best walking route to North Adelaide is up King William Road past the Festival Centre (nearly every bus from outside the Festival Centre also goes this way). From Elder Park, the pretty 1874 Adelaide Bridge crosses the river to Creswick Gardens, home of the **Adelaide Oval** cricket ground (free guided tour Thurs 10am; 2hr) and with superb views of **St Peter's Cathedral** (daily 9am–5pm; free guided tours Wed 11am & Sun 3pm) in Pennington Gardens. The Anglican cathedral was built in 1869 in French Gothic-revival style; its main entrance is suggestive of Notre Dame in Paris. The *Cathedral Hotel*, opposite, is Adelaide's second oldest hotel, built in 1850; it has a humorous "Quasimodo" theme and very good-value meals. At the top of King William Road, the peaceful and shady **Brougham Gardens** boast palm trees against a backdrop of the Adelaide Hills. Continuing straight up, the commercial strip of O'Connell Street has an embryonic restaurant scene to rival that of Rundle Street.

If you want to see a wide range of early colonial architecture you might do better to head north via Morphett Street and Montefiore Road to **Jeffcott Street** (buses #233 & #253 from King William Street follow this route). **Lights Vision**, on Montefiore Hill, is a bronze statue of Colonel William Light pointing proudly to the fine views of the city he designed. In Jeffcott Street itself look out for the neo-Gothic 1890 mansion **Carclew**, with its round turret, and the **Lutheran Theological College**, a fine bluestone and redbrick building with a clock tower and cast-iron decoration; a towering palm adds a lush note. In peaceful **Wellington Square** the gorgeous 1851 *Wellington Hotel* retains its original wooden balcony. Turning into tree-lined **Gover Street** you'll find rows of simple **bluestone cottages**; in contrast, **Barton Terrace West**, two blocks west, has grand homes facing the parklands.

The third route from the city to North Adelaide is via Frome Road (past the zoo) to **Melbourne Street** (buses #204, 206, 209, 272 & 273 from King William Street), an upmarket strip of good cafés, antique stores, restaurants, designer clothing boutiques and speciality shops. Although the traffic is heavy, lots of trees, plants and vine-covered awnings give the narrow street a shady, relaxed feel. *The Banana Room* (☎239 0755) along here is probably the best retro-chic clothes store in Australia, with an immaculate range of designer dresses from the 1920s on; a 1926 Coco Chanel dress is on display. Don't expect bargains – most things are over $100, with a smattering over $300 – but it's fascinating to browse.

## The suburbs

Adelaide spreads a long way beyond the small inner-city enclaves, but few visitors see much of this. Most will at some stage venture down to the sea – **beaches** stretch from Henley via **Glenelg** to Brighton, while **Port Adelaide** has some excellent museums to set off its dockside atmosphere – but the inner suburbs remain uncharted territory. Some of them are well worth breaking the mould for, with local character, inexpensive restaurants and out-of-the-ordinary shopping.

**Norwood**, just east of the city, has two interesting streets; Magill Road (bus #106 from Currie Street), with a concentration of antique shops, and The Parade (buses #122–124 from Currie Street), a lively shopping strip with some great cafés and pubs and good bookshops. On weekends the small **Orange Lane Market** (Sat & Sun 10am–5pm), in a tin-roofed shed at the corner of Edward Street and The Parade, is a sedate place to browse among secondhand and new clothes, books, jewellery and bric-a-brac, as well as handicrafts, and there are Asian or fry-up food stalls. In January the lively **Italian Festival** (☎366 4555 for details) takes over Norwood Town Hall.

In **Thebarton**, west of the city, the lively **Brickworks Market** (Fri–Sun 9am–5pm; bus #112, #113, #115, from Currie and Grenfell Streets) radiates out from the 1912 Brickworks Kilns at 36 South Road. There are plaza shops and indoor and outdoor stalls, mostly selling new clothes, and it's always busy with buskers and crowds of people grazing their way around the varied food stalls or enjoying the small amusement park.

Immediately south of the city **Unley Road** (bus #191, #192 or #192B from King William Street) is known for its antique shops and expensive boutiques. Parallel King

William Road at **Hyde Park** (bus #202 or #203 from King William Street) is a fancy parade of upmarket fashion shops and some of Adelaide's best cafés and restaurants.

## Port Adelaide and around

The unfortunate early settlers had to wade through mud at Port Misery when they arrived; nowadays **PORT ADELAIDE** takes the strain. Established not far from Port Misery in 1840, by 1870 it was a substantial shipping area with solid stone warehouses, wharves and a host of pubs. The area bounded by Nelson, St Vincent and Todd streets and McLaren Parade is a well preserved nineteenth-century streetscape; several ships' chandlers and shipping agents show it's still a living port, a fact confirmed by the many corner pubs with decorative iron-lace balconies. There's no tourist office, but the *Port Adelaide Info Service* provides up-to-date details of attractions over the phone (☎47 6000).

To get here, take a train from central station or bus #258 or #259 from North Terrace; the best day to visit is Sunday, when the **Fishermen's Wharf Markets** (8am–5pm) take over a large waterfront warehouse on Queens Wharf and several **cruises** are available on the water. The market (mainly bric-a-brac) adds some life to the waterfront, but the once-varied food stalls now seem to be dominated by purveyors of meat pies and steak sandwiches. Outside is the quaint red-painted metal **lighthouse** (1869) that originally sat at the entrance to Port River; it can be climbed and inspected as part of your explorations of the Maritime Museum (below), as can the museum's two floating vessels moored 300 metres away, the steam tug *Yelta* and the coastal trader *Nelcebee*. *Jessica Lauren River Cruises* (☎47 1170) has two-hour Sunday afternoon trips from the lighthouse while the *MV Foxy Lady* (☎341 1194) has Sunday cruises of Port River (2pm & 3.30pm) as well as Wednesday and Saturday trips at 1.30pm.

The pick of Port Adelaide's several museums is the **South Australian Maritime Museum** on Lipson Street (Tues–Sun 10am–5pm, plus Mon during school holidays; $7, or combined with the Port Dock Railway $11). Located in the **old Bond Store** with its massive timber posts and wooden floors, the museum is concerned with the migrants who came through the port and the South Australian **coastal ketch trade**. Starting from the basement, the migration section has faithfully reconstructed three typical steerage or economy cabins from 1840, 1910 and 1950; you can wander through them, lie on a bunk, listen to sails creaking or hear "new Australians" remembering their journey. Level two explores the various ways that South Australia relates to the sea, from seaside scenes with displays on bathing and a working penny arcade, to pleasure cruises on the gulf, fishing and ship model-making. On the ground floor you can board a real ketch; upstairs is a more traditional collection.

**Port Dock Station Railway Museum** (daily 10am–5pm; $6), further along Lipson Street, is a trainspotter's delight, with a collection of over twenty steam and diesel locomotives. The model train displays include a fantastic one with a South Australian setting complete with the Adelaide Hills, the Flinders Ranges and a model of Port Adelaide; and there are seven fully decked-out trains, some with stores and kitchens, others with upmarket dining rooms and lounges. The train ride, which runs on demand, costs $2 extra and is glorified by steam on Sundays.

The **Historical Aviation Museum** (Sat & Sun 10am–5pm; $3), in an old flour mill at 11 Mundy Street, has World War II aircraft and aviation memorabilia among its collection. A more interesting war-related place to visit, though, is **Fort Glanville** (every third Sun 1–5pm, Sept–May; $5), 3km west in Semaphore, at 359 Military Road. This is the only complete example of the many forts built in Australia when fear of Russian invasion reached hysterical heights after the Crimean War.

## Glenelg and the beaches

The most popular and easily accessible of the city's beaches is **Glenelg**, 11km southwest of the city. The half-hour tram ride out there from Victoria Square is part of the experience, in beautiful 1929 trams with original fittings – red leather seats and leather hanging straps, and airy panelled-wood interior compartments.

Glenelg was the site of the landing of Governor Hindmarsh and the first colonists; the **Old Gum Tree** where he read the proclamation establishing the government of the colony still stands in McFarlane Street (bus #167 or #168 from Grenfell Street, downtown), and there's a re-enactment here on Proclamation Day (Dec 28) every year.

Nowadays, Glenelg is busy even off season. **Jetty Road**, the main drag, is crowded with places to eat (for the obligatory seaside fish 'n' chips, *Bay Fish Shop* at no.27 is the best) and there's lots of accommodation (see pp.575–576). The tram terminates in **Moseley Square** with its elegant town hall and clock tower. On the opposite corner the original *Pier Hotel*, now part of the *Ramada Grand Hotel*, follows in the Victorian tradition of imposing seafront hotels, and is crowded with drinkers on Sunday, when Glenelg is at its most vibrant. From Moseley Square, the jetty juts out into the bay, and in summer the beach on either side is crowded with people swimming in the calm waters; it's also a popular windsurfing spot year-round. On the foreshore, **Glenelg Tourist Information** (daily 9am–5pm; ☎294 5833) can help with anything you might need; next door, *Beach Hire* (☎294 1477) rents out deck chairs, umbrellas, surf skis and boogie-boards. Rollerblading and cycling are other popular Glenelg activities, with a **bike track** south of the square and mountain and touring bikes to rent from *Holdfast Cycles* on the Anzac Highway at no. 768 (☎294 4537); seek rollerblades at *Coastal Creatures*, 6/61 Jetty Road (☎295 2266).

North of Glenelg, **West Beach** (#276 bus from Currie Street, 25min) is a rather soulless spot with a caravan park and a drive-in. It does have a good, long, sandy beach, but atmospheric **Henley Beach**, further north still, is a better option (bus #132 or #133 from Currie Street, 20min; #286 or #287 from North Terrace, 35min). Here there are restaurants, cafés and pubs, while Henley Square, opposite the pier, is like an amphitheatre. On either side are classic federation-style buildings, and across Seaview Road is the beautiful *Ramsgate Hotel* with its elegant iron-lace balcony. The next beach along, **Grange**, is really charming, with a row of Victorian terraced houses facing the beach (bus #112 or #135 from Grenfell Street, 30min; Grange line train, 20 min).

To the south of Glenelg, **Brighton** has an old-fashioned, almost 1950s air, and is reached via the Noarlunga Centre train (25min). Along the Esplanade, the *Tram Stop Café* (perfect fish and chips) and the *Esplanade Hotel* look straight out of that era. The focus of the seaside suburb is the jetty beyond the stone Arch of Remembrance where families and couples wander; along the Esplanade joggers, cyclists and skateborders strut their stuff.

## Eating and drinking

Adelaide has roughly one restaurant for every thirty people, so not surprisingly **eating out** is a local obsession, and it's incredibly inexpensive. Moonta Street, closed to traffic between Gouger and Grote streets, is a small **Chinatown**, with several Chinese restaurants and supermarkets; there are many other restaurants on **Gouger Street**, at their busiest on Friday nights when the nearby Central Market is open till 9pm. **Café** society is based around the alternative zone of Rundle Street in the city, and in North Adelaide on O'Connell Street and the upmarket, decidedly chic Melbourne Street. Finally, eating in **pubs** in Adelaide doesn't just mean the usual steak and salad bar but covers the whole spectrum, from some of the best "contemporary Australian" food in town to bargain specials in several pubs along King William Street.

As for drinking, South Australian wine features heavily – which is just as well, since by general consensus, **tap water** in Adelaide tastes dreadful. Although it's perfectly safe, there's usually only a small charge for spring water, which is what everybody drinks.

## Restaurants

**Amalfi**, 29 Frome St (☎223 1948). Creative Italian; upbeat, jazzy and young with experimental sauces and traditional ones given a hot edge. Crowded and open very late, closed Sun.

**The Boathouse**, off Victoria Drive (☎223 5863). Serving mouth-watering but pricey "contemporary Australian" cuisine, this is a very popular venue for Sunday lunch overlooking the river.

**Colonial Café**, 2 Durham St, Glenelg (☎294 8224). Simple light meals by day, fancier contemporary Australian food at night; peaceful, light and airy. Expensive. Closed Mon & Tues.

**Flinders Stuben Restaurant**, 223 Flinders St (☎223 2539). As a visitor to Adelaide, you can be signed in to this German club. Small and friendly, with inexpensive, filling German food.

**Fortuna Garden**, 68 Moonta St (☎231 2231). Popular, large Cantonese restaurant in Chinatown. Every Friday there's a lunch and dinner special with all you can eat for $8.50.

**Gouger Café**, 98 Gouger St (☎231 2320). Unreconstructed, down-to-earth fish caff with original 1950s decor and classic neon sign; dinner nightly, lunch weekdays only.

**Noodles**, 119 Gouger St (☎231 8177). Popular southeast Asian restaurant serving Thai and Malaysian food. Non-smoking. Lunch Thurs & Fri, dinner nightly.

**Rakuba African**, 33A O'Connell St, North Adelaide (☎267 3227). Sudanese chef cooks regional dishes; occasional live music, and noticeboard with other African happenings around town. BYO. Daily except Mon 5.30–11pm.

**Red Ochre Grill**, 129 Gouger St (☎212 7266). Slightly pricey top-notch contemporary Australian cuisine, with bush tucker on the menu. Relaxed vine-shaded outdoor eating area.

**Shibata**, 135 Melbourne St, North Adelaide (☎267 3381). Japanese, specializing in *nabe mono*, one-pot dishes. Daily 6–11pm.

**The Snake Charmer**, 46 Unley Road, Unley (☎272 2624). Upmarket Indian.

**Zambracca**, 94 Melbourne St (☎239 1345). Lively bistro crowded with the smart set; superb Mediterranean food in spacious slick surrounds. Daily 9am–late.

## Cafés and cheap eats

**Al Frescoes**, 260 Rundle St. If you only go to one café in Adelaide, come here. Packed every night, the young Italian community have made it their own, and it's *the* place to see and be seen. Great coffee, *biscotti*, delicious *gelati* made on the premises and *focaccia* and *calzone* to eat. Daily 6.30am–late, which means around 4am at weekends.

**Café Aqua**, 164 Military Rd, Semaphore. Gay- and lesbian-friendly café with outdoor dining facing the sea. Light meals with a cosmopolitan twist.

**Anders**, 61 Jetty Rd, Glenelg. Small, busy German-run bakery and café. Sells sweet treats, as well as savoury pastries.

**Buongiorno Café**, 145 The Parade, Norwood. Large, always lively café reaches a crowded and noisy crescendo Sunday night; anything imaginable Italian to eat or drink. Daily 8am–1am or later.

**Café La Mer**, 8 Jetty Rd, Glenelg. Gleaming Italian café/restaurant/bar is noisy yet relaxed; anything from *gelati* to *focaccia* to pasta. Daily noon–late.

**Café Paradiso**, 150 King William Rd, Hyde Park. Long-established favourite; great coffee and real Italian al fresco dining, from pasta to *osso buco*. Daily 8.45am–11.30pm.

**Café Piccante**, 128 King William Rd, Hyde Park. All stone and chrome, a cool haven in summer; fashion-conscious right down to the pizzas with goat's cheese. Daily 11am–late.

**Clearlight Café**, 203 Rundle St. Vegetarian wholefood place where everything is clean and healthy; even the paint is non-toxic – and the food is delicious. Mon–Thurs 9am–4pm, Fri & Sat 9am–9pm.

**Cowley's Pie Cart**. An Adelaide institution, this mobile pie cart is positioned outside the GPO on Franklin Street nightly. It's famous for its "pie floaters", a gruesome concoction of hot pork pie afloat in a sea of peas and slathered in tomato sauce. Sun–Thurs 6pm–1am, Fri & Sat 6pm–3.30am.

**The Elephant Walk**, 76 Melbourne St, North Adelaide. Carved wooden elephants and bamboo dividers make private little lounge areas; lively but intimate. Daily 8pm–late.

**Fasta Pasta**, 61 O'Connell St, North Adelaide, and in the city at 131 Pirie St and 465 Pulteney St. Part of a chain which serves authentic, inexpensive fresh pasta with interesting sauces, ordered informally at the counter, and served with bread and a dish of parmesan.

**Flash Coffee Gelateria**, 87 Hindley St, next to the *Plaza Hotel*. Tiny Italian coffee bar opened in 1957 and hardly changed, still serving the best coffee and *gelati* in town; also croissants and *focaccia*.

**The Gallerie**, 20 Gawler Place. Excellent Asian food court in the basement of this arcade. Mon–Fri 9am–5.30pm.

**Gilles Street Snack Bar**, 269 Gilles St. Friendly, family-run and close to the hostels; breakfast from 6.30am. Closed weekends.

**Hawkers Corner**, corner of Wright St and West Terrace. Chinese, Thai, Malaysian and North Indian stalls. Try the Malay seafood *laksa*. Tues–Sat 5–10.30pm, Sun 11.30am–8.30pm.

**Jerusalem Sheshkebab House**, 131A–131B Hindley St. Dimly lit Lebanese BYO that serves fresh and tasty Middle Eastern dishes.

**Marcellina Pizza Bar**, 273 Hindley St. At the quieter western end, this all-night pizza, steak and pasta bar is always full of the spill-out from the area's clubs and pubs; the pizzas are among the best in town. Closed Sun.

**Minim's Café**, 199 Hutt St. One of several good cafés along this street near the Gilles Street hostels; great breakfast plus the usual Italian-style fare. Licensed and BYO.

**Ruby's Café**, 255B Rundle St. A popular market caff in the 1950s, the decor hasn't changed except in the bar. Cocktails, arts noticeboard and changing exhibitions feature, along with Sunday breakast, which is served all day (9am–5pm); otherwise, it's open evenings only, 6.30pm–late.

**Sandbank on the Bay**, 1st Floor, Tourism Commission Building, The Foreshore, Glenelg. Verandah seats overlooking the water and with the benefit of refreshing sea breezes; great for coffee and letter writing.

**Tiki Snack Bar**, Victoria Square. Right next to the GPO and opposite the shady square with pavement tables, a perfect spot for devouring mail and a good salad sandwich. Weekdays only 6.30am–5.30pm.

**Vego and Lovin' It**, 1st Floor, 240 Rundle St. Vegan café with mock tacky decor and seriously low prices.

**Zumma Café**, 56 Gouger St. With its back entrance opening onto the Central Market, this place positively buzzes during market hours. Cheap breakfasts, plus quiche and salads. Mon–Thurs 7am–6pm, Fri 7am–9pm, Sat 7am–late.

## Pubs

**Ambassadors Hotel**, 107 King William St. Slightly sleazy pub, but ridiculously cheap simple pub lunch put on to attract the drinkers.

**Austral Hotel**, 205 Rundle St. Counter meals here, with Malaysian, Thai, Mexican and Italian dishes, as well as good old Aussie steaks, burgers and seafood, are something else. A restaurant section, frequented by twenty-somethings, does upmarket versions.

**The Bull and Bear Ale House**, 91 King William St. Snazzy bar in basement of the *State Bank Centre*, a cool retreat on a hot day for sticky stockbrokers; imported ales and sophisticated meals.

**The Earl of Aberdeen**, 316 Pulteney St, Hindmarsh Square (☎223 6433). Gazebo full of greenery serves huge portions of pasta, steak, fish and kangaroo, imaginatively cooked. Attentive service.

**The Oxford Deli Bar**, *The Oxford Hotel*, 101 O'Connell St, North Adelaide. The *Deli Bar* is good value: order at the counter and eat in the groovy pub. There are plenty of meals under $5, with full marks going to the Oxburger and fries at $5.50.

**The Oz Rock Café**, *Ramada Grand Hotel*, The Foreshore, Glenelg. There are some great bistro-style places to eat inside *The Grand*, including this one which serves up kangaroo, crocodile, emu and octopus, plus plenty of homegrown beef.

# Entertainment and nightlife

*Well it's one more boring Thursday night in Adelaide*
*And it looks like everybody must've died . . . .*

Redgum

Dead as Adelaide can appear at night, there's actually quite a lot going on – bands, clubs, film and theatre – if you know where to look. The best place to find out **what's on** is *The Guide*, a pull-out weekly with film and theatre listings and reviews in Thursday's *Advertiser*. There's also a thriving **free press**: top of the culture stakes is

## THE ADELAIDE FESTIVAL AND WOMADELAIDE

The **Adelaide Festival** takes over the city for three weeks at the beginning of March of every even-numbered year, a huge event attracting an extraordinary range of international and Australian theatre companies, performers, musicians, writers and artists. Around the main festival has grown an avant garde and experimental **Fringe**, which for many is more exciting than the main event. The official festival began in 1960 and since 1973 has been based at the purpose-built **Festival Centre**; there's late night cabaret after the evening's events in the Festival Fez-top, a tent pitched outside. **Writers' Week**, the literary festival, is held in marquees in the Pioneer Women's Memorial Gardens; there are free outdoor concerts and opera, even films. Other venues around town host **Artists' Week**, exploring visual arts, and a small **film festival**. Programmes are available from *Tourism South Australia* offices, or write to Adelaide Festival, PO Box 1269, Adelaide 5001 (☎08/216 8600).

The **Fringe Festival** begins, with a wild street parade on Rundle Street, a week before the main event and ends a day after. Based at the **Lion Arts Centre**, on the corner of North Terrace and Morphett Street, and at venues all over town, it unleashes buskers en masse into Rundle Mall. Twenty-four hour licensing laws are taken advantage of, as the Sydney and Melbourne arts scenes join the locals for some serious partying: late every night the Fringe Club has bands, cabaret and comedy. For more details on the Fringe, call ☎08/231 7760, or pick up a programme from any *STA Travel* office.

**Womadelaide** is an outdoor world music weekend that began in 1992 as part of the Arts Festival but has now developed its own identity and is held every alternate (odd-numbered) year to the festival. It takes place in late February in Botanic Park: the full weekend (Fri night through to Sun night) costs around $98, but day and session passes are also available (☎08/216 8635 for information).

*The Adelaide Review*, a highbrow monthly covering visual and performing arts, film, literature, history, wine and food, available from bookshops, museums, galleries and just about everywhere else. At the more populist end of the scale, *Rip It Up* is a gig listings magazine, out every Thursday, with film, theatre and music reviews and interviews, while if you're into clubbing, dance and fashion, get hold of *The Core* every Wednesday; both of these can be picked up at most record stores and bookshops.

At night, the place to head is **Hindley Street**, where the concentration of clubs and live music venues are always buzzing – though it can get sleazy as the night wears on. And, of course, there's the **Adelaide Casino** (Mon–Thurs 10am–4am, non-stop Fri 10am–Mon 10am; neat dress required), near the train station. As unpromising as this might sound, it's worth at least one visit: the marble entrance with its dome is stunning and, although this elegance isn't matched by the glitzy gaming rooms, the Austrian crystal chandeliers are jaw-slackening.

## Pubs and bars

**The Austral**, 205 Rundle St (☎223 4660). More consciously arty and music-oriented than the *Exeter* (see below), the *Austral* is frequented by students for the independent local bands. Thurs–Sun, usually free.

**Boltz Bar and Café**, 286 Rundle St (☎232 5234). Café downstairs dips into every culture for its fab food; bar upstairs has pool table, amusement machines, and live techno/soul/funk thrice weekly. Young fairly hip crowd. Daily 10.30am–3am.

**The Earl of Aberdeen**, 316 Pulteney St (☎223 6433). Young uptempo bar with jazzy, funky sounds on the sound system.

**The Exeter Hotel**, 246 Rundle St (☎223 2623). "No renovations, no bullshit" is the slogan at this long-established hang-out for Adelaide's artists and writers. Bluesy bands Tues–Sun; free.

**The Oxford**, 101 O'Connell St, North Adelaide (☎267 2652). Slick marble and music-video bar.

**Rio's**, 111 Hindley St (☎212 2744). The tackiest bar in town; open 24 hours.

The Talbot Hotel, 104 Gouger St (☎231 9780). Out the back, one tiny bar (open weekends only) has intimate booths and classic Thirties decor.

Universal Wine Bar, 258 Rundle St (☎232 5000). Stylish bar run by a winemaker aiming to educate folk about South Australia's wines.

## Clubs and live music

Cargo Club, 213 Hindley St (☎231 2327). Club that features jazz soul, funk and R&B acts; classic cool meets Nineties post-modernism in the decor. Tues night "Boplicity" is devoted to jazz.

Fezbah, Festival Theatre Piano Bar. Music cabaret plays ambient and acid jazz, attracting an older after-work crowd. Fri from 11pm.

Heaven, *New Market Hotel*, 1 North Terrace (☎211 8533). Commercial dance club catering to the mainstream. Resident DJs as well as visiting international acts and one-off events.

Liberty, 90 Hindley St. Big-name alternative Australian and overseas bands. Dance club Fri and Sat.

Nexus Cabaret, Lion Arts Centre, North Terrace (☎212 4276). "Café Musica" hosts irregular programmes of World Music run by the Multicultural Artworkers Committee.

Old Lion Hotel, 165 Melbourne St, North Adelaide (☎267 3766). Formerly the Lion Brewery, this place serves real ale, and is an impressive cabaret-style venue for interstate and international acts.

Producers Hotel, 235 Grenfell St (☎223 5026). Local Adelaide as well as Melbourne bands play alternative/grunge music; the cover charge ranges from $2–7. Wed night is "Brackets in Jam", a loud jam session of local musos.

Synagogue, 9 Synagogue Place, off Rundle St (☎22 3433). Industrial-chic venue in a converted temple. Three rooms with music ranging from underground and progressive house/garage to funk and retro disco upstairs.

Vibe Shift at *Café Tapas*, 242A Rundle St (☎223 7564). Resident DJs Yo Daddy Mac and Yusef Wilson III play acid jazz and funk. On Saturday nights there's flamenco music and dancing, and retro music on Sundays.

## Gay and lesbian nightspots

Beans Bar, 258 Hindley St. Predominantly lesbian bar, though only Friday 5–9pm is strictly women only. Intimate, relaxed atmosphere during the week, DJ at weekends, women's pool competition Thurs. Tues–Sun till late.

Centralia Hotel, Front Bar, 65 North Terrace. Predominantly male bar, a good place to meet up before getting down. Mon–Sat 5pm till late.

Edinburgh Castle Hotel, 233 Currie St. Friendly mixed venue with a juke box, dance floor, and open fireplaces.

Mars Bar, 122 Gouger St (☎231 9639). An Adelaide institution, albeit a tired one. Drag acts and a big, mixed crowd. Daily 9pm–late.

## Film

As well as several city and suburban mainstream film complexes, Adelaide now has three arthouse/retro cinemas to its credit. The discount day for mainstream cinemas is Tuesday; some have introduced cheap Thursdays as well. There are still several **drive-ins**; the one at Military Road, West Beach is the closest to the centre.

Academy, Hindmarsh Square (☎223 5000). Mainstream downtown multiscreen.

Capri, 141 Goodwood Rd, Goodwood (☎272 1177). Alternative and arty films; budget day Tues.

The Chelsea, 275 Kensington Rd, Kensington Park (☎31 5080). Big new movies and a wonderful, innovatory "Crying Room" for parents and babies. Cheap day Tues.

Greater Union 5, 128 Hindley St (☎231 5961). Big mainstream complex at the heart of the action.

Hoyts Regent Cinema, Regent Arcade, 101 Rundle Mall (☎223 2233). Central multiscreen cinema.

Mercury Cinema, 13 Morphett St (☎410 1934). Arthouse and retro films, with late-night screenings on weekends. Cheap Mon.

New Trak Cinema, 375 Greenhill Rd, Toorak Gardens (☎332 8020). Good alternative cinema.

The Piccadilly, 181 O'Connell St, North Adelaide (☎267 1500). Prestige new releases. Cheap day Tues.

## GAY AND LESBIAN ADELAIDE

South Australia was the first state to legalize gay sex and remains one of the most tolerant of lesbian and gay lifestyles. Adelaide has a more modest gay community than Sydney or Melbourne but the scene enjoys a serenity the bigger cities can't match. Apart from the city's more mainstream annual festivals, there are a clutch of strictly gay and lesbian fiestas: the **Stonewall Celebrations** in June, including *the* dance party and various cabarets; the **Sleaze Ball** in August; and the **Festival of Life** every November. The first **Rainbow Pride Festival** was held in 1994 as part of the Adelaide Fringe Festival.

To find the action, start with a copy of the *Adelaide Gay Times* to add to our listings below.

### Publications and bookshops

**Adelaide Gay Times**, 55 Halifax St (☎232 1544). Free from venues, $1 from bookshops – you'll definitely find it at *Imprints* at 80 Hindley Street.
**Liberation**, c/o *Women's Studies Resource Centre*, 64 Pennington Terrace, North Adelaide. Periodic women's newsletter, good for contacts.
**Murphy Sisters Bookshop**, 240 The Parade, Norwood (☎332 7508). Feminist/lesbian bookshop.
**Sisters by the Sea Bookshop**, 14 Semaphore Rd, Semaphore (☎341 7088). Specializes in lesbian and feminist books, and has a good noticeboard.

### Organizations and support groups

**AIDS Council of South Australia (ACSA)**, 64 Fullarton Rd, Norwood. Education, support and counselling (information line ☎362 1611; outside the city ☎ free call1800/88 8559).
**Clinic 275**, 1st Floor, 275 North Terrace (☎226 6025). Free health testing and counselling Mon, Thurs & Fri 10am–4.30pm, Tues & Wed noon–7.30pm.
**Darling House Gay and Lesbian Community Library**, 64 Fullarton Rd, Norwood (☎362 3106). Fiction, non-fiction and newspapers. Mon–Fri 9.30am–5.30pm, Sat 2–5pm.
**Gay and Lesbian Counselling Service** (☎362 3223 or free call 1800/182 233). Counselling, information, needle exchange. Counselling line 7–10pm daily plus 2–5pm weekends.
**Legal assistance** (☎268 9266) 24-hour service.
**Lesbian & Gay Community Action**, PO Box 6183, SA 5000 (☎362 3106). Rights organization responsible for Stonewall and Festival of Life.
**Lesbian Line** (☎223 1982). Support and information, Fridays 6–9pm.

### Travel agent

**Parkside Travel**, 70 Glen Osmond Rd, Parkside (☎274 1222). Hotel reservations and travel services.

*See also p.577 for gay- and lesbian-friendly places to stay and opposite for gay and lesbian nightspots.*

## Theatre and performance

Out of festival time, theatre, ballet, opera, contemporary dance, comedy and cabaret continue to thrive at the Festival Centre, and more experimental theatre still finds its base at the Lion Arts Centre, home of the Fringe Festival. Almost anything that's on can be booked through *Bass* (☎13 1246).

**Café Tapas**, 242A Rundle St (☎223 7564). Occasional poetry readings; see the *Vibe Shift* listing under "Clubs and live music", above, for other happenings here.
**Doppio Teatro** (☎231 0070). Bilingual theatre company trying to extend the understanding of Italian-Australian culture; performances at the *Lion Theatre* and elsewhere.
**Festival Centre**, King William Rd (☎216 8600). Three major auditoria.

**La Mama**, 4 Crawford Lane, Hindmarsh (☎346 4212). Tiny theatre staging experimental works with new directors and actors.

**Lion Arts Centre**, corner North Terrace and Morphett St (☎231 7760). The *Lion Theatre* is the main venue here, and there's always lots going on.

**Theatre 62**, 145 Burbridge Rd, Hilton (☎234 0838). Small experimental space which often has women's performances.

# Listings

**Airlines** *Ansett*, 142 North Terrace (reservations ☎233 3111; information ☎13 1515), also sell tickets for *Kendell Airlines* (flying from Adelaide to Broken Hill, Ceduna, Mt Gambier, Port Lincoln, Whyalla, Cooper Pedy, Olympic Dam, Woomera, Ayers Rock and Kingscote); *Cathay Pacific* (☎13 1747); *Malaysia Airlines* (☎231 6171); *Qantas*, 144 North Terrace (domestic ☎13 1313, international ☎237 8541), also sells tickets for *Augusta Airlines* (flying to Port Augusta, Leigh Creek, Innaminka, Birdsville and Boulia); *Singapore Airlines* (☎238 2747).

**Airport bus** *Transit Airport–City Bus* (☎381 5311) will pick you up if you book; also services Keswick train station.

**Banks and exchange** All the major banks are located on King William St. Exchange services available at *Thomas Cook*, 45 Grenfell St (☎212 3354) and at *American Express*, 13 Grenfell St (☎212 7099). The accounting office of the Rundle Mall *Myer Centre* will change money on Saturday; ask at the Information Desk on the ground level.

**Bikes and bike rental** *Pulteney Street Cycles*, 307–309 Pulteney St (☎232 5826), central and easygoing with quality mountain and racing bikes; *Bike Moves*, 10 Canterbury Terrace, Black Forest (☎293 2922), 3km out but will deliver for small charge; *Freewheelin' Cycle Tours and Mountain Bike Hire*, 314 Gilles St (☎232 6860), offers bike tours to the McClaren Vale as well as rental of bikes and touring gear. *Bicycle SA*, 1 Sturt St (☎213 0637), is a cycling organization which has all sorts of information and organizes regular touring trips and an annual 9-day bike ride in early October.

**Bookshops** *Imprints*, 80 Hindley St, small highbrow bookshop; *Unibooks*, Adelaide University, contemporary literature; *Angus and Robertsons*, 112 Rundle Mall, large mainstream store; *Europa Books*, 16 Pulteney St, foreign-language literature and magazines; *O'Connell's Bookshop*, Leigh St, excellent secondhand bookshop that will buy or exchange your books; *Backpages Books*, 248 The Parade, Norwood, quality secondhand shop.

**Buses** *Greyhound.Pioneer* have offices at the Central Bus Terminal, 111 Franklin St (☎13 2030), while *Firefly Express* are based at 185 Victoria Square (☎231 1488). State services include *Stateliner* (☎233 2755) to the Riverland, Whyalla, Port Lincoln, Ceduna, Arkaroola, Alice Springs and Broken Hill; *Premier* (☎415 5555) to the Yorke and Fleurieu peninsulas; and *Bonds* (☎231 9090) to Mount Gambier. The *Bus Booking Centre*, at *Intercity Travel*, 33 King William St (☎212 2733), arranges travel on any bus service.

**Camping equipment** Rundle St is the place: try *Paddy Pallin*, at no. 228 (☎232 3155); *Scout Outdoor Centre*, no. 192 (☎223 5544); or *El City Rubber*, at no. 186.

**Car rental** Try *Action* (☎352 7044); *Excel* (☎234 1666); *Hertz* (☎231 2856); *Koala* (☎352 7299); *Thrifty* (☎211 8788). Cheaper, older cars from *Cut Price Car Rentals* (☎43 7788); *Hire a Hack* (☎271 7820); *Rent-a-Bug* (☎234 0911).

**Disabled contacts** *Disability Information and Resource Centre*, 195 Gilles St (☎223 7522); *Access Cabs* (☎234 6444).

**Environment and conservation** The *Conservation Council of South Australia*, 120 Wakefield St (☎223 5155), is a good place to find out what's going on; there's a noticeboard, bookshop and library. *The Wilderness Society* has its campaign office at 116 Grote St (☎231 6586) and its shop at 44 Grote St (☎231 0625).

**Hospitals** *Royal Adelaide Hospital*, North Terrace (☎223 0230); 24-hr Medical Centre, Shop 2, 60 West Terrace (☎231 8800).

**Laundries** *Adelaide Launderette*, 152 Sturt St (daily 7am–8pm; service washes 8am–5pm); *Gilles St Laundromat*, 316 Gilles St (daily 6am–11pm; unattended).

**Left luggage** Adelaide Train Station has 24-hour lockers.

**Maps** *The Map Shop*, 16A Peel St (between Hindley and Currie streets; ☎231 2033), has the largest range of local and state maps; if you're a member of an affiliated automobile association overseas, you can get free regional maps from the RAA, 41 Hindmarsh Square (☎223 4555).

**Motorcycle rental** *Show & Go Motorcycles*, 236 Brighton Rd, Smithton Park (☎376 0333).

**Newspapers** The newspaper booth at 33 King William St sells papers from around the world. Adelaide's *The Advertiser* doesn't have very good coverage of world or even Australian news, but is useful on Thurs for entertainment listings, Wed and Sat for classifieds.

**Post office** corner of King William and Franklin streets (Mon–Fri 8am–6pm, Sat 8.30am–noon).

**Rape and sexual assault** ☎267 8282 or free call 1800/81 7421, after-hours emergency line ☎267 8292.

**Shopping** The usual 9am–5 or 6pm Mon–Sat hours apply, with late-night shopping until 9pm on Fri in the city and Thurs in the suburbs, plus Sunday trading (11am–5pm) in the city only. You can find most things in Rundle Mall. For alternative fashion, Rundle St, and particularly *Miss Gladys Sym Choon* at no. 235, is the place to go. Some enjoyable retro clothes stores are *Mabs*, 207 Grenfell St, and *Port of Call*, round the corner in Frome St. For Aboriginal arts and crafts, try *Tandanya*, 253 Grenfell St, or the *Otherway Shop*, 185 Pirie St.

**Sport and outdoor activities** *North Adelaide Aquatic Centre*, Jeffcott Rd, North Adelaide (daily 9am–5pm; ☎344 4411), indoor centre with pool, gym, sauna and spa; *Canoe n' Kayak Hire*, 29 Angus St, Goodwood (☎271 6354); *Coastal Creatures*, 6/61 Jetty Rd, Glenelg (☎295 2266), rollerblade rental.

**Taxis** *Adelaide Independent* ☎234 6000; *United Yellow Cabs* ☎223 3111; *Suburban Taxi Service* ☎211 8888. There's a cab rank on the corner of Pulteney and Rundle streets.

**Telephones** Rundle Mall has lots, including credit-card phones. For peace and quiet, try the *Phone Room* in the GPO.

**Tours** *Wayward Bus* (☎232 6646 or free call 1800/882 823) does an excellent one-way small-group tour from Adelaide to Melbourne via the scenic coastal route, for around $125 per day; they also run one-way tours to Alice Springs (8 days, $480) and Perth (14 days, $770). *Trekabout Australia*, 30 Berryman Drive, Modbury (☎396 2833), does 4WD personalized tours to the Simpson Desert and the Flinders Ranges. See also "Bikes and bike rental" for details of cycling tour operators.

**Trains** *Australian National Travel Centre*, Station Arcade, North Terrace (☎13 2232; Mon–Fri 8.30am–5.30pm), for interstate train enquiries and tickets.

**Travel agents** *Adelaide YHA Travel*, 38 Sturt St (☎231 5583); *Flight Centre*, 54 King William St (☎211 7246) & 136 North Terrace (☎231 0044); *Peregrine Travel*, upstairs at 192 Rundle St (☎223 5905); *STA Travel*, 235 Rundle St (☎223 2426); *Thor Adventure Travel*, upstairs at 228 Rundle St (☎232 3155).

**Travellers' Aid**, Adelaide Train Station (Mon–Fri 9am–5pm, Sat 9am–12.30pm).

**Women's Adelaide** The *Women's Studies Resource Centre*, 64 Pennington Terrace, North Adelaide (☎267 3633; Mon–Thurs 9am–6pm, Fri 9am–5pm), is a good meeting place with library, video and computer facilities; at the same address is the *Adelaide Women's Community Health Centre* (☎267 5366 for appointment; Mon & Wed–Fri 8.30am–5pm, Tues 8.30am–6.30pm) for free contraception, pregnancy tests, health information and referrals. The *Women's Information Switchboard* (122 Kintore Avenue, corner North Terrace; ☎223 1244, free call ☎1800/188 158, daily 9am–9pm; office open to callers 9am–5pm) has loads of practical information. *Women of the Wilderness*, PO Box 340, Unley, SA 5061 (contact the YWCA for further information ☎340 2422) specialize in outdoor expeditions and workshops: bushwalking, cycling, rafting, sailing, skiing, surfing, all affordably priced.

**Work** *Commonwealth Employment Service*, 55 Currie St (☎231 9444). Unemployment is high in Adelaide itself, but it's a good place to find out about casual fruit-picking work in the Riverland.

# Around Adelaide

Escaping Adelaide for a day or longer is easy and enjoyable, with a choice of beaches, hills and wine, or any combination thereof. Closest at hand are the **Adelaide Hills**, southeast of the city, popular for weekend outings and with numerous small national and conservation parks to walk in, as well as other less strenuous tourist attractions. To the south, the **Fleurieu Peninsula** stretches out towards Cape Jervis, with plenty of fine beaches as well as a number of small wineries. If wine is your priority, though, head for the **Barossa Valley**, Australia's premier wine-producing region, with over thirty excellent wineries to visit less than 50km from Adelaide. The valley is easily visited in a day out from the city, or on a tour, but it's also a great place to stop over and unwind. The **Yorke Peninsula**, across the gulf from Adelaide, is far less known, though many locals holiday here: as well as beaches, it has the remains of an old copper-mining industry and an excellent national park.

---

### TELEPHONE NUMBERS

In **August 1996**, all seven-digit numbers in the ☎08 code region will have an extra 8 added to the beginning of the number.

In **February 1997**, all numbers in the ☎085 code region will have the prefix 85 added; and numbers in the ☎088 code region will have the prefix 88 added.
These later changes will coincide with the implementation of the ☎08 **area code** across the whole of South Australia.

---

## The Adelaide Hills

The beautiful **Adelaide Hills** are the part of the Mount Lofty Ranges closest to the city, just half an hour's drive from Adelaide, and for the most part accessible by local bus and train services. Many people live in the hills, and there are some grand old summer houses taking advantage of the cooler air up here. The **Heysen Trail** long-distance walk cuts across the hills, with a series of YHA hostels along it; most are run on a limited-access basis and the key must be obtained from the Adelaide office (38 Sturt St, ☎08/281 55873) first. In mid-summer there's a high fire risk here, and the trail itself is closed from mid-December to April as a precaution.

Leaving the city by Glen Osmond Road you soon start to wind steeply up on the way to the South Eastern Freeway, the main road to Melbourne. This was the traditional route to Melbourne too – there's an old toll house not far out of the city and several fine old coaching hotels like the *Crafers Inn*. At **CRAFERS** itself, you can leave the freeway for scenic Summit Road, which runs along the top of the hills, past the **Mount Lofty Botanic Gardens** (daily 10am–4pm) to the **Mount Lofty lookout**, the highest point on the range (727m).

The turn-off to **Cleland Wildlife Park** (daily 9.30am–5pm; $7) is the first on the left after the lookout. Part of the Cleland Conservation Park, it offers the usual opportunity to cuddle a koala and see other Australian fauna: the two-hour guided night-time walks are the best way to see the mainly nocturnal animals at their most active ($9; booking essential; ☎08/339 2444). North of here, the **Morialta Conservation Park** is most easily reached by taking the #105 bus from Grenfell Street (35min). It goes right into the park along the scenic Morialta Falls Road; from the entrance to the park it's a two-kilometre bushwalk to a lovely waterfall, with a kiosk halfway. Further along Norton Summit Road, the *Scenic Hotel*, clinging to the side of the hill at Norton Summit, is a great place for a drink.

South of Crafers, and virtually in the southern suburbs of Adelaide, is **Belair National Park**; getting there is half the pleasure, on a suburban train that makes its way upwards through tunnels and valleys with views of Adelaide and the Gulf (35min). Alighting at Belair Station, steps take you to the valley and the grassy recreation grounds and kiosk. With its joggers, manmade lake, hedge maze, forest nursery and restored summer retreat (Old Government House; Sun 12.30–4pm) this seems more of a garden than a national park, though there are also some more secluded bush trails through gum forests.

## Hahndorf

**HAHNDORF**, 28km from the city, is the most touristy destination in the hills (*Mount Barker Passenger Service* bus from 101 Franklin Street; 40min; ☎08/391 2977), and is always crowded at weekends. Australia's oldest German settlement, founded in 1839, it still has the look of a nineteenth-century village. The Bavarian-style restaurants and coffee houses, craft, antique and gift shops are thoroughly commercial, of course, but it's still enjoyable, especially in autumn when the chestnuts and elms lining the main street are golden and the German-style food is just right for the season. **Hahndorf Tourist Information Centre** at 41 Main Street (daily 10am–4pm; ☎08/388 1185) can provide information about the entire area, though you won't need much help in the village itself: there's basically just one street and all the buildings have blue plaques recounting their history. The **Hahndorf Antique Clock Museum** (daily 9.30am–5pm; $3) has an impressive and noisy working collection, while the **Hahndorf Academy** ($2) is devoted to the paintings of nineteenth-century artist **Hans Heysen**, mostly of the local area (the Heysen Trail is named after him).

For a glass of authentic locally brewed pilsner, head for the lovely wooden bar of the *German Arms Hotel*, with a roaring log fire and photos of old Hahndorf, plus a good **restaurant**. *Karl's German Coffee House* serves marginally lighter meals, while *The German Cake Shop* is a crowded bakery and coffee shop whose speciality is *bienenstich*, a yeast cake topped with honey and almonds, and filled with cream, butter and custard. For a picnic, head for *Hahndorf Gourmet Foods*, famous for their homemade *wurst*.

### Further out: Mount Torrens and Birdwood

Further out, but still barely 50km east of Adelaide, the **Torrens River Gorge** and upper valley is one of the loveliest areas of the Adelaide Hills. You can get here with *ABM Coaches* (101 Franklin Street; ☎08/349 5551; Mon–Fri twice daily). This scenic route takes in **CUDLEE CREEK**, with its private **Gorge Wildlife Park** where big cats and deer strike a strange chord in a mainly native bird and animal park with walk-through enclosures, and **GUMERACHA** where *The Toy Factory*, 389–108 Birdwood Road, sells wholesale wooden toys, games and puzzles to the public and has a giant rocking-horse kids can climb up (daily 9am–5pm; free). It also goes past **BIRDWOOD** and Australia's largest collection of veteran, vintage and classic cars, trucks and motorcycles at the **National Motor Museum** on Shannon Street (daily 9am–5pm; $7).

## The Barossa Valley

The **Barossa Valley**, producing internationally acclaimed wines, is only an hour's drive from Adelaide. Small **Lutheran churches** dot the valley, which was settled in

---

### WINE TASTING – SOME TIPS

**Smaller wineries** tend to have more charm and intrinsic interest than the larger, more commercial operators and it's here you'll often get to talk to the wine maker face to face. Generally you'll get the best reception as a couple: wineries have become increasingly distrustful of groups intent on getting drunk for free, and some have begun to charge a nominal tasting fee to discourage this, but it's still rare.

For a novice, wine-tasting can be an intimidating experience. On entering the **tasting area** (or **cellar door**) you'll be shown a list of wines that may be tasted, printed in the order that the winemaker considers best on the palate. Unless you know what you're doing, it's not done to alter this order. To get the full taste, sniff the wine first to appreciate the aroma or bouquet, and then sip, rolling it around on your tongue before swallowing; there's usually a spitoon if you don't want to swallow. Don't be shy about discussing the wines with the person serving – their purpose is to dispense chat and wisdom, and even wine snobs are down-to-earth Australians at heart.

---

the 1840s by German Lutherans fleeing from religious persecution: by 1847 over 2500 German immigrants had arrived and after the 1848 revolution more poured in. The German dialect in the area was strong until World War I, when the spoken language was frowned upon and German place names were changed by an Act of Parliament. The towns, however – most notably Tanunda – remain thoroughly German in character even without the large doses of oom-pah tourist hype that they all serve up, and the valley is well worth visiting for the vineyards and wineries, the architecture, and the bakeries and butcher shops where old German recipes have been handed down through generations. It's a popular **day-trip** from Adelaide, and many of the big commercial wineries are besieged by busloads of tourists intent on a day's free drinking. On a quick whizz along the Barossa Valley Highway, the area seems thoroughly touristy and traffic-laden; the peaceful backroads, however, yield more interest, with small, family-owned wineries to explore. Many provide picnic areas and barbecues, and even children's playgrounds.

The first vines were planted in 1847 at the Orlando vineyards, an estate which is still a big wine producer. Today, however, there are over forty **wineries**, from multinationals to tiny specialists. Because of the variety of soil and climate, the Barossa seems able to produce a wide range of wine types of consistently high quality; the white Reislings are among the best. The region has a typically Mediterranean climate, with dry summers and mild winters. The best time to visit is autumn (March–May) when the vines turn russet and golden and the harvest has begun in earnest; a lot of grape-picking is still done by hand and work is available from February. This is also the time of the week-long **Vintage Festival**, beginning on Easter Monday of every odd-numbered year (☎085/63 0600 for more information).

### Exploring the valley

For obvious reasons, a **car** is not the ideal way to explore the Barossa – not if you want to taste the wines anyway. Once here, you can always rent a bike or take a tour. The main **route** from Adelaide follows the Main North Road through Elizabeth and Gawler, and then joins the **Barossa Valley Highway** to Lyndoch. A more scenic drive would take you through the Adelaide Hills to Williamstown or Angaston, while from the **Sturt Highway** you can turn into the Valley at Nuriootpa.

Getting to the valley by **bus** is also reasonably easy: the *Barossa-Adelaide Passenger Service* (☎085/64 3200; 3 daily Mon–Fri, 1 on Sat & Sun) stops at the main Barossa towns en route to Nuriootpa, or the daily *Greyhound.Pioneer* Sydney-bound services can drop you at Nuriootpa. If you're **cycling**, you might want to consider taking the **train** to Gawler, 14km from Lyndoch.

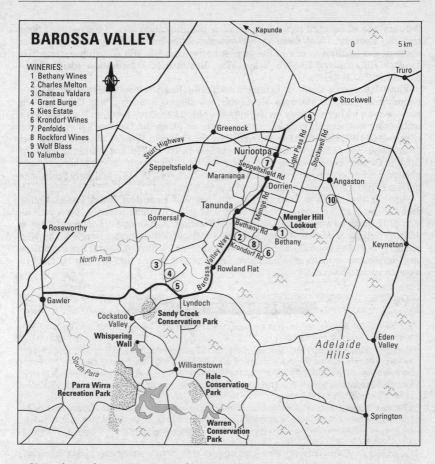

**BAROSSA VALLEY**

WINERIES:
1 Bethany Wines
2 Charles Melton
3 Chateau Yaldara
4 Grant Burge
5 Kies Estate
6 Krondorf Wines
7 Penfolds
8 Rockford Wines
9 Wolf Blass
10 Yalumba

If you do need a **car** to get around, you can **rent** one from the *Caltex* service station, 8 Murray Street, Tanunda (☎085/63 2677). The best alternative is **cycling**, with a sealed bike track avoiding the busy highway between Tanunda and Nuriootpa: cycle rental is available at *Zinfandel's*, 58 Murray Street, Tanunda (☎085/63 2822), and *The Bunkhaus*, Barossa Valley Way, Nuriootpa (☎085/62 2260); both charge about $10 per day. There's also a range of **tours**: *Valley Tours* (☎085/62 1524; $24) run a minibus which picks up from accommodation in Lyndoch, Tanunda, Angaston and Nuriootpa in the morning, returning you at 3.15pm, with four wineries, lunch and an unpretentious commentary in between. From Adelaide, *E & K Mini Tours* (☎08/365 3816; $29) operate an inexpensive day-tour including the Adelaide Hills, the Whispering Wall, a 3-course bistro meal and three large wineries, with the emphasis on a free grog-up.

### Lyndoch and around
"A beautiful place, good land, plenty of grass and its general appearance open with some patches of wood and many kangaroos," recorded **Colonel William Light** in 1837 on first sight of the **LYNDOCH** area; settled in 1839, it's one of the oldest towns in South Australia. Although vineyards were established from the beginning, the primary

industry was wheat until 1896 when someone had the bright idea of converting a flour. mill into a winery. Today there are ten wineries in the immediate Lyndoch area, from some of the smallest to one of the largest in the Barossa, still all family-owned. *Kies Lyndoch Hills Cellars*, Barossa Valley Way, has **tourist information** (daily 10am– 4.30pm; ☎085/24 4110).

Eight kilometres south of Lyndoch off **Yettie Road** is the **Whispering Wall**, a retaining wall for the **Barossa Reservoir**; it's shaped in such a way that a spoken message can be heard plainly on the opposite side 140 metres away, as if a ghost were whispering in your ear. Four kilometres northeast along the Barossa Valley Way, the village of **ROWLAND FLAT** is dominated by the **Orlando Winery** complex (Mon–Fri 10am–5pm, Sat & Sun 10am–4pm), the oldest in the valley and home of some of Australia's best known wines, sold under the "Jacob's Creek" label. Johann Gramp planted the first commercial vines at nearby Jacob's Creek in 1847, and forty years later his son expanded the winery and moved it to Rowland Flat.

Another 4km north of Rowland Flat, the peaceful **Krondorf Road/Hallet Valley** area runs east of the Barossa Valley Way, with four charming wineries, each with its own philosophy of winemaking and tasting: *Krondorf*, *Rockfords*, *St Hallets* and *Charles Melton*. Behind *St Hallets Winery*, you can watch skilled coopers at work at the **Keg Factory**, St Hallet Road (Mon–Sat 8am–4.30pm; Sun 10.30am–4.30pm); huge stainless steel fermentation tanks aren't suitable for the many wines that need to be aged in wood to impart flavour.

## BAROSSA WINERIES

It's hard to choose between so many wineries, almost all of them worth a look, but the ten below should start you off.

**Bethany Wines**, Bethany Rd, Bethany. Set in an old quarry, a hillside winery with views over historic Bethany village; five generations of the Schrapel family have grown grapes here. The ports are worth trying, especially the unusual white variety. Mon–Sat 10am–5pm, Sun 1–5pm.

**Charles Melton**, Krondorf Rd, Tanunda. Small, friendly winery concentrating on traditional dry red styles. Daily 11am–5pm.

**Chateau Yaldara Estate**, Gomersal Rd, Lyndoch. The ruins of a nineteenth-century flour mill transformed into a Baroque-style chateau. Tours (daily 10.15 & 10.45am and 1.15pm 2.15pm & 3.15pm) focus on the chateau's antiques collection. European-style wines, specializing in sweet and sparkling whites. Daily 9am–5pm.

**Grant Burge Wines**, Barossa Valley Way, Jacob's Creek . Small, quality winery, established in 1988 on this historical site. Daily 10am–5pm.

**Kies Estate Lyndoch Hill Cellars**, Barossa Valley Way, Lyndoch. Small-scale winery, which has been in the same family since 1857. Daily 10am–4.30pm.

**Krondorf Wines**, Krondorf Rd, Tanunda. Revamped 1860s winery and vineyard, with a reputation for quality and integrity of its mostly white wines. Daily 10am–5pm.

**Penfolds Wines and Kaiser Stuhl**, Barossa Valley Way, Nuriootpa. Largest winery in the Barossa churns out mass-produced wines, not all made from local grapes. Tour (Mon–Fri 10am, 11am, 1.30pm & 2.30pm; $4) focusses on wine production and bottling, and ususally includes a demonstration of coopering skills. Mon–Fri 9am–5pm, Sat & Sun 10am–5pm.

**Rockford Wines**, Krondorf Rd, Tanunda. No-nonsense approach and big unfussy wines using old-fashioned techniques and grapes; good Grenache and Basket Press Shiraz. Daily 11am–5pm.

**Wolf Blass Wines**, Bilyara Vineyards, Sturt Highway, Nuriootpa. Set up in 1973 by German winemaker Wolfgang Blass, a bow-tied, self-promoting character. Prize-winning wines with a reputation for quality and consistency. Mon–Fri 9.15am–4.30pm, Sat & Sun 10am–4.30pm.

**Yalumba Wines**, Eden Valley Rd, Angaston. Largest and oldest family-operated Barossa winery. Lovely building and gardens. Mon–Fri 8.30am–5pm, Sat 10am–5pm, Sun noon–5pm.

Parallel to Krondorf Road to the north, Bethany Road runs east off the Barossa Valley Way to **BETHANY**, the first German settlement in the Barossa. The land is still laid out in the eighteenth-century *Hufendorf* style, with long narrow farming strips stretching out behind the cottages, and the creek running through each property. The old stone cottages remain well cared for with pretty gardens, the bell still rings at the **Herberge Christi Church** each Saturday at dusk to mark the working week's end, and Bethany still feels like a peaceful rural village without even a pub or shop. The common where cattle were grazed is now the Bethany Reserve, with a picnic spot by the creek. Opposite the reserve in a restored cottage is *Bethany Art and Craft Gallery* (daily 10am–5pm).

## Tanunda

**TANUNDA**, the Barossa's most quintessentially German town, announces itself as a tourist destination as you head along the Barossa Valley Way and enter through the Orlando archway that spans **Murray Street**. This tree-lined main street, with several old and beautiful buildings, is too manicured to be quite real, with German music at its most pedestrian wafting out of small wooden kegs above the shops. More authentic atmosphere can be found in the narrow streets on the western side of town, towards the river. Here **Goat Square** was the site of the first town market and is bordered by the original cottages; during the Vintage Festival, the early market is re-enacted. Many **wineries** dot the town, the largest concentration along Para Road, beside the river

For a good overview of the history of the valley, visit the **Barossa Valley Historical Museum**, 47 Murray Street (Mon–Fri 1–5pm, Sat & Sun 2–5pm; free). Less relevant but more fun is the **Kev Rohrlach Technology Museum** on Barossa Valley Way (daily 10am–5pm; $5), a do-it-yourself museum created by a self-made man who started collecting tractors, then progressed through motorcycles, buggies and tanks to solar-powered cars; added to this is Kev's booty from trips to the South Pole, the Himalayas and Mount Kilimanjaro. **Norm's Collie Dogs**, at "Breezy Gully" off Gomersal Road (Mon, Wed & Sat 2pm; $5) could only be in Australia; forty sheep dogs are put through their paces by Norm and a herd of sheep. **Mengler's Hill Lookout**, east of Tanunda along Basedow Road and then the Mengler's Hill Road Scenic Drive, provides an unmatched view of the valley and its vineyards: there's a **Sculpture Garden** with white marble sculptures on the slopes below, and at night you can see the lights of Adelaide from here.

**Seppeltsfield**, off the highway 4km northeast of Tanunda, must be the most spectacular of the wineries (tastings Mon–Fri 9am–5pm, Sat 10.30am–4.30pm, Sun 11am–4pm). During the Great Depression the Seppelt family paid their workers in food to plant an avenue of date palms from Marananga to Seppeltsfield. The local saying is that where the palms end, so did the Depression. Halfway along the gorgeous palm-lined avenue, the **Seppelt family mausoleum** (for male family members only!) sits on top of a hill, with smaller palms leading up to it and wonderful views of the estate. The estate itself was founded in 1851 when Joseph Seppelt, a wealthy merchant, arrived from Silesia bringing his workers with him: he turned to winemaking when his tobacco crop failed. **Seppelts** became the largest winery in the colony, with everything from a port-maturation cellar to a distillery, vinegar factory and brandy bond store. All have been preserved in their original condition and there's a **tour** focussing on the historical buildings (hourly Mon–Fri 11–3pm, Sat & Sun 11.30–2.30pm; $2).

## Nuriootpa and Angaston

Just seven kilometres from Tanunda, **NURIOOTPA** is the Valley's commercial centre: appropriately the town's name is an Aboriginal word for "meeting place", as this was where local Aborigines gathered to barter. It's not the most attractive of towns, but it still serves its purpose. The **Barossa Information Centre** (Mon–Fri 8.30am–5pm, Sat & Sun 9.30am–1.30pm; ☎085/62 1866) occupies **Coulthard House,** a gracious two-storey building commissioned by the area's first settler, William Coulthard. The town grew around his red-gum slab hotel, now the site of the *Vine Inn* community hotel. Together with the Community Store (where co-op members purchase shares and share in the profits), this finances many developments in the town like the fine **swimming centre** in Coulthard Reserve by the shady, gum-lined North Para River.

**ANGASTON**, southeast of Nuriootpa, is a pretty little town situated in the **Barossa Ranges**, an area of predominantly grazing land of red gums and rolling ranges, although a few of the Barossa's oldest winemakers have been here for more than a century. This is the side of the Barossa that drew the British pioneers, including one George Fife Angas, after whom the town is named. The **Collingrove Homestead** (Mon–Fri 1–4.30pm, Sat & Sun 11am–4.30pm; closed Fri July–Sept; $3), 6km from town on Eden Valley Road, is an Angas home surrounded by lush gardens, owned by the National Trust. Angas also lived at nearby **Lindsay Park**, now the **Lindsay Park Stud**, Australia's leading racehorse breeding and training complex.

At **SPRINGTON**, 20km south of Angaston, the big attraction is the **Herbig family tree**, a tree in which a pioneer German couple began their married life and had two of their sixteen children. Inevitably, Springton's old buildings have undergone the "boutiquing" process: the blacksmith shop is now a winery, and the early post office has been transformed into an art and craft gallery.

## Barossa accommodation

There's comfortable accommodation, B&Bs and caravan parks throughout the valley, and you should never have a problem finding somewhere good. The following are some of the better-value places.

**Barossa Brauhaus Hotel**, 41 Murray St, Angaston (☎085/64 2014). Good-value basic pub rooms and cheap singles. Breakfast available. ③.

**Barossa Gateway Motel and Hostel**, Kalimna Rd, Nuriootpa (☎085/62 1033). If the *Bunkhaus* is full this is the slightly scruffier alternative. Motel units ③, dorms ①.

**Barossa House**, Barossa Valley Way, halfway between Tanunda and Nuriootpa (☎085/62 2716). Best-value B&B with en-suite rooms. ④.

**The Bunkhaus**, Barossa Valley Way, 1.5km south of Nuriootpa (☎085/62 2260). On 12 hectares of vineyards, a comfortable friendly hostel with a pot-belly stove perfect for drinking wine around in winter. Work may be available. Bike rental. Self-contained cottage ③, dorms ①.

**Collingrove Homestead**, Eden Valley Rd, 6km from Angaston (☎085/64 2061). B&B accommodation in the old servants' quarters, set in English-style gardens. ⑦.

**Langmeil Cottages**, Langmeil Rd, Tanunda (☎085/63 2987). German-style stone cottage, peaceful setting and views of the Barossa Ranges; extras include breakfast, champagne, bicycles, barbecue and heated pool. ⑥–⑦.

**Lawley Farm**, Krondorf Rd (☎085/63 2141). On a quiet road ideal for walking and cycling, these restored stone cottages are shaded by pepper trees. With a full breakfast in the farmhouse kitchen and a hot spa in the garden, this makes a great base in walking distance of the best wineries. ⑦.

**Seppeltsfield Holiday Units**, Seppeltsfield Road (☎085/62 8240). These well-equipped log cabins offer some of the best-value accommodation in the valley, set on a rural hillside overlooking the *Seppelt* winery. ⑤.

**Tanunda Caravan and Tourist Park**, Murray St, Tanunda (☎085/63 2784). Set in parkland among beautiful waratah trees. On-site vans ③.

**Tanunda Hotel**, 51 Murray St, Tanunda (☎085/63 2030). Built from local stone and marble in 1845 with Edwardian additions and decor inside. ④–⑤.

**The Vine Inn**, 14 Murray St, Nuriootpa (☎085/62 2133). Recently renovated motel-style units. ⑥.

**Vineyards Motel**, corner Stockwell and Nuriootpa roads, Angaston (☎085/64 2404). Spacious units with queen-size beds. ⑤.

## Barossa food

To go with the wine, and to cater for all the tourists, there are excellent restaurants throughout the valley, as well as plenty of picnic spots and barbecue areas.

**Barossa Bistro**, 37 Murray St, Angaston (☎085/64 2361). Inexpensive, filling set lunch; more expensive dinner menu features bush tucker.

**Château Yaldara Garden Bistro**, Gomersal Rd, Lyndoch (☎085/24 4200). Affordable prices aimed at families; pasta dominates. Daily 10am–4pm

**Giovanni's Italian Bistro**, Barossa Junction Resort, Barossa Valley Way, Tanunda (☎085/63 3400). Reasonably priced pasta in a family atmosphere.

**Heinemann Park Restaurant/Café**, 2a Murray St, Tanunda (☎085/63 3500). Stone bungalow set in a park with al fresco eating; affordable southeast Asian cuisine. Daily except Tues 11am–late.

**Linke's Bakery and Tea Rooms**, 40 Murray St, Nuriootpa. Bakery with filling soups and inexpensive German fare to eat in.

**Lyndoch Bakery**, Barossa Valley Highway, Lyndoch. Best German bakery in the Barossa; also moderately priced licensed restaurant with hearty, traditional dishes. Closed Mon.

**1918 Bistro and Grill**, 94 Murray St, Tanunda (☎085/63 0405). Fresh food and local ingredients, with a Mediterranean twist. Local wines are inexpensive cleanskins (unlabelled), or BYO. Tues–Sun noon–10pm.

**The Pheasant Farm**, Samuel Rd, off Seppeltsfield Rd, near Nuriootpa (☎085/62 1286). Set by a lake full of yabbies (crayfish), trout, ducks and geese, this highly regarded restaurant specializes in game, producing fresh adventurous food. Expensive. Lunch Wed–Sun, dinner Sat.

**Tanunda Hotel**, 51 Murray St, Tanunda (☎085/63 2030). Interesting food a cut above the usual hotel fare with plenty for vegetarians, moderately priced.

**Tanunda Wurst Haus**, 28 Bridge St, Tanunda. Specializing in traditional Barossa *Mettwurst*, this delicatessen enables you to eat cheaply but tastily. Good cappuccino.

**The Vintners Restaurant**, corner of Nuriootpta & Stockwell roads, Angaston (☎085/64 2488). Winemakers' hangout with interesting, elaborate menu and suitably impressive wine list. Expensive. Lunch Tues–Sun, dinner Fri & Sat.

**Zinfandel Tea Rooms**, 58 Murray St, Tanunda. Breakfast available on the verandah, German and Australian dishes for lunch and a delicious choice of strudels and cakes. Daily 8.30am–6pm.

# The Fleurieu Peninsula

The **Fleurieu Peninsula**, thirty minutes south of Adelaide by car, is bounded by Gulf St Vincent to the west and the Southern Ocean in the south, the two connected by the Backstairs Passage at **Cape Jervis** (where the ferry leaves for Kangaroo Island, see p.603). There are fine beaches on both coasts and, inland, more wineries in the rolling **Southern Vales**. It's pleasantly undeveloped: many of the towns were settled from the 1830s on and there's much well-preserved **colonial architecture**, often housing restaurants and B&Bs. For a round trip, leave the city via the Adelaide Hills and cut down through Mount Barker to Strathalbyn and Goolwa, on the south coast, circling round through Victor Harbour, Willunga and McLaren Vale.

*Premier* (☎08/415 5555) has at least two daily services from Adelaide to Goolwa via McLaren Vale, Willunga, Victor Harbour and Port Elliot. *Freewheelin Cycle Tours* do a day trip beginning in Hahndorf, then through the Southern Vales wine area (☎08/373 3482; $46 includes Adelaide pick-up and return, bikes and lunch).

## Goolwa and Port Elliot

**GOOLWA** lies twelve kilometres upstream from the ever-shifting sand bar at the mouth of the Murray. Boaties love its position adjacent to vast Lake Alexandrina yet accessible to the Coorong (see p.609) and the ocean, and its situation has always been its fortune: although so close to the coast, Goolwa feels like a real river town, and it thrived above all in the days of the Murray paddle-steamer trade, when it was the final offloading port. Then a rip-roaring river town with over 88 taverns, it had the biggest police station in South Australia. The railways brought the good days to an end, and today only a few reminders remain, many of them clustered along Railway Terrace with its buildings painted in federation colours. Here you'll find the **Goolwa Tourist Information Centre** (daily 10am–4pm; ☎085/55 1144).

**Cruises** to the mouth of the Murray (passing through the barrages which keep saltwater out of the freshwater system) and to various other destinations leave from the end of the wharf: details from *Goolwa Cruises* (☎085/55 2203). Also on the wharf is **Signal Point Interpretative Centre** (daily 10am–5pm; $5), an innovatively designed exhibition telling the story of the Murray and the river trade. A free 24-hour vehicular ferry crosses from Goolwa to the mostly bare, flat and tranquil **Hindmarsh Island**, between the river mouth and the lake.

*River's End Resort Motel* (☎085/55 5033; ⑤), on Noble Avenue 3km northeast of Goolwa, has an eco-tourism slant, with **motel** units, pool, sauna, tennis court, bar and an inexpensive dining room. The alternative in town is the *Corio Hotel* on Railway Terrace (☎085/55 2011; B&B ③), also a popular local eating place. Campers can head for *Goolwa Camping and Tourist Park*, Kessel Road (☎085/552 144; on-site vans ②).

**PORT ELLIOT**, on the coast 14km west of Goolwa, is a pleasant little town with some fine old buildings and a wonderful find, the *Sitar Indian Restaurant*, 12 The Strand, which serves traditional Northern Indian food & vegetarian specials (nightly 5.30–10pm & Sunday lunch). There's good **surf** between here and Victor Harbour – you can rent gear from *Southern Surf*, at 36 North Terrace. *Chiton Rocks Surf Lifesaving Club* on Seagull Avenue (☎085/54 2047) overlooks the surf of **Chiton Rocks**, and has hostel-style accommodation (①) open to all. The best beach for relatively easy surfing is **Middleton**, while **Waipinga Pass** offers more thrills to experienced surfers. For the latest surf report, call ☎085/54 2047.

## Victor Harbor

**VICTOR HARBOR** on Encounter Bay was once a popular holiday destination for Adelaidians. In the 1920s there were 65 guesthouses and thousands poured in during the peak season; an uncomfortable four-hour train ride only added to the adventure. Then, as decent roads and the motor car brought it within an hour's drive, less people came – it was too easy, too close to home. Now, however, thanks to whales, Victor Harbour is experiencing a resurgence.

In the 1830s there were three whaling stations here, hunting **southern right whales.** They were so called because they were the "right" ones to kill: slow moving because of their high oil content, which fortuitously also made them float after the slaughter. They came to Encounter Bay to breed between June and September, heading close to shore where they became easy targets. After the peak 1830–1840 period, their numbers began to decline: the last one taken here was in 1878, and by 1930 they'd been hunted almost to extinction. Now, however, they've started to recover, and to return to Encounter Bay. In 1991, forty were seen in the bay, sometimes coming right up to the shore, and 80,000 people flocked to see them. Since then, Victor Harbor has gained its very own **South Australian Whale Centre** on Railway Terrace (daily 9am–5pm; $5; ☎085/52 2266) with interpretative displays and exhibits on whaling history, natural history of whales and the marine environment. It also acts as a monitoring station, locating and tracking whales, and confirming sightings; visit the centre for information on whale locations, or call the whale information hotline (☎0055/31 636, charged at 70c per minute).

Other local attractions include the **Cockle Train** (school holidays only; $12; ☎08/231 1707), a steam train running on the otherwise disused line to Goolwa and back. You can walk the 500 metres along the narrow causeway to **Granite Island** or ride the *Granite Island Horse Tram* ($2, $3 return), a traditional holiday ride; included in the price is a chair lift to the crest of the island up a steepish slope, although it's hardly a strenuous walk. Fairy penguins come onto the island to nest, roost and moult: the best time to see them is a couple of hours after dusk when they come back from feeding. If you're travelling with restless children, **Greenhills Adventure Park**, Waggon Road, alongside the Hindmarsh River (☎085/52 1222), has activities from canoeing to go-kart racing, while **Urimburra Wildlife Experience** (daily 10am–5pm; $5; ☎085/54 6555), 5km north on Adelaide Road, is an open-range park with native animals from around Australia.

For further **information**, head for the *Victor Harbour Tourist Information Centre* on Torrens Street (daily 10am–4pm; ☎085/52 4255); they can also help you with accommodation. The best **place to stay** is *Anchorage Guest House*, 21 Flinders Parade (☎085/52 5970; B&B ⑤), an original beachfront guesthouse, lovingly restored and serving excellent meals; the same people run the surprisingly gloomy and spartan *Warringa Hostel* next door (①). Alternatives are *Villa Victor Bed and Breakfast*, 59 Victoria Street (☎085/52 4258; B&B ⑤); *Clifton Motel and Lodge*, 39 Torrens Street (☎085/52 1062; ④–⑤); *Family Inn Motel*, 300 Port Elliot Road (☎085/52 1941; ④–⑤); and *Adare Caravan Park*, Wattle Drive (☎085/52 1657), in the grounds of lovely Adare House – run by the Uniting Church, so no alcohol allowed. Good places to **eat** include *Nino Solari's Pizzeria*, 16 Albert Place (☎085/52 3501), where you can plough into some generous pasta too, and the old-fashioned *South Coast Fish Café*, 10 Ocean Street (☎085/52 2573). The *Hotel Crown* at 2 Ocean Street serves cheap bar meals and has big-name bands on weekends.

## The Southern Vales

The wineries of the **Southern Vales**, in the northwest of the peninsula, are virtually in Adelaide, and the suburban fringes of the city now push right up to **REYNELLA**, where the first vineyards were planted in 1838. Among the earliest is *Hardy's Reynella Winery* (Reynell Rd; daily 10am–4.30pm), where the tasting room occupies the original ironstone and brick building among botanical gardens. There are several other wineries in Reynella but the largest concentration, often in bush settings, are around the small town of **McLAREN VALE**, with about forty wineries, mostly small and family-run. Since the 1960s there's been a trend for grape growers to switch from supplying winemakers to producing their own wine in a bid for independence, and as a result there's a swathe of "boutique" wineries.

McLaren Vale is itself a "boutique" town, with its many B&Bs and restaurants catering for the wine-buff weekend crowd. The liveliest time is in October when the **Bushing Festival** celebrates the new wines, and the Bushing King or Queen, the winemaker who has produced the wine judged to be the best of the vintage, is crowned. Among the **B&Bs** are *McLaren Vale*, 56 Valley View Drive (☎08/323 9351; ⑤), which is very homey and serves a full breakfast; *Southern Vales*, 13 Chalk Hill Road (☎08/323 8144; ⑤, including 5-course breakfast), a more modern and hotel-like place with gorgeous vineyard views; and *Samarkand*, Branson Road (☎08/323 8756; ⑥), a separate wing of a log cottage. Most **places to eat** are fairly fancy, and many of the wineries also have restaurants attached; simpler meals can be had at *Koffee n Snax*, 150 Main Road, an unpretentious coffee shop, while the *Hotel McLaren*, 208 Main Road (☎08/323 8208) does good-value counter meals. Restaurants include *The Barn*, on the corner of Main Road and Chalk Hill Road (☎08/323 8618), a rustic old barn with a vine-shaded courtyard and a walk-in cellar where you choose your own local wine: moder-

## SOUTHERN VALES WINERIES

Half a dozen favourites from a wide choice of excellent wineries.

**Chapel Hill**, Chapel Hill Road, McLaren Vale. In an old stone chapel, this is a small but very civilized winery. Winemaker Pam Dunsford was McLaren Vale's first Bushing Queen; her wines have won several prizes. Mon–Fri 9am–5pm, Sat & Sun 11am–5pm.

**D'Arenberg**, Osborn Road, McLaren Vale. Family winery set up in 1928 with a simple tasting room in an unglamorized farm setting; friendly people and very reasonably priced wine. Mon–Fri 8am–5pm, Sat 10am–5pm, Sun noon–4pm.

**Kays Brothers**, Kays Road, McLaren Vale. Wonderful family winery established in 1890; old photos of the family and the area cover the oak casks containing port. Picnic area among towering gum trees overlooks grazing cattle. Mon–Fri 10am–5pm, Sat & Sun noon–5pm.

**Oliver Hill**, Seaview Road, McLaren Vale. Small, slightly off-beat winery/restaurant (bookings ☎08/323 8211) started in 1973 by Berlingieri Vincenzo, a real character. A perfect place for pasta like his grandmother used to make – sitting at chunky red cedar gum tables and imbibing wine. Daily 10am–5pm.

**Scarpantoni**, Scarpantoni Drive, McLaren Flat. Run by an Italian family: someone's always happy to chat about wine, over a glass, or an espresso if you prefer. Daily 10am–5pm.

**Woodstock**, Douglas Gully Road, McLaren Flat. Tiny peaceful tasting room looks out to a garden; Sunday lunch with guest chefs in the *Coterie* next door (bookings ☎08/383 0156). Mon–Fri 9am–5pm, Sat & Sun noon–5pm.

ately priced contemporary cuisine is served daily noon to midnight. On the corner of Willunga and McMurtie roads, the *Salopian Inn* (☎08/323 8769) is an atmospheric 1851 stone inn with a seasonally varied menu, while the BYO *Pipkins*, 199 Main Road, serves morning tea and light lunch.

### Gulf St Vincent beaches

A series of superb swimming beaches, often known as the **wine coast**, runs along the Gulf St Vincent shore roughly parallel to the Southern Vales, from **O'Sullivans Beach** down to **Sellicks Beach**, beyond which the coastline becomes rockier. They're all easily accessible from Adelaide on public transport: take the train to Noarlunga Centre and then buses to the various beaches.

   **PORT NOARLUNGA** is the main town, surrounded by steep cliffs and sand hills: its jetty is popular with anglers, and with wetsuit-clad teenagers who dive bomb from it; at low tide a natural reef is exposed. Lifesavers patrol the local beaches, and you can rent surf and snorkelling gear at *Ocean Graffix Surf and Skate Centre*, 21 Salt Fleet Point. **Moana**, two beaches south, has fairly tame surf perfect for novices. The southern end of **Maslins Beach**, south again, broke new ground by becoming Australia's first legal **nude** bathing beach in 1975. The wide, isolated beach is reached via a long, steep walking track down the colourful cliffs from the Tait Road car park, deterring all but the committed. **Port Willunga**, the next stop down, offers interesting diving around the wreck of the *Star of Greece*. **Aldinga Beach** is the last to which public transport runs – you'll need a lift or transport of your own to reach the 6km of firm sand at **Sellicks Beach**.

## The Yorke Peninsula

The **Yorke Peninsula** was almost the last section of the Australian coastline to be mapped by Matthew Flinders in 1802, and it still seems a bit of an afterthought: flat plains stretch out to the sea, so extensively cleared for farming that only tiny areas of original vegetation remain, in the Innes National Park at the very tip of the peninsula and in a couple of conservation parks. Much is now made of the northern peninsula's **Cornish heritage**, but the miners from Cornwall who flocked to the area when **copper** was discovered in 1859 have left behind little but their names and the ubiquitous Cornish pasty. The three towns of the Copper Triangle or "**Little Cornwall**" – Kadina, Wallaroo and Moonta – make the most of it at the *Kernewek Lowender* (Cornish Festival), held over the long weekend in May of every odd-numbered year, though in fact the mining boom ended seventy years ago, and they've been plain country towns ever since.

Just two hours' drive from Adelaide, the peninsula offers peace for a weekend as well as good **fishing**. The east coast ports of Ardrossan, Port Vincent and **EDITHBURGH** on the Gulf St Vincent were visited first by ketches and schooners, and later by steamers transporting wheat and barley to England. Now the remaining jetties are used by anglers. They're all pleasant to visit, but Edithburgh offers most facilities: once a substantial salt-production town and grain port, it still has a few fine old buildings. There's a tidal swimming pool set in a rocky cove, and from Troubridge Hill you can see across to the Fleurieu Peninsula and to **Troubridge Island Conservation Park** with its iron lighthouse and fairy penguin population: guided tours are available from Chris Johnson (☎08/852 6290; $20). *Edithburgh Lodge*, 24 O'Halloran Parade (☎08/852 6262; ①), is a big old four-bedroom house sleeping sixteen where you can stay if it's not booked out with groups; the same friendly people run *The Anchorage* next door, with its modern foreshore motel units (④).

Right at the tip of the peninsula, the **Innes National Park** with its contrasting coastline of rough cliffs and sweeps of beach, its sand dunes and interior of mallee scrub, is untouched except for the ruins of the gypsum-mining town of **INNESTON** near **Stenhouse Bay**. The **National Park Visitor Centre** is here, offering facilities including hot showers, and selling entry permits ($2 per car) and **camping** permits ($3–6 per group). The main camping area is at **Pondalowie Bay**, which happens to have some of the best surf in the state; there are several other good surfing spots around the national park and heading north to Corny Point. Other, more sheltered coves and bays are good for snorkelling, with shallow reef areas of colourful marine life, while on land you might see emus, western grey kangaroos, pygmy possums and mallee fowl.

*Premier* (☎08/415 5555) have a daily **bus** service from Adelaide to Moonta, via Kadina and Wallaroo. The *Yorke Peninsula Bus Service* (☎08/391 2977) runs from Adelaide to Yorketown, alternating daily between the east coast via Ardrossan, Port Vincent and Edithburgh and the centre via Maitland and Minlaton. There's no transport to the national park itself.

# Kangaroo Island

As you head towards **Cape Jervis** along the west coast of the Fleurieu Peninsula, **KANGAROO ISLAND**, only 13km offshore, first appears behind a vale of rolling hills. Once on the island its size and emptiness leave a strong impression. This is actually Australia's third largest island after Tasmania and Melville Island (north of Darwin), and with 450km of coastline and mostly unsealed roads, exploring the island takes time. Although it's been promoted as a tourist destination for over ten years, the island is still very unspoilt and only at the peak holiday period (Christmas to the end of January, when most of the accommodation is booked out) does it feel at all busy. Once out of the few small towns, you won't see shops, roadside stalls or filling stations; what you will see are long, straight stretches of road through undulating fields, dense forests of gum or mallee scrub, and the sea. There's often a strong wind off the Southern Ocean, so bring something warm whatever the season, and take care when **swimming**: there are strong rips

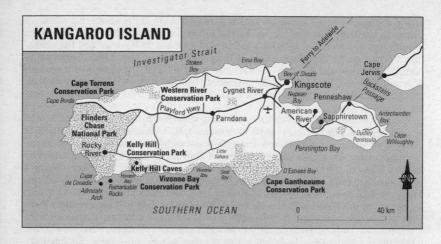

**KANGAROO ISLAND**

on many of the beaches. Safe swimming spots include Island Beach, Stokes Bay, Antechamber Bay, Hogg Bay, Emu Bay and Vivonne Bay.

Kangaroo Island is possibly the best place in Australia to see an astonishing range of **wildlife**, largely untroubled by disease or natural predators, and with a quarter of the island protected as **national or conservation parks**. Many have entry fees and extras for guided tours; a one-year Island Pass ($15) covers all these costs plus camping, and is worth it if your tour is an extended one. Get them from the NPWS office at Dauncy Street, Kingscote (Mon–Fri 8.45am–5pm; ☎0848/22 381), which also dishes out general tourist **information**, or from the parks themselves. When Matthew Flinders came across the island in 1802, "black substances" seen on shore in the twilight turned out to be **kangaroos**, prolific and easily hunted. Kangaroos still abound, lending the island its name, as do **wallabies**. **Koalas** were introduced at Flinders Chase National Park in 1923, and have spread widely. There are also **echidna** and **platypuses**, the two monotremes; **fur seals**, **sea lions** and **fairy penguins** on the shore and surrounding rocks and islets; and even the occasional appearance of a **southern right whale**, as well as over 200 kinds of bird, **snakes**, and **wild pigs** and **feral goats** which are the successors of those left here by early seafarers. There are also over a million **sheep** on the island, most of them **merino**.

---

### TELEPHONE NUMBERS

In **February 1997**, to coincide with the implementation of the ☎08 area code across the whole of South Australia, all phone numbers in the ☎0848 code region will **change by area** as follows:

**American River** will change from ☎0848/33 xxx to 08/8553 7xxx
**Cygnet River** will change from ☎0848/29 xxx to 08/8553 9xxx
**Harriet** will change from ☎0848/94 xxx to 08/8559 4xxx
**Karratta** will change from ☎0848/37 xxx to 08/8559 7xxx
**Kingscote** numbers beginning 22 will change from ☎0848/22 xxx to 08/8553 2xxx, and numbers beginning 23 will change from ☎0848/23 xxx to 08/8553 3xxx
**Penneshaw** will change from ☎0848/31 to 08/8553 1xxx
**Stokes Bay** will change from ☎0848/36 xxx to 08/8559 2xxx

*(If in doubt, phone the* **Telstra hotline** *on free call* ☎*1800/88 8888.)*

# Island transport

There are frequent **ferries** to Kangaroo Island, plying across the Backstairs Passage from Cape Jervis to Penneshaw – often a rough journey, though mercifully short. *Sealink* have two large vehicle ferries which run at least three times daily and up to six times during peak holiday periods, taking about an hour to cross: buses connect the service with Adelaide (7am daily) and on the other side there are buses to American River and Kingscote if you book ($29 one way, $42 including bus; cars $58; bikes $5; ☎13 1301). The *Valerie Jane* takes only 30 minutes to cross, twice daily, but doesn't carry vehicles ($38 includes bus from Adelaide; ☎0848/31 233) while departing from Port Adelaide, the *MV Island Seaway* brings food and other supplies to Kingscote once a week (7hr 30min; $25; cars $61; bikes $4.80; ☎0848/22 273). A new service between Glenelg and Kingscote, *Kangaroo Island Fast Ferries* (2hr; $24–29 one way; ☎08/295 2688) departs once daily, with a ticket office opposite the tram stop on the foreshore.

In addition, there are lots of cheap **packages** including accommodation and tours or car rental worth checking out, often with special backpacker rates. At one end of the scale, *Sealink* (☎13 1301) do a whirlwind $130 one-day tour leaving Adelaide at 7am and getting back at 10.30pm, but it's pretty exhausting; *Fast Ferries* (☎08/295 2688) run a similar tour from Glenelg for around $99. More leisurely options include *Sealink*'s "Backpacker Adventure Tours" and those offered by specialized island-based operators (see "Getting around" below), but check the noticeboards in Adelaide hostels for the latest.

It takes 30 minutes to **fly** to Kangaroo Island from Adelaide and costs $45–63 one way. *Air Kangaroo Island* (☎08/234 4177) flies to Kingscote, as do *Albatross Airlines* (☎0848/22 296; 3 daily; courtesy bus to Kingscote), *Kendell Airlines* (free call ☎1800/33 8894) and *Emu Air* (free call ☎1800/18 2353; 2 daily); *Emu* also fly to Penneshaw. Car rental companies have offices at Kingscote Airport and there's a bus to town for about $6; for other destinations call *Airport Coach Services* (☎0848/22 678).

## Getting around

Once you're on the island, you really need your own transport. As there are just three **car rental** firms, to be sure of a vehicle it's best to book – that way you'll also be met with the vehicle off the ferry or plane. *Budget Rent a Car* (☎0848/23 133), and *Kangaroo Island Rental* (☎0848/22 390 or free call 1800/088 296), are both fairly expensive at around $69 a day, $420 a week; *Kangaroo* also have 4WD landcruisers. For cheaper deals, try *Low Rate Car Rentals* (☎0848/23 198), who also rent motorcycles and camping gear.

There are few sealed **roads** on the island – the main one being the Playford Highway from Kingscote through Cygnet River and Parndana to the edge of Flinders Chase National Park; at the eastern end of the island, sealed roads feed off it to the airport and main settlements, including Penneshaw. The rest are unsealed: constructed of ironstone rubble on red dirt, they can be very dangerous. The recommended speed on these roads is 60kph; driving slowly also reduces the risk of colliding with the native fauna. The same roads make **cycling** a tough proposition – you'll need a mountain bike and a tolerance for long bone-rattling stretches and choking clouds of red dust. Note that the rental bikes available on the island (from *Wisteria Lodge Motel*, Kingscote ☎0848/22 707 or *Linnets Island Club*, American Beach ☎0848/33 053) are for fun only, and useless over long distances. *Kangaroo Island Bike Hire* at American Beach (☎0848/31 026) rents out **mopeds**.

Most people lump for **bus tours**, which you can make flexible with a bit of planning, and are good value if bought as part of a package (see above). *Kangaroo Island Explorer Tours* (☎0848/22 640) will drop off and pick up people who want to take their excellent south coast tour in stages, camping along the way; they also have north coast and other tours. More specialized outfits include *Adventure Charters Kangaroo Island* in Kingscote (☎0848/29 119), run by a former national park ranger who offers 4WD tours with an emphasis on fine food, wine and accommodation as well as nature; expensive but worth it for those who can afford it. Based in Stokes Bay, the intriguingly-named tour outfit *Up the Creek with Kate* (☎0848/36 251), are day bushwalks led by Kate Stanton, discovering wildflowers and wildlife. *Diving Safaris* (☎1800/06 1887) run dive tours for licensed divers, with special backpacker rates.

## Around the island

Most people arrive on Kangaroo Island with the ferry at **PENNESHAW**, set on low, penguin-inhabited cliffs. This is also the best place to base yourself for your stay, with comfortable accommodation and plenty of places to eat (see "Practicalities" below). At night, the fairy penguins cross the beach at Hogg Bay and practically run wild through the town; a national park guide provides an informative commentary on their antics (departing from the *Sorrento Motel*; 8.30pm nightly except Tues & Sun; $3.50). There's good, safe swimming at Eastern Cove, American Beach (where *Adventureland Diving* provides residential scuba courses as well as rock-climbing, abseiling and canoeing; ☎0848/31 072) and at Antechamber Bay. Just past the bay, there are a couple of ancient lighthouses worth exploring: you can even stay in the sandstone homes of the original keepers (see "Practicalities" below).

The **Dudley Peninsula**, on which Penneshaw stands, is attached to the rest of the island by a narrow neck of sand; at the isthmus 511 steps lead up **Mount Thisby** (Prospect Hill), a 99m hill of sand with views across to the mainland, to **Hungry Beach**, **Pelican Lagoon** and **American River** on the island's north coast, and in the opposite direction to **Pennington Bay** with its good surf, but a dangerous undertow, and sponge-textured weathered rocks to clamber over. **American River** is actually a sheltered bay, and many small fishing boats moor here aiming to catch some of its abundant **whiting**: boats can be chartered for local fishing.

### Kingscote and the north coast

It's a 45-minute drive (60km) from Penneshaw to **KINGSCOTE**, the island's main town with banks, shops, a hospital, library and the only high school. It also has a small sandy beach with grassed terraces and a sea pool with a waterslide and grassy playground. You can walk to the **Reeves Point Historic Site** along the Esplanade, and less than a kilometre up the hill above on Seaview Road is **Hope Cottage Folk Museum** (daily 2–4pm; closed July & Aug), the restored 1859 home of a pioneering family.

The beaches of the north coast are more sheltered than those facing south. **Emu Bay**, 21km from Kingscote, is a secluded and quiet spot with no shops, a few holiday homes, and a wide, clean, white sandy beach, jetty and basic **campsite** with toilet facilties only (☎0848/22 325). Secluded **Stokes Bay** is reached through a natural tunnel between overhanging boulders. There's a delightful calm rock pool, a perfect semi-circle of rounded black stones, which conveniently provides protection from the dangerous rip in the bay. Outside the tunnel, the *Hungry Hide-out Kiosk* (daily 10am–5.30pm; ☎0848/36 277) looks after the beachfront **campsites** and also sells milk and bread.

### The south coast

Several conservation parks are strung along the exposed south coast. The largest is **Cape Gantheaume**, an area of low mallee scrub supporting prolific birdlife around **Murrays Lagoon** (ranger station), the largest freshwater lagoon on the island. Adjacent **Seal Bay Conservation Park** is home to several hundred sea lions, the second largest breeding population in Australia. The sea lions here are unusually tolerant of humans and you can walk quietly among the colony at Seal Bay accompanied by a national park guide (9am–4.30pm every 45min; $3.50).

**Vivonne Bay**, with its long sandy beach and bush setting, is a great place to camp. The *Vivonne Bay Store* (☎0848/94 252) collects the fee for the beachfront **campsite** (toilets, water, barbecues). It's safe to swim near the jetty or boat ramp or in the Harriet River, but the bay itself has a dangerous undertow. Between Seal Bay and Vivonne Bay, **Little Sahara** is fifteen kilometres of perfect white sand dunes rising unexpectedly out of mallee scrub.

The main feature of the **Kelly Hill Conservation Park** is the **Kelly Hill Caves**, ten hectares of limestone cave formations (guided tours hourly 10am–4pm, plus 5pm in summer; 45min; $3.50). The tour explores only the largest cave, which is not your usual damp, bat-filled cavern but very dry with a constant temperature of sixteen degrees. If you want to explore other caves there are *Adventure Caving Tours* (☎0848/ 37 231 for details and booking). The 18-km return **Hanson Bay Trail** goes from the caves to the sea, passing freshwater lagoons and dune systems: allow at least eight hours –longer if you're tempted by the fine swimming at the bay.

## Flinders Chase National Park

FLINDERS CHASE NATIONAL PARK, South Australia's largest, occupies the entire western tip of the island. It became a park as early as 1919, and in the 1920s and 1930s koalas, platypuses, emus and Cape Barren geese were introduced. The land is mainly sugar gum forest, but the Rocky River **visitors' centre** (daily 9am–5pm; ☎0848/37 235) is surrounded by open grasslands grazed by large numbers of Cape Barren geese and kangaroos. Koala signs lead to a glade of trees with the creatures swaying high up, within binocular range; following the **Black Stump walking track** for 3km you'll reach a platypus viewing area which requires endless patience. The winding road through the park, rough to very rough, will take you on to the most spectacular feature, the huge and weirdly shaped **Remarkable Rocks** on Kirkpatrick Point, where fur seals bask in the sun on the rocks below.

# Practicalities

In addition to the **campsites** and caravan parks listed below, don't forget the basic beachside tent sites at Emu, Stokes and Vivonne bays – detailed in the "Around the island" section above. Town-based **accommodation** is most easily found in **Penneshaw**. *Tandarra Lodge and Penguin Hostel* (☎0848/31 018; dorms ①, basic motel rooms ④–⑤), is much more relaxed than the modernized *Penneshaw Youth Hostel* (☎0848/31 233; ①). *Sorrento Resort* (☎0848/31 028; ⑥) is the upmarket alternative, with a heated pool among palm trees, a spa, sauna and tennis court, plus a good restaurant. There's camping at Brown Beach or *Penneshaw Caravan Park*, Talinga Avenue, to the left off the ferry (☎0848/31 075; on-site vans ③), a pleasant seaside spot. You can also stay in the two **lighthouse keepers' cottages** at Cape Willoughby (☎0848/37 235; ④).

The best **restaurant** in town is the relaxed *Old Post Office Restaurant* (nightly except Mon, licensed; ☎0848/31 063) with vegetarian and home-style meals, while the *Penneshaw Hotel* is small and friendly. *Condon's Takeaway and Launderette* (daily 7.30am–7.30pm; laundry 24hr), attached to the youth hostel, does fast food and a breakfast fry-up and sells a small range of groceries, but you'd be better off going to *Muggleton General Store* opposite the hotel which sells virtually everything and has a takeaway and a sit-down café. The *Sealink* office is at 7 North Terrace (Mon–Fri 8am–6pm, Sat & Sun 8am–1pm & 3pm–6pm; ☎0848/31 122). There's no bank in Penneshaw, but the **post office** (Mon–Fri 9am–1pm & 2–5pm, Sat 9am–11pm) acts as an agent.

At **American River**, *Matthew Flinders Terraces* (☎0848/33 100; ⑦) is a beautifully situated motel with good restaurant, or try the *Wanderers Rest* (☎0848/33 140; ⑦), an upmarket B&B. Holiday units here include the budget *Casuarina Units* (☎0848/33 020; ③), and the more expensive *Ulonga Lodge* (☎0848/33 171; ⑤–⑥) and *Cooinda Holiday*

*Village* (☎0848/33 063; ⑤–⑥). The *Linnets Island Club* (☎0848/33 053; tent sites, plus holiday flats ④, motel units ⑤–⑧) has a wide range of facilities including sauna, pool, spa, camp kitchen, playground, barbecues and tennis court.

In **Kingscote** the waterfront *Ozone Hotel* (☎0848/22 011, or free call 1800/08 3133; ⑤–⑥) established in 1907, is an institution, and the best place to eat in town with a café, bistro and restaurant. The *Queenscliffe Family Hotel* (☎0848/22 254; ⑤) is another old pub offering rooms and meals, or try *Ellisons Seaview Motel*, Chapman Terrace (☎0848/22 030; ⑤). For the budget-conscious, there's the *Kangaroo Island Central Backpackers Hostel* on 19 Murray Street (☎0848/22 787; ①). Campers have a choice between the small and central *Kangaroo Island Caravan Park* (☎0848/22 325; on-site vans ②, cabins ③–④) and the *Nepean Bay Caravan Park* (☎0848/22 394; on-site vans ②, cabins ③–④) at Brownlow Beach, 3km away, which is more inviting and better equipped. The nearby *Brownlow Holiday Units* (☎0848/22 293; ④) also offer good value.

In the **Flinders Chase National Park** the main camping area is at Rocky River where there are also two cottages, the four-bedroom Old Homestead (④) and the one-room Mays Cottage (③): details from the visitors' centre (☎0848/37 235). *Flinders Chase Farm Hostel* (☎0848/37 223; ①) is ideally placed on the edge of the park; it provides mellow budget accommodation, meals can be arranged, and bike rental is available.

# The southeast: the Princes Highway

For most travellers, the southeast is an area to be passed through as quickly as possible between Melbourne and Adelaide. From Tailem Bend, on the Murray River some 85km out of Adelaide, three highways branch out. The **Ouyen Highway** is the quintessential road to nowhere, leading through the sleepy settlements of Lameroo and Pinnaroo to the insignificant town of **Ouyen** in Victoria's mallee country. The **Dukes Highway** is the fast, boring route to Melbourne via the South Australian mallee scrub and farming towns of **Keith** and **Bordertown**, before continuing in Victoria as the Western Highway across the monotonous Wimmera. If you want to break this journey, the **Coonawarra** and **Naracoorte** lie between the Dukes Highway and the coastal route: the former is a tiny wine-producing area that makes some of the country's finest red wine and has plenty of wineries to visit, among them the famous *Wynn's*; the latter a fair size town with a freshwater lagoon system that attracts prolific birdlife, and a conservation park with impressive World Heritage-listed caves.

The **Princes Highway** (Highway 1) is much less direct but far more interesting; it follows the extensive coastal lagoon system of **the Coorong** to **Kingston SE**, whence it runs a short way inland to **Mount Gambier** before crossing into Victoria. On this last stretch, another possible route – Alternative Highway 1 – sticks closer to the coast. *Bonds Mount Gambier Bus Service* (☎08/231 9090) has two routes between Adelaide and Mount Gambier, one inland via Keith, Bordertown, Naracoorte, Coonawarra and Penola; the other along the coast via Meningie, Kingston, Robe and Millicent.

## Coorong National Park

From Tailem Bend, the Princes Highway skirts Lake Alexandrina and freshwater Lake Albert, where **MENINGIE** is a popular fishing centre, before skirting the edge of the **Coorong National Park**. The coastal saline lagoon system of the Coorong (from the Aboriginal *Karangk* meaning long neck) is separated from the sea for over 100km by the high sand dunes of the **Younghusband Peninsula**: the famous Australian children's film *Storm Boy*, about a boy and his friendship with a pelican, was filmed here, and the state's most prolific pelican breeding-ground is brilliant for observation of these awkward yet graceful birds.

The Coorong is also good for beach **camping**: with a permit (see below), you can camp anywhere along the beach between high and low watermark, but cars must be parked in designated places, marked by green posts. There are no facilities in the park and no drinking water, though the latter is available at the **Salt Creek Visitor Centre** (Mon–Fri 8am–4pm) on the edge of the park about 60km south of Meningie. General **information** and camping **permits** ($3 per group of five or fewer) can also be obtained here, or at the national park **headquarters** in Meningie (34 Main Street; Mon–Fri 10am–4.30pm; ☎085/75 1200); after hours, permits can be bought from the *Melaleuca Centre*, 74 Princes Highway (Sat & Sun 11am–3.30pm) or at the roadhouses at Policemans Point and Salt Creek. If you want to stay in more comfort, there are plenty of **motels** at Meningie.

**Camp Coorong**, run by the *Ngarrindjeri Lands and Progress Association*, is 12km south of Meningie. This cultural centre attempts to explain the heritage and culture of the Ngarrindjeri Aborigines who were one of the largest groups in South Australia, occupying the land around the Coorong and the lower Murray River and lakes. There's a museum, and you can camp here or stay in the well set-up **bunkhouse** (booking required on ☎085/751 5557; ①). Weekend **cross-cultural tours** are available from Adelaide with Ngarrindjeri guides taking you through the Coorong, where you feast on bush tucker and stay overnight at Camp Coorong (*Osprey Expeditions*, ☎08/370 9337).

## Alternative Highway One

**KINGSTON SE**, on Lacepede Bay, is the first town past the Coorong: here the Princes Highway turns inland, while Alternative Highway 1 continues along the coast, to rejoin the main road at Millicent. As the **Big Lobster** signifies, Kingston has an important lobster industry: buy them at *Lacepede Seafood* on Marine Parade (daily 9am–5pm) for around $25 a kilo, or at restaurants around town. On Hanson Street, the *Royal Mail Hotel*, resolutely unrenovated, also serves fresh Coorong mullet. Lobsters apart, you're better off continuing down the coast: if you do need to stay, you have the choice of the usual motels, the *Bunkers Backpackers Hostel*, 21 Holland Street (☎087/67 2185; ①), or the *Kingston Caravan Park*, Marine Parade (☎087/67 2050; on-site vans ②).

**ROBE**, on the south side of Guichen Bay 44km from Kingston, was one of South Australia's first settlements, established as a deep-water port in 1847. After 1857, over 16,000 Chinese landed here and walked to the goldfields, 400km or so away, to avoid the poll tax levied in Victoria at the time. As trade declined and the highway bypassed town, Robe has managed to maintain both dignity and charm, and during the busy summer period the population of less than 800 expands to over 11,000; Adelaidians love the place and some even drive the 366km for a weekend. It's all deliberately low-key: the main street of Victoria Street is tree-lined and semi-residential, the shops blending unobtrusively with the houses. **Tourist information** is incorporated in the library on the corner of Smiley and Victoria streets (Mon–Fri 10am–noon & 1–5pm, Sat 8.30am–12.30pm); they have walking and driving maps and a Historical Interpretation Centre. If you walk north along the bay to Cape Dombey, with its boldly striped obelisk, you can watch fairy penguins on the rocks.

There's a choice of dozens of places to stay, including two superior **pubs**: the *Robe Hotel*, Mundy Terrace (☎087/68 2077; ④–⑤), is an old stone beachfront hotel with modern touches; the *Caledonian Inn*, Victoria Street (☎087/68 2029; B&B ④), is a charming ivy-covered stone building in the English village mould, and serves excellent food. *Robe Backpackers*, Victoria Street (☎087/68 2445; ①), is clean and comfortable and has bikes for rent, or the *Guichen Bay Motel*, opposite (☎087/68 2001; ⑤), offers more luxury with picnic tables outside the rooms and a pool. *Sea Vu Caravan Park*, 1 Squire Drive (☎087/68 2273; on-site vans ③, cabins ④) is family-run, close to town with a swimming beach just below. Besides the pubs, a good place to **eat** is *Wilson's at Robe* on Victoria Street (☎087/68 2459).

Between Robe and **BEACHPORT** are four lakes: for part of the way you can take the Nora Criena Scenic Drive through **Little Dip Conservation Park**, 14km of coastal dune systems. The drive gives views of Lake Eliza and Lake St Clair before returning to Alternative Highway 1 and Beachport, which boasts one of the longest jetties in Australia and many lobster fishing boats at anchor on Rivoli Bay. *Bompa's*, overlooking the bay at 3 Railway Terrace (☎087/35 8333; B&B ④–⑥), was the town's first licensed hotel in 1879, and is now a pleasing **guesthouse** and coffee shop, which also serves evening meals to guests. Other places to stay on the foreshore are the *Beachport YHA* (☎087/35 8197; ①) and *Beachport Caravan Park* (☎087/35 8128; on-site vans ③), both on Beach Road. Back on Railway Terrace, the *Beachport Hotel* (☎087/35 8003; ④) is a big 1880s beachfront establishment with simple rooms and good **meals**. *Beachport Motor Inn*, Railway Terrace (☎087/35 8070; ⑤), has several self-catering units.

## Mount Gambier

**MOUNT GAMBIER** is the southeast's commercial centre; not far from the Victorian border, the town sprawls up the slopes of an extinct volcano with three craters, each with its own lake surrounded by heavily wooded slopes. The **Blue Lake** is the largest of them, up to 204m deep and 5km in circumference; from November to March it's a stunning cobalt blue, reverting to duller grey in the colder months. There's a scenic drive around the lake and several lookouts. For information on this and other attractions, including a couple of art galleries, head for the *Lady Nelson Tourist Interpretative Centre* (daily 9am–5pm; ☎087/241 730), right on the highway.

You probably wouldn't stop here too long, but Mount Gambier is a good place to break for something to **eat**, and there are heaps of places to **stay** if you need to, with motels lining the highway either side of town. Right in the centre of town, *Jens Hotel*, 40 Commercial Street (☎087/25 0188; ④), is a classic, wide-balconied old boozer with good basic meals and accommodation. The *Mount Gambier Hotel*, 2 Commercial Street, has more upmarket food, or try the classic Italian *Café Capri Pastacceria & Geletaria*, 13 Commercial Street (daily 8am–6pm).

# The Riverland

The **Riverland** is the long irrigated strip on either side of the Murray from Blanchetown to the border. The Canadian Chaffey brothers had already developed successful irrigation settlements in California when they were invited to Australia to look into possibilities for the Murray, establishing an **irrigation colony** at **Renmark** in 1887. The Riverland's deep red-orange alluvial soil – helped by this extensive irrigation – is very fertile, making the area the state's major supplier of oranges, stone-fruit and grapes. Fruit stalls along the roadsides add to the impression of a year-long harvest, and if you're after fruit-picking work it's an excellent place to start. The area is also Australia's major **wine**-producing region, though the technologically advanced wineries with huge production bases make mainly mass-produced wines for casks and export. Many are open to visitors, but their scale and commercialism make them less enjoyable for a wine-tasting trawl than, say, the Southern Vales (see p.601).

From Waikerie to Renmark all the **towns** feel pretty much the same, with a raw edge, little charm or sophistication, and an undercurrent of violence most apparent on

## THE MURRAY RIVER

The **Murray** is Australia's Mississippi. A fraction of the size, perhaps, but in a country of seasonal, intermittent streams it's a great river. Like the Mississippi too, the Murray helped open up a new continent, first to explorers, later to trade. Fed by melting snow from the Snowy Mountains, it has enough volume to flow through the arid plains, eventually reaching the Southern Ocean southwest of Adelaide. For much of its length it forms the border between New South Wales and Victoria, slowing its course on reaching South Australia to meander and produce extensive alluvial plains where irrigation areas are now established. Almost half of South Australia's water comes from the Murray: even far-off Woomera relies on it.

Historically, the riverland was densely populated by various **Aboriginal peoples**. They navigated the river in bark canoes, the bark being cut from river red gums in a single perfect piece; many trees along the river still bear the scars. Nets and spears were used to catch fish, duck and emu; mussels were also an important food source. The Ngarrindjeri people's Dreamtime story of the river's creation explains how Ngurunderi (a Dreamtime hero) travelled down the Murray from its confluence with the Darling, looking for his two runaway wives. Then the Murray was just a small stream. As Ngurunderi searched, a giant Murray cod surged ahead of him, widening the river with swipes of his tail. Ngurunderi tried to spear the fish, which he chased right through to the ocean: the thrashing cod carved out the pattern of the Murray River during the chase.

The explorers **Hume** and **Hovell** came across the Murray at Albury in 1824. In 1830, **Sturt** and **Mitchell** navigated the Murray and Darling in a whale boat, Sturt naming it after the then Secretary of State for the Colonies (coincidentally *Murrundi* was the Aboriginal name for part of the river). Their exploration opened up the interior and from 1838 the Murray was followed as a **stock route** to South Australia by drovers or "overlanders" taking sheep and cattle to newly established Adelaide. In 1853 the first **paddle steamer** on the Murray, the "Mary Ann", was launched near Mannum. Goods were transported far inland, opening up new areas for settlement; in return wool was carried to market. River transport reached its peak in the 1870s, but by the mid-1930s it was virtually finished – bowing to the superior speed and flexibility of the railways.

### SEEING THE RIVER

Several old **paddle-steamers** still cruise the Murray for pleasure. The *PS Mundoo* (☎085/55 2203) cruises the South Australian length of the river, leaving Goolwa at the river mouth annually on the first of July for a three-week return journey to Renmark; you can pick up the boat as a day-trip between towns. Many shorter cruises, in a variety of craft, are offered in the riverside towns.

Hiring a **houseboat** is a relaxing and enjoyable way to see the river. All you need is a driving licence, and the cost is not astronomical if you can get a group of people together and avoid the peak holiday seasons. A week in a ten-berth houseboat out of season should cost around $600–1000. *South Australian Tourism Commission* (☎08/212 1505 or free call 1800/88 2092) have pamphlets with costs and facilities; they can also book for you.

A more hands-on way to explore the wetlands and creek systems is in a **canoe**. *Leisure Directions* (☎08/213 0555) produce free brochures on canoeing and excellent canoeing maps. The best place to rent canoes and kayaks is *Riverland Canoeing Adventures*, Alamein Avenue, North Loxton (☎085/84 1494), which also rents camping equipment and bikes. The flat country, short distances between towns and dry climate are perfect for **cycling**, and bikes can also be rented at various hostels along the way.

drunken Friday nights. Time here is best spent on or around the river, with the towns seen as departure points for river cruises, places to eat and stay. Each has only one hotel, even the 7000-strong towns of Berri and Renmark. These huge and graceless **community hotels** are a Riverland feature: owned and run by the town, their profits are ploughed back into the hotel or channelled into the community, generally into sporting groups.

The **Sturt Highway**, the major route between Adelaide and Sydney, passes straight through the Riverland. Leaving Adelaide, it bypasses Gawler and cuts across the north-ern end of the Barossa Valley, reaching the Murray at Blanchetown, about 130km from the city. *Stateliner* run a daily service along the highway from Adelaide to Renmark via Blanchetown and Waikerie, and also go daily except Tuesday to Loxton. *Greyhound.Pioneer* drop off and pick up at the Riverland towns on their interstate routes.

## Blanchetown to Waikerie

The river takes a huge meander away from the road between Blanchetown and **WAIKERIE**, little over 40km away in a straight line, which is the first of the real Riverland towns. It's also the heart of the largest citrus-growing area in Australia and the first thing you notice is **Waikerie Co-op Producers**, a huge complex taking up both sides of a street – the "largest fruit-packing house in the southern hemisphere". This apart, it's a pleasant town with many fine sandstone buildings. If you detour around the river loop you'll pass through **MORGAN**, at the farthest point, once one of the busiest river ports in South Australia and still with twelve-metre-high river wharves.

### Loxton

About 35km further along the Sturt Highway, the Murray makes another large loop away from the highway, with Loxton at its southernmost reach. Leaving the highway at Kingston OM, you pass the **Moorook Game Reserve**, a large swamp fringed with river red gums and home to many waterbirds; at the other end of the loop there's a 24-hour free ferry across the river to Berri (see below). In **LOXTON** itself, the **Tourist & Travel Centre** is at 45 East Terrace (Mon–Fri 9am–5pm, Sat 9–11.30am; ☎085/84 7919), where you can also book for the *MV River Rambler* (2pm weekends and school holidays; 2hr; $12; direct bookings on ☎085/84 6359) which cruises upstream to the **Loxton Historical Village** (Mon–Fri 10am–4pm, Sat & Sun 10am–5pm; $4), a replica of a turn-of-the-century Riverland town. Opposite Loxton, **Katarapko Game Reserve** is where Katarapko Creek and the Murray have cut deep channels and lagoons, creat-ing an island. Access is by water only and it's perfect for canoeing and observing the prolific birdlife; to camp you need a permit from the NPWS, 2 Wilson Street, Berri (☎085/95 2177). *Loxton Riverfront Caravan Park*, Habels Bend (☎085/84 7862; dorms ①, on-site vans ②, cabins ③–④), is the next best thing, a peaceful spot opposite the game reserve, with backpacker accommodation in the "Loxton Katarapko Lodge", plus canoes for rent and safe swimming.

Back in town, the *Loxton Hotel-Motel*, East Terrace (☎085/84 7266; ④–⑤), is inex-pensive, friendly and down to earth, with decent counter meals and bargain single rooms. On the same street there are two cafés to eat at, the *Colonial* and *Annies*, as well as the *Loxton Palace Chinese Restaurant*.

### Barmera

If you haven't followed the river to Loxton, **BARMERA**, on the shores of Lake Bonney, is the next major stopping point along the highway. Its claims to fame are varied and dubi-ous: at **Pelican Point**, on the lake's western shore, there's an official nudist beach, while every June the **South Australian Country Music Awards** are held in the lovely old

*Bonney Theatre.* If you want to get on the water here, *Riverland Leisure Canoe Tours*, Thelma Road (☎085/88 2053) also rent out canoes. For more about the music awards, and **tourist information** in general, contact the *Barmera Travel Centre*, Barwell Avenue (Mon–Fri 8.30am–5pm, Sat 9–11.30am; ☎085/88 2289). The *Barmera Hotel/Motel* (☎085/88 2111; ③–④) is much the worst of all the Riverland community hotels, and probably not somewhere you'd feel comfortable staying; Friday night bands let loose downstairs until 2am. A cut above is the expensive *Barmera Country Club*, on Hawdon Street (☎085/88 2888; ⑥), overlooking the golf course with a pool, spa and tennis courts, and a restaurant. The extensive *Lake Bonney Caravan Reserve* on Lakeside Drive (☎085/88 2234; on-site vans & cabins ③, cottage ④) is a scenic alternative.

## Berri

The scene for **BERRI** is set by the **Big Orange**, symbol of the fact that this is the town where the orange juice comes from. Which is about as good as it gets: visit *Berrievale Orchards*, for more juice, or the **Wilabalangaloo Flora and Fauna Reserve** (Mon & Thurs–Sun 10am–4pm; $2) with scenic river walks above coloured sandstone cliffs, a native animal enclosure and a local history museum. In town the *Berri Hotel Motel*, Riverview Drive (☎085/82 1411; pub rooms ④, motel units ⑤), is a huge riverfront pub that grows ever tackier and ritzier – though it's not a bad place to stay, with swimming pool, tennis courts and good food. *Berri Backpackers*, on the Sturt Highway opposite the Berri Club (☎085/82 3144; ①), has an eccentric owner, pool, and a good chance of picking up work if you want it; they also rent out bikes and offer an affordable canoe tour in the summer. For **food**, *Down to Earth*, 5 William Street, is a decent healthfood store, *The Berri Canton Palace* on the same street is a good Chinese serving lunch and dinner daily except Monday. *Denny Street Deli*, 22 Denny Street, does breakfast, lunch and tea. If you want to launch yourself on the river here, *Swan Houseboats* (☎085/82 3077) rent out dinghies and canoes. For more information on Berri, head for the **tourist office** on Vaughan Terrace (☎085/82 1655).

## Renmark

**RENMARK**, on a bend of the Murray 254km from Adelaide, is the last major town before the New South Wales border. The **Renmark Tourist and Heritage Centre** on Murray Avenue (Mon–Fri 9am–1pm & 2–5pm, Sat & Sun 10am–1pm & 2–4pm; ☎085/86 6704) books river cruises and houseboats. Outside, the *PS Industry* is moored: one of only six wood-fuelled paddle-steamers left on the Murray, it's gradually being renovated. **Cruises** from Renmark (book at the tourist centre) are on the *Waterway Safari*, an aluminium tri-hull that explores the river's backwaters and lagoons on anything from a two-hour cruise to a five-day camping trip; the paddle-steamer *Murray Princess* does three-day round-trip cruises from Renmark via Berri and Loxton (from $400).

Opposite the tourist office, the huge **Renmark Community Hotel** is a focal point for the town. Built in 1897, the hotel was given its classic facade in the 1930s and modernized inside too. *Da Vincis* is a beautiful bar with Art Deco features, while the rest of the hotel is tacky Seventies style. Adelaide bands play at the hotel on Friday nights; any other entertainment will be found at the **Chaffey Theatre** on 18th Street (☎085/86 5462), an impressive performing arts centre hosting amateur and professional plays, films and concerts. **Olivewood** (Mon & Thurs–Sun 10am–4pm, Tues 2–4pm; $2), the former home of the Chaffey brothers at the corner of Renmark Avenue and 21st Street, is now owned by the National Trust. A palm-lined drive leads through a citrus orchard and olive trees to the house, which is a strange hybrid of Canadian log cabin and Australian lean-to. The attached museum is the usual hotch-potch of local memorabilia, unrelated to the Chaffeys or their ambitious irrigation project.

The obvious **place to stay** is the landmark *Renmark Community Hotel* (☎085/86 6755; ③–⑦), where rooms range from budget to deluxe with various shades in between, and there's an outdoor swimming pool and spa, and a bistro. Other options include the *Renmark YHA* on 16th Street (☎085/86 6937 weekdays, ☎085/86 6839 weekends; ①): there's no resident manager, but keys can be collected from the L J Hooker office on Renmark Avenue, across the road from the bus drop-off point. *Renmark Caravan Park*, on Patey Drive 2km east of town (☎085/86 6315; on-site vans & cabins ③–④), enjoys an idyllic setting along a kilometre of riverfront, but the *Riverbend Caravan Park* is closer to town, on the highway (☎085/95 5131; on-site vans ②, cabins ③–④). Two good **restaurants** are *Ginger Mick's Pizza*, 124 Murray Street, open late every night except Sunday, and *Sophie's Restaurant*, 202 Renmark Avenue (in the *Caltex* service station) for Greek food.

# The mid-north

The area north of the **Sturt Highway**, bounded by **Port Augusta** (see p.619) and the **south Flinders Ranges**, is a fertile agricultural region known as the **mid-north**. Only 14km north of the Barossa Valley, **Kapunda** became the country's first mining town when **copper** was discovered in 1842. It can also be reached as a short detour from the **Barrier Highway** en route to Broken Hill, a route that continues through the larger mining town of **Burra** and the self-proclaimed "frontier to the Outback", **Peterborough**. **Clare**, the centre of the mid-north's wine area, is 45km southwest of Burra, and is on the alternative route to Port Augusta, the Main North Road. The **Heysen Trail** runs through Kapunda, Burra and then, via **Crystal Brook**, into the foothills of the Flinders. Heading north to Port Augusta on **Highway 1** for the Northern Territory or Western Australia, you'll pass through the ugly lead-smelting city of **Port Pirie**, and thence on to the south Flinders Ranges.

Getting around the area by **bus** is problematic: while most of the major towns have transport links to Adelaide, there's virtually none between towns, however close. *Greyhound.Pioneer*, on its Adelaide–Broken Hill route, goes via the Clare Valley (Auburn, Watervale, Sevenhill, Clare), Jamestown and Peterborough, while its Adelaide–Sydney service stops at Burra. *Stateliner* serves the same Clare Valley towns. There's no public transport to Kapunda. All interstate buses to Darwin or Perth take Highway 1 through Port Pirie; if you get off 27km before this, it's only a couple of kilometres walk to Crystal Brook and the Heysen Trail.

## Copper-mining towns

In 1841 South Australia was in serious economic trouble; the discovery of **copper** at Kapunda the following year rescued the young colony and put it at the forefront of Australia's mining boom. The early finds were soon overshadowed by those at Burra 65 kilometres north: the Burra "**Monster Mine**" was the largest in Australia until 1860, creating fabulous wealth, and attracting huge numbers of Cornish miners in particular. The boom ended as suddenly as it began, as resources were exhausted – mining finished at Burra in 1877 and Kapunda in 1878.

Heading to **KAPUNDA** from the Barossa, the landscape changes as vineyards are replaced by crops and grazing sheep. As you come into town, you're greeted by a colossal sculpture of a Cornish miner entitled *Map Kernow* – "son of Cornwall". A place that once had its own daily newspaper, eleven hotels and a busy train station is now a rural service town, pleasantly undeveloped and with many old buildings decorated with locally designed and manufactured iron lacework.

If you have your own transport, you can follow a 10-km **heritage trail** that takes in the ruins of the Kapunda mine, with panoramic views from the mine chimney lookout: details from the **Kapunda Information Centre** on Hill Street (☎085/66 2902). On the same street the **Kapunda Museum** (daily Sept–May, otherwise Sun & holidays only, 1–4pm) occupies the mammoth Romanesque-style former Baptist church. The best time to come to Kapunda is during the **Celtic festival** over the first weekend in April, when Celtic music, bush and folk bands feature at the four pubs.

If you want to **stay**, *Oliver's at Ford House*, 80 Main Street (☎085/66 2280; ⑤), has colonial-style B&B; the *Sir John Franklin Hotel*, also on Main Street (☎085/66 2106; ④), has simple, clean rooms and is the most popular pub for inexpensive **meals**; campers are catered for at *Dutton Caravan Park*, 11 Montefiore Street (☎085/66 2094).

## Burra

In 1851 **BURRA**, a little over 50km north, had 5000 residents and was mining five percent of the world's copper; when the mines closed in 1877 it became a service centre for the surrounding farming community. It also takes advantage of its position on the Barrier Highway, using the copper heritage to draw visitors. Plenty of money is spent restoring and beautifying the place, even to the extent of topping up pretty, gum-shaded **Burra Creek** to ensure it's always running. The creek divides the town grid in two: the mine is in the north, while the southern section has the shopping centre, based around **Market Square**, where you'll also find the **tourist office** (daily 10am–4pm; ☎08/8892 2154). Their main function is loan of the **Burra Passport Key** to people driving the 11km **heritage trail**; for about $15 per car (plus deposit), the key lets you into six major sites en route – though you still have to pay for admission to the museums.

Heading north along Market Street you come to the **Burra Monster Mine** site, where there are extensive remains and interpretative walking trails as well as the *Enginehouse Museum* (Mon noon–2pm, Tues–Fri 11am–2pm, Sat & Sun 11am–4pm; $3). Continuing north, the **Bon Accord Mine Complex** on Linkson Street (Mon–Fri 12.30–2.30pm, Sat & Sun 12.30–3.30pm; $3) was a short-lived failure compared to its hugely successful neighbour; there's a scale model of the monster mine and a shaft and mining relics on view. Other key-pass places in the northern section of the town are the old **police lock-up and stables**, **Redruth Gaol** and **Hampton**, a private township in the style of an English village, now deserted. Back in the main part of the town, there's entry to the **Unicorn Brewery Cellars** (1873) and the fascinating two remaining **Miners' Dugouts**: around 1851 nearly 2000 people lived in homes clawed out of the soft clay along Burra Creek, because of a shortage of housing. There are two further **museums**: the *Market Square Museum* (Sat 2–4pm, Sun 1–3pm; $2) was a general store, post office and home from 1880 to 1920; *Malowen Lowarth* on Kingston Street (Sat 1–3pm, Sun 10.30am–12.30pm; $3) is one of the **Paxton Square Miners' Cottages**, decorated in 1850s style.

You can **stay** in other miners' cottages in the Paxton Square row (☎08/8892 2622; ④): it's fairly rudimentary accommodation with a modern kitchen; the stone cottages are freezing in winter but there's a fireplace and plenty of blankets (bring your own linen). Other accommodation in town includes *Burra View House*, Mount Pleasant Road (☎08/8892 2648; B&B ⑤), and *Burra Motor Inn*, Market Street (☎08/8892 2777; ⑤). All the **hotels** also have rooms, and most provide breakfast; there are no restaurants, so the hotel dining rooms take the strain. Best of the lot is *Kooringa Hotel*, Kingston Street (☎08/8892 2013; ④), a pleasant place with excellent food; while the cheapest is the *Royal Exchange Hotel*, Bests Place (☎08/8892 2392; ②), or if you have a tent you could try *Burra Caravan Park*, Bridge Terrace (☎08/8892 2442). *Price's Bakery*, Market Square, serves homemade soups, gourmet hot dogs, and inexpensive **meals**.

# The Clare Valley

The wine industry in the **Clare Valley**, west of the Barrier Highway between Kapunda and Burra, was pioneered by Jesuit priests at **Sevenhill** in the 1850s. There's no tourist overkill here: bus trips are not encouraged, and because it's a small area with just over twenty wineries, you can learn a lot about the local styles of wine – the area is recognized especially for its fine Rhine Rieslings. Often, too, you'll get the personal treatment, with the winemaker presiding at the cellar door. In the cool uplands of the North Mount Lofty Ranges, the valley is really a series of gum-fringed ridges and valleys running roughly 30km north from **Auburn** to the main township of **Clare**, on either side of the Main North Road. Huge sheep runs were established here in the nineteenth century and the area, which is prime merino land, still has an obvious pastoral feel; several stations can be visited, as well as the wineries. There are also beautiful old villages and some well-preserved mansions on view, with plenty of restaurants and B&Bs.

Heading north through the valley, the first place you come to is **AUBURN**, 120km from Adelaide, which began life as a halfway resting point for wagons laden with copper ore en route from Burra to Port Adelaide. In the old Mechanics Institute building *Miss Mabel Cottage Living* (Thurs–Sun 10am–5pm; ☎08/8849 2208) has **tourist information**, as well as *Miss Mabel's Tea Room* and the *Dennis Cottage* (⑦), a luxurious **place to stay** with a spa and paraphernalia associated with C J Dennis – the popular poet who was born here in 1876. The *Rising Sun Hotel* (☎08/8849 2015; ④) is one of many great **pubs** in the valley, first licensed in the 1850s. It has a fancy restaurant (Thurs–Sat 7–10pm), as well as small bedrooms and motel-style accommodation.

The next tiny village is **LEASINGHAM**, worth stopping at for *Crawley's Restaurant & Leasingham Village* (☎08/8843 0136; dorms ①, cabins ③; linen available), a popular place for grape-pickers to stay from March through to mid-April; wineries often phone and ask for workers. At nearby **WATERVALE**, there are four small **wineries**: *Watervale Cellars*, North Terrace (daily 11am–5pm), is one of the most enjoyable in the valley, while the *Watervale Hotel* (☎08/8843 0109; ④) is a no-frills country local with inexpensive pub grub.

About a kilometre before the village of Sevenhill (see below), you can turn off east to **MINTARO**. On the way, *Paulett Wines* (daily 10am–4.30pm) has fabulous views, its verandah overlooking the Polish Hill River area (a dry creek for eleven months of the year). Mintaro itself is a ghost town that has been resurrected by the National Trust, extolling the virtues of the Georgian-style **Martindale Hall** (Mon–Fri 11am–4pm, Sat & Sun noon–4pm; admission $4; ☎08/8843 9088; B&B ⑧). There's a romantic story attached to the hall, which you'll hear if you can afford $200 to **stay the night**; you get the full run of the place (except the smoking room), but it's freezing in winter.

Back on the main road, the village of **SEVENHILL** has the valley's oldest winery, *Seven Hills Cellars,* on College Road (Mon–Fri 8.30am–4.30pm, Sat 9am–4pm). This is still run by a religious order and mainly makes sacramental wine, though the brothers have diversified into table wines, sweet sherry and port, doing everything from growing the grapes to bottling. The old sandstone building has a tasting room with lots of character and history, and there's an early Catholic church in the grounds. Nearby on College Road, *Thorn Park Country House* (☎08/8843 4304; ⑧) is an 1850 stone and slate building in a gorgeous setting, and offering beautifully indulgent dinner, **bed and breakfast**, but at a price – $200-plus per night. *Seven Hills Hotel* on the Main North Road is a classic country pub serving lunches. To the west of the Main North Road, **Spring Gully Conservation Park** has the last remnant of red stringybark forest in South Australia. There are steep gullies, waterfalls, wildlife and, in spring, lovely wildflowers; free camping is allowed outside of fire-ban season.

## Clare

**CLARE** itself is a surprisingly ordinary town, with few concessions to the weekend visitors who pour in from Adelaide: it consists primarily of Main Street, and everything is closed on Sunday. **Tourist information** (daily 10am–4pm; ☎08/8842 2131) is at the

Town Hall, 229 Main North Road, where they can book accommodation and restaurants and have an excellent free visitors' guide with map and information; you can also book here for *Clare Valley Scenic Tours*, who run various tours, including one of local wineries (Mon & Fri 1pm; $15).

**Wineries** around town include *Tim Knappsteins*, 2 Pioneer Avenue (Mon–Fri 9am–5pm, Sat 10am–5pm, Sun 11am–4pm), an ivy-covered sandstone building with a verandah and an open log fire in winter; *Jim Barry*, Main North Road (Mon–Fri 9am–5pm, Sat & Sun 10am–4pm), a friendly, family-run place; and *Leasingham*, 7 Dominic Street (Mon–Fri 8.30am–5pm, Sat & Sun 10am–4pm), a large commercial winery established in 1893. There are also lots of stations open for tours and **farmstays**. The pick of the bunch is *Bungaree Station* (☎08/8842 2677; camping, plus BYO-bedding shearers' quarters ①, cottages ⑥; tours available), a working merino station 12km north on the Main North Road, and one of the oldest properties in the district.

Places to **stay** in Clare itself are all along Main Street: try *Clare Valley Motel* (☎08/8842 2799; ⑤), *Clare Central Motel* (☎08/8842 2277; B&B ⑤), or one of the hotels; *Bentleys* (☎08/8842 2815; rooms ④, dorms ①) is very friendly and has bike rental and good food, the *Clare Hotel* (☎08/8842 2816; ④) has pleasant rooms and meals, and the *Taminga Hotel* (☎08/8842 2808; ③) has bargain basic pub rooms. You can camp at *Christison Caravan Park*, Main North Road (☎08/8842 2724), 4km south.

The *Clare Valley Café* on Main North Road is a good place for fast **food** in 1950s-style booths, while *Brice Hill Vineyard Restaurant* (☎08/8842 2786), 3km south on Wendouree Road, has more innovative food.

## Port Pirie

From Clare, the Main North Road heads to **Jamestown**, 65km north. To the west, a road branches off towards Crystal Brook where there's a hikers' lodge at Bowman Park providing basic overnight shelter for hikers on the Heysen Trail. From here it's not far up Highway 1 to **PORT PIRIE**, the fourth-largest urban centre in South Australia. An ugly industrial city, its skyline is dominated by smelters' chimneys: as the nearest seaport to Broken Hill, the lead and zinc smelting industry here dates back to the discovery of the rich vein of lead-silver-zinc found there in 1883. The new **Port Pirie Tourism and Arts Centre** (☎086/33 0439), on Mary Elie Street, opposite the silos, promotes the world's largest smelting works as a prime attraction, reason enough not to stop unless a tour of the Pasminco Metals BHAS **smelting plant** (10am Wed & Sat; free) is high on your list. Beyond Port Pirie, Telowie Gorge and Mount Remarkable National Park in the southern reaches of the Flinders Ranges (see pp.620–621) are in easy reach.

# OUTBACK SOUTH AUSTRALIA

*...a country such as I firmly believe has no parallel on earth's surface.*
                                        The explorer Charles Sturt, 1844.

All routes in the Outback radiate out from **Port Augusta** and, with few connecting roads, interstate destinations will probably dictate which direction you leave town. Buses cover the highways but elsewhere you'll need to have your own transport or take a safari. To the west, the **Eyre Highway** runs 950km to the border of Western Australia, with desert scenery all the way unless you detour around the coast of the Eyre Peninsula. The rail line west runs further inland, through even more extreme desolation. North, the **Stuart Highway** and **New Ghan rail line** link Port Augusta with the Northern Territory through 890km of progressively drier scenery where regular markers along the roadside record the distance covered as well as how far there is to go. **Prohibited zones** surround much of the highway, though about the only places you'd want to leave it anyway are **Woomera** and **Coober Pedy**, both outside military zones and the boundaries of Aboriginal Land.

All other roads north head from Augusta along the route taken by the legendary but now defunct **Old Ghan** (see box on p.467) to the country towns of **Quorn** and **Hawker**, where routes diverge: northeast through the **Flinders Ranges** and along the **Strzelecki Track** to **Innamincka**; or due north to **Marree**, at the head of the **Birdsville** and **Oodnadatta tracks**. **Sealed roads** end at Lyndhurst on the way to Marree, and Wilpena Pound in the central Flinders; check conditions if you plan to go any further – in dry weather conventional vehicles often make it to Innamincka and Oodnadatta, but none of the north's remoter tracks should be attempted during the searing summer months. **Buses** run the length of the Stuart Highway, between Woomera and Andamooka, and from Port Augusta to Marree and Arkaroola in the northern Flinders.

A **Desert Parks Pass** is required for legal entry into Innamincka Regional Reserve, Lake Eyre National Park, Witjira National Park and the Simpson Desert: $50 per vehicle allows twelve months' unlimited access and use of campsites, and also includes copies of the detailed NPWS *Desert Parks Handbook* and *Westprint Heritage Maps*' surveys. Passes are available from agencies throughout the north or by post from NPWS, Far North Office, 60 Elder Terrace, Hawker 5434 (☎086/48 4244).

**Independent travellers** share common concerns throughout the north. Plastic is often carried in preference to wads of **cash**; many roadhouses and fuel pumps have EFTPOS facilities. **Water** is vital: with few exceptions, lakes and waterways are dry or highly saline, and most Outback deaths are related to dehydration or heatstroke – bikers seem particularly prone. As always, stay with your vehicle if you break down. Summer **temperatures** are lethally hot, winters pleasant during the day, sub-zero at night; rain can fall at any time of year, but is most likely between January and May.

Recent RAA **road maps** are good but lack surface detail; if you're spending any time in the north pick up the excellent *Westprint Heritage Maps* and cluttered *Landsmap Outback: Central and South Australia*. The *South Australia Tourist Association* put out a road map of the Flinders Ranges, but it's inadequate for walking, so **hikers** traversing the Flinders on the Heysen Trail need topographic maps of each section and advice from the nearest NPWS office. Conditions of minor **roads** are so variable that maps seldom do more than indicate the surface type – local police and roadhouses will have current information.

---

### TELEPHONE NUMBERS

In February 1997, all **phone numbers** in the ☎086 code region (which covers most of the numbers from here to the end of this chapter) will have the prefix 86 added, to coincide with the implementation of the new area code of ☎08 for the whole of South Australia.

So, for example, what was ☎086/xx xxxx will become ☎08/86xx xxxx.

---

# Port Augusta and the west

How you see **Port Augusta** depends on where you've come from: arriving from the Outback the trees, shops and hotels can be a real thrill, but compared with the southeast, it's pretty dismal. However, being a transport bottleneck has saved the town from destitution and, while you're deciding where to head next, there's some good **bushwalking** country around **Mount Remarkable**, at the tail end of the Flinders Ranges. The direct route west from Port Augusta, the **Eyre Highway**, begins its daunting journey towards Western Australia across the top of the **Eyre Peninsula**, but going this way, you'll see virtually nothing. An alternative route detours around the peninsula's coastline (via the Lincoln and Flinders highways) before rejoining the highway at **Ceduna** on the brink of the **Nullarbor Plain**, while the rail line parallels the coast some 100km inland.

## Port Augusta

Dubbed "Porta Gutter" by Adelaide's smart set, who paint dire pictures of a town rife with petty crime, **PORT AUGUSTA** sits at the tip of the Spencer Gulf and on the edge of everywhere else. Despite the name, the docks closed long ago and more recent employment mainstays such as the power station and railways were drastically scaled down during the 1980s – the former rail buildings have been converted to CES offices.

Attractions in town are few and far between: during the summer, you should make the most of the small **swimming beach** below the bridge at the end of Young Street to escape the dust and heat – the old wooden pile crossing, now a footbridge, makes a good perch for fishing. The chief source of **information** on other attractions is the **Wadlata Outback Centre** at 41 Flinders Terrace (Mon–Fri 9am–5.30pm, Sat & Sun 10am–4pm; $5.50; ☎086/42 4511), which is well worth a look in its own right. Audio-visual technology, didgeridoo loudspeakers and a giant model of Akurra, the Dreamtime snake, are deployed to explain Aboriginal bushcraft and Flinders Ranges' creation myths, while geological displays and tales of the hardships suffered by nineteenth-century explorers Eyre, Sturt (and his boat), Stuart and Giles fill in the background. It might also be worth enquiring here about the ambitious **Arid Lands**

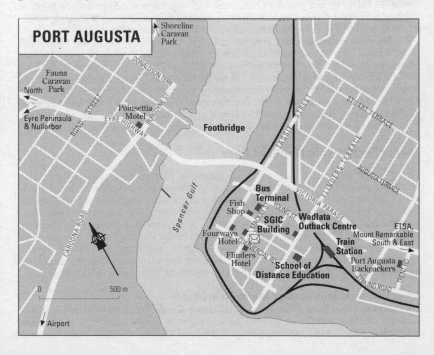

**Botanic Gardens**, a planned showcase for regional and international desert flora; though still under construction, a boardwalk gives views over plants in place so far.

If you're still in a tour mode after Wadlata, drop in on the **School of Distance Education**, also on Flinders Terrace, opposite Commercial Road (☎086/42 2695; term time Mon–Fri 10am; donation), and listen to a lesson conducted over the airwaves. Interaction is pretty lively and might explain the better than average academic record for remote area students using the school.

### Practicalities

The centre of town overlooks the east side of the Spencer Gulf, more like a river where it divides the town. Arriving, the **airport** (☎086/42 3100) is 5km west of the centre on Caroona Road – you'll need to get a taxi in (☎086/42 4466). Both bus and train stations are a short walk from the shops, **banks** and services along Tassie Street and narrow Commercial Road (with the post office): the **bus terminal** is at 21 Mackay Street (all services ☎086/42 5055); **trains** pull in at Stirling Road (☎086/41 8111). If you need **maps and information** beyond what's available at the Outback Centre, try the SGIC Building at 9 Mackay Street, home to both the Department of Lands (for maps; ☎086/48 5300) and the helpful NPWS (☎086/48 5310), for outback information, park maps and permits; the RAA, at 91 Commercial Road (☎086/42 2576), will also provide maps for its members. Local **tours** can be arranged through *Butlers Outback Safaris*, 2 Woodstock Street (☎086/42 2188; 2- to 7-day 4WD trips to the Flinders and Innamincka), or you can do it yourself with a **rental car** from *Budget*, 16 Young Street (☎086/42 6040).

The shambolic *Port Augusta Backpackers* at 17 Trent Street (☎086/41 1063; ①; free pick-up) and friendly *Flinders Hotel*, 39 Commercial Road (☎086/42 2544; ①–③), offer central budget **beds**, or there's the comfortable *Poinsettia Motel*, 24 Burgoyne Street (☎086/42 2411; ④), just over the Gulf on the highway. Closest **campsites** are north of the bridge at *Big 4 Fauna Caravan Park* (junction of Eyre and Stuart highways; ☎086/42 2974) or *Shoreline Caravan Park* (end of Gardiner Avenue; ☎086/42 2965).

**Meals and entertainment** abound at hotels, but opening hours are vague and often depend on demand. Seafood addicts should head for the fish shop in Marryatt Street, which sells fresh fish, as well as the fried sort with chips; *Barnacle Bill's* on Victoria Parade has $8 all-you-can-eat deals Monday and Tuesday night, while *Basic Foods* in Commercial Street is a wholesome vegetarian café. The central *Commercial Hotel* offers more fights than feeds, but *Fourways* promotes $5 lunches and **Cagneys nightclub** (Fri & Sat; pretty seedy unless there's a band playing). *Transcontinental*, Port Augusta's weekly rag, will have details of anything that's happening around town.

## Mount Remarkable National Park

The Flinders run low in their southern extremes, more heavily timbered than the desert ranges but otherwise similar in formation. **Mount Remarkable National Park** lies in two sections, circled by a ring road that starts 45km southeast of Port Augusta and runs via Wilmington, Melrose and Port Germein. The larger **western** slice contains Mambray Creek and Mount Cavern, and connecting tracks from them to Alligator Gorge; Mount Remarkable and sections of the Heysen Trail rise to the **east** behind Melrose. If time is short, Alligator Gorge is easy going, the Mount Cavern circuit considerably harder, but both make good day trips from Augusta. *Stateliner* buses ply daily to Mambray Creek and thrice weekly to Wilmington and Melrose.

### Alligator Gorge, Melrose and Mount Remarkable

The 11km dirt road from Wilmington to **Alligator Gorge** ($3 visitor's permit available on entry; further permission needed to overnight at gorge) ends at a picnic area perched on a spur above two **campsites** at Teal and Eaglehawk dams. Stairs descend the gorge wall with several walking options once you reach the floor: a three-hour circuit north to the ranger's office past the rippled **Terraces** – remains of a fossilized lake shore – or south along the creek for an hour through a tight red canyon alive with frog calls, moss gardens and echoes. These narrows are sometimes flooded, though usually there are enough stepping stones to avoid wet feet. Longer hikes down to Mambray Creek need maps and approval from the NPWS in Augusta.

**MELROSE** is a quiet former copper-mining town with two hotels, pleasant creek-side **caravan park** (☎086/66 2060) and a few cottage industries. The **smithy**, recently restored to original 1865 condition, is part museum (Sat & Sun 11.30am–4.30pm) and part restaurant with superb à la carte menu (Thurs–Sun from 6.30pm; book on ☎086/665 2173). The van park hands out walking maps for historic buildings, old mines and ascents to **Cathedral Rock** in the national park. The unremarkable summit of **Mount Remarkable** can be reached via the **Heysen Trail**, starting a couple of kilometres north of town from the showground.

## Telowie Gorge, Mambray Creek and Mount Cavern

Small and appealing, **Telowie Conservation Park** lies to the south off the Port Germein to Murray Town road. A very short path leads between the gorge walls, but, unless you're properly equipped for a long hike over to Wirrabara Forest and the Heysen Trail, you'll get more of a flavour of the area by camping along the creek and spending dawn and dusk looking for animals.

The access track to **Mambray Creek** is east off the highway, halfway between Port Germein and the Wilmington road. There's a campsite (water, toilets) and National Park headquarters, but it's often deserted. Mambray Creek is the start of some serious walks either into the park's north along the **Battery Track** and **Alligator Creek**, or on the tough but shorter Mount Cavern circuit. Follow the path anti-clockwise along the Black Range to **Mount Cavern** and soaring views, with wedge-tailed eagles gliding around the rim. The descent is down a loose stone slope held together by grasstrees, entering cool woodland at Mambray Creek Gorge, where you might encounter large groups of **emus** at close quarters.

# The Eyre Peninsula

Far from the rigours of the true Outback and long appreciated by Adelaidians as an antidote to city stress, the **Eyre Peninsula**'s broad triangle is protected from the arid climes further north by the **Gawler Ranges**. The area began to be farmed late last century; fishing communities sprang up at regular intervals and iron ore, discovered at the turn of the century, is still mined around **Whyalla**. The detour **around the coast** brings you in contact with imposing scenery and superlative **surfing** and **beach fishing**, especially where the Great Australian Bight's elemental weather hammers into the western shore – a chance to give your senses a workout before the Nullarbor's deadening horizons. Unfortunately, *Stateliner* only run down the east coast to **Port Lincoln** at the southern tip, so you'll need your own transport to tackle the west side.

> Locals don't rate Eyre Peninsula tap **water** as worth drinking; you might want to avoid it.

## Whyalla and the east coast

First visible an hour from Port Augusta as a smudge of grey over Long Sleep Plain, **WHYALLA**, the state's second city and headquarters of its heavy industry, is not the prettiest of places. BHP have their massive "long products" **steelworks** here (tours 9.30am Mon, Wed & Fri; $5; 2hr 30min; book through the information centre mentioned below) and tankers queue offshore to fill up at Santos' gas refinery and distillery. Until they closed in 1980, local **shipyards** turned out a few famous vessels, notably the minesweeper *Whyalla* which now guards the northern entrance to town. The accompanying **maritime museum** and **information centre** is open daily 10am to 4pm; $4 for tour of ship; (☎086/45 7900).

The highway curves through town as Whitehead Street and Darling Terrace; you'll find post office, **banks**, **bus station**, hotels and shops in the immediate area, all periodically covered in red fallout from BHP's mysterious pellet plant. **Accommodation** options include the *Foreshore Caravan Park* on Broadbent Terrace (☎086/45 7474; cabins ③) and *Derham's Motel* on Watson Terrace (☎086/45 8877; ⑥), both a ten-minute walk away on a surprisingly nice beach with fishing potential off the jetty; otherwise try your luck at one of the hotels – *Spencer* on Forsyth Street (☎086/45 8411; ④) has rooms, good food and weekend music. Seafood marinara at *Spagg's*, 83 Essington Lewis Avenue (☎086/45 2088), is a welcome change from counter meals; after eating, walk past the rows of fifty-year-old workers' homes to the top of Hummock Hill for a view of the industrial complexes by night.

Whyalla aside, the east coast is an unassuming run of sheltered beaches and villages nestled beneath towering grain silos, the sort of places to ignore completely or get waylaid for a week. **COWELL** is known for obliging whiting and for black jade or nephrite, but Arno Bay, Port Neil and even larger Tumby Bay lack any specific attractions.

## Port Lincoln and the lower peninsula

A tuna port and resort town built on a hillside above Boston Bay, **PORT LINCOLN** has the busiest atmosphere of anywhere on the peninsula; its harbour is dotted with yachts and trawlers and seafront Tasman Terrace and Liverpool Street are full of eateries and far from genteel taverns. Possible **accommodation** prospects are the handful of terraced tent sites at *Kirton Point Caravan Park* (far end of Tasman Terrace; ☎086/ 82 2537) or motel lodgings along Tasman Terrace and the highway.

Lincoln has an unsuspected artistic streak – *Arteyrea Gallery* in Washington Street (☎086/82 4771; look for the bike-riding fish) is worth a peek – but most attractions are under water. With bait and tackle from any service station you're ready to **fish** off the town jetty; for heavier game contact *Sea Charters* (☎086/82 2425). The trip to Boston Island is unexciting – you're better off tagging along with *Dangerous Reef Cruises* for seals, birdlife and sharks: book this and check out other local attractions at the **information centre** on Tasman Terrace (Mon–Fri 9am–5.30pm, Sat 9am–noon; ☎ free call 1800/629 911). **Divers** after Great White thrills should contact *Got One* (80 Tasman Terrace; ☎086/83 0021) and organize a foursome to split the $800-a-day tab; a shark cage is employed if you're "lucky" enough to make contact. Gentler local diving can find you among seals and dolphins, or collecting **lobster** (*Port Lincoln Diving*, 73 Mortlock Terrace; ☎086/82 4428).

Onshore, a 4WD comes in handy for exploring **Lincoln National Park**, a rough peninsula of sandy coves, steep cliffs and mallee scrub, which is home to the discreet rock parrot. The NPWS in Liverpool Street (☎086/88 3177) can supply maps and advice on road conditions. Similar scenery 32km south at **Whalers Way** is open to all traffic once a permit and key have been collected from the information centre in Port Lincoln at Tasman Terrace ($15, plus $3 deposit); the name derives from the whaling station which once operated at Cape Wiles – relics are stacked up around the gate. If you've ever felt the need to be impressed by the sea's power, head for **Cape Carnot**: giant waves and frosty blue surf force through **blowholes** which sigh as they erupt in sync with the swell.

An hour's drive from Lincoln at the bottom of the west coast, **Coffin Bay National Park** is a landscape of dunes and saltmarsh. Though parts are open to conventional traffic, you ought to see the NPWS in Port Lincoln before venturing here: you will be rewarded by isolation, sand sculptures at Sensation and Mullalong beaches, and the quality of the fishing. Semi-circular stone walls on the northern shore are **Aboriginal fish traps** – fish were chased in at high tide and then the gaps in the side blocked with nets as the water receded.

## The west coast

To catch the best of the west coast and the townships along the way, you'll need to detour off the main road between Coffin Bay township and Ceduna. The coastal communities are an unlikely mix of conservative farmers and "alternative" surfies who come to ride the endless succession of strong, hundred-metre-long crests rolling into Waterloo Bay at **ELLISTON**, one of the state's most highly regarded **surf beaches**. Bold **murals** at the Community Hall between the café and campsite address local themes – including a long-suppressed incident when Aboriginal people were driven over the cliffs. South of Venus Bay, rocks have been hollowed by the sea to form the **Talia Caves** but the lengthy beach is more compelling – camping is prohibited but you'd probably get away with sleeping in the car. Turning coastwards about 10km north of Port Kenny takes you past the strangely flared **Murphy's Haystacks**, a group of low granite monoliths that look like giant mushrooms; push on to **Point Labatt** for a look at mainland Australia's only colony of fur seals. Binoculars or a telephoto lens help to distinguish mother seals teaching pups to swim from the torpid, bulkier males basking on the rocks. Then it's back to the highway at Streaky Bay, the only place with a real centre on the west coast, and drier country as you approach Ceduna and the Nullarbor.

## The Eyre Highway and Gawler Ranges

Taking the **Eyre Highway** directly across the top of the peninsula ensures an easy, comfortable crossing to Ceduna, speeding past the mines at **Iron Knob** and a dry scrub populated by green ring-necked parrots. Unusual geology appears southwest of Wudinna, where **Ucontichie Hill** is an isolated granite mound (an inselberg) with curved forms including a **wave rock** similar to Hyden's in Western Australia (see p.524).

Iron Knob can be the start of forays along dirt tracks into the **Gawler Ranges**, rejoining the highway at Wirrulla. While you might not need 4WD, it is a remote area that requires advance preparation and advice from the NPWS. The ranges are low, rounded volcanic ridges coloured orange by dust, with occasional speckled boulders poking through a thin grass cover; it's worth frightening the sheep and pink Major Mitchell cockatoos by walking up one of the peaks for a closer look. *Mount Ive Homestead* (☎086/48 1817; ④) advertises **farm accommodation**, but don't turn up unannounced. The track into the ranges passes **Lake Gairdner**, largest of the Gawler's **salt lakes**, with the ruins of Pondanna Homestead on a lonely plain at its southern end.

---

### HIGH IMPACT – THE ACRAMAN METEORITE

In the mid-1980s, a band of red earth from 600-million-year-old deposits in the Flinders Ranges was bafflingly identified as coming from the Gawler Ranges, 400km away. Investigations and satellite mapping suggested that 35km-wide **Lake Acraman** in the Gawler Ranges was an eroded **meteorite crater**, while Lake Gairdner and fragmented salt pans (such as Lake Torrens, see p.625) further east were set in ripples caused by the force of the strike. Estimates suggest that to have created such a crater the meteorite must have been four kilometres across; the mystery band in the Flinders was dust settling after impact.

# Ceduna and the Nullarbor Plain

**Nullarbor** may not be strictly correct Latin for "treeless", but it's an apt description of the plain which stretches flat and infertile for over 1200km across the Great Australian Bight. Taking the **train**, or **motorbiking** the rail service track (which requires a back-up crew, fuel, and provisions dumps), brings you closer to the dead heart than the **road**, which allows some breaks in the monotony of the journey to scan the sea for southern right whales and visit at least one Aboriginal site.

You know where you are in **CEDUNA**: all the shops from camping store to super-market are unambiguously named and a lone signpost in the centre points west, labelled simply "Perth". Despite being small enough to walk around in twenty minutes, there's no lack of **van parks**, **banks** or **service stations**, with almost every brand of fuel on offer – some places even hand out discount cards for use at their pumps along the way. The *Foreshore Van Park* on South Terrace (☎086/25 2290; cabins ③) and *Community Hotel/Motel* on O'Loughlin Terrace (☎086/25 2008; ④) are right next to the jetty if you want to fish for whiting on the turn of the high tide. Before your early morning start – it's a long way to anywhere – call in at the **information centre** on Poynton Street (☎086/25 2780) and the NPWS on McKenzie (☎086/25 3144) for the latest on the Nullarbor's attractions. Incidentally, it almost never rains on the plain, and there's always a charge for **water**, which has to be distilled from underground reserves, so carry your own.

## The Plain

Ceduna to the Western Australian border is 480km, easily covered in under five hours if you want; Dali-esque fridges standing along the highway in the early stages are actu-ally makeshift mailboxes for remote properties. The last chance to **catch some waves** is at **Cactus Beach/Point Sinclair** south of Penong; there's a campsite and basic store (12.30–2pm). Pull in two hours later at **Yalata Community**, settled by Maralinga peoples cleared off their ancestral land by the British atomic bomb tests at Maralinga in the 1950s, for permits to cross community borders and reach the **Head of the Bight**, *the* place to see **whales** when they migrate up here in June. The Head is a stir-ring setting where in less than a kilometre powdery dunes rise to absurdly melodra-matic cliffs – you can't help feeling that this is how early cartographers must have envisaged the edge of the world; the southern right whales (see p.600) make things easy by sporting idly with their calves in the water below. Twenty minutes away, the **Nullarbor Roadhouse** (☎086/25 6271; ③) has **beds**, a campsite and the last fuel before Border Village; the famous triple yellow sign on the highway warning of camels, wombats and kangaroos for the foreseeable future marks the start of the completely treeless run. Ironically, rabbits – no longer controlled by farmers now the area is a national park – have almost crowded out the wombats.

Curiously enough for a land with minimal rainfall, the Nullarbor is undermined by flooded limestone **caverns** explored recently by scuba divers and visited 25,000 years ago by Aborigines looking for water and chalcedony to make tools. From the outside **Koonalda Cave** is a large hole with recently planted fruit trees growing in the mouth; inside, a tremendously deep network of tunnels leads to an underground lake, the shafts grooved by fingers being dragged over their soft walls. Although the patterns are clearly deliberate, their meaning is unknown; the cave is closed off to protect the engravings, but Ceduna NPWS (see above) might be able to arrange a visit.

**Border Village** is just another roadhouse (☎090/39 3474; ④) with a natty fibreglass kangaroo in the car park – certainly the largest between here and Antarctica. Eucla (see p.534) and the rest of the Nullarbor's pleasures lie 16km over the line in Western Australia on a noticeably worse road and in an earlier time zone.

# The Stuart Highway: Woomera and beyond

Two hours north of Port Augusta on the Stuart Highway, **WOOMERA** was closed to the public until 1982. An uncharismatic barracks town, it sits at the southeastern corner of a 500km corridor known locally as "the Range" and ominously highlighted on maps as **Woomera Prohibited Area**. Don't expect to find out why at the mostly military **Heritage Centre** (March–Nov daily 9.30am–4.30pm; $2.50) on the crossroads of Dewrang and Banool avenues. Models and plenty of pictures emphasize Woomera's value as a satellite launch site and joint intiatives with NASA, but the reasons for the creation of the Prohibited Area – weapons testing and the British-run Maralinga/Emu Junction **atomic bomb tests** between 1953 and 1963 – are skirted around. For a first-hand account, read Len Beadell's *Outback Highways* (see *Contexts*, p.843), cheerful tales of the bomb tests and the construction of "some sort of rocket range – or something" by the chief engineer. Currently, the range is used as a nuclear waste dump, and there are plans to land Japan's prototype space shuttle here.

Named after the *E*uropean *L*auncher *D*evelopment *O*rganization which designed rockets in the 1960s, the *Eldo Hotel* in Kotara Crescent (☎086/73 7867; ④) can provide **beds**, food, booze and conversation with US troops stationed here. The welcoming *Woomera Travellers Village* on Wirruna Avenue (☎086/73 7800; ②) is a good alternative – **camping** on the lawn is better than a bed in the dreary ex-barracks. The **shopping centre** has a bank, café and noticeboard.

### A detour: Roxby Downs, Andamooka and Lake Torrens

Instead of returning to the highway, consider carrying on past Woomera to the strangest two companion towns in Australia (**bus** on Thurs, Fri & Sun evenings). **ROXBY DOWNS**, 80km away, is completely modern, a service centre built in 1986 for miners working the copper, gold, silver and uranium deposits at nearby Olympic Dam Mine (tours March–Nov daily at 9.45am from *Olympic Dam Tours* **information office**, next to the *BP* service station, Olympic Way; ☎086/71 0788; $13). Another half-hour on an unsurfaced road lands you at **ANDAMOOKA**, an **opal**-mining shanty town of block and scrap iron construction whose red earth high street becomes a river after rain. The soil proved too loose for the underground homes which became de *rigueur* at Coober Pedy (see below), but mud lean-tos built in the 1930s are still standing opposite the post office. Facilities include fuel, a supermarket, *Tuckerbox Restaurant* (11am–late), two hotel/motels, two campsites and the *Opal Creek Showroom* which distributes maps and advice. If you fancy your luck "noodling", head to **German Gully**, where the local opal is more strongly coloured than Coober Pedy's, but little has been found for years.

**Lake Torrens**, a sickle-shaped salt lake related to the Acraman Meteorite (see box on p.623), is another half-hour ride in a 4WD – birdwatchers find it a worthwhile trip in wet years for for the waterfowl. The lake is also renowned in paleontological circles for traces of the 630-million-year-old **Ediacaran fauna**, the earliest known evidence of animal life, which was first found in Australia. Delicate fossil impressions of jellyfish, sea pens and obscure organisms are preserved in layered rock; the South Australian Museum in Adelaide has an extensive selection, but rarely issues directions to the site, which has been plundered by collectors since its discovery in 1946 by geologist Reg Sprigg.

## Coober Pedy

**COOBER PEDY** is the most enduring symbol of the harshness of Australia's Outback and the determination of those who live there; a place where the terrain and temperatures are so extreme that homes – and even churches – have been built underground, yet which managed to attract thousands of opal prospectors. In a virtually waterless

## WATER AND POWER

An evaporation rate of four metres a year has made **water** a critical consideration in Coober Pedy – wasting it is criminal. Rain, if any, falls in January, May and September and briefly fills nearby waterholes; the rest of the time saline artesian supplies are pumped from the Esso Bore outside town and purified at the osmosis plant on Hutchison Street. An ambitious town sewerage system is being planned to produce fertilizer and replace the disconnected jumble of private piping. **Power** is supplemented by solar panels and an experimental wind generator, but even so the town is often blacked out on hot days by everyone using their air-conditioners at once.

desert 270km from Woomera and considerably further from anywhere else, the most remarkable thing about the town – whose name stems from an Aboriginal phrase meaning "white man's burrow" – is that it exists at all. **Opal** was discovered by William Hutchison on a gold-prospecting expedition to the Stuart Range in February 1915; the town itself dates from the end of World War I, when returning servicemen headed for the fields to try their luck and used their trench-digging skills to excavate dwellings.

Summer sees Coober Pedy seriously depopulated but, if you can handle the intense heat, it's a good time to look for bargain opal purchases – though not to scrat around in the inferno for them yourself: gem-hunting is better reserved for the "cooler" winter months. At the start of the year, spectacular **dust storms** often enclose the town in an abrasive orange twilight for hours.

The local scenery might be familiar if you're a film fan: the unique landscape was used to great effect in *Mad Max III* and Wim Wenders' epic *Until The End Of The World*. There's not much to it, just a plain disturbed by conical pink mullock (or slag) heaps, with clusters of trucks and home-made contraptions off in the distance, and

## FINDING AND BUYING OPAL

**Opal** is composed of fragile layers of silica, and derives its colour from the refraction of light – characteristics that preclude the use of heavy mining machinery, as one false blow would break the matrix and destroy the colour. Deposits are patchy and located by trial and error: the last big strikes at Coober Pedy petered out in the 1970s and, though bits and pieces are still found – including an exceptional opalized fossil skeleton of a pliosaur (the reptilian equivalent of a seal) in 1983 – it's anybody's guess as to where, or if, there are any more major seams. Because so much depends on luck, you'll hear little about mining technique and more about beating the system. For instance, it's illegal to mine in town, but there's nothing to prevent home extensions; similarly, non-mining friends are often roped in to register claims and sidestep the "one per person" rule. Working another's claim (the "night shift") is a less honourable short-cut.

Unless you're serious (in which case you'll have to pay $35 to the Mines Department for a **Miner's Permit** to peg your claim, and $110 to keep it for a year), the easiest way to find something is by **noodling** over someone's diggings – ask the owner first. Miners use ultraviolet lamps to separate opal from **potch** (worthless grey opal), so you're unlikely to find anything stunning, but look out for shell fossils and small chips.

The best time to **buy opal** is outside the tourist season, but don't expect wild bargains and don't deal through grizzled prospectors in the hotel unless you're very clued up. There are three categories: **cabochon**, a solid piece; **doublet**, a thin wafer mounted on a dark background to enhance the colour; and **triplet**, a doublet with quartz lens. While cabochons are most expensive and triplets least valuable, it takes some experience to price accurately within each category as size, clarity, strength of colour, brightness and personal aesthetics all contribute. With close on fifty dealers in town, it's up to you to find the right stone; reputable sources give full written guarantees.

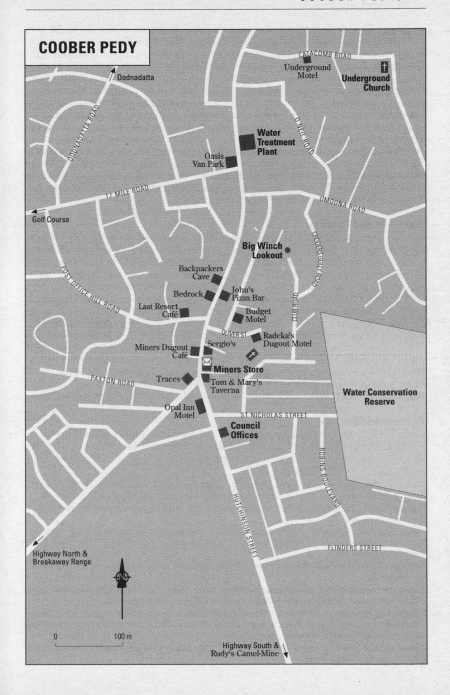

# COOBER PEDY

Oodnadatta

CATACOMB ROAD

Underground
Motel

Underground
Church

OODNADATTA ROAD

D'NEIL ROAD

Water
Treatment
Plant

Oasis
Van Park

17 MILE ROAD

UMOONA ROAD

Golf Course

POST OFFICE HILL ROAD

CROOERS GULLY ROAD

Big Winch
Lookout

Backpackers
Cave

CLUB ROAD

John's
Pizza Bar

Bedrock

Budget
Motel

Last Resort
Café

OLIVER ST

Radeka's
Dugout Motel

Miners Dugout
Café

Sergio's

Miners Store

PAXTON ROAD

Traces

Tom & Mary's
Taverna

Water Conservation
Reserve

Opal Inn
Motel

ST NICHOLAS STREET

Council
Offices

ROBINS BOULEVARD

HUTCHINSON STREET

Highway North &
Breakaway Range

FLINDERS STREET

N

0          100 m

Highway South &
Rudy's Camel-Mine

**warning signs** alerting you to treacherously invisible unfenced 30m shafts. Be very careful where you tread: even if you have transport, the best and safest way to explore is to take a tour, examine a map, then go back on your own. Past the diggings, the **Breakaway Range** is a brightly coloured plateau off the highway about 11km north of town, of interest for the views, close-ups of the hostile terrain, and bushwalking through two-century-old stands of mulga. In the centre of town, the **Big Winch look-out** gives a grandstand view of the mix of low houses and hills pocked with ventilation shafts; the welded metal "tree" up here was assembled before any grew in the area.

For more on **mining**, check out one of several mine displays and museums: try *Old Timers Mine*, Crowders Gully Road (☎086/72 5555), or *Umoona* on Hutchison Street (☎086/72 5288). Numerous **tours** are on offer for around $15: they all feature a town drive, a spot of noodling and a visit to an underground home – which you might find embarassingly like visiting a zoo; book through your accommodation, or give *Abu Waru Tours* (☎086/72 5333), *Prospectors Opal Tours* (☎086/72 5338), or *Gem City Tours* (☎086/72 5408) a go.

## Transport and services

Just about everything you'll need in Coober Pedy lies around the 500m strip between the *Opal Inn Hotel* and the water treatment plant on **Hutchison Street** (also known as Main Street) which leads north off the highway. **Buses** drop off on Hutchison Street (*Greyhound.Pioneer* and *Stateliner* at the *Ampol* service station, ☎086/72 5151; *McCafferty's* at *Johns Pizza*, ☎086/72 5561); from the **airport** you may be able to get a lift with one of the hostel buses that meet most flights, or make an advance reservation to ensure that someone meets you. The council offices on Hutchison Street, opposite the hotel (Mon–Fri 9am–5pm, some weekends; ☎086/72 5298) are a mine of local information; *Underground Books* (☎086/72 5558), on Post Office Hill Road opposite the *Mobil* service station, is a good alternative source – it stocks packs of local sketch maps which are a useful back-up to road maps. The *Miners Store* on Hutchison Street (☎086/72 5051) is the major **supermarket**, **post office** and *Commonwealth* **bank** agent (there's also a *Westpac* branch nearby); everyone shops on Thursday as fresh meat and veggies arrive in a refrigerated lorry Wednesday night and are scarce by the weekend.

## Accommodation

Coober Pedy leans heavily on tourist income and organizing **lodgings** should prove no problem. Some people find the idea of sleeping underground disturbing but, while not all accommodation is subterranean, it's worth spending at least one night in naturally cooled tunnels for the experience.

**Bedrock and Backpackers Cave**, below the *Opal Cave*, Hutchison Street (☎086/72 5028). Tunnels bored straight into the hillside and lined with bunks; basic and offering little privacy. ①.

**Budget Motel**, Oliver Street (☎086/72 5163). Very friendly and tidy above-ground accommodation; three to a room. ①.

**Oasis Van Park**, opposite the water treatment plant, Hutchison Street (☎086/72 5169). Seems to have the monopoly on Coober Pedy's few trees; films about the area screened Mon, Wed & Sat, 7pm. Cabin rooms ③.

**Opal Inn Motel**, Hutchison Street (☎086/72 5054). Standard motel block behind the hotel of the same name. ④.

**Radeka's Dugout Motel**, Oliver Street (☎086/72 5223). One of Coober Pedy's oldest dwellings, but amenities have recently been improved to make it the best budget option. ①.

**Riba's: the Travellers' Nest**, take William Creek Road from the highway (4km south of the Hutchison Street turn-off) and *Riba's* is down a track 800m on the right (☎086/72 5614). Out of the way but friendly campsite; cheapest place in town.

**Underground Motel**, Umoona Road (☎086/72 5324). Clean, tiled rooms with views over the desert from the front porch. ⑤.

## Cafés and restaurants

Restaurants in town are good value and portions huge; beware of over-ordering. All the following are on Hutchison Street.

**John's Pizza Bar** Takeaway fast food and coffee.

**Last Resort Café** Upmarket place with pavement tables, excellent pastries and coffee.

**Miners' Dugout Café** Kangaroo dishes and budget specials.

**Sergio's** Home-style Italian restaurant with red and white tablecloths and impeccable pasta.

**Tom and Mary's Taverna** Souvlaki morning to midnight.

**Traces** Greek grills and dance, 4pm–late daily.

## Beyond Coober Pedy

The Stuart Highway ploughs another 350km north from Coober Pedy to the border. From **MARLA** township you could head east to Oodnadatta across the **Painted Desert** at Arkaringa Hills, a larger version of the Breakaway Range, or west into Aboriginal land to the state's newest opal strike at Mintabie – seek permission from Marla's police.

If it's **Oodnadatta** you're after, there's also a direct 200km dirt road from Coober Pedy across the pan of Giddi-Gidna, the **Moon Plain**, covered by the mail run which departs from *Underground Books* at 9am Monday ($20 one-way; 3hr) and Thursday ($40 one-way; 6hr). Different routes to Oodnadatta are followed on the two days, but if you're just in it for the experience and the scenery, there's a $49 day-trip that returns you to Coober Pedy.

Australia's hottest 4WD journey has to be west from Coober Pedy to the **atomic bomb sites** at **Emu Junction**: concrete slabs cap pits where contaminated equipment lies buried, and sand fused into sheets of glass by the blasts covers the ground – the area is still highly radioactive and you'd be advised to pass through quickly. Beyond lies the virgin **Unnamed National Park** and routes across Aboriginal land to the **Warburton Road**; Ceduna NPWS (11 McKenzie Street; ☎086/25 3144) supplies practical details and permits to 4WD convoys only.

# The Flinders Ranges and the northeast

The first stop between Port Augusta and the **Flinders Ranges National Park** is **QUORN**, whose stone buildings and village atmosphere are a last vestige of the south. Best known for the **Pichi Richi railway**, the sole operational section of the Old *Ghan*, Quorn was a major rail centre until the line was rerouted through Port Augusta in the 1950s. Enthusiasts restored the service twenty years later and started taking passengers on a two-hour return haul to Woolshed Flats through the **Pichi Richi pass** – whose name has been variously attributed to a medicinal herb or an Aboriginal word for "gorge". Punctuated by a break at Woolshed Flats for cream tea, it makes a relaxing and mildly scenic journey; contact the station for a timetable (☎086/48 6598). There's a caravan park in Quorn but a night spent at the *Transcontinental Hotel* (☎086/48 6076; ①–④) is much more congenial, with an easy-going crowd of truckies and drovers from the north for company. If you want to explore some of the country round here, *Intrepid Tours*, 29 First Street (☎086/48 6277), run a 4WD bash any day they can fill a vehicle.

There's good local bushwalking off the back road to Hawker in a string of ridges and cliffs, outrunners from the main body of the central Flinders 100km north. **Dutchmans Stern** is closest to Quorn, a solid day's hike for the reasonably fit from the car park to various lookouts. Less dedicated walkers will find **Warren**, **Buckaringa** and **Middle gorges** more accessible; Buckaringa's vertical face is the most reliable place in the ranges to see the rare and ravishingly pretty **yellow-footed rock wallaby**. Closer to Hawker, it's also worth taking in the well-preserved remains of **Kanyaka Homestead**, abandoned after a drought in the 1880s, and **Yourambulla Cave**, which has some unusual charcoal symbols in a high overhang, reached by ladder. Both are signposted from the road.

**HAWKER** is somewhere to fuel up, make use of the last banks and shops for a while, have a meal at the *Old Ghan Restaurant* down past the hotel, and organize a **flight over the Flinders** (through *Hawker Caravan Park*, on the Wilpena exit; ☎086/ 48 4006) and seek advice from the regional NPWS office about far northern parks and roads (60 Elder Terrace, Mon–Fri only; ☎086/48 4242). Decisions have to be made in Hawker about whether to press on into the Flinders and the northeast or continue following the former *Ghan* line north towards Marree; the bitumen on the latter route extends past the Leigh Creek coalfields to Lyndhurst, start of the Strzelecki Track. *Stateliner* buses pass through Tuesday, Thursday and Friday, continuing to Wilpena and Arkaroola in the Northern Flinders (Tues, Fri) or Marree (Thurs).

## Flinders Ranges National Park

The procession of glowing red mountains at **Flinders Ranges National Park**, folded and crumpled with age, produce some of the Outback's most spectacular and timeless scenery, rising from flat scrub to form abrupt escarpments, gorges and the famous elevated basin of **Wilpena Pound**. The hard contrast between sky and ranges is softened by native cypresses and river red gums, and in spring the plains are burnished by **wildflowers** of all colours. Bushwalkers, photographers and painters flock here in their hundreds, but with a system of graded **walking tracks** ranging from a few minutes to several days duration, not to mention roads of varying quality, the park is busy without being crowded.

Orient yourself at **WILPENA** – a motel, store, campsite and NPWS **information centre** situated at the end of the bitumen and marking the start of the main routes into Wilpena Pound. Wilder places to set up camp for a few days further into the park include the National Park campsites at **Bunyeroo** and **Brachina Gorge** in the west, **Trezona** and **Oraparinna** in the centre, and **Wilkawillana Gorge** in the extreme northeast, all accessible on unsealed roads. Even more formal **lodgings** tend to be basic; for a longer stay you might consider renting a holiday cottage, which can be a bargain during the summer – contact *Flinders Outback Tourism* (☎08/373 3430 or 08/ 8373 3430 from Aug 1996). Back in "town", the *Wilpena Pound Motel* (☎086/48 0004; ⑥) is a comfortable but overpriced base: there's a good, surprisingly exotic restaurant – the chalet-like bar makes an atmospheric setting for an *après*-hike drink, and 4WD tours and flights over the pound can be arranged. *Wilpena Campsite*, next door, is wooded and well-equipped. Other places nearby include *Rawnsley Park* (☎086/48 0030; fuel, store, 4WD trips, horse-riding, mountain bike rental; tent spaces, plus cabins ④), 35km north of Hawker on the edge of the National Park, in a beautiful setting with Rawnsley Bluff and Wilpena Pound rising behind; *Willow Springs* (☎086/48 6282; ②), 17km north of Wilpena before the Wilkawillana Gorge junction, a working sheep station with blockhouse dormitories; and *Oraparinna Homestead* (☎086/48 4244, or book with the Hawker NPWS; ③), in the centre of the park off the Blinman Road, 24km north of Wilpena, with self-contained shearers' quarters and cabins.

Most **walking tracks** lead into Wilpena Pound, though you can also pick up the Heysen Trail and follow it north from Wilpena for a couple of days around the ABC Range to **Aroona Ruins** on the northern edge of the park. Wilpena NPWS offer booklets, maps (sometimes the 1:50,000 topographical series) and latest information on the routes; you're required to log out and back with them on any walk exceeding three hours. Realistically, hiking is restricted to cooler winter months between May and

### FLINDERS DREAMING

The almost tangible spirit of the Flinders Ranges is reflected in the wealth of Adnyamathanha ("hill people") **legends** associated with them. Perhaps more obvious here than anywhere else in Australia is the connection between landscapes and Dreamtime stories, which recount how scenery was created by animal or human action – the distinction is often blurred. A central character is **Akurra**, a gigantic maned serpent (or serpents) who guards waterholes and formed the Flinders' contours by wriggling north to drink dry the huge salt lakes Frome and Callabonna. Ochre paintings are one type of **art** often encountered at sites, but there's a more extensive, older engraved tradition: circles generally depict a campsite, with additional lines and rings representing stages in initiation rites.

October as scant shade and reflective rocks raise summer temperatures well into the forties. Don't underestimate conditions: even on short excursions, you'll need good footwear, a hat, sunscreen and **water** – at least half a litre per hour is recommended. **Camping out**, a waterproof tent, groundmat and fuel stove are essential, and note that the **weather** is very changeable; wind-driven rain can be a menace along the ridges and heavy downpours make tracks dangerous.

## Wilpena Pound

**Wilpena Pound**'s two major hiking destinations are **St Mary's Peak** on the rim and **Edowie Gorge** inside the pound, easily tackled individually or joined into an overnight circuit if time allows. For the round-trip, leave the peak until last and head off across the Pound's flat, grassy bowl to the remains of **Hill's Homestead** – further evidence of the region's unsuitability for farming – then follow the track northwest to **Cooinda Camp**, about two hours from the start. Assuming you left early enough, there's time to pitch a tent and spend the rest of the day following the creek upstream past **Malloga Falls** to **Glenora Falls** and views into Edowie Gorge before heading back to Cooinda – there might be places to swim after rain. Next morning, it's a steep climb to **Tanderra Saddle** below the peak, but not as bad as the last burst to St Mary's summit which often involves scrambling on all fours. The effort is rewarded by unequalled views west to Lake Torrens and north along the length of the ABC Ranges towards Parachilna; on exceptional mornings the peak stands proud of low cloud inside the Pound. The direct descent from the saddle back to Wilpena campsite is initially steep but shouldn't take more than three hours. Splitting the tracks into separate return walks from Wilpena, allow nine hours for Edowie Gorge, eight hours for a straight ascent of St Mary's, and ten hours for a circuit via St Mary's and Cooinda Camp but omitting Edowie Gorge.

Shorter routes lead up **Mount Ohlssen Bagge** (a tiring four hours) and **Wangara Lookout** (2hr) for lower vistas of the Pound floor, and southwest across the Pound to **Bridle Gap** (6hr) following the Heysen Trail's red markers. Things to look out for are euro wallabies, emus and parrots inside the Pound, and cauliflower-shaped fossil **stromatolites** – algal corals – on the Mount Ohlsen Bagge route, similar to those still living at Hamelin Pool in Western Australia (see p.540).

## Art sites, more gorges and onwards

Two **Aboriginal galleries** worth seeing are Arkaroo Rock and Sacred Canyon, both a short drive from Wilpena. **Arkaroo** is back off the main road towards Rawnsley Park and involves an hour's walk up the outside of Wilpena Pound to see mesh-protected rockfaces covered in symbols relating to an initiation ceremony and the Pound's formation, some dating back 6000 years. Snake patterns depict St Mary's Peak as the head of a male Akurra coiled round the Pound. To reach **Sacred Canyon**, briefly take the road from Wilpena into the north of the park past the **Cazneaux Tree** – a river red gum made famous by Harold Cazneaux's prize-winning 1930 photograph Spirit of Endurance – before turning right and following a bumpy track to its end. Rockhop up the narrow, shattered gorge to clusters of painted swirls covered in a sooty patina and clearer engraved emu prints and geometric patterns; the best examples are in the vicinity of the second cascade.

The main road through the park heads straight out to Blinman, but there's a detour track to **Bunyeroo** and **Brachina gorges** on the western limits. The gorges make good campsites: you have to walk into Bunyeroo but the track passes through Brachina on its way to the surfaced Hawker to Marree road. If you're pressing directly on to the Northern Flinders, you can avoid Blinman by turning right off the main road about 20km from Wilpena, heading to **Wirrealpa Homestead**.

# The Northern Flinders

The Wilpena to Blinman road passes through a low group of hills, thin in timber but still swarming with euro wallabies, red kangaroos and galahs. **BLINMAN** is a few houses, three fuel pumps, and a hotel (☎086/48 4867; ④) with log fires, games room, and a pool; the keys to everywhere else in town are kept at the bar. They have few guests and you get the feeling that you'd be remembered if you went back in five years time. The main track heads west through **Parachilna Gorge** to Parachilna on the Hawker to Marree stretch (where you can pick up tours with *Prairie Hotel Tours*; ☎086/48 4895); the route into the Northern Flinders lies east, joining up with the direct road from Wilpena and then running north to the **Gammon Ranges National Park** and Arkaroola.

## Chambers Gorge and Big Moro

**Chambers Gorge** and **Big Moro** are remote, little visited sites on the road to the Gammon Ranges, worth every groan and twang of your vehicle springs for their stark beauty and Aboriginal significance. The 10km access track into **Chambers Gorge** (east, 28km after Wirrealpa) is decidedly dodgy after rain when you'll need 4WD, but at other times conventional vehicles might reach a natural campsite at the foot of **Mount Chambers**, within twenty minutes' walk of the gorge mouth. Stories tell how Yuduyudulya, the fairy wren, threw a boomerang which split Mount Chambers' eastern end and then circled back to form the crown. An indistinct left fork before the gorge leads to a dense gallery of **pecked engravings**; most are circles though a goanna stands out clearly on the right, facing the main body of art. Chambers Gorge itself is huge and silent, the broad stony entrance guarded by high, perpendicular cliffs and brilliant green waterholes; it would take days to explore properly.

**Big Moro** is sacred to the Adnyamathanha as the residence of an akurra. The creek trickles through a crumbling gorge into two clear green pools; limestone outcrops on the south side hide miniature caves. The gorge is west down an exceptionally tortuous 15km 4WD track opposite **Wertaloona Homestead**, 60km from the Mount Chambers junction. Pay attention to any signs and leave the three gates as you find them.

## The Gammon Ranges

Arid and bald, the **Gammon Ranges** are the Flinders' last fling, a vicious flurry of compressed folds plunging abruptly onto the northern plains. Balcanoona is the NPWS headquarters for the otherwise undeveloped **Gammon Ranges National Park**, a thick band of sandstone cliffs – check with the Hawker NPWS for current conditions. Two ways to experience the area are to either carry on to Arkaroola (outside the park) or take the road west across the park through **Italowie Gorge** to Copley on the Hawker–Marree road. The steep red walls of the gorge are home to iga, native orange trees which symbolize the Adnyamathanha as a people. There are **bush campsites** here and shearers' quarters at Balcanoona (book through Hawker NPWS; ②).

**ARKAROOLA** (Mount Painter Sanctuary) is a private **resort** (☎086/48 4848; ①–⑤) and a source of fuel, provisions, meals, rooms and a campsite. Scene of Australia's most recent volcanic activity, the area is a geologist's paradise: **Paralana Hot Springs** (two hours away in a 4WD) bubble out radioactive radon gas, and walks into the rough hills surrounding the resort turn up fossils and semi-precious minerals galore. The area is so rugged that conventional mining isn't really a profitable venture – drilling rigs are airlifted in, then ferried around on the lower half of a Chieftain tank – and mining giant *CRA Zinc* concentrates on mapping uranium and copper deposits in order to show progress and keep their licence. The resort's $50 **Ridgetop Tour** brings you closest to the heart of the scenery: four hair-raising hours in an open 4WD (wear something warm) following precipitous contours to **Sillers Lookout** and views east to the shimmering salt lakes of **Frome** and **Callabonna**. Remains of the hippopotamus-sized marsupial diprotodon have been found at Callabonna; the diprotodon survived well into Aboriginal times, but died out as the climate changed after the last Ice Age.

Arkaroola marks the limit of public transport; the *Stateliner* bus returns to Port Augusta on Wednesday and Saturday. Some vehicles (with either high clearance or very careful drivers) can continue directly north to join the **Strzelecki Track** at Mount Hopeless, a little under halfway to Innamincka. If you're unsure, the track can also be reached via Lyndhurst on the Hawker–Marree road, but this involves a 300km detour from Arkaroola.

## The Strzelecki Track

The 460km **Strzelecki Track** between Lyndhurst and Innamincka was laid down in 1870 by **Harry Redford**, better known as Captain Starlight, who stole a thousand cattle from a property near Longreach in Queensland and drove them south across the Strzelecki Desert and down to Adelaide. Later used for more orthodox purposes, the track had a reputation as one of the roughest stock routes in the country, a serious obstacle for transport. Much of its epic nature has since been flattened, along with the road surface, by companies draining the **Moomba gas and oil fields**, and it's negotiable in any sound vehicle when dry.

Start at Lyndhurst by filling the tank – the **next fuel** is at the other end – and heading off around the northern tip of the Flinders; once past them, the journey becomes flat and pretty dull. At around the 105km mark you cross the 4850km-long **Dog Fence** (or Great Dingo Fence), which stretches from the Nullarbor Plain east into New South Wales and is intended to keep dingoes from southern flocks. Although its value is debatable, you do frequently see desiccated canine corpses poisoned by "1080" bait. The road from Arkaroola connects within sight of **Mount Hopeless** (a pathetic rise, appropriately named), and the next place to stop and perhaps camp is at the hot outflow from **Montecollina Bore**, 30km on. From here the scenery picks up slightly as the road runs between dunes, and it's hard to resist leaving footprints along one of the pristine red crests.

At **Strzelecki Crossing** there's a choice of routes: you could abandon the track and head east to where Queensland, New South Wales and South Australia meet at **Cameron's Corner**, where there's a store with **fuel**, campsite and a small bar (☎080/91 3872, 08/8091 3872 from Mar 1997); or you could continue to Innamincka either via Moomba or by following the direct but less frequented **Old Strzelecki Track**. Cameron's Corner and the old track are 4WD only, and all of the routes are crossed by straight **seismic test lines** which run off to dead ends in the bush – you risk becoming permanently lost if you accidentally follow one, so take care. **Moomba**'s jumble of pipes and lick of flame are sometimes marked as a township on maps but, though visible from the road, the refinery is closed to the public; within an hour you've crossed into the **Innamincka Regional Reserve** and are approaching Innamincka's charms.

## Innamincka

Cooper Creek, which runs through Innamincka, is best known for the misadventures of explorers Burke and Wills, who ended their inept 1861 expedition (see p.389) by dying here. On much the same spot **INNAMINCKA** was later founded as a customs house to collect taxes on stock being moved between Queensland and South Australia. Never more than a handful of buildings, it found fame mainly because John Flynn's Flying Doctor Service ran a mission here and because the hotel piled up decades of empties into a legendary 180-metre-long bottle dump before the town was abandoned in 1952. Recreational four-wheel-driving has led to a renaissance: a new **hotel** (☎086/75 9901; ⑤) has weekend barbecues, video jukebox and impromptu dance sessions on Friday and Saturday nights; *Innamincka Trading Post* (☎086/75 9900) stocks provisions and fuel; the mission was rebuilt in 1994 as a **museum**; and opposite is a solar-powered telephone and spotless toilet/shower block. Pelicans, parrots and inquisitive dingoes will be your companions if you camp out for free along the creek.

It only takes an hour to look around the museum and hunt for evidence of the bottle dump before you're ready for other distractions: walking, **fishing** for yellowbelly, bream and catfish, and swimming along the creek might fit the bill, or the *Trading Post* has canoes for rent. With a vehicle you could strike out 20km west to **Wills' grave** or 8km east to where **Burke** was buried (both bodies were removed to Adelaide in 1862). Another 8km beyond Burke's cairn is **Callyamurra waterhole**, the largest permanent body of water in central Australia, and a footpath to rock engravings of crosses, rainbow patterns and bird tracks; 4WD vehicles can also tackle the 110km track north to shallow **Coongie Lakes** with abundant birdlife and swimming opportunities. An hour east of Innamincka along a suddenly bad track is Queensland, the **Dig Tree** and a fuelless route to Quilpie (see p.388).

# The far north: Marree and beyond

**MARREE** is a despondent couple of mud streets and tattered houses which somehow outlived the Old *Ghan's* demise in 1980, leaving carriages to rust on sidings and rails to be used for tethering posts outside the hotel. First a camel depot, then a staging post for the overland telegraph line and finally the point where the rail line skirted northwest around **Lake Eyre**, today all traffic comes by road and is bound for the **Birdsville Track** into Queensland or the **Oodnadatta Track**, which follows the former train route to Oodnadatta and beyond into the Northern Territory or Simpson Desert.

**Accommodation** is limited to the hotel on the main street (☎086/75 8344; ④) or the caravan park outside town (☎086/75 8371; cabins ④); the latter is decent but unpopular locally for setting up a store and fuel pump actually on the highway. Two doors past the hotel, *Oasis Café* is a well stocked shop and fast-food outlet; across the track and heading towards Oodnadatta, the post office doubles as a *Commonwealth Bank* agent. If it's open, visit the *Arabana Community Centre* just up from the café for some insights into the region's Aboriginal history.

## Lake Eyre

**Lake Eyre** is a massive salt lake caught between the Simpson and Strzelecki deserts in a region where the annual evaporation rate is thirty times greater than the rainfall. Most years a little water trickles into the lake from its million-square-kilometre catchment area, which extends well into central Queensland and the Northern Territory, but floods have filled the basin only four times since white settlement of the region – most dramatically in 1974 when the lake expanded to 140km long. A hypnotic, glaring **salt crust** usually covers the southern bays, thick enough in 1964 to be used as a range for Donald Campbell's successful crack at the world land speed record. A mysterious, spiritual landscape with harsh surrounds paved by shiny gibber stones and walled by red dunes, some wildlife manages to get by in the incredible emptiness. The resident Lake Eyre dragon is a diminutive, spotted grey lizard often seen skimming over the crust, and the rare flooding attracts dense flocks of birds, wakes the plump water-holding frog from hibernation and activates plants into explosions of colour.

While you can **fly** over the lake (make bookings through Marree's van park), only four-wheel drives can reach the shore 95km north of Marree, though the track to the campsite at a gum-shaded waterhole, just over halfway at **Muloorina Homestead**, is good. Timber at the lake is sparse and protected, meaning that there's little shade and no firewood. There's no help if something goes wrong, so don't drive on the lake's crust – the grey slush below is impossible to extricate your vehicle from should you fall through.

## The Birdsville Track

Assuming there's been no rain, the 520-km **Birdsville Track** is no obstacle to careful drivers during the winter: the biggest problem is getting caught in dried wheel ruts and pulled off the road. Tearing north, the distant tips of the Flinders Ranges dip below the horizon behind, leaving you on a bare plain with the road as the only feature. Look for the **MV Tom Brennan**, a vessel donated to the area in 1949 to ferry stock around during floods, but now bearing an absurd resemblance to a large grey bath tub. Before the halfway house at Mungeranie Gap, a scenic variation is offered by the **Natterannie Sandhills** (150km), once a severe obstacle but now graded by digging out the soft sand and replacing it with clay. **Mungeranie roadhouse** (☎086/75 8317) provides the only services on the track (fuel, beds and snacks), but seems to be unattended on Sunday when you'll have to slog up the hill to the manager's house. In a 4WD you can head west from the roadhouse to **Kalamurina campsite** near Cowarie Homestead (58km) for the thrill of **fishing** (in a desert!) on Warburton Creek.

Back on the track, a windmill at **Mirra Mitta bore** (37km from the roadhouse) draws piping hot water out of the ground beside long-abandoned buildings; the water smells of tar and drains into cooler pools, providing somewhere to camp. By now you're crossing the polished gibber lands of the **Sturt Stony Desert**, and it's worth going for a walk to feel the cold wind and watch the dunes dancing in the heat haze away to the west. The low edge of **Coonchera Dune** to the right of the track (190km from the roadhouse) marks the start of a run along the mud pans between the sandhills; look for desert plants and dingoes. Two more hours should see you pulling up outside the Birdsville pub (p.390).

## The Oodnadatta Track

The road from **Marree to Oodnadatta** is the most interesting of the three famous Outback tracks, mainly because abandoned sidings and fettlers' cottages from the Old *Ghan* provide frequent excuses to get out of the car and explore. Disintegrating sleepers lie by the roadside along some of the route, otherwise embankments and rickety bridges are all that remain of the line. As with the roads to Birdsville and Innamincka, with care any sound vehicle can have a go in good winter weather.

About 100km into the journey near **Curdimurka ruins** the road runs within sight of **Lake Eyre South**, giving a flavour of its bigger sister if you can't get out there. On alternate Septembers (even-numbered years) the **Curdimurka Outback Ball** sees 3000 souls from everywhere between Alice Springs and Port Pirie don their finest threads for a night of mayhem under the stars. Twenty-five kilometres later, a short 4WD track south ends below three conical hills – two of which have hot, bubbling **mound springs** at the top, created when water escaping from the artesian basin deposits heaps of mud and minerals. The perfectly symmetrical **Blanche Cup** looks out across a plain stripped of every shred of greenery by rabbits and cattle to **Hamilton Hill**, an extinct spring, while further south the **Bubbler** gently spits out fine sand. Important to the Arabana, these springs were used by Sturt in the 1850s and later by the telegraph and rail depots, but tapping the artesian basin for bore water has greatly reduced their flow.

One of these bores is just across the road at **Coward Springs**, where a corroded pipe spilling into ponds beside the track has created an artificial environment of grasses and palms behind a **campsite**, with toilet blocks and cabins built from sleepers. The ground can be boggy after rain but it's still a tempting stop; donations are requested for overnight stays. **William Creek**, 75km on, has a resident population of just ten – and a source of fuel, camping and relaxation in the **hotel**. Bar, walls and ceiling are heavily decorated with cards and photographs of 4WD disasters, and is the hang-out for stockmen from **Anna Creek Station**, which, covering an area the size of Belgium, is the world's largest cattle property. A solar-powered phone outside faces the battered remains of a *Black Arrow* **missile** dragged off the Woomera Range, just a few minutes' drive away. Off-road drivers can take a 70km track from here to Lake Eyre's western shore.

After William Creek the track gets rougher, crossing sand dunes and then moving into stony country cut by frequent creeks – shallow for most of the year. Hardy mulgas line the banks, their soft yellow blooms giving off a distinctive acrid scent. On the last stretch to Oodnadatta, stay alert for a sight of the extraordinary red and black crescent petals of **Sturt's desert pea**, the state emblem, growing by the roadside.

### Oodnadatta

Unless you stay long enough to meet some locals, you'll probably feel that, like Marree, **OODNADATTA** survived the *Ghan's* closure with little to show for it. A few logically arranged but untidy streets lacking atmosphere or purpose, Oodnadatta was founded as a railhead in 1890, and mail and baggage for further north had to make do with camel train from here until the line to Alice Springs was completed in 1928. Now that has gone, the town has become a base for the Aranda community – *utnadata* ("mulga blossom") is the Aranda name for a local waterway – and 4WD crews heading into the Simpson Desert. After rain you'll even need 4WD for the last slippery kilometre into town past the racecourse. If your visit coincides with the **race weekend** in May, helicopters will be circling the track on the left trying to dry it out and the town will be deserted, so stop at the track, buy a pass and join in. With neat clothes and some sort of tie, you'll even get into the "formal" ball afterwards.

Camp at the *Pink Roadhouse* (☎086/70 7822), unless the relative luxury of a bed at the *Intercontinental Railway Hotel* (☎086/70 7804; ④) appeals. The roadhouse acts as a store, bank, post office and café, and sells detailed sketch maps of the area. The hotel holds the key to the **Railway Museum** opposite, where you'll find a strangely timeless photographic record of the town – scenes are hard to date because so little seems to have changed. Stock up with provisions and then drop into the **police station** (☎086/70 7805) for a report on the roads and next fuel supplies if you plan to head north towards Dalhousie Springs and the Simpson Desert (4WD only) or west to the Stuart Highway at Coober Pedy or Marla.

## Dalhousie Springs and desert crossings

If you don't follow the track out to the Stuart Highway, the area north of Oodnadatta is strictly for ambitious four-wheel-driving, with Dalhousie Springs in the Witjira National Park a worthwhile destination, or the Simpson Desert for the ultimate challenges. The route directly north, initially towards Finke and the Northern Territory, is fairly good – in 4WD terms – as far as **Hamilton Homestead** (110km), though Fogarty's Claypan, over halfway, might present a sticky problem. Convoys can turn east at Hamilton for a direct route to Dalhousie Springs (75km) past empty blockhouses at **Pedirka**, but solo drivers should take the longer route via **Eringa ruins** (160km) which avoids a deep creek crossing; gibber plains on both tracks make punctures all too common. Just after Eringa, there's a right turn to a trampled cattleyard at **Bloods Creek bore** on the edge of **Witjira National Park**; from there you can detour 30km north to **Mount Dare Homestead** (fuel, accommodation, food and provisions; ☎089/52 5355, 08/8952 5355 from April 1996, and ask for "Mount Dare"; ①–⑤) or continue to the springs. **Dalhousie Springs** were first described by the explorer Giles, who crossed through in the 1870s, before the artesian basin had been extensively tapped by pastoralists:

> *The ground we had been traversing abruptly disappeared, and we found ourselves on the brink of limestone cliffs... From the foot of these stretched an almost illimitable expanse of – welcome sight – waving green reeds, with large pools of water at intervals, and dotted with island cones topped with reeds or acacia bushes.*

Though reeds and water are less lavishly distributed today, Giles' account still rings true. The collection of over one hundred mound springs form Arabian-like oases, an impression enhanced by the green circle of date palms clustered around many of the pools. The

## THE SIMPSON DESERT CROSSING

Crossing the 550-odd kilometres of steep north–south dunes through the **Simpson Desert** between Dalhousie and Birdsville in Queensland is the ultimate challenge for any off-roader; in June, 4WD groups are joined by bikes attempting to complete the punishing **Simpson Desert Cycling Classic**. Winter sees a steady stream of vehicles moving from west to east (the easier direction since the dunes' east slopes are steeper and harder to climb) but there's no help along the way so don't underestimate the difficulties. Convoys need to include at least one skilled mechanic and, apart from the usual spares, a long handled shovel and a strong tow-rope. You'll also need more than adequate food and water (six litres a day per person) while keeping weight to a minimum, and of course fuel – around 100 litres of diesel if you take the shortest route, or 200 litres of petrol. **Dune ascent techniques** start with reducing tyre pressures to around 15psi to increase traction; select the gear and build up revs before starting. Don't attempt a gear change on the way up. If you don't make it over, slide down and try again; lighter vehicles may end up towing overburdened trucks. If all else fails, detours bypass many dunes.

The most testing, direct route follows the **French Line**, with the **Rig Road** detouring around the worst section but adding substantial distance (and fuel requirements) to the crossing. The enjoyment is mostly in the driving, though there's more than sand to look at: trees and shrubs grow in stabilized areas and at dusk you'll find dune crests patrolled by reptiles, birds, small mammals and insects. Photographers take advantage of clear night skies to make time exposures of the stars circling the heavens. **Purni Bore**, 70km from Dalhousie, is another uncapped spout (though this may change with growing concerns over diminished ground water) where birdlife and reeds fringe an 80°C pool. A post battling to stay above shifting sand at **Poeppel Corner** (269km) marks the junction of Queensland, South Australia and the Northern Territory; lakes here vary in their salt content and sometimes have to be skirted around. After the corner the dunes become higher but further apart, separated by claypans covered in mulga and grassland. **Big Red**, the last dune, is also the tallest; once over this it's a clear 41-km run to Birdsville.

*Note: Parts of the Simpson Desert will become Aboriginal Land in 1996; this may affect access between Dalhousie and Birdsville – check with the NPWS in Hawker (☎086/48 4242) or Birdsville (Graham Street; ☎076/56 3249) before setting out.*

largest spring, next to the **campsite** (which sports a solar-powered phone), is cool enough to swim in, hot enough to unkink your back, and what survives of the vegetation simmers with birdlife: budgerigars, galahs, and the fairy wren's eye-catching livery of purple, blue and red. As nothing flows into the springs, the presence of **fish** – some, like the Dalhousie hardyhead, unique to the system – has prompted a variety of improbable explanations. One theory is that fish eggs were swept up in dust storms and later fell with rain at Dalhousie, but it's more likely that fish were brought in during an ancient deluge or that the population survives from when the area was an inland sea.

While the main springs area is flat and trampled by years of abuse from campers and cars, trudging out to other groups over the salt and samphire-bush flats armed with a packed lunch and camera gives you an idesa of what Giles was describing, and a good vantage of the region from the top of well formed, overgrown mounds. More views can be had from the stony hills to the west, and from **Dalhousie Homestead**, 16km south of the springs along the Pedirka road. The homestead was abandoned after the *Ghan* line was laid down, and today the stone walls, undermined by rabbit burrows, are gradually falling apart in the extreme climate.

## travel details

### Trains

**Adelaide** to: Alice Springs (*Ghan*, 1 weekly; 11hr 30min); Melbourne (*Overlander*, 1 daily, 12hr; combined bus/train, 6 weekly, 10hr 45min); Perth (*Indian Pacific*, 2 weekly; 37hr); Sydney (*Indian Pacific*, 2 weekly, 27hr; combined train/bus, 1 daily, 21hr).

### Buses

**Adelaide** to: Arkaroola (2 weekly; 11hr 15min); Ayers Rock Resort (2 daily; 20hr); Broken Hill (1–2 daily; 7hr); Ceduna (2 daily; 12hr); Fleurieu Peninsula (2–5 daily; 1hr); Loxton (6 weekly; 3hr 30min); Melbourne (4 daily; 9hr 30min–14hr); Mount Gambier (6 weekly; 6hr); Perth (2 daily; 34hr); Port Augusta (several daily; 6hr 30min); Port Lincoln (1–3 daily; 10hr); Renmark (1–2 daily; 4hr); Sydney (4 daily; 21–24hr); Whyalla (2–5 daily; 6hr); Yorke Peninsula (1–4 daily; 3–4hr).

**Coober Pedy** to: Oodnadatta (2 weekly; 5hr).

**Port Augusta** to: Arkaroola (2 weekly; 7hr); Blinman (2 weekly; 3hr 15min) Coober Pedy (4 daily; 6hr 10min); Hawker (4 weekly; 1hr 30min);

Mambray Creek (for Mount Remarkable; several daily; 1hr); Marla (4 daily; 10hrs); Marree (2 weekly; 5hr); Melrose (3 weekly; 1hr); Port Lincoln (1 daily; 10hrs); Quorn (2 weekly; 40min); Wilpena Pound (4 weekly; 2hr 15min); Wilmington (3 weekly; 45min); Woomera (4 daily; 2hr).

**Woomera** to: Andamooka (3 weekly; 2hr); Roxby Downs (3 weekly; 1hr 10min).

### Flights

**Adelaide** to: Alice Springs (2 daily; 2 hr); Ayers Rock Resort (2 daily via Alice; 3hr 45min); Brisbane (3–12 daily; 4hr); Broken Hill (1–4 daily; 1hr 40min); Cairns (4 daily; 4hr); Canberra (8 daily; 3hr 10min); Coober Pedy (at least 1 daily; 1hr 30min); Darwin (1 daily; 5hr); Gold Coast/ Coolangatta (2–10 daily; 4hr 45min); Hobart (8 daily; 3hr); Kangaroo Island (1–4 daily; 30min); Melbourne (10 daily; 1hr); Perth (4 daily; 5hr); Sydney (12 daily; 2hr 10min).

The **Channel Mail Run** is a weekend in a light aircraft taking in 47 stops between Port Augusta and Boulia in southwestern Queensland – contact Port Augusta airport (☎086/42 3100).

# CHAPTER NINE

# VICTORIA

A ustralia's second smallest state, **Victoria** is the most densely populated and industrialized, but has a wide variety of attractions packed into a small area. It may not be a state to tour comprehensively, but Australians, at least, lap up the legends of their history that are thick on the ground: you're never too far from civilization, but everywhere there's a wild past of **gold prospectors** and **bushrangers**.

All routes in the state radiate from **Melbourne**, bang in the middle of the coastline on the huge Port Phillip Bay, and no point is much more than five hours' drive away. Yet all most visitors see of Victoria is its cultured capital, the fairy penguins on nearby **Phillip Island**, and perhaps the idyllic **Wilsons Promontory National Park** (the "Prom"), a couple of hours away on the coast of the mainly dairying region of **Gippsland**. Some may also venture to the **Goldfields**, where the nineteenth-century goldrushes left their mark in the grandiose architecture of old mining towns such as **Ballarat** and **Bendigo**. There's a great deal more to the state than this, however, including one legendary route, the **Great Ocean Road**, a winding 280 kilometres of spectacular coastal scenery with wave-carved rock formations capable of wowing the most insensate. And although the state doesn't have a reputation for being sun-blessed, its weather is more volatile than poor and it gets its fair share of sunshine; beach culture is alive and well on this coastline with some of the best **surfing** in Australia.

Marking the end of the Great Dividing Range, the massive sandstone ranges of the **Grampians**, with their Aboriginal rock paintings and dazzling array of springtime flora, rise from the monotonous wheatfields of the **Wimmera** region and the wool country of the western district. To the north of the Grampians is the wide flat region of the **Mallee** – scrub, sand dunes and dry lakes heading to the **Murray River**, where **Mildura** is an irrigated oasis supporting orchards and vineyards. In complete contrast, the **Victorian Alps** in the northeast of the state have several winter **ski slopes**, high country that provides perfect bushwalking and horse-riding territory in summer. In the foothills and plains below, where bushranger **Ned Kelly** once roamed, are some of Victoria's finest **wineries** (wine buffs should pick up a copy of the excellent 100-page brochure, "A Touring Guide to the Wine Regions of Victoria", available from the tourist information centre in Melbourne and other towns).

Public transport, by road and rail, is with **V/Line**, one of Australia's best, with many country trains and buses to fill the gaps; excellent value *V/Line* **passes** offer a fortnight's unlimited first-class travel for $130.

---

## ACCOMMODATION PRICES

All the accommodation listed in this book has been categorized into one of eight price bands, as set out below. The rates quoted represent the cheapest available double or twin room in high season – except for category ①, which are per-person rates for a dorm bed, and the prices given for units, cabins and vans, which are the daily charge for the whole unit.

| | | | |
|---|---|---|---|
| ① Under $16 | ② $16–26 | ③ $ 27–36 | ④ $ 37–54 |
| ⑤ $55–74 | ⑥ $75–94 | ⑦ $95–124 | ⑧ $ 125 upwards |

For more accommodation details, see pp.31–34.

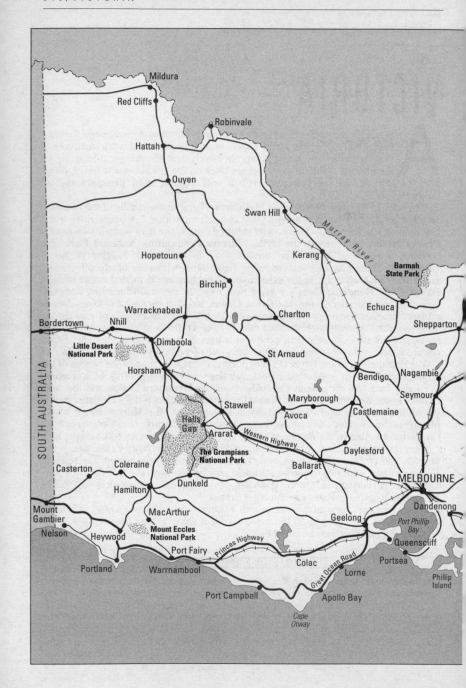

NEW SOUTH WALES

Rutherglen

Wangaratta

Wodonga

Beechworth

Glenrowan

Mt
Beauty

Benalla

Bright

Euroa

Mt Bogong

Mt Buffalo

McKillops
Bridge

Mansfield

Mt Hotham

Omeo

Mt Buller

Bonang

Buchan

Mitchell River
National Park

Cann River

Orbost

Mallacoota

Bairnsdale

Croajingolong
National Park

Mt Baw Baw

Lakes
Entrance

Princes Highway

Sale

Warragul

Ninety Mile
Beach

Morwell

Tarra Bulga
National Park

Korumburra

Leongatha

Yarram

Welshpool

Wilsons
Promontory
National Park

Snowy River

Hume Hwy

0          200 km

## Some history

Semi-nomadic **Koories** have lived in this region for at least 40,000 years, and from earliest times developed sophisticated hunting and gathering methods, creating rock art, weaving baskets, making possum-skin cloaks to protect against the cold, and establishing semi-permanent settlements such as those of circular stone houses and fish traps found at Lake Condah in western Victoria.

For the colonists, Victoria did not get off to an auspicious start: there was an unsuccessful attempt at settlement in the **Port Phillip Bay** area in 1803 but Van Diemen's Land (Tasmania) across the Bass Strait was deemed more suitable. It was in fact from Launceston that Port Phillip Bay was eventually settled, in 1834; other Tasmanians soon followed and **Melbourne** was established. This occupation was in defiance of a British government edict forbidding settlement in the territory, then part of New South Wales, but **squatting** had already begun the previous year when Edward Henty arrived with his stock to establish the first white settlement in **Portland** on the southwest coast. A pattern was created of land-hungry settlers – generally already men of means – responding to Britain's demand for wool, so that during the 1840s and 1850s what was to become Victoria evolved into a prosperous pastoral community with squatters extending huge grazing runs.

From the beginning, the Koories fought against the invasion of their land: 1836 saw the start of the **Black War**, as it has been called, a bloody guerrilla struggle against the settlers. By 1850, however, the Aborigines had been decimated – by disease as well as war – and felt defeated, too, by the apparently endless flood of invaders; their population is believed to have declined from around 15,500 to just 2300.

By 1851 the white population of the area was large and confident enough to demand separation from New South Wales, achieved, by a stroke of luck, just nine days before **gold** was discovered in the new colony. The rich goldfields of Ballarat, Bendigo and Castlemaine brought an influx of hopeful migrants from around the world. More gold came from Victoria over the next thirty years than was extracted during the celebrated Californian goldrush. From 1850 to 1880, gold transformed Victoria from a pastoral backwater into Australia's financial capital; following federation in 1901, Melbourne was even the political capital – a title it retained until Canberra became fully operational in 1927.

# MELBOURNE

**MELBOURNE** is Australia's second largest city, with a population of around three million – about half a million less than Sydney. Rivalry between the two cities – in every sphere from cricket to business – is on an almost childish level, though, in purely monetary terms, Sydney is now clearly in the ascendancy, having taken over as the nation's financial centre, while Melbourne's industrial-based economy is in the doldrums. Melbourne, however, makes a strong claim to being the nation's cultural capital, and its less brash charms have repeatedly earned plaudits as "the world's most liveable city". Magnificent landscaped gardens and parks in the English style provide green spaces hard by the centre, while beneath the skyscrapers of the CBD, an understorey of solid, if somewhat boastful, Victorian-era facades ranged along tree-lined boulevards presents the city on a more human scale. The air of approachability is further enhanced by the numerous arcades, lanes and alleys in which are hidden some of the country's best cafés, pubs and speciality shops. This is a city that grows on you, one that is undeniably a good place to live, and enjoyable to visit too.

Much has changed since Ava Gardner came to film *On the Beach* here in 1959 and reputedly said, "It's a story about the end of the world, and Melbourne sure is the right place to film it". Large-scale **immigration** since World War II has, in a sense, brought the world to Melbourne, shaking up the formerly self-absorbed, parochial WASP mind-set for good. Whole villages have come here from Lebanon, Turkey, Vietnam and all over Europe, most especially from Greece, furnishing the well-worn statistic that Melbourne is the third largest Greek city behind Athens and Thessaloniki. The European influence is perhaps clearest in winter, as ancient wooden trams rattle past warm cafés and bookshops, and promenaders dress stylishly against the chill. Not surprisingly, the immigrant blend has transformed the city into a foodie mecca, where tucking into a different **cuisine** each night – or new hybrids of East, West and South – is one of the great treats. **Sport** too, especially Aussie Rules Football, is almost a relig-ion here. The Melbourne Cup in November is a public holiday celebrated with gusto, and the city's fine sporting venues, many left over from the 1956 Olympics, are well used. Laced with a healthy dash of counter-culture, Melbourne's **artistic life** also thrives: besides heavyweight seasons of classical music and theatre, a whacky array of small galleries, and enough arthouse movies to last a lifetime, the city has the leading role in Australian literary life, based around the Writers' Festival in October.

The only real drawback is the frequently cursed **climate**. Winter is mild, and the occasional heatwaves in summer are mercifully limited to a few days at most, but the problem is that of unpredictability. Cool, rainy "English" weather can descend in any season, and spring and autumn days can be immoderately hot. But even this can be turned to advantage: as the local saying goes, if you don't like the weather, just wait ten minutes and it'll change.

# Arrival and information

Melbourne's **Tullamarine Airport** is 22km northwest of the city on the Tullamarine Freeway; the *Skybus* service (half-hourly from the airport 5.40am, with the last bus at 11.30pm; $9; ☎9335 2811) will take you to Franklin Street Bus Terminal and Spencer Street Train Station; courtesy bus connections to hotels and other city stops can be arranged. A taxi from the airport costs around $25 to the city centre, $30 to St Kilda. *Greyhound.Pioneer* buses arrive at the **Melbourne Bus Terminal**, on the north side of the city centre at 58 Franklin St, whereas *McCafferty's*, *Firefly* and *V/Line* use the **Spencer Street Bus Terminal** on the west side. **Spencer Street Station** nearby handles country and interstate trains. Many hostels pick up from these terminals, and from the Bass Strait **ferry from Tasmania**, which docks at Station Pier in Port Melbourne. About 4km southwest of the city centre, this is served by the #109 tram to Collins Street in the CBD, and the *Skybus* service.

### Information

Unfortunately, the **Victorian Information Centre** has been lumped together with the RACV, Victoria's motoring organization, at 230 Collins St (Mon–Fri 9am–6pm, Sat 9am–1pm; ☎9650 1522), and functions mainly as a travel agency. There are pamphlets galore but staff are not terribly helpful; the RACV section upstairs, however, has a good selection of travel books, and useful maps of the city and state, which are free if you belong to an affiliated motoring organization. **Information Victoria**, 318 Little Bourke St (Mon–Fri 8.30am–5.30pm), has free maps and brochures, as well as a noticeboard of city events, and a shop selling the city's largest range of local maps.

More likely to be useful are the two staffed **Visitor Information Booths** (Mon–Thurs 9am–5pm, Fri 9am–7pm, Sat 10am–4pm, Sun 11am–4pm) at City Square and Bourke Street Mall; and the **VISITS information terminals** – interactive touch-screen

The **telephone code** for Melbourne is ☎03.

machines where you can look up anything from a cab phone number to a Chinese restaurant – at locations including Flinders and Spencer Street stations, the Victorian Arts Centre, *Southern Cross Hotel*, Town Hall and Bourke Street Mall.

**Alternative sources of information** include the *Department of Conservation and Natural Resources*, 240 Victoria Parade (Mon–Fri 10am–5pm; ☎9412 4011), for anything about national parks and conservation areas in Victoria; and the *National Trust* office, Tasma Terrace, 6 Parliament Place (Mon–Fri 9am–5pm; ☎9654 4711), which sells several guides to walking tours of historical Melbourne. *Melway,* available from all newsagents, is the best **street directory**. Friday's *Age* contains an excellent pull-out **listings** section, *EG*, detailing the week's entertainment as well as fairs and markets, art and craft exhibitions, sport, and other events in and around town.

# City transport

Melbourne's efficient public transport system of trams, trains and buses is called **The Met**, on which a range of interchangeable **tickets** is available. Unless you're going on a day trip to the outskirts, you can get anywhere you'd need to, including St Kilda and Williamstown, on a zone 1 ticket. An ordinary zone 1 ticket costs $2.10, a short hop $1.40; these tickets are valid for two hours, or all night if bought after 7pm. A day-ticket ($4.10) is better value if you're making more than one trip in zone 1; also worth considering are weekly tickets ($18 for zone 1) and cards valid for ten trips within zone 1 ($12). The Explorer's Pass – three zone 1 day-tickets, booklet and map for $15 – is less of a bargain. Regular and day-tickets can be bought on board trams and buses, while the full range is available at selected shops (usually newsagents and milk bars), train stations and the *City Met Shop*, 103 Elizabeth St. For further information, call the **Met Transport Information Centre** (Mon–Sat 7.30am–8.30pm, Sun 9.15am–8.30pm; ☎13 1638).

Services operate from Monday to Saturday from 5am to midnight, and on Sunday from 8am to 11pm, supplemented in the early hours of Saturday and Sunday by **NightRider buses** (hourly 12.30–4.30am; $5), which head from the City Square on Swanston Walk along the suburban train routes; each bus is equipped with a mobile phone, on which the driver can book a taxi to meet you at a bus stop.

### Trams

Melbourne's **trams** give the city a distinctive character and provide a pleasant, environmentally friendly way of getting around: the **City Circle** (see box below) is particularly convenient, and free. Trams run down the centre of the road, and stops are signposted (the "Central Melbourne" map on pp.652–653 shows the main routes in the centre); they often have central islands where you can wait, but if not take care crossing the

---

**VINTAGE TRAMS**

Many of the trams traversing Melbourne's streets on a daily basis are vintage wooden ones. None are quite as old as the system, which dates from 1885, but some from the 1930s are still in use, and one dates from 1929. On Sundays between 10am and 6pm restored vintage trams run between Elizabeth Street and the zoo, Swanston Street and St Kilda Beach, and from St Kilda Beach to Kew. The vintage **City Circle Trams** run free of charge in a loop along Flinders Street, Spring Street, LaTrobe Street and Spencer Street (daily except Christmas Day and Good Friday, every 10min between 10am and 6pm). The **Colonial Tramcar Restaurant** is a converted 1927 tram offering traditional silver and white-linen restaurant service as you trundle around Melbourne ($40–85, depending on meal, all drinks included; book as early as possible on ☎9696 4000).

## DRIVING AND CYCLING IN MELBOURNE

**Driving** in Melbourne requires some care, mainly because of the trams. You can only overtake a tram on the left and must stop and wait behind it while passengers get on and off, as they step directly into the road (there's no need to stop if there's a central pedestrian island). A peculiar rule has developed for major intersections in the city centre to accommodate trams: when turning right, you pull over to the left-hand lane and wait for the lights to change to amber before turning – a so-called "hook turn". Signs overhead indicate when this rule applies.

**Cyclists** should also watch out for tram lines – tyres can easily get wedged in them. This apart, Melbourne is perfect for cycling and you'll be in good company as it's a popular way of getting around. A cycle map of Melbourne is available from *Bicycle Victoria*, 15–17 O'Connell St, North Melbourne (Mon–Fri 9am–5pm; ☎9328 3000) – as is a free "Great Rides" brochure detailing Australia-wide bike rides.

road. It can be uncomfortable waiting in the middle of a busy road, especially for a woman alone at night – you may feel less vulnerable waiting on the footpath, where there's often a shelter anyway. Some trams, especially during peak hours, have a ticket machine and can only be boarded at the front, but most can be boarded through either the front or middle doors and have a conductor to check and sell tickets.

### Trains

**Trains** are the fastest way to distant suburbs. An underground loop system feeding into seventeen suburban lines connects the city centre's five **train stations**: Spencer Street, which also serves as the station for interstate and country trains; Flagstaff on the corner of Latrobe and William streets; Museum beween Elizabeth and Swanston streets; Parliament on Spring Street; and Flinders Street. The last is the **main suburban station**, with its clocks detailing the times of all train departures (and its traditional "under the clocks" meeting place). Bikes can be carried free, except Monday to Friday between 7 and 9.30am and 4 and 6.30pm, when an extra adult concession fee has to be paid. Surfboards are carried free.

### Buses

**Regular buses** often run on the same route as trams, as well as filling gaps where no train or tram lines run, but they are likely to be the least useful mode of public transport for visitors. However, **Explorer Buses** might be the easy answer to sightseeing headaches – and footaches. At present they take two slightly different routes, both starting at Flinders Street Station; tickets are bought from the driver. The *City Explorer* (hourly 10am–4pm; one-day ticket $13, two-day ticket $24; ☎13 1304), runs up the eastern side of the city to Lygon Street and the zoo, then down the western side and on to the Shrine of Remembrance and the Victorian Arts Centre. The *City Wanderer* (daily 10am–3pm; two-day ticket $15; ☎9563 9788), a red double-decker, has more stops in the city centre, and then heads west over the Westgate Bridge to Scienceworks and on to Williamstown.

# Accommodation

When looking for somewhere to stay in Melbourne, your basic choice is between the **city centre** (plus adjacent suburbs **North Melbourne**, **Carlton** and **Fitzroy**) and down by the sea around **St Kilda**. Some of the cheap accommodation areas on the fringes of the city centre are fairly dead at night, but they are within easy reach of all the action. St Kilda is very lively, though a bit rough around the edges, with loads of hostels and inexpensive hotels and motels. **Richmond**, **South Melbourne** and **South Yarra** offer a good compromise, handy for both the centre and St Kilda's nightlife, but with enough tasty eating options of their own to keep you going.

The most exclusive **hotels** are downtown around Collins Street. Most of the large hotels around Spencer Street Station, which had degenerated into seedy cheapies, have now been revamped; it's still noisy and not terribly attractive though. There's an increasing amount of **backpacker accommodation** in Melbourne, ranging from little better than doss houses (especially around druggy St Kilda) to salubrious Victorian-era mansions with dorms attached. Hostel beds in St Kilda can go as low as $8, though the average is more like $11; in the city, the average price is $15. Campsite cabins and vans are an alternative worth considering for those with their own transport (see p.649).

## City centre

**Adelphi Hotel**, 187 Flinders Lane (☎9650 2709). Melbourne's most stylish hotel: a striking exterior and a sparse, ultra-modern interior design that extends to the large guest rooms, all topped with a huge pool on the roof. ⑧.

**Astoria City Travel Inn**, 288 Spencer St (☎9670 6801). Three blocks north of Spencer St Station, the spacious and bright motel suites here have been recently decorated. In-house amenities include a pool, guest laundry, and a licensed Italian restaurant. ⑥.

**Batmans Hill**, 66 Spencer St (☎9614 6344). An elegant Edwardian exterior belies a functional and modern interior, but a wide range of facilities include bars, a restaurant and 24-hour room service, and it's handy for the station. ⑧.

**City Centre Private Hotel**, 22 Little Collins St (☎9654 5401). Good position in a quiet street near the *Windsor Hotel*, 100m from Parliament Station. Some rooms have fridges, all share bathrooms, and facilities include small, basic kitchens, a TV lounge and laundry. ③–④.

**Hotel Enterprize** (formerly *John Spencer Hotel*), 44 Spencer St (☎9629 6991). Right by the station, this solid old-fashioned hotel has good economy rooms with shared facilities and no frills, plus well-appointed en suite rooms. Room service and undercover parking available. ④–⑦.

**Exford Hotel**, 199 Russell St (☎9663 2697). In an extremely central position above a pub, this brightly renovated hotel is secure and very clean, and has a small courtyard with barbecue; doubles are especially good value. Rooms ④, dorms ①.

**George St Apartments**, 101 George St (☎9419 1333). Serviced self-catering studio apartments 1km from the centre, on a quiet street running off the east side of Fitzroy Gardens; off-street parking. Light breakfast included. ⑤.

**Kingsgate Budget Hotel**, 131 King St (☎9629 4171). Although the foyer has been renovated, budget rooms are very basic and slightly gloomy; en-suite rooms, charged at B&B rates, offer better value, with fridges, air-conditioning, heating, and tea- and coffee-making facilities. There's a guest laundry and a TV room, but no kitchen facilities. ⑤–⑥.

**The Meeting Place**, 319 Elizabeth St, opposite *Daimaru* (☎9602 2888). Large, clean rooms above the busy *Meeting Place Tavern*, some en suite; no parking or lifts. ⑤–⑥.

**Miami Hostel & Private Hotel**, 13 Hawke St, off the north end of King St (☎9329 8499). Lodging house, with a TV lounge, pool table and games room, offering B&B in fairly basic rooms – though it's full of students in term-time. Good-value weekly rates include dinner Mon–Fri. ④.

**Queensberry Hill YHA**, 78 Howard St, off Victoria St (☎9329 8599). Ultra-modern hostel – more like a smart hotel – with family rooms, double rooms and small dorms, as well as a cafeteria, TV rooms and a huge, well-equipped kitchen. The office opens 7.30am–10.30pm, but access is 24-hr. An easy 10-min walk from Melbourne Bus Terminal; *Skybus* will drop off here on request. Rooms ④, dorms ②.

**Terrace Pacific Inn**, 16 Spencer St (☎9621 1922, or free call 1800/81 6168). Popular with business people, this very pleasant, well-maintained hotel constitutes excellent value, with en suite rooms (B&B only), rooms with shared facilities, a bar, restaurant and elegant breakfast room. ④–⑤.

**Toad Hall Guesthouse**, 441 Elizabeth St (☎9600 9010). Very good choice close to Melbourne Bus Terminal: friendly, secure and clean, with good facilities and car parking available. Rooms ④, dorms ①–②.

**The Victoria Hotel**, 215 Little Collins St (☎9650 0441, or free call 1800/33 1147). Huge, old, but refurbished hotel in an unbeatable central location, with its own café and bar; all rooms – with or without their own bathrooms – have telephones, heating, tea- and coffee-making facilities. Undercover parking available for $6 per day. ④–⑦.

**The Windsor Hotel**, 103 Spring St (☎9653 0653). This opulent Victorian-era hotel, a landmark opposite Parliament House, is classified by the National Trust, but you'll pay over $300 a night for the privilege. ⑨.

**YWCA**, 489 Elizabeth St (☎9329 5188). Practically opposite Melbourne Bus Terminal and close to the Victoria Market, these recently renovated premises consist mostly of en suite private rooms, some with fridge, telephone, colour TV and air-conditioning. The few dorms (maximum stay 3 nights) are overpriced. Guests have access to a kitchen, laundry, licensed restaurant, swimming pool, gymnasium and undercover parking. Both sexes welcome. Rooms ⑤–⑥, dorms ②.

## North Melbourne, Carlton, Fitzroy and Preston

**Carlton College**, 101 Drummond St, Carlton (☎9663 1644). Ideally located near the Lygon St cafés and shops, this student accommodation in Italianate terraces turns into a backpacker hostel from mid-November to the end of February. The small dorms, singles, twins and doubles are simple, but excellent value. All rates B&B. Rooms ②–③, dorms ①.

**Chapman Street YHA**, 76 Chapman St, North Melbourne (☎9328 3595). More intimate than the new Queensbury Hill YHA, but nearly 3km from the centre – take tram #50, #57 or #59 heading north on Elizabeth St. All rooms are twins; car parking available. Rooms ③, dorms ①.

**Ciro's Family Motel**, 204–218 Lygon St, Carlton (☎9639 3322). Small, simple, old-style motel run by a friendly Italian family. Room rates include dinner. ⑤.

**Downtowner on Lygon**, 66 Lygon St, Carlton (☎9663 5555). Attractively refurbished rooms with all mod cons (some with spa) in the heart of Carlton, plus a restaurant and undercover parking. ⑦.

**The Nunnery**, 116 Nicholson St, Fitzroy (☎9419 8637; #96 tram from Bourke St). Half of this ex-convent is an attractive guesthouse, half a not-so-special hostel with rather crammed dorms. A small courtyard and a tiny rooftop area are the only outdoor sitting areas, but the atmosphere is busy and friendly; there's also a big TV lounge and a kitchen. Two doors away is a great pub and within five minutes' walk are the cafés of Brunswick St. Rooms ④, dorms ①–②.

**The Terrace**, 418 Murray Road, Preston (☎9470 1006). 10km from the centre, but very close to a train station, bus and tram stops, and a cheap market, and handy for excursion areas further north and northeast. The large hostel in a rambling (and in parts ramshackle) Victorian-era mansion has extra facilities such as a games room and spa, but its real strength is the good work contacts of the owner-manager. Free pick-up from the airport, city or Tasmanian ferry. Rooms ②–③, dorms ①.

## Richmond, South Melbourne and South Yarra

**Central House**, 337 Highett St, Richmond (☎9427 9826; tram #75 or #48 from Spencer St or Flinders St to bus stop no. 25). Luxury apartments have been converted into a small, well-equipped hostel, not spotlessly tidy, but with a homely, friendly atmosphere. Accommodation is mostly in dorms (some women-only), with a few twin and double rooms. The owner has good employment contacts. Pick-up from the airport, bus terminals or Tasmanian ferry. Rooms ③, dorms ①.

**Lords Lodge Backpackers**, 204 Punt Rd, South Yarra (☎9510 5658; #6 or #72 tram from Swanston St). Small, non-smoking hostel in an old mansion, with a friendly, personal atmosphere, centrally positioned in a fashionable area. As well as singles and doubles, there are medium-sized dorms (some women-only), each with a fridge, and two with their own small kitchen. Office hours are 8am–noon & 5–10pm. Rooms ③, dorms ①.

**Richmond Hill Guesthouse**, 353 Church St (between Bridge Rd and Swan St), Richmond (☎9428 6501; tram #75 or #48 from Spencer St or Flinders St). Clean and well-run ex-YWCA in an old mansion with very pleasant sitting rooms, large kitchens and a small courtyard. Opt for either a dorm (some women only), or a simple single, twin or double. Rooms ③–④, dorms ①.

**Hotel Victoria**, 123 Beaconsfield Parade, South Melbourne (☎9690 3666). Downstairs at this grand seafront hotel, built in 1888, has been meticulously restored, but accommodation is in a more modern style, some of it facing a noisy dual carriageway. Choose between en suite doubles and cheaper rooms with shared facilities. ⑤–⑧.

**West End Hotel**, 76 Toorak Rd West, South Yarra (☎9866 3135; tram #8, or train to South Yarra). Close to the heart of exclusive South Yarra, an old-fashioned B&B overlooking a shady park. ④.

## St Kilda and Elwood

**Bayside Motel**, 63 Fitzroy St, St Kilda (☎9525 3833). The triples are especially good value among these motel units with all mod cons – opt for a room at the back, as those facing the street are a bit noisy. Secure car park available. ④.

**Bayside Private Hotel**, 65 Ormond Esplanade, Elwood (☎9531 9238). Run-down, but clean and safe seaside hotel, where rates for the well-equipped rooms include meals; excellent weekly full-board deals are also offered ($135). ⑤.

**Enfield House**, 2 Enfield St, St Kilda (☎9534 8159). A few dorms, a TV lounge and reading rooms have been carved out of a stately Victorian-era mansion, with a bewildering number of very basic dorms and rooms out the back in former flats that have clearly seen better days. Alcohol and smoking are banned from the rooms, but guests have access to kitchens, a courtyard and rooftop terrace, and there's a good noticeboard and lots of activities. Transport is provided to the train and bus stations and the Tasmanian ferry, and to and from the airport on demand. Rooms ③, dorms ①.

**Florida Lodge**, 37 Grey St, St Kilda (☎9534 3842). These Fifties-style brick apartments (each with 2 bedrooms, a lounge and bathroom) are rented out as singles, twins, doubles or dorms, providing very cheap accommodation for budget travellers, couples and people on working-holiday visas. Most are clean and bright, though tackily furnished, but the state of the flat naturally depends on whom you share it with. Especially good-value weekly rates. Rooms ③–④, dorms ①.

**Kookaburra Cottage**, 56 Jackson St, St Kilda (☎9534 5457). A friendly and secure atmosphere characterizes this small, clean and well-run hostel, which is continually being renovated. All rooms have a handbasin and a fridge. Office hours are 8.30am–12.30pm and 6–8.30pm, but there is an answering machine. Pick-ups from the Tasmanian ferry, trains and buses. Rooms ③, dorms ①.

**Leopard House**, 27 Grey St, St Kilda (☎9534 1200). Large, pleasant old house, with lockable dorms, either segregated or mixed, and a good noticeboard. The office is open Mon–Sat 8–11am & 4–7pm. ①.

**Olembia Bed and Breakfast**, 96 Barkly St, St Kilda (☎9537 1412). Fine old building with open fireplaces (though it's a no-smoking establishment), fresh flowers and other luxuries, two cosy lounges and a well-equipped kitchen. Singles, twins and doubles are very appealing, while the dorms (some women only) have handbasins and clothes-hanging space. Free pick-up from the bus terminals and Tasmanian ferry at certain times, from the airport once a day. Rooms ④, dorms ①.

**Regal Private Hotel**, 149 Fitzroy St, St Kilda (☎9534 5063). Old-style boarding house that has so far survived the gentrification trend that is transforming this end of Fitzroy St. Rooms are very simple, but clean, and the weekly rates constitute especially good value. ③.

**The Ritz**, 169 Fitzroy St, St Kilda (☎9525 3501). You're above a busy nightclub at this fairly new, well-furnished, and friendly hostel, but within range of plenty of cheap restaurants and milk bars.

---

### GAY AND LESBIAN ACCOMMODATION

**Californian Motor Inn**, 138 Barkers Rd, Hawthorn (☎9818 0281 or free call 1800/33 1166). Gay-friendly motel accommodation close to the city, with parking available. ⑤–⑥.

**Exchange Hotel**, 119 Commercial Rd, South Yarra (☎9867 51444). Accommodation at traditional gay men's pub. ④.

**Fitzroy Stables**, 124 Victoria St (off Brunswick St), Fitzroy. Lovely self-contained unit with a cathedral ceiling, mezzanine bedroom and small kitchen, facing a courtyard with a cottage garden; for a gay couple or single. ⑥.

**Laird Hotel**, 149 Gipps St, Collingwood (☎9417 2832). Rooms for gay men only. ⑦.

**The Melbourne Guesthouse**, 26 Crimea St, St Kilda (☎9525 4746). Gay-friendly, small Victorian-style hotel near the city, with a kitchen, laundry, courtyard and garden. ⑤.

**163 Drummond Street**, 163 Drummond St, Carlton (☎9663 3081). B&B guesthouse. ④.

**Prince of Wales Hotel**, Fitzroy St, St Kilda (☎9534 8251). Rooms above a busy gay and lesbian pub. ⑤.

**Share-a-Home** (☎1800/80 3468). Arranges house shares for gays and lesbians.

**The Victoria Hotel**, 380 Victoria St, Brunswick (☎9380 1853). Women-only café-bar with B&B accommodation.

Rooms are simple but spotless, and there are two TV lounges, a dining room and a tiny kitchen. Rooms ③, dorms ①.

**St Kilda Coffee Palace Backpackers Inn**, 24 Grey St, St Kilda (☎9534 5283). Well-run, very large, but somewhat impersonal place, with good security. Some of the spacious dorms are women-only, and there are plenty of twins and doubles, and a good rooftop garden. Pick-up service from the Tasmanian ferry and the bus terminals in the morning or on demand. Rooms ③, dorms ①.

**Warwick Beachside St Kilda**, 363 Beaconsfield Parade, St Kilda (☎9525 4800). Three minutes from the cafés and pubs of Fitzroy St, these Fifties-style brick buildings contain well-equipped 1- and 2-bedroom units, all with colour TV, direct-dial telephones and complete kitchen facilities. Good weekly rates. ⑤–⑥.

## Camping and caravan parks

There are no campsites anywhere close to the centre; the nearest is *Melbourne Caravan and Tourist Park*, with scenic *Hobsons Bay* not much further.

**Crystal Brook Holiday Centre**, corner of Anderson's Creek and Warrandayte roads, East Doncaster (☎9844 3637). Modern campsite and holiday park with tennis courts and a pool, 21km northeast of the city centre (20min via the Eastern Freeway). Cabins ④–⑤, on-site vans ③–④.

**Hobsons Bay Caravan Park**, 158 Kororoit Creek Rd, Williamstown (☎9397 2395). Pitch your tent facing St Kilda across Hobsons Bay. Cabins ③.

**Melbourne Caravan and Tourist Park**, 265 Elizabeth St, Coburg East (☎9354 3533). Ten kilometres north of the city, the closest spot to camp, with a kitchen and a swimming pool. Cabins and on-site vans ④–⑤.

# The City

Melbourne is a city of few sights and much lifestyle, a place to sit and enjoy a coffee or stroll in a park rather than traipse round museums and tourist attractions. The Central Business District, bounded by Latrobe, Spring, Flinders and Spencer streets, offers little beyond some fine public buildings and lots of shops, though the **Old Melbourne Gaol** exerts a ghoulish fascination. On all sides, save the downtown west, the CBD is surrounded by gardens; few cities can have so much green space so close to the centre. To the north a wander through lively, century-old **Queen Victoria Market** will repay both serious shoppers and people-watchers, while **Carlton Gardens** is probably the pleasantest of Melbourne's leafy refuges. In the east the CBD rubs up against **Eastern Hill**, with its government buildings and landscaped **Fitzroy Gardens**, from where it's a short walk to the venerable **Melbourne Cricket Ground**, a must for sports fans. To the south is the muddy, much-maligned **Yarra River**, best appreciated on a **boat cruise**, though its banks are fast being regenerated as pleasure grounds. South of the river, the Victorian Arts Centre, whose highlights are the **National Gallery** and the **Performing Arts Museum**, forms a cultural strip on one side of St Kilda Road, while on the other Government House and the impressive Shrine of Remembrance front the **Royal Botanic Gardens**, where along with the soothing greenery you'll get a dose of horticultural education.

## The CBD

Seen from across the river or from the air, Melbourne's **Central Business District** offers up a spectacular, modern skyline; at ground level, however, what you notice are the florid nineteenth-century facades, grandiose survivors of the great days of the gold-rushes and after, when Melbourne consolidated its position as a financial centre. The former **Royal Mint** on William Street near Flagstaff Gardens is one of the finest examples, but the main concentrations are on Collins Street, and along Spring Street to the east. At the centre of the CBD, trams still jolt through busy **Bourke Street Mall**, so it's not quite a pedestrian haven; Swanston Street, bounding the Mall to the east, has also been closed to all traffic bar trams between Flinders and Latrobe streets and renamed Swanston Walk. A stone's throw from these central thoroughfares, narrow lanes, squares and arcades add a less predictable feel to a stroll through the city.

## Collins Street

**Collins Street** is *the* smart Melbourne address – especially if you're an international banker – becoming increasingly exclusive as you climb the hill from the rather grimy and noisy Spencer Street end. Starting from this less rarefied end, the brand-new Stock Exchange squares up to the **Rialto Building** opposite, an Italianate Gothic complex built in the 1890s, which now houses a luxury hotel, the *Meridien*. The building was the site of long-running disputes between developers and conservationists in the 1980s over the development of the massive **Rialto Towers**, Melbourne's tallest structure. The eventual compromise – though some hate it all the same – is a classic skyscraper, the reflective surface of its twin towers lending the skyline a bit of oomph. On clear days, especially in the evening, a trip in the lift up to the **Rialto Observation Deck** on the 55th floor is a must (Mon–Fri 11am–11pm, Sat & Sun 10am–11pm; $6); on Saturdays and Sundays there's an arts and crafts market at the towers from 10am to 6pm. Nearby at 333 Collins St, the former **Commercial Bank of Australia** has a particularly sumptuous interior that you're welcome to admire during business hours, with its domed banking chamber and awesome barrel-vaulted vestibule.

The 1890s **Block Arcade**, at nos. 282–284, is Melbourne's grandest shopping arcade, its name appropriately taken from the tradition of "doing the block" – promenading around the city's fashionable shopping streets. Restored in 1988, the L-shaped arcade sports a mosaic-tiled floor, ornate columns and mouldings, and a glass-domed roof. **Australia on Collins**, a modern alternative next door, has set its sights firmly on the street's glitzy shopping crown: it boasts a very upmarket food court, and, on the top level, "Collins Street in the Sky", designed to give the feel of Collins Street as it used to be, with trees, street lamps and café.

On the corner of Collins and Swanston streets, Neoclassical Melbourne Town Hall faces boring **City Square**, the result of years of argument about Melbourne's need for a focal point – it failed dismally to provide one. An unmissable landmark on the south side of City Square is the splendid **St Paul's Cathedral**, built in the 1880s according to the Gothic-revival design of English architect William Butterfield, who never actually visited Australia. Across from the cathedral on Swanston Walk, *Young and Jackson's Hotel* is now protected by the National Trust, not for any intrinsic beauty but as a showcase for a work of art which has become a Melbourne icon: **Chloe**, a full-length nude now reclining upstairs in *Chloe's Bar and Bistro*, exhibited by the French painter Lefevre at the Paris Salon of 1875, was sent to an international exhibition in Melbourne in 1881, and has been here ever since.

Back on Collins Street, the pompous Melbourne Athenaeum next to the town hall is an important ingredient in the rising streetscape leading up past **Scots Church**, whose Gothic-revival design merits a peek, though it's famous mainly as the place where Dame Nellie Melba first sang in the choir. Further up, beyond expensive boutiques and even more expensive souvenir shops, Collins Place and the towering **Regent Hotel** dominate the upper part of Collins Street, known as the "Paris end". The (male) toilet of *Le Restaurant* on the 35th floor of the *Regent* is known as the "loo with a view", but the **view** from the tables by the window isn't bad, either – though it doesn't come cheap (see "Eating and drinking", p.663). Yet another **arts and crafts market** plies its wares in Collins Place on Sundays between 8am and 5pm. Opposite, overshadowed by the *Regent* tower, stands one of the last bastions of Australian male chauvinism: the very staid, men-only Melbourne Club.

## Bourke Street and Chinatown

**Bourke Street Mall**, lined with trees and seats but not quite traffic-free, is the most-captivating part of Bourke Street, with the wonderful Victorian-era **General Post Office** to set against department stores and crowded shops. Running off the mall, the lovely **Royal Arcade** is Melbourne's oldest (1839), paved with black and white marble and lit by huge fanlight windows – a clock on which two seven-foot giants, Gog and Magog, strike the hours adds a welcome hint of the grotesque. As you climb the hill east of here, Bourke Street keeps up the interest, with several cafés and bars that put out pavement tables at night – including *Pellegrini's*, Melbourne's first espresso bar and still buzzing – as well as late-opening book and record stores.

North of Bourke Street, running parallel, is **Little Bourke Street**, with the majestic **Law Courts** at the western end by William Street, and **Chinatown** in the east between Exhibition and Swanston streets. Australia's oldest continuous Chinese settlement, Melbourne's Chinatown began with a few boarding-houses in the 1850s (when the goldrushes attracted Chinese people in droves, many from the Pearl River Delta near Hong Kong) and grew as the gold began to run out and Chinese fortune-seekers headed back to the city. Today the area still has a low-rise, narrow-laned, nineteenth-century character, and it's packed with Chinese restaurants and stores. The **Museum of Chinese Australian History**, in an old warehouse in Cohen Place (Sun–Fri 10am–4.30pm, Sat noon–5pm; $3), is concerned particularly with the Chinese role in the foundation and development of Melbourne.

## Museum of Victoria and Melbourne Central

The **Museum of Victoria** (entrance on Swanston Street; daily 10am–5pm; $5) is essentially an old-fashioned, stuffed-animal-type collection, with snippets of Egyptology and dinosaurs, exhibited around a two-tiered central hall. They've even stuffed the legendary racehorse **Phar Lap** – winner of the Melbourne Cup in the early 1930s who met an untimely death when he was allegedly poisoned in the United States. Newer displays, focussing on social history, inject a bit of life: the excellent, permanently evolving **Koorie exhibition** concentrates on unusual angles such as the role of Aboriginal women. Forget the dull children's museum but head for the much more exciting **Planetarium** if you're around at show time (weekdays at 3pm, weekends & holidays at noon, 1 & 3pm; $8, including museum entrance). The museum has been seeking its own more spacious home (away from the State Library with which it shares the block) for years, and may soon make a break for freedom to the Exhibition Buildings in Carlton.

Opposite the museum, **Melbourne Central** is an ultra-modern shopping complex that has skilfully incorporated an old redbrick shot tower under its pointed glass dome. Among the shops here is the *Daimaru* department store, which offers a fascinating taste of things Japanese – not least in the food hall.

## Old Melbourne Gaol

The **Old Melbourne Gaol** (daily 9.30am–4.30pm; $6; no disabled access), on Russell Street, a block north of the museum, is probably the most worthwhile of all the downtown sights. Certainly it's the most popular, largely because Australian folk hero and bushranger **Ned Kelly** was hung here in 1880 – his famous suit of armour, the site of his execution and his death mask are all on display (for more on Ned Kelly's exploits, see p.741).

The bluestone prison was built in stages from 1841 to 1864 – the goldrushes of the 1850s caused such a surge in lawlessness that it kept having to be expanded. A mix of condemned men, remand and short-sentence prisoners, women and "lunatics" (often, in fact, drunks) were housed here; long-term prisoners languished in hulks moored at Williamstown, or at the Pentridge Stockade. Much has been demolished since the gaol was closed in 1923, but the entrance and boundary walls at least survive, and it's worth

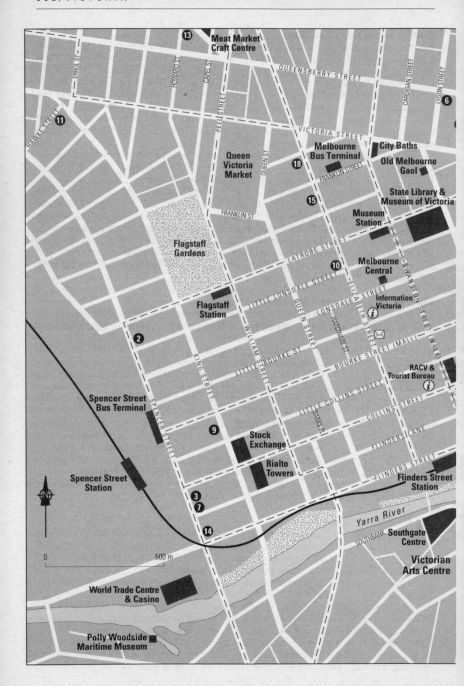

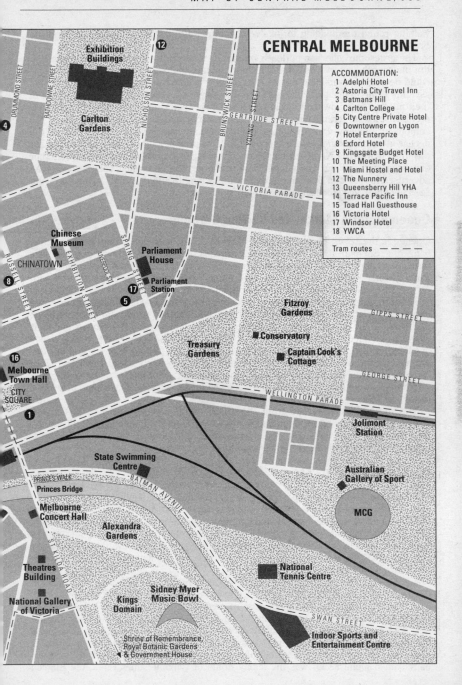

# CENTRAL MELBOURNE

**ACCOMMODATION:**
1 Adelphi Hotel
2 Astoria City Travel Inn
3 Batmans Hill
4 Carlton College
5 City Centre Private Hotel
6 Downtowner on Lygon
7 Hotel Enterprize
8 Exford Hotel
9 Kingsgate Budget Hotel
10 The Meeting Place
11 Miami Hostel and Hotel
12 The Nunnery
13 Queensberry Hill YHA
14 Terrace Pacific Inn
15 Toad Hall Guesthouse
16 Victoria Hotel
17 Windsor Hotel
18 YWCA

Tram routes — — — —

Exhibition Buildings

DRUMMOND STREET

RATHDOWNE STREET

NICHOLSON STREET

BRUNSWICK STREET

GERTRUDE STREET

YOUNG STREET

Carlton Gardens

VICTORIA PARADE

Chinese Museum

RUSSELL STREET

CHINATOWN

EXHIBITION STREET

SPRING STREET

LYGON ST

Parliament House

Parliament Station

Fitzroy Gardens

GIPPS STREET

Conservatory

Captain Cook's Cottage

Treasury Gardens

Melbourne Town Hall

CITY SQUARE

GEORGE STREET

WELLINGTON PARADE

State Swimming Centre

Jolimont Station

Australian Gallery of Sport

PRINCES WALK

BATMAN AVENUE

Princes Bridge

MCG

Melbourne Concert Hall

Alexandra Gardens

ST KILDA ROAD

Theatres Building

National Tennis Centre

National Gallery of Victoria

Kings Domain

Sidney Myer Music Bowl

SWAN STREET

Indoor Sports and Entertainment Centre

Shrine of Remembrance, Royal Botanic Gardens & Government House walking round the building to take a look at the formidable arched brick portal on Franklin Street.

The gruesome collection of **death masks** on show in the tiny cells bears witness to the nineteenth-century obsession with phrenology, the belief that people's characters could be read by examining the features of their heads. Inmates of prisons and mental asylums came under particular scrutiny: the shape of someone's brow, the length of their nose or even how their ear lobes joined their head could be deemed to indicate a predisposition to criminality or insanity. Accompanying the displayed heads are compelling, bloody case histories of the usually murderous crimes which the deceased's cranial bumps were supposed to have predetermined. Most fascinating are the women: **Martha Needle**, who poisoned, among many others, her husband and her daughters with arsenic; and young **Martha Knorr**, the notorious "baby farmer" who advertised herself as a "kind motherly person, willing to adopt a child" – after receiving £2–5 per child, she killed and buried them in her backyard.

## Queen Victoria Market and Carlton Gardens

Opened in the 1870s, **Queen Victoria Market** (Tues 6am–2pm, Thurs 6am–6pm, Fri 6am–1pm, Sat 6am–4pm, Sun 9am–4pm) remains one of the best loved of Melbourne institutions. Its collection of huge, decorative open-sided sheds and high-roofed halls is fronted along Victoria Street by restored shops, their original awnings held up with decorative iron posts. Although undeniably quaint and tourist-friendly, the market is a boisterous, down-to-earth affair where you can buy practically anything from new and secondhand clothes to fresh fish at bargain prices. Stallholders and shoppers seem just as diverse as the goods on offer: Vietnamese, Italian and Greek greengrocers pile their colourful produce high and vie for your attention, while the huge variety of deliciously smelly cheeses effortlessly draws customers to the old-fashioned deli hall. Saturday morning is the most chaotic and interesting of all, a weekly social ritual as half of Melbourne turns out for some serious food shopping. On Sundays most of the food sections are closed, and the atmosphere is more recreational as people shop mainly for clothes and shoes.

The most pleasant escape from the CBD, at its northeast corner, is **Carlton Gardens**, especially by the fountain at the Royal Exhibition Buildings. Built for the International Exhibition of 1880, the buildings originally covered the whole of the park, but now only the magnificent Neoclassical Main Hall remains.

## Eastern Hill and the MCG

The **Eastern Hill** area beyond Spring Street has many fine public buildings, centred around **Parliament House**. Erected in stages between 1856 and 1930, the parliament buildings (40-min guided tours on non-sitting days Mon–Fri 10 & 11am, 2, 3 & 3.30pm; free) have a theatrical presence, with a facade of giant Doric columns rising from a high flight of steps, and landscaped gardens either side. Just below, the old Treasury Building (1857) and adjacent State Government office, facing the beautiful Treasury Gardens, are equally imposing.

To the east, the broad acres of **Fitzroy Gardens** run a close second to Carlton Gardens as a getaway from the CBD. Originally laid out in the shape of the Union Jack flag, the park's paths still just about conform to the original pattern, but in between the formal style has been fetchingly abandoned. The flowers, statuary and fountains are best appreciated on weekdays, as at the weekend you'll spend most of your time dodging the video cameras of wedding parties. The gardens' much-touted main attraction is really only for kitsch nostalgists: **Cook's Cottage** (winter daily 9am–5pm; summer daily 9am–5.30pm; $2.50) was the family home of Captain James Cook, the English navigator who explored the southern hemisphere in three great voyages and first "discovered" the east coast of Australia. It was purchased in 1933, shipped over from Yorkshire piece by piece and presented as a gift to the state of Victoria for its 1934 centenary. Redbrick and ivy-covered, the cottage attempts to recreate the atmosphere of eighteenth-century England, reinforced by displays about the ill-fated discoverer himself. Elsewhere in the gardens, a tacky model Tudor village continues the "olde worlde" theme, but you'll probably find the **Conservatory**'s flower displays (daily 9am–5pm; free) more interesting, and can refresh yourself at the kiosk or the tearoom.

## The MCG

**Yarra Park**, home of the hallowed **Melbourne Cricket Ground**, lies across Wellington Parade from the southeastern corner of Fitzroy Gardens – also easily reached by tram along Wellington Parade or train to Jolimont Station. Home to the Melbourne Cricket Club since 1853, the MCG is now a vast and ugly stadium, as only the historic members' stand survived the complete reconstruction that made the ground the centrepiece for the 1956 Olympic Games. As well as hosting state and international cricket matches and some of the top Aussie Rules football games, the MCG contains the **Australian Gallery of Sport** (daily 10am–4pm; $7) and the **Olympic Museum**. Tours of the ground itself (hourly 10am–3pm, except on match days) are included in the admission fee; highlight of these is the members' pavilion – home of the most traditional and elitist club in Australia – packed with fascinating cricketing memorabilia. The Gallery of Sport covers all other games from cycling to tennis to footie – complete with an entertaining machine that plays the various footie-club songs. The Olympic Museum covers all the twentieth-century Olympiads but concentrates on Melbourne 1956, generally regarded as a hugely successful event that brought the city to the attention of the world.

## The Yarra River and the south bank

The notoriously muddy **Yarra River** is an essential part of Melbourne, traditionally home to the docks, now the focus of leisure activity. In the early days, tidal movements of up to two metres meant frequent flooding, a problem only partly solved by artificially straightening the river and building up its banks – but with the incidental benefit of reserving tracts of low-lying land as recreational space, now pleasingly criss-crossed by paths and cycle tracks.

Four **bridges** cross the river from the CBD: Spencer Street Bridge at the end of Spencer Street, Kings Bridge on King Street, Queens Bridge, not quite at the end of Queen Street, and Princes Bridge which carries Swanston Street across; there's also a pedestrian bridge from the bank below Flinders Street Station to the Southgate Centre. The best way to see the Yarra is on a **cruise**: *Williamstown Bay and River Cruises* (see p.663) ply the lower section from Williamstown to the World Trade Centre or Southgate, while *Melbourne Cruisers* depart half-hourly for various cruises (1hr 30min–2hr 30min; $11–22; book on ☎9629 7233 Mon–Fri, ☎9650 2055 Sat & Sun) from Princes Walk below the northern end of Princes Bridge. Their "River Gardens Cruise" and the "Melbourne Highlights Coffee Cruise" will both take you past affluent South Yarra and industrial Richmond to **Herring Island**, which it's hoped will soon be protected as a wildlife reserve.

On the south side of Princes Bridge you can rent **bikes** to explore the salubrious left bank; on fine weekends especially, the Yarra comes to life, with people messing about in boats, cycling and strolling, and family groups gathered for barbecues. The **Southgate Centre**, immediately west of Princes Bridge, is a highly successful recent development: once dingy and industrial, it's now a shopping complex with rows of smart cafés and bars whose outdoor tables are packed at weekends. Newcomers to

Australia may want to attend the **Sensorvision Experience Show** (hourly 11.30am–4.30pm, with additional late show at 5.30pm Sat & Sun; $6) at Southgate's Australiagate Theatre, which offers an informative, state-of-the-art slide show about Australia's landscapes, history and peoples, with voice-over, sound effects, and "smell effects" of eucalypt forests, bushfires, dusty wool sheds and the like.

## Docks and sports

Immediately downstream of the city centre, beyond Spencer Street Bridge, is the old **dock area**, much of it now earmarked for commercial and leisure development. Although Melbourne is still the busiest container port in the southern hemisphere and the fifth largest in the world, few ships now come up the river, preferring to offload at deepwater Port Melbourne. The excellent **Polly Woodside Maritime Museum** (daily 10am–4pm; $7) is tucked into a small old dock here; to reach it cross Batman Bridge, turn right and then second right into Phayer Street. The focus is the *Polly Woodside* itself, a small, barque-rigged sailing ship, built in Belfast in 1885 for the South American coal trade and only retired in 1968, when it was the last deep-water sailing vessel in Australia still afloat. Facing the museum across the Yarra are the World Trade Centre and Melbourne's latest and most controversial attraction, the Crown Casino, where gamblers queue up practically around the clock to play their favourite game.

Upstream from the CBD, the parklands on the north bank were developed for the 1956 Olympics and are still the focus of **sport** in Melbourne. Following Batman Avenue along the river from Princes Bridge you pass the **State Swimming Centre**, a place for serious laps, embellished with a glass-sided diving pool. Between Swan Street and the MCG is the **National Tennis Centre** which hosts international tournaments; dirt is heaped inside for occasional motorcross events. Bordered by Swan Street and the river are the "Glasshouse" or **Indoor Sports and Entertainment Centre**, home of the Melbourne Giants basketball team, and the Olympic **velodrome**, now more often the setting for greyhound races and American Football.

## Victorian Arts Centre

The **Victorian Arts Centre**, just off St Kilda Road, comprises the National Gallery of Victoria, the Melbourne Concert Hall and the Theatres Building, topped by its hideous spire. The "Arts Tower", as it's sometimes called, is meant to represent the pinnacle of the arts in Melbourne, its curved surfaces supposedly evoking the flowing folds of a ballerina's skirt. Germaine Greer's attempt at explanation was that "stunned by the bad taste of the Sydney Opera House, the Melbournians have clearly decided to fight fire with fire ..."

There are guided **tours** (Mon–Fri noon and 2.30pm, Sat 10.30am & noon, $8; backstage tour Sun 12.15pm & 2.15pm, $10) of the **Concert Hall** and **Theatres Building**, which are worth going on mainly to see the collection of art in the various foyers. The highlight of the Arts Centre if you're not seeing a performance, however, is the fun and accessible **Performing Arts Museum** (Mon–Fri 11am–5pm, Sat & Sun noon–5pm; $5), which covers everything from opera to TV and rock 'n' roll and has wonderful temporary exhibitions, normally on aspects of popular culture.

The **National Gallery of Victoria** (daily 10am–5pm; $6, free on Mon; guided tours Mon–Fri noon & 2.30pm) is altogether a more serious contender: Australia's finest state gallery, with the best collection of Australian art – colonial to contemporary – in the country. Seventy thousand works, rotated regularly, form the permanent collection, and special exhibitions are frequently staged. The **Heidelberg School** is very well represented, as well as more contemporary artists such as Arthur Boyd, Sidney Nolan, William Dobell, Fred Williams and Margaret Preston; the **Aboriginal art** section is also strong. On Sundays between 9am and 6pm the pavement and other areas of the Arts Centre play host to a good arts and crafts market.

## Kings Domain

Across St Kilda Road from the National Gallery, the **Kings Domain** is a grassy open park encompassing the **Sidney Myer Music Bowl**,which serves as the outdoor music arena for the Victorian Arts Centre. South of the Bowl, and behind imposing iron gates with stone pillars and a British coat of arms, you glimpse the flag flying over **Government House**, the ivory mansion of the Governor of Victoria, set in extensive grounds. The National Trust run **guided tours** (subject to availability Mon & Wed 10 & 11.30am, 1 & 2.30pm, booking compulsory on ☎9654 4711; closed Dec 16–Jan 25; $6), the highlight of which is the state ballroom. This occupies the entire south wing and includes a velvet-hung canopied throne, brocade-covered benches, gilded chairs, ornate plasterwork and three huge crystal chandeliers. Next to Government House is the **Old Melbourne Observatory**, where around the time of the new moon you can view the night sky through the huge old telescope (details and bookings through the Museum of Victoria, ☎9669 9942; open night first Saturday of every month 8–10pm).

Just south of the Government House grounds, **Latrobe's Cottage** (daily except Fri, 11am–4.30pm; $3) has been re-erected as a memorial to Lieutenant-Governor Latrobe, who lived in this tiny house throughout his term of office (1839–54). The whole thing was sent over from England in prefabricated form, and as the first governor's residence it's a telling contrast to the later one. Inside are interesting historical displays on Latrobe and the early days of the colony. Across Dallas Brooks Drive from here, the **Australian Centre for Contemporary Art** (Tues–Fri 11am–5pm, Sat & Sun 2–5pm; free) has consistently challenging exhibitions of contemporary international and Australian art.

The **Shrine of Remembrance**, in formal grounds in the southwestern corner of the Domain, is aligned with St Kilda Road – which describes a gentle arc around it – so that its forbidding mass looms ahead as you enter or leave the city. It's a rather Orwellian monument, apparently half Roman temple, half Aztec pyramid, given further chill when a mechanical-sounding voice booms out and calls you in to see the symbolic light inside. The shrine is designed so that at 11am on Remembrance Day (Nov 11) a ray of sunlight strikes the memorial stone inside – an effect that's simulated every half-hour.

## Royal Botanic Gardens

The **Royal Botanic Gardens** (Nov–March 7.30am–8.30pm, April 7.30am–6.30pm, May–Oct 7.30am–5.30pm) contain more than 10,000 different plant species and varieties in a landscaped setting of 36 hectares. Melbourne's much-maligned climate is perfect for horticulture: cool enough for temperate trees and flowers to flourish, warm enough for palms and other sub-tropical species, and wet enough for anything else. The **visitors' centre** (daily 10am–4pm; free guided walks Tues–Fri & Sun 10am & 11am) at the National Herbarium, just across Dallas Brooks Drive from Latrobe's Cottage, is the best place to start your wanderings, with displays, maps and brochures.

Highlights include the **herb garden** (daily 10am–4pm), comprising part of the medicinal garden established in 1880; the **fern gully**, a lovely walk through shady ferns, with cooling mists of water on a hot summer's day; and the large ornamental **lake** full of ducks and black swans. On summer evenings, bucolic plays such as *Wind in the Willows* or *A Midsummer Night's Dream* are often performed in the gardens (see p.675 for booking information).

# Melbourne suburbs

Far more than in the city centre, in Melbourne's **inner suburbs** you'll get a feel for what life here is really all about. Many have quite distinct characters and personalities, whether as ethnic enclaves or self-styled artists' communities. What's more, they're all easily reached on a pleasurable tram ride. Day-trips to places further afield around Melbourne are detailed on pp.679–690.

Café society finds its home to the north among the alternative galleries and second-hand shops of **Fitzroy**, and to the south in **St Kilda**, which has a trendy but raucous nightlife, and the added advantage of the beach. On Lygon Street in **Carlton**, which fuelled the Beat Generation with espresso, there are now as many boutiques as book-stores and art centres. Grungy **Richmond**, to the east, can claim both Vietnamese and Greek enclaves, and a diverse music scene in its many pubs, while across the river is the place to shop till you drop: wealthy **South Yarra**, flanked by self-consciously groovy **Prahran** and snobby **Toorak**.

Browsing through markets and shops, cruising across Hobsons Bay, sampling world foods and, of course, sipping espresso, are the primary attractions of the suburbs, but if you want to firm up your itinerary with something more concrete, make for the **Meat Market Craft Centre**, just outside the city centre in North Melbourne, the well-designed **zoo** in Carlton, **Scienceworks**, a hugely enjoyable interactive museum in Spotswood, or Eltham and its artists' colony of **Montsalvat**.

## North Melbourne

The suburb of **North Melbourne**, beyond Queen Victoria Market, is barely out of the centre at all, but it's already distinctly different, with two-storey **terraced houses** embellished with iron-lace balconies and awnings (especially on Errol, King, Chetwynd and William streets), and many unpretentious Italian cafés along Victoria Street. Head up Capel Street to Courtney Street and you'll find the **Meat Market Craft Centre** (Tues–Sun 10am–5pm) in the second block along. Inside this converted nineteenth-century brick abattoir, with its open rafters and gruesome-looking hooks still on display, you can watch craftspeople at work and buy their products. The centre also boasts an excellent café, and a noticeboard that's a good source of information on craft workshops and contacts.

## Carlton

**Carlton** is not much further from the city than North Melbourne (tram #21 or #15 from Swanston Street), but it feels yet more separate, possibly because its character is reinforced by the presence of Melbourne University and a long-established Italian café scene. **Lygon Street** is the centre of the action, and it was here that espresso bars were really introduced to Melbourne, in the 1950s; exotic spots like the *Caffe Sport*, *La Gina*, *University Caffe*, *Don Basilio*, *La Cacciatora* and *Toto's* (which claims to have intro-duced pizza to Australia) had an unconventional allure in staid Anglo-Melbourne, and the local intelligentsia soon made the street their second home. Victorian terraced houses provided cheap living, and this became the first of the city's "alternative" suburbs. These days Carlton is no longer particularly bohemian; its residents are older and wealthier, and Lygon Street has gone very definitely upmarket, though the smart fashion shops still jostle with arts centres, bookshops, and excellent ethnic restaurants and cafés.

Lygon Street itself is the obvious place to explore, but the elegant architecture also spreads eastwards to Drummond Street, and, flanking Carlton Gardens, Rathdowne and Nicholson streets. In the grounds of **Melbourne University**, you'll find cheap food and useful noticeboards (for accommodation and things for sale) in the Union Building. Running along the western side of the university, Royal Parade gives onto **Royal Park**, with its memorial to the explorers Burke and Wills, and from there it's a short walk through the park to the zoo.

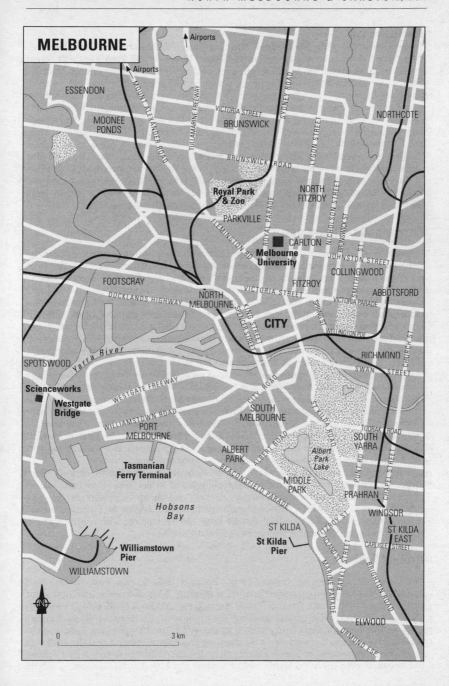

**MELBOURNE**

↑ Airports

↑ Airports

ESSENDON

MOONEE PONDS

MOUNT ALEXANDER ROAD

TULLAMARINE FREEWAY

VICTORIA STREET

BRUNSWICK

SYDNEY ROAD

NORTHCOTE

BRUNSWICK ROAD

LYGON STREET

**Royal Park & Zoo**

NORTH FITZROY

PARKVILLE

FLEMINGTON RD

ROYAL PARADE

CARLTON

**Melbourne University**

NICHOLSON STREET

BRUNSWICK ST

JOHNSTON STREET

COLLINGWOOD

FOOTSCRAY

DOCKLANDS HIGHWAY

NORTH MELBOURNE

VICTORIA STREET

FITZROY

SMITH STREET

VICTORIA PARADE

ABBOTSFORD

KING STREET

SPENCER STREET

**CITY**

SPRING ST

WELLINGTON PDE

CHURCH ST

SPOTSWOOD

Yarra River

RICHMOND

SWAN STREET

**Scienceworks**

WESTGATE FREEWAY

**Westgate Bridge**

WILLIAMSTOWN ROAD

PORT MELBOURNE

CITY ROAD

SOUTH MELBOURNE

ALBERT ROAD

ST KILDA ROAD

TOORAK ROAD

SOUTH YARRA

**Tasmanian Ferry Terminal**

ALBERT PARK

*Albert Park Lake*

CHAPEL STREET

PUNT RD

BEACONSFIELD PARADE

MIDDLE PARK

PRAHRAN

*Hobsons Bay*

WINDSOR

**Williamstown Pier**

ST KILDA

**St Kilda Pier**

FITZROY ST

ST KILDA EAST

CARLISLE STREET

WILLIAMSTOWN

BARKLY STREET

MARINE PARADE

BRIGHTON ROAD

ELWOOD

0            3 km

ORMOND ESP

## Melbourne Zoo

When it opened in 1862, **Melbourne Zoo** (Jan–March daily 9am–9pm; April–Dec daily 9am–5pm; $11.50; tram #55 or #56 from William Street or #68 from Elizabeth Street; volunteer guides available from the guide office 10am–4pm) was the first in Australia. Some of its original features are stil in evidence, including Australian and foreign trees, landscaped gardens, and a few restored Victorian-era cages, but almost all the animals have been rehoused in better, more natural conditions. The Australian area contains a central lake with waterbirds, open enclosures for koalas and other animals, and a bushland setting where you can walk among emus, kangaroos and wallabies. Strolling along the boardwalks of the Great Flight Aviary, you'll come across areas of rainforest, wetland, and a scrub area with a huge gum tree where many birds nest. The dark **platypus habitat** (11am–4pm) is also worth a look, since they're notoriously difficult to see in the wild – even here there's no guarantee you'll be lucky. Highly enjoyable too is the **Butterfly House** (Mon–Fri 9.30am–4.30pm, Sat & Sun 9.30am–5pm), a steamy tropical hothouse with hundreds of colourful Australian butterflies flitting about.

## Fitzroy and Collingwood

In the Seventies, **Fitzroy** took over from Carlton as the centre for artistic noncomformity; its focus is **Brunswick Street**, especially between Gertrude Street, home to an excellent women's bookshop and Turkish takeaways, and Johnston Street, with its lively Spanish bars and restaurants. In the shadow of Housing Commission tower blocks, welfare agencies and charity shops rub shoulders with funky secondhand clothes and junk shops, ethnic supermarkets and restaurants, cafés full of students and equally grungy artists, writers and musicians, and thriving bookshops that stay open late, often as crowded as the many bars and music-scene pubs. Most of the rough old hotels have been done up to match the prevailing mood: the *Provincial* is a good example, with its distressed paint-job and deli/café/bar inside.

The plethora of small **galleries** in Fitzroy reflects the area's fringe art leanings: some to look out for are *Gore Street*, 258 Gore St (Tues–Fri 10am–5pm, Sat noon–4pm), for conceptual art; the *Women's Gallery*, 375 Brunswick St (Wed–Fri 2–8pm, Sat & Sun 11am–6pm), run by a committee of women and showing women artists; the *Victorian Centre for Photography*, 205 Johnston St (Wed–Sun noon–5pm); and *Panorama* on Brunswick Street, an arthouse cinema with a gallery in the foyer. The **Fitzroy Pool**, in the north of the suburb on the corner of Young and Cecil streets, is a summer meeting place where people occasionally swim between posing sessions.

While not as trendy as Brunswick Street, formerly shabby **Smith Street**, which forms the boundary between Fitzroy and **Collingwood** to the east, is fast catching up. You still find many charity shops, ethnic butchers and cheap supermarkets, but New Age bookshops, quirky little cafés and revamped pubs are edging in. Collingwood and the adjacent suburb of Abbotsford have a large gay population, with a clutch of gay bars and clubs, particularly in Peel and Glasshouse streets.

## Around Prahran

Prahran Council, covering South Yarra, Prahran and, to the east, Toorak and Armadale, oversees an extensive area of **shopping**, both downbeat and upmarket. Chapel Street is the main drag: in South Yarra it extends for a Golden Mile of trendy shopping and *very* chic cafés; heading south beyond Commercial Road through Prahran and Windsor it gradually moves downmarket, until Dandenong Road and the *Astor Cinema* mark the start of St Kilda. Crossing Chapel Street at right angles in South Yarra, Toorak Road boasts equally ritzy designer boutiques, and, if that's possible, becomes even more exclusive east of Grange Road, as it enters Toorak, a suburb synonymous with wealth in Melbourne. Below Toorak, High Street Armadale, between Kooyong and Glenferrie roads, holds a concentration of antique shops. **Trams** #6 and #7 from Swanston Street will get you from the city to Chapel Street.

### South Yarra and Toorak

Among the boutiques and speciality shops, bistro bars for the beautiful people and drop-dead-cool nightclubs, the **Jam Factory** shopping complex, named after its former incarnation, is worth making a beeline for, on the **South Yarra** stretch of Chapel Street. **Como House**, overlooking the river from Como Avenue in South Yarra (daily 10am–5pm; $7), is a good example of the townhouses built by wealthy nineteenth-century landowners. The elegant white mansion, a mixture of Regency and Italianate architectural styles, has been restored by the National Trust. To reach the house, walk east along Toorak Road from Chapel Street, and then north on Williams Road, or, from the city centre, take tram #8 from Swanston Street.

Toorak has never been short of a bean: when Melbourne was founded, the wealthy chose to build their stately homes here on the high bank of the Yarra, leaving the flood-prone lower ground for the poor. This old money has in recent years been joined by new; many European Jews who worked hard after arriving penniless in Australia celebrated their new wealth by moving to Toorak in the 1950s and 1960s. There's little to see or do in the suburb: the hilly, tree-lined streets are full of huge mansions in extensive private gardens, while so-called Toorak Village is stuffed with wickedly expensive designer boutiques.

### Prahran

Beyond Commercial Road in **Prahran** proper, Chapel Street still focuses on fashion, but in a more street-smart vein, becoming progressively more downmarket and more interestingly ethnic the further south you go. Landmarks include **Prahran Market** (Tues & Thurs 8am–5pm, Fri 6am–6pm, Sat 7am–1pm), round the corner in Commercial Road, an excellent, though slightly expensive food emporium (fish, meat, fruit, vegetables and delicatessen). **Chapel Street Bazaar**, back on the main drag, has good secondhand clothes, Art Deco jewellery, furniture and bric-a-brac. **Greville Street**, off Chapel Street in the heart of Prahran, is a former hippy hangout turned respectable, with antique shops, antiquarian bookstores, retro clothes and groovy designer shops – very young and full of itself. On Saturdays and Sundays, small **Greville Street Market** hawks secondhand clothes, jewellery, arts and crafts, on the corner of Gratton Street in Gratton Park (noon–5pm).

## South Melbourne and Albert Park

If it's the bay you're heading for, then St Kilda is the obvious destination, but the quickest and most interesting way there is on the #96 tram from Bourke or Spencer Street, which runs on a light rail track via South Melbourne and Albert Park. Both are worth checking out in their own right if you have the time. **South Melbourne**'s focus is the **South Melbourne Market** on Coventry Street (Wed 7.30am–2pm, Fri 7.30am–6pm, Sat 7.30am–1pm, Sun 7am–4pm), an old-fashioned value-for-money place with new and secondhand clothes and books, as well as fruit and veg, and delicatessen stalls. Pleasant cafés line Coventry Street opposite the market, while not far away on Clarendon Street a few ancient shops survive virtually unaltered, complete with corrugated-iron awnings and iron-lace pillars.

**Albert Park** has the feel of a small village, with many lovely old terraced houses and Dundas Place, a shopping centre of mouth-watering delis and bakeries. In the shadow of the St Kilda Road office buildings lies Albert Park itself, the highly controversial site for the **Australian Grand Prix**, which Melbourne has snatched from

Adelaide. Many trees have been cut down already, but the developers will have to get a move on if they're to complete the track and grandstands in time for the first scheduled race in November 1996.

# St Kilda and around

The former seaside resort of **St Kilda** has an air of shabby gentility, which enhances its current schizophrenic reputation as a sophisticated yet seedy suburb, largely residential but blessed with a raging nightlife. Running from St Kilda Road down to the esplanade, **Fitzroy Street** is Melbourne's red-light district – usually pretty tame, though late at night not a comfortable place for women alone – and epitomizes this split personality: it's lined with dozens of thoroughly pretentious cafés and bars to gawp at the strip's goings-on. On weekend nights these and others throughout St Kilda are filled to overflowing with a style-conscious but fun crowd. During the day there's a very different feel, especially on **Acland Street** with its wonderful continental cake shops and bakeries. Ogling the mouthwatering window displays is a favourite way of passing the time on Sundays.

Also on Sunday, the **St Kilda Craft Market** (9am–5pm, in winter until about 4pm) lines the waterfront on Upper Esplanade. It's mainly arts and crafts, and not really good enough to justify the hordes of strollers, but it's part of the ritual, along with taking a look at the beach, feeding your face, ambling into a few shops, listening to a busker, and perhaps calling at the covered market on Albert Street. **Luna Park** on the Esplanade is a well-loved landmark, a tacky, old-fashioned fairground entered through a huge laughing clown's face. Wandering around is free, but you pay for individual rides, or $14 (child $11) for unlimited rides. You can sit under the palm trees of **O'Donnell Gardens**, next door, or nearby **St Kilda Botanical Gardens**, and eat your Acland Street goodies. The **beachfront** is a popular weekend promenade summer or winter, with separate cycling and walking paths stretching down to Elwood and Brighton, and a long pier thrusting out into the bay.

On Saturdays, Sundays and public holidays, **boat trips** from the pier across Hobsons Bay to Williamstown (*Williamstown Bay and River Cruises*; departures 11.30am, 12.30, 1.30, 2.30 & 3.30pm; 20min; $6 or $10 return; ☎9397 2255) are rewarded with lovely views of St Kilda and the city. A longer alternative is a cruise with *Penguin Waters Cruisers* (hourly departures until around midnight; 1hr; $15–20; ☎015/31 1922), on which, with a little luck, you'll catch a glimpse of **fairy penguins**, without the crowds that accompany them on Phillip Island (see pp.684–685).

If you want to get a bit more serious, call in at one of the busy bookshops on Acland Street, or check out the local arty community at the **Linden Gallery** (Tues–Sun 1–6pm), based in a fine Victorian-era mansion at 26 Acland Street, where painting, installations and video art are displayed.

## Elwood and Elsternwick

The next stop south along the bay, **Elwood**, is a quieter version of St Kilda, still with a faintly alternative air. Ormond Road's original shopfronts conceal a health-food store, an organic greengrocer, a couple of cafés and an alternative-therapies centre. Ormond Esplanade runs past thickly wooded parkland through which occasional paths run down to the beach.

East of Elwood, **Elsternwick** (train to Ripponlea) is a largely orthodox Jewish area, with a strong hippie presence as a sub-plot. The original 1918 fittings and facade of *Brinsmead Chemist* at 73 Glen Eira Rd are protected by the National Trust, as is **Ripponlea House** at 192 Hotham St (daily 10am–5pm; $7), which shows how Melbourne's wealthy elite lived a century ago. The 33-room mansion has magnificent gardens, complete with ornamental lake and fernery, and a way-over-the-top interior. The grounds are popular for picnics at weekends, when the tearoom is also open.

## Spotswood and Williamstown

Docks and industry dominate the area west of the city centre, reached by suburban train or by heading out on the Westgate Freeway across the huge Westgate Bridge. A good reason for visiting **Spotswood**, the first suburb across the Yarra, is **Scienceworks**, at 2 Booker St (daily 10am–4.30pm; $8). Inside the Space Age building, set in an appropriately desolate wasteland, the displays are ingenious, fun and highly interactive. Part of the exhibition consists of the original Spotswood Pumping Station, an unusually aesthetic early industrial complex with working steam pumps.

On a promontory at the mouth of the Yarra, **Williamstown** is a strange mix of very rich and very poor, of industry, yachting marinas and working port. Expensive cafés ring Nelson Place, but the down-to-earth *Yacht Club Hotel* here offers the cheapest meal in town – prices have been fixed since the 1970s and it's always packed on Sundays, especially when the **Williamstown Market** is held along the waterfront (third Sunday of every month). The most enjoyable way to get to Williamstown is by **boat** from St Kilda (see opposite). The trip up the Yarra from Williamstown to the World Trade Centre (Sat, Sun and public holidays at 4.15pm; $8; also *Williamstown Bay and River Cruises*; ☎9397 2255) passes through the docks and under Westgate Bridge, among others, ending up just below Spencer Street Bridge: it's fascinating and pleasantly uncommercial, with no commentary or pressure to buy anything.

## Eltham

**ELTHAM** is much further out, a bushy suburb 24km northeast of the city that's known as a centre for arts and crafts. Its reputation was established in 1935 when the charismatic painter and architect **Justus Jorgensen** moved to what was then a separate town and founded **Montsalvat**, a European-style artists' colony. Built with the help of his students and followers, the colony's eclectic design was inspired by medieval European buildings with wonderful quirky results; Jorgenson died before it was completed and it has deliberately been left unfinished. He did, however, live long enough to see his community thrive, and to oversee the completion of the mudbrick Great Hall, whose influence is evident in other mudbrick buildings around Eltham. Today Montsalvat, a two-kilometre walk from Eltham Station, is still operating as a colony of painters, potters and craftspeople, and can be visited daily (sunrise–sunset; $5). It's also used as a venue for concerts, the most important being the three-day **Montsalvat Jazz Festival** on the last weekend in January (☎9439 8771 for details).

# Eating and drinking

Melbourne is Australia's premier city for eating out: Sydney may be more stylish and Adelaide cheaper, but Melbourne has the best food and the widest choice of it, almost all exceptionally good value. In March each year, the city celebrates its pre-eminence with a **Food and Wine Festival**, in which the distinct ethnic areas host culinary street parties. In the **city centre**, Greek cafés line Lonsdale Street between Swanston and Russell streets, while Little Bourke Street is the home of Chinatown. Lygon Street in inner-city **Carlton** is just one of many pockets across the city with a concentration of Italian restaurants. Johnston Street in **Fitzroy** is the Spanish strip, while nearby up-and-coming Smith Street and arty Brunswick Street both have a huge variety of cuisines. Greek restaurants fill Swan Street in inner-city **Richmond**, and Vietnamese places dominate Victoria Street. Fitzroy and **St Kilda**, another gastronomically mixed bag, are the centres of café society; St Kilda also has great bakeries and delis, as does Jewish **Balaclava**.

Most of Melbourne's restaurants are BYO, and even the licensed ones generally allow you to bring your own drink – though check first, and note that a corkage fee ($1–2 per person) often applies. If you're going to be around for a while, *The Age Cheap Eats in Melbourne*, and its more upmarket companion, *The Age Good Food Guide*, are worthwhile investments.

## City centre

The centre is full of old-fashioned **coffee lounges**, the type of place where you can get a milky cappuccino and grilled cheese on toast, with a mini-jukebox at your table. In the department stores, both the *Myer* and *David Jones* food halls are excellent for upmarket picnic ingredients, while *Daimaru* has several good eating places on different levels, including a sushi bar and a Japanese restaurant.

**Cafee Baloo's**, 260 Russell St. An odd mixture of Italian pasta and Indian curries, but inexpensive and tasty. BYO. Open until 11pm.

**Cafe Segovia**, 33 Block Place, near Little Collins St. Very pleasant Spanish-style café, serving good coffee and excellent food. Licensed and BYO. Mon–Thurs 7.30am–7.30pm, Fri 7.30am–10pm, Sat 8.30am–5pm, Sun 10am–5pm.

**Campari Bistro Café**, 25 Hardware St. Casual and characterful, this daytime spot pulls in lawyers from the nearby courts with excellent southern Italian food: pasta weighs in at around $10, steaks and fish around $15, and breakfast is available. Closed Sun.

**Curry Bowl**, 250 Elizabeth St. Sri Lankan fast food to eat in or take away. Closed Sun.

**Florentino**, 80 Bourke St (☎9662 1811). A Melbourne institution, which divides loyalties between the cellar café-bar (Mon–Sat 8am–11.30pm), serving inexpensive, home-style pasta dishes, drinks and good coffee, and the very pricey and elegant Italian-French restaurant upstairs (closed Sat lunch and Sun). Licensed.

**Gopals**, 139 Swanston St. Cheap veggie place run by the Hare Krishnas. Closed Sun.

**Hopetoun Tea Rooms**, Block Arcade, near Collins St. Tea, scones and delicious cakes have been served in these elegant surroundings for more than 100 years, but new-fangled delicacies like *focaccia* with pesto sauce have now wheedled their way onto the menu. Closed Sat afternoons and Sun.

**Hyatt International Food Court**, 123 Collins St. Spacious, airy place, good for breakfast, where customers choose imaginative salads and other dishes from various stalls, and bars serve alcohol. Occasional jazz in the evening. Open Mon–Thurs until midnight, Fri & Sat until 2am.

**India House**, upstairs at 401 Swanston St. Tandoori and north Indian food, including inexpensive vegetarian dishes, in a relaxed atmosphere with friendly staff. Licensed and BYO. Lunch Mon–Fri, dinner Mon–Sat.

**Kappo Okita**, 17 Liverpool St (☎9662 2206). Modest Japanese café with excellent and inexpensive food, especially sushi and sashimi. Best to reserve for weekend evenings. BYO. Lunch Mon–Fri, dinner Mon–Sat.

**Medallion**, 209 Lonsdale St. Popular Greek café, once shabby, now with an over-the-top disco-style interior, but still serving authentic, cheap food. Daily until late (3am Fri & Sat).

**Metropolitan Cafe**, 36 Little Latrobe St. Upstairs café in a warehouse setting, serving good food with a vegetarian emphasis; popular for lunch. Licensed. Mon–Thurs 8am–6pm, Fri & Sat until 1am (kitchen closes at 10pm).

**Mietta's**, 7 Albert Place, off the upper end of Collins St near the *Regent* (☎9654 2366). Opulent restaurant serving French cuisine of very high standard. As an alternative to the *Windsor* (see below), you can take afternoon coffee and cake here in a rather more "continental" setting.

**Ong International Food Court**, basement of the *Welcome Hotel*, 256 Little Bourke St. Authentic Asian food court with stalls selling Chinese, Vietnamese, Malaysian/Singaporean and Thai food. licensed. Daily 10am–10pm.

**Pellegrini's Espresso Bar**, 66 Bourke St. Melbourne's first espresso bar is still an institution, crowded after work with chat and clatter: classic 1950s interior and great pasta. Open daily.

**Pure and Natural Food Company**, opposite Flinders St Station. Local chain whose motto is "fast food that's good for you" has twenty outlets in Melbourne; inexpensive, health-conscious and mainly vegetarian. Mon–Fri 6am–5.30pm, Sat 8.30am–2.30pm.

**Le Restaurant**, 35th Floor, *The Regent*, corner of Collins and Exhibition streets (☎9653 0000). Luxurious restaurant with silver service and fantastic views over Melbourne and Port Phillip Bay. Carefully prepared seasonal dishes, together with Australian produce such as barramundi and yabbies, at a price – expect to pay in the region of $70 per head (not including drinks). Dinner only, Tues–Sat from 7.30pm.

**Rosati's**, 95 Flinders Lane. Large bar-restaurant with the look of a revamped station waiting room; stylish though, and a good meeting place after the movies or theatre. Licensed. Daily 11am–12.30am (lunch not served on Sat).

**Satay Inn**, 250 Swanston Walk. Excellent affordable Malaysian, close to the big department stores. BYO. Daily lunch and dinner.

**Southgate**, across the river from Flinders St Station. With fine views of the river and the city skyline, this centre has developed into a very popular feeding and watering hole. On Fri and Sat nights advance booking is essential for the restaurants. Just to name a few good spots: *The Blue Train Café* (☎9696 0111), which serves drinks and tasty and very inexpensive light meals attracting a young, hip crowd; *Egusto* (☎9690 9819), which does "modern Australian" cuisine with an Italian slant; heading more upmarket, try *Walter's Wine Bar* (☎9690 9211), or *Simply French* (☎9699 9804), for excellent French food – leave some space for the brilliant desserts.

**Tokio Japanese Take Away**, Shop 16, The Causeway, off Bourke St Mall. Run by a young Japanese couple and tucked away in a side lane: good, very cheap Japanese food to eat in or take away. Closed Sunday.

**Tsindos**, 197 Lonsdale St. All the Greek classics from taramasalata to moussaka and souvlaki at reasonable prices, plus live bouzouki music every night except Sunday. Licensed and BYO. Lunch Mon–Fri, dinner Mon–Sun.

**Vialetto Caffe**, 75 Hardware St. Good-value weekday breakfasts (8–11am): freshly squeezed juices, muesli, croissants, and *focaccia* and free-range eggs as you like them with grilled bacon.

**Waiters Restaurant**, 20 Meyers Place, off Bourke St. Long-established Italian, once a waiters' favourite for its late hours; generous servings, low prices, no frills. BYO. Lunch Mon–Fri, dinner Mon–Sat till midnight.

**William Angliss College**, Latrobe St (☎9606 2111). Licensed restaurant with fine food and service. Incredibly cheap, but you're at the mercy of the catering students. Essential to book.

**The Windsor Hotel**, 103 Spring St (☎9653 0653). Afternoon tea in this Victorian-era hotel is absolutely traditional; plan to spend an hour or more luxuriating in the opulence.

## Chinatown

*Dim sum* (a series of small delicacies, served from trolleys) is available at lunchtime almost everywhere; on Sundays it's a crowded ritual.

**Camy Shanghai Dumpling and Noodle Restaurant**, Tattersalls Lane (between Little Bourke and Lonsdale streets, close to Swanston St). Extremely cheap, partly self-service spot, dishing up very simple, but delicious dumplings and noodles. No alcohol. Mon–Thurs 11am–8pm, Fri & Sat 11am–9pm.

**Empress of China**, 120–122 Little Bourke St (☎9663 1883). Expensive but good value, with lots of lesser-known dishes on offer. Licensed. Closed Sat lunchtime.

**Flower Drum**, 17 Market Lane, between Bourke and Little Bourke streets (☎9662 3655). Among some very good Chinese restaurants, this is simply outstanding: sophisticated Cantonese cuisine, including exquisite seafood and fish, but also expensive – about $110 for two, plus drinks. Licensed. Closed Sun lunchtime.

**King of Kings**, 209 Russell St. Simple, inexpensive Hong Kong-style food, including congee, and lots of dishes with pork and offal. BYO. Lunch and dinner daily, open until 2.30am.

**Kun Ming Cafe**, 212 Little Bourke St. A bustling café, one of the cheapest around. BYO. Open daily for lunch and dinner.

**Little Malaysia**, 26 Liverpool St. Cheap and good Malaysian hawker fare. BYO. Open daily for lunch and dinner.

**Shark Fin House**, 131 Little Bourke St. Converted warehouse with three storeys devoted to about fifty kinds of *dim sum*, all through the week, night and day.

# Carlton and North Melbourne

As well as an Italian strip of restaurants and cafés on Lygon Street, between Gratton and Elgin streets, Carlton is home to some great Asian restaurants; while, to the south of Carlton, North Melbourne harbours a gem of a Balinese place.

**Café Notturno**, 78 Lygon St. 24-hr pizza spot, crowded, noisy and smoky late at night.

**Ciro's**, 204 Lygon St. Best-value Italian in the area, with no frills.

**Nyonya**, 191 Lygon St. Authentic Nyonya cuisine, a blend of Malaysian and Chinese cooking, at moderate prices. BYO. Lunch and dinner daily.

**Shakahari**, 329 Lygon St. Excellent, imaginative vegetarian food, influenced by various Asian cuisines, at moderate prices. BYO. Mon–Thurs noon–10.30pm, Fri & Sat noon–11.30pm.

**Tiamo**, 303 Lygon St. One-time beatnik hang-out, still popular with students, with layers of browning 1950s posters, and a good-value blackboard menu. Mon–Sat 8am–11pm, Sun noon–8.45pm.

**Toto's Pizza House**, 101 Lygon St. Melbourne's first pizzeria, dating from the 1950s – cheap, cheerful and noisy. Daily noon–1.30am.

**Warung Agus**, 305 Victoria St (☎9329 1737). Authentic Balinese restaurant with superb, affordable food. BYO. Lunch Fri, dinner Tues–Sat.

# Fitzroy and Collingwood

Adjacent Fitzroy and Collingwood probably have the widest choice of cuisines in the city, and are good places to wind up at night, always with lots going on. Spanish bars and restaurants, often with flamenco music and dance, vie for attention on Johnston Street between Brunswick and Nicholson streets.

## Brunswick Street

**Afghan Gallery**, 327 Brunswick St. Amid Afghan hangings and rugs, cheap and authentic food, very popular with students. BYO. Dinner daily.

**Baker's Cafe**, 384 Brunswick St. In a lively, relaxed atmosphere – flickering candles at night and upbeat music – the huge, irresistible blackboard menu offers very good value. BYO. Daily 7am–10pm.

**Black Cat Cafe**, corner of Brunswick and Greeves streets. The prototype of the groovy Brunswick Street café: Fifties theme, jazz music, great noticeboard. Try the bagels and a "Spider", a speciality ice-cream soda. Daily 9am–1am.

**Mario's**, 303 Brunswick St. European-style café where you can eat breakfast – until midnight – lunch and dinner or just have a coffee or a drink. Dauntingly smart staff and decor, but not expensive or dressy; the clientele are an interesting mixture of posers, celebrities and scruffs.

**Nyala**, 113 Brunswick St. This, and its quieter branch in a historic bluestone terrace house in Greeves St (off Brunswick St), are the only places in Melbourne serving Ethiopian food, a tasty mix of Middle Eastern influences with Indian spices thrown in. BYO. Dinner Tues–Sat.

**Rhumbaralla's**, 342 Brunswick St. The neon sign in the window is one of the street's landmarks, and the inside of this stylish café is just as vibrantly coloured. The place hums to the sound of the ceiling fan, jazz music and conversation. Breakfast till midday – eggs benedict the favourite – then anything from *focaccia* to steak. Licensed and BYO. Daily 9am–1am.

**Shanti**, 285 Brunswick St. Unlike most other Melbourne Indian restaurants, this one specializes in southern Indian food, using coconut milk rather than cream and yoghurt, and offers lots of vegetarian options and seafood at moderate prices; the *dosas* are especially good value. Licensed and BYO (wine only). Lunch Mon–Fri, dinner daily.

**Thai Thani**, 293 Brunswick St (☎9419 6463). One of Melbourne's best Thai restaurants, on two crowded levels, with moderate prices. BYO. Dinner daily.

**The Vegie Bar**, 378 Brunswick St. Simple, fresh food cooked to order. Cheap, popular and hip rather than hippie: jazzy soul sounds and poster-covered walls. Daily noon–10pm.

## Johnston Street

**Carmen Bar**, 74 Johnston St. The best-value tapas bar in the area, usually full of Spanish people. Live flamenco Wed–Sat. Open Mon–Sat 6pm–late.

**Kahlo's**, 36 Johnston St. Smallish, cosy tapas bar. Wed–Sat 6pm–1am.

**Pinchos**, 11–13 Spring St, off Johnston St (☎9416 0303). Large Spanish restaurant and tapas bar, good for groups. Flamenco Thurs–Sat. Open Tues–Sun to 1am.

**La Tasca**, 42 Johnston St. Wines and sherries by the glass, and reasonable tapas. Live flamenco Thurs–Sun.

## Smith Street

**The Attic Bar**, 123 Smith St. Spacious café-bar, great for a late-night coffee or drink, with interesting, but slightly uncomfortable saw-log tables. Extensive blackboard menu of light meals, very good desserts and a good wine list – many available by the glass. Licensed. Lunch 11am–3pm, dinner 5.30pm–2am.

**Blonds, the Swedish Place**, 279 Smith St. Not everything on the menu is Swedish, but the excellent *gravlax* (marinated salmon), yeast dough rolls, beers and vodka certainly are. Rustic decor and cheery atmosphere. Licensed. Daily 9am–11pm.

**Cafe Coco**, 129 Smith St. Cosy spot, where the blackboard menu of inexpensive light meals, excellent cakes and good coffee, changes regularly. Licensed.

**Cafe Zahara**, 261a Smith St. Good-value Indonesian (Lombok- and Sumatra-inspired) and Malaysian dishes, such as *soto ayam* and *laksa*. No alcohol. Lunch Mon–Thurs & Sat, dinner daily to midnight.

**Caribbean Cafe**, 224 Gertrude St (just around the corner from Smith St). Simple, homely place, run by an ex-cricketer from Trinidad, doling out West Indian dishes like fish soup, coco mussels and goat curry, at moderate prices. BYO. Lunch Wed–Fri, dinner Mon–Sat.

**Ly Ly**, 183 Smith St. Simple Vietnamese café, serving excellent soups and some Chinese dishes. Closed Sun.

**Soul Food Vegetarian Cafe**, Smith St. Comfortable cafeteria-style place with wooden trestle tables, pine walls, and a good noticeboard at the back. Mon–Sat until 10pm.

**Vatan Gida Foodstore**, 131 Smith St. Excellent Turkish deli among a bevy of Turkish cafés.

# Richmond and eastern suburbs

Swan Street, running from Church Street towards Wattle Park, is home to Melbourne's best Greek restaurants. On the north side of Richmond, Victoria Street is lined with Vietnamese supermarkets, clothes shops, and dozens of cheap, authentic restaurants. In contrast, Hawthorn East harbours one of Melbourne's temples to gastronomy.

**Agapi**, 262 Swan St (☎9428 8337). Long-established inexpensive Greek restaurant. Licensed and BYO. Daily lunch and dinner.

**Hellas Cake Shop**, 324 Lennox St, off Swan St. Yummy Greek cakes and biscuits, which the friendly staff are happy to name and explain. Daily 9am–6pm.

**Stephanie's**, 405 Tooronga Rd, Hawthorn East (☎9822 8944). Renowned chef Stephanie Alexander's restaurant, considered one of the finest in the city and producing intensely flavoured, imaginative dishes. Located in a grand old mansion, this is the place to mark a very special occasion: it *is* expensive at about $170 per person for dinner, plus drinks, but lunch can be surprisingly affordable – around the $60 mark. Lunch Tues–Fri & Sun, dinner Tues–Sat. Booking essential.

**Tho Tho's Bar-restaurant**, 66 Victoria St. Much more upmarket than its Vietnamese neighbours, but usually packed and noisy. Inexpensive food, with the lunch specials offering especially good value. Licensed and BYO. Daily 11am–midnight.

**Thy Thy 1**, upstairs at 142 Victoria St (☎9429 1104). The most sought-after Vietnamese in the street always has queues: basic but great food. BYO.

**Thy Thy 2**, 116 Victoria St. Slightly upmarket from *Thy Thy 1*, but similar and also very popular. BYO. Daily 9am–11pm.

**Vao Doi**, 120 Victoria St. Another much-frequented Vietnamese place, with set lunch menus for the uninitiated.

## South Yarra, Prahran and Windsor

**Betelnut**, Shop 10, 168 Commercial Rd, opposite Prahran Market (☎9510 5760). Small, but very smartly designed café, though inconspicuous from the outside. Very tasty, reasonably priced Indonesian-Malaysian food. BYO. Dinner Mon–Sat until 10pm; booking recommended Fri and Sat.

**Cafe Feedwell**, 95 Greville St, Prahran. Melbourne's oldest vegetarian café, but certainly not an "alternative" cheapie any more. Tofu-based dishes, healthy pies and the like make a hefty meal, and they do good sandwiches, made from excellent homemade bread. BYO.

**Caffe e Cucina**, 581 Chapel St, South Yarra (☎9827 4139). One of Melbourne's coolest eating spots draws a smart clientele and dishes up fantastic pasta. Licensed.

**The Continental Cafe**, 132–134 Greville St, Prahran. Hugely popular restaurant and nightclub, with waistcoated waiters and an equally smart, arty clientele; breakfast all day, very good pasta dishes, and a wide range of wines and liqueurs. Licensed. Daily 7am–midnight.

**Falafel House**, 196 Toorak Rd, South Yarra. Middle Eastern takeaway, perfect after pubbing or clubbing. Daily 9am–5am.

**Giardino's Trattoria**, 341–345 Toorak Rd, South Yarra (☎9824 1444). Italian restaurant with huge servings, casual service, and lots of families.

**Helens Polish Coffee Lounge**, 134 Chapel St, Windsor. Simple, authentic Polish place open breakfast to dinner; great cakes (try the poppy-seed chocolate cake) and full meals.

**Lacota**, 278 Toorak Rd, South Yarra (☎9826 9030). This stylish eatery serves an intricately multicultural cuisine – sort of "East meets West meets South" – but it really works. Very good wine list, with many wines by the glass. Licensed. Daily 7am–1am.

**Poppy's**, 580 Chapel St, South Yarra. Delicious, inexpensive Thai fare with a good range of vegetarian dishes. Mon–Fri 9am–9pm, Sat noon–9.30pm, Sun 6.30–9.30pm.

**Samos Greek Taverna**, 120 Chapel St, Windsor (☎9510 4561). Plastic vines and fishing nets set the scene; excellent, moderately priced Greek food with music on the weekends, when you'll need to book.

**Tamani Bistro**, 156 Toorak Rd, South Yarra (☎9866 2575). Dimly lit, crowded Italian cheapie.

## South Melbourne, Albert Park and Port Melbourne

There's not much of a night-time scene in these suburbs, but cafés and delicatessens dish up a mouthwatering selection of Italian food during the day.

**Albert Park Deli**, 129 Dundas Place, Albert Park. Superb delicatessen takeaway, specializing in delicious breads and *arancini* (Italian rice balls).

**The Avenue Foodstore**, 69 Victoria Ave, South Melbourne. Brightly lit, breezy café with a huge glass-fronted counter piled with food. Daily 8am–8pm.

**Cafe Bombay**, 396 Bay St (continuation of City Rd), Port Melbourne. Long-running Indian restaurant that serves consistently good food, including plenty of vegetarian dishes. Licensed and BYO. Lunch Tues–Fri, dinner daily.

**Coventry Street Foodstore**, 315 Coventry St, opposite South Melbourne Market. Breakfast, cakes, savoury snacks and light lunches are all homemade, using natural ingredients. BYO. Tues–Thurs 8am–3.30pm, Sat & Sun 9am–5pm.

**Dundas Place Café**, 131 Dundas Place, Albert Park. Packed and noisy on weekday lunchtimes, for both its music and Italian gourmet delights.

**Villagio Continental Delicatessen**, Dundas Place, Albert Park. Gleaming shop full of all kinds of Italian food, with tables outside where you can eat your selections and drink coffee. Closed Sun.

## St Kilda

The current cool area of St Kilda is Acland Street, from *Greasy Joe's* to the *Dog's Bar* (see "Bars and pubs" below). Walk past on a Sunday and you'll be eyed up and down by the crowds sitting at the outdoor tables; late breakfast is a less intimidating obsession.

**Cicciolina**, 130 Acland St. Plain decor, lots of tables crammed in, Italian food with an interesting twist: the recipe for a roaring success. Licensed and BYO (wine only). Mon–Sat 9am–11pm, Sun until 10pm.

**Cleopatra's**, 1 Fitzroy St. Excellent Lebanese takeaway.

**Deluxe International Delicatessen**, 94 Acland St. Traditional deli jazzed up by new owners, with local artists brought in to work on the decor. Great espresso, adventurous food and excellent breakfasts. There are only a few stools, but in summer you can sit in the courtyard.

**The Esplanade Hotel**, 11 Upper Esplanade. The veggie restaurant at the back is casual and slow, with slapdash decor to match, but the excellent food is worth the wait.

**The Excellent**, 109 Acland St. Old-fashioned café, unconcerned with style, but still going strong: excellent for coffee and good old toasted sandwiches.

**Galleon Café**, 9 Carlisle St. Breakfast, served until 4pm, is the big thing here, especially popular at weekends; there's also a useful noticeboard. Mon–Fri 9am–midnight, Sat & Sun from 9.30am.

**The George**, corner of Fitzroy and Grey streets. Ultra-cool French-style brasserie that turned this seedy part of Fitzroy St around. Dinner is moderate to expensive, but breakfast is good value, and during the day or after dinner time you can come in just for a café au lait and one of their fantastic desserts. Licensed, with a great wine list (there's also a wine and bread shop). Daily 7am–11pm.

**Greasy Joe's**, 68 Acland St. Good greasy breakfast until 6pm, and a range of meaty and veggie burgers, which you can eat at pavement tables. At night it's little more than a bar. Daily until 1am.

**Monarch Cake Shop**, 103 Acland St. Mouth-watering continental patisserie.

**Nullfaur**, 213 Barkly St. Good and very inexpensive northern Indian food such as tandoori chicken, naan and samosas; there's zero decor, but most people take away. No alcohol. Tues–Sun noon–10pm, Mon from 4pm.

**The Pavilion**, 40 Jacka Boulevard (☎9534 8221). Upmarket (and expensive) seafood restaurant, though the menu does include some non-fish dishes. Situated in the old changing sheds, this is one of the few Melbourne restaurants with a view.

**Stokehouse**, 30 Jacka Boulevard. Located by the beach and packed in warm weather, the restaurant divides into two sections: downstairs is affordable with lots of unusual pizzas and pastas, fantastic cakes, coffee and wines; upstairs has better views of the bay, but is beyond most budgets. Licensed. Downstairs open Mon–Fri noon–11pm, Sat noon–1am, Sun 10am–11pm.

**Topolinos**, 87 Fitzroy St. A dimly lit, noisy and smoky St Kilda institution, which pumps out pizzas, good cocktails and generous pasta dishes until dawn.

**Waldorf Cafe Restaurant**, corner of Fitzroy and Grey streets. In the same location as *The George* (see above), but less pretentious: moderately priced, homely Italian food, or just coffee and cake. Licensed. Daily lunch and dinner.

**Wild Rice**, 211 Barkly St. Vegan macrobiotic café with a lovely courtyard garden. Daily noon–10pm.

## Elwood and Balaclava

Elwood's easygoing haunts are similar to St Kilda's, while Balaclava, to the east along Carlisle Street, specializes in inexpensive kosher food.

**Cafe Tarrango**, 15 Ormond Rd, Elwood. Indian-run café, with delicious organic, biodynamic vegetarian food but not much atmosphere.

**Cafe Zuni**, 402 Barkly St (near Ormond Esplanade), Elwood. Variety of breakfasts are served until 5pm; lunch and dinner is typical Melbourne "East meets West" cuisine, such as lamb curry and olive gnocchi. Licensed and BYO. Daily from 7am until late.

**Glicks**, 330A Carlisle St, Balaclava. Very friendly spot, renowned for bagels and traditional Jewish savouries: try *kreplach*, *latkes* or *gefilte fish*. Sun–Thurs 6am–9pm, Fri till sunset, closed Sat.

**Haymisha Kosher Bakery**, 320 Carlisle St, Balaclava. Jewish bakery with good wholemeal and rye breads, bagels, onion rolls, cakes, doughnuts and a large variety of cookies. Closed Sat.

**Mussels Fish and Chippery**, 37 Glenhuntly Rd, Elwood. Perfect for a beach lunch, a takeaway with an emphasis on quality – you can even get marinated grilled baby octopus.

**Tibetan Himalaya Restaurant**, 8–10 Glen Eira Avenue, off Glen Eira Rd, near Ripponlea Station. Inexpensive Tibetan cuisine in a very friendly, no-frills restaurant. BYO. Dinner Tues–Sun.

**Turtle Café**, 34 Ormond Rd, Elwood. Relaxed old corner café with soft jazz and good food.

# Nightlife and entertainment

Melbourne prides itself on being a cultural city with intellectual leanings, so there's a rich arts and music scene and always plenty to do in the evening. To find out **what's on** check out *The Age* on Friday, when it publishes a comprehensive entertainment guide, *EG* – much better than *Sun-Herald*'s Thursday supplement. *Melbourne Events* is a handy, and surprisingly hip, free monthly guide to all sorts of happenings, published by Melbourne Council and available at tourist information outlets.

Annual festivals further enliven the scene: the **Melbourne International Festival** in October concentrates on mainstream visual and performing arts, with a sprinkling of good concerts and opera; the much more experimental and innovative **Melbourne Fringe Festival** happens more or less at the same time, as does the **Melbourne Writers' Festival**. The heavily promoted **Moomba Festival**, held during the first half of March, has events including firework displays and dragon boat races on the banks of the Yarra in Alexandra Gardens, but is actually rather drab and commercial. Three music festivals occupy the first half of the year: the **Montsalvat International Jazz Festival** in the last week of January, at venues in Eltham and the city centre; the **Melbourne Music Festival** in February, one of the largest Australian festivals of contemporary music; and the **Brunswick Music Festival** in the third week of March, concentrating on folk and world music. The **Next Wave Festival**, held over two weeks in the second half of May, celebrates Victoria's young artists, writers and musicians.

**Tickets** for most things can be booked through *Bass* (☎11500, for credit card bookings only), which has an outlet at the Victorian Arts Centre (Mon–Sat 9am–9pm). You can buy tickets half-price on the day of performance from the *Half Tix* booth, in the Bourke Street Mall (Mon & Sat 10am–2pm, Tues–Thurs 11am–6pm, Fri 11am–6.30pm; cash only; ☎9654 9420).

## Bars and pubs

The distinction between restaurant, bar, café and nightclub is often blurred, but not at the handful of pub breweries, where a range of beers is made on the premises. Most hotel bars are closed on Sunday in the city centre, though not in the suburbs. (See also "Live music" below.)

### City centre

**Charles Dickens Tavern**, downstairs, Block Court, 290 Collins St. A place for homesick Brits with bitter and Guinness on tap, pint glasses and live soccer. Licensed to 3am.

**DBs Food Court and Bars**, *Sportsgirl Centre*, Collins St. Crowded and lively Friday night spot with free up-and-coming bands and a happy hour 5–9pm.

**Giardini Café Bar**, 14 Bourke St. Small wine bar painted with frescos in bold, Mediterranean colours, which serves breakfast and light meals.

**Le Monde**, 18 Bourke St. Slick café-bar, dishing up tasty food, at the lively end of Bourke St. Open 24hr.

**The Lounge**, 243 Swanston Walk. Genuine all-rounder, attracting an arty-grungy crowd: bar, nightclub (see "Clubs" below) with live music, and good, cheap food in the upstairs restaurant – eat al fresco on the terrace.

**Mitre Tavern**, 5 Bank Place. Long-established watering-hole, popular with office workers.

**Ruby Red**, 9 Drewery Lane (off Lonsdale St, close to Melbourne Central). Bar and Cajun restaurant, often featuring good jazz and blues.

### North Melbourne, Carlton and Fitzroy

**Gypsy Bar**, 334 Brunswick St, Fitzroy. Intimate bar crammed with Brunswick Street's finest, especially for jazz on Sunday nights; great coffee and food. Daily 9.30am–1am.

**Lemon Tree**, 10 Grattan St, Carlton. Upmarket bar which often features live jazz and has a fine beer garden.

**Lord Newry**, 543 Brunswick St, North Fitzroy. The cosy front bar with an open fire is a good place for conversation; delicious food is served upstairs, where anything from poetry readings to jazz might happen.

**Pumphouse Hotel**, 128 Nicholson St, Fitzroy. Pub brewery, very popular with backpackers from the nearby hostel, *The Nunnery*.

**The Redback Brewery**, 75 Flemington Rd, North Melbourne. Slick boutique brewery packed out on weekends with the striped-shirt brigade, but worth persevering as *Redback*, the house beer, is one of the tastiest around.

### Richmond, South Yarra and Prahran

**All Nations Hotel**, 64 Lennox St, off Swan St, Richmond. Old-style Aussie pub with exceptional bar meals and a relaxing beer garden.

**Arcadia**, corner of Punt St and Toorak Rd, South Yarra. Silent black-and-white movies are projected while a jukebox blasts through the café atmosphere; play board games in the reading room, pool or pinball, scoff cake, or swig coffee and boutique beer to escape. Daily 11am–1am.

**Black Match**, 545 Church St, Richmond. Favourite university students' haunt with neo-punk decor.

**Fawkner Club**, 52 Toorak Rd, South Yarra. Swanky pub with a great beer garden, though it's hard to get a seat on a sunny day.

**Station Tavern and Brewery**, 96 Greville St, Prahran. Look out for the train dramatically bursting through the facade – it's rumoured Kylie used to drink here, and the place is still full of young wannabes.

### St Kilda

**Angelucci's**, 42 Fitzroy St, St Kilda. Pretentious bar-restaurant that replaced the *Catani Bar*, purveying reliable pastas and wine.

**Cafe Menis**, 16 Fitzroy St, St Kilda. Café-bar, crowded on weekends, serving everything from drinks, through snacks to full meals.

**Dog's Bar**, 54 Acland St, St Kilda. The coolest spot on St Kilda's strip.

**The George**, corner of Fitzroy and Acland streets, St Kilda. Hip, but one of St Kilda's roughest pubs, retaining the classic "hose-down" tile interior.

## Live music

Melbourne has a thriving band scene, in which just about every pub puts some sort of music on at some time in the week, often free. The pubs listed are also good places for a drink, and always contain at least two bars so you can escape the din if you want to. Grungy Richmond has a big concentration of music pubs with several into African and reggae music; Fitzroy and St Kilda are the other areas to head to for a range of live music. The free listings magazines, *Beat* and *Inpress*, are good sources of info about the local band scene; you can pick them up at most record shops. Local FM stations *Triple R* (102.7) and *PBS* (106.7) air alternative music and tell you what's on where.

### City centre and the northern suburbs

**Africa Bar & Club**, 99 Smith St, Collingwood. African restaurant that turns into a nightclub Fri and Sat, featuring African and world music.

**Bennetts Lane**, 25 Bennetts Lane (a small alley off Little Lonsdale St in the CBD, between Exhibition and Russell streets). One of Melbourne's most interesting jazz venues, in a cramped, Fifties-style cellar.

**Brunswick East Club Hotel**, 280 Lygon St, Brunswick East. Headquarters of the Melbourne Folk Club.

**The Club**, 132 Smith St, Collingwood. Well-known Australian bands play downstairs; free entry to jazz and blues in the upstairs bar until 2am. Fri and Sat 9pm–7am.

**Dan O'Connell's**, 225 Canning St (between Rathdowne and Nicholson streets), Fitzroy. Irish music Wed–Sun; free.

**Grace Darling Hotel**, 114 Smith St, Collingwood. Pleasant watering hole, which sometimes features live jazz and R&B.

**Jazz Lane**, 290 Lonsdale St, city centre. New jazz venue in a basement bar-bistro.

**McCoppins Hotel**, 166 Johnston St, Fitzroy. Live R&B, blues and jazz in the Music Room.

**The Punters Club**, 376 Brunswick St, Fitzroy. One of the nerve centres of the Melbourne band scene, with well-known independent bands nightly; usual cover charge $5.

**The Rainbow**, 27 St David St, Fitzroy. Mellow atmosphere, interesting crowd and decor in an intimate bar with free music – eclectic jazz, funk and fusion – every night.

**The Tote**, 71 Johnston St, Fitzroy. Hardcore thrash.

## Richmond and the southern suburbs

**Bridge Hotel**, 642 Bridge Rd, Richmond. Jazz, reggae and African music.

**Central Club Hotel**, 293 Swan St, Richmond. Alternative independent bands.

**Cherry Tree Hotel**, 53 Balmain St, Richmond. Scores of tribute bands trying to make their vicarious mark.

### GAY AND LESBIAN MELBOURNE

Melbourne's gay scene may not be as upfront as Sydney's, but it's almost as formidable; this is such a diverse city that gays and lesbians seem just two more of the different groups that give the city its easy-going, multifarious feel.

The scene in Melbourne is less ghettoized than in Sydney. That said, **Fitzroy**, **Collingwood** and **Carlton**, north of the river, and **St Kilda**, **South Yarra** and **Prahran**, to the south, boast a strong male presence; lesbians are everywhere, but **Fitzroy**, **Northcote** and **Clifton Hill** are Melbourne's recognized stomping grounds. There are two gay and lesbian free **papers** to help you navigate new waters: the well-established *Melbourne Star Observer*, published weekly, and the sparky, fortnightly newcomer, *Brother Sister*. There's also a monthly lesbian newsletter, *Labrys*, available from *Shrew Women's Bookshop* ($5).

Big **events** are mostly organized by the *ALSO Foundation*, including two over the Australia Day weekend at the end of January – Red Raw and WOW (Women's Own Warehouse). The scene's annual highlight, however, has to be the fabulous **Midsumma Festival** in late January and early February. Already in its seventh year, Midsumma provides an umbrella for a wide range of sporting, artistic and theatrical events and coincides with the **International Lesbian and Gay Film and Video Festival**. The Queen's Birthday in June is celebrated at the Winter Daze party and while the whole city is taking a day off to celebrate Melbourne Show Day in September, the Show Off dance party is the place to be.

#### ORGANIZATIONS, SUPPORT GROUPS AND BOOKSHOPS

Melbourne is blessed with a dazzling variety of gay and lesbian organizations, support services and businesses, the most important of which are listed below. Everything else, from gay vets to lesbian psychologists, can be found in the *ALSO Directory*.

**AIDS organizations and medical care** *ACTUP Melbourne*, Carlton Community House, corner of Wilson & Park streets, North Carlton (☎9650 3812), meets Monday evenings; *Gay Men's Health Centre* (☎9483 6777), 117 Johnston Street, Collingwood; *People Living With Aids* (☎9525 4455); *Positive Women* (☎9347 0244), run by and for women with HIV, through the *Melbourne Sexual Health Centre* (see p.677); *Victoria AIDS Council* (☎9483 6700), 117 Johnston Street, Collingwood; *Victoria AIDS Line* (☎9419 3166), telephone-counselling, referral and information Mon–Fri 11am–10pm, Sat & Sun 11am–2pm & 7–11pm.

**ALSO Foundation** 4th Floor, 247 Flinders Lane, city centre (☎9650 8157): organizes events and publishes the *ALSO Directory*, free from community outlets.

**Continental Cafe**, Greville St, Prahran. Smart venue for established and up-and-coming artists.

**The Esplanade Hotel**, 11 Upper Esplanade, St Kilda. The "Espie" is the soul of St Kilda and of Melbourne's eclectic band scene (huge bouncers make it look rougher than it actually is). Interesting nightly menu of free bands in the front bar; admission charged to see bands in the Gershwin Room.

**The Palace**, Lower Esplanade, St Kilda (next to the *Palais*). Entertainment complex with big-name bands in the main room, smaller bands in the pool room, and a club at the rear.

**Prince of Wales Hotel**, Fitzroy St, St Kilda. Seedy late-nighter with good bands; gay bar upstairs.

## Clubs

Promoters hand out passes for reduced or free admission to a rapidly changing array of clubs on the corner of Bourke and Russell streets, or you can pick them up in record shops like *Gaslight* further up Bourke Street. King Street, in the CBD between Collins Street and Flinders Lane, has a handy concentration of clubs.

**The Bull Ring**, 95 Johnston St, Fitzroy. The best place to dance to Latin rhythms; the band starts at 10.30pm, the dancefloor show at 11pm.

**Gay and Lesbian Party Line** ☎190/12494.

**Gay and Lesbian Switchboard** ☎9650 7711: telephone-counselling, information and referral.

**Gay and Lesbian What's On** ☎190/12505 (24hr recorded information).

**Gay Information Line** ☎190/12504 (24hr recorded information).

**Hares and Hyenas**, 135 Commercial Rd, Prahran (☎9824 0110). Gay and lesbian bookshop.

**Lesbian Information Line** ☎190/12506 (recorded information 24hr).

**Lesbian Line** ☎9416 0850: run by the *Women's Liberation Switchboard*, counselling and support Thurs 6–10pm.

**Midsumma Festival** Offices at the *Cosmopolitan Motor Inn*, 6 Carlisle St, St Kilda (☎9534 0781); hotline ☎190/10190.

**Shrew Women's Bookshop** 37 Gertrude St, Fitzroy (☎9419 5595).

**Victorian Network** ☎9650 5103 (for under 26s).

**Women's Book Exchange**, 10 Smith St, Fitzroy (☎9417 7989).

**Women's Information and Referral Exchange (WIRE)** ☎9654 6844: information about lesbian groups, referral to feminist doctors, solicitors, etc.

CAFÉS AND MEETING PLACES

**The Angel Café**, 362 Brunswick St, Fitzroy (☎9417 2271). Run by women, this place is extremely popular with the Fitzroy lesbian scene. 7am–11pm; closed Tues.

**Café Baghdad**, 151 Commercial Rd, Prahran (☎9826 5336). Small but beautifully formed gay and lesbian café – worth waiting, especially when the belly dancers are unveiled. Daily till 1am.

**Globe Café**, 218 Chapel St, Prahran (☎9510 8693). Good choice for a well-deserved treat after a hard morning's browsing on Chapel Street.

**Oscar's Wilde Café**, 147 Commercial Rd, Prahran (☎9827 6260). Cosy, inexpensive café in the heart of gay Prahran; international dishes (Cajun, curries, stir-fries and Mediterranean) served in generous portions. Licensed and BYO (wine only).

**Street Café**, 23 Fitzroy St, St Kilda (☎9525 4655). Upmarket café, bar and restaurant located in the heart of the St Kilda scene.

*See also p.648 for gay- and lesbian-friendly places to stay and p.674 for gay and lesbian nightspots.*

**Carousel**, Aughtie Drive, South Melbourne. Dance venue playing good acid jazz and funk.

**Chasers**, 386 Chapel St, South Yarra. One of several clubs full of bright young things on this fashion-conscious street.

**Lizard Lounge**, *The Union Hotel*, 90 Chapel St, Windsor. Alternative indie club. Thurs–Sat 9pm–3am.

**The Lounge**, 243 Swanston Walk, city centre. Grungy club with bands, films, pool, dance floor and a cool-off balcony. 6pm–3am most nights, to 6am Fri and Sat.

**The Metro**, 20 Bourke St, city centre. Huge old theatre on three floors with eight bars and three dance floors, all very lavish. Enormous queue of spivved-up kids on Friday night. Fri & Sat $10.

**The Ritz**, 169 Fitzroy St, St Kilda. Dressy twenty- and thirty-somethings dance to Seventies rock.

## Gay and lesbian nightspots

**Club 80**, 10 Peel St, North Melbourne. Melbourne's largest, sleaziest male cruising bar. Seven days till late – weekdays from 8pm, weekends from 2pm. Cover charge.

**Flavour**, 28 Warburton Lane, off Little Bourke St, city centre. Gay and lesbian piano and cocktail bar, with drag shows and other live entertainment. Daily.

**Girl Bar**, *Commerce Club*, 328 Flinders St, city centre. Every second Friday.

**Glasshouse Hotel**, 51 Gipps St, Collingwood (☎9419 4748). Sociable pub which attracts a mixed crowd during the week. Saturdays are women-only, Sundays for men; 11am till late.

**Laird Hotel**, 149 Gipps St, Collingwood (☎9417 2832). Well-equipped boys' venue, with two bars, DJs, a beer garden and games room. Bootscooting (country line-dancing) and barbecues on Sun. Popular with the leather crowd. Daily from 5pm, cheap drinks until 10 pm.

**Peel Hotel**, 113 Wellington St, off Johnston St, Collingwood (☎9419 4762). Bar, dance floor and recovery garden, drawing a large and appreciative crowd of gays and lesbians. Daily 8pm till late.

**Prince of Wales Hotel**, Fitzroy St, St Kilda. This gay pub is the venue for some of the city's best club nights, including *Sailors* on Sun – great live shows and laser displays – and *Scandal* for women on the third Sat of each month. Cover charges.

**Stewarts Hotel**, corner of Elgin & Drummond streets, Carlton (☎9387 2862). Mixed dance venue with live entertainment. Women-only on Friday nights, 8pm–1am. No cover.

**Tasty**, 328 Flinders Lane, city centre. Mixed crowd takes over the bar and pool room Sat 10pm–late.

**3 Faces**, 143 Commercial Rd, South Yarra (☎9826 0933). Excellent dance club with weekly menu of top-notch drag shows, karaoke nights and talent quests. Tues–Sun 8pm–3am. No cover.

**The Tote**, corner of Wellington & Johnston streets, Collingwood (☎9419 5320). Women's night Thurs 8pm–3am.

**12 Bar**, 12 MacKillop St, city centre (☎9670 0445). Newly opened restaurant-bar, with a dance floor and pool tables. Daily noon until late, mixed.

**The Victoria Hotel**, 380 Victoria St, Brunswick (☎9380 1853). Women-only bar with a café menu and live music; B&B accommodation available.

**Xchange Hotel**, 119 Commercial Rd, South Yarra (☎9867 5144). Traditional male-dominated joint showing videos and drag acts. Daily from midday.

# Comedy

Melbourne is the **comedy capital** of Australia, home of the madcap *Doug Anthony All Stars*, *Wogs Out of Work* and comedians from TV shows like *The Big Gig* and *The Comedy Company*. The highlight of the comedy year is the **Age Comedy Festival** (April), based at the *Athenaeum Theatre*, 88 Collins St, and the *Universal Theatre*, 13 Victoria St, Fitzroy, with performances at several other venues around town; as well as local and interstate acts, you're liable to see some of the best stand-up comedians from overseas.

**The Comedy Café**, 177 Brunswick St, Fitzroy (☎9419 2869). The most established comedy club.

**Comedy Club**, 380 Lygon St, Carlton (☎9348 1622). Slick, cabaret-style space which features largely mainstream comedians.

**The Esplanade Hotel**, 11 Upper Esplanade, St Kilda. Occasional stand-up comedy shows on weekends.

**The Last Laugh**, 64 Smith St, Collingwood (☎9417 7711). Theatre-restaurant that's been hosting comedy for years.

# Theatre

Melbourne has a rich dramatic life from fringe to mainstream, with venues all over the place. Watch out for outdoor performances in summer; there's usually an al fresco Shakespeare and something for children through December and January in the Royal Botanic Gardens (☎9655 2300 for details; credit-card bookings on ☎11500).

**CUB Malthouse**, 113 Sturt St, South Melbourne (☎9685 5111). The renovated malthouse contains two venues: the Beckett and the larger Merlyn Theatre. The resident company is the *Playbox Theatre Centre* which produces contemporary Australian plays; guest performances include opera, dance, concerts and readings.

**La Mama**, 205 Faraday St, Fitzroy (☎9347 6142). Plays by new writers, as well as poetry and play readings.

**Napier St Theatre**, 199 Napier St, South Melbourne (☎9699 9720) Small theatre which stages modern plays.

**Playhouse Theatre**, Victorian Arts Centre, 100 St Kilda Rd (☎9617 8211). Mainstream productions, mainly from the *Melbourne Theatre Company*.

**Princess Theatre**, 163 Spring St, city centre (☎9662 2911). Lavish musicals in a fabulously ornate old theatre.

**Russell Street Theatre**, 19 Russell St, city centre (☎9654 4000). Combination of new Australian drama, productions of recent overseas plays and classics.

**Theatreworks**, 14 Acland St, St Kilda (☎9534 4879). Ground-breaking new Australian plays.

## Classical music, opera and dance

The **Melbourne Symphony Orchestra** has a season from February to December based at the Melbourne Concert Hall and at the Melbourne Town Hall on Collins Street, while the **State Orchestra of Victoria** performs less regularly at the Concert Hall, often featuring works by Australian composers. If you can't afford to go, you can listen to Symphony Orchestra concerts broadcast on Tuesday at 7pm on *Radio 3MBS* (103.5FM).

**George Fairfax Studio**, Victorian Arts Centre, 100 St Kilda Rd (☎9617 8211). Modern dance and plays.

**Her Majesty's Theatre**, 219 Exhibition St, city centre (☎9663 3211). Occasionally hosts some of the great foreign ballet companies.

**Melbourne Concert Hall**, Victorian Arts Centre, 100 St Kilda Rd (☎9617 8211). Big-name concerts.

**State Theatre**, Victorian Arts Centre, 100 St Kilda Rd (☎9617 8211). Venue for the Victoria State Opera and the Australian Ballet Company.

## Film

The **International Film Festival** in June (☎9417 2011) has been going for over forty years and is the centrepiece of Melbourne movie life, based at the glorious Art Deco *Astor Theatre* and other cinemas around Melbourne. Everyday mainstream cinemas are concentrated on Bourke Street, where discount day is usually Tuesday; independent cinemas tend to discount on Mondays.

**Astor Theatre**, corner of Chapel St and Dandenong Rd, St Kilda (☎9510 1414). Classic double bills and prestige new releases; on Saturday nights there's a pianist and singer between films.

**Brighton Bay Twin Cinemas**, 294 Bay St, Brighton (☎9596 3590). Very comfortable setting for European and arthouse films. Cheap Mon.

**Carlton Moviehouse**, 235 Faraday St, Carlton (☎9347 8909). Over 70 years old, the inner city's oldest cinema has a lot of charm; arthouse and foreign films. Cheap Mon.

**Chinatown Cinema Complex**, Bourke St, between Swanston and Russell streets, city centre. Two theatres showing Chinese films, all subtitled.

**Cinema Nova**, Lygon Court Plaza, 380 Lygon St, Carlton (☎9347 8909). Arthouse and European films; come just before the show starts to avoid prolonged exposure to the awful crimson and purple bordello decor.

**Como**, Gaslight Gardens, corner of Toorak Rd and Chapel St, South Yarra (☎9827 7533). In the same chain as the *George Cinema* in St Kilda and *Brighton Bay Twin* – and shows similar films.

**The George**, 133–137 Fitzroy St, St Kilda (☎9534 6922). Latest releases on the border between arthouse and mainstream.

**Glasshouse Cinema**, Royal Melbourne Institute of Technology, 360 Swanston St, city centre (☎9417 5320). On-campus cinema for arthouse and experimental film.

**Kino**, 45 Collins St, city centre (☎9650 2100). In the opulent Collins Place atrium, with several cafés and bars in the complex. Stylish, arty new-release films. Half-price Mon.

**Longford Cinema**, 59 Toorak Rd, South Yarra (☎9867 2700). Exclusive release for quality films, somewhere between arthouse and mainstream. Late films Fri and Sat. Cheap Mon.

**Lumiere**, 108 Lonsdale St, city centre (☎9639 1055). Arthouse movies.

**State Theatre**, 1 MacArthur St, city centre (☎9651 1301). The *AFI* (*Australian Film Institute*) cinema buff's cinema; often shows Australian films.

**Trak Cinema**, 445 Toorak Rd, Toorak (☎9827 9333). European films.

**Valhalla Cinema**, 89 High St, Northcote (☎9482 2001). Art Deco period piece, decorated by the planner of Canberra, Walter Burley Griffin. Cult classics, new releases and late shows.

# Listings

**Airlines** The offices of several domestic airlines are in Franklin St near the interstate bus terminal. *Air New Zealand* (☎9602 5900), *Alitalia* (☎9670 0171), *Ansett* (☎13 1300), *British Airways* (☎9672 1100), *Canadian Airlines* (☎9629 6731), *Cathay Pacific* (☎13 1747), *Continental* (☎9321 6858), *Garuda* (☎9654 2522), *Japan Airlines* (☎9654 2733), *Kendell* (☎9670 2677), *KLM* (☎9654 8344), *Lufthansa-Lauda Air* (☎9602 5144), *Malaysian Airlines* (☎9279 9999), *Olympic* (☎9629 2411), *Philippine Airlines* (☎9654 3633), *Qantas* (international ☎9805 0111; domestic ☎13 1313), *Singapore Airlines* (☎9602 4555), *Thai International* (☎9650 7522), *United* (☎9602 2544).

**Airport bus** *Skybus* (☎9335 2811) departs roughly every half hour from bay 30 at Spencer Street Bus Terminal (see "Arrival and information", p.643 for more).

**American Express** 105 Elizabeth St (Mon–Fri 8.30am–5.30pm, Sat 9am–noon).

**Banks and foreign exchange** All major banks can be found in Collins St; the *Bank of Melbourne* is open later than others (Mon–Fri 9am–5pm, Sat 9am–noon). Even longer hours for foreign exchange at *Thomas Cook*, 261 Bourke St (Mon–Fri 8.45am–5.15pm, Sat 9am–4pm, Sun 10am–4pm, public holidays 10am–3pm; ☎9654 4222).

**Bicycles** There are few outlets for renting bikes. *Hire a Bicycle* (☎9758 5160) park a truck-full of cycles beneath Princes Bridge daily 11am–5pm in fine weather – basically for trundling along the river bank, but they may do a longer-term deal. Bike shops include *St Kilda Cycles*, 11 Carlisle St, where you can rent bikes (☎9534 3074); and *Melbourne Bicycle Centre*, 179 High St, Prahran (☎9529 3910).

**Books** Mainstream bookshops, all of them with many branches all over the city and suburbs, are: *Angus & Robertson*, 107 Elizabeth St; the discount shop *Book City*, 191 Bourke St; *Collins Booksellers*, 115 Elizabeth St; and *Dymocks*, corner of Bourke and Swanston streets. One of Melbourne's best literary bookshops is *Readings*, 338 Lygon St, Carlton, now with several branches. In Fitzroy, Brunswick St has the very good *Brunswick St Bookstore*, no. 305 (daily 10am–11pm), and *Grub St Bookshop* at no. 317 for secondhand books, while at 37 Gertrude St is the *Shrew Women's Bookshop*. Toorak Rd, South Yarra, has another good *Readings* at no.153, and *Black Mask Books* at no. 78, which has a general selection but specializes in mystery and crime fiction. St Kilda also has several bookshops including the comprehensive *Mary Martin*, 160 Acland St; the more intriguing *Cosmos Books and Music*, 112 Acland St; and secondhand bookshop *The Book Cave*, 183 Barkly St (daily 10.30am–6pm), which specializes in New Age and mystery, but also has a small selection of other books. In the city centre, *The Paperback* at 60 Bourke St is tiny but crammed and open until 11pm nightly; also very good is *The Hill of Content*, 86 Bourke St; *Bowyangs*, 372 Little Bourke St (Mon–Fri 9am–5.30pm, Sat 10am–2pm) specializes in travel books and maps; and the *Australiana*

*Book and Map Shop*, 46 Bourke St, is as its name suggests (other branches at 27 Elizabeth St and 274 Lonsdale St).

**Buses** Each of the bus companies which operate out of Spencer Street and Franklin Street terminals maintains an office at the relevant terminal, where you can buy last-minute tickets (*V/Line* reservations daily 7am–9pm; ☎13 2232). However, it's much easier to go to the *Bus Booking Centre*, 44 Spencer St (☎9629 3848), or to *Interstate and Country Bus Services*, Shop 14, 177 Flinders St, opposite Flinders St Station (☎9654 8477), who will shop around for you (with no booking fee); they can generally unearth the cheapest deals, and also sell bus passes and make bookings for the several good minibus tours to Sydney or Adelaide (see "Tours", below). City bus information from the *Met Transport Information Centre* (see p.644).

**Cameras** *Camera Action*, 217 Elizabeth St (☎9670 6901), is an excellent all-round camera shop.

**Car rental** *Budget*, 398 Elizabeth St (☎9639 2344); *Delta*, 85 Franklin St (☎9662 2022); *Dollar*, 206 Barkly St, St Kilda (☎9525 5511); *Hertz*, 97 Franklin St (☎9663 6244); *Murphy*, 341 Burnley St, Richmond (☎9427 7711); *National*, corner of Queensberry & Peel streets (☎9329 5000; one-way rentals possible); *Network*, corner of Willsmere Rd & Earl St, Kew (☎9853 6766; one-way rentals possible). Used-car companies with cheaper rates include *Rent-A-Bomb*, 507 Bridge Rd, Richmond (☎9428 0088), and *Ugly Duckling,* 197 Inkerman St, St Kilda (☎9525 4010). Campervans are available from *Motorhome Rentals* (☎9787 7943 or free call 1800/33 8817).

**Consulates** *Denmark*, 7 Acacia Ave, Brooklyn (☎9894 1383); *Netherlands*, 499 St Kilda Rd (☎9867 7933); *Norway*, 120 Collins St, Armadale (☎9654 8020); *UK*, 90 Collins St (☎9650 4155); *USA*, 553 St Kilda Rd (☎9526 5900).

**Disabled travellers** *Disabled Persons Information Bureau*, 115 Victoria Parade, Fitzroy (☎9412 7176); *Disability Resource Centre*, 381 Burnley St, Richmond (☎9428 8911); *Para Quad Association*, 208 Wellington St, Collingwood (☎9417 7400 or ☎ free call 1800/80 5384). The *Disability Services* of the Public Transport Corporation can be called on for assistance in using public transport (☎ free call 1800/01 3920 for metropolitan and suburban stations, ☎9619 2251 for Spencer St and country stations). Melbourne City Council produces a free mobility map showing access and facilities in the city centre, available from the Town Hall.

**Diving** *Associated Divers*, 1292 Centre Rd, Clayton (☎9544 9002) have equipment and run courses.

**Emergency** ☎000 for fire, police or ambulance.

**Environment and conservation** *Australian Trust for Conservation Volunteers* (☎9532 8446); *Department of Conservation and Natural Resources*, 240 Victoria Parade, East Melbourne (☎9412/ 4011); *Environment Centre Bookshop*, 247 Flinders Lane; *The Wilderness Centre*, 59 Hardware St (Mon–Thurs 9am–5.30pm, Fri 9am–7pm, Sat 9am–3pm).

**Ferry** If you're heading for Tasmania on the Bass Strait ferry (*Spirit of Tasmania*; three times a week; 14hr; reservations ☎13 2010), you need to get to Station Pier in Port Melbourne; take the #109 tram from Collins St in the city. The airport bus *Skybus* also runs to the pier.

**Health** *Royal Melbourne Hospital*, Grattan St, Parkville (☎9342 7000); *St Vincent's*, Victoria Parade, Fitzroy (☎9807 2211); *Royal Dental Hospital*, corner of Elizabeth St and Flemington Rd, Parkville (☎9341 0222); *Melbourne Sexual Health Centre*, 580 Swanston St, Carlton (☎9347 0244).

**Laundries** *City Edge Launderette*, 39 Errol St, opposite North Melbourne Town Hall (daily 6am–11pm); *The Soap Opera Laundry & Cafe*, 128 Bridport St, Albert Park (Mon–Fri 7.30am–9.30pm, Sat 8am–8pm, Sun 9am–9pm) – coffee and snacks while you wash.

**Left luggage** Spencer St Station has lockers (daily 6am–10pm; $2; emptied nightly) and attended left luggage ($8 overnight). Flinders St Station has lockers (Mon–Fri 8am–8pm; $2). The lockers at the Melbourne Bus Terminal in Franklin St are accessible 24 hr ($3 or, for larger ones, $4).

**Library** *State Library of Victoria*, 328 Swanston Walk: the General Reference and Information Centre keeps popular Australian and overseas magazines, while the Newspaper Room has foreign papers (Mon 1–9pm, Tues 10am–6pm, Wed 10am–9pm, Thurs–Sun 10am–6pm).

**Markets** *Queen Victoria Market*, the *Victorian Arts Centre* crafts market, and local markets at Prahran, South Melbourne and St Kilda, are discussed above in "The City" and "Melbourne Suburbs". *Camberwell Market*, Station St (Sunday 6am–1pm; train to Camberwell), is a large flea-market with lots of good secondhand clothes, books and records as well as bric-a-brac, and with plenty of food vans and cafés.

**Motorbikes** The northern end of Elizabeth St in the city centre has a string of motorbike shops. *Garner's Hire Bikes*, 179 Peel St, North Melbourne (☎9326 8717), do rentals, and sell secondhand machines with buy-back deals.

**Newspapers** Melbourne's *The Age* is arguably Australia's best daily paper; the pulpy *Sun-Herald* is the city's only other daily. Foreign newspapers can be perused at the State Library (see above), or bought from *McGill's Newsagency*, 187 Elizabeth St.

**Pharmacy** *Henry Francis Chemists*, 215 Elizabeth St (open 7 days); *Mulqueens Pharmacy*, Swanston St, opposite the Town Hall (open 7 days until late); *Leonard Long*, corner of Williams Rd and High St, Prahran (open 7 days until midnight).

**Rape** *Sexual Assault Crisis Line*, Royal Women's Hospital (☎9344 2210); *Telephone Service Against Sexual Assault* (weekends, public holidays, and after hours Mon–Fri; ☎9349 1766). *CASA House*, 270 Cardigan St, Carlton (☎9344 2210), provides medical care, support and counselling for victims of sexual assault.

**Record shops** Three are very close to each other at the upper end of Bourke St: *Virgin Megastore*, 152 Bourke St (Mon–Wed 9.30am–6pm, Thurs 9am–9pm, Fri & Sat 9.30am–midnight, Sun 11am–5pm), the largest music store in Australia; *Gaslight*, 85 Bourke St (Mon–Sat 9am–late, Sun noon–late), with a superb range, including imports and Australian independents, of everything except classical; and *Thomas's Records*, a small, but very good store at 31 Bourke St. *Au-go-go*, 349 Little Bourke St (Mon–Sat 9.30am–7pm, Sun 11am–5pm), sells independent and rare recordings, and displays notices for room shares and what's on. *The Basement Discs*, 24 Block Place, off Little Collins St, has a great range of jazz and world music.

**Shopping** The big two department stores, *David Jones* and *Myer*, are located off the Bourke Street Mall. *Daimaru* in Elizabeth St is Japanese-owned, with a very sophisticated feel. Chapel St, South Yarra, is the home of interesting upmarket fashion, getting younger and less expensive towards Prahran. Greville St, Prahran, has lots of retro chic, although Brunswick St in Fitzroy is the best spot for secondhand clothes. *Dangerfield* (at 238 Flinders Lane in the city centre, and Greville St, Prahran) has modern funky clothes, including lots of great hats and jewellery. Little Bourke St (from no. 349 upwards) and Hardware St, round the corner, are the places to go for travel equipment, such as maps, camping gear and outdoor clothing.

**Skiing** *Melbourne Ski Centre*, 17 Hardware St (☎9670 2855), can advise on skiing conditions at Baw Baw, Buffalo, Mount Hotham, Buller, Falls Creek and at Thredbo in NSW.

**Swimming** *State Swimming Centre and Gymnasium*, Batman Ave (☎9654 1100): 50-m indoor heated pool and diving pool (Mon–Fri 5.30am–7.30pm, Sat & Sun 9am–3pm), gymnasium (Mon–Wed 6am–9pm, Thurs & Fri until 8pm, Sat & Sun 9am–3pm), solarium and sauna. *City Baths*, corner of Swanston and Franklin streets (Mon–Fri 6am–10pm, Sat & Sun 8am–6pm; ☎9663 5888), has a 30-m heated indoor pool for swimming plus a pool for water aerobics, a sauna and spa, in a lovely Victorian redbrick building.

**Taxis** Taxi rank on Swanston St outside Flinders St Station, and plenty to flag down. *Arrow* (☎9417 1111), *Astoria* (☎9347 5511), *Regal Combined Taxis* (☎9810 0222), *Silver Top* (☎9345 3455).

**Telephones** Melbourne is well stocked with functioning public telephones. For quiet, try the *Telecom Calling Centre* on Elizabeth St.

**Tours** Reliable operators who have been around for some time include: *Autopia Tours* (☎9326 5536), tours to the Great Ocean Road, Phillip Island and Hanging Rock; *Dreamtime Outback Safaris* (☎1800/64 6871), 5-day 4WD camping tours in Victoria and southwest NSW that focus on Aboriginal culture; *Echidna Walkabout* (☎9419 8637), wildlife-spotting in the Brisbane Ranges and You Yangs among other options; *Let's Go Bush* (bookings via *Dial-a-Coach Booking Centre*, 177 Flinders St; ☎9654 8477), tours to Dandenong Ranges, Great Ocean Road and Otway National Park; and *Mac's Backpacker Tours* to Great Ocean Road and Phillip Island (book through hostel or the YHA – see "Travel agents" below). One-way tours are a good way to take in the sights en route: *Aussie Expeditions* (☎1800/63 5058) run a 5-day "Alpine Wilderness Adventure" between Mellbourne and Sydney (weekly departures Oct–April); see box on p.25 for other one-way options.

**Trains** Spencer St Station has a staffed information desk where you can get hold of all *V/Line* train (and bus) timetables and quotes on prices; buy your ticket at the busy ticket room opposite or on ☎9619 5000 (7am–9pm). If you're travelling with a bicycle, come at least thirty minutes earlier to book it on the train. Suburban train information from the *Met Transport Information Centre* (see p.644).

**Travel agents** *Flight Centre*, at 19 Bourke St (☎9650 2899) and many branches; *STA Travel*, 273 Little Collins St (☎9654 8722), and 142 Acland St, St Kilda (☎9525 3188); *Outdoor Travel Centre*, 1st Floor, 55 Hardware St (☎9670 7252); *YHA Victoria*, 205 King St (Mon–Fri 9am–5.30pm, Sat 9am–noon; ☎9670 9611).

**Travellers Aid Centres** Lower ground floor, Spencer St Station (Mon–Fri 7.30am–7.30pm, Sat & Sun 7.30am–11.30am; ☎9670 2873), and 2nd Floor, 169 Swanston St (Mon–Fri 8am–5pm, Sat 10am–4pm): both provide nappy-changing facilities, showers (for a fee), toilets, lounge rooms, wheelchairs for rent, assistance for disabled and frail persons, and information; in Swanston St there are also tearooms and lockers ($1).

**Women** *Women's Information and Referral Service* (*WIRE*; Mon–Fri 9am–9pm; ☎9654 6844, free call ☎1800/13 6570) is a telephone information service run by women for women. *Healthsharing Women Health Resource Centre,* level 3, 373 Little Bourke St, runs a drop-in and telephone service for health information and advice (Mon, Tues, Wed & Fri 10am–4pm, Thurs 1–7pm; ☎9670 0669, free call ☎1800/13 3321). *Shrew Women's Bookshop*, 37 Gertrude St, Fitzroy (☎9419 5595), has a folder of women's contacts.

# AROUND MELBOURNE

There are many possible day-trips out of Melbourne, mainly around the shores of the huge **Port Phillip Bay**, encircled by the arms of the Bellarine and Mornington peninsulas. The **Mornington Peninsula** on the east side is home to some of the city's most popular beaches, packed on summer weekends; Western Port Bay, beyond the peninsula, encloses two fascinating islands – little-known **French Island**, much of whose wildlife is protected by a state park, and **Phillip Island**, where the waddling ashore of masses of fairy penguins every night is among Australia's biggest tourist attractions. Inland to the east, the **Yarra Valley** and the **Dandenong Range** offer beautiful countryside, wine-tasting and bushwalking. The **Bellarine Peninsula** and the western side of Port Phillip Bay are less exciting, but they do give access to the west coast and the Great Ocean Road.

# The Mornington Peninsula

The **MORNINGTON PENINSULA** curves right around Port Phillip Bay, culminating in Point Nepean, well to the southwest of Melbourne. The shoreline facing the bay is beach-bum territory, though the well-heeled denizens of the main resorts, **Sorrento** and **Portsea**, might well resent that tag. On the largely straight, ocean-facing coast, **Point Nepean National Park** encompasses some fine seascapes, with several walking trails marked out. **French Island**, off the eastern side of the peninsula, is further away from the beaten track and offers a pleasant retreat in the form of camping, cycling and wildlife-watching.

As well as the beaches, the peninsula's **community markets** selling local produce and crafts attract many city dwellers: most are monthly affairs, so there's usually one every weekend. One of the biggest and best is Red Hill Community Market, held on the first Saturday of every month (7am–noon, but not June–Aug), at Red Hill Recreation Reserve, Red Hill Road, 10km east of Dromana.

The peninsula is easily accessible by **public transport** from Melbourne (zone 3 ticket). Take the train to Frankston and change there for Stony Point, or catch bus #788 from Frankston to Sorrento and Portsea. From Sorrento there's a community bus to Dromana via Blairgowrie, Rye and Rosebud (4 daily Mon–Fri) but no transport to Arthurs Seat.

## The western coast

The peninsula essentially starts at suburban Frankston, 40km from central Melbourne, and from here on down, the western coast, flanked by the Nepean Highway, is beach after beach, all crowded and traffic-snarled in summer. Twelve kilometres beyond Frankston, the old fishing port of **Mornington** preserves some of its heritage in fine

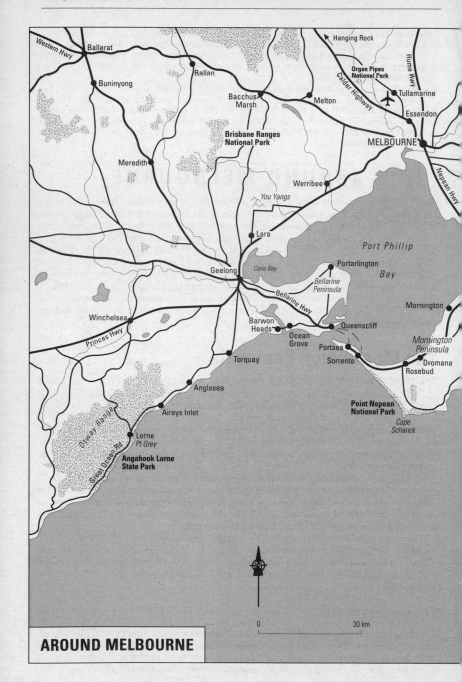

**AROUND MELBOURNE**

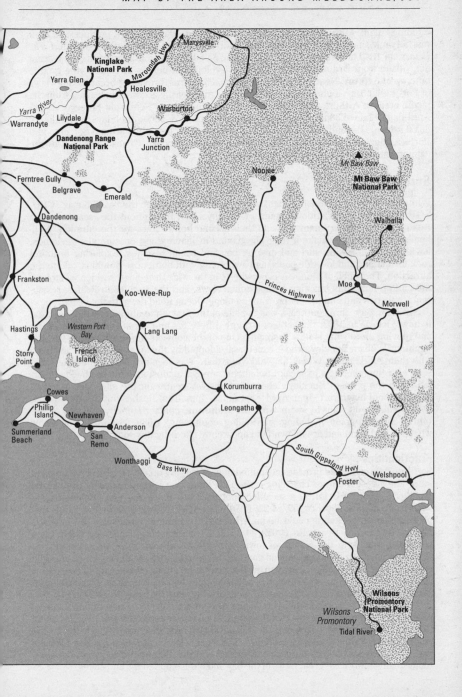

buildings along Mornington Esplanade; every Wednesday there's a produce and craft market on Main Street. **Mount Martha**, 11km on, is another old settlement, where *The Briars*, an 1840 homestead (daily 11am–5pm, $4.50) gives an inkling of the pioneering life. Inland from Dromana, where seaside development begins in earnest, the granite outcrop of **Arthurs Seat State Park** rises to 305 metres, providing breathtaking views of Port Phillip Bay: a **chairlift** makes the vista more easily accessible, leaving from the picnic area on Arthurs Seat Road, just off the Mornington Peninsula Freeway (Sept–April daily 11am–4.30pm; May–Aug weekends, public & school holidays, same hours; $5.50 return). Beyond, the peninsula arcs and narrows: the sands around Sorrento and Portsea offer a choice between the rugged surf of the ocean ("back" beaches) or the calmer waters of the bay ("front" beaches).

# Sorrento

With some of the most expensive real estate outside the Melbourne CBD, **SORRENTO** is the traditional haunt of the city's rich throughout the "season", from Boxing Day to Easter; many move to their second homes here for the duration. Well-heeled outsiders also make it their playground in January and summer weekends, flocking here to swim, surf and dive on bay and ocean beaches. Exploring beautiful rock formations and low-tide pools, and swimming with bottlenose dolphins, add to the attraction. The smell of money is everywhere, in the wide, tree-lined residential streets, the clifftop mansions boasting million-dollar views, and the town-centre cafés, restaurants, galleries and antique shops, running along Ocean Road down to the beach.

**Sullivan Bay**, 3km southeast, was the site of the first white attempt to settle in what is now Victoria in 1803; the settlers struggled here for four months before giving up and moving on to what is now Tasmania. One of the convicts in the expedition was the infamous William Buckley, who escaped, was adopted by the local Aborigines and lived with them for 32 years. When the "wild white man" was seen again by settlers he could scarcely remember how to speak English; his survival against all odds has been immortalized in the phrase "Buckley's chance". A display centre on the site (Oct–Mar Sat, Sun & school holidays 1–4pm; April–Sept Sun 1–4pm; free) fleshes out the story of the settlement. If you want to **swim with the dolphins**, contact *Polperro Dolphin Swims* (4hr; $50 per person including snorkelling equipment; ☎059/88 8437), who know where to find them and are known (and apparently liked) by the dolphins.

## Practicalities

Sorrento's three **hotels** provide accommodation of varying quality, but all serve up good food. The oldest and most charming is the 1871 limestone *Sorrento Hotel*, 5 Hotham Rd (☎059/84 2206; B&B ⑥), in a secluded spot on a hill above the jetty. Below, on the waterfront, *Koonya Hotel* (☎059/84 2281; ⑤) has less character, and the live bands that play the bar at weekends could be an irritant. A welcome alternative to the hotels is *Carmel*, 142 Ocean Beach Rd (☎059/84 3512; ⑤), a charming sandstone **B&B** (non-smoking), smack in the middle of town. *Sorrento Backpacker's Hostel*, 3 Miranda St (☎059/84 4323; ①), is a modern and comfortable **hostel** with small en-suite dorms and stacks of local information. **Caravan parks** tend to be either closed (out of season) or completely booked up and twice the normal price: two of the more reasonable are *Nautilus* (☎059/84 2277; on-site vans ③) and the *Foreshore Reserve* (☎059/84 2797).

As you might expect, all this glitz needs to be nourished by plenty of fancy **eating places**. More modest options include getting a takeaway to eat on the benches along Ocean Road or on the beach: try the *Village Bakehouse*, 29 Ocean Beach Rd. In the moderate price range, *Buckley's Chance*, 174 Ocean Beach Rd, is a relaxed pancake parlour, which also serves burgers and steaks; and the century-old *Sorrento Tearooms* (daily 10am–5pm) have great views of the bay and old-fashioned tea and cakes.

**Ferries** run across the mouth of the bay from Sorrento to Queenscliff on the Bellarine Peninsula. The *Peninsula Searoad Ferry* (☎052/58 3244) carries passengers and vehicles year-round (about every two hours 8am–6pm, in summer until 8pm; advance bookings for cars recommended). The *Sorrento Ferry Co.* (☎059/84 1602; call to check times) runs a passenger ferry on Saturdays and Sundays from Boxing Day to April 25, and during school holidays, calling at Portsea en route.

## Portsea and Point Nepean

**PORTSEA**, just beyond Sorrento, is a mecca for divers, with excellent dives up to 40m in depth off Port Phillip Heads; trips operate from the pier throughout the summer and there are a couple of good dive shops. Portsea Front Beach, on the bay by the pier, is wall-to-wall beautiful people, as is Shelley Beach, which also attracts playful dolphins. On the other shore, Portsea Ocean Beach has excellent surfing, and a hang-gliding pad on a rock formation known as London Bridge. Back on the bay side, the extensive lawns of *Portsea Hotel*, a hugely popular drinking spot with weekend bands, overlook the beautiful people's beach.

The tip of the peninsula, with its fortifications, quarantine station and army base (still operational), was off limits to the public for a century until the establishment of the **Point Nepean National Park** in 1988, whose orientation centre is just one kilometre west of Portsea (daily 9am–5pm; $7 park entry fee; ☎059/84 4276). Because of its fragile sandy environment, cars are not allowed into the park and visitor numbers are limited, so you need to book to visit.

An open-air **transporter** (hourly 9.30am–12.30pm & 2–3pm) runs the 7km to the fortifications at the point, with two optional drop-offs for walks: the first (suitable for wheelchairs; 1km return) leads through coastal vegetation to the Port Phillip Bay shoreline; the second (1km return, steep in sections) leads to the top of Cheviot Hill, where you can look across to Queenscliff, and takes you on to views of **Cheviot Beach** where Harold Holt, Australia's prime minister of the time, went for a swim in the rough Bass Strait surf on December 17, 1967 and disappeared, presumed drowned: his body was never found. A third walk takes you around **Fort Nepean** right at the point. Built at the same time as Fort Queenscliff opposite to protect wealthy post-goldrush Melbourne from an imagined Russian invasion, the fort is essentially a two-storey building below ground. It takes an hour or so to explore the tunnels, which lead down to the Engine House at water level. On the first weekend of each month there's no transporter and the park is opened up to cyclists, an extremely popular outing ($5; cyclists must start before 2pm). The old **quarantine station** offers guided tours at weekends.

The rest of Point Nepean National Park, which spreads itself along the ocean coast, is freely open to the public. A great two-day walk (26km) runs from London Bridge along the coast to **Cape Schrank**, site of an 1859 lighthouse and an information centre. Here a timber staircase and walkways lead down to the sea along a narrow neck of land, providing magnificent coastal views. Also worth embarking on in this area is the **Bushrangers Bay Nature Walk** (6km return; 2hr) from the cape to Main Creek, which begins as a leisurely walk along the clifftop, then leads down to a wild beach facing Elephant Rock.

## French Island

About half of **French Island**, once a prison farm, is now a state park and, except for some farming areas, the rest is undeveloped, with a flourishing koala population among its rich wildlife. Virtually vehicle-free, it's a great place to cycle, and this is encouraged, with all walking tracks open to bikes; aim to be self-sufficient and bring camping gear. *Bay Connections Passenger Ferries* normally leave daily from Stony Point

(9am, 10am, 4pm and 5pm, departing from the island half an hour later; $14 return, ☎059/79 3722), but at the time of writing there was some doubt about their continuance. The alternatives are chartering a ride with *Arch Cruise* (☎059/79 3774) from Stony Point, going on a day-tour from Western Port Marina, Hastings, with Alan Chandler (☎059/80 1210), or crossing from Cowes on Phillip Island (see p.686). Lois Airs (☎059/80 1241), a long-time resident of the island, gives information about the island and also runs very inexpensive morning or afternoon **tours**. If you want to camp at the state park camping ground, Lois will transport your luggage there, leaving you free to cycle.

# Phillip Island

**PHILLIP ISLAND**, with its southern edge facing Bass Strait and its northern in the calm waters of Western Port Bay, is a hugely popular holiday destination from Melbourne, famous above all for the nightly roosting of hundreds of **fairy penguins** at Summerland Beach. Most visitors only come for the Penguin Parade, but spending a few days on the island will allow you to explore some dramatic coastal scenery and fine beaches, and a couple of well-organized wildlife parks. **Cowes**, on the sheltered bay side, is the main town and a lively and attractive place to stay.

A daily **V/Line bus** to Cowes departs from Melbourne in the afternoon, with an additional evening service on Fridays; the bus drivers will usually drop you off where you request in Cowes. Since there's no public transport when you get there however, it can be tricky trying to get to the Penguin Parade, over 10km from Cowes. Planning to stay at the *Amaroo Park YHA* makes sense: not only do they have a **free bus** to and from Melbourne's *Queensbury Hill YHA* on Tuesdays and Fridays (booking essential), they also organize a minibus for their guests to the parade ($5). The easy way to see the island is on a **tour** from Melbourne. The best is with *Autopia Tours* (☎03/9326 5536), who pick up from central Melbourne or St Kilda: their one-day tour (daily, 11am–midnight; $40) takes in the Wildlife Park, Koala Conservation Centre and Penguin Parade as well as the Nobbies. Phillip Island is also a departure point for cheap **flights to Tasmania**.

If you have your own vehicle, head southeast from Melbourne on the Princes Highway to Dandenong, then follow the South Gippsland Highway to Lang Lang and from there the Bass Highway to Anderson where the road heads directly west to San Remo and the bridge across to the island, a drive of three hours or so in total. The scenic lookout about 3km before San Remo is worth stopping at, for fantastic views of Western Port Bay and the surrounding countryside. **SAN REMO** itself has lots of motels, a picturesque fishing fleet by its wharf and a co-operative selling fresh fish and crays. Not surprisingly you can get delicious fish and chips; the best are from 121 Main St.

The first settlement on the island, **NEWHAVEN**, has a large **tourist information centre** (daily 9am–5pm; ☎059/56 7447), where you can pick up a free map and buy tickets for the Penguin Parade, ferry tours, and for **Churchill Island** (daily noon–5pm; $4.50), barely a kilometre out of town via a rickety bridge. Your admission allows you to look round a historic homestead and cottage in English-style gardens, surrounded by ancient moonah trees, abundant birdlife and an unspoilt coastline.

## Phillip Island Reserve: the Penguin Parade

The **Phillip Island Reserve** includes all the public land on the **Summerland Peninsula**, the narrow tip of land at the island's western extremity. The reason for the reserve is the **Fairy (or Little) Penguin**, smallest of the penguins, which is found only in southern Australian waters and whose largest colony breeds at Summerland Beach (around 2000 penguins in the parade area, and 20,000 on the island altogether). The **Penguin Parade** (nightly after dusk; $6.50; ☎059/56 8691) may sound horribly commercial – and with 4000 visitors a night at the busiest time of the year (immediately after Christmas), it can hardly fail to be; spectators sit in concrete-stepped stadia looking down onto a floodlit beach, with taped narration in Japanese, Taiwanese and English. But don't be too hard on it: ecological disaster would ensue if the penguins weren't managed properly, and visitors would still flock here, harming the birds and eroding the sand dunes. As it is, all the money made goes back into research and looking after the penguins, and into facilities like the excellent **Penguin Parade Information Centre** (admission included in the parade ticket, open from 10am): the "Penguin Experience" here is a simulated underwater scene of the hazards of a penguin's life, and there are also interactive displays, videos and even nesting boxes to which penguins have access from the outside, where you can watch the chicks.

The parade itself manages to transcend the setting in any case, as the penguins come pouring onto the beach, waddling comically once they leave their preferred environment. They start arriving soon after dark; fifty minutes later the floodlights are switched off and it's all over, at which time (or before) you can move on to the extensive boardwalks over their burrows, with diffused lighting at regular intervals, enabling you to watch their antics for hours after the parade finishes – they're active most of the night. If you want to avoid the worst of the crowds, the quietest time is during the cold and windy winter (you'll need water- or windproof clothing at any time of year). Remember too that you can see fairy penguins close to St Kilda Pier in Melbourne (see p.662) and many other beaches in southern Australia, not in such large numbers perhaps, but with far fewer onlookers.

### The Nobbies and Seal Rocks

At the tip of the Summerland Peninsula is **Point Grant**, where **The Nobbies**, two huge rock stacks, are linked to the island at low tide by a wave-cut platform of basalt, affording views across to Cape Schrank on the Mornington Peninsula. From the point a boardwalk leads across spongy greenery – vibrant in summer with purple and yellow flowers – along the rounded clifftops to a lookout over a blowhole. This is a wild spot, with views along the rugged southern coastline towards Cape Woolamai, a granite headland at the eastern end of the island. From September to April you may see shearwaters (muttonbirds) here – they arrive in September to breed and head for the same burrows each year, after an incredible flight from the Bering Strait in the Arctic Circle. Further off Point Grant, **Seal Rocks** are two rocky islets with the largest known colony of Australian fur seals; in December, peak breeding season, they number at least 5000. The seals can be viewed through a coin-operated telescope at the *Nobbies Kiosk* (daily 10am–dusk); ferry tours to Seal Rocks are available from Cowes (see below).

## Phillip Island Wildlife Park and the Koala Conservation Centre

Two further parks complete Phillip Island's rich collection of wildlife attractions. **Phillip Island Wildlife Park**, on Thompson Avenue just 1km south of Cowes (daily 9am–dusk; $6), is a shady shelter for Australian animals, most of them enclosed and not all native to Phillip Island. Highlights include the beautiful pure-bred dingoes, Tasmanian devils, fat dozy wombats to hold and feed, if they're awake (but watch out, they bite), as well as a free-flight aviary and a koala reserve. Free to range are emus, Cape Barren geese, wallabies, eastern grey kangaroos and pademelons.

A better place to see koalas in a natural environment is the **Koala Conservation Centre**, on Phillip Island Road between Newhaven and Cowes (daily 10am–5.30pm; $2.50), which aims to keep the habitat as natural as possible while still giving people a close view. The centre's purpose is to breed disease-free koalas, as on Phillip Island they're infected with chlamydia. You can learn about koalas in the excellent interpretative centre (though without koala cuddling sessions, which are illegal in Victoria), and can consult a board showing where they've been spotted that day. For a decent view, rent a pair of binoculars.

## Cowes and Rhyll

In the centre of the north coast, where the sandy bays are sheltered enough for good swimming, **COWES** is Phillip Island's main town. Several good places to eat and stay can be found here on The Esplanade, a lively strip facing the jetty. Based in the old Rotunda, *Cowes Ferry Service* (☎018/55 3136) offers several **cruises** from the jetty, the best being the tour to Seal Rocks (see above; Tues, Thurs, Sat & Sun 2.15pm, depending on the weather; 2hr; $35) to watch the Australian fur seals close up; or choose a more sedate harbour cruise (12.30pm & 4.30pm, with extra cruises in summer; 1hr; $12). The same company links Cowes to Stony Point on the Mornington Peninsula and to French Island (Tues, Thurs, Sat & Sun, daily in January), and also runs ferries to French Island and Stony Point. Worth considering as a quieter place to base yourself is **RHYLL**, about 6km to the east.

### Practicalities

The main reason to come to Cowes or Rhyll is if you're planning to stay on the island: out of season you should have no trouble, but during the peak Christmas–Easter season accommodation nearly doubles in price and some places demand minimum weekly bookings. Starting from the budget end, the YHA **hostel**, *Amaroo Park,* at the corner of Church and Osborne streets right in the centre of town (☎059/52 2548; dorms ①, rooms ③), has a convivial bar, cheap meals and a swimming pool as well as laying on various good day-trips, bike rental, and, best of all, a free bus to and from Melbourne (see p.684). In shady grounds which give onto a quiet swimming beach, *Kaloha*, on the corner of Chapel and Steele streets (☎059/52 2179), has everything from **camping** sites, through on-site vans and cabins (④), to motel units with cooking facilities (④–⑤). Among the **motels**, the *Seahorse*, 29–31 Chapel St (☎059/52 2003; ④–⑤), and the *Coachman*, at 51 Chapel St (☎059/52 1098; ⑤–⑦), the latter with the added benefits of a heated pool and spa, are both above average. *The Continental Phillip Island*, a conveniently central **hotel** at 5–8 The Esplanade (☎059/52 2316; ⑤–⑦), also has a heated pool and offers accommodation in en-suite rooms, some with seafront balconies. **B&Bs** range from *Narrabeen Cottage*, 16 Steele St (☎059/52 2062; ⑦–⑧), a delightful guesthouse where gourmet dinners can be arranged, to the simpler, but quite agreeable, *Flynns Reef*, on the corner of Backbeach and Ventnor roads (☎059/56 8673; ④). The pick of **Rhyll**'s accommodation is the *Bains Holiday Units*, 8 Beach Rod (059/56 9263; ⑤), right on the waterfront

**Restaurants** include the expensive but relaxed *Jetty* on Cowes' Esplanade (☎059/52 2060), which specializes in fresh local seafood, and *Isola Di Capri*, 2 Thompson Ave (☎059/52 2435), for convivial, affordable Italian. Simpler **cafés** abound, like the *Praha Coffee House* and *Fountain Place* (excellent ice cream), both on Thompson Avenue. The *Isle of Wight Hotel* on The Esplanade has several places to eat, including a good-value bistro with sea views, as well as **bars**, a lively beer garden and entertainment on summer weekends. In **Rhyll**, eat at *Poppy's Restaurant*, 14 Lock Road, where lunches, teas and tasty dinners are served in a beautiful old wooden house.

# The Yarra Valley and the Dandenongs

Northeast of Melbourne, the **Yarra Valley** stretches out towards the foothills of the Great Dividing Range, with **Healesville** as a target for excursions into the wine country and to the superb forest scenery beyond. To the east, and still within the suburban limits, the cool, high **Dandenong Range** is as pretty as anywhere in Australia, with quaint villages, fine old houses and beautiful flowering gardens.

You can get plenty out of exploring the Dandenongs by public **transport**, but to get the most out of the Yarra Valley, you really need your own vehicle. Healesville, at least, comes within the orbit of the suburban transport system, accessible by train from Melbourne to Lilydale and then by bus. Trains also run via Ferntree Gully to Belgrave in the Dandenongs. *McKenzies Bus Lines* run a daily service from Spencer Street Station through Healesville to Marysville and beyond. The *V/Line* bus to Eildon follows a similar route via Healesville and Marysville daily, the one to Mansfield passes through Lilydale and Yarra Glen daily, and there are local buses from Belgrave to Emerald.

## The Yarra Valley

Just half an hour from Melbourne by car, many of Victoria's best small **wineries** – about two dozen, several with restaurants – lie en route to or beyond Healesville. Wine country starts at **Yarra Glen**, which also boasts the splendidly restored *Grand Hotel* and, not far away on the Melba Highway, the National Trust **Gulf Station** (Wed–Sun & public holidays 10am–4pm; $5), a collection of ten 1850s slab farm buildings set in sixteen hectares of farmland. Around Yarra Glen you can check out wineries (all signposted) on one of three routes – the Melba Highway northwards, the Maroondah Highway through Healesville, or the Warburton Highway further south.

One worth visiting from the **Melba Highway** is *De Bortoli*, at Pinnacle Lane, Dixon's Creek, which has the added benefits of an Italian restaurant and views over the gentle valleys. On the **Maroondah Highway**, *Domaine Chandon*, near the town of Coldstream, is owned by the French champagne house *Möet et Chandon*, producing fine *méthode champenoise* sparkling wine, which you can taste in an 1880s homestead. From the **Warburton Highway** you can detour to several, including *Yarra Burn* on Settlement Road at Yarra Junction, which operates a good restaurant on weekends.

From Yarra Junction it's not far to **WARBURTON** itself, a pretty, old-fashioned town on the Upper Yarra River, and starting point for the **Upper Yarra Track**, which follows old timber tram and vehicle tracks upstream for over 80km. The track can be covered as a series of short walks or as a continuous five- to seven-day trek, finishing in the Baw Baw National Park where it joins the Alpine Walking Track; for more information contact the *Department of Conservation and Natural Resources* in Healesville (☎059/62 4900). Guided **canoe trips** on the Upper Yarra can be arranged through *Upper Yarra Travel and Tours*, 5 Lower Homestead Road, Wonga Park (☎03/9722 1387 or 9722 1956).

### Healesville and beyond

**HEALESVILLE** is a pleasant enough town, site of a **tourist information centre** (at the beginning of town when you come from Melbourne, in a little shack just off the Maroondah Highway; daily 10am–5pm), and the renowned **Healesville Sanctuary** (daily 9am–5pm; $12; free voluntary guides 10am–3pm if booked in advance; ☎059/62 4022). This is a true sanctuary, established over fifty years ago to provide care for injured and orphaned animals which are then either returned to the wild or become part of the collection for education and breeding of endangered species. It's a fascinating place in a beautiful setting, with a stream running through park-like grounds, dense with gum trees and cool ferns, and 3km of paths to follow past picnic and barbecue areas. Many of the animals are in enclosures, but there are paddocks of emus, wallabies and kangaroos you can stroll through. Don't miss the excellent "Animals of the Night" enclosure (10am–4.30pm); other star attractions include the open aviaries (9am–4.30pm), a scary Reptile House, and a brand-new Platypus Display Centre.

Continuing north towards the mountains on the Maroondah Highway, the scenery just gets better and better, especially if you take the detour to **Marysville** along Lady Talbot Drive. In the luxuriant forest dotted with waterfalls, trees include messmate, manna gum, tall mountain ash, and myrtle beech covered in moss and ferns. Further north still, the Maroondah Highway passes through the aptly named **Cathedral Range State Park**, where high umbrella ferns shelter beneath beautiful soaring gums.

## The Dandenongs

Often called the **Blue Dandenongs**, this high mountain range (up to 633m) shares with NSW's Blue Mountains the natural phenomenon of a blue haze rising from forests of gum trees. Abundant rain ensures the area stays cool and lush, while fine old houses and gardens add to the scenery. Easy bushwalks in the **Dandenong Range National Park** start from Ferntree Gully, accessible by train or by car via the Burwood Highway. The best way to enjoy the forests and fern gullies, however, is to take a ride on the **Puffing Billy** (55min; $15; ☎03/9870 8411) which runs for 13km between Belgrave (on a suburban train line from Melbourne) and Emerald Lake, stopping at Menzies Creek and Emerald. The steam train has run more or less continuously since the early 1900s, though its operation now depends on dedicated volunteers; on total fire ban days, diesel locomotives are used. Timetables vary seasonally but there are generally several services daily until late afternoon; local buses also cover the Belgrave–Emerald route.

Just outside Emerald, man-made **Emerald Lake** has paddle-boats to rent and a swimming pool with waterslide, as well as trails through bushland continuing into the nearby state reserve. If you need **accommodation**, *Emerald Backpackers*, 49 Emerald Lake Road (☎059/68 4086; dorms ①, rooms ③), has a country setting and a casual party atmosphere; the owners will help long-stay guests look for local rural work. *Choo Choos Restaurant and Bar*, at 32 Monbulk Road in Emerald (food to midnight, bar to 1am; ☎059/68 4145), is a friendly, reasonably priced oddity, serving **meals** on authentic railway crockery in old railway dining carriages.

# Geelong and the Bellarine Peninsula

Heading west towards Geelong – for the Bellarine Peninsula or the Great Ocean Road – it's just a short detour off the Princes Freeway to **WERRIBEE** (or a half-hour train ride from Melbourne; zone 3), where the extraordinary **Werribee Park Mansion and Zoological Gardens** are located on K Road. Built by two Scottish squatters made rich beyond their wildest dreams, the mansion (Mon–Fri 10am–3.45pm, during daylight saving until 4.45pm; weekends and public holidays 10am–4.45pm; $10) is fully cast with people in nineteenth-century period costume, adding to the period flavour. In the extensive grounds beyond the formal gardens (daily 10am–3.30pm, during daylight saving until 4.30pm) roam giraffes, rhinoceroses, hippopotamuses and other creatures (50-min safari bus tours, $8). Continuing along the freeway you can detour west again through Little River to the **You Yangs**, small but rugged volcanic peaks which loom sharply out of the surrounding plains. Scramble to the top of the highest, Flinders Peak (348m), which Matthew Flinders climbed in 1802, and you're rewarded with fine views of Geelong and Port Phillip Bay. The You Yangs, as well as the nearby **Brisbane Ranges**, are excellent for keeping vigil for kangaroos, wallabies, koalas and possums at dusk.

# Geelong

GEELONG is not an attractive town, too industrial to appeal as a coastal resort: the fact that the National Wool Museum is the main attraction gives you some idea. You may have heard of it, however, because it's a wealthy place – on wool money – and site of an exclusive boarding school. Heading for the Bellarine Peninsula, *Bellarine Transit* **buses** depart from the railway station (an hour from Melbourne) for Point Lonsdale via Queenscliff and for St Leonards via Portarlington. If you want to explore, head down Railway Terrace alongside palm-filled Johnstone Park and you'll reach Malop Street, the main shopping strip; there's a helpful staffed **tourist information** stall in Market Square. Many of the best of the town's Victorian buildings are nearby on Little Malop Street, including the elegant **Geelong Art Gallery** (Tues–Fri 10am–5pm, Sat & Sun 1–5pm; $3).

From Malop Street, Moorabool Street leads down to the water, with views of shipping traffic and, across the water, an industrial skyline with hills behind; swimming is permitted on a tiny section of the eastern beach. The main **Tourist Information Centre** (daily 10am–5pm; ☎052/22 2900 or 23 2399), with free maps of town and peninsula, is at the corner of Brougham and Moorabool streets, in the Geelong Wool Exchange, the National Trust-listed building which also houses the **National Wool Museum** (daily 10am–5pm; $7). Wool is still auctioned off on the top floor of the exchange on thirty days in the year; the museum concentrates on the social history surrounding it, with reconstructions of typical shearers' quarters and a millworker's 1920s cottage.

If you want something to **eat** there's plenty of choice, especially along Little Malop Street, where possibilities include *Bamboleo*, *Cats* and *Yours Naturally*. To check out what's going on, pick up a copy of the free **listings magazine** *Forte*, available from the Performing Arts Centre opposite the art gallery, which covers the whole of southwest Victoria; as well as entertainment it has information on surfing, scuba-diving and other activities. There's a surprisingly healthy local band scene in Geelong: the *Barwon Club Hotel*, Moorabool Street, and *Lamby's Bar*, downstairs at the National Wool Museum, are worth a look at weekends.

# Queenscliff and around

From Geelong, the Bellarine Highway runs 31km southeast to **QUEENSCLIFF** through flat and not particularly scenic grazing country. Queenscliff is essentially a quiet fishing village on Swan Bay – with several quaint cottages on Fishermens Flat – that became Melbourne's favourite holiday resort in the nineteenth century, fell out of favour, and has recently enjoyed something of a revival – a popular place for a weekend away or a Sunday drive. Its position near the narrow entrance to Port Phillip Bay made it strategically important: a **fort** here faces the the one at Point Nepean, defending Melbourne against an enemy that never materialized. Now the home of the Australian Army Command and Staff College, the fort can be visited on weekend tours.

Full details of other things to do are available from the **Queenscliff Information Centre**, 76 Hesse St (Mon–Sat 9am–5pm, Sun 11am–4pm; ☎052/58 3403). Among these is the **Queenscliff Martime Centre**, Weerona Parade (Sat & Sun 10.30am–4.30pm; during school holidays daily 10.30am–4.30pm; $2), which concentrates on the many wrecks caused by The Rip, a fierce current through the mouth of the bay. Outside, a tiny fisherman's cottage is set up as it would have been in 1870, and there's a shed where an Italian fisherman painted, in naive style, all the ships he'd seen pass through from 1895 to 1947 (imaginatively including the *Titanic*). Next door, the **Marine Discovery Centre** (school holidays daily 10am–4pm; $1.50; ☎052/58 3344) opens its aquarium, stocked with local marine life, to the public during school holidays, when it also runs marine biology cruises, rock pool rambles, snorkelling tours and twilight walks. Back on the main street, the **Queenscliff Historical Centre** (daily 2–4pm; free) helps puts the rest of the town into context. Every Sunday, the **Bellarine Peninsula Railway** operates steam trips from the old Queenscliff Railway Station to Drysdale, 20km northwest (11am & 2.30pm, more often during school holidays; $5; ☎052/58 2069). Queenscliff market is held on the last Sunday of every month in Symonds Street.

### Point Lonsdale and Portarlington

From Queenscliff it's about 5km to peaceful **Point Lonsdale**, whose most noticeable feature is a magnificent 1902 lighthouse, 120m high and visible for 30km out to sea. Below the lighthouse, on the edge of the bluff, is "Buckley's Cave" where William Buckley is thought to have lived at some stage during his thirty-year sojourn with the Aborigines. At **Portarlington**, which sits on Port Phillip Bay about 14km north of Queenscliff, there's a beautifully preserved steam-powered flour mill, four storeys of solid stone owned by the National Trust (Sept–Dec & Feb–May Sun 2–5pm; Jan Wed, Sat & Sun 2–5pm).

### Practicalities

Three grand **Victorian-era hotels** are popular settings for romantic breaks: the *Vue Grand*, 46 Hesse St (☎052/58 1544; ⑧), has a Spanish-style exterior and a fabulously ornate Victorian interior with very expensive restaurant, though rates include breakfast and dinner; the clifftop *Ozone Hotel*, 42 Gellibrand St (☎052/58 1011; B&B ⑦), has sea views from two iron-lace decorated verandahs, and a gorgeous dining room; while the refined *Queenscliff Hotel*, 16 Gellibrand St (☎052/58 1066; ⑧), including breakfast and evening meal), is perhaps the best of all, and certainly the least intimidating; if it's free, go for the romantic octagonal room in the tower. **Budget alternatives** include the *Queenscliff Inn*, 59 Hesse St (☎052/58 3737; B&B ⑨–⑥), a pleasant Victorian guesthouse, and *Beacon Resort Motel*, 78 Bellarine Highway (☎052/58 1133), which has tent sites, cabins (④), holiday units (⑤), motel rooms (B&B ⑥), a heated pool and tennis courts. Among the town's **eating places**, the best fish and chips come from *Queenscliff Fish and Chips*, 77 Hesse St; for a seafront coffee and croissant you can't beat *Promenade Café*, 1 Symonds St; and for old-fashioned tea and scones turn to *Colonial Arcade Tearoom* in the Queenscliff Arcade, at 79 Hesse St. *Squidly's Café*, 80 Hesse St (☎052/58 3613) does casual lunch and dinner from Wednesday to Sunday – it's worth booking on a Saturday night.

**Ferries** run from here across the mouth of Port Phillip Bay to Sorrento (see p.683).

# THE GREAT OCEAN ROAD AND THE FAR WEST COAST

The **Great Ocean Road**, Victoria's famous southwestern coastal route, starts at **Torquay**, just over 20km south of Geelong, and stretches 285km west to Warrnambool. Built between 1919 and 1932, the idea was to construct a scenic road of world repute, equalling California's Pacific Coast Highway – and it does. The road was to be both a memorial to the soldiers who had died in World War I, and an employment scheme for those who returned. Over three thousand ex-servicemen laboured with picks and shovels, carving the road into cliffs and mountains along Australia's most rugged and densely forested coastline; the task was pushed on with the help of the jobless during the Great Depression. From Torquay to **Apollo Bay**, hugging the coast-

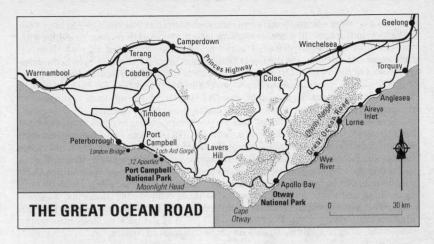

**THE GREAT OCEAN ROAD**

line, it passes through the popular holiday towns of **Anglesea** and **Lorne**, set below the Otway Range. From Apollo Bay the road heads inland through the towering forests of the **Otway National Park**, before rejoining the coast at Princetown, to wind along the shore for the entire length of the **Port Campbell National Park**. This stretch from Moonlight Head to Port Fairy, sometimes referred to as the "Shipwreck Coast", is the most spectacular – over eighty ships have gone down here, victim of the rough Southern Ocean and dramatic rock formations like the **Twelve Apostles**, which sit out to sea beyond the rugged cliffs. The often windy and stormy weather enhances the jagged coastline, and even at the height of summer you can't rely on sun here.

If all you're doing is heading from Melbourne to Warrnambool in a hurry, the **Princes Highway** is a much faster way and, of course, a much duller one. The only place you might consider a short stop is Colac, where **Lake Colac** and vast **Lake Corangamite** support a profusion of birdlife, with botanical gardens and a bird sanctuary.

From **Warrnambool**, the small industrial coastal city where the Great Ocean Road ends, the Princes Highway continues along the coast, through quaint seaside **Port Fairy** and industrial **Portland**, before turning inland for the final stretch to the South Australian border. If you're determined to stick to the coast, you can continue along the Portland–Nelson road, with Mount Richmond National Park and Discovery Bay Coastal Park on the coastal side, and Glenelg National Park on the other, ending up at the little town of **Nelson** on the peaceful Glenelg River, just before the South Australian border and with the spectacular Princess Margaret Rose Caves nearby.

The **Great Southwest Walk**, a circuit spanning 250km from just outside Portland to the Glenelg River and Nelson, then back through the two coastal parks to Portland, is magnificent. There are campsites all along the route; for further information and maps, consult the *Department of Conservation and Natural Resources*, 240 Victoria Parade, East Melbourne (☎03/9412 4011), or local offices along the way.

### Transport

If you don't have your own car or a **lift** (it's always worth checking hostel notice-boards), you might want to consider one-way **car rental**, usually available from the big-name companies. There are plenty of parking spots where you can pull over and admire the view, but even so the unfortunate driver will miss out on a lot of the scenery; with narrow roads, steep cliffs and incessant hairpin bends you need to keep your eyes glued to the road. In summer **cyclists** take to the road in droves, an exhilarating ride but only for the experienced and fearless. One-way **tours** that ply between Melbourne and Adelaide, via the Great Ocean Road, are a good way to take in the scenery: *Wayward Bus* (☎1800/88 2823) does it in three-days, while *Heading Bush* (☎1800/ 63 9933) takes five days. *Autopia Tours* (☎03/9670 9611) and *Let's Go Bush* (☎03/9654 8477) both do affordable overnight tours of the Great Ocean Road, returning to Melbourne. Note that some tours only run during the summer months.

*V/Line* has a "Great Ocean Road" **bus** service from Geelong to Apollo Bay, calling at Torquay, Anglesea, Lorne and points in between. Their "Coast Link" bus service from Apollo Bay heads to Warrnambool along the Great Ocean Road on Fridays only (plus Mondays in December and January). *Port Campbell Shuttle Service* can pick you up in Apollo Bay ($50 for one person, $25 a head for two or more; ☎055/98 6369) and show you all the sights on the way to Port Campbell. There's a **train** service from Melbourne via Geelong and Colac to Warrnambool (2–4 times daily), with connecting buses to Port Fairy, Portland and Heywood (2–3 times daily) and on to Mount Gambier in South Australia (once daily). From Warrnambool you can also get back to Melbourne on the inland road, or up to Ballarat. There's no public transport to Nelson.

# Torquay

**TORQUAY** is the centre of **surf culture** on Victoria's "surf coast", which extends from Point Lonsdale on the Bellarine Peninsula to Aireys Inlet; two local beaches, **Jan Juc** and **Bells Beach**, are solidly entrenched in Australian surfing mythology. If you're not here for the surf, then there's not really a lot happening: in hot weather the place is boisterously alive, out of season it's somnolent and low-key. Easter is the big event, when the **Surf Classic** at Bells Beach brings national and international contestants to Torquay, along with thousands of spectators. Local **buses** run between Geelong and Torquay via Jan Juc – call *Bellarine Transit* (☎052/23 2111) for the latest information.

Entering Torquay along the Great Ocean Road (Geelong Road within the town), you'll see the **Surf Coast Plaza** shopping centre, a must-see if you're at all into surfing or surf gear. The new **Surfworld Museum** (daily 10am–5pm; $5), at the rear of the plaza, is devoted to Torquay's main industry – and a prosperous one it is, turning over more than $200 million a year. *Surfworld* features a wave-making machine, interactive videos that explain how waves are created, and displays about the history of surfing. Many of the biggest surfing businesses are based in Torquay, and every surf accessory conceivable is sold somewhere. The biggest and the oldest is *Rip Curl*, 101 Geelong Rd (daily 9am–5.30pm), who started making surfboards here in 1969 and now stock all the major brands, as well as their own boards and gear. Based at the same shopping centre are showcase outlets for other big names: *Billabong, Piping Hot* and *Quiksilver*, to name just a few. Bargains can sometimes be found at *Bojo's Factory Outlet* and *Baines Beach Surf Seconds* around the corner in Baines Street (fourth factory on the right).

A grassy public reserve shaded by huge Norfolk Island pines (with electric barbecues and picnic tables) runs along rocky **Fisherman's Beach** (the "front beach"). Here you'll find an occassionally staffed **tourist information booth** (☎052/61 3310), but a noticeboard in the window provides local information when it's shut. The **Mary Elliott Pottery**, 80 Geelong Rd, also supplies tourist information and is open daily. The **Surf Beach** (or "back beach"), further out, is bound by rugged cliffs and takes a full belting from the Southern Ocean; it's patrolled in summer. **Jan Juc**, across the golf course, is also patrolled in season and has better swimming and surfing. The **South Coast Walk** to Aireys Inlet via Anglesea begins from here (25km; 8hr); the sector to **Bells Beach** is a one-hour, three-kilometre walk.

## Practicalities

**Accommodation** in Torquay is limited to a couple of motels and several caravan and camping parks: one of the most central options is the *Torquay Hotel/Motel*, at 36 Bell St (☎056/61 2001; ④). There's a great deal more choice when it comes to **food**, with some excellent, typically casual, places designed to satisfy a surfer's hunger. *Coastal Cottage Foods*, Shop 2, 57 Geelong Rd (daily 9am–5.30pm), serves healthy, cheap snacks with tables outside to eat them at; finish off next door at the *Great Australian Ice Creamery*. *Micha's Mexican*, 23 The Esplanade (☎052/61 2460; licensed and BYO; open daily for dinner), is a long-time favourite, with inexpensive drink – you'll need to book on summer weekends. The surfers' all-time favourite, however, is *Yummy Yoghurt*, a tiny café at 3 Gilbert St, its walls covered with testimonials from surfing champions, which doles out simple vegetarian stuff, shakes and frozen yoghurt. For **entertainment** surfies head for the *Torquay Hotel*, 36 Bell St, where live bands play at weekends. At Jan Juc, *Pabs Tavern* on Stuart Avenue is also a favourite hangout, with good food too.

# Anglesea and Aireys Inlet

Just beyond Bells Beach, the turn-off to **Addis Point** is well worth a detour. The road goes right onto the headland where, from the car park, you look down onto the waves crashing onto the point. Steps lead down to an even better vantage point, with heaving surf below you, and Bells Beach stretching out to the northwest.

First impressions of **ANGLESEA** are not promising: long before you reach town, you're greeted by the smell of an open-face brown-coal mine and power station generating electricity for *Alcoa Australia*'s aluminium-smelting works at Geelong. Past the power station, however, it's a perfectly pleasant place, with the Anglesea River running through to the sea, and picnic grounds along its banks. Despite tourist development, the beach still has sand dunes and a wild feel. The surf itself is fairly gentle, safe for children but with enough oomph for body surfers to have some fun. Anglesea's main claim to fame is that a large population of **kangaroos** grazes its golf course.

From Anglesea the road goes inland through scrubby bush for a few kilometres. Beyond, a lovely white lighthouse with a red cap overlooks the small town of **AIREYS INLET**. There's little more here than a general store (which sells heavily discounted fuel) and the *Aireys Inlet Caravan Park* opposite (☎052/89 6230; on-site vans ③, cabins ④). On the way out of town, the *Lighthouse Keepers Inn* (☎052/89 6666; ⑤–⑦) offers more upmarket accommodation, in keeping with the huge and ritzy houses that jostle for ocean views on the way to Lorne; one, just before Fairhaven, is so desperate for a vista that it sits on a concrete stem, like a wine-glass.

# Lorne

Picturesquely located at the foot of the heavily forested **Otway Range**, on the banks of the Erskine River, **LORNE** has long been the premier holiday town of the Great Ocean Road, so much so that the state government has pronounced it to be a place of "special significance and natural beauty". Only two hours' drive from the city, it's hugely popular with Melbourne weekenders who relish its well-established café society and whiff of Sixties counter-culture, overlaid on an essentially middle-class 1930s resort. To complete the picture, the **Angahook-Lorne State Park**, with its walking tracks, plunging falls and fern gullies, surrounds the town.

About nine hundred people live in Lorne, but from Christmas until the end of January twenty thousand more pour in – arrive unannounced and you'll have no hope of finding even a camping spot. The highlight of the peak season is the **Pier to Pub**

**Swim** in early January: the largest blue-water swimming event in the world, it attracts as many as two thousand competitors to race the 1200m from Lorne Pier to the main beach. The atmosphere around this event is a lot of fun, but generally Lorne is much more enjoyable when it's less crowded, which means coming during the week and outside the peak summer season.

Throughout the town, old guesthouses nestle alongside modern holiday flats. The main beachfront drag, Mountjoy Parade, is enlivened by the likes of the *Grand Pacific Hotel*, still with a recognizable 1870s facade, and by the modern, terraced *Cumberland Resort*, the so-called "Pink Palace". Between the street and the beach is a foreshore with tennis courts, trampolines and pool; the surf **beach** itself is one of the safest in Victoria, protected from the Southern Ocean by two headlands. In summer, this beach gets very crowded, and the secluded unofficial nude beach of **Jamiesons** (about 13km south by the Jamieson Creek), hidden by ferns and gullies, is a real find.

## Angahook-Lorne State Park

The **Angahook-Lorne State Park** extends from Aireys Inlet to Kennett River along some fifty kilometres of coastline. Pockets of temperate rainforest, towering blue-gum forests, cliffs and waterfalls characterize the Lorne section of the park, south of the Erskine River. The **Erskine Falls**, one of the most popular attractions, drop thirty metres into a fern-fringed pool – reach them along a winding eight-kilometre road (some of it gravel), which has a sting in its tail with a final short descent on a very steep but sealed section. From the car park the falls are a two-minute walk through majestic trees and tall umbrella ferns; another 150m leads down to the quiet, rocky Erskine River. It's also possible to walk through the bush from Lorne to the falls (7.5km one way; 4hr), starting from the *Erskine River Caravan Park* and following the river; after a kilometre you'll pass the Sanctuary, a natural rock amphitheatre, then Splitter Falls and Straw Falls, before reaching the crowning Erskine Falls.

Closer to town, **Teddy's Lookout** in Queens Park is either a quick drive from the Great Ocean Road, up Otway Street and then along George Street, or a three-kilometre walk. You end up high above the sea, with a view of the St George River below and the Great Ocean Road curving itself around the cliffs.

## Practicalities

Lorne's **tourist office**, at 144 Mountjoy Parade (Mon–Fri 9am–5pm, Sat & Sun 10am–3pm; ☎052/89 1152), is very helpful and has a good stock of leaflets packed with local information, including several free driving maps and details of walks within the state park. *Mocean*, 55 Mountjoy Parade (daily 9.30am–5.30pm), rent out quality surf- and boogie-boards and wetsuits, as well as making top-notch customized boards of their own. Any other services you might need – banks, post office, shops – can easily be found in the centre of town.

### Accommodation

Lorne has plenty of motel, hotel and self-catering accommodation, most of it in the upper price brackets. If you want to keep costs down (but don't fancy the dorms at *Great Ocean Road Cottages*), contact the *Lorne Foreshore Committee*, which has an office on Ocean Road by Erskine Bridge (☎052/89 1382) and runs four **caravan parks** around the town, with on-site vans for around ④.

**The Anchorage**, 32 Mountjoy Parade (☎052/89 1891). Self-catering accommodation with barbecues, pool and heated spa. ⑤–⑥.

**Cumberland Resort**, Mountjoy Parade. Luxurious but pricey 1-bedroom apartments, some with ocean views, and a plethora of complimentary facilities, including tennis courts, indoor pool, spa, sauna, windsurfers, boogie-boards and bicycles. ⑧.

**Erskine Falls Cottages**, off Erskine Falls Road, about 4km north of town (☎052/89 2666). Luxurious 2-bedroom cottages in a quiet bushland setting in the hills above Lorne, with superb views, a pool, heated spa, tennis court and barbecue. ⑦–⑧.

**Grand Pacific Hotel**, 268 Mountjoy Parade (☎052/89 1609). Faded grandeur concealing reasonably priced motel-style accommodation. ⑤.

**Great Ocean Road Cottages**, 3 Erskine Ave (☎052/89 1809). In a lovely forested setting beside the Erskine River, with a backpacker section and well-designed, comfortable self-catering cottages. Dorms ②, cottages ⑤–⑦.

**Lorne Coachman Inn**, 1 Deans Marsh Rd (☎052/89 2244). Fairly luxurious motel beside the Erskine River. ⑥–⑦.

**Lorne Hotel**, Mountjoy Parade (☎052/89 1409). Very large rooms, some with balconies and sea views, but noisy at weekends. ⑥.

**Ocean Lodge Motel**, 6 Armytage St (☎052/89 1330). Run-of-the-mill but good-value motel accommodation. ⑤–⑥.

## Food and entertainment

There are great places to eat and drink everywhere. In the evening, *Kosta's* often has **music**; the *Lorne Hotel* has bands on Friday and Saturday nights and the public bar, with its pool table and pinball machine, is a favourite with the young crowd. *Lorne Theatre* (☎052/89 1272) has **films** all week in summer.

**Angelo's at the Pier**. Seafood and charcoal-grilled steaks. Licensed and BYO.

**The Arab**, Mountjoy Parade. An original beatnik hangout, which opened two weeks before the Olympic Games in 1956 and has been going strong ever since. Now sporting a minimalist decor, but still good for snacks during the day and fancier meals at night.

**Burger It**, 58 Mountjoy Parade. The self-proclaimed source of "Australia's Original Gourmet Burger"; the range includes lentil, rabbit, emu and croc burgers.

**Kosta's**, 48 Mountjoy Parade. Popular, Greek-influenced bar and eating house, decorated with surrealist wall paintings, and looking onto a courtyard with ducks. Closed May–Sept.

**Lorne Hotel**, Mountjoy Parade. Best pub meals in town, with a dining room overlooking the ocean.

**Normandy Fare**, Mountjoy Parade, near the corner of Grove Street. Pleasant café serving Devonshire teas and dinner.

# Apollo Bay and the Otway Range

**APOLLO BAY** has a lovely setting, at the foot of gently rounded green hills, pounded by surf on the other side. **Fishing** – commercial and recreational – is the big thing here; if you're interested in doing a bit yourself, the *MV Revolution* departs from Fishermen's Wharf for fishing trips (daily 10am & 2pm; enquire on board, or call ☎03/9793 3405). The town has an enjoyably alternative feel – a lot of musicians live here and both local pubs have music on the weekends. For information on local activities, head for the Apollo Bay and Otway **information centre**, 55 Great Ocean Rd (☎052/37 6529; daily 10am–5pm), where they'll also book accommodation. Taking to the air is increasingly popular here: the *Wingsports Flight Academy* (☎052/37 6486) offers courses in **hang-gliding** and **paragliding**, and allows those with no prior experience to get a taster by **flying** with a fully qualified pilot along the coast in a powered hang-glider. Or you can fly in a Tiger Moth operated by *Torquair Airpark* (☎052/61 5100); a flight to the Great Apostles and back will set you back $50 (minimum 3 passengers). If **horse-riding** is more your thing, book a trail ride with *Wild Dog Trails* (☎052/37 6441; 1hr 30min $18, day-rides $70).

Apollo Bay has an especially wide variety of **accommodation**. Numerous holiday flats, cosy B&B cottages, guesthouses and farmstays are to be found in the area, many of them picturesquely located in the hills and valleys around town. The information centre has full details: one that's particularly worth seeking out is *Wongarra Heights*,

Sunnyside Road, Wongarra (☎052/37 0257; ⑥), which offers B&B accommodation on a farm 12km out of town, with great views. Apollo Bay's main street is lined with rather drab **motels** like the inexpensive *Iluka Motel* (☎052/37 6531; ④), at 65 Great Ocean Rd above the greasy spoon *Iluka Café*. There are several **caravan parks**, the closest to town being *Waratah Caravan Park* at 7 Noel St (☎052/37 6562; on-site vans ③, cabins ④). For foreshore **camping** in more natural, secluded surrounds, try the *Marengo Camping Reserve*, Marengo Crescent (☎052/37 6162), or *Skenes Creek Camping Reserve*, 6km back along the Ocean Road, where a caretaker calls every day. There's a YHA-affiliated **hostel** 2km north of the town centre at *Pisces Caravan Resort* (☎052/37 6749; dorms ①, cabins ②–⑥).

The most interesting places to **eat**, in terms of good food as well as scenic views, are outside town. Located in the hills up the coast above Skenes Creek, *Chris's Beacon Point Restaurant*, 2km up Skenes Creek Road (☎052/37 6411), is renowned for its Mediterranean cuisine and especially its seafood. The *Tanybryn Tea House and Gallery*, on the corner of Skenes Creek and Wild Dog roads, is also worth the drive (15min) for its well-stocked craft shop, café and fine panorama. In town, the eating places are strung along the Great Ocean Road as it passes through. You can eat in or take away at the self-explanatory *Wholefood Deli* at no. 61 (daily 10am–7pm); *Bay Leaf Gourmet Deli* at no. 131 is more atmospheric and sophisticated; for pancakes or crepes go to *Flipz* at no. 21–23. The *Apollo Bay Hotel* has great seafood, and also cheaper counter and bistro meals. Two other simple restaurants are *Buffs Bistro* near the information centre, for seafood, pasta, nachos and dips; and the *Otway Restaurant*, a bit further up at 210 Great Ocean Rd (lunch and dinner daily; BYO) which rustles up inexpensive, home-style dishes like roasts, grilled meats and fish.

## Otway National Park

From Apollo Bay, the Great Ocean Road soon enters **Otway National Park**, curving and bending upward through temperate rainforest with occasional glimpses of cleared hilltops and sheep grazing in the distance. An easy stroll on a boardwalk from **Maits Rest** car park, 17km west of Apollo Bay, takes you through a lovely fern gully and gives a good idea of the dense rainforest that once covered the entire Otway Range. A little further down the road towards Lavers Hill there's a turn-off to the **Cape Otway Lighthouse**, 14km away along an unsealed road, whose grounds you can explore (daily 10am–4pm; public tours inside the lighthouse five times daily on Tues, Thurs, Sat & Sun, $5). About halfway along this track, *Bimbi Park* (☎052/37 9246; on-site vans ③) is the only **caravan park** actually within the national park. While the setting is gorgeous, on a small farm with paddocks of horses and cows surrounded by bushland, the place is generally shabby and neglected. They do, however, offer excellent **horse rides** – half an hour to Station Beach, for example, a three-kilometre-long beach with freshwater springs and waterfalls.

Back on the Great Ocean Road, you momentarily return to the ocean at **Castle Cove**, a good lookout point across green, undulating dairy country. Returning inland, stepped hills rise sharply from the road as it passes turn-offs to **Johanna**, one of Victoria's best-known surf beaches, and winds up towards **LAVERS HILL**, high in the Otway Range. The town is epitomized by its craft shop and fern nursery, and the cosy tearooms at *Gardenside Manor* and the *Blackwood Gully Tourist Centre*, both of which serve light snacks and Devonshire teas from 10am daily. The *Otway Junction Motor Inn* (☎052/37 3295) offers more solid **meals**, both German and Australian, as well as motel-style **accommodation** (⑤–⑥). An alternative place to sleep is the *Lavers Hill Roadhouse* (☎052/37 3251), where you get the choice between bunkhouse (②) and on-site vans (③).

Three kilometres further, **Melba Gully Conservation Park** – one of the wettest spots in Victoria – is home to the Big Tree, a 300-year-old Otway messmate, its base covered in moss; at night glow-worms are a common sight.

# From Moonlight Head to Peterborough

The 130-kilometre stretch of coast between lonely, windswept Moonlight Head and Port Fairy is known as the **Shipwreck Coast** – all of it protected within the **Port Campbell National Park**. The stretch from Princetown to Peterborough is the most obviously hazardous to shipping, with its sheer limestone cliffs and massive eroded stacks. The first worthwhile stop beyond Princetown is to walk down **Gibsons Steps**, steep and slippery, to a small, kelp-covered beach sitting beneath the towering cliffs. From here on, the spectacle gets more and more extraordinary, with plenty of handy stopping points where you can gawp at the amazing formations. The most jaw-dropping are the **Twelve Apostles**, gigantic limestone pillars, some rising 65 metres out of the ocean, which retreat in rows as stark reminders of a wasting coastline (the cliff faces are still being eroded at a rate of about two centimetres per year). Sunset here is a popular time for photographers; in summer that's about 9pm, in winter about 5.45pm.

Next comes **Loch Ard Gorge**, where the **Historic Shipwreck Trail** begins. Extending from here to Peterborough, the trail links the sites of dozens of shipwrecks with path signs and information plaques. The *Loch Ard*, an iron-hulled square rig, was carrying immigrants from England in June 1878 when it hit a reef and foundered. Of fifty-three on board, only two survived: Eva Carmichael and Tom Pearce, both 18 years old, were swept into the long gorge with its narrow entrance, high walls and small beach; Tom dragged Eva into a cave in the western wall of the gorge before running for help. A walkway leads down to the beach, fetchingly covered with delicate pink kelp, and you can scramble over craggy rocks to the deep, sandy cave where Eva sheltered, now a nesting site for small birds. The Loch Ard cemetery, where the rest of the ship's complement are buried, is on the clifftop overlooking the gorge. Driving on takes you past yet more scenic points, with resonant names like the Blowhole and the Thundercave, before reaching Port Campbell.

## Port Campbell

**PORT CAMPBELL** is a small and companionable settlement on the edge of the park. The **Port Campbell National Park Information Centre** on Tregea Street (daily 10am–noon & 1–4.30pm; ☎055/98 6382) has all sorts of displays and information, as well as leaflets detailing the self-guided **Port Campbell Discovery Walk** (90min), which will lead you along the clifftop to a viewpoint above Two Mile Bay. Port Campbell **beach** is a small sandy curve, safe for swimming and patrolled in season.

The town climbs up the hill behind the beach. The *Port Campbell Trading Company*, a small **art gallery** at 27 Lord St, displays works by local artists and craftspeople. Opposite, the **Loch Ard Shipwreck Museum** (daily 9am–5pm; $3) has exhibits and videos relating the stories of five of the South West Coast shipping disasters (the *Loch Ard, Fiji, Schomberg, Falls of Halladale* and *Newfield*), as well as artefacts salvaged from some of the wrecks. If you're really fascinated by the wrecks, *Schomberg Diving Services* at 29 Lord St (daily 9am–6pm; ☎055/98 6499) lead **dives** to some of them, as well as renting out diving and snorkelling gear. *Shipwreck Coast Scenic Flights* (☎055/ 98 6369) offer a different perspective – they **fly** from Peterborough but can pick up and drop off at Port Campbell. *Port Campbell Shuttle Service* (☎055/98 6369) provides custom-made **tours** (maximum 6 passengers) to all attractions along the coast in air-conditioned 4WD vehicles.

## Practicalities

*Nelson's Store* (daily 8am–6pm winter; 7am–7pm summer) is the town's **general store** and just about everything else: post office, newsagent, bookshop, youth hostel keyholder and home of an EFTPOS system that takes every imaginable card. If you're looking for **somewhere to stay**, *Port Campbell Hotel* on Lord Street (☎055/98 6320; B&B ⑤) has old-fashioned rooms, a lively bar, and a bistro serving lunch and dinner daily. Opposite at 37 Lord St, *Port O'Call* (☎055/98 6206; ⑤) is a good, inexpensive motel. *Port Campbell Youth Hostel*, 18 Tregea St, run by the *Surf Life Saving Club* (☎055/98 6379), has basic but adequate dorms (①), while *Port Campbell Caravan Park* (☎055/98 6369) offers on-site vans (③) and cabins (④) right on the beach.

Places to **eat** include *Emma's BYO*, 25 Lord St, which operates from Tuesday to Saturday as tearooms by day (11am–4pm) and restaurant at night (7–11pm); the *Great Australian Bite*, on Lord Street opposite the beach; and the *Port Campbell Take Away Cafe* also near the beach.

## Beyond Port Campbell

At one time, tourists could walk across the double-arched rock formation called **London Bridge**, a short way west of Port Campbell, to the outer end facing the sea. In mid-January 1990, however, the outer span collapsed and fell into the sea, minutes after two extremely lucky people had crossed it – they were eventually rescued from the far limestone cliff by helicopter. Another good place to stop, just before Peterborough, is the **Grotto**, where a path leads from the clifftop to a rock pool beneath an archway.

Moving on, there's little to detain you in the last stretch of the Great Ocean Road from Peterborough, on Curdies Inlet, to Warrnambool, which is largely undulating dairy country. If you're a cheese fan, you might consider a detour to **Timboon**, 18km inland from Port Campbell: at *Timboon Farmhouse Cheese* (daily 10am–4pm), on the corner of Ford and Fells roads, you can taste and buy excellent, bio-dynamic cheese and wine.

# Warrnambool and onwards

**WARRNAMBOOL** seems unable to decide whether it's an industrial city or a charming, seaside agricultural town. Coming into town on the Great Ocean Road you get the positive side: a lovely coastal setting, with *Alansford Cheeseworld* to indicate that this is the centre of rich dairy country. Approach from the west, however, and the Princes Highway, lined with car lots and motels, brings you in through heavy traffic past an ugly factory belching smoke.

**Lady Bay**, where Warrnambool is sheltered, was first used by sealers and whalers in the early nineteenth century, and permanently settled from around 1839. Southern right whales, hunted to the brink of extinction, have in the last few years returned and been sighted in the surf off **Logans Beach** between May and October. The bay was never a good port, exposed to unpredictable weather, reefs and shallow water, and there were 28 shipwrecks here between 1836 and 1908. The excellent **Flagstaff Hill Maritime Village** on Merri Street (daily 9.00am–4.30pm; $9.50) delves into these and other shipwrecks along the treacherous coast, particularly exploring the *Loch Ard* disaster (see above). The recreated nineteenth-century village is set around a fort erected in 1887, a time when, improbably, the fear of Russian invasion permeated Australia.

Downtown, Warrnambool is a bustling city, with a major shopping centre on Liebig Street, several galleries and museums, and some fine old churches. Perhaps the best of the sights is the **Warrnambool Art Gallery** on Liebig Street (Tues–Sun noon–5pm), a fine provincial gallery with collections of Western District colonial paintings and contemporary Australian prints. The **Botanic Gardens** on Botanic Road are also worth visiting, designed by William Guilfoyle, then Director of the Melbourne Botanic Gardens, in 1877. The classically designed gardens are peaceful and beautiful, with glimpses of the sea.

## Practicalities

**Warrnambool Tourist Information**, at 600 Raglan Parade (Mon–Fri 9am–5pm, Sat & Sun 10am–4pm; ☎055/64 7837), is modern, large and well organized, and also books accommodation and acts as a travel agency. If you want to **stay**, *The Stuffed Backpacker*, operated by *Flaherty's Chocolate Shop*, 52 Kepler St (☎055/62 2459; ①) has very cheap B&B in basic dorms. The *Surf Side One Caravan Park* on Pertobe Road (☎055/62 4897; dorms ①, cabins ④) also has backpacker accommodation and is right on the beach, less than a kilometre from town. More comfortable rooms can be found at the *Lady Bay Hotel*, also on Pertobe Road (☎055/62 1544; ④); failing all of these, motels line the Princes Highway either side of town.

There are plenty of good places to **eat** on Liebig Street. The requisite seaside fish and chips are freshly cooked at *Seafoods*, at no. 126. The *Victoria Hotel* (at the corner of Lava Street) has bar meals, or there's classier cuisine at the *Sherwood Rooms Restaurant* in the *Tatts Hotel* at no. 191. *Dimitri's*, at 92 Liebig St, is a casual good-value Greek restaurant, while *Rios Deli* at no. 142 does good sandwiches, bagels and cakes. *Rogers Bar* at the *Whalers Inn*, on the corner of Liebig and Timor streets, is where the young and trendy of Warrnambool go to **drink**, with its slick modern-looking bar.

## Onwards: Tower Hill Game Reserve and Koroit

About 13km west of Warrnambool along the Princes Highway, **Tower Hill Game Reserve** is located in the crater of a volcano which last erupted about 18,000 years ago. In the last century the pioneer settlers stripped Tower Hill of its trees and used it as grazing land, but since the 1960s it has been reforested and the wildlife has gradually returned. Visit the island in the middle of the crater lake at dusk and you'll encounter emus and koalas and probably more kangaroos and wallabies than you can count. Unfortunately, **access** to the game reserve may soon be restricted to 8am–5pm, and on days of extreme fire danger the reserve is sometimes completely closed (enquire on ☎055/65 9202). The **Natural History Centre** (daily 9.30am–4.30pm) on the island has displays about the area's geological history and the revegetation program, while a bird hide nearby enables you to spy on the abundant birdlife. There are also five self-guided short **walks** around the reserve (30min–1hr).

Just north of here, **KOROIT** is a tiny, old-fashioned town with the largest concentration of people of Irish descent in Australia; naturally the Catholic Church is impressive, but the building that dominates the town (no more surprisingly) is the elegant two-storey *Koroit Hotel*. It's been run by the same family since 1922, and little has changed in that time. Other buildings along the main street are faded one-storey Victorian and Edwardian shop-fronts with shady corrugated-iron awnings, and there's also a deserted train station. If you cut north from here to the Hamilton Highway you'll know you're getting into wool country when you see sheep walking down the main street of Woolsthorpe.

# Port Fairy and Mount Eccles

**PORT FAIRY**, the next stop along the coast, was an early port and whaling centre that's now a quaint crayfishing town with a busy jetty, a harbour full of yachts, and over fifty National Trust-listed buildings. Heavy southern breakers roll into the surrounding beaches, and there's a muttonbird rookery on Griffiths Island where you can watch the muttonbirds (shearwaters) roost at dusk from a specially constructed lookout. For a historic town, it's also quite a happening place, with numerous events: in summer the six-week-long **Moyneyama Festival** focusses on the great outdoors with events like a raft race on the Moyne River and reaches its climax with the Moyneyama New Year's Eve procession; at Easter the annual Queenscliff to Port Fairy yacht race ends here in a huge party. The biggest event, however, is over the Labor Day long weekend in March, when the huge **Port Fairy Folk Festival** takes over the town, with Australian and overseas acts playing world, roots and acoustic music – everything from Koorie to country, and from blues to Celtic; up to twenty thousand people pour into town for the festival, and accommodation is scarce. For more information and festival bookings call the Port Fairy **tourist information centre**, on Bank Street (Mon–Fri 10am–4pm, weekends 10am–12.30pm &1.30–4pm; ☎055/68 2682). They also book accommodation and produce an excellent free map of the Port Fairy Heritage Walk, which leads you around the town's numerous fine buildings. The **History Centre**, located in the Old Courthouse in Gipps Street by the river, exhibits costumes, historic photographs, shipwreck relics and other items relating to the town's pioneer history (Wed, Sat & Sun 2–5pm, daily during school holidays & long weekends; $2).

## Port Fairy practicalities

With its villagey atmosphere, Port Fairy is a good place for a stopover between Melbourne and Adelaide, and has a variety of **accommodation** options, as well as good pubs, tea rooms, and restaurants. The *Port Fairy Youth Hostel*, 8 Cox St (☎055/68 2468; ①), is in a lovely old house right in the centre of town, though the inside of the hostel is rather run-down and shabby. The *Seacombe House Motor Inn* at 22 Sackville St (☎055/68 1082; ④–⑦), one of the many National Trust-listed buildings, has a few inexpensive rooms in the old hotel, as well as modern motel units and historic cottages. In fact, there are numerous quaint colonial cottages and B&B places, offering accommodation for one night or longer stays, such as *Whalers Cottages*, corner of Whalers Drive and Regent Street (☎055/68 1488; ⑤–⑥), *Cottages of the Port*, 96 Gipps St (☎055/68 1838; ⑥–⑦), and *Lough Cottage*, 216 Griffith St (☎055/68 1583; ⑤). Full details of all such properties, and of Port Fairy's six caravan parks, can be obtained from the tourist information centre.

*Lunch* is an appropriately named **café** in the old Borough Chambers, 20 Bank St, with eclectic and very enjoyable food (Wed–Sun 9am–5pm, extended hours during the holiday season). **Tea** is served at *Mott's Cottage*, 5 Sackville St (10.30am–4.30pm; closed August, & Mon except during holidays), a fine example of a modest dwelling. *Culpepper's*, 24 Bank St, is a healthfood shop which also serves Devonshire teas and **light meals**. For an upmarket licensed **restaurant**, try *Dublin House Inn*, 57 Bank St, or the very good *Stag Inn Restaurant* at the *Seacombe House Motor Inn*. The best place to **drink** is the *Caledonian Inn* on the corner of Banks and James streets, the oldest continually licensed pub in Victoria (since 1844).

# Mount Eccles National Park

Just over fifty kilometres north of Port Fairy is the wonderful **Mount Eccles National Park**. Mount Eccles (though it hardly deserves to be called a mountain) is an extinct **volcano** with lava caves, channels and a crater lake amid rugged, stony country; there used to be a quarry here and you can see the various layers of different lava flows where the mountain has been cut. **Lake Surprise** is the delightful crater lake, shimmering blue in summer. Walks include a two-kilometre (1hr) walk around the rim of the crater, or you can descend and walk around the shoreline (with a chance to swim in the lake, which is 21°C in summer); there's also a two-hour walk along a lava canal leading to a lava cave.

**Birdlife** around the lake includes wedge-tail eagles, kookaburras, tawny frog-mouths, dog birds, barn owls and boobooks. The trees are loaded with koalas which can be seen at any time of the day. There are also eastern grey kangaroos, echidnas, bats, tiger snakes, copper-head snakes and blue-tongued lizards. Mid- to late spring is a good time for wild flowers, from orchids to native geraniums, and wattle. Look out for a tree in the southwest corner of the park that has had an Aboriginal shield cut out of it with a sharpened stone tool. The **visitors' centre** (☎055/76 1014) has an informative display to help you explore and learn about the park, and the history of the volcano and of the area's Aborigines. You can also **camp** here: there are toilets, water, and wood is supplied.

# Portland to South Australia

**PORTLAND**, the Princes Highway's final call on the Victoria coast, is a large and unattractive industrial and fishing port. Huge ships dock in **Portland Bay**, where a vast heap of sandy brown bauxite sits beside the *Alcoa* smelter, in full view of the Esplanade. **Aluminium** is Australia's largest single export, and in 1980 big business met **Aboriginal resistance** here, when a legal battle developed over the siting of the smelter on land that had great importance for the Gunditj Mara. There were traces of over sixty Aboriginal campsites and workshop areas on the proposed site, and sacred places including a burial ground. The smelter eventually went ahead, but *Alcoa* was forced to pay the Gunditj Mara 1.5 million dollars' compensation, which was used to buy back land in the area of the Lake Condah mission (see below).

Battles with local Koories were nothing new for Portland. Even before the area was permanently settled by whites – and it's the oldest settlement in Victoria – there had been conflict between whalers and Aborigines, which resulted in the decimation of an entire tribe. Anything found dead on the shore, including whales, had traditionally been claimed by the local Aborigines; when the whalers found them cutting up and eating their catch they indulged in a punitive **massacre** from which few escaped. The first **squatters** in Victoria, the Hentys, came to the Portland area in 1834 to graze sheep over vast landholdings, and they too soon came into conflict with the Koories – from 1838 clans began to use their traditional burning-off process in an attempt to drive the Hentys away. During the 1840s a sustained guerrilla war, known as the **Eumeralla War**, was fought against settlers occupying land around Port Fairy, Mount Napier and Lake Condah. In the end it was only the deployment of the Aboriginal **Native Police Corps** in 1842 that finally broke the resistance – and even they took four years.

In Portland they do their best to ignore the seamier side of things, with the seafront Esplanade lined with fish and chip shops and cafés as if the view of the smelter, and its history, didn't matter, and numerous drab museums and historical buildings that mainly celebrate the white settlement. Portland does support a **tourist office** (daily 10am–4.30pm; ☎055/23 2671) on the waterfront, but it's unlikely that you'll want to linger, let alone stay.

The best of the surrounding area lies along the coast to the southwest, where, once you get away from the smelter, the scenery, around craggy **Cape Nelson** and stormy **Cape Bridgewater**, is stunning: there are caves, freshwater lakes close to the cliff coast, a petrified forest of limestone columns where ancient trees used to stand, blow-holes and the beach of **Bridgewater Bay**, which stretches in a wide, sandy arc between the two capes. The best way to explore these features is along walking tracks from the Blowholes car park, which is signposted left off the road to Cape Bridgewater. Bring good walking shoes as the volcanic rocks can be very sharp, and take food and drink.

# Lake Condah Mission

**Lake Condah Mission** is some 50km northeast of Portland, on the western edge of Mount Eccles National Park. In this traditional Aboriginal area, with its plentiful game and fish, a mission was established in 1867, and surviving Aborigines from the area were brought here, but were forbidden to speak their own language or practise their culture. At its height in 1880, there were over twenty timber and stone buildings. Although the mission officially closed in 1919, a large community stayed on until the 1950s, when they were gradually dispossessed as land was given to returned soldiers under the soldier settlement scheme; perhaps the greatest injustice occurred when several Aboriginal returned soldiers who had lived on Lake Condah applied for land, only to be knocked back. With the money paid in settlement of the *Alcoa* dispute (see above), the land was finally bought back in the 1980s.

As well as the ruins of the mission, remains of older stone huts and fish traps are visible; you're welcome to wander about the 1600 hectares of land, though there's little to explain what you can see. Plans to operate the mission as a tourist venue, with accommodation and guided tours, seem to have been shelved for the time being.

# Lower Glenelg National Park and Nelson

From Portland, the **Princes Highway** makes its way via Heywood to Mount Gambier in South Australia fairly uneventfully. After 120km, it crosses the **Glenelg River** (which has its source in the Grampians) at Dartmoor, a popular point to begin a four-day canoeing trip down to the river mouth at Nelson. For most of the journey, the clear, blue river flows through unspoilt **Lower Glenelg National Park**, in a sixty-kilometre gorge cut through limestone. The spectacular **Princess Margaret Rose Caves** (guided tours hourly) lie beside the river as it loops round by the South Australian border, and can be reached by canoe, car (unsealed roads lead here from both sides of the border), or on a cruise from Nelson.

**NELSON** is at the end of the coastal road and virtually on the border, less than 40km from Mount Gambier. A peaceful, friendly little hamlet, it feels caught in a time warp, and there's little to do but **fish** on the Glenelg. *Nelson Boat Hire* in Kellet Street (daily 8.30am–6pm, closed Wed out of season; ☎087/38 4048) sell bait and can tell you what you're likely to catch and where; you'll also need a licence from *Nelson Kiosk* (daily 8am–6pm), the local filling station and post office. Fishing shelters line the river or you can rent a boat of virtually any kind, from a Canadian canoe to a cruiser sleeping six. *Nelson Endeavour*, on the opposite bank of the river on Old Bridge Road, operates **cruises** to the Princess Margaret Rose Caves (☎087/38 4191; Wed & Sat 1pm, twice daily during summer school holidays; $15; 3hr 30min), as do *Glenelg River Cruises* (☎087/38 4192).

The **Lower Glenelg National Park and Information Centre** (daily except Tues 9am–4.30pm; ☎087/38 4051) is signposted just off North Nelson Road; it also covers the Discovery Bay Coastal Park, which protects the shoreline almost all the way from Portland to the border. Here you can get camping permits (book in advance in peak seasons) and information on walks and activities. The one-storey *Nelson Hotel*, Kellet Street, is a classic untouristy pub, which has budget **accommodation** (☎087/38 4011; ③) and very inexpensive counter meals. Halfway between Portland and Nelson, *Nioka Farm Home Hostel* (☎055/20 2233; ②; booking essential) offers backpacker accommo-

All ☎087 **phone numbers** in **Nelson** will change in February 1997: the area code will change to ☎08, and the number will have the prefix 87 added. So, for example, what was ☎087/xx xxxx will become ☎08/87xx xxxx.

*(For more on changes to phone numbers Australia-wide, see p.40.)*

dation on a huge sheep farm bordering the Lower Glenelg National Park. The rate includes breakfast and evening meal with the family, and they'll pick you up from Portland if you arrange it in advance.

# CENTRAL VICTORIA:
# THE GOLDFIELDS

Central Victoria is classic Victoria: a rich pastoral district, chilly and green in winter and parched a brownish yellow in summer, with two grand provincial cities, **Ballarat** and **Bendigo**, their fine buildings funded by gold. Nowadays both are major tourist centres on the gold trail. The many surrounding country centres like **Maryborough** and **Castlemaine**, once prosperous gold towns in their own right, now seem too lowly for their extravagant architecture.

There's fairly good **transport** in this direction, with regular *V/Line* trains and buses to Bendigo, Ballarat and the other major centres, and local buses filling most gaps. If you're driving, the best way to tour the area is to follow the **Goldfields Tourist Route** with its chocolate-brown signs marked by a distinctive circled capital G. The route links the major cities – Bendigo, Castlemaine, Ballarat, Ararat and Stawell – with many smaller places in between.

### Towards the Goldfields: the Calder Highway

Though you could take the Western Freeway or the train directly to Ballarat, the route **towards Bendigo**, 150km northwest of Melbourne along the Calder Highway, is far more interesting. The railway to Bendigo, which continues to Swan Hill, follows the same route, calling at the main towns. At Diggers Rest, 22km from Melbourne, a short detour to the east will take you to tiny **Organ Pipes National Park**, so designated for its outstanding geological interest. The rock formations here are a series of basalt

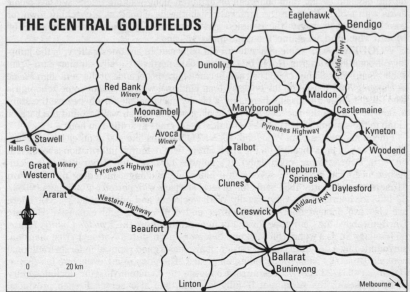

THE CENTRAL GOLDFIELDS

## THE GOLDRUSHES

The Californian goldrushes of the 1840s captured the popular imagination around the world with tales of the huge fortunes to be made gold prospecting, and it wasn't long until Australia's first goldrush, near Bathurst in New South Wales in 1851. Victoria had been a separate colony for only nine days when gold was found at Clunes on July 10, 1851; the **goldrush** began for real when rich deposits were found in Ballarat nine months later. The richest goldfields ever known soon opened at Bendigo, and thousands poured into Victoria from around the world. The golden decade of the 1850s saw Victoria's population increase from eighty thousand to half a million, half of whom stayed permanently in the state. The British and Irish made up a large proportion of the new population but over forty thousand Chinese came to make their fortune too, along with experienced American gold seekers and others as various as Russians, Finns and Filipinos. Ex-convicts and native-born Australians, of course, also poured into Victoria, leaving other colonies short of workers; even respectable policemen deserted their posts to become "diggers", and doctors, lawyers and prostitutes poured into the haphazard new towns in their wake. The goldfields were a great equalizer; all you needed was a shovel and perseverance, and a fortune was as likely yours as the next man's.

In the beginning, the fortune seekers panned the creeks and rivers searching for **alluvial gold**, constantly moving on at the news of another find. But gold was also deep within the earth, where ancient riverbeds had been buried by volcanoes; in Ballarat in 1852 the first **shafts** were dug, and because the work was unsafe and arduous, the men joined in bands of eight or ten, usually grouped by nationality, working a common claim. For deep mining, diggers stayed in one place for months or years, and the major workings rapidly became stable communities with banks, shops, hotels, churches and theatres, evolving more gradually, on the back of income from gold, into grandiose towns.

columns, formed by lava cooling in an ancient riverbed, and rising up to twenty metres above Jacksons Creek. The park (daily 8am–4.30pm; weekends, public holidays and during daylight saving until 6pm) can be explored along walking tracks and has picnic areas with tables. Back on the highway, Gisborne developed as a coaching town for travellers on their way to the Bendigo and Castlemaine goldfields; it's dominated by **Mount Macedon**, an extinct thousand-metre volcano.

**WOODEND**, with some characterful old pubs and an antiques gallery, is the jumping-off point for **Hanging Rock**, in a reserve 6km northeast (daily summer 8am–7pm; winter 8am–6pm; $5 per car). The rock became famous because of the eerie film *Picnic at Hanging Rock* (based on the book by Joan Lindsay), which is about some schoolgirls who mysteriously go missing here after a picnic; many people falsely believe the story to be true, though the rock itself is not at all spooky. You can walk around the base or climb to the summit with its massive boulders and crags in around an hour.

Fifteen kilometres from Woodend, **KYNETON** seems like just another boring country town as you pass through on the High Street (where tourist information is located at no. 6, in *Dapples Store*, open daily). It's notable, however, for **Piper Street**, a picturesque historical strip with several fine bluestone buildings, including the **Kyneton Museum**, a two-storey 1855 bank, full of local artefacts with period outbuildings (☎054/ 22 1433 for hours, which vary; usually Wed, weekends and public holidays; $3). There are also two ancient flour mills at either end of the town and expansive **Botanic Gardens** above the Campaspe River. For **accommodation**, the *Kyneton Country House*, 66 Jennings St, is a wonderful weekend hideaway in a restored National Trust mansion, surrounded by a beautiful cottage garden; it also has a good reputation for its traditional cooking (☎054/22 3556; ⑨, including all meals). The price of a Devonshire tea ($5) at *Babette's* (☎054/22 2581), a **restaurant** opposite the Kyneton Museum, includes entry to the museum; the restaurant is fully licensed, and also serves French provincial cuisine from Wednesday to Saturday evenings. A few houses further down, the *Bluestone Cottage*, 78 Piper St, serves scrumptious Devonshire teas and hearty, country-style lunches.

# Bendigo

Rich alluvial gold was first discovered in **BENDIGO** in 1851, and once it was exhausted shafts were sunk into a gold-bearing quartz reef. Bendigo became the greatest goldfield of the time, with the world's deepest mine. Mining continued here right up to 1954, long after the rest of central Victoria's goldfields were exhausted, so it's a city that developed over a prosperous century: the nationwide department store *Myer* began life here, as did Australia's first building society in 1858. Though in many ways it's even more magnificent than Ballarat (see p.712), Bendigo is considerably lower key, never having turned itself into a purely tourist town. Its most visited sights are legacies of the mining days – the **Chinese Joss House** and the **Central Deborah Mine** – but there are a myriad less obvious attractions.

At the heart of town are two cathedrals – rich on gold-digging, local Catholics were able to bring stonemasons from Italy and England to work on the full-on Gothic **Sacred Heart Cathedral** – and vast **Rosalind Park**. Wanting to give Bendigo a sophisticated London air, its newly prosperous citizens gave its central crossroads the incongruous name of **Charing Cross**. **Pall Mall** runs to the east of here, while **View Street** climbs to the north with many fine old buildings. South, Mitchell Street runs to the **train station** and, to the west, High Street (the Calder Highway) runs out of town. The other important street is Hargreaves, one block south of Pall Mall, with its impressive town hall and obligatory, rather dreary shopping mall.

## The Town

Many of Bendigo's finest goldrush buildings are along **Pall Mall**, including the ornate Italianate post office (1887) and law courts (1896) – neither of which would seem out of place in a capital city – and the quite amazingly decorative **Shamrock Hotel** opposite; four storeys of gold-boom architecture at its most extreme. **View Street**, climbing the hill beside Rosalind Park, has more in the same vein. The *Bendigo Arts Centre* here is a massive Neoclassical pile, joined to the much more homely redbrick fire station which now does duty as the Community Arts Centre. The **Art Gallery**, in an ugly 1960s building at no. 42 (Mon–Sat 10am–5pm, Sun & public holidays 2–5pm; $2), has an extensive collection of Australian painting from Bendigo's goldfield days to the present, as well as nineteenth-century British and European art, acquired with all that gold. Several commercial galleries, antique shops, restaurants, cafés and bars add to the arty feel of the street, which also has its credibly dog-eared side with a charity shop, community café and Red Cross Centre. The Queen Elizabeth Oval with its old redbrick stadium backs onto Rosalind Park; you can watch Aussie Rules football here on a cold winter Sunday.

**Bridge Street**, one of the oldest in Bendigo, was once **Chinatown**, home to thousands of Chinese who poured into Victoria's richest gold area in the 1850s, and who knew Bendigo as "the golden mountain"; when the gold ran out, many turned to market gardening in the area. Right up to the 1960s you could still have seen the old Chinese shops with their faded signs, but now you have to be content with the **Golden Dragon Museum** (daily 9.30am–5pm; $5), whose impressive collection of Chinese processional regalia includes what are said to be the world's longest and oldest Imperial dragons, Sun Loong and Loong. A history exhibition tells the full story of Bendigo's Chinese community since the goldrush. The **Joss House**, on Finn Street in

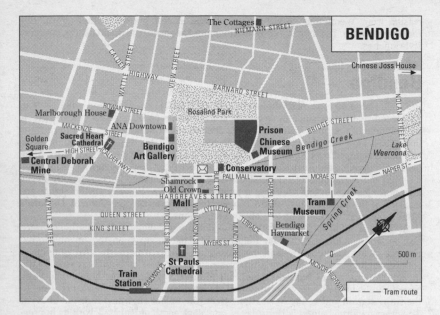

North Bendigo (daily 10am–5pm; $3; bus #7, approx. hourly, Mon–Fri only), was built by the Chinese of Emu Point in the 1860s, and is the oldest Chinese temple still in use in Australia, now operated by the National Trust. The route to the shrine passes man-made Lake Weeroona, where there's a **Chinese Tea House** in the picnic grounds.

### The Central Deborah Goldmine

The **Central Deborah Goldmine**, at the corner of Violet Street and the Calder Highway (daily 9am–5pm; underground tour $11), was the last mine to close in the Central Goldfields. The hour-long underground tour is worth taking if you've never been down a mine before, and as long as you're not claustrophobic; everybody is issued with a reassuring hard hat, complete with torch and generator. Going down to a depth of sixty metres takes 85 seconds in the lift – to reach the bottom of some of the deepest shafts would take 30 minutes. The further down you go the hotter it gets, but at sixty metres it's quite warm and airless enough for most people, dripping with water and muddy underfoot.

You're free to wander about on the surface, taking a look at the engine room with its steam-driven air compressor, and the various methods of processing the quartz. Other things to look at are a room set up like a modest miner's house from the 1840s, a model of the mine, and a museum with photographs and stories in the old changing rooms.

## Practicalities

**Bendigo Tourist Information** is about 3km south of the centre at 26 High St, Kangaroo Flat (daily 9am–5pm; ☎054/47 1383). They don't book tours or accommodation but do provide lots of brochures and maps – the free *Bendigo* booklet, including a walking map, is very useful (you'll also find "Heritage Walk" panels outside significant buildings). *Mully's Café*, in the city centre at 32 Pall Mall, also dispenses tourist information.

A good way to get an impression of town is to take the **Talking Tram Tour**, though the taped commentary can be rather irritating (hourly departures from the Central Deborah Goldmine on High Street 9.30am–3.30pm; 1hr; $6). The ticket includes entrance to the Bendigo Tram Museum towards the other end of the ride; Bendigo had electric trams even before Melbourne, but they shut down in 1972. **Buses** have taken their place as everyday transport – they all leave from the corner of Mitchell and Hargreaves streets, with a flat fare of $1.30 for two hours (*Christians Bus Company* ☎054/47 2222). *Woods Airport Service* provides a transport service to Melbourne's Tullamarine Airport (☎054/35 3756; $32 one way; departures three times daily, booking essential).

## Accommodation

In terms of atmosphere and style, the **bed and breakfast guesthouses** and **cottages** that dot Bendigo and the whole goldfields area are a much better option than the average, somewhat sterile motel room.

**ANA Downtown Motor Inn**, 46 View St (☎054/43 9155). Excellent position next to the Performing Arts Centre; some units have spas. ⑤–⑥.

**Bendigo Haymarket Motor Inn**, 5 McIvor Rd (☎054/41 5654). Ultra-modern motel with one disabled-accessible unit, a swimming pool and sauna; some rooms have spas. ⑤.

**Central City Caravan Park**, 362 High St (☎054/43 6937). Good hostel accommodation in three cabins with separate kitchen and common room, plus camping, vans and cabin units. Dorms ①, vans ③, cabins ④.

**The Cottages**, corner of Niemann and Anderson streets (☎054/41 5613). B&B in two small, self-contained weatherboard cottages. ⑤–⑦.

**Elm Motel**, 454 High St, Golden Square (☎054/47 7522). Inexpensive motel, conveniently located next to the interstate bus terminal with a public bus into town at the front door. ④.

**Marlborough House**, 115 Wattle Street (☎054/41 4142). Beautifully furnished en-suite guestrooms in a grand goldrush mansion, just up the hill from the Sacred Heart Cathedral. B&B ⑤–⑦.

**Old Crown Hotel**, 238 Hargreaves St (☎054/41 6888). Centrally located, comfortable pub accommodation with a light breakfast included in the tariff. ④.

**Rupertswood Country Home**, Mandurang Road, Mandurang, about 7km south of Bendigo (☎054/39 5532). Quiet location in a picturesque valley; en-suite guestrooms and private sitting rooms. ⑤–⑦.

**Shamrock Hotel**, Pall Mall (☎054/43 0333). Fabulous Victorian hotel that has everything from budget, shared-facility rooms to executive suites. ④–⑧.

## Eating, drinking and nightlife

The town offers a fairly good choice when it comes to **eating** and **drinking** and there is plenty of student-influenced **nightlife** during term-time. Entertainment at the Latrobe campus is open to non-students – call ☎054/44 7478 to find out if anything is happening. Several pubs have bands, including the *Golden Vine*, 135 King St, on Friday and Sunday nights, and the *Limerick Tavern*, 44 Williamson St, on Thursday nights. The *Rifle Brigade Hotel*, 137 View St, is a brewery pub with a wrought-iron verandah which attracts a young crowd. A nightclub popular with students is *Hot Gossips*, 264 Hargreaves St, open late every night except Monday.

**Black Sheep**, 58 Bull St. Upmarket joint serving Tex-Mex and veggie burgers. Licensed.

**Clogs**, 106 Pall Mall. Modern, lively, reasonably priced brasserie. Daily from 5pm, plus lunch on Sun.

**Cumberland Hotel**, 56 Williamson St. Family bistro open daily for lunch and dinner.

**Gold Mines Hotel**, 89 Marong Rd. Good bistro meals in a refurbished old hotel on the Calder Highway towards Bridgewater: near the Deborah Hold Mine, turn into Lily Street, drive up to the end and turn left.

**Karl's Kaffee House**, 95 View St. German pastries and savouries, and great coffee in cosy surrounds. Daily to 5pm.

**Matilda's Café**, 29 Charing Cross. This community café staffed by volunteers is the cheapest place to eat in town, serving filling veggie and non-veggie food in a relaxed homely atmosphere. Mon–Fri 9.30am–5.30pm.

**Metropolitan Brasserie**, corner of Bull and Hargreaves streets. This transformed 1860s pub has won several awards for its food which features bush tucker. Daily noon–midnight for meals or drinks.

**Shamrock Hotel**, Pall Mall. Lovely café-bar for a coffee or drink, or inexpensive bistro meals.

**Whirakee Restaurant and Wine Bar**, 17 View Point, at the beginning of View St, just opposite the fountain. Outstanding, though expensive, French-inspired cuisine, with an excellent wine list featuring local wines.

# Castlemaine and around

**CASTLEMAINE** is at the centre of the area once known as the Mount Alexander Goldfields; between 1851 and 1861, 105,000 kilogrammes of gold were found in the area when its gullies were among the richest in the world (more modest quantities are still found at Wattle Gully mine at nearby Chewton, the oldest working gold mine in Australia). Castlemaine became the headquarters of the Government Camp for the area in 1852, and all its impressive buildings were built within the next ten years. With no deep mines to sustain it however, Castlemaine has developed little since then.

The town's finest building is the **Old Castlemaine Market** on Mostyn Street (daily 10am–5pm; $3), a wonderfully over-the-top piece of Neoclassicism. Inside, a historical display portrays the history of the Mount Alexander Goldfields and Castlemaine. The **Theatre Royal** in Hargraves Street, one of the oldest theatres in Australia, is also rather magnificent; it's said that when the famous Lola Montez performed here, miners threw nuggets of gold at her in appreciation. Now it's an unusual **cinema** (☎054/72 1196) with a cabaret-style section downstairs and a licensed bistro; upstairs it has traditional movie-house seating. Theatre groups and live bands sometimes perform here, and there's even a disco till 3am, Thursday to Saturday.

Another unusual attraction, a little way from the centre, is **Buda** (42 Hunter Street; daily 9.30am–5pm; $5), a gracious nineteenth-century home and garden originally built in 1861 by a retired Baptist missionary in the style of an Indian villa. It was added to by its new owner Ernest Leviny, a Hungarian silversmith, in the 1890s. House and gardens give an insight into the good life of the goldrush days, and much of Leviny's and his family's work is on display, along with early photography and the family art collection. The **Castlemaine Art Gallery and Museum**, Lyttleton Street (Mon–Fri 10am–5pm, Sat & Sun 10am–noon & 1–5pm; $3), also merits a visit. Established in 1913 in a classic Art Deco building, the gallery specializes in Australian photographs and paintings, with many works of the Heidelberg School, notably Frederick McCubbin and Tom Roberts. Partly due to the big **Castlemaine State Festival**, held in even-numbered years over ten days from the last week of October, this is quite an arty place, with several other galleries around town. As a counterbalance in odd-numbered years, lots of small and large gardens in the Castlemaine district open their doors to visitors, during the **Festival of Gardens**, which takes place on the weekend prior to the Melbourne Cup in November.

A **Sunday Market** is in full swing from about 9am to 5pm in the old Technical College building at the corner of Hargraves and Forest streets, and, if you're here on a Saturday, trek the 2km out to **Wesley Hill Market** on the Melbourne Road, a giant fleamarket (8am–1pm), with local produce and crafts. A recently established tourist attraction is the **Dingo Farm** between Castlemaine and Chewton where about 70 dingoes are kept in fenced-in enclosures on five hectares of bushland (☎054/70 5711; daily 9am–5pm, $5); watch out for signs on the Pyrenees Highway.

## Practicalities

The **Castlemaine Information Centre** is on Duke Street – the Pyrenees Highway – designed to catch weekenders as they drive in (weekends, public & school holidays 10am–4.30pm; ☎054/72 4574). In town you can get brochures during business hours from the Development Committee, 13 Hargraves St (☎054/72 3222).

**Places to stay** include *Campbell Street Lodge*, 33 Campbell St (☎054/72 2377; ⑤–⑥), with motel-style rooms in a National Trust-classified house, and the charming *Bookshop Cottage*, 242 Barker St (☎054/72 1557; ④), behind the *Castlemaine Bookshop*. *The Criterion Hotel*, 163 Barker St (☎054/72 1114; ①), is the local hangout, with pool tables, bands at weekends, cheap counter meals and really basic rooms upstairs. The *Commercial Hotel* at the corner of Hargraves and Forest streets (☎054/72 1173; ①) also has cheap backpacker accommodation; phone for pick-ups from the train station. At the other end of the market, *Ellimatta*, 233 Barker St (☎054/72 4454; B&B ⑦), is a guesthouse in a beautifully restored former hotel with an award-winning restaurant.

**Food** here is excellent, with a wide variety of places. *Bings Café*, 71 Mostyn St, opposite the market (Mon–Fri 9am–4.30pm, Sat 9am–1pm), has breakfast all day, and everything from full meals to veggie burgers to sandwiches. *Togs Place*, 58 Lyttleton St, provides good food in a peaceful atmosphere, with a courtyard to sit out in summer; or sample Mexican fare in a 140-year-old bakery, at *Simpatico Mexican Restaurant*, 32 Johnstone St (dinner Wed–Sun). Top of the range is the *Ellimatta Restaurant* (☎054/72 4454; licensed; lunch daily, dinner Thurs–Sat).

## Maldon

**MALDON** is a tiny, peaceful town of tearooms, antique shops and bed and breakfasts surrounded closely by low hills. In 1965 the National Trust declared it the best-preserved gold-era settlement in Victoria. Gold was found here in 1853 and the rich, deep alluvial reefs were mined until 1926, almost rivalling Bendigo for longevity. As you come into town you'll be greeted by dilapidated old farmhouses and dogs that sit in the middle of the road scratching their heads for want of anything better to do. The main shopping street largely preserves its original appearance, with single-storey shopfronts shaded by awnings and decorated with iron-lace work. It's a popular weekend getaway simply to relax and unwind.

The easiest way to get here from Melbourne, especially if you're relying on **public transport**, is via Castlemaine: trains depart Melbourne 8.35am and 3.50pm Mon–Fri, and the connecting *Castlemaine Bus Lines* buses (☎054/72 1455) depart Castlemaine train station at 10.15am and 5.45pm. Return buses depart from the *Grand Hotel*, Mon–Fri 6.35am and 9am, to connect with trains to Melbourne. On Sundays and holidays there are also **steam train** rides from Maldon to Castlemaine (hourly 1–4pm; $7).

Apart from the town's architecture, things to see are distinctly limited: the **Maldon Museum** (Mon–Fri 1.30–4pm, weekends & public holidays 1.30–5pm; $1) is a typical pioneer memorabilia museum, and you can also tour underground at **Carman's Tunnel Goldmine**, off Parkin's Reef Road, 3km south of town (weekends, school and public holidays 1.30–4pm; $2; 30min). For advice on other activities, check out the **Visitor Centre**, opposite the museum (Mon–Fri 11am–3pm, weekends & public holidays 10am–4pm).

An excellent place to **stay** if you're hankering for a little luxury is *The Barn* (☎054/75 2015; ⑥), a self-catering place with whitewashed stone walls, open fire and french windows. At the *Heritage Cottages*, 25 Adair St (☎054/75 1094, ⑤–⑥), you'll sleep in a pretty two-bedroom cottage with period furnishings and open fires. In a town of **tearooms**, *Berryman's* is the best value. *McArthur's* further up has a very pleasant courtyard, and the mango cheesecake is highly recommended.

# Maryborough and around

**MARYBOROUGH** was relatively late onto the gold bandwagon – with the first find here in 1853 – but it didn't take long to exploit it. Now it's a large, solid and rather dull country town, interesting only for remnants of architecture far too pompous for so quiet a place. The **train station** is exceptional: when Mark Twain visited Maryborough he described it as a train station with a town attached. The booking hall still feels like the entrance to a grand cathedral, though sadly much of the detail, including the marble toilet fittings, has been lost. The **Civic Centre** at the heart of town is a classic nineteenth-century square with an elegant post office and gracious town hall and court-house. **Maryborough Tourist Information** is nearby on Tuaggra Street (Sun–Fri 10am–3pm, Sat 9am–3pm; ☎054/61 2643).

If you want to **stay**, try the *Albion Hotel/Motel*, 57 High St (☎054/61 1035; ④); or the *Railway Hotel* at the corner of Burnes and Terara streets (☎054/61 1025; dorms ①, rooms ③), a quiet, comfortable and clean place, with a good library in the lounge room and breakfast included. Downstairs the bistro has inexpensive **meals**.

**DUNOLLY**, 21km to the north, is an attractive town with kurrajong trees lining the main street and many distinctive old buildings. The goldfields here produced more nuggets than any in Australia, including "Welcome Stranger" from nearby Moliagul, the largest ever found. Fourteen kilometres south of Maryborough, **TALBOT** is a tiny settlement which consists of little more than a restaurant, a pub and a corner store. It's hard to believe now that the town once housed 33,000 people and had 56 hotels. The expensive but excellent *Bull and Mouth Restaurant* (☎054/63 2325; licensed; dinner Thurs–Sun, lunch Sun only) is housed in an 1859 bluestone hotel, filled with fresh flowers, which also has cabins for rent (⑤). **AVOCA**, 26km southwest of Maryborough on the Pyrenees Highway, was another rich source of alluvial gold. It boasts a collection of nineteenth-century buildings including a chemist shop established in 1854 and believed to be the oldest in Victoria. These days, the area around Avoca, known as the Pyrenees region, is increasingly known for its **vineyards**. A cluster of them is located in or near Moonambel, a hamlet 17km northwest of Avoca: one to aim for is the *Warrenmang Winery*, Mountain Creek Road (☎054/67 2233; daily 9am–5pm), which has a picturesque setting, a good restaurant, and also offers accommodation (B&B ⑦).

# Daylesford and Hepburn Springs

The attractive, hilly country around Daylesford and Hepburn Springs is known as the "spa centre of Australia", with a hundred **mineral springs** within a thirty-mile radius. Daylesford grew from the Jim Crow gold diggings of 1851, but the large Swiss-Italian population here quickly realized the value of the water from the mineral springs, which had been bottled since 1850. People have been taking the waters at Hepburn Springs for almost as long – the spa complex was built in 1895. **Tourist information** for the area is found at *Spa Centre Tourist Centre*, 49 Vincent St, Daylesford (daily 9am–5pm; ☎053/48 3707), with loads of brochures for the many places offering **bed and breakfast** and a board that lists vacancies at weekends, when they tend to fill up. You can get a **bus** to Hepburn Springs outside (Mon–Fri, 7 daily between 8.30am–5pm). *V/Line* buses run from Melbourne or Ballarat to Daylesford.

## Daylesford

The town of **DAYLESFORD** has a New Age, alternative atmosphere, with a large gay community, and several gay-friendly guesthouses. Its well-preserved Victorian and Edwardian streets rise up the side of Wombat Hill, where the **Botanical Gardens** sit between Hill Street and Central Springs Road, with fantastic views all around from the lookout tower. Not far away, on the corner of Daly and Hill streets, the **Convent Gallery** (daily 10am–6pm; $2) is a rambling ex-convent where seven individual galleries sell quality arts, crafts and antiques and a Mediterranean-style café is open for lunch and coffee. There's a great Sunday market at the train station to the east of here.

The main street, Vincent Street, heads south towards **Lake Daylesford** where the **Central Springs Reserve**, with several walking tracks, has old-fashioned water pumps allowing you to drink the water of the mineral springs. Here the *Lake Daylesford Book Barn*, open daily, has to be one of the most picturesquely situated bookshops ever: with its extensive range of secondhand books, pot-bellied stove and views, you could be in here for hours. The picturesque *Boathouse Café* (☎053/48 1387) has lakeside dining (breakfast Sat & Sun 9–10.30am, lunch and dinner daily), as well as dinghies, canoes and paddle-boats for rent.

In town, all your esoteric needs are effortlessly taken care of at places like *Books and Buddhas*, 107 Vincent St, with its crystals, tarot readings and free meditation sessions, *Spa Centre Organics*, and the *Himalaya Bakery*, 73 Vincent St (heavy but nutritious dark bread and entirely virtuous cakes). Less puritan offerings are available at *Sweet Decadence*, 57 Vincent St (chocolates, coffee and cake in the characterful old bar of what was the *Victoria Hotel*), at *Le Bon Bon* chocolate and confectionery shop in the foyer of the *Alpha Galleria*, 63–65 Vincent St, or at *Jack's Licensed Café* (open Thurs–Mon 10am–5pm) in the same building, which serves espresso, indulgent cakes and gourmet sandwiches. The *Harvest Café*, at 29 Albert St (Thurs–Sun, breakfast–dinner), is a friendly non-conformist haven where you can eat practically anything, and listen to folk and acoustic music Sunday nights. For a real splurge, head for *Lake House* on King Street near the lake, an outstanding, and correspondingly expensive, **restaurant** (☎053/48 3329; coffee, brunch and dinner daily).

To stay around here, **bed and breakast** is the way to go: *The Balconies*, 35 Perrins St (☎053/48 1322; ⑥), a rambling mansion with several balconies giving lake views, is a favourite with gay visitors; *35 Hill Street* (☎053/48 3878; ⑤) is an early Victorian brick cottage just below the Botanic Gardens; while *Wombat Hill Cottage*, 35 Central Springs Rd (☎053/48 1184; ⑥), has a self-contained unit sleeping four that backs directly onto the gardens. *Walsh's Daylesford Hotel*, Burke Square (☎053/48 2335; ⑤), has pleasant pub rooms.

## Hepburn Springs

**HEPBURN SPRINGS** is not really a town at all, but a collection of guesthouses, a wonderful Art Deco resort hotel, and a café, in a green, hilly and peaceful spot – only 4km north of Daylesford. From the bus stop, walk through the shady Soldiers Memorial Park to the **Mineral Springs Reserve** where old pumps let you taste three kinds of mineral water and the revamped *Hepburn Springs Spa Complex* (☎053/42 2034; Mon–Fri 10am–8pm, weekends 9am–8pm) is located. For $7 you can spend as long as you like here in the relaxation pool (32°C) and mineral-water spa (38°C); or indulge yourself with twenty minutes in your own aero-spa bath, with essential oil added, for $15. The southern wing has massage, saunas, flotation tanks, and therapy and couch pools. Advance bookings are necessary.

*The Springs Hotel*, Main Road (☎053/48 2202; rooms ⑤, cabins ⑥; breakfast included) is a classic 1930s **resort** with guest rooms, and small cabins out the back with bush views from their verandahs. There's a good-value buffet lunch in the dining room and an interesting, more expensive, dinner menu; counter meals are also available in the bar. *Dudley House*, 101 Main Rd (☎053/48 3033; ⑤–⑥), is a lovely federation-style weatherboard house offering elegant **bed and breakfast**. At the budget end of the scale, the *Continental Guest House*, 9 Lone Pine Ave (☎053/48 2005; ①–②, BYO linen), has **dorms** or shared twins, a kitchen (vegetarian only), and a vegetarian café on Saturday nights. The *Springs Cosy Corner Café* on Tenth Street is a groovy place with eclectic cuisine, open noon to midnight Thursday–Sunday.

# Ballarat

BALLARAT is a grandiose provincial city that makes a strong impression whichever direction you approach it from. From the west, the Western Highway runs along the **Avenue of Honour**, over 22km of trees on either side of the road, dedicated to soldiers who fought in World War I, and ending with the massive **Arch of Victory** through which you drive to enter Sturt Street and the city. From the east the Western Highway – Victoria Street – runs between lawns, trees and colourful flowerbeds. The train brings you in to elegant Ballarat Station (1889), with its domed clock tower.

The Ballarat area was already settled before gold was discovered, and preserves a rural life for which the city is the supply centre. Nonetheless it's gold which again has marked the place indelibly: over a quarter of all the gold found in Victoria came from Ballarat and its fantastically rich reef mines before they were exhausted in 1918. Nowadays, besides the more obvious tourist attractions – especially Sovereign Hill – and fine architecture, the town is interesting in its own right, with a fairly large student population and some cultural presence and nightlife as a result. Most people don't stay here overnight however, as it's only a little over an hour's drive away from Melbourne.

## The Town

Sturt and Victoria streets terminate on either side of the Bridge Street Mall, the central shopping area at the base of quaint **Bakers Hill** with its old shop-fronts. Southeast of the city centre, Eureka Street runs off Main Street towards the site of the **Eureka Stockade**, with several museums and antique stores along the way. Main Street becomes Ballarat-Buninyong Road, and six blocks down is crossed by Bradshaw Street where **Sovereign Hill**, the recreated gold town, is found. Northwest of the centre, approached via Sturt Street, are the **Botanical Gardens** and **Lake Wendouree**.

The most complete nineteenth-century streetscape is probably along Lydiard Street, which runs from the centre up past the train station, with its two-storey terraced shop-fronts with verandahs and decorative iron lace, mostly of the period 1862–1889. The 1888 former **Mining Exchange** has been recently renovated and looks particularly fine, as does *Her Majesty's Theatre* (1875). The **Ballarat Fine Art Gallery**, 40 Lydiard St (daily 10.30am–5pm; $3; guided tours Mon–Fri 2pm, Sat & Sun 2.30pm), another superb building, is the oldest provincial art gallery in Australia, established in 1884. Its collection is extensive, and known especially for colonial and Heidelberg School paintings; the original **Eureka Flag** (see "Eureka Stockade" box, below) is also here, tatty and ragged. Displayed alongside are the watercolours of S T Gill, a self-taught artist, who painted scenes of goldrush days in Ballarat. In another part of the gallery, the drawing room of the famous Lindsay family (whose best known members are Norman Lindsay the artist, and Jack Lindsay the writer) from nearby Creswick, has been reconstructed, complete with several of their paintings. There's also a representative modern collection, and a good café. Nearby, on Sturt Street, check out the imposing Classical revival **Town Hall**, which dominates the centre. For current happenings on the Ballarat art scene, try the **Arts Post Gallery**, 21 Main St (daily 10am–5pm), which also has a café.

There are still over fifty **hotels** in Ballarat – survivors of the hundreds that once watered the thirsty diggers. Some of the finest are on Lydiard Street: *Craig's Royal Hotel* at no. 10 and the *George Hotel* at no. 27 are an integral part of Ballarat's architectural heritage. Sadly, during the 1970s, the council forced most of the old pubs to pull down their verandahs on the grounds that they were unsafe, so very few survive in their original form. One that does is attached to the *Golden City Hotel*, 427 Sturt St, which took the council to the Supreme Court to save its magnificent wide verandah with original cast-iron decoration; it's now open on weekends as a bar and appreciatively packed out in summer.

## The Botanical Gardens

The **Ballarat Botanical Gardens**, laid out in 1858, comprise forty hectares alongside **Lake Wendouree**, just to the northwest of the city centre (#15 bus from Sturt St, by *Myers*). Begonias grow so perfectly in Ballarat that a Begonia Festival runs for ten days in March and the glasshouse here is used to display them. Otherwise, highlights are the Avenue of Big Trees, with a Californian redwood among its monsters, and the classical statuary, donated by rich gold-miners, scattered about the gardens. Pride of place goes to Benzoni's *Flight from Pompeii*, housed in the Statuary Pavilion. Prime Minister Avenue has a bust of every prime minister of Australia.

## Eureka Street

As you head towards Eureka Street and the Eureka Stockade (bus #8 will take you there from outside the *ANZ Bank* on Sturt St if you don't want to walk the couple of kilometres), take a look at the dozens of antiques and alternative shops along Main

---

### THE EUREKA STOCKADE

The **Eureka Rebellion** is one of the most celebrated events of Australian history, regarded as the only act of white armed rebellion the country has seen. It was provoked by conditions in the goldfields, where diggers had to pay exorbitantly for their right to prospect for gold (as much as thirty shillings a month), without receiving in return any right to vote, to decent roads, transport, police protection, or any chance of a permanent right to the land they worked. Checks for licences were ruthless and brutal, and corruption rife. Protest meetings calling on diggers to refuse to pay drew huge crowds at Ballarat, Bendigo and Castlemaine; in response, in November 1853 the government reduced the fee a little.

The administration at Ballarat was particularly repressive, and in November 1854 local diggers formed the **Ballarat Reform League**, demanding full civic rights and the abolition of the licence fee, and proclaiming that "the people are the only legitimate source of power". The end of the month saw a group of 200 diggers gather inside a **stockade** of logs, hastily flung together, and determined to resist further arrests for non-possession of a licence. They were attacked at dawn on December 3 by police and troops; thirty died inside, and five members of the government forces also lost their lives.

The movement was not a failure, however: the diggers had aroused widespread sympathy, and in 1855 licences were abolished, replaced by an annual **Miner's Right** which carried the right to vote and to enclose land. The leader of the rebellion, Irishman Peter Lalor, went on to become a member of parliament.

The **Eureka Flag**, with its white cross and five white stars on a blue background, has become a symbol of the left, and indeed of almost any protest movement: shearers raised it in strikes during the 1890s; wharfies used it before World War II in their bid to stop pig-iron being sent to Japan; and today the flag is flown by a growing number of Australians who support the country's transformation to a republic. On a deeper level, all sorts of claims are made for the Eureka Rebellion's pivotal role in forming the Australian nation and psyche. The diggers are held up as a classic example of that Australian (male) ethos of mateship and anti-authoritarianism, while the goldrush in general is credited with overthrowing the hierachical, colonial order, as servants rushed to make their fortune, leaving their masters and mistresses to fend for themselves.

Street – many of the shop buildings are antiques in themselves. The site of the **Eureka Stockade** in Eureka Memorial Park is marked by a simple interpretive board and a replica of the stockade; everywhere else in Ballarat, though, seems intent on cashing in on the Eureka story. Perhaps the most blatant attempt is the **Eureka Exhibition** (daily 9am–5pm; $5) in the museum opposite the park, an overpriced electronic exhibition where you pass through a series of computer-controlled scenes of the stockade – save your money. The same admission fee of $5 is levied at **Montrose Cottage**, 111 Eureka St (daily 9.30am–5pm), the last original miner's cottage in Ballarat – it's been furnished in 1850s style and fitted out with a social history display.

## Sovereign Hill

A kilometre and a half from the centre of town, on Bradshaw Street, **Sovereign Hill** (daily 9.30am–5pm; $16 1-day Gold Pass includes admission to Sovereign Hill, the Gold Museum and a tour through the underground mine; 2-day Gold Pass $18; bus #9 or #10 from outside the *ANZ Bank* on Sturt St) is a recreated gold-mining township, with seventy buildings and shops based on the Ballarat main street of the 1850s, fully cast with characters wandering about in the dress of the period. The township was planned around an actual mine shaft from the 1880s, where guided underground tours are available. There are diggings where you can learn how to pan for gold (and perhaps get a small memento) and a mining museum with steam-operated machinery. The intricately detailed **Chinese village** is the most interesting but, unlike the bustling main street, this fringe settlement is strangely deserted since no Chinese people have been co-opted into the roles.

Sovereign Hill puts on a spectacular outdoor sound and light show, "**Blood on the Southern Cross**" (Sept–May Mon–Sat nights, June–August three nights per week, during school holidays every night; 1hr 20min; $17), which makes use of the whole panorama of Sovereign Hill to tell the story of the Eureka Stockade.

## The Gold Museum

Opposite Sovereign Hill, the **Gold Museum** (daily 10am–5.20pm; $4.50) offers a good view of the recreated settlement. It has an outstanding display of real gold, and explores the history of gold and its uses with a large collection of coins and more. The museum's other purpose is to look at the social history of Ballarat: its **Eureka Exhibition** details life on the goldfields and explains the situation that provoked the Eureka Rebellion. Central to the exhibition is a large painting by George Browning, an artist of the time: it sets the scene of the Eureka Stockade with red-coated soldiers in the foreground shooting at the rough-looking crew behind their stockade. It's interesting to see quite a few black faces portrayed in the stockade, which is generally labelled as the only white armed uprising to have taken place in Australia.

# Practicalities

**Ballarat Visitor Information Centre**, on the corner of Sturt and Albert streets in the heart of the city (Mon–Fri 9.15am–5pm, Sat & Sun 10am–4pm; ☎053/32 2694), has free information and maps of the town. If you want to get a quick impression, try the *Begonia City Explorer* (☎053/39 3922; $7), a one-hour city tour that can be joined here or at Sovereign Hill; *Golden Heritage Walks* (☎053/33 1632) offer **walking tours** from the tourist office. Regular **buses** can take you anywhere you don't feel like walking – *Ballarat Transit System* (☎053/31 7777) has a flat two-hour fare of $1.20. Bus routes pass right by Sovereign Hill and other tourist attractions, stopping on Sturt Street outside *Myers Department Store* or outside the *ANZ Bank* on the corner of Lydiard Street; timetable and network information is posted at both. You can use the system to get as far as Creswick (see below), 18km north.

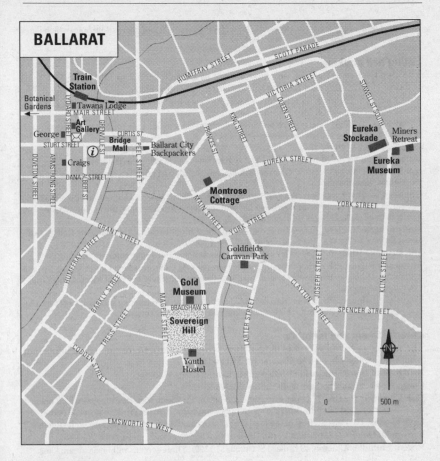

## Accommodation

There's an abundance of accommodation in all price ranges in Ballarat, from hostels to motels to grand hotels, so there shouldn't be a problem finding a room to suit.

**Ballarat City Backpackers**, *Bridge Mall Inn Hotel*, 92 Bridge Mall (☎053/31 3132). Good budget accommodation with a pool table. Noisy live bands play Wed–Sat, free to guests. ①.

**Craigs Hotel**, 10 Lydiard St South (☎053/31 1377). Grand Victorian-era hotel; ask for the wonderful two-level North Tower suite if your budget will stretch that far. B&B ⑤–⑧.

**George Hotel**, 27 Lydiard St (☎053/33 4866). The front section of this 1850s hotel, with colonial-style decor, houses an inexpensive bistro and rooms, some with four-poster beds; out the back are motel units, with breakfast included. Rooms ④, motel units ⑥.

**Goldfields Caravan Park**, 108 Clayton St (☎053/32 7888). Well-placed right next to Sovereign Hill, with good facilities for campers including a camp kitchen. On-site vans ③, cabins ④.

**Miners Retreat Motel**, 602 Eureka St (☎053/31 6900). Standard motel units, just 100m from the site of the Eureka Stockade; light breakfast included. ④.

**Sovereign Hill Accommodation**, Sovereign Hill (☎053/33 3409). YHA hostel modelled on the pre-1855 set-up, which is often booked out by school groups, but usually has room at weekends and during school holidays. There's also motel-style accommodation (breakfast included), with access to the hostel kitchen and comfortable common room. Dorms ①, motel units ⑤–⑥.

**Tawana Lodge**, 128 Lydiard St (☎053/31 3461). Fine accommodation in a private hotel which dates from 1886 and is listed by the National Trust. ④.

### Eating and drinking

You won't starve in Ballarat, nor die for want of a drink, with over fifty pubs. Fast food is found in *McDonald's* on Bakery Hill and *Pizza Hut* opposite.

**Cafe Pazani**, 102 Sturt St. Slick Italian café serving expensive food and excellent coffee. Licensed. Tues–Sat 9am–1am, Sun & Mon 9am–5.30pm.

**L'Espresso**, 417 Sturt St. Hip place for coffee, doubling as a music store selling world music, jazz, soul, and funk – good sounds but meagre servings.

**Eureka Pasta & Pizza House**, 23 Sturt St. The best place for pasta in town: a lively, crowded atmosphere for big, good-value servings and vegetarian options. Licensed. Daily to 5pm.

**Golden City Deli**, 423 Sturt St. Gourmet sandwiches, salads and other wholesome unfussy food in an original stone chapel.

**Golden City Hotel**, 427 Sturt St. This historic hotel, built in 1856, packs them in with an "all you can eat" lunch and dinner menu. Relaxed bar with espresso machine, pool tables, music video and locally brewed Ballarat Bitter (or Ballarat Bertie).

**Masons at the Gallery**, 40 Lydiard Street North. Pleasant little café at the Fine Arts Gallery, with lots of flowers and imaginative food. Daily 10.30am–4.30pm.

**The Pancake Kitchen**, 2 Grenville St. Pancakes day and night in a cosy goldrush building.

**Porters Bar and Café**, corner of Mair and Peel streets. Old pub transformed into a stylish bar and restaurant, dishing up moderately priced food with diverse influences and local wines. Lunch Tues–Fri, dinner Mon–Sat.

**Tokyo Grill House**, 109 Bridge Mall (☎053/33 3945). Teppanyaki cooking means it's prepared on hot plates in front of you, but the high-quality ingredients make it expensive.

### Entertainment and nightlife

The music scene in Ballarat is bigger than you might expect; for up-to-date info about what's on locally, check *The Courier* on Thursday.

**Bridge Mall Inn**, 92 Bridge Mall. Independent touring bands Wed–Sat.

**Camp Hotel**, 38 Sturt St. Tues night jam sessions.

**Her Majesty's Theatre**, 17 Lydiard St (☎053/33 5800). Elaborate Victorian theatre, which opened in 1875 with a performance by Australia's first opera company. Touring productions of all sorts.

**Hot Gossips**, 120 Dana St. Best of the local clubs, set in an old church, and popular with students.

**Provincial Hotel**, 121 Lydiard St North. Open to 4am nightly; bands, and a disco Wed–Sat.

**Regent Multiplex Cinema**, 49 Lydiard St (☎053/31 1399). Three screens with mainstream films.

## Around Ballarat

Rich alluvial gold was found at **CRESWICK**, 18km north of Ballarat, in 1851, and it became an important mining centre. Now it's a quiet little town, where the only reminder is the wildly out-of-place Victorian architecture. The *American Hotel* and the *British Hotel* face each other across the main street, a hangover from mining days when the different nationalities of miners stuck to their segregated groups. Not much further out, to the northeast, **CLUNES** was the site of the first worthwhile Victorian goldfield in 1851. The reefs here were too deep for small-scale mining, and the Port Phillip Company took over operations. The only profitable British gold mine in Australia, it was most productive between 1857 and 1881. The main street has many solid old buildings and rows of original shop-fronts which are sadly vacant – entrepreneurial attempts to attract the tourist trade with antique and craft shops have foundered. The **Clunes Museum** (weekends & school holidays 11am–4.30pm; $2) details the gold-mining era of the town. The *Club Hotel*, 34 Fraser St (☎053/45 3250; ④), has inexpensive **accommodation**, with a buffet breakfast included, and, for lunch and dinner, rustles up rump **steaks** at unbelievably low prices.

# WESTERN VICTORIA AND THE MALLEE

Several roads run west from the goldfields to the South Australian border through the seemingly endless wheatfields of **the Wimmera**. To the west of the farming centre of **Ararat** is the major attraction of the area, the **Grampians (Gariwerd) National Park**, the southwestern tail-end of the Great Dividing Range. **Stawell** and **Horsham**, regarded as the capital of the Wimmera, are good bases here but **Halls Gap**, right inside the park, is even better. North of Horsham, **Nhill** and **Dimboola** are situated close to the **Little Desert National Park** and, like Warracknabeal further north, are wheat centres. Beyond here is the least populated part of the state, the wide, flat **Mallee** with its twisted mallee scrub, sand dunes and dry lakes. This region, with several state and national parks, extends from the **Wyperfeld National Park** in the south, right up to Mildura's irrigated oasis on the Murray. South of the Grampians is sheep country; following the Hamilton Highway from Geelong you'll end up at **Hamilton**, the major town and wool capital of the western district, also accessible via **Dunkeld** on the edge of the Grampians.

## Transport

*V/Line* has a bus service once daily to Hamilton from Ballarat via Dunkeld (connecting train to Ballarat from Melbourne), heading on to Mount Gambier in South Australia, and a bus service from Warrnambool (connecting train to Warrnambool from Melbourne via Geelong) from Monday to Friday. The "Grampians Link" consists of a train service from Melbourne to Ballarat and a connecting coach to Halls Gap, via Ararat and Stawell, once daily. At the time of writing the *V/line* night train ("Overlander") from Melbourne to Adelaide via Ballarat, Ararat, Stawell, Horsham and Dimboola was not running due to trackwork, being replaced by a daily "Daylink" connection: a train from Melbourne to Bendigo, and from there a connecting bus via Horsham and Dimboola to Adelaide. The "Daylink" may soon, however, be restricted to three services a week – for up-to-date timetable information phone *V/Line* ☎13 2232. The interstate buses to Adelaide run on the Western Highway via Ballarat, Ararat, Stawell, Horsham, Dimboola and Nhill.

# Hamilton

Three highways converge on **HAMILTON**, where you can see the Grampians from the edge of the main street. It's a civilized little city whose main claim to fame is that it's the "Wool Capital of the World". The only reason you're really likely to be here is passing through, en route from the Goldfields to South Australia, or from the mountains to the coast. There's plenty to distract you while you're here however, and the **Hamilton District Tourist Office**, in Lonsdale Street (☎055/72 3746; daily 9am–5pm), will do its best to persuade you to take a look – a friendly and helpful place that will also book accommodation.

The most worthwhile of the town's five museums and galleries is the **Hamilton Art Gallery**, on Brown Street (Tues–Fri 10am–5pm, Sat 10am–noon & 2–5pm, Sun 2–5pm; free), one of the finest provincial art galleries in the state. Its collection of eighteenth-century watercolours of English pastoral scenes by Paul Sandby is the biggest outside the royal collection; there are also ninety Hogarth engravings, eighteenth-century English furniture, and more. The influence of the rich, local Ansett family (of airline fame) is obvious; many of the excellent contemporary paintings were acquired through the Ansett Hamilton Art Awards, sponsored by *Ansett* transport.

Also in the town centre are the **Hamilton History Centre** (daily except Sat 2–5pm; $1), located in the Mechanics Institute Building at 43 Gray St, and the **Aboriginal Keeping Place** (admission by appointment, call ☎055/72 3368; $1) in the same building. A good deal more interesting than the main history centre, the latter has displays and dioramas highlighting aspects of the rich Aboriginal culture of western Victoria. East of town on the Ballarat Road, the **Sir Reginald Ansett Museum** (daily 10am–4pm; $1) charts the history of the *Ansett* flight network which started here, while the **Hamilton Pastoral Museum** (limited hours or by appointment, ☎055/72 2489; $5) displays all sorts of fascinating agricultural bits and pieces in an old church building.

There's also some refreshing greenery in the town centre: the **Botanical Gardens** are just one block from the main street on the corner of French and Thompson streets, while the banks of the **Grange Burn** as it flows through town are home to the eastern barred bandicoot, the only known population in mainland Australia. Grange Burn flows into man-made **Lake Hamilton**, with a safe, sandy swimming beach, and thousands of trout.

### Practicalities

If you want to **stay**, there's a wide variety of accommodation. The *Commercial Hotel*, 145 Thompson St (☎055/72 1078; dorms ①, rooms ③), is the cheapest option but it's basic with few comforts; a better choice for budget travellers is *Lake Hamilton Caravanpark and Lodge*, Ballarat Road (☎055/72 3855; dorms ①, cabins ③, rooms ④), with backpacker accommodation and comfortable, heated rooms, plus a pretty camping area, local information and occasional tours. Nearby is the luxurious *Grange Burn Motor Inn*, 142 Ballarat Rd (☎055/72 5755; ⑥). The relaxed *Grand Central Hotel*, 141 Gray St (☎055/72 2899; ④), is a good place to both eat and sleep: motel-style rooms include breakfast and there's a decent, unpretentious bistro; Melbourne bands play here at weekends. *Living Naturally*, 92 Thompson St, does café-type food during the day, and the pleasant *Gilly's Coffee Shop & Grill*, 106 Gray St, is open daytime and evening.

## Around Hamilton

Hamilton is situated on the fringe of the extensive volcanic plain that runs across western Victoria and into South Australia. **Mount Napier** (439m) to the south and Mount Rouse at Penshurst to the east were the sources of most of the lava flow covering the Hamilton area. Byaduk Caves Road towards MacArthur gives a very good view of Mount Napier, directly ahead as you drive. Lava flows are still clearly visible here, with black wattle trees flourishing on many of them. The **Byaduk Caves** are actually fern-filled lava tubes; three of the twelve are easy enough to get into but the others require the use of ropes. As you explore, watch out for stinging nettles and rough terrain, with frothy textured lava rocks scattered around, porous and covered in moss.

Heading towards South Australia along the Glenelg Highway, **COLERAINE**, 35km from Hamilton, is picturesquely sited in the Wannon River Valley, between two table-lands. The **Points Aboretum** here is the nation's official eucalypt collection, with the largest number of species anywhere in the world. At **CASTERTON**, 29km further west on the Glenelg River, the 1843 **Warrock Homestead** is one of the most interesting in the country: more than thirty buildings are still used by the descendants of the original settlers and are open to visitors. From here it's less than an hour's drive to South Australia and the Coonawarra wine region (see p.608).

# Ararat and the Western Highway

Heading west from Ballarat towards the mountains, **ARARAT**, some 90km away, is still very much a goldfields town, with more overbearing Victorian architecture than the sleepy place seems to have use for. It was founded in 1857 when a group of seven hundred hopeful Chinese, making the slow trudge from South Australian ports to the central Victorian goldfields, stumbled across a fabulously rich, shallow alluvial gold-field, the **Canton Lead**. As the the only town founded by the Chinese in Australia, a project is underway in Ararat to build a **Chinese museum**, "Gum San", at the site of the old mine entrance. Few other signs of the embryonic Chinese settlement survive in what soon became a rich, planned town: the main street was laid out so as to show off the best profiles of **Mount Ararat** in the west and the **Pyrenees Range** with **Mount Cole** to the east.

These days Ararat is the commercial centre for a sheep-farming and wine-producing area; reasonably priced **wineries** in the immediate area include *Montara Vineyards*, 3km south along the Chalamabar Road (Mon–Sat 9.30am–5pm, Sun noon-4pm) and *Boroka Vineyard* on the Pomonal Road near Halls Gap, at the foot of the Grampians (Mon–Sat 9am–5pm). Next door to the town hall, with its clock tower and fountain, **Ararat Tourist Information** on Barkly Street (Mon–Fri 9am–5pm; ☎053/52 2096) has loads of information on the Grampians as well as a list of places to stay in town. Nearby, the **Langi Morgala Museum** (Sat & Sun 2–4pm; $1) occupies an old brick building with bluestone at the base and around the huge arched windows and doors; the name is supposedly an Aboriginal one meaning "yesteryear". Along with the usual pioneering stuff, there's an important collection of Aboriginal artefacts here.

If you're ready for **food**, make your way to Barkly Street, where all the following can be found. *Kaman's Koffee Lounge* serves classy sandwiches and good-value meals; there's also a healthfood store and a decent delicatessen. The *Ararat Hotel* has bar meals; the *Caffe Dominica*, in a Victorian mansion, has a coffee shop, bistro and pricey restaurant, open late; and the *Pyrenees Country Kitchen* is another award-winning, but expensive, restaurant.

## Great Western and Stawell

Between Ararat and Stawell is the small settlement of **GREAT WESTERN**, the centre of a wine-producing area whose most famous wineries are right in town, on the Moyston Road. **Seppelt's Great Western** (Mon–Sat 9am–5pm; Sun noon-4pm), established in 1865, and **Best's Great Western** (Mon–Fri 9am–5pm, Sat 9am–4pm), established in 1866, are both renowned for their sparkling, *methode champenoise* wines; *Seppelt's* also boasts extensive underground cellars classified by the National Trust.

**STAWELL**, most famous for being the home of the **Stawell Gift**, a foot race with big prize money conducted every Easter since 1877, is also the closest major town to the Grampians and the departure point for the **bus** to Halls Gap. There's a helpful **Grampians Information Centre** on 54 Western Highway (☎053/58 2314), and the *Stawell Gift Hall of Fame* on Main Street (Mon–Fri 10am–4pm) charts the history of the race itself. The town has a pleasant, old-fashioned feel, and it's a much less expensive place to stay than Halls Gap. The many **motels** along the highway all charge much the same (④) for similar facilities. A couple of bed and breakfasts and a caravan park are the only real alternatives: pricey *Bellellen Rise* (☎053/58 2750; ⑦), on a sheep-grazing property 11km out of town on the Bellellen Road; *Clovelly House* (☎053/58 2986; ⑥), 7 Clifton Ave, in town; and *Stawell Grampians Gate Caravan Park*, Burgh Street (☎053/58 2376; on-site vans ③), the closest camping area to town.

# The Grampians (Gariwerd) National Park

Rising from the flat plains of western Victoria's wheat and grazing districts, the sandstone ranges of the **GRAMPIANS**, with their weirdly formed rocky outcrops and stark ridges, seem doubly spectacular. To their scenic splendour you can add a dazzling array of **flora**, with a spring and early summer bonanza of wildflowers, **Aboriginal rock art** and **Brambuk**, an impressive Aboriginal cultural centre, **waterfalls** and **lakes**, and over fifty **bushwalks** along 100km of well-marked tracks. There's also several hundred kilometres of road, from sealed highway to rough track, allowing for **scenic drives** and **4WD** tours.

**HALLS GAP**, 26km from Stawell, on the eastern fringes, is the only settlement within the national park. Its setting, in the long flat strip of the Fyans Valley surrounded by the soaring bush and rock of the Mount Difficult and Mount William ranges, is gorgeous; koalas are frequently seen in the surrounding trees. Packed with accommodation and other facilities catering to park visitors, this is the obvious place to base yourself, especially if you don't have your own transport. The newsagency in town acts as agent for the *ANZ* bank, and its **post office** section services *Commonwealth* passbooks.

Just over 2km south of Halls Gap along the Grampians Road (sometimes also known as the Dunkeld Road or the Dunkeld–Halls Gap Road) is the **National Park Visitors' Centre** (daily 9am–4.45pm), the best place to start your visit, with an interesting display and videos which trace the development of the Grampians over 400 million years. They sell books, including the excellent *Grampians Touring Guide*, ideal for short walks, and more detailed topographic maps: although most of the walking tracks are clearly defined and well signposted, it's a good idea to buy the *Natmap* or *Vicmap* and carry a compass if you're planning an overnight trek. Details of bushwalks are posted and there are masses of free leaflets; before doing extended walks, call into the visitors' centre and register. Some **walks** start from the camping ground at Halls Gap, while others branch off the Victory and Grampian roads making them difficult to get to without a car.

The **best times to come** are spring and early summer when the waterfalls are flowing well and the wildflowers are in full bloom (although something will be in flower whenever you come), or in autumn. Between June and August it rains heavily and can get extremely cold; many tracks are closed then to avoid erosion. Summers are very hot, with water scarce and the threat of bushfires ever present. If you're undertaking extended walks in summer, you should carry a small radio to keep tabs on the fire risk: on **total fire ban days**, no exposed flames, not even that of a portable gas stove, are allowed.

## ROCK ART IN THE GRAMPIANS

It's estimated that **Koorie** Aborigines lived in the area known to them as **Gariwerd** at least 5000 years ago. The area offered such rich food sources that the Koories didn't have to devote all their time to hunting and food gathering, and could give due weight to religious and cultural activities. Evidence of this survives in rock paintings, usually executed in a single colour, either red or white, in a linear style, but sometimes with hand prints or stencils. You can visit some of the rock shelters where Aborigines camped and painted on the sandstone walls, although many more are off-limits. In the northern Grampians one of the best is **Gulgurn Manja** (also known as Flat Rock), 5km south of the Western Highway near the Hollow Mountain camping ground; from Flat Rock Road there's a signposted fifteen-minute walk. The name means "hands of young people", as many of the handprints here were done by children. In the southern Grampians, **Billimina** (Glenisla Shelter) is a fifteen-minute walk above the Buandik camping ground; it's an impressive rock overhang with clearly discernible, quite animated red stick figures. Guided tours are organized from the **Brambuk** cultural centre to several other sites.

# Brambuk

Located behind the visitors' centre, **Brambuk** (daily 10am–4.45pm; $3.50, redeemable in shop or café; ☎053/56 4452) grew from an idea for a rock-art facsimile centre that would draw the tourist traffic away from the fragile art sites themselves. From that beginning, it developed into a full-blown **cultural centre** for western Victorian Aboriginal culture: a place where visitors could learn and Koories could gain employment, with a management committee composed entirely of Koories. One of its achievements, unfortunately rather short-lived, was the restoration of indigenous place names in the park. These were appended to the European names in 1991, only to be discreetly dumped when the Liberal Party came to power after the Victorian state elections of 1992. The building, with its undulating red-ochre tin roof, blends wonderfully with the backdrop of bush and rocky ridge – it was designed in consultation with the five Koorie communites responsible for the centre and incorporates many symbolic features. Outside, landscaped grounds reflect the major plant communities in the national park.

Inside, a small **exhibition** area has a poignant photographic history of the area's Aborigines, and there's a visual display of traditional Aboriginal foods and lifestyles, plus a section devoted to Central Australian land rights. A continuously run video consists of interviews with different Koories about aspects of their lives, past and present. Downstairs is a **shop** selling Aboriginal music, books and souvenirs, while the *Koori Gugidja Gugidjela Restaurant* (see "Grampians food, drink and entertainment" below) is a highlight of Brambuk, and alone justifies a trip here.

# Bushwalks, scenic drives and tours

The scenery and wildlife of the Grampians is tremendously varied, and the diversity of **vegetation** in the park boosted by the fact that this is the meeting place of the ecosystems of the forested areas of the south and east of Victoria and the dry mallee country of the north. It's significantly warmer in the northern Grampians, an area of arid bushland with bent and twisted trees and scrubby undergrowth. In the cooler south, vegetation ranges from stringybark forests and red-gum woodland in the wet Victoria Valley to luxuriant fern gullies like Delleys Dell in the Wonderland area. There are also subalpine communities of plants in exposed sites like Mount William and areas of stunted heaths on the Major Mitchell Plateau.

Roads through the park enable you to **drive** to major points and then get out and walk. Take care though, as animals are often killed, especially on the Grampians Road south of Halls Gap and the Mount Abrupt Road north of Dunkeld. The most popular section for visitors is the **Wonderland area** to the west of Halls Gap. From the Halls Gap campsite you can head directly to **Venus Baths** (2km), **Mackeys Peak** (1km), or the **Pinnacles** (10km), the most popular lookout in the Grampians with a narrow rock ledge nearby – the **Nerve Test** – that many try out. **Delleys Dell** is another Wonderland walk (5km), through canopies of tree ferns; start at Rosea picnic area. The other major features are the Balconies, Mackenzie's Falls and Zumsteins, all accessible via the Mount Victory Road northwest of Halls Gap. The walk to the **Balconies** (1.6km return), also known as the **Jaws of Death**, begins from the Reid Lookout car park, through a stand of lichen-covered tea trees. The weird formation consists of one ledge above another, and if you're brave enough you can stand right on the edge of the lower jaw and be enthralled by splendid views over the forested Victoria Valley. The much-photographed formation can also be seen from a distance from the **Reid Lookout** itself.

The camping area at **Zumsteins** (5km east of Mount Victory Rd) has been closed down because of problems with effluent from the sewage system getting into drinking-water supplies. There's still a picnic area and car park, however, where western grey kangaroos stand passively, waiting for food. They're tame enough to pat, but can be a serious nuisance when you bring out your food; don't encourage them by feeding them.

## THE MAJOR MITCHELL TRAIL

The first Europeans to reach the Grampians were **Major Thomas Mitchell** and his exploration party in 1836. Mitchell was the New South Wales Surveyor General, whose glowing reports of his explorations subsequently attracted many squatters in the early 1840s. The **Major Mitchell Trail**, a signposted 1700-kilometre "long-distance cultural trail" along back roads and sometimes bush tracks, allows you to follow his route through Victoria, from Mildura along the Murray to Swan Hill, then south to Horsham, detouring into the Grampians to ascend Mount William, and thence to the coast at Nelson and Portland. Heading back, it runs inland via Hamilton and Dunkeld on the southern edge of the Grampians, through Central Victoria via Castlemaine, and then across the northeast via Benalla and Wangaratta, crossing back into New South Wales at Wodonga. A **handbook** of the walk is available from the *Department of Conservation and Natural Resources* in Melbourne (see p.644) and at its offices and some tourist offices along the trail.

A three-kilometre walk runs along the Mackenzie River Gorge from here to the base of thundering **Mackenzie's Falls**, which you can also reach more directly from the Mount Victoria Road. There's parking above the falls and a short strenuous walk to the base.

If you're reasonably fit, consider tackling the walk to the peak of **Mount William** (1168m; 3.5km return), the highest point in the park. This starts from the Mount William Road car park, for which you turn off 16km south of Halls Gap. More challenging overnight walks include one to the **Major Mitchell Plateau**, starting from the same car park but involving a difficult 500-metre climb to the plateau; and the **Mount Difficult** walk across a large undulating rocky plateau, which starts from Roses Gap.

### Tours

**Grampian Tours** (☎053/56 6221), operated by the same people who run the youth hostel, organize excellent day-tours of the national park in a minibus with 4WD capability, stopping often so you can go for short walks to points of interest. The price ($50–70) includes lunch in the bush; tours start in Halls Gap, but they'll also pick up from Stawell. **Grampians Joyflights**, departing from Pomonal airstrip between December and June, give the definitive overview of the park, with sky-high prices to match; book through the *Grampians Store*, Pomonal, between 9am and 6pm (☎053/56 6294).

## Grampians accommodation

During school holidays, particularly in January and at Easter, the Grampians are packed: although Halls Gap has a plethora of **accommodation** of every kind, you'll need to have booked far in advance then, and many places will insist on long stays.

In town, *Mountain Grand*, Grampians Road (☎053/56 4232; ⑤), is a very friendly **guesthouse** with excellent bistro, restaurant and bar catering to walkers' appetites and pockets. The *Kookaburra*, on Heath Street (☎053/56 4395; ⑥), is one of the better **motels**, with an excellent restaurant (see above), while the cheapest is the *Grand Canyon Motel* (☎053/56 4280; ④), less than 1km north of the town centre on Grampians Road. **Self-catering** accommodation also abounds: if you don't want to spend a lot of money, *Kingsway Holiday Flats*, Grampians Road (☎053/56 4202; ④–⑤), are a good deal, spartan but clean, comfortable, and have TV and a full kitchen. If you can splurge a bit, the *Grampians Wonderland Cabins*, Ellis Street, just off the Grampians Tourist Road on the way to Brambuk (☎053/56 4264; ⑥) are beautiful, new two-bedroom timber cabins set in ten hectares of bushland.

The **youth hostel** in Halls Gap, on the corner of Buckler Street and Grampians Road (☎053/56 6221; ①), is very popular in spring and summer, but in winter it's pleasantly quiet, with a wood-burning stove to fend off chills. There's no resident manager so you book by phone or just turn up and put your name beside a bed number on the chalk-board; staff turn up in the evening to collect money. An old house at the back takes the overflow in summer, and the same people run *Lake Fyans Holiday Park* (☎053/56 6230; on-site vans ③, cabins ④) at Pomonal where they take the overflow of the overflow, bringing guests back to Halls Gap in the morning; it has good cabins, basic caravans and tent sites, in a lakeside setting with canoes, and tennis and volley ball courts.

There's no booking for the **campsites** in the national park – they operate on a first-come, first-served basis. A permit is required: fill in a form and put your money into the box at the site, or buy one from the National Park Visitors' Centre or from tourist offices in surrounding towns. **Bushcamping** is allowed in the park except in the Wonderland Range and within 100 metres of a dam, river or creek and within 50 metres of a road.

Besides the basic national park camping sites, there are tons of **caravan parks** in the vicinity. The most convenient, *Halls Gap Caravan Park* (☎053/56 4251; on-site vans ③, cabins ④), is right opposite the shopping centre and consequently less than secluded, but it's well equipped, and many walks start right here. *Roses Gap Recreation Centre* (☎053/59 5264; cabins ④, cottages ⑤), across at the northern end of the national park, is well set up for camping with a camp kitchen and sheltered barbecue, and also offers cabins and cosy cottages with fireplaces.

## Grampians food, drink and entertainment

The **Koori Gugidja Gugidjela Restaurant** (reservations preferred, ☎053/56 4452), attached to the Brambruk cultural centre (see above), is one of the Grampians' culinary highlights. During the day it's a simple café where you can sample a roo burger, an emu sausage or a muttonbird pie, followed by a "wattlecino". On Thursday, Friday and Saturday nights it turns into a full-blown restaurant (licensed and BYO), complete with candlelight, white tablecloths, napkins and soft didgeridoo music playing in the back-ground. It's one of few places in Australia where you can sample **bush tucker**, serving indigenous meat seasoned with native berries, seeds, nuts and plants: try smoked muttonbird, kangaroo fillets with Illawarra plum relish, or panfried emu with herbs and banksia honey. For the less adventurous, there's also chicken, rabbit, duck and pasta.

There's no shortage of places to eat in **Halls Gap** either, including the *Stony Creek Bakery* (daily 8am–5pm), which has fresh bread daily and also sells eggs; *Caffe Nico* for bagels, pizzas and pastas as well as fish and chips; and the rather expensive *Flying Emu Café. Stony Creek Pizzeria*, open to 8.30pm nightly, does passable pizza as well as pancakes, salads, soups and pasta. *Chez Suzy at Budja Budja*, Lot 5, Dunkeld Road (9am–late), is a pleasant, moderately priced restaurant and bar where you can get anything from breakfast and Devonshire teas to a full-blown meal, imaginatively prepared using locally produced ingredients. *The Kookaburra Restaurant and Motor Inn*, Grampians Road (daily from 6.30pm), also comes highly recommended for its inexpensive café-style dishes, mainly pasta, and for its restaurant food, which features dishes such as venison, western district lamb, and locally caught fish.

The opening of the *Halls Gap Pub* on the Stawell Road broke a 24-year-old "drought"; it has a bistro with a great view of the Grampians and a drive-in bottleshop. A tiny **cinema** operates during school holidays, and there's even a film festival at the begin-ning of November.

# The Wimmera

**The Wimmera**, dry and hot, relies heavily on irrigation water from the Grampians for its vast wheatfields; before irrigation and the invention of the stump jump plough, the area was no more than mallee scrub, similar to the lands beyond **Warracknabeal**, the northernmost wheat-growing centre.

**HORSHAM** is somewhere you might want to stop for a break en route to Adelaide, with an idyllic picnic spot complete with barbecues by the Wimmera River; there's little else to attract you in the capital of the wheatfields, though **Mount Arapiles**, 40km west, is one of the most important rock-climbing centres in Australia, and the Grampians (Gariwerd) National Park (see above) is within striking distance to the southeast. If you need **food** or a **bed**, the *Royal Hotel*, 132 Firebrace St (☎053/82 1255; ③), does the former surprisingly well and the latter adequately: established in 1881, it's a grand old place with many original features. *Roundabout Lunchtime*, 66 Firebrace St, offers healthy food cooked on the premises and real coffee. Run by the same people who manage the *Horsham Hostel* (☎053/82 0068; ①) next door, *Cafe Bagdad* at 48 Wilson St (closed Mon) has a slightly studenty, alternative feel and serves espresso, cakes and ice creams, as well as soups, salads and *focaccia*. There are dozens of other places to stay, if you have the time and inclination: **Wimmera Tourism** on O'Callaghan Parade (irregular hours; ☎053/82 3778) can advise.

Continuing along the Western Highway, **DIMBOOLA**, deep in the dreary flatlands, is the sort of place that frustratingly closes down for lunch just as the interstate buses stop for a break, running to its own dusty clock. There's one motel (☎053/89 1177; ④), one hotel (☎053/89 1630; ④) and a caravan park (☎053/89 1416; on-site vans ②). **NHILL** and Kaniva, further along the highway, are similiarly undistinguished. All three towns are within a few kilometres of the **Little Desert National Park**, with Nhill being the best starting point if you plan to explore. *Whimpey's Little Desert Lodge* (☎053/91 5232; dorms ②, units ④), 16km southeast of the town on the Harrow Road, lies on the fringe of the park and runs good 4WD **tours**; it has camping, bunk rooms and units, plus a bar and restaurant. In fact, far from being a desert, the national park has a great variety of plants with colourful wildflower displays in spring; much of the vegetation is low mallee scrub (**mallee** is a low-growing, bush-like type of eucalypt), among which the now rare mallee fowl can be found. You can **camp** within the national park by following the Kiata South Road 13km from Kiata, east of Nhill (call the ranger for more information on ☎053/91 1275 or 89 1204).

# The Mallee

**The Mallee**, the most sparsely populated area of Victoria, begins north of Warracknabeal, from where the **Henty Highway** heads up to join the Sunraysia Highway and forge its way to Mildura, on the New South Wales border. This is an area worth visiting in winter, when it's drier and warmer than the rest of Victoria, but not too hot to make bushwalks unbearable. You really need your own transport to see anything; just about the only **public transport** is the small *Henty Highway Coach* from Horsham to Mildura (☎053/82 4260; $40; 4hr; departs Horsham every Tues, Thurs and Fri), which mainly carries freight. Along the way are small dusty towns like Brim, Bealah and **HOPETOUN** ("gateway to the Mallee"), whose shops still have their old awnings and apparently their original window displays too.

Hopetoun is at least somewhere you might have a reason to stop, as the approach to **Wyperfeld National Park**, 51km away. At 356,800 hectares it's Victoria's third largest and has a chain of normally dry lake beds, mallee scrub, river red gum and black box woodlands and rolling sand plains, with emus, kangaroos and mallee fowl among its wildlife. There's a shady camping and picnic area with water and toilets near the **information centre** (☎053/95 7221) where you can find out about the many walks in the park; this is also a good area to explore on a mountain bike. The **Big Desert Wilderness** is directly west of Wyperfeld, but can only be reached by a track that runs between Broken Bucket Tank, northwest of Nhill, and Murrayville on the Mallee

Highway west of Ouyen; there are no tracks, roads or facilities in the park, just more sand dunes and mallee scrub and stacks of wildlife. You'll need 4WD and considerable dedication to get the most out of it.

Beyond Hopetoun, the Henty Highway merges into the Sunraysia Highway; heading north on the Sunraysia there's tourist information at the **general store** in the small town of **SPEED** – which could hardly have a less appropriate name. From here the mallee scrub clings to the edges of the highway tenaciously, threatening to invade the red soil of cleared fields on either side, and the equally red dust of the unsealed road. **OUYEN**, "heart of the Mallee", is another undistinguished small town where two highways cross. Heading west along the Mallee Highway, the access track to the picturesque **pink salt lakes** of the Murray-Sunset (Yanga-Nyawi) National Park sprouts northwards from Linga. Continuing north on the Calder Highway from Ouyen, the **Hattah-Kulkyne National Park**, with its gum-lined lakes system, dry mallee scrub and native woodland, lies east of the highway: Lake Hattah is reached by turning off the highway at Hattah, 34km north of Ouyen, onto the Hattah-Robonvale Road.

From Hattah it's less than 70km to Mildura and the Murray.

# THE MURRAY REGION

From its source close to Mount Kosciusko high in the Australian Alps, the **Murray River** forms the **border** between Victoria and New South Wales until it crosses into South Australia (someone got a ruler out for the rest of the border to the coast); although the actual watercourse is in New South Wales, the Victorian bank is far more interesting and more populous. After the entire length was navigated in 1836, the river became the route along which cattle were driven from New South Wales to the newly established town of Adelaide, and later in the century there was a thriving paddle-steamer trade on the lower reaches of the river, based at Wentworth on the New South Wales side (see p.611 for more on early Murray navigation). In 1864, **Echuca** was linked by railway to Melbourne, stimulating the river trade in the upper reaches. Echuca thus became a major inland port, the furthest extent of the navigable river. At the height of the paddle-steamer era, **Mildura** was still a run-down, rabbit-infested cattle station, but in 1887 the Chaffey brothers (see p.610) instituted irrigation projects that now support dairy farms, vineyards, vegetable farms and citrus orchards throughout northwestern Victoria. Between Mildura and Echuca, **Swan Hill** marks the transition to sheep, cattle and wheat country; the **Pioneer Settlement** here explores the extraordinarily hard lives of the early settlers. Above Echuca the Murray loses much of its magic as it flows through the more settled northeast.

**Paddle-steamers** cruise for leisure now, and are an unbeatable way to enjoy the river and admire the magnicent **river red gums** lining its banks, and the huge array of birds and other wildlife that the Murray sustains. Renting a **houseboat** is also a relaxing (if expensive) way to go.

# Mildura

**MILDURA** has the mirage-like aura of an oasis, its vineyards and orange orchards standing out from a hot, dry landscape. To the southwest especially is an almost entirely empty area, evocatively named **Sunset Country**, with nothing but gnarled mallee scrub, red sand and pink salt lakes (reached via Linga on the Mallee Highway, see above). Mildura's wide streets are lined with palms, giving a balmy impression even in the mild winter sunshine. It makes a good winter getaway, but summer can be stiflingly, unremittingly hot – the green grape vines in the surrounding countryside and the flowers and towering red gums that line Deakin Avenue, the main thoroughfare, offer some relief, but you'd do best to avoid the area then.

**Deakin Avenue** runs northwest through town to the river, with 7th Street and the train station facing the parklands that run along the river. Like any self-respecting small city, Mildura has its mall, which runs parallel to Deakin Avenue between 8th and 9th streets; here you'll find the **Mildura Information Centre** (Mon–Fri 9am–5pm, Sat & Sun 10am–4pm; ☎050/23 3619) which has particularly good information on the surrounding national parks and a free map of the town.

Sights are thin on the ground here, and probably the most interesting thing to do is head for the river and watch traffic passing through the seventy-year-old **Mildura Weir** system, designed to provide stable pools for irrigation and to enable navigation throughout the year. There's a pretty picnic ground by lock 11 (the trickiest), just beyond the art gallery. If there's nothing happening on the river, wander down to the **Mildura Arts Centre**, 199 Cureton Ave (Mon–Fri 9am–5pm, Sat & Sun 2–4.30pm; $2), which consists of a historic home, Rio Vista, and the provincial art gallery. **Rio Vista** was built in 1890 for William Chaffey, who lived here with his first and second wives (both called Hattie Schell, the second the niece of the first) until he died in 1926. It's a lovely house, though rather ill-suited to the climate, and inside are various displays about the Chaffeys and the development of Mildura. The art gallery's most important piece is the **Edward Degas** pastel *Woman Combing Her Hair at the Bath*; it also has some excellent sculpture.

## Tours and activities

The best **short river cruise** is on the *PS Melbourne* (daily 10.50am & 1.50pm; $14; 2hr 10min; ☎050/23 2200), Mildura's only genuinely steam-driven paddle-steamer. Built in 1912, it still has its original boiler and engine, which you can watch in action during the trip. Upstairs the captain, in full regalia, gives a sensible commentary – and keeps quiet plenty of the time too. The same company runs *Paddleboat Rothbury*, built in 1881 when it was the fastest steamboat on the river, but now converted to diesel and undertaking cruises to local attractions like Golden River Zoo and Trentham Estate Winery. *Showboat Avoca* (☎050/21 1166), another historic paddler, does lunch and dinner cruises. For **longer cruises**, the PS *Murray River Queen* (free call ☎1800/88 8524) has three-night cruises from $276 and six-nighters from $552. *Paddleboat Coonawarra* (☎050/23 3366 or free call ☎1800/03 4424) has similar deals and also cheaper stand-bys. All cruises leave from **Mildura Wharf** at the end of Madden Avenue, west of the train station. For information about renting your own vessel, see "Around Mildura" below.

Away from the river, *Mallee Outback Experiences* (☎050/21 1621) do a town **tour** on Thursdays, as well as tours to the surrounding **national parks**: the popular one-day trip (Wed & Sat) with a former park ranger 110km across the border to the **Mungo National Park** (see p.236) is recommended. *Camerons*, 72 Lime Ave (☎050/21 2876), rent out sports gear and arrange **hot air balloon flights** daily, weather permitting, from $100 per person. *Crossroads Sporting Complex* on 15th Street has an indoor heated **pool**, and there's an outdoor Olympic pool on 12th Street for a refreshing plunge. If you want to swim in the river – there's a sandy **swimming beach** with lifeguards in summer at Chaffey Bend – take local advice and beware of dangerous currents; people have drowned here.

## Practicalities

Mildura is 555km from Melbourne, about as far as you can go in this small state; right on the border of New South Wales, and little over 100km from South Australia, it's ideally located for **onward transport** to either. Buses on the Sturt Highway, the major route between **Adelaide** and **Sydney**, pass through several times daily, at least one of them continuing all the way to **Perth**. North up Silver City Highway, **Broken Hill** can be reached by train or the local "Silver City Link" bus via Wentworth (departing Mildura train station Mon, Wed & Fri 7.50am; 3hr; ☎050/21 1166). Bookings for any of the above can be made through *Chaffey's Travel*, 71 Deakin Ave (☎050/23 5044). From **Melbourne**, there's a *V/Line* train-bus connection via Bendigo and Swan Hill at least once daily (☎13 2232 for bookings). **Local transport** includes buses to Red Cliffs and across the river to Wentworth, NSW (see p.235), or you can **rent a car** from *Maw Auto-Rent*, Koorlong Street, Irymple (free call ☎1800/65 6200).

Mildura has a reputation as a place to get **work** picking fruit; the only guaranteed time is February for the grape harvest, however, when the heat is at its most intense. If you think you could handle it, turn up around the second week of February for the six-week season. The CES, 87 Langtree Ave (Mon–Fri 8.45am–5pm; ☎050/21 9500), opens a **Harvest Office** each year; some growers have accommodation but normally you'll need your own transport and a tent.

## Accommodation

Mildura has stacks of accommodation and competition has kept prices low, especially at the motels.

**Apex Caravan Park**, Chaffey Bend (☎050/23 2309). Well-equipped site, right on the Murray by the beach, where guests can rent bikes. On-site vans ③, cabins ⑤.

**Carn Court Holiday Flats**, 826 15th St (☎050/23 6311). Good, inexpensive choice if you want to self-cater, with an outdoor pool. ④–⑤.

**City Colonial Motor Inn**, 24 Madden Ave (☎050/21 1800). New, well-appointed motel near the waterfront, with a solar-heated pool; some rooms have spas. ⑤–⑥.

**Mildura Grand Hotel**, 7th St, opposite the train station (☎050/23 0511). Fancier than its bland pub appearance suggests: a range of accommodation from basic to highly luxurious, with a dining room (breakfast is included), games room, spa, sauna, and outdoor swimming pool. ⑥–⑧.

**Murray View Motel**, 82 7th St (☎050/21 1200). Family-run, good-value modern motel, with a solar-heated pool. ④.

**Rosemount Holiday House**, 154 Madden Ave (☎050/23 1535). Old-style guesthouse that doubles as an affiliate YHA. Good facilities, breakfast, an outdoor swimming pool and work contacts. Dorms ①, rooms ②–④.

**Three States Motel**, 847 15th St (☎050/23 3735). Very popular motel with bargain rates, a pool, common spa, and tennis court. ④.

## Food

Healthy food abounds in Mildura's cafés and restaurants. If you have a vehicle, it's fun to buy fruit and vegetables from surrounding farms: if not, *The Vegie Mart*, 145 9th St, has a good range and also sells meat, cheeses, fish and poultry.

**Bananas Vegetarian Restaurant**, corner of 7th St and Chaffey Ave by the Arts Centre. Exotic and moderately priced, offering the tastiest dishes from various cuisines. BYO. Daily from 6pm.

**Hudak's Bakery**, Langtree Mall. Good continental breads and delicious zucchini slice. Open daily.

**Le Zizzles**, 30 Langtree Ave. Seafood, steak, ribs and all-you-can-eat salad and sweets bar. Fully licensed. Daily for lunch and dinner.

**Hotel Mildura**, 124 8th St. Bistro with classic Australian food, as well as Chinese-inspired dishes.

**Stefan Cantina**, in *Mildura Grand Hotel*, 7th St, opposite the train station (☎050/23 0511). This place is tucked away in the old cellar and there's no menu, but the excellent Italian food just keeps coming. Lunch and dinner Tues–Sat, booking essential.

**Yummies**, 136A 8th St. A sort of healthfood café, mostly – but not strictly – vegetarian; yummy fruit smoothies. Mon–Fri 7am–5.30pm, Sat 9am–2.30pm.

## Nightlife

Mildura's nightlife may not be the world's greatest, but there's plenty to keep you occupied. Perhaps the best thing to do is to try out one of the **clubs**, where you can be signed in as a visitor, and inexpensive food and drink are deployed to lure people onto the gambling machines. One of many is the *Mildura Workingman's Club*, on Deakin Avenue between 9th and 10th streets. Established in 1895, the club reputedly has the world's longest bar, a continuous undulating island 91 metres long; unfortunately you no longer get the full effect as the end of the bar is closed off for poker machines. Another good place for a drink is the vibrantly coloured and modern *Sandbar* (open to 1am nightly; light meals until 10pm), its yellow walls covered with bright papier-mâché menageries and other zany paraphernalia; bands play here on weekends and through the week in summer. The *Hotel Mildura*, 124 8th St, has a dance club called *Maddenz* (Thurs–Sat 9pm–3am) frequented by a young crowd, with free entry and pub prices, but don't come wearing your sneakers; the hotel's *Tavern Bar* is rough and best avoided.

## Around Mildura

The easiest excursion from Mildura is to **RED CLIFFS**, some 15km south, with its vineyards and tree-lined streets. There's a **Sunday market** along the highway near the train station, selling everything from local produce to second-hand junk, crafts and new clothes. The huge *Lindemans Karadoc Winery* is one of the largest **wineries** in Australia, where 50,000 tonnes of grapes are crushed every year. The range of wines for tasting is extensive, and the prices very reasonable (Mon–Fri 9am–5pm, Sat & Sun 10am–4.30pm).

Across the Murray from Mildura at **BURONGA** (actually in NSW, but more readily accessible from this side of the river) you can rent your own vessel to really get to grips with the river. *Buronga Boatmen* (☎050/23 5874), next to the bridge, have **fishing boats** from $10 per hour and **canoes** from $6 per person per hour. Or phone *The Rivermen* (free call ☎1800/80 9152) about renting a **houseboat**: weekly rates range from about $500 to nearly $2000, but they can accommodate from four to twelve people, so if you get a group together it can be quite reasonable – all you need to provide is a driver's licence and some food. The nearby *Floating Cafe* (daily 10am–6pm) is a colourfully shaded pontoon in a lovely spot with pelicans and ducks floating by. Also at Buronga is the **Stanley Winery** (Mon–Fri 10am–4pm, Sat 10.30am–4pm, Sun noon–4pm) producer of that great Aussie institution, cask wine. It's the largest cask winery in New South Wales – you can taste the wine here or just pose outside the big wine cask outside.

Thirty-one kilometres west of Buronga is the river town of Wentworth; located on the main Silver City Highway to Broken Hill, its attractions are fully covered in the *New South Wales and ACT* chapter (see p.235).

# Swan Hill and around

Heading for Swan Hill, you can aim south down the Calder Highway, turning east at Hattah onto the Hattah-Robinvale Road and continuing past the Hattah Kulkyne National Park (see p.725). Alternatively, you can cross the Murray into New South Wales and follow the Sturt Highway, re-crossing the river at **ROBINVALE**, a small rather characterless fruit-growing town, but idyllically situated within a great loop of the river. Wine buffs should make a stop at *Robinvale Winery*, Sea Lake Road (Mon–Sat 9am–6pm, Sun 1–6pm), where a wide range of **wines** including some Greek varieties are biodynamically produced. Horses can be hired from *Gadsen's Horse Hire* (☎050/26 4155) to explore **riverside trails**.

Twenty-five kilometres from Swan Hill you reach the highly productive stone-fruit and vegetable growing area of **NYAH**. Bushcamping with no water or facilities is allowed in the nearby Nyah and Vinefera **state forests** along the Murray; for full details, contact the *Department of Conservation and Natural Resources*, McCallum St, Swan Hill (Mon–Fri 8am–4.30pm; ☎050/33 1290). Eight kilometres beyond Nyah, **Tyntynder Homestead** (daily except Sat 9am–4.30pm; $6) is worth a visit, a classic 1846 bungalow among flowering gardens, furnished in wealthy squatter style. There's also a museum section with Aboriginal artefacts among its collection.

As you approach **SWAN HILL** itself, the landscape changes – this is cattle and sheep country, with wheat fields further north. The Murray here is shallow and tricky to navigate, so there's not much river traffic. A service centre for the pastoral industry, Swan Hill has a typically solid, conservative atmosphere. Perhaps surprisingly, it's quite a multicultural sort of place, with ten percent of Victoria's Aboriginal population, and a large Italian community: elderly Italian matrons gossip on street corners, the pizzas and bread are suitably good, and ornate mausoleums dominate the cemetery. The Pioneer Settlement (see below) is undoubtedly Swan Hill's main attraction, but while you're here, you could also take a look at the **Swan Hill Regional Contemporary Art Gallery** (daily 9am–4.30pm; $1), which specializes in folk and Aboriginal art, and the **Murray Downs Homestead** (daily 9am–4.30pm; $6.50) an impressive Victorian mansion at the heart of a 4,000-hectare station – it's over the bridge in New South Wales, but barely a kilometre from town.

## Pioneer Settlement

Swan Hill's **Pioneer Settlement** (daily 8.30am–5pm; $9), a reconstruction of a pioneering community at Horseshoe Bend, about a kilometre south of the train station, was the first of its kind in Australia and is still one of the best. The buildings are all authentic, having been transported from various sites near and far. One of the most interesting came from South Melbourne, where it was lived in until 1967: the **Iron House** is an example of nineteenth-century "kit homes", which were sent out from Britain in their thousands during the housing crisis that accompanied the goldrush – Victoria had whole streets of them, stinking hot in summer and freezing cold in winter.

In the settlement's streets many of the **shops** are functional – the baker, the printer, the haberdashery and the porcelain doll shop – with assistants dressed in vaguely period costume. Generally, though, it's low-key and peaceful: buildings like the barber's shop and the stock and station agents are open for you to wander around undisturbed. The pharmacy has a large collection of old medicines with a gruesome dentist's surgery out back; the church is made from old bricks of the original courthouse; and there's even a rather creepy Masonic Lodge, which is still used. The **Mechanics Institute** has a traditional collection of books and a wonderful working "Stereoscopic Theatre" dating from 1895: the wooden cylinder has 25 viewfinders each with a leather seat from which you can admire the 3D scenes. **Rides** around the settlement are offered in a 1924 Dodge and a horse-drawn carriage. In the evening, the **sound and light show** (nightly from dusk; $6) is strikingly effective.

The settlement is situated on the banks of the Marraboor River, a branch of the Murray. Across the river, a wooden bridge leads to **Pental Island**'s assortment of native flora and fauna. Meanwhile, an old paddle-steamer, the *Pyap*, **cruises** from the settlement upriver past Murray Downs every day at 10.30am and 2.30pm ($6; 1hr).

## Practicalities

The **Tourist Information Office**, 306 Campbell St (Mon–Fri 9am–5pm, Sat 10am–1pm), has a free map of the town with detailed information on local attractions; it also sells tickets for the Pioneer Settlement sound and light show.

There's a strip of **motels**, all with swimming pools, along Campbell Street, where in fact you'll find almost everything in town. *Swan Hill Resort Motor Inn* at no. 405 (☎050/32 2726; ⑥) is the most luxurious, with indoor and outdoor pool and spa plus gym and other sports facilities; it's easily located because of its restaurant, *The Silver Slipper*, which has a huge rotating stiletto outside and gets even tackier inside. *Pioneer Station Motor Inn* at no. 421 (☎050/32 2017; ④) is older and better value; at no. 182, the *White Swan Hotel* (☎050/32 2761; ③) has simple, shared-facility rooms as well as more luxurious ones; the *Commercial Hotel* at no. 91 (☎050/32 1214; ④) has the cheapest singles but is otherwise less good. In a central location at 1 Monash Drive, *Riverside* (☎050/32 1494; on-site vans ③–④, cabins ④–⑤) is a good **caravan park** right on the riverfront.

The large Italian population in Swan Hill has had a beneficial effect on the **food**: *Bartalotta's Hot Bread Kitchen*, 178 Campbell St, is excellent, and there are three pizzerias – *Pizza Graffitti* in Campbell Street is the best, while *Quo Vadis*, Campbell Street again, also has a restaurant serving good pasta. Both health food and junk food are doled out during the day at the *Old Royal*, a slightly alternative café at 176 Campbell St; at no. 225, *Teller's Licensed Deli-Café* is a slick-looking city-style brasserie in an old bank.

**Car rental** is available from *McDonald Caltex Service Station*, 402 Campbell St (☎050/32 2695). The *Richard Swimming Centre*, Monash Drive (Oct–April daily 7am–9pm), has several **swimming pools** and a waterslide.

## Swan Hill to Gunbower Island

From Swan Hill, the Murray Valley Highway heads southeast, away from the river, following the rail line past a series of fifty-odd freshwater lakes. At the first of these, **Lake Boga**, just 16km from Swan Hill, *Lake Boga Jet Ski Hire and Parasailing* rent out jet skis and offer parasailing. Also by the lake – follow the signs – is *Best's St Andrew's Winery*, a large, commercial **winery**, the oldest in the Swan Hill region, which offers conducted tours (Mon–Fri hourly 10am–3pm) and tastings. The lakes end at **Kerang**, a sizeable town on the Loddon River in a citrus-growing area. **Lake Reedy** near here is one of the largest ibis breeding grounds in Australia and has a public viewing hide; the birds are widespread in the area, though, so you'll probably see them anyway.

From Kerang, the Murray Valley Highway continues east to Cohuna, in a rich dairying area, and from there towards **Gunbower Island**, a further 23km. The "island", encircled by the Murray River and Gunbower Creek, is a state forest of huge red gums and Gunnawarra wetlands, with 160 bird species and much wildlife. It's most easily approached from Cohuna (follow the signs on the Kerang–Koondrook road); details of walks and camping can be obtained from the *Department of Conservation and Natural Resources* in the Civic Centre, Edward Street, Cohuna (☎054/56 2266).

# Echuca

**ECHUCA**, a lively and progressive place, is the most easily accessible river town from Melbourne, only three hours or so by bus or car, making it a popular weekend getaway. The largest inland port in Australia after the railway line connected it to Melbourne in 1864, the **Port of Echuca**, with its massive wharves and collection of old buildings, is a major tourist attraction, and several cruises trawl along the river from here. The town itself is not too touristy though, and has retained much of its charm. There are two primary streets: High Street, the old main street, leads to Murray Esplanade and the wharf and is the centre of tourist activity, with lots of cafés and boutiquey shops, while Hare Street, the modern main street, remains satisfyingly functional.

# Port of Echuca

To enter the old wharf area (daily 9.15am–5pm; $5), you need to get hold of a "**passport**", either from the tourist office (see "Practicalities" below) or from the *Star Hotel*, opposite the wharf; it also allows entry to the *Star Hotel* and the *Bridge Hotel*. The **Star Hotel** was first licensed in 1867 and is a typical pioneer pub, a tiny one-storey building with a tin roof and verandah. As the river trade declined, the *Star* was delicensed (in 1897) along with many of the other 79 hotels in town. Drinking on the premises became illegal, so the loyal clientele dug a tunnel to the street through which they could escape at the the first whiff of a police raid – you can examine this, along with the cellar and a small museum.

The magnificent red-gum **wharf** was nearly a mile long in its prime and is still fairly extensive. Three landing platforms at different levels allowed unloading even during flooding, and from the top, high over a bend in the river, the views are wonderful. Goods were transferred from train to steamer via this top level, and old train carriages sit on sidings here, piled high with trunks of red gum. You can wander below to the other levels, through a network of thick river-red-gum piles standing 12 metres high. At the lowest level, several **old boats** undergoing restoration are moored, including the *Pevensey*, a 1911 steam-driven cargo boat which you can wander aboard – it offers one-hour cruises on the last Sunday of every month (☎054/82 4248). In the wharf cargo shed there's a a a scale model of the working port and a ten-minute audio-visual presentation with historical narration.

Back outside the wharf complex, along Murray Esplanade, opposite Hopwood Gardens, is the **Bridge Hotel**, opened in 1858 but delicensed in 1916. It was built by the founder of Echuca, Henry Hopwood, an ex-convict who also started a punt service across the Murray; the story goes that if the pub wasn't doing well he'd close the ferry down for a few hours, leaving prospective passengers with little else to do but have a few drinks. Other things to see in the old port area include the **Red Gum Works** (daily 9am–5pm), housed in a large loading shed and wonderfully scented by the wood as it's transformed from tree-trunk to souvenir; there's also a steam-operated sawmill and a blacksmith at work. **Echuca Wharf Pottery** (daily 9.30am–6pm) also has demonstrations daily. The **World in Wax Museum**, 630 High St (☎054/82 3630; daily 9am–5pm; $5), displays sixty wax figures of "world-renowned personalities", with Australia rather unimaginatively represented by Paul Hogan and Dame Nellie Melba.

## Njernda Koori Aboriginal Museum

When the **missions** began to close in the 1930s, many Aboriginal families, especially Yorta Yorta people from Cummeragunga mission, and Wemba Wemba from Moonacullah mission, migrated to the Echuca area. Since they weren't made welcome in the towns, the migrants were forced to live on the fringes in poor, flood-prone housing, just close enough to be able to get to work and seek education. Women commonly worked in canneries and hospitals; the men packed fruit, sheared and laboured.

The **Njernda Koori Museum** (Tues–Sun & public holidays 10am–4.30pm; $2.50) in the Old Court House, on Law Place near the wharf, tells the story of the Wemba Wemba and the Yorta Yorta Aborigines. Run by the Echuca Aboriginal Co-operative, it aims to explain Koorie culture and community ways; a cultural officer is on hand on Wednesdays to explain and interpret the history presented in the museum. With fascinating videos and photo exhibitions, it's well worth seeing.

## River cruises

A wide choice of **cruises** are on offer, departing from berths just beyond the old wharf, best approached from Murray Esplanade. One-hour port cruises are available on the *PS Pride of the Murray* (daily 9.45am, 11am, noon, 1.15 pm, 2.30pm; $8; ☎054/82 5244) and the *PS Emmylou* (daily 10.15am, 11.45am, 1.15pm, 2.45pm; $9; ☎054/82 3801); the latter is a wood-fired paddle-steamer which also offers two-night cruises (from $345 per person including all meals). Other vessels include the *PS Canberra* (daily 10am, 11.30am, 1.30pm, 3pm; 1hr; $8), and *MV Mary Ann* (☎054/82 6000) which does lunch and dinner cruises.

## Practicalities

The **Tourist Information Centre**, at the corner of Leslie Street and Murray Esplanade (Mon–Fri 9am–5pm, weekends 10am–4pm; ☎054/80 7555), is in the old redbrick Customs House in the historic wharf area; they sell tickets to the port complex and for cruises, as well as booking accommodation. The *Echuca Travel Centre*, 203 Hare St, sells *V/line* and interstate **bus** tickets.

The best **budget accommodation** in town is *Echuca Riverboat Hostel*, 103 Mitchell St (☎054/80 6522; ①), right on the edge of the Banyule Forest, ten minutes' walk through red gums to sandy river beaches where you can swim; it's a friendly place with facilities including a spa, bike rental and some tours. The *Steam Packet Inn*, corner of Leslie Street and Murray Esplanade (☎054/82 3411; ⑤), is a National Trust-classified inn in the heart of the old port area, now a **motel**. *Echuca Hotel*, 571 High St (☎054/82 1087; ④), the town's first pub, still has some original features and offers simple accommodation in large pleasant rooms. Upmarket **bed and breakfast** accommodation can be found in several pretty, historic homes: one that stands out is *The River Gallery Inn*, 578 High St (☎054/80 6902; ⑥–⑦), where all the self-contained rooms have open fireplaces, and some have spas. *City of Echuca*, in Victoria Park, Crofton Street (☎054/82 2157; on-site vans ③, cabins ④), is a well-equipped **caravan park** right on the riverfront, and there are a couple of **nudist resorts** around Echuca. *River Valley Nudist Resort* (☎054/82 6650; ④) is in a bushland setting along the Goulburn River, and *Wyanda Park Nudist Resort* (☎058/67 3236; ④) is thirty minutes' drive from town. Enquire at the tourist office about the many **houseboats** available to rent in the area.

With hungry Melbournites to feed, there's no shortage of decent **eating places**. *Sutton* on Hare Street is an old-fashioned bakery with a shaded bench outside where you can eat your haul. *The Blue Pacific*, also on Hare Street, does good-quality freshly cooked fish and chips; equally traditional though rather more refined, *Town Hall Tea Rooms*, on the High Street, serve genteel teas and hot meals. *Roma Restaurant*, 191 Hare St, is open late every night for decent pasta and pizza, while the *American Hotel*, on the same street, serves good, plain counter meals. On the other side of the river, the *Philadelphia Bar & Grill* at the *Moama Motor Inn*, Cobb Highway, specializes in Cajun and creole cooking.

**Nightlife** is better than you might expect; the *American Hotel*, a small and friendly local on the corner of Hare and Heygarth streets, is a good place to start with a drink. The *Royal Hotel*, 183 Hare St, draws a youngish crowd and plays host to live bands on weekends. At 2 Nish St, *The Mill* is a glitzy and expensive nightclub in a converted mill just over the railway line. *Paramount Arts Activity Centre* on Hare Street has **films** on Friday and Saturday nights, and plays occasionally; check the local paper for details. If you're around in late October, check out the **Rich River Festival**, ten days of balls, street parades, pageants and markets; in mid-February there's a self-explanatory **Jazz, Food and Wine Weekend**.

## Around Echuca

Thirty kilometres southeast of Echuca, the main attraction of Kyabram is **Kyabram Fauna Park** (daily 10am–6pm; $5), a community-owned wildlife park divided into grassland for free-ranging kangaroos, wallabies, emus and others, and a huge wetland area. You can wander around the grassland area and through several aviaries; a two-storey observation tower affords views of the more than eighty species of native birdlife on the water. Diamond pythons, tiger snakes, crocodiles and other not-so-pleasant members of the Australian fauna can be viewed from a safe distance at the new Reptile House.

**BARMAH**, some 30km upstream on the Murray, is most easily reached by crossing into NSW at Echuca and heading north on the Cobb Highway, then turning east. This small river town is associated with red-gum milling, and with sleeper cutting in the early railway days. *Barmah Caravan Park* (☎058/69 3225; ①–③) has a great site on the banks of the river among red gums, with a small sandy beach for swimming. Ten kilometres out of town, **Barmah State Park** has Australia's largest stands of **river red gum**, some of them 40m tall and 500 years old. The forest runs along the Murray for over 100km and stands in an extensive flood plain: **canoeing** between the trees at flood time is magical (July–Nov; canoe rental and transport from *Echuca Boat and Canoe Hire* ☎054/80 6208). During the wet season, more than 200 species of waterbird come here and there's plenty of other wildlife; you might even see brumbies (wild horses). When it's dry, there are well-established walking tracks to take advantage of: the place was of special significance to the Yorta Yorta Aborigines and you can still see fish traps, middens and scars on trees where the bark has been used for canoes. During the Barmah Cattle Muster every April, 2000 head of cattle grazed in the forest are mustered in a frenzied, exciting atmosphere.

Yorta Yorta culture and lore is explained in the park's **Dharnya Centre** (daily 10am–5pm; free), which also has archeological information and artefacts. The *MV Kingfisher* **cruise** (Mon, Wed, Thurs & Sat, plus other days during busy times; $15; 2hr; reservations essential ☎054/82 6788 or 058/69 3399) leaves from here – a flat-bottomed boat that glides over Barmah Lake and through stands of red-gum. *Echuca Sightseeing* (☎054/82 1335) does a good half-day **tour** which includes the *Kingfisher* cruise and a visit to the *Dharnya Centre* (Wed 8.30am & Sun 11.30am; $29).

# GIPPSLAND

**GIPPSLAND** stretches southeast of Melbourne from Western Port to the New South Wales border, between the Great Dividing Range and the Tasman Sea. Green and well watered, it's been the centre of Victoria's dairy industry since the 1880s. **South Gippsland** is also, in contrast, the site of vast brown-coal deposits between Moe and Traralgon in the Latrobe Valley, where power stations generate most of the state's electricity, while offshore, Bass Strait wells exploit natural gas and crude oil reserves, with several gas processing and oil stabilizing plants marring the coastline.

For those more predisposed to natural delights, South Gippsland also has Victoria's most popular national park, **Wilsons Promontory**. "The Prom" is a hook-shaped land mass jutting out into the sea, with superb scenery and bushwalks. In the east the industry disappears around the **Gippsland Lakes** and **Ninety Mile Beach**; and running to the NSW border is the unspoilt coastline of the **Croajingolong National Park**.

## Transport

*V/Line* trains run from Melbourne to Bairnsdale, basically following the Princes Highway through South Gippsland. From Bairnsdale, buses leave for Orbost, stopping at Lakes Entrance. The "Sapphire Coast Link" is a train-bus connection between Melbourne and Narooma on the south coast of NSW: take the train to Sale, then a connecting bus along the Princes Highway via Lakes Entrance, Orbost, Cann River, and Genoa. The "Capital Link" connects Melbourne with Canberra: take the train to Sale, then a bus via Lakes Entrance, Orbost and Cann River (Mon, Thurs & Sat).

Bookings for both the above should be made through *V/Line* (☎13 2232). There's a daily *Greyhound.Pioneer* service along the coast from Melbourne to Sydney, but it's not very convenient if you want to get off at stops in East Gippsland: the bus leaves Melbourne in the evening and gets to Lakes Entrance around midnight, to Cann River at about 3.30am.

# Wilsons Promontory and Tarra Bulga

**WILSONS PROMONTORY**, the most southerly chunk of the Australian mainland, was once joined by a land bridge to Tasmania. Its barbed hook juts out into the Bass Strait, surrounded by a rocky coastline interspersed with sheltered sandy bays and coves; the coastal scenery is made even more stunning by the backdrop of granite ranges. It's understandably Victoria's most popular **national park**. Though the main campsite gets packed in summer, there are plenty of walking tracks and opportunities for bushcamping; the park's big enough to allow you to escape the crowds, with about 130km of coastal scenery, and inland areas packed with tall forests, heathlands and salt marshes. You can swim at several of the beaches and even surf: *Wilsons Prom Surf School* operates courses for all ages and abilities, with all equipment provided (☎056/808 512 or ☎059/525 512).

There's no public **transport** to Wilsons Promontory; the nearest you can get is with the *V/Line* bus from Dandenong, which will take you as far as Foster on the South Gippsland Highway. If you're coming from Phillip Island, *Amaroo Park Backpackers* in Cowes (☎059/52 2548) have a good inexpensive **tour**. With your own vehicle, the easiest way to get here from Melbourne without getting lost is to follow the South Gippsland Highway to Meeniyan, turning right onto route 189 which takes you all the way to the park entrance. Once you get into the park, it's 30km to Tidal River on a good sealed road. At the entrance you pay $6 per car – if you stay overnight, this is deducted from the cost.

The **information centre** (daily 8.30am–4.30pm; ☎056/80 8538) at **Tidal River** is an obvious first stop. They have plenty of information, though not all of it is on display, so ask: the small booklet *Discovering the Prom on Foot* is pricey but invaluable if you're attempting any of the overnight walks. Tidal River, situated by a small river on Norman Bay, is the park's main camping and accommodation centre; colourful rainbow lorrikeets fly about the place and land to be fed from people's hands. There's also a **general store** here (daily 9am–7pm), with a pricey supermarket section, takeaway food, fuel pumps and LP gas. **Accommodation** is arranged through the information centre, but for the Christmas, summer and Easter holiday period it is well-nigh impossible to get anything at all; many places are booked up to a year in advance. Self-contained holiday units (☎056/80 9500) are available by the week ($200–540, depending on the season); there are also cabins (④) and a 500-site camping area that has all the creature comforts – hot showers, shops, a laundry and summer outdoor cinema.

Many **short walks** begin from Tidal River, including a track for the mobility disabled: one of the best is the **Squeaky Beach Nature Walk** (1hr return) which crosses Tidal River, heads uphill and through a tea-tree canopy to end up on a beach of pure quartz sand that is indeed squeaky underfoot. **Overnight walks** allow you to discover the peace of the southern half of the park, with pit toilets and water available at the campsites. All of the tracks are well marked and relatively easy, often boardwalked. The most popular is the two- to three-day (36km) Sealers Cove–Refuge Cove–Waterloo Bay walk, beginning and ending at the Mount Oberon car park. Crowds are even thinner in the remote north of the park, where there are no facilities and limited fresh water: this is the province of experienced, properly equipped bushwalkers.

## Tarra Bulga National Park

If you're in the mood for national parks, another good one can be reached from Yarram, 50km beyond Foster on the South Gippsland Highway. **Tarra Bulga National Park**, in the heart of the Strzelecki Ranges, is dominated by forests of mountain ash and myrtle beech with a lower canopy of ferns, a cool green environment alive with colourful lyrebirds, crimson rosellas and yellow-breasted robins among the rich bird-life. There's a **Visitors' Information Centre** (☎051/96 6127) at Balook on the Grand Ridge Road, between the two separate sections of the park, where you can find out about several bushwalks. The Grand Ridge Road (mostly unsealed) winds along the top of the Strzelecki Ranges through fern gullies and towering trees, giving gorgeous views of South Gippsland. *Tarra Bulga Guest House* (☎051/96 6141; ⑥), on a beef and lamb property on Grand Ridge Road just 50m from the visitors' centre, has all creature comforts including a library, games room and all meals.

# The Gippsland Lakes region

The **Gippsland Lakes**, Australia's largest system of inland waterways, are fed by the waters of the Mitchell, Nicholson and Tambo rivers, and separated from the sea by Ninety Mile Beach. East of Yarram, the beach stretches long and straight towards **Lakes Entrance**, the tacky focal point of the area and one of Victoria's most popular holiday spots, with the foothills of the high country within easy reach to the north.

**SALE**, at the junction of the South Gippsland Highway and the Princes Highway, is a good point from which to head off to explore the coastal park and Ninety Mile Beach. From Seaspray, 35km south, a coastal road hugs the shore for 20km to Golden Beach, from where a scenic drive heads through the **Gippsland Lakes Coastal Park** to **Loch Sport**. Here you're faced with the enviable dilemma of lakes on one side, and ocean beaches with good surfing on the other – an unsealed road continues on to Sperm Whale Head in the **Lakes National Park**. Sale's **Tourist Information Centre** (daily 10am–4pm; ☎051/44 1108), on the Princes Highway, can fill you in on all the details.

Moving on, **BAIRNSDALE** is the next major town on the highway, and another jumping-off point for the lakes; local information comes from the **tourist office** on Main Street (Mon–Fri 9am–5pm, Sat & Sun 10am–4pm; ☎051/52 3444). Northwest of Bairnsdale, the **Mitchell River National Park** is home to the **Den of Nargun**, a small cave haunted, in Aboriginal legend, by a *nargun* – a creature half made of stone. The cave is located in a small, beautiful valley; follow the loop track from the park picnic area via a lookout to the Mitchell River (30 min), then take the track along Woolshed Creek to the cave and climb up the steep path back to the starting point (40 min).

## Lakes Entrance and Metung

The sandy barrier between the Gippsland Lakes and the sea was formed about 6000 years ago; when first seen by white men in the 1840s the outlet to the sea was a seasonal, intermittent gap, unsuitable for reliable trade. In 1889 the present stable entrance was opened 6km east of the old one: the artificial entrance effectively cuts off access to the length of **Ninety Mile Beach** from the town, and means that it's no longer really ninety miles either.

As you might expect from the area's holiday popularity, **LAKES ENTRANCE** is a big, rather tawdry, tourist town, with loads of motels at either end of town as you enter from the highway. There are all sorts of attractions aimed at keeping holidaying kids happy – from *Fun Park* through *Seashell Museum* to mini-golf – on the Esplanade, which fronts onto an arm of Lake King. Lakes Entrance is also a big **fishing port**: the

Fishermans Cooperative Wharf has a viewing platform where you can watch the catch being unloaded, and a tantalizing fish shop.

Beaches are the big attraction, of course. **Lakes Entrance Surf Beach**, a substantial stretch of white sand patrolled in season by lifesavers, can be reached via a footbridge across the lake to Hummocks Reserve, then a two-kilometre walking track. Of the many **lake cruises** on offer, a justifiably popular choice is the trip from the Club Jetty at the western end of town, up North Arm to the *Wyanga Park Winery* on the fringe of the Colquhoun Forest, in the winery's own boat, *The Corque* (several cruises daily; book at the tourist office, or through the winery on ☎051/55 1508). Other diversions are provided by local **tour operators** such as *Gippsland High Country Tours* (☎051/57 5556) and *4 WD Coastal Tours* (☎051/55 32 56) run 4WD day-trips through the Snowy River National Park, the Errinundra Plateau and Croajingolong National Park, as well as shorter trips. *Phoenix Flights* (☎051/52 4617), based at the Bairnsdale Aerodrome, do cheap, kiss-me-quick scenic **flights** over the extensive waterways (from $15 per person for 10min, minimum two people).

If the commercialism of Lakes Entrance turns you off, head for the more refined charms of **METUNG**, a pretty, upmarket boating and holidaying village with hot mineral pools. Just 10km west along the shoreline, it is reached via a side road off the highway towards Bairnsdale.

## Practicalities

**Lakes Entrance Tourist Information** (daily 10am–5pm; ☎051/55 1966), on the Esplanade, provides local advice and tickets for cruises on the lakes, and can also book **accommodation**, a useful service in summer, when the place is very crowded. *Lakes Main Caravan Park*, at 7 Willis St at the eastern end of town, is a helpful place with on-site vans, backpacker accommodation in four-bed dorms, and tents to absorb any overflow; bikes can be rented here (☎051/55 2365; dorms ①, on-site vans ②). The **motels** are as tacky as their names suggest: probably the best of the lot is the brand-new *Coastal Waters Motel* on the Esplanade (☎051/55 1792; ⑤–⑦), which has its own saltwater pool. A better, and usually cheaper, option are **cabins** or **cottages**. *Lazy Acre Log Cabins*, 35 Roadknight St (☎051/55 1323; ⑤–⑦) are a good bet, with a pool and common spa, and facilities for the disabled. Places to **eat** in Lakes Entrance include *Tres Amigos*, 521 Esplanade, for good Mexican food; *Caffe 567*, 567 Esplanade, for delicious coffee and Italian-style ice cream; and *Fish-a-Fare*, 509 Esplanade, an excellent fish and chips shop.

A typically good-value option in **Metung** is *Maeburn Cottages*, 33 Mairburn Road, where you have a choice between attractive two-bedroom cottages and a six-bed bunkhouse (☎051/56 2736; dorm ②, cottage ④–⑤; BYO linen). At 155 Metung Rd, *McMillans Holiday Village* comprises eleven very comfortable, fully equipped cottages of different sizes in a garden setting, with a solar-heated pool, tennis court and a private jetty (☎051/56 2283; ⑤–⑧). The *Metung Hotel* has inexpensive accommodation and bistro **meals** (☎051/56 2206; ④); or wine and dine at the pricey but excellent *Morcomb's of Metung* on the waterfront (lunch Sat, Sun & public holidays, dinner Wed–Sun).

# Buchan and the Snowy River Loop

Nowa Nowa is the inauspiciously named town where you turn off the Princes Highway for Buchan, in the foothills of the Victorian Alps, and a satisfying loop through the Snowy River National Park. The little town of **BUCHAN** has impressive underground limestone formations, viewable on guided tours of two **caves**: the Royal Cave (daily 10am, 1pm & 3.30pm; 45min; $6.50) and the Fairy Cave (daily 11.15am & 2.15am; 45min; $8), with additional tours at peak times. In the extensive park surrounding them there's an icy, spring-fed swimming pool, playground, walking tracks, wildlife and a campsite.

The road continues north from Buchan through hilly country, following the Murrindal River and slowly winding its way up to the plateau of the Australian Alps. The melodramatically named **Shades of Death Cave** (aka Murrindal Cave), 14km north of Buchan, is a 14-million-year-old vertical or "pothole cave": you work your way down to the bottom cavern on concrete pathways. Guided tours are organized during school holidays from 11am to 4pm, at other times by appointment (☎051/55 9458; $7). The sealed road ends just before the *Seldom Seen Roadhouse*. From here you can continue right up to Jindabyne in the Snowy Mountains of NSW, but about two thirds of the way are unsealed and can be very rough; check road conditions before attempting this.

## Snowy River National Park

Turning right at Wulgumerang, about 55km north of Buchan, enables you to describe a scenic arc through the northern end and around the eastern fringe of the **Snowy River National Park**, following the unsealed road towards Bonang (check road conditions beforehand as this is an unsealed road which can deteriorate badly in adverse weather conditions). **Little River Falls** are well worth a stop on this stretch: a short walk leads from the car park past snow gums to a lookout with breath-taking views of Little River Gorge and the falls.

Further on, you descend to the valley of the Snowy River, which you cross at **McKillops Bridge**, set in the landscape that inspired Banjo Patterson's famous ballad, *The Man from Snowy River*. The river's sandy banks are a favourite camping area, and also the place to set out on a **rafting** trip through deep gorges, caves, raging rapids and tranquil pools; *Snowy River Expeditions*, located in Buchan (☎051/55 9353) offer good - value expeditions. If you want to play at being the man from Snowy River, *Snowy River Trail Rides*, based in Buchan, have daily **horse rides**, as well as extended camping trips in the high country (☎051/55 9245).

## Bonang and the Errinundra National Park

The road through the national park continues until it meets the Bonang–Orbost road. *The General Store* (☎064/58 0265) at **BONANG**, a former goldrush town, books guided tours of the restored **Aurora Gold Mine**, as well as trail rides and scenic flights; you can also get takeaway food, groceries and fuel here. The rustic *Delegate River Tavern*, about fifteen minutes' drive north towards the NSW border from Bonang, is open daily for counter **meals** and has good-value B&B **accommodation** in log cabins (☎064/58 8009; ③).

The road down to the coast, still mostly unsealed, leads past the **Errinundra National Park**, with magnificent wetland eucalypt forests containing giant, centuries-old specimens, and Victoria's largest surviving stand of rainforest. All the roads in the area are heavily used by logging trucks – watch out.

## Orbost

The road from Bonang eventually emerges at the old-fashioned town of **ORBOST**, back on the Princes Highway where it crosses the Snowy River. There's a tranquil picnic spot opposite the *Orbost Caravan Park*, on the corner of Lochiel and Nicholson streets (☎051/54 1097; on-site vans ②), with huge gums lining one bank and cows roaming the paddocks on the other. On Nicholson Street the **tourist office** (Mon–Fri 8.30am–5pm, Sat & Sun 9am–4pm) is housed in an authentic pioneer slab hut. The town's biggest attraction is the new **Orbost Rainforest Centre** (Nov–May Mon–Fri 9am–5pm, Sat & Sun 10am–5pm; June–Oct Tues–Fri 9am–5pm, Sat 10am–5pm; free), with an audio-visual display and landscaped gardens showing examples of the three types of rainforest in Victoria: cool temperate, warm temperate and dry rainforest. They also have information on the national parks in the area, and on the latest road conditions; several good bushwalking books as well as *Natmaps* are on sale.

# Croajingolong National Park

From Orbost to **CANN RIVER** the Princes Highway continues well inland, not to reach the coast again until Eden, across the border in New South Wales. The *Department of Conservation and Natural Resources* **information centre**, on the Princes Highway in Cann River (Mon–Fri 9am–5pm; ☎051/58 6351), provides information on the **Croajingolong National Park**, which begins south of the town at Sydenham Inlet and for 100km follows the coast to the state border; foothills cloaked in warm temperate rainforest stretch down to the unspoilt "Wilderness Coast". There are several camping spots in the park – all astoundingly popular in summer and allocated way in advance by a ballot system. Cann River itself offers very good value **accommodation** at three motels, the cheapest being the *Cann River Motel* on the Princes Highway (☎051/58 6255; ④), and at the *Cann River Caravan Park* at the junction of Princes and Cann Valley highways (☎051/58 6369; ②), which has cabins for rent. On the way out of town, it's worth checking out the *Nulluak Gundji Aboriginal Arts and Craft Centre*, which is signposted from the highway.

## Mallacoota and around

**MALLACOOTA** is a holiday resort actually within the Croajingolong National Park, on the lake system of the **Mallacoota Inlet**. It's approached via Genoa, 47km from Cann River along the Princes Highway. About 10km from Genoa, a turnoff to the left leads to **Gipsy Point**, an idyllic spot near the confluence of the Genoa and Wallagaraugh rivers on the upper reaches of the Mallacoota Inlet, and a fine place to spend a blissful day or two (see "Practicalities" below for somewhere to stay and eat here).

Your logical first step on arriving in Mallacoota itself is to head for the **Mallacoota Information and Booking Service**, 57 Maurice Ave (Christmas–Easter daily 8.30am–7.30pm; other times Mon–Fri 9am–5.30pm, Sat 9am–noon; ☎051/58 0788) where you can sort out your accommodation and buy tickets for leisurely **cruises** via Bottom Lake and Top Lake and Wallagaraugh River up to the NSW border. If that sounds too lazy, you can rent a boat or canoe for your own explorations from *Buckland's Jetty Boat Hire* (☎051/58 0660). The *Department of Conservation and Natural Resources* office, on the corner of Allan and Buckland drives (☎051/58 0219) has details of secluded camping spots and local **bushwalks**.

Come summer time, Mallacoota, although seemingly remote, teems with avid holidaymakers, most conspicuously teenagers making use of their first cars to get a taste of freedom. Mallacoota's small population of just over a thousand trebles again for the Easter "Carnival in Coota" **arts festival**, which includes all sorts of music, theatre and comedy, a community market, and fascinating sand sculptures.

### Practicalities

You'll probably enjoy Mallacoota more if you **stay** away from the centre at somewhere like *Mareeba Lodge*, 59 Mirrabooka Rd (☎051/58 0378; ⑤), a friendly B&B. **Mudbrick** houses have really caught on here, so much so that Mallacoota is sometimes referred to as the "mudbrick capital of Australia". One of the trendsetters was Peter Kurz, owner of *Adobe Holiday Flats*, 17 Karbeethong Ave, 4km northwest of town in Karbeethong (☎051/58 0329; ④–⑤; BYO linen): these cosy mudbrick flats boast beautiful views of the lake and lots of birdlife. *Jingalong Lodge* (☎051/58 0352; ⑥) offers self-catering (everything supplied) on a cattle property on the eastern shore of the inlet, with access only by water from Mallacoota Jetty; call and they'll pick you up.

In terms of **food**, there isn't much choice: the *Tide Bistro* is probably the best place in town, or there are counter meals at the *Mallacoota Hotel*. Other distractions include **bands** at the local pub every night in January, and a summer **cinema** at the

Mallacoota Community Centre, Allen Drive. The only **bank**, *Westpac*, 58 Maurice Ave, is open Mon–Fri 9.30am–12.30pm & 1.30–3.30pm, but there are EFTPOS facilities at the *Mobil* service station and the *Bait and Tackle Shop*.

**Gipsy Point**, about 20km northwest, harbours the friendly *Gipsy Point Hotel*, set in a garden by the water; it has counter meals and accommodation in good en-suite rooms or holiday units (☎051/58 8200; ④–⑦). Nearby, the *Gipsy Point Lodge* on McDonald Street has B&B rooms and cottages (☎051/58 8205; ④–⑤) and arranges birdwatching and bushwalking excursions.

# THE NORTHEAST

The direct route between Melbourne and Sydney, the **Hume Highway** cuts straight through Victoria's northeast: what has become known as **Ned Kelly country**. **Euroa**, **Benalla** and **Glenrowan** – where the outlaw was finally seized after a bloody shoot out – all have traces of the masked bushranger's activities, with Glenrowan wholeheartedly cashing in. West of the Hume, **Rutherglen**, right up against the state border, is Victoria's oldest established wine-producing region. There are also vineyards in the rich fruit-growing region of the **Goulburn Valley**, along the Goulburn Valley Highway from **Seymour**.

**Bushwalking** in the Warby Ranges State Park, just outside Wangaratta, and the Mount Buffalo Plateau south of Myrtleford, is most easily organized by going through an outdoor tour operator such as *Bogong Jack Adventures* (☎057/27 3382), who also offer small-group bicycle **tours** of the Rutherglen wineries, as well as other less active options in northeast Victoria.

*V/Line* run several train and bus routes through the northeast. The Melbourne to Albury train service goes via Seymour, Euroa, Benalla, Glenrowan, Wangaratta, Chiltern and Wodonga at least twice daily. There's also a train or bus from Melbourne to **Tocumwal** via Seymour, Nagambie and Shepparton two to four times daily. Buses depart from Benalla to Yarrawonga (once or twice daily), as well as three times a week to Shepparton and Bendigo, and to Wangaratta for Rutherglen.

# The Goulburn Valley

The **Goulburn River** rises at Lake Eildon and flows through Seymour, Nagambie and Shepparton to join the Murray just east of Echuca. The rich plains of the Goulburn Valley yield much **fruit**, with an important fruit-canning industry based at Shepparton as well as several **wineries**.

**SEYMOUR** is the first major stop on the Hume Highway out of Melbourne; an important train interchange, it's an uninspiring place for the visitor. The Goulburn Valley Highway begins here, heading north to **NAGAMBIE** on the shores of the man-made Lake Nagambie. The town itself is uninteresting but two prominent **wineries** nearby add some welcome flavour. **Chateau Tahblik** (Mon–Sat 9am–5pm, Sun noon–5pm; ☎057/94 2555), 6km southwest, is the oldest continually operating winery and vineyard in Victoria: it opened in 1860 and survived the phylloxera blight that devastated the Australian wine industry in the 1890s. The Shiraz and Marsanne are still made from the old vines that have seen more than 130 harvests. The whitewashed buildings have been well preserved and there are extensive grounds to explore. In complete contrast, **Mitchelton Winery** (Mon–Fri 9am–5pm, Sat & Sun 10am–5pm; guided tours Sat & Sun, 1hr, $4; ☎057/94 2710), 10km southwest of Nagambie along the Goulburn Valley Highway, is ultramodern: its distinctive sixty-metre observation tower features on the Mitchelton label. Again there are large grounds, this time on the river with a pool and barbecues, which draw the crowds on summer Sundays when a $2 fee is charged. From May to October **river cruises** depart from the winery (daily except Mon & Fri 2pm; $6.50; 1hr), and there's a moderately priced restaurant over-looking the river, open for morning and afternoon teas as well as lunch.

The **tourist office** in Nagambie, at 143 High St (Mon–Fri 9am–5pm, Sat, Sun & public holidays 10am–2pm; ☎057/94 2647), deals with bookings for *V/Line*, since the station is unattended; tickets are also available at the newsagency. As few people stop over in town, **accommodation** is very inexpensive: try *Nagambie Goulburn Highway Motel*, 143 High St (☎057/94 2681; ③–④), or *Nagambie Caravan Park*, next door (☎057/94 2681; on-site vans ②).

The small city of **SHEPPARTON** is the centre for the *SPC* and *Ardmona* canned fruit companies' operations, with peaches, pears, apples and plums tinned and exported worldwide; it's also a good rest stop on the way to Echuca, with pleasant riverside picnic spots. **Tourist information** (daily 9am–5pm; ☎058/31 4400) is dispensed on the Goulburn Valley Highway to the south of town, beside Victoria Park Lake.

# The Hume Highway and Kelly Country

Forty-seven kilometres beyond Seymour, **EUROA** is a far more attractive place – a friendly small town with many fine redbrick buildings. The *Euroa Community Exchange Centre*, 50 Binney St (Tues–Fri 9am–5pm), is a relaxed place, with a small café and **information** on the town. The street itself has a pleasant, old-fashioned feel, with the colourful and airy *Blue Dorset Deli* providing fresh coffee, gourmet sandwiches and other just-baked treats. The **Apex Bicentennial Walk** follows Seven Creeks through the bush, with the Strathbogie Ranges as a scenic backdrop. For **accommodation**, *Euroa Caravan Park*, Kirkland Ave (☎057/95 2160; ②), sits by the creek among huge gum trees, while the *Euroa Motel* (☎057/95 2211; ④) on the Old Hume Highway has inexpensive, if ageing, units. Opposite the motel you can't miss *Morrisons of Euroa*, the famous bush-clothing outfitters started up by a former shearer twenty-five years ago. Although operations have now moved to Melbourne, the original store remains, selling samples and seconds of their range as well as other bush classics.

**BENALLA** is a rather civilized town on the lake of the same name, formed by the Broken River which runs through town. The **Tourist Information Centre**, 14 Mair St (daily 10am–5pm; ☎057/62 1749), is helpful, offering lots of pamphlets and information on the region; it's a pleasant place to stop anyway, overlooking Lake Benalla with a self-service tearoom and craft shop. The **Costume and Pioneer Museum** ($1.50) in the same building features fabulous frocks from the Thirties, but more fittingly has a range of Ned Kelly relics, including the green silk cummerbund he was awarded as a child for saving a friend from drowning, and which he proudly wore when captured. More Kelly memorabilia can be found at the *Kelly Museum*, 101 Bridge St ($1). Across the lake, the *Benalla Art Gallery* (daily 10am–5pm; $2) enjoys a lovely setting. The town is also a major **gliding** and **ballooning** centre; call the *Gliding Club of Victoria* (☎057/62 1058), *The Right Altitude Hang-Gliding School* (☎057/62 6227) or *Balloon Flights Victoria* (☎057/98 5417) for flights in the respective craft. For a bite to **eat**, try *Hides Bakery* at 115 Bridge St, with great vegetarian pies, salads and sandwiches, or the *Toast Office* at 3 Bridge St.

## Glenrowan and Kelly's last stand

**GLENROWAN**, 29km on from Benalla, was the site of the **Kelly Gang's last stand**. You're never allowed to forget it: a gigantic effigy of the man himself, in full iron regalia, greets you as you enter town, and there are lots of other tawdry attractions

## THE NED KELLY STORY

Even before Ned Kelly became widely known, folklore and ballads were popularizing the free-ranging bush outlaws as potent symbols of freedom and resistance to authority. By the time he was eleven, **Ned Kelly**, son of an alcoholic rustler and a mother who sold illicit liquor, was already in constant trouble with the police, who considered the whole family troublemakers; constables in the area were instructed to "endeavour, whenever the Kellys commit any paltry crime, to bring them to justice . . . the object [is] to take their prestige away from them".

Ned became the accomplice of the established bushranger, **Harry Power**, and by his mid-teens had a string of warrants to his name. Ned's brother, Dan, was also wanted by the police and, hearing that he had turned up at his mother's, a policeman set out, drunk and without a warrant, to arrest him. A scuffle ensued and the unsteady constable fell to the floor, hitting his head and allowing Dan to escape. The following day warrants were issued for the arrest of Ned (who was in New South Wales at the time) and Dan Kelly for attempted murder; their mother was sentenced to three years' imprisonment.

Now the **Kelly gang**'s crime spree really began, and following the death of three constables in a shoot-out at Stringybark Creek, the biggest manhunt in Australia's history was under way, with a £1000 reward offered for the gang's apprehension. On December 9th, 1878 they robbed the bank at Euroa, getting away with £2000, before moving on to Jerilderie in NSW, where another bank was robbed and Kelly penned the famous **Jerilderie Letter** describing the "big, ugly, fat-necked, wombat-headed, big-bellied, magpie-legged, narrow-hipped, splay-footed sons of Irish bailiffs or English landlords which is better known as Officers of Justice or Victoria Police" who had forced him onto the wrong side of the law.

After a year on the run, the gang formulated a grand plan: they executed Aaron Sherritt, a police informer, in Sebastopol, so attracting a trainbound posse from nearby Beechworth; this train was to be derailed at Glenrowan with as much bloodshed as possible before the gang moved on to rob the bank at Benalla and barter hostages for the release of Kelly's mother. In the event, having already sabotaged the tracks, the gang commandeered the *Glenrowan Inn* and, in a moment of drunken candour, Kelly detailed his ambush to a schoolteacher who escaped, managing to save the special train. As the armed troopers approached the inn, the gang donned the homemade **iron armour** that has since become their motif. In the ensuing gun fight Kelly's comrades died or killed themselves as the inn was torched, while Ned himself was taken alive, tried by the same judge who had incarcerated his mother, and sentenced to hang.

Public sympathies lay strongly with Ned Kelly, and a crowd of 5000 gathered outside Melbourne Gaol on November 11, 1880 for his execution, believing that the 25-year-old bushranger would "die game". True to form, his last words are said to have been, "Such is life."

along the highway, such as the *Last Stand Show* (daily 9.30am–4.30pm; 40min; $12), a "computerized animated theatre" using dummies shuffling around on cue to dramatize the story of the siege – save your money. The last stand itself took place in Siege Street near the Glenrowan Train Station. Along the rail lines north of town, a small stone monument marks the spot where Kelly forced railworkers to rip up a section of the track, to try to derail the trainful of troopers he had lured to the town; overlooking the town to the west is Mount Glenrowan which the bushrangers used as a lookout.

More interesting and far better value than the *Last Stand Show* is **Kate's Cottage and Ned Kelly Memorial** (daily 9am–5.30pm; $2), a replica of the Kelly home. With its bare earth floor, bark roof and newspaper-lined walls, it speaks volumes of the deprivation that drove the family towards crime. An evocative audiotape narrates Ned's story from childhood and is interspersed with folk songs inspired by his life. The original homestead, 9km west along Kelly Gap Road, is now nothing more than rubble and a brick chimney.

# Wangaratta

The small city of **WANGARATTA**, at the junction of the Ovens and King rivers, 16km from Glenrowan, is a convenient overnight stopover between Sydney and Melbourne, but there are few other reasons to hang around. The highway either side of "Wang" is lined with motels, and the **Wangaratta Tourist Information**, on the corner of Handley Street and Tone Road (daily 10am–4pm; ☎057/21 5711), is on the ball, booking local tours and accommodation and offering stacks of leaflets about the area. *Wangaratta Arts Centre* in Ovens Street (☎057/22 0865) is a fine old redbrick building where the **Exhibitions Gallery** (Wed–Sun noon–5pm; free) has ever-changing shows and occasional Sunday-afternoon music recitals. The **Wangaratta Jazz Festival** on the weekend prior to the Melbourne Cup (usually the last weekend in October) is considered the premier jazz festival in the country; book somewhere to stay well in advance if you're planning to attend.

Among a vast range of **accommodation**, good bets include the *Wangaratta Central Motel*, 11 Ely St, next to Merriwa Park (☎057/21 2188; ④); the *Billabong Motel*, 12 Chisholm St (☎057/21 2253; ④), with good-value singles; and the very modern *Warby Lodge Motor Inn*, 55 Ryley St (☎057/21 8433; ⑤), with a pool. For **food**, the *Owls Roost Rock 'n Roll Café* at 19 Faithfull St is done out in classic Fifties style, *Pure And Natural Food Company* have one of their fast healthfood outlets at 22 Murphy St, but overall the *Hollywood Pizza Restaurant*, on the corner of Ford and Murphy streets, is probably your best bet, open till 2am on weekends.

*V/Line* operate a daily **bus service** from Wangaratta to Bright via Beechworth and a thrice-weekly service to Rutherglen.

# Beechworth

Thirty-five kilometres east of Wangaratta, off the Ovens Highway, **BEECHWORTH** was once the centre of the rich **Ovens gold-mining region**. Sited picturesquely in the foothills of the Victorian Alps, the entire town has been acknowledged as being of historical significance by the National Trust, and the surrounding area has been designated a **historic park** by the *Department of Conservation and Natural Resources*.

Like much of the northeast, Beechworth is rich in **Ned Kelly** history. The **government buildings** (daily 1–4pm; $2) on Ford Street house the grim cell where he was imprisoned as a teenager (same hours; $0.20), as well as the imposing HM Training Prison where he and his mother were incarcerated before the 1880 trial, and the courthouse where the fatal trial was held. Also on Ford Street is the **Burke Memorial Museum** (daily 9am–4.30pm; $2) with relics of the goldrush, and the story of the Chinese miners who flocked here. The museum is dedicated to the explorer Robert O'Hara Burke, one-time Superintendent of Police in Beechworth, who perished with William John Wills on their historic journey from Melbourne to the Gulf of Carpentaria (see box on p.389). On William Street there's the century-old **Murray Brewery Cellars** (daily 10am–4pm; $1), with old bottles and brewery machinery displayed, and on Railway Avenue, in the goods shed of the old train station, is the National Trust **Carriage Museum** (daily 10am–12.30pm & 1.30–4pm; $1.50), with twenty beautifully restored examples, including a *Cobb & Co* stagecoach.

A free **map** of the town is available from the **tourist information** outlet at *The Rock Cavern*, on the corner of Ford and Camp streets (daily 9am–5.30pm; ☎057/28 1374), where you can pay $2 to see some lacklustre mineral displays. The *Department of Conservation and Natural Resources* on Ford Street (☎057/28 1501) has information on the five-kilometre **Gorge Scenic Drive** which you can also walk or, better still, cycle; call in at *Beechworth Bicycle Hire*, 79 Ford Street (☎057/28 2066). The one-way route begins from Sydney Road and returns to Bridge Street, alongside the western edge of the town. It takes in the famous Spring and Reid creeks, which supported 8000 diggers in 1852, as well as natural features such as Flat Rock, Telegraph Rock and Woolshed Falls. The route also passes the granite *Powder Magazine* (daily 10am–12.30pm & 1.30–4pm; $1), formerly a storehouse for blasting powder and now a National Trust musuem.

## Practicalities

Not surprisingly, bed and breakfast **accommodation** abounds in Beechworth. *Burnbrae*, on Gorge Road (☎057/28 1091; ⑤), just over a kilometre south of town, is a nineteenth-century cottage with verandahs and rambling gardens overlooking Beechworth Gorge; *Rose Cottage*, 42 Camp St (☎057/28 1069; ⑤), is also old and quaint. Other historic and good-value places are the *Hibernian Hotel* on the corner of Camp and Lochiel streets (☎057/28 1070; B&B ④), and the historic *Tanswells Commercial Hotel*, 30 Ford St (☎057/28 1480; B&B ④). The latter has been continuously licensed since 1853 and has pleasant **bars** and bistro **food**. The *Beechworth Bakery*, 27 Camp St (daily 6.30am–6pm), has delicious pies, bread, cakes and pastries, and on sunny days you can have breakfast on the balcony. A good, though expensive, place for lunch or dinner is *The Parlour & Pantry* at 69 Ford St (BYO and licensed; lunch daily, dinner Thurs–Mon, daily during the holiday season), where only local produce is used in the imaginative dishes, which are complemented by an extensive wine list. If you really want to splurge, head for the *Bank Restaurant*, 86 Ford St in the *Bank of Australia* building (☎057/28 2233; licensed), where from Thursday to Saturday dinners are formal, candlelit affairs, while from Monday to Wednesday and on Sunday simpler, more rustic fare is offered; sometimes a jazz band plays on Sunday afternoons in the courtyard.

*V/Line* has a **bus service** from Wangaratta to Beechworth (2–3 daily Mon–Fri, 1 daily Sun), and *Beechworth Buslines* (☎057/22 1843) have a Monday–Saturday service from Beechworth to Albury/Wodonga.

## Chiltern

**CHILTERN**, a low-key former gold-mining centre with a well-preserved, mid-nineteenth-century streetscape, lies just off the Hume Highway 40km or so from Wangaratta. The setting – with a bit of recent architectural licence in Conness Street – has been used in several period films. Although no longer licensed, the **Star Hotel** is still set up with the original bar and taps, an authentic background to a rather more ordinary souvenir and craft shop. For $2 you can take a peep out the back at a **monster vine**: planted in 1867 and reputedly Australia's largest, it once produced a single yield of over six kilos of grapes. The 1866 **Athenaeum** (Sat & public holidays 1–4pm; $2) is now a local history museum that includes a collection of paintings by the obsessive local artist Alfred Eustace, who would use any available medium to paint on: paper, cardboard, even large gum leaves. Chiltern's most interesting attraction, however, is **Lake View** (weekends and school holidays 10am–noon & 1–4pm; $2) on the shores of Lake Alexander, near the train station. Built in 1870, it was, for a short while, the home of the writer Ethel Florence Lindesay (1870–1946) who, under the pseudonym of **Henry Handel Richardson**, immortalized the house in the novel *Ultima Thule*, the last book in the trilogy *The Fortunes of Richard Mahoney*. For **refreshment**, there are the *Barambogie Tearooms* and the *Mulberry Tree Restaurant and Tearooms*, both on Conness Street.

## Rutherglen

**RUTHERGLEN**, 18km west of Chiltern and 32km west of Wodonga on the Murray River Highway, is at the heart of Victoria's oldest wine-producing region, renowned for its excellent fortified wines, Rutherglen Muscat and Tokay. Fifteen **wineries** are situated in the area, most of them third- or fourth-generation establishments with cellars full of character. The landscape is a bit of a disappointment, largely consisting of flat paddocks of cattle and sheep where you'd expect undulating vineyards. In fact, wine-making has always been just one of a range of farming activities in an area where diver-sification remains the key to survival. The weather partly accounts for the quality of Rutherglen's fortified wines: the long, mild autumns allow the grapes to stay on the vines for longer, producing higher levels of sugar in the fruit. All the wineries are open for free **tasting** and cellar door sales from 10am to 5pm, Monday to Saturday – Sunday hours differ from place to place.

The *Vintage Cellar*, 84 Main St (☎060/32 9784), opposite the post office, acts as a **tourist information centre**, as well as selling local wines and renting out bicycles. You can pick up the "Winemakers of Rutherglen" **map** and guide to the area here, or from any of the wineries themselves. On the Queen's Birthday weekend in June the town hosts the **Winery Walkabout**, when the new season's releases are presented to the public – one of Australia's biggest wine-tasting festivals. Another festive event is held over the Labour Day weekend in mid-March: **Tastes of Rutherglen** sees some of the best restaurants in the region guest-starring at the wineries, in a celebration of fine food and wine.

### Practicalities

Rutherglen is a popular weekend getaway from Mebourne, so **accommodation** can be hard to find then; during the week you'll have no problem. The focus of the small town is the National Trust-listed *Victoria Hotel*, 90 Main St (☎060/32 9610; ④), where you can both eat and sleep. On the walls of the bar is a framed cover of the June 28, 1880 *Melbourne Herald* chronicling the capture of the Kelly Gang, which makes for fascinat-ing reading while you imbibe. In the cosy back bar, the **bistro** serves reasonably priced food and local wines. The rowdier *Star Hotel* in Main St (☎060/32 9625; dorms ①, rooms ④) is cheaper though, and warmer in winter. The *Walkabout Motel* (☎060/32 9572; ④–⑤) on the Murray Valley Highway is a modern establishment with an outdoor pool.

# The Snowfields and the High Country

The **Victorian Alps**, the southern extension of the Great Dividing Range, bear little resemblance to their European counterparts; they're too gentle, too rounded, and above all too low to offer really great **skiing**. Nonetheless in July and August there is usually plenty of snow, and the resorts are packed out. Most people are here for down-hill skiing, though the **cross-country skiing**, which is rapidly growing in popularity, is excellent: **Lake Mountain**, 21km from Marysville, is the region's premier cross-country destination. **Snowboarding**, a relatively new alpine sport, was first encouraged at Mount Hotham and is now gaining ground everywhere, especially with "cross-over" skateboarders and surfers. **Falls Creek**, **Mount Hotham** and **Mount Buller** are the largest, most commercial skiing areas, particularly the last which is within easy reach of Melbourne; smaller resorts like **Mount Baw Baw** are more suited to beginners. While you wouldn't come to Victoria especially to ski, you might as well give it a go if you're here at the right time of year, though be warned that accommodation prices may take your breath away.

In summer, the alps are ideal **bushwalking** territory, with most of the high moun-tains (and the ski resorts) contained within the vast **Alpine National Park**. The most famous of the walks is the 400-km **Alpine Trail**, which begins in Baw Baw National Park, near Walhalla in Gippsland, and follows the ridges all the way to Mount Kosciusko in the Snowy Mountains of New South Wales. If you are doing any serious bushwalking, you'll need to be properly equipped: even in summer it can be *very* cold up here, especially at night; the weather can change suddenly and unexpectedly; and it's often surprisingly hard to find water. **Mansfield** and **Bright** are good bases for exploration of the alps and, with their fresh mountain air, great places to unwind in their own right. The ski resorts can be ugly and half-closed in summer, but there are often great bargains to be had on rooms.

If you're **driving**, you'll need snow chains in winter (they're compulsory in many parts), and should take local advice before venturing off the main roads.

## Mansfield, Merrijig and Mount Buller

**MANSFIELD** sits at the junction of the Maroondah and Midland highways just a few kilometres north of Lake Eildon, 140km east of Seymour and 63km south of Benalla. As the main approach to Mount Buller, it's a lively place with good pubs, restaurants, even a cinema. *V/Line* has a year-round **bus** service from Melbourne to Mansfield (1–2 daily; 3hr). **Mansfield Tourist Information** (daily 10am–4pm; ☎057/75 1464), at the Old Railway Station, Melbourne Road, has full details of everything that's going on, and of walks in the surrounding country and accommodation. Mostly what's going on is **strenuous activity**: if it's not skiing (there's a **ski centre** at 32 High St; ☎057/75 2095), it's horse-riding, hiking, climbing, abseiling, hang-gliding, rafting or canoeing. Among the many local outfits are *Stoney's Bluff and Beyond Trail Rides*, Mount Buller Road (☎057/75 2212), for great trail rides, and *Mountain Adventure Safaris* (☎03/9817 4683) for rafting, canoeing and many other pursuits.

The *Alzburg Inn Resort*, 39 Malcolm St (☎057/75 1694; ⑤–⑥, more expensive in winter), is a popular **hotel** for skiers, while at the other end of the scale *Mansfield Backpackers*, 112 High St (☎057/75 1800; ①), organizes all sorts of activities, particularly hang-gliding. The area around Mansfield is renowned for **luxurious B&Bs**, the most famous and expensive being *Howqua Dale Gourmet Retreat* (☎057/77 3503; ⑧), south of town near Howqua, which is run by two chefs and feted for its outstanding food; cooking courses are sometimes held here. On a more modest scale are the lovely *Wombat Hills Cottage* (☎057/76 9507; ⑦), each with three bedrooms and a private courtyard, plus tennis courts, or *Alpine Country Cottages* (☎057/75 1694; ⑦), two cottages sleeping four people each, with spa.

### Merrijig

The small town of **MERRIJIG**, a little under halfway to Mount Buller, is largely responsible for the great number of **riding** outfits around here. The breathtaking high-country scenery nearby was used as the location for the film of *The Man from Snowy River*, and visitors have been trying to live out their fantasies ever since. If you want to combine riding with lodge **accommodation**, try *Merrijig Tail Rides*, Mount Buller Road (☎057/77 5590; ⑤, including breakfast).

### Mount Buller

**MOUNT BULLER ALPINE VILLAGE** is 48km from Mansfield, up a smooth, sealed and gradually climbing road. With 7000 beds, 24 modern ski-lifts and 80km of runs, it has the greatest capacity of any Australian ski resort. Extras like an outdoor **ice skating rink** in winter (10am–10pm; $7) make it fun for those who just want to muck about in the snow. For **cross-country skiing**, nearby **Mount Stirling** is a better bet: there's no village here, just a complex containing *Mount Stirling Ski Hire* (☎057/77 6441), the ski school and bistro, 8km along Mount Stirling Road from the Telephone Box Junction.

In **summer**, other activities are on offer: the friendly young couple at the youth hostel operate *Kangulandai Alpine Activities* (☎057/77 6181), with guided **walks** through the bush; and the *Abom Restaurant* on Summit Road diversifies into tennis courts, horse rides and mountain-bike rental. Views from the **summit** of Mount Buller are spectacular, with a panoramic view westward to the lakes, northwards to farmlands and east to Falls Creek and Mount Hotham.

The official start of the ski **season** is the Queen's Birthday long weekend in June, though decent snow may not arrive until August, lasting through to October. Day-trip or week-end **packages** are the best way to go, far cheaper than trying to do it yourself. *YHA Victoria* travel agency in Melbourne, for example (205 King St; ☎03/9670 9611), offers packages based around their youth hostels at Mount Buller and Mount Baw Baw. Day-trips include *Mount Buller Snow Caper Day Tours* (free call ☎1800/03 3023), leaving Spencer Street Station at 4am and arriving at Mount Buller at 9am, returning the same night – around $95 including a lift day-pass and beginner's ski lesson. It's also worth checking out the area around Hardware Street in Melbourne, where *Melbourne Ski Centre*, at no. 17 (☎9670 2855), can advise on skiing conditions at the resorts, and several places offer a variety of deals and equipment rental.

The **Alpine Resorts Commission** (☎03/9895 6900) administers the resorts and charges an entry fee of $15 per car. *Australian Alpine News* is a free publication which is good for facts; for **weather** and snow conditions, call the *Mountainline Snow Report* (☎190/32009); and for accommodation, contact *Victorian Alpine Accommodation and Information Centre* (☎03/9826 8966). As a rough guide to **costs**, a day-pass at Mount Buller is around $55, ski school $30 a day, and full equipment rental $30.

During the season *Mansfield–Mount Buller Bus Lines*, 133 High St, Mansfield (☎057/ 75 2606), operates a **ski transport service** to Mount Buller and *Stirling Experience* (☎057/77 3541) runs an on-demand service from Mansfield and Merrijig to Mount Stirling (pre-booking essential; price depends on number of people). In Bright, the *Bright Ski Centre*, 22 Ireland St, takes bookings for *Bright Alpine Tours* (☎057/55 1093) who run ski buses to Mount Hotham and Falls Creek; there's no transport to Mount Buffalo.

*Mansfield–Mount Buller Bus Lines*, 133 High St, Mansfield, offer **year-round transport** to Mount Buller if booked 12 hours in advance (☎057/75 2606), but services are predominantly geared to skiers (see "Ski Practicalities" box above). The *Central Reservation Service* books **accommodation** all year (free call ☎1800/03 9049). The life of the resort village revolves around the *Abom Restaurant*, Summit Road (open all year), with its café-bar, restaurant and great views, and the huge *Arlberg Hotel*, 53 Summit Rd (☎057/77 6260; ⑤ summer, ⑧ winter), offering entertainment in ski season and every-thing from fast food to an expensive restaurant; the pizzeria is best. For the budget-conscious, the *Mount Buller Youth Hostel*, The Avenue (☎057/77 6181; dorms winter ④, summer ①), is right in the centre of the village, and has self-catering facilities.

# Bright and around

**BRIGHT** is at the centre of the picturesque Ovens Valley, between Mount Buffalo and Mount Beauty about 75km southeast of Wangaratta on the Ovens Highway. It began life as a gold-mining town in the 1850s, and still has a faintly elegant air, with tall European trees lining the main street and filling the parks. A clear stream flows through Centennial Park, opposite the tourist office, and in autumn the glorious displays of the changing leaves make a very un-Australian scene.

The ski fields of Mount Hotham, Mount Buffalo and Falls Creek are less than an hour's drive away and consequently the town is popular as a **ski base** in winter, while in summer **outdoor activities** such as paragliding, hang-gliding, bushwalking, horse-riding and cycling are all on the agenda. *Alpine Paragliding* at the *Sports and Squash Centre* (☎057/55 1753) offers tandem flights for novices, introductory and full courses leading to a licence, while *Mountain Air Joy Flights* (☎057/53 5250) offers a bird's eye-view of the gorgeous mountain scenery from a more sedate small plane. *Freeburgh Trail Rides* on Harrietville Road, Freeburgh (☎057/55 1370), do very good short rides for beginners as well as longer rides and overnight safaris with bushcamping. *High Country Expeditions* (☎057/55 1475) offer half- or full-day 4WD trips and camping tours into the high country.

For a change of pace, visit *Boynton's of Bright*, a relatively new **winery**, 10km northwest of Bright at Porepunkah, which specializes in cool-climate wines (☎057/56 2356; daily 9am–5pm). It's on the northeastern slopes of the valley, with picnic areas on the lawns, and has spectacular views of Mount Buffalo.

## Practicalities

*V/Line* operates a **bus** service to Bright from Wangaratta (daily except Sat; 1hr 15min); to **get around**, you can rent a motorbike from *Bright Rent-a-Mobile*, 76 Gavan St (☎057/55 1238), or a mountain bike from the *Sports and Squash Centre*, 47 Gavan St (☎057/55 1339). *Bright Accommodation and Travel Service*, 1A Delany Ave, doubles as the **Bright Tourist Information Centre** (daily 10am–4pm; ☎057/55 2275 or 55 1509); they give the low-down on happenings in town and book accommodation – useful when things are tight in winter, or for bargains in summer.

One of the best **places to stay** is the *YHA Bright High Mountain Country Hostel* in the *Bright Shire Caravan Park*, Cherry Avenue (☎057/55 1141; dorms ①, cabins ③–④), a modern hostel built on the foundations of an old lodge. East of town, the *Ellenvale Holiday Units*, 68 Delany Ave (☎057/55 1582; ⑤–⑥), are excellent, including a solar-heated pool and spa, tennis court and barbecues. Also good, and with similar facilities, are *Mystic Valley Cottages*, 9 Mystic Lane, 2km southeast on the way to Wandiligong (☎057/55 1045; ⑤–⑥), on a hill overlooking the valley. Slightly further out (8km from Bright), but set in the beautiful Wandiligong Valley itself, **B&B** is available at the "Wandi Pub", aka the *Mountain View Hotel* (☎057/55 1311; B&B ④), which also serves classic Aussie pub food. The best-value **motels** are the centrally located *Elm Lodge*, 2 Wood St (☎057/55 1144; ④), and the charming century-old *Alpine Hotel*, 7 Anderson St (☎057/55 1366; ④). The latter is the focal point of town, with a rowdy bar, good-value bistro meals and excellent breakfast; the back bar has **bands** on Friday nights, and outside there's a sunny beer garden.

Other good **places to eat** are *Alps*, 94 Gavan St, a casual, moderately priced choice for pizza, pasta and Mexican dishes, and the *Cosy Kangaroo*, across the street. *Simone's* at the *Ovens Valley Motor Inn*, corner of Ovens Highway and Ashwood Avenue (☎057/ 55 2027; dinner daily; licensed), ranks as one of the top Italian restaurants in Victoria: no run-of-the-mill pizza or pasta dishes here – we're talking pumpkin, ricotta and walnut ravioli, or veal cutlets brushed with truffle oil, followed perhaps by chestnut tiramisu.

## Mount Hotham and around

Heading southeast out of Bright on the Alpine Tourist Road, it's 18km to **HARRIETVILLE**, tucked just below Mount Hotham and Mount Feathertop. Another former gold town, it's now a pretty little village of wide, tree-lined streets, and a popular skiing base: there are outlets to rent skis and chains, a seasonal shuttle bus up to the resorts, and several places to stay and eat. Beyond Harrietville, it's a steep ascent to **MOUNT HOTHAM** in the Alpine National Park, the "powder snow capital of Australia". This being the state's highest ski area, the snow can be marginally less sticky than elsewhere, but the Rockies it ain't. **Dinner Plain**, a resort 8km from the summit and about 1500m above sea level, has much more of a cosy, alpine village feel – complete with architect-designed timber houses that are meant to resemble cattlemen's mountain huts – than the somewhat unsightly Hotham "village". There are cross-country trails from Hotham to Dinner Plain. Hotham is also considered the home of Victorian **snowboarding**, with special facilities, rental and lessons available. In the ski season, free tractor-driven carts ferry you around the village, all day till late. It's a rather drab place in summer, but the *General Hotel* does stay open with its bar, bistro, bottleshop and fantastic mountain views. For full details and latest prices of the mainly lodge-style **accommodation**, ring the *Mount Hotham Alpine Resort Booking Centre* (free call ☎1800/65 7547).

### Falls Creek

Thirty kilometres east of Bright, in the Upper Kiewa Valley, the town of Mount Beauty lies at the base of the state's highest peak, **Mount Bogong** (1986m). **FALLS CREEK** is 32km further, on the edge of the Bogong High Plains. This is probably Victoria's **best skiing**, with an extensive snow-making system to supplement any shortage of the real stuff, a wide variety of downhill pistes, and good cross-country trails. A snowboarders' park has also been established in the Vertigo Valley near Scott's Chair. For **accommodation** bookings and information, ring the *Mount Beauty Accommodation Service* (free call ☎1800/6362 39).

### Mount Buffalo National Park

Six kilometres northwest of Bright, back along the Ovens Highway, you can turn off into **Mount Buffalo National Park** ($5 entrance fee per car, $9 when ski lifts are operating), which encompasses a huge plateau around Mount Buffalo. **Skiing** here is for beginner to intermediate skiers only – there's a tiny resort around the *Tatra Inn* (☎057/55 1988; ⑨, including breakfast and evening meal) – but it's a gorgeous place to learn, among surreal-looking snow-covered gum trees. Relatively inexpensive packages, including accommodation, ski lessons and other fees, can be arranged through *Mount Buffalo Reservations* (free call ☎1800/03 7038).

The park looks at its best in **summer** though, when there are wildflowers and waterfalls, and it's a great place for walking, watersports and active enjoyment of all sorts. Among the main attractions is **Mount Buffalo Chalet** (☎057/55 1500; ⑨, including all meals), built by the Victorian government in 1910, and about forty minutes' drive on a sealed road from the Ovens Highway turn-off. It's very Australian in appearance, with its bottle-green tin roof, but European in feel, surrounded by flowers and magnificent views. There's croquet on the lawn, a sauna, billiards, games room and tennis court, plus horse-riding (summer only), and canoes and mountain bikes for rent. The *Chalet Café* (daily 9.30am–4.30pm) is a no-frills, no-views cafeteria; if you want to eat properly, book ahead for the main dining room. On the way to the chalet, you pass **Lake Catani**, where there's the only **camping** in the park (June–Oct; ☎057/55 1466, booking essential), as well as swimming, canoeing, kayaking and fishing for trout – the chalet rents out equipment. **Bent's Lookout**, opposite the chalet, has tremendous views over the Ovens Valley, with small stone cabins doing duty as winter picnic areas. There's a **hang-gliding ramp** near here: if you're experienced and want to leap into the void, enquire at *Eagle School of Hang-Gliding* (☎057/55 1724). Beyond the chalet a sealed, not too steep road continues to Mount Buffalo itself (1721m).

## Mount Baw Baw

The ski village at **MOUNT BAW BAW**, near the edge of the Baw Baw National Park, is well south of all the others, and strictly speaking in Gippsland. It's a quiet little resort, consisting mainly of private lodges and the Mount Baw Baw **youth hostel** (☎051/65 1129; dorms in summer ①, in winter ④ including meals). Skiing is limited, but it's relatively cheap, with a lift day-pass costing about $35. The place is deserted in summer and there's little point in coming up at this time, although the views of Gippsland from the summit are magnificent. The other drawback is that the resort can be hard to get to: there's no public transport to the mountain and the closest town is Noojee, 48km away. The roads are narrow, steep, winding and unsealed, with lots of logging trucks, so take care if you're driving.

## travel details

*V/Line* monopolizes transport within Victoria, with a comprehensive combination of **train** and **bus** services, Melbourne and Ballarat being the two train interchanges. Below are the main *V/Line* Victorian and interstate services and private interstate services; local buses are detailed in the text.

### Trains

**Melbourne** to: Adelaide (1 daily; 12hr); Alice Springs (2 weekly; 37hr); Ballarat (5–9 daily; 2hr); Bendigo (3–5 daily; 2hr); Geelong (15–25 daily; 1hr 15min); Perth (2 weekly; 50hr); Sydney via Albury (1 daily; 13hr); Warrnambool (2–5 daily; 3hr).

### Buses

**Melbourne** to: Adelaide (4 daily; 10hr); Brisbane and the Gold Coast (3 daily; 25hr); Perth via Adelaide (daily; 46hr); Sydney (4 daily; 13hr); Sydney via Canberra (3 daily; 14hr); Sydney via Bega (1 daily; 17hr).

### Ferries to Tasmania

**Melbourne** to: Devonport, Tasmania (3 weekly; 14hr).

### Flights

*Qantas & Ansett* fly from **Melbourne** to: Adelaide (5–8 daily; 40min); Alice Springs (2 daily; 4hr); Ayers Rock Resort (1 daily except Fri; 5hr); Brisbane (6–8 daily; 2hr); Cairns (4 daily; 4hr 30min); Canberra (6 daily Mon–Fri, 2 on Sun; 55min); Coolangatta (7 daily Mon–Fri, 10 daily Sat & Sun; 3hr); Darwin (2 daily; 7hr 30min); Hobart (4 daily; 1hr); Launceston (6 daily; 1hr); Mackay (2–3 daily; 4hr 15min); Perth (5 daily Mon–Fri, 2 on Sun; 4hr); Rockhampton (4 daily Mon–Fri, 2 daily Sat & Sun; 3hr 30min); Sydney (20 daily Mon–Fri, 3 on Sun; 1hr 10min); Townsville (3 daily; 4hr 30min).

*Kendell Airlines* fly from **Melbourne** to: Albury (4 daily Mon–Fri, 2 daily Sat & Sun; 45min); Burnie (9 daily; 1hr); Cooma (1 daily; 1hr 50min); Devonport (12 daily; 1hr 10min); King Island (3 daily; 45min); Merimbula (1 daily; 1hr 10min); Mildura (3 daily Mon–Fri, 1 daily Sat & Sun; 1hr 20min); Mount Gambier (3 daily Mon–Fri, 1 daily Sat & Sun; 1hr); Portland (3 daily Mon–Fri, 1 daily Sat & Sun; 50min); Wagga Wagga (3 daily Mon–Fri, 2 daily Sat & Sun; 1hr 20min).

# CHAPTER TEN

# TASMANIA

There's an otherworldly quality to **Tasmania**; romantics can see a gothic landscape of rain clouds and brooding mountains, revelling in the island's isolation and heavily wooded wilderness. The gothic notion extends to the ruins, evident everywhere, of a colonial past with a rich lode of a rather vicious British history, a prison island whose name – Van Diemen's Land – was so redolent with horror that when convict transportation ended in 1852 it was immediately changed. Another view, quite different, presents a tamed landscape roughly the size of Ireland, its distances comprehensible to a European traveller, with resonant echoes of England: cream teas, old-fashioned bed and breakfasts, and friendly, homespun people.

In winter, when the grass is green, the gentle and cultivated **midlands**, with their rolling hills, dry stone walls and old stone villages, can be reminiscent of England's West Country, though in summer the light is too harsh and the grass too yellow to bear comparison. Town names, too, invariably invoke the British Isles – Perth, Swansea, Brighton and Somerset among them. It's a "mainlander's" joke that Tasmania is twenty years behind the rest of Australia, and it *is* very old fashioned. This can at times be charming, but on other occasions is just frustrating and parochial.

Tasmania is the closest point in Australia to the Antarctic circle, and the **west coast** is wild, wet and savage, bearing the full brunt of the Roaring Forties. Inland, the **southwest** has wild rivers, impassable temperate rainforests, buttongrass plains and glacially carved mountains and tarns that have been linked to create the vast **World Heritage Area**. Crossed only by the Lyell Highway, this stretches from the South West National Park to the Franklin Lower Gordon Wild Rivers National Park and across to the Cradle Mountain Lake St Clair National Park, providing some of the world's best wilderness walking and rafting, and the stage for some dramatic conflicts between conservationists and the logging and mining communties. It's still one of the **cleanest places** on earth, though, despite attempts at industrialisation, and a wilderness walk breathing in fresh air and drinking freely from tannin-stained streams is a genuinely bucolic experience.

A north-south axis divides the settled areas, with the two major cities, **Hobart**, the capital, in the south, and **Launceston** in the north. The **northwest coast**, facing the mainland across the Bass Strait, is the most densely populated region, the site of

---

### ACCOMMODATION PRICES

All the accommodation listed in this book has been categorized into one of eight price bands, as set out below. The rates quoted represent the cheapest available double or twin room in high season – except for category ①, which are per-person rates for a dorm bed, and the prices given for units, cabins and vans, which are the daily charge for the whole unit.

| | | | |
|---|---|---|---|
| ① Under $16 | ② $16–26 | ③ $ 27–36 | ④ $ 37–54 |
| ⑤ $55–74 | ⑥ $75–94 | ⑦ $95–124 | ⑧ $ 125 upwards |

For more accommodation details, see pp.31–34.

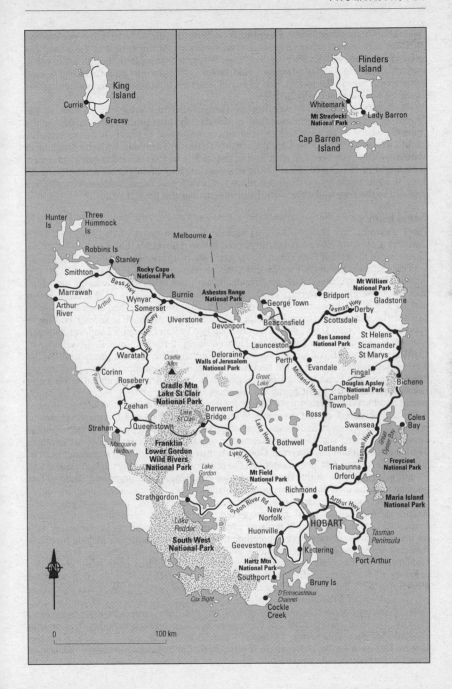

Tasmania's two other cities, **Devonport** (where the Bass Strait ferry docks) and **Burnie**, and several other large, conservative towns. At the centre of Tasmania, the **central plateau**, with its thousands of lakes, is sparsely populated, though full of week-ender fishing shacks. The sheltered **east coast** is the place to go for sun and coastal pleasures, a mostly flat terrain with plenty of deserted beaches, safe for swimming, set against a backdrop of bush-clad hills.

Don't expect boiling hot **weather** in Tasmania. It rarely tops 25°C, even at the height of summer, and the weather is notoriously changeable, particularly in the uplands, where it can sleet and snow at any time of year; February is the most stable month. However, the UV rays are particularly strong in Tasmania, with the ozone layer thinning every year over this area, and in the middle of a summer day can burn unprotected skin in 15 minutes. Wear plenty of sunscreen and a hat. Winter is a bitterly cold time to visit unless you choose the more temperate east coast; wilderness walks are best left to the very well experienced and equipped at this time of year.

## Some history

**Abel Tasman**, the Dutch navigator, sighted the west coast of the island in 1642. Landing a party on its east coast, he named it **Van Diemen's Land** in honour of the Governor of the Dutch East Indies. Early maps show it connected to the mainland, and several eighteenth-century French and British navigators, including William Bligh and James Cook, who claimed it for the British, did not claim otherwise. It was not until 1798 that Matthew Flinders circumnavigated the island, his discovery of the **Bass Strait** cutting a week off the journey to Sydney. In 1803, after the French had been seen nosing around the island's southern waters, it was decided to establish a second **colony** in Australia. Lieutenant David Bowen was despatched to Van Diemen's Land, settling with a group of convicts on the banks of the Derwent River at Risdon Cove. In the same year, Lieutenant-Colonel David Collins set out from England with another group to settle the Port Phillip district of what would become Victoria; after a few months they gave up and crossed the Bass Strait to join Bowen's group. Hobart Town was founded in 1804 and the first **penal settlement** opened at Macquarie Harbour in 1821, followed by Maria Island and Port Arthur; they were mainly for those who had committed further offences while still prisoners on the mainland. With harsh conditions and a repressive, violent regime, Van Diemen's Land became part of British folklore as a place of terror, a prison-island hell. Collins was Lieutenant-Governor of Van Diemen's Land until his death in 1810, but it is Lieutenant-Governor **George Arthur** (1824–1836) who stands out most in the island's history. His ideas influenced the prison settlement at Port Arthur and he was in charge at the time of the **Black Line** (see box below), the organized white militia used against the indigenous Aboriginal population.

Tasmania was not part of the postwar industrialization that transformed the mainland. A small, isolated and neglected state, it even missed out on postwar immigration and consequently remains predominantly Anglo-Saxon in character, with an insular – often conservative – population. Its **natural resources** include forests – covering forty percent of the island – and water, and the mountainous terrain and fast-flowing rivers meant that hydroelectricity schemes began early here, under the auspices of the huge Hydro Electricity Commission (HEC). The flooding of **Lake Pedder** in 1972 led to the formation of the *Wilderness Society*, a protest organization whose successful **Franklin Blockade** in 1982 managed to save one of the last wild rivers. Controversy over these issues divides the state into "Greens" and a pro-logging, pro-dam working class scared for their jobs. In 1989, enough ordinary Tasmanians showed that they didn't want Tasmania's natural assets destroyed by voting for the **Green Independents**, giving them a short-lived but possibly repeatable balance of power in parliament.

## THE ABORIGINAL PEOPLES OF TASMANIA

The attempted genocide of the Aboriginal peoples of Tasmania is one of the most tragic episodes of modern history. Ironically, if not for the American and British sealers and whalers who had operated from the shores of Van Diemen's Land since 1793, abducting Aboriginal women and taking them to the Furneaux islands in the Bass Strait as their slaves and mistresses, the Tasmanian Aborigines would have disappeared without trace. Until recently, school books taught that the last Aboriginal Tasmanian was **Truganini**, who died at Oyster Cove in 1876. However, a strong Aboriginal movement has grown up in Tasmania in the last twenty years, with over 6000 descendants proclaiming their heritage and pushing for land rights.

The **Aboriginal people of Tasmania** appear to have been racially distinct from those of the mainland, although their beliefs and rituals were similar. Isolation seems to have led to separate cultural development: they couldn't make fire but kept alight smouldering fire sticks; their weapons were simpler – no boomerangs; and although seafood was a main source of food, eating scaly fish was taboo. In appearance, the men were startling, wearing their hair in long ringlets smeared with red ochre, while women wore theirs closely shaved. To keep out the cold, they coated their bodies with animal fat and charcoal.

At the time of the establishment of the first **white settlement** there were reckoned to be about 5000 Aboriginal people in Tasmania, with a fierce attachment to their land and a determination to defend it, by force if necessary. Confrontation was inevitable as the settlers attempted to enclose and clear land, and by the 1820s the white population was in a frenzy of fear – even though, for ever settler who died, twenty Aborigines met a similar fate. In 1828 Governor Arthur declared martial law, expelling all Aboriginal people from the settled districts and, in practice, giving settlers a licence to shoot on sight. The British Government, alarmed by these events, planned to round up the remaining Aborigines and confine them to Bruny Island. In 1830, a mass militia of 3000 settlers formed an armed human barrier, the **Black Line**, which was to sweep across the island, clearing Aborigines before them, in preparation for "resettlement".

The line failed, and in the end only 135 Aboriginals were found alive to be moved to a makeshift settlement on exposed and barren **Flinders Island** in 1834. Within four years most of these people also died, of despair, disease, or as a result of the harsh conditions. In 1837, the 47 survivors were transferred to their final settlement at Oyster Cove where, no longer a threat, they were often dressed up and paraded on official engagements. The skeleton of the last survivor, "Queen" Truganini, was on show in the Museum of Tasmania until 1976, when her remains were finally cremated and scattered in the D'Entrecasteaux Channel as she had wished.

Recent campaigns have been aimed at stopping logging in particularly sensitive areas, and ending **woodchipping** (pulping trees for paper) for export to Japan; currently ninety percent of the wood taken from Tasmania's forests ends up this way. It's claimed the Tasmanian state government are subsidizing the industry, selling woodchips off at a third of the going rate to keep Tasmanians in work. Two other high-profile conservation issues seem set to send the Green party into asendancy again: the **Pedder 200 Campaign** to return submerged Lake Pedder to its natural state, which is whipping up media interest nationally (see p.818), and the proposed "tourist road" between Heemskirk and Zeehan through the wild **Tarkine area** on the northwest coast. In January 1995, an incredibly vast and ancient Huon Pine was found in the area, as big as a city block and thought to date from 8000 BC. Conservationists are sceptical that **"the road to nowhere"**, as they've dubbed it, is being used as a cover to open up the area, currently state forest, for logging – thereby destroying its ability to be put forward for World Heritage listing.

# Tasmanian practicalities

Make sure you give yorself enough **time** to see Tasmania; although it is small in Australian terms, the main reason to come here is the great outdoors. If you only want to see its cities you could just spend a few days here, but really you need a couple of weeks or longer to get a flavour of the countryside. **Tasmanian Travel Centres** in the major cities offer **information** and can also book all transport, tours and accommodation; their free information paper, *Travelways*, is extremely useful, with detailed and comprehensive information on accommodation, attractions, bus timetables, car rental, adventure tours and national parks.

## Getting there

The traditional way to get to Tasmania is across the Bass Strait on the *TT Line Spirit of Tasmania* **ferry** from Port Melbourne to Devonport (free call ☎1800/03 0344; in Port Melbourne ☎03/9644 5233; in Devonport ☎13 2010; departs Port Melbourne Mon, Wed & Fri at 6pm, arriving at 8.30am; leaves Devonport Sat, Tues & Thurs at 6pm). If a rough, fourteen-hour overnight trip doesn't worry you too much, this is still the way to go. Everyone gets a bed on the boat – there's a hostel section as well as private cabins from basic to deluxe – and there are restaurants, bars and entertainment. You'll need to book in advance in summer, especially if you want to take a vehicle over: prices start at around $85 for a low-season hostel bed ($110 in high season), with standard cabins from about $140 per person low season rising to $160 in high season, and luxury suite cabins range seasonally from $200 to $275 per person. Whatever standard of accommodation you choose, you'll pay $125–175 to take a car across, and $20 for a cycle.

Several airlines **fly** from the mainland to Hobart, Launceston, Wynyard (Burnie Airport), Devonport, Queenstown, Smithton and Strahan, as well as to King and Flinders islands. To give you an idea of costs, the cheapest fare from Sydney to Hobart return is $309, but *Ansett* in particular have been offering special peak-season $199 returns. *Airlines of Tasmania* (☎003/91 8755) fly from Sale and Traralgon in Victoria's Gippsland to Hobart ($224 one-way), King Island ($199 one-way) and Flinders Island ($105 one-way), and within Tasmania to all local airports including the Bass Strait islands; ask about the standby backpacker fares from Victoria to Launceston for around $70 one-way, $140 return. *Kendell Airlines* (☎03/9670 2677 or free call 1800/338 894) offers substantial discounts to overseas passport holders on their routes from Melbourne to King Island, Devonport and Burnie Airport; *Aus-Air* (☎03/9580 6166 or free call 1800/33 1256) flies from Moorabbin, just outside Melbourne, to Burnie, Devonport and Flinders Island for $142 one-way, or to Launceston ($168 one-way) and King Island ($110 one-way). *Hazelton Air Services* (☎02/235 1411/02/9235 1411 from July 1996) fly from Sale in Victoria's Gippsland to Launceston ($370 return). The cheapest flights are standbys from Phillip Island with *Phillip Island Air Service* (☎059/56 7316) to Burnie Airport or Devonport for $189 return.

The only **international flights** are from Christchurch in New Zealand to Hobart, with *Qantas* ($576–613 return), and with *Air New Zealand* for roughly the same price.

## Accommodation

On the whole, **accommodation** is cheaper than on the mainland, with few **motels** outside the main towns, but high-quality **hotel (pub)** accommodation, usually serving breakfast, and plentiful British-style **B&Bs**. **YHA hostels** tend to be basic and old-fashioned, with mainly dorm beds, but are gradually being modernized – the plus is prices start from as low as $9 and you'll find them off the beaten track; in the major tourists areas, **backpackers hostels** have sprung up, with plenty of twin and double rooms, and prices starting from about $12. **Campers** will find lots of free sites, often with minimal facilities of a pit toilet and tap water.

## Getting around

Passenger train services no longer exist in Tasmania. Instead, three local **bus companies** reach most destinations between them: *Tasmanian Redline Coaches* (☎002/31 3233, free call 1800/03 0033), *Hobart Coaches* (☎002/34 4077, free call 1800/03 0620), and *Tasmanian Wilderness Transport* (☎003/34 4442). You cannot use a mainland bus pass on any of these, and services are limited, especially on the east and west coasts, and in winter and spring buses can be downright inconvenient. Regular scheduled services are offered by the two large operators, *Redline* and *Hobart Coaches,* with several smaller local operators on the east coast, like *Bicheno Coach Service* (Coles Bay–Bicheno), *Peakes Coaches* (St Marys–Swansea) and *Sun Coast* (Derby–St Helens), helping to fill in the gaps. *Tasmanian Wilderness Transport* specializes in bushwalkers' transport, getting you to some of the more remote places all over the state in their minibuses. Prices are quite high, considering the short distances – for example, Hobart to Launceston will cost you around $16, to Devonport just under $30. Buying a local **bus pass** is one way of trimming costs: *Redline* offers a *Tassie Pass* (7-day $111, 15-day $139, 30-day $177), though this won't get you to more out-of-the-way places; *Hobart* and *Wilderness* offer a joint *Wilderness & Highway Pass* (7-day $99, 14-day $140, 30-day $179), which does get you to all the major bushwalking areas as well as the main cities and towns.

You may find that **renting a car** is more of a viable option, particularly if you can get a group together, with reasonable weekly rates available from local operators (see the city "Listings" sections for suggestions). **Driving** is fine, except that there's so little traffic in places that locals automatically drive slowly and in the middle of the road. Few cars on the road also make **cycling** an attractive option, especially in summer, and on the flatter midlands and east coast routes – otherwise there are plenty of gruelling hills to keep you in shape; several operators in Hobart, Launceston and Devonport, again detailed in the text, rent bikes set up for touring.

## National parks and bushwalking

Finally, all **national parks** in Tasmania charge daily **entry fees**, often on an honour system, at $2.50 per person or $8 per vehicle: if you plan to go bush for long periods, then the bi-monthly (car $25, person $10) or annual passes (car $40 all parks, $15 one park) night be better value. Tasmania's wilderness has always attracted thousands of **bushwalkers**, and many of the tracks have become churned-up and are gradually being boardwalked; keeping to set paths to avoid further erosion is just one of the national park's minimum-impact guidelines, available in a leaflet from *Department of Parks, Wildlife & Heritage*, 134 Macquarie Street, Hobart (write to GPO Box 44A, Hobart 7001, or call ☎002/33 6197). It must be emphasized that walking in the wilderness can be dangerous if you're ill-prepared: you should never walk alone and should always register your walk details with a park ranger, or inform others of your intentions. The free "Bushwalking Trip Planner for Tasmania's World Heritage Area" sets out the clothing and equipment you'll need in an area where the weather can change rapidly; even a warm summer's day can bring hail, sleet or snow, and walkers who disregarded warnings have died of hypothermia. As a minimum, you need wet-weather gear, walking boots, a decent tent and a fuel cooking stove, maps and a compass (which you should know how to use). If you don't have all the necessary, you can rent gear from outdoor shops in Devonport, Hobart and Launceston – again, see "Listings" sections of these city accounts.

# HOBART AND THE EAST

The **Derwent River** flows from Lake St Clair at the heart of Tasmania, past **Mount Field National Park**, Tasmania's oldest and most popular national park, through well-preserved **New Norfolk** towards Tasmania's capital at **Hobart**. Here, the river estuary forms a fine harbour before flowing into the waters of **Storm Bay** and out to the Tasman Sea. Hobart is Australia's most southerly city, battered by winds roaring in from the Antarctic in winter, while the coastline around it looks as if someone has poured acid onto the map. Hook-shaped **South Arm**, at the entrance to Storm Bay, is echoed on a larger scale by the **Tasman Peninsula**, with its infamous convict settlement at **Port Arthur**. To the south, the two tenuously connected halves of **Bruny Island** protect the waters of the **D'Entrecasteaux Channel**. On the mainland here the **Huon Valley** is fertile and cultivated, but as you head further south the coastline becomes increasingly wild: there are caves and thermal springs, the **Hartz Mountain National Park** inland, and rafting possibilities on the **Picton River**. The last settlement is **Cockle Creek**, from where the **South Coast Track** sets off towards the **South West National Park**, the great mass of wilderness which forms Tasmania's southwest corner.

North of Hobart, the **east coast** of Tasmania is the tamest and most temperate part of the island, providing a popular cycling route past numerous sandy and deserted beaches and some lovely national parks. The **Tasman Highway** follows this coastline from Hobart to Launceston, heading inland through the northeast at **St Helens**, the east coast's largest town. The northeast corner is virtually unpopulated, with **Mount William National Park** a haven for the Forrester kangaroo. Heading inland are old tin-mining towns, and some superb rainforest remnants and mountain scenery at **Weldborough Pass**, beyond which you pass through rich agricultural and forestry country to Launceston.

# Hobart

**HOBART** is tiny but beautifully sited, and any approach is exhilarating: speeding across the expressway on the Tasman Bridge over the wide expanse of the **Derwent River**, or swooping down the Southern Outlet with hills and harbour, docks and houses spread out below. The green- and red-tin-roofed timber houses climb up the lower slopes of **Mount Wellington**, snow-covered for two or three months of the year, and look down on the expansive harbour. It's a water-focussed city, the centre only a few minutes' walk from the waterfront, where fresh seafood can be bought straight from fishing boats in **Sullivans Cove**; here yachties hang out at old dockside pubs or head for an early morning café selling scallop pies – Hobart's speciality. Yacht races and regattas mark the year, while weekends see the water alive with boats; you can choose any conceivable craft to take a **harbour cruise**, a perfect activity in the dry and rarely too hot summers. In winter, though, the wind roars in from the Antarctic and temperatures drop to 5°C and below.

Australia's second oldest city after Sydney, Hobart has managed to escape the clutches of the developers with its early architectural heritage remarkably well preserved – more so than any other Antipodean city. In 1803, **Lieutenant John Bowen** led a party of 24 convicts from Sydney to settle on the eastern shores of the Derwent River at Risdon Cove. A year later, **Lieutenant-Colonel David Collins** arrived with his three-hundred or so convicts, a contingent of marines to guard over them, and thirty or more free settlers including women and children; and founded Hobart Town on Sullivans Cove, 10km below the original settlement and on the opposite shore. Collins was to serve as Lieutenant-Governor of the colony for ten years. For the first two of those years, food was scarce, and settlers relied on hunting local game, creating an early gun culture that was later to have terrible effects on the Aboriginal population. The fine deep-water port helped make the town prosperous: whaling, ship-building, and the transport of crops and wool earning money for a rich merchant class. Between the late 1820s to the 1840s was a golden age for building, with government architect **John Lee Archer** and convict **James Blackburn** responsible for some of Hobart's finest buildings. There's a wealth of colonial Georgian **architecture**, with more than ninety buildings classified by the National Trust, sixty of them in Macquarie and Davey Streets. **Battery Point**, a village of workers' cottages and grand houses set in narrow, irregular streets, has hardly changed in the last 150 years.

## Arrival, information and transport

Hobart **airport** is 26km northeast of the city at Cambridge (flight information ☎13 1515). *Redline* runs an airport **shuttle bus** ($6) to the city, dropping off at central accommodation, as well as at the *Adelphi Court YHA* in New Town; a **taxi** will cost around $20. If you're coming in by **bus**, you'll arrive in Collins Street, either at *Redline*'s new **Transit Centre**, centrally located at 199 Collins Street (Mon–Fri 6.15am–6.15pm, Sat 8am–4pm, Sun 9am–6.15pm; ☎34 4577), where there are phones, newsagents, toilets, showers and left-luggage facilities, or at the more basic *Hobart Coaches* depot, at 4 Liverpool Street (☎34 4077). If you're **driving** in, take a good look at your map to plan your route, as most of the streets are one-way. There's plenty of cheap streetside parking available.

### Information

The first stop for general information is the **Tasmanian Travel & Information Centre**, 80 Elizabeth Street (Mon–Fri 8.45am–5pm, Sat 8.45am–noon, Sun 8.45am–11am; ☎30 8233), which also doubles as a comprehensive travel and booking agent. The **National Trust Shop**, Galleria 33, Salamanca Place (Mon–Fri 9.30am–5pm, Sat 9.30am–1pm), has inexpensive architectural guides detailing the bewildering range of listed buildings. On a more alternative note, the **Tasmanian Environment Centre**, 102 Bathurst Street (Mon–Fri 9am–5pm; ☎34 5566), is a relaxed resource space with lots of books and information on Tasmania and noticeboards of environmental events, rooms to let and things for sale. Organizations like *Bicycle Tasmania* and the *Hobart Walking Club* (visitors can join their walks) use it as their base, and the centre operates its own walks and talks programme throughout the year. For **bushwalking information** and maps head for the *Land Information Bureau* at 134 Macquarie Street (Mon–Fri 9am–4.45pm; ☎33 8011); upstairs, the *Department of Parks, Wildlife & Heritage* (☎30 2620) has park information sheets and can refer you to a parks officer for advice.

### City transport

Hobart's public transport system, the **Hobart Metro**, is useful for getting to less central accommodation and some more distant points of interest. You can pre-purchase

---

**TELEPHONE NUMBERS**

The **telephone code** for Hobart is ☎002, but this will change to ☎03 in November 1996. Also in November 1996, all **Hobart numbers** will have the prefix 62 added; so, for example, what was ☎002/xx xxxx will become ☎03/62xx xxxx.

*(For more on changes to phone numbers Australia-wide, see p.40.)*

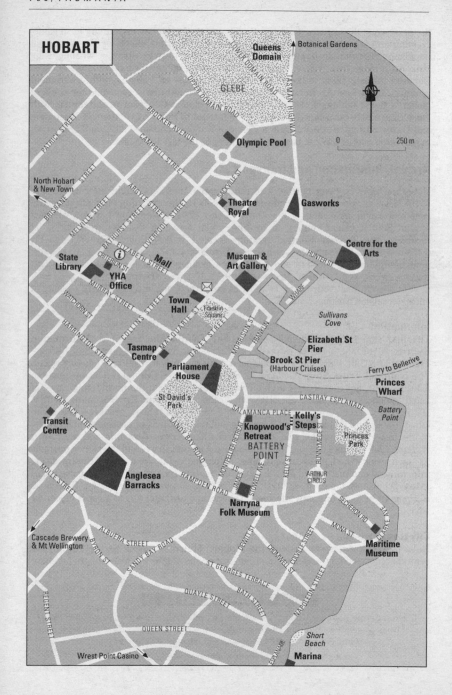

# HOBART

Queens Domain

▲ Botanical Gardens

GLEBE

North Hobart & New Town

Olympic Pool

Theatre Royal

Gasworks

Centre for the Arts

State Library

YHA Office

Mall

Museum & Art Gallery

Town Hall

Franklin Square

Sullivans Cove

Elizabeth St Pier

Brook St Pier
(Harbour Cruises)

Ferry to Bellerive ▶

Tasmap Centre

Parliament House

St David's Park

Princes Wharf

Battery Point

Transit Centre

Kelly's Steps

Knopwood's Retreat

BATTERY POINT

Princes Park

Anglesea Barracks

ARTHUR CIRCUS

Cascade Brewery & Mt Wellington

Narryna Folk Museum

Maritime Museum

Short Beach

Wrest Point Casino ▲

Marina

*Metro Tens* (a pack of ten discounted tickets) and get timetables (30c each) from the *Metroshop*, 18 Elizabeth Street, opposite the GPO; this is the bus interchange, from where you can catch any bus (timetable hotline ☎13 2201). Single **tickets**, available from the driver, are valid for 90 minutes and cost from $1.10 (for a one- or two-zone journey); off-peak, day-rover passes are $2.80. Buses run until around 11pm from Monday to Thursday, until midnight on Friday and Saturday, and until about 7pm on Sunday. A weekday peak-hour **ferry** service operates to Bellerive, on the eastern shore, from Brooke Street Pier. You can hail a **taxi** on the street, or there are taxi stands around the city, with the major one outside the town hall on Elizabeth Street.

For **cruises**, see the box on p.762; and for city **tours**, see "Listings", p.768.

# Accommodation

There's plenty of **accommodation** in Hobart, but during the peak season in January, when the yachties hit town, prices can shoot up and inexpensive places are hard to find. City and dockside **pubs** are the best option for clean, affordable private accommodation, and there's always a bed at one of Hobart's several **hostels**. Battery Point is full of (sometimes pricey) **B&Bs**, and there are also several good **self-catering** holiday apartments in this area, with costs comparable to a motel. Most **motels** are situated in Sandy Bay, about 3km from the centre, or along the Brooker Highway, but private hotels and guesthouses tend to offer better value.

## Hotels and motels

**Argyle Motor Lodge**, corner of Lewis and Argyle streets, North Hobart (☎34 2488). Situated in a quiet area twenty minutes' walk from the city centre. Some self-catering units also available. ⑤–⑥.

**The Black Prince Hotel**, 145 Elizabeth St (☎34 3501). Central, with budget motel-style rooms. ⑤, including breakfast.

**Customs House Hotel**, corner of Murray and Morrison streets, opposite Watermen's Dock (☎34 6645). Sedate, old-style waterfront hotel with great views, popular with yachties. ④–⑤, including breakfast.

**Fountainside Motor Inn**, corner of Liverpool St and Brooker Ave (☎34 2911). Multi-storey motel set on a noisy intersection, but featuring room service and the 24-hour *Jellies Coffee Shop*. ⑤.

**Hobart Macquarie Motor Inn**, 167 Macquarie St (☎34 4422 or free call 1800/80 2090). This very central high-rise is friendlier than it looks, with pool, sauna, spa and under-15s staying for free. ⑥.

**Midcity Inn**, 96 Bathurst St (☎34 6333). A central location and facilities that include a bistro, restaurant and two bars. Pleasantly decorated rooms, all with views. ⑦.

**Theatre Royal Hotel**, 31 Campbell St (☎34 6925). Basic hotel with plain but presentable rooms in a great position; some singles available. Excellent bar and bistro downstairs, too. ④, including light breakfast.

**Wrest Point Hotel–Casino**, 410 Sandy Bay Rd, Sandy Bay (☎25 0112). Upmarket four-star hotel with riverside rooms. Heated indoor pool, sauna, and 24-hr room service. ⑧.

## Private hotels and guesthouses

**Astor Private Hotel**, 157 Macquarie St (☎34 6611). This old-fashioned, family-run guesthouse is very central. ④, including breakfast.

**Colville Cottage**, 32 Mona St, Battery Point (☎23 6968). Peaceful Victorian weatherboard B&B, with en suite rooms and a pleasant garden. ⑥.

**The Lodge on Elizabeth**, 249 Elizabeth St (☎31 3830). Good-value non-smoking B&B in a Georgian-style mansion. ⑤.

**Red Chapel House**, 27 Red Chapel Ave, Sandy Bay (☎25 2273). Friendly, family-run non-smoking guesthouse. ⑥.

**Wellington Lodge**, 7 Scott St, Glebe (☎31 0614). Weatherboard B&B classified by the National Trust; close to Queens Domain park and city centre. Non-smoking. ⑥.

## Hostels and budget rooms

**Adelphi Court YHA**, 17 Stoke St, New Town (☎28 4829). Modern motel-like hostel and guest-house in a quiet suburban street; the main drawback is it's a long way from the centre – about a 25-minute walk from town and ten minutes to the nearest shops or pub. Cramped kitchen facilities, but catered breakfasts are popular and relieve the strain. Bus #25–42, #100 or #105–128 from Elizabeth St, then walk, or #15 or #16 from Argyle St. Rooms ③–④, dorms ①.

**Bellerive YHA**, 52 King St, Bellerive (☎44 2552). Set in a quiet seaside residential area, this is a cosy hostel in an 1869 sandstone building with lots of books, games and a fireplace. Best reached with your own transport; otherwise take a ferry from Sullivans Cove (weekdays only during peak hours), or the longer way round by bus : #83–87 from Elizabeth Street. ①.

**Central City Backpackers**, 2nd Floor, Imperial Mansions, 138 Collins St (☎24 2404 or free call 1800/81 1507). Hobart's best hostel – a former hotel with large improved kitchen and dining area – exudes a shabby, friendly charm. More budget accommodation than a backpackers, with families welcome. ①.

**Duke of Wellington**, 192 Macquarie St (☎23 5206). A non-smoking backpackers hostel above a pub; friendly management offer free entry to see bands and discounts on pub meals. Rooms ③, dorms ①.

**Jane Franklin Hall**, 6 Elboden St, South Hobart (☎23 2000). Student rooms available in the holidays; many single rooms. Excellent facilities include kitchen, free laundry, TV lounge, gym and pool. ④.

**Ocean Child Backpackers**, *Ocean Child Inn*, 86 Argyle St (☎34 6730). Comfortable hostel with clean rooms for two, three or four. The *Inn* has a quiet bar and offers good budget meals. ①.

**Tasmanian Backpackers**, *New Sydney Hotel*, 87 Bathurst St (☎344 4516). Clean and central, but with limited facilities – and sometimes noisy bands playing downstairs. It's always lively though, and you can get $5 budget meals in the pub. ①.

**Transit Centre Backpackers**, 199 Collins St, above the *Transit Centre* (☎34 7874). Modern, well-equipped and spacious, but lacking in atmosphere. ①.

**Telegraph Hotel**, 19 Morrison St (☎34 6254). Great location on Sullivans Cove, with backpacker bunks including linen. ①.

## Caravan parks and self-catering apartments

**Battery Point Holiday Flats**, 15 Secheron Rd, Battery Point (☎23 6592). Well-equipped units on a quiet street overlooking the water. ⑤.

**Crelin Lodge**, 1 Crelin St (☎43 6555). In the centre of Battery Point, with up to five-bed units. ⑤.

**Graham Court Holiday Villas**, 15 Pirie St, New Town (☎78 1333). One- to three-bedroom apartments. ⑤–⑥.

**Sandy Bay Caravan Park**, 1 Peel St, Sandy Bay (☎25 1264). The closest caravan park to the city centre (3km), in salubrious Sandy Bay. Full range of facilities, including playground and camp kitchen. On-site vans ③, cabins ④.

**Treasure Island Caravan Park**, 671 Main Rd, Berriedale (☎49 2379). Large park, 12km from town, with kitchen and pool. On-site vans ③, cabins ④.

# The City

Hobart is small and easy to find your way around, with the streets arranged in a grid pattern running southeast towards **Sullivans Cove**. You can walk anywhere in the mostly flat city centre, although some pretty steep hills surround it. The civic centre is **Franklin Square**, bounded by **Macquarie** and **Davey** streets, which between them have a concentration of listed buildings. The main shopping area is **Elizabeth Street Mall**, roughly in the centre of the **CBD** (the City Business District, as the city centre is known); Elizabeth Street slopes down from **North Hobart**, with its collection of restaurants, to the Elizabeth Street Pier on **Franklin Wharf**. Here, at the harbour, fishing boats and yachts are moored, while cruises leave from Brooke Street Pier. **Salamanca Place**, with its row of Georgian warehouses, is on the waterfront on the southern side of the cove; a steep climb up Kelly's Steps leads to **Battery Point** to the south. Following the river around from Battery Point, you reach salubrious **Sandy Bay**, with its casino and Royal Yacht Club. To the north of the centre are the parklands of the **Queens Domain**, with the **Royal Botanical Gardens** along the waterfront; from the Domain, the **Tasman Bridge** crosses the Derwent River to the residential eastern shore.

There are relatively few sights in Hobart beyond the streets themselves, but these are enough to fill hours of wandering, with a few museums and parks to give you something to aim for. While walking through the city, it's worth glancing up occasionally to the street signs; the streets are often named after an important local figure, and carry a biography and portrait. Around the docks area and Battery Point, there are also interpretive boards pointing out historical and architectural features.

## Franklin Square to the Tasmanian Museum and Art Gallery

Starting from **Franklin Square**, and the imposing sandstone **Town Hall**, you can head past many of the finest old buildings on Davey Street on the way to St Davids Park, or make for the Tasmanian Museum on Macquarie Street. **St Davids Park** was originally the graveyard of St Davids Cathedral (at the corner of Murray and Macquarie streets), but was converted to a park early this century. It's a quiet spot where some of the more important monuments have been preserved, including a huge memorial to the first Governor, David Collins. Other gravestones have been removed and set into two undulating sandstone walls at the bottom of the park.

The **Tasmanian Museum and Art Gallery**, 40 Macquarie Street (daily 10am–5pm; free), has a collection of photographs of the Tasmanian Tiger, thought to have been extinct since 1936. It was a peculiar, flesh-eating, dog-like marsupial with a rigid tail, stripes, and backwards opening pouch that was hunted out of existence – although unconfirmed reports of them still occur from time to time. There's also an Aboriginal room which features a full account of their near-extermination, and an excellent convict section: if you can't get to Port Arthur, Richmond Gaol or any of the other convict ruins, this display will convince you of the brutality of the regime. On a lighter note, the "Megafauna" room is good fun, with life-sized reconstructions of the giant marsupials that once roamed Australia. In the **art gallery**, the colonial art section has several portraits painted in the 1830s and 1840s of the well-known "final" Aborigines – Manalargenna, Tanleboneyer, Truganini and Wooredy – and superb early Tasmanian landscapes by W C Piguenit.

Another central museum worth a look is the **Allport Library and Museum of Fine Arts** (Mon–Fri 9.30am–5pm; free) on the ground floor of the **State Library**, at 91 Murray Street (library hours Mon–Tues 9.30am–6pm, Wed–Fri 9.30am–8pm), a private collection of eighteenth- and nineteenth-century furnishings, ceramics, silver and glass, paintings, prints and rare books relating to Australia and the Pacific.

Campbell Street, heading in the other direction from Franklin Square, is another area that's worth exploring. The **Theatre Royal**, at the corner of Sackville Street (☎bookings ☎34 6266), is Australia's oldest surviving theatre, built in 1837. It has an intimate interior with beautiful Regency decor, and the best way to see it is to attend a performance. Otherwise, try your luck and ask if you can have a look around. Further up, at the corner of Brisbane Street, the **Penitentiary Chapel and Criminal Courts** (hourly tours, daily 10am–4pm; $5; ☎31 0911) comprise a complex of early buildings with two courtrooms, underground tunnels and cells.

## The Waterfront

The focus of Sullivans Cove is busy **Franklin Wharf**, the first commercial centre of Hobart, where merchants erected large warehouses as the colony grew wealthier. In

## HARBOUR CRUISES

**Cruise Company**, Brooke Street Pier (☎002/34 9294). Fast catamarans allow you to see a lot: best cruise on the Derwent is their *Iron Pot Cruise* to the river mouth and across the top of Bruny Island (Sat 2pm; 2hr; $20). The very chocolatey *Cadbury's Cruise* heads upriver to the chocolate factory at Claremont; it's essential to book in advance as chocoholics treat this as a pilgrimage (Mon–Thurs 10am, Fri 9.15am; 4hr; $30). A one-hour cruise goes just beyond the Tasman Bridge (3 daily; $10).

**Lady Nelson**, Elizabeth Street Wharf (☎002/34 8522; summer only). This replica of the brig in which Matthew Flinders made his exploratory journeys is a sail-training vessel, but also offers after-

noon pleasure trips (Mon, Sat & Sun 1–4pm; $20). When the ship leaves Hobart at the end of summer for longer journeys on the eastern seaboard, you can join as a paying passenger (about $130 per day).

**Lady Theresa**, Watermans Dock (☎002/25 0922). Small, wood-fired steam boat that does a slow chug round the harbour (daily 10.30am, noon, 1.30pm, 2.30pm & 4pm; $12; 1hr).

**Rhona-H**, Watermans Dock (mobile ☎018/13 3396). A sailing experience on a fifty-year-old gaff-rig ketch made of Huon Pine, with a lively skipper; you're encouraged to participate. Harbour cruise (3hr; $25), Storm Bay (8hr; $50), and longer overnight cruises (around $130 a day), too.

the 1830s, Hobart was one of the world's great whaling centres, and to cater for growing volumes of shipping, the New Wharf – **Princes Wharf** – was built, featuring a row of handsome sandstone warehouses on Salamanca Place. As the new wharf became the focus of port activity, the old wharf developed into an industrial centre of flour mills and factories. The *Henry Jones Jam Factory*, between Victoria and Macquarie Dock on Hunter Street, is now the **Centre for the Arts**, the University of Tasmania's art school – an indication of the direction the area is now taking. You walk through the jam factory facade into a courtyard with several large pieces of sculpture and the high-tech new face of the art school. Inside, the **Sir James Plimsoll Gallery** (daily noon–5pm; free; ☎38 4300 for details of exhibitions) has several shows a year featuring the work of contemporary Australian artists.

The old docks along Franklin Wharf are also thriving: **Constitution Dock** has boats selling fresh and cooked seafood, and, right by it, the *Mures Fish Centre* is two levels of fish-eating heaven (see "Eating and drinking", p.765). At **Victoria Dock**, lobster boats are moored and there's also, strangely, a very ancient Sydney Harbour Ferry with a coffee shop, and sometimes exhibitions, on board. From Brooke Street Pier and Watermens Dock, any number of **cruises** depart (see box above ).

On **Salamanca Place** the old warehouses, shipping offices and storerooms are now full of art and craft galleries, speciality shops and cafés, interspersed with characterful waterfront pubs. Several of the narrow lanes and arcades are worth exploring. Heading down Montague Lane, you stumble upon a pleasant courtyard with picnic tables, buildings on three sides and, on the fourth, an unexpected cliff. On Saturdays, the area bursts into life for the jam-packed open-air **Salamanca Market** (8am–2pm), an event with an alternative feel, wonderful food, quality Tasmanian crafts, secondhand clothes, books and bric-a-brac. It's also – unusually for Tasmania – a rare chance to people-watch with all the prime tables outside *Knopwoods Retreat* and the *Retro Café* snapped up early. Another, much more commercial market happens on Sundays (9am–3pm) at the recently renovated old **Gasworks**, just beyond Sullivans Cove at no. 2 Macquarie Street. The restored stone building is wonderful, but the slick shops, restaurants and enterprises within – many are part of chains – are trying too hard to attract tourists for it to feel like much of an experience.

## Battery Point

Kelly's Steps lead from Salamanca Place to **Battery Point**, with its enduring village atmosphere. With the building of the new wharf, a working-class community grew up behind Salamanca Place, transforming what had been farmland into a residential area; it takes its name from the battery of guns that were once sited on present-day **Princes Park**, protecting the harbour below. The newly developing area was first home to small cottages for waterfront workmen and, later, fine merchants' houses began to be built here: the old pubs, with names like the *Shipwrights Arms* and *Whalers Return,* leave no doubt about the nature of the population. The narrow streets, closely packed cottages, the green of **Arthurs Circus** and the "corner store" nature of the shops enhances the nineteenth-century village feel. There's a particular concentration of early buildings on De Witt and Cromwell streets. **St George's Church** on Cromwell Street was the joint work of John Lee Archer (responsible for the nave) and James Blackburn (the tower), the early colony's two most famous architects. If you want chapter and verse on the history and architecture, join the good value **Battery Point Walking Tour** (Sat 9.30am–12.30pm departs from the Wishing Well, Franklin Square; $5 includes morning tea; ☎237 570 for bookings), led by admirably knowledgeable National Trust volunteers.

**Hampden Road** has more fine nineteenth-century mansions, including one at no. 103 known as **Narryna** (Mon–Fri 10am–5pm, Sat & Sun 2–5pm; $5), furnished with period antiques. It houses the **Van Diemen's Land Folk Museum**, with a display of entertaining miscellany, while out the back there's a blacksmiths, a vehicle shed housing old traps, and a coach house full of brewery equipment. Tucked away at the end of Secheron Road, a dead end where leafy gardens surround elegant two-storey homes, the **Maritime Museum** (Mon–Fri & Sun 1–4.30pm, Sat 10am–4.30pm; $2) occupies Secheron House, built in 1831 for the Surveyor General of the colony, George Frankland; the verandah, where you can sit and look at the harbour, was added in the 1840s.

# Around the harbour

The estuary of the **Derwent River** is the deepest (and second busiest) natural port in Australia. Heading upstream, the scenery is increasingly industrial, with a huge zinc-processing plant and, at Claremont in a more unspoilt setting, the **Cadburys Factory**. Tours of the factory include as much chocolate as you can eat and are understandably popular (Mon–Fri 9am, 9.30am & 10.30am, 11.15am & 1pm; 2hr; $10; tickets must be booked and paid for in advance at Tasmanian Travel Centre); take bus #24–29 to Springfield then #39 to Claremont, and then walk. Failing that you can take a cruise all the way – see box above.

The eastern side of the river is more residential, and looking across you'll see swelling, bush-clad hills with a modest line of homes below. The **Tasman Bridge** connects the eastern shore with the city: it was out of action for over two years from January 1975 when the 20,000-tonne tanker *Lake Illawarra*, heading for the zinc smelting works, crashed into it and wiped out two pylons. The ship is still down there with its two-and-a-half million dollars worth of zinc concentrate, as are the bodies of seven crew members and five people in four cars.

Over on the eastern shore, the **Kangaroo Bluff Battery** at Bellerive – along with its counterparts at Sandy Bay (Alexandra Battery) and Battery Point (Mona Street Battery) – was erected in response to a Russian scare in the late nineteenth century, but it never saw active service. **Bellerive**, which you can reach by ferry from Brooke Street Pier, has a long sandy beach at the Esplanade; some swim from it but the water can be polluted. There's cleaner water and surf beaches across the promontory from Belerive at **Oppossum Bay** (bus #95 or #99 from the city centre); while **Seven Mile**

**Beach** on Frederick Henry Bay offers calmer swimming (bus #92 or #93). Ten kilometres east of Bellerive, **Risdon Cove** was the site of the first European settlement of Van Diemen's Land; interpretive boards set out the early history. To get there, take bus #24–29 to Springfield, then the #68 (or #67 at weekends).

## The Queens Domain

The **Queens Domain**, just north of the city centre, looks attractively green on the map but is considerably less inviting in reality: a sparse, bush-covered hill traversed by walking and jogging tracks but caught between two very busy highways. At the base of the hill on the Derwent, where the trees suddenly become lush and green, the **Royal Botanical Gardens** (daily 8am–4.45pm) are formal gardens of flower displays and orderly trees. Pick up a leaflet detailing features of the garden at any entrance or from the **Information Centre** at the main entrance (Mon–Fri 9am–noon & 1–4.30pm), on the western side of the park. It's easy enough to walk to the Domain, following Davey Street or Liverpool Street from the city centre, but the gardens are some way in: half an hour's walk in all. Any bus to Eastern Shore, including the #64 and #98, will drop you at Government House, in the centre of the Domain near the gardens, but there's no transport back.

## Sandy Bay

**Sandy Bay** is a leafy, well-heeled suburb east of Battery Point, home to an upmarket shopping centre, the Royal Yacht Club, and the **Wrest Point Casino** on Sandy Bay Road. An ugly 1970s' high-rise, the casino strives hard to be glamourous, but groups of slacks-clad pensioners and tour groups wearing name tags set the tone in the small gambling area. The **Sandy Bay Regatta**, in January, sees yachts moored all around Sandy Bay's marinas, and sailing on the water, with a fun fair along the waterfront. Weekends, too, see lots of yachts on the water.

# Inland to Mount Wellington

Heading inland, the route south and west towards Mount Wellington takes you through South Hobart, on to Cascade Road and past the pretty **Cascade Gardens**. Here, the magnificent seven-storey **Cascade Brewery** is the oldest in Australia, still using traditional methods and taking advantage of the pure spring water which cascades – of course – down Mount Wellington. There's a traditional north/south divide between beer drinkers in Tasmania: in Launceston and the north you drink *Boags*, in Hobart you drink *Cascade*, although in fact the two breweries merged in 1922. **Tours** run on weekdays only (9am & 1pm; 2hr; bookings essential: ☎24 1144; $7), and at a fairly gruelling pace, but you do get a couple of (light) beers at the workers' bar, and a bottle of *Premium Lager* at the end in the brewer's original residence. The small museum of brewing paraphernalia includes a couple of childhood pictures of Hollywood star Errol Flynn, who was brought up in the Cascades area.

In any image of Hobart, **Mount Wellington** (1270m) is always looming in the background. Access is up a winding road of dozens of hairpin bends, lined with houses as far as Fern Tree, where the tavern offers teas and meals at the bottom of the walking track up the mountain (2hr up, 1hr down): thick bush thins out as you ascend, and by the top it's bare and rocky. Pure, drinkable water cascades from rocks as you climb, and halfway up, just after the first lookout, there's a grassy picnic area with barbecues, toilets and information boards. At the top, the stone **Pinnacle Observatory Shelter** (daily 8am–6pm) has details of the magnificent panorama spread before you. From here, it surprising how empty the land around Hobart really is, seemingly nothing but uninhabited bush and plains of grass. Despite opposition, there are controversial plans afoot to build a cable car to the top, but for the moment it's fairly unspoilt. In January, the *Metro* runs special **buses** right up Mount Wellington from Macquarie Street, opposite the post office (Mon–Fri 2 daily; $4); at other times take Fern Tree bus #48 from Macquarie Street, get off at stop 27 and walk back to Fern Glade, where the walks begin. *Wandering Albatross*, 288 Davey Street (☎24 1577) offers a $30 tour that includes a visit to the summit, breakfast and then a 20-kilometre downhill mountain-bike ride.

The views are also terrific from the Old Signal Station on **Mount Nelson** (340m) above Sandy Bay. The Station was established in 1811 to announce the appearance of ships in Storm Bay and the D'Entrecasteaux Channel; the signalman's residence now contains tea rooms, open daily until 6pm and later on weekends for dinner, with the sparkling city lights below. Mount Nelson buses #57 and #58 from Macquarie Street run to the top.

## Eating and drinking

Hobart's steadfastly Anglo-Saxon fare can't compare with the mainland cities' ethnically eclectic range of cuisines, but its food is becoming more cosmopolitan, and at least there's excellent **seafood**. Fishing boats moor at Victoria Dock, right in the city, and sell their catch direct to the public. There are several "Asian" restaurants around, but few are authentic and those that are are often pricey.

**Ali Akbar**, 321 Elizabeth St, North Hobart (☎31 1770). Good quality BYO Lebanese restaurant.

**The Astor Grill**, 157 Macquarie St (☎34 3809). Reminiscent of an old-fashioned English grill room, specializing in steaks, Tasmanian crayfish and fresh local oysters. Expensive. Lunch Mon–Fri, dinner nightly.

**Cha Chas**, 91 Elizabeth St (☎34 6018). Easy-going, licensed brasserie with plenty of choice. Lunch Mon–Fri, dinner Tues–Sat.

**Concetta's** 207 Harrington St (☎34 4624). Home-style Italian cooking in a boisterous, family-run establishment. Dinner Mon–Sat.

**Da Angelo Ristorante**, 47 Hampden Rd, Battery Point (☎23 7011). Great village spot for a more upmarket Italian with good service and generous portions, tasty too.

**Etna Pizzeria**, 345 Elizabeth St (☎34 4105). Late-night pizzeria with delicious *gelati*. Open until 1am Fri & Sat.

**The Europa Restaurant**, 121 Collins St (☎31 1000). Café/bar serving European meals, accompanied by live music. Closed Sun.

**Flippers Seafood**, Constitution Dock. Takeaway seafood from a boat moored in the dock; best fish and chips in town. Daily 10am–8pm

**Garden of Earthly Delights**, 247 Sandy Bay Rd, Sandy Bay (☎23 4471). Good home-cooking, vegetarian and meat. Daily 11am to late.

**Groovy Grub Wholefood Café**, 39 Barrack St. For serious vegetarians and vegans; Mon–Thur 10am–9pm, Fri to 9.30pm.

**Hara Wholefood Café**, 181 Liverpool St. Relaxing, slightly offbeat feel, less puritanical than the name suggests. Closed Sun.

**Harbour Lights Café**, 29 Morrison St. Mildly curried scallop pies are a favourite yachties' breakfast; a couple of stools to sit at, but mainly takeaways. Mon–Fri 6.30am–3.30pm.

**Kaos Cafe**, 237 Elizabeth St. Trendy gay-friendly coffee spot. Mon–Sat until midnight, Sun to10pm.

**La Cuisine**, 85 Bathurst St & Trafalgar Centre, 110 Collins St. Café-patisserie with great cappuccino and excellent pastries. Mon–Fri 9am–6pm.

**Mummy's Coffee Shop**, 38 Waterloo Crescent, Battery Point. Tiny café that fits in with the village atmosphere of Battery Point.

**Mures Fish Centre**, Victoria Dock. Two-level food centre set among yachts and fishing boats, with three restaurants, a fishmonger, bakery and café. *Mures Upper Deck* is an upmarket restaurant with lovely views; *Mures Lower Deck* has bistro food and prices; *Orizuru* serves authentic sushi. Closed Sun.

**Orient Express**, 147a Little Collins St. Good, cheapish servings of Malaysian, Indian and Thai food in this small, arty café. Closed Sat & Sun.

**Red Lion Tavern**, 19 Macquarie St. African food; lunch and dinner Tues–Sat.

**Renown Milkbar**, 337 Elizabeth St, North Hobart. A Hobart institution with windows full of imported chocs. Good for coffee or a snack. Daily 8am–11.30pm.

**Retro Café**, 31 Salamanca Place. Serving the best espresso in town, and the place where Hobart's arty types observe each other. Mon–Sat 8am–6pm (until midnight on Fri), Sun 10am–5pm.

**Shipwright's Arms Hotel**, corner of Colville and Trumpeter streets, Battery Point. Old pub, popular with the yachtie crowd and dishing up a legendary fresh seafood platter.

# Entertainment and nightlife

There isn't a lot of **nightlife** in Hobart, and if you've come here to have a wild time you're in the wrong place. Car-loads of rowdy young lads drive up and down Liverpool Street, with its smattering of pubs and clubs, on Friday and Saturday night. A large but less obnoxious crowd gathers on Friday nights at Salamanca Place, outside the historic *Knopwood's Retreat*, while the more conservative *Wrest Point Casino* at Sandy Bay is open late every night for gambling, drinking and dancing.

If you want to know **what's on**, Thursday's *Mercury* has a "gig guide", and check Friday and Saturday's entertainment section, too. As far as **live music** goes, Tasmania is too small to attract many bands, so it's mostly local ones playing the pubs: the few big events that do occur attract an extraordinarily varied audience, as everybody goes to everything. For anything more interesting, keep an eye on what's happening at the University of Tasmania. **Dance** places, with one exception, are glitzy, Seventies-style discos.

## Bars, clubs and live music

**Cafe Who**, 251 Liverpool St (☎31 2744). Hip bar that regularly hosts good local bands, including late-night jazz acts. Excellent food – Australian contemporary, with wallaby salad among its offerings.

**The Doghouse**, corner of Goulburn and Barrack streets (☎34 4090). Somewhat sleazy and druggy but a good venue for indie music, with occasional interstate bands.

**Duke of Wellington Hotel**, 192 Macquarie St (☎23 5206). Old hotel, now with music Thurs–Sat 10.30pm–2.30am; a very drunk crowd stream in after midnight. There's a popular bar with pool tables upstairs.

**The Hobart Saloon**, 7 Watchorn St (☎34 5165). Barn-like bar with American West theme. Lively and packed on Fri & Sat nights.

**Knopwood's Retreat**, 39 Salamanca Place (☎23 5808). Pub that's a favoured student hang-out, with a relaxed coffee parlour-cum-bar feel and magazines and newspapers on hand. Open till midnight Fri, closed Sun.

**The Lodge**, 251 Liverpool St (☎31 2744). Hobart's most alternative dance club; DJs play alternative, hardcore dance music; free on Thurs. Open Thurs–Sat 10pm–4am; $5. Slick café/bar downstairs.

**The New Sydney Hotel**, 87 Bathurst St (☎34 4516). Hobart's Irish pub with traditional music Wed 9pm–midnight and on Sat afternoon. Sun evening there's jazz/blues from 4–8.30pm. Good value meals, too.

**Rockerfeller's Café & Bar**, 11 Morrison St (☎34 3490). Cocktails, Sunday night jazz and an American-style menu. Closes at midnight (2am Fri & Sat).

**Round Midnight**, 2nd floor, 39 Salamanca Place (☎23 2491). Intimate but not intimidating late-night venue for R&B and indie bands. Bar opens at 9.30pm and bands start after 11pm. Closed Mon.

**St Ives Hotel**, Sandy Bay Rd, Sandy Bay (☎23 3655). "Boutique" hotel with its own brewery. The excellent bottle shop out the back has a good range of Tasmanian wines.

**Theatre Royal Hotel**, 31 Campbell St (☎34 6925). Despite the trendily upmarket renovations, the public bar is as down to earth as ever. People spill in here from the theatre next door. Recommended bistro too. Open until midnight; closed Sun.

**Stoppy's Waterfront Tavern** (☎23 3799). Salamanca Place. Boozy unpretentious pub that hosts live bands every weekend.

## GAY AND LESBIAN HOBART

Male homosexuality is still a criminal offence in Tasmania, although gays are not actively pursued by the police: there is a Sexual Privacy Bill that gays can use in court in their defence, and national and international pressure may well lead to changes in the law in the future. The 1995 Mardi Gras parade in Sydney saw the Tasmanian float heavily cheered. Every Saturday the **Tasmanian Gay and Lesbian Rights Group** (GPO Box 1733, Hobart, TAS 7001) has a stall at Salamanca Market with a petition to urge the reform of the law; they also sell the group's magazine, *Pink Thylacines*. The **Gay Information Line** (☎34 8179) is a five-minute recorded message that provides pointers for gay visitors and numbers for further information. The only **gay and lesbian club** is tame but enjoyable: *La Cage*, 2B Gladstone Street (Thurs–Sat from 11pm; ☎23 8337); there's also the gay-friendly *Kaos Café*, 237 Elizabeth St (☎31 5699).

## Film and theatre

**AFI State Cinema**, 375 Elizabeth St, North Hobart (☎34 6318). Arthouse and foreign films; cheap tickets Wed.

**Salamanca Arts Centre**, 77 Salamanca Place (☎23 4544). Home base of several performance companies: the *Terrapin Puppet Theatre* puts on touring shows, including a puppet picnic at the end of December in St Davids Park. Puppeteers are welcome to come in and look around. The *Peacock Theatre* produces mainly traditional theatre while the *Zootango Theatre Company*, is the one for contemporary theatre: in January they put on wonderful outdoor plays in the Botanical Gardens. There's also an interesting contemporary art gallery upstairs.

**Theatre Royal**, 29 Campbell St (☎34 6266). This lovely old place is not too expensive or stuffy: comedy nights as well as serious drama.

**Village Cinema Centre**, 181 Collins St (☎34 7288). Seven screens showing mainstream new releases.

## Listings

**Airlines** *Airlines of Tasmania* (☎48 5030); *Ansett*, 61 Elizabeth St Mall(☎38 0800); *Par Avion* (☎48 5390); *Qantas*, 77 Elizabeth St Mall (☎35 4900); *Tasair* (☎48 5088).

**Airport shuttle bus** Information from *Redline* (☎31 3233).

**Banks** Major banks all have branches on Elizabeth Street.

**Bike rental** *Wandering Albatross* (☎24 1577) rents out bikes for touring.

**Bookshops** *Ellison and Hawker Bookshop*, 90 Elizabeth St (☎34 2322). The best bookshop in Hobart, with an excellent travel section upstairs. *Fullers Bookshop*, 140 Collins St (24 2488), is also a goodie.

**Buses** *Tasmanian Redline Coaches*, 199 Collins St (☎31 3233); *Hobart Coaches* and *Wilderness Transport*, 60 Collins St (☎34 4077).

**Campervan rental** *Tasmanian Campervan Hire*, Hobart Airport (☎002/48 9623), from $550 per week.

**Car rental** *Annie's Auto Rent*, 32 Burnett St, North Hobart (☎31 1077); *Avis*, at the airport (☎48 5424); *Marquee Car Rentals*, 19 Tasman St, North Hobart (☎31 3820); *Rent-a-Bug*, 105 Murray St (☎31 0300); *Thrifty*, 39 Campbell St (☎34 1341).

**Disabled travellers** *Aged and Disability Care Information Centre*, 192 Macquarie St (☎24 2322 or free call 1800/806 656), is an excellent source of information for visitors with disabilities; free mobility maps of Hobart. *Maxi Taxis* ☎34 8061 is the best taxi firm to use.

**Hospitals** *Royal Hobart Hospital*, 48 Liverpool St (☎38 8308).

**Newspapers** *Ellison & Hawker Newsagency*, 92 Elizabeth St (☎34 4099), is the island's only foreign newspaper outlet.

**Outdoors and sport** *Jolly Swagman*, 107 Elizabeth St (☎34 3999), is a good outlet for camping gear rental; *Sport and Rec Shop*, Macquarie St, has information and a bookshop on Tasmania's sporting and outdoor opportunities run by the *Department of Tourism, Recreation and Sport* (☎33 8011); *Paddy Pallin*, 76 Elizabeth St (☎31 0777), for quality outdoor equipment to buy and rent, as well as bushwalking information; *Southern Tas Divers*, 212 Elizabeth St (☎34 7243), for diving charters and gear rental; *Sport and Dive*, 109 Elizabeth St (☎34 3798), for fishing charters and diving gear.

**Pharmacies** *Macquarie Pharmacy*, 180 Macquarie St (open until 10pm daily).

**Post office** GPO, at the corner of Elizabeth and Macquarie streets; Mon–Fri 8am–6pm. Have mail addressed to:- Poste Restante, Hobart GPO, TAS 7000.

**Rape** *Sexual Assault Support Service* (☎31 1811).

**Taxis** *City Cabs Co-op* ☎34 3633; *Combined Services* ☎13 2227.

**Tours** *Hobart Coaches*, 60 Collins St (☎34 4077), which runs a *City Sights Tour* through the city, docks, Battery Point, Anglesea Barracks, Mount Wellington and the Botanical Gardens (Tues 9.15am & Thurs 1pm; 3hr; $23); *Hobart Sightseeing*, 199 Collins St (☎31 3511), has a similar tour without the Botanical Gardens (Tues 9.30am, Sat 1.30pm; 3hr; $23). Both companies offer tours to surrounding areas: Port Arthur, Richmond, the Huon Valley, Russel Falls and Bruny Island.

**Travel agents** *Hobart Flight Centre*, 138 Collins St (☎24 0311); *Tasmanian Travel and Information Centre*, corner of Davey and Elizabeth streets (☎30 8233).

**Women** There's a women's information service at the *Office of the Status of Women*, 3rd Floor, Franklin Square Building, Macquarie St (☎34 2166, outside Hobart free call ☎1800/001 377), and the *Hobart Women's Health Centre*, 326 Elizabeth St, North Hobart. Women's expeditions are led by Vicky Bonwick, 126 Strickland Ave, South Hobart (☎24 0253).

**Work** *Willing Workers on Organic Farms* (*WWOOF*; ☎66 0283) arrange voluntary work on organic farms.

**Youth Hostel Association of Tasmania**, Head Office, 28 Criterion St (☎34 9617), Mon–Fri 9am–4.30pm.

# Around Hobart

South of Hobart is picturesque channel, orchard and island country, with forests thrown in for good measure. The D'Entrecasteaux Channel region and the Huon Valley form Tasmania's premier **fruit-growing** district, and once millions of apples were exported from Port Huon to England; since the UK joined the European Community, however, two thirds of the apple orchards have been abandoned. The region is also heavily forested and, around Geeveston, magnificent forests are still logged. From **Geeveston**, Hartz Mountain National Park and the Picton River are easily accessible to the west. Heading back down the southeast coast, caves, thermal springs and an operational railway are available en route to **Cockle Creek**, the southernmost point you can drive to in Australia, with access by foot into the South West National Park. Offshore, across the D'Entrecasteaux Channel, **Bruny Island** – Truganini's birthplace – has deserted beaches and coastal bushwalks. To the north, you can head inland to New Norfolk and on to the **Mount Field National Park**, while to the east lies historic **Richmond**, and, on the Tasman Peninsula, the old penal settlement at **Port Arthur**.

## South: the D'Entrecasteaux Channel and Huon Valley

The **Channel Highway** hugs the coastline from Hobart, a lovely drive around the shores of the **Huon Peninsula**, circling back along the shore of the Huon River to Huonville: heading to Huonville directly, it's only 37km on the Huon Highway. **Rafting** is possible all year on the Huon River, with day trips led by *Rafting Tasmania* (☎002/27 9516) for around $95. The Channel Highway takes you first to **KINGSTON**, a leafy residential suburb with a wide, sandy beach; there are more good beaches, like Blackmans Bay, on the little promontory below Kingston. At **KETTERING**, a thriving fishing port, there's an attractive marina full of boats, and the ferry for Bruny Island. The famous *Woodbridge Hotel* (☎002/67 4604; B&B ⑤) is right on the water, not far from here – with one of the best restaurants in Tasmania (inevitably pricey), and good views from the rooms upstairs.

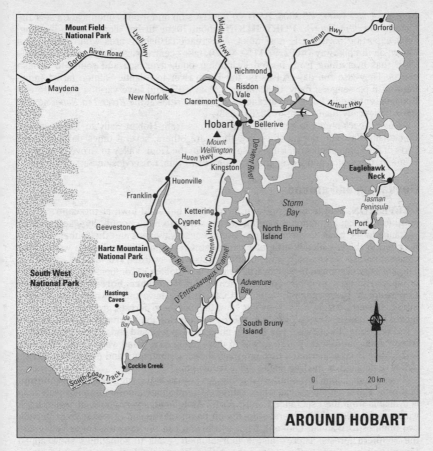

### AROUND HOBART

On the other side of the peninsula, **CYGNET**, at the centre of a major fruit-growing region, is a likely spot to look for **fruit-picking work** in the harvest season of March and April. *Balfes Hill Hostel*, 340 Craddoc Road (☎002/95 1551; ①), is a particularly good place to stay if you hope to do this, as they have all the contacts. It's 4km from Cygnet and you'll need to catch a bus from Huonville (*Cygnet Couriers*; ☎002/95 1371) if you don't have your own transport; you can rent a bike from the hostel.

**HUONVILLE**, on the Huon River, is the region's commercial centre, and – again – its money comes from apples. At **GROVE**, 6km back towards Hobart on the Huon Highway, the **Huon Valley Apple and Heritage Museum** (daily 9am–5pm; $3) celebrates the local produce once shipped en masse to Britain before it joined the European Community, an industry now seriously curtailed; the museum is surprisingly interesting, with hundreds of varieties of apples, assorted apple paraphernalia from what was once a huge export industry, and plenty of things to taste. Back in Huonville, forty-minute **jet boat rides** through the rapids, or gentler pedal boat rental can be arranged through the kiosk on the Esplanade (☎002/64 1838).

Beyond Huonville, the road shadows the west bank of the Huon to **FRANKLIN**, a handsome place right on the river, with several fine old buildings. You can stay in

*Franklin Lodge* (☎002/66 3506; B&B ⑤), or just stop off for an economical meal at the historic *Franklin Tavern*. **PORT HUON**, about 10km further along, was a bustling, apple-exporting port, but is now quiet, a recreational fishing area where *Port Huon Resort*, on the highway (☎002/97 1110; ⑤–⑦), takes centre stage. Its riverfront "Sports Club" has everything from heated swimming pool, gym, spa and sauna to squash courts. They also run day-cruises on the Huon river to Atlantic Salmon farms (minimum of 6 passengers; daily 10.30am & 2.30pm; $15) and have various places to eat. You can rent paddle boats and arrange $30 jet boat rides at the *River Tea Room* next to Apex Park (daily 10am–5pm; ☎002/64 1838).

*Hobart Coaches* operates several **bus** services from Hobart daily to Kingston and Blackmans Bay, and during the week there are others, several times daily, to most parts of the Huon peninsula. Buses also run down the Houn Valley to Grove, Huonville, Franklin, Geeveston and Dover (5 daily Mon–Fri, 1 Sun; no service on Sat).

## Geeveston and around

**GEEVESTON**, 8km from Port Huon, is a sleepy but solid town at the centre of the Southern Forest, a traditional logging centre, with two huge upright logs acting as an entrance to the town. Confrontation between conservationists and the timber industry here led to the so-called "Battle of Farmhouse Creek" in 1986, a dispute won by the conservationists, after which some of the forests were awarded World Heritage listing. The Forestry Commission was awarded millions of dollars in compensation, to be used on special forestry projects, one of which is the **Esperance Forest and Heritage Centre** (daily 10am–4pm; $4; ☎002/97 1836), in the Geeveston Town Hall on Church Street. It starts out lovingly showing how the Southern forests grow, but gradually moves on to the history of logging in the area – covering the Farmhouse Creek dispute – and concludes by showing you how to chop down a tree and end up with woodchips. After visiting the centre, you're meant to drive along Arve Road, where several boardwalks have been constructed through magnificent swamp gum and eucalyptus forests – they're detailed on the free leaflet that's handed out.

Twenty-four kilometres southwest along Arve Road is the rugged **Hartz Mountain National Park**, with its glacial lakes, rainforests and alpine moorlands; a day-walk map is available from the Esperance Centre. From Arve Road, a very stony, unsealed track winds up for 12km, with several stopping-off points, at the end of which you can walk two minutes to Waratah Lookout, from where you can see over the Huon Valley and the Southern forests. There's also a four-kilometre walk to sometimes snowcapped Hartz Peak, for views to the west of the Arthur Range: the walk is on a tricky alpine track, wet and boggy underneath and with the potential for fog and icy winds at any time – recommended for well-prepared walkers only.

The **Picton River** skirts the Hartz Mountains from its source deep in the South West National Park and continues towards the **Tahune Reserve**, at the junction with the Huon River, just north of the Hartz Mountain park. With its bouncy rapids, intermittent gentle sections and magnificent wilderness scenery, it's a popular, short (and affordable) rafting alternative to the Franklin. *Peregrine* (☎002/31 0977) operates a one-day rafting trip from Hobart (Dec–April on demand; $105); while *Wandering Albatross* (☎002/24 1577) has a good $95 one-day trip or a two-day excursion (around $220), rafting up to Tahune Reserve to camp, and spending the next day walking to the top of Hartz Peak.

## Dover and around

**DOVER**, 21km from Geeveston, is a beautiful fishing village on a lovely large bay – **Port Esperance**. There are trees everywhere, and lush hills surround the town with the clear, virtually triangular, outline of **Adamsons Peak**, snowcapped in winter, as a backdrop. Boats moor off a picturesque jetty in the bay, where two tiny tree-covered islets look wonderful silhouetted against the sky at dusk. The hub of Dover is the *Dover Hotel* on the highway (☎002/98 1210; dorms ①, rooms ④, motel units ⑤), with its old-fashioned dining room overlooking the water; at the back of the pub, on a long stretch of grass beside an apple orchard and rolling fields, is an excellent lodge housing the backpacker rooms. *Dover Beachside Caravan Park*, Kent Beach Road (☎002/98 1301; on-site vans ③) is also scenically situated near the jetty, beside a creek. Although you can find fuel and supplies 20km further south at Southport (the last of either) you're better off doing so in Dover, where there's more choice and better value.

Thirty-one kilometres from Dover, the Hastings Caves lie in the foothills of Adamsons Peak, with the **Thermal Springs State Reserve** en route. The springs (daily 9am–6pm, until 7pm in Jan; $2.50) are in a lush setting, and there are several walks in the grounds, one through a fern glade. The pool itself is very disappointing, though – small, shallow and tepid (ranging from 20 to 30°C), and not at all the steaming waters you might imagine. The pebbly base has recently given way to a concrete floor. **Hastings Caves**, a few kilometres further on, are more worthwhile, with all the usual underground wonders: Newdegate Cave, the best, is open daily for tours (11.15am, 1.15pm, 2.15pm, 3.15pm & 4.15pm, with extra tours at peak periods; 45min; $8); it's always cold inside, and wet, so bring something warm to wear.

Other attractions in the immediate area include the **Ida Bay Railway** (4–10 daily; 1hr 20min; closed July & Aug; $9; ☎002/93 3110), a vintage, narrow-gauge bush railway, running since 1914, which travels for 16km along the southern edge of Southport to the beautiful beach at Deep Hole Bay. Services wait for twenty minutes here, or you can take a later service back and perhaps take a walk to the Southport Lagoon Wildlife Sanctuary. The railway has **camping** sites or very basic cabins (②) in the settlement of Ida Bay. Alternatively, the *Lune River Youth Hostel* (☎002/98 3163; ①), a few kilometres away in a rambling weatherboard homestead, has a reputation for being something of an outdoor activities centre, organizing caving and renting out mountain bikes. If you notify the hostel in advance, they can pick you up from Dover for a small charge; **Lune River** isn't a town but rather a collection of houses and a post office, while the river itself is popular with gem fossickers. Between July and January, there are cruises on the river on the vintage 1918 cutter *Olive May* with the *Southwest Passage Cruising Co* (☎002/98 3247; $30 half-day).

To get to the area, you can utilize *Wilderness Transport*'s Hobart to Cockle Creek run which stops at Huonville, Dover, Hastings Cave and Lune River (no service June–August, otherwise one service Fri plus extra Mon & Wed services 1 Dec–20 April).

## Cockle Creek

Beyond Lune River and Ida Bay, the unsurfaced Cockle Creek Road takes you past picturesque sheltered bays and scenic coastal forests, where wildflowers bloom in summer, to **COCKLE CREEK** on lovely, unspoilt **Recherche Bay** (prounounced "research" by locals). There are lots of camping spots along the shore and some people love it so much they live here semi-permanently in shacks and old buses, mainly fishing-obsessed retirees after the abundant crays, cockles and fish in the bay. Pit toilets and water are the only facilities – no showers. The most popular walk around here is to follow the muddy but boardwalked start (or, more usually, the end) of the **South Coast Track** to the beach at South Cape Bay and back (4hr): the entire length of the track is for the very experienced only, but this gives you a small taste (see p.819 for details of the whole walk). *Wilderness Transport* operates a **bus** service to Cockle Creek from Hobart (schedules at end of "Dover and around" account, above).

# Bruny Island

For beautiful lonely beaches and superb bushwalking, you can't beat **Bruny Island**. Almost two distinct islands joined by a narrow isthmus (where you can sometimes see fairy penguins), it's roughly 71km from end to end, with a population of only 400, and few cars. The cost of taking a car across on the ferry deters casual visitors, so the island is never very full. The ferry from Kettering goes to substantially rural North Bruny, although most of the settlements, and the places to stay and eat, are on South Bruny: with its state forests and reserves, the south is also the more scenic half. At the northern end of the isthmus, a small monument to Truganini (the "last" Tasmanian Aborigine, who was born here) caps the tallest sand dune, offering superb views of the southern part of the island. You can see **Fluted Cape State Reserve** to the east of Adventure Bay; here, a steep climb to the top of the Cape (2hr 30min return) offers still better views. **Labillardiere State Reserve** takes up the western "hook" of South Bruny Island; a winding, bumpy road leads to the **Cape Bruny Lighthouse**, a route providing a seven-hour circuit walk of the peninsula.

The **ferry from Kettering** sails nine times daily or more (7.15am–6.30pm, later on Fri; ☎002/33 5363 for exact times; $18 per car return, foot passengers and bikes free) – the *Ferry Road Store* (☎002/67 4474), opposite the jetty, can supply you with Bruny Island **information**, including a free map. If you catch the 9.30am (Mon–Fri) ferry, the *Mail Bus* can take you to settlements on the island (ask at the store for return times); otherwise there's no transport – and no town – when you arrive on the ferry. Renting a car or bicycle in Hobart or planning to walk the island are the only alternatives; *Hobart Coaches* operate services from Hobart to Kettering which connect with a couple of the ferries.

The main settlement on **North Bruny** is **BARNES BAY**, where the *Lyndenne Restaurant* (book in advance on ☎002/60 6264) offers expensive, freshly caught seafood and steak in a friendly atmosphere, and also serves morning and afternoon tea. *Camel Treks Tasmania* (☎002/60 6335; daily 10am & 2.30pm, 4-hr trip $48; 7-hr $85; overnight $100) is also based here: it might seem an odd spot for camel trekking, but it's fun, the routes are interesting, and the food is delicious. At **Dennes Point**, in the far north, *House Sofia* (☎002/60 6277; ⑥) is a wonderful guesthouse with a family atmosphere and views of the bay from the verandah; the price is for full board with home cooking.

On **South Bruny**, **ADVENTURE BAY** is the main centre on the east coast, with safe swimming and a general store (open daily to 8pm), and the **Bligh Museum of Pacific Discovery** (daily except Wed 10am–3pm; $2). Bruny Island has always been linked with early explorers, for whom it provided a safe refuge after the arduous jorney across the Southern Ocean, and this place has maps, documents, paintings and artefacts relating to landings there. The *Penguin Tea Rooms* have freshly baked food, while the best place to stay is the helpful *Lumeah Hostel*, on Quiet Corner off Main Road (☎002/93 1265; rooms ④, dorms ①). The *Captain Cook Caravan Park*, Adventure Bay Road (☎002/93 1128; on-site vans ③), is next to the beach; the *Adventure Bay Holiday Home*, Quiet Corner (☎002/43 6169; minimum 2 nights ⑤), in a shady spot by a small stream, has self-contained units. Over on the Channel coast, **ALLONNAH** is Bruny's main settlement. As well as a general store, there's *Bruny Hotel*, Bruny Main Road (☎002/93 1148; ④), with good-value counter meals. *Alonnahup Holiday Flats*, Ritchie St (☎002/93 1339; ⑤), are fully equipped, with TV and breakfast ingredients supplied, and boats are available for rent. Five kilometres south at **LUNAWANNA**, the *Whalers Inn* on Light House Road (☎002/93 1271; ⑤) has individual villas on a tree-covered hillside. *St Clairs Restaurant* (☎002/93 1300) serves satisfying meals and features entertainment at weekends.

# New Norfolk and Mount Field National Park

Heading inland from Hobart towards the Mount Field National Park, the A10 hugs the Derwent for 50km to the well-preserved colonial buildings of **NEW NORFOLK**, a sizeable town which has been at the centre of the hop-growing industry for 150 years; there are still oast houses in the surrounding hop fields. The broad stretch of the Derwent up here is clean, beautiful and swimmable, disturbed only by thrill seekers on jet boats. The *Bush Inn* on 49 Montagu Street (☎002/61 2011; B&B ④), the main road, claims to be Australia's oldest continuously licensed **hotel**: virtually untouched, with stained wooden floorboards, huge stone fireplaces, and a small ballroom with chandeliers and piano, it's a lovely place to stay. As is the *Old Colony Inn* on the same street at no. 21 (☎002/61 2731; ⑤), a simple, whitewashed, two-storey building housing a collection of antiques and artefacts (daily 9am–5pm; $1.50) – you get in free if you eat here. *Hobart Coaches* has several buses daily (Mon–Fri only) to New Norfolk; one service daily continues to Maydena via the entrance to Mount Field National Park. *Redline* runs to New Norfolk from Hobart once daily in summer (10 Sept–31 May), the rest of the year on Tuesday, Wednesday, Friday and Sunday only.

## Mount Field National Park

It's 37km from New Norfolk to **Mount Field National Park**, a high alpine area with tarns created by glacial activity where, in winter, there's enough snow to create a small ski field. The magnificent stands of **Swamp Gum**, the tallest species of eucalypt and the tallest hardwood in the world, help make this Tasmania's most popular park; there are several **waterfalls**, and extended walks along the tarn shelf, with basic huts provided. Most people come here to see the impressive two-level **Russell Falls**, close to the entrance, a destination for tour buses whose clients appreciate the easy, well-graded thirty-minute circuit walk. Longer walks continue on to **Horseshoe Falls** (1hr) and **Lady Barron Falls** (circuit 3hr). The best short walk is the **Tall Trees Track** (1hr 30min) where huge Swamp Gums dominate; the largest date back to the early 1800s. To get away from the tour-group mob, there are plenty of longer walks, including extended circuits that take several days; the walk to **Twilight Tarn**, with its historic hut, is one of the most rewarding. Most treks start from **Lake Dobson**, 16km inside the park, and unless you're very keen you'll need your own transport to reach any of them, although sometimes the ranger can offer you a lift.

For information on the walks, to register for overnight ones and to chat with the ranger to make sure you're properly prepared, drop into the **Mount Field Ranger Station** (☎002/88 1149) at the entrance to the park. There's also information here about walks in the South West National Park, several of which can be commenced from Scotts Peak Road, which runs off the Gordon River Road to the west of Mount Field (see p.817). If you want to **stay** in the vicinity, the tiny settlement of **NATIONAL PARK** on Maydena Road consists of the *National Park Hotel* (☎002/88 1103; B&B ④), with basic ground-floor pub accommodation, and the easy-going homestead housing the *National Park Youth Hostel* opposite (☎002/88 1369; ①); there's plenty of interaction, including pool tournaments, between the two. Within the park itself, there's a campsite near the ranger station, with civilized amenities including a laundry and a small kiosk. Near the main camping area, you can catch your dinner at the **Russell Falls Trout Farm** (daily 9.30am–5pm; $2), or stay in more comfort at *Russell Falls Cottages* (☎002/88 1198; ④), in fully self-contained units.

**Junee State Reserve** is prime platypus territory; you can reach it from Mount Field if you have a car or bike, and in summer the ranger often organizes guided walks. Head 11km southwest to Maydena, then right into narrow, winding Junee Road for 3.5km. At the reserve, the Junee River flows into **Junee Cave**, ten minutes' away walk through regenerating forest. Platypuses are very common on the Junee River, but that doesn't mean you'll see any – they're extremely elusive. The trick is to arrive at dawn or dusk, well camouflaged, and sit quietly for at least an hour. Peta Britton (☎002/88 2206) leads **trail rides** from Junee Road through the reserve, checking out the caves along the way.

# Richmond

**RICHMOND**, on the Coal River some 25km north of Hobart, is one of the oldest and best-preserved towns in Australia, surrounded by undulating rural countyside. Settlers received land grants in the area not long after the fledgling colony had been set up in 1803, and in 1824 Lieutenant Governor Sorell founded the town, on the route between Hobart and the east coast. Soon, traffic to the new penal settlement at Port Arthur began to pass through, and Richmond's strategic location made it an important military post and convict station – and, by the 1830s, the third-largest town in Tasmania. In 1872, however, the **Sorell Causeway** was opened, and Richmond was bypassed, becoming a rural community with little incentive for change or development. Most of the fifty-odd nineteenth-century buildings – plain and functional stone dwellings – date from the 1830s and 1840s, many now used as galleries, craft shops, cafés, restaurants and guesthouses. Attractions along Bridge Street include the wooden **Richmond Maze** (daily 10am–5pm; $2.50), thé **Old Hobart Town Model Village**, a large-scale outdoor model of Hobart in the 1820s (daily 9.30am–5.30pm; $4.50); and the **Richmond Toy Museum** (daily 10am–5pm; $2.50), with toys dating from the 1890s to the 1960s.

Tourist fluff aside, the grey-stone, slate-roofed **Richmond Gaol** (daily 9am–5pm; $3), an intact example of an early prison, is Richmond's most authentic attraction. For most of its life, the prison's function was to house prisoners in transit or awaiting trial, and to accommodate convict road gangs working in the district; the east wing was designed to house female convicts, who could not be accommodated at Port Arthur. Informative signs explain the various features of the gaol, which now seems incongruously pretty, set around a central square with grass, flowers and a tree.

In addition to the gaol, Richmond has the distinction of having both Australia's oldest Roman Catholic Church – of **St John**, which dates in part from 1837 – and its oldest bridge. **Richmond Bridge** was constructed in 1823 under harsh conditions using convict labour; there's a legend that it's haunted by the ghost of the brutal flagellator, George Grover, who was beaten to death by the convicts and thrown into the river during its construction.

## Practicalities

*Hobart Coaches* runs four services from Hobart on Monday to Friday, stopping at Richmond on the way to the east coast. **Accommodation** is mainly very pricey bed and breakfast in quaint colonial buildings. *Emerald Cottage*, at 23 Torrens Street (☎002/60 2192; ⑦, with breakfast ingredients supplied), is a converted stable where you get a whole cottage to yourself. For something grander, you'll notice *Prospect House* (☎002/60 2207; ⑦) on your left as you come into town on Cambridge Road: a Georgian country mansion set in twelve hectares of landscaped grounds, with its own licensed restaurant. Further out, 6km from Richmond along Prossers Road, *Richmond Country Bed and Breakfast* (☎002/60 4238; ⑤) is non-smoking and reasonably priced, a comfortable homestead with a quiet farm setting. The cheapest place to stay is *Richmond Cabin and Tourist Park*, Middle Tea Tree Road (☎002/60 2192; on-site vans ③, cabins ④), on the outskirts of town as you come in from Hobart, with shady grounds and a heated indoor pool.

On the **food** front, Bridge Street has reliable pub meals on offer at the *Richmond Arms Hotel*; probably the best pies in Tasmania from the *Jolly Miller Bakery* behind the *Bridge Inn*; and a sort of upmarket brasserie in the *Richmond Wine Centre* (10am–6pm, to 8pm Fri & Sat), where the emphasis is on quality Tasmanian produce.

## The Forestier and Tasman peninsulas

The fastest route from Hobart to the **Tasman Peninsula** heads northeast along the Tasman Highway before crossing the **Sorell Causeway**; on the huge expanse of Pittwater, windsurfers are out in force on a sunny day. From the small town of **SORELL**, the Arthur Highway heads across the narrow isthmus to the **Forestier Peninsula**, and from there on to the hook of the **Tasman Peninsula**.

**Port Arthur**, right at the bottom, is the major attraction, but the two scarcely developed peninsulas offer several good **bushwalks**, and on their rough ocean sides are some impressive rock formations. The narrow point where the two land forms join is the infamous **Eaglehawk Neck**, once guarded by vicious dogs to turn the Tasman Peninsula into a kind of prison island. Around here are some of the finest coastal features: just to the north, there's the the **Tessellated Pavement**, which you can climb down onto at low tide; and to the south, off the highway, a fierce **Blowhole**, the huge **Tasman Arch** and the **Devils Kitchen**, a sheer rock cleft with the sea surging in and a peaceful fishing cove nearby. The **Tasman Trail** is a great coastal walk that starts from Devils Kitchen and ends at **Fortescue Bay**, with its good camping area (otherwise the bay is 12km down a dirt road east off the Arthur Highway). South of Port Arthur, several walking tracks begin from **Remarkable Cave**: to Crescent Bay (5hr return), Mount Brown (5hr return) and Maingon Blowhole (3hr return); you used to be able to walk through it when the tide was out but the steps in have recently been washed away. *Eaglehawk Neck Backpackers* (☎002/50 3248; ①), 687 Old Jetty Road, is the perfect place to stay to explore these places, 1km west of the Arthur Highway on the Forestier Peninsula side of the Eaglehawk Neck. It's a spacious, non-smoking, friendly and green place; bikes are lent (for a small donation) to enable you to get about, and there are canoes to use, too.

In nearby **DOO TOWN** (where all the houses have names with "doo" in them, like *Love Me Doo* and *Doo Little*, as something to distract the busloads of tourists who pour through – but never stop – on their way to Port Arthur), *Ocean Sports* (☎002/50 3425) offers dive-boat charters, equipment included, at low rates. For something to **eat** in the area, the *Eaglehawk Neck Cafe* on the Arthur Highway, near the turn-off to the Blowhole, is run by a French woman, and offers tasty, reasonably priced food, from vegetarian to traditional meat dishes, plus coffee and cakes; it's open for breakfast, lunch and dinner.

## Port Arthur

> *The most unceasing labour is to be extracted from the convicts . . . and the most harassing vigilance over them is to be observed.*
>
> Governor Arthur

The ex-prison town of **PORT ARTHUR** was popularized by Marcus Clarke's romantic tragedy, *For the Term of his Natural Life*, written in 1870. Port Arthur was chosen as the site for a prison settlement in September 1830; its first 150 convicts worked like slaves to establish a timber industry in the wooded surroundings. The regime was never a subtle one: **Governor Arthur**, responsible for all the convicts in Van Diemen's Land, believed that a convict's "whole fate should be…the very last degree of misery consistent with humanity". Gradually, Port Arthur became a self-supporting industrial centre: the timber industry grew into shipbuilding, there was brickmaking and shoe-making, wheat-growing, and even a flour mill. From the 1840s until transportation ceased in 1853, Port Arthur received most of Britain's convicts, and the penal settlement grew steadily, with brick and stone buildings replacing the early timber constructions. The lives of the labouring convicts contrasted sharply with the prison officers and their families, who had their cricket fields, ornamental gardens with fountains shaded with English oaks, brass bands, drama club and library. The years after transportation ended were in many ways more horrific than what had preceded them, as psychological punishment replaced physical beatings. In 1852, the **Model Prison**, based on the spoked-wheel design of Pentonville Prison in London, opened. Here prisoners could be kept in tiny cells in complete isolation and absolute silence; they were referred to by numbers rather than names, and wore hoods whenever they left their cells. The prison continued to operate until 1877, by now incorporating its own **mental asylum** full of ex-convicts as well as a geriatric home for ex-convict paupers.

Not long after Port Arthur had closed down as a prison settlement – in 1877 – the public became fascinated by its buildings and the tragedy behind them, and guided tours were offered by ex-convicts. In the 1890s the town around the prison was devastated by bushfires that left most buildings in ruins. A major conservation and restoration project began in the 1970s and today the **Port Arthur Historic Site** (daily 9am–5pm; $12.50 includes a 40-min guided tour) covers a huge area with over sixty buildings, some furnished and restored, others picturesque ruins, dotted about green lawns with paths and shady trees sloping down to the cove. With the water lapping gently alongside, it all looks more like a serene old-world university campus than a prison. You can also take the *MV Bundeena* across the bay from Port Arthur jetty to the **Isle of the Dead** (noon–5pm; $5), which was Port Arthur's cemetery from 1832 to 1877: a tour of the graveyard, with its 1769 unhappy convict souls, is included.

## Practicalities

If you don't have transport, the best way to see Port Arthur is on a **tour**: there are plenty, and most of them take in some of the Tasman Peninsula sights along the way. *Hobart Sightseeing* and *Hobart Coaches* offer day-tours for around $40. If you prefer to travel here by regular **bus**, you'll have to stay two nights if you want to see anything: *Hobart Coaches* travel down from Hobart twice a day during the week. "Convict Country Bus Service", operated by *Redline,* departs Hobart once daily during the week.

If you're staying the night at Port Arthur, join the nightly lantern-lit **Ghost Tour** (2hr; $7.50; bookings on ☎002/50 2539), which features lovingly researched and hauntingly retold tales of the settlement's past as you wander in and out of the ruins. Every night (Nov–May 7.30pm; $5) in the *Broad Arrow Café* you can also see the 1926 silent movie *For the Term of his Natural Life*, which was filmed around the Port Arthur area.

There are various **places to stay** on the edges of Port Arthur. The *Port Arthur Motor Inn*, Remarkable Cave Road (☎002/50 2101; ⑥), is pleasant enough, with a bar open to the public and reasonable counter meals. Just across the road is *Roseview Youth Hostel* on Champ Street (☎002/50 2311; ①; booking essential Jan & Feb). Spacious *Port Arthur Villas* (☎002/50 2239; ⑤) has the amenities of a motel but with a full kitchen, just across Remarkable Cave Road from the historic site.

A couple of good places to **eat** in Port Arthur are the *Frances Langford Tea Rooms*, in the restored 1930s policemen's quarters, and the *Port Arthur Food and Wine Centre* in the parsonage. Down by the bay, a punt is moored most days (closed Jun–Aug), selling locally caught, freshly cooked seafood.

# The east coast: the Tasman Highway

On much of its journey following the sunny **east coast,** the **Tasman Highway** gently rises and falls through grazing land and bush-covered hills. In summer, there's something of an unspoilt Mediterranean feel about this coast, with its long white beaches, blue water stretching to a blue cloudless sky, scenic hills in the background, and a strong local fishing industry. Because the east coast is sheltered from the prevailing westerly winds, and has warm offshore currents, it has one of the most temperate climates in Australia. This, and the mainly safe swimming beaches, means it's a popular destination for Tasmanian families in the school holidays – prices go up and accommodation is scarce from Christmas to the middle of February. Even so, it's still relatively undeveloped and peaceful; there are four national parks, which include a whole island – **Maria Island** – and an entire peninsula – the glorious **Freycinet National Park**.

The east coast is also Tasmania's best **cycling route**: it's relatively flat and the climate is mild enough to tackle it in winter, too. Towns are well spaced and there's a string of youth hostels so you don't need to camp, while the small population means even fewer cars than usual. **St Helens** is the largest town on the east coast, with a population of just over a thousand; situated on **Georges Bay**, it's a good base for exploring the northeast corner and **Mount William National Park**. The oldest town, **Swansea**, lies sheltered in **Great Oyster Bay**, facing the Freycinet Peninsula. To the north, **Bicheno** is a small fishing town with fantastic diving, a good base for visiting both the Freycinet National Park (and its tiny settlement of **Coles Bay**) and the **Douglas Apsley National Park** inland. The highway detours inland at **St Marys**, although a new road means you can choose to follow the coast, missing out on a high climb with spectacular views of the surrounding coastline.

Because the east coast is not heavily populated, there's a lack of **banking facilities**, particularly ATMs; banks themselves only open on one or two days a week. There's an EFTPOS machine at Bicheno, and full banking at St Helens, while small settlements have post offices which are *Commonwealth Bank* agents, but it's important to make sure you always have enough cash.

**Transport** services don't operate daily either – another good reason to cycle. *Hobart Coaches* run down the east coast, with departures from Hobart via Richmond or Sorell to St Helens; there are none on Tuesday, and Saturday services in January and February only. *Redline Coaches* has a regular Monday to Friday service between Hobart and Bicheno plus one Sunday service if booked, and between Launceston to St Helens via St Marys. The local bus company, *Sun Coast* (☎003/76 1807), operates between Derby and St Helens, and *Peakes* (☎003/72 5390) between St Marys, Bicheno and Swansea; again, both of these are Monday to Friday services only. If you don't fancy getting stuck somewhere for a couple of days, check timetables carefully.

## Maria Island

As the Tasman Highway meets the sea at **ORFORD**, a small holiday resort on the estuary of the Prosser River, you get your first views across to **Maria Island**. The entire island, fifteen kilometres off the east coast, is a national park, uninhabited save for its ranger. Its wide tracks are ideal for mountain biking, an activity encouraged here – as no other vehicles are allowed you can ride in perfect safety. The coast road has no gradient, but inland there are a few hills to persevere with. **Birdlife** is prolific, with over 130 species.

The ferry lands at historic **DARLINGTON** where the structures of the **penal settlement** still stand, including the commissariat store with its visitor information boards, the convict barn, the cemetery, the mill house and the penitentiary. The latter is now a **bunkhouse**; units have bunks with mattresses and wood stoves; they're always in demand and are often booked up six months in advance, so call the ranger (☎002/57 1420) before turning up. The **campsite** here is among the island's best, with a public phone, toilets, fireplaces, cold water taps and tank water for drinking; there's a small fee for camping here – the ranger will come around and collect it. As there is little water elsewhere on the island, free-range camping is best done at **Frenchs Farm** or at **Encampment Cove**, two campsites with a rainwater supply and fireplaces; the latter, on Shoal Bay, is the more picturesque of the two.

There are many short **walks** on the island, as well as longer bushwalks: free pamphlets are available from the ranger's office at Darlington (☎002/57 1420). If you have a couple of days to spare you can walk past the narrow isthmus to the rarely visited **southern end** of the island, with its unspoilt forests and secluded beaches, but come prepared – there's no water at all down here.

### Getting there: Triabunna

**Ferries** leave for the island from the *Eastcoaster Resort* at Louisville, halfway between Orford and Triabunna, and from **TRIABUNNA** itself. The *Eastcoaster Express* (☎002/57 1589), a fast catamaran taking only twenty minutes, leaves the resort daily at 10.30am, 1pm and 3.30pm, returning from Maria Island at 11am, 1.30pm and 4pm, with extra trips between 26 December and 28 January (day-trips $16, campers $19, bikes and kayaks $3). The laidback *Triabunna YHA* in Spencer Street, 1km outside Triabunna (☎002/57 3439; rooms ②, dorms ①), is a good base for a day-trip to the island. You can also charter a **flight** to the island from Triabunna with *Salmon Air* (☎002/57 3186).

# Swansea

From Triabunna it's a fairly uneventful drive north to **SWANSEA**, overlooking **Great Oyster Bay**, with views across to the Freycinet Peninsula. If you're lucky you might see dolphins frolicking in the bay from Franklin Street (the main street), which runs along the waterfront. One of Tasmania's oldest settlements, it's an administrative centre, fishing port and seaside resort, with well-preserved architecture dating from the 1830s to the 1880s. The focus of town is still **Morris's General Store** on Franklin Street, run by seven generations of the family since 1868; the imposing three-storey building is even older than that. Now there's the rather ugly additon of a *Riteway Supermarket* to one side, but the drapery and hardware is still found on the ground floor of the old store. Other historical traces can be seen at the **Community Centre** (Mon–Sat 8.30am–5.30pm; $2), also on Franklin Street, a former school whose miscellaneous collection includes a billiard table built from a single log of blackwood – you can have a game on it for $2. One of the main draws of the town is a recently established **ferry** which takes you the 20km from the Swansea Jetty straight across Great Oyster Bay to Coles Bay – and Freycinet National Park – in just 45 minutes, cutting out the long 60-km drive right around the lagoon; book at *Swansea Backpackers* (☎002/57 8399; $9 one-way, $15 return).

*Hobart Coaches* local depot is at the *Shell Service Station* on the Tasman Highway (☎002/34 4077); *Redline Coaches* stop at the *Swansea Corner Store* (☎002/57 8118); there are also local services with *Peakes* (☎003/72 5390) from *Morris's Store*. If you want to stay the night, budget **accommodation** consists of the comfortable *Swansea YHA*, 5 Franklin Street (☎002/57 8367; ①; bikes and fishing lines for rent); the well-run *Central Swansea Backpackers*, 20 Franklin St (☎002/57 8399; dorms ①, rooms ③), housed in a quaint 1860s building; and the *Swan Motor Inn*, 1 Franklin Street (☎002/57 8102; ⑤–⑥), a fine old hotel with a redbrick motel addition and a bistro. There's also B&B at *Meredith House*, 15 Noyes Street (☎002/57 8119; ⑥), or the *Oyster Bay Guest House*, 10 Franklin Street (☎002/578 110; ⑤–⑥); and two waterfront **caravan parks** with excellent facilities: *Swansea Caravan Park* on Shaw Street, opposite the Old Bark Mill (☎002/57 8177; on-site vans ③, cabins ⑤) and *Kenmore Caravan Park*, 2 Bridge Street (☎002/57 8148; on-site vans ③, cabins ④).

As for **food**, downstairs at the *Oyster Bay Guest House*, the *Shy Albatross Restaurant* (Tues–Sat from 7pm) serves interesting and not too pricey contemporary Australian cuisine. *Just Maggies*, a relaxed café at 26 Franklin Street (daily 9am–5pm), is a prime spot for dolphin watching, while *Kabuki By the Sea* (book for dinner on ☎002/57 8588) is a fine Japanese restaurant 12km north on the Tasman Highway – its views are stunning. The *Westpac* **bank** on Franklin Street is open Thursdays, as well as Tuesdays during January and February (☎002/57 8147 to double-check, as opening times may change).

# The Freycinet Peninsula

Heading for Coles Bay and **Freycinet National Park**, you turn off the Tasman Highway 33km north of Swansea, following the Coles Bay Road. Roughly eight kilometres down, a side road (3km of unsealed road) leads you to the **Friendly Beaches**, a new addition to the national park, taking in a length of unspoilt shoreline backed by eucalypt forest. If you're **cycling**, you can save forty kilometres by riding along Nine Mile Beach Road, at the end of which a ferry will take you across the Swan River to **SWANICK**, about 6km out of Coles Bay. The trip costs about $8 and must be booked in advance; it doesn't operate from June to September; contact Kirk Dalwood (☎002/57 0239). The only place to stay at Swanick is *Swan River Cottages* (☎002/57 0216; ⑥), each of which can accommodate up to six people.

COLES BAY, on the edge of the Freycinet National Park, is a sheltered inlet with fishing boats moored on deep blue water against the striking backdrop of **The Hazards**, three pink granite peaks – Amos, Dove and Mayson – rising straight from the sea. The hamlet of Coles Bay has been the base for the park, and for fishing and recreation, since the 1930s. As a result, there are numerous fishing shacks and **holiday houses** available to rent: call Mrs Kempnich (☎002/57 0333), Mrs Michlik (☎002/57 0116) or Mrs McCambridge (☎002/57 0176). One kilometre from the general store, *Iluka Holiday Centre,* on the Esplanade (☎002/57 0115; ③–④), has on-site vans, good bedsitting units and larger cottages with wood fires, as well as landscaped tent sites. Attached is a small supermarket, an excellent eat-in bakery selling pastries, *focaccia,* pizza and decent cappuccino (daily 7am–10pm), plus a restaurant and tavern. The *Coles Bay Caravan Park,* Coles Bay Road (☎002/57 0100; on-site vans ③) is further out – 4km west – and also has backpacker accommodation (①), with a free shuttle bus to the national park. **Supplies** of all sorts are available at *Coles Bay Trading* on Garnet Avenue; this is also the post office, petrol station, boat rental outlet and tourist information centre. Next door there's a decent coffee shop serving breakfast (8.30am–10am), then regular meals until about 6pm. *Coles Bay Licensed Restaurant* (daily 9am–8.30pm), across the road, is unassuming but the food is surprisingly good, with a takeaway at the front.

*Redline* and *Hobart Coaches* only drop off at the turning to Coles Bay on the Tasman Highway, leaving you to walk the final 31km, or wait for the *Bicheno Coach Service* (3 daily Coles Bay–Bicheno; ☎002/57 0293), which can take you right to the start of the walking tracks and also back from Coles Bay to the highway to make the *Redline* and *Hobart Coaches* connections.

### Freycinet National Park

The **national park office** (daily over summer & Easter 8.30am–12.30pm & 1–5pm, otherwise daily 9am–noon; ☎002/57 0107), where you can get advice on bushwalking and buy booklets on day walks and maps, is just a kilometre out of Coles Bay. Opposite, the national park **campsite**, with water and toilets but no showers, shelters among bush and dunes behind Richardson's Beach; it's packed in holiday season, when you'll need to book ahead through the park office. Otherwise, you can walk into the national park and camp for free. At the other end of Richardsons Beach, *Freycinet Lodge* (☎002/57 0101; ⑧) has luxurious wooden cabins spread through bushland, and offers guided bushwalks and a tennis court; the dining room, open to the public all day, overlooks the beach. There's also *Coles Bay YHA* in the national park, but you can only stay here if you've booked in advance through the Hobart office (☎002/34 9617; ①), and even then it's often full with groups.

Tracks into the park begin at the **Walking Track Car Park**, a further 4km from the office. **Water** is scarce, so you must carry all you'll need, although the ranger can advise you if there are any streams safe to drink from at a particular time. The shorter walks are well marked and not too difficult: exquisite **Wine Glass Bay**, with its perfect curve of white beach, is the aim of most walkers, just over an hour each way. The **peninsula circuit** is a joy, ten hours of walking, best spread over two days, and a good practice run for the big southwest hikes. There's a campsite at **Cooks Beach**, with a pit toilet, water tank, and a rough hut you can stay in; plus lots of mischievous marsupials after your food, so wrap it up tight.

**Schouten Island**, off the tip of the peninsula, was included as part of the national park in 1967: it's perfect for really secluded camping, as you're quite likely to have it all to yourself. *Freycinet Sea Charters* (Mike Dicker ☎002/57 0355) will drop you off there for $45 return, or you could try *Keno Sea Fisheries* (Chris Holloway ☎002/57 0344) for flexible boat charter; alternatively, if you're charming enough, you might get a ride from a fisherman at Coles Bay. There are campsites with pit toilet, a hut and two water tanks at **Moreys Bay**, and the creek at **Crocketts Bay** has reliable upstream water. Although there are no proper tracks on the island, walking is easy.

# Bicheno

Halfway up the east coast, **BICHENO** (pronounced "bish-eno"), sheltered in **Waubs Bay**, is a busy crayfishing and abalone port. The same conditions that make Bicheno ideal for fishing also make it a perfect spot for **diving**. The usually clear waters are rich with a variety of marine life, and there's a **Marine Reserve** on the eastern side of **Governor Island**, with spectacular large caves and extraordinary vertical rock faces with swim-throughs and drop-offs. *Bicheno Dive Centre*, 4 Tasman Highway (☎003/75 1138), offers diving courses and gear rental. **Information** on other activities around Bicheno is available from *Bicheno Penguin Tours*, Foster Street (daily 9am–5.30pm; ☎003/75 1333), which arranges diving, horse-riding, cycling, and a wide variety of local tours, the most popular being the summer visits to **Diamond Island** to observe the local **penguin** population. They would like to discourage visitors from going there alone as it's becoming a successful penguin breeding ground; it's also worth bearing in mind that people who don't know what they're doing have drowned trying to get back after the tide has come in. The **Sea Life Centre** (daily 9am–5pm; $4), on the Tasman Highway, has a rather dingy aquarium and an excellent, cheap seafood restaurant.

Bicheno makes for a pleasant place to stay a while, with plenty of **accommodation**. *Camp Seaview*, 29 Seaview Street (☎003/75 1247; dorms ①, family units ⑤), is open to backpackers in the school holidays, with superb facilities. The simple *Bicheno YHA*, 3km north on the highway (☎003/75 1293; ①), has a great beachfront location opposite Diamond Island; fresh oysters and ice-cream for sale are yummy extras. Other places include the *Beachfront Motel*, Tasman Highway (☎003/75 1111; ⑤), with lots of free sport and a pool; *Bicheno Cabin and Tourist Park*, 4 Champ Street (☎003/75 1117; on-site vans ④, cabins ⑤); and *Bicheno Gaol*, on the corner of James and Burgess streets (☎003/75 1430; ⑥–⑦), with B&B cottage accommodation right in the old prison. **Food** is excellent, too: *Waubs Bay House*, 16 Tasman Highway, is a brasserie-style place for anything from coffee to inexpensive French food; the pricier and more formal *Cyrano French Restaurant*, 77 Burgess Street (☎003/75 1137; daily from 6.30pm) is also in the classic French vein. The *Longboat Tavern* on the Tasman Highway has counter meals, and the *Galleon Coffee Lounge*, 45 Foster Street (daily 8am–7.30pm), is a good place for breakfast.

For **buses** to Freycinet National Park, the *Coles Bay–Bicheno Coach Service* (☎003/75 1461) leaves from the *Night Owl* takeaway, at 52 Burgess Street (3 daily Mon–Sat).

## The Douglas Apsley National Park

Continuing north along the Tasman Highway from Bicheno, **Douglas Apsley National Park** is Tasmania's newest national park. Proclaimed in 1990, its unique feature is the state's only remaining large dry sclerophyll forest. The temperate weather of the east coast means the park's two-day walk – undertaken north to south, is a good one at any time of the year. This is a low-maintenance, untouristy park and facilities are minimal – which means back to basics bush camping. As the length of national park ends, 27km north of Bicheno, **Chain of Lagoons** – with its great fresh seafood roadside stall and wonderful waterfront camping on a farmer's property at nearby Piccaninny Point – marks the turn-off for St Marys, 17km inland. You can choose to continue along the coastal Tasman Highway – or detour inland for a high climb with spectacular views of the surrounding coastline. Dramatic **Elephant Pass** shouldn't be missed, not least for the laidback *Mount Elephant Pancake Barn*, run by a relaxed young Dutch couple (☎003/72 2263), where the coffee, food, views and atmosphere are magical – and if you like it that much, you can even stay here in a startlingly individual guestroom (B&B ⑤).

## St Marys and St Helens

From the pass the road heads on to **ST MARYS**, a picturesque little town surrounded by state forest and waterfalls with a quiet, old-fashioned feel, plus a slight alternative edge – and some fine bushwalks. The best thing about it is the *Seaview Farm Lodge* (☎003/72 2341; rooms ②, dorms ①), 8km uphill on German Town Road, a characterful farm hostel well known for its Green credentials and connections, with walking trails and views over the surrounding countryside; there are several private cabin rooms or you can stay in the farmhouse, and you can even arrange a pick-up in advance if you don't have your own transport.

Heading downhill back to the coast, **ST HELENS**, the largest town on the east coast and the last before the Tasman Highway turns inland, is situated on **Georges Bay**, a long narrow bay with two encircling arms. Both town and bay are fairly dull – it's the surrounding coastline that's of interest. Local **information** is available from the *St Helens History Room*, 55 Cecilia Street, opposite the Post Office (Mon–Fri 9am–4pm; $2; ☎003/76 1744), providing maps and suggested walks as well as details of the area's mining history; and from *St Helens Secretariat*, 20 Cecilia Street (Mon–Fri 9am–5pm; ☎003/76 1329). The noticeboard outside the *Tigerbarn Supermarket* car park has information on Mount William National Park and details of walks in the area.

The southern arm of Georges Bay is occupied by **St Helens Point Recreation Area** with its large lagoon – Diana's Basin – which the highway skirts as it leads into town. On the ocean side the **Peron Sand Dunes** stretch for several kilometres, and at the point there's good surfing at **Beer Barrel Beach**. Ten kilometres north of Georges Bay, **Binalong Bay**, with its beach of bright sugary sand, is an easy cycle ride with only a couple of small climbs: it's another popular surf spot (with a strong current, so beware) – there's safer swimming in the large lagoon tucked behind, where people go boating and water-skiing. You can camp here as well as further along at the **Bay of Fires Coastal Reserve**. The unsealed road along the coastal reserve ends at **The Gardens**, where a couple of artists live, show their work, and serve snacks and cups of tea at *The Gallery*. The southern half of **MOUNT WILLIAM NATIONAL PARK** is approached on a different road; it's 54km from St Helens to the pink granite tower of the Eddystone Lighthouse. You reach the northern end of the park, with it's campsite at **Great Musselroe Bay**, via Gladstone. There are no real tracks in the park, but plenty of beach and headland walking, and lots of Forrester kangaroos.

## St Helens Practicalities

The *St Helens Hotel*, 49 Cecilia Street (☎003/76 1133), has plain food plus **accommodation**: budget rooms aimed at backpackers (③) and spacious but drab family rooms (⑤). *St Helens YHA*, 5 Cameron Street (☎003/76 1661; ①), is clean and friendly; or try the salubrious *Warrawee Guest House* (☎003/76 1987; B&B ⑤–⑥) on the Tasman Highway, the friendly *Cecilia House*, 78 Cecilia Street (☎003/76 1723; B&B ⑤), or the cheaper *Artnor Lodge*, 71 Cecilia Street (☎003/76 1234; B&B ④). The *Bayside Inn*, 2 Cecilia Street (☎003/76 1466; ⑤–⑥), is a modern hotel/motel with a restaurant, pool and drive-in bottle shop, right on the water. *Eastlines Hire Service*, 28 Cecilia Street (☎003/76 1720), enable you to enjoy the outdoor and water-based activities in the area, offering fishing trips and diving courses, as well as renting out diving gear and a dinghy. For **transport** to and from St Helens, *Suncoast Agencies*, 30 Cecilia Street (Mon–Fri 9am–5pm; ☎003/76 1533), books and sells tickets for *Hobart Coaches*: buses depart outside. *Redline*'s agent is the newsagency at 32 Cecilia Street.

# St Helens to Scottsdale: the Tasman Highway

From St Helens, the **Tasman Highway** cuts across the northeastern highlands towards Launceston, 170km away. It's mostly dairy country, with the odd patch of surviving rainforest and the remnants of a tin-mining industry, based around the **Blue Tier**, a mountain which in the 1870s saw a mining boom. Many **ghost towns** were left after the mines finally closed in the 1950s.

Twenty-six kilometres out of St Helens is the turn-off for **PYENGANA** and **St Columba Falls**. In Pyengana it's worth calling in to *Healey's Pyengana Cheese Factory* (daily 9am–6pm; ☎003/73 6157), where you can watch the stuff being made and buy all the materials for a picnic at the falls. Further along, the "Pub in the Paddock", *St Columba Falls Hotel* (☎003/73 6121; dorms ①, B&B ④), looks like a farmhouse; a real country local with huge farm-grown steaks, free camping out the back, and a minibus in which they offer tours of the old tin mines. At the end of the road – the last bit on dirt – the **Columba Falls State Reserve** is an area of cool, temperate rainforest. The short walk to the viewing platform at the base of the falls is easy, through a forest of manferns and under a canopy of sassafras and myrtle. Columba Falls are the tallest in Tasmania, pouring with tremendous force 110m over cliffs – truly thunderous in winter, when the viewing platform is shrouded in mist.

Back on the main road approaching the Blue Tier, **GOSHEN** is the first of the ghost towns: little more than an old school and the ruins of the *Oxford Arms Inn*. A little further on is the turn-off for **GOULDS COUNTRY**, with the remaining buildings, all wooden, of what was once a town, and **LOTTAH**. The **Weldborough Pass** (595m) is probably the most beautiful part of the drive, with views across the valleys to the sea – it's worth taking the twenty-minute walk through the **Weldborough Pass Scenic Reserve**, predominately myrtle forest with man ferns and occasional tall blackwoods. **WELDBOROUGH** itself, once the centre of a Chinese mining community, now consists of the *Weldborough Hotel* (☎003/54 2223; ③), where you can get a feed and a basic pub room for the night; ask about pitching a tent out the back.

**DERBY**, on the Ringarooma River, was made prosperous by the profitable **Briseis Tin Mine** which operated in the town between 1876 and 1952. The **Derby Tin Mine Centre** (daily 10am–4pm; $4) is now the only sign of development in a town that's been closing down since the 1950s: it has interesting relics of Chinese miners and examples of gemstones fossicked in the area.

**SCOTTSDALE**, 99km from St Helens in all, is a large, pleasantly situated town servicing the agricultural and forestry industries of the northeast, but it's none too exciting. Better to head 21km northwest to **BRIDPORT**, a fishing town and holiday spot where the *Bridport Caravan Park* (☎003/56 1227) stretches for about a kilometre along Anderson Bay: it feels just like bush camping, but with all the amenities. The beaches are lovely, especially the wide sandy expanse where the Bird River flows into the sea among sand dunes. *Bridport Seafoods* (daily 10am–7pm), attached to the fish processing plant on the Main Street, does excellent sit-down meals.

# NORTHERN AND CENTRAL TASMANIA

The **north** of Tasmania is rich and settled agricultural country, and the fertile soil of the **Tamar Valley** in particular made this a prosperous area during the early colonial period. **Launceston** quickly grew as a port and city, 30km inland at the confluence of the Tamar and the North and South Esk rivers; around the area are still found gracious early houses and well-preserved villages. Also settled early, due to its fine and open land, was the mostly flat, gently undulating **midlands** stretching between Launceston and Hobart, with the old coaching route between the two cities still more or less followed by the **Midlands Highway**. With its stone walls, hedgerows, haystacks and small villages and towns, this rural stretch from the Tamar Valley through to Hobart is softly appealing but not particularly exciting. In contrast, the area around **Deloraine**, 45km west of Launceston, is spectacular: The early colonial town is surrounded by rich farmland and dramatically located in hilly country below the crest of the **Great Western Tiers** – a mecca for bushwalkers. From Deloraine, the **Lake Highway** heads steeply south up over the Western Tiers and on to the **Central Plateau**, a scarcely populated lake-filled region dominated by the **Great Lake** and its shambolic fishing shacks.

# Launceston and around

**LAUNCESTON** is dominated by the **Tamar River**, and approaching from the north along the Tamar Highway, zooming through haystacked countryside, it's a lovely sight, with grand Victorian houses nestling on hills above the banks. Approaching from the south, however, on the dreary Southern Outlet, a perhaps more accurate picture emerges of a dull but worthy provincial town. It's Tasmania's second-largest city, with a population of over 92,000, but despite its much-vaunted English look – especially in its many formal parks and gardens – only the surrounding countryside of the **Tamar Valley** (see p.793) really makes a visit pay dividends.

As the third-oldest city in Australia, first settled in 1804, Launceston has hung on to disappointingly little of its elegant colonial Georgian architecture. Existing examples are mainly utilitarian structures like merchant warehouses and mills, now converted into museums, galleries or tourist attractions. What the city does have in abundance, however, are many fine examples of colonial Victorian architecture: the 1870s and 1880s were prosperous times for Launceston, years of mineral exploration spurred on by the mainland gold rush. Building boomed and many massive and dignified public buildings date from this period – though unfortunately, the often florid facades were simply attached to Georgian structures.

Launceston's real attractions, though, are its natural assets. Situated at the confluence of the narrow **North Esk** and **South Esk rivers**, the South Esk has carved its way through rock to reach the Tamar and created the breathtaking **Cataract Gorge**, only ten minutes' walk from the city centre. On the water, yachts and outboard motors have around 50km of river to play on, while beyond the western side of the city, bush-covered hills fold back into the distance to **Ben Lomond**, where in winter the locals can be skiing within an hour.

# Arrival, information and transport

There are direct flights from Melbourne and Hobart to **Launceston Airport**, actually almost in the town of Evandale, 20km south of the city. A bus service ($6) to the city is provided by *Redline Coaches,* which meets all flights and drops off at the casino, the depot, or at your chosen accommodation. A **taxi** costs about $18 or you could **rent a car** – the four main car companies are represented at the airport.

**Buses** arrive at centrally located depots within a block of each other. *Redline Coaches* (☎31 3233) will drop you off at accommodation as far out as the caravan park, or else at their depot at 112 George Street. *Wilderness Transport* (☎34 4442) drops you within the city centre or at their office at 101 George Street; *Hobart Coaches* (☎34 3600) has a depot at 83 Cimitiere Street. There's no problem with **parking** in the city centre – if the short-term metered parking is full, there are loads of **car parks** around the city, charging just 50¢ an hour. Most streets operate on a **one-way system**: Cameron Street is blocked by Civic Square, and Brisbane Street by the Mall.

## Information

For **information**, first stop should be the *Tasmanian Travel Centre*, on the corner of St John and Paterson streets (Mon–Fri 8.45am–5pm, Sat 9am–noon; information ☎36 3122, reservations ☎36 3133), which can book accommodation, as well as travel tickets. Aside from street and regional **maps**, pick up the "Walk About Launceston" brochure and the free community newspaper, *Launceston Week.* For an alternative viewpoint, the *Wilderness Society Shop*, at 174 Charles St, opposite Princes Square (Mon–Sat 9.30am–5.30pm; ☎34 2499), is a good source of information about wilderness issues and the environment. You can put your name down here for the summer walks programme – weekends and day walks – into areas under threat by logging. The *Launceston Environment Cente*, 34 Paterson Street (Mon–Fri 10.30am–4.30pm; ☎31 8406), is another worthy source of information, with a library which has useful background on Tasmania.

## City transport

Launceston is very compact and most accommodation is within walking distance of the city centre, though **public transport** (the *MTT*) is useful for a couple of scattered attractions and some outlying accommodation. The **MTT bus interchange** (fare and timetable information ☎31 9911), where all buses arrive and depart, is at St John Street, on either side of the **Brisbane Street Mall**. Single fares are inexpensive, but it may be worth buying a *Day Rover* ($2.60) for unlimited travel between 9am and 4.30pm and then again after 6pm.

# Accommodation

**Accommodation** in Launceston is very good value and rates don't tend to be hiked up in the busy December to February period; most places have parking available, too. However, **hostel** beds are scarce, though there is a temporary YHA hostel in the summer; contact the Tasmanian YHA (☎002/34 9617) for details and location, which may change from year to year. There's a concentration of **motels** along Brisbane Street.

## Hotels, motels, B&Bs and self-catering

**Ashton Gate**, 32 High St (☎31 6180). Classified by the National Trust, the weatherboard house has been taking guests for 40 years. Bedrooms, painted a calming blue, are large and light. B&B ⑤–⑥.

**Batman Faulkner Inn**, 35–39 Cameron Street (☎31 7222). Established in 1822, and offering bargain single en-suite rooms for VIP or YHA cardholders. Larger, flashier rooms (with a light breakfast) available to all comers. Backpacker rooms ②, otherwise ⑤–⑥.

**The Edwardian**, 227 Charles St (☎31 4089). A lovely, two-storey redbrick Edwardian house with self-contained suites. Breakfast provisions are provided. ⑤–⑥.

**Lloyds Hotel**, 23 George St (☎31 4966). Plain, old-fashioned hotel. Rooms are en suite; hot drinks and TV in the guest lounge. The dining room downstairs does plain economical meals. The hotel is closed on Sun, when enquiries can be made and keys got from the *Commercial Hotel* opposite. ④.

**Motel Maldon**, 32 Brisbane St (☎31 3211). Elegant Victorian building, featuring chandeliers, engraved glass and carved wooden staircase but with modern motel-style accommodation. ⑤.

**North Lodge Motel**, 7 Brisbane St (☎31 9966). More like apartments than motel rooms, all with two bedrooms and cooking facilities. It's very central, overlooking City Park, and rates often drop when business is slack. ⑤.

**Prince Albert Inn**, corner of William St and Tamar St (☎31 7633) A delightfully eccentric place to stay: the dining room, where you breakfast from blue-and-white china on immaculate white table-cloths, is full of stuffed animals, while old photographs and colonial prints cover the walls. Non-smokers only. ⑥–⑦.

**The Royal Hotel**, 90 George St (☎31 2526). Although a noisy pub, closing at 2am most nights, the accommodation is inexpensive and rather civilized. B&B ④.

**Sportsman's Hall Hotel**, 252 Charles St (☎31 3968). A pleasant pub run by a friendly woman, who takes a lot of care over the well-furnished, comfortable rooms (shared bathrooms). The price includes breakfast. ④.

**Windmill Hill Tourist Lodge**, 22 High St (☎31 9337). Pleasant, two-storey house with bay windows and an old-fashioned 1940s feel. Huge rooms with small kitchen alcove and bathroom. ⑤.

## Hostels and caravan parks

**Launceston City Backpackers**, 173 George St (☎34 2327). Small and friendly hostel in a big old federation house that's nicely decorated and well equipped. It's on the same street as the *Redline* and *Wilderness Transport* depots, a couple of minutes' walk heading south. For access between 8am and 5pm, go to *Wilderness Transport* office. Dorms ①, rooms ③.

**Launceston City Youth Hostel**, 36 Thistle St, South Launceston (☎44 9779). A rather gloomy institutional place, with rules and regulations everywhere and a midnight curfew. However, there's bike and camping equipment rental, and the manager is very knowledgeable about bushwalking. Despite the name, this is not a YHA hostel. Take bus #20, #21, #22, #24 or #25 and get off at Wellington St (stop 8); *Redline* coaches also drop off here. ①.

**Parkside Backpackers**, 103 Canning St (☎31 4615). There's been good reports of this centrally located 50-bed hostel with a laundry, TV room, recreation area, garden and barbecue. ①.

**Treasure Island Caravan Park**, 94 Glen Dhu St, South Launceston, 2km south (☎44 2600). The small park, sloping up a hillside, looks right over the freeway. It's noisy, the ground is hard and uneven and it's crowded in summer – but there's nowhere else to camp in the Launceston area. Public transport as for *Launceston City Youth Hostel*, above. On-site vans ③, cabins ④.

# The City

The **Brisbane Street Mall** marks the centre of the city, which is arranged in a typical grid pattern around it. **Brisbane Street**, with the mall as its focus, is the main shopping precinct; heading east along the street, two other pedestrian shopping areas feed off it: **Quadrant Mall** and **Yorktown Square**. The city is small and easy to find your way around, but if you want some background information, *Launceston Historic Walks* (Monica Harris ☎31 3679) departs Monday to Friday at 9.45am ($10; 1hr) outside the tourist office on Paterson Street.

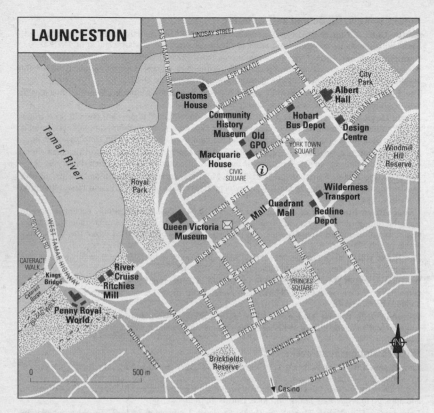

**LAUNCESTON**

City Park
Albert Hall
Customs House
Community History Museum
Hobart Bus Depot
Design Centre
Old GPO
York Town Square
Macquarie House
Windmill Hill Reserve
Civic Square
Royal Park
Wilderness Transport
Quadrant Mall
Redline Depot
Queen Victoria Museum
River Cruise
Ritchies Mill
Kings Bridge
Cataract Walk
Penny Royal World
Brickfields Reserve
Princes Square
Casino

Tamar River

0   500 m

## City Park and the old wharf area

City Park, with its entrance of impressive wrought-iron gates on Tamar Street, is a real treasure. Established in the 1820s, the impression of a formally organized, very English park is reinforced by the **John Hart Conservatory**, full of flowers and ferns, and by the lovely wrought iron drinking fountain erected here for Queen Victoria's Diamond Jubilee in 1897. Referred to by the locals as "Monkey Park", the park is the closest thing Launceston has to a zoo: its Japanese macaques (over 20 of them), romp around their small moat-surrounded island daily between 9am and 5.30pm. The **City Park Train** (10.30am–4pm), a vehicle with several tiny carriages, whizzes kids and adults twice around the five-acre park for around a dollar a ride.

Within City Park, on the corner of Tamar and Brisbane Streets, is the **Design Centre of Tasmania** (Mon–Fri 10am–6pm, Sat 10am–1pm, Sun 2–5pm; free), established in 1976 to support and encourage Tasmanian designers. For a state that's always been perceived as lagging behind by the mainland, it's a source of pride that Tasmanian designers helped furnish the new Parliament House in Canberra; "Furniture Focus", a permanent display of contemporary, innovative furniture, includes some of their work.

Backing onto City Park, on the corner of Tamar and Cimitiere streets, is **Albert Hall**, a grand building in the ornate High Victorian style. Built for the Tasmanian Industrial Exhibition of 1891, the steps of the symmetrical stone building fan out invitingly. You can wander up the steps and have a look inside the Great Hall (restored to its original state) and at the Brindley water-powered organ, imported from England in 1861 and the only one of its kind in the world.

Further along Tamar Street, on the corner of William Street, the extremely elaborate Victorian facade of the three-storey **Prince Albert Inn** hides the original Georgian facade. The 1855 building was once a tavern frequented by the sailors from the clippers that berthed at the **Old Launceston Wharves**, a hundred metres away. The wharves on the North Esk River have vanished, but the massive Neoclassical **Customs House** is still there on the the Esplanade. Restored by the Federal Government, it now houses their offices. The **old wharf area**, around William Street and the Esplanade, has several other interesting old industrial buildings, including the **Esk Brewery Oast House** (1881) and the **Monds and Alfflek Mill** (1860).

## St John Street

The now defunct **General Post Office**, on the corner of Cameron Street and St John Street, is a two-storey, Queen Anne-style, redbrick structure built in 1889. The tower was an afterthought (1903), and it shows, throwing out the proportions of the building. Opposite the old post office, the grand white building, with its giant colonnade of nine Corinthian columns, is the **Town Hall**, erected in 1864. A new, ultra-modern post office is now situated at 170 Brisbane Street.

A block north of the GPO, on the corner of Cimitiere Street, is the **Community History Museum** (Mon–Sat 10am–4pm, Sun 2pm–4pm; $2; ☎37 1391), housed in the old Johnston and Wilmot store, built in 1842. It has changed little over the last 150 years, with its bare rafters, old wooden floors and staircases and rough, wooden pillars holding up the ceiling. Upstairs, a room completely lined with tin – floors, walls and ceiling – was designed to be cool and rodent-proof; Johnstone and Wilmot kept chocolate in here. The building also used to house the old Maritime Museum, and the remains of that are here, too, with artefacts relating to whaling and sealing.

Five blocks south of the GPO, bounded by Frederick and Elizabeth Streets, is peaceful **Princes Square**, a park since 1859, after previous lives as a brickfields and then as a parade ground.

## The shopping area

The main Brisbane Street shopping thoroughfare centres on the **Brisbane Street Mall**, a modest affair taking up one small city block. It was completed in 1975, the first stage of the pedestrianization policy for the central city, and is pleasant enough with its trees and seating. Just off here, **Quadrant Mall** is unusually shaped, bounded by Brisbane Street and St John Street, with several lanes and an arcade feeding off it. *Gourlay's Sweet Shop* is a Launceston institution with row upon row of glass jars full of imported and local sweets – for something really local, try the leatherwood honey drops. **Yorketown Square** – designed to have a yesteryear feel – can be accessed by cobbled lanes off Cameron, George, and Brisbane streets, with the businesses lining the square mainly cafés and restaurants, most with outdoor tables. On Sundays the "village market" sells mainly crafts (9am–2pm). Nearly opposite the George Street entrance to the square is *The Old Umbrella Shop* (Mon–Fri 9am–5pm, Sat 9am–noon; ☎31 9248) at no. 60, a National Trust information centre housed in a rare example of a mid-Victorian shop, built in the 1860s and lined with Tasmanian Blackwood.

## From Civic Square to the museum

Shady, grassy **Civic Square**, closed to traffic, does convey a tidy spirit of civic mindedness. Here, **Macquarie House** (Mon–Sat 10am–4pm, Sun 2–4pm; free), a branch of the Queen Victoria Museum (see below), was built as a warehouse in 1830 for Henry Reed, a wealthy merchant. These days, its emphasis is on convict history and the history of Launceston, the entrance level featuring some portraits from the famous series of photographs taken of the convicts of Port Arthur, the penal settlement near Hobart, three years before it closed in 1874. Upstairs the focus is on architecture – worth checking out before embarking on walking tours of the city.

**Cameron Street** was one of the first streets formed after the city's settlement in 1806, and the stretch from Civic Square to Wellington Street contains an almost perfectly preserved nineteenth-century streetscape. On the corner of Cameron and Charles streets are a conglomeration of warehouses and stables built in 1840 in Regency style, a building form quite rare in Australia. The rest of the block contains examples of mainly Victorian buildings, including the typically imposing Supreme Court building and, opposite, a row of very fine Victorian redbrick terrace houses with beautiful wrought-iron work.

## The Queen Victoria Museum and Art Gallery

The **Queen Victoria Museum and Art Gallery** on Wellington Street (Mon–Sat 10am–5pm, Sun 2–5pm; free) was opened in 1891 to mark half a century of Queen Victoria's reign. Its great treasure is the Chinese joss house from Weldborough, built in the 1870s by Chinese workers introduced to the east coast tin mines to provide cheap labour.

Elsewhere, there's a history of mining in Tasmania, made more accessible by interpretive displays; and if you poke around you'll also turn up displays of stuffed animals, accounts of the geology of Launceston and the local area, a **Planetarium** (Tues–Sat at 2pm and 3pm; $3, children $2), and the "Discovery Plus" room with its microscopes and specimen trays – live, giant burrowing cockroaches from Northern Queensland, the largest in the world at eight centimetres, are kept in a viewing box. Upstairs, the **Art Gallery** has some gothic and wild Tasmanian landscapes by the nineteenth-century painter Piguenit, while the *Queen Vic Café*, downstairs, is one of the best cafés in Launceston.

## Royal Park to Penny Royal World

Behind the museum, across Bathurst Street, **Royal Park** has extensive formal parklands running down to the Tamar River; there's even a croquet lawn here, if you were in any doubt about its English character. Between Royal Park and Cataract Gorge a concentrated tourist area unfolds. **Ritchies Mill Arts Centre**, at 2 Bridge Road, was converted from a nineteenth-century flour mill and millers' cottage; situated on the Tamar River, it has two galleries, an al fresco café and some varied **artists' studios** and exhibition space.

**Penny Royal World** (daily 9am–4.30pm; closed two weeks in July; $19.50, child $9.50), opposite Ritchies Mill, has been developed on the site of an old bluestone quarry, which closed forty years ago. In 1971 a decaying ironstone watermill and farmhouse, built by settler Andrew Gatenby in 1840 at Barton near Cressy (54km from Launceston), were transported here stone by stone. Named after the Penny Royal Creek, the buildings were redeveloped: Gatenby's 1825 wooden cornmill was replicated from studying its ruins, and the original machinery, including two French Burr grindstones, are now operational. The standard entrance fee includes the *Lady Stelfox* cruise and a ten-minute ride on a restored Launceston tram, though you can buy separate tickets to the various attractions and just see the bits, if any, that interest you.

The landing stage behind the Arts Centre is where the **paddle steamer**, *Lady Stelfox*, departs for her forty-minute cruises along the Tamar and into the mouth of Cataract Gorge (daily 10.10am–3.10pm hourly; $6.50, children $3.50). The cruise gives a close-up view of the *Launceston Yacht Club*, as well as the salubrious sight of the wealthy suburb of Trevallyn, with its classic Victorian mansions strung along the hillside among leafy trees. Returning, you cruise close to the port and shipping western side of the Tamar, before briefly entering the natural beauty of Cataract Gorge (see below).

## Cataract Gorge and beyond

Few, if any, cities have such a magnificent natural feature within fifteen minutes' walk of the centre as **Cataract Gorge**. Turn left at Penny World and walk to the decorative **Kings Bridge**, a wrought-iron bridge, fabricated in Manchester and transported to Launceston in 1863, that has a span of sixty metres. Standing here, the mouth of the gorge is a beautiful sight, the cliffs rising almost vertically from the smooth water of the South Esk River as it empties itself into the Tamar. The natural spectacle is even more dramatic after dusk when this end of the gorge is floodlit.

There are two walking routes along the Gorge, both taking about twenty minutes. The **Zig Zag walk**, on the Penny Royal side of the bridge, is the more strenuous. Running steeply along the top of the gorge, it joins Kings Bridge to the **First Basin**, a large, deep canyon worn away by the river and full of water. Crossing the bridge, the more sedate **Cataract Walk** begins by the tiny toll house, with its iron-lace decoration, and leads to the gardens of the **Cliff Grounds**. As you walk along either side, particularly on weekends and during summer, you'll see people canoeing, abseiling or even jumping off the cliffs into the water. If you want to join in, between November and May, *Whitewater Experiences Tasmania* (☎34 7999) have daily half-day (8.30am & 1pm; $75) and full-day (Wed, Sat & Sun; $105) rafting trips in the gorge.

Enter from the **First Basin** end (where there's a car park; or catch bus #51 or #53) and you'll find an enormous swimming pool, built partly to discourage people from swimming in the basin itself, where some have died. Nevertheless, people do still swim in the basin, despite big signs warning them of the dangers of hypothermia; diving is not recommended as there are submerged rocks and logs.

To get across the First Basin to the Cliff Grounds, you can take the **Launceston Basin Chair Lift** (daily 9am–4.30pm; $3, child $2.50), which takes an exhilarating six minutes to cover 457 metres – it's claimed to have the longest single span (308m) of any chair lift in the world. The views are wonderful but if you're scared of heights you might find it a bit much and you should cross the First Basin via the **Basin Walk** directly under the chair lift. The other alternative, the narrow **Alexandra Suspension Bridge**, is fairly alarming, too. Called the "swinging bridge" by locals, it's even shakier when crowded with joggers after work.

The **Cliff Grounds**, on the shady northern side of the gorge, are fanciful gardens, whose ferns, native and exotic plants are arranged rather artfully around a lovely rotunda, which dates from 1896. The rotunda contains an interpretative centre with early photographs and displays covering the history and botany of the gorge, while the swish *Gorge Restaurant*, in the grounds, features fine food, Tasmanian wines and crisp white tablecloths. Less expensive Devonshire teas are served from the kiosk out the back of the restaurant, and you get an equally good view from the outside tables.

## Trevallyn Dam

It's possible to undertake longer bushwalks from Cataract Gorge Reserve, with a track going from the Alexander Suspension Bridge, following the river through unspoilt bush to the narrower **Second Basin** and the disused **Duck Reach Power Station**. The walk takes ninety minutes (return) or you can walk a little further and reach the 450-hectare **Trevallyn State Recreation Area** (daily 8am–dusk; no camping) on the South Esk River and the **Trevallyn Dam**. This is 6km west of the city centre: to reach it by road, go via the suburb of Trevallyn, following Reatta Road.

There's an **information centre** at **Aquatic Point**, where there are grassy areas, a children's playground, toilets and barbecues. The rest of the reserve is made up of open eucalypt forest, with marked bushwalks and nature trails that you'll share with horse riders. In summer, canoes and windsurfers can sometimes be rented; ask at the information office.

### Waverly Woollen Mills and Franklin House

The city's three woollen mills are all open for inspection, though easily the most interesting is the **Waverly Woollen Mills** (Mon–Fri 9am–4pm; $3), on Waverly Road, 5km west of the city centre; take bus #34 or #35 from city stop G to Waverly Road turn-off and it's a 500m walk. It's the oldest woollen mill in Australia, established in 1874, and much of the cloth is still manufactured on old-fashioned machinery.

**Franklin House**, at 413 Hobart Road (6km towards Hobart on the Midland Highway; bus #20, #22 or #25 from city stop C; daily Sept–May 9am–5pm, June–Aug 9am–4pm; $4.50), was built in 1838 for Britton Jones, a local brewer who had obviously done well. Furnished as an early Victorian home, it became a leading school for boys four years after it was built, a role it retained for half a century. Although it's been beautifully furnished and restored, the most outstanding feature of the interior is the woodwork – made entirely of unusual New South Wales cedarwood.

## Eating

**Arpar's Thai Restaurant**, corner of Charles and Paterson streets (☎31 2786). Licensed and BYO Thai establishment with a good reputation; daily 5.30pm to late.

**Calabrisella**, 56 Wellington St (☎31 1958). A real find – a crowded, nosiy, atmospheric and affordable Italian restaurant. Dinner nightly except Tues; BYO.

**Cucina Simpatica**, corner of Margaret and Frederick streets, opposite Brickfields Reserve (☎34 3177). Launceston's hip café, with a colourful Mediterranean feel, is a good place to relax with a coffee and a newspaper. The menu is distinctly Italian; nothing is over $15 and the emphasis is on fresh Tasmanian produce. Daily 9am–late; BYO.

**Gourmet on Brisbane**, 86 Brisbane St. A big, bright delicatessen doubles as a crowded café; you can sit outside on a nice day. Daily to 9pm.

**Hard Times**, 135 George St. Arty licensed café with eclectic decor and mainly nibbly dip foods such as nachos, guacomole and houmous, as well as pasta.

**Janet's**, 2 Patterson St. A tiny, homey café run by friendly women; freshly baked trays of lasagne or egg and bacon pie are displayed; sandwiches and great salads, too. Mon–Fri 8am–5pm

**Montezuma's**, 63 Brisbane St (☎31 8999). Typical Mexican; mains from $13, but tacos and nachos are filling enough. Good-value margaritas too. Daily from 6pm, plus Wed–Fri noon–2pm.

**O'Keefe's Hotel**, 124 George St (☎31 4015). People crowd into the lounge bar for pub meals they claim are the best in Tasmania, with an award-winning chef. Vegetarians can usually opt for pasta.

**Pepper Berry**, George St. Café serving stunning Australian food with creations like wallaby pie and pumpkin and macadamia nut flan to slaver over; affordable prices between $2 and $10. Mon & Tues 10.30am–6pm, Wed–Sat 10.30am–10pm.

**Ripples Café**, Ritchies Mill Arts Centre, Paterson St. Very popular riverside café with outdoor tables under umbrellas; the locals hang out here with newspapers on Saturdays, sipping the excellent coffee with *biscotti* (Italian biscuits).

**Satay House**, Innocent St, Kingscourt Shopping Centre, behind *Roelf Voss Supermarket*, Kings Meadows (☎44 5955). You'll have to venture into suburban Launceston for this authentic Indonesian restaurant, but it's worth it. Family-run, the chef uses her grandmother's recipes. Lunch Thurs & Fri, dinner Mon–Sat; BYO.

**Shrimps**, corner of George St and Patterson St (☎34 0584). A Launceston institution, with the best seafood in town. Formal but not stuffy, and an imaginative menu. Lunch Mon–Fri, dinner Mon–Sat.

**Tairyo Japanese Restaurant**, 25 Yorketown Square (☎34 2620). The special discount lunch of ramen, sushi or tempura, served with soup and rice, make this a popular daytime spot. Prices go up in the evening. Lunch Tues–Fri, dinner Mon–Sat; BYO.

## Entertainment and nightlife

The *Examiner*, based in Launceston, is the newspaper for the north of Tasmania – Thursday's edition contains an entertainment section. However, there's never very much going on in this quiet city and no particularly lively area. The **Princess Theatre** has performances by the *Tasmanian Symphony Orchestra* every month, while the **Silverdome**, out of town on the Bass Highway at Prospect, holds big entertainment events, exhibitions and sports events. Book through *Centretainment*, 68 Charles St (☎34 3033). The only **cinema**, the *Village 4*, 163 Brisbane Street (☎31 5066), has four screens showing mainstream films.

## Pubs, clubs and venues

**The Royal Hotel**, 90 George St (☎31 2526). A lively pub, with music video and pool table.

**Launceston Hotel**, 107 Brisbane St (☎31 9211). The "Lonnie", to locals, has several bars that turn day into night, as well as a disco (Wed–Sat) and local cover bands at weekends. Closed Sun.

**Batman Fawkner Inn**, 35–39 Cameron St (☎31 7222). Stylish historic hotel with several bars. On Fri & Sat nights the *Wall Street* bar has a disco.

**The Star Bar**, 113 Charles St (☎31 9659). Launceston's only boutique brewery is surprisingly sophisticated with its slick modern decor and brasserie-style Mediterranean food and coffee.

**Country Club Casino**, Country Club Ave, Prospect Vale; 9km out of town off the Bass Highway (☎35 5777). From the outside it looks as exclusive as its name suggests, but it's not really – just don't wear sandshoes or T-shirts after 8pm. Live entertainment nightly in the *Lanai Bar*. Sunday buffet lunch in *The Grill Room* (around $25 a head) is a bit of a Launceston tradition, with stacks of seafood, prawns and oysters. Open Mon–Thurs & Sun noon–3am, Fri & Sat until 4am. Catch bus #61; if you want to stay late you'll have to catch a taxi back ($10–12).

# Listings

**Banks** *Commonwealth Bank*, 97 Brisbane St (☎37 4444).

**Bike rental** *Rent-A-Cycle Tasmania*, from *Launceston City Youth Hostel* (☎003/44 9799). All bikes are fully equipped with rear panniers, puncture kit, tools,and helmets. From $65 a week; mountain bikes start at $90.

**Camping equipment** The best place to rent camping gear is at *Launceston City Youth Hostel* (☎003/44 9779), which you'll find has everything from tents to woollen trousers. *Allgoods* come a close second at their *Tent City* store, 60 Elizabeth St (☎31 3644); their main store at 71–79 York St, has a comprehensive range of camping gear from the bottom of the market up. *Paddy Pallin*, 110 George St (☎31 4240), focusses on the top end of the market and also sells fuel, a wide range of freeze-dried foods, guide books and maps.

**Car rental** *Apple Car Rentals*, 192 Wellington St (☎43 3780); *Advance Car Rentals*, 42 Thistle St (☎44 2164); *Auto Rent Hertz*, 58 Paterson St (☎35 1111).

**Hospital** *Launceston General*, Charles St (☎32 7111).

**Left luggage** *Wilderness Transport*, 101 George St. For $5, you can leave baggage for as long as you like (within reason). Most hostels will also mind baggage for you.

**Parking** Launceston has metered street parking and its car parks are dirt cheap. *Kings Quadrant Car Park* (☎34 2456) – entrance on York St near George St corner – has a weekly rate of $12; if you want to go on the Overland Track (a one-way walk), you can safely leave it here. Normal rates are $2.20 per day (Open Mon–Fri 7.30am–6.30pm, Sat 7.45am–1pm).

**Pharmacy** *Centre Pharmacy*, 84 Brisbane St (☎31 777); daily 8.30am–10pm.

**Tour operators** *Tasmanian Wilderness Transport*, 101 George St (☎34 4442), has a summer programme of day tours (1 Dec–20 April) in small minibuses to Cradle Mountain ($40), Asbestos Range National Park ($40 includes barbecue), Mole Creek caves and wildlife park ($50), Evandale Market ($15) and the Tamar Valley ($35). *Launceston Sightseeing* (☎31 3233; YHA discounts) offer more conventional trips in large coaches to Cradle Mountain ($39), Mole Creek ($40), Tamar Valley ($33) and probably the best, to the Bridestow Estate Lavender Farm when it's flowering in late December to mid-Jan ($24).

# Around Launceston

Before launching yourself into the beauty of the Tamar Valley, there are several local destinations worth visiting **around Launceston**, most notably the historic town of **Evandale**, just 20km from the city. If you're here in winter, you might consider joining the ski crowd who descend upon the **Ben Lomond National Park**, southeast of Launceston; out of season, this is fine bushwalking country.

## Entally House

**Entally House** (daily 10am–12.30pm & 1–5pm; $4.50) at **HADSPEN**, 18km west of Launceston on the Bass Highway, is the oldest National Trust-owned property in Australia. A large homestead, built in 1819 by Thomas Haycock Reibey, it would have remained a classic, colonial Georgian cottage if not for a later second-storey addition, reached up rickety stairs. The extensive grounds, running down to the river, are a perfect picnic setting and you don't have to pay to wander in them.

## Evandale

Twenty kilometres southeast of Launceston, just beyond Launceston Airport, is **EVANDALE**, a classified historic town whose good food and weekly market are real draws. At the **Evandale Tourism and History Centre** (daily 11am–3pm; ☎003/91 8128) pick up a "Heritage Walk" brochure ($1); if it's closed, there's a map pointing out historic features opposite the *Ingleside Bakery*, while many of the old buildings have descriptive plaques. **Solomon House** (1836) is a whitewashed two-storey brick building with a green tin roof, which operated as *Clarendon Stores* for about 130 years. The bakehouse at the rear once supplied early settlers, though now it's an excellent tearoom. The **Clarendon Arms Hotel**, 11 Russell Street, was built in 1847 on the site of the former convict station, its interior walls covered in murals depicting the early history of Tasmania. There's a portrait of the infamous bushranger Mathew Brady and his gang, and portraits of Aborigines King Billy and Truganini, among others.

Further down Russell Street, the **Evandale Market** (Sun 10am–2pm) attracts big crowds to its 140 summer stalls. A lot of local vegetable-growers – particularly organic producers – bring their produce straight here; you'll also find a flea market, and some pretty exotic food stalls for Tasmania. Although there's no public transport here, *Wilderness Transport* (☎003/34 4442)can take you on a relaxed tour to the markets for $15 (departing Launceston Sun 9.30am); a visit to nearby historic **Clarendon House** is extra and optional.

## Skiing in Ben Lomond National Park

The high plateau of the **Ben Lomond Range**, over 1300 metres high and 84 square kilometres in area, lies entirely within **BEN LOMOND NATIONAL PARK**, 50km southeast of Launceston. A small ski village sits below **Legges Tor**, the second highest point in Tasmania (1572m); the bumpy outline of the range's steep cliffs dominate the horizon and can be reached in an hour from Launceston (or just half an hour from Evandale). The ski season runs from mid-July to the end of September, and although **accommodation** is limited, the region's accessibility means there's no real need to stay. If you're determined, the pricey *Ben Lomond Creek Inn* (☎003/72 2444; ⑦, including breakfast and dinner) is usually booked out at weekends. Meals are available here, or there's fast food from the ski resort kiosk.

*Alpine Enterprises* (☎003/72 2499) runs the **ski lifts**; an all-day pass costs $25. They offer some ski rental on the mountain but a better range is available at *Launceston Sports Central*, at 88a George Street (☎003/31 4777), which can also advise on ski packages that include transport, gear rental and lift pass for $37. Finally, *YD Watersports* at 67 Elizabeth Street, Launceston (☎003/31 6791) rents out snowboards at $25 a day.

If you're driving, be warned that the final 20km to the ski village is unsealed and the last leg, **Jacobs Ladder**, is very steep, with several hairpin bends, sheer drops and no safety barriers. You must carry wheel chains, which can be rented from the snowline. If you wish to skip the hair-raising final section, there's a **shuttle bus** from the bottom of Jacobs Ladder offered by *Wilderness Transport* (☎003/34 4442), who also have a hassle-free transport service from Launceston, for $25 return.

Outside of the ski season, all services cease and the businesses close down, but **bushwalkers** are lured by the magnificent scenery and the alpine vegetation. There's a twelve-and-a-half-kilometre track from Carr Villa on the slopes of Ben Lomond to Legges Tor. Bush **camping** is permitted anywhere in the national park but Carr Villa is an informal camping area with pit toilet. For more information, contact the ranger (☎003/90 6279).

# The Tamar Valley

To the north of Launceston is the beautiful **Tamar Valley**, where – for 64km – the tidal waters wind through orchards, vineyards, forested hills and grazing land. Only the Batman Bridge, near Deviot, and the APPM Wood Mill and Bell Bay Power Station near George Town at the river's mouth, spoil the idyllic pre-industrial scenery.

## West of the Tamar

The West Tamar Highway follows the line of the Tamar River from Launceston to Beauty Point, passing through **Grindlewald Swiss Village**, really a suburb of Launceston. Further along, **Brady's Lookout State Reserve** provides magnificent views of the Tamar Valley and Ben Lomond; you can see as far as Low Head, 34km away. As an alternative to heading straight along the highway, you can detour for a stretch through **ROSEVEARS**, on a picturesque sweep of road along the river banks, popular with cyclists. Along the way, stop at **St Matthias Vineyard** for some wine tasting, or a coffee, some Tasmanian cheeses and great views.There's also the **Waterbird Haven Trust** (daily 10am–4pm; $4), stretching for half a kilometre along the waterfront, and drinks available at the **Rosevears Tavern** – built by William Rosevears in 1831. A few kilometres west of Rosevears, reached by turning west off the highway at Legana, is **Notley Gorge State Reserve**, while **BEACONSFIELD**, back on the highway, was at the centre of Tasmania's former **gold-mining** area – the mining ruins are still visible.

## South of the Tamar: George Town and Low Head

Leaving Launceston on the southern banks of the Tamar, it's only a few minutes before you're zooming through scenic countryside, with cows feeding in paddocks at the base of the bush-covered hills at Dillston. After Hillwood, you're headed for the port of **GEORGE TOWN**, the third-oldest town in Australia, where Colonel Paterson landed in 1804 to begin settlement of northern Tasmania. However, it isn't particularly old or interesting, with only one colonial building to look at – **The Grove**, at 25 Cimitiere Street (daily 10am–5pm; $5), an elegant stone Georgian mansion. However, more interesting is **LOW HEAD**, 5km north, with 24 National Trust-listed buildings, whitewashed cottages and rambling houses, all sitting amid extensive parkland. The original convict-built **Pilot Station** now houses the **Old Watch House Museum** (daily 8am–5pm; free), with maritime memorabilia.

If you need a **place to stay**, there are several choices. *Gray's Hotel*, 77 Macquarie Street (☎003/82 2655; ⑤), the oldest pub in George Town, was built in 1835 but has few discernible traces of those times in its motel rooms. *Pier Hotel*, 5 Elizabeth Street (☎003/82 1300; ⑥), is a pretty wooden hotel on the waterfront with rooms in the old part upstairs, modern motel rooms on the waterfront, and self-catering units. The food here is very good, with the extensive menu including pasta and Asian curries. Opposite, at 4 Elizabeth Street, is the *George Town YHA* (non-resident managers, call ☎003/82 1399 9am–5pm; dorms ①, rooms ④). *Belfont Cottages*, 178 Low Head Road (☎003/82 1841; ⑥, with breakfast provisions supplied), is next door to a small, white tower with a red light. *Low Head Caravan Park*, Low Head Road (☎003/82 1573) has on-site vans (③) and cabins (④). An alternative to eating at the pubs is the *George Town Deli*, 65 Macquarie Street (closed Sat & Sun), which sells healthfoods and deli items and serves light lunches.

### Around George Town: some vineyards

You could spend a pleasant day out from George Town exploring the **vineyards** around the **Pipers River area**, which produce distinctly flavoured, crisp fresh wines. At **Rochecombe Vineyard** at Pipers River, 2km off the B82 on a sealed road (turn off just before the filling station at Pipers River), a Swiss husband-and-wife team make European-style wines – the climate here is supposedly similiar to the Loire Valley. There are tastings and a restaurant in the original weatherboard farmhouse (tastings daily 10am–3pm, restaurant 9am–5pm). The friendly small-scale **Delamere Winery**, on Bridport Road, Pipers Brook (daily 10am–5pm; ☎003/82 7190), also has tastings, while **Pipers Brook Vineyard** (Mon–Fri 10am–4pm, Sat & Sun 11am–5pm), 2km off the B82, about 10km from Pipers River, is a well-established winery in a modern complex, with self-guided tours.

# The Midlands Highway

The **Midlands Highway** is a fast three-hour route between Hobart and Launceston and more or less follows the old coaching road, although detours are necessary if you're to visit some of the historical towns en route. *Redline* has several daily **bus** services between Hobart and Launceston, stopping at the major midlands towns. *Hobart Coaches* service is express and doesn't stop.

## Campbelltown and Ross

Beyond **CAMBELLTOWN** – which has a suitably Scottish dourness about it – sheep grazing land, with hills on either horizon, continues until the turn-off to **ROSS**, 2km east of the highway. Another town settled by Scots, this has a very secluded, rural feel. Church Street, lined with deciduous trees, ends quite abruptly and overlooks miles of fields, farmland and hills. Walking through the church grounds, there are views of the Macquarie River, spanned by the sandstone **Ross Bridge**, designed by John Lee Archer and built by convicts in 1836; the intricate stone carvings on its three arches earned the convict stonemason a free pardon. There's a fairly melancholy walk in the other direction from the church down to the original Ross burial ground, past the site of the **Female Prison**, where female convicts were held before being sent to properties as assigned servants. You can **stay** in several of the old cottages dotted about town; one couple look after three cottages (☎003/81 5354; ⑤, including breakfast provisions). The old sandstone *Man O'Ross Hotel* on Church Street (☎003/81 5240; ④) has several intimate rooms to eat or drink in, and basic accommodation upstairs.

## Oatlands

Back on the Midlands Highway, it's 88km to **OATLANDS**, which sports Australia's greatest concentration of colonial Georgian buildings: 140 in two square kilometres, most built by convicts. Many are now occupied by antique and bric-a-brac shops, tearooms and colonial accommodation places, and only the **Carrington Mill** and outbuildings are open to the public (daily 9am–5pm; admission by donation). The partly restored windmill was built in 1837 and operated until 1892; today, from the top, you can get fine views of the town and the surrounding countryside. Probably the best way to see the town is to go on one of Peter Fielding's guided **heritage walks** (☎002/54 1135; or ask at 7 Gay St); he has the keys to several of the other buildings, including the Old Gaol and the courthouse; there's a spooky evening **convict tour** (nightly 5pm; $6) and the later **ghost tour** (nightly 8pm; $8).

For **food**, *Oatlands Roadhouse*, on High Street (daily 7.30am–9pm), sells tasty Lebanese dishes; the *Crinoline Kitchen*, at the centre of High Street, has original 1850s' features and light lunches; dinner here is more upmarket. A couple of good **places to stay** are *Oatlands Lodge*, 92 High Street (☎002/54 1444; ⑥), a colonial-style B&B right in the centre of town, and, further out, the tiny *Oatlands Youth Hostel*, 9 Wellington Street (☎002/54 1320; ①), a popular overnight stop for cyclists zooming through the midlands.

# The Western Tiers and Central Plateau

**Deloraine** is a delightful town on the **Meander River**, nestled in a valley of rich farmland dominated by **Quamby Bluff** (1256m) and the **Western Tiers**, where the Central Plateau drops abruptly to the surrounding plains. On the Bass Highway, it's equidistant from Devonport and Launceston (45km). From Deloraine, the **Lake Highway** begins, rising up over the Western Tiers to the Central Plateau, with its thousands of lakes. To the west of Deloraine, heading for Cradle Mountain, are the extensive cave systems around **Mole Creek**, while **Walls of Jerusalem National Park** is accessed from **Western Creek**, 32km southwest of Deloraine.

## Deloraine and Around

**DELORAINE** is a hilly town, often shrouded in mist, even on summer mornings, and sliced in two by the bubbling **Meander River**. It's a classified historic town, the area settled by Europeans in the 1830s, although the town didn't begin to develop until after 1846. **West Parade** follows the river, facing the park; at no. 17, **Bonney's Inn** is the town's oldest remaining building (now a restaurant), dating from 1830 and of solid Georgian design, with an elegant portico. At the next block, Westbury Place rises up steeply from West Parade; if you climb the hill you'll reach **St Marks Church** (1860) with its tall spire; continuing to the top of the hill, there's a scenic lookout which gives a panoramic view over the town and the Western Tiers to the south.

With such close accessibility to prime **bushwalking** areas, Deloraine is becoming a walkers' base. Popular walking tracks are to **Quamby Bluff**, renowned for its myrtle rainforest; the Liffey River track (4–5hr) to **Liffey Falls**; and to **Meander Falls**, about 25km south of Deloraine. At **MOLE CREEK**, 24km to the southwest, you can inspect two rather spectacular underground caves: **Marakoopa Cave** with its huge caverns, streams, pools and glow-worms, and the smaller but more richly decorative **King Solomons Cave** with its stalactites and stalagmites (Marakoopa daily 10am, 11.15am, 1pm, 2.30pm & 4pm, 50–80min; Solomons 10.30am, 11.30am, 12.30pm, 2pm, 3pm & 4pm, 40–60min; $8 single cave, $12 for both). Nearby, the **Mole Creek Wildlife Park** (daily 9am–5pm; $7.50, child $3.50) is Tasmania's best such park. Informed park keepers will explain things and enlighten visitors. There are plentiful animals, including Tasmanian Devils, most of which have been rescued.

In Deloraine itself there's a **Visitor Information Centre** in town at 29 West Church Street (Mon–Fri 8am–6pm, Sat 9am–noon; *Redline* tickets sold; ☎003/62 2046), with maps, walking times and walk conditions. Several **operators** also lead outdoor activities in the area, including the *Cadman and Norwood Environmental Consultancy* (day walks $50–85; ☎003/69 5150), based in nearby Meander, whose bushwalks are guided by field naturalists with botany or ecology qualifications. *Adventuremania* (☎003/31

8102) features abseiling, rock-climbing, canoeing, caving and bushwalking activites in the area, including a three-day bushwalk in the Western Tiers. *Central Highlands Trail Rides* (☎003/69 5298) have three-hour rides around Quamby Bluff ($45) or a six-hour ride to Jackys Marsh, with its tall eucalypt forests ($65 includes lunch); overnight camping trips to the top of the plateau can also be arranged. *Bonney's Farm* (☎003/62 2122) offer tailor-made "soft" tours to areas around Deloraine like Mole Creek Caves and Liffey Falls ($20 half-day, $40 day) and to Cradle Mountain (day-tour $45). Finally, *Wild Caves Tours* (Oct–April only; ☎003/67 8142), based at nearby **Mole Creek**, offers $50 half-day, $100 full-day tours of the Mole Creek caves, underground streams and subterranean systems.

## Practicalities

A couple of **places to stay** also focus on outdoor activities. The best is the wonderful timber *Highview Lodge YHA Hostel*, 8 Blake Street (☎003/62 2996; ①), set on a hill with unparalleled views of the mountains from its patio; well-run and very clean, with bikes for rent. *Bonney's Farm*, off Weetah Road, 4km northwest of Deloraine (☎003/62 2122; ⑤), has a guesthouse and self-contained two- or three-bed units, as well as tours around the area (see above). In the centre of town, *Bonney's Inn*, 17 West Parade (☎003/62 2974; B&B ⑥), has very spacious apartments; *Kev's Kumphy Korner Backpackers*, 24 Bass Highway (☎003/62 3408; ①), is okay but lacks atmosphere; while the *Bush Inn*, 7 Bass Highway (☎003/622 365; ②), is comfortable and inexpensive. You can **camp** at the *Apex Caravan Park*, 51 West Parade (☎003/622 345; on-site vans ②).

Deloraine's developing into a bit of a café town and there are plenty of great **places to eat**, several on the main street, Emu Bay Road. *Reuben's*, 21 Emu Bay Road, has a casual atmosphere, with newspapers, espresso, vegetarian options and affordable lunch and dinner. *Wild Things Café*, 55 Emu Bay Road, is a colourful place with good-value food. For economical pub meals, the pleasant old *Bush Inn* is best – you can play pool here and see bands at the weekends.

The three **bus** companies all stop regularly at Deloraine: *Redline* on its Launceston to Burnie service (3–5 daily), stopping outside the Visitor Information Centre; *Hobart Coaches* on its Hobart to Burnie run (2–5 daily), stopping outside *Sams Supermarket*; and *Wilderness Transport* en route to Lake St Clair from Launceston and Devonport (summer 1 daily, winter Wed only), and to Cradle Mountain from the same (summer 1 daily, winter 4 daily), stopping outside *Sullivans Restaurant*. *Wilderness Transport* also runs to the start of the walk to the Walls of Jerusalem (see below) from Launceston, via Deloraine, Mole Creek and King Solomons Cave (Tues & Fri in summer).

# Walls of Jerusalem National Park

The **WALLS OF JERUSALEM NATIONAL PARK** is on the western side of the Central Plateau, a series of five mountain peaks which enclose a central basin, an isolated area noted for its lakes, pencil pines, and the biblical names of its various features. The best time to visit is late spring or early summer; people have died here of exposure, so make sure you're well prepared. You'll need a National Park Map ($8 from *Tasmaps*), with walking notes on the reverse.

The Walls of Jerusalem is the only national park you can't drive to, so the walk begins even before you enter. From King Solomons Cave, head south, following the Mersey River and the unsealed road east of Lake Rowallan; the car park is at Howells Bluff. It's a wilderness walk into the park, which is isolated and without a ranger (although rangers do patrol), nor even the most basic facilities. However, the track is well kept with boardwalks now over sensitive boggy areas, and there's plenty of clean water from streams and lakes to drink. If you just want to walk into the park to the central basin (through **Herods Gate**, with views of Barn Bluff and Cradle Mountain to the northwest), camp and walk back, it's a 14-kilometre-return hike, which takes about five to seven hours each way at a steady pace over two days. There are numerous walks to the various peaks and lakes – from **Damascus Gate** you get stunning views of Cradle Mountain–Lake St Clair National Park immediately west – and a keen and experienced, well-equipped and preferably accompanied walker could make a few days of it. *Wilderness Transport* offer transport to the start of the walk from Launceston (1 Dec– 20 April Tues & Fri).

## The Central Plateau

At its northern and eastern edges, the **Central Plateau** is rimmed by the long crest of the Great Western Tiers (1440m). At over a thousand metres above sea level, in winter the plateau is subject to snow, sleet and frost. The **Great Lake** lies on the plateau about 8km from the escarpment, and only 40km from Deloraine, along the mostly unsealed Lake Highway which continues to **BOTHWELL**, the plateau's only town, ending at Melton Mowbray. At **LIAWENEE**, on the Lake Highway on the edge of the Great Lake, there's a **tourist office** for the area. The major lakes can be accessed from roads leading off the Lake Highway. To the west, between Cradle Mountain–Lake St Clair National Park and below the Walls of Jerusalem National Park, is the inaccessible "Land of Three Thousand Lakes".

The Central Plateau has few inhabitants – the permanent population is only around 780 – but it's full of **fishing shacks**, and on a fine weekend the population sometimes swells to 25,000. It's also the stronghold of the **Hydro Electricity Commission** (HEC): the countless high-altitude lakes are used as water storage for the generation of electricity. HEC villages, set up for hydroelectricity workers, come and go on the plateau, and once abandoned they're often transformed into lodge-style acommodation, like *Bronte Park Highland Village* (☎002/89 1126; hostel ①, lodge & cabins ⑤), on the bone-shattering Marlborough Highway (B11), which runs southwest off the Lake Highway as it curves around the bottom of the lake to **MIENA**. *Bronte Park* is ideally situated for **Lake St Clair** (25km), and **Lake Big Jim**, popular for trout fishing. There's every type of **accommodation** available in the village, from self-contained cottages and the chalet, with its cosy bar and dining room, to a hostel and campsite. Call in advance, and they'll meet the *Redline* Hobart to Strahan bus that passes the turn-off on the Lyell Highway; failing that, *Wilderness Transport* comes this way between Lake St Clair and Launceston (summer 1 daily, winter Wed only) – a route which also passes the Great Lake.

# THE WEST

The western half of Tasmania is, except for the rich beef, dairy and vegetable land along the northwest coast, an untamed area. The wild **west coast**, densely forested and battered by the rough southern ocean and the "Roaring Forties", its shores strewn with huge dead trees washed down from the southwest's many rivers, would probably still be uninhabited if it weren't for its **logging** and **mining** industries. This is pro-logging, pro-damming country, with the densely populated (by Tasmanian standards) northwest coast skimmed by the **Bass Highway**, passing through two unattractive and industrial cities, **Devonport** and **Burnie**. The **Rocky Cape National Park** and the historic town of **Stanley** (originally built by the *Van Diemen's Land Company – VDL –* which still owns the northwest corner of the state) yield the most interest.

From here, the highway heads inland to **Smithton**, the beginning of a thickly forested region and a logging heartland. The Bass Highway ends at the tiny settlement of **Marrawah**, on the west coast (popular with surfers), and an unsealed road extends to sleepy **Arthur River**: from here, the west coast stretches south, uninhabited and virtually inaccessible for its entirety, except for the town of **Strahan**, on the vast **Macquarie Harbour**. To reach Strahan, you have to head back along the northwest coast to Somerset, from where the Lyell Highway (A10) heads south through a copper- and lead-mining backwater. **Queenstown**, on the way, has been subject to an ecological disaster; its surrounding rainforest has been destroyed, and in its place are bare and chalky hills.

Strahan sits on the edge of the **southwest wilderness**, the wettest part of Australia after the tropical lowlands of north Queensland, with rugged coastlines, wild rivers, open plains, thick rainforest and spectacular peaks. It's mostly inaccessible, except to very experienced and well prepared bushwalkers, but **cruises** leave from Strahan up the **Gordon River**, offering a glimpse of the magnificent scenery. A plan to dam the **Gordon River** below the point where it joins the **Franklin River** put Strahan at the centre of a struggle between environmentalists and the state government. Eventually the federal government stepped in, and, following a landmark High Court ruling in 1983, the whole of the southwest – including the **South West National Park**, the **Franklin Lower Gordon Wild Rivers National Park**, and the adjoining heavily glaciated **Cradle Mountain–Lake St Clair National Park** – became a vast, protected **World Heritage Area**, taking up twenty percent of the state. From Queenstown, en route to Hobart, the **Lyell Highway** provides limited access to the mainly inaccessible Franklin Lower Gordon park, and to Lake St Clair at **Derwent Bridge**.

# The northwest coast

A succession of the island's larger towns dot Tasmania's conservative, agricultural **northwest coast**, including the cities of **Devonport** and **Burnie**, and the historical smaller community of **Stanley**, on a peninsula jutting into the Bass Strait. The **Bass Highway** which connects them becomes spectacularly beautiful beyond Wynyard, passing Table Cape, Boat Harbour Beach, and Rocky Cape National Park, though it skirts the very northwestern tip (privately owned by the *Van Diemen's Land Company*). At its end is **Marrawah**, from where you can head to Arthur River for a cruise. *Redline* has daily services (except Sun) from Launceston, stopping at all points along to the Bass Highway to Smithton, but there is no public transport to Marrawah or Arthur River.

## Devonport and around

The industrial port of **DEVONPORT**, which in 1959 replaced Launceston as the terminal of the **Bass Strait Ferry**, is not an inspiring first point of contact with Tasmania. As the ship makes its slow progress up the Mersey River, you might almost be in a 1950s' English seaport, but for the tin-roofed weatherboard bungalows and the brittle quality of the light. As a jumping-off point for Cradle Mountain, the Overland Track, and the rugged west coast, Devonport has developed a significant tourism infrastructure, with

---

### TELEPHONE NUMBERS

In February 1997, all **phone numbers** in the ☎004 code region (which covers most of the numbers from here to the end of this chapter) will have the prefix 64 added, to coincide with the implementation of the new **area code** of ☎03 across the whole of Tasmania and southeastern Australia.

So, for example, what was ☎004/xx xxxx will become ☎03/64xx xxxx.

car rental, bus companies, camping stores and backpacking information, but it's hardly a destination in itself. Most visitors simply see it through a bus window en route to Hobart or Launceston, but there's something quite endearing about its insistence on still moving to its own slow rhythm, with shops, offices and restaurants adhering to crazily restricted opening hours.

## Arrival and information

Up to 900 people arrive in Devonport at 8.30am each Tuesday, Thursday and Saturday morning on the *Spirit of Tasmania* **Bass Strait ferry** (☎13 2010), which docks at East Devonport just across the River Mersey from the city centre. Resisting the free coffee and pamphlets at the "Showcase of Devonport" here, most passengers head straight for the waiting **buses**: *Hobart Coaches* leave the terminal at 8.50am, *Redline* at 8.45am, both bound for Launceston and Hobart.

If you decide to stay, a short walk north, the ferry *Torquay* crosses the river to the centre (every 15–30min Mon–Thurs 7.30am–6.30pm, Fri 7.30am–9.30pm, Sat 8.30am–5pm, no service Sun; $1.20, bicycles 40¢; ☎004/24 0911).

*Airlines of Tasmania, Kendell, Phillip Island Air* and *Aus Air* fly into **Devonport Airport**, 10km east of the city along the Bass Highway. Taxis into town cost about $10, and the *Wilderness Transport* shuttle bus connects with all flights.

**Car rental** firms located at the airport and ferry terminal include *Hertz* (☎004/24 1013), *Avis Tasmania* (☎004/27 9797), *Budget* (☎004/24 7088) and *Thrifty* (☎004/27 9119); among cheaper alternatives are *Lo-Cost Auto Rent*, 23 King Street (☎004/24 4692) and *Range Rent-A-Bug*, Murray Street, East Devonport (☎004/27 9304). You can rent **bicycles** from *Hire A Bicycle*, 5 Raymond Avenue (☎004/24 3889).

Tourism **information** officials are on hand at the ferry terminal until 9.30am on arrival days; *Tasmanian Travel* also has an office at 5 Best Street (Mon–Fri 8.30am–5pm, Sat 9am–noon; ☎004/21 6222). Staff here can book accommodation, tours and travel, but for anything more unusual, head for the *Backpackers Barn*, 10–12 Edward Street (daily 9am–6pm; ☎004/24 3628), which specializes in planning, equipment and transport for bushwalkers and backpackers. The best place to **rent equipment** is *Allgoods*, 10 Rooke Street (☎004/24 7099).

## Accommodation

Devonport has plenty of **accommodation**, mainly intended for ferry passengers. Hotels, motels and B&Bs take advantage of the summer trade to raise their prices.

**Abel Tasman Caravan Park**, 6 Wright St, East Devonport (☎004/27 8794). A short walk from the ferry terminal on East Devonport Beach. On-site vans ③, cabins ④.

**Alexander Hotel**, 78 Formby Rd (☎004/24 2252). Neat but faded basic rooms. Light breakfast in the dining room. ④.

**Gateway Motor Inn**, 16 Fenton St (☎004/24 4922). Although this ugly brick 1970s building is Devonport's highest standard hotel, many unrenovated rooms remain stuck in that era. ⑦.

**Macwright House YHA**, 115 Middle Rd (☎004/24 5696). Over half an hour's walk from the town, but there's a $3 shuttle service to and from the ferry terminal. A large and friendly hostel, with a heated pool and a big garden, plus camping equipment for rent, and tours to Cradle Mountain. ①.

**Radclyffe Hall**, 139 Tarleton St, East Devonport (☎004/27 9219). Women-only accommodation in a lovely Victorian-era home from home, a short walk from the ferry terminal. Reasonably priced breakfasts and dinners are available; other useful amenities include cycle rental and a good notice-board. Radclyffe Suite ④, dorms ①.

**Tasman House Backpackers**, 169 Steele St (☎004/23 2335). Highly recommended hostel five minutes' walk from the town centre. The people who run it are well-travelled musicians who encourage participation in regular barbecue nights ($5), and once a month everyone in the hostel is encouraged to cook a dish from their home country for sharing. The managers also operate licensed tours, and bargain $5 breakfasts are available. Rooms ②–③, dorms ①.

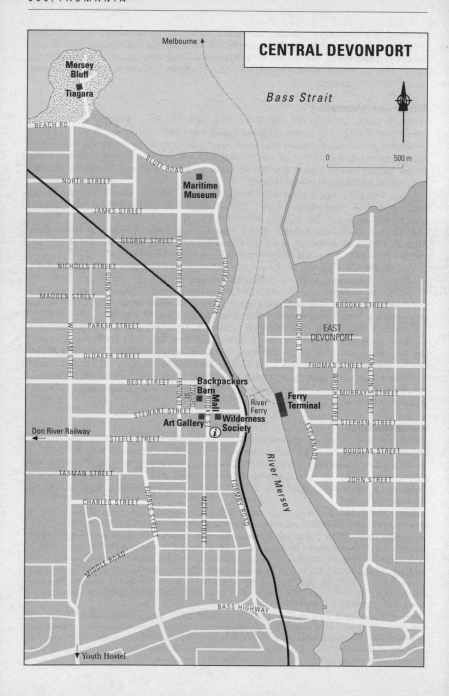

Melbourne ▲

**CENTRAL DEVONPORT**

**Mersey Bluff**
■ **Tiagara**

*Bass Strait*

N

BEACH RD.

BLUFF ROAD

0                    500 m

NORTH STREET

■ **Maritime Museum**

JAMES STREET

GEORGE STREET

FENTON STREET

NICHOLLS STREET

VICTORIA PARADE

GUNN STREET

MADDEN STREET

BROOKE STREET

PARKER STREET

WILLIAM STREET

CHURCH ST.

EAST DEVONPORT

OLDAKER STREET

THOMAS STREET

TARLETON STREET

WRIGHT STREET

BEST STREET

FENTON ST.

EDWARD ST

**Backpackers Barn**
Mall

MURRAY STREET

STEPHEN STREET

**Ferry Terminal**

STEWART STREET

BROOKE ST.

River Ferry

Don River Railway

**Art Gallery**
**Wilderness Society**
(i)

ESPLANADE

DOUGLAS STREET

STEELE STREET

JOHN STREET

TASMAN STREET

*River Mersey*

CHARLES STREET

FORBES STREET

MCFIE STREET

FORMBY ROAD

MIDDLE ROAD

BASS HIGHWAY

▼ Youth Hostel

**Tramahere Hotel**, 34 Best St (☎004/24 1898). Central backpacker accommodation, with minimal facilities but decent rooms well away from the noise of the bar. Rooms ③, dorms ①.

**Wenvoe Heights**, 44 McFie St (☎004/24 1719). Rambling two-storey turn-of-the-century B&B with sea views from a wrought-iron balcony. ⑤.

## The City

**Central Devonport** is bounded by the Mersey River; Formby Road runs alongside it, while Stewart Street, at right angles to it (with the post office at the corner), is dominated by the bulk of the *Abel Tasman* when it's in port. The *Wilderness Shop* at no. 6 (☎004/24 7393) serves as an excellent source of alternative tourist information, as well as selling posters, cards, T-shirts, and books. The **Devonport Art Gallery**, in a converted church at no. 45, holds changing exhibitions by artists and has a small permanent collection of Tasmanian ceramics (Mon–Fri 10am–5pm, Sun 2–5pm; free).

Away from the city centre, the National Trust-run former home of Sir Joseph Lyons, the only person ever to be Premier of Tasmania (1923–1929) and Prime Minister of Australia (1932–1939), can be seen at **Home Hill**, 77 Middle Road (Tues–Thurs, Sat & Sun 2–4pm; $4.50). His widow, Dame Enid Lyons, became a federal minister after his death. At the river mouth, the model ships in the **Tasmanian Maritime and Folk Museum**, 47 Victoria Parade (Sun–Mon & Wed–Fri, Oct–March 1–4.30pm, April–Sept 2–4pm; $1), range from sailing vessels to modern passenger ferries.

The **Tiagarra Tasmanian Aboriginal Culture and Art Centre**, at Mersey Bluff north of the town centre, preserves around 270 Aboriginal rock engravings (daily 9am–4.30pm; closed July; $2.50; ☎004/24 8250). Only eleven of the coiled lines and concentric circles, motifs of snakes, abalone shells, emus, crayfish and other creatures, are exposed to view, but a **Display Centre** provides generalized (and rather rushed) background information on how the Tasmanian Aborigines lived.

Although commercial passenger services on Tasmania ended in the 1970s, the **Don River Railway** runs excursions along the Don River to the popular surfing spot of **Coles Beach** from Don Recreation Ground (hourly 11am–4pm; 30min; $3 one way, $6 return; ☎004/24 6335). Steam locomotives pull the carriages on Sundays, public holidays, and from Christmas to the end of January; otherwise it's diesel power.

## Asbestos Range National Park

In **Asbestos Range National Park**, 30 km east of Devonport, re-introduced **Forrester kangaroos** come down to feed at **Bakers Beach** at dusk. The park is renowned for its occasional spectacular storms accompanied by strong winds powering along the beach. There's a self-registering fee-paying **campsite** (ranger ☎004/28 6277), and the beach is good for swimming, and for oyster-hunting from the rocks at low tide. The excellent dusk *Tasmanian Wilderness Transport* **tour** here (departing Launceston daily 6pm; $40; ☎003/34 4442) includes plenty of wildlife spotting, a swim, and a night-time barbecue where the guide usually manages to lure out an opportunistic semi-tame and entertaining **tasmanian devil** who crunches his fearsomely strong jaws through the proffered bones as if they were jelly.

## Eating and drinking

**Alexander Hotel**, 78 Formby Rd (☎004/24 2252). Refurbished riverfront pub, popular with 18–30s. Decent music and an excellent bistro menu.

**The Greendoor**, 10 Oldaker St (☎004/24 6000). Upmarket restaurant serving European- and Asian-inspired food in a shady courtyard. Closed Sun & Mon.

**Golden Panda Chinese Restaurant**, 38 Formby Rd (☎004/24 9066). Standard Cantonese cuisine.

**Klaas's Bakehouse**, 11 Oldaker St (☎24 8866). European-style bakery (daytime only) using only the best ingredients. There's a token table outside where you can sip espresso with your pastry.

**Rialto Gallery**, 159 Rooke St (☎24 6793). Reasonably priced Italian dishes from the Venetian region, usually including a vegetarian special. Lunch only Mon–Fri, dinner Sat & Sun.

# Ulverstone

Dull, conservative **ULVERSTONE**, 20km west of Devonport where the **Leven River** flows into the sea, is chiefly notorious for an **anti-gay rally** in 1989 when 800 hysterical homophobes chanted "kill them, kill them" at seventy gay and lesbian protestors. However, it's also a popular family holiday spot, with unpolluted **beaches** and plenty to occupy children, including the **Ulverstone Waterslide** (Dec 18–Feb 14 10am–7pm; $2.50). *Hobart Coaches* pull in at the *Anotole Milkbar*, 60 Reibey Street (☎004/25 3396); the *Redline* depot is at 33 Victoria Street (☎004/25 5776).

**Accommodation** possibilities include B&B in the pleasant two-storey *Ocean View Guesthouse*, 1 Victoria Street (☎004/25 5401; B&B ⑤), and the splendid 1903 redbrick *Furners Hotel*, 42 Reibey Street (☎004/25 1488; B&B ⑤), complete with carved blackwood staircase and an excellent **bistro**; or try the waterfront *Ulverstone Caravan Park* (☎004/25 2624; on-site vans ③, cabins ④).

## Around Ulverstone

In the picturesque hop-growing countryside south of town, the **Gunns Plains Caves** (daily 10am–4pm hourly; 50-min tour $6; ☎004/29 1388) are worth visiting for their remarkable limestone formations. Huge "pieces of bacon" drape from the ceiling, looking like streaky rashers but as big as blankets; when lit from behind they glow a succulent red. A permanent stream feeds an underground lake, and platypuses and possums enjoy the cool cave temperatures.

The scenic drive west from Ulverstone follows the old Bass Highway along the coastline, passing the Three Sisters and Goat Islands bird sanctuaries, and Penguin Point where fairy penguins roost. **PENGUIN** itself, 12km along the highway, is a neatly tended town with three safe swimming beaches. Blue and white penguin-shaped garbage bins line the main street, culminating in the two-metre-high "big penguin" in the foreshore park.

# Burnie

**BURNIE**, on Emu Bay 15km west of Penguin, is an ugly and frankly smelly paper-manufacturing centre, deceptively situated amid rich farming land. There's no real need to come here – especially considering "Burnie" Airport is 19km away in more salubrious Wynyard – but you may well pass through at some stage.

The **Tasmanian Travel Centre** at the Civic Square precinct, off Little Alexander Street (Mon–Fri 8.45am–5pm, Sat 8.45am–noon, Sun 8.45–11am; ☎004/34 6111) can direct you towards Burnie's few points of interest. The Civic Centre on Wilmot Street holds both the **Pioneer Village Museum**, with its reconstructed turn-of-the-century street (Mon–Fri 9am–5pm, Sat & Sun 1.30pm–4.30pm; $4), and the **Burnie Regional Art Gallery** (Tues–Fri 10.30am-5pm, Sat & Sun 1.30–4.30pm; free).

If you have to **stay**, the cheapest, very basic, hotel is the *Regent Hotel*, 26 North Terrace (☎004/31 1993; ③); the least expensive motel is the *Ocean View Park-A-Tel*, 253 Bass Highway (☎004/31 1925; ④–⑤) at Cooee on the way out of town towards Wynyard. The *Glen Osborne House* at 9 Aileen Crescent (☎004/31 9866; ⑥) is a pricey Victorian B&B with a lovely garden of lawns, roses and fruit trees. As well as a *McDonald's* and a *Pizza Hut*, Burnie offers, in the *Rialto Gallery* at 46 Wilmot Street (☎004/31 7718), a popular and affordable Italian restaurant. The *Redline Coaches* depot is at 117 Wilson Street (☎004/31 2660); *Hobart Coaches* are at 54 Cattley Street (☎004/31 1971).

# Wynyard and around

**WYNYARD**, another 19km along the old Bass Highway from Burnie and a whole lot more pleasant, snuggles comfortably into the lush pasture lands between the **Inglis River** and the sea. Most of the action in the town itself revolves around the wharf area off Goldie Street, with its fishing boats and fresh fish shop, but the adjacent coastline has much to entice visitors. At **Fossil Bluff**, an easy three-kilometre walk along the bicentennial track, layers of sedimentary rock containing fossilized sea shells can be easily examined at low tide, while the beach has good views of the 170-metre sea face of **Table Cape**.

Eleven kilometres west of town, a turn-off from the Bass Highway winds downwards to **Boat Harbour Beach**, the prettiest on the northwest coast with pale blue water, white sand and very gentle waves. It's perfect for diving, too; equipment can be rented from the *Scuba Club* at 62 Scenic Drive in Wynyard (☎004/42 2247), who also organize excursions. The milk bar on the beach is the place to ask about camping nearby, and also rents **boogie-boards** and **wave skis**. Next door, the *Harbour Restaurant* (☎004/45 1371; closed Sun night & Mon) serves pricey seafood dishes. The spacious dorms at the new *Boat Harbour Backpackers*, back up the hill on Strawberry Lane (☎004/45 1273; ①), make a great place to stay.

Nearby **Sisters Beach** is another attractive beach, as well as being the site of the **Birdland Native Gardens** on Wattle Avenue (daily 9am–5pm; $2.50; ☎004/45 1270), where 93 species (not always very conspicuous) are protected in their natural habitat.

## Rocky Cape National Park

Stretching along the coast for a mere 12km of rugged hills and cliffs from Sisters Beach to Rocky Cape, **Rocky Cape National Park** is Tasmania's smallest national park, created in 1967 to preserve some remarkable Aboriginal archeological finds. The mainly quartzite hills are pockmarked with caves, of which the two major ones, North Cave and South Cave, contain huge shell middens, bones and stone tools dating back as far as 8000 years, when the sea was several fathoms below its current level.

Although North Cave can be visited – it's a fifteen-minute-return walk from the road, reached by driving 5km into the park and turning left at the lighthouse fork – the main activity here is walking along various easy tracks. The whole length of the park takes seven hours; you have to carry all your water, and there are no toilets, which renders camping more difficult. Rocky pools, safe swimming beaches and picnic areas scatter the route, while spring and summer sees a profusion of wildflowers on the scrubby heathland, including some unique native orchids. At dusk, you may well see wallabies, echidnas, and assorted birds.

## Practicalities

*MTT* **public transport buses** connect Wynyard with Burnie (around $1.80 for a day ticket), stopping at 38 Jackson Street. *Redline Coaches* call at the *BP* service station (☎004/42 2205). Wynyard's "Burnie" **airport**, just five minutes' walk from the town centre, has daily services to Melbourne and cheap flights to and from Phillip Island, off the coast of Victoria; tickets can be booked through *Wynyard Travel Service*, 84 Goldie Street (☎004/42 2391).

Helpful volunteers at **Wynyard Tourist Information**, 45 Jackson Street (Mon–Fri 10am–4pm, Sat & Sun 1–4pm), have information on local activities and **accommodation**. *Wynyard YHA*, 36 Dodgin Street (☎004/42 2013; ①), is the best choice for budget travellers, but is rather drab. Rates at the shabby but comfortable *Federal Hotel*, 82 Goldie Street (☎004/42 2056; ④), include a cooked breakfast. The *Inglis River Hotel Motel*, 4 Goldie Street (☎004/42 2344; ④) is the best value of the few motels, while the *Alexandria*, Table Cape Road (☎004/42 2094; ⑥), is a classy B&B.

The best **place to eat**, drink coffee and relax is *Mare's Place*, 8 Goldie Street (daily 10.30am–5.30pm), in a building that once housed the general store. Occupying a great position opposite the river, it offers delicious espresso and a blackboard menu ranging from toasted sandwiches through homemade fettucine. Antiques, jewellery and crafts are for sale downstairs, while upstairs is a gallery for local artists. *Peppers Restaurant*, 43 Jackson Street (☎004/42 1177), is a more predictable (and expensive) à la carte restaurant, and *YT's Fish Place*, on the Wharf, is good for fresh fish (daily 9.30am–6.30pm).

# Stanley

The tiny historical town of **STANLEY**, 6km off the Bass Highway and 32km west of Rocky Cape, was the first settlement in northwest Tasmania, being the original 1826 headquarters of the *Van Diemen's Land Company*. It occupies a picturesque setting on a small foot-shaped peninsula, right at the base of an unusual rock formation – "The Nut", described by Flinders as a "cliffy round lump in form resembling a Christmas cake" – that rises plumb from the ocean to nearly 150m. **Circular Head**, as it's officially called (the name also for the surrounding municipality) is thought to be a volcanic plug, with the softer sediments around it eroded away.

Although it's still possible to do the strenuous ten-minute walk up the grassy **Nut** itself, it can be explored in comfort thanks to an exhilarating **chair lift**, erected in 1986 and reached via the ramp opposite the post office (daily summer 9.30am–6.30pm, winter 9.30am–4pm weather permitting ☎004/58 1286 to check; $3.50 one-way, $5.50 return). A short walk around the **Nut State Reserve** at the top (constantly bracing yourself against the wind) affords views over the town and port, and southeast as far as Table Cape. Directly below is the exquisitely deserted **Godfrey's Beach**, with its calm and translucent crystal-blue waters.

Stanley's main street, **Church Street**, runs at the foot of the Nut, with its restaurants and crafts shops high enough above the beach, wharves and the rest of the town to command excellent views. The 1850s Georgian **Plough Inn Museum** here holds an expensive assortment of historical artefacts (daily 10am–5pm; $4.50; ☎004/58 1266), though entrance to the impressive ground-floor crafts and antique shop is free. Items include beautifully crafted wooden bowls made from huon pine, swamp gum bark, Tasmanian myrtle burls, blackwood and musk. They also rent bikes and provide tourist information.

Wandering down to the foreshore area, the slate-roofed stone **Van Diemen's Land Company Store** in **Marine Park** is the headquarters and venue for the three-day **Circular Head Arts Festival**, held in early September. It combines visual art with plenty of entertainment: mime artists, street theatre, and bands. From the nearby **port area**, at low tide, you can see the remnants of a 1923 shipwreck, a victim of the "furies" of the Bass Strait.

## Practicalities

Fitting in with its historical aura, Stanley has several "colonial" **B&Bs**, such as the *Touchwood Colonial Cottage*, 33 Church Street ( ☎004/58 1348; ⑥, with breakfast provisions supplied) and *Wisteria Cottage* (☎004/58 1186; ⑤). The weatherboard *Harbour Masters Cottage* at 42 Alexander Terrace (☎004/58 1209; ⑥) is particularly luxurious, though the accommodation here is self-catering. The *Stanley Motel*, Dovecote Road (☎004/58 1300; ⑤), is less expensive, while for budget travellers, *Stanley YHA* is at the *Caravan Park*, Wharf Road (☎004/58 1266; dorms ①, on-site vans ③, cabins ④), near the *BP* service station which serves as Stanley's *Redline* depot.

Probably the best place to **eat** in Stanley is *Hurseys Seafoods*, next to Marine Park. In fact, it has to be the best fish 'n' chip shop in Tasmania: inside are huge holding tanks where you can select live fish and crays; as well as around twenty kinds of fish, they

## THE VAN DIEMEN'S LAND COMPANY

*. . . how is it that an absentee owner across the world got this magnificent and empty country without having paid one glass bead?*

Cassandra Pybus

The **Van Diemen's Land Company** was the brainchild of a group of prominent and well-connected private individuals, who in 1824 managed to obtain by Royal Charter 250,000 acres of the mainly thickly forested, unexplored northwest corner of Tasmania. Their plan was to create their own source of cheap wool in the colonies, which could be relied upon even if Europe was subject to political upheaval; the *Tranmere* arrived at Circular Head in 1826, with the personnel, livestock, supplies and equipment to create the township of Stanley.

The first flocks were grazed at Woolnorth on Cape Grim, a plateau of tussock grass and ti tree that might have been made for the purpose but, in fact, was prime Aboriginal hunting land. When hunting parties began to take sheep, whites indiscriminately killed Aborigines in retaliation, and a vindictive cycle of killing began. The most tragic incident occurred around 1826 or 1827: a group of Aboriginal men seeking revenge for the rape of their women speared a shepherd and killed one hundred sheep; these deaths were ruthlessly avenged when a group of thirty unarmed Aborigines muttonbirding near the same spot were killed by shepherds, and their bodies thrown over a cliff (now euphemistically called "Suicide Cove"). Ultimately, the Aboriginal people of the northwest were systematically hunted down, with the last being captured near the Arthur River in 1842.

The *Van Diemen's Land Company* was detested by free settlers, for always using its influence to get the pick of convict labour, and always preferring this labour to that of free men. In the 1840s the company changed its emphasis from wool production to the sale and lease of its land; it is still registered on the London Stock Exchange, and its major stockholders have probably never laid eyes on the land they own.

have freshly cooked local muttonbirds (also known as shearwaters) – they're not to all tastes, though, being very oily. Among other good options, all on Church Street, are the fresh seafood in the lounge bar at the *Union Hotel*, the generous home-style cooking at *Sullivans Restaurant* (☎004/58 1144), or a snack and espresso at the relaxed *Stranded Whale Coffee Shop*.

## Smithton and Woolnorth

The only way to see Tasmania's rugged northwest tip, which remains under the control of the *Van Diemen's Land Company* (VDL), is to arrange a tour from the unattractive logging town of **SMITHTON**, at the mouth of the Duck River 22km west of Stanley. Trips to **Woolnorth**, the original VDL cattle and sheep property, depart on alternate days at 9.30am from the *Bridge Hotel Motel* on Montague Road, where you can also stay (☎004/52 1389; ④–⑥). The tour ($50, including a barbecue lunch; book on ☎004/52 1252) also takes in Cape Grim, where the air is reputed to be the cleanest in the world – it's the site of one of only six global "baseline air-monitoring stations". Smithton's one other attraction is the **Lacrum Dairy** (closed July–Oct), 6km north at Mella, where tours of the modern milking plant (3pm & 5.30pm; $5; ☎004/52 3500) include afternoon tea, served with Tasmanian cheeses.

South of Smithton, ten **forestry reserves** range from rainforests to blackwood swamps and giant eucalypt forests; all are accessible from a circular route via Kanunnah Bridge and Taytea Bridge on the C218, a 90km round trip. The *Forestry Commission*, at the corner of Nelson and Smith streets (☎004/52 1317), can provide maps and route information; the most rewarding reserves are the **Julius River Forest Reserve** and the **Milkshakes Hills Forest Reserve**.

## Marrawah

From Smithton the Bass Highway cuts across the northwest corner to the rich farming settlement of **MARRAWAH** on the west coast. Thirty kilometres along the way, a 1500-metre trail leads through a swamp at the grumpily named **Dismal Swamp Nature Reserve**. Marrawah itself has a small store, and the *Marrawah Tavern* serves plain but filling meals. **Greenpoint Beach**, which has been voted one of the three best **surfing** beaches in Australia, is just 2km from Marrawah, and has the town's only accommodation in the shape of a small camping area. The curve of Ann Bay here is shrouded by the hump of Mount Cameron West to the north. Three kilometres north of this bluff, at the end of a long exposed beach, is the most complex **Aboriginal art** site in Tasmania: rock carvings of geometric or non-figurative forms cover slabs of rock at the base of a cliff.

## Arthur River and the Arthur Pieman Protected Area

Just over 20km south of Marrawah, the scattering of holiday homes at **ARTHUR RIVER** mark the start of one of the Tasmanian coast's last great **wilderness areas**, where mighty trees that have washed down the Arthur River crash and batter against the windswept shoreline. All the west coast was once like this, but the progressive damming of its rivers has left the **Arthur Pieman Protected Area** as a unique reminder, complete with a spectacular array of bildlife, such as black cockatoos, Tasmanian rosellas, orange-breasted parrots, black jays, wedge-tail eagles, pied heron, and azure kingfishers. Trees on the steep banks of the river include myrtle, sassafras, celery-top pines, laurels and giant tree ferns. It would be madness to attempt to swim in the wild conditions (with occasional freak waves) of the protected area – even walking along the beach, picking your way over the scattered lumber, can be something of an obstacle course. It's essential therefore to brief yourself in advance with the latest information from the base office of the *Department of Parks, Wildlife & Heritage* on Arthur River Road (Mon–Fri 8am–5pm; daily during fire season Dec–April; ☎004/57 1225).

The small **shop** on Gardiner Street is the only source of supplies in Arthur River; attached is the area's only accommodation, the *Arthur River Holiday Units* (☎004/57 1288; ⑤). However, **camping** can be a joy, with facilities varying from the fully serviced caravan park near the base office to secluded areas among shady trees in the dips and hollows behind the dunes, equipped merely with water taps.

If you want to get out on the river, take a cruise (see below) or contact *Arthur River Canoe Hire* (☎004/57 1312) which has canoes and boats available for rent: one-person canoes are $5 per hour/$30 per day, two-person canoes $6/$40, and boats $15/$100.

### The Arthur River Cruise
Perhaps the biggest attraction of the entire northwest coast is the five-hour **Arthur River Cruise** (daily 10am, returning 3pm; no trips June–Aug; adults $35, under-16s $15, under-6s free; reservations ☎004/57 1158, or book through *Tasmanian Travel Centres*), on the *George Robinson*, which sails 19km upriver to the confluence of the Arthur and Frankland rivers at Turks Crossing. En route you cruise past a wedge-tail eagle's nest, and even see a pair of enormous sea eagles being hand-fed, as well as experiencing the transition from coastal scrub woodland to temperate rainforest. After a barbecue lunch in a clearing, there's a four-kilometre bushwalk.

# The route to the west coast

From Somerset, a suburb of Burnie on the shores of Emu Bay, the A10 **heads to Queenstown** in the heart of Tasmania's west coast mining area. This major route to the west coast is relatively recent; prior to 1932 the coast was accessible only by sea. If you're not driving, you can use the affordable *Struthers Transport* freight service (☎004/33 0393) to get from Burnie to Savage River and to Waratah.

Following the highway, after 10km you pass **YOLLA**, a picturesque little town surrounded by rich farming country; there are a couple of places to fill up with fuel. A few kilometres past the Tewkesbury turn-off, the rural landscape ends and the road rises and winds through temperate rainforest to the **Hellyer Gorge State Reserve**. In twenty minutes, you can walk through spicy ferns and dense myrtle forest to the Hellyer River and back on a wide and easy track.

Once through the forest, the landscape is starkly shocking: mile after mile of felled trees and stumps ravaged by logging. By the time you reach the B23 turn-off west to Waratah, on the way to the Pieman River, the forest is beginning to reassert itself.

## West to Waratah and the Pieman River

Tiny windswept **WARATAH**, set in mountain heathland 8km off the A10, reached its peak in the early 1900s after thirty years of tin-mining at **Mount Bischoff**, when it was linked to Burnie by the **Emu Bay Railway**, built to facilitate access to the silver fields of Zeehan and Rosebery. Though the mine closed in 1935, Waratah is still a miners' town, with recent mining developments at the Que River. Little more than a scattered collection of scruffy weatherboard cottages, it's pretty soulless, but if you're desperate you can camp at the exposed site behind the Municipal Council buildings on Smith Street; get the key for the hot showers and pay ($5 per site) at the *Waratah Road House* (daily 6am–8pm), further along Smith Street. You can find **meals** at the big old two-storey pub up on the hill, a relic of former boom times. Beyond Waratah, the last fuel stop on the road is **Savage River**, an operational mining town with accommodation and meals on offer at the *Savage River Motor Inn* (☎004/46 1177; ④–⑤).

The beautiful, unspoilt **Pieman River**, within **Pieman River State Reserve**, is reached from the old gold-mining settlement of **CORINNA**. It's hard to believe that 2500 people occupied what's now just a few shacks and dense bush. Corinna even had its own port, despite the difficulties of getting through the narrow **Pieman Heads** from the coastline. The river here is too dangerous for swimming: it's very cold, with an average drop of nearly twenty metres from the banks. The reserve used to be a logging area and it still holds one of the biggest and best of the remaining huon pine stands – saved because the water here was too deep to allow a dam to be built. The river can be enjoyed, and the wild west coast reached, via the **MV Arcadia II Cruise** (daily 10.30am–2.30pm; $30, including morning tea; ☎004/46 1170). *Arcadia II* was built in Hobart (from huon pine) as a luxury pleasure cruiser but has been through several other lives since 1939, including active service off the Philippines. From the boat you can see huon pine, leatherwood and pandanus ferns among the **temperate rainforest** of the river's north bank; the drier southern bank has mainly brown stringy-bark eucalypts.

The trip gives you an hour and a half to wander on your own along the west coast: by the landing are several intriguing **holiday shacks**, ramshackle affairs of tin verandahs variously propped up by raw tree posts and an old bus. A wide sandy path leads to a beach between two outcrops of jagged orange sedimentary rock, where the dark blue sea is tinged by the tannin-stained river water.

The affable brothers who run the cruise virtually run the town too. They open the **kiosk** daily whenever they have time, but bring food along if you intend to use the **campsite** (no showers) or the *Retreat Cabins* (④, BYO linen), also both operated by the brothers. From the car park there's a walking track leading to a huge 600-year-old **manfern**, one of only four of such antiquity known to exist in Tasmania.

# Zeehan

Back onto the A10, the highway continues through the comparatively large town of **Rosebery**. **ZEEHAN**, 6km off the A10, was clearly once a prosperous town, boasting a population of 8000 at its zenith. However, the silver-lead mines which opened in the 1880s had already begun to fail by 1908, and the town only revived in the 1970s with the opening of the Renison Bell tin mines. Several "boom" period buildings can still be seen in town, including the elaborate facade of the **Gaiety Theatre**, once the largest theatre in Australia, which hosted Houdini and Caruso but now houses a hairdresser. The **West Coast Pioneer Memorial Museum** (daily April–Sept 8.30am–5pm, Oct–March 8.30am–6pm; free) on Main Street has displays on mining history. Basic pub **accommodation** and decent counter meals can be had at the *Cecil Hotel*, Main Street (☎004/71 6221; ④); the caravan park (☎004/71 6633; on-site vans ③, cabins ④) is a kilometre from the centre on Hurst Street.

From here it's possible to go straight to Strahan (47km) on a sealed road, bypassing Queenstown.

# Queenstown

**QUEENSTOWN** used to be promoted vigorously by *Tourism Tasmania* during the 1970s when its famous (now infamous) **"lunar landscape"** was seen as a prime attraction. Though nowadays people are sent instead to **Strahan** to experience wilderness on the Gordon River, Queenstown illustrates the grim reality of blind progress in such a sensitive environment and the devastation it causes. As you approach down the hill from Strahan you're confronted by the hideously ugly **Mount Lyell Copper Mine**; from Hobart, the road winds down to the town around reddish-brown bare rock.

With its wide streets, two-storey hotels and identical, poky tin-roofed weatherboard houses, Queenstown has been a mining centre ever since 1883, when gold was discovered at Mount Lyell. In 1893 the *Mount Lyell Mining and Railway Company* was formed and began to mine copper at Mount Lyell, which it has continued to do ever since. This is redneck territory, with a completely different atmosphere to nearby Strahan; twenty years ago, the people of Queenstown claimed to be inordinately proud of their bare hills. Those weird mountains, chalky white and almost totally devoid of vegetation, are the result of a lethal combination of tree-felling, sulphur, fire and rainfall. Between 1896 and 1922 the eleven furnaces at the Mount Lyell smelters devoured huge amounts of timber, and the surrounding hills' rainforest covering has taken decades to begin to re-establish itself; even then, the sulphur fumes emitted by the same smelters have killed off the regrowth. Because sulphur had been absorbed into soil and tree stumps, bush-fires swept the hills summer after summer, and rainfall finally eroded the remaining soil. Since the smelters closed in 1969 there has been some token regrowth on the lower slopes. There is further evidence of environmental damage – if more were needed – to be seen in the grey sludge of the Queen River, which spews eventually into Macquarie Harbour, where it forms an unsightly grey delta.

The mining company has an exemption to pollute until 1996; though closed down for a short time, it is fully expected to re-open at the end of 1995 under new ownership – and very strict anti-pollution requirements. There are still daily tours of the **Mount Lyell Mine** (Oct–April 9.15am, 2.30pm & 4.30pm; May–Sept 9.15am & 4pm; 1hr 30min; $8) and, though the plans for reforestation are explained, it's hard to stifle lingering cynicism. Bookings and departures are from the *Western Arts and Crafts Centre* at 1 Driffield Street (☎004/71 2388), which provides tourist information, but the *RACT Office*, 18 Orr Street (Mon–Fri 9am–5pm), is Queenstown's official **tourist information** office, and more reliable on the town's dubious attractions.

Right next door to the mine is the *National Parks and Wildlife Service* office (☎004/71 2511), the base for the Franklin Lower Gordon Wild Rivers National Park and the place to pick up the department's rafting and bushwalking guidelines. While in town, you could also check out the old photographic displays in the **Galley Museum** (Mon–Fri 10am–12.30pm & 1.30–4.30pm, Sat & Sun 1.30pm–4.30pm; $2), housed in the old *Imperial Hotel*. You wouldn't really choose to stay in Queenstown, but it can be a cheap alternative if Strahan is overflowing. The *Empire Hotel* at 2 Orr Street (☎004/71 1699; ③) is a lovely, old-fashioned place with a variety of reasonable rooms, including several budget singles, and good-value meals. *Mountain View Holiday Lodge*, 1 Penghana Road (☎004/71 1163; motel units ④, backpacker dorms ①), has been converted from the mine's single men's lodgings.

# Strahan

**STRAHAN** is easygoing, relaxed and even progressive. The only town and port on the west coast, it sits in the huge **Macquarie Harbour**, site of **Sarah Island**, a harsh secondary convict settlement in use between 1822 and 1830. The entrance to Macquarie Harbour, named **Hells Gates** by arriving convicts, is only 80m wide. **Houn pine**, perfect for shipbuilding, grows abundantly in the area and this became the convicts' trade. After 1830 the timber continued to attract loggers, but it wasn't until 1882 that Strahan began life as a port for the nearby copper and lead fields. Tasmania's third-largest port in 1900, its unreliability had closed it by 1970 and the population dwindled to 300. It's now a small **fishing village**, chasing abalone, crayfish and shark, though the basing of the **Franklin Blockade** campaign here in 1982 shook up the town and brought the Australian media flocking for two months (see p.812). **Cruises** on the **Gordon River** were already running then, but the declaration of a **World Heritage Area** has meant that busloads of tourists now regularly pour in to see the river, creating a briefly hectic atmosphere, after which the town rapidly reverts to its usual peaceful state.

## Accommodation

You can **camp** along the beach for free at Ocean Beach and Henty Dunes (see "Around Strahan", below), you'll need transport and there are no facilities, but free hot showers can be had in the toilet block opposite the post office. **Accommodation** is expensive and gets booked up in the summer; to be safe, **book ahead** or bring a tent – otherwise you might have to push on to Zeehan or Queenstown.

**Franklin Manor**, The Esplanade (☎004/71 7311). Sedate and elegant two-storey weatherboard B&B, surrounded by trees and flowers. Beautiful and lovingly maintained interior, the guest lounge is always filled with fresh flowers and classical music. ⑦–⑧.

**Gordon Gateway Chalet**, Grining St (☎004/71 7165). Peaceful harbourfront spot looking across to the town and its fishing boats; spacious rooms with kitchenettes. ⑥.

**Hamers Craypot Inn**, The Esplanade (☎004/71 7191). This renovated 1930s hotel has clean, modern rooms with washbasins, colour TV, and sea views. The café-style lounge bar serves seafood and good fresh salads and there's also a public bar. ⑤, including a light breakfast.

**Strahan Motor Inn**, Jolly St (☎004/71 7160). Expensive motel complex on a hill overlooking the town, with some wheelchair-accessible units; the restaurant has sea views. ⑦.

**The Strahan Village**, The Esplanade (☎004/71 7191). Newly built colonial-style motel rooms, attached to *Hamers*. ⑦.

**Strahan Wilderness Lodge**, Ocean Beach Rd (☎004/71 7142). Best value place to stay, set in spacious grounds criss-crossed by walking tracks, just out of town. Comfortable lodge in an old homestead (B&B, ③), plus very private cottages with balconies (self-catering, ④).

**Strahan YHA**, Harvey St (☎004/71 7255). Recently renovated, clean and friendly hostel with new toilet block and improvements planned for the rather cramped kitchen. Dorms ①, cabins ③.

**West Strahan Caravan Park**, The Esplanade (☎004/71 7239). Simple, inexpensive campsite.

## The Town

Strahan is ready for the tourist invasion, with a wharf redevelopment plan that's already begun with the innovative wooden and iron **Strahan Visitor Centre** (daily summer 10am–8pm, winter 10am–6pm; $4.50; ☎004/71 7488), whose design aims to echo the area's boatbuilding and timber industries, its interior featuring a huge glass wall overlooking the harbour. The centre is provocative and challenging, with the quote on the vestibule wall immediately striking an **ecological** note. The exhibition's seven main themes are Aborigines, convicts, logging, ecology, economy, wilderness and conflict – a satisfyingly radical departure from the usual local museum fodder.

Adjacent to the visitor centre is the large corrugated-iron shed of **Morrison's Saw Mill** (daily 8am–5pm), where Tasmanian timbers are processed; you can visit the mill and buy well-designed and crafted furniture, and smaller items like picture frames. Also on The Esplanade, the old **Customs Bond Store** houses the post office and the **World Heritage Area Visitor Centre** (daily 8am–5pm; free), but it's not a patch on the other centre.

The **Strahan Historic Foreshore Walkway** is a pleasant gravel track following the harbour around to **Regatta Point**, where the defunct 1899 train station was used by the Queenstown-based *Mount Lyell Railway and Mining Company* to transport ore to the port. En route there's the **People's Park** with its rainforest walk to **Hogarth Falls** (40min; 2km return).

## The Gordon River

The **Gordon River** is deep, its waters dark from the tannin leaching out of buttongrass plains – even the tap water in Strahan is brown (though perfectly fine to drink). Cruise boats used to travel as far as Sir John Falls, 30km upriver, but the speed required was causing the river banks to erode, and boats now go only the 14km to **Heritage Landing**, where there's a chance to see a slice of real rainforest, with a boardwalk above the rainforest floor enabling you to see the thick undergrowth without disturbing it in the process. Trunks and branches of ancient myrtles and huon pines provide homes for mosses, lichens and liverworts on their bark, and ferns and fungi grow from the trunks – even the dead trees support some forms of life, however lowly. The wet and swampy conditions are ideal for **huon pines**, found only in Tasmania, and the second-oldest living things on earth after the bristlecone pines of North America. The pines can grow from seed but more often regenerate vegetatively, putting down roots where fallen branches touch the soil. Always highly sought after, by virtue of being one of the few green Tasmanian timbers that floats, huon pine logs were floated down to the boom camp and there formed into huge rafts to be rowed across Macquarie Harbour. The **Boom Camp** is still set up and anyone can stay for free; just bring bedding and food. The *Heritage Wanderer* (see below) will drop you off and pick you up if you've arranged it with them first.

The *Heritage Wanderer* (no service mid-June to Aug, otherwise departs daily 9am, returning about 4.15pm; $36; snacks and lunch available on board; ☎004/71 7174; stops off at Sarah Island for a wander around the ruins) is just one of an array of **river cruises** but it's one of the best, aboard a smaller boat with a more relaxed feel, and in no great rush to get anywhere. The big operator is *Gordon River Cruises* (☎004/71 7187; daily 9am–1.45pm, $42 includes morning tea; plus Nov 1–April 30 9am–3.30pm, $60 includes lunch), with faster boats that whizz thrillingly through Hells Gates.

## Around Strahan

Outside the town, **Ocean Beach** is at 30km the longest beach in Tasmania and was, in the early 1990s, the site of the stranding of several **pilot whales** from Antarctica. Rescue operations were sadly unsuccessful and the whale skeletons, half-buried in the sand, can still be seen. Come at dusk for marvellous sunsets and to watch – from

November to February – the migratory **muttonbirds** roost. The extensive **Henty Dunes**, 12km out of town on the Zeehan Road, are also worth seeing; there's **camping** available at the picnic area.

For getting around, *Wilderness Photographics* on the Esplanade rent ten-speed **mountain bikes** ($3 per hour, $18 for 24hr; ☎004/71 7323), or there's a plethora of organized tours. *Strahan Wilderness Tours*, at *Wilderness Photographics* on the Esplanade (☎004/71 7401), run three walks a day (2hr 30min; $30), and their four-wheel-drive tours include bouncing along a six-hour track to the Franklin River. *Teepookana and King River Wilderness Tours* (☎004/71 7103) do a four-wheel-drive tour of the ghost towns of **Pilliger** and **Teepookana**.

*West Coast Yacht Charters*, on the Esplanade (closed July–Sept; ☎004/71 7422 or free call 1800/03 0505), run wonderful evening **crayfish dinner sails** on Macquarie Harbour (6–8.30pm; $40 includes wine and fresh cray supper) in the characterful 1905 cutter *Wraith of Hamble*, plus morning fishing trips with all gear supplied; you can even stay on board the cutter for B&B with a difference (④). *Wilderness Air*, on Strahan Wharf (daily summer 8.30am–8.30pm, winter 8.30am–5.30pm; 1hr 20min flight; $98; ☎004/71 7280), run spectacular **seaplane flights** over Macquarie Harbour and the wilderness area, from which you're privy to the unforgettable image of the smooth dark ribbon of the wild river easing through dense forest below. The seaplanes land further upriver than the cruise boats can reach at **Sir John Falls Landing** – the highlight of the trip is a dramatic landing on the glassy calm of the Gordon River.

### Eating and drinking

Strahan's best **restaurant** is the dining room of the stylish *Franklin Manor* across from the centre of the town on The Esplanade (☎004/71 7311), where for $30 you can get a set dinner menu featuring lots of fresh seafood; in the daytime they also serve up afternoon teas in refined surroundings. Less expensive and formal, and the focus of the town's social life, *Hamers Craypot Inn*, also on The Esplanade but in the centre (☎004/71 7191) has a fine bistro which serves up a suitably wide selection of seafood, as befits a fishing village. The *Harbour Café* on the corner of Esk Street and The Esplanade is Strahan's greasy-spoon caff, with views of the fishing boats – and copious hamburgers and breakfasts. *Strahan Butchery Delicatessen*, on The Esplanade in the town centre, sells fresh and smoked fish, crays, meats and cheeses – perfect picnic fodder.

### Transport and services

The *Harbour Café* (☎004/71 7209) is the place to enquire and book for the weekend-only *Wilderness Transport* services to Cradle Mountain, Launceston, Devonport and Hobart (all depart Strahan on Sunday and return on Saturday). *Redline* has more frequent services, connecting with Strahan on the Hobart to Devonport route via Queenstown and Cradle Mountain daily except Sunday; their agent is *Strahan Newsagency* (☎004/71 7263). There are EFTPOS facilities and a small supermarket and newsagent in town.

# The World Heritage Area

Right up until the last century, the concept of **wilderness** was overwhelmingly that of a malevolent force, untamed by man. In the late twentieth century, especially for jaded inhabitants of the technologically-swamped developed world, the image is increasingly becoming a benign one: the natural as opposed to the artificial, virgin forest as opposed to polluted streets, the spiritual versus the material. It's the lure of this ideal of wilderness that attracts a certain type of traveller to Tasmania, to commune with nature at its most unspoilt. The state's vast wilderness areas of the Southwest National Park,

Franklin Lower Gordon Wild Rivers National Park and the adjacent Cradle Mountain–Lake St Clair National Park make up the **World Heritage Area**, recognized by UNESCO.

## Some history

In 1972, the flooding of the beautiful and unique **Lake Pedder** led to the formation of the *Wilderness Society*, which began a relentless campaign against the *Hydro Electricity Commission*'s next plan for the southwest, to build a huge dam on the Lower Gordon River that would efface Tasmania's last wild river, the Franklin. Pro-HEC forces included Tasmanian Premier Robin Gray. Years of protests and campaigns ensued, but in 1981 the whole southwest area was proposed for the World Heritage list. The **Franklin Blockade**, organized by the *Wilderness Society* and led by **Dr Bob Brown**, began on December 14, 1982, the day the southwest officially joined the list – a fact the Tasmanian government was choosing to ignore.

For two months, blockaders from all over Australia travelled upriver from their Strahan base to put themselves in front of the bulldozers at the site, in non-violent protest. The blockade attracted international attention, notably when the British botanist David Bellamy joined in the protest and was among the 1200 or so arrested for trespassing. During the course of the campaign, the Labor Hawke Government was voted in, and in March 1983, following a trail-blazing High Court ruling, the federal government forbade further work by the HEC.

Locals who supported the "Greenie" protesters showed a lot of courage, in the face of antagonism within the community. Though the blockade itself had failed to stop work on the dam, it had changed or at least challenged the opinion of many Australians. Particularly on Tasmania's west coast, communities and families were split over the Franklin issue, as resentment grew towards the mainlanders, who were regarded as denying potential employment to Tasmanians. Recent *Wilderness Society* campaigns have only added to these tensions.

# Cradle Mountain–Lake St Clair National Park

**Cradle Mountain–Lake St Clair National Park** is Tasmania's best known, its northern **Cradle Mountain** end easily accessible from either Devonport, Deloraine or Launceston, and its southern **Lake St Clair** end from Derwent Bridge on the Lyell Highway between Queenstown and Hobart. One of the most glaciated areas in Australia, with many lakes and tarns, it covers some of Tasmania's highest land, with craggy mountain peaks like **Mount Ossa**, the state's highest point. At its northern end, Lake St Clair is the country's deepest freshwater lake at over 200m, occupying a basin gouged out by two glaciers. Betwen Cradle Mountain and Lake St Clair, the 85km **Overland Track**, attracting walkers from all over the world, is the best way to take in the stunning scenery – spread over six or more mud- and leech-filled days of physical, albeit exhilarating, exhaustion.

*Redline* pass by Derwent Bridge on their Hobart–Queenstown route (daily except Sun) but you'll have to walk several kilometres or take a taxi ($4) to Lake St Clair. On the Burnie–Queenstown route, they go as far as *Cradle Mountain Lodge* (daily in summer, winter Tues, Thurs & Sat). *Wilderness Transport* run to Lake St Clair from Hobart via Mount Field National Park (summer daily, winter Tues & Sat; returning to Hobart daily in summer, Tues & Sun in winter), and from Launceston, Deloraine and Devonport right to the *Cradle Mountain Visitor Centre* or Lake Dove (summer daily; winter/spring Tues, Thurs, & Sat; returning the same days plus Sun in winter/spring). You can also try *Maxwell's Cradle Mountain Lake St Clair Charter Bus and Taxi Service* (☎004/92 1431) connecting Devonport and Launceston to Lake St Clair ($40), Launceston and Devonport to Cradle Mountain ($40).

## The Overland Track

In the summer, hundreds flock here to walk the **Overland Track**, probably Australia's greatest extended bushwalk: 85km unbroken by roads and passing through buttongrass plains and forests of deciduous beech, Tasmanian myrtle, pandanus, King Billy pine and wildflowers, with side walks to climb various mountain peaks and view waterfalls and lakes. Much of the track is boardwalked, but you'll still end up thigh-deep in mud. There are several huts along the route, but no guarantee that they won't be full, so you must carry a good tent. The walk generally takes six days, five if you catch a boat from Narcissus Hut across Lake St Clair, and ten allowing time for side walks. You should take enough food and fuel to last, plus extra supplies to cover you in case of accidents or bad weather setting in; there's always plenty of unpolluted fresh water to drink from streams. The best time is February, when the weather has stabilized, but it's bound to rain at some point and may even snow. Most people walk north to south, but you can pay the **fee** at either end in the **national park office** (see "Cradle Mountain and Lake St Clair practicalities" sections below), where you must also register, get an obligatory briefing and have your gear checked to make sure it's sufficient. The Cradle Mountain–Lake St Clair National Park **map** and notes (*Tasmap*; $8) is an essential purchase. Once you end up at Derwent Bridge, exhausted and covered in mud, you can use the hot showers at the campsite (50c for 6min).

### THE OVERLAND TRACK: A PERSONAL ACCOUNT

The steep climb away from the car park at Lake Dove immediately sets the mood for what is to follow. The cars, day-trippers and litter soon vanish and the shapes, noises and smells of the landscape take control of our imagination. The steep craggy form of Cradle Mountain looms to the left, its outline in stark contrast to the smooth glacial pools of Lake Dove, Lake Hanson and Lake Wilks. Once on the plateau the first boardwalk appears, allowing us to plod along with comfortably dry feet. There is about 60km of boardwalk along the length of the track, since a huge number of people now tramp up and down it.

Walking through the cirques and glacial troughs, the formations around Waterfall Valley Hut remind me of school textbooks of dinosaurs and prehistoric man: the dramatic peak of Barn Bluff emerging from the moist clouds; Mount Ossa silhouetted against the sky, inviting us to scale its rocky flank. Summer offers no predictable weather patterns: hot sun, cold rain and biting winds, all within a few hours, are common. The night's damp chill requires good sleeping bags, even in the huts with their warm coal stove. Conversation here is lively; energized by fresh air and physical activity, people really talk.

Most of the day is spent dealing with what is immediately around us, driving rain on Pine Forest Moor, muddy slopes at Frog Flats, leeches everywhere, and a rumbling stomach. The large numbers of wallabies and snakes add to a sense that man has not managed to interfere too much with this particular place. Being able to drink clean water (the colour of tea) from a stream is a bonus most people appreciate. Frequent rain washes down the mountainsides and over buttongrass plains, filling the various rivers and spectacular waterfalls southwest of Kia Ora Hut.

The last stretch of the track is along the length of Lake St Clair. For a more remote final day, we took the track behind Mount Olympus. The scenery is less spectacular than at the Cradle Mountain end but equally impressive, with Bryons Gap giving wonderful views of the Franklin Lower Gordon Wild Rivers National Park and of Frenchmans Cap. Without the guiding trail of boardwalk a good eye for post spotting is needed. This part is particularly leech-infested and even more like a set from *The Land That Time Forgot*. We take our time savouring the tranquil beauty of Lake Petrarch, disturbing a sleeping snake and watching it uncoil and escape. The forests of Ghost Gums sway with the coming of a storm and a sleepless night is spent underneath a creaking bough as thunder rattles along the valley.

---

**TELEPHONE NUMBERS**

In November 1996, all numbers in the ☎002 **code region** will have the prefix 62 added; and in February 1997, all numbers in the ☎004 **code region** will have the prefix 64 added.

These later changes will coincide with the implementation of the ☎03 **area code** across the whole of Tasmania and southeastern Australia.

*(For more on changes to phone numbers Australia-wide, see p.40.)*

---

**Guided tours** are available, the best offered by *Craclair Tours* (☎004/24 7833; Oct–April; 8-day $895); you'll still have to camp and carry six kilos, however. For the real soft option, try *Cradle Mountain Huts* (22 Brisbane St, Launceston; ☎003/31 2006; 6-day $1250), staying in private lodges with hot showers, beds and delicious meals.

## Cradle Mountain practicalities

At **Cradle Mountain**, the impressive modern *Cradle Mountain Visitor Centre* (daily 8am–5pm; ☎004/92 1133) provides information on the many day walks available in this area of the park, and acts as a registration point for the Overland Track. It's a few kilometres from the visitor centre to **Lake Dove**, where several walks start, including the famous track, and in summer there's a shuttle bus ($5; every 90min). The same shuttle also runs to Waldheim, where there's **accommodation**, booked through the *Cradle Mountain Camping Ground* (☎004/92 1395; huts ④, bunkhouse $20 per person), actually a couple of kilometres outside the park along the road to the entrance; there are basic, picturesquely-sited huts (④), plus a couple of 24-bed bunkhouses, plus the *Cradle View Restaurant*; fuel is available here. More luxurious is the classy *Cradle Mountain Lodge* (☎004/92 1303; rooms in chalet ⑥, self-contained log cabins ⑦), signposted about a kilometre from the campsite and just outside the park entrance; there's also a restaurant, bar and grocery store here.

## Lake St Clair practicalities

There's another ranger station at Cynthia Bay on **Lake St Clair** (daily 8am–5pm), where the unspoilt lake is surrounded by bush; this also functions as a registration point for Overland Track walkers. The *MV Ida Clair* cruises on the lake dropping off at Narcissus Hut to begin the track from the other end, or just for a day walk (Cynthia Bay 9am, 12.30pm & 3pm, Narcissus 9.30am, 1pm, 3.30pm; $15 one-way, $20 return). The kiosk (☎002/89 1137) where you buy tickets for the boat also rents dinghies with outboard motors ($55 per day) and organizes the **campsite** – where there's also some cabins to stay in complete with wood stoves ($30). *Maxwells* (☎004/92 1431) $4-shuttle to Derwent Bridge leaves on demand and connects with *Redline* buses at **Derwent Bridge** on the Lyell Highway, or you can get a taxi direct there ($5), or take advantage of a return minibus run (6.30pm–9.30pm; $8) to the *Derwent Bridge Hotel* (☎002/89 1125; B&B ⑦), for **food** and drink; you can also stay here in pricey lodge-style **accommodation**.

# Franklin Lower Gordon Wild Rivers National Park

The **Franklin Lower Gordon Wild Rivers National Park** was declared in June 1980 and by 1982 had been included with the adjoining parks on the World Heritage List. This park exists more than anything for its own sake, most of it being virtually inaccessible. You can cruise up the Gordon, or fly over it, but the really adventurous can explore by **rafting the Franklin** and walking the **Frenchmans Cap Track**, both accessible from the **Lyell Highway**, which extends from Strahan to Hobart and runs through the park between Queenstown and Derwent Bridge. There are also plenty of short walks leading from the highway to rainforests, rivers and lookouts.

The **Franklin River** is one of the great rivers of Australia, and the only major wild river system in Tasmania that's not been dammed. It flows for 120km from the Cheyne Range to the majestic **Gordon River**, from an altitude of 1400m down to almost sea level. Swollen by the storms of the "Roaring Forties" and fed by many other rivers, it can at times become a raging torrent as it passes through ancient heaths, deep gorges and rainforests. The discovery in 1981 of stone tools in the **Kutikina Cave** on the lower Franklin has proved that during the last ice age southwest Tasmania was the most southerly point of human occupation on earth.

## RAFTING ON THE FRANKLIN

One of the most rugged and inaccessible areas left in the world, the surrounds of the Franklin River can't really be seen on foot – there are few tracks through this twisted, tangled and above all wet rainforest. **Rafting** is the only way to explore the river and, even then, it's possible just between December and March. The Franklin is reached by rafting down the Collingwood River from the Lyell Highway, 49km west of Derwent Bridge. The full trip takes eight to fourteen days, ending at the Gordon River, where rafters head back to Strahan by ferry from Heritage Landing (*Gordon River Cruises* ☎004/71 7187) or by seaplane from Sir John Falls Camp (*Wilderness Air* ☎004/71 7280).

One of the most dangerous rivers to raft in Australia, with average **rapids** of grades 3 to 4, up to grade 6 in places, the Franklin requires an expedition leader with great skill and experience (though even guides have died in the rapids). It's also very remote and in the event of an accident help can be days away; however, this haunting isolation is part of the attraction for most visitors. The weather, too, can be harsh – and the water is cold. It's inadvisable to attempt the trip **independently** unless everyone in the party has white-water experience and the group leader has made a Franklin River trip before; groups are required to have at least two rafts and to stay in contact with the **ranger** at Queenstown. Bear in mind that there's nowhere to rent rafting equipment in Tasmania. The **tour operators** don't require you to be experienced, just fit with lots of stamina and courage. **Prices** are high, but this is an experience of a lifetime, with the flight back to Strahan thrown in. For the shorter five-day trip from Propsting Gorge to the Gordon, expect to pay around $880; from $1325 for the full eleven-day trip from the Collingwood to the Gordon. The two Tasmanian-based operators, running trips from December to early April, are *Rafting Tasmania* (☎002/27 9516), and *Peregrine Adventures* (☎002/31 0977).

The sketchy "Franklin River Rafting Notesheets" are available free from the Queenstown Ranger Station, PO Box 21, Queenstown, Tasmania 7467 (☎004/71 2511), and the *Wilderness Society* publishes "Notes for Franklin River Rafters and Bushwalkers". There are **campsites** all along the Franklin, but most have room for only two or three tents.

### THE ROUTE

From the **Collingwood River**, it takes about three days to raft to the **Frenchmans Cap Track**. This is the **Upper Franklin**, alpine country with vegetation adapted to survive snow and icy winds. Look out for two endemic pines, **pencil pine** and **King Billy pine**. There are lots of intermediate rapids along this stretch and a deep quartzite ravine and large still pool at Irenabyss.

The **Middle Franklin** is a mixture of pools, deep ravines and wild rapids as the river makes a 50km detour around Frenchmans Cap. Dramatic **limestone cliffs** overhang the **Lower Franklin**, which involves a tranquil paddle through dense myrtle beech forests with flowering leatherwoods overhead. The best raftable white water is here at Newlands Cascades. It's a short distance to **Kutikina Caves** and **Deena Reem**; only rafters can gain access to these Aboriginal caves.

Flying over the national park from Strahan, you can see the confluence of the two rivers – the planned site of the ill-fated dam – surrounded by thick forest, much of it impenetrable and probably never walked by human feet. The Gordon appears wide and slow compared to the narrow, winding Franklin. From above, the forest reveals its beautiful combination of textures and colours, the delicate white and greens of the myrtle, pines and other trees a complete contrast to the typical Australian scene of dusty green gums shading to blue in the distance.

## Along the Lyell Highway

Heading east from Queenstown, the Lyell Highway enters the **Franklin Lower Gordon Wild Rivers National Park**, reaching Nelson River bridge after 4km, from where **Nelson Falls** is an easy twenty-minute-return walk through temperate rainforest. From here, the road begins to wind and rise up to **Collingwood River**, the starting point for raft or canoe trips down the Franklin (see box above), with some basic camping facilities. It's another ten minutes' walk from here to the **Alma River Crossing**.

In fine weather, the white quartzite dome of **Frenchmans Cap**, looking a little like snow, can be seen from the highway. For a more spectacular viewpoint that takes in the Franklin River Valley, **Donaghy's Hill Wilderness Lookout Walk** begins further along the highway on the left. Walk from the parking area along the old road to the top of the hill, where a sign marks the beginning of the forty-minute-return track. Further along the highway, the **walking track to Frenchmans Cap** (see below) begins with a fifteen-minute stroll to the "flying fox" that gets bushwalkers across the river. Continuing on the Lyell, there's soon another chance to see the Franklin on a ten-minute **Nature Trail**, with the river tranquil at this point, running around large boulders. At the start of the trail there's a picnic area and a wooden shelter with an **interpretative board** about the Franklin River. Beyond this point, you come across wonderful open buttongrass plains, huge uninhabited expanses fringed with trees. This is **Wombat Glen**, which looks as though it's been cleared into grazing country until you step out into it and discover its true, bog-like identity.

At the foot of **Mount Arrowsmith**, the highway begins to ascend, winding around the mountain's southern side above the U-shaped glacial Surprise Valley. The **Surprise Valley Lookout** offers a good view of the valley and, across to the southwest, another excellent aspect of Frenchmans Cap. Continuing down, you come to King William Saddle, another fine lookout point with views of the **King William Range** to the south and **Mount Rufus** to the north.

## The Frenchmans Cap Track

The most prominent mountain peak in the Franklin Lower Gordon Wild Rivers National Park is the white quartzite dome of **Frenchmans Cap** (1443m). Its southeastern face has a sheer 500-metre cliff and from its summit there are uninterrupted views of Mount Ossa in the Cradle Mountain Lake St Clair National Park, Federation Peak, Macquarie Harbour and, on a fine day, the whole of the southwest wilderness. It takes three to five days to do the 54km return trip to the summit, and the best time to go is between December and March, though you'll be in the company of all the other seven hundred or so people who walk the track at this time each year. Frenchmans Cap is much more demanding than the relatively straightforward Overland Track, with some very steep extended climbs and sections of mud, and should be attempted only by skilled bushwalkers – preferably with prior experience of other Tasmanian walks. Weather is temperamental: it rains frequently, and even in summer can snow. Beyond Barron Pass, the track is above 900m and at any time of the year might cop high winds, mist, rain, hail and snowfalls.

The track begins at the Lyell Highway, 55km from Queenstown, served by *Redline* (☎002/31 3233), *Wilderness Transport* (☎003/34 4442), and *Maxwell's Coaches* (☎004/ 92 1431). It's not advisable to leave a car unattended in the car park at the start – park at Lake St Clair and pick up transport from there instead. A fifteen-minute walk from the road brings you to the aerial cableway or **"Flying Fox"** across the river for the start of the walk. Record your trip intentions in the registration book here and again in the logbook at the two **huts** at Lake Vera and Lake Tahune that provide basic accommodation, though this is usually full and you must bring tents and stoves along. There are composting toilets at both huts and plenty of camping spots along the way; water along the track is safe to drink. From the Franklin River to Lake Vera, the well-defined track crosses plains and foothills, then becomes steep and rough as it climbs to Barron Pass for magnificent views, becoming easier again on the way to Lake Tahune, close to the cliffs of Frenchmans Cap. From here it's a steep kilometre's walk to the summit, before returning the same way.

For further **information**, get the free "Frenchmans Cap Track Bushwalker Notes" from the Communications Section of the *Department of Parks, Wildlife & Heritage*, 134 Macquarie Street, Hobart 7000; buy the "Frenchmans Cap Map and Notes" ($8, *Tasmap*); or contact the Queenstown Ranger Station (☎004/71 2511).

## The South West National Park

Tasmania's **southwest** is an area of contrast: arrow-sharp crested ranges of white quartzite cut across buttongrass plains. The isolation, rough terrain and unpredictable weather, even in summer – the southwest has over 200 days of rain a year – mean this is an area for experienced bushwalkers only. Being able to use a compass and read a map are important, but so is a tolerance of trudging through deep mud and swampy buttongrass while heavily laden with supplies and plagued by leeches.

"South Coast Walks" (*Tasmap*; $8) covers the southern gateways to the World Heritage area: Cockle Creek through Port Davey to Scotts Peak as well as Moonlight Ridge and South West Cape, including notes on track conditions, weather and campsites. For the rest of the area you'll need to purchase topographic local **maps**, and for detailed information, refer to John Chapman's *South West Tasmania*.

Two airlines operate **flights** into the national park from Cambridge aerodrome, 15km from Hobart. *Par Avion* (☎002/48 5390) run eighty percent of southwest flights, with a daily service to Melaleuca, weather permitting ($85 one-way; 4hr scenic flight $130); you can register your walk at the airstrip, where the same company operates a **Wilderness Camp** ($445 for 2 days, including flight, accommodation and meals). *Tas Air* (☎002/48 5088) fly to Melaleuca, Cox Bight or Scotts Peak ($90; which can cut out the trudge from Melaleuca), and they also offer joy rides over the whole of the World Heritage Area for $135. If you're planning an extended walk, you can arrange for either airline to drop food supplies for you ($3 per kilo).

Unless you're flying in or beginning at **Cockle Creek**, south of Hobart, access to the South West National Park is via the **Strathgordon Road** which passes Mount Field National Park. The ranger for this end of the park is based at Mount Field and you should drop in or call (☎002/88 1213) to check conditions and that you're adequately prepared. The good sealed road heads through state forest and the South West Conservation Area, with the amazing craggy landforms of the **Frankland Range** looming and signposts helpfully pointing out the names of the features. There's a $4.50 toll on the road between **Lake Pedder** and the **Gordon Dam** (power station tours daily 9.30am–3pm; 40min; $3.50), payable at the toll gate 4km out of **Maydena**. The road to **Scotts Peak**, where the walks commence, is very poor but *Wilderness Transport* run a service there and to Condominium Creek from Hobart, via Mount Field (summer Tues, Thurs, Sat & Sun; winter Thurs only; no service June–August).

## PEDDER 2000: THE RESURRECTION OF LAKE PEDDER

To Dr Bob Brown, Tasmania's foremost Green activist, Lake Pedder "was one of the most gently beautiful places on the planet". In the Frankland Range in Tasmania's south-west, the glacial lake had an area of 9.7 square kilometres until 1972, when it and the surrounding valleys were flooded as part of a huge hydroelectric scheme, creating a reservoir covering a massive 240 square kilometres and reached by the Lake Gordon Road via Maydena. Before then, the lake was so inaccessible that it could only be visited by light aircraft, which used to land on the perfect sand of the lake beach.

**Pedder 2000** is a campaign spearheaded by the *Wilderness Society* to drain the current Lake Pedder by the turn of the century and restore the lake to its former glory. In late 1994 a scientist revealed that, beneath the water, the sandy beach remained; and in 1995 divers filmed underwater, revealing the still-visible impressions of tyre tracks from the light aircraft that once landed there. The cost of draining the lake would be high and the current Tasmanian Premier, Ray Groom, leader of the Liberal Party, is opposed to the idea, citing his government's position that a "large and smelly puddle" would be the only result. Certain scientists and conservationists, however, *do* consider it possible for the lake to revert to its former state, even though it might take 20 or 30 years. A decision to drain the stored water would need the vision and permission of both the state and federal governments, and it may yet come to a tussle between the two governments in the High Court in Canberra.

## Western Arthurs Traverse

The most spectacular bushwalk in Tasmania, only 20km in length and 5km in width, **Western Arthurs Traverse** contains 25 major peaks and 30 lakes. The last glacial period gouged into this range, leaving sharp quartzite ridges, craggy towers and impressive cliffs, and carving cirque valleys that are now filled by dark, tannin-stained lakes, with surrounding buttongrass plains in complete contrast. Violent storms, mists and continuous rain can plague the route in summer since it's in the direct path of the "Roaring Forties". Crossing these ranges makes for a superb but difficult walk: though there's no manmade track, the route starting at Scotts Peak Road is not hard to follow; it involves scrambling over roots and branches and short descents and ascents into gullies and cliff lines, and you'll need to use a rope at some point. The whole walk takes between nine to twelve days and camping areas are limited.

The **Eastern Arthur Range** contains the major goal for intrepid southwest walkers, often considered the most challenging peak in Australia. This is **Federation Peak**, its steep, almost perfectly triangular outline rising starkly to outclass the surrounding rugged peaks and ridges. It was named by a surveyor in the year of federation, when most of the major landmarks in the southwest were still unvisited, and this peak was not in fact successfully scaled until 1949, its thick scrub, forests and cliffs keeping walkers at bay. Although the walk is now easier, the terrain having been "broken in", every year many walkers are turned back by the worst weather in Tasmania; and one person has died tackling the route. All the ascents are extremely difficult and most parties take between seven and ten days to reach the peak and return; minor rock climbing is required to get to the summit. The walk starts at the same point as the Port Davey Track (see below).

## Mount Anne Circuit

The highest peak in the southwest (1423m), **Mount Anne** is part of a small range capped with red dolerite in contrast to the surrounding white quartzite. Views from the summit are spectacular in fine weather but the route is very exposed and prone to bad weather even in summer. It's only suitable for experienced walkers carrying a safety rope. The three- to four-day walk begins 20km along Scotts Peak Road at

Condominium Creek (where there are camping facilities), and ends 9km south at Red Tape Creek, so a car shuttle might be advisable, or you can arrange to be picked up by *Wilderness Transport* (☎003/34 4442).

## Port Davey Track
Going straight through the heart of the World Heritage Area from Scotts Peak Dam south to Melaleuca (where you fly out) at Port Davey, the **Port Davey Track** is a wet, muddy four- to five-day track over buttongrass plains, with views of rugged mountain ranges. It's less interesting than some of the other walks in the area and most groups combine it with the **South Coast Track** for a mega ten- to sixteen-day wilderness experience, requiring a drop-off of food supplies. This combined walk is often called the **South West Track**.

## The South Coast Track
The **South Coast Track** is known for its magnificent beaches and spectacular coastal scenery of Aboriginal middens, rainforest and buttongrass ridges. At 85km it's one of the longest tracks in the South West National Park, a five- to ten-day moderate to difficult walk, usually from Melaleuca to Cockle Creek. Since the route is mostly coastal, the climate is milder than in many parts of the World Heritage Area, but you'll still need your wet weather gear as it tends to rain every other day. Though the track is regularly maintained, you do need to plough through sections of mud and across the exposed Ironbound Range (900m), the latter only to be attempted in fine weather. There are no huts along the way except at the Melaleuca airstrip. The best **approach** is to fly direct to Cox Bight, cutting out the boring buttongrass plains walk from Melalueca, then head for Cockle Creek. Alternatively, you can begin at Cockle Creek and get flown out at Melaleuca, or arrange for extra food supplies to be flown in at Melaleuca and continue along the Port Davey Track across the water using the row boats provided.

*Tasmanian Expeditions* (☎003/34 3477 or free call ☎1800/030 230) is the only company running an extended **organized walk** of the South Coast Track (Dec–Feb; $1040). You need to be very fit for the nine-day trip as each party member (10 maximum) carries a share of the food and tents, making the pack weight 18–20kg.

## South West Cape
The granite South West Cape juts out for 3km into the wild Southern Ocean and in effect forms the beginning of the southwest. Walking is fairly easy here, though the rough unmarked tracks across open countryside require sound navigation, and some high windy ridges have to be crossed. All routes start and end at Melaleuca or Cox Bight but there are a variety of ways to the cape and beyond, taking in different beaches and bays. Depending on which you choose, a simple route will take from three to seven days and the full circuit between six and nine. Note that its growing popularity has led to some overcrowding in the summer months.

## travel details

### Between Tasmania and the mainland states

#### Ferries
*Spirit of Tasmania* Bass Strait **ferry**: from Port Melbourne (Mon, Wed & Fri 6pm), returning from Devonport (Tues, Thurs & Sun 6pm); journey time 14hr 30min.

#### Flights
Mainly through Sydney or Melbourne, with smaller companies operating from Sale, Traralgon and Phillip Island, all in Victoria's Gippsland region. Flights within the state are available with *Tasmanian Air*, but as distances are so short, they're not really essential.

**Melbourne** to: Hobart (10 daily; 1hr); Launceston (10 daily; 1hr); Burnie (9 daily; 1hr); Devonport (12 daily; 1hr); King Island (3 daily; 45min); Flinders Island (3 weekly; 1hr 30min); Queenstown (2 weekly; 2hr 35min); Smithton (2 weekly; 1hr 20min); Strahan (2 weekly; 2hr 10min).

**Sydney** to: Hobart (4 daily; 2hr 20min); Launceston (4 daily; 2hr 35min).

## Transport on the island
### Buses

**Devonport** to: Burnie (2–3 daily; 50min); Cradle Mountain (summer 1 daily, winter 3 weekly; 2hr 15min); Deloraine (5–7 daily; 40min); Hobart (2–3 daily; 5hr 30min); Lake St Clair (summer 1 daily, winter 1 weekly; 4hr 45min); Launceston (3–5 daily; 1hr 30min); Queenstown via Strahan (5 weekly; 7hr); Strahan (1 weekly; 6hr 40min).

**Hobart** to: Burnie (2–3 daily; 4hr 45min); Cockle Creek (1–3 weekly, except June–Aug; 3hr); Devonport (2–3 daily; 5hr 30min); Dover (Mon–Fri 4 daily, 1 Sun; 55min); Kettering (Mon–Fri 5 daily; 40min); Lake St Clair (summer 1 daily, otherwise 2 weekly; 3hr); Launceston (5–9 daily; 2hr 30min); New Norfolk (3–9 daily; 30min); Port Arthur (Mon–Fri 2 daily; 2hr); Queenstown via New Norfolk, Derwent Bridge and Strahan (5 weekly; 7hr 45min); Richmond (Mon–Fri 4 daily; 30min); St Helens via Bicheno (5 weekly; 4hr); Scotts Peak (1–5 weekly, except June–Aug; 30min); Strahan (1 weekly; 7hr 45min).

**Launceston** to: Bicheno via the midlands (Mon–Fri 1 daily; 2hr 40min); Burnie (3–4 daily; 3hr); Cradle Mountain (summer 1 daily, winter 3 weekly; 4hr); Deloraine (2–3 daily; 40min); Devonport (3–5 daily; 1hr 30min); George Town (1–3 daily except Sat; 1hr); Hobart (5–9 daily; 2hr 30min); Lake St Clair (summer 1 daily, winter 1 weekly; 3hr 15min); Smithton (Mon–Sat 1–2; 4hr 40min); St Helens via St Marys (Mon–Fri 1 daily; 2hr 45min); Strahan (1 weekly; 7hr 30min); Walls of Jerusalem (summer 2 weekly; 3hr 30min).

# PART THREE

# THE
# CONTEXTS

# A HISTORY

The first European settlers saw Australia as *terra nullius* – empty land – on the principle that Aborigines didn't "use" the country in an agricultural sense; a belief which remained uncontested in law until 1992. However, decades of archeological work, the reports of early settlers and oral tradition have established a minimum date of 40,000 years for human occupation, and evidence that Aboriginal peoples shaped, controlled and used their environment as surely as any farmer. Even so, it's difficult for visitors to form a unified idea of pre-colonial times, as two centuries of European rule shattered traditional Aboriginal life, and evidence of those earlier times mostly consists of cryptic art sites and legends – though if you're lucky enough to get beyond the tourist image, you'll realize that Aboriginal culture, though being redefined, is far from confined to the past. The very simplified outline of Aboriginal history below is intended mainly as a background to accounts given in the guide, followed by a fuller description of the years since European colonization.

## FROM GONDWANA TO THE DREAMTIME

After the break up of the super-continent **Gondwana** into India, Africa, South America, Australasia and Antarctica, Australia moved away from the South Pole, reaching its current geographical location about fifteen million years ago. Though the mainland was periodically joined to New Guinea and Tasmania, there was never a land link with the rest of Asia, and the country developed a unique fauna – most notably the **marsupials**, or pouched mammals, but also a whole range of giant animals, the **megafauna** – which flourished, along with widespread rainforests, until about 50,000 years ago. Subsequent Ice Ages dried out the climate, and though some of the megafauna survived into Aboriginal times, by 6,000 years ago the seas had stabilized at their present levels, and Australia's environment was much as it appears today: an arid centre with a relatively fertile eastern seaboard.

**Humans** had been in Australia long before then, of course, most likely taking advantage of low sea levels to cross the Timor Trough into northern Australia, or island hopping from Indonesia onto what is now the Cape York Peninsula via New Guinea. Exactly when this happened, how many times it happened and what the colonists did next are debatable: there's no direct evidence for either distinct or continuous migrations from Asia, but since the earliest dated sites are found in the south of Australia, it seems reasonable that human occupation goes back further than scientists' current 40,000-year estimates. The oldest known remains from central Australia are only 22,000 years old, so it's also fairly plausible that initial colonization occurred around the coast, followed by later exploration of the interior – though it's just as likely that corrosive rainforests, which covered the centre until about 20,000 years ago, obliterated all trace of human habitation. The presence of the dingo and disappearance of the **thylacine** (Tasmanian tiger) on the mainland but not (until recently) in Tasmania indicates that there was a further influx of people and **dogs** more recently than 12,000 years ago, after Tasmania had become an island.

The earliest inhabitants used crude **stone implements**, gradually replaced by a more refined technology based around lighter tools, **boomerangs**, and the use of core stones to flake "blanks" which were then fashioned into spearheads, knives and scrapers. As only certain types of stone were suitable for the process, tribes living away from quarries had to trade with those living near them. **Trade** networks for rock, **ochre** (a red clay used for ceremonial purposes) and other products — shells and even wood for canoes — eventually reached from New Guinea to the heart of the continent, following river systems away from the coast. **Rock art**, preserved in an ancient engraved tradition and more recent painted styles, seems to indicate that cultural links also travelled along these trade routes — similar symbols and styles are found in widely separated regions.

It's probable that the disappearance of the megafauna was accelerated by Aboriginal hunting, but the most dramatic change wrought by the original Australians was the controlled use of **fire** to clear areas of forest. Burning promoted new growth and encouraged game, indirectly expanding grassland and favouring certain plants — cycads, grasstrees, banksias and eucalypts — which evolved fire-reliant seeds and growth patterns. But while modifying the environment for their own ends, the Aboriginal belief that land, wildlife and people were an interdependent whole engendered a sympathy for the natural processes, and maintained a balance between population and natural resources. Tribes were organized and related according to complex kinship systems, reflected in the 300 different **languages** known to exist at that time. Legends about the mythical **Dreamtime**, when creative forces roamed the land, provided **verbal maps** of tribal territory and linked natural features to the actions of these Dreamtime ancestors, who often had both human and animal forms. This spiritual and practical attachment to tribal areas was expedient in terms of use of resources, but was the weak point in maintaining a culture after white dispossession: separated from the lands they related to, legends lost their meaning — and the people their sense of identity.

## THE FIRST EUROPEANS

Prior to the sixteenth century, the only regular visitors to Australia were the **Malays**, who established seasonal camps while fishing the northern coasts for *bêche de mer*, a sea slug, to sell to the Chinese. In Europe, Spain and Portugal had carved up the globe between them in 1494 under the auspices of Pope Alexander VI at the **Treaty of Tordesillas**,

and all maritime nations subsequently kept their nautical charts secret to protect their discoveries. So it's likely, but not certain, that the inquisitive **Portuguese** knew of **Terra Australis**, the Great Southern Land, soon after founding their colony in East Timor in 1516.

But while contemporary politics later confused the issue of "discovery", various nations were making forays into the area: the **Dutch** in 1605 and 1623, who were appalled by the harsh climate and inhabitants of Outback Queensland, and the **Spanish** in 1606, looking for plunder, and pagans to convert to Catholicism. Guided by the Portuguese **Luis Vaes de Torres**, they blithely navigated the strait between New Guinea and Cape York — as if they knew it was there. Torres probably did; there's evidence that the Portuguese had **mapped** a large portion of Australia's northern coastline as early as 1536.

The rest of the seventeenth century saw the Dutch navigators **Dirk Hartog**, **Van Diemen** and **Abel Tasman** add to maps of the east and northern coasts, but eventually discard "New Holland" as a barren, worthless country. **British interests** were first stirred in 1697 by **William Dampier**, a buccaneer who wrote florid accounts of his visit to Western Australia, but it wasn't until the British captured the Spanish port of Manila in the Philippines in 1762 that detailed maps of Australia's coast fell into their hands; it took them only six more years to assemble an expedition to locate the continent. Sailing in 1768 on the *Endeavour*, captain **James Cook** headed to Tahiti (where scientists observed the movements of the planet Venus), then proceeded to map New Zealand's coastline before sailing west in 1770 to search for the Great Southern Land — unsure whether this was New Holland or an as yet undiscovered landmass.

They sighted the continent in April that year, and sailed northwards from Cape Everard to **Botany Bay**, where Cook commented on the Aborigines' initial indifference to seeing the *Endeavour*. When a party of forty sailors attempted to land, however, two Aborigines attacked with spears and had to be driven off by musket fire. Continuing on up the Queensland coast, they passed Moreton Bay and Fraser Island before entering the treacherous passages of the Great Barrier Reef where, on June 11, the *Endeavour* ran aground off

Cape Tribulation. Cook managed to beach the ship safely at the mouth of the Endeavour River (present-day Cooktown), where the expedition set up camp while the ship was repaired.

Contact between Aborigines and whites during the following six weeks was tinged with a mistrust that never quite erupted in a serious confrontation, and Cook used the opportunity to make notes in which he tempered romanticism for the "noble savage" with the sharp observation that European and Aboriginal values were mutually incomprehensible. The expedition was intrigued by some of the wildlife but otherwise unimpressed with the country, and were glad to sail onwards on 5 August. With imposing skill, Cook successfully managed to navigate the rest of the reef, finally claiming Australia's eastern seaboard – which he named **New South Wales** – on 21 August in the name of King George III, at Possession Island in the Torres Strait, before sailing off to Timor.

## CONVICTS

The expedition's reports still didn't arouse much enthusiasm in London, where echoes resounded of the Portuguese and Dutch opinions of the previous century. The outcome of the **American War of Independence** in 1783, however, saw Britain deprived of anywhere to transport convicted criminals; they were temporarily housed in prison ships or "hulks" moored around the country while the government tried to solve the problem. Sir **Joseph Banks**, botanist on the *Endeavour*, pushed Botany Bay as an ideal location for a penal colony which could soon become self-sufficient. The government agreed (perhaps also inspired by the political advantages of gaining a foothold in the Pacific), and in 1787 the **First Fleet**, consisting of between 750 and 821 convicts (the numbers are disputed) on eleven ships under the command of Captain **Arthur Phillip**, set sail for Australia. Reaching Botany Bay in January 1788, Phillip deemed it unsuitable for his purposes and instead founded the settlement at **Sydney Cove**, on Port Jackson's fine natural harbour.

Early years were not promising: the colonists suffered erratic weather and starvation, Aboriginal hostility, soil which was too hard to plough and timber which dented their axes. In 1790, supplies ran so low that a third of the population had to be transferred to a new colony on **Norfolk Island**, 1500 kilometres east; even so, in the same year Britain dispatched a second fleet with 1000 convicts – 267 of whom died en route. To ease the situation, Phillip granted packages of farmland to marines and former convicts before he returned to Britain in 1792. The first **free settlers** arrived the following year, while war with France reduced the numbers of convicts being transported to the colony, allowing a period of consolidation.

Meanwhile, **John Macarthur** manipulated the temporary governor into allowing his **New South Wales Corps**, which had replaced the marines as the governor's strong arm, to exercise considerable power in the colony. This was temporarily curtailed in 1800 by Philip King, who slowed an illicit rum trade, encouraged new settlements, and speeded production by allowing convicts to work for wages. Macarthur was forced out of the corps into the **wool industry**, importing Australia's first sheep from South Africa, but he continued to stir up trouble which culminated in the **Rum Rebellion** of 1808, when merchant and pastoral factions, supported by the military, ousted Governor **William Bligh**, formerly of the *Bounty*. Britain finally took notice of the colony's anarchic state, and resolved matters by appointing the firm-handed Colonel **Lachlan Macquarie**, backed by the 73rd Regiment, as Bligh's replacement in 1810; he settled the various disputes – Macarthur had fled to Britain a year earlier – and brought the colony eleven years of disciplined progress.

Macquarie has been labelled the "Father of Australia" for his vision that the country could rise above its convict origins; he implemented enlightened policies towards former convicts or **emancipists**, enrolling them in public offices. He also attempted to educate, rather than exterminate, Aboriginal people, and was the driving force behind New South Wales becoming a productive, self-sufficient colony. But he offended the landowner **squatters**, who were concerned that emancipists were being granted too many favours, and also those who regarded the colony's prime purpose as a place of punishment. In fact, conditions had improved so much that by 1819 New South Wales had become the major destination for voluntary emigrants from Britain.

In 1821 Macquarie was replaced as governor, and his successor, Sir Thomas Brisbane, was instructed to segregate, not integrate, convicts. To this end, New South Wales officially graduated from being a penal settlement to a new British Colony in 1823, and convicts were used to colonize newly explored regions – Western Australia, Tasmania and Queensland – as far away from Sydney's free settlers as possible.

## EXPLORERS

**Matthew Flinders** had already circumnavigated the mainland in 1803 (suggesting the name "Australia") in his leaky vessel, *Investigator*, and with the colony firmly established, expeditions began probing inland from Sydney. In 1823, John Oxley, the Surveyor General, having previously explored newly discovered pastoral land west of the Blue Mountains, chose the **Brisbane River** (in Queensland) as the site of a new penal colony; this opened up the fertile **Darling Downs** to future settlement. Meanwhile, townships were founded, leading to the creation of separate states to add to that of **Van Diemen's Land** (Tasmania), settled in 1803 to ward off French exploration: Albany (1827) and Fremantle on the west coast (1829), the Yarra River (Melbourne) in 1835, and Adelaide in 1836.

But it was the possibilities of the **interior** – which some maintained concealed a vast inland sea – that captured the imagination of the government and squatters. Charles **Sturt** left Adelaide in 1844 to try and cross the centre; forced to camp for six months at a desert waterhole, where the heat melted the lead in his pencils and unthreaded screws from equipment, he managed to reach the aptly named Sturt's Stony Desert before scurvy forced him back to Adelaide. At the same time, **Ludwig Leichhardt**, a Prussian doctor, had more luck in his crossing between the Darling Downs and Port Essington (near Darwin), which he accomplished in fourteen months. Unlike Sturt, Leichhardt found plenty of potential farmland and returned a hero; however, he vanished in 1848 while attempting to cross the continent again. The same year saw the ill-fated **Kennedy** expedition just managing the trek from Tully to Cape York in northern Queensland, but with the loss of most of the party – Kennedy included – as a result of poor planning, starvation and Aboriginal attack.

Similarly, **Burke and Wills'** successful 1860 south-to-north crossing between Melbourne and the Gulf of Carpentaria in Queensland was marred by the death of the expedition leaders (see box on p.389 for the full sorry tale). Finally, Australia's centre was located by John MacDouall **Stuart** in 1860, who subsequently managed a safe return journey from Adelaide to the north coast the next year. Hopes of an inland sea were quashed, and the harsh reality of a dry, largely infertile interior dawned on developers.

## ABORIGINAL RESPONSE

European advances had been repulsed from the colony's first year, when Governor Phillip sadly reported that "the natives now attack any straggler they meet unarmed". Forced off their traditional hunting grounds, which were taken by the settlers for agriculture or grazing, the Aborigines took to stealing crops and spearing cattle. Response from the whites was brutal; a relatively liberal Lieutenant-Governor Arthur ordered a sweep of Tasmania in 1830 to round up all Aboriginal people and herd them into reserves, a symbolic attempt to clear "the uncivilized" from the paths of progress. More direct action, such as the **Myall Creek Massacre** in 1838 (see box on p.216), when twenty-eight Aborigines were roped together and butchered by graziers, created public outcry, but similar "**dispersals**" became commonplace wherever indigenous people resisted white intrusion. More insidious methods, such as poisoning waterholes or lacing gifts of flour with arsenic, were also employed by pastoralists angered over stock losses.

Aboriginal peoples were not a single, unified society, and Europeans exploited tribal divisions by creating the notorious **Native Mounted Police**, an Aboriginal force who ruthlessly aided and abetted the extermination of rival groups. By the 1890s, adhering to a perverted Darwinian concept which held that Aboriginal people were less evolved than whites and so doomed to extinction, most states had followed Tasmania's example of "protectionism", relocating survivors into reserves which were frequently far from traditional lands: in Queensland for instance, Rockhampton Aborigines were moved to Fraser Island, 500km away.

## GOLD

The discovery of **gold** in 1851 by Edward Hargraves, fresh from the Californian fields, had a dramatic bearing on Australia's future. The first major strikes in New South Wales and Victoria saw an immediate rush of hopeful miners from Sydney and Melbourne and, once the news spread overseas, from the USA and Britain. The British government, realizing the absurdity of spending taxes on shipping criminals to a land of gold when there were plenty of people willing to pay for their passage, finally **ended transportation** in 1853. Gold also opened up Australia's interior far more thoroughly than explorers had done; as returns petered out in one area, prospectors moved on to find more. Western Australia and Queensland (which was saved from bankruptcy by gold in 1867) experienced booms up until 1900 and, while mining initially followed in the path of pastoral expansion, rushes began to attract settlements and markets into previously uncultivated regions.

A new "level society", based on a work-and-mateship ethic, evolved on the goldfields, where education had little bearing on an ability to endure hard work and spartan living conditions: but the **diggers** were all too aware of their poor social and political rights in other arenas. At the end of 1854, frustrations over mining licences erupted at **Eureka** (see p.713), near Ballarat in Victoria, where workers built a stockade and ended up being charged by mounted police. In the aftermath, rights, including the vote, were granted to miners. The Victorian goldfields also saw **racial tensions** directed against a new minority – the **Chinese** – who first arrived there during the 1850s. Disheartened by diminishing returns and infuriated by the Chinese ability to find gold in abandoned claims, diggers stormed a Chinese camp at **Lambing Flat** in 1861; troops had to be sent in to stop the riots, but the ringleaders were acquitted by an all-white jury. Throughout the country, goldfields became centres of **nationalism** (despite the fact that the Chinese improved life by running stores and market gardens in mining towns), peaking in Queensland in the 1880s where the flames were fanned by the importation of **Solomon Islanders** to work on sugar plantations. Ostensibly to prevent slavery, but politically driven by recession and growing white unem-

ployment, the government forced the repatriation of Islanders, taxed the Chinese out of the country, and passed the 1901 Immigration Act, which heralded the **White Australia policy** – greatly restricting non-European immigration, and prevailing right up until 1958.

## FEDERATION AND WAR

Central government was first mooted in 1842, but new states were not keen to return to being controlled by New South Wales, lose interstate customs duties, or share the new-found mineral wealth which had consolidated separation in the first place. But by the end of the century they began to see advantages to **federation**, not least as a way to control indentured labour and present a united front against French, German and Russian expansion through the Pacific. A decade of wrangling by the states, to ensure equal representation irrespective of population, saw the formation of a High Court and a two-tier parliamentary system consisting of a House of Representatives and Senate, presided over by a Prime Minister. Each state would have their own premier and Britain would be represented through a Governor-General. Approved by Queen Victoria shortly before her death, the **Commonwealth of Australia** came into being on January 1, 1901.

It's notable that the Immigration Act (see above) was the first piece of legislation to be passed by the new parliament, and reflected the nationalist drive behind federation. Though the intent was to encourage an Australia largely of European – and preferably British – descent, the policy also sowed the seeds for Australian independence from the "Mother Country". The first pull away came as early as 1912, when the Commonwealth Bank opened; Australia was trying to become less financially reliant on Britain. A negative aspect of the White Australia policy was that Aboriginal people were not even included in the national census, or allowed to vote until 1967. On the progressive side, the new government gave **women** the vote in 1902, and the Australian Labor Party, which had grown out of the depression and union battles with the government during the 1890s, established the concept of a minimum wage in 1907.

Defence had also been a moving force behind federation. But, even forewarned by the war between Japan and Russia in 1904,

Australia was largely unprepared for the outbreak of hostilities in Europe a decade later, owning little more than a navy made up from secondhand British ships. Promising to support Britain to "the last man and the last shilling", there was a patriotic rush to enlist in the army, and an opportunistic occupation of German New Guinea by Australian forces. Surprisingly, the issue of compulsory conscription raised by the Prime Minister **Billy Hughes** was twice defeated in referenda during the war.

From the Australian perspective, the most important stage of the war occurred when Turkey sided with Germany in 1915. **Winston Churchill** formulated a plan to defend British shipping in the Dardanelles by occupying the **Gallipoli Peninsula**, and diverted Australian infantry bound for Europe. Between April and December 1915, wave after wave of Australian troops were mown down as they landed on the beaches below Turkish gun emplacements; by the end of the year it became clear that Gallipoli was not going to fall, and the survivors were "evacuated" to fight on the Western Front. The long-term effect of the slaughter was the first serious questioning of Anglo-Australian relationships: should Australia have committed and sacrificed so much to help a distant country further its European policies? Conversely, as Australia's debut on the world stage, Gallipoli still remains a symbol of national identity and pride.

## 1918–1939

After World War I, the Nationalist Party joined forces with the **Country Party** to assume government under the paternalistic and fiercely anti-socialist guidance of **Earle Page** and **Stanley Bruce**. The Country Party had formed over the widening divisions between a growing urban population and farmers, who felt isolated and unrepresented politically. Under the coalition, pastoral industries were subsidized by overseas borrowing, allowing them to compete internationally, and technology began to close the gap between city and Outback: radio and aviation developments saw the birth of *Qantas* – the Queensland And Northern Territory Air Service – and the **Royal Flying Doctor Service** in Queensland's remote west. In the cities, work started on the Sydney Harbour Bridge, and the new Commonwealth Capital, Canberra, was completed.

On the social front, the US stopped mass immigration in 1921, deflecting a flood of people from a depressed **southern Europe** to Australia – which the government countered by encouraging British immigrants with assisted passages. While progressive in some areas, proposing a dole for the unemployed, sick, pensioners and mothers, the government over-reacted to opposition, illustrated by the **seamen and dockers' strike** of 1928. Citing the arch-villain "communism" as being behind the dispute, they attempted to stretch the scope of the Immigration Act to allow action against politically motivated disturbance. However, the implications that the law could be altered against anyone who disagreed with the government contributed to the downfall of Bruce and Page the following year. The themes of their rule – differences between rural and urban societies, questions of Australian identity, union disputes, and the effects of heavy borrowing to create artificially high living standards, unsupported by Australia's actual capabilities – are still current issues.

As the **Great Depression** set in during the early Thirties, Australia faced collapsing economic and political systems, with all the parties divided; pressed for a loan, the Bank of England forced restructuring of the Australian economy. This scenario, of Australia still financially dependent on Britain but clearly regarded as an upstart nation, came to a head during the 1932 "**Bodyline**" cricket series. The loan was virtually made conditional on Australian cricket authorities dropping their allegations that British bowlers were deliberately trying to injure Australian batsmen during the tour.

Meanwhile, worries about communism were succeeded by the rise of fascism, as Mussolini and Hitler took power in Europe and Japanese forces invaded Manchuria – the **Tanaka memorial** in 1927 actually cited Australia as one of Japan's future conquests. Although displaying a certain ambivalence to fascism, Australia assisted the immigration of refugees from central Europe, and after a prolonged union battle, halted iron exports to Japan. When the Prime Minister Joseph Lyons died in office, **Robert Menzies**, a firm supporter of British notions of civilization, was elected to the post in time to side with Britain as hostilities were declared against Hitler in September 1939.

## WORLD WAR II AND AFTER

Like the First World War, World War II saw Australia developing its identity through participation in global affairs, but this time without Britain's help. Menzies' United Australia Party barely lasted long enough to form diplomatic ties to the United States – in case Germany overran Europe – before internal divisions saw the government crumble, replaced by Labor and **John Curtin** in 1941.

Curtin, concerned with Australia's vulnerability after Pearl Harbor, made the radical decision of shifting the country's commitment in the war from defending Britain and Europe to fighting off an invasion of Australia from Asia. After the **fall of Singapore** in 1942 and the capture of 20,000 Australian troops, Curtin succeeded in ordering the immediate recall of Australians fighting in the Middle East, despite opposition from Churchill, who wanted them for the Burma campaign. In February, the Japanese unexpectedly bombed Darwin, launched submarine raids against Sydney and Newcastle, and invaded New Guinea; feeling abandoned by Britain, Curtin appealed to the US, who quickly adopted Australia as a base for co-ordinating Pacific operations under **General Douglas Macarthur**. Meanwhile, Australian troops in New Guinea halted Japanese advances along the **Kokoda trail** at **Milne Bay**, while the Australian and US navies routed the Japanese fleet in the **Battle of the Coral Sea**.

Australia came out of the Second World War realizing that, politically as well as geographically, the country was closer to Asia than Europe, that it could not count on Britain to help in a crisis (Churchill had been ready to sacrifice Australian territory to protect British interests elsewhere), and that it was able to form political alliances independently of the Mother Country. From this point on, Australia began to look on the US and the Pacific, as well as Britain, for direction. Another consequence of the war was that immigration was speeded up, fuelled by Australia's recent vulnerability. Under the slogan "Populate or Perish", the government re-introduced assisted passages from Britain – the "ten-pound-poms" – also accepting substantial numbers of European refugees; even Torres Strait Islanders, previously banned from settling on the mainland, were allowed to move onto Cape York in northern Queensland.

With international right-wing extremism laid low by the war, the old bogey of **communism** returned. When North Korea, backed by the Chinese, invaded the south in 1950, Australia, led by a revitalized Menzies and his new Liberal Party, was the first country after the US to commit troops to counter communist forces. A staunch supporter of British interests, Menzies also sent soldiers and pilots to Malaysia, where communist rebels had been fighting the British colonial administration almost since the end of World War II, under the anti-communist SEATO (Southeast Asia Treaty Organization) banner. At home, he opened up central Australia to British **atomic bomb tests** in the 1950s, because, in the tradition of the first European colonists, "nobody lived there". Some Aborigines were cleared to reserves, others – along with British troops involved in the tests – suffered the effects of fall-out and had their traditional lands rendered uninhabitable for the foreseeable future. Wrangles with the British government over compensation and the clearing of the test sites at **Maralinga** and **Emu Junction** were finally settled in 1993.

Menzies was still in control when the US became involved in **Vietnam**, and with conflict in Malaysia all but over, Australia volunteered "advisers" to Vietnamese republican forces in 1962. Once fighting became entrenched, the government introduced conscription and, bowing to the wishes of US President **Lyndon Johnson**, sent a battalion of soldiers into the fray in 1965, events that immediately split the country. Menzies quit politics the following year, succeeded by his protégé **Harold Holt**, who, rallying under the catchphrase "All the way with LBJ", gladly increased Australian commitment to the Vietnamese conflict. But as the war dragged on, world opinion shifted to seeing the matter as a civil struggle, rather than as a fight between western and communist ideologies, and in 1970 the government began scaling down its involvement. In the meantime, Aboriginal people were finally granted civil rights in 1967, and Holt mysteriously disappeared while swimming in the sea off Victoria, leaving the Liberals in turmoil and paving the way for a Labor win under **Gough Whitlam** in 1972.

Whitlam's three years in office had far-reaching effects: he ended national service and participation in Vietnam, granted independence to **Papua New Guinea**, and instituted free healthcare and higher education systems. In doing so, however, he alienated the mostly conservative Senate, and when the government attempted to finance mining interests with an illicit overseas loan in 1975, the opposition prevented the Senate from functioning. In an unprecedented move, the Governor-General **John Kerr** (until then, a largely decorative representative of the Crown overseeing Australian affairs) dismissed the government – a move that shocked many into questioning the validity of Britain's ultimate hold on Australia – and called an election, which Labor lost. By contrast, the following eight years were uneventful, culminating in the return of Labor under the charismatic Bob Hawke, a former trade union leader, in 1983.

## CURRENT EVENTS

To date, Labor have won a record four terms, three of them under Hawke, who was deposed in 1991 by his treasurer **Paul Keating**. A politician rather than a policy maker, Keating is best-known for his bullying rhetoric and his desire to turn Australia into a **republic** by the year 2001. Though now accepted by all parties, the notion of a republic was launched by Labor just prior to the 1992 general election, successfully dividing the opposition which lost after making a Goods and Services Tax part of their manifesto. **John Hewson**, the Coalition leader at the time, was forcibly replaced in 1994 by **Alexander Downer**, a move immediately regretted by the party as a string of blunders proved him an inept figurehead. Downer resigned in January 1995 and was succeeded by the once-and-future leader, **John Howard**.

Despite the Coalition's defeat at the last election, Keating is widely unpopular and many see his republican leanings as a smokescreen for the party's inability to deal with the country's problems – a massive balance-of-payments deficit and the severe drought in eastern Australia. The state governments, too, are becoming divisive and confused; corrupt or simply inept policies have seen a rash of **Royal Commissions** into state management, while Victoria's ruinous bid for the 1996 Olympics has brought the state to its knees.

Overseas, Australia is becoming more dedicated to its role as part of Asia, rather than Europe or the United States; though it was the first country to back the US during the Gulf War, continual bickering over trade agreements with the US has seen a cooling in relations. An Asian bias makes good economic sense, but has led to an often appallingly conciliatory attitude towards events in that region; as early as 1975, Australia didn't protest the annexation of Timor by Indonesia, and response to the Dilli Massacre and Khmer Rouge renaissance has been pitifully weak. Further afield, Australia's main strength in primary production seems certain to be undermined by South Africa's gradual re-emergence into international trade, though the effects will be moderated by Australia's increasingly secure stake in the Asian markets.

There have been advances though, most notably in the field of **Aboriginal rights**. A thorough but ineffective inquiry into the number of Aboriginal deaths in custody was overshadowed in June 1992 when the High Court handed down the landmark **Mabo Decision**, legally overturning the concept of *terra nullius*. The Mabo claim, set around **Murray Island** (Mer) in the Torres Strait, acknowledged the Merriam as traditional landowners and sparked furious debate between miners, pastoralists and the state and federal governments as to interpretation. A **Native Title Tribunal** has been set up to consider whether claims made under the Mabo legislation are valid. Among other conditions, claimants have to prove constant association with the land in question since white occupation, but it is likely that progress through the courts will be slow and painful. In the short term, Mabo seems certain to engender legislation confirming that Aboriginal peoples have land rights; exactly what these are may take years to establish.

# AUSTRALIA'S INDIGENOUS PEOPLES

**White Australians and the international community have grouped Australia's indigenous peoples under the term Aborigines since the British invaded in 1788. At the recent insistence of these indigenous groups, we are coming to recognize many separate surviving indigenous cultures and lament the loss of others by deliberate or accidental genocide since invasion.**

**Today these surviving cultures include highly urbanized Koorie communities in Sydney and Melbourne, semi-nomadic groups such as Pitjantjatjaras and Warlpiris living a relatively traditional lifestyle on the fringes of Central Australia's Great Victoria Desert, and the seafaring Merriam and other peoples of the Torres Strait Islands north of the mainland. If there is any thread linking these groups it is the cultural revival experienced over the last twenty years. Under the banner of national political movements, all of these groups have renewed their commitment to organizing their social world according to extensive kin networks, to re-establishing close religious and legal relationships to the land, and to maintaining and revitalizing their cultures and languages.**

## COLONIZATION

To understand the magnitude of the progress towards revival made in Australia, it is necessary to understand how dreadful the impact of colonization has been. The estimated 750,000 indigenous inhabitants of Australia in 1788 were unilaterally dispossessed of their lands and livelihoods by the British colonists who failed to recognize them as inhabitants and owners. Australia was annexed to the British Empire on the basis that it was *terra nullius*, or wasteland. This legal fiction persisted until the High Court judged in the 1992 **Mabo** case that native title to land still existed in Australia unless it had been extinguished by statute or by some use of the land that was inconsistent with the continuation of native use and ownership.

Upon deciding that the country was unoccupied, successive waves of new settlers hastened to make it so. Violent conflicts between indigenous and recently arrived Australians resulted in the decimation of Aboriginal groups. The most notorious of these conflicts was the **unofficial war** waged against Tasmania's Aboriginal peoples which resulted in the near destruction of indigenous Tasmanians. Grisly souvenirs of this war, including skeletons and preserved body parts, still shame the collections of museums throughout the world. Historians estimate that 20,000 Aborigines may have died in these mostly unrecorded battles.

**Disease** has also been a powerful if unintentional weapon in the war against indigenous Australians, and proved more effective than shooting or poisoning. Whole populations were wiped out by smallpox and malaria epidemics, and as recently as the 1950s desert peoples were severely affected by outbreaks of influenza and measles. The lack of immunity to these introduced diseases was exacerbated by the trauma of dispossession, the lack of availability of traditional food and water supplies, and the unhygienic results of being required to wear European-style clothing.

Australia's Aboriginal peoples have also been subjected to various forms of **incarceration**, ranging from prisons to apartheid-style reserves. In some parts of Australia these reserves were established on traditional lands, allowing people to continue to live relatively undisturbed. In other parts of the country, notably Queensland, people were forcibly removed from their home areas and relocated in reserves all over the state. Families were brutally broken up and the ties with the land and religion shattered. This treatment persisted in some areas until the late 1960s. Aboriginal people are still ridiculously over-represented in Australia's prison population, a situation which led to a **Royal Commission into Aboriginal Deaths in Custody**, which reported to the Federal Parliament in 1991. It called for wide-ranging changes in police and judicial practice, and substantial changes to social programmes aimed at improving the lot of Aboriginal peoples in the areas of justice, health, education, economics and empowerment.

Also since the 1950s, Aboriginal children have been legally removed from their black mothers and given into the care of state institutions and white foster parents as a part of a policy of assimilation. The practice began in Victoria in 1886 and has continued until remarkably recently (1969). This period of **"taking the children away"** still haunts the lives of many Aboriginal Australians who have lost contact with their natal families and their culture. The policy is currently the subject of a major government inquiry, bringing the issue to wider attention for the first time.

The result of two centuries of brutal mistreatment is that by almost every statistical indicator the Aboriginal population is **highly disadvantaged** in both absolute terms and compared to non-Aboriginal groups.

## REVITALIZATION

The revitalization of Aboriginal peoples effectively began in 1967 when a constitutional referendum recognized indigenous Australians as voting citizens. After over a hundred years of agitation, **land rights** were accorded to Aboriginal groups in the Northern Territory in 1976 under federal legislation. Since then, other states have legislated to vest title over various pieces of state-owned land to their traditional Aboriginal Owners. Tasmania and Western Australia remain the only states not to have made provisions for any Aboriginal land rights. Various representative bodies were set up by successive federal governments throughout the 1970s and 1980s, culminating in the **Aboriginal and Torres Strait Islanders Commission** (ATSIC), established in 1990. This statutory authority gives elected Aboriginal representatives effective control over many of the federal funding programmes directed at Aboriginal organizations and communities. Since the late-1980s, substantial funds have been directed towards training for employment.

With ownership of land and control over funding have come opportunities for economic self-sufficiency and expansion previously unavailable to Aboriginal groups. In many parts of the country this has allowed Aborigines to buy the cattle stations on which they worked without wages for many years. In central Australia, Aboriginal enterprises include TV and radio stations, transport companies, small airlines, publishing companies, tourist businesses and joint-venture mining operations.

Co-operative agreements with the Federal Australian Nature Conservation Agency have led to Aboriginal ownership and joint management of two of Australia's most important conservation reserves, **Uluru-Kata Tjuta** and **Kakadu national parks** in the Northern Territory. These arrangements recognize that Aboriginal owners retain an enormous amount of intricate knowledge about the ecology of their traditional lands that can be of great assistance in the development of comprehensive land management plans. The Uluru Fauna Survey, a joint scientific survey between Pitjantjatjara and Yankunytjatjara landowners and the scientific research authority, CSIRO, represents a landmark in the application of indigenous knowledge to solving conservation problems. In the wake of the Mabo Decision, other state and territory governments are looking at the Uluru model of co-operative park management as a way of accommodating Aboriginal land interests while providing for more effective conservation strategies.

## CITIZENSHIP AND ITS PROBLEMS

Despite these successes, Australia's indigenous peoples are still struggling against considerable disadvantages. Along with citizenship in 1967 came the right to purchase and consume alcohol, which has proved disastrous. **Alcohol** is heavily implicated in the destructive downward spiral often observed by visitors to Outback towns in Australia: there is a synergistic relationship between the disempowerment of Aboriginal people in general and self-destructive drinking behaviour in the individual. The negative repercussions are evident in sickness and death, violence and despair, exclusion from education and meaningful employment, as well as families and communities in disarray. The vast over-representation of Aboriginal people in the criminal justice system is directly attributable to the mediation of alcohol: large numbers of Aboriginal people are apprehended by police and held in police cells owing to drunkenness, even where public drunkenness is no longer a criminal offence.

Government response to Aboriginal drinking has typically been racist until recent years. Statutes like the notorious **two-kilometre**

**law** in Alice Springs, which made it an offence to consume alcohol in a public place within two kilometres of licensed premises, were directed specifically at getting Aboriginal drinkers out of sight of visitors to the town centre. In recent times, most governments have begun moving away from racist and draconian measures and towards providing Aboriginal communities and families with the legislative supports to limit drinking within their towns and homes, and have invested money in sobering-up shelters and alcohol **rehabilitation** programmes.

On the positive side, many families and communities are confronting the problems that alcohol is causing. This is possible because although some Aboriginal people equate drinking rights with racial equality, most have a negative view of alcohol abuse. A large proportion of Aborigines, particularly women and those who don't live in towns, abstain altogether; furthermore, Aboriginal people themselves are beginning to put pressure on problem drinkers to limit their drinking, and are now able to use new laws to reduce the damage that alcohol is doing to their families and communities.

A **case study** illustrates these efforts. Imanpa is a small Pitjantjatjara community between Alice Springs and the tourist mecca Uluru (Ayers Rock). Seeing their community racked by alcohol-related violence and death, Imanpa residents looked at ways to limit availability of alcohol to residents. With neighbouring communities, they successfully lobbied the Northern Territory Liquor Commission to limit the amount of takeaway alcohol that could be purchased at highway roadhouses to six cans of beer. They reached co-operative agreements with the licensees of these roadhouses that they would not serve takeaway alcohol to anybody travelling to, or living on, Aboriginal communities. Imanpa drinkers can still travel the 300 kilometres to Alice Springs to purchase drink and the community is looking at the possibility of pressuring government to reduce the number of takeaway outlets in Alice Springs: with approximately seventy outlets for a population of 20,000, Alice Springs has the highest per capita availability of alcohol in the world. They are also supporting efforts of their neighbours in the Mutitjulu community near Ayers Rock Resort. At the resort, habitual drinkers persist in persuading well-meaning tourists to buy alcohol on their behalf. The community is working with the resort to try to educate the tourists out of being tricked or intimidated in this way, and of the benefits of limited alcohol supply for the community's future.

Poor health continues to substantially reduce the life expectancy of Aborigines. In 1989, the first comprehensive National Aboriginal Health Strategy was put in place. Better and greater health education, better and greater access to quality housing, more specifically Aboriginal health services and better immunization programmes are all parts of the strategy. As with most areas of social service, health services for Aboriginal people have been the province of white professionals until very recently; an essential focus of the new strategy is empowering Aboriginal people by giving resources to them directly.

## THE FUTURE

Improvements in health and education, combined with the hope and reality of restoration of some of the land appropriated since 1788, have led to a **revival of interest** in their own culture for many Aboriginal people. **Languages** that have slipped into disuse are being relearned. **Ceremonies** and **art forms** that have been forgotten are being revived through research and reconstruction. Links with land and family that have been torn apart are being reforged. The benefits of this revitalization flow on to visitors to Aboriginal Australia. Aboriginal tour companies are introducing visitors to the ancient law, cultural history and culinary possibilities of the land. Aboriginal **dance** theatres are producing new and vivid works, and reinterpreting ancient dance forms for modern audiences. Aboriginal **authors and poets** are publishing major new works that present unique and indigenous viewpoints. Aboriginal **painters and sculptors**, using a mix of traditional and modern techniques and forms, are producing vivid and exciting works of art. Aboriginal **national parks** are introducing visitors to an ancient and alternative view of the natural landscape. There has never been a time when these most ancient of cultures have been more accessible to visitors.

# WILDLIFE

**Despite 40,000 years of human pressure and manipulation, accelerated in the last century by the effects of introduced species, Australia's ecology and wildlife remain among the most unique, and most endangered, on earth. Hoofed mammals brought in by European colonists have desertified an unsuitable environment and feral cats, hunting for pleasure as much as need, are still decimating the country's indigenous birds and small marsupials.**

Australians love to tell stories about the **dangers** that the bush holds for the inexperienced (see the "Health" section of *Basics*, p.20, for general advice on coping with hazardous wildlife). In reality, fearsome "drop bears" lurking in gums, fallen tree trunks that turn out to be giant snakes, bloodthirsty wild pigs and other rampaging terrors are confined to hotel bars; the product of suburban paranoia laced with a surprising naivety about the great outdoors. Apart from a couple of avoidable exceptions, there's nothing to fear from Australia's wildlife, and if you spend time in the bush at any stage you'll undoubtedly end up far better informed than the yarn-spinners.

Reptiles and birds abound, and while those variations on the mammalian theme, marsupials and monotremes, may not be exclusively Australian – they're also found in New Guinea and South America – it's here that they reached their greatest diversity and numbers.

## MARSUPIALS AND MONOTREMES

**Marsupials** are generally nocturnal mammals that give birth to a partially formed embryo which itself then develops in a pouch on the mother; this allows a higher breeding rate in good years. Easiest to find because they actively seek out people, ridiculously cute **ringtail** and **brushtail possums** are common in suburbs and campsites, often approaching if there's a chance of food. With a little persistence, you should encounter one of the several species of related **glider possums** in forest margins at dusk. **Kangaroos** and **wallabies** are the Australian answer to antelopes, and range from tiny, solitary rainforest forms to the gregarious 2m-tall **red kangaroo** of the

central plains – watching herds bounce effortlessly across the Outback is an extraordinary sight. Being smaller, less active and more sensitive to disturbance has made arboreal, eucalyptus-chewing **koalas** and tubby, ground-dwelling **wombats** elusive, and placed them on the endangered list as their habitat is cleared. **Carnivorous marsupials** are mostly shrew-sized today (though a lion equivalent probably survived into Aboriginal times); two of the largest are spotted **native cats** or **quolls**, and Tasmania's own **Tasmanian devil**, a terrier-sized scavenger.

Platypuses and echidnas are the only **monotremes**: egg-laying mammals which suckle young through specialized pores. Once considered a stage in the evolution of placental mammals, they're now recognized as a specialized branch of the family. Neither is especially rare, but being nocturnal, shy, and in the case of the platypus, aquatic, makes them difficult to find. **Echidnas** resemble a thick-spined hedgehog or small porcupine, occur throughout the country and are one of the few ant-eating mammals in Australia. **Platypuses** are confined to the eastern ranges, and look like a blend of duck and otter, with a grey, rubbery bill, webbed feet, short fur, and a poison spur on males. This mix was too unlikely for nineteenth-century biologists, who initially denounced stuffed specimens as a hoax assembled from pieces of other animals.

## INTRODUCED FAUNA

Of the **introduced mammals**, **dingoes** are descended from dogs, introduced to Australia by Aboriginal people in the last 12,000 years. To keep them away from flocks, graziers built the world's longest fence, which stretched from South Australia into northwest Queensland and down again to New South Wales. **Camels** have also taken Australia in their stride since their introduction in the 1840s, and thrive in the central deserts – Australia is the only place where dromedaries still occur in the wild, and they are regularly exported to the Middle East. The blight that **hoofed** mammals – horses, cows, sheep and goats – have perpetrated on Australia's fragile fauna is immense. Much of the country has been prematurely desertified by their eating habits, abrasive hooves and demand for water that, once extracted from below ground, is not replenished, alters the mineral balance and kills remaining plantlife. The damage caused by **rabbits** is well-known, but it is the feral **cat**, which hunts for sport as well as necessity, which is seen as the greatest threat to the indigenous fauna, primarily small marsupials and birds.

## REPTILES, BIRDS, BATS AND MARINE LIFE

**Reptiles** come in all shapes and sizes. In the tropics, pale **lizards** wriggling across the ceiling on velcro-like pads are **geckos**, and you'll find fatter, sluggish **skinks** everywhere. Other widespread species are **frill-necked lizards**, known for fanning out their necks and running on their hind legs when scared, stumpy **blue-tongued lizards**, often seen sunning themselves near paths, and the ubiquitous **goanna** family, which includes the monstrous perentie, third largest lizard in the world. In central Australia, look out for the extraordinary **thorny devil**, an animal that seems part rock, part rose-bush. **Crocodiles** are confined to the tropics and come in two styles. The shy, inoffensive **freshwater** crocodile grows to around three metres in length and lives off fish and frogs. The larger, bulkier, and misleadingly named **saltwater** or **estuarine crocodile** grows to seven metres, ranges far inland (often in fresh water), and is the only Australian animal which constitutes an active threat to humans. Highly evolved predators, they should be given a very wide berth (see box on p.433 for specific croc-country precautions). **Snakes** inevitably receive bad press and Australia has the lot, from constricting **pythons** through to three-quarters of the most venomous species in the world.

With a variety of terrain that reaches from temperate well into tropical zones, Australia's **birdlife** is prolific and varied. **Fairy penguins** and **albatrosses** are resident along the south coast, while **riflebirds**, related to New Guinea's **birds of paradise**, and the **cassowary**, a colourful version of the ostrich, live in tropical rainforest. The drabber **emu** prefers drier plains further west. Among the birds of prey, the countrywide **wedge-tail eagle** and the **white-breasted sea eagle** of the northern wetlands are most impressive in their size. Both share their environment with the **brolga**, an Australian crane, and the even larger stork, the **jabiru**, with its deep green plumage. **Parrots**, arguably the country's most spectacular birds, come in over forty varieties, and whether they're flocks of green budgerigars, outrageously coloured rainbow lorikeets or white sulphur-crested cockatoos, the experience is noisy. Equally raucous are **kookaburras**, giant kingfishers found near permanent water and whose owl-like cousin, the **tawny frogmouth**, has one of the most disgruntled expressions known to birdkind.

Huge colonies of **bats**, in orange, fruit and horseshoe varieties, congregate in caves or fill entire trees all over Australia.

In addition to what you'll see on the Barrier Reef (covered in the chapter on tropical Queensland), whales, turtles, dolphins, seals and dugongs (sea cows) are part of the country's **marine life**, with **southern right whales** recently making a welcome return to the southern coasts after being hunted close to extinction.

## FLORA

Australia's most distinctive and widespread **trees** are those which developed resistance to, or even dependence on, **fire**. Some, like the ubiquitous, seemingly limitless varieties of

## AUSTRALIA IN THE PAST

Australia has a **fossil record** which makes up in range what it lacks in quantity. Imprints of invertebrates from South Australia's **Ediacaran fauna**, dated to over 600 million years, are the oldest evidence of animal life in the world, while on a larger scale, footprints and fragmentary remains of several **dinosaur** species have been uncovered, and **opalized marine fossils** are unique to the country. Most intriguing perhaps is evidence of the **megafauna**, giant marsupials which flourished until about 30,000 years ago, overlapping with Aboriginal occupation. Climatic changes were probably responsible for their demise, but humans definitely did clear out the **thylacine**, a dog-like marsupial with an oversized head which vanished from the mainland after dingoes arrived, surviving in Tasmania until 1936 – the year it received government protection.

eucalypts or **gum trees**, need extreme heat to burst open button-shaped pods and release their seeds, even encouraging fires by shedding bark and leaves to deposit a thick layer of tinder on the forest floor. Other shrubs with similar habits are banksias, grevillias and bottlebrushes with their distinctive bushy flowers and spiky seed pods, while those prehistoric survivors, palm-like **cycads** and grasstrees, depend on regular conflagrations to promote new growth. Aboriginal people possibly enhanced these fire-reliant traits by organizing controlled burn-offs of vegetation; new shoots tempted animals into the locality.

Despite the country's extensive arid regions, there is no native equivalent to the cactus although the dry, spiky **spinifex**, or porcupine grass, the succulent samphire with its curiously jointed stem, and the aptly named **saltbush**, come closest in their ability to survive extreme temperatures. Following rain, smaller desert plants rush to bloom and seed, covering the ground in a spectacular blanket of colour, a phenomenon for which the southwest of Western Australia is well known.

On a larger scale, the Outback is dotted with stands of hardy **mulgas** and **wattles**, which superficially resemble scrawny eucalypts with gnarled bark, as well as scattered groups of bloated, spindly-branched **bottle trees**. The similar but far larger **boab**, found in the Kimberley and northeastern Northern Territory, is thought to be an invader from East Africa. **Mallee** scrub is unique to the southeastern Outback, where clearing of these tangled, bush-sized eucalypts for grazing has endangered both scrub and those animals who rely on it – the mound-building mallee fowl being the best known.

**Mangrove swamps**, found along the tropical and sub-tropical coasts, are tidal zones of thick grey mud and mangrove trees, whose interlocked, aerial roots make an effective barrier to exploration. They've suffered extensive clearing for development, and it wasn't until recently that their importance to the estu-arine life-cycle won them limited government protection – though Aboriginal people have always found them a rich source of animal and plants products.

**Rainforest** once covered much of the continent and, although today surviving in a fraction of its former abundance, you'll find pockets everywhere, from Tasmania's richly verdant wilderness to the monsoonal examples of northern Queensland and the Top End. Trees grow to gigantic heights as they compete with each other for light, supporting themselves in the poor soil with aerial or buttressed roots. The extraordinary **banyan** and **Moreton Bay fig** trees are fine examples of the two types. They support a superabundance of plant species, with vines tangling in the lower reaches while **orchids**, elkhorns and other **epiphytes** use larger plants as roosts. **Palms**, cabbage trees and tree ferns, with their giant, delicately curled fronds, occur in more open forest where there's regular water.

Some forest types illustrate the extent of Australia's **prehistoric flora**: Antarctic beech, found south of Brisbane's latitude as well as in South America, native **pines**, and kauri or karri from Queensland and WA which also occur in New Zealand – are all evidence of the supercontinent Gondwanaland which broke up into separate landmasses fifty million years ago. Other "living fossils" include primitive marine **stromatolites** – algae corals – still found around Shark Bay, Western Australia, or fossilized in the central deserts.

As long as you don't eat them or fall onto the pricklier versions, most Australian **plants** are harmless; though in rainforests you'd want to avoid entanglement with spiky **lawyer cane** and **wait-awhile** vines. However, watch out for the large, pale green, heart-shaped leaves of the **stinging tree** (gympie) – a scraggly "regrowth" plant found on the margins of cleared tropical rainforest. Even a casual brush delivers an agonizing and prolonged sting; if you're planning on bushwalking in the tropics, learn to recognize and avoid this plant.

# AUSTRALIAN FILM

**No visitor to Australia these days will be unaware of the rise in popularity of and respect for the Australian film industry since the early Seventies. It is generally agreed (with deference to a 1900 Salvation Army promo, *Stations of the Cross*) that *The Story of the Kelly Gang*, made in 1906 by Charles Tait, was the world's first feature-length film. Australians' well-known antagonism towards figures of authority soon led to a hugely popular series of bushranger movies, eventually to be banned in 1912 by the NSW police on the grounds that their unsympathetic portrayal in these pictures was corrupting youngsters.**

This **early heyday** of Australian film-making predated Hollywood and persisted with various World War I morale-boosting productions, despite the creation of a distribution duopoly (known as the "combine") which showed little interest in independent Australian films outside of its control. With the ending of the war and its many cinematic testaments to the heroic disaster of Gallipoli, Australian silent cinema reached a creative peak. **Raymond Longford** was Australia's Spielberg of Silents at this time, and his 1919 production of *The Sentimental Bloke* and its sequel *Ginger Mick*, a year later, were popular and notably naturalist dramas of a woman's taming of her larrikin husband's proclivities. Along with the already established contempt for authority, Longford's films featured a distrust of sophistication and formality and, even then, the mythic spell of "the Bush" began making its mark in Australian productions.

## HOLLYWOOD DOMINATION

Gradually, however, the combine squeezed the life from Australian cinema, which continued to decline as the powerful Hollywood studios got into their stride and entered the Golden Age of Talkies. In 1933 the mildly reformed wild boy from Tasmania, **Errol Flynn**, starred in his first feature film, *In the Wake of the Bounty*, directed by **Charles Chauvel**, a leading figure in Australian film-making until the late Fifties.

World War II saw a return to newsreels and documentaries, with the legendary cameraman, Damien Parer, earning **Australia's first Oscar** for his account of the fighting in New Guinea (*Kokoda Front Line*, 1942). Following the War, however, Hollywood's global cine-domination was unassailed, and Australian cinema just about fell off the edge of the globe. Nevertheless, **Chips Rafferty** turned up as Australia's answer to John Wayne, appearing in an unremarkable series of formula films such as the scenically superb epic of bovine migration, *The Overlanders* (1946).

In the Fifties the British Ealing Studios and MGM set up production companies in Australia, knocking out the odd outback drama watered-down for international consumption (but not success). This era produced few notable Australian films other than Cecil Holmes' hop back onto the bushranger bandwagon, *Captain Thunderbolt* (1953), and his similarly leftist study of mateship, *Three In One* (1957). Chauvel's remarkable *Jedda* (1955) was more unusual in that it tackled the tricky issue of an Aboriginal girl's white upbringing, sexual temptation and subsequent abduction back to tribal life, where a tragic death inevitably awaited her. If there is one subject Australian cinema still has difficulty dealing with (the New Wave having finally got to grips with women as individuals), it is Aborigines.

Australia was by now nothing more than an exotic, marsupial-speckled location for "**kangaroo westerns**" and other dramas where British and American actors could exercise their skills. *On the Beach* (1959) saw Stanley Kramer directing Nevil Shute's post-holocaust drama with Ava Gardner, Gregory Peck and Fred Astaire tiptoeing through the fall-out; a year later Zimmerman directed an affectionate classic of outback itinerant labour, *The Sundowners*, starring Deborah Kerr and Robert Mitchum.

## THE NEW WAVE

The **New Wave**'s birth was a response to the burgeoning counter-culture of the late Sixties. Among the many notable reforms of Gough Whitlam's Labor government was support for the long-neglected arts. Film-makers in particular were given a shot in the arm with the introduction of extremely generous grants to more than cover the cost of production. While in its early years this financial support helped produce some of the crassest male-fantasy "sex romps" ever seen (Tim Burstall's 1973 *Alvin Purple* and Terry Bourke's *Plugg* are matchlessly dire), the opening of the **Australian Film School** in 1973 allowed genuine talents such as Gillian Armstrong, Bruce Beresford and Paul Cox to flourish.

Two years later the **Australian Film Commission** evolved from previous similar organizations to help produce and market Australian films, and although the grants have been regularly reduced ever since, their introduction kick-started the moribund industry so that these days there exists a diverse pool of directors and technicians to keep things going.

Peter Weir's unsettlingly eerie *Picnic at Hanging Rock* (1975) remains an early jewel, the decade ending with further acclaim for his *Gallipoli*, Phillip Noyce's extraordinary *Newsfront* and Gillian Armstrong's first feature, *My Brilliant Career*. Auspicious futures were launched for Armstrong, and actors Sam Neill, Judy Davis and Mel Gibson, whose post-apocalyptic *Mad Max* trilogy saw a gradual stylistic evolution to suit the huge American market.

With *Crocodile Dundee*'s international box office success in 1985, Australia briefly became a fashionable destination – indeed Kakadu National Park owes as much to Peter Faiman's fish-out-of-water fairy tale for its present popularity as does Uluru (Ayers Rock) to the famous Dingo Baby case; *Evil Angels* (released in the UK under the title *A Cry in the Dark*) saw Meryl Streep miscast as Lindy Chamberlain in Fred Schepisi's 1987 version of those events.

---

### HOT SPOTS FOR FILM BUFFS AND SOAP GROUPIES

The majestic scenery of the Northern Territory has featured in many films: **Kakadu National Park** provided the setting for many of the scenes in *Crocodile Dundee*: familiar spots might include **Anbangbang Billabong** (see p.439) and **Waterfall Creek** (see p.440). *We of the Never Never* was set in the **Mataranka** region, which, predictably, has been re-christened "Never Never" country (see pp.453–454); some costumes worn in the film are on display in the Old Courthouse and Residency in **Alice Springs** (see p.464).

Desolation and Outback grandeur have a stranglehold on the science-fiction and post-apocalyptic genres: *Mad Max II* locations include the **Silverton** area of New South Wales (see p.244); as his parting shot, Mel Gibson upscuttled the semi-trailer on the nearby **Mundi Mundi Plains**. In South Australia, the pock-marked scenery of **Coober Pedy** (see pp.625–626) has found favour with many filmmakers, including Wim Wenders, who made his epic *Until the End of the World* here, while the lunar-like landscape was

also an invaluable element in creating the atmosphere of *Mad Max III*. And *that* Outback pub in *Crocodile Dundee* was none other than the Walkabout Hotel, at **McKinlay** in Queensland, (see p.398).

Lusher surroundings have also caught the imagination: in Victoria, the eponymous **Hanging Rock** (see p.704) which featured in *Picnic at Hanging Rock*, is within striking distance of Woodend, but is disappointingly lacking in eeriness.

Inevitably, the **Sydney** area has its fair share of hallowed ground for TV addicts: *Skippy, the Bush Kangaroo*, or at least son of Skippy, is the star of **Waratah Park** (see p.121). *Sylvania Waters*, somewhat surprisingly, is not fictitious, but a waterside nouveau-riche suburb of **Botany Bay** (see p.98) that the BBC "discovered" for their fly-on-the-wall documentary, while the soapy teenage angst and surfie bonhomie of *Home and Away* revolves around **Palm Beach** in Sydney's northern beaches (see p.97), with the Barrenjoey Lighthouse and headland regularly in shot.

Contemporary Australian cinema is perhaps most exceptional for establishing a number of **women directors** and **producers** and providing a handful of strong women's roles. Inevitably only the mainstream hits, like the uplifting *Strictly Ballroom* and *Death in Brunswick* have achieved wide overseas release while many equally fine "small" films pass largely unseen. It is these quirky, uniquely Australian films of which the rejuvenated industry can be most proud. The prestige of numerous and consistent awards at the Cannes Film Festival and others proves that Australia's long-established cinematographic heritage has, more than any other art form, helped rid the country of its former philistine reputation. Confident and uncompromising films like *Malcolm, Celia, Sweetie, The Year My Voice Broke*, are just a few which complement their better known siblings with 1994 seeing a media-led "renaissance" in Australian film. Stephan Elliot's sartorially outrageous *Adventures of Priscilla, Queen of the Desert* was the country's biggest box-ooffice success and won international acclaim, while Rolf De Heer's jet-black satire, *Bad Boy Bubby*, though not being the best choice for a first-date movie, put lead actor Nicholas Hope on the map. Best of all was P J Hogan's wonderful *Muriel's Wedding*, perfectly encapsulating the indigenous film-making idiom, and proving that Australia's cinematic talent can still come up with financially viable and idiosyncratic gems.

## FILMS TO WATCH OUT FOR

While you'd be lucky to catch all the recommendations below on the big screen (although keep an eye on the programmes of **arthouse**, or repertory, **cinemas** in the major cities), many of the titles below can be found in **video** rental stores.

### HUMOUR, BLACK COMEDY & SATIRE

**The Adventures of Priscilla, Queen of the Desert** (Stephan Elliot, 1994). A Queer romp across the Outback, prying into some musty corners of Australian social life along the way.

**Babakiueria** (1988). Culture-reversing spoof starts with Aborigines invading Australia during a roadside barbie and continues with an anthropological-style study of white Australia. Rare but well worth the search.

**Death in Brunswick** (John Ruane, 1990). Black comedy concerning the misfortunes of a hapless dishwasher who becomes embroiled in a gangland killing.

**Les Paterson Saves the World** (George Miller, 1986). Barry Humphries plays the repugnant cultural attaché in a lame spoof of monumental bad taste.

**Malcolm** (Nadia Tass, 1985). Charming, offbeat comedy about a slow-witted tram driver in Melbourne.

**Muriel's Wedding** (P J Hogan, 1994). Kleptomanic frump Muriel wastes away in an Abba-and-confetti dreamworld until ex-schoolchum, Rhonda, masterminds her escape from her awful family. Great performances.

### ADOLESCENT AND MISFIT ROMANCE

**Flirting** (John Duigan, 1989). Sequel to *The Year My Voice Broke* follows young boy's adventures in boarding school. Superior coming-of-age film.

**Lonely Hearts** (Paul Cox, 1981). Following the death of his mother, 50-year-old Peter buys a new toupee and joins a dating agency. Sensitive portrayal of the ensuing, at times awkward, relationship. Other Paul Cox features worth looking out for include *Man of Flowers, My First Wife* and *Cactus*.

**Strictly Ballroom** (Baz Luhrmann, 1991). Feel-good hit at Cannes and the box office follows mismatched dancers who, together, dare to defy the prescribed routines.

### URBAN DYSFUNCTIONALS

**Careful, He Might Hear You** (Carl Shultz, 1982). Absorbing tug-of-love drama set in 1930s Sydney.

**The Devil's Playground** (Fred Schepisi, 1975). Burgeoning sexuality oozes between pupils and their tutors in a Catholic seminary.

**The Last Days of Chez Nous** (Gillian Armstrong, 1991). Middle-aged woman slowly loses her grip on her marriage and family.

**Monkey Grip** (Ken Cameron, 1981). Bleak but candid portrayal of rootless lives and love in mid-Seventies Melbourne.

**Proof** (Jocelyn Moorehouse, 1990). Uncomfortably cold film about a blind cynic rejecting his equally maladjusted housekeeper's advances.

**Romper Stomper** (Geoffrey Wright, 1991). Violent account of the racial hatred and gradual disintegration of a gang of Melbourne skinheads.

**Sweetie** (Jane Campion, 1988). Part black comedy, part bleakly disturbing portrait of a bizarre suburban family.

## OCKERDOM & HOONERY

**The Adventures of Barry McKenzie** (Bruce Beresford, 1972). Ultra-ocker comes to England to teach the "pommie sheilas about real men". Ironically, Humphries' satire got beer-spurting ovations from the very people he despised and also set Beresford back a couple of years.

**Crocodile Dundee** (Peter Faiman, 1985). Acceptable side of genial, dinky-di ockerdom saw Hogan sell Australian bush mystique to the mainstream.

**The FJ Holden** (Michael Thornhill, 1977). Portrayal of west Sydney hoons' joyless hedonism as they ricochet between police, bars and girls.

**Wake in Fright** aka **Outback** (Ted Kotcheff, 1970). A horrifying gem in its uncut, 114min version; *Deliverance* or *Straw Dogs* Down Under. Coast-bound teacher blows his fare in Outback Hicksville and slowly degenerates into a brutal, beer-sodden nightmare.

## GRITTY AND DEFIANT WOMEN

**Celia** (Ann Turner, 1988). Wonderful allegory mixes Fifties' rabbit eradication programme with communist witch-hunt. Stubborn Celia is determined to keep her bunny.

**The Getting of Wisdom** (Bruce Beresford, 1977). Spirited Laura rejects polite sensibilities and snobbery of an Edwardian boarding school.

**Heatwave** (Phillip Noyce, 1981). Sweltering urban machinations as Judy Davis uncovers dirty dealings surrounding a proposed development in heatstruck Sydney.

**My Brilliant Career** (Gillian Armstrong, 1978). Early feminist questions and defies the expectations of 1890s Victoria.

**Puberty Blues** (Bruce Beresford, 1981). Two teenage beach girls refuse to accept their push-chair-and-shopping-trolley destiny.

**Shame** (Steve Jordell, 1986). Lone woman lawyer on a motorbike gets stuck in an Outback town full of creeps and delves into its dirty secret.

**We of the Never Never** (Igor Auzins, 1981). Good-looking version of Jeannie Gunn's autobiographical classic of turn-of-the-century station life in the Top End.

## MEN IN RUGGED CIRCUMSTANCES

**Gallipoli** (Peter Weir, 1980). Deservedly classic buddy movie in which a young Mel Gibson strikingly evokes the Anzacs' cheery idealism and the tragedy of their slaughter.

**The Last of the Knucklemen** (Tim Burstall, 1978). Tensions build up in a remote Outback mine and explode in bare-fisted punch ups.

**The Man from Snowy River** (George Miller, 1981). Men, horses and the land from A B ("Banjo") Paterson's seminal and dearly loved poem caught the overseas' imagination. A modern kangaroo western.

**Plains of Heaven** (Ian Pringle, 1982). Spookily atmospheric story of two weathermen in a remote meteorological station slowly losing their minds.

**Sunday Too Far Away** (Ken Hannam, 1973). Simple tale of macho shearers' rivalries in Outback South Australia.

## OUTBACK NIGHTMARES & WEIRDNESS

**Evil Angels** (*A Cry in the Dark*) (Fred Schepisi, 1987). A dramatic retelling of the Azaria Chamberlain story; dingoes will never seem quite the same again.

**Picnic at Hanging Rock** (Peter Weir, 1975). Richly layered tale of the disappearance of a party of school girls and its traumatic aftermath.

**The Lost Weekend** (Colin Eggleston, 1977). The beautiful bush closes in menacingly on an insensitive and ecologically unsound couple camping on a remote beach.

**Razorback** (Russell Mulcahy, 1984). Darkest of comedies exploiting urban paranoia of the Outback, and featuring a remote township, a gigantic, psychotic wild pig, and some bloodthirsty nutters who run the local abbatoir.

**Walkabout** (Nicholas Roeg, 1971). Following their deranged father's suicide during a bush picnic, two children wander through the wilderness until an Aboriginal boy guides them back to civilization.

## ABOUT ABORIGINES

**The Chant of Jimmie Blacksmith** (Fred Schepisi, 1977). Based on Thomas Keneally's excellent book set in the 1800s about a half-white Aboriginal boy who is forced onto the wrong side of the law.

**The Fringe Dwellers** (Bruce Beresford, 1985). Aspiring daughter persuades her family to move from the bush into a suburban white neighbourhood with expected results.

**Jedda** (Claude Chauvel, 1955). An orphaned Aboriginal girl brought up by a "civilized" white family cannot resist her "tribal" urges and is semi-voluntarily abducted by a black outlaw.

**Manganinnie** (John Honey, 1980). Set during the "black drives" of 1830s Tasmania, a young Aboriginal girl gets separated from her family and meets a white girl in similar straits.

## PORTENTS OF DOOM

**Cane Toads: An Unnatural History** (Mark Lewis, 1988). Bizarre and amusing documentary about the mixed feelings Queensland's poisonous amphibians arouse and the real threat they may pose to Australia's ecology.

**The Last Wave** (Peter Weir, 1977). Spooky chiller about a lawyer defending an Aborigine accused of murder – and the powerful, elemental forces his people control.

**Mad Max II** (George Miller, 1981). The best of the trilogy, set in a near future where loner Max protects oil-producing community from fuel-starved crazies. Great machinery and stunts.

**Newsfront** (Philip Noyce, 1978). Nothing portentous whatsoever but an excellent movie set among mid-Fifties Melbourne's newsreel crews, concerning the disparate political and professional aspirations of two brothers.

# BOOKS

Australian writing came into its own in the 1890s, when a strong nationalistic movement leading up to eventual federation in 1901 produced writers like Henry Lawson and balladeer "Banjo" Paterson, who romanticized the bush and glorified the mateship ethos, while outstanding women writers, like Miles Franklin and Barbara Baynton, gave a feminine slant to the bush tale and set the trend for a strong female authorship. In the twentieth century Australian novelists have come to be recognized in the international arena, with Patrick White awarded a Nobel Prize in 1973, and Peter Carey taking the Booker Prize in 1988. More recently, writers who have made a name for themselves within Australia, such as David Malouf and Tim Winton, have begun to arouse curiosity further afield.

These days Australian writing is flourishing: as in the United States, the **short story** thrives in Australia, with popular magazines such as *Australian Short Stories* and literary journals such as *Meanjin* providing a forum and exposure for short fiction and new writers. Eagerly read anthologies, on every theme imaginable and with a healthy emphasis on multiculturalism and women's writing, are constantly coming out; for a taste of the latest, the annual *Picador New Writing* is worth seeking out.

You'll be surprised at the range available in Australian **bookshops**, though be prepared to pay more than you would at home. We've given the publishers of each book, where available, in the United Kingdom (UK), the United States (US), and Australia (Aus); obviously most Australian-interest books are more widely available in Australia. O/p signifies an out-of-print – but still highly recommended – book. University Press is abbreviated as UP.

## TRAVEL

**Bruce Chatwin** *Songlines* (Picador UK, Aus; Penguin US). Semi-fictional account of an exploration into Aboriginal nomadism and mythology that turns out to be one of the clearest and most inspiring expositions of this complex subject. A must.

**Linda Christmas** *The Ribbon and the Ragged Square* (Penguin US). Pushy English journalist's travels and observations around the "ragged square of Australia" in the Eighties.

**Robyn Davidson** *Tracks* (Vintage UK; Pantheon US). Powerfully compelling account of a young woman's journey across the Australian desert, accompanied only by four camels and a dog. Davidson manages to break out of the heroic-traveller mould to write with compassion and honesty of the people she meets in the Outback and the doubts, dangers and loneliness she faces on her way. A classic of its kind.

**Howard Jacobsen** *In the Land of Oz* (Penguin UK, Aus). Jacobsen focusses his lucidly sarcastic observations on a round-Australia trip that gets rather close to some home truths for most Australians' tastes.

**Jan Morris** *Sydney* (Penguin UK; Random House US). Morris revises her former sour opinion in an insightful and informative account of Australia's favourite city.

## BIOGRAPHY

**Blanche D'Alpuget** *Robert J Hawke* (Penguin Aus). Definitive, much-praised biography of the colourful, tearful ex-Prime Minister of Australia, made even more interesting by the revelation that Blanche has since become his girlfriend. Read between the lines. For an update, you could try Bob Hawke's own effort, *The Hawke Memoirs* (Reed Aus), which the critics have mostly panned.

**Albert Facey** *A Fortunate Life* (Viking UK; Viking Penguin US o/p; Penguin Aus). Hugely popular autobiography of a battler, tracing his progress from a bush orphanage to Gallipoli, through the Depression, another war and beyond.

**Dorothy Hewett** *Wild Card* (Virago UK; Trafalgar US; Penguin Aus). One of Australia's most famous playwrights and poets, Hewett is also one of its more unconventional and outspoken. Her autobiography explores the first part of her life (1923–58): born in Perth, the beautiful, passionate writer threw her energies into the Australian Communist Party and into her love life, challenging political and sexual convention. Leaving her husband, she married a boiler maker and moved to Sydney, where she lived in working-class areas and took a job in a factory – on which she based her novel *Bobbin' Up* (Virago UK).

**Barry Humphries** *More Please* (Penguin UK, Aus). Autobiography of the face behind the many outrageous Australian caricatures.

**Clive James** *Unreliable Memoirs* (Picador UK; Knopf US o/p). The ex-pat satirist humorously recalls his post-war childhood and adolescence in Sydney's southern suburbs.

**David Malouf** *12 Edmondstone Street* (Penguin Aus). An evocative autobiography-in-snatches of one of Australia's finest literary novelists, describing, in loving detail, the eponymous house in Brisbane where Malouf was born, expanding to a view of the wider world: life in the Tuscan village where he lives for part of each year, and his first visit to India.

**David Marr** *Patrick White: a life* (Vintage UK, Aus; Knopf US). Superb biography of Australia's Nobel prize-winning author. The late Patrick White (1912–1990) is brought to life: a difficult, complex man whose terrible rages and homosexuality are frankly explored.

**Hazel Rowley** *Christina Stead: a biography* (William Heinemann Aus). Stead (1902–1983) has been acclaimed as Australia's greatest novelist, but years of living abroad gave her a wide range of settings for her novels. After years of living in Paris, London and New York with her American husband, she returned to Australia in her old age. Her masterpiece, *The Man Who Loved Children* (Flamingo UK; H Holt & Co US), ostensibly set in Chesapeake Bay in the USA, is regarded very much as the Sydney of her childhood, with the character of the title based on her famous naturalist father.

## SOCIETY AND CULTURE

**Krim Benterrak, Stephen Muecke and Paddy Roe** *Reading the Country* (Fremantle Arts Centre Press Aus). Intellectual exploration of Roebuck Plains in northwest Western Australia as an arena for contending discourses, ranging from the perceptions of seventeenth-century English explorer Dampier to the area's representation in Benterrak's paintings, in Roe's oral tales and Muecke's postmodern deconstruction.

**Geoffrey Blainey** *Triumph of the Nomads* (Macmillan UK o/p; Overlock Press US; Sun Aus). Fascinating account portraying Aboriginal people as masters and not victims of their environment. One of the best books on the subject.

**John Bryson** *Evil Angels* (Penguin UK o/p, Aus; Bantam US). The trial and witch hunt of Lindy Chamberlain, convicted of murdering the infant daughter whom she maintained was carried off by a dingo. Account of a miscarriage of justice that delves into the grubbier regions of Australian psyche and the law.

**David Headon** *North of the Ten Commandments* (Hodder & Stoughton UK, Aus). Anthology of NT writings from all perspectives and sources – an excellent literary souvenir for anyone who falls for the charms of Australia's "one percent" territory.

**Donald Horne** *The Lucky Country* (Angus & Robertson UK o/p; Penguin Aus). Although nearly thirty years old, this seminal analysis of Australian society has yet to be matched and is still often quoted.

**Pybus and Flanagan** (eds) *The Rest of the World is Watching: Tasmania and the Greens* (Sun Aus o/p). Poignant essays by prominent Green figures. Well-argued viewpoints on Tasmania's key Green issues and their importance on a global scale.

## HISTORY AND POLITICS

**Len Beadell** *Outback Highways* (Weldon Aus). Extracts from Len Beadell's half-dozen books, cheerfully recounting his life in the Central Australian deserts as a surveyor, and his involvement in the construction of Woomera and the atomic bomb test sites at Emu Junction and Maralinga.

**Michael Cannon** *Who Killed the Koories?* (Heinemann Aus o/p). Account of the violent 1840s in New South Wales as colonists and pioneers moving inland clashed with the Koorie Aborigines.

**Paul Carter** The Road to Botany Bay (Faber & Faber UK; U Cambridge P US). Fascinating and original analysis of "discovery" as cultural imperialism, and the metaphysics of exploration.

**Manning Clarke** A Short History of Australia (Penguin Aus). Condensed version of leading historian's multi-volumed tome focusses on dreary successions of political administrations over two centuries, cynically concluding with the "Age of Ruins".

**Miriam Dixon** The Real Matilda (Penguin Aus). Scholarly analysis of women's invisible role in Australia's history.

**Alan Frost** Botany Bay Mirages: Illusions of Australia's Convict Beginnings (Melbourne UP Aus). Historian Frost's well-argued attempt to overturn many long-cherished notions about European settlement. Among his contentions is that Australia was settled primarily as a means of supplying the British navy with scarce flax and wood for masts rather than as a dumping ground for convicts.

**Harry Gordon** Voyage of Shame: the Cowra Breakout and Afterwards (U Queensland P Aus). A revision of Gordon's excellent account, originally published as Die Like the Carp and rewritten to mark the 50th anniversary of the World War II breakout of prisoners of war.

**Stephen Hawke and Michael Gallagher** Noonkanbah (Fremantle Arts Centre Press Aus). Account co-authored by the then Prime Minister's son of the Labor Party's double standards and Aboriginal resistance to oil exploration on their land near Fitzroy Crossing in the early Eighties.

**Robert Hughes** The Fatal Shore (Pan UK, Aus; Random US). Minutely detailed epic of the origins of transportation and the brutal beginnings of white Australia.

**John Molony** The Penguin History of Australia (Penguin UK, Aus). Less scholarly but more accessible and interesting account than Manning Clarke's obligatory text.

**Patrick O'Farrell** Through Irish Eyes (Jesuit Publications Aus). Celebration of the Irish experience Down Under: a vivid collection of nineteenth- and twentieth- century photographs depicts the lives of the spirited immigrants who came in search of a better life.

**John Pilger** A Secret Country (Vintage UK; Knopf US; Random Aus). Australian-born Pilger challenges the country's sunny self-image with accounts of dirty dealings: mistreatment of Aborigines, racist immigration policies, British nuclear experimentation, Vietnam and the cosy mateship among politicians and industrialists.

**Cassandra Pybus** Community of Thieves (Minerva Aus). Fourth-generation Tasmanian's deeply felt account of the near annihilation of the island's Aboriginal people attempts to reconcile past and future.

**Henry Reynolds** The Other Side of the Frontier and The Law of the Land (Penguin Aus). Revisionist historian demonstrates that Aboriginal resistance to colonial invasion was both considerable and organized. His later work critically reassesses the arguments used to justify European settlement of Australia.

**Bill Rosser** Up Rode The Troopers: The Black Police in Queensland and Dreamtime Nightmares (U Queensland P Aus). Two accounts of harsh methods used in nineteenth-century Queensland to "disperse" Aborigines, postulating reasons why Aborigines were unable to mount widescale organized resistance.

**Babette Smith** A Cargo of Women (Sun Aus). Smith painstakingly traces the subsequent lives of one ship's "cargo of women" convicts transported to Sydney; eye-opening and sad.

**Ann Summers** Damned Whores and God's Police (Penguin Aus). Stereotypical images of women in Australian society are explored in this ground-breaking reappraisal of Australian history from a feminist point of view.

## CONTEMPORARY FICTION

**Jessica Anderson** Tirra Lirra by the River (Penguin US, Aus). Richly evocative novel follows an old woman's recollection of her troubled life as she returns from Britain to her childhood home in Brisbane.

**Thea Astley** It's Raining in Mango (Penguin Aus). Set in far northern Queensland, this saga traces the history of one rambunctious family from the 1860s to the 1980s, with each generation blithely plumbing new depths of failure.

**Murray Bail** Holden's Performance (Faber & Faber UK o/p; Penguin Aus). Satirical story of an Adelaide bouncer's rise to become bodyguard to the Australian Prime Minister. Wonderfully wide-ranging cultural references and caricatures.

**Rosa Cappiello** *Oh Lucky Country* (U Queensland P Aus). Powerful novel of the migrant experience from a young woman's point of view, translated from the Italian.

**Peter Carey** *Bliss* (Faber & Faber UK; HarperCollins US; U Queensland P Aus o/p). One of Carey's best novels is also his first: a story somewhere between fantasy and reality of a Sydney ad executive who drops out to New Age NSW. Other gems to search out are his early collection of bizarre short stories, *The Fat Man in History* (Faber & Faber UK; Vintage US; U Queensland P Aus); *Illywhacker* (Faber & Faber UK; HarperCollins US; U Queensland P Aus), the picaresque tale of a phenomenal liar; and Booker Prize-winning *Oscar and Lucinda* (Faber & Faber UK; U Queensland P Aus).

**Brian Castro** *Birds of Passage* (HarperCollins UK; Allen & Unwin Aus). Tale of a young, blue-eyed Chinese Australian interwoven with that of his immigrant ancestor; a richly metaphoric tale about a search for identity.

**Peter Corris** *The Empty Beach* (Unwin UK, Allen & Unwin Aus). Australia's answer to Raymond Chandler. Corris's hard-boiled novel is set in a glittering yet seedy Sydney where a soft-centred private eye investigates murder and exploitation in an old people's home.

**Christopher Cyrill** *The Ganges and its Tributaries* (Penguin Aus). Impressive first novel which swoops between India and Australia, charting a family's migration from Calcutta to Melbourne's St Kilda.

**Robert Drewe** *The Savage Crows* (Picador Aus). From one of Australia's best writers, this first novel is among his most powerful. A writer, whose own life is falling apart in a cockroach-ridden contemporary Sydney, sets out to discover the grim truth behind Tasmania's "final solution".

**Ben Elton** *Stark* (Warner UK). As the Earth reaches ecological meltdown corporate bread-heads pull the plug and prepare to abandon the planet. Mostly set in Western Australia, a hilarious, thought-provoking eco-apocalyptic thriller.

**David Foster** *Moonlite* (Penguin UK o/p, US o/p, Aus). Amusing social satire set in the Australian goldfields. An albino Scottish high-lander meets his black counterpart and finds the Aboriginal world, like his own traditional Celtic way of life, in conflict with the material-istic nineteenth century.

**Helen Garner** *Postcards from Surfers* (Bloomsbury UK; Penguin US, Aus). Recommended short stories by one of Australia's finest women writers. Her first novel, *Monkey Grip* (Penguin Aus), is a classic Seventies tale of obsession, love and heroin in inner-city Melbourne.

**Kate Grenville** *Lillian's Story* (Allen & Unwin Aus). A literary sensation when it was first published, the tragi-comic tale of Lillian Singer is loosely based on the life of Bea Miles, the eccentric Shakespeare-sprouting, tram-stopping, taxi-hijacking Sydney bag lady. Its sequel, *Dark Places* (Picador Aus) lacks any of *Lillian's Story*'s light, being told from the point of view of altogether nasty Albion Gridley Singer, a fact-loving patriarch who propels his daughter Lillian into madness.

**Rodney Hall** *Kisses of the Enemy* (Faber & Faber UK; Farrar, Strauss & Giroux US; Penguin Aus). Satirical analysis of power set in the near future. Under fat President Buchanan, puppet of a huge multinational company, the Republic of Australia slips from British into American hands.

**Barbara Hanrahan** *The Scent of Eucalyptus* (Trafalgar US; U Queensland P Aus). First novel of the prolific South Australian writer who consistently pushed reality to the edge of fantasy in her work, this captures the essence of Adelaide in the 1960s.

**Janette Turner Hospital** *Charades* (Virago UK; H Holt & Co US; U Queensland P Aus). Modern bedtime stories recounted by the beau-tiful Charade to her ageing doctor, moving backwards and forwards through time and space – Boston, Toronto, Melbourne and a childhood in the rainforest of North Queensland.

**David Ireland** *City of Women* (Penguin Aus). Producer of weird visions of Sydney, here a futuristic, violent city from which men are banished; *Archimedes and the Seagle* (Penguin UK, Aus) provides a delightful philosophical discussion between a dog and a bird as they roam the Domain and Woolloomooloo.

**Elizabeth Jolley** *Woman in a Lampshade* (Penguin UK). Set around Perth, this is an excel-lent collection of short stories to start you off on Jolley's original and quirky work, which thrives on black humour. Her characters suffer from isolation of the heart: *The Sugar Mother*

(Penguin Aus) examines what happens to a faithful husband when his wife goes on sabbatical and a young woman and her mother turn up on his doorstep demanding shelter.

**Dorothy Johnson** *Maralinga My Love* (Penguin Aus). Playing on the title of *Hiroshima Mon Amour*, the 1959 Alain Resnais film, this controversial novel written in the late Eighties is set around the secret British atomic tests in the Australian desert during the Conservative Menzies years of the late 1950s.

**Andrew McGahan** *Praise* (Allen & Unwin Aus). Running through one hot summer of unemployment, heroin, alcohol, sex, love and abortion in Brisbane, the detached narrator and his friends live life without much of a purpose. Unflinchingly, McGann dwells on the seedier details, creating a vivid portrait of self-destructing youth, with no moral to the tale.

**David Malouf** *Johnno* (Penguin Aus). The story of the outrageous Johnno from boyhood to manhood as told by his straighter friend Dante, this makes a fine introduction to one of Australia's most important contemporary writers. Try also *Remembering Babylon* (Picador UK), his Booker-nominated saga dealing with the real and symbolic settlers' relationship with Aborigines.

**Drusilla Modjeska** *The Orchard* (Picador Aus). The highbrow hit of 1994, Modjeska's delicate insightful book blends literary criticism and philosophy with three interconnected stories of women and girls, using as a central metaphor the garden and its growth, cultivation and change.

**Frank Moorhouse** *Room Service and Other Stories* (Penguin Aus). One of Australia's best satirists and an innovative crafter of the short story; this hilarious collection ranges from a look at Hiltons around the world to childhood fibs.

**Dorothy Porter** *The Monkey's Mask* (Hyland House Aus). Never afraid of experimentation, poet Porter combines three unlikely forms: the novel in verse, a detective thriller and erotica. Tough lesbian private investigator Jill Fitzpatrick trawls through the Sydney literary scene on the hunt for a murderer: all the suspects are male poets struggling under the weight of hugely inflated egos. Disturbing, full of suspense – and very witty.

**Tim Winton** *The Riders* (Picador UK; Macmillan Aus). The latest offering from one of Western Australia's finest writers, whose novels are richly metaphorical and tinged with the magical. *The Riders* sees Winton's first fictional jaunt to Europe, a desperate chase from Ireland through Greece, France, Italy and Holland as the rough-faced, kind-hearted and bloody-minded Australian Scully and his one-of-a-kind young daughter Billy track the beautiful (and ultimately mysterious) wife and mother who has abandoned them. Earlier novels, such as *Cloudstreet* (Picador UK; Graywolf US; Penguin Aus), brilliantly evoke the WA landscape.

## AUSTRALIAN CLASSICS

**Barbara Baynton** *Bush Studies* (HaperCollins US & Aus). A collection of nineteenth-century bush stories from the female perspective.

**Ralf Boldrewood** *Robbery Under Arms* (Penguin UK o/p; HarperCollins US & Aus). Story of Captain Starlight, a notorious bushranger and rustler around the Queensland borders.

**Marcus Clarke** *For the Term of his Natural Life* (Penguin UK; HarperCollins US & Aus). Written in 1870 in somewhat overblown prose, this romantic tragedy is based on actual events in Tasmania's once notorious prison settlements.

**Eleanor Dark** *The Timeless Land* (Angus & Robertson UK; HarperCollins Aus). Historical novel which recounts the beginnings of Australia.

**Miles Franklin** *My Brilliant Career* (Virago UK; Harper Collins US & Aus). Novel about a spirited young girl in turn-of-the-century Victoria who refuses to conform.

**May Gibbs** *Snugglepot and Cuddlepie* (HarperCollins Aus). A timeless children's favourite, the illustrated adventures of two little creatures who live inside gumnuts.

**Xavier Herbert** *Capricornia* (HarperCollins Aus). Indignant and allegorical saga of the brutal and haphazard settlement of the land of Capricornia (tropical NT thinly disguised).

**George Johnston** *My Brother Jack* (Angus & Robertson UK, HarperCollins US & Aus). First in a disturbing trilogy set in Melbourne suburbia between the wars, which develops into a semi-fictional attempt to dissipate the guilt Johnston felt at being disillusioned with, and finally leaving, his native land.

**Thomas Keneally** *The Chant of Jimmie Blacksmith* (Penguin UK, US, Aus). Prize-winning novel delves deep into the psyche of an Aboriginal outlaw, tracing his inexorable descent into murder and crime. Sickening, brutal and compelling.

**D H Lawrence** *Kangaroo* (Penguin UK, US). The famous English author wrote this novel while holed up in a cottage in Thirroul, on the New South Wales south coast, in 1922. Themes of political confrontation and vivid pictures of Australia show just what an imagination he had, since he spent barely a fortnight in Perth and a day in Sydney.

**Henry Lawson** Ballads, poems and stories from Australia's best-loved chroniclers come in a wide array of collections. A few to try are: *Henry Lawson Bush Ballads* (Angus & Robertson Aus), *Henry Lawson Favourites* (Penguin Aus) and *While the Billy Boils – Poetry* (HarperCollins Aus).

**Norman Lindsay** *The Magic Pudding* (HarperCollins Aus). Whimsical tale of some very strange men and their grumpy, flavour-changing and endless pudding; a children's classic with very adult humour.

**Ronald McKie** *The Mango Tree* (HarperCollins Aus). Gentle account of boyhood and first love in tropical Queensland.

**Ruth Park** *The Harp in the South* (Penguin Aus). First published in 1948, this is a well-loved tale of inner-Sydney slum life in 1940s Surry Hills. The spirited Darcy family's battle against poverty provides memorable characters, not least the Darcy grandmother with her fierce Irish humour.

**A B ("Banjo") Paterson** *The Collected Verse* (Angus & Robertson UK, Aus; HarperCollins US). Australia's most famous bush balladeer, author of *Waltzing Matilda* and *The Man from Snowy River*, who helped romanticize the bush's mystique.

**Henry Handel Richardson** *The Getting of Wisdom* (Virago UK; Trafalgar US; Minerva Aus). A gangly country girl's experience of a snobby boarding school in turn-of-the-century Melbourne; like Miles Franklin (see above), Richardson was actually a female writer.

**Nevil Shute** *A Town Like Alice* (Mandarin UK & Aus). A wartime romance which tells of a woman's bravery, endurance and enterprise, both in the Malayan jungle and in the Australian Outback where she strives to create the town of the title.

**Christina Stead** *For Love Alone* (Virago UK; Harvest US o/p; HarperCollins Aus). Set largely around Sydney Harbour, where the late Stead grew up, this novel follows the obsessive Teresa Hawkins, a poor but artistic girl from a large, unconventional family who scrounges and saves to head for London and alone.

**Randolph Stow** *The Merry-go-Round in the Sea* (Penguin Aus). Endearing tale of a young boy growing up in rural Western Australia during World War II.

**Kylie Tennant** *Ride on Stranger* (HarperCollins Aus). First published in 1943, this is a humorous portrait of Sydney between two world wars, seen through the eyes of newcomer Shannon Hicks. A determined young woman, she comes across more than her fair share of fanatics and charlatans in the course of her up and down career.

**Patrick White** Considered dense and symbolic – even visionary (though some claim misogynistic) – White's novels can be heavy going, but try and plough through *The Tree of Man, Voss, A Fringe of Leaves* or *The Twyborn Affair* (all Penguin, UK, US & Aus), the last a contemporary exploration of ambiguous sexuality.

## ANTHOLOGIES

**Mary Lord** (ed) *Best Australian Short Stories* (Penguin Aus). 130 years of short story writing, from Henry Lawson to Helen Garner. Ideal interstate bus companion.

**Dale Spender** (ed) *The Penguin Anthology of Australian Women's Writing* (Penguin UK, Aus). Brick-sized book with all the best of Australian women's writing from Elizabeth Macarthur to Germaine Greer.

**John Tranter and Philip Mead** (eds) *The Penguin Book of Modern Australian Poetry* (Penguin Aus). Poetry has a popular and active appeal Down Under; this century's best are collected in this anthology.

**Beth Yahp** (ed) *Family Pictures* (Angus and Robertson Aus). A fine book exploring the notion of the Australian family: multicultural and delightfully jumbled, with portraits and family secrets slipped from some of the country's best and newest writers.

## ABORIGINAL WRITING

**Faith Bandler** *Welou, My Brother* (Wild & Wooley Aus o/p). Novel by a well-known black activist describes a boy's early life in Queensland, and the tensions of a racially mixed community.

**Jack Davis et al** *Paperbark* (U Queensland P Aus). Accessible introduction to Aboriginal writing, from legends to modern poetry and prose.

**Nene Gare** *The Fringe Dwellers* (Sun Aus). Story of an Aboriginal family on the edge of town and society.

**Colin Johnston** *Wildcat Falling* (Angus & Robertson Aus). The first novel by an Aboriginal writer to be published (in 1965), this is the story of a black teenage delinquent coming of age in the 1950s. The author's later works are published under his Aboriginal name, Mudrooroo.

**Ruby Langford** *Don't Take Your Love to Town* (Penguin Aus). Autobiography demonstrating a black woman's courage and humour in the face of tragedy and poverty lived out in northern New South Wales and the inner city of Sydney.

**Sally Morgan** *My Place* (Virago UK; Little US; Fremantle Arts Centre Press Aus). Widely acclaimed and bestselling account of a Western Australian woman's discovery of her black roots.

**David Mowaljarlai and Jutta Malnic** *Yorro Yorro* (Magabala Books Aus). Starry-eyed photographer Malnic's musings while recording sacred Wandjina sites in the west Kimberley and, more interestingly, Mowaljarlai's account of his upbringing and Ngarinyin tribal lore.

**Mudrooroo** *Doctor Wooreddy's Prescription for Enduring the Ending of the World* (Hyland House Aus). Details the attempted annihilation of the Tasmanian Aborigines, drawing a strong parallel between the rape of Tasmanian women and of the people's land and heritage.

**Adele Pring** *Women of the Centre* (Pascoe Aus). Tales of women's lives from the central deserts.

**Paddy Roe** *Gularabulu* (Fremantle Arts Centre Press Aus). Stories from the west Kimberley,

both traditional myths and tales of a much more recent origin.

**Kath Walker** *My People* (Jacaranda Wiley Aus). Collection of verse by an established campaigning poet (now known as Oodgeroo Noonuccal).

**Glenys Ward** *Wandering Girl* (Virago UK, Fawcett US). The author, from Western Australia, tells her own story of growing up in a white world.

**Sam Watson** *The Kadaitcha Song* (Penguin US, Aus). Brutal, fast-paced thriller; a modern parable of warring good and evil, mixed with ancient sorcery.

**Archie Weller** *The Day of the Dog* (Allen & Unwin Aus). Written in 1981 for a competition, Weller's violent first novel came out in an angry burst after being released, at 23, from a spell in Broome Gaol. The protagonist, in a similiar situation, is pressured back into a criminal world by his Aboriginal peers and by police harassment. Searing pace and forceful writing.

## SPECIALIST AND WILDLIFE GUIDES

Australians are passionate and active travellers, and in every regional centre you'll find **specialist guides** to surfing, diving, cycling and numerous other activities: many of these are detailed in the text. There are few guides to Australia's **wildlife** designed for field use, though National Parks and Wildlife Service shops often stock booklets on local flora and fauna. As any visit to a remainder bookshop will prove, coffee-table works are legion.

**Jack Absalom** *Safe Outback Travel* (Five Mile Press Aus). A bible for Outback driving and camping, full of sensible precautions and handy tips for preparation and repair.

**The Australian Museum Trust** *Complete Book of Australian Mammals* (Angus & Robertson UK). Excellent photographic record but far too heavy to cart around. *Key Guide to Australian Mammals* (Reed Aus) offers a more portable selection of colour illustrations.

**Wally Caruna** *Aboriginal Art* (Thames and Hudson UK, US). Excellent illustrated paperback introduction to all styles of Aboriginal art.

**John Chapman** *Bushwalking in Australia* (Lonely Planet, UK, US & Aus). Long-established guide to trails throughout Australia.

**Josephine Flood** *The Riches of Ancient Australia* (U Queensland P Aus). Indispensable and lavish guide to Australia's most famous landforms and sites. The same author's *Archeology of the Dreamtime* (Collins) provides background and evidence on the development of Aboriginal society.

**Clifford and Dawn Frith** publish a range of meticulously photographed booklets on Australia's tropical wildlife from rainforest to reef (Frith & Frith Aus); the set form a fine overview of the north's fauna.

**The Great Barrier Reef** (Readers Digest UK). Complete rundown on the Reef, lucid and lavishly illustrated. Available in coffee-table format and in a slighter, more portable, edited edition.

**Blue Sky, Blue Bush and Silver** (Blue Bush Press Aus). Subtitled *"A guide to the Art, Artists and Galleries of Broken Hill, Australia"*, this beautiful book makes a wonderful souvenir of Broken Hill for art aficionados.

**Leigh Hemmings** *Bicycle Touring in Australia* (Mountaineer Books UK & US). Detailed illustrated guide focusses on a region in each state/territory with gradient profiles and maps plus sections on packing and maintenance.

**Tim Low** *Bush Tucker: Australia's Wild Food Harvest* (Angus & Robertson Aus). A guide to the bountiful supply of bush tucker that was once the mainstay of the Aboriginal diet.

**Oliver Mayo** *The Wines of Australia* (Faber & Faber UK, US; Penguin Aus). Good introduction to Australian wines and wine makers.

**Peter and Pat Slater** *Field Guide to Australian Birds* (Weldon Aus). Pocket-sized and easiest to use of the many available guides to Australian birds.

**Tyrone Thomas** *Regional bushwalking guides* (Hill of Content Aus). This series of five local guides are excellent trail companions.

**Mark Warren** *Atlas of Australian Surfing* (Angus & Robertson UK; Harper Collins US, Aus). Comprehensive guide to riding the best of Australia's waves .

**Mary White** *The Greening of Gondwana* (Reed Aus). Classic work on the evolution of Australia's flora and geography.

# AUSTRALIAN ENGLISH

The colourful variant of Australian English, or strine (which is how Australian is pronounced with a very heavy Australian accent), has its origins in the archaic cockney and Irish of the colony's early convicts as well as the adoption of words from the many Aboriginal languages. For such a vast country, the accent barely varies to the untutored ear – from Tasmania to the Northwest you'll find little variation in the national drawl, with its curious, interrogative ending to sentences – although Queenslanders are noted for their slow delivery. One of the most consistent tendencies of strine is to abbreviate words and then stick an "-o" or, more commonly, an "-ie" on the end: as in "bring your cozzie to the barbie this arvo" (bring your swimming costume to the barbecue this afternoon). This informality extends to the frequent use of "bloody", "bugger" and "bastard", the latter two used affectionately. Attempting to abuse someone by calling them a bastard will most likely end up in an offer of a beer. There's also an endearing tendency to genderize inanimate objects as, for example, "she's buggered, mate" (your inanimate object is beyond repair) or "do 'im up nice and tight" (be certain that your inanimate object is well affixed).

The popularity of dire Australian TV soap operas has seen strine spread overseas, much as Americanisms have pervaded the English-speaking world. Popular strinisms like "hang a U-ey" (make a U-turn) and the versatile and agreeable "no worries" are now commonly used outside Australia.

**Anzac** Australia and New Zealand Army Corps; every town has a memorial to Anzac casualties from both World Wars.

**Arvo** Afternoon.

**Back o' Bourke** Outback.

**Banana bender** Resident of Queensland.

**Barbie** Barbecue.

**You beauty!** or **beaut** Exclamation of delight.

**Beg yours?** Excuse me, say again?

**Beyond the Black Stump** Outback, back of beyond.

**Billabong** Waterhole in dry river bed.

**Billy** Cooking pot.

**Bitumen** Sealed road as opposed to dirt road.

**Blowies** Blow flies.

**Bludger** Someone who does not pull their weight or a scrounger as in "dole bludger".

**Blue** Fight, also a red-haired person.

**Bottle shop** Off-licence or liquor store.

**Brumby** Feral horse.

**Buckley's** No chance; as in "hasn't got a Buckley's".

**Bugs** Moreton Bay bug – type of crayfish indigenous to southern Queensland.

**Bunyip** Monster of Aboriginal legend; bogeyman.

**Burl** Give it a go; as in "give it a burl".

**Bush** Unsettled country area.

**Bushranger** Runaway convict, outlaw from the nineteenth century.

**Bushwhacker** Someone lacking in social graces, a hick.

**BYO** Bring your own. Restaurant which allows you to bring your own alcohol.

**Chook** Chicken.

**Chunder** Vomit.

**Cocky** Small farmer **Cow cocky** Dairy farmer.

**To come the raw prawn** To try and decieve or make a fool of someone.

**Coo-eee**! Aboriginal long-distance greeting now widely adopted as a kind of "yoo hoo!".

**Cozzies**, **bathers**, **swimmers**, **togs** Swimming costume.

**Crim** Criminal.

**Crook** Sick or broken.

**Crow eater** Resident of South Australia.

**Cut lunch** Sandwiches.

**Dag** Nerd **Daggy** unattractive.

**Daks**, **strides** Trousers/pants.

**Dam** A man-made body of water or reservoir; not just the dam itself.

**Damper** Soda bread cooked in a pot on embers.

**Dekko** To look at, as in "take a dekko at this".

**Deli** Delicatessen, corner shop or sandwich bar.

**Derro** Derelict or destitute person.

**Didgeridoo** Droning musical instrument made from a termite-hollowed branch.

**Digger** Old timer, especially an old soldier.

**Dill** Idiot.

**Dob in** To tell on someone, as in "she dobbed him in".

**Drongo** Fool.

**Drover** Cowboy or station hand.

**Dunny** Outside pit toilet.

**Esky** Portable, insulated box to keep food or beer cold.

**Fair dinkum**, **Dinky di** Honestly, truly.

**Fossick** To search for gold or gems in abandoned diggings.

**Galah** Noisy or garrulous person.

**Garbo** Garbage or refuse collector.

**G'day** Hello, hi.

**Give away** To give up or resign, as in "I used to be a garbo but I gave it away".

**Grog** Alcoholic drink, usually beer.

**Gub**, **Gubbah** Aboriginal terms for a white person.

**Gutless wonder** Coward.

**Hoon** A yob, delinquent.

**Humpy** Temporary shelter used by Aborigines and early pioneers.

**Jackeroo** Male station hand.

**Jilleroo** Female station hand.

**Joey** Baby kangaroo still in the pouch.

**Koorie** Collective name for Aboriginal people from southeastern Australia.

**Larrikin** Mischievous youth.

**Lay by** Practice of putting a deposit on goods until they can be fully paid for.

**Lollies** Sweets or candy.

**Manchester** Linen goods.

**Mexicans** Residents of NSW and Victoria.

**Milk bar** Corner shop and often small cafe.

**Never Never** Outback, wilderness.

**New Australian** Recent immigrants, often a euphemism for Australians of non-British descent.

**No worries** That's okay, It doesn't matter, Don't mention it.

**Ocker** Uncultivated Australian male.

**Outback** Remote, unsettled regions of Australia.

**Paddock** Field.

**Panel van** Van with no rear windows and front seating only.

**Pashing** Kissing or snogging.

**Perve** To leer or act as a voyeur, as in "What are you perving at?"

**Piss** Beer.

**Pissed** Drunk.

**Piss head** Drunkard.

**Pokies** One-armed bandits, gambling machines.

**Pommie**, **Pom** Person of English descent – not necessarily abusive.

**Rapt** Very pleased, delighted.

**Ratbag** An eccentric person, also term of mild abuse.

**Ratshit** or **Shithouse** How you feel after a night on the piss.

**Rego** Vehicle registration document.

**Ridji Didge** The real thing or genuine article.

**Ripper!** Rather old-fashioned exclamation of enthusiasm.

**Rollies** Roll up cigarettes.

**Root** Vulgar term for sexual congress.

**Rooted** To be very tired or to be beyond repair; as in "she's rooted, mate" – your [car] is irreparable.

**Ropable** Furious to the point of requiring restraint.

**Sandgroper** Resident of WA.

**She'll be right** or **She'll be apples** Everything will work out fine.

**Shoot through** To pass through or leave hurriedly.

**Shout** To pay for someone or to buy a round of drinks; as in "it's your shout, mate".

**Sickie** To take a day off work due to (sometimes alleged) illness; as in "to pull a sickie".

**Singlet** Sleeveless vest.

**Skivvy** Polo neck.

**Smoko** Tea break.

**Snag** Sausage.

**Spunk** Attractive or sexy person of either gender; as in "what a spunk!"

**Squatter** Historical term for early settlers who took up public land as their own.

**Station** Very large pastoral property or ranch.

**Sticky beak** Nosey person or to be nosey as in "let's have a sticky beak".

**Stockman** Cowboy or station hand.

**Stubby** Small bottle of beer.

**Swag** Large bedroll or one's belongings.

**Tall poppy** Someone who excels or is eminent. "Cutting down tall poppies" is to bring over-achievers back to earth – a national pastime.

**Thongs** Flip-flops or sandals.

**Throw a wobbly** Lose your temper.

**Tinnie** Can of beer or small aluminium boat.

**Ute** Short for "utility" vehicle; pick-up truck.

**Wacko!** Exclamation of enthusiasm.

**Walkabout** Temporary migration undertaken by Aborigines; also has the wider meaning of a journey.

**Gone walkabout** To go missing.

**Warm fuzzies** Feeling of contentment.

**Waxhead** Surfer.

**Weatherboard** Wooden house.

**Whinger** Someone who complains – allegedly common among Poms.

**Wog** Derogatory description for those of Mediterranean descent.

**Wowser** Killjoy.

**Yabber** To talk or chat.

**Yabbie** Freshwater crayfish.

**Yakka** Work, as in "hard yakka".

**Yobbo** Uncouth person.

# INDEX

**Note:** where a place name alone might cause confusion, the standard abbreviation for the state has been added in parentheses; these are ACT (Australian Capital Territory), NSW (New South Wales), NT (Northern Territory), QLD (Queensland), SA (South Australia), TAS (Tasmania), VIC (Victoria), WA (Western Australia).

---

### ROUGH GUIDE FAVOURITES
#### Outback/country towns

---

**ROUGH GUIDE FAVOURITES**
**Scenic drives**

| | |
|---|---|
| Eyre Highway, SA/WA | →p.533 |
| Finke Gorge, NT | →p.474 |
| Great Ocean Road, VIC | →p.690 |
| Lyell Highway, TAS | →p.816 |
| Stirling Ranges, WA | →p.522 |
| Ross River Highway, NT | →p.475 |
| Simpson Desert Crossing, QLD/NT | →p.637 |

---

**ROUGH GUIDE FAVOURITES**

**Walks**

| | |
|---|---|
| Alpine Walk, VIC | →p.744 |
| Blue Pool/Canungra Creek Track, QLD | →p.290 |
| East Coast Trail, Hinchinbrook Island, QLD | →p.348 |
| Heysen Trail, SA | →p.572 |
| Kings Canyon, NT | →p.479 |
| Overland Track, TAS | →p.813 |
| Six Foot Track, NSW | →p.143 |
| Wilpena Pound, SA | →p.631 |

| ROUGH GUIDE FAVOURITES | |
|---|---|
| **Beaches** | |
| Belongil Beach, NSW | →p.201 |
| Bondi Beach, NSW | → p.94 |
| Cable Beach, WA | →p.557 |
| Lorne, VIC | →p.694 |
| Whitehaven Beach, Whitsunday Island, QLD | →p.334 |
| Wine Glass Bay, TAS | →p.780 |

### THANKS

**Thanks** are due to all those who wrote in with comments, suggestions and criticisms of the previous edition: Anne and Robert (the Mission Beach Scots), Andrew Bathurst, Paul Bew, Peter Brandis, Annie Chandler, Mirna Dzamonda, Kirsten Eady, Michelle Groat, Naomi Halbert, Richard Hart, Jay Houghton, Liz Hughes, V. Hunt, Andrew Hutter, Mark Ignativ, Jean-Luc, Mic Jessop, Hans-Peter Lorenz, R. Lothholz, Lara McCarthy, Tony Marshall, Alexander Mead, Dominic Mobbs, Aaron Morin, Sarah Pepper, Simon Oliver Peter, Conny Peterseil, Julian Richards, Russell Rose, Laura Slade, Angela Tsen and Richard Turner. With apologies to any we've missed . . .

### HELP US UPDATE

We've gone to a lot of effort to ensure that this edition of *The Rough Guide to Australia* is completely up-to-date and accurate. However, things do change – places get "discovered", opening hours are notoriously fickle – and any suggestions, comments or corrections would be much appreciated.

We'll credit all contributions, and send a copy of the next edition (or any other *Rough Guide* if you prefer) for the best letters. Please mark letters: "Rough Guide Australia Update" and send to:

Rough Guides, 1 Mercer Street, London WC2H 9QJ

or Rough Guides, 375 Hudson Street, 3rd Floor, New York NY 10014.

# direct orders from

| | | | | |
|---|---|---|---|---|
| Amsterdam | 1-85828-086-9 | £7.99 | US$13.95 | CAN$16.99 |
| Andalucia | 1-85828-094-X | 8.99 | 14.95 | 18.99 |
| Australia | 1-85828-141-5 | 12.99 | 19.95 | 25.99 |
| Bali | 1-85828-134-2 | 8.99 | 14.95 | 19.99 |
| Barcelona | 1-85828-221-7 | 8.99 | 14.95 | 19.99 |
| Berlin | 1-85828-129-6 | 8.99 | 14.95 | 19.99 |
| Brazil | 1-85828-102-4 | 9.99 | 15.95 | 19.99 |
| Britain | 1-85828-208-X | 12.99 | 19.95 | 25.99 |
| Brittany & Normandy | 1-85828-224-1 | 9.99 | 16.95 | 22.99 |
| Bulgaria | 1-85828-183-0 | 9.99 | 16.95 | 22.99 |
| California | 1-85828-181-4 | 10.99 | 16.95 | 22.99 |
| Canada | 1-85828-130-X | 10.99 | 14.95 | 19.99 |
| China | 1-85828-225-X | 15.99 | 24.95 | 32.95 |
| Corsica | 1-85828-089-3 | 8.99 | 14.95 | 18.99 |
| Costa Rica | 1-85828-136-9 | 9.99 | 15.95 | 21.99 |
| Crete | 1-85828-132-6 | 8.99 | 14.95 | 18.99 |
| Cyprus | 1-85828-182-2 | 9.99 | 16.95 | 22.99 |
| Czech & Slovak Republics | 1-85828-121-0 | 9.99 | 16.95 | 22.99 |
| Egypt | 1-85828-188-1 | 10.99 | 17.95 | 23.99 |
| Europe | 1-85828-159-8 | 14.99 | 19.95 | 25.99 |
| England | 1-85828-160-1 | 10.99 | 17.95 | 23.99 |
| First Time Europe | 1-85828-270-5 | 7.99 | 9.95 | 12.99 |
| Florida | 1-85828-184-4 | 10.99 | 16.95 | 22.99 |
| France | 1-85828-124-5 | 10.99 | 16.95 | 21.99 |
| Germany | 1-85828-128-8 | 11.99 | 17.95 | 23.99 |
| Goa | 1-85828-156-3 | 8.99 | 14.95 | 19.99 |
| Greece | 1-85828-131-8 | 9.99 | 16.95 | 20.99 |
| Greek Islands | 1-85828-163-6 | 8.99 | 14.95 | 19.99 |
| Guatemala | 1-85828-189-X | 10.99 | 16.95 | 22.99 |
| Hawaii: Big Island | 1-85828-158-X | 8.99 | 12.95 | 16.99 |
| Hawaii | 1-85828-206-3 | 10.99 | 16.95 | 22.99 |
| Holland, Belgium & Luxembourg | 1-85828-087-7 | 9.99 | 15.95 | 20.99 |
| Hong Kong | 1-85828-187-3 | 8.99 | 14.95 | 19.99 |
| Hungary | 1-85828-123-7 | 8.99 | 14.95 | 19.99 |
| India | 1-85828-200-4 | 14.99 | 23.95 | 31.99 |
| Ireland | 1-85828-179-2 | 10.99 | 17.95 | 23.99 |
| Italy | 1-85828-167-9 | 12.99 | 19.95 | 25.99 |
| Kenya | 1-85828-192-X | 11.99 | 18.95 | 24.99 |
| London | 1-85828-231-4 | 9.99 | 15.95 | 21.99 |
| Mallorca & Menorca | 1-85828-165-2 | 8.99 | 14.95 | 19.99 |
| Malaysia, Singapore & Brunei | 1-85828-103-2 | 9.99 | 16.95 | 20.99 |
| Mexico | 1-85828-044-3 | 10.99 | 16.95 | 22.99 |
| Morocco | 1-85828-040-0 | 9.99 | 16.95 | 21.99 |
| Moscow | 1-85828-118-0 | 8.99 | 14.95 | 19.99 |
| Nepal | 1-85828-190-3 | 10.99 | 17.95 | 23.99 |
| New York | 1-85828-171-7 | 9.99 | 15.95 | 21.99 |
| Pacific Northwest | 1-85828-092-3 | 9.99 | 14.95 | 19.99 |

# around the world

| | | | | |
|---|---|---|---|---|
| Paris | 1-85828-235-7 | 8.99 | 14.95 | 19.99 |
| Poland | 1-85828-168-7 | 10.99 | 17.95 | 23.99 |
| Portugal | 1-85828-180-6 | 9.99 | 16.95 | 22.99 |
| Prague | 1-85828-122-9 | 8.99 | 14.95 | 19.99 |
| Provence | 1-85828-127-X | 9.99 | 16.95 | 22.99 |
| Pyrenees | 1-85828-093-1 | 8.99 | 15.95 | 19.99 |
| Rhodes & the Dodecanese | 1-85828-120-2 | 8.99 | 14.95 | 19.99 |
| Romania | 1-85828-097-4 | 9.99 | 15.95 | 21.99 |
| San Francisco | 1-85828-185-7 | 8.99 | 14.95 | 19.99 |
| Scandinavia | 1-85828-039-7 | 10.99 | 16.99 | 21.99 |
| Scotland | 1-85828-166-0 | 9.99 | 16.95 | 22.99 |
| Sicily | 1-85828-178-4 | 9.99 | 16.95 | 22.99 |
| Singapore | 1-85828-135-0 | 8.99 | 14.95 | 19.99 |
| Spain | 1-85828-240-3 | 11.99 | 18.95 | 24.99 |
| St Petersburg | 1-85828-133-4 | 8.99 | 14.95 | 19.99 |
| Thailand | 1-85828-140-7 | 10.99 | 17.95 | 24.99 |
| Tunisia | 1-85828-139-3 | 10.99 | 17.95 | 24.99 |
| Turkey | 1-85828-242-X | 12.99 | 19.95 | 25.99 |
| Tuscany & Umbria | 1-85828-243-8 | 10.99 | 17.95 | 23.99 |
| USA | 1-85828-161-X | 14.99 | 19.95 | 25.99 |
| Venice | 1-85828-170-9 | 8.99 | 14.95 | 19.99 |
| Vietnam | 1-85828-191-1 | 9.99 | 15.95 | 21.99 |
| Wales | 1-85828-245-4 | 10.99 | 17.95 | 23.99 |
| Washington DC | 1-85828-246-2 | 8.99 | 14.95 | 19.99 |
| West Africa | 1-85828-101-6 | 15.99 | 24.95 | 34.99 |
| More Women Travel | 1-85828-098-2 | 9.99 | 14.95 | 19.99 |
| Zimbabwe & Botswana | 1-85828-186-5 | 11.99 | 18.95 | 24.99 |
| *Phrasebooks* | | | | |
| Czech | 1-85828-148-2 | 3.50 | 5.00 | 7.00 |
| French | 1-85828-144-X | 3.50 | 5.00 | 7.00 |
| German | 1-85828-146-6 | 3.50 | 5.00 | 7.00 |
| Greek | 1-85828-145-8 | 3.50 | 5.00 | 7.00 |
| Italian | 1-85828-143-1 | 3.50 | 5.00 | 7.00 |
| Mexican | 1-85828-176-8 | 3.50 | 5.00 | 7.00 |
| Portuguese | 1-85828-175-X | 3.50 | 5.00 | 7.00 |
| Polish | 1-85828-174-1 | 3.50 | 5.00 | 7.00 |
| Spanish | 1-85828-147-4 | 3.50 | 5.00 | 7.00 |
| Thai | 1-85828-177-6 | 3.50 | 5.00 | 7.00 |
| Turkish | 1-85828-173-3 | 3.50 | 5.00 | 7.00 |
| Vietnamese | 1-85828-172-5 | 3.50 | 5.00 | 7.00 |
| *Reference* | | | | |
| Classical Music | 1-85828-113-X | 12.99 | 19.95 | 25.99 |
| Internet | 1-85828-198-9 | 5.00 | 8.00 | 10.00 |
| Jazz | 1-85828-137-7 | 16.99 | 24.95 | 34.99 |
| Opera | 1-85828-138-5 | 16.99 | 24.95 | 34.99 |
| Reggae | 1-85828-247-0 | 12.99 | 19.95 | 25.99 |
| Rock | 1-85828-201-2 | 17.99 | 26.95 | 35.00 |
| World Music | 1-85828-017-6 | 16.99 | 22.95 | 29.99 |

# Good Vibrations!

# Qantas flies to 53 destinations in Australia.

## (Yes, there are 53.)

From Britain you can fly with Qantas to any of Australia's seven international gateways. Which means Sydney, Melbourne, Brisbane, Darwin, Cairns, Perth or Adelaide. But where you arrive is nowhere near the half of it. Because that's where our domestic service takes off to forty six further destinations. To everywhere that's anywhere in Australia, in fact. So your stay in the land of Dreamtime couldn't have a more appropriate start. For details of our fares and schedules please call your local Qantas travel office or see your travel agent.

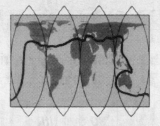

# THE ONLY WAY TO 'GETTAROUND' DOWN UNDER IS TO 'GETTABUS'

**Aussie Pass**

**From Just $1 a Day!**

## THE BEST WAY TO SEE AUSTRALIA

If you really want to see Australia and experience the magnificence
of this diverse continent,
*'getta bus pass'* and relax in comfort aboard one of our air-conditioned coaches.
Not only does a bus pass offer excellent value for money,
it's the ideal way to travel independently,
with convenient 'pick-up' and 'put-downs' at selected hostels.
And remember, when bought in the UK, most bus pass prices are cheaper
than those sold down under.

For further details, ask your local travel agent or call
Greyhound International on (01342) 317317 Fax: (01342)328519
Greyhound International, Sussex House, London Road, East Grinstead, West Sussex RH19 1LD.

# THE LOWEST PRICE CAR RENTAL AROUND THE

# AND THAT'S A PROMISE†

For convenient, low-price car rental – all around the world – choose Holiday Autos. With a network of over 4,000 locations in 42 countries, when you're off globetrotting you won't have to go out of your way to find us.

What's more, with our lowest price promise, you won't be flying round and round in circles to be sure you're getting the best price.

With Holiday Autos you can be sure of the friendly, efficient service you'd expect from the UK's leading leisure car rental company. After all, we've won the Travel Trade Gazette 'Best Leisure Car Rental Company' award and the Independent Travel Agents' 'Top Leisure Car Rental Company' award time and time again. So, we've quite a reputation to maintain.

With Holiday Autos you simply don't need to search the globe for down-to-earth low prices.

For further information see your local Travel Agent or call us direct on **0990 300 400**

# Holiday Autos
**WE KNOW YOU HAVE A CHOICE**

†Our lowest price promise refers to our pledge to undercut by £5 any other equivalent offer made at the same price or less by an independent UK car rental company for a booking made in the UK prior to departure. Holiday Autos undercut offer is valid unless and until withdrawn by Holiday Autos.

# AT WIZARD PRICES

**FLY TO ANYWHERE IN AUSTRALIA** from London or Manchester and take advantage of our special fares. Return tickets are generally valid for 12 months, with **STOPOVERS** allowed in Asia or the USA. They're **FLEXIBLE** too, allowing you to change your mind as you go. You'll find us in over **100 BRANCHES** across Australasia, Asia, USA and Europe offering advice based on 25 years of experience.

## FARES START FROM ONLY
# £330 O/W & £550 RTN.

**CALL 0171 361 6200 FOR YOUR FREE COPY OF THE STA TRAVEL GUIDE**

**Europe: 0171 361 6161, Worldwide: 0171 361 6262
or 0161 834 0668 (Manchester)**

*LONDON, MANCHESTER, LEEDS, BRISTOL, CAMBRIDGE, OXFORD, GLASGOW*

**STA TRAVEL**

*BIRMINGHAM, CARDIFF, COVENTRY, LOUGHBOROUGH, NOTTINGHAM, SHEFFIELD, WARWICK, DURHAM, CANTERBURY*